The Insider's Guide to the Colleges

The Insider's Guide to the Colleges

41st Edition

2015

**Compiled and Edited
by the Staff of the
Yale Daily News**

St. Martin's Griffin
New York

Readers with comments or questions should address them to Editors, The Insider's Guide to the Colleges, c/o Yale Daily News, 202 York Street, New Haven, CT 06511-4804.

Visit *The Insider's Guide to the Colleges* Web site at www.yaledailynews.com/books.

The editors have sought to ensure that the information in this book is accurate as of press time. Because policies, costs, and statistics do change from time to time, readers should verify important information with the colleges.

The Library of Congress Cataloging-in-Publication Data is available upon request.

ISBN 978-1-250-04806-6 (trade paperback)
ISBN 978-1-4668-4835-1 (e-book)

First Edition: July 2014

10 9 8 7 6 5 4 3

Contents

Preface

Welcome to the 2015 edition of *The Insider's Guide to the Colleges!* Choosing the right school and navigating through the application process may seem overwhelming, but you are beginning your search on the right foot simply by picking up this book. In the 41st edition of the *Insider's Guide*, we provide you with an accurate picture of day-to-day college life. For each school profile, we rely on hours of personal interviews with actual students to give you a true sense of the college and its student body.

We tell you what we wanted to know when we were in your shoes. College is going to be one of the most exciting and rewarding experiences of your life. It is about opening yourself up to new experiences, haphazardly putting together something edible in the dining hall when the lines are long and the food is bad, and making the kinds of friends who will skip class to give you a hand when you need it. It is about pulling all-nighters on papers due the next morning or talking to your roommates until the sun comes up. It is about driving halfway across the country to see your football team win, getting blasted for an opinion piece you wrote for the college newspaper, or volunteering at the local elementary school when you still have to do 300 pages of reading. College is gallons of coffee, stress, and laughter.

But first, you need to choose a school. Among the thousands of colleges that span the continent, you can apply to no more than a handful. Maybe you have a vague idea of what you want, but how do you begin to narrow your choices?

That is where the *Insider's Guide* comes in. For this 41st edition, we have revamped our entire book to ensure that it provides an accurate portrayal of college experience at each of the more than 300 institutions we feature. We give you the inside scoop directly from the students who attend these schools. We research each college by interviewing friends, friends of friends, and a selection of student leaders. These unique perspectives offer insights that you won't find on the glossy pages of admissions brochures or by browsing schools' Web sites. It also means that we are only as accurate as the opinions of our sources. After all, the college experience is unique for every individual. Indeed, one student's closet-sized dorm room may be another student's palace.

In addition to college profiles, the *Insider's Guide* includes a number of special features to help you in your search. The "College Finder" gives you a rundown on various schools according to key attributes, such as student body size and graduation rate. "Getting In" takes you step-by-step through the intricacies of the admissions process. In "The College Spectrum," we discuss some of the most important factors to consider when choosing between schools, as well as giving you a look at current trends in college life. "Introduction for International Students" provides tips on applying to American schools for those living outside of the United States, while "Students with Disabilities" informs those with learning or physical disabilities about issues they should consider when applying. "Study Abroad" gives you a peek at the overseas adventures that students undertake during their college years. We have revised our "Insider's Packing List" and our "Insider's Quiz." Our editors have also added new items to the ever-popular "Editors' Choice" feature, a ranking of colleges in categories spanning from ugliest school colors to biggest rivalries. These lists are based on student interviews as well as our own research and assessment. We hope that this feature will offer you a new perspective or introduce you to a school you may not have otherwise considered.

We know how stressful the college selection process is for you. After all the hard work of preparing and applying, acceptances often appear to be offered randomly, with little regard to merit. You may not be able to attend your top college choice. Nevertheless, you should try not to worry, however difficult it may sound. Ultimately, the majority of students love their college experiences. In part, this is because they applied to schools that were right for them. But most importantly, every single college will provide you with new people to meet, new paths to explore, and new experiences to enjoy. Wherever you end up, just remember one thing: those four years fly by, so make the most of them!

Acknowledgments

We would like to particular give thanks to Matt Martz, our editor at St. Martin's Press. His leadership and understanding have been essential, and without his organizational and creative vision, the 2015 *Guide* could never have been published. To Emad Haerizadeh and Jeff Marsh at the *Yale Daily News*, we give considerable thanks for their time and patience. We would also like to thank all the interviewees who were gracious enough to give us a peek into their lives and their colleges: Without you, this book would not have been possible. Finally, we are especially thankful to those Yalies who, over 40 years ago, decided to devote their time and energy toward creating a helpful guide for high schoolers about to go to college. We hope you enjoy the book!

How to Use This Book

How We Select the Colleges

One of the most difficult questions we wrestle with here at *The Insider's Guide* is which schools to include in the upcoming edition. From more than 2,000 four-year institutions nationwide, we only cover slightly over 300 colleges. We examine a number of criteria in deciding which colleges to select, but our first priority is always the quality of academics offered by the institution. Another key factor in our decision is the desire to offer a diversity of options in *The Insider's Guide*. Thus, we have included schools from all 50 states as well as several top institutions in Canada. In our school choices, we have also taken into account the range of extracurricular options available to students, including publications, teams, and ethnic organizations. Each year we review our list of schools, research potential additions, and try to include new colleges that have not been featured in the past. Our goal is to provide you with the latest and the most comprehensive insider information.

We have made a point to review the largest state-affiliated institutions because of the significant number of students who apply to and matriculate at their states' schools. These universities tend to offer a particularly wide range of opportunities. We have also made every effort to include a broad cross section of smaller colleges because of the unique education they offer. Many of these schools are liberal arts colleges, generally clustered in the Northeast, offering a broad but personalized education. To add to the diversity of schools reviewed by *The Insider's Guide*, we have also included selections from the most prominent technical schools and creative and performing arts schools. These institutions provide specialized education, combining general knowledge with a concentration in a particular field. The sampling of schools in this category is by no means comprehensive, and we encourage students interested in specialized institutions to explore their options more deeply through additional research.

In sum, this book covers the colleges we believe to be among the most noteworthy in both the United States and Canada. This selection does not imply in any way that you cannot get a good education at a school not listed in the *Guide*. We strongly encourage students to use strategies discussed within this book to explore the wide variety of schools that we did not have space to include here, including community colleges, state schools, international schools, and professional schools. In addition, it's not guaranteed that you will have a blissful four years if you attend one of the schools we feature! Rather, we believe that every school in the *Guide* offers students the raw materials for constructing an excellent education.

It's All Up to You

Now that you have picked up a copy of *The Insider's Guide*, it's up to you how to use it. A few dedicated readers scrutinize the book from start to finish, determined to gain the most complete understanding of the college process and the schools that are out there. Others flip through the *Guide* for only a few minutes to look at **FYIs** from schools that interest them or to read funny quotes taken from nearby colleges. Another good strategy is to use the **College Finder**, **Editors' Choice lists**, and statistics that begin each article to learn more about colleges that you may not have heard of before. It might be worthwhile to read up on colleges that you wouldn't initially consider—you just may find yourself intrigued by the student perspectives. Take advantage of the opening features of the book—they are designed to help you zero in on schools that meet your search criteria. You can also explore these beginning sections to learn what is unique and important about schools you are already considering. We encourage all these approaches. Above all, we hope that the *Guide* is fun to read, educational, and a useful aid in helping to make the college selection process less stressful.

While our **Editors' Choice lists** use a mix of statistics and subjectivity to provide an alternative perspective on the schools we include, we have avoided the temptation to pigeonhole the colleges with some kind of catchall rating system, or worse, to numerically rank them from first to last. Our reason is that the "best" college for one person may come near the bottom of the list for another. Each student has his or her own particular set of wants and needs, so it would be impossible for us to objectively rank the schools from "best" to "worst." Whereas most rankings focus solely on academic factors, the college experience is a balance of academics, social life, extracurricular activities, and much more.

Even so, some may wonder why we don't rate the colleges solely on the basis of academic quality. We think that attempting to come up with such a ranking is both impossible and undesirable. There are too many variables—from the many factors that contribute to the quality of a department and school as a whole to the articulateness and accessibility of the professor who happens to be your academic advisor. Furthermore, it's useless to try to compare a college of 2,000 students with a university of 10,000 (or a university of 10,000 with a state school of 40,000 for that matter) on any basis other than individual preference. Despite these reasons not to, some reportedly reputable sources such as national magazines often insist on publishing numerical rankings of colleges. We advise you not to take these lists too seriously. Oftentimes the determining factor in the rankings is a statistic such as "percent of alumni who donate money," something that means very little to most college applicants.

For over 40 years, *The Insider's Guide* has been dedicated to the belief that the best rankers of schools are students themselves, not magazine writers. Our goal, therefore, is to help you train your eye so you can select the college that is best for you. Remember, we may describe, explain, interpret, and report—but in the end, the choice is always yours.

Getting In

Applying to college can seem as intimidating as reading through this thick book, but neither should be a chore. In the spring of your sophomore year of high school, your Aunt Doris, whom you have not seen in seven years, pinches your cheek and asks you where you are going to college. "How the heck should I know," you think to yourself. That fall, your mom tells you that the girl down the street with the 4.0 grade point average is taking the SAT prep course for the fifth time to see if she can get a perfect score and win thousands in scholarship money. You reply that you are late for school. You keep ducking the subject, but the hints come with increasing regularity. Not only has dinnertime become your family's "let's talk about Lauren's college options" hour, but friends at school are already beginning to leaf through college catalogs. Soon you find the guidance counselor's office crowded with your wide-eyed peers, and it's clear they aren't asking for love advice. Panicking, you decide to make an appointment with the counselor yourself.

When you first talk to your counselor, preferably in the early part of your junior year, you may not yet feel completely comfortable in high school, let alone prepared to think about college. The entire prospect seems far away, but choosing the right school for you takes a good amount of thought and organization—and a visit to your counselor is a solid start. You may even be wondering if college is the path you want to take after high school. And you're not alone. A good number of people choose to take a year or two off to work or travel before pursuing a college education.

One important resource in making a decision about any post-graduation plans is your counselor. College counselors have a wealth of information and experience from which to draw, and they can help you lay out a plan for whatever direction you wish to take. If you decide that college is your next step, you will have a lot of options. Although many schools are surveyed in this book, we have not included professional schools or community colleges, all of which also offer a wide variety of opportunities. With research of your own and the aid of your counselor, you should be able to find a school that will give you what you're looking for.

In your hunt for the best college, it is wise to do a little exploring of your own before sitting down with your counselor. Counselors can be invaluable advisors and confidants throughout the college admissions process, but sometimes counselors inadvertently limit your search by only recommending noncompetitive schools, or, conversely, by assuring you that you'll get into whichever school you want. A few may even try to dissuade you from applying to colleges that you are seriously considering. These cases aren't common, but they do happen. Regardless of your counselor's perspective, it is best if you already have an idea of what you are looking for, as it will help both you and your advisor sort out all the options. You can refer back to these initial goals as you learn more. In the end, always follow your instincts.

As you begin to wade through the piles of brochures, ask yourself questions. What factors about a school make a difference to you? What do you want in a college? A strong science department? A Californian landscape? A small student body? A great social life? Although each college is a mix of different features, it is wise to place your academic needs first. Check out the general academic quality of the school, as well as what kind of programs they offer. Please note: since many students change their majors repeatedly before finally settling down, it's a good idea to look for schools with programs in a number of areas that interest you.

Of course, it's impossible to think of all the angles from which you should approach your college search. You can't predict what your interests will be three or four years from now, or what things will prove most important to you at the college you attend. After all, those realizations are a big part of what the college experience is all about. But by taking a hard look at yourself now, and proceeding thoughtfully, you can be confident that you are investigating the right colleges for the right reasons.

As you begin the search, schools will start to seek you out as well. In the early winter of your junior year, you'll receive your PSAT scores, and unless you request otherwise, your mailbox will soon become inundated with letters from colleges around the country.

The College Search Service of the College Board provides these schools with the names and addresses of students who show promise, and the schools crank out thousands of form letters to send, and often to students with backgrounds that they feel are underrepresented in their student population.

While sorting through these masses of glossy brochures, you'll probably notice that most of them contain lofty quotes and pictures of a diverse, frolicking student body. One of the best ways to find out if these ideals are actually truths is to visit the college. But before that, you can verify some of what you read by comparing it to nationally published articles and statistics. You will probably find the colleges that most interest you through your own research, and many of these schools wait for you to contact them before they send information. In that case, create a form letter that briefly expresses your interest in the college and requests materials. You'll get your name on their mailing lists, and they'll appreciate the fact that you took the initiative.

Throughout this process, make sure to listen to those who know you well and often have sound advice to share—namely, your parents and elder siblings. Besides having some ideas of schools you might enjoy attending, your parents also have great insight into how your education can and will be financed. If you come to an early understanding with your family about prospective colleges and financial concerns, things will move much more smoothly down the road. But be warned—the college search can be one of the most trying times in any parent-child relationship, and some parents become more or less involved in the process than students want. The best advice we can give is to remember that calm, patient discussions are a better tactic than yelling matches.

When consulting others about your college search, it is helpful to keep a few things in mind. Every piece of advice you receive will be a reflection of someone's own life experiences, and it is likely to be highly subjective. Most adults will suggest schools located in regions they know or colleges they have visited or attended themselves. Also, opinions are often based on stereotypes that can be false, outdated, or just misleading. Still, the more people you talk to, the better perspective you will gain on the colleges you are considering. Once you have a few outside ideas, this book can give you some inside information. If you like what you have heard about a particular school, follow up with some research and find out if it's still a place that calls to you.

As you approach the time when your final college list must be made, you will probably have visited college fairs and attended various college nights. Real-life representatives from the schools are always good to meet. Talking to current college students is an even more important step, as is visiting the schools that make it to your last list. During these encounters, ask the questions that are on your mind. Be critical and observant. When it's time for the final leg of the college selection process, you'll be calm and satisfied if you know you've really looked hard into yourself and all your options.

Visit

Whether your list of schools has been set for months or fluctuates on a daily basis, college visits are a great way to narrow down your choices and prioritize your list of options. Try to plan campus visits so you'll be finished by the fall of your senior year, especially if you are considering early application programs. Additionally, aim to see as many schools that interest you as possible—there's no better way to get a feel for where you'd like to spend the next four years of your life.

When you visit a campus, try to keep in mind why you are there. You have probably already seen the college viewbook with glossy pictures of green lawns and diverse groups of students in seminar-size classes. Now is the time to find out what the campus is really like. Is the student population truly that diverse? Do people really gather and play Frisbee on plush green lawns? What do the dorms actually look like? And most importantly, do you feel comfortable there?

If you are visiting a campus for an interview, make sure you schedule one in advance. Making the decision not to interview on campus may be a good one, however. While some schools require an on-campus interview, some insiders recommend that you request an alumni interview instead. Alumni interviews tend to be more convenient and less grueling than on-campus interviews. In any case, make sure you check a school's policy regarding interviews before you arrive, and schedule your visit accordingly.

While some prefer to visit colleges over summer vacation, we think the best time to visit is during the academic year, when regular classes are in session. During the summer months very few students are on campus, so it will be much more difficult to get a feel for the student culture and vibrancy (or lack thereof). Times of unusually high stress also will not give you a good idea of what ordinary life is like. For this reason, you'll also want to avoid exam periods and vacations. During the academic year, your questions about the campus are much more likely to be answered. You'll get a feel for the type of people at the school, and you'll get an idea of what it is like to be a student living on campus. It's important to get a good sense of what your daily life will be like if you end up attending the school.

Before you look at any college, take a little time to prepare. Perhaps you will want to come up with some kind of system to evaluate the schools you will visit. Putting together a list of characteristics that are important to you will make it easier to compare one school to the next, whether they be academics, the size of the campus, or the surrounding area's vibrancy and atmosphere. Make sure you jot down some notes on the schools during and after your trips. Although colleges may seem easy to differentiate at the time, your impressions of each may blur together when you are back at home, sitting in front of 10 seemingly identical applications.

An overnight stay with undergraduates can provide you with a more inside look at campus life. Most admissions offices have students on call who are happy to show you around campus, take you to some classes and parties, and let you crash in their dorms. If you have friends there, they are good resources as well. Either way, staying with students will help you see what an undergraduate's academic and social life is really like. One student said, "I found that it didn't matter much if I stayed over or not, as long as I got to talk to students. But if you do stay over, Thursday or Friday night is the best time." Sometimes it is hard to connect with students during a single day when everybody is rushing around to classes. Try to spend a night late in the week when students will have more time for you and the nightlife will be more vibrant. It is always possible that you will end up with hosts that are difficult to relate to or socially withdrawn. Don't let a bad hosting experience completely dictate your feelings about the college—just do everything you can to get out into the student body and explore what the school has to offer.

Keep in mind that college life doesn't consist entirely of classes. Sample the food,

which is, after all, a necessity of life. Check out the dorms. Take the campus tour. Although you are sure to be inundated with obscure facts about the college that may not interest you, it can be useful to have a knowledgeable guide to show you the buildings themselves and the campus as a whole. If you have any questions, do not hesitate to ask. Tour guides are often students and are a great resource for any information you want about the school.

Should you bring your parents along? Maybe. Some students prefer to leave them at home. Although parents don't mean any harm, they can sometimes get in the way. Your discomfort at having them around when you're trying to get along with new students may cloud your opinion of a school. However, most students do bring along at least one family member. If you go this route, don't completely discount the advice or opinions they may have about the school. Parents can be great resources to bounce ideas off of, particularly regarding the pros and cons of the various colleges you have seen. You might want to take the campus tour with them, and then break away to explore the campus on your own and talk with students one-on-one. When you enter college your parents will not be there with you, so it's a good idea to get a feel for what that will actually be like.

Most importantly, keep in mind your sense of the campus atmosphere. How does it feel to walk across the main quad? Does the mood seem intellectual or laid-back? Do T-shirts read "Earth Day Every Day" or "Coed Naked Beer Games"? Look for postings of events; some campuses are alive and vibrant while others seem pretty dead. Check your comfort level. Imagine yourself on the campus for the next four years and see how that makes you feel. Focus on these characteristics while you are on campus—you can read about the academic requirements when you get back home. Most of all, enjoy yourself! The campus visit is an exciting peek into a world that will soon be your own.

The Interview

Just about every college applicant dreads the interview. It can be the most nerve-racking part of the college application process. But relax—despite the horror stories you might have heard, the interview will rarely make or break your application. If you are a strong candidate, don't be overly self-assured; if your application makes you look like a hermit, be lively and personable. Usually the interview can only help you, and at some schools it is nothing more than informational. "I was constantly surprised at how many questions they let me ask," one applicant reported.

Consider the interview your chance to highlight the best parts of your application and explain the weaker parts without being whiny or making excuses. Are your SAT scores on the low side? Does your extracurricular section seem a little thin? An interview gives you the opportunity to call attention to your successes in classes despite your scores, or explain that of the three clubs you listed, you founded two and were president of the third.

There are a few keys to a successful interview.

1. The first and most important is to stand out from the crowd. Keep in mind that the interviewer probably sees half a dozen or more students every day, month after month. If you can make your interviewer laugh, interest him or her in something unusual you have done, or somehow spice up the same old questions and answers, you have had a great interview. Don't just say that you were the president of something; be able to back up your titles with interesting and genuine stories. On the other hand, don't go overboard and shock your interviewer with spring break stories, for example. That will most likely work against you.

2. Do not try to be something you are not. Tell the truth and give the interviewer a feel for who you really are—your passions, your strengths, and your challenges. By doing so, you will be more relaxed and confident. Even if you feel that the "real you" isn't that interesting or amazing, take time to reflect on your high school experience—the stories that surface in your mind may just surprise you.

3. A few days before the actual interview, think about some of the questions you might be asked. Some admissions officers begin every interview by asking, "Why do you want to go to this school, and why should we let you?" You should not have memorized speeches for every answer, but try not to get caught off guard. Make sure you really know why you want to attend this college. Even if you are not sure, think of a few plausible reasons and be prepared to give them. Students often make the mistake of giving a canned answer, which is okay since most answers are similar, but admissions officers look to admit students who want to take advantage of all that is available at their school. Your answer must include the three essential elements of a good reply: your interests, whether academic or extracurricular; what you believe the school will provide; and how and why you are excited about the opportunity to take advantage of them. Other common questions include those about your most important activities, what you did with your summers, and what vision you may have for your future.

4. A note of caution: If your interview takes place after you have submitted your application, the interviewer might ask you questions about some of the things you included. One student wrote on his application that he read *Newsweek* religiously. During his interview, the admissions officer asked the student about a story in a recent issue of the magazine. The student had no idea what the interviewer was talking about. He was not accepted. While this was only one of many factors that the admissions officer had to consider, it is still important. So be ready to back up your claims. It is always an excellent idea to indicate that you have a special interest in something, but make sure the interest is genuine—you may wind up in an hour-long conversation on the topic. Do not start talking about how you love learning about philosophy if you have only dabbled in it once. An open, thoughtful manner can do as much as anything else to impress your interviewer, although an overly negative attitude will make just as much of an impression.

5. Being spontaneous in a contrived situation usually amounts to having a successful interview. If you are nervous, that's okay. Said one applicant, "I felt sick, and I didn't eat for a day before the interview." The most common misconception is that admissions officers are looking for totally confident individuals who know everything and have their entire future planned out. Almost the opposite is true. An admissions officer at a selective private college said, "We do not expect imitation adults to walk through the door. We expect to see people in their last year or two of high school with the customary apprehensions, habits, and characteristics of that time of life." Admissions officers know students

get nervous. They understand. If everything in your life is not perfect, do not be afraid to say so when appropriate. For example, if the conversation comes around to your high school, there is no need to cover up if problems do exist. It is okay to say you did not think your chemistry lab was well equipped. An honest, realistic critique of your school or just about anything else will make a better impression than false praise ever could.

6. If something you say does not come out quite right, try to react as you would with a friend. If the interviewer asks about your career plans, it is alright to say that you are undecided. As a high school student, no one expects you to have all the answers—that is why you are going to college. Above all, remember that the admissions officer is a person interested in getting to know you as an individual. A person who may be a parent to someone, a friend of someone's, a sibling of someone's. They empathize. As one interviewer explained, "I'm not there to judge the applicants as scholars. I'm just there to get a sense of them as people."

7. Do not get so worried about saying all the right things that you forget to listen carefully to the interviewer. The purpose of the interview is not to grill you, but to match you with the school in the best interest of both. Sometimes the interviewer will tell you, either during the interview or in a follow-up letter, that you have little chance of getting in. If she says so or implies it, know that such remarks are not made lightly. On the other hand, if she is sincerely encouraging, listen to that, too. If an interviewer suggests other schools for you to look into, remember that she is a professional and take note. Besides, many interviewers appreciate a student's ability to listen as well as to talk.

8. Your interviewer might ask you whether you have a first choice, particularly if her college is often seen as a backup. If the school is really not your first choice, feel free to sidestep that question as gracefully as possible. Not only is it more than likely that you haven't made up your mind, but your first choice is your business, not theirs. If the school really is your first choice, though, feel free to say so, and give a good reason why. A genuine interest can be a real plug on your behalf.

9. Also know that you can direct the conversation. Do not worry about occasional lapses as some interviewers wait to see

how you will react to a potentially awkward situation. Take advantage of the pause to ask a question or bring up a relevant topic that really interests you. It is your job to present the parts of you and your background that you want noted.

10. Selective colleges need reasons to accept you. Being qualified on paper is not always enough. Think of the interviewer's position: "Why should we accept you instead of thousands of other qualified applicants?" The answer to that question should be evident in every response you give. Use the interview to play up and accentuate your most memorable qualities. Show flashes of the playful sense of humor that your English teacher cites in his recommendation; impress the interviewer with the astute eye for politics about which your history teacher raves.

11. Too many applicants are afraid to talk confidently about their accomplishments. If the interviewer is impressed by something, do not insist that it was not much, or he might believe you. If he is not impressed by something you think is important, tactfully let him know that he should be. But do not, under any circumstances, act like you are too good for the college. One well-qualified applicant to a leading college was turned down when the interviewer wrote, "It obviously isn't going to be the end of his world if he doesn't get in. And it won't be the end of our world, either." If there is any quality you want to convey, it is a sincere interest in the school.

12. Almost all interviewers will eventually ask, "Do you have any questions about our school?" Come to the interview armed with a couple of good questions, and not ones whose answers are easily found in the college's viewbook or on the school Web site. Do not ask if they have an economics department, for example, or ask the average class size in introductory economics courses. It may help to do some extra preparation ahead of time. Are you interested in studying abroad? If so, know what kind of programs the school offers and ask a few questions about them. If you are excited to learn more about the school and have already done some homework, it goes a long way in the eyes of the interviewer. Also, if the interviewer is an alumnus, a good question is to ask what they would have done differently during their time at the college. You can be sure that they will need a moment of reflection, and you'll have time to relax!

13. You will probably wonder what to wear. This is no life or death decision, but remember that your appearance is one of the first things the interviewer will notice about you. Wear something you will be comfortable in—a jacket and a tie or a nice dress is fine. Do not, however, be too casual. Faded jeans and a T-shirt will give the impression that you are taking the interview too lightly. But, if your interview is at Starbucks as opposed to someone's office building, take their choice in location as a cue for dress.

14. One crucial point: Keep your parents a thousand feet and preferably a thousand miles away from the interview session. It will be harder to relax and be genuine with an additional set of eyes on you, and you might hold back some interesting information. When parents sit in, interviews tend to be short, boring, and, worst of all, useless. If the interviewer feels you cannot handle an hour without your parents, she might be concerned about your ability to survive the pressures of college life. Take the risk of hurting your parents' feelings and ask them to wait outside.

Once the interview is over, it is perfectly alright for your parents to ask any questions they may have if the interviewer walks with you back to the waiting room. Even if this makes you uncomfortable, do not let it show. Admissions officers can learn as much about you by the way you treat your parents as they do in the interview. The interviewer is not judging your parents. As long as you conduct yourself calmly and maturely, you have nothing to worry about.

15. It is a good idea to send a thank-you note after the interview. It doesn't need to be extensive, just let the interviewer know that you appreciate the time she or he spent with you and that you enjoyed learning more about the school. While it doesn't seem like much, a simple note can leave a lasting impression. Be sure to say something specific to your interviewer. If you shared a laugh or if the interviewer mentioned something about his or her job, try to slip something personal into the note. All of this advice applies for interviews given by alumni as well as those conducted by admissions staff. Alumni interviewers sometimes carry slightly less weight with the admissions office, but they are valuable contacts with the schools and should not be taken lightly.

Expect on-campus interviews to be a bit more formal than alumni interviews.

What if you do not have an interview at all? Perhaps you live too far away, and you cannot get to the school itself. Or, perhaps you feel that your lack of poise is serious enough that it would work against you in any interview you had. Talk it over with your guidance counselor. In general, geographic isolation is a valid excuse for not having an interview, and most colleges will not hold it against you. Ask if they will allow a phone interview instead. Yet, if the college is fairly close and makes it clear that applicants should have an on-campus interview if at all possible, make the effort to go. Otherwise, the college will assume that for some reason you were afraid to interview, or worse, that you simply did not care enough to have one. If the prospect is genuinely terrifying, schedule your first interview for a safety school, or ask your guidance counselor to grant you a practice interview. You might discover that the process is not as horrible as you originally thought.

The Tests

Whether you are an Olympic hopeful, a musical prodigy, or a third-generation legacy, it doesn't matter. You cannot avoid taking standardized tests if you want to go to college. Ninety percent of all four-year institutions now require some type of admissions test. Certainly, tests do not tell the whole story—grades, recommendations, extracurricular activities, the application essays, and personal interviews round out the picture. However, standardized test scores are often the only uniform criteria available to admissions committees. They are meant to indicate the level of education you have had in the past, as well as your potential to succeed in the future. Unfortunately, while they aren't perfect, they are a necessary evil.

Virtually all of the nation's colleges require applicants to submit SAT Reasoning Test or ACT scores. In addition, many colleges will ask their applicants for SAT Subject Test scores. If you are an international student with a native language other than English (or recently moved from an education system using a foreign language), you may be required to take the TOEFL as well. If you take AP tests or are in an IB program, your scores could help you earn college credit if they fulfill the score requirements of the college to which you are applying. Does all this seem overwhelming to you? Read this section and hopefully we can help you understand each test a little better.

The SAT Reasoning Test, formerly known as the Scholastic Aptitude Test (SAT), is the most widely chosen admissions test by college applicants. Administered by the Educational Testing Service (ETS) and created by the College Board, the SAT Reasoning Test currently has a math section, a critical reading section, and a writing section. A nearly four-hour test, there are a total of 10 sections; three are writing, three are verbal, three are math, and there is an unscored variable section (math or critical reading) thrown in somewhere to try out new question formats. The math section includes material up through Geometry and Algebra II, and, to your benefit, you are allowed to use calculators. It has five-choice multiple-choice questions and questions where you produce the answer yourself. In the critical reading section, you will find sentence completions and short and long passages with reading comprehension questions. The writing section involves an essay in response to a prompt and multiple choice questions that require you to identify grammar and usage errors and improve sentence and paragraph structure.

The SAT scores the math, critical reading, and writing sections separately on a 200 to 800 scale. Therefore, your combined score can be a minimum of 600 and a maximum of 2400. One disadvantage with the SAT is that you are penalized for wrong answers, so avoid guessing haphazardly. However, if you can eliminate a few answer choices, it is often better to guess than to leave the question blank. The average score for each section is a 500 based on the recentered scale that the ETS implemented starting in 1995. When the SAT was originally calibrated, it was done so that the average score for the math and verbal sections would each be 500. Over several decades, the average dropped—some say as a result of the declining American education system. However, others argue that the perceived "decrease" is not surprising considering that today's over two million SAT-takers are much more representative of American education as a whole than the 10,000 primarily affluent prep-school students who took the test when it was implemented in 1941. As a result, the scoring was recentered in 1995 in order to redistribute scores more evenly along the 200 to 800 scale. All colleges and scholarship institutions are aware of this new scoring

calibration, so even though it may be easier to get that rare 800 section score, your percentile rank among other students who took the exam will not change.

There are five ways to register for the SAT. The two most common methods are to complete an online registration at www.college board.com or mail in a registration form, which you can get from your high school counselor's office. If you've registered for an SAT Program test before, you can complete the registration over the phone. For those students living outside of the United States, U.S. territories, and Puerto Rico, there is an option to fax in your registration. International students have the option of registering through a representative found in the International Edition of the SAT Registration Bulletin. The SAT is administered seven times a year domestically, and six times a year overseas.

Before you take the test, be sure to take advantage of two services offered by the College Board upon registration. The first is called the Student Search Service. It allows universities, colleges, and scholarship programs to get general information about you, as well as what range your score falls into. You will receive a flood of information about different schools and scholarship programs in the mail in addition to information regarding financial aid opportunities. While you'll begin to see most of these letters as junk mail, some of them will help you come up with the list of colleges to which you intend to apply. As a second service, the College Board will mail your test scores to a maximum of four specified schools or scholarship programs for free. You can send additional score reports for a fee. Be aware that if you have taken the SAT more than once, all of your previous scores will be sent when reporting to schools and scholarship programs. If you have second thoughts and want to cancel your scores, you must do so by the Wednesday following your exam via e-mail, fax, or mail.

The American College Test (ACT) was required mostly by colleges in the southern and western regions of the country but is now accepted by most colleges across the nation. The exam covers English, reading, mathematics, and science reasoning in the format of 215 multiple-choice questions. It also offers an optional writing component. One distinguishing feature of the ACT is that it measures what you have learned in the high school curriculum rather than your aptitude.

The ACT, unlike the SAT, does not deduct any points for incorrect answers, so be sure to fill in a bubble for every question. You will receive a score on a scale of 1 to 36 for each of the four subject areas; your Composite score is just an average of the four scores rounded to the nearest whole number. Based on the over 1.3 million students who choose to take the test, the average Composite score is around 21. Registration is much like the SAT, with a mail-in option, online registration at www.act.org, or telephone preregistration. There is a stand-by registration option for those who forget to register. As far as score reporting goes, you can choose up to six schools or scholarship programs on your registration to have the scores sent to for free. The great thing about the ACT is that you can choose to send just one testing date's scores instead of having your whole history of scores sent, as is done with the SAT.

Many of the more selective colleges also require up to three SAT Subject Tests, formerly called SAT IIs. Available subjects include English, a variety of foreign languages, math, history, and several of the sciences. Due to the recent addition of the writing section to the SAT Reasoning Test, there is no longer a writing Subject Test available. One thing about the SAT Subject Tests is that you don't have to choose which tests you want to take until you're at the test center on the test date. The scores are reported on a 200 to 800 scale, with Score Choice as an option that allows students to not submit all of their scores. Score Choice has been controversial because students can choose to submit only their best scores, without revealing the total number of tests they have taken or the number of times they took each test.

The Test of English as a Foreign Language (TOEFL) is an English proficiency test provided for international students who want to study in the United States, Canada, or other English-speaking countries. It is administered by paper and pencil, on a test-center computer, or over the internet. The score scale for the test varies depending on which form of the test you choose to take. Furthermore, the essay is scored separately and has a separate scoring scale. The TOEFL will test your listening, structured writing, and reading skills—giving a better picture of your English to the schools you apply to.

Advanced Placement (AP) exams are another animal altogether since their purpose is not only to get you into college, but also to earn you credits once you get there. Administered in May, each test covers a specific subject area and scores your performance from 1 to 5. Different schools require different scores for granting college credit. Some will offer credit but still require you to take classes in a subject that you aced on the AP exams. Since the tests require in-depth knowledge of specific subjects, do not put off studying for them. The general practice is to take the exam in a particular subject the May right after you have finished (or are in the midst of finishing) a course in that area. Not only can you get college credit with a high score, but you can also help your college applications with AP exams taken before your senior year.

If you attend an International Baccalaureate (IB) school, you might be able to receive college credit for your coursework depending on your score. A score of 4 or 5 is the required minimum by a college for credit and/or placement, but many institutions require a score of 6 or 7. Although not as popularly embraced by colleges and universities across the nation for giving college credit, they will definitely recognize you for the rigorous work you have completed in the program and can enable you to take higher-level courses in certain subject areas.

You may have already taken the PSAT/NMSQT, which is usually administered to sophomores or juniors through their high school. This is a great practice exam for the SAT Reasoning Test because it has a lot of the same type of questions. It is also a good way to qualify for merit scholarships if you get a high score. The PSAT changed its format to incorporate writing skills in the fall of 2004 to complement the new SAT in 2005.

The most reliable way to keep up-to-date on test dates, testing sites, and registration deadlines is through your high school guidance office. After the PSAT, you will be on your own about when and where you take the tests. Find out way ahead of time which ones are required by the colleges you are interested in; deadlines have a way of sneaking up on you. It is a good idea to begin taking the tests by the spring of your junior year. If you take the SAT Reasoning Test in March or May of your junior year and do not do as well as you think you should, you will have a couple of other opportunities to improve your score. The required SAT Subject Tests should be taken by June of your junior year so that if you decide to apply to an early-action or early-decision program, you will have completed the required testing.

Avoid postponing required testing until November, December, or January of your senior year. One new college student, who put off his exams until the last minute, recalled his college freshman faculty advisor saying to him, "I just don't understand it . . . you went to one of the best high schools in Chicago and did very well. How could your SAT scores have been so low?" He told her how lucky he felt just getting into college; he had contracted a nasty flu and thrown up before, during, and after the test! On the other hand, do not repeat tests over and over. The ETS reports that students gain an average of 25 points on both the math and reading sections of the SAT Reasoning Test upon taking the test a second time. Two or three shots at the SATs should be sufficient. If you've got the time and money, you may want to consider taking a prep course given by a professional test-preparation service. National test-prep companies like Kaplan and the Princeton Review, as well as dozens of local companies, attempt to give helpful tips on how to take tests for those willing to shell out hundreds of dollars. If you do decide to take a prep course, take it seriously. You may have six or seven high school classes to worry about, but you cannot hope to get your money's worth if you do not attend all of the sessions and complete the homework in these prep courses.

Many people choose not to take practice courses. A good student who is confident about taking tests can probably do just as well studying on his or her own. Practice exams are available online and in commercially marketed practice books. Get acquainted with the tests you plan to take beforehand; you should not have to waste time during your exam rereading instructions and trying to figure out what to do. It's a good idea to even simulate an actual test by timing yourself with no interruptions on a real test that was previously administered.

The College Board puts out a book called *The Official SAT Study Guide* that proves to be one of the most effective ways to prepare for the SAT Reasoning Test. True to its title, the book has official SATs from the past, along with hints, test-taking strategies, and exercises to help you improve your test score. The ACT has a similar book called *The Real ACT Prep Guide* with three complete exams plus ACT's own analyses and explanations designed to help you with the test. Getting the chance to practice exams in a real test-like situation (no phones, family, or friends to distract you) will help you to get a keener sense of the overall structure of the test and help you work faster during the actual exam. It might also help you calm down!

Do not cram the night before the exam. Get plenty of sleep and relax. "My teacher encouraged us to go out and have a good time the day before," recalled one first-year college student. "So I went to the movies as a distraction. I think it worked!" On the day of the test, eat a full breakfast that isn't too heavy, dress comfortably, and do not forget to bring two pieces of ID, a calculator, a couple of number two pencils and a pencil sharpener. Make sure you are up early and know where you will be taking the test as well as how to get there. The test center may be overcrowded, there may be no air-conditioning or heat, and a hundred construction workers may be drilling outside the nearest window—be prepared for anything!

The key to success on any of these exams is to keep calm. During the exam, keep track of how many problems there are and allot time accordingly. Read and attempt to answer every question since you do not get more credit for the hard ones than the easy ones. If you are stuck on a question, try to eliminate as many answers as possible and select from the remaining choices. Only if you really have no clue about the question should you leave it blank on the SAT.

A word of warning: Do not even think about cheating. It is not worth it, and your chances of getting caught and blackballed from college are high. To weed out cheaters, the ETS uses the mysterious K-index, a statistical tool that measures the chance of two students selecting the same answers. If your K-index is suspect, a form letter goes out to the colleges you are interested in, delaying your score until you retake the exam or prove your innocence. Know that looking at another person's test is not the only activity that the ETS considers cheating. Going back to finish work on a previous section is also against the rules. Do not tempt fate—a low score is better than no score at all.

At the beginning of this section, we stressed that standardized tests are important. How important? It varies depending on the school you are applying to. At many state schools, admission depends almost entirely on test scores and grades; if you score above the cutoffs, you are in. With the more selective schools, scores are usually only one of many important factors in the admissions process. According to the dean of admissions at Harvard University, "If scores are in the high 500 to low 700 range, they probably have a fairly small impact on our decisions."

Each of the schools in this book lists a mean score range for the SAT. Remember that there are students who score below this range and above this range that were accepted to that college. Unless you score far below or far above the mean of your desired college, most likely your SAT Reasoning Test score will not make or break your chances of getting in. If you attended an inner-city school or a school in an area of the country where education standards are below the norm, your apparent deficit might, in fact, indicate a strength—as long as you are above the minimum levels.

Many students mistakenly believe that the SAT is the only test that "really matters" in competitive college admissions. In fact, SAT Subject Test scores taken as a whole are usually of equal importance. Colleges will often view these scores as a more accurate predictor of future performance than the SAT Reasoning Test. Aside from tests, it is important to remember that your high school record is weighed heavily. If you bomb your admissions tests, but have decent grades, there's a chance that your high school performance can outweigh the bad test scores. However, a poor GPA is hard to overlook, even if your scores are high. Remember that your admissions test scores are just a portion of the whole picture you present to the colleges. So try your best to make it advantageous to you, and don't worry if you don't get a perfect score!

The Application

I t's the fall of your senior year of high school. You've done your research and found a few schools that you're interested in. You've taken the standardized tests, you've visited the campuses, and you may even have had some on-campus interviews. You still have one major hurdle ahead of you, however: The Application. Although the piles of paperwork may seem daunting, with some advance planning you can make the application process as painless as possible. As you go through the often challenging process, keep in mind that it's all worth it in light of your ultimate goal: acceptance.

First, you have to decide where you want to apply. You should have this done no later than the first few weeks of your senior year. After talking to students and visiting campuses, try to narrow down your original list of colleges to somewhere between five and 15. Applying to any more schools than this is

probably overkill. Not only is it a waste of time to apply to more schools than necessary, it is also a waste of money to apply to any school you won't be happy attending—application processing fees can be pricey. However, you want to apply to enough schools that you'll be sure to get accepted somewhere.

It's also important to think about the selectivity of the schools you apply to. Don't be scared to apply to your dream school even if your SAT score or GPA is a bit low. On the other hand, make sure to apply to at least one or two "safety schools," where you'll be both happy and stand an excellent chance of getting accepted. A good rule of thumb is to apply to at least one "reach" school, a school that may be a long-shot to get into, but one where you'd love to go, at least one "safety school," and a few "good fit" schools in between.

After you've listed the schools where you'll apply, get the applications and figure out when each of them is due. It may be a good idea to make a list of deadlines, both early and regular, and hang it somewhere in your room. Many schools allow you to download their applications from their Web sites. Others send them to you in the mail; if this is the case, make sure you request the application in plenty of time to fill it out carefully and send it in. Whatever you do, make sure you get your applications in on time. Many schools won't even look at applications they receive late, so make deadlines a priority.

Different schools accept applications in a variety of ways. A brief description of the major types of applications follows:

- Rolling Admissions: Most large public schools and many less-selective colleges accept "rolling applications," which means they process applications continuously, in the order they receive them. You hear back from the school a few weeks after you send in your application. Though these schools often accept applications into the spring, it is important to send in your application early because admittance often becomes more challenging as these schools accept more and more students. Try to send in applications to schools with rolling deadlines as early as you can.

- Regular Decision: Colleges that don't offer rolling admissions typically require all your application materials to be sent by a specific date, usually in December or early January. The applications are processed and evaluated all at the same time, so while it is still a good idea to send in your application materials early, there is no automatic advantage to applying as soon as you can, as there is with rolling admissions. Whereas with rolling admissions, you'll hear back from the college within a few weeks, with regular decision all applicants hear back from the school at the same time. Many schools have separate parts of the application with different deadlines, so be prepared to organize your calendar so as not to miss any deadlines. Acceptances and rejections get mailed in late March or early April.

- Early Decision: Some schools offer an early decision option as part of their regular decision program. However, a recent push by presidents of several top universities (including Harvard, Stanford, Yale, and others) is working to erode this option since it may hurt economically disadvantaged students who would need to compare financial aid packages in making their decision. Typically available at more selective colleges, the early-decision program allows you to apply to one school by mid-October or November. The school will then respond by mid-December either with an acceptance, rejection, or deferral. An acceptance to a school under an early decision program is binding. This means that when you apply early decision, you sign a contract stating that you absolutely commit to attending that school if you are accepted. Failure to comply with the agreement can lead to unpleasant consequences like being blackballed from other schools. Rejections are final. A deferral means that the admissions committee will wait to make a decision about your application until they see what the regular pool of applicants is like. If you are deferred from an early decision acceptance but are accepted with the regular pool, the contract is no longer binding, and you may choose to attend a different school.

  Early decision does have some advantages. By expressing a clear interest in one school, you may gain some advantage in admissions, and if accepted you'll already know where you're going to school in December. However, by no means feel that you need to apply to a school under an early decision commitment. You should not apply to a school early decision unless you are totally, completely, positively sure that the school is your first choice, and you should not apply early decision if you feel like your credentials will improve significantly during your first semester of your senior year. Rejections under early decision are final, so if you think your application will be stronger after another semester, you should wait until you can provide the best application possible.

- Early Action: Early action has become an increasingly common option at schools across the country. Like early decision, early action offers applicants a chance to find out in December if they've been admitted. However, the acceptance is not binding; if you get accepted to another school in April that you would prefer to attend, you're welcome to do so. This provides a convenient alternative for students who want to hear back from a school as soon as possible, but aren't ready to commit to attending a particular school right away. Some institutions, such as Stanford and Yale, now offer single-choice early action programs. Under these plans, acceptance is still nonbinding, but students may not submit an early application (early action or early decision) to any other institution. This allows early applicants to compare financial aid packages from the regular round of admissions before making a decision.

Once you know when your applications will be due, it's time to start filling out the paperwork, either on actual paper or online. The latter is becoming increasingly common. There are a few general guidelines to follow. First, read the entire application carefully before you begin. Plan what you are going to say in each section before you write anything. It is a great idea to make a photocopy of the application to "practice" on before you fill out the official form, although applying online means you can go back and change your answers before the final submission. Always fill out or type the application yourself. If you're going to handwrite the application, try to use the same pen for the entire thing, to remain consistent in ink color and thickness. If you're going to use a printer, use a standard font like Times New Roman or Arial, and use the best printer you can find. Presentation and neatness count. If the application specifically suggests that you handwrite anything, be sure to do so, but draft exactly what you're going to write on scrap paper so that you don't have to make any corrections on the actual application.

More and more colleges nationwide are coming to accept the Common Application in lieu of applications specifically tailored for their schools. With a standard format and several general essays, you can fill out this application—online or on paper—once and submit it to any of the participating schools. It makes the application process somewhat less burdensome and time-consuming, although you may still want to consider tweaking essays to better fit the demands of each individual college. Some colleges will also have a Supplement to the Common Application specific to each college with additional questions.

Applications are usually divided up into several sections. All of them are important, and you should use all of them to your advantage. The following explanations of the application sections include some things you should remember when filling out your application:

- Personal Information: This section is fairly straightforward. It asks for general information about you, your school, and your family. Since all applications will ask for pretty much the same information, it's a good idea to keep it all on an index card so that you can easily reference it whenever you need to. This section often includes a question about race. Although this question is optional, you can go ahead and answer it; it won't hurt you, and the answer could help you. If you do answer, don't try to stretch the truth; answer it the way you would on a census form. Legal debates about affirmative action have gotten a lot of attention in recent years, but you still should not worry about answering this question.

- Standardized Tests: This is another relatively easy section to fill out. Most applications require you to fill in your test scores here, but also require you to have copies of your scores sent from the testing companies to the admissions offices. Make sure you do this in enough time for the test scores to arrive at the admissions office well before applications are due. Also, be sure you pay attention to which tests are required by your school. Some schools don't require test scores at all, others require either SAT Reasoning and Subject Tests or ACT scores, and still others specify which they want. Be sure your school receives all of the scores that it needs.

- Extracurricular Activities: This is the first section where your personality and accomplishments can shine through; be sure to make the most of it. Your extracurriculars allow the admissions office to see what you do when you're not studying. Sports, clubs, publications, student government, jobs, and volunteer positions are examples of some of the activities that fall into this category. Make sure to follow directions carefully when filling out this section. Some schools want you to write your activities directly on the form; others allow you to attach a typed list to the application instead. If you have the option to type a list, it's a good idea to do so, even if the rest of your application is handwritten. It looks neater, you'll have more space for all your activities, and you can just print out a copy of the list for each school that requests it. Just make sure to adapt the list to the particular requirements of the school. If the application instructs you to list your activities in chronological order, do so. Otherwise it is best to list activities in order of their importance to you.

A few final words about extracurriculars—quality is more important than quantity. It is infinitely better to have long-term involvement and leadership positions in a few activities than it is to join a thousand groups to which you devoted only an hour a month. Admissions officers can tell when you're just trying to pad your résumé with activities. They look more highly on passion and commitment to a few activities that reflect who you are and what interests you. You're also more likely to stand out to admissions officers if you have dedicated your time to an activity or subject that few others have explored. Admissions officers come across countless tennis captains and student-body presidents, but few national kayaking champions.

- Transcript: Your transcript is a window into your academic history. Admissions officers look at your grades and class rank, along with the types of classes you've taken. A high GPA is important, but so is the number of AP or Honors courses you've had. Colleges look for students who challenge themselves. At this point you can't go back and fix that C you got in freshman biology, but you can do a few things to make your transcript look as good as possible. First, make sure everything is accurate. Check that your grades are correct and that every honors class you have taken is listed as such. Second, remember that colleges will see your grades from senior year. Don't pad your schedule with blow-off courses; make sure to continue to take challenging classes. Try not to let yourself develop a serious case of "senioritis," because admissions committees will think that you don't take academics seriously. Also, if you received a poor grade in a particular class because of a certain situation, or you struggled all of sophomore year because someone you loved passed away, feel free to write an additional essay explaining any vast discrepancies. Lastly, request transcripts from your high school as soon as you can. They can take a while to print, and you don't want your application to be late because you did not get your transcript in time.

- Recommendations: Many schools request letters of recommendation from teachers, coaches, or other adults who know you well. These letters let the admissions officers see how others view you and your potential. Most people will be happy to write a good recommendation for you. If a teacher doesn't feel comfortable recommending you, he or she will most likely not agree to write a letter for you. So don't worry about a teacher trashing you behind your back; it probably won't happen.

Do think carefully about whom you choose to write these letters, though. You want to choose teachers who know you personally and with whom you have a good relationship. It's a good idea to choose teachers in your strong subjects, but it's also important to demonstrate some diversity of interest. For example, it is better to have your English teacher and your physics teacher write recommendations than it is to have two math teachers write them. Whomever you choose, make sure to provide them with plenty of time to write and revise a strong recommendation. You may even want to contact them before the summer of your senior year and let them know you'd like them to write on your behalf. That will give them ample time to write a shining letter! Many colleges want your teachers to send recommendations in separate from the rest of your application. If so, don't forget to give teachers a stamped and addressed envelope in which to send it. Be assertive; there's nothing wrong with reminding your teachers about the recommendation, and asking before the deadline if they'd gotten it done. Most teachers are careful about these deadlines, but it does not hurt to make sure. And don't forget to thank the people who have done such a big favor for you!

Additionally, most recommendation forms have a line asking you to waive your right to see the recommendation. You should probably sign it. Signing the waiver shows confidence that your teachers respect you and gives the recommendation more credibility. Finally, though most schools only require two recommendations from teachers, some allow you to send additional recommendations from others who know you well. Though by no means required or necessary, this is a good opportunity for students with significant activities outside of school-affiliated activities to get people like coaches, art tutors, or employers to say something helpful. Don't go overboard on these though; one extra recommendation is more than enough. Content is more important than the person who writes it. It's not impressive to get your state senator to write a recommendation for you if he's never met you before.

- The Essay: The college essay strikes fear in the hearts of high school seniors every fall, but you should not think about it as something scary. Instead, consider it an opportunity to show your wonderful, special, unique personality while telling the admissions officers a bit about yourself. If you give yourself plenty of time and have some fun with it, it can actually be the most enjoyable part of your application.

Think about your topic carefully, but do not kill yourself trying to come up with a topic that you think an admissions officer will like. It's always a good idea to write about something that is meaningful to you. If you feel strongly about the topic, it will show through in your writing, and that will catch an admissions officer's attention. Too many students write about a class project or winning the state championship—try to describe experiences that are less common. You want your personality and your passion to shine through. Though it might seem obvious, it's worth restating that you should be sure to answer whatever question the application asks. Sometimes you can reuse an essay for more than one school, but don't try to make an essay fit a topic just so you don't have to write another one. And be prepared to write several different essays if you're applying to a lot of schools.

Once your topic is chosen, give yourself enough time to write a good rough draft. It's sometimes intimidating to begin writing, but just put your pen to paper (or fingers to keyboard) and start. It doesn't matter what your draft looks like at first; you'll have plenty of time to correct and edit it later. Since the essay is the part of the application where you can be yourself, write in a way that feels natural to you, whether that's humorous, serious, or something completely different. Your essay should give colleges an idea of who you really are. Being honest with yourself and schools makes it more likely you'll end up somewhere that is a good fit. You should never submit a first draft to a college. Revise your essay a few times, both for style and for content. If the application gives you a word limit, stick to it.

Once you feel confident about the essay, it's a good idea to have a teacher, parent, older sibling, or counselor look over it for you. They can help you both find technical mistakes in spelling and grammar and point out places where you could be more clear in your content. By all means have others help you out with your essay in these ways, but under no circumstances should you ever, ever let anyone else write your essay for you. Not only is this dishonest, admissions officers read thousands of essays every year and have a good eye for essays that do not seem to be written by a particular student. While they probably won't be able to pinpoint why they're uncomfortable with a particular essay, they could be left with a negative feeling about your application. Once your essay has been drafted, revised, edited, and perfected, you can either handwrite it on the application form, or, if the school allows, you can attach a typed version to the form. However, almost all college applications are also available online, allowing you to simply insert the text into the online form or upload the document.

Once your application is complete, put a stamp on the envelope (or click that "submit" button that's been haunting you) and pat yourself on the back. Your application was honest, well-thought-out, neat, and will show the admissions committee who you are. Although you should make sure that the admissions office has received all of your materials, whether through a confirmation email or a phone call, there is not much left to stress out about. Once the application is in the mail, it's out of your hands, so kick back, relax, and enjoy the end of your senior year. After all that work, you deserve it.

The Wait

There is probably nothing anybody can say to you at this point to make you feel secure and confident regarding your applications. Your worries of the last few months about application deadlines and teacher recommendations are now petty concerns, replaced with the general unease that comes with the uncertain ground of your applications and your fate resting in the hands of various admissions offices across the state and country. You are finished with the applications but have only just begun the long road of anxiety.

Well, all is not lost. While it is nearly impossible to distract you from the near-constant pressure of the uncertainty regarding your future, we can at least let you know a little more about what is going on in the office.

Your application will arrive and most likely be put into an anonymous-looking, plain envelope. It will then be given to the admission officer who is in charge of your district or school. In some larger schools, you will not get much individual attention: There are often grade and SAT/ACT score cutoffs that they use to determine who gets admitted. With limitations on resources and thousands of applications pouring in, this is usually the only way they can manage the process in the given time frame. In smaller, private schools that can afford it, your application will be considered much more closely. Generally, your application will be read by up to three or four officers. Some schools use a numbering system to rate your academic record, your standardized test scores, and your extracurricular activities. There are some "bonus points" that you may end up with for uncontrollable variables such as your economic or racial background, or your relationship to an alumnus of the school.

Mostly, your application will speak for itself. While some schools weigh academics over extracurriculars, others might want to see high levels of community involvement or strong standardized test scores. This is where things are entirely out of your control. Each school is looking for a diverse group of students. The schools keep their academic standards relatively high, while looking for people from every possible background with every possible interest. If there happen to be 20 other students just like you from Houston, Texas, with 2100 SATs, a 3.5 GPA, roles in several school plays, and playing time on the varsity basketball team, all 20 will probably not be accepted. Likewise, if you happen to be the only student applying with a 1740 SAT, 2.8 GPA, and who founded a nonprofit organization to help teach English to needy children in Africa, you would probably look more unique and attractive to the admissions officer. It is fantastically frustrating, but in the end much of this process is out of your control. You are not only competing to be good enough for a school, but you are competing against everybody else who is applying to the school. Admissions officers are quick to admit that they turn away an incredible number of qualified applicants every year; enough, in fact, to more than fill two separate classes of equal strength. The decision process, therefore, often seems arbitrary. You may end up on the wait list of one of your safety schools, and find yourself accepted at the strongest school you applied to. You simply cannot know what is going to happen until you receive the letters. Most schools are constantly adjusting their criteria in order to admit what they see as the most accomplished and vibrant student body possible.

When the decision has been made, the myth is generally true: Big, thick envelopes often have big admit letters inside. The thin ones often bring bad news. You will probably be receiving a mix of these, so don't let a poor first response get you down. You may end up knowing the decision before the envelope ever reaches your mailbox. Each year, more schools are letting students find out their acceptance status online.

The good news is that thin envelopes sometimes bring news of a place on the wait list. The last thing you want to do in this situation is anger the admissions office. Surely, a place on the wait list is disappointing. There are only two things that can help you get off, however. First and foremost, the best you can hope for is a lot of luck. Your eventual admission depends a lot on how many people reject their offers of admission. The second factor is how you act: Admissions offices like to see people eager to attend their school. A simple letter stating your excitement about the school and your eagerness to attend may help nudge things in your direction. Anything pestering or negative directed at the admissions office will ensure you a rejection letter. In the end, you should choose the school where you feel most comfortable. The best advice we can offer you is to follow your instincts. If you get some kind of feeling about a school, go with it! There is no better reason out there to make a decision. For now, sit back and relax. It's your senior year, your very last semester in high school. While you can't start failing your classes now, there is plenty of room left for you to chill out. Do what you can to forget about your applications and instead think about how you can make the most out of your last couple months of high school. Be proud that your applications are finished and go out and have some fun!

The Money

Best case scenario: you get into the college of your dreams. But what if you get into the college of your dreams only to realize you cannot pay for it. With many of the nation's most expensive colleges quickly passing the $35,000 annual tuition mark, adding up to $140,000+ for a four-year education (not to mention room and board), it is no wonder that many students are talking as much about finances as they are about SAT scores. Although few families can afford this expensive price tag, especially if there is more than one member of the family attending college, there are many resources to aid families in paying for college. You should never hesitate to apply to a college simply because of its "sticker price." Many colleges meet most, if not all, of a family's financial need with a combination of scholarships, grants, loans, and work-study programs.

The most important step you can take as a student is to openly discuss your family's financial situation at the outset of your college search. Talk about how much your family is able to pay for college, how much your parents are willing to take out in loans, and other financial topics. By initiating this discussion with your family, you are showing them that you are both responsible and sensitive to your family's financial situation.

Your biggest advantage in the financial aid game is to be organized. As you will find out, there are many forms that you must fill out in order to even begin applying for financial aid. Getting organized helps you to see exactly where you stand in the financial aid process. The money is not going to land on your doorstep, so you have to be proactive in looking for it. There are plenty of resources available to you, but you have to know where to look for them.

A good place to start is with your high school guidance counselor. Counselors have knowledge and experience in helping students like yourself get into college and pay for college. Oftentimes, they receive information from colleges regarding scholarships and will post them around the school. Take note of these announcements and fill out the applications as soon as possible. The applications can be time-consuming, but if you are well-organized, there should be no problem. The following Web sites also provide useful information for students seeking financial aid: www.finaid.org and www.fastweb.com. The more persistent and diligent you are in your search, the better your chances will be for finding the resources you need.

The best sources for financial aid are the colleges themselves. Colleges oftentimes earmark large sums of money specifically for financial aid. Many colleges also receive money from federal and private sources for financial aid purposes. Scholarships come in a variety of forms, including need-based, merit, and achievement awards. You will need to look at what types of financial aid the schools that you are considering offer. Be aware of which colleges offer only need-based financial aid packages and which colleges offer merit and/or achievement scholarships. The policies and practices at each school can vary significantly, so it is important that you have the information you need.

Carefully read the bulletins provided by the colleges you are considering. If you have any questions, e-mail or call the admissions office or financial aid office right away. Find out what the colleges' admissions policies are regarding financial aid applicants. Some of the nation's wealthier schools have need-blind admissions, which means that you are considered for admission without taking into account your family's ability to pay. However, at some schools, financial need may play a part in the final admission decision, especially in borderline cases where preference may be given to those with the ability to pay. Even if you do not think you can afford it, apply to the school and for the financial aid. Then, just wait and see. You might be pleasantly surprised. Sometimes it is cheaper to attend a more expensive college because they often provide superior aid packages. Of course, this is not always the case, but it does prove that you should never decide against a school because of money until you have a financial aid offer (or rejection) in your hand.

As a financial aid applicant, you will soon notice all that paperwork involved. Most schools require you to file a standardized need analysis form to determine an expected family contribution (EFC). Depending on the school, the form will either be the College Board's Profile form or the U.S. Department of Education's Free Application

for Federal Student Aid (FAFSA), or in some cases, both. The school will also have its own financial form for you to fill out, which you have to send along with your family's income tax forms for verification. The school will determine a reasonable family contribution for one year. (The student is also usually expected to contribute at least $1,000 from summer earnings.) To come up with an estimate, a formula established by Congress is used. The formula takes into account family income, expenses, assets, liabilities, savings accounts, and other data. The cost of attendance minus this expected family contribution yields an approximate financial need. The school then designs a financial aid package that may consist of a low-interest, federally-guaranteed loan, a work-study job, and a combination of different types of grants. This would lead one to believe that all packages would be similar, yet this is not always the case. Even though all schools receive the same input data, they do not all use the same formula. The family contribution will thus vary slightly, but there should not be a big difference. The difference in aid packages comes mainly from the way the school issues money. Some schools may require you to get more loans, or they might give you more money.

Some schools will always make better offers than others. Some wealthier schools guarantee to meet the full "demonstrated" need of every applicant that they accept. At other colleges, however, the financial aid package may leave an "unmet" need that you will have to cover on your own. In unfortunate cases like these, students can bear the extra financial burden or choose a college that gives them a better offer.

There are a few things that you can do to improve your chances of receiving an adequate financial aid package from a school. First of all, be efficient in getting all of the forms in as early as possible. Some schools have a limited supply of funds available for financial aid, and the earlier they look at your application, the better your chance of receiving a larger share. Getting your forms in early shows a good-faith effort on your part, and schools are more likely to be cooperative with you if they feel you are being cooperative with them. Another thing you can do is write a letter to the financial aid office explaining any special family circumstances that are not reflected on the financial aid forms. These can include a recent death in the family or the need to support an aging relative. If you do not let the school know about such situations, there is no way they can take them into account.

If a school offers you a financial aid package that you consider inadequate despite your best efforts to let them know about your family situation, all is still not lost. After you have been accepted at the school, make a polite call to the school's financial aid office. If you noted any special circumstances either on the financial aid form or in a separate letter, ask if they took them into account when determining the award. Sometimes letters or comments get overlooked in the haste to get the aid awards out on time. If they say they took the circumstances into account, or if you did not mention any, tell them you would really like to attend the school but do not think it will be possible without more aid. If another school has offered you more aid, mention that, especially if the school is a competitor of the one you're talking to. Calling may not help, but they are not going to withdraw your acceptance once you are in.

If you are eligible for money on the basis of need, then the school may list some federal government assistance. The first of the types of federal government assistance are grants. Grants do not have to be paid back, unlike loans, but they are also harder to obtain. The federal government offers two grants: the Federal Pell Grant and the Federal Supplemental Education Opportunity Grants. You have to demonstrate "exceptional" financial need for either, but the latter is harder to obtain since the government does not guarantee as much. A Pell Grant is as high as $4,050, and the FSEOG is as high as $4,000 annually.

The federal government also offers lower-interest loans. If you demonstrate "exceptional" financial need, you may be eligible for a Perkins Loan, which can be loaned at 5 percent interest up to a maximum of $4,000. There are two types of Stafford Loans, one subsidized and the other unsubsidized. The subsidized Stafford Loan is only for people who demonstrate financial need, and it has a fixed rate of 6.80 percent interest. The government pays for the interest while you are in school and during the grace period after you graduate. The unsubsidized loan is for those who do not demonstrate financial need, and they have to pay interest the whole time. There is also a new loan called the Federal Direct Student Loan which is just like the Stafford except that the lender is the federal government and not a bank.

There is also a federal government sponsored loan for parents called the PLUS loan. It is particularly valuable for those who qualify for little or no financial aid. Each year, parents are allowed to borrow the full amount of tuition less any financial aid the student receives. The loan requires good credit, repayment while the child is still in school, and interest rates that are not far from market rates. Still, it can help to ease the burden on middle-class families.

You will also probably be required to take a job through the federal work-study program. Many applicants worry that working part-time will detract from studying or, equally important, playtime. Yet, if you work on campus, you certainly will not be the only one: Most colleges report that about half of their students hold term-time jobs. It is possible to take a full load of courses, participate in extracurricular activities, and work 10 or 15 hours per week, all while maintaining a good grade point average. Although freshmen tend to get the least exciting jobs on campus, in later years you may well find yourself working on interesting research, in a lab, or in a library.

Many private colleges also provide scholarships based on academic, athletic, or artistic ability. As competition among colleges for the best students intensifies, more and more colleges are offering lucrative merit awards to well-qualified students. There are many excellent schools, including many state universities, that offer merit scholarships in ever-increasing numbers. The best sources for information are your high school counselor and state Department of Education.

Be sure not to overlook the millions of dollars of aid available from private sources. Organizations ranging from General Motors to the Knights of Columbus offer money for college, often as prizes to assist students from your community. Sometimes large companies offer scholarships to children of their employees, so have your parents find out if their employers have such programs. There are also several scholarships out there related to specific majors, religions, or even ethnic heritage. Or if you scored very high on the PSAT, you could be in the running for a National Merit Scholarship. There is often a catch to merit-based awards, however: If you qualify for awards from private sources, your school will often deduct some or all of the amount from any need-based aid you receive.

In the past two decades there has also been a revival of interest in ROTC (Reserve

Officers Training Corps) programs. These scholarships from the four branches of the armed forces help pay for tuition, books, and room and board during college. When you graduate, you are committed to anywhere between four and eight years of reserve or active duty, depending on the program. As the supply of financial aid declines and the cost of college education continues to climb, more and more students are coming to see ROTC scholarships as worthwhile. However, be very thorough when investigating ROTC programs at different schools. Some colleges tend to be more antimilitary, and you may find yourself part of a controversial program. Even so, the benefits of the program can be substantial for a student who joins after careful consideration and research.

More and more, federal aid is being reserved exclusively for the very needy. Many families with incomes over $35,000 who qualify for PLUS loans must now pass a needs test to get Stafford Loans. Yet, if you play your cards right, your family should not have to undergo severe financial hardship to put you through school.

Advice for Transfers

If you are already in college and are thinking about transferring to another school, the preceding advice is mostly old news to you. Theoretically you know what to do now, but there are actually a number of new considerations that all potential transfers should keep in mind.

There are plenty of reasons students cite for transferring. Perhaps you don't feel comfortable in the social or political environment at your school. Maybe your academic interests have changed, and the programs available at your current college are not extensive enough. It could also be an issue of being too far from or close to home. Whatever the reason, it's important to figure out what it is about your college experience that doesn't work, so you can find one that does.

You're about to embark on a daunting and sometimes disappointing process, so be sure to think it through beforehand. It can be easy to blame your school if you are unhappy. But issues with the college experience itself, such as roommate problems or work overload, may be the real source of your dissatisfaction. If so, you may be able to work out these troubles without transferring.

Don't assume that you'll necessarily be happy at another university. One student left Stanford in search of "greener pastures." Instead, she found New England "cold, gray, and without pastures at all." According to another student, "It's a big risk. You have to really want to leave where you are or really want to go where you will be." There are no guarantees that you will be better off at another school, and the process itself may make things even less satisfactory for you. You might want to take a semester or two off to reevaluate your situation, or think about giving a more wholehearted effort to making your current situation work.

Most schools accept transfer students who have up to two years of credit at another university. It may be safer, however, to transfer after your first year, because your old university will be more likely to take you back if you change your mind. One student advised that it is better to take a leave of absence from your original school than to withdraw completely.

The application process is also slightly different for transfer students. Be aware that colleges tend to consider a transfer student in a different light from a high school senior. To your advantage, admissions officers tend to look upon transfer applicants as mature and motivated candidates who have the potential to make a significant impact on campus. However, few students tend to leave top private universities, so the acceptance rate for transfers at top schools is much, much lower than that for first-time applicants. The situation can be different at larger state schools.

Each school looks for different students, but grades, recommendations, and the essay that explains why you want to transfer are usually the three most important parts of the application. Make sure that you find classes with professors who will be able to write you good recommendations. Standardized test scores and extracurriculars are less important. One exception to this may be if you decide to take time off and do something exceptional during your time away from school. Keep in mind that your college transcript is incredibly important. As much as you might want to leave your school, do not ease up on your academics. If staying an extra semester will help boost your academic record, you may want to consider holding off on your move.

Because colleges will expect you to prove that you have developed during your first year or two of college and to show why you absolutely cannot stay at your old school, your essay (and interview if you can arrange one) is critical. Be definite and clear about your reasons for transferring and what you expect to find in a new environment. Academic reasons are best; personal ones are only as convincing as you can make them. It also helps if the department in which you want to major is undersubscribed at the new school.

Make sure you know a lot about the school you are applying to. Not only will this show through in your application, but you will also be much more prepared for the experience ahead. If what you need is an active, social campus in which to get involved, then make sure that you will be guaranteed on-campus housing. If you are going to need financial aid, check and see that it will be available for transfer students. Also, be sure you look into how your credits will transfer at the new school. Will you get credit toward a major, or only toward graduation? If you don't have a major already picked out, it can be very difficult to graduate in four years.

Before submitting the paperwork, make sure that you are confident in your decision to transfer, and be ready for anything. It's important to have a backup plan for the upcoming year in case you don't get accepted. Come up with a plan for what you would do with a year off, or be prepared to make another run at getting the most out of your school. If everything does work out for you, make sure you have covered all of the bases before you commit to the new school. Making the decision to transfer is not a walk in the park, but you shouldn't let this deter you. If you are truly unhappy with your current situation, it can be a very rewarding and worthwhile route.

The College Spectrum

At first glance, the sheer number of colleges included in this book may seem a bit overwhelming—clearly you would never consider applying to over 300 schools. Since colleges and their student bodies vary in so many ways, it can be difficult to identify schools at which you would feel comfortable. One piece of advice is to be aware of the general social, political, and academic trends many schools are currently experiencing. Issues such as affirmative action, the fairness of standardized testing, expanding financial aid and early application programs have become heated topics of discussion on countless college campuses. It can be helpful to figure out where certain schools stand in terms of these trends. Another way to get some perspective on different colleges is to identify where they stand in terms of various criteria—to figure out where they fall on a continuum that we call the College Spectrum. Most importantly, it is not our place to judge which types of schools are best, but instead to present a variety of perspectives and observations that can help you with the decision-making process. Here are some of the many areas you can consider in comparing different schools.

Size

The total undergraduate enrollments of the schools in this book range from 26 at California's Deep Springs College to nearly 40,000 at Ohio State University. Considering the size of the campus you want to attend is helpful in the initial narrowing-down process; the feel of a school can be very dependent on the number of students around. There are two main parts of your experience that will be affected by the size of the school you choose: academics and social life.

Academically, class size and the accessibility of senior faculty are two important areas of comparison that tend to vary between large and small schools. In this case, smaller colleges decidedly have the advantage simply because a smaller population usually translates into smaller classes. Students at small schools have great opportunities for one-on-one student-faculty interaction. At large schools, students are more likely to complain of impersonal instruction and "being treated as a Social Security number."

To make up for this apparent disadvantage, many larger schools offer special programs intended to create a more intimate sense of community among professors and students. Different universities have different approaches. Some offer honors programs for a limited number of students, and some house all the students who are in special programs together. Generally, students in such programs all take the same or similar courses—most of which are small, discussion-oriented classes. Bear in mind that many honors and special programs are highly selective; do your best to make a realistic assessment of your chances to be accepted. Additionally, don't be taken in by the glossy pictures in admissions booklets: If you are considering a large university, take a close look at the quality of its special programs. If you are seriously considering one of these programs, try to speak with an undergraduate currently participating in the program—he or she may be able to paint a more accurate picture of what it is like. Another important factor to remember is that no matter how large a school is, not all of the classes it offers will be huge and overcrowded, and some of the bigger classes will break into smaller discussion groups. Thus, although most schools do have some very large classes, you can almost always find small ones of interest. But in this case, it is important to remember that in bigger schools, it is often difficult to get into small classes as an underclassman.

Also, pay attention to who teaches the classes. At most liberal arts colleges, only professors do. Many large universities pad their student-faculty ratios by including graduate students, or they advertise discussion classes that turn out to be taught by people who are still working toward a Ph.D. By reading guides such as this one and by talking to students, you can find out roughly how many graduate students teach and whether or not senior professors teach undergraduates at all. Keep in mind that having younger, less experienced professors teach is not always a bad thing. Many times, courses taught by graduate students allow for a rapport between teachers and students that does not develop with some of the stodgier old professors. However, if graduate students appear to dominate the teaching, even if only for the freshman year, you should definitely consider this as you make your decision. These facts will also give you a sense of how much personal attention the typical undergraduate student receives from the administration.

For highly specialized fields that require extensive facilities, the resources at small schools are generally limited. Larger universities usually have the funding to sponsor more expensive research facilities and to draw renowned professors to their specialized programs. For facilities not associated with academics, such as the gym or the library, size and showiness are not nearly as important as accessibility. You will not care how many racquetball courts the gym has as long as one is available when you want to play and it's not a three-mile walk away. Instead of asking how many volumes there are in the library, find out whether everyone has full access to all its resources, and if the library holds long hours. Since they cater to so many students with diverse interests, large universities most often offer a wide range of facilities.

Social life, too, is affected by the size of the school. Consider carefully what kind of social life you plan to have and which type of school would be more conducive to your interests. The setup of freshman housing will play a significant role in your social experience; your first-year roommates and hallmates often become some of your closest friends. It's likely that the people you associate with will also be determined by your extracurricular interests—a sports team, a student newspaper, or student government. This tends to be especially true for universities that do not provide more than one year of campus housing.

The key is finding your own comfortable niche within any school. While there are usually more niches to be discovered in large colleges, finding yours may require some initiative. The larger the school, the more subgroups there are likely to be within the student body. Frats and sororities tend to be more abundant and popular on bigger campuses. An advantage to being a member of a very large community is that the supply of new faces never runs out. If you get tired of one circle of friends, you can always find another. But it is also important to keep in mind that when you are on your own in the midst of all those unfamiliar people, it is also possible to feel very lonely. On the other hand, small environments can be more welcoming and friendly. Small schools often have a greater sense of community and people can find that making friends is easier. But some students find that small schools can be a little too small, because "everybody knows everybody else's business." In that case, you may want to consider studying at a school where you won't necessarily know everyone's name.

One common misconception about smaller schools is that they are inevitably more homogenous and have less school pride or spirit. On the contrary, many of them, especially the more selective ones, have just as many different types of people as do most large universities, only in smaller numbers. Although larger schools, especially those with a big emphasis on athletics, may have tremendous school spirit, smaller ones foster their own brand of pride, usually stemming from rich tradition and a strong sense of community.

Schools come in all different sizes. No matter how big or small a school is, make sure it prioritizes what is important to you. Be sure to keep in mind both academic and social consequences of the size of your school: Both have the potential to drastically change your college experience.

Location

At some point, if not right away, you will find yourself thinking about the towns in which each of your college choices is located. Can you see yourself living there for four years? What sounds more appealing to you—a college where your dorm is surrounded by towering oak trees, or a college with easy access to shops and malls? Before you answer these questions, be sure you really understand the difference between urban and rural settings, and more importantly, how this difference will impact your college experience.

Often, what some students perceive to be "city life," "suburban life," or "life on the farm" is not the reality of what living at a college in one of these areas would be like. Many factors need to be considered in order to get an accurate idea of how location will affect your whole college experience.

Whether you've found your way through cornfields for 18 years, or you've wandered around Times Square by yourself since you were 10, going away to college, while exciting and rewarding, can also be an intimidating experience. Many people arrive at school the very first day completely oblivious to the opportunities and the challenges of being out of their town, their state, or their region. If you are from a rural area and are considering the big move to the city, expect adjustment (to noise, traffic, people, crime, the hectic pace), but try not to make or accept any assumptions about "the horrors" of city life. If you are from an urban area and are considering the peace and quiet of a smaller school tucked in the woods somewhere, also expect adjustment (to relatively silent nights, no movie theater or department store, the slower pace), but also try not to make or accept any assumptions about "life with the cows." Your thoughts about the location of the school should be balanced by the fact that every school will inherently have some sort of community; is this community, along with the city the school is located in, right for you?

College is a great time to try new things, including a new location—a new city, a new state, maybe a whole new region of the United States or beyond. In general, you do need to be aware of certain broad characteristics of each type of campus. At a campus in a big city, for example, there is a greater chance that on-campus nightlife will be non-existent, as everyone will head to clubs and bars to relax. Yet after a week of academic work, extracurricular activities, dorm parties, visiting speakers, football games, and the multitude of other school-sponsored events, being in an urban environment means there is still the option of seeing a Broadway show or going to a world-renowned museum. As for a campus in a smaller town, the exact opposite may be true. Without anything to do around town, students will have all of their activities and create all of their own nightlife on campus. While you may sometimes wish you did have the major clubs and bars, the tight-knit community that forms among students at the school may very well more than compensate for those longings. Whichever setting you do end up choosing should depend on your own reflections on how you would feel in those surroundings.

Another point to consider is how comfortable you would be living so close to or so far away from home. Does leaving the Pacific Ocean for the Atlantic Ocean sound like a real adventure, or does being even two hours away from your family make your hands start to tremble? Are you at a point in your life where you still want to be with all of your friends going to the same school near your hometown, or can you not wait for all of your new friends and your "whole new life" far from home? Distance is one of those factors that require thinking about everything in context. Your life will change in college, whether you pack your bags to travel far away or keep your room at home. Anywhere you end up, even if you do stay close to home, your old relationships will change at least a little bit. Make sure you are honest with yourself about your reasons for choosing a particular school. It may be helpful to talk to current students at the school to get a sense of where they came from and what they think about the location. It may also be helpful to come up with a list of positive and negative aspects of the school's location. Include everything that will affect your life: the weather, the people, the travel expenses, and the homesickness, without forgetting to take into account the school's own community. Life at college will require at least some adjustment, but it may be that exact adjustment which completes your college experience.

Private vs. Public

The question of whether to attend a public or private school is best answered through a cost-benefit approach. Don't worry, we know you haven't had Econ 101, so consider this a free lesson. Let's first divide the universities in the United States into three categories: large private, public, and small private.

The most obvious distinction between a private and a public university is the price tag. As the cost of a private school education continues to climb, public school is becoming an increasingly attractive option. However, in recent years the tuition gap has significantly diminished for those who are eligible for financial aid, as private schools have allocated increasingly more funds to aid packages. These packages are almost always a combination of loans and grants, meaning that they do not always diminish the cost of college, but simply postpone it to a future date.

Most top-tier private institutions have adopted need-blind admissions policies which means that they admit regardless of your ability to pay and then work with you to create a financial aid package that will allow you to attend. Princeton led the pack in this respect by announcing that it would replace loans with outright grants; soon many other colleges followed suit.

Smaller private schools, however, do not have the high-powered endowments necessary to fund such need-blind policies. In this area, public universities definitely have an advantage. Subsidized by state taxpayers, they offer an outstanding education at a fraction of its actual cost—everyone is basically a financial aid recipient.

If you do decide to break the bank and attend a private school, you will often be rewarded with smaller class sizes and greater student-teacher interaction. There is, however, a not-so-obvious advantage to small private colleges. At larger private or state universities much of the teaching duty has been increasingly placed on the shoulders of teaching assistants (graduate students). Additionally, at large private universities, professors must often devote a significant amount of time to research in order to stay ahead in their field. Small private colleges offer teaching environments in which the professors are not burdened with this dictum of publish or perish; they can devote all their time to teaching the material instead of contributing to it.

At college you will learn as much from your fellow students as you will from your professors, so it's important to consider the quality and diversity of the student body. This is an important consideration because at any good college, public or private, much of the valuable learning takes place outside of the classroom.

When deciding which type of school to attend, make sure you look beyond its label as either public or private. While some applicants consider attending a state university second-best when compared to an elite private school, others make a public institution their first choice. It is important to consider department-specific academic strengths along with the reputation of the university as a whole. Public schools such as UC Berkeley, UCLA, and University of Michigan rank among some of the top academic institutions, public or private, in the country. In the end, you should never be swayed too much by a school's private or public designation. Instead, try to choose the school that's best suited to you.

Coed or Single-Sex?

Since coeducation became the norm at American universities in the 1960s, the number of single-sex schools in the nation has dropped significantly. There are only four men's colleges remaining in this book: Deep Springs College, Hampden-Sydney College, Morehouse College, and Wabash College. The students here chose to attend mainly because of their belief that the absence of the opposite sex allows greater dedication to academics and a friendlier, more fraternal atmosphere. Tradition prevails at these all-male institutions, and men that work best in these atmospheres find themselves very content.

Women's colleges have similar reasons for existence as all-male colleges, but with a few twists. There are many more women's colleges, as the whole movement for women's education came later and is still firmly rooted in feminist beliefs. The most famous all-female schools are the Seven Sisters, a group of seven Northeastern colleges that self-organized in 1927 to promote single-sex education. The Seven Sisters—Barnard, Bryn Mawr, Mount Holyoke, Radcliffe (now folded into Harvard), Smith, Vassar (now coed), and Wellesley—hoped to compete with the image of the Ivy League schools.

Most women who attend single-sex colleges cite the supportive, nurturing environment as their college's greatest asset. In an arguably male-dominated culture, women's schools provide a learning environment where there is support for developing one's female identity, no academic competition with men, and numerous leadership opportunities. Women's colleges are usually very liberal, with a focus on current events and debates on different points of view.

There is no debate, however, about the fact that life at a single-sex institution is very different from life at a coed one. Because single-sex schools tend to be smaller, there are often fewer academic programs and resources than at larger coed colleges. Also, the atmosphere is somewhat contrived, since one of the sexes is missing. There are always outlets through which students can find the opposite sex, such as "brother universities," but the social life and vivacity of the campus is usually at a much "calmer" level than coed schools. For students who want the best of both worlds, there are a few colleges that are part of coed consortia. Women at Mount Holyoke and Smith can take classes at the neighboring Amherst and Hampshire Colleges and the University of Massachusetts; the women at Barnard are paired with the coed Columbia University; and Bryn Mawr allows its female students to explore academic offerings at Haverford and Swarthmore College.

Besides the actual experience, another thing to keep in mind is a certain stigma attached to many single-sex schools. Since the majority of these schools are extremely liberal, they are generally known for strong activism in women's and gay rights. This reputation exists despite the more conservative nature of some of the top academic single-sex schools. Whether accurate or not, this is another factor to consider in your choice.

Single-sex atmospheres can be ideal for some students, but not everyone seeks out such a college experience. Most college-bound seniors end up enrolling in coeducational schools, an environment that requires little adjustment. Issues of coed bathrooms and dormitories may concern you, but there are many different housing options, including single-sex floors and Greek houses, and administrators work to make you comfortable. Most campuses also feature organizations that encourage members of the same sex to bond with each other, including fraternities and sororities as well as advocacy groups (usually female). So after choosing whether a single-sex or coed college is right for you, wait for your institution to send you information on handling all the details.

Advising and Tutoring

The first few weeks of college can be confusing. There are placement tests to take, forms to fill out, questions about AP credits to ask, and parents to kiss goodbye. Many freshmen are often unaccustomed to the breadth of courses from which to choose. Also, it's hard to plan your academic year when you're in the midst of meeting new friends, moving into your dorm room, trying to go to as many parties as possible, and asking out that cute girl from pre-orientation. However, do not be daunted.

Almost all colleges provide students with faculty advisors for at least the first year. Their function is twofold: they can both rubber-stamp your schedule and be used as reference for everything from course selection to general questions about the college. Though most students agree that faculty advisors are usually only good for placing their John Hancocks on your schedule, there are a few who are adamant that faculty advisors do have some value. If you do not know what you want to major in from day one, don't worry, your advisor can help you plan your schedule and think things through.

If you still have unanswered questions, ask upperclassmen (often the best source of good, quick information). They can point you toward interesting classes, often-overlooked majors, and talented professors—but remember their advice is very much based on their personal experience. For more detailed, department-specific questions about graduation/major requirements, ask a faculty member in that department.

Once you have chosen your classes, remember that this is only half the battle! Fortunately, most colleges and universities offer tutoring resources free of charge to help you succeed. If you find yourself in a large class with a professor who rushes through the most important points in the last five minutes of lecture or have a nervous or unhelpful TA, you should consider getting a tutor. Professors' office hours are usually insufficient for detailed explanations. Even the brightest students can benefit from going over the subject matter now and again.

Many times tutors are graduate students or particularly advanced undergraduates proficient in that specific academic discipline. Having recently learned the material, they can often make it more accessible than a professor who has taught it for decades. When exam time rolls around, look to upperclassmen for old study guides and more general insight into acing specific courses.

A Minority Perspective

As a minority student or a person of color, there might well be some additional factors to consider in your decision. You may, for example, be searching for a school with a high population of students from a particular background or for a school with high overall diversity. A school with a large minority population may prove to be more supportive and even more comfortable. Regardless of size, a strong minority community can be helpful during the next four years and can even help reduce ignorance on some campuses.

Another factor to consider is the general attitude of both the administration and the student body. Unfortunately, racism still exists in many parts of society, but do not assume a defensive attitude while visiting schools. Instead, be aware of possible situations and attitudes that may make you feel excluded and uncomfortable. What might have seemed like a diverse college in the brochures may not seem so open-minded after all. Take note of how integrated the minority community is and what the school does to recognize and support other cultures. Some schools may foster a pressure to conform; if the school has a large population of a certain race, there may be a distinct sense of separatism. For some this may provide a stronger sense of belonging, while for others it will only increase the stress of college life.

To determine the true attitude of the administration, look at how it attempts to support the minority communities. Some schools assign ethnic counselors to help minority students adjust to college life. Some students appreciate this; others resent it. One student reported that her school was doing so much to accommodate her minority status she felt separated rather than integrated. Many students, however, get used to the idea of special resources and ultimately find them supportive. Another thing to look at is the extracurricular life. What kinds of organizations are there for specific minority groups or minority students in general? The school may have cultural centers and politically-oriented associations that focus on the traditional arts and dances of their culture. Examples of popular organizations that foster a sense of community among minority students include Movimiento Estudiantil Chicano de Aztlán (MEChA) for Chicano students; Native American Student Associations at campuses around the country; and Asian American Student Associations.

Besides cultural centers and politically-oriented associations, many schools have Greek organizations centered on celebration of heritage. This category includes the predominantly Jewish fraternity Alpha Epsilon Pi, the Asian sorority Sigma Phi Omega, and African American fraternity Alpha Phi Alpha. Other minority students choose to organize themselves around professional aspirations (National Association of Black Journalists) or religion (Asian American Christian Fellowship).

For African American students, an important decision may be whether to attend a predominantly black college over another school. Despite the improving financial situations of most private black colleges, you are likely to find better facilities and larger academic departments at other schools. Unfortunately, the continuing decline of federal funding is likely to exacerbate this situation,

since black colleges rely heavily on such resources. Nevertheless, many students choose to attend a predominantly black college for many of the same reasons other students choose to attend a single-sex school. Some black students find them a more congenial and accepting community that is more conducive to personal growth. Likewise, students often have a better chance to attain key leadership positions at a college where they do not have minority status. At a predominantly black school, the African American experience is one of the central issues on campus. What does it mean to be a black person in 21st century America? Of what importance is African American heritage? At predominantly black schools, these questions are addressed in a manner and with a commitment unrivaled by other institutions.

In this book, we include reports on five of the best-known predominantly black schools in the United States: Howard University in Washington, D.C.; Spelman and Morehouse Colleges in Georgia; Florida A&M University; and Tuskegee University in Alabama. For a more complete listing, we suggest you consult *The 100 Best Colleges for African American Students*, written by Erlene B. Wilson and published by Plume. An online resource under the name of Black Excel may also prove useful for African American students. Another school with an ethnic majority is the University of Hawaii, which is predominantly made up of Asian students.

Ultimately, you have to decide where you will feel most comfortable. Whatever your choice, it is important to remember that your ethnicity is an integral part of yourself and is not something you should have to compromise in choosing a school.

Sexual Minorities

The first question that a gay, lesbian, bisexual, or transgender student should ask when considering a college is the same one that straight students ask: where will I be the happiest and most comfortable for four years? Students planning on being openly gay at college will want to choose a campus where they can come out to their roommates, friends, and even professors without worrying about the consequences. But how can you tell after one or two trips to a college whether or not you'll get a positive reception?

The good news is that, as one transfer student put it, "there are sensitive people everywhere—at large schools and small ones." Another student said she sought out a campus with diversity, guessing that a diverse population "would create more understanding." But beyond these general guidelines, there are other aspects of campus life to observe. Check out a school's listing of organizations, for instance. A school with several gay alliances and clubs, for example, probably has a more accepting environment, even if you don't think you'll end up being active in any of them. One student pointed out that the surrounding community can be just as important. "Knowing that there were gay bars and events in the town made me more comfortable in my choice." The more town-gown interaction there is, the more important it is that a prospective student feels comfortable being gay in that city.

In looking for a school, all students search for a place with unlimited options. As a gay or lesbian student, the best college is going to be one where your opportunities are not constrained by your sexual orientation. As one gay member of a fraternity pointed out, "I wanted to join a frat in college, so it was important that I found a place where my sexuality wouldn't be as big a deal. . . ." In other words, there are countless schools where gay and lesbian students participate in every aspect of campus life—and fortunately it isn't too hard to track them down. This is not to say life for gay students is always perfect; gay students do risk running up against prejudices, but it is reassuring to know that gay and lesbian students at large and small schools, public and private, have managed to find their niche, be active members of the undergraduate community, and simply have a good time.

Politics

The level of political activism on a campus may affect how comfortable you are there. You will find that many schools have clubs of all alignments, and political journals of all bents as well, from the left-wing liberals to the Green Party to the ultraconservatives. Generally these partisan organizations are most active in presidential election years. If this is what interests you, you will have no trouble finding your political niche.

Forty years ago, political activism permeated college campuses. Today, the number of students strongly involved in politics on campus is generally a minority. One student remarked that a majority of her fellow students stay away from politics for social reasons: many people at her university look down on those with strong convictions because they assume them to be closed-minded. Instead of joining political organizations, many students channel their activism into volunteer programs that confront specific problems such as urban blight or environmental destruction. Usually, small liberal arts schools are the most politicized colleges. "At my school, you don't just put your name on name tags, you put your cause, your oppressor, your god, and your sexual orientation," said one student. Before selecting a school, you may want to see if it has a political forum that brings in outside speakers and organizes discussions and lectures.

Only ten years ago, campus activism was moving toward being institutionalized and domesticated. In recent years, however, concerns with the recent wars, healthcare reform, and environmental initiatives have since provoked an increasing amount of activity on behalf of students. Student protests, petitions, and marches have garnered much support as well as media recognition. Additionally, certain incidents and issues, particularly those involving racism and sexuality, receive community-wide attention. The gay and lesbian-rights activists at some schools sponsor a kiss-in where same-sex couples cluster around the campus's central promenade and make out. Gay rights, AIDS awareness, and race-related issues are commonly on the collegiate slate of activist causes. Today, to be politically correct (PC)—manifested by a tolerance for others' ideas and political affiliations and an attempt to be inoffensive to any and all groups in speech as well as in print—is something of a secondary issue. Although PC was a hot topic on campuses in the nineties, the debates on the spelling of "woman" and whether your roommate is disabled or "differently-abled" seem to have faded.

However, the PC movement's focus on the implications of language has pushed people—particularly educators—to reconsider the lens through which academic disciplines are typically approached. Many schools now require students to take courses that focus on non-Western cultures, or courses aimed at raising sensitivity to minority issues and concerns. More and more schools have started classifying "Women and Gender Studies" as a major, as well as "Latin American Studies" and "African American Studies." Courses and programs exploring Native American Studies have also begun to emerge.

By visiting a college you can quickly pick up on how important politics are to the student body. Read posters and skim student newspapers to gauge whether or not the political climate on that campus is right for you. The best schools may be those that can absorb all viewpoints, so that no matter what you think, there will be others who will embrace your thoughts, challenge them, or respect your decision not to vocalize them.

Pre-professionalism vs. Liberal Arts

Pre-professionalism is a term you will see repeated throughout this book. Not all curriculums are the same, and whether you will receive either a preprofessional or liberal arts education is determined both by the school you attend and the major you choose there.

Majors that do not lead directly to a specific career fall into the liberal arts category. Even if a student plans to be an accountant, for example, he or she might get a liberal arts degree in philosophy or English, and then go on to study accounting at the appropriate professional school. The goal of a liberal arts education is to teach students how to think creatively and analytically, preparing them to pursue any career.

There are pros and cons to both tracks. Some argue that a liberal arts education is the key to a solid education and to becoming a well-rounded individual. Others believe that a liberal arts degree can be a waste of four years and thousands of dollars for those who already have their career plans mapped out. Students from a liberal arts background may also have a more difficult time securing a job immediately after graduating, as they tend to lack both experience and specific skills. Many preprofessional programs require students to take general education courses in liberal arts departments. In fact, almost all colleges insist that you take some courses outside your chosen field.

If you don't yet know your interests well enough to decide which option is for you, you may be pleased to learn that the largest colleges and universities have both liberal arts and preprofessional students. The University of Michigan, for example, has a strong undergraduate school of business;

many students in Michigan's liberal arts school also plan to go into business eventually but are pursuing a B.A. in a more general field first. The case is similar with Cornell.

If you do know what you want from a school in terms of career preparation, then you may prefer to attend a preprofessional institution. But keep in mind that getting a liberal arts education and getting a good job are not mutually exclusive. Moreover many report that the learning environment at a preprofessional university is more competitive, and would therefore not be as enjoyable to a student who enjoys the intellectual exchange more common to liberal arts campuses.

Greek Life and Other Social Options

When choosing a college, you are choosing a place in which to live and learn. In this way the social life at colleges becomes a large factor in choosing your school and many people claim that when they visited colleges, the people they met made them love or hate the campus more than any other aspect. You will find that sometimes you just click with the students at a particular school. Although most schools are large enough to ensure you will find your social niche, it is also important to consider how the overall social atmosphere will affect you while you are there.

Collegiate life in the United States often conjures images of a social scene dominated exclusively by fraternities and sororities. While this is true of some schools, there are many schools where Greek life is either nonexistent or less central to college life than some would believe. Greek life can run the gamut from a dominating institution to a relatively unknown and tame element of college life. It is also true that while many fraternities and sororities have high levels of membership, some of the numbers are dropping across the country. This is due mostly to increasingly strict policies on campuses to curb hazing as well as alcohol abuse that has made Greek life so infamous in today's media.

Although the most widely publicized side of Greek organizations has to do with their partying habits, belonging to a Greek organization is not just for those who like to party. In fact, many organizations have reformed their policies to reduce or eliminate such practices as pledge hazing and many require that Greeks be dry at official functions (although that does not mean they cannot party together outside of meetings).

Beyond being a social group, Greek organizations offer many advantages to students including a nationwide network of alumni, community service opportunities, and housing (which is often very difficult to find for upperclassmen). The emphasis on community service is particularly important to most Greek organizations and most chapters have an office dedicated specifically to organizing the chapter to participate in local charitable activities. On some campuses, the fraternities and sororities are the most active social-service organizations.

In terms of housing considerations, most organizations are on campus and thus are financially supported by the school, national chapter, and students. Because of this, Greek houses are often some of the nicest housing available, as freestanding buildings with manicured lawns and beautifully decorated interiors. However, an increasing trend among colleges is to kick Greek organizations off campus. This trend is especially marked among fraternities that gain the reputation of being unkempt and raucous. Without campus funding, many of the organizations lose large amounts of their financial support and thus cannot run as well as those that are on campus.

Whether Greek life appeals to you or not, it is essential to know just how influential the Greek organizations are at each school you are considering. At some campuses, not rushing could seriously limit your social options. On the other hand, there are many schools where fraternities and sororities are most certainly not part of campus life and are regarded as conformist. There are also schools, especially among the Ivy League, where although Greek life is present, there is a strong residence system that fills many of the social functions that Greek organizations occupy elsewhere. As a rule of thumb, Greek life is more dominant at the largest schools where practical concerns keep the organizations strong and smallest at the most specialized schools where campus life is intimate enough that smaller social organizations may prove stifling.

However, even at the most Greek-dominated campuses, there are always other social outlets. Your interests will largely determine who your friends are. Therefore, you should choose a school that has groups that represent your interests. Greek organizations, athletics, cultural organizations, or theater groups can all be part of your college experience. The people you meet in these organizations often become some of your closest friends. Ultimately, the best way to tell if a school's social scene is right for you is to visit the campus or talk to friends who go there. Most college applicants worry that they will not find people like themselves when they get to college, but, when they get there, they realize that making friends was much easier than expected. Find what you think will be the right combination of organizations, Greek or otherwise, and you will meet the right people.

Security

Students are in college to learn and to take advantage of what their schools have to offer, and campus security efforts are one reflection of a school's commitment to making that possible. Crime in general is increasing on campuses across the country, from recent tragedies that made students question the safety of their own classrooms to the rising number of sexual assaults. In response to this trend, federal legislation has made it mandatory for all colleges receiving federal aid (which is almost every one) to publish crime statistics in several categories. At your request, the appropriate office (usually the public relations or admissions offices) at any college or university should release to you the crime count for the last calendar year. Many colleges have also taken measures to beef up security. If you visit a campus and notice very stringent security measures (at the University of Pennsylvania, for example, you have to show your ID just to get into the quadrangle), remember that this means two things: there is a need for security measures, and the administration is responding to this need.

There are a number of features that any safety-conscious campus should have. Doors to individual dorm rooms and to the building entrances should be equipped with locks. All walkways should have bright lights, not only so that you yourself can see, but so friends and classmates would be able to see you from a distance in case of danger. Another important security measure is a safety phone system with one-touch access to an emergency line. Each safety phone should have a distinct light to make it easily recognizable at night. Ideally, there should be enough units so that you are never more than half a block from a phone. For getting around campus late at night, colleges should provide bus service or student safety escorts, free of charge. At least one of these services should be available 24 hours a day and should travel to every possible destination on campus. Every school should employ some type of security guard, whether unarmed monitors in or near the dorms or full-time police officers responsive solely to students and the affairs of the college. At the beginning of the year, make sure you enter these phone numbers into your cell, although they should be clearly posted as well.

Security problems are not limited to urban campuses. Some rural schools have crime rates as high as the urban ones. The sad truth is that most nonviolent crimes are committed by other students, not outsiders. Why is campus crime such an issue now? College students are ideal targets—they keep expensive stereo and computer equipment in poorly guarded areas, and they often walk alone across dark, seemingly safe campuses.

It is important to understand that you cannot judge the safety of a campus simply by eyeing it from the safe confines of a brochure. Yet, by using a little common sense and preventive measures, the security problems of a given school should not prevent you from attending. By making yourself aware of potential problems and following the school's security guidelines, you can improve your chances of enjoying a safe four years.

Computers

Whether you are an art major, a computer science major, or an expert procrastinator, computers will be an important part of your college experience. Looking up information for that research paper due in 12 hours, searching for your classmate's e-mail address in the online directory, and downloading the next problem set from the class Web site are just a few examples of the countless ways that computers are a part of everyday life on campus. With that in mind, here are a few things to look for when evaluating a college's computing facilities:

24-Hour Computer Clusters: Make sure that there are at least a few accessible computer clusters to rely on when your computer or printer stops cooperating once you finally sit down to start your homework. Many people also like to work on their papers in computer clusters to get away from the distractions of their own room. Easily

accessible clusters with numerous, fast computers are always a plus.

Macs vs. PCs: Although compatibility issues are largely a thing of the past, the networks at some schools may be preferentially built for Macs or PCs. If you are looking into bringing your computer, double-check that your school provides adequate support for your machine.

Support Staff: Another important thing to consider is the availability of technical assistance. Many schools hire students or other staff to troubleshoot the problems you may encounter with networking, hardware, or software licensed by the school. This can be especially helpful at the beginning of each semester when you have to register your computers with the school network and install the necessary software.

Internet and E-mail Access: Nearly every school now provides Ethernet access from dorm rooms and e-mail accounts that you can use both during the semester and on your breaks. Another feature to look for is the availability of wireless Internet access at your school, which is also becoming more and more universal. In addition to getting rid of an extra wire on your desk, it also allows you to check your e-mail or chat with your roommate from anywhere on campus, including common rooms, labs, classrooms, and nearby coffee shops. But make sure you don't get too caught up in reading *The New York Times* online when you should be taking notes during a lecture!

Academic Usage of the Internet: Professors at most schools now use the Internet (in some form) as an important resource for their classes. Being able to find class notes, handouts, homework assignments, or even taped lectures posted on a Web site can be worth considering when choosing a class or a school. Although not every professor at every school is willing to put extensive course information online, finding a school where it is more common will help make your life slightly easier over the next four years.

A Final Note About Quality of Life

If you started at the first page and you've read up to here, you are probably thinking there are just way too many things to think about in choosing a college! Certainly, you already have many reasons why, right off the bat, you would add a college to, or eliminate a college from, your list. Perhaps the school has the best zoology program in the nation. Or maybe you have always wanted to be in the stands cheering as your school's basketball team wins the championship game. Either way, a final but crucial criterion for your decision is the overall quality of life you can expect to have at college.

Everyone goes to college to learn more, right? Yes, of course. Continuing your academic education will provide you with even more ways of thinking as well as more opportunities after graduation. You have to remember, though, college is someplace you will be for three or more years of your life. Academics are the most important reason to go to college, but when it comes down to everyday life, the college you choose will basically be your new world. Everything from extracurricular activities to housing, social life, and even weather will affect the way you eat, dress, study, and relax. Don't consider UMass if you can't stand the cold; and don't go to Florida State if the heat makes you miserable. Have you always thought about joining a fraternity or a sorority, and there just aren't any on campus? Or perhaps your favorite weekend activity is to curl up on a chair in a coffee shop; is the college in such a small town that there is no coffee shop? What about the housing situation? Could you see yourself coming "home" every day to that closet-sized room you share with three other students? Speaking of the other students, would you be comfortable being around them—or any of the people walking down the street? All of these factors can and will make a difference in how you feel about a school. The best way to really get an idea of what it would be like to be a student at the college is to visit the school, maybe stay over for a night or two, talk to the students around you, and browse through the student newspaper. Do you like what you see and how it feels to be there?

As you figure out what you like about a college, you may also want to check that those aspects of the school will still be there when you enroll. When the economy is doing poorly, an increasing number of schools, both public and private, face a shortage of funds; administrations at the schools have no choice but to make budget cuts. Without adequate funding, programs or even entire departments may be eliminated, the number of tenured professors may be reduced, campus renovations and additions may be delayed, extracurricular activities and sports teams may be cut, or worse yet, a combination of all of these possibilities may take place. If you are the star of your high school's varsity swimming team and want to continue swimming in college, check with the coach or the current swimmers to make sure the team is not rumored to be next on the list of programs to be cancelled. If you know that you want to major in biomedical engineering, make sure the department is big enough so that it is not one of the smaller and less popular departments that would be first to go. As recent newspaper headlines will tell you, even the best-endowed schools are tightening their purse strings.

We hope that we have given you a stronger sense as to what to think about and what to focus on as you continue to search for the college that's right for you. Just remember, in the end, you are the one who will be attending the college, so you should be the one who is happy. Best of luck!

Introduction for International Students

International students looking to apply to colleges in the United States may discover a daunting and unfamiliar path ahead of them. More so than in many other countries, admission to U.S. colleges depends not only on grades and scores, but on the whole package: what you have done outside of schoolwork, what your teachers have to say about you, and what you have to say about yourself. In addition to the typical trials of the application process, students from abroad may also have to deal with linguistic and cultural differences, scarce resources, and communication delays that their American counterparts do not. Yet you should not let yourself be deterred by these challenges—some basic planning can eliminate many potential obstacles and pave the way to a unique and rewarding college experience.

An "international student" formally refers to anyone who is applying to American universities from an address outside of the United States. This means U.S. citizens and permanent residents applying from abroad are still placed in the international category. Many colleges review this applicant pool differently from the domestic applicants—admissions committees might place less emphasis on SAT scores, for example. Many schools also look for geographical and cultural diversity, which could work in your favor if only a few students are applying from your country, or against you if there are many other applicants.

With these advantages and disadvantages in mind, here are some tips about the application process that might be especially helpful. You should also read the **Getting In** section of this book for more general information. The best advice is: get started early. Deadlines for American universities can be as early as October for fall admissions. As one student said, "Make sure you take care of everything well ahead of time—last-minute surprises are harder to deal with abroad."

Pre-Application Preparations

If you decide that you want to go to an American university, start getting involved. While extracurricular activities are not considered in the admissions processes for schools in many countries, American universities place emphasis on what you achieve outside of the classroom. Extracurricular experiences can include a variety of activities such as taking piano lessons, writing for the newspaper, doing volunteer work, or working part-time. These activities might highlight your leadership, talent, or determination. If your school does not offer many extracurricular activities, look for opportunities to get involved in the community or take the initiative to organize something yourself. When application time rolls around, be sure to list everything to which you have devoted your time.

Academically, international students might want to think about taking Advanced Placement (AP) tests and courses related to them if they are not already following the International Baccalaureate (IB) program. Although not required for college admission, AP exams measure the level of your knowledge in the subject as compared to American high school students. As an added bonus, high scores might let you bypass some classes in college or accelerate and graduate early. Arranging to take an AP test internationally might be difficult since testing sites are less ubiquitous than in the States; try to see if an American school in your area will arrange it. If you can take it and have recently completed a course corresponding to one of the tests, it would be a risk-free way to increase your chances at admission—students can choose whether to report individual AP scores. Students studying under the IB system, and even students who do not take either of these tests, might be able to negotiate for acceleration in their first year of college. Acceleration policies vary greatly, however, from college to college.

Deciding that you want to go to college in the United States and figuring out where to apply might be a rocky starting point for many international students because of the relative lack of information. But research is an essential part of the college application process and what many internationals said they wished they had spent more time doing. The United States is a huge country, and it will make a difference whether you are in California or Massachusetts, whether you are in a city or a rural area. There are also many schools with excellent programs, beyond the names that people outside of the United States would recognize. If you have a guidance counselor at your school who is knowledgeable about admissions to U.S. schools, take advantage of the resource. However, many advisors are not. One international student, now a senior, warned, "don't trust your high school counselors too much; they probably don't know as much about the schools you're applying to as you might assume they do—including application deadlines."

If your advisor is unable to offer you the help you need, seek out a counselor outside of the school. You might also want to speak with someone who has recently gone through a similar decision-making process, or talk to an American expatriate. Libraries and the Internet are prime sources of information. College Web sites provide accurate, up-to-date information, and sometimes feature special application guidelines for international students. If possible, try to visit the colleges. It could make a big difference in your opinions.

You may also want to consider the size of the international population at the schools you are deciding between. Colleges with a larger number of students from abroad tend to have more organizations and activities geared toward international students. These schools will likely have more extensive resources available for you at the administrative level as well. However, this may not be an important factor in your decision, and it all depends on what kind of college environment you are looking for.

Testing

Most American colleges require international students to take the SAT Reasoning Test, a selection of SAT Subject Tests, and the TOEFL. The Educational Testing Service (ETS) has many international test sites, although the tests might still be hard to come by in certain countries. Students from such diverse countries as Israel, Japan, and Guatemala all said signing up was easy, particularly with online registration. However, some people might have to travel hours out of the way to get to the testing center. To avoid any unnecessary travel, register for these tests early before popular testing centers fill their seats. To find out where the nearest testing center is located, write to ETS or visit their Web site, www.ets.org.

Many colleges require the TOEFL (Test of English as a Foreign Language) if English is not your first language or the language of instruction in your high school. While taking another test might seem like a hassle, TOEFL is easier than the SAT and could work to your advantage since many schools will substitute a TOEFL score for the SAT Verbal score. If you are satisfied with your SAT Critical Reading scores, you should probably not bother taking TOEFL—although a near perfect score could never hurt. The recently instituted SAT Writing section's essay will pose a further hurdle to nonnative English speakers, and while colleges are likely to take your native abilities into account when making admissions decisions, the essay will most likely require more test preparation on the part of such students.

Application Package

In getting teachers to write recommendations for you, be sure to approach those who not only know your work but know you and are willing to write enthusiastically about you. International teachers tend to be more reluctant to award superlatives or write a personalized recommendation than their American counterparts. If you attended a school taught in a non-English language, you can ask the teachers to write you recommendations in English, have them translated, or send them to the colleges to have them translated. It is often better to have the recommendations translated in your own country than to send them to colleges to be translated by someone there. You might offer to work with your teacher to translate the letter into English, especially if you have a higher level of proficiency.

The essay is a personal reflection of yourself and an opportunity to have the different parts of your application come together. Think of what will be interesting to the admissions officers reading the essay, and allow for more creativity than might be acceptable in college applications in your own country. Many internationals choose to write about living in different countries or experiencing cultural differences, which might be more interesting than the fact that you won a national academic award—the latter point can be listed elsewhere in the application. You want to give the admissions officers a strong sense of who you are and how you will add to the college community.

Financial Aid and Visas

While some large and wealthy colleges can afford to be need-blind in their admission of international students, the consensus is that there is very little financial aid available for non–U.S. citizens and residents. If you will definitely need aid, you should research the financial aid policy of each college before applying. Depending on which country you are from, you might be able to look to sources in your home country for financial support. If, on the other hand, you are an American citizen applying from abroad, the financial aid process is the same as for any other American student.

As soon as you mail that final college application, most of your hard work will be over. Although regulations differ from country to country, you shouldn't have any problems obtaining a student visa once you are accepted to a U.S. school. The visa will allow you to work inside the university, but be forewarned that finding an outside job will be very difficult.

International students face a number of challenges when applying to U.S. universities, but some advance research and planning can help make the process as painless as possible. There are numerous benefits to pursuing an American education—you'll have a vast array of academic options, enjoy access to high-tech facilities, and be exposed to students with backgrounds quite different from your own. Attending a U.S. college is a chance to expand your horizons, and you shouldn't let the application obstacles hold you back. One international student summed it up by saying, "Although it is an endless process, it is worth it!"

Students with Disabilities

The college search process is a difficult one, but it can be even more so for students with disabilities. Whether the disability is physical or learning-related, the need for special resources means that, on top of evaluating academics and social life, students need to be certain that a school will help them learn and live as comfortably as any other student. Early preparation, along with careful planning for the transition from high school to college, will make life at college much easier.

Planning Is Key

Above all, students should choose a school for its merits. The director of the Resource Office on Disabilities at Yale said that her most important advice was to "check out the school first, but also consider the disability services office, as a second choice, very important." Even a high quality of services cannot remedy a school at which the student is unhappy—but weak or nonexistent disability services can be very detrimental to one's college experience.

High schools must accommodate students as fully as possible under the Individuals with Disabilities Education Act. However, colleges are classed under the Americans with Disabilities Act, which mandates that they provide "reasonable accommodations" for those in need; the definition of "reasonable" will vary from school to school. The best place to figure out what a school offers as "reasonable accommodation" is at the school's designated office for students with disabilities; the people there will be able to tell you what they have on hand and can arrange.

Before visiting the school, be sure to alert the admissions office. They can usually work with the disabilities office to make sure, for instance, that your tour has a sign interpreter or that it only visits wheelchair-accessible sites. When you visit, you will see how good a fit the school is for you in terms of accommodations. If at all possible, make time to visit the disabilities office while you are there. Have an honest discussion with the staff about the accommodations that are necessary for your disability; and get a feel from them about what they believe can be provided.

During the applications process, you can disclose or not disclose your disability at your discretion; admissions officers from multiple selective schools have made clear that "when we learn of an applicant with a disability, we check to make sure that our school has the resources available to accommodate the individual before we ask the traditional questions: Have they made the most of their high school career? Would they contribute to the school's community? And so on."

As soon as you decide on a school, you should contact the people at the school's disabilities office immediately, mid-May at the latest. The first thing they will need is documentation of the disability, and they will work from there. They will work with the housing department to provide necessary living accommodations, such as ground-floor rooms or flashing fire alarms. Often, the people in the disabilities office will ask more questions over the summer than you do to find out what you need and what other resources you can use. Don't be afraid to check back with them over the summer; working closely with the office will make it more likely that you're comfortable at the school in the fall.

Before coming to college, you should prepare yourself for the transition. Make sure that everything you need has been set up ahead of time. The first few weeks of college are such a whirlwind that dealing with small problems like malfunctioning hearing aids or mislaid walking sticks will take away from the experience of your new life away from home. And if things do not go as planned, the disabilities office will be one of your best resources for handling the unexpected.

If You Have a Physical Disability

For physical disabilities, the actual layout of the campus may matter most. If you are blind, you will want to make sure that the campus is easy to familiarize yourself with, and that there are multiple ways available to orient yourself. If you are in a wheelchair, you will need to know which buildings are accessible for you, including dorms, classroom buildings, and administrative buildings. Older campuses, especially those built in the eighteenth or nineteenth centuries, will need to be examined more thoroughly, and it may be necessary to ask the disabilities office to make sure that classes you have preregistered for are located in accessible buildings. One student pointed out that "schools that are truly committed to making their campuses accessible for wheelchair users will not only have many ramps available, but those ramps will be attractive and blend in naturally with the immediate environment." Elevators should be available when necessary. Many campuses will also provide special shuttle transport services for disabled students.

If You Have a Learning Disability

For learning disabilities, providing documentation starts with a diagnosis. If you don't have a formal diagnosis, check to see if the school of your choice offers diagnostic services; some even offer those services free. Given that information, the school will often work directly with the professors to make sure that those disabilities are accommodated. This might include extended testing time, typing rather than writing, or a private room for testing. These accommodations may also be available for students with temporary disabilities, such as severe recurrent migraine headaches or short-term injuries. The specific accommodations depend on the circumstances.

It is common for schools to offer alternate methods for course reading. Blind students might need the texts in Braille, while dyslexic students might prefer the text as an audio recording.

Note-taking services are offered at nearly every school. Because lectures can be fast-paced and seminars can be intensive, it may make more sense for students to receive notes from another person in the class. This option is also offered for those experiencing minor injuries: if a right-handed student breaks her right wrist, she will need a note-taker until she can write again.

Final Thoughts

Social life is an area in which students tend to be more independent: having a sign interpreter in class is common, but having a sign interpreter outside the academic sphere usually does not fall under "reasonable accommodation." Check, however, to see whether your school provides escort services if you are blind, or whether they will provide personal care assistants if you have a severe mobility disability; in that case, they may work with Vocational Rehabilitation services in your home state to help pay for those accommodations.

Usually, you will not have to pay for these services since they fall under "reasonable accommodations" mandated by the state. For specialized services, it will vary by school. Remember, it is entirely your decision whether or not to disclose your disability up front. Above all, you should find a school that is best suited to you individually, and then make sure that the school can help you and provide you with resources to be a successful student.

Terms You Should Know

Advanced Placement (AP)—College credit earned by students while still in high school. Many high schools offer specially designed AP courses that prepare students for the College Board's AP Exams. Administered in May, they can qualify students who score well for advanced standing when they enroll at certain colleges.

all-nighter—As in, "pulling an all-nighter." The process by which students attempt to learn a semester's worth of course material or crank out a paper of considerable length in a short period, often 24 to 48 hours. Soda, coffee, and/or caffeine pills are the staples of most all-night cramming sessions.

American College Test (ACT)—Test administered to high school juniors and seniors by the American College Testing Program. Traditionally it has been used as an admissions criterion used primarily by Midwestern schools in the past, but has gained national stature as a college admissions test. The ACT is currently the biggest rival to the SAT.

American College Testing Program (ACTP)—The organization that produces the American College Test (ACT) and the Family Financial Statement (FFS). Many Midwestern universities use the ACT and the FFS in admissions instead of the SAT and the Financial-Aid Form (FAF). (See also "Family Financial Statement" and "Financial-Aid Form.")

arts and sciences (also called liberal arts)—A broad term that encompasses most traditional courses of study, including the humanities, social sciences, natural sciences, mathematics, and foreign languages. A liberal arts college is also a college of arts and sciences. (See also "humanities" and "social sciences.")

beer pong—A party game usually played with Solo cups and cheap beer. The 10 cups on each side of the table are arranged in a triangular formation, and attempts are made by the teams to direct ping pong balls into the other team's cups, either by a perfected toss or with a ping pong paddle. When the other team's ball lands in your cup, you must drink the contents. A frat house staple.

candidate's reply date—The May 1 deadline, observed by most selective colleges, by which the applicant must respond to an offer of admission, usually with a nonrefundable deposit of several hundred dollars. Colleges that require students to respond by May 1 in almost all cases notify them of their acceptance on or before April 15.

College Board—The organization that sponsors the SAT, the SAT Subject Tests, the Advanced Placement tests, and the Financial-Aid Form (FAF). College Board admissions tests are developed and administered by the Educational Testing Service (ETS). (See also "Advanced Placement" and "Financial-Aid Form.")

Common Application—A form produced by a consortium of over 300 colleges that may be filled out and sent to member colleges in lieu of each school's individual application. Colleges often require that a supplemental application specific to the particular school be submitted as well.

comprehensive exams (comps)—Also known as "generals," these tests, administered by some colleges (usually during the senior year) are designed to measure knowledge gained over a student's entire college career. Schools that give comps usually require students to pass the test in their major field in order to graduate.

computing assistant (CA)—A university employee, often an undergraduate, who helps students with all varieties of computing problems, from using a word processor to downloading games from the network.

consortium—A group of colleges affiliated in some way. The extent of the association can vary widely. Some consortiums—usually among colleges in close proximity—offer a range of joint programs that may include cross-registration, interlibrary loans, residential exchanges, and coordinated social, cultural, and athletic events.

co-op job—A paid internship, arranged for a student by his or her college, that provides on-the-job training, usually in an occupation closely related to the student's major.

core curriculum—A group of courses all students in a college must take in order to graduate. Core curricula are becoming widespread.

deferral—A college's postponement of the decision to accept or reject an early admissions applicant. The applicant's file is entered in with those of regular-action candidates in the spring and is reviewed once again, this time for a final decision.

discussion section—A smaller group of students who meet regularly with the guidance of a teaching assistant to discuss the material covered in a large lecture. Designed to make sure students do not get lost in large classes. The teaching assistant answers questions, fosters discussion, and usually grades assignments.

distribution requirements—Requirements stipulating that students take courses in a variety of broad subject areas in order to graduate. The number and definition of subject areas and the number of courses required in each varies from school to school. Typical categories include the humanities, social sciences, fine arts, natural sciences, foreign languages, and mathematics. Unlike a core curriculum, distribution requirements do not usually mandate specific courses that students must take. (See also "humanities," "social sciences," and "core curriculum.")

drunk dial—To make a phone call to an old boyfriend or girlfriend, former hook-up (see below), or current love interest in an inebriated state. Drunk texting is a newer phenomenon where similar exchanges take place via text message rather than calling.

dry—as in "dry campus." A school that does not allow alcohol for any students in its dorms or other campus facilities.

early action—A program that gives students early notification of a college's admissions decision. Unlike early decision, it does not require a prior commitment to enroll if accepted. Early action has become increasingly popular and is now available at many colleges covered in this book. Some institutions, including Stanford and Yale, offer "single-choice" early-action programs. These plans work the same way as regular early action, except that students cannot apply early anywhere else. Deadlines for both types of early-action applications are usually in late fall, with notification in December, January, or February. An applicant accepted under early action usually has until May 1, the candidate's reply date, to respond to the offer of admission. (See also "early decision" and "candidate's reply date.")

early decision—A program under which a student receives early notification of a college's admissions decision if the student agrees in advance to enroll if accepted. Students may apply early decision to only one college; it should be a clear first choice. Application deadlines for early decision are usually in November, with decision letters mailed by mid-December.

Facebook—An online directory launched in 2004 that connects individuals through high school, college, and residential networks. Invaluable tool for procrastinators.

Facebookstalk—The process of "researching" the likes of a crush, former high school sweetheart, or ex-boyfriend's girlfriend through Facebook. (See Facebook.)

family contribution—The amount of money that a family can "reasonably" be expected to pay toward a student's education, as determined by one of the two standardized needs-analysis forms. (See also "Financial-Aid Form" and "Family Financial Statement.")

Family Financial Statement (FFS)—The financial-needs analysis form submitted to the American College Testing Program (ACTP), which, like the FAF, determines the expected family contribution. Colleges that use the American College Test (ACT) for admissions purposes usually require a copy of the FFS report from students applying for financial aid. (See also "American College Testing Program," "family contribution," and "Financial-Aid Form.")

fee waiver—Permission, often granted upon request, for needy students to apply for college admission without having to pay the application fee.

Financial-Aid Form (FAF)—The financial-needs analysis form submitted to the College Board by students applying for financial aid. Like the Family Financial Statement (FFS), it yields the expected family contribution. Colleges that require the Scholastic Assessment Test (SAT) for admission typically use the FAF as the basis for financial-aid awards. (See also "Family Financial Statement," "family contribution," and "College Board.")

financial-aid package—The combination of loans, grants, and a work-study job that a school puts together for a student receiving financial aid.

five-year plan—The practice of completing a four-year degree program over a five-year period.

flex dollars—Miscellaneous credit, usually part of a purchased meal plan, that can be used at campus stores and sometimes restaurants on and off campus, rather than cash. Especially convenient for late-night snacking and study breaks.

four-one-four—An academic calendar consisting of two regular four-month semesters with a short "winter" or "January" term in between. Variations include four-four-one and three-three-two. In most cases, these numbers refer to the number of courses a student is expected to complete in each segment of the year, although at some schools they refer to the number of months in each segment.

freshman 15—A reference to the number of pounds students often gain during the freshman year. Usually caused by a combination of too little exercise, unlimited helpings in the dining hall, too many late-night runs for pizza, and overconsumption of alcoholic beverages.

gap year—The option of taking a year off between high school and college. Usually spent traveling, working, or volunteering.

government aid—Money that federal or state governments make available to students, most of which is administered through the colleges on the basis of need. Government aid can come in the form of grants, loans, and work-study jobs. Stafford Loans (formerly Guaranteed Student Loans) and PLUS parent loans are made available through commercial lending institutions. For further information on government aid programs, contact the state and federal departments of education.

grade inflation—A situation in which average work is consistently awarded a higher letter grade than it would normally earn. At most schools, the grade for average work is about B–/C+. But in classes or entire colleges with grade inflation, it can be as high as B or even B+.

Greek system—The fraternities and sororities on a particular campus. They are called "Greek" because most take their names from combinations of letters in the Greek alphabet.

gut—A course widely known to be very easy, often with enrollments well into the hundreds. Guts are traditionally favorites among second-semester seniors, but they can also help to balance a term that includes very difficult courses.

hipster—a member of the student body who appears to be more artsy, literary, emotionally attuned, and/or nicotine-addicted than the rest of the class. Known to sport vintage and/or ill-fitting clothing.

hook-up—To enjoy a person's nonplatonic company, often used in reference to a one-night event. A very vague term that can range from an innocent kiss to sex, depending on usage.

humanities—Subjects in which the primary focus is on human culture. Examples include philosophy, language, and literature. (See also "social sciences.")

independent study—A course, usually in a student's major field, in which he or she studies independently and meets one-on-one with a professor on a topic of the student's choosing. Some colleges require an independent study essay or research paper for graduation.

interdisciplinary major—A major that combines two complementary subjects from different fields, such as biology and psychology. Students completing these majors take courses in each area as well as courses that explicitly join the two.

International Baccalaureate (IB)—A high school program found across the world which, like AP courses, can earn a student advanced standing upon college enrollment.

intramurals—Athletic leagues informally organized within a college. Students are free from the burden of tryouts and play with and against fellow classmates.

jungle juice—A potent mix of liquor (often grain alcohol) and juice served at college parties out of a large water cooler or punch-bowl. Freshmen who underestimate the juice's power due to its fruity taste, inevitably regret consumption the morning after.

language requirement—A rule at many colleges that requires students to study a foreign language before graduation. Two years on the college level are usually required, although credit from Advanced Placement or SAT Subject Tests often allows students to bypass the requirement.

legacy—An applicant whose mother or father is a graduate of a particular school. On occasion, students with legacy status are given extra consideration in admissions.

merit scholarship—A financial grant for some part of college costs, usually awarded for academic achievement or special skill in an extracurricular activity and not based on need. Private corporations and many colleges offer merit scholarships.

Natty Light—Cheap beer, a staple of college parties, sometimes referred to by its brand name, Natural Light. Often accompanied by its comrade "The Beast" (Milwaukee's Best), as well as a variety of inexpensive hard liquors.

need-based aid—Money awarded solely on the basis of need, usually administered through the colleges. Some schools agree to pay the difference between their total fees and the expected family contribution; others pay only part of it, leaving some "unmet" need. Most financial-aid packages consist of some combination of three components: grants, loans, and work-study jobs. Some of the money comes from the college's own resources, although part is financed by federal and state governments. (See also "government aid.")

need-blind admissions—A policy in which the applicant's ability to pay does not affect the college's consideration of his or her application. Some schools with need-blind admissions also guarantee to meet the full demonstrated financial need of all accepted applicants as determined by one of the two standardized needs-analysis forms; others do not. (See also "family contribution," "Family Financial Statement," and "Financial-Aid Form.")

office hours—A period during which a professor agrees to be available in his or her office for the purpose of talking with students about their coursework. Professors are not always required by their colleges to have office hours, but most do regardless.

open admissions—A policy under which any applicant with a high school diploma is accepted. State universities that have this policy usually limit open admission to state residents.

parietals—Regulations that govern the times when students of one sex may visit dorms or floors housing the opposite sex. Now usually found only at the most conservative schools.

pass/fail or CR/F or CR/D/F—An option offered by some schools in certain classes. A student may enroll in a class and simply receive credit or failure (or a D in "CR/D/F") for it on his or her transcript instead of a specific grade. While students often are not allowed to take required classes CR/D/F, the option allows them to take classes out of their comfort range without the fear of being punished with a bad grade for experimenting.

Phi Beta Kappa—An academic honor society to which students with the best grade point average in each class are elected. Less than the top 10 percent of a class, and usually far fewer, receive this honor.

PLUS parent loans—A component of the Stafford Loan, for parents. (See also "government aid.")

pre-frosh—A visiting high school student, potential college recruit, or admitted student who has yet to enroll.

pregame—To prepare for a party, bar, show, or another event by imbibing beforehand. Saves time and money.

problem set (pset)—An annoying weekly assignment that is usually inevitable in science or quantitative classes. This thankless task will keep you up till 2 a.m. Sunday nights but can count for anywhere between 1/50 of your grade or one-half. Previously known as homework.

quad—An abbreviation for "quadrangle"; many dorm complexes are built in squares (quadrangles) with a courtyard in the middle. Quad can also refer to a suite of dormitory rooms in which four students live together.

quarter system—An academic calendar dividing the school year into four quarters, three of which constitute a full academic year. Less common than the semester system, it is most often used by large universities with

extensive programs in agricultural and technical fields.

resident advisor/assistant (RA)—A student, usually an upperclassman, who lives in a dorm and helps to maintain regulations and enforce school policy, as well as offering advice and support to dorm residents. RAs receive compensation from the school for their services, usually in the form of free room and board.

rolling admissions—A policy under which a college considers applications almost immediately after receiving them. Decision letters are mailed within a month after the application is filed. Colleges with rolling admissions continue to accept applications only until the class is filled, so it is best to apply early.

Scholastic Aptitude Test (SAT)—Test administered to high school juniors and seniors by the College Board of the Educational Testing Service, with math, verbal, and written-language sections. Used as an admissions criterion at most colleges nationwide.

section all-star—A member of a discussion section who distinguishes him or herself by volunteering contributions in an excessively obnoxious or earnest manner. Sometimes encouraged by the TA, always reviled by other section members. Known for quoting from the original Greek and becoming belligerent during debates.

senior project—Many majors at many colleges require seniors to complete a special project during their senior year. This could involve a thesis (anywhere from 15 to 100 pages), a research project, some sort of internship, or all of the above. Some colleges offer seniors a choice between taking comps or doing a project. (See also "comps.")

sexile—There are two people in the bedroom you share with your roommate, and you are not one of them. If you are lucky, you have a common room with a comfortable couch.

social sciences—Subjects that deal systematically with the institutions of human society, most notably economics and political science. The behavioral sciences, which include psychology, sociology and anthropology, are often included in this group as well.

Sophomore Slump—A period, usually the first semester of sophomore year, when students experience unprecedented levels of stress and angst. Often results from the disillusionment and increased workload following freshman year.

study break—An institutionalized form of procrastination involving food and talk. Often informally arranged—"I'm sick of calculus, let's take a study break at (insert name of local hangout)"—but can be sponsored by RAs, cultural groups, or even school administrators. Some nights, study breaks can take more of your time than the actual studying.

teaching assistant (TA)—A graduate student who assists a professor in the presentation of a course. Usually the professor gives two to four lectures a week for all the students in the class; the TAs hold smaller weekly discussion sections.

three-two program (3–2)—A program that allows students to study for three years at one school, followed by two at another, more specialized school. Upon completion, many of these programs award both the bachelor's and the master's degrees.

town-gown relations—The contact between a college (students, employees, buildings) and its host town (citizens, businesses, local government) and the set of issues around which this contact revolves. Such issues include taxes, traffic, local employment practices, and government services such as road maintenance, sewage, and trash collection.

townie—A resident of a college town or city who is not enrolled in the college, but who might sit beside you at the local pub. Often involves a them-versus-us mentality.

trimesters—An academic calendar that divides the school year into three terms of approximately equal length. Schools on the trimester system generally have one term before the winter break and two after.

tutorial major (also self-designed or special major)—A program offered by many schools in which a student can plan his or her own major, combining the offerings of two or more traditional majors, usually in consultation with a faculty member. An example is Medieval Studies, in which the student might study the history, literature, philosophy, and art of the period, taking courses from a number of departments. (See also "interdisciplinary major.")

waiting list—A list of students who are not initially accepted to a certain school, but who may be admitted later, depending on the number of accepted students who enroll. Most colleges ultimately accept only a fraction of the students on the waiting list, who are notified during the summer.

work-study—Campus jobs, for financial-aid recipients, that are subsidized by the federal government. Work-study jobs are a component of most need-based financial-aid packages. Students typically work 10 to 20 hours a week to help finance their education.

Editors' Choice

Biggest Jock Schools

University of Florida
University of Notre Dame
Ohio State University
Michigan State University
University of Iowa
University of Nebraska-Lincoln
University of Texas
University of Connecticut
Pennsylvania State University
University of North Carolina

"Sports are vital to the University because the teams bring in millions of dollars a year and create a sense of pride and tradition. The jocks get treated like the second coming of Christ."—Alexandria Butler, University of Connecticut

Easiest Course Load

Arizona State University
Seton Hall University
University of Alaska-Fairbanks
University of Hawaii
Salve Regina University
Hampshire College
Louisiana State University
University of Texas, Austin
Benedict College
University of California/Santa Cruz

"Hampshire is full of self-motivated kids with extraordinarily high goals. Hampshire does not have majors; you choose what to take. This creates a lot of pressure to choose the 'right' thing. We do have requirements, but they are just broader and include areas like multicultural perspectives and community service."—Jill Erwich, Hampshire College

Most Blondes

University of Southern California
University of Mississippi
Southern Methodist University
Pepperdine University
Arizona State University
University of California/Santa Barbara
Vanderbilt University
University of Notre Dame
Baylor University
Auburn University

Most Difficult Requirements

Columbia University
Claremont McKenna College
Stanford University
United States Air Force Academy
Colorado School of Mines
United States Military Academy
Harvey Mudd College
United States Naval Academy
Reed College
United States Coast Guard Academy

"I think it's completely true. Reed is ridiculously hard and truly belongs with the Harvards and Yales of the world. Going to Reed is like the Bataan Death March except we're not in the Philippines and the march never ends."—Alex Gersovitz, Reed College

Schools That Never Sleep

New York University
Arizona State University
University of Southern California
Hunter College
Columbia University
Tulane University
Yale University
Princeton University

University of Chicago
Parsons School of Design

"Contrary to popular belief, New York City sleeps . . . everywhere. Try taking the F train at 8 a.m.: it's all suits and snores. However, there's always a bunch of stuff you can busy yourself with so you can return home with pretty incredible stories for your friends stuck on those 'campus' things."—Jenna Rosenberg, New York University

Happiest Students

Stanford University
Brigham Young University
Yale University
University of Colorado
Clemson University
Bowdoin College
Whitman College
Claremont McKenna College
Brown University
Rice University

Most Behind the Times

College of William and Mary
Oral Roberts University
Bob Jones University
University of North Dakota
Union College
George Mason University
Davidson College
Brigham Young University
Washington and Lee University
Princeton University

"Princeton's attempt to spearhead a grade-deflation policy has received no followers among the Ivy League, which single-handedly puts us behind the times. Also, the obsession with both traditions and the creation of a Fitzgerald-era class of elitism and exclusivity definitely acts counter to the diversification efforts of most other institutions."—Ota Amaize, Princeton University

Strongest Undergraduate Focus

Princeton University
Carleton College
Grinnell College
Williams College
Yale University
Amherst College
Swarthmore College
Dartmouth College
Occidental College
Wellesley College

"Our professors are always available for office hours and spend significantly more time actually teaching than many others in the Ivy League. In addition, Yale has significant resources geared toward making undergraduate life as smooth and exciting as possible."—Ayibitari Owi, Yale University

Most Millionaire Graduates

Harvard University
University of Pennsylvania
Yale University
Massachusetts Institute of Technology
Dartmouth College
Princeton University
Stanford University
Northwestern University
Duke University
Brown University

Best Study Abroad Programs

University of Virginia
Baylor University
New York University
Tufts University
Georgetown University
American University
Middlebury College
Macalester College
Bates College
DePauw University

"There are a bunch of study abroad locations. I plan on going to Ghana junior year because I've heard some pretty wonderful things from upperclassmen. I'm excited for the great artist community and the food is supposed to be pretty incredible."—Jenna Rosenberg, New York University

Biggest Rivalries

Duke University/University of North Carolina
West Point/United States Naval Academy
Harvard University/Yale University
Stanford University/University of California/Berkeley
University of Florida/Florida State University
University of Washington/Washington State University
University of Texas/Austin/Texas A&M University
Ohio State University/University of Michigan
University of Southern California/University of California/Los Angeles
University of South Carolina/Clemson University

"Our rivalry with UNC is a great part of the Duke experience and quantifies the passion we bring to everything. There are some students that really bleed blue as they sleep in tents outside of Cameron Indoor Stadium for weeks on end in order to reserve seats for the big game."—Rajhai Wilson, Duke University

Place Most Likely to Find Your Spouse

Middlebury College
Connecticut College
Williams College
Princeton University
Brigham Young University
Clemson University
Florida State University
Wheaton College (Illinois)
University of Southern California
University of Mississippi

Best College Town

University of California/Berkeley (Berkeley)
University of Michigan (Ann Arbor)
University of Wisconsin (Madison)
Princeton University (Princeton)
Indiana University (Bloomington)
University of Florida (Gainesville)
North Carolina State (Raleigh)
University of Texas (Austin)
University of Miami (Oxford)
Boston College (Chestnut Hill)

"Chestnut Hill is a great college town because it combines the benefits of a big city with the feel of a suburban college campus. Just be sure to bring money, because Boston is expensive."—Gordon Bell, Boston College

Best Local Restaurants

Columbia University
New York University
University of Pennsylvania
Tulane University
University of California/Los Angeles
Boston University
Georgetown University
Harvard University
Yale University
University of Chicago

"New Haven's restaurants are fantastic. Even though it's a small city, New Haven possesses the diverse cuisines of a metropolis 10 times its size, including Japanese, Thai, Cuban, Italian, French, vegetarian, and even vegan."—JonPaul McBride, Yale University

Ugliest School Colors

Clemson University (Burnt Orange and Purple)
University of Oregon (Green and Yellow)
Bowling Green State University (Brown and Orange)
Rice University (Blue and Gray)
University of Washington (Purple and Gold)

Florida State University (Maroon and Dark Gold)

Rowan University (Brown and Yellow)

University of Tennessee (Bright Orange and White)

University of Wyoming (Brown and Gold)

Auburn University (Burnt Orange and Navy Blue)

(Anteaters)

University of California/Santa Cruz (Banana Slugs)

North Carolina School of the Arts (Fighting Pickles)

Rhode Island School of Design (Scrotie)

Whittier College (Poets)

University of Hawaii (Rainbow Warriors)

Connecticut College (Camels)

Craziest Mascot

Xavier University (Blue Blob)

Evergreen State College (Geoducks)

University of Maryland (Terrapins)

University of California/Irvine

"An anteater is definitely a strange mascot because most people want a mascot to be intimidating. Instead, we have an anteater. At the same time, I guess it's cool because we always know that no one else will."

—Student at University of California/Irvine

College Finder 2015

Regions

New England:
Connecticut
Maine
Massachusetts
New Hampshire
Rhode Island
Vermont
Eastern Canada

Mid-Atlantic:
Delaware
District of Columbia
Maryland
New Jersey
New York
Pennsylvania
West Virginia

Midwest:
Illinois
Indiana
Iowa
Kansas
Kentucky
Michigan
Minnesota
Missouri
Nebraska
North Dakota
Ohio
South Dakota
Wisconsin

Southeast:
Alabama
Arkansas
Florida
Georgia
Louisiana
Mississippi
North Carolina
South Carolina
Tennessee
Virginia

West:
Alaska
Arizona
California
Colorado
Hawaii
Idaho
Montana
New Mexico
Nevada
Oklahoma
Oregon
Texas
Utah
Washington
Wyoming
Western Canada

Schools with Fewer than 1500 Undergrads

New England:
College of the Atlantic
Marlboro College
Bennington College
United States Coast Guard Academy
Hampshire College
Bard College

Mid-Atlantic:
St. John's College
Trinity College
Haverford College
Bryn Mawr College
Swarthmore College
Goucher College
The Cooper Union for the Advancement of
    Science and Art
Sarah Lawrence College
The Juilliard School

Midwest:
Wabash College
Centre College
Cornell College
Earlham College
Knox College
Kalamazoo College
Alma College
Beloit College
Lake Forest College
St. Mary's College
Lawrence University
Principia College

Southeast:
New College of Florida
Randolph College
Sweet Briar College
Hollins University
Agnes Scott College
Milsaps College
Hampden-Sydney College
Wofford College
Birmingham-Southern College

West:
Deep Springs College
Harvey Mudd College
Mills College
California Institute of the Arts
Scripps College
California Institute of Technology
Pitzer College
Claremont McKenna College
Whitman College
Reed College
University of Dallas
Hendrix College
Whittier College

1500–5000 Undergrads

New England:
Amherst College
Babson College
Bates College
Bowdoin College
Clark University
Colby College
College of the Holy Cross
Connecticut College
Middlebury College
Mount Holyoke College
Rhode Island School of Design
Salve Regina University
Simmons College
Smith College
Trinity College
Wellesley
Wesleyan
Wheaton College
Williams College
Worcester Polytechnic Institute

Mid-Atlantic:
Alfred University
Allegheny College
Barnard College

Catholic University
Clarkson University
Colgate University
Dickinson College
Drew University
Franklin and Marshall College
Gettysburg College
Hamilton College
Hobart and William Smith Colleges
Lafayette College
Manhattanville College
Muhlenberg College
Skidmore College
St. Bonaventure University
St. Lawrence University
St. Mary's College of Maryland
Stevens Institute of Technology
Susquehanna University
Union College
Ursinus College
Vassar College

Midwest:
Albion College
Carleton College
College of Wooster
Denison University
DePauw University
Grinnell College
Gustavus Adolphus College
Kenyon College
Macalester College
Oberlin College
Ohio Wesleyan University
Rose-Hulman Institute of Technology
St. Olaf College
Wheaton College
Wittenberg University

Southeast:
Florida Institute of Technology
Florida Southern University
Furman University
Morehouse College
Rhodes College
Rollins College
Spelman College
Stetson University
Tuskegee University
University of Richmond
Washington and Lee University

West:
Colorado College
Colorado School of Mines
Lewis and Clark College
Occidental College
Pepperdine University
Pomona College

Rice University
St. Mary's University
Trinity University
University of Puget Sound
University of Redlands
University of Tulsa
Willamette University

University of Colorado/Boulder
University of Houston
University of Texas/Austin
University of Washington
University of Western Ontario

Over 20,000 Undergrads

New England:
University of Massachusetts/Amherst
University of Toronto

Mid-Atlantic:
Penn State University
Temple University
University of Maryland/College Park

Midwest:
Indiana University
Iowa State University
Michigan State University
Ohio State University
Purdue University
University of Illinois/Urbana-Champaign
University of Iowa
University of Kansas
University of Michigan
University of Minnesota
University of Missouri/Columbia
University of Wisconsin/Madison

Southeast:
Florida State University
Louisiana State University
North Carolina State University
University of Florida
University of Georgia
University of South Florida
University of Tennessee/Knoxville
Virginia Polytechnic Institute

West:
Arizona State University
Brigham Young University
Texas A&M University
Texas Institute of Technology University
University of Arizona
University of California/Berkeley
University of California/Davis
University of California/Los Angeles
University of California/San Diego

Single-Sex Schools

Female:
Mills College
Scripps College
Agnes Scott College
St. Mary's College
Mount Holyoke College
Spelman College
Barnard College
Smith College
Wellesley College
Trinity College (D.C.)
Bryn Mawr College
Sweet Briar College
Hollins University
Simmons College
Wells College

Male:
Deep Springs College
Wabash College
Hampden-Sydney College
Morehouse College

Predominantly Male Schools (>66%)

California Institute of Technology
Clarkson University
Colorado School of Mines
Florida Institute of Technology
Georgia Institute of Technology
Harvey Mudd College
Michigan Technological Institute
Rensselaer Polytechnic Institute
Rochester Institute of Technology
Rose-Hulman Institute of Technology
Stevens Institute of Technology
United States Air Force Academy
United States Coast Guard Academy
United States Military Academy
United States Naval Academy
Worcester Polytechnic Institute

Predominantly Female Schools (>66%)

Adelphi University
Bennington College
College of the Atlantic
Drew University
Eugene Lang College of The New School
    University
Goucher College
Howard University
Hunter College
Manhattanville College
Parsons The New School for Design
Rhode Island School of Design
Salve Regina University
Sarah Lawrence College
St. Mary's University
Wells College

High Minority Enrollment (>35%)

New England:
Amherst College
Babson College
College of the Atlantic
Dartmouth College
Harvard University
Massachusetts Institute of Technology
Mount Holyoke College
Rhode Island School of Design
Smith College
Trinity College (CT)
Wellesley College
Wesleyan University
Yale University

Mid-Atlantic:
Adelphi University
American University
City University of New York/City College
City University of New York/Queens College
Columbia University
The Cooper Union for the Advancement of
    Science and Art
Cornell University
Howard University
Hunter College
Johns Hopkins University
New York University
Princeton University
Rutgers/The State University of New Jersey

State University of New York/Stony Brook
Trinity University
University of Maryland/College Park

Midwest:
DePaul University
Loyola University
University of Chicago
University of Illinois/Chicago

Southeast:
Florida A & M University
Morehouse College
Spelman College
Tuskegee University
University of Miami
University of South Florida
University of Tampa

West:
California State University/Fresno
California Institute of Technology
Claremont McKenna College
New Mexico State University
Occidental College
Pepperdine University
Rice University
Scripps College
St. Mary's College of California
Stanford University
University of Alaska/Fairbanks
University of California/Berkeley
University of California/Davis
University of California/Irvine
University of California/Los Angeles
University of California/Riverside
University of California/San Diego
University of Hawaii/Manoa
University of Houston
University of New Mexico
University of Southern California
University of Texas/Austin
University of Washington
Whittier College

Schools Accepting <25% of Applicants

The Juilliard School
Yale University
United States Naval Academy
Harvard University
United States Military Academy
The Cooper Union for the Advancement of
    Science and Art

Stanford University
Princeton University
Columbia University
United States Air Force Academy
California Institute of the Arts
Massachusetts Institute of Technology
Brown University
Dartmouth College
Amherst College
Williams College
Pomona College
California Institute of Technology
University of Pennsylvania
Duke University
Washington University in St. Louis
Rice University
Claremont McKenna College
Georgetown University
United States Coast Guard Academy
University of California/Los Angeles
Middlebury College
Bowdoin College
Cornell University

Schools Accepting 25–40% of Applicants

University of California/Berkeley
Swarthmore College
University of South Carolina
Pepperdine University
Barnard College
Wesleyan College
Tufts University
Haverford College
Carleton College
Vassar College
Hunter College
Northwestern University
University of Notre Dame
Washington and Lee
Bates College
Boston College
Colgate University
Hamilton College
Bucknell College
Rhode Island School of Design
College of William and Mary
Connecticut College
Johns Hopkins University
New York University
Vanderbilt University
Oberlin College
Emory University
Trinity College

Bard College
Colby College
Wellesley College
Babson College
University of Virginia
Harvey Mudd College
California Polytechnic State University San
    Luis Obispo
George Washington University
Kenyon College
Pitzer College
Macalester College
Brandeis University
University of Chicago
University of Richmond
Lehigh University
Carnegie Mellon University
City University of New York/Queens
    College
University of California/San Diego
University of Miami
Northeastern University
Elon University
State University of New York/Binghamton
Denison University
Colorado College
University of Tennessee/Knoxville
College of the Holy Cross
Sarah Lawrence College
Franklin and Marshall College
Reed College
Occidental College
Tulane University
University of Delaware
Wheaton College
Muhlenberg College
Gettysburg College
Spelman College
Howard University
Bryn Mawr College
Wake Forest University
Union College
University of Rochester
The College of New Jersey
Skidmore College
Kansas State University
Stevens Institute of Technology
Scripps College
Wabash College
University of Pittsburgh
Dickinson College
Rhodes College
University of Maryland/College Park
Fordham University
University of Connecticut
Whitman College
State University of New York/
    Stony Brook

Large Fraternity/ Sorority Systems (More than 30%)

Albion College
Birmingham-Southern College
Bucknell College
Case Western Reserve University
Centre College
Colgate University
College of William and Mary
Cornell College
Dartmouth College
Denison University
DePauw University
Emory University
Franklin and Marshall College
Furman College
Gettysburg College
Hamilton College
Hampden-Sydney College
Lehigh University
Massachusetts Institute of Technology
Millsaps College
Northwestern University
Ohio Wesleyan University
Rensselaer Polytechnic Institute
Rhodes College
Rollins College
Rose-Hulman Institute of Technology
Stevens Institute of Technology
Texas Christian University
Tulane University
University of Richmond
University of the South/Sewanee
University of Virginia
Ursinus College
Vanderbilt University
Wabash College
Wake Forest University
Washington and Lee University
Whitman College
Willamette University
Wofford College

Schools with No Fraternities or Sororities

Agnes Scott College
Alfred College
Amherst College

Antioch College
Bennington College
Boston College
Bowdoin College
Brandeis University
Brigham Young University
Bryn Mawr College
California Institute of Technology
California Institute of the Arts
Carleton College
Claremont McKenna College
Clark University
Colby College
College of the Atlantic
Connecticut College
Deep Springs College
DePaul University
Drew University
Earlham College
Eugene Lang College of The New School
    University
Evergreen State University
Fairfield University
Fordham University
Georgetown University
Goucher College
Hampshire College
Harvey Mudd College
Haverford College
Ithaca College
Lewis and Clark College
Macalester College
Marlboro College
Mills College
New College of South Florida
Pitzer College
Principia College
Rhode Island School of Design
Rice University
Sarah Lawrence College
Scripps College
Seton Hall University
Simmons College
Skidmore
Smith College
St. Bonaventure University
St. John's University/College of
    St. Benedict
St. Mary's College
St. Olaf College
Sweet Briar College
Trinity University
United States Air Force Academy
United States Coast Guard Academy
United States Military Academy
United States Naval Academy
University of Dallas
University of North Carolina/Chapel Hill

University of Notre Dame
University of Washington
Vassar College
Wellesley College
Wells College
Williams College

Schools with Very High Four-year Graduation Rates (>85%)

Amherst College
Bates College
Bucknell College
Carleton College
Claremont McKenna College
College of the Holy Cross
College of William and Mary
Columbia University
Dartmouth College
Davidson College
Duke University
Georgetown University
Harvard University
Haverford College
Johns Hopkins University
Lafayette College
Middlebury College
Muhlenberg College
Oberlin College
Oxford University
Pomona College
Princeton University
Principia College
St. Olaf College
Swarthmore College
Tufts University
United States Air Force Academy
United States Coast Guard Academy
United States Naval Academy
University of Chicago
University of Michigan
University of Notre Dame
University of Pennsylvania
University of Virginia
Vanderbilt University
Vassar College
Villanova University
Wake Forest University
Washington and Lee University
Washington University in St. Louis
Wellesley College
Whitman College
Williams College
Yale University

Under $10,000 (Out of State)

Brigham Young University
City University of New York/City College
College of William and Mary
Deep Springs College
Michigan State University
Millsaps College
Mississippi State University
New Mexico State University
Ohio University
Queen's University
Rutgers/The State University of
    New Jersey
United States Air Force Academy
United States Coast Guard Academy
United States Military Academy
United States Naval Academy
University of Arizona
University of Kansas
University of Michigan
University of Minnesota
University of South Alabama
University of South Dakota
University of Utah
University of Virginia
University of Waterloo
University of Western Ontario
West Virginia University

Under $10,000 (In State)

Arizona State University
Auburn University
Bowling Green State University
California Polytechnic State University/San
    Luis Obispo
California State University/Chico
California State University/Fresno
City University of New York/City College
Clemson University
Colorado School of Mines
Evergreen State University
Florida A & M University
Florida State University
George Mason University
Hunter College
Illinois State University
Indiana University, Bloomington
Iowa State University
Kansas State University
Louisiana State University

Marshall University
McGill University
Mississippi State University
New College of South Florida
New Mexico State University
Ohio State University
Oklahoma State University
Oregon State University
Southern Illinois University/Carbondale
State University of New York/Albany
State University of New York/Binghamton
State University of New York/Buffalo
State University of New York/Stony Brook
Texas A&M University
Texas Tech University
United States Air Force Academy
United States Coast Guard Academy
United States Military Academy
United States Naval Academy
University of California/Berkeley
University of California/Davis
University of California/Irvine
University of California/Los Angeles
University of California/Riverside
University of California/San Diego
University of California/Santa Barbara
University of California/Santa Cruz
University of Alabama
University of Alaska/Fairbanks
University of Arkansas
University of Cincinnati
University of Colorado/Boulder
University of Connecticut
University of Delaware
University of Florida
University of Georgia
University of Hawaii/Manoa
University of Houston
University of Idaho
University of Illinois/Chicago
University of Illinois/Urbana-Champaign
University of Iowa
University of Kansas
University of Kentucky
University of Maine/Orono
University of Maryland/College Park
University of Massachusetts/Amherst
University of Mississippi
University of Missouri/Columbia
University of Missouri/Kansas City
University of Montana
University of Nebraska/Lincoln
University of Nevada/Reno
University of New Mexico
University of North Carolina/Chapel Hill
University of North Dakota
University of Oklahoma
University of Oregon
University of Rhode Island

University of South Alabama
University of South Carolina
University of South Dakota
University of Tennessee/Knoxville
University of Texas/Austin
University of Washington
University of Wisconsin/Madison
University of Wyoming
Virginia Polytechnic University
Washington State
West Virginia University

Over $35,000

Amherst College
Bard College
Barnard College
Bennington College
Boston College
Boston University
Bowdoin College
Brandeis University
Brown University
Bucknell University
Carnegie Mellon University
Claremont McKenna College
Colgate University
Columbia University
Dickinson College
Franklin and Marshall College
George Washington University
Georgetown University
Hamilton College
Hampshire College
Haverford College
Kenyon College
Middlebury College
New York University
Pitzer College
Reed College
Sarah Lawrence College
Scripps College
St. John's University
St. Lawrence University
St. Olaf College
Stevens Institute of Technology
Swarthmore College
Trinity College
Tufts University
Tulane University
University of Pennsylvania
University of Richmond
Vassar College
Wheaton College
Whitman College

Insider's Quiz

What kind of college is right for you?

Which high school stereotype would best describe you?
a. Athlete
b. Intellectual
c. Hipster
d. Prepster
e. Emo or granola-loving Hippie

Which of the following statements do you best relate to?
a. I want everyone to have heard of my college!
b. It's okay if people haven't heard of my college before. I know it's a great school.
c. In college I want to have the big city at my fingertips!
d. I want my classmates to dress like me—classic and colorful with collars always up.
e. I can't wait to go to school with people who understand me!

You wouldn't like a college that:
a. Is too far away from home.
b. Isn't in the quintessential college town.
c. Isn't in a big city.
d. Has too many students who don't summer in Nantucket or Martha's Vineyard.
e. Doesn't care about political issues.

What do you expect walks to class will be like in college?
a. I'll see lots of people that I have never met before.
b. I'll see half my friends on the way and know almost all the people I see who are in my year.
c. I'll be surrounded by the noises, people, and cars that fill a busy, buzzing city.
d. It will look like a Ralph Lauren fashion show.
e. I'll be almost too busy reading all the posters about political activism events that are going on around campus to walk!

You imagine that varsity athletics at your dream school will be:
a. A huge draw.
b. Not as popular as intramural sports.
c. Not as well attended as the professional athletic events in the city.
d. Important depending on the sport—lacrosse and crew will be bigger than football and basketball.
e. What do you mean by varsity athletics?

Where do you see yourself meeting up with your college friends?
a. At the student center, the hub of campus activity.
b. On the quad, where people are hanging out on the lawn.
c. At one of the zillion Starbucks that are on every corner.
d. The squash court.
e. At social activism meetings.

When you run into your professor outside of class, what do you think you'll discuss?
a. Whether he/she saw the big game this weekend.
b. The intense argument about Kant that took place between the 10 students who make up the class.
c. Recommended local concert venues.
d. The best conditions for yachting.
e. Whether we could all just sit in a circle on the floor in the classroom and not at the desks.

You're running late to class, so you pull your tried-and-true wardrobe staple out of the closet:
a. Your school sweatshirt.
b. A sweater you permanently borrowed from your best friend.
c. Skinny jeans.
d. A Polo shirt.
e. A hand-dyed scarf obtained in an obscure country.

What will your dream job be like?
a. I'll be working at a big company with a dynamic atmosphere.
b. I'll work at a smaller company where I can have a big influence.
c. I'm not sure, but I know it will be in a big city.
d. I'll either be a high-power consultant or a trophy wife/husband.

e. Who knows? I don't plan for the future. I just go with the flow.

What will you be doing in your free time 10 years after college graduation?
  a. Cheering on my alma mater at home games.
  b. Reading books in the local coffee shop.
  c. Going to museums and cultural events during the day and clubbing at night.
  d. Relaxing at my getaway home, sailing, and gossiping about my old classmates.
  e. Going to rallies and protests.

Results

What kind of college is right for you?

If you answered mostly a's, a Big State School like University of Florida or Ohio State University.

If you answered mostly b's, a Small Liberal Arts school like Williams College or Vassar College.

If you answered mostly c's, an Urban School like New York University or Georgetown University.

If you answered mostly d's, a Preppy School like Washington and Lee University or Hamilton College.

If you answered mostly e's, an Alternative School like Wesleyan University or Reed College.

Insider's Packing List

Recreational

___Twister
___Deck of cards
___Dice
___A white T-shirt to write on
___Shot glass
___Board games
___Fan
___Feather boa
___Cowboy hat
___Picnic blanket
___Cute Facebook photo
___Bottle opener
___Corkscrew
___Water guns
___Water balloons
___Sexy underwear
___Bathing suit
___*Us Weekly* subscription
___Hookah
___Frisbee
___Volleyball/Basketball/Baseball (pretty much anything you can throw)
___Body paint
___Wig
___Game console (preferably a Nintendo Wii)

Practical

___Red cups
___Clorox wipes
___Airborne
___Shower shoes
___Febreze
___Tool kit
___iPod
___Duct tape
___Iron
___Layers
___Compact umbrella
___Brita
___Cough drops
___ATM card
___Checkbook

___Stamps
___Stationery
___Homemade cookies
___bleach pen
___Energy-saving lightbulbs
___Hand sanitizer
___Thai bowls
___Microwaveable mac & cheese
___One pair of shoes that you don't mind ruining
___One pair of shoes that you'd hate to ruin
___At least one nice outfit
___Social Security number (memorized)
___Best high school friends' e-mails and school addresses
___Markers
___Organized jewelry holder
___Lots of towels
___Hair straightener
___Plastic utensils
___Day planner
___Mirror
___Punch bowl
___Nalgene water bottle
___North Face fleece
___Ethernet cord
___Alarm clock
___Overnight bag
___As many pairs of socks and underwear as possible (to put off laundry day)
___Standing and/or desk lamp
___Hangers
___Scissors
___Digital camera
___Rechargeable batteries

Academic

___Laptop
___USB flash drive
___1-subject notebooks
___Index cards
___An endless supply of pens, highlighters, No. 2 pencils, etc.

Decorative

___Photos of your family
___Photos of your high school friends
___Christmas lights
___Sticky tack (for posters)
___Throw pillows
___Plastic hooks
___Corkboard
___Whiteboard

Things to Leave at Home

___Varsity jackets
___High school yearbooks
___Pleasure reading
___More than two stuffed animals
___A high school sweetheart
___SAT scores
___Trophies
___Stamp/baseball card/Absolut ad
    collections
___Dry-clean-only clothes
___College T-shirts

A Word About Statistics

Do you want to narrow your search, size up a school quickly, or check out your chances of getting admitted? Statistics are a useful place to start when you are browsing colleges, and they are also helpful in creating that perfect list of reach, mid-range, and safety schools to which you will apply. A statistical profile precedes every college in *The Insider's Guide*. The colleges themselves typically provide the data. The letters "NA" (not available) either represent data that the school did not report, or those that could not be found on the school's Web site. For the most up-to-date information, as well as for all data not included in *The Insider's Guide*, you should contact the colleges directly.

As a rule, the statistics provided are from the most recent year for which the college has information. In most cases, this means the last two academic years. In general, percentages have been rounded to the nearest whole-number percent. Statistically speaking, there is no significant difference between an acceptance rate of 30 percent and 30.4 percent; in fact, even a difference of 3 to 5 percent would hardly be noticeable.

Below the name of each school, the **address,** undergraduate **admissions phone number,** and undergraduate **admissions e-mail** address are listed; this is the contact information that a school's admissions office prefers applicants to use when corresponding.

A **Web site URL** is listed for each school, which we recommend you visit to get a quick sense of the school online.

Year Founded is the year that the school first accepted students.

The designation **private or public** refers to private schools versus publicly funded state schools. Tuition is often lower for public schools, especially for in-state students. This label cannot in any way be applied to refer to the quality of education.

Religious affiliation indicates whether a school is affiliated in any way with a particular religious establishment. This affiliation may vary—simply being a part of the school's history to being the religion predominantly practiced on campus.

Location describes the setting of the college, which is either rural, suburban, in a small city, or urban. This description gives only a general idea of the surroundings, and remember, like the rest of the statistics, it is given by the school itself.

Number of applicants is the number of completed first-year undergraduate applications received by the university.

The **percent accepted** figure is the number of applicants accepted for the most recent entering freshman class (in this case, usually the class of 2014) divided by the total number of applicants. This is an imperfect measure of a college's selectivity, and does not necessarily reflect academic quality, since many factors can influence acceptance rates. One example of this is that some schools with reputations for being easy after admission tend to attract larger numbers of applicants. For another example, public schools offer lower tuition to in-state residents, which is an attractive incentive for those applicants. Even winning sports teams can increase application numbers. There are many other factors that can influence the quality and size of the applicant pool even from year to year. Despite these caveats, the percent accepted figure is a revealing statistic. Colleges that accept relatively small numbers of applicants are usually in the best position to maintain high academic standards. When the acceptance rate is less than one-third, you can be assured that the school is one of the best around.

Percent accepted who enroll is the number of students who enroll divided by the number of students accepted. This figure, commonly called the "yield" by the admissions offices, is another way to assess how well a school attracts qualified applicants. Since many applicants have to decide between several schools, the yield is a good indicator of which schools are first-choice and which are "safety" schools. The latter usually have yields below 40 percent. The main use of yields is to compare colleges that have similar applicant pools. State universities tend to have high yields because some applicants are in-state students who do not apply elsewhere.

Number entering includes the total number of first-year students on campus at the beginning of the year.

Transfers reports the number of students who were accepted for transfer to that institution each year. The transfers accepted is a better indication of an applicant's chances of gaining admission than the actual number of transfers matriculated, since often the number of transfers accepted is large compared to the number of matriculating transfer students. Keep in mind that "NA" here does not mean that there were no transfers, only that the schools did not report a number. Of course, not every school accepts transfer students, but those that do may restrict the number or have as many students leaving as transferring. Many big state schools are known for accepting lots of transfers from local community colleges. For these reasons, the number of transfers is not a good measure of a school's popularity.

The College Board prefers schools to use the **middle 50% SAT** range when discussing scores. This represents the range in which half of a particular school's new freshman students' scores fell. A mathematics range of 550 to 650 would mean that half the incoming freshmen had SAT mathematics scores between 550 and 650. The middle 50 percent range are the numbers between the twenty-fifth and seventy-fifth percentile boundaries; someone whose SAT score falls on the seventy-fifth percentile scored higher than 75 percent of the people who took that particular test. The same applies for someone whose score falls on the twenty-fifth percentile; the median is a score at the fiftieth percentile. Therefore, if your SAT score falls within the middle 50 percent range, you are on par with the SAT scores of last year's successful applicants. This does not mean that you have a 50–50 chance of getting in. Instead, view this figure as an indication of your own competitiveness against the overall applicant pool that the school evaluates.

Schools in the South and Midwest often prefer the American College Test (ACT). We report the **middle 50% ACT** in addition to the **middle 50% SAT** ranges for this reason. The scale for this test is 1 to 36, and the middle 50 percent range for this test means the same as it does for the SAT.

There has been a growing population of students applying early to college to demonstrate commitment or to increase chances of admission using **early decision** or **early action**. A school's policy for early admission may include "early action" (EA) or "early decision" (ED). Both programs have application due dates far in advance of regular admission, so check with the school to make sure your application will arrive on time. Remember that while early action is advance

acceptance with the option of applying and matriculating elsewhere, early decision requires a commitment to matriculate and to rescind all outstanding applications to other schools. The fact that these programs exist should not exert any pressure on an applicant to commit to an institution early.

The **EA and ED deadlines** are dates for the submission of early applications, while **Regular Deadline** is the final date for completed applications (except for second-term grade reports and late admissions tests) for freshman students. Early decision and early action programs have different deadlines, and rolling admissions may have priority deadlines after which an application is at a disadvantage. Transfer student applications usually are due one or two months after freshman applications. Nevertheless, submitting your application early gives the admissions committee more time to become familiar with your application and increases your chance of getting in.

The **application fee** is the processing fee for an application and is due at the same time as the other application materials. Check with individual schools to see if the application fee can be waived for economic reasons or for in-state applicants.

Full-Time undergraduate enrollment is the number of full-time undergraduate students for the most recent year available at the time of publication, whereas **Total enrollment** gives the total number of students, including part-time and full-time undergraduates, graduate students, and professional students. Often the ratio of undergraduate to graduate students gives an indication of the relative emphasis an institution places on each.

Percent male/female (M/F) gives the percentage of undergraduates of each sex.

Percent minority is the percentage of enrolled students who indicated on their applications that they consider themselves members of a minority group. This figure is broken down by percentages of students in four broad minority groups—**African American, Asian/Pacific Islander, Hispanic, and Native American**—to give a measure of the ethnic diversity of the school. **Other** includes any student who is a member of a minority group but not one of the four listed above. Many students of different ethnicities, such as international students and biracial students, are not included in this section. You may want to contact the college directly for more specific information.

Percent in-state/out-of-state is the percentage of enrolled undergraduates who are residents of the state in which the school is located. For Canadian schools, the percentage is that of students from within Canada. This figure gives an approximation of the regional diversity of the school. Obviously, the in-state numbers will usually be much higher for public schools than for private schools, although in most cases, states provide incentives for private schools to take in-state students.

Percent from public HS is, of course, the percentage of students whose secondary education took place in a public school.

The **Retention rate** is the percentage of first-year students who remain enrolled at a given institution for their second (sophomore) year. This statistic is an indicator of the quality of life, resources, and general satisfaction of the students at a particular college. Like the statistics on percent accepted who enroll, these numbers are most useful in comparisons between schools of the similar academic caliber, size, and student body.

The **Graduation rate** represents the percentage of students who graduate successfully over a certain time period. Schools were asked for both their **four-year** and **six-year** graduation rates. Many students take at least five years to obtain their bachelor's degree, and in this case the six-year graduation rate would be higher than the four-year rate. Contact a school directly to find out how long the average student takes to complete the requirements for his or her degree. Generally students are more likely to take over four years to graduate in public schools than private schools.

Percent Undergraduates in on-campus housing gives the portion of students living in school-controlled housing. Some smaller schools guarantee on-campus housing for all students if they choose to remain on campus. At most institutions, a large percentage of the freshman class lives on campus, while most of the rest of the student body lives off campus. There are often opportunities for upperclassmen to live on campus if they choose to do so, as Resident Assistants (RAs) or in other student leader positions. Be prepared to seek off-campus housing arrangements early if a school's housing percentage is less than 90 percent or if no figure is listed.

The **number of official organized extracurricular organizations** figure represents the number of extracurricular organizations recognized by the college administration.

This is just another indicator of what student life is like outside of classes.

Three most popular majors lists the top programs of study among the seniors in the most recent graduating class for which the college has data. Remember, though, that popularity is not necessarily a measure of quality. Also, the exact number of students majoring in any given field can vary widely from year to year. Certain schools, however, are well-known for specific programs (e.g., criminology, biomedical engineering, government, journalism).

The **Student/Faculty** ratio indicates how many students there are in comparison to professors. While this statistic certainly varies by department, and has no real implication in the possibility of faculty-student interactions, many people like to know it. A more useful statistic is the **Average class size** for undergraduate classes, but beware, as often this includes small classes or sections not taught by a professor.

Percent of students going to grad school represents the percentage of students going on to graduate or professional school after graduation. Schools vary on whether this number represents those who go immediately after graduation, or after a few years. If you are interested in a particular graduate or professional degree, you may want to check with individual schools as to preparation programs they offer.

Tuition and fees and cost for **room and board** figures are given for the most recent year available. In cases where costs differ for **in-state** and out-of-state students, both figures are listed. Also, many public schools charge tuition that varies with the course load taken. Remember that these figures are meant as an estimate of the cost for a year at a given institution, and do not include travel, books, and personal expenses. These figures tend to increase every year. Use these figures as a relative index of how expensive one college is compared to another. For Canadian schools, these figures are reported in Canadian dollars.

For **percent receiving financial aid out of those who apply, first year**, schools are asked to report the percentage of the entering class receiving need-based financial assistance from the institution out of those applying for aid. This does not include students receiving only merit-based scholarships, federal loans not given out by the institution, and students who did not apply for aid. These figures are most relevant for comparing similar institutions. As to the **percent receiving financial aid among all students**, the number indicates the ratio of number of students receiving financial aid over undergraduate enrollment. Questions about schools' particular financial aid programs should be addressed directly to their financial aid offices.

Finally, **Canadian schools** report their statistical information in a very different manner from American schools, so some statistics such as average SAT scores are not reported. However, it is important to know that Canadian universities are familiar with applicants from the United States, since a large number of Americans do travel north for college education. As you get deeper into your search, it will be important to contact Canadian colleges directly since most schools in Canada also report their deadlines and statistics by individual program of study rather than for the college or university as a whole. Furthermore, admissions procedures, competitiveness, and tuition fees are often very different based on whether the student is a Canadian or international citizen, as well as the specific type of academic program. Our advice is to visit the schools' Web sites for detailed statistical information on the specific programs.

Alabama

Auburn University

Address: Quad Center, Auburn, AL 36849
Phone: 800-282-8769
E-mail address: admissions@auburn.edu
Web site URL: www.auburn.edu
Year Founded: 1856
Private or Public: Public
Religious Affiliation: None
Location: Suburban
Number of Applicants: 17,798
Percent Accepted: 69%
Percent Accepted who enroll: 34%
Number Entering: 4,160
Number of Transfers Accepted each Year: 1,980
Middle 50% SAT range: M: 520–630, CR: 500–610, Wr: Unreported
Middle 50% ACT range: 22–27
Early admission program EA/ED/None: None

Percentage accepted through EA or ED: NA
EA and ED deadline: NA
Regular Deadline: Rolling
Application Fee: $40
Full time Undergraduate enrollment: 19,812
Total enrollment: 23,187
Percent Male: 52%
Percent Female: 48%
Total Percent Minority or Unreported: 15%
Percent African-American: 9%
Percent Asian/Pacific Islander: 2%
Percent Hispanic: 2%
Percent Native-American: <1%
Percent International: 1%
Percent in-state/out of state: 69%/31%
Percent from Public HS: 86%
Retention Rate: 86%
Graduation Rate 4-year: 34%

Graduation Rate 6-year: 62%
Percent Undergraduates in On-campus housing: 14%
Number of official organized extracurricular organizations: 300
3 Most popular majors: Business, Education, Engineering
Student/Faculty ratio: 18:1
Average Class Size: 25
Percent of students going to grad school: 35%
Tuition and Fees: $18,260
In-State Tuition and Fees if different: $6,500
Cost for Room and Board: $8,260
Percent receiving financial aid out of those who apply: 64%
Percent receiving financial aid among all students: 54%

There's much more to Auburn University than its storied football rivalry with the University of Alabama. Students at the South's first land grant university benefit from exceptional academic resources across 12 undergraduate schools. The first school in the nation to offer a Bachelor's in Wireless Engineering, Auburn isn't afraid of innovation, but is also steeped in almost 200 years of tradition. The Southern friendliness that permeates campus makes the Auburn family a close-knit group. Students and alums alike often address each other with a "War Eagles" greeting, the official battle cry of Auburn's beloved football team.

Get Schooled

Auburn has 12 schools for undergraduates, a mix of liberal arts and pre-professional programs. The schools of Architecture and Veterinary Medicine are particularly prestigious, but most undergrads take their classes at the College of Liberal Arts or the Ginn College of Engineering. Freshmen often end up in larger core classes like English Composition or Biology 101. Students generally don't find academic requirements, which are "designed to be flexible," too taxing. One hard-and-fast rule, though, is 12 credit-hours a semester; most students take around 15, usually across five courses. Those courses aren't easy, either: one Honors College student says teachers definitely "make you earn your grade." Auburn's most popular majors are Business, Engineering, and Education, and while class size "depends on your major," classes generally tend to shrink in the upper grades. Despite the school's large size, professors are known to make themselves available, often through their office hours. At the same time, "it's the student's responsibility to take that step forward," according to one senior. TAs don't have quite the same accessible reputation, and students say some have trouble speaking clear English.

Most Auburn students don't complain of being overworked. Come finals, though, Draughton Library gets "packed," and the Student Government Association provides massages and donuts to stressed-out students. The SGA also organizes on-campus events and concerts throughout the year.

Studying abroad isn't huge at Auburn, although the university offers a range of programs. One student estimates that about one in 10 participate in some sort of program outside the country, but it's largely dependent on major, with foreign language majors more likely to study abroad.

Each of the 12 schools does advising on its own, and "some are better than others," but students can take advantage of career services or more general student counseling. Overall, students feel they can always find someone to talk to.

Tiger Den
Most of Auburn's students live off campus. Housing is not guaranteed for anyone, even freshmen, but apartments near campus are comfortable and easily accessible, thanks to the university's Tiger Transit system. Those who stay on campus end up in one of three residence hall clusters—The Hill, The Village, or the Quad—each of which has easily accessible laundry facilities, kitchens, and social space. Construction on another cluster is set to finish in the summer of 2013, as the university continues to expand its housing capacity. But the proximity of nearby apartment buildings, combined with the fact that 69% of students have a car on campus, means that the dearth of housing doesn't bother too many Auburn students. The same can't be said for parking, which can be a "nightmare," although the university is working to add more spaces. Other campus facilities include the Student Activities Center and the Health and Wellness Center, which includes a climbing wall and a tiger paw–shaped whirlpool.

Auburn students are generally content with their dining options, and the food is "always good quality," according to a sophomore. Terrell Dining Hall and the War Eagle Food Court feed the bulk of campus, with the university offering options like fajitas, make-your-own pasta, and other dining hall mainstays. Some commercial eateries operate on campus, and students can use their Tiger Card "like a debit card" for others in town. Food trucks are increasingly visible, and some local restaurants are so famous that they have become legends. One sophomore says that Momma G's deli, with its buffalo chicken nachos, is a "staple of Auburn tradition."

Southern Comfort
Auburn is a Southern school in more ways than one. The majority of students are "Southern born and bred," with roughly 60% from Alabama alone, and the region's rural vibe and agricultural history still permeate campus, according to one senior. Auburn students embody "Southern politeness," a stereotype they're proud to confirm even when face-to-face with rival football fans, who are "shocked at how welcoming we are." "On the whole," qualifies one student, "Auburn fans are polite and pleasant to interact with." That congeniality is perhaps best embodied by "Hey Day," an event organized by administration during which students are encouraged to wear nametags and "say hey" to their fellow Tigers.

Students here are fairly preppy and "dress more formally," while the campus as a whole is very conservative. Not surprisingly, around 20% of guys and 30% of girls at Auburn are Greek. Social life can revolve around frats, where many students will go to party all year round, but they certainly don't "control the whole campus," says one student. For of-age students, favorite local watering holes include Sky Café and the Bank Vault. Drinking is fairly prominent at Auburn, and campus police are said to be relaxed, but "Auburn isn't typically known as a drinking school." Given the number of cars on campus, drunk driving is a concern, but a volunteer designated-driver program offers rides to discourage risky behavior.

Students who are not in frats can find their niche in any one of the more than 300 student organizations on campus, ranging from Habitat for Humanity to WEGL, the student radio station. But part of Auburn's charm is its small-school feel, being a part of the "Auburn Family," and kids feel at home in the student population in general.

Set, Hike!
Part of what makes that community is, of course, football. On Saturdays throughout

the fall and often extending well into winter, Jordan-Hare Stadium brims with 85,000 screaming, orange-and-blue clad Tigers who turn out to support their team. The tailgate scene is always a highlight, and students will dress up before heading to the games, sundresses and all. The school's official cheer is a rousing "War Eagle!" screamed at kickoff, and Auburn has had plenty to cheer for over the past few years. They even captured the BCS National Championship in 2010 behind Heisman winner—and current Carolina Panthers quarterback—Cam Newton, the latest in a long line of great Auburn athletes like Bo Jackson and Charles Barkley. After games, revelry spills out of the stadium to Toomer's Corner and its celebrated oaks, which students drape with toilet paper—a ritual known as "rolling"—after an Auburn win. The Iron Bowl, a game between Auburn and Alabama every year, is not to be missed.

> **"Even for those who don't care much about football, the experience and atmosphere are still wonderful."**

When football season ends, campus refocuses around other hangout spots. The Foy Student Union houses War Eagle food court, a CD and game store, an ATM, and a mail drop, as well as lounge space for students to kick back. At the other end of campus is the Haley Center, an academic nucleus containing lecture halls and the Auburn bookstore. Students also hang out at the library, said to be a social hub. In the spring, students gravitate towards off-campus apartment complexes in Auburn, where "there's usually something going on."

Something for Everyone

Auburn boasts the best of both worlds. With 12 schools and plush facilities, it offers anything that a large university can, housing aside. It's always easy to find something to do, and with nearly 20,000 undergrads, students are sure to meet someone who shares their interests. Auburn also offers something few other schools can: a highly competitive football team in college sports' toughest conference. At the same time, the southern friendliness that permeates campus makes the Auburn family a close-knit group. From the football field to the film club, veterinary school to liberal arts, everyone finds something they love at Auburn. That is, if they can find a parking spot first.—*David Whipple*

FYI
If I could change one thing about Auburn, I'd "add more parking."
Typical weekend schedule: "Tailgate a football game, win a football game, celebrate at Toomer's corner, and then head to the frats at night."
Three things all Auburn students should do before graduating are "get a picture with Aubie (Auburn's mascot), climb to the top of Sanford tower and sign your name, and roll Toomer's corner."

Birmingham-Southern College

Address: 900 Arkadelphia Road, Birmingham, AL 35254	**Percentage accepted through EA or ED:** NA	**Graduation Rate 6-year:** 69%
Phone: 800-523-5793	**EA and ED deadline:** NA	**Percent Undergraduates in On-campus housing:** 77%
E-mail address: admission@bsc.edu	**Regular Deadline:** Rolling	
Web site URL: www.bsc.edu	**Application Fee:** $40	**Number of official organized extracurricular organizations:** 70
Year Founded: 1856	**Full time Undergraduate enrollment:** 1,389	
Private or Public: Private	**Total enrollment:** 1,389	**3 Most popular majors:** Business Administration/Management, Health/Medical Preparatory Programs, Pre-Law Studies
Religious Affiliation: United Methodist	**Percent Male:** 59%	
Location: Urban	**Percent Female:** 41%	
Number of Applicants: 2,227	**Total Percent Minority or Unreported:** 16%	
Percent Accepted: 60%	**Percent African-American:** 9%	**Student/Faculty ratio:** 10:1
Percent Accepted who enroll: 23%	**Percent Asian/Pacific Islander:** 2%	**Average Class Size:** 15
Number Entering: 292	**Percent Hispanic:** 2%	**Percent of students going to grad school:** 50%
Number of Transfers Accepted each Year: 101	**Percent Native-American:** <1%	**Tuition and Fees:** $25,586
Middle 50% SAT range: M: 520–650, CR: 520–640, Wr: Unreported	**Percent International:** Unreported	**In-State Tuition and Fees if different:** No difference
Middle 50% ACT range: 22–28	**Percent in-state/out of state:** 67%/33%	**Cost for Room and Board:** $8,595
Early admission program EA/ED/None: None	**Percent from Public HS:** 65%	**Percent receiving financial aid out of those who apply:** 80%
	Retention Rate: 86%	**Percent receiving financial aid among all students:** 46%
	Graduation Rate 4-year: 60%	

Nearby universities compete for dominance on the football field, but Birmingham-Southern College is Alabama's undisputed academic powerhouse. The private liberal arts college challenges its 1,389 students to think broadly and deeply, offering small classes and close relationships with faculty and professors. Outside of the classroom, students are part of a close-knit community that offers plenty of options for entertainment, socializing, and getting involved in clubs and organizations—all set on a leafy campus featuring Federalist architecture, expansive quads, and a lake that becomes a popular hang-out spot on sunny days. The parks, bars, and restaurants of downtown Birmingham are just three miles away, but many students find they rarely want to leave the "bubble" of the gated campus, known as "the Hilltop."

"It all comes down to academics"

Students at Southern agree that the college's academics are rigorous, and claim that nearly everyone on campus makes schoolwork a priority. "You could be the star of the football team at BSC, but you're going to get respect for being a great student," said one senior history major. Although he and others bemoan their workloads, generally agreed to be significantly heavier than those of friends at nearby schools, they feel that the quality of teaching makes the additional work "worth it."

BSC's general education requirements, called the "Explorations" curriculum, are fairly significant and force students to take courses across a range of disciplines with the goal of producing graduates who can "communicate effectively, solve problems creatively, engage their social and political world, connect their coursework to the wider world, and engage in self-directed teaching and learning." To that end, students must take classes in writing and critical thinking, creative expression, quantitative analysis, scientific methodologies, foreign language, the analysis of peoples and societies, and ethics. Although the curriculum is extensive, students say it is flexible enough to be manageable. One junior business administration major took a painting class to satisfy the creative expression requirement and discovered a "hidden talent" for the arts, something she thinks would have been unlikely at a different school.

BSC offers 30 majors and 23 minors, along with a number of special academic programs, including the selective Harrison Honors program that allows students to complete an interdisciplinary research project and participate in special seminars. Business and biology are among the most popular majors. The hard sciences and mathematics majors are known for being difficult, especially chemistry and physics. A senior who plans to graduate with a double major in mathematics and economics recalled that many prospective mathematics majors were weeded out during challenging introductory courses. One senior English major noted that although the hard sciences are considered more difficult, the humanities and social science majors are "equally intellectually challenging." All majors offer difficult courses, but some introductory courses, such as Introduction to Sociology and Introduction to Education Studies, require less work.

The rigor of BSC stems from its small class sizes and active professors. The average class has 15 students, the student to faculty ratio is 10:1, and full professors teach every class, with teaching assistants providing help with grading and planning. Nearly every student at BSC values his or her close relationships with professors, who are always available via email and generally take an active interest in their students' growth and intellectual development. While the instructors are demanding, students agree they are willing to help by freely offering their time, meeting with students after class, answering questions, and explaining concepts. One junior communications major texted some of her professors upon finding out that she'd secured an internship for the January interim term and was impressed by the fact that they were all "so excited and happy" for her.

In addition to their regular coursework, BSC students must complete at least two "January term" classes during their four years at the college. "J-term" offers students the chance to explore a fun or unusual topic in a class on campus, study abroad with professors, or get an internship. Students fondly recalled a trip to Italy with a beloved professor of art history, a course on barbeque, and studying art history by applying Queer Theory. They must also obtain at least 24 "culture credits" by attending guest lectures and performances on campus.

Small and cozy but tolerant and inclusive

Students say the college's liberal arts ethos both attracts and creates young adults who are generally tolerant and open-minded. One sophomore business administration major said that his best friend, a senior, is a member of both the College Republicans and Allies, the LGBTQ advocacy organization on campus. But while intellectual diversity is extensive (surprisingly so, given the school's Deep South location, said one senior from a small town in Alabama), socioeconomic and racial diversity is limited. The school has a reputation as a "rich white kid's" college, and many students fit the "preppy" stereotype. Students said the college is working to change this image. Under the leadership of President General Charles Krulak, BSC has begun a drive to attract greater numbers of international students, and one senior from Sri Lanka said he'd already noticed an increase in the number of internationals, who generally number around 45. Domestic minorities remain underrepresented, but a senior history major was quick to note that the student body had elected a Latino as its student body president.

Because the majority of students live on campus, including all freshmen and most students in other classes, students say the dorms are a good way to meet people. Women in the freshman class are housed in either Margaret Daniels Hall or Cullen Daniels Hall, while men live in the New Men's dorm. Each dorm houses students in halls of fully furnished doubles with communal bathrooms and a common room on each floor. Students are assigned roommates after completing housing questionnaires, and athletes are generally placed with teammates. In terms of facilities, "It's obviously not the most glamorous," said one senior biology major who remembers "freaking out" about rooming and being pleasantly surprised that his room was larger than a coffin. One sophomore recalled that his freshman year room was "pretty average, nothing to complain about, just a regular dorm."

After freshman year, students enter a housing lottery with preference given to older students and to students with the highest GPAs within each year. "Once you're a sophomore, befriend the smart seniors," advised the senior biology major—students enter the lottery in pairs or groups, and the group is given the draw time of the best-positioned member. Options range from stand-alone doubles to suites of five singles to apartments outfitted with kitchens and private bathrooms. The apartments are a favorite choice for many students, allowing additional space and a feeling of independence while still being close to campus. One senior gloated that the bedroom came furnished with a king-sized bed.

All students who live on campus are required to purchase a meal plan. Dorm residents may purchase a seven-day plan, which includes unlimited access to the dining hall—known as The Caf—or a five-day plan, so they can eat at The Caf during the week and use "Panther Bucks" to buy food from the on-campus Subway or convenience store on weekends. Apartment residents buy a reduced meal plan that mixes Panther Bucks with 150 meals in The Caf. Food is said to be "not half-bad," though one Hindu junior said she has trouble finding satisfying vegetarian options, "And I can only imagine how hard it is for vegans," she added. The Caf's "Flat-top Grill" and "Homezone" rotate their menus each day, while pizza, pasta, burgers, and the salad bar are dining hall staples. One Subway employee, Mrs. Queenie, is a "campus legend," and several students said befriending her should be on every student's college bucket list.

The neighborhood surrounding BSC, Arkadelphia, offers relatively little in terms of dining and entertainment. "Well, there's two gas stations and a Wal-Mart a little ways off," said one junior who admitted to spending most of her free time on the Hilltop. Although Arkadelphia is "not the safest neighborhood," students feel secure because campus is gated. "There's literally one entrance," noted a senior. When they do leave campus, students drive three miles down the highway to downtown Birmingham—transportation is never a problem because most students have cars. Downtown, students enjoy local breweries, barbeque spots, and ethnic restaurants offering everything from top-notch Thai to $2 tacos.

Life in "The Bubble"

Some Birmingham residents deride BSC as an exclusive bubble, but students don't seem to mind that designation. They find that their insular campus has plenty to offer, including on the weekends, when performances, parties, and sporting events abound. Greek organizations dominate BSC

social life. About half of the student body joins one of the six fraternities or six sororities on campus, and many more attend parties and socials at the houses. "The Row," where all the fraternity houses are located, is a fixture of campus nightlife. For fraternity members, almost every weekend night is spent partying or unwinding with brothers at the house. Sorority sisters tend to go out to parties or socials as a group.

Rush begins informally during the summer before freshmen arrive, with frats and sororities hosting meet-and-greets for incoming students. Two weeks after school starts, the three-day official rush period begins, culminating in bid night, which turns into a massive party on The Row for the entire campus. Since the rush period is relatively short, it feels less like "a circus" than at other Southern schools, but periodically calls arise for a delayed rush that begins during the second semester; these calls are generally ignored.

The Greek scene dominates campus social life (and even intramurals, with most teams sponsored by a frat or sorority), but since parties are open to all, it never feels exclusive or intimidating, said one non-Greek junior. "It just never occurred to me to rush, and I've never regretted not rushing," she added. One sophomore Sigma Chi brother said the frat has plenty of pseudo-members who frequently hang out at the house but never went through the formal rush process, "and that's fine."

Since most partying occurs at The Row, drinking in dorms and apartments is limited. And although BSC isn't conservative by Alabama standards, most students oppose drug use. One brother recalled that anyone caught using drugs during the pledging period was immediately dismissed from the fraternity. Binge drinking is also not seen as a problem—plenty of students drink, but most "know how to handle themselves." The college treats students like "mature adults," said one senior mathematics major. "If you're acting stupid in public, you'll probably get in trouble," he said. But the college recognizes that students drink and doesn't "harass" them or shut down parties. Alcohol is allowed in dorms, provided students are over 21, and although "it depends on the RA," most RAs are fairly relaxed and more focused on planning study breaks than on confiscating illicit alcohol.

Aside from the Greek parties, the Student Government Association's entertainment board, called Quest II, organizes back-to-school formal dinners at the start of each semester, a Christmas party each December, a Mardi Gras ball, and two weekend concert series—E-Fest in the fall and SoCo in the spring—that feature local and national acts. "We had the Yin-Yang Twins, Hoodie Allen, and a couple of years ago The Fray came," said a senior biology major. The campus-wide events are free and well-attended, and faculty members often attend with their families. At the Christmas party, students help faculty children decorate gingerbread houses and student bands provide entertainment.

As is common throughout the South, BSC students are big sports fans, coming out regularly to tailgate and cheer for their Division III teams. Basketball, lacrosse, baseball, and football are among the most popular teams, although the football team is somewhat overshadowed by the powerhouse programs at Auburn and the University of Alabama. That doesn't matter a bit on homecoming weekend, when "everybody comes out to cheer for the football team," and many alumni return to the Hilltop with their families.

> "You could be the star of the football team at BSC, but you're going to get respect for being a great student."

To the students at BSC, small is beautiful, enabling them to form close relationships with professors and with each other. Every downside of the campus's size—limited class offerings, "everybody knows everybody," etc.—is outweighed by the benefits of a tight-knit community, and students say they wouldn't trade their time on The Hilltop for all the SEC football championships in the world.—*Isabelle Taft*

FYI

If you come to Birmingham-Southern, you'd better bring: good walking shoes, because it's very hilly!

If you come to Birmingham-Southern, you'd better leave behind: recklessness. If you make fool of yourself at The Row during your first week, you'll get a bad reputation, and on a small campus, that can stick for a while.

Three things every Birmingham-Southern student should do before graduating are: 1. Befriend Mrs. Queenie at Subway. 2. Stay out late at The Row and then get food from Al's. 3. Go to an art opening featuring the work of students or local artists.

Tuskegee University

Address: 120 Old
Administration Building,
Tuskegee, AL 36088
Phone: 334-727-8500
E-mail address:
adm@tuskegee.edu
Web site URL:
www.tuskegee.edu
Year Founded: 1881
Private or Public: Private
Religious Affiliation: None
Location: Rural
Number of Applicants: 2,471
Percent Accepted: 64%
**Percent Accepted who
enroll:** 44%
Number Entering: 701
**Number of Transfers
Accepted each Year:** 378
Middle 50% SAT range:
M: 380–490, CR: 400–500,
Wr: Unreported
Middle 50% ACT range:
17–22
**Early admission program
EA/ED/None:** None

**Percentage accepted
through EA or ED:** NA
EA and ED deadline: NA
Regular Deadline: Rolling
Application Fee: $25
**Full time Undergraduate
enrollment:** 2,411
Total enrollment: 2,479
Percent Male: 44%
Percent Female: 56%
**Total Percent Minority or
Unreported:** 99%
Percent African-American:
84%
**Percent Asian/Pacific
Islander:** <1%
Percent Hispanic: <1%
Percent Native-American:
<1%
Percent International: 1%
**Percent in-state/out of
state:** 28%/72%
Percent from Public HS:
Unreported
Retention Rate: 71%
Graduation Rate 4-year: 25%

Graduation Rate 6-year: 50%
**Percent Undergraduates in
On-campus housing:** 55%
**Number of official organized
extracurricular
organizations:** 36
3 Most popular majors:
Electrical, Electronics and
Communications
Engineering, Veterinary
Medicine
Student/Faculty ratio: 12:1
Average Class Size: 15
**Percent of students going to
grad school:** 23%
Tuition and Fees: $17,070
**In-State Tuition and Fees if
different:** No difference
Cost for Room and Board:
$7,950
**Percent receiving financial
aid out of those who apply:**
80%
**Percent receiving financial
aid among all students:**
92%

Tuskegee University has historically been home to many generations of African American men and women searching for an outstanding academic experience in addition to a unique cultural enrichment. Tuskegee's close-knit student community lives and studies in one of the country's most historic African American universities.

Changing Tradition
Tuskegee affords its undergraduates the opportunity to pursue a true liberal arts education through the College of Liberal Arts and Education. Although it was founded with the intention of giving African Americans a more technical, career-specific education to give them an edge in specific job markets, the curriculum has gradually changed to ally Tuskegee with other liberal arts schools. Still, some traditions remain: all freshmen are required to take an orientation course, which consists of University history, including the mandatory reading of Booker T. Washington's *Up from Slavery*, and advice for adapting to college life. Freshmen will also discover that their other basic requirements include physical education and English courses.

The University includes five colleges in total: the College of Agriculture, Environmental and Natural Sciences; the College of Business and Information Science; the College of Engineering, Architecture and Physical Sciences; the College of Veterinary Medicine, Nursing and Allied Health; and the College of Liberal Arts and Education. Thus, despite the shift toward a more liberal arts–oriented academic environment, many Tuskegee students are engineering or science majors. The school often receives acclaim for its pre-vet, pre-med and nursing programs, and students confirm high numbers of enrollees in each of these disciplines. Lower level lectures tend to enroll between 40 and 50 students, but the average class size overall is about 20 students. Students like the class sizes, and report that "whatever class size you prefer, you can usually pick accordingly." The smaller class sizes and minimal use of TAs keep student-faculty interaction high. Students generally give Tuskegee's academics a high rating. There were those who disagreed, remarking that "it can be easy to feel lost in the larger classes that don't have TAs," but on the whole, many agreed that the school is "demanding but rewarding." Tuskegee's history is clearly visible around its campus. A senior commented that "It's very cool, some of the brick buildings were built by students when the school was founded."

Still Living in the Past

The residential life on campus is one of students' more frequent complaints. In addition to being "ancient" and "without much furniture," dorms are not coed and students are required to live on campus both freshman and sophomore years. The older dorm buildings have a reputation for being in poor physical condition, and one student called the dorms "older than rocks." "You had better bring things that make you feel at home," said one undergrad, because "there's no real cozy feeling." The on-campus apartment situation is slightly better; the Commons apartments offer students the amenities of a kitchen in addition to rooms that they can make their own with decorations. Students' biggest problem, however, is with the University housing regulations. Because of the school's conservative nature, men's and women's dorms are separated by a 10-minute walk to prevent students from visiting those of the opposite gender. The University staff also keeps a close eye on dorms; students are not allowed to be on the "wrong" side of campus after 11 p.m. and, if caught, face punishment.

> "The town of Tuskegee offers nothing except seclusion from the modern world, but you learn a lot trapped in the wilderness."

Many upperclassmen choose to move off campus. One student said of the coed policies, "I love my campus, but I had to leave it because of the rules." Students tend to meet in the student union, which contains a movie theater, a grill, a game room and offices for student organizations. The student cafeteria is another popular meeting place, and serves as a place where Tuskegee's many clubs and organizations can meet to bring students together. Some of the biggest clubs are the state clubs, which unite students hailing from the same state to plan activities relating to their home turf. African American groups like the National Society of Black Engineers and several prominent fraternities and sororities are also present on campus. There is an active chapter of ROTC, which helps some students to fund their education. Students are active in community service, and the nearby hospital employs a number of Tuskegee students.

Football and basketball games generate great excitement at Tuskegee. In particular, the rivalries with Morehouse College and Alabama State University tend to draw the largest crowds to sporting events. Homecoming is one of the biggest social events of the year. The weeklong tradition incorporates performances by student groups, the Miss Tuskegee Gala and a number of pep rallies to boost school spirit. In the spring, the school hosts "Springfest," an event drawing many students together for shows, concerts and a dance.

The Typical Tuskegee Student

While the Greek system is a visible presence on campus, students report that they do not feel an urge to rush. There is little animosity between the fraternities, but they reportedly have a "friendly rivalry." Officially, alcohol is prohibited on campus and students who are caught with it face fines or other penalties. As a result, drinking generally tends to occur off campus. Students said they considered the town of Tuskegee "slow," but most agree that it has most of the things necessary for college life. And, as one student put it, "Tuskegee has a lot of potential to grow," adding, "but you come for the school, not the town." Tuskegee students also added that their campus is safe, with a large body of security officers and a closely monitored electronic keycard system.

Tuskegee is more than just an academic college experience; it is also one of cultural and historical enrichment. The school's fundamental mission remains an avid part of why students attend, and the school's community and tradition are enough to overcome some of its more conservative and comparatively strict policies. The experience tends to bind people in a lasting way. As one student said, "There are a lot of good people here and you can meet a lot of great minds—not to mention we're friends for life. People might complain about things here, but in the end, you don't want to leave."—*Melissa Chan and Staff*

FYI

If you come to Tuskegee, you'd better bring "a car to survive here because the nearest mall is 20 minutes away. The town of Tuskegee offers nothing except seclusion from the modern world, but you learn a lot trapped in the wilderness."

What's the typical weekend schedule? "Go to a football game if we're playing at home and then party at a fraternity at night."

If I could change one thing about Tuskegee I'd "change the administration. It seems to have no respect or regard for the students, the registration process takes three days, and the dorms are really run-down."

The three things every student should do before graduating from Tuskegee are "try the food at the Chicken Coop, go to Homecoming, and visit the George Washington Carver Museum on campus."

University of Alabama

Address: P.O. Box 870132, Tuscaloosa, AL 35487-0132
Phone: 205-348-5666
E-mail address: admissions@ua.edu
Web site URL: www.ua.edu
Year Founded: 1831
Private or Public: Public
Religious Affiliation: None
Location: Suburban
Number of Applicants: 20,112
Percent Accepted: 54%
Percent Accepted who enroll: 51%
Number Entering: 5,489
Number of Transfers Accepted each Year: 2,006
Middle 50% SAT range: M: 500–620, CR: 490–620, Wr: 480–600
Middle 50% ACT range: 22–29
Early admission program EA/ED/None: None

Percentage accepted through EA or ED: NA
EA and ED deadline: NA
Regular Deadline: Rolling
Application Fee: $40
Full time Undergraduate enrollment: 22,866
Total enrollment: 24,882
Percent Male: 48%
Percent Female: 52%
Total Percent Minority or Unreported: 19%
Percent African-American: 12%
Percent Asian/Pacific Islander: 1%
Percent Hispanic: 2%
Percent Native-American: 1%
Percent International: 2%
Percent in-state/out of state: 69%/31%
Percent from Public HS: Unreported
Retention Rate: Unreported
Graduation Rate 4-year: 35%

Graduation Rate 6-year: 62%
Percent Undergraduates in On-campus housing: Unreported
Number of official organized extracurricular organizations: 348
3 Most popular majors: Accounting, Finance, Marketing/Marketing Management
Student/Faculty ratio: 19:1
Average Class Size: 15
Percent of students going to grad school: 24%
Tuition and Fees: $21,900
In-State Tuition and Fees if different: $6,400
Cost for Room and Board: $8,564
Percent receiving financial aid out of those who apply: 65%
Percent receiving financial aid among all students: 62%

The University of Alabama, with a thriving football culture and Greek life, is no stranger to tradition. Founded in 1831, UA now enrolls roughly 33,000 students as the state's largest university. Nicknamed "the Capstone" by its students, the college consistently ranks among the top 50 public universities. Surviving the destruction of the Civil War and the chaos of the Civil Rights movement, the University of Alabama has earned its cherished chant: "roll, tide, roll."

Greek Galore

UA boasts the largest Greek community in the country. More than 7,000 students decide to join one of the 56 sororities and fraternities on campus. Along with the Crimson Tide football team, Greek life dominates the social scene. One student describes the sorority rushing process as "very intense and demanding." As one senior reports, "If you don't find your niche, it can be difficult."

But with a smorgasbord of extracurricular options, most students have no trouble finding that niche. Beyond Greek life, the Student Government Association is especially popular on campus. The Crimson White, the student-run newspaper created in 1894, continues to be a popular source of campus news and has a history of investigative journalism still alive today.

Despite the prominent Greek social scene, students insist that alcohol is not necessary for a fulfilling social life. "Drinking is a personal choice. No one judges others on their decision," one student says. But another student admits, "It is prominent. It is here." Along the same lines, one student sums up the campus environment surrounding drugs: "If you're looking for it, you're going to find it."

Many students take advantage of the university's location in the heart of Tuscaloosa. "The Strip," as a student hotspot, offers bars, restaurants and shops about a mile from campus. With no shortage of options, students say there's something for everyone. Among the numerous restaurants, students name Bento, Mellow Mushroom and Buffalo Phil's as favorites.

On campus, the university's dining options still seem to satisfy most students. Three main dining halls serve traditional buffet-style meals, while the Ferguson Center Student Union—shortened to "the Ferg" by students—houses an extensive food court (including the largest Starbucks in the nation!).

With an extensive campus police presence, students say they feel safe walking around campus at night. Freshmen are required to live on campus, and there is a wide range of housing options. Given the diversity of options—traditional rooms or suite-style living, coed or gender-specific—the dorms "provide a very nice home away from home," according to one student. To make room for continually growing class sizes, the university unveiled its newest housing addition, the "Presidential Village," in August 2012.

Asked about the diversity on campus, students say there are significant numbers of out-of-state and international students. But, as one student says, a sense of southern hospitality seems universal.

An Academic Grab Bag

The University of Alabama houses eight undergraduate colleges: Arts and Sciences, Commerce and Business Administrations, Communications and Information Services, Education, Engineering, Human Environmental Sciences, Nursing and Social Work. Between them, the colleges offer 80 majors and a mix of liberal arts and pre-professional

tracks—a true grab bag of educational opportunities. In fact, the academic diversity at the University of Alabama is a source of individuality in an otherwise homogenous school. "We are a small college within a big university," said one senior in the Communications school. "It's really the best of both worlds."

For those unfulfilled by the usual offerings, the Honors College and the New College provide additional options. While the Honors College is selective—entering freshmen must have a 3.3 high school GPA and a composite ACT of 28 or SAT of 1250 (verbal and quantitative)—University of Alabama students can apply late, as long as they have a minimum GPA of 3.3. Admission into the Honors College allows students to take departmental honors courses, which are limited to Honors students and are typically smaller than their counterparts. There are no special Honors majors, but Honors students do graduate with Honors distinction on their diploma.

A haven of progressive education, the New College allows students to design their own major or minor, or to pursue one of two preset minors in Interdisciplinary Environmental Studies or Leadership and Civic Engagement. The New College emphasizes independent research and facilitates close relationships between students, faculty and administrators. One student, a minor in Leadership and Civic Engagement, said he has been invited over to professors' houses and called them at one or two in the morning; the "administration, faculty and staff really have a vested interest in our lives, academic and personal," he said. "They do whatever they can to help you succeed."

Despite the general accessibility of professors, classes at the University of Alabama can be large, with an average size of 30 to 50 students, according to one student. One senior recalled 500 students in her freshman "Mass Communications" lecture, but added that classes since then have been as small as 20 students. As classes become smaller, professors grant more attention to students and grading becomes more personalized, with fewer multiple-choice tests. Hands-on experiences are a common way to challenge students, especially in the pre-professional schools. One Public Relations major said that as a class project, "we have a client and we perform a PR campaign for one client. This client has real money and a real job, and you create a campaign for someone's business."

"College is all what you make of it," said one student. By all measures, the University of Alabama can provide a rigorous education for curious and driven students. In 2012, the university even ranked first among public universities nationwide in terms of the number of National Merit Scholars enrolled.

"Students at the University of Alabama live and breathe football."

Crimson Tide

The university is home to the powerhouse Crimson Tide football team, one of the oldest and most decorated teams in the nation. "Students at the University of Alabama live and breathe football," said one freshman girl. "During the fall, football is the main focus of pretty much all students and alumni." This is no exaggeration: "Football rules the social scene," said one graduating senior. "I've already got the football schedule for next season in my calendar."

Many school traditions revolve around football. "There is always a pre-game video that involves legendary coach Bear Bryant," said one student. "Each sorority house is required to create a huge pomp for the Homecoming game," she added. But while the annual homecoming parade and bonfire are especially important occasions for fraternities and sororities, football games are "day-long events" that bring together all of campus. In the fall, students are reluctant to go home on weekends lest they miss an opportunity to cheer on the Crimson Tide.

Given such talk of Game Day and Greek dominance, UA may conjure a conventional image of college life. While students refuse to sacrifice their southern spirit, there is more to the University of Alabama than football and frats. Academically diverse, bubbling with extracurricular life and set in a thriving city, the University of Alabama truly has something for everyone.—*Hayley Byrnes and Yuval Ben-David*

FYI
If you come to the University of Alabama, you'd better leave your winter coat behind.
Three things every student at the University of Alabama should do before graduating are 1. Attend a football game 2. Eat breakfast at Rama Jama's 3. Go to a tailgate on the Quad.
What surprised me the most about the University of Alabama when I arrived was that there are so many out-of-state students.

University of South Alabama

Address: 307 University Boulevard North, Mobile, AL 36688-0002
Phone: 251 460-6101
E-mail address: admiss@usouthal.edu
Web site URL: www.southalabama.edu
Year Founded: 1963
Private or Public: Public
Religious Affiliation: None
Location: Suburban
Number of Applicants: 4,473
Percent Accepted: 87%
Percent Accepted who enroll: 48%
Number Entering: 1,879
Number of Transfers Accepted each Year: 1,734
Middle 50% SAT range: M: 420–560, CR: 435 570, Wr:420–560
Middle 50% ACT range: 19–25
Early admission program EA/ED/None: None

Percentage accepted through EA or ED: NA
EA and ED deadline: NA
Regular Deadline: 10-Aug
Application Fee: $35
Full time Undergraduate enrollment: 11,578
Total enrollment: 14,769
Percent Male: 46%
Percent Female: 54%
Total Percent Minority or Unreported: 44%
Percent African-American: 29%
Percent Asian/Pacific Islander: 3%
Percent Hispanic: 3%
Percent Native-American: 1%
Percent International: 2%
Percent in-state/out of state: Unreported
Percent from Public HS: 92%
Retention Rate: 70%
Graduation Rate 4-year: 13%

Graduation Rate 6-year: 31%
Percent Undergraduates in On-campus housing: 21%
Number of official organized extracurricular organizations: 185
3 Most popular majors: Health Professions, Business/Marketing, Education
Student/Faculty ratio: 22:1
Average Class Size: Unreported
Percent of students going to grad school: 20%
Tuition and Fees: $14,760
In-State Tuition and Fees if different: $7,380
Cost for Room and Board: $6,270
Percent receiving financial aid out of those who apply: 7%
Percent receiving financial aid among all students: 57%

Located in Mobile, Alabama, the University of South Alabama—"USA" or "South" to students—combines the conservative hospitality of the South with the warm sunny climate of the Gulf Coast. Mobile itself is a historic port city and boasts wildlife-rich deltas and estuaries, antebellum homes with hanging Spanish moss, its own popular Mardi Gras celebration and of course, 21 golf courses and a variety of nearby beaches. The University, located in the heart of the city, caters to both traditional and nontraditional students alike and offers a variety of degree options for adults of any age returning to earn their bachelors' degrees.

Academics: Something for Everyone

The University of South Alabama offers a variety of special programs to accommodate the diverse groups that comprise its student body. Those maintaining at least a 3.5 GPA in high school can apply for the university Honors Program, which includes participation in small honors seminars and the completion of an Honors Senior Project. Each honor student is assigned a faculty mentor from the department of his or her major; these mentors offer advice on everything from course selection to future careers within the field, and both mentor and student participate in group community service projects. New students jump into college life through USA's First Year Experience Program, in which all freshmen living in the dorms are required to participate. The program includes a mandatory freshman seminar designed to teach "effective study skills, exam preparation, college level research skills, writing effectively and student health issues," among other topics, as well as providing tutors, a campus meal plan, and access to student RAs who can offer advice and counsel about campus life. In addition, many USA courses in a variety of disciplines are offered online, allowing students to attend class from home and submit homework in their pajamas.

A branch campus of the University in Fairhope, Alabama, located in Baldwin County—USABC—also offers undergraduate, graduate and nondegree courses and opportunities for public service involvement for students who, for a variety of reasons, might prefer a different location. This branch campus primarily supports undergraduate majors in business, both elementary and secondary education, nursing and adult interdisciplinary studies. USABC is not a residential campus—students enrolling here generally commute from their homes in Baldwin County—and boasts its own computer lab and performance center but shares the libraries and other research resources with the main University campus across Mobile Bay.

> **"The university, located in the heart of the city, caters to both traditional and nontraditional students alike."**

All students must fulfill the core curriculum before graduation, which requires taking several courses in each of the major academic disciplines—humanities and fine arts; natural sciences and mathematics; and history, social and behavioral sciences—as well as two classes in written composition. South is divided into nine different colleges encompassing a variety of fields of study. Those related to healthcare—the Colleges of Medicine, Nursing and Allied Health Professions—are considered to be particularly strong and rigorous. The joint BS/MS degree programs in these majors are popular, but to gain admission, students must have GPAs in the 3.8 range and apply during their junior year.

BYOB

South's architecture is fairly nondescript like many college campuses built in the late twentieth century. One student described it as "nothing fancy . . . built to last, not to look pretty." Few students live in the dorms all four years, but for those who do, it can be a rewarding experience and provide the opportunity to meet many new friends quickly. "Living in dorms is a terrific way to meet people," enthused one junior. "Most of the people I hang out with now I met freshman year in dorms." The residence halls offer various rooming options in the form of suites and apartments; for first-time students, the most popular options are the Epsilon and Delta two-person suites with private baths. All students living on campus are required to purchase a meal plan, but limited weekend operating hours for the on-campus

eateries can reportedly cause frustration. USA also offers married students housing in the form of unfurnished single-family houses in the neighborhood of Hillsdale Heights.

Most of South's 11,400 undergraduate students come from nearby cities and towns in Alabama, making the University primarily a commuter school in which much of the student body drives to class every day. Many clubs, for example, hold meetings in the afternoons to accommodate members who leave campus in the evening. Because of this, the campus activities and night life can be somewhat lacking; as one student complained, "there is no campus life at South!" However, the University is taking steps to correct this problem, and programs such as the Freshman Year Experience help new students to make friends and connections. The RAs in each dorm occasionally sponsor activities to foster a community spirit, and interested students can join intramural sports and other organizations to stay involved.

The social scene that does exist at USA revolves around the Greek system, and most events that take place on campus are sponsored by one of the college's 19 fraternities and sororities. Although total membership is not huge, the Greeks have a strong presence on campus, due mainly to their widespread involvement in other clubs and organizations. Because South's campus is officially dry (although, as one student put it, this is true "in name only"), the frats do not usually supply alcohol at their parties, so Greek and non-Greek partiers alike are encouraged to bring their own beverages.

The Jaguar Life

The University recently approved the addition of a football team in fall 2009; it gained full Division 1 FBS status in 2013. In the past, many students have lamented the lack of school spirit that results from not having a football team. In the sport's absence, the crowd-pleasing sports to watch are men's and women's varsity basketball; die-hard Jaguar fans can also watch these games live via Internet streaming. Students can also indulge their competitive sides in an assortment of intramural sports based out of USA's state-of-the-art Intramural Field Complex, including inner tube water polo, soccer, flag football, basketball, volleyball and softball. The Student Recreation Center is home to two basketball courts, a weight-lifting room, a track and a game room containing table tennis and a pool table as well as free SouthFit aerobics and dance classes. The University has also recently announced plans to build a brand-new recreation center with additional facilities.

South also boasts a sizeable Student Center that hosts lounge areas, a computer lab, office space for student groups, a big-screen TV, a variety of small eateries located in the Market area and a large ballroom that can be reserved for student use. Jaguar Productions, the Student Activities Board, meets here as well, and provides a relatively popular way for students to become involved with the university and help to plan campus-wide concerts, film screenings, lectures, vacation trips and more. Over 200 clubs and organizations also offer a chance to meet fellow students and include everything from pre-professional organizations to groups for sports, music,

meteorology and video gaming enthusiasts. Jag TV, USA's student-run television station, is broadcast in all of the residence halls and other buildings throughout the campus.

The University of South Alabama offers numerous benefits to its many students, from its location in the welcoming Deep South city of Mobile to its variety of special degree and enrichment programs. Non-traditional students especially find its continuing education programs to be accommodating and flexible, while those living in the residential dorms appreciate the social atmosphere and the friendly RAs. The University's shortcomings, most notably a lack of school spirit, can be overcome through a determination to stay involved, and South's recent efforts to this end have made strides in improving the sense of community.—*Kristin Knox*

FYI

If you come to USA, you better bring "a desire to get involved and make the most of the college experience."

What is the typical weekend schedule? "Go to a frat party at night, catch up on work during the day."

Three things every student at USA should do before graduating are "play oozeball (volleyball in a knee-deep mud pit), go to an event in the Mitchell Center, and take advantage of the fine-arts offerings."

Alaska

Started in Fairbanks, the University of Alaska has now expanded onto 19 campuses across the picturesque state of Alaska. With its largest hubs in Fairbanks (UAF), Anchorage (UAA) and Juneau (UAS), the widespread university has nearly 33,000 full and part-time students enrolled at its various campuses. With an almost unprecedented 500 degree, certificate or endorsement options, students can enroll in workforce training, master's and bachelor's degrees, or go a step further to doctorates. A prominent research institution, UA boasts research projects amongst the best and only such projects done in their fields. In addition to its large emphasis on research, the locations of the schools make them highly desirable destinations for those aiming to either live within one of the most breathtaking campuses in the country or delve into natural sciences.

Natural Sciences, and Much More

The first notable fact about the college is the disconnect between Alaska and the rest of continental USA. With its large land mass and low population, Alaska offers unique opportunities for students who wish to explore the lesser known side of the country—the one connected to wilderness and nature, and less to the virtual world that most campus students immerse themselves in.

Due to the location of UA—with the Arctic circle passing through the state—UA's strongest and most interesting programs focus on exploiting the resources available exclusively in the Arctic landmass. Thus, students have the opportunities to collect first-hand information about natural phenomena, such as climate change. As one student said, "Alaska is the thermometer for climate change." Since the effects of climate change are first felt near the polar regions, students have an edge in being the first to study and see the effects that global warming has on the climate. They have the option of looking into fields as diverse as glacial melting, atmospheric modeling of the climate and sea ice retreat. Another popular field of research is the effects of the melting permafrost on the environment.

Scientific research institutes at UA include the Geophysical Institute, Arctic Region Supercomputing Center and School of Fisheries and Ocean Sciences. As the UA has the prestigious position of being granted all three—land, sea and space—grant programs, the university is affiliated with national institutes such as NASA.

While one student said that it is "definitely focused on the sciences," students agree that the liberal arts programs are not lacking in strength. Another student said that the strength of the communications program drew him in while he came to Alaska with the ROTC. "While it was initially simply a place to go explore with the ROTC, who gave me a chance to go anywhere in the country, I decided to stay and pursue my degree at UAF because of the unique chance I got here to mix academics and nature."

Because students are heavily involved in outdoor activities, students said that teachers tend to grant concessions to students, in terms of the workload. One student said that he was allowed to submit an assignment late since he was hiking over the weekend, and that the curriculum is based on the understanding that the university cannot be compared to, or based on, the average American university. As one student said, "Do not come here if you are not prepared to enjoy the sights that surround you."

Not Just a Place to Study

"Whether or not it's negative 40 outside, the students must go outside and collect data," one professor said. Since Fairbanks and the other cities of Alaska are now competing with Antarctica for being the coldest place in the world, the education at UA takes advantage of the harsh climate. One student said, "Since the extreme cold is felt in Alaska, tests of US army gear and equipment is done through a cold climate research laboratory. This provides an excellent opportunity to get

tied into research with the Department of Defense."

While the weather may scare many away, those brave enough to venture to Alaska have the chance to do research on fascinating subjects such as cold weather hunting and aurora lights. As one professor said, "There is nothing called bad climate in Alaska, only bad clothing." Added benefits are extreme outdoor activities such as ice climbing, snowboarding, skiing and winter hunting. However, with over 80 student groups, students participate in a variety of extracurricular activities that go beyond just sports; night photography (especially of aurora lights) is preferred, while students also explore their creative sides through painting, poetry, theater and music. One student said, "Alaska is a state where the beauty of your surroundings pushes you into introspection, and the urge to create something with your mind and body."

> "Do not come here if you are not prepared to enjoy the sights that surround you."

UA has an on-campus dining option called Seawolf Dining along with cafes and food courts. The Cuddy Coffee House, aka the "Daily Grind," offers delectable organic coffee. The food court has Asian cuisine, including fresh sushi. Students can also get food from Gorsuch Commons, which has a convenience store and an eatery.

UA housing options are equally plentiful. Its three Residence Halls—with 200 students in North, East and West—feature singles, doubles, quads and communal spaces. Templewood Apartments, which houses about 80 students, provides in-suite bathrooms and local phone service. Students residing in Gorsuch Commons have access to a fitness center and computer lab.

Only 698 out of a population of around 2,000 freshman come to UA directly from high school. This shows that, as one student said, "The spirit of adventure lies within the students who venture to Alaska." However, the negative side to this atypical college experience is that most of the freshmen come from within the Alaskan state, with only 12% coming from outside Alaska, and of those, only 2% are international students. Regardless, the students that are seen on campus are those who "either come to experience something exotic, run away from the typical

American lifestyle or have a fascination with the unknown."

All in all, UA will not provide the usual American college experience. While the university is like most universities—where the undergraduates enjoy going out on the weekends and frequenting the university pubs—the experience is more influenced by the air, water and soil surrounding the university than any other. A positive that comes from the distinction of Alaska from the rest of consumer-driven, mechanical America is that Alaska boasts of its own local beer breweries. As one student said, "Alaska is a place where the people are unusual and the beer is unusually good."—*Devika Mittal*

FYI
If you come to UA, you'd better bring "lots of warm clothes."
What is the typical weekend schedule? "Outdoor field trips, and also college parties."
Three things every student at UA should do before graduating are "enjoy the scenery, go hiking, and participate in a environmentally related research project."

Arizona

Arizona State University

Address: PO Box 870112, Tempe, AZ 85287

Phone: 480-965-7788

E-mail address: admissions@asu.edu

Web site URL: www.asu.edu

Year Founded: 1885

Private or Public: Public

Religious Affiliation: None

Location: Suburban

Number of Applicants: 27,089

Percent Accepted: 95%

Percent Accepted who enroll: 35%

Number Entering: 8,458

Number of Transfers Accepted each Year: 5,258

Middle 50% SAT range: M: 480–610, CR: 470–600, Wr: Unreported

Middle 50% ACT range: 20–26

Early admission program EA/ED/None: None

Percentage accepted through EA or ED: NA

EA and ED deadline: NA

Regular Deadline: Rolling

Application Fee: $25

Full time Undergraduate enrollment: 53,298

Total enrollment: 65,804

Percent Male: 48%

Percent Female: 52%

Total Percent Minority or Unreported: 35%

Percent African-American: 5%

Percent Asian/Pacific Islander: 6%

Percent Hispanic: 15%

Percent Native-American: 2%

Percent International: 2%

Percent in-state/out of state: 78%/22%

Percent from Public HS: Unreported

Retention Rate: 80%

Graduation Rate 4-year: 29%

Graduation Rate 6-year: 54%

Percent Undergraduates in On-campus housing: 78%

Number of official organized extracurricular organizations: 512

3 Most popular majors: Journalism, Multidisciplinary Studies, Psychology

Student/Faculty ratio: 22:1

Average Class Size: 15

Percent of students going to grad school: Unreported

Tuition and Fees: $17,949

In-State Tuition and Fees if different: $5,661

Cost for Room and Board: $8,790

Percent receiving financial aid out of those who apply: 70%

Percent receiving financial aid among all students: 66%

Located in Phoenix, Arizona, the nation's fifth largest city, Arizona State University (ASU) educates more than 67,000 students on four different campuses. These four campuses are unified by their goal of being centers for academic excellence and innovative research. Under the leadership of one of *Time* magazine's "10 Best College Presidents," Michael Crow, ASU has been shedding its reputation as one of America's top party schools and evolving into a research institution that attracts a diverse, motivated student body. The students are responding positively towards the change. As one student states, "I'd like to change the stereotype/reputation that ASU has maintained over the years designating it *only* as a party school with low education standards." While the "play hard" culture at ASU is still an option to those who desire it, Arizona State is moving toward an environment that is lauded for its advances in academia rather than a university defined by the popularity of weekend parties.

Study like a Sun Devil

Within the undergraduate degree program, ASU offers over 250 academic majors on its four campuses: Downtown Phoenix, Polytechnic, Tempe, and West campus. According to one student, "There's such a wealth of opportunities available because we are so large. Anything you want to do, you can do it at Arizona State. Any major, any organization, any research project, any study abroad program—literally anything, you can make it happen here."

Students declare a major when they apply

and are admitted to one of the fifteen different schools. The largest schools are the College of Liberal Arts and Sciences and the W.P. Carey School of Business. Professor Edward Prescott, the 2004 Nobel Prize winner in Economic Sciences, teaches classes at the business school while the former executive editor of the *Washington Post*, Professor Len Downie, educates students at the Walter Cronkite School of Journalism and Mass Communication. Students studying at the renowned Cronkite School receive valuable hands-on experience through numerous internship opportunities in the nation's twelfth largest media market. This school is located at the new Downtown Phoenix Campus and is easily accessible by the recently constructed Light Rail.

Barrett, the Honors College at ASU, enjoys the reputation of being one of the nation's premier undergraduate honors colleges. Barrett students live in a $130 million residential community that was opened in fall of 2009. Students seem to love the ability to experience the small college feel in Barrett while still being able to enjoy the resources and athletic programs of a large university. A well-liked Honors class is Human Event. A mandatory freshman course for honors students, this class focuses on "tracing the written word from the beginning to the present day across various cultures and disciplines."

Of the 277 different academic fields, "marketing, political science, communication, business, sustainability (ASU's School of Sustainability is the first degree-granting institution of sustainability in the entire country), and journalism" are some of the most popular majors at ASU. With all of these options, students agree that it is "not really" difficult to enroll in classes at Arizona State, especially given the fact that most classes are "huge." According to one student, "Some classes that have a famous professor or a class that pertains to a special topic may fill up fast, but there is usually a variety of class sections offered." Popular classes at ASU include Professor Matt McCarthy's Computer Applications and Information Technology course and Professor David Capco's Biology and Chinese Medicine course. Another student raves, "American Political Thought and Political Ideologies were the most fun classes for me personally because I'm a political science major!"

Arizona State University has attracted a wide array of prominent visitors in the past few years. As one student states, "Because we are such a large campus, we always have great speakers and cultural events happening. We have dozens of off-Broadway shows and famous symphonies." ASU also hosts a wide variety of guest lecturers. According to one Sun Devil, "In the last few years, we've had dozens of famous people make stops here—Nancy Pelosi, Jonathan Alter, Bill Clinton, Al Gore, and Ron Paul. President Barack Obama has visited ASU numerous times, most recently when he was our commencement speaker." Additionally, Professor Donald Johanson, the founder of the Institute of Human Origins at Arizona State who found the skeleton known as "Lucy," has given talks about his discovery.

Social Life of Sun Devils

Students at ASU love their university's size. Making friends is easy because "there is ALWAYS something going on around campus and friendly faces everywhere." As one Sun Devil states, "I don't think there's any bad part about going to a school [ASU's] size because it's easy to find smaller communities and to make connections with other students and professors."

> "Any major, any organization, any research project, any study abroad program—literally anything—you can make it happen here."

On the weekend, students enjoy hanging out with their friends at parties hosted by the different Greek houses. According to one student, Greeks comprise a "small percentage of the population but are a very visible and active one, so they have a dominant presence on campus. Greeks have such a large presence on campus because they're usually always doing some sort of community service, holding leadership positions in other organizations, and making themselves visible. It's different than at other schools because most chapters have untraditional housing (no sorority houses, just dormlike housing)." About "nine percent" of the undergraduates are in fraternities or sororities. According to one student, "Recruitment for ASU's 13 Panhellenic sororities and rush for ASU's 22 fraternities begins around Labor Day. Spring rush is only for fraternities and some houses."

For those who want to escape the Greek scene, students can spend time on Mill Avenue during the weekends. Sun Devils also flock to Tempe Marketplace. Both are popular spots for nightlife, shopping, and dining. Another popular destination is Old Towne Scottsdale, which contains shopping, entertainment, arts, and dining attractions. Many students have cars, although Sun Devils agree that parking is difficult and often expensive. Students love the ability to take road trips, and many travel to Las Vegas, California, or Mexico during their four years as an ASU student.

At Arizona State, "most students live on campus their freshman year and then live off campus." Students agree that it is not really difficult to find housing. As one student described it, "Housing at ASU is solid." Students rave about the new residence halls, especially the new Honors complex designed exclusively for honors students to live in throughout their junior and senior years. According to one Sun Devil, "It's changing the way students live on campus."

If students live on campus, they are required to be on a meal plan. Students at ASU find that the dining hall options are good. However, there are complaints about the cost of meal plans and the dining hall hours. One student states, "The quality is ok, but the variety gets old fast."

Sun Devil Spirit

ASU students have a wide variety of ways to become involved in campus life. The oldest student organization on campus is Devils' Advocates, a group of students who talk to high school students about the opportunities and benefits of attending ASU. Other prominent groups on campus include the Undergraduate Student Government, the Resident Hall Association, and the Programming and Activities Board. The Greek community and the Sports Club Association also attract a sizeable number of students.

When students at Arizona State are asked about what sets their university apart from other schools, they generally reply with the three Ss: "size, social scene, and sports." Sun Devils love being a part of the Pac-12. Although one student laments, "If I could

change one thing about ASU, we would have a better football team."

School spirit runs high during the "Duel in the Desert." Since 1899, Arizona State and the University of Arizona have been battling it out on the football field. Students at ASU also participate in Lantern Walk, the school's oldest tradition. At this homecoming event, "thousands of students take lighted candles and walk up to the 'A' mountain (a mountain with the big gold A on it)." The ceremony is accompanied by a big pep rally. Other fun traditions at ASU include: Oozeball—a campus wide mud volleyball tournament; Undie Run—a tradition where students take off their clothes, donate them to charity, and run around campus half naked to celebrate the end of classes; and the whitewashing of "A" Mountain—a part of Freshman Orientation when the newest class of Sun Devils hikes to the mountain and whitewashes the coveted letter gold to ring in the new school year.

Without a doubt, Sun Devils love their school. According to one student, "I love that ASU was founded by the people of Arizona—we were literally established by a ballot initiative. I think that fuels our desire to be the best public university. We were established by the citizens of Arizona, and we open our doors to people who want to learn." Students truly feel like ASU is setting the standards for any public educational institution. Even though the university can be characterized as "fast-moving and untraditional," students appreciate the culture at ASU. As one Sun Devil states, "The culture really differentiates our school from others. Administration, students, and faculty are pretty laid back relative to traditional schools on the East Coast." Students truly love studying under the bright Arizona sun, and they appreciate the new direction their institution has taken. "There are so many new and innovative ideas coming out of ASU. I think that we are constantly growing and achieving, and we are not slowing down."—*Alexa Sassin*

FYI

If you come to ASU you'd better bring: "sunscreen, maroon and gold, and flip flops."

What's the typical weekend schedule: "People begin going out Thursday evenings. Students typically visit the different house and frat parties. Class fills up Friday afternoons until the evening when the partying picks up again. Saturdays are spent at the pool or an ASU athletic event, followed by a night on Mill Avenue. On Sundays, students spend the day catching up on homework."

If I could change one thing about ASU I would: "have it by the beach."

Three things a student should do before graduating: "Climb 'A' mountain, attend Sigma Chi's Hallowrave party, have a meal at the Chuckbox."

University of Arizona

Address: PO Box 210040, Tucson, AZ 85721-0040

Phone: 520-621-3237

E-mail address: appinfo@arizona.edu

Web site URL: www.arizona.edu

Year Founded: 1885

Private or Public: Public

Religious Affiliation: None

Location: Urban

Number of Applicants: 26,629

Percent Accepted: 75%

Percent Accepted who enroll: 32%

Number Entering: 6,464

Number of Transfers Accepted each Year: 2,846

Middle 50% SAT range: M: 490–620, CR: 480–610, Wr: Unreported

Middle 50% ACT range: 21–27

Early admission program EA/ED/None: None

Percentage accepted through EA or ED: NA

EA and ED deadline: NA

Regular Deadline: 1-May

Application Fee: $50

Full time Undergraduate enrollment: 26,909

Total enrollment: 30,592

Percent Male: 48%

Percent Female: 52%

Total Percent Minority or Unreported: 39%

Percent African-American: 4%

Percent Asian/Pacific Islander: 7%

Percent Hispanic: 19%

Percent Native-American: 3%

Percent International: 4%

Percent in-state/out of state: Unreported

Percent from Public HS: 90%

Retention Rate: Unreported

Graduation Rate 4-year: 57%

Graduation Rate 6-year: Unreported

Percent Undergraduates in On-campus housing: 20%

Number of official organized extracurricular organizations: 727

3 Most popular majors: Cellular and Molecular Biology, Political Science and Government, Psychology

Student/Faculty ratio: 19:1

Average Class Size: 25

Percent of students going to grad school: 42%

Tuition and Fees: $24,574

In-State Tuition and Fees if different: $8,364

Cost for Room and Board: $8,540

Percent receiving financial aid out of those who apply: Unreported

Percent receiving financial aid among all students: 63%

Located in Tucson, Arizona—one of the oldest towns of the Wild Wild West—the University of Arizona provides the perfect historical backdrop for the party-seeking Wildcats of today. Known for its active Greek life and lively social scene, the school attracts thousands of students who "like having a good time." With stellar academics, unique extracurricular activities, and over 300 days of nearly non-stop sunshine added to the mix, the University of Arizona is a good choice for students looking for fun-filled yet rigorous undergraduate experience.

Wildcats at Work

When Wildcats aren't partying at a fraternity or bathing in the Arizona sun, they are scrambling to finish homework assignments or studying in the Mansfield Library. "We're actually a really smart school for as much as people party here," said one junior. UA is home to the prestigious Eller College of Management, and its business programs attract 16 percent of the undergraduate population. Other popular majors include psychology, engineering, and programs pertaining to the medical field, such as pre-physiology and pre-nursing. Offering students over 100 undergraduate degree options, UA gives Wildcats plenty of opportunities to explore their academic interests, and students can choose from a variety of disciplines, from a major in biomedical engineering to a minor in hip-hop. While students agree that UA is "stronger in the sciences than the humanities," Wildcats can take a break from labs and chemistry lectures with a wide variety of intriguing humanities classes, including guitar lessons, courses in African dance, and a Slavic Studies class about werewolves and vampires.

Despite its party-school reputation, UA is not all fun and games. Courses—graded on a "hard grading system" of A to E—are generally not curved "unless everyone fails their exams," which is common in more difficult science courses such as physics and math. Wildcats must maintain at least a 2.00 GPA to graduate, and must take an average of 5 classes per semester. UA also requires that students fulfill general education requirements within four course categories. Described by one junior as "random classes" the university "wants you to take to put your toe in the water," general education classes include Foundations courses in English, math, and a foreign language; Tier One and Tier Two classes centered on culture, arts and natural sciences; and Diversity Emphasis classes focused on gender, ethnicity, social class, or sexual orientation. According to one physiology major, noting that science majors don't have to fulfill the natural science requirement, "general education requirements differ for each major." Students say the typical workload also "depends on the major," with chemistry, biochemistry, engineering, and physiology majors bearing the brunt of UA's schoolwork. Studious Wildcats can also opt to join the Honors College by applying before their freshman year, and enjoy a more challenging curriculum of over 250 honors courses. However, students may also take an "easier" route by becoming a business or humanities major. "Business majors have no class on Friday," remarked one junior. "I hear they get to party more."

Going Wild

Regarded by Wildcats as "a pretty big party school," the University of Arizona lives up to its wild reputation. "The campus is dead on the weekends during the day," a student said. "But nighttime's for having fun." Students generally go out on Fridays, Saturdays, and "Thirsty Thursdays," while more adventurous Wildcats party more frequently throughout the week. "It sounds kind of crazy, but we do party a lot on Tuesdays," said one sorority girl. But rather than capturing the rowdiness of the weekend, Tuesdays are designated as "wine nights," and involve casual drinking and "hanging out at frats."

When Wildcats go on the nightly prowl, they migrate to Greek Row, home to over 50 fraternity and sorority houses. Students agree that "Greek life's pretty big here," and partying at frats is "the huge thing" on campus. Of course, living in Arizona is an added perk for the Wildcat social scene. Living under sunny skies for most of the year, fraternities host pool parties as early as March, one student claimed. Larger fraternities, such as Sigma Alpha Epsilon, Phi Gamma Delta, and Pi Kappa Phi, also hold "Weekenders," in which members and their dates go on weekend trips to Las Vegas or nearby Mexico.

Though Greek life is a big part of the campus's social scene, the University of Arizona offers many other options to go wild. "The only people that go to the frats usually are sophomores and freshmen," said one sorority girl. "Juniors and seniors are usually at bars." Older Wildcats can be found socializing in bars and restaurants along Union Boulevard and Fourth Avenue, such as Gentle Ben's Brewing Company and Frog & Firkin. But one activity that Wildcats of all ages can enjoy is the university's annual Spring Fling. The largest student-run carnival in the nation, UA's Spring Fling has everything from a "fun house" and a "pirate ship that swings" to "rides that shoot you up really fast like the Superman [rollercoaster]." Students can also unleash their wild sides earlier in the school year at Viva La Paz, a fall-semester "drag queen show," or Hoggoween, an alcohol-free Halloween costume party hosted in Graham-Greenlee residence hall.

Living in the Wild

Freshmen can choose from 23 brick residence halls, each with its own unique personality. Likins Hall, the "athletic, party dorm," and Árbol de la Vida, the Honors Dorm, are the newest and most expensive residence halls. Parker House and Maricopa Hall are the school's all-girl dorms, and one RA compares the latter to "a grandma's house—quiet, with chandeliers, and not loud and crazy." Coronado Hall, on the other hand, is the university's designated party dorm, with 776 residents and "people drinking in study rooms." UA employs over 200 RAs, many of whom are "lenient, but follow the rules." Alcohol and drug policies are strongly enforced, and one freshman said RAs do not usually tolerate alcohol in the dorms. "There are certain things that I'm kind of strict with," one RA said. "But as long as you're not making a scene, I don't really care that much. I know that you're in college experiencing new things."

Fun in the Sun

For many University of Arizona students, "sports are really the biggest thing." A member of the formidable Pacific-12 college athletic conference, UA takes athletics seriously. The school has even gained nationwide recognition, with its talented baseball team seizing the championship title in the 2012 collegiate World Series. At UA football or basketball games—two of the most widely attended sporting events—stands are filled with spirited Wildcats who sing "Born to Be Wild" and make "unsportsman-like chants" toward the opposing team. "The students here have a vast amount of school spirit and pride," one junior remarked. "You can find that at most other universities, but not to the same extent." Wildcats are encouraged to buy a "Red" ZonaZoo Pass, which allows students to attend any home sporting event for a price of $150. Wildcats also go to University Boulevard to enjoy "Bear Down Fridays," a Friday night celebration before every home football game that includes live music, pep rallies, and family-friendly activities.

Athletes train at any one of 12 athletic facilities, such as the Hi Corbett Field and the Jimencz Practice Facility. Most students and non-athletes work out at the Student Recreation Center, which provides students with two gyms, an indoor track, a 30,000 square-foot weight room, 18 athletic courts, and "a lot of equipment." UA also caters to students with less of an athletic bent, offering over 500 extracurricular activities where Wildcats can discover their passions. "Anything you can imagine is here," one student said. Aspiring writers can work for *The Daily Wildcat*, while other students can rush one of the 51 fraternities and sororities that dominate the social scene. From religious groups and ultimate Frisbee to sushi-making and Quidditch, the University of Arizona can always assure students of a good time. "We're really fun—I'm obsessed with my school," remarked a freshman Wildcat. "The second I'm done with classes, there's so much to do. I'm never bored."
—*Rosa Nguyen*

FYI

If I could change one thing about the University of Arizona, I'd change "the meal plan food. We have a lot of fast food places instead of a dining hall. They talk about the whole freshman fifteen thing and [the food] doesn't help."

What's the typical weekend schedule? "Go to a frat party, go to a Saturday night basketball game, and get homework done on Sunday."

If you come to University of Arizona, you'd better bring "flip flops, a swimsuit, and shades, because the sun is always in your eyes."

Arkansas

Hendrix College

Address: 1600 Washington Avenue, Conway, AR 72032
Phone: 501-450-1362
E-mail address: adm@hendrix.edu
Web site URL: www.hendrix.edu
Year Founded: 1876
Private or Public: Private
Religious Affiliation: Methodist
Location: Rural
Number of Applicants: 1,420
Percent Accepted: 94%
Percent Accepted who enroll: 32%
Number Entering: 433
Number of Transfers Accepted each Year: 41
Middle 50% SAT range: M: 550–660, CR: 580–690, Wr: Unreported
Middle 50% ACT range: 25–31
Early admission program EA/ED/None: None

Percentage accepted through EA or ED: NA
EA and ED deadline: NA
Regular Deadline: 1-Jun
Application Fee: $40
Full time Undergraduate enrollment: 1,342
Total enrollment: 1,342
Percent Male: 45%
Percent Female: 55%
Total Percent Minority or Unreported: 6%
Percent African-American: 4%
Percent Asian/Pacific Islander: 3%
Percent Hispanic: 4%
Percent Native-American: <1%
Percent International: 2%
Percent in-state/out of state: 49%/51%
Percent from Public HS: 71%
Retention Rate: 85%
Graduation Rate 4-year: 62%

Graduation Rate 6-year: 68%
Percent Undergraduates in On-campus housing: 84%
Number of official organized extracurricular organizations: 80
3 Most popular majors: Biology/Biological Sciences, General English Language and Literature, General Psychology
Student/Faculty ratio: 12:1
Average Class Size: 18
Percent of students going to grad school: 92%
Tuition and Fees: $25,780
In-State Tuition and Fees if different: No difference
Cost for Room and Board: $7,950
Percent receiving financial aid out of those who apply: 100%
Percent receiving financial aid among all students: 100%

O n a warm fall evening in Arkansas, a group of several dozen young men clad in Oxford shirts strides out onto a brick plaza filled with pecan trees. They are here to dance, but this is no formal ball. Their classy shirts and ties are complemented by nothing more than their boxers. At the first beat of a subwoofer they drop to the ground and tear through an elaborate hip-hop dance in perfect unison. They are followed by a group of girls in fancy tops and volleyball shorts who perform a routine that would turn heads at any dance club. All the while, their entire school is there watching, cheering them on and howling with friendly laughter. "Shirttails," one of Hendrix College's oldest traditions, initiates freshmen into the life of the college and serves as a fitting introduction to the close-knit community that they will be a part of for the next four years.

An Academic Odyssey

Don't let the booty-shaking antics of Shirttails fool you; Hendrix students take their academics very seriously. "I don't think I knew how academically intense Hendrix would be," a junior said. Over the last decade, Hendrix has revamped its curriculum to provide a unique liberal arts education that emphasizes experiential learning.

All freshmen must take a class from the "Engaged Citizen" seminar program, which offers more than a dozen classes taught by pairs of professors that all explore the greater theme of involvement in a community. Freshmen are also required to take a once-weekly class called "Explorations" which aims to introduce them to academic life at Hendrix and sharpen their research and discussion skills.

The flagship component of the Hendrix curriculum is its unique Odyssey Program, which guarantees that all students will have multiple hands-on learning experiences before they graduate. "Odyssey is one of the main reasons I came to Hendrix. It's fantastic," a senior said.

To graduate from Hendrix, students must complete three projects from three of six categories: Artistic Creativity, Global Awareness, Professional and Leadership Development, Service to the World, Undergraduate Research, and Special Projects. Hendrix's Committee on Engaged Learning has awarded over $2 million in grants to Odyssey projects since the program began in 2007. One anthropology major said that she had recently received funding to study the American expatriate community in Bangkok, while some her peers have projects planned such as "*An Investigation of Milk Snakes, A Coral Snake Mimic*," "*Professional Field Experience with Peticolas Brewing Company,*" and "*A Japanese Journey: Retracing Basho's Narrow Road.*" The Odyssey Program is a big part of why Hendrix sends a higher percentage of their student body to the National Conference on Undergraduate Research than any college in the United States. Students can also earn Odyssey credits from special Hendrix courses and extracurricular activities. One junior said that he planned to fulfill his requirements with an art class, a business management capstone course, and taking a position as the Student Senate bookkeeper.

Hendrix students astound each other with the variety and ambition of their projects. "People will talk about their friends saying, 'Oh my God! Did you hear what they did? That's so cool!'" a student said. She added that the competition for Odyssey funding is never cut-throat or unpleasant. "Everyone roots for each other."

Professors are at the heart of the Hendrix learning experience, supervising projects and making themselves "insanely accessible" to students in their classes. One senior counted five of her professors as good friends as well as mentors. "They will stay late, they will work one-on-one with you. They are tough, but they will do whatever it takes to help you meet their standards."

However, one student said that sometimes an extra effort is necessary to get that special attention. "They're not always going to seek you out," she said.

According to one senior, "There's a good mix between the professors that are really nice, and those that seem stern but are really supportive." One student cautioned that a popular history professor "will call you stupid, but he's great because he demands a lot."

Classes at Hendrix are very small; the largest only have around 30 students. Getting into some classes can be difficult, especially the introductory psychology course. Social sciences like psychology and anthropology are among the most popular majors at Hendrix, along with biology, biochemistry, English, and international relations. There is some tension on campus between science majors and humanities majors on campus, with both groups believing that they are given a heavier workload. But it's definitely not enough to keep students from making friends outside of their major.

Living at Hendrix: Pick Your Best Fit

Freshman orientation at Hendrix is a fun-filled week before the beginning of classes that starts on campus and ends with the class dividing into 22 small groups to go on an amazing variety of orientation trips. Students can go on outdoor adventures, explore towns and cities around the Southeast, do community service, or even go to an amusement park. Then students will return to campus and move into their dorms. Hendrix offers five single-sex dorms and one co-ed dorm to freshmen, each of which has acquired a unique reputation over the years. Veasey and Galloway (which houses mostly sophomores) attract girls who are looking to party, and Martin Hall is sometimes referred to as "the frat boy dorm" (although Hendrix does not have any fraternities or sororities). Beasey and Hardin offer quieter environments for men and women, respectively, and the co-ed Couch Hall also has fewer parties. Because most freshmen visit Hendrix before matriculating, they can learn about the different reputations of the dorms and typically request one which fits their lifestyle. All freshmen share a floor with a senior RA who makes sure the environment is safe, but their alcohol policy is usually relaxed.

Most upperclassmen move into on-campus apartment complexes and tend to stick with their friends from dorm life (one complex is known as "the Martin Retirement Home"). One senior said that she enjoyed living in her apartment. "It's big enough for a party and no one cares if you have one. It's also far away enough that you can just stay there and work without distractions."

Hendrix students are content to stay on campus on weekends. Drinking and casual partying with friends is the most popular activity, but "it's easy to not drink at any age," a senior said. Conway is in a dry county, so the only places for upperclassmen to get drinks off campus are at restaurants like Zaza's, which serves gourmet pizza and salad and hosts a "Thirsty Thursday" Karaoke night.

> "People will talk about their friends saying, 'Oh my God! Did you hear what they did? That's so cool!'"

Life in the Natural State

Conway, a city of 60,000 people, offers "quite a few things to do, but not so much for college kids," according to one student. However, Conway residents take great pride in their city and eagerly invite the help of Hendrix students with public works projects. One student said that during her time at Hendrix, she had helped clear walking trails and plan sidewalks, and took a tour of the city's revamped recycling facility. "For being a small town in Arkansas, it's pretty progressive," she said.

Many Hendrix students hail from Arkansas and take their college friends on weekend adventures. Students can hike in the Ozark Mountains and raft down winding rivers, or go on less rustic trips to concerts in Little Rock or football games at the University of Arkansas in Fayetteville. Fall in Conway is warm and lovely, and winter can be surprisingly chilly despite the southern latitude. Multiple students interviewed said that the spring can be very humid and rainy and the sub-par drainage system on campus can produce major puddles. One said that she wished she had known "how strong the correlation between your happiness and wearing rain boots on rainy days is."

Hendrixtracurriculars

Hendrix students take part in dozens of clubs and organizations, some of which have a great influence in the social life on campus. Shirttails, held in the fall, is coordinated by the Shirttails Serenade committee, and the concert that follows the dance-off is organized by Hendrix's online radio station,

KHDX. The spring's biggest event is Charity Week, which benefits Campus Kitty, the largest charitable organization at Hendrix. Charity Week raises money through fun dances and events like "Miss Hendrix," which pits eight men against each other in a goofy drag show, and it ends with a concert as well. Hendrix seems to have a knack for bringing in stars of the hipster-rap scene; both Chiddy Bang and Macklemore have performed at recent shows. Two more campus parties, the Halloween Ghost Roast and an annual toga party planned by the Student Senate, bring out most of the college as well as students from around Arkansas. Of course, not every organization at Hendrix takes on the task of planning campus-wide parties. Students can write for the campus magazine, *The Profile*, cook international dishes at the Culinary Club, take in classic films with the Film Society, and pursue just about any interest in Hendrix's other organizations.

Knights on the Field

Hendrix fields varsity teams in eleven women's sports and ten men's sports, which compete in the Southern Athletics Association. In September of 2013, the Hendrix Knights played their first varsity football game since 1960. Hendrix's teams often struggle to beat their tough competition in the Southern Athletic Conference, but they are provided with top-notch facilities to help them work towards winning a championship. The new Wellness and Athletics Facility, open to all students, provides a 7,000 square foot fitness room, basketball courts, an indoor track, and an eight lane pool.

Food, Fun, and Friendship

Hendrix only has one dining hall, but it offers enough options to keep students content for many meals. "Hendrix food is fantastic and it gets better all the time," a senior said. The dining hall offers customizable pizza and burger stations, a wok, and a smoothie station along with standard cafeteria fare. Dining hall workers get to know the names of just about every student, and give them a special treat on their birthday.

In the intimate environment of Hendrix College, it's impossible to be overlooked. And this is never clearer than on students' birthdays. If spotted in the dining hall on their birthday, Hendrix students will be treated to a cake and a song from the culinary staff and everyone else in the cafeteria. Another birthday tradition is to be thrown into a fountain by your friends, no matter the weather. Hendrix students say that the friendship and encouragement from the people around them define their college experience. In the words of one senior, "Everyone on campus is excited to continue growing, and we push each other. Hendrix gives you the freedom to continue to discover yourself."—*Josh Mandell*

FYI
What's the typical weekend schedule? Exercise/homework in the morning followed by shananigans with friends at night
Where's the best place to go for late night food?. Nothing's better than Waffle House at 2AM.
What you should know to have fun at Hendrix College: You can have plenty of fun at parties without getting too crazy! Themed parties are huge here, so get ready to dress up and dance!

University of Arkansas

Address: 232 Silas Hunt Hall, Fayetteville, AR 72701
Phone: 479-575-5346
E-mail address: uofa@uark.edu
Web site URL: www.uark.edu
Year Founded: 1871
Private or Public: Public
Religious Affiliation: None
Location: Urban
Number of Applicants: 14,019
Percent Accepted: 60%
Percent Accepted who enroll: 45%
Number Entering: 3,780
Number of Transfers Accepted each Year: 1,686
Middle 50% SAT range: M: 520–640, CR: 500–610, Wr: Unreported
Middle 50% ACT range: 23–28
Early admission program EA/ED/None: EA

Percentage accepted through EA or ED: Unreported
EA and ED deadline: 15-Nov
Regular Deadline: 1-Aug
Application Fee: $40
Full time Undergraduate enrollment: 15,001
Total enrollment: 17,247
Percent Male: 52%
Percent Female: 48%
Total Percent Minority or Unreported: 21%
Percent African-American: 5%
Percent Asian/Pacific Islander: 2%
Percent Hispanic: 4%
Percent Native-American: 2%
Percent International: 3%
Percent in-state/out of state: 70%/30%
Percent from Public HS: 84%
Retention Rate: 83%

Graduation Rate 4-year: 32%
Graduation Rate 6-year: 56%
Percent Undergraduates in On-campus housing: 30%
Number of official organized extracurricular organizations: 340
3 Most popular majors: Finance, Journalism, Marketing/ Marketing Management
Student/Faculty ratio: 18:1
Average Class Size: 25
Percent of students going to grad school: Unreported
Tuition and Fees: $16,320
In-State Tuition and Fees if different: $5,888
Cost for Room and Board: $8,330
Percent receiving financial aid out of those who apply: Unreported
Percent receiving financial aid among all students: 64%

For it's A-A-A-R-K-A-N-S-A-S for Arkansas! Fight! Fight! Fi-i-i-ght!" Don't even think about setting foot in Fayetteville, Arkansas, without knowing the words to the Razorback fight song. Athletics aren't just for the jocks at this Southern university. If you are looking for a community with school pride, are unsure if you want to rush Pi Beta Phi or just go to their parties, and are interested in anything from engineering to agriculture, the University of Arkansas is calling your name.

Welcome to Fayetteville
Located in the Ozark Mountains, Fayetteville is the home of 345 acres of University of Arkansas campus. The city has a population of about 73,600 people for now, but Northwest Arkansas is considered one of the fastest-growing regions in the United States, according to the U.S. Census.

Upon arrival in Fayetteville, freshmen are introduced to their academic advisers, who "really know what they're doing," according to one senior. During orientation period, freshmen are clued in to all university policies and academic requirements. "It's hard to fall through the cracks freshman year," students said. "There are advisers and older students who really take pride in helping the younger ones." Make sure you ask about Advanced Placement status in classes, or how to "CLEP-out" of the University's second-language requirement by taking proficiency tests or foreign language classes. Oftentimes high school AP credits can cut down your "core" course load. The completion of core classes is required for graduation, and according to a senior, the readily accessible advisers are helpful in "letting us know exactly what we need" in order to graduate on time.

By sophomore year undergrads are usually enrolled in a specific college at the University of Arkansas. Students may choose between the Dale Bumpers College of Agricultural, Food & Life Sciences, the School of Architecture, the Fulbright College of Arts & Sciences, the Sam M. Walton College of Business, the College of Education and Health Professions, and the College of Engineering, depending on the student's academic interests. With over 200 academic degree programs, UA covers virtually all academic bases.

Most students are quick to say that the professors are all easy to reach, and hold convenient office hours, often meeting students for coffee on campus. However, as the freshmen core courses (such as Chemistry and Communications) are usually numbered at around 200 or 300 students, they are mostly taught by Teaching Assistants, not actual professors. One senior business major explained, "Once you get more into your major by junior and senior year, you get more of the professors, and people who actually wrote the books you are reading."

Deemed the hardest major at Arkansas by a number of students, engineering is only a hair less harrowing than molecular biology. Nonetheless, students claim that the difficulty of the subjects really shouldn't deter any undergrads from taking them. "Help is really just around the corner," one sophomore said. "I have tutors in a few subjects, and they are really flexible, and helpful around midterms and finals especially."

Life as a Razorback

While students are required to live on campus their freshman year, this is certainly not viewed as a bad thing. The dorms are described as "traditional" and "spacious" but beware: they are not all created equal.

Humphreys (aka "the Hump-Dump") is coed and in the middle of campus. However, it has no air-conditioning and is "miserable" at the beginning of school because "it can get pretty hot here in Arkansas." A better dorm is Pomfret, which "everyone who lives there loves" and "they have a lot of fun." Its location isn't as convenient, however, as it sits at the "very bottom of a great big hill." (Don't come to Fayetteville without good walking shoes; students say "we have a ton of huge hills!")

By sophomore year many students choose to live off campus in any of Fayetteville's many apartment complexes. The city is "overflowing" with them, and the crowding in the city has also created a huge parking problem. Students call the city parking "awful" and "downright impossible." Luckily for future classes, the city just built the biggest parking deck in the state of Arkansas, which holds more than 500 automobiles.

Greeks and Non-Greeks

Sophomore year is also the first year that students who choose to "Go Greek" can live in their fraternity and sorority houses. While Greek life is a large part of the Arkansas social scene, it is certainly not something that students feel pressured to join. "If you do it, great, but if you don't want to do it, that's great too," one Razorback senior commented. Greek or not, students can still attend frat parties, where the serving of alcohol to minors is reportedly "not a problem whatsoever." Students who live in off campus apartments and houses often open up their houses for parties and keggers, and offer a stress-free night for students who are underage.

The Greek houses are also all on campus, making party-hopping very convenient. With Sorority Row on Maple Street and Fraternity Row on Stadium Drive, undergrads don't have to look far for a "typical huge, beautiful, southern-style Greek house" offering plenty of cold beer and Southern hospitality.

Students are quick to add that there are no lines drawn between dorm-dwellers and off campus renters. UA offers over $100 million of financial aid each year, and many students receive this in the form of free room and board. The cafeterias received mixed reviews from Razorback undergrads. While some students lived on campus for four years and "never got tired of it" others don't think they will "step foot into a dining hall" for a whole year, even if they live in the dorms.

"Arkansas sporting events are huge, women's or men's, it's just a culture."

On campus or off, students mix and mingle the nights away on Fayetteville's Dickson Street. Running straight through campus, the street offers so many bars and clubs that "it's hard to keep up with the new names and owners," explains one seasoned senior. Go to George's Majestic Lounge and rub elbows with University of Arkansas alums recounting the nights they spent at the waterhole 50 years ago. Gypsy, Alligator Ray's, and Grubb's are just a few of the places that shouldn't be missed during an educational stint in Razorback Country. Even underage students can party with the rest of them on certain nights. Clubs and bars often offer 18-and-over nights, and on big weekends (think Homecoming Weekend versus South Carolina, or 'Bama and Texas games) the whole street is closed off.

A University of Arkansas education is incomplete without the inclusion of Arkansas athletics. Their unstoppable track program, which is known to have won 17 consecutive indoor titles, and their powerhouse football and basketball teams are just a few examples of nationally dominant Razorbacks sports. "The weekends are all about sporting events," students explain. "You have to get real geared up for the game, and no matter what, you MUST know the fight songs."

"Suuuey, Hogs"

With no professional sports teams to root for in the area, the entire Fayetteville community supports their hogs on game day. From the parquet in the Bud Walton Arena to the green grass of the Donald W. Reynolds Razorback Stadium, the thrill of victory (and the stench of keg beer) lingers in the sweet Southern air. Arkansas sports aren't simple weekend entertainment for UA Students. Students reported that "Arkansas sporting events are huge. Women's or men's, it's just a culture."

If a Division I athletic career isn't a personal option, undergrads can still quench their competitive spirits within the confines of HPER (the UA Health, Physical Education, and Recreation building). The $14 million facility is the largest in the area and features 10 racquetball courts, four basketball gyms, an indoor track, an Olympic-size swimming pool, a climbing wall, men's and women's saunas, a computer lab, thousands of lockers, and a human performance lab.

Greek or non-Greek, on campus or off, athlete or academic, Razorbacks are all about one thing: having one hell of a time. If you are looking for a school with tons of school pride nestled in a true Southern college city, then University of Arkansas is the place to be. When you are leaving home, don't forget to pack your Razorback football jersey. You won't regret it.—*Meredith Hudson*

FYI

If you come to Arkansas, you'd better bring "your car or enough money to buy one."

What's the typical weekend schedule? "Friday: hit up a frat party; Saturday: go crazy at the football game, head to the bars at night; Sunday: sleep in, catch up on studying."

If I could change one thing about the University of Arkansas, I would "send more funds to the science department instead of to athletics. Sometimes we lack a sufficient amount of chemicals to perform chemistry experiments."

Three things every student should do before graduating are "attend a Razorback football game and 'call the hogs,' take a class that is taught in Old Main, and eat at Herman's restaurant."

California

California Institute of Technology

Address: 1200 East California Boulevard, Pasadena, CA 91125

Phone: 626-395-6341

E-mail address: ugadmissions@caltech.edu

Web site URL: www.caltech.edu

Year Founded: 1891

Private or Public: Private

Religious Affiliation: None

Location: Urban

Number of Applicants: 5,225

Percent Accepted: 13%

Percent Accepted who enroll: 37%

Number Entering: 244

Number of Transfers Accepted each Year: 10

Middle 50% SAT range: M: 762–800, CR: 700–790, Wr: 700–790

Middle 50% ACT range: 33–35

Early admission program EA/ED/None: EA

Percentage accepted through EA or ED: 36%

EA and ED deadline: 1-Nov

Regular Deadline: 3-Jan

Application Fee: $65

Full time Undergraduate enrollment: 978

Total enrollment: 978

Percent Male: 60%

Percent Female: 40%

Total Percent Minority or Unreported: 9%

Percent African-American: 1%

Percent Asian/Pacific Islander: Unreported

Percent Hispanic: 6%

Percent Native-American: 1%

Percent International: 9%

Percent in-state/out of state: 31%/69%

Percent from Public HS: Unreported

Retention Rate: 98%

Graduation Rate 4-year: 81%

Graduation Rate 6-year: 90%

Percent Undergraduates in On-campus housing: 92%

Number of official organized extracurricular organizations: 150

3 Most popular majors: Mathematics, Mechanical Engineering, Physics

Student/Faculty ratio: 3:1

Average Class Size: 14

Percent of students going to grad school: Unreported

Tuition and Fees: $31,437

In-State Tuition and Fees if different: No difference

Cost for Room and Board: $10,146

Percent receiving financial aid out of those who apply: 60%

Percent receiving financial aid among all students: 60%

Many people across the nation just think of football and New Year's parades when they think of Pasadena, but this sunny Southern California suburb is home to more than just the Rose Bowl. For those who are familiar with science, they know that Caltech is home to one of the world's premier research institutions. And for students who are serious about math and science, and looking for opportunities for world-class research, they'll find what they're looking for in the small, close-knit community of Caltech. At this school, students take their education seriously, but they also have fun in an off-beat way, all while sharing the campus with Nobel Prize winners and professors who are the leaders in their fields.

Not for the Faint of Heart

To be blunt, Caltech is not for everyone, and students don't pretend otherwise. Caltech students say that the academics are rigorous and a love for learning and science is definitely necessary. The core curriculum required of all students includes five terms each of math and physics, in addition to classes in chemistry and biology. But don't think students can get through without taking any English classes—although Caltech places an obvious emphasis on math and science, it also requires students to take 12 courses in the humanities and social sciences. For many, making the transition from high school to Caltech's level of academics may be a bit challenging; students describe classes as especially hard. Luckily, students take all classes pass/fail for their first two terms to help them transition and, beyond freshman year, collaboration is always a big part of Caltech life. People typically work in small groups for homework, and exchange answers between groups. "You wouldn't pass if you didn't work with other people," one sophomore said.

Students say most of the work involves lots of problem-solving as opposed to just plug-and-chug with numbers. One student described freshman classes as very intellectual—calculus is proof-based and chemistry classes go beyond the typical high school approach. "I expected that I would be one of the people left behind, since there are so many smart people, but everyone really starts off in the same place," one freshman said. "Most people haven't seen the new material covered since we basically start from scratch—it's much more of a theoretical approach."

Students admit that Caltech's academics can get overwhelming, but that help is readily available for those who seek it, whether it's from friends, classmates, RAs, or free tutors. "You can get help in whatever class you need and if you're sick and can't finish a set, you can get an extension from the health department," one student said. "People are glad to help and it's mutual because even if you're one of the few people who know how to do a problem, you're going to need help on other ones."

A big part of Caltech's academic community is the Honor Code, which in effect makes almost all exams take-home and trusts undergraduates to time themselves and be honest. One student said, "Undergrads are given a lot of free range and people take it pretty seriously." Students say the honor code is designed not to punish, but to eliminate unfair advantage. "I really like the honor code because it goes into all aspects of Caltech life," said one freshman, who hadn't had any proctored tests yet. "There are open kitchens, and you can leave your door unlocked because people won't steal your stuff unless it's for a prank, but then you'll get it back." And it's exactly this kind of trust that builds a small, close-knit undergraduate community.

Ditching the Books for the Stacks

Sleep deprivation due to late-night problem sets is a regular part of Caltech culture, but don't think that Caltech students skip out on fun. Pranks are very much a part of Caltech culture, and they happen very often. But these go beyond your typical college pranks. A classic example of Caltech fun is the annual Pumpkin Drop, where students use liquid nitrogen to freeze pumpkins and drop them off the tallest building on campus. One of the most popular days on campus is Ditch Day, when school essentially stops—professors even extend set deadlines so that everyone can participate in the fun. The senior class plays hooky for a day, and in order to prevent underclassmen from ransacking their rooms, they block their doors with "stacks." Originally, these were physical blocks made of plywood and concrete intended to prevent anyone from entering, but they've since become complex sets of puzzles planned months or years in advance, intended to occupy the underclassmen's attentions while the seniors are away.

> **"It's a lot of hard work, in not very much time, but it's fun."**

Students say that Ditch Day consists of people running around solving problems—essentially high-tech, brainy scavenger hunts. "Last year, I worked on a stack that involved rearranging electrical circuits," one sophomore said. "There was one stack where undergrads were given a reprogrammed TI-83 [calculator] to plug in numbers and get clues to run around campus."

Houses Are Where the Heart Is

Caltech's social scene is dominated by houses, which students describe as a cross between frats and dorms. All students go through Rotation during their first days at Caltech, a process when every freshman eats a meal in each of the eight houses. After getting a feel for the houses, which each have different personalities, the freshmen rank their top three choices and get assigned to the house where they will live for the rest of their time at Caltech. Students say they meet many if not most of their friends through their houses—living in the same dorm and having family-style dinners every day creates a strong bond. "The house system is great because it gives you an instant sense of connection," one student said. "It's not so great for people who don't like the houses they're in, but it works for almost everyone, and you can switch house affiliation."

And at the heart of the housing system are the students of Caltech. Although students admit Caltech has a much higher density of nerds and geeks than your typical school, and that there is an uneven mix of genders, they say that the students make the close-knit community very comfortable. "It's an exceptional group of students," one sophomore said. "People are really interested in science, but you can typically talk to people about any topic and they'll be knowledgeable." Students say there are a certain number of students who stay in their rooms and study all day, but that most people are very outgoing and willing to help out with house events. In response to the stereotype of awkward nerds, one freshman said, "If anything, that helps us bond better, because if there's someone just like you, you're more likely to bond." Even if they're working, most students will leave their doors open and many leave messages on dry-erase whiteboards, keeping the small community connected.

Under Construction

"Our idea of fun is definitely different from most colleges," one freshman said. Students say that partying in the typical college sense of the word isn't very prevalent on campus, but when Caltech students party, they go all out—in an off-beat way, of course. Students don't just go to the local store for red Solo cups; they go to Home Depot to buy two-by-fours for major construction. For all large parties, the houses spend two to three weeks building elaborate structures in their courtyards. One freshman described her house's courtyard: "We built a dance floor about five feet off the floor, and then flooded the entire courtyard two to three feet. We also had fountains and waterfalls." For

Interhouse, one of the biggest parties of the year, all the south houses build similarly elaborate structures in their courtyard, and if students aren't happy with one party, they can hop on over to another party close by. On other days of the year, there are camping trips and pool games and even margarita Mondays.

But despite the fun, students are brought back by the reality of the demands of school. Students point out the high rate of 5–6 year graduations, dropouts and transfers, and say that students need to be able to perform under high pressure. "Even if you're the best, you can still not do well here," one sophomore said. "Being smart and working hard don't guarantee success, and you can't let that drag you down." But if students can get beyond the challenges of hard classes, they'll find a rewarding experience and will have some fun along the way. In fact, they may become one of the many famous physicists, engineers or scientists who have graduated from Caltech and gone on to make a name for themselves in science-related fields, whether in academia, industry or research. Students have the opportunity to sample the big leagues as part of professors' research projects, or by getting hands-on experience at the famous Jet Propulsion Laboratory, which Caltech operates for NASA.

Summing up the Caltech experience, one sophomore said, "It's a lot of hard work, in not very much time, but it's fun." This sunny Southern California school may not be for everyone, but if you're dedicated to math and science, willing to work really hard, and can persevere with a sense of humor, then this just might be the school for you. Caltech is a unique experience and, upon graduation, students enjoy the unique benefit of a world-class education and the respect of anyone familiar with the fields of math and science. One student said, "It's not for everyone, but anyone can come here and be accepted, no matter who you are."—*Della Fox*

FYI

If you come to Caltech, you'd better realize "it's not so much what you bring, but what you take out, and how you stay through in the middle."

What's the typical weekend schedule? "Saturday is typically relaxed: playing Frisbee and maybe catching up on sleep a bit. Sunday you work until midnight when you order pizza, and then you work more."

If I could change one thing about Caltech, I'd "make the classes easier so we would have more time to engage in extracurricular activities. And make pass/fail last longer than two terms."

Three things every student at Caltech should do before graduating are "participate in Ditch Day, do SURF (Summer Undergraduate Research Fellowship), and explore the tunnels underneath the campus, which help you get into buildings you wouldn't normally be able to get into."

California Institute of the Arts

Address: 24700 McBean Parkway, Valencia, CA 91355
Phone: 661-255-1050
E-mail address: admiss@calarts.edu
Web site URL: www.calarts.edu
Year Founded: 1961
Private or Public: Private
Religious Affiliation: None
Location: Suburban
Number of Applicants: 1,186
Percent Accepted: 32%
Percent Accepted who enroll: 40%
Number Entering: 151
Number of Transfers Accepted each Year: 188
Middle 50% SAT range: Unreported
Middle 50% ACT range: Unreported
Early admission program EA/ED/None: None

Percentage accepted through EA or ED: NA
EA and ED deadline: NA
Regular Deadline: 4-Jan
Application Fee: $70
Full time Undergraduate enrollment: 820
Total enrollment: 1,317
Percent Male: 54%
Percent Female: 46%
Total Percent Minority or Unreported: 30%
Percent African-American: 9%
Percent Asian/Pacific Islander: 9%
Percent Hispanic: 12%
Percent Native-American: <1%
Percent International: 8%
Percent in-state/out of state: 66%/44%
Percent from Public HS: Unreported
Retention Rate: Unreported
Graduation Rate 4-year: 57%

Graduation Rate 6-year: Unreported
Percent Undergraduates in On-campus housing: 40%
Number of official organized extracurricular organizations: 5
3 Most popular majors: Acting; Film, Video and Photographic Arts; Visual Performing Arts
Student/Faculty ratio: 7:1
Average Class Size: 12
Percent of students going to grad school: Unreported
Tuition and Fees: $32,860
In-State Tuition and Fees if different: No difference
Cost for Room and Board: $5,236
Percent receiving financial aid out of those who apply: Unreported
Percent receiving financial aid among all students: 38%

C alifornia Institute of the Arts, a school self-contained in a single building, was supposed to be a haven for artists in the middle of nowhere. Besides the fact that a strip-mall town grew up around it, Cal Arts is pretty much just that: a place for artists to gather and work on their skills. Students who go to Cal Arts love it, but more importantly, they love what they do, making the focused nature of the school perfect for self-motivated artists.

Math and Science? Not really . . .

The nearly 900 undergraduates enrolled in Cal Arts are members of one of six schools, in a range of highly selective BFA programs. One student said that the music technology program accepts around six to eight students each year. Cal Arts only has Bachelor of Fine Arts and Master of Fine Arts programs. To graduate, students not only need to take a certain number of classes within their "métier," what the students interviewed called their discipline, but also need to complete a Critical Studies requirement. Critical Studies are academic subjects, spread over a number of distributional requirements. There are also core classes required of students: a Writing Arts course, which discusses the relationship between art and society, and Foundation courses, which could be on a number of topics. The Foundation courses are geared specifically toward a certain discipline. One photography and media major said that the Foundation course required of all fine arts majors entitled "What Makes it Art," was "kind of a lame class," and featured the only teacher he did not like.

The categories for distributional requirements, the Breadth requirements, include humanities, social sciences, cultural studies, natural sciences, quantitative, métier studies in the student's métier and métier studies in a separate métier. Yes, there is even a quantitative requirement. "But it's art school math, so it's pretty friendly," one student said. Even in the Critical Studies classes, which students take on Wednesdays, there is usually an art bent, the same student said. She said that her paper topic for her philosophy class was to pick three pieces of art and "philosophize about them." Another student said Critical Studies is "kind of the fun way to do something that is out of your métier."

While the classes within the métiers are usually capped at around eight to 10 students, Critical Studies classes can have up to about 30. Despite this, students said that there are no 800-student lectures, and all classes are taught with students sitting "in a round," emphasizing student participation. One student, who transferred to Cal Arts from NYU's Tisch School of the Arts, said she preferred the Critical Studies classes at Cal Arts as opposed to the distributional requirements at NYU. The student, who is in the School of Theater's BFA Acting program, said that it was hard to be in classes at NYU with majors in non-art subjects. "The academics are set up for artists and they are very artist friendly," she said. That being said, students agreed that the Critical Studies classes are not particularly challenging. "I can definitely say it is not as challenging as it could be and sometimes I do find myself a little bored," one student said.

> "You have to love what you do, because that is basically all you do."

For students at Cal Arts, most of their time both inside and outside of the classroom is spent concentrating on their métier. "I'm a violin performance major and for my major all I do is focus on music," one student said. Most students interviewed said that the classes within their métier are challenging and require a lot of work outside the classroom. One student stressed that to succeed in métier classes one has to be self-motivated. "The department classes are going to be challenging," the student in the acting program said. "You are going to work really hard. It's easy to sit back, but the kids who do that don't last very long."

Each student is given a mentor in his or her field, and, since the student body is relatively small, that professor only has a small number of students he or she is mentoring, which makes relationships quite casual. Students always call their instructors by their first names. Students praise the instructors, who for the most part are all working professionals. "They have great insight," one

student in the dance program said. "It's really different than having someone who has sort of had their career that is sort of over and is teaching. Another student said he liked the fact that while you are showing a teacher your work, that teacher will often turn around and show you theirs as well.

No ABCs
Students at Cal Arts are graded on a pass/fail basis. Upon finishing a course students receive a mark of High Pass, Pass, Low Pass, No Credit or NX (insufficient attendance). No Credit is essentially the equivalent of failing. If a student chooses to take the class in which he or she received a No Credit again, the previous class will go off their record. Additionally, if a student receives an "Incomplete," he or she is required to finish that class at some point in time. One student, who came to Cal Arts from a high-stress-level private school, said she appreciates the system of grading. "I take so much more pride in my work because I feel like I am getting positive feedback as opposed to feeling like there is someone out to get me in the grading."

Let's put on a show!
Students at Cal Arts in the performing arts are required to be involved in performances outside of their classroom work, and the facilities are state of the art. The student in the acting program raved about the Disney Modular Theater. The theater—there is only one other like it in the entire world—can transform into anything a production wants it to be. The stage can be raised if that is necessary, or a production can even have a waterfall, like one recent show did. There are also smaller and more casual ways for students to perform. Most students interviewed mentioned the Coffee House, which puts on performances that are student-run, directed, produced and performed. At Cal Arts students interviewed said the focus is interdisciplinary. One student described an instance in which a student in the world music program helped out his friend who is a dance major.

An artists' commune in a conservative town
There are two dorm complexes, one for undergraduates and one for grad students. In Ahmanson, the dorm for graduate students, most of the residents are older, and many have families. Every freshman is required to have a meal plan, but some students end up cooking in their dorm rooms. Since there is

no guaranteed housing for undergraduates, many students live off campus. But that doesn't mean they spend a lot of time in Valencia. While students love the Cal Arts campus, the surrounding town of Valencia receives less than rave reviews. "The town of Valencia is like one giant strip mall," one student said. "Basically everything is a chain." She added that students go to Abbey Lane Café, one of the few restaurants that is not a chain in the neighborhood. Cal Arts remains isolated from the town. "The town never knows what is going on," another student said. "It's like the house on the hill in *Edward Scissorhands*."

> **"All of the action happens at Cal Arts. It's like the Vatican."**

Despite the fact that Valencia is a suburb of Los Angeles, one student said he does not get the opportunity to go there often since transportation is difficult. There is no easy form of public transportation to get to the city, and once there it is hard to get around without a car. While some students have cars, others who don't often don't want to feel like they are begging rides off of them. "If you don't have a car you can feel like you are in a bubble," he said. "All of the action happens at Cal Arts," another student said. "It's like the Vatican."

The Red Cup Rule
Even though there are not a lot of the big parties that come with Greek life, there is a fair amount of alcohol and drug use on and off campus among students. Most students interviewed agreed that school policy on drug and alcohol use is fairly lax. One student mentioned what she knows as the "red cup rule." The "red cup rule" is an unspoken rule between school security and students. The rule implies that as long as the liquid is protected in a plastic red cup, students can drink anything. "If a security guard sees you with a red cup they can't tell you to throw it away," she said. Another student said, "there is obviously a lot of pot." While there is a lot of pot, harder drugs are rare, although one student said you will hear about the isolated instances of a student going to rehab.

While most students socialized with others in their métier, art gallery openings on Thursdays are a chance for all students to get together. At the gallery openings there is wine and beer for students over 21 years old, and sometimes live music or a DJ. There are also a few famed parties that most students at the school attend, such as the Halloween party. Despite the popularity of the art gallery openings and the Halloween party, one student said that most of the "hardcore parties" are off-campus.

The place for artists
Most students interviewed had trouble finding things to complain about at Cal Arts. For students who really care about their art and want to pursue it as their career, Cal Arts seems to be the perfect place. While there are so many opportunities for artists that one student said a "workaholic" tendency can take over, she emphasized that "it's a really good school if you are self-motivated."— *Esther Zuckerman*

FYI
If you come to Cal Arts, you'd better bring "receptivity, a willingness to work. If you aren't willing to do the work then you are not going to do very well."
What is the typical weekend schedule? "If I were in a show there would be rehearsal on Saturday and rehearsal on Friday night. Sundays would be off and your free time is your free time. I'd rehearse at some point for a scene in my acting class. At night it's a social hour or it's work."
If I could change one thing about Cal Arts, I'd "have online class sign-ups. Everyone just runs for it."
Three things every student at Cal Arts should do before graduating are "put on your own show, live in the dorms for one year and make sure to chill on the hill a lot."

California State University System

The California State system boasts that it comprises the largest and most diverse universities in America. It offers the chance to study everything from marine navigation and technology to mathematics and engineering among its 23 campuses. Geographically too, the University spans from San Diego State, just 18 miles from the Mexican border, to Humboldt State, 774 miles north in Eureka, Calif.

Founded in 1960 and administered by a governor-appointed 25-member Board of Trustees, the CSU system coexists with the University of California system and California Community Colleges to form a trifecta of higher education in the Golden State.

Where to go
With so many options in regards to location, the third-largest state may seem a bit intimidating. To help out, www.csumentor.com eases the application and decision process for prospective undergrads. Each campus offers different programs and has different sized student bodies. Along with the UCs and Community Colleges, the three systems allow a place for every California resident to pursue a degree. Financing an education is easy too—tuition ranges from $4,000 to $21,000 depending on living situation, and campus and financial aid opportunities are plentiful.

The wide array of campuses, along with their geographical differences offers prospective students enough choice to satisfy even the most fickle of tastes.

In the Classroom
Though the UC system retains the spotlight, Cal States are no slouch in academics. The system maintains a focus on undergraduate education, as opposed to the larger universities' research-oriented approach.

California Polytechnic/San Luis Obispo's College of Engineering, for example, was ranked No. 1 by *U.S. News and World Report* for public undergrad engineering schools. One of the first Cal State universities, San Francisco State, offers a world-class cinema department. Cal-Maritime Academy offers the opportunity to study Coast Guard and Naval operations without the requirement of military service.

The Cal State system offers a variety of academic opportunities, boasting, "We prepare graduates who go on to make a difference in the workforce."

Sunshine and Sports
All 23 campuses, except CSU–Channel Islands, have either a Division I or Division II sports program. Recently, Cal State Dominguez Hills sent their No. 9 ranked men's soccer team to the national semifinals before the Toros' championship run was cut short in a 3–2 double overtime defeat to Tampa. CSU–Northridge, affectionately known as cee-sun, boasts a long sports tradition. The Matadors men's basketball squad finished second in the Big West to UC–Santa Barbara.

Many CSU schools compete in the Big West league while six campuses participate in the Mountain Pacific Sports Federation. With the sun shining year-round, IM and club sports are also popular.

With the draw of a diverse student body, numerous options in location and academic course of study, the California State University system retains a vital role to California's higher education.—*Brittany Golob*

California Polytechnic State / San Luis Obispo

Address: Admissions Office,
San Luis Obispo, CA 93407
Phone: 805-756-2311
E-mail address:
admissions@calpoly.edu
Web site URL:
www.calpoly.edu
Year Founded: 1901
Private or Public: Public
Religious Affiliation: None
Location: Suburban
Number of Applicants:
33,352
Percent Accepted: 34%
**Percent Accepted who
enroll:** 31%
Number Entering: 3,501
**Number of Transfers
Accepted each Year:**
1,623
Middle 50% SAT range:
M: 570–680, CR: 530–630,
Wr: Unreported
Middle 50% ACT range:
24–29
**Early admission program
EA/ED/None:** ED

**Percentage accepted
through EA or ED:**
Unreported
EA and ED deadline:
31-Oct
Regular Deadline: 30-Nov
Application Fee: $55
**Full time Undergraduate
enrollment:** 18,516
Total enrollment: 19,777
Percent Male: 56%
Percent Female: 44%
**Total Percent Minority or
Unreported:** 24%
Percent African-American:
1%
**Percent Asian/Pacific
Islander:** 11%
Percent Hispanic: 11%
Percent Native-American:
<1%
Percent International: 1%
**Percent in-state/out of
state:** 96%/4%
Percent from Public HS:
Unreported
Retention Rate: 90%

Graduation Rate 4-year:
23%
Graduation Rate 6-year:
70%
**Percent Undergraduates in
On-campus housing:** 29%
**Number of official organized
extracurricular
organizations:** 375
3 Most popular majors:
Engineering, Business,
Agriculture
Student/Faculty ratio: 19:1
Average Class Size: 24
**Percent of students going to
grad school:** 20%
Tuition and Fees: $15,213
**In-State Tuition and Fees if
different:** $5,043
Cost for Room and Board:
$9,369
**Percent receiving financial
aid out of those who apply:**
43%
**Percent receiving financial
aid among all students:**
Unreported

San Luis Obispo, one of the oldest cities in California, is home to one of the most prestigious institutions of the California State University system, California Polytechnic State, also known as Cal Poly. A large land-grant university of nearly 20,000 students, Cal Poly is a prominent research institution that focuses on engineering and agriculture, even though it also offers an array of liberal arts programs of study. As a technical school, research is also an important part of the university. In addition, the affordability of the school for Californian residents means that it is a highly desirable destination for many students from the Golden State.

Engineering and Beyond

Although the College of Engineering is recognized across the country, Cal Poly includes five other divisions: Agriculture, Food, and Environmental Sciences; Architecture and Environmental Design; Business, Liberal Arts; and Sciences and Mathematics. Given the university's name, it is clear what topics are the most important to Cal Poly. Students generally agree that engineering and architecture are particularly prestigious. It shows with the enrollment. In fact, the engineering school accounts for nearly one-third of the undergraduate student body. The College of Liberal Arts, however, only has 3,000 students, which is less than one-sixth of the student population. "We are definitely a technical school," said one student. "Compared to other schools, we don't have that many liberal arts majors."

An important distinction in the application process for Cal Poly is that it requires students to declare their majors on their applications. Therefore, most students going into the school have a specific career in mind. Each major has its own high school requirements to ensure that all students have the basic skills to succeed in the field. The school has over 60 majors from which the students can choose when they apply. The admissions office then selects the best candidates from the application pools of each major. To prevent people from applying to easy majors and then changing them during the course of their study at Cal Poly, the university has very strict standards in transferring from one major to another. "Most people here know exactly what they want to do, and they are really focused," said one student. Indeed, given the technical nature of the university, Cal Poly is best for prospective students who have mapped out their next few years both academically and professionally.

> "Most people here know exactly what they want to do, and they are really focused."

Despite the technical aspect of the university and the specialized nature of many majors, students are required to take a number of general education courses in order to ensure that they have some knowledge of other academic fields. "The required courses can be annoying because you have to take them," said one student. "But after you have taken them, you are glad because you always learn something new in those classes." The general education classes are divided into communication, science and mathematics, arts and humanities, society and individual, and technology. The requirements are also different for students depending on their college. For example, those in the College of Engineering have to take fewer classes in humanities than those who are in the College of Liberal Arts.

The coursework at Cal Poly can be difficult, especially for those who are not ready to work hard. Given the large number of engineering students and the mathematical proficiency needed for technical majors, many students can face some difficulties at the beginning. However, as they become more familiar with college living, students generally make enough adjustments to manage their workload. "I had a hard time in freshman year," said one student. "But I have been doing well since then because I found better work methods." Furthermore, the engineering and science majors can be difficult and competitive, while some business and agriculture programs of study are more relaxed.

Over the years, Cal Poly has been highly regarded as one of the best technical schools in the country. Among western universities for which the highest program offered is the master's degree, Cal Poly is consistently ranked in the top 10 by the *U.S. News and World Report*. It is also consistently recognized as having a top engineering program, not to mention an outstanding architecture school. All of this means that the application process is highly competitive. The acceptance rate has recently fallen under 40 percent.

A Historic City

San Luis Obispo traces its current settlement to 1772 with the beginning of a Spanish mission in the area. Today, the city remains relatively small, with a population of only 44,000, and much of the activity in the city is centered on Cal Poly. The town is small, but, given the scope of the university, it offers a number of restaurants and bars close to campus to serve and entertain students. The natural location of the city is very convenient for all those enjoying the outdoors. The Los Padres National Park is only five miles to the east, while the Pacific Ocean is less than 10 miles to the West. Big cities, however, are less accessible, since San Luis Obispo is almost at the midpoint between San Francisco and Los Angeles. "I enjoy living here," said one student. "But you won't find too many interesting places to go to during weekends."

The housing at Cal Poly is highly limited. Most of the on-campus residential halls are reserved for freshmen. There is a special arrangement of six freshmen residences called Living-Learning Program halls. The idea is for the university to combine living with academics. Therefore, students of the same college live together. This way, they can support each other in their academics and make useful connections for future endeavors. For all those who are interested in bringing alcohol to the dorms, it might not be a very good idea, as the university is strict about the usage and possession of alcohol. Freshmen in dorms must purchase a meal plan. The campus has 19 different food venues for students, though many of them are quite small and limited. More than half of the student body live off campus after their first year. It is generally easy to find reasonable housing around the campus area in San Luis Obispo.

Given the small number of students living on campus and the dry dorm policy, most parties and weekend socializing opportunities happen in off campus housing, Greek houses, or local restaurants and bars. Although the

Greek life certainly exists, it is only one small portion of the social scene. Despite all of this, given the size of the university, students agree that they can no doubt find many interesting events to attend during the weekends.

Diversity and Festivity

While the school has a mix of students from all ethnic groups, it is not particularly as diverse as many other universities within the California public education system. Nevertheless, most people are happy with the makeup of the student body. One issue, however, is that more than 90 percent of the students are from within California. After all, it is a public university designed to serve Californians. Nevertheless, students do not believe that this aspect of the school has any effect on their college experience.

For students who have a clear vision of what they want to do during their college years and who are willing to work hard, Cal Poly certainly represents a very good destination. Many of its technical programs are highly prestigious, and it can be relatively affordable for residents of California. Therefore, if you don't mind living in a small, historic town away from big cities, Cal Poly is certainly a great college option.—*Xiaohang Liu*

FYI
If you come to Cal Poly, you'd better bring "a car."
What is the typical weekend schedule? "Parties! What else?"
If I could change one thing about Cal Poly, I'd "build more dorms."
Three things every student at Cal Poly should do before graduating are "go hiking, swimming, and study hard."

California State University / Chico

Address: 400 West First Street, Chico, CA 95929-0722
Phone: 530-898-4428
E-mail address: INFO@csuchico.edu
Web site URL: www.csuchico.edu
Year Founded: 1887
Private or Public: Public
Religious Affiliation: None
Location: Urban
Number of Applicants: 15,069
Percent Accepted: 87%
Percent Accepted who enroll: 21%
Number Entering: 2,765
Number of Transfers Accepted each Year: 3,082
Middle 50% SAT range: M: 460–570, CR: 450–550, Wr: Unreported
Middle 50% ACT range: 19–24
Early admission program EA/ED/None: None

Percentage accepted through EA or ED: NA
EA and ED deadline: NA
Regular Deadline: 30-Nov
Application Fee: $55
Full time Undergraduate enrollment: 15,804
Total enrollment: 17,034
Percent Male: 48%
Percent Female: 52%
Total Percent Minority or Unreported: 22%
Percent African-American: 2%
Percent Asian/Pacific Islander: 6%
Percent Hispanic: 13%
Percent Native-American: 1%
Percent International: 2%
Percent in-state/out of state: 98%/2%
Percent from Public HS: Unreported
Retention Rate: 79%
Graduation Rate 4-year: 15%

Graduation Rate 6-year: 52%
Percent Undergraduates in On-campus housing: 1%
Number of official organized extracurricular organizations: 192
3 Most popular majors: Business Administration, Liberal Arts, Psychology
Student/Faculty ratio: 22:1
Average Class Size: 23
Percent of students going to grad school: Unreported
Tuition and Fees: $14,178
In-State Tuition and Fees if different: $4,008
Cost for Room and Board: $8,718
Percent receiving financial aid out of those who apply: 88%
Percent receiving financial aid among all students: 87%

A member of the California State University system, the largest system of higher education in the United States, California State University, Chico has an enrollment of nearly 17,000 students, the great majority of whom come from the Golden State. Founded in 1887 as Northern Branch State Normal, Chico State has now become a major educational institution in California, offering both bachelor's and master's programs. The school is especially popular with Californian students who are able to receive a solid education at relatively low costs and enjoy the college town atmosphere offered by Chico.

A Research Institution

Chico is divided into nine colleges, covering all major academic and professional areas. The schools include Agriculture, Business, Behavioral and Social Sciences, Communication and Education, Engineering, Humanities and Fine Arts, Natural Sciences, Graduate Studies, and Continuing Education. This means a large selection of academic programs for students. "We are a pretty big state school," said one student. "We have people of diverse interests, and I think Chico does a good job in having something for everyone in terms of academics."

The university offers nearly 150 undergraduate majors in more than 50 departments, which is a very large number for any academic institution. Some of the unique majors include Recreation Administration, Kinesiology, and Applied Computer Graphics, which are hard to find in most other universities. The specialized nature of many majors means that a high percentage of students at Chico State are focused on career preparation when they enter the school. "There are always a lot of people who don't know what they want to do even when they are seniors," said one student. "But there are also a lot of people who came in here to focus on specific professions." According to students, the classes at Chico State are mostly "pretty good" in preparing students for future careers.

For the most part, students do not complain about workload. "You always meet a bunch of professors who give us a lot of work and grade really harshly," said one student. "But from my experience, as long as you don't fall too far behind, you will do just fine in most of your classes." Ultimately, the difficulties of classes depend on the students' choices. Similar to many other colleges, a number of classes in engineering can be particularly challenging, especially for those who do not have strong backgrounds in mathematics.

As with most universities, Chico State has a list of general education requirements for all undergraduates. They are designed to expose students to a number of important disciplines so that they will have a wide range of knowledge and skills. The first part of the requirements ensures that students have basic abilities in communications, mathematics, and logic, three topics that are highly valuable for undergraduates in any majors. The rest of the requirements focus on knowledge, meaning that all graduates of Chico State must have some understanding of social sciences, natural sciences, and humanities. Although many students may find some of the classes rather interesting and enlightening, others believe that it can be burdensome and boring. "I didn't like the required classes," said one student. "I will never use some of the stuff that they teach in those classes."

The lectures at Chico State can be very large. However, compared to many other large institutions, the university is very good at ensuring a number of small classes. "I think the professors and the students do get to know each other," said one student. "And I never think the classes are too big." One of the best ways to have a small, more intimate academic experience is through the honors program, which ensures that its members will be able to attend classes with less than 25 students. Other benefits include living in Honors House during freshmen year and priority registration for classes, which can be valuable for students to enroll in some of the more popular courses. There are even opportunities for some upper-level classes to have two professors per course, so that students can hear different viewpoints on subjects.

The City of Roses

Chico, also known as the City of Roses, is at the foot of the Sierra Nevada Mountains. It is surrounded by a few other midsized towns and cities, but for the students at Chico State, the city is rather small and not too interesting. The location, however, is highly appreciated by outdoors enthusiasts who are able to take advantage of the different expeditions to the surrounding parks, creeks, and hills. Chico is also home to Bidwell Park, the largest municipal park in the United States. "I am not bored by Chico," said one student. "But if you are, you can get out of here and go hiking and rafting."

The dormitory system is mostly occupied by freshmen. In fact, the dorms provide housing to slightly over 1,200 students. Besides the traditional housing facilities, the university also provides a number of themed houses. Most of them are based on the academic programs of students. For example, there is one program for students in agriculture and another for those in engineering. Alcohol policy is very strict, as alcohol is generally forbidden from university facilities. The meal plans provide sit-down dining services in two locations as well as a number of coffee shops and convenience stores. Of course, given the size of Chico State, there are few dining locations. It does not disturb most students, however, as they generally live off campus anyway.

> "On the weekends, you can definitely find places where you can have a good time."

The reason for the large number of students living off campus is that the apartments and houses around the area can be found at reasonable prices. In addition, the university's housing office also provides resources to students in their search for dwellings. The great majority of upperclassmen move off campus, which also allows for a greater degree of freedom. One student said,

"I prefer living off campus because you feel more like you are on your own."

The parties at Chico State are generally found in the fraternities and sororities, as well as in off campus houses. Furthermore, even though the city is relatively small, it still offers a number of bars, restaurants, and clubs for late-night entertainment, especially during the weekend. "We have some really cool parties here," said one student. "On the weekends, you can definitely find places where you can have a good time."

Enjoying Life
Chico State does have a very good athletic program. Most teams compete in NCAA Division II, and the men's baseball team has made several appearances in the championship series during the last two decades. One drawback, however, is that the football program was disbanded in 1997 as a way to cut costs.

Chico State is primarily an institution of Californians, as most students are from the state. However, as one student pointed out, "it's not like everybody looks at you differently when you say you are not from California." For students from anywhere, the university provides a very good education with hundreds of options. At the same time, despite being located in a relatively small city, the social aspect of Chico State is still highly inviting, making it a very good destination for students.—*Xiaohang Liu*

FYI
If you come to Chico State, you'd better bring "hiking boots."
What is the typical weekend schedule? "Parties are on Thursday, Friday, and Saturday. If you want to go outdoors, you should probably go on Saturday."
If I could change one thing about Chico State, I'd "get more people to live on campus."
Three things every student at Chico State should do before graduating are "go hiking, enjoy the weekends, and just have fun."

California State University / Fresno

Address: 5150 North Maple Ave. M/S JA 57, Fresno, CA 93740-8026
Phone: 559-278-2261
E-mail address: admissions@csufresno.edu
Web site URL: www.csufresno.edu
Year Founded: 1911
Private or Public: Public
Religious Affiliation: None
Location: Urban
Number of Applicants: 14,537
Percent Accepted: 70%
Percent Accepted who enroll: 27%
Number Entering: 2,823
Number of Transfers Accepted each Year: 2,798
Middle 50% SAT range: M: 410–540, CR: 400–510, Wr: Unreported
Middle 50% ACT range: 16–22
Early admission program EA/ED/None: None

Percentage accepted through EA or ED: NA
EA and ED deadline: NA
Regular Deadline: 1-Feb
Application Fee: $55
Full time Undergraduate enrollment: 19,245
Total enrollment: 21,728
Percent Male: 43%
Percent Female: 57%
Total Percent Minority or Unreported: 56%
Percent African-American: 6%
Percent Asian/Pacific Islander: 16%
Percent Hispanic: 34%
Percent Native-American: <1%
Percent International: 1%
Percent in-state/out of state: Unreported
Percent from Public HS: 99%
Retention Rate: 82%
Graduation Rate 4-year: 15%

Graduation Rate 6-year: 46%
Percent Undergraduates in On-campus housing: 6%
Number of official organized extracurricular organizations: 250
3 Most popular majors: Health Sciences, Liberal Arts and Sciences
Student/Faculty ratio: Unreported
Average Class Size: 25
Percent of students going to grad school: Unreported
Tuition and Fees: $13,857
In-State Tuition and Fees if different: $3,687
Cost for Room and Board: $8,590
Percent receiving financial aid out of those who apply: 80%
Percent receiving financial aid among all students: Unreported

You might think that nothing clashes with Southern California like math, science, and engineering, but California State University, Fresno, ("Fresno State") would prove you wrong. For students with a particular interest in STEM fields or agriculture, Fresno state offers a great combination of academic opportunities, Greek life, and independence off campus.

One unit at a time

Fresno State awards course credit via a "unit" system, where one unit is equal to one hour in the classroom. Most majors require 120 units to graduate, but some majors, such as engineering, require more units for the bachelor's degree. Of the 120 units required, 51 of them must be classified as "general education requirements," classes that students take after introductory courses often during the junior or senior year. But be warned: even though general education classes are required, according to one student, "enrollment will give you a headache," since registration depends on seniority. Each major asks different numbers of units of its students; the mass communications and journalism major, for instance, requires 33 units in the major, while the English education major requires 48 units in the major. Most students average about 15–16 units per semester, and finish gaining the 120 units to graduate by taking fun and interesting electives, like "History of Jazz and Rock and Roll."

According to one student, Fresco State's STEM majors and programs are known for being more difficult than studies in the humanities, but are also stronger and more popular than their humanities counterparts. In particular, the school's agriculture major, for which it is known, is regarded as particularly difficult. But, "each major has that one professor who is known for having a great class that students want to be enrolled in," making all kinds of classes desirable.

> **"Each major has that one professor who is known for having a great class that students want to be enrolled in."**

Free Speech—In and Out of the Press

Greek life has a definite presence on campus, with over 1,000 participating students. However, the university does follow an "anti-alcohol stance," and is dry, besides for a campus bar that hosts university sponsored events.

Sports games, particularly in basketball and football, feature high turnouts, especially when Fresno State's Bulldogs are barking at rival teams. In addition to varsity sports, club and intermural sports have a supportive following. However, because Fresno State is mostly a commuter campus and many students have additional, full-time jobs, according to one student, "After 5PM, the campus empties out."

For the students who do decide to live on campus, four housing options are available: the "community style," the "suite one room," the "suite two rooms," and the "suite three rooms." Community style living features coed rooms with gender-designated bathrooms branching out from a hallway, whereas suites are gender-designated and feature common rooms shared by multiple bedrooms.

Students are most often found in the two walkways that circle the student union, called the "Free Speech" area. The Free Speech area is not only the campus's nucleus because it is centrally located (in addition to surrounding the student union it also is near the library and campus bar) but also because it features booths set up by Fresno State's various fraternities and sororities.

Safety is a primary concern for Fresno State, as the western side of its campus borders "Sin City," a dangerous area for students to walk alone, particularly at night, due to high crime rates. The eastern side of campus, however, where dorms are located, is generally regarded as being much safer.

For students living on campus, obtaining a meal plan is mandatory. However, most students, because they live off-campus, don't eat dining hall food and instead grab lunch at a nearby Taco Bell or the recently built student mall, which features restaurants amenable to a quick bite, like Subway.

For students who choose to participate in extracurriculars, a plethora of options are available: from student government, to the campus's newspaper, *The Collegian*, to community service. In addition, each department runs a plethora of academic-specific clubs and organizations for students to delve into.

Fresno State enables its students to combine academics and extracurriculars with a career outside of campus. Together, a successful campus life and non-campus life can give students a positive college experience and strong sense of self. —*Phoebe Kimmelman*

FYI
If you come to Fresno State, you'd better bring "gas money."
The biggest college-wide tradition/event at Fresno State is "football. Go Bulldogs!"
One thing you wish you would've known before coming to Fresno State is "the student newspaper requires two intro courses."

The Claremont Colleges

The Claremont Colleges consist of five small independent liberal arts colleges and two graduate schools found in the tree-lined streets of Claremont, California. Claremont McKenna, Harvey Mudd, Pitzer, Pomona, and Scripps form the 5-Cs, the undergraduate liberal art colleges, while the graduate institutions are the Claremont Graduate University and the Keck Graduate Institute, which are separated from the undergraduate institutions/colleges. While each of the 5-Cs is independent, the close proximity of the other colleges of the consortium enables students to enjoy both the resources of a large university and the intimacy of a small liberal arts college.

Academic Unity
The colleges are distinct in the sense that students receive their degrees from their own college and the colleges' administration and admissions departments are independent from each other. However, partly due to the highly specialized nature of each of the colleges, raging from the humanities and the social sciences to engineering and math, students from individual institutions can take classes in colleges other than their own. Cross-registration is very common and students can even take most of their classes in colleges other than their own. Due to the high degree of specialization in the colleges,

students might even choose to do an off campus major and major in a different college, if they find that their own college's emphasis no longer satisfies their academic interests.

The colleges also share many programs and academic departments such as the Women's Union, the Intercollegiate Department of Media Studies, and the Five-College Theater Department. Shared facilities include counseling centers and the Libraries of the Claremont Colleges, all of the dining halls, and the campus bookstore.

Campus interests
In addition to academic integration, the colleges also share many athletic and social activities. Pitzer and Pomona make up an NCAA Division III team while the other three colleges form another. At the same time, all undergraduates can use most of the 5-Cs athletic facilities.

The schools' social scene is quite integrated in the sense that students often attend parties in other colleges. Many times however, their dorms function as the students' social circles with parties inside rooms although there are often all-college parties hosted by the colleges.

Many of the student organizations are integrated in the sense that their membership draws from all five colleges.—*Katerina Karatzia*

Claremont McKenna College

Address: 890 Columbia Avenue, Claremont, CA 91711
Phone: 909-621-8088
E-mail address: admission@ claremontmckenna.edu
Web site URL: www .claremontmckenna.edu
Year Founded: 1946
Private or Public: Private
Religious Affiliation: None
Location: Suburban
Number of Applicants: 3,670
Percent Accepted: 22%
Percent Accepted who enroll: 40%
Number Entering: 320
Number of Transfers Accepted each Year: 86
Middle 50% SAT range: M: 660–750, CR: 630–740, Wr: Unreported
Middle 50% ACT range: Unreported

Early admission program EA/ED/None: ED
Percentage accepted through EA or ED: 28%
EA and ED deadline: 15-Nov
Regular Deadline: 2-Jan
Application Fee: $60
Full time Undergraduate enrollment: 1,211
Total enrollment: 1,211
Percent Male: 54%
Percent Female: 46%
Total Percent Minority or Unreported: 28%
Percent African-American: 4%
Percent Asian/Pacific Islander: 12%
Percent Hispanic: 11%
Percent Native-American: <1%
Percent International: 6%
Percent in-state/out of state: 46%/54%
Percent from Public HS: Unreported

Retention Rate: 97%
Graduation Rate 4-year: 90%
Graduation Rate 6-year: 94%
Percent Undergraduates in On-campus housing: 98%
Number of official organized extracurricular organizations: 280
3 Most popular majors: Economics, International Relations, Political Science
Student/Faculty ratio: 8:1
Average Class Size: 17
Percent of students going to grad school: Unreported
Tuition and Fees: $37,060
In-State Tuition and Fees if different: No difference
Cost for Room and Board: $11,930
Percent receiving financial aid out of those who apply: 45%
Percent receiving financial aid among all students: 51%

C laremont McKenna College is part of the Claremont College Consortium with Scripps College, Pitzer College, Pomona College, and Harvey Mudd College in Claremont, California. CMC, formally Claremont Men's College, has about 1,200 undergraduates on the 50-acre campus. Its focus on social sciences and strong faculty consistently make it one of the highest-ranked US liberal arts colleges. Known for the relaxed and intellectual spirit of the campus, Claremont McKenna is also known to have some of the happiest students in the country.

Five Colleges of Classes

There is a strong focus on the social sciences at Claremont McKenna, with about 80 percent of students majoring in Economics or Government. The Government Department and the Robert Day School of Economics and Finance are the largest within their fields in the Claremont College Consortium, so they attract students from the other four colleges as well. "Because there's an emphasis on the social sciences, there's a very pragmatic sense to our liberal arts education. CMC puts a huge emphasis on internships and real-world experience," one student with a dual major in International Relations and Religious Studies stated. She said this emphasis on real-world applications, while eye-opening, can make it more difficult for students who might be looking for an "intellectual bubble" during their college experience. "If you want to escape to 19th-century British literature, for example, it's going to be a bit harder to do here," she said.

CMC students can take classes at any of the five colleges in the Claremont Consortium. It's common for some of the smaller departments, like languages, to be centered in certain colleges: CMC students take Russian at Pomona, for example, and Arabic at CMC. One senior said, "I find that the spread of resources has been the most rewarding experience at Claremont. I've had at least one class at Pomona or Harvey Mudd every semester I've been here." CMC students can take up to two-thirds of their classes at the four other colleges.

Students and professors can build strong relationships inside the classroom that extend into daily life at CMC. About 80 percent of classes at CMC are capped at 20 students to allow students to get to know their professors. Faculty members are equally accessible outside of class; CMC owns about 70 houses at the edge of campus for faculty and senior staff members, who often host classes or visits with students in their homes. "It's often said that if you don't go to a professor's home by winter of sophomore year, you're doing something wrong," said the senior class president, who has dinner at her favorite professor's house every month. Students can also get involved in their professors' research projects, because faculty members who conduct research through the college often take on sophomores or juniors as research assistants.

As well as general education requirements, all students must complete a senior thesis in either the first or second semester of their senior year. For their requirements, students must take a course in science, a course in math, two Humanities courses, three social sciences courses, and two foreign language courses, literary analysis courses, or humanities seminars. In addition, students have to take three terms of a physical education course or two semesters of a varsity intercollegiate sport. One student explained, "When CMC was Claremont Men's College it was really military-based, so they really stress physical education here." Students normally take four courses per term. However, one first-semester freshman said that if the four-course workload seems manageable enough, students can plan to "overload" (take an approved schedule of five classes) for the next term.

CMC grades on a 12-point system, with an A being 12 points, an A- being 11 points, and so on. One senior said she didn't think there was much grade inflation on campus, especially in the Economics department, which is on a "perfect bell curve." While CMC doesn't have minors, students can take a sequence, which is a similar interdisciplinary study to supplement a student's major. The sequences, which one senior described as "focused on the social sciences," include ethics, computer science, legal studies, leadership, financial economics, Asian-American studies, gender studies, and human rights, genocide, and holocaust studies.

Claremont McKenna is well known for its strong social science curriculum, but also has a strong science program in conjunction with Pitzer College and Scripps College. Almost half of students study abroad at some point through one of many options offered by CMC.

Outside of the Classroom

Extracurricular clubs and organizations, for the most part, stretch across all five of the Claremont Colleges. It is normal to be "hyper-involved" in extracurriculars at CMC. One senior said that most students became involved in at least two or three things freshman and sophomore years before rising to leadership positions junior and senior years. "People aren't pressured to join extracurricular activities, but I think [getting involved] is definitely the environment of the school," she said. Clubs like the *a capella* groups and On the Loose, the outdoors club, are made up of students from all five colleges, but there are a few specialized activities for CMC students only, like the student investment fund, which handles part of the CMC endowment. The senior class president said activities are an integral part of coming into oneself during college. "Everyone kind of knows each other and knows what they're involved with. In that regard people start building identities for themselves," she explained.

The Marian Miner Cook Athenaeum, a speaker series that brings a different lecturer to campus each night, is open to everyone. Students attend a dinner in formal business attire with the speakers, who include physicists, politicians, musicians, and more. Speakers have included President Bill Clinton, Spike Lee, Desmond Tutu, Bono, and Salman Rushdie.

Though the school was founded less than a century ago, CMC has many traditions. One senior mentioned "ponding," which entails getting thrown into a fountain by your friends on your birthday. "Wherever you are, they'll find you, hoist you up, carry you to a fountain, and throw you in," she said, and added that one of the fountains on campus was built for "the express purpose of ponding," because CMC students used to throw people into the pond at Scripps and damage the underwater life. Another tradition is that upperclassmen will drag freshmen out of their dorms on the first night of freshman year for a surprise water fight.

The social scene also extends across the five colleges. "I think the best thing about the social scene is that it's five college-inclusive," one freshman said. "Everyone meshes—there's no exclusivity. It's great." Grades and different friend groups will all attend the same parties, which are often sponsored by the student governments or dorms, but there is not a Greek system on campus. Each week, students receive the "Party Inform," an email that lists all the social events and parties in the five colleges for the upcoming weekend. "Everyone is always in anticipation of the Party Inform because it's fun to read," said one student. Thanks to the "Thursday Night Club," CMC students are able to begin their weekends early. Saturdays are also a big night to go out. Big parties of the year include the Pirate Party (complete with Pirate-themed inflatables), the 24-hour party (for a whole day), and the Halloween Party. Not all students drink, however, and there is a substance-free dorm for those who choose not to do so.

Athletics are a main part of CMC life, with many top-five Division III teams, including tennis, soccer, and golf. The five colleges split up their athletic programs into Claremont McKenna, Harvey Mudd, and Scripps, and Pitzer and Pomona. The CMS and PP rivalry "always gets a lot of fanfare," said one student. There are "tailgates, a proliferation of t-shirts, and a lot of competitions, so that stuff gets pretty intense," one senior said. A member of the golf team said there isn't as much cheering for intercollegiate sports, though there are a lot of student athletes at CMC. While they don't take over athletes' lives, sports are a big time commitment for students. The golf player said, "Next semester for golf is going to be practice six days a week. It's going to be intense. If you're in-season, you're pretty busy." Sports are a great way to meet people at CMC, since "you become really good friends with all the people on the team," the member of the golf team added.

> "As far as the academics, the consortium has defined a lot of my experience. For the most part, they academically and socially mix a lot."

Intramurals within CMS are also a big part of campus life. Sports include innertube water polo, flag football, and three-on-three soccer. Dorms, groups of friends, and other organizations can throw their hats into the ring with their own teams.

With its happy students, top-rated academics, and the vast resources of the Claremont Consortium, it's no wonder that Claremont McKenna College is such a popular destination for high school seniors. CMC students enjoy particularly close connections with their professors and a vibrant extracurricular life. The school's beautiful campus in California only completes the impression of CMC as a true academic paradise.—*Julia Zorthian*

FYIs:
What surprised me the most about Claremont McKenna College when I arrived was "how tight knit the five colleges are."
If I could change one thing about Claremont McKenna College, I'd "add a music or arts program."
What differentiates Claremont McKenna College the most from other colleges is "how relaxed and genuinely happy everyone is."

Harvey Mudd College

Address: 301 Platt Boulevard, Claremont, CA 91711

Phone: 909-621-8011

E-mail address: admission@hmc.edu

Web site URL: www.hmc.edu

Year Founded: 1955

Private or Public: Private

Religious Affiliation: None

Location: Suburban

Number of Applicants: 3,144

Percent Accepted: 21%

Percent Accepted who enroll: 29%

Number Entering: 194

Number of Transfers Accepted each Year: 10

Middle 50% SAT range: M: 740–800, CR: 690–770, Wr: 690–770

Middle 50% ACT range: 32–35

Early admission program EA/ED/None: ED

Percentage accepted through EA or ED: 29%

EA and ED deadline: Early Decision I–Nov 15, Early Decision II–Jan 2

Regular Deadline: 2-Jan

Application Fee: $60

Full time Undergraduate enrollment: 776

Total enrollment: 776

Percent Male: 58%

Percent Female: 42%

Total Percent Minority or Unreported: 29%

Percent African-American: 1%

Percent Asian/Pacific Islander: 29%

Percent Hispanic: 6%

Percent Native-American: 1%

Percent International: 7%

Percent in-state/out of state: 40%/60%

Percent from Public HS: 69%

Retention Rate: 98%

Graduation Rate 4-year: 83%

Graduation Rate 6-year: 89%

Percent Undergraduates in On-campus housing: 99%

Number of official organized extracurricular organizations: 109

3 Most popular majors: Computer Science, Engineering, Math

Student/Faculty ratio: 9:1

Average Class Size: 18

Percent of students going to grad school: 36%

Tuition and Fees: $42,410

In-State Tuition and Fees if different: No difference

Cost for Room and Board: $13,858

Percent receiving financial aid out of those who apply: 84%

Percent receiving financial aid among all students: 50%

Harvey Mudd College is one of the five prestigious Claremont Colleges located in sunny southern California. Although many may not have heard of this small college, which only enrolls about 200 students per class, Harvey Mudd is one of the best math, science, and engineering colleges in the nation—all while maintaining its identity as a liberal arts college. Harvey Mudd is home to some of the brightest and quirkiest students in the country.

The List of Majors: Short and Sweet

At Harvey Mudd, there are only nine majors: biology, biology/chemistry, chemistry, computer science, engineering, mathematics, mathematics/computer science, mathematical biology, and physics. In addition, there is the Independent Program of Study and the Off-Campus Major. The limited number of majors demonstrates how serious Harvey Mudd is in its commitment to teaching math, science, and engineering, but the students there do not find themselves restricted. Students at Harvey Mudd are free to take humanities classes either at Harvey Mudd or at any of the other four Claremont colleges. The core requirements required of all Harvey Mudd students are four semesters of math, three semesters of physics and physics lab, two semesters of chemistry and chemistry lab, two semesters of humanities and social sciences, an engineering course, a biology class, and a computer science class.

Since there really is no such thing as an easy class at Harvey Mudd, no particular major is considered harder than the others. Getting into classes for one's major is quite easy; one student noted, "I have never *not* gotten into a class I wanted to be enrolled in." Just as the list of majors is short, classes are likewise very small. Classes are at the most 200 students for freshmen core lecture classes, and upper division classes tend to be around 30 students at the most. An engineering major said, "Upper division classes tend to weed people out and have smaller class sizes." In fact, there are certain engineering classes known as "weed-out" classes, intended to determine which students *really* want to major in that field.

Once students get through these most difficult courses, however, they are rewarded. Mudd offers a Clinic program, which gives upperclassmen the opportunity to work on real-world industrial projects in teams of four or five under the guidance of a student team leader, a faculty advisor, and a liaison from a sponsoring organization. While other schools have engineering senior projects, Mudd "actually gets companies to pay something like $40,000 to have a few Mudd students do a project for them, so it's cool to get that real world experience before graduating."

A Liberal Arts/Math and Science School

On top of the classes required for their major, Mudd students are required to take 10 additional humanities and social sciences classes, which students fondly call "hum/soc classes" (pronounced hum-sock). They must also pick a concentration in the humanities as well, which ensures that Harvey Mudd students aren't knowledgeable only about numbers and equations. Even though they are at a math and science school, students tend to be quite well rounded. A sophomore said, "We get to take a lot of really cool humanities classes from the other Claremont colleges."

Students agree that, although Harvey Mudd is the best of the five Claremont Colleges, it is definitely nice to have the other colleges around. With four other colleges in such close proximity, students are offered countless opportunities. One student listed the classes he took outside of Harvey Mudd: "I've taken voice lessons, music theory, and Chinese at some of the other colleges."

All My Professors Know My Name

Because classes tend to be so small, students are usually very close to their professors and professors are very involved in their students' academic pursuits and personal lives. Professors want students to achieve academic excellence, but at the same time believe in personal development. First-semester freshmen do not have grades for their classes but receive either high pass, pass, or fail marks. If a freshman "high passes" all or too many of their classes, they are promptly sent a good-natured letter from their dean: "We are very happy with

your academic achievement but, please, get a life!" The Dean's words are humorous, but true. Professors and deans truly want their students to be happy and have fun—Mudd throws famous annual parties funded by the school such as "Tequila Night."

In addition, professors are provided with a financial fund to take students out for lunch or dinner. One student noted that her professor was "in competition" with another professor to see who could take out the most students for a meal. Opportunities like these encourage interaction and foster relationships between students and professors outside of the classroom. Students say professors tend to be "down to earth" and very accessible for help or questions. Students agree that professors truly want to help their students and will often seek out those who are not doing well in their classes to help them. Nonetheless, even though professors are kind and good-natured, they still are hard graders. One student said, "Getting A's is hard and there is definitely grade deflation at our school."

So What Do You Do Outside of Studying?

Outside of studying and doing endless problems for their five or more classes, Mudd students play as hard as they study. They may be some of the brightest students in the nation, but Mudd students do many of the same things any college student would do: "hang out with people, play guitar, procrastinate." The people that Mudd students tend to hang out with are determined on proximity—the dorms that Mudd students are assigned to often function as their social circles as well. Because dorms are considered "extremely spacious," pretty much everyone lives on campus, even as upperclassmen.

Dorm life is exciting and packed with personality. North dorm folk, or "Northies," know how to party and will often have a game or two of beer pong going. The school is strict on underage drinking, but often "turns a blind eye" and cares more about their students' well-being. West dorm folk have their own traditions: "Their courtyard often has broken electronics, appliances, who-knows-what lying around, and often a fire going on at night." East dorm is quieter and composed mainly of CS majors, and one can always join them for a competitive video game or two. The South dorm is also considered quieter, although they are quite a musical bunch; one can often find a few Southies in the courtyard playing guitar together. Across the street from Mudd is Scripps College, which is a small, all-girls liberal arts college. Students comment that there is definitely a lot of interaction between the schools, "enough to make the Mudd girls jealous sometimes."

Mudd also throws some pretty wicked parties which are kindly funded by the school. Parties that all students must attend at least once include the LTG (Long Tall Glasses), a formal party hosted in the North dorms. Suds is another popular party open to all the Claremont colleges involving foam generating machines and a lot of partying.

Besides partying, Mudd students are very active and involved in their extracurricular activities. For those who are artistically inclined there is a jam society that maintains a jam room with a drum set and other musical equipment. There is also a Mudd art club which exhibits a lot of student artwork. Mudd students can also join organizations at other Claremont colleges as well. For the physically active, there is the "Foster's Run," which is an annual nine-mile unicycle ride to a local donut shop which gives students free strawberry donuts "which are quite tasty." Overall, Mudd students are a diverse and involved group of people who seem to find their niche in the school pretty quickly.

The Joke's on You

Harvey Mudd may not have a Greek scene or a football team, but it does have some of the nation's best pranksters. Pranks play a huge role on campus and myths are passed on from upperclassmen to underclassmen about past accomplishments. However, there are rules to pulling a prank such as the "24-hour reverse rule" in which the prank must be reversible in 24 hours. Therefore, a student fondly noted, "you can't shave off someone's eyebrows while they're sleeping because it won't grow back in 24 hours."

Individuals enjoy pranking each other, but there is also a rivalry between Mudd, Caltech, and MIT. Mudd was the first college to steal Caltech's campus cannon, followed by MIT. Perhaps due to the nature of their pranks, Mudd students are not allowed to prank other Claremont colleges. Despite the prankster nature of students, the administration trusts students and there is a school-wide honor code. Students are given 24-hour access to the academic buildings, including labs and machine shops. The campus is filled with unlocked bikes, skateboards and scooters because students respect each other's property and well-being.

> "Although school and work can get hard, it's good to know that everyone's working as hard as you. Everyone is doing something amazing."

Mudd students all learn to accept the fact that they are nerds. In fact, they are proud of it. A sophomore remarked that her physics professor "quacks when he's lecturing" because he uses penguins to describe special relativity. Professors and students alike are quirky, but friendly. Freshmen are encouraged to find their interests immediately on campus and dorm with upperclassmen, who often help them integrate into the campus. Students agree that "although school and work can get hard, it's good to know that everyone's working as hard as you. Everyone is doing something amazing."—*Emily Chen*

FYI

If you come to Harvey Mudd, you'd better bring "a Brita water filter, since the tap water isn't too good to drink."

What is the typical weekend schedule? "Slack off as much as possible on Friday and Saturday, and then do pretty much all my weekend work on Sunday. It seems to work pretty well. I think many manage to not even have classes on Friday, so their weekend probably starts a bit earlier."

If I could change one thing about Harvey Mudd, I'd "make studying abroad easier."

Three things every student at Harvey Mudd should do before graduating are "learn to unicycle, explore the random basements in the academic buildings, and pull a prank on someone."

Pitzer College

Address: 1050 North Mills Avenue, Claremont, CA 91711
Phone: 909-621-8129
E-mail address: admission@pitzer.edu
Web site URL: www.pitzer.edu
Year Founded: 1963
Private or Public: Private
Religious Affiliation: None
Location: Suburban
Number of Applicants: 3,812
Percent Accepted: 26%
Percent Accepted who enroll: 27%
Number Entering: 268
Number of Transfers Accepted each Year: 20
Middle 50% SAT range: M: 600–680, CR: 590–670, Wr: Unreported
Middle 50% ACT range: Unreported
Early admission program EA/ED/None: ED

Percentage accepted through EA or ED: Unreported
EA and ED deadline: 15-Nov
Regular Deadline: 1-Jan
Application Fee: $60
Full time Undergraduate enrollment: 1,033
Total enrollment: 1,080
Percent Male: 40%
Percent Female: 60%
Total Percent Minority or Unreported: 59%
Percent African-American: 6%
Percent Asian/Pacific Islander: 9%
Percent Hispanic: 16%
Percent Native-American: 1%
Percent International: 3%
Percent in-state/out of state: 47%/53%
Percent from Public HS: Unreported
Retention Rate: Unreported

Graduation Rate 4-year: 74%
Graduation Rate 6-year: Unreported
Percent Undergraduates in On-campus housing: 74%
Number of official organized extracurricular organizations: 120
3 Most popular majors: Film/Cinema Studies, Psychology, General Sociology
Student/Faculty ratio: 11:1
Average Class Size: 15
Percent of students going to grad school: Unreported
Tuition and Fees: $37,520
In-State Tuition and Fees if different: No difference
Cost for Room and Board: $10,930
Percent receiving financial aid out of those who apply: 77%
Percent receiving financial aid among all students: 42%

Pitzer, one of the five Claremont Colleges, is known as the most liberal of colleges within the consortium. An intimate community located a world from the cold New England winter, Pitzer is a breeding ground for creative and adventurous young people determined to make a change. Students very much march to the beat of their own drum, and enjoy the freedom and creativity of academic life at Pitzer. As one student said, "Pitzer students aren't looking for a formula, they're looking to create their own."

Creative Academics

Along the grassy mounds of Pitzer, the words "academic requirements" and "department" are conspicuously absent. Instead, students are discussing how they'll meet their "objectives" and which "field group" they plan on majoring in. Pitzer students have the ability to choose from and combine a variety of majors, and many design their own. Some student-created majors include Theater for Social Change, Media Studies and Gender Studies, and Visual Pragmatics. For students

focused on the humanities and social justice, the possibilities are endless. As one student put it, "Pitzer has made me think of academics as something that's creative. They are so much your own."

Pitzer's unique academic philosophy and strong programs in the behavioral sciences set it apart from the other Claremont colleges. Its most popular programs include Psychology, Sociology, and Media Studies. The school's mission statement requires that students commit themselves to the pursuit of social justice, intercultural understanding, and environmental sensitivity in academic life. Pitzer's strong sense of community and social responsibility gives it a special flavor. "I don't know anyone who's not passionate about what they're learning," said a Sociology major.

Students rave about interactive classes in which they are able to engage with different communities. "A lot of the professors were or are activists in the community. Because of that, classes are very geared towards how to make social changes," observed one student. At Pitzer, a Sudanese Lost Boy teaches a class on African politics. A community organizer takes his Rural and Urban Social Movements class to La Paz, where the Farm Movement's union headquarters are located, and students meet the leaders who they had learned about in the classroom. A creative writing course collaborates with a juvenile detention facility, and culminates in a joint poetry reading on campus. Pitzer students agree that the courses are student driven, and that the small class sizes allow for these sorts of opportunities.

> "Pitzer students aren't looking for a formula, they're looking to create their own."

Because the school is so heavy on the humanities and behavioral sciences, Pitzer students are grateful for the opportunities provided by the five college consortium. It's very easy to take classes at the other schools, which include Pomona, Harvey Mudd, Claremont McKenna, and Scripps. "I have a friend who's majoring at Pomona because they didn't have the major at Pitzer. It's very flexible," explained a sophomore. "It's possible to take all of your courses at another 5-C if you want to," said another student.

While the resources of the consortium are available, don't think of Pitzer as an academic "backdoor" to the other Claremont Colleges. Pitzer admissions have become increasingly competitive. One student on the academic advisory council noted that, "the most recent freshmen and sophomores are more academically competitive than in years past. More and more you're seeing Pitzer kids studying in the library on Friday nights along with students from the other 5-Cs." However, the students are not competing with one another. "I don't know how my friends do in school, but I know what they're interested in and involved in."

Hipsters—Not Hippies

There is the old stereotype of Pitzer as the hippie, pot smoking Claremont College, a product of its conception in the ultraliberal era of the sixties. While the student body is certainly creative, and there is a laid-back, liberal feel to campus, don't expect to see peace signs, pot, and tie-dye everywhere you look. "There are a lot of HIPSTERS—not hippies," joked one student. She added that Pitzer students are "very passionate and very independent. They're also usually pretty quirky."

While you won't find students pre-gaming for a wild frat party, the social life is definitely active and also more intimate than at other schools. "Because the school is so small, it's hard not to be friends with and know who everyone is," said one sophomore, "and everyone's always hanging out and down to do something." When not at relaxed dorm parties, Pitzer students will go to dance parties and concerts at the Grove House, a unique old house built in 1902 and transported to campus that now serves as a center of social life. Grove House "is my favorite place on the planet," gushed one student. Aside from "Groove at the Grove," there are 5-C events every weekend, and for those who are worried about the small size of Pitzer, students say that it is not an issue. "You have the other schools if you feel claustrophobic or want a new scene," said a student. Overall, "Pitzer kids like to have a good time, but it's more laid-back fun," said another.

Some other major events on campus include Kohoutek, a giant music festival that occurs every spring and is a highlight of the year. A smaller festival, called Reggae Fest, happens in the fall. Students also enjoy hiking and skiing at Baldy Mountain, and throw themselves into the 120 on-campus extracurricular activities. At Pitzer, students are more likely to cheer for their friends playing intramural sports than the Sagehens, the official mascot of the joint Pomona-Pitzer athletic program. Internships in the surrounding area during the school year are also very popular. Through the Ontario program, students can design an independent study project in a local community in conjunction with a class. Students also play a role in all of the college's decisions as voting members of Pitzer's governing bodies.

And as for that stereotype? "Yea, there's the idea that we're all pot smoking hippies," said one student. "But if you look at the extra-curriculars on campus, and what students are doing, the reality doesn't mesh with the old stereotype."

Dorm Life

Pitzer's campus grounds consist of grassy mounds and cacti amidst a gorgeous backdrop of the San Gabriel mountains. California weather is certainly an appeal. On campus, student murals containing political and social messages, approved by a student committee, adorn some of Pitzer's building walls. The nearest town is a sleepy suburb containing little shops and restaurants that primarily cater to residents.

Most students stay on campus all four years in one of five residence halls. Three of Pitzer's newest halls are certified gold standard—recognized by the U.S. Green Building Council as some of the leading sustainable buildings in the United States. Upperclassmen typically live in Meade, and enjoy common rooms and suites of eight. Freshmen dorms are horseshoe shaped, making it "easy to know what people are up to." During a student's first year, he or she will live in a double joined to another double by a common bathroom. Each hall has a mentor and an RA. Mentors help the students feel comfortable and hold small bonding events, whereas RAs monitor the halls. As for the prevalence of drugs and alcohol on campus, one student said, "I don't know if there's more here than at other schools, but alcohol and pot are definitely present."

The Gold Center is another central feature of campus. It holds a fitness center, a gallery, and multi-purpose rooms. Students frequent the Center's Shakedown café, an organic eatery run by creative student chefs. The center also holds various events that bring students together, ranging from hosting speakers on campus to holding "snacky-snack time," when they bring restaurant food to students at 10 pm on Tuesday nights.

While students have the luxury of being able to get anywhere on campus within five minutes of walking, they also benefit from the unique student-run Green Bike Program. The program allows students to enter a lottery system, and winners enjoy a free bike, repairs included, for the rest of the year. Pitzer students founded the Green Bike Program as an eco-friendly way to travel between the Claremont Colleges.

Pitzer and the World

Pitzer's small student population certainly lends itself to a nurturing and "comforting" environment. With the amenities of the five-college consortium, personalized academic attention, and idyllic California weather, Pitzer students are living in the perfect college bubble. Yet, students are constantly stretching themselves, engaging with different communities and designing hands-on projects. Students are able to enjoy the support of a personal community as they explore academia and the world beyond. One student said, "While Pitzer is its own world, it makes an effort to show how you can fit into the bigger picture."—*Raphaella Friedman*

FYI
If you come to Pitzer, you'd better bring "a sense of initiative so you can take control of your own education and ideals."
What's the typical weekend schedule? "Parties at the other 5-Cs on Thursday and Friday nights, a musical event, playing Frisbee, maybe going into L.A., and studying on Sunday."
If I could change one thing about Pitzer, I would change "the level of student apathy—I really wish the average student would care more about the environment and stop sinking into the Southern California lifestyle."
Three things every student at Pitzer should do before graduating are: "Go to the hot springs, have an internship with a social justice group in L.A., and go on a Pitzer Outdoor Adventures trip."

Pomona College

Address: 333 N College Way, Claremont, CA 91711
Phone: 909-621-8134
E-mail address: admissions@pomona.edu
Web site URL: www.pomona.edu
Year Founded: 1887
Private or Public: Private
Religious Affiliation: None
Location: Suburban
Number of Applicants: 7,207
Percent Accepted: 14%
Percent Accepted who enroll: 39%
Number Entering: 394
Number of Transfers Accepted each Year: Unreported
Middle 50% SAT range: M: 690–770, CR: 680–780, Wr: 680–780
Middle 50% ACT range: 31–34
Early admission program EA/ED/None: ED

Percentage accepted through EA or ED: 29%
EA and ED deadline: 1-Nov
Regular Deadline: 2-Jan
Application Fee: $65
Full time Undergraduate enrollment: 1,572
Total enrollment: 1,586
Percent Male: 49%
Percent Female: 51%
Total Percent Minority or Unreported: 54%
Percent African-American: 6%
Percent Asian/Pacific Islander: 10%
Percent Hispanic: 13%
Percent Native-American: <1%
Percent International: 5%
Percent in-state/out of state: 32%/68%
Percent from Public HS: 70%
Retention Rate: 99%
Graduation Rate 4-year: 90%

Graduation Rate 6-year: 95%
Percent Undergraduates in On-campus housing: 98%
Number of official organized extracurricular organizations: 280
3 Most popular majors: Biology/Biological Sciences, General Economics, General, English Language and Literature
Student/Faculty ratio: 8:1
Average Class Size: 15
Percent of students going to grad school: 80%
Tuition and Fees: $39,572
In-State Tuition and Fees if different: No difference
Cost for Room and Board: $13,227
Percent receiving financial aid out of those who apply: 53%
Percent receiving financial aid among all students: 56%

P omona College might not be the most recognizable of names outside the state, but it has an appeal all its own. This small liberal arts college tucked into Southern California boasts "very curious and passionate" students and a location that's "one hour from snow, one hour from the beach, and one hour from Disneyland." As one of the members of the Claremont College Consortium, the college is able to have the benefits of an undergraduate focus without sacrificing the resources of a large research university. Combining strong academics, an idyllic setting, and an intimate atmosphere, Pomona boasts some of the happiest students in the country. One student summed up Pomona's unique appeal: "Pomona gives you a liberal arts education as good as anything on the East Coast, but I think the people here are a lot more cheerful, a lot friendlier, and just really happy."

A Truly Liberal Education

Students at Pomona say their classes are "demanding," but that they ultimately have a lot of freedom to design their own educations.

To graduate, Pomona requires all students to take thirty-two courses and fulfill the Breadth of Study Requirements, which one junior described as "take five classes you like and then, done." Every student takes at least one course in each of five disciplines: Creative Expression; Social Institutions and Human Behavior; History, Values, Ethics, and Cultural Studies; Physical and Biological Sciences; and Mathematical Reasoning. In addition, students have to participate in physical education and take an intermediate language class or its equivalent. While upperclassmen can pick any of forty-five different majors to concentrate in, freshmen start out by taking a required first-year seminar. These Critical Inquiry classes, with unique topics ranging from "Facebook, Fairness, and Forgery" to "The Heart of a Doctor," have a capped enrollment of fifteen students and are "writing-intensive."

Although the most popular majors at Pomona are said to be in the social sciences and humanities, especially politics and economics, many students focus on the natural sciences, which are notoriously difficult.

"It's a big jump place for medical school, and there are lots of premeds," said one freshman. But non-science majors need not fear; Pomona offers a variety of science courses that are relatively easier and more interdisciplinary, such as geology classes and "Physics and Music." In general, students are interested in a range of areas and are easily able to find classes to fulfill their requirements: "Here, you can really like religious studies even if you're a chemistry major," one senior said.

Students at Pomona frequently mentioned having casual meals with their professors, getting advanced research opportunities as underclassmen, and learning about their professors' quirkier sides. "Classes are small enough that you get to know your professors as people," a junior said. In addition to having accessible professors, Pomona students can take advantage of small discussion-based classes that are taught seminar-style. According to one student, a "big" class consists of thirty students, and "most of them are small enough that they can be definitely interactive." While upperclassmen have priority in picking classes, a freshman said that he hadn't had problems registering for the courses he wanted.

One of Pomona's most distinctive features is its membership in the Claremont Colleges consortium (Pomona even shares athletic teams and a mascot, the Sagehen, with Pitzer College), which gives Pomona students the option of registering in courses offered by the other colleges—Claremont McKenna, Harvey Mudd, Pitzer, and Scripps. Many students sample the rigorous science courses at Harvey Mudd, the media studies program at Pitzer, and the business program at Claremont McKenna. "If it were just Pomona, I would feel a little limited by class options," said one girl. However, freshmen aren't allowed to cross-register, and even upperclassmen must take at least two courses at Pomona every semester. Popular courses at Pomona itself include the English seminar "Obscure and Eclectic Fiction" and "The U.S. Congress," in which students participate in simulations of the U.S. legislature along with other Claremont students. In general, students say the workload is intense but "open-ended," with much more collaboration than competition. "It's definitely challenging, but it's never too much. You get a lot of collaboration here," said one. Another added, "There's almost nonexistent competition between students here. Individually, they are really high-achieving, they are motivated,

they have goals in life, and they work really hard, but it's not like if you get an A, I can't get an A."

Surfing, Skiing, and Partying

"The smart and personable people you will meet at Pomona and love for the rest of your life—that's really the best thing about it," declared a senior. Students say Pomona does an excellent job of welcoming its freshmen right from the beginning and continues to support them for the rest of their undergraduate years. Before classes start, freshmen go on student-led Orientation Adventure trips throughout California. Freshmen say they "really start to bond" with their classmates over four days of hiking around Yosemite, surfing in Santa Barbara, or just exploring Southern California while doing community service. But one of the most praised features of freshman year is the sponsor group program, in which freshmen are divided into groups of ten to twenty. Guided and mentored by two sophomores who are "like their brothers and sisters," these groups live in the same hall together and become "like family."

The consortium system offers Pomona students not only academic options, but also a variety of social scenes. "There definitely is a big party scene, but there are basically no frats," said a freshman. "Parties are usually inside the rooms, or there's always a big party at the other colleges." In addition, Pomona students receive a daily "student digester e-mail" listing all of the day's events and activities, including official college-sponsored parties, shows, movie screenings, and even "politics talks," in which politics professors and students gather to drink wine, eat cheese, and discuss current events. Although "the alcohol scene is definitely present," and "pretty much everyone" drinks, students have the option of choosing substance-free housing. A sophomore said, "I've generally found that there are more nondrinkers than one would think and it's not hard to find stuff to do without drinking heavily."

Pomona's alcohol policy is considered "not super-rigid." Drinks are allowed everywhere on campus; however, no hard liquor is allowed on South Campus, where underclassmen live. RAs are known to be stricter on South Campus, but are mostly there to make sure students understand how to handle alcohol responsibly, and "if there's an emergency they'd know how to respond to it."

The college often sponsors parties, and when it comes to big annual events, "the administration treats students like royalty."

These events are a large part of Pomona's quirky culture and lore, or "Pomoniana." Along with traditional parties like the "screw your roommate dance," in which students set up their roommates on blind dates, Pomona organizes an annual "Death by Chocolate" event on the last day of classes before fall semester finals. "Basically, they just fill one of our auditorium rooms with chocolate—fondue, cocoa, cake, everything," explained a junior. On Snow Day, another pre-finals event, the college hires a snow machine to fill the quad with snow, so students can enjoy snowball fights and snowmen in the middle of Southern California. Of course, ski resorts aren't that far from Pomona, and one of the college's most beloved traditions is Ski-Beach Day: "In the morning, Pomona pays for us to go skiing and snowboarding in the mountains, and in the afternoon, we drive down to the beach and hang out in the sun." Despite its closeness to both beaches and mountains—not to mention that it's just an hour away from L.A.—most students stay on campus. That's because there's plenty to do at Pomona itself, students say, but for those who would like to venture off campus, there's a Metrolink station a few blocks away, and "people will drive or ride up to go see games and concerts."

Students say that hall life is very social, with residents keeping their doors open most of the time. "The students here are pretty easygoing and pretty content and smiley," said a junior. "People will go out all the time and do homework in the sun on the lawn or on the 'beach,' which is this sandy area with a beach volleyball court." While some students praised the feel of a small, intimate community—"everyone knows everyone else, everyone knows where everyone else lives"—one freshman said he already felt that the community was "too small." Even in this small community, students have a wide variety of passions and come from a variety of ethnic backgrounds and states. However, most students are considered "really liberal" and middle- to upper-class.

A Sagehen's Habitat
Housing at Pomona is guaranteed for all four years, and only a few seniors live off campus. About two-thirds of freshmen are in doubles, and the rest are in singles. Most underclassmen live on South Campus in hall-style dorms, but housing improves with seniority. North Campus, where upperclassmen live, has many two-room doubles, which are two singles connected by a small

entryway and a door. Juniors and seniors generally have singles or even suites, and "one of our nicest dorms has fireplaces and balconies, with really spacious rooms."

In addition, students can also choose to live in a few themed dorms, including substance-free housing, and "Unity Dorm," which consists of one floor of students who "really actively want to be engaged in their dorm, so they do barbecues and field trips and stuff together." Students who want to immerse themselves in a foreign language can live in one of six special language halls in Oldenborg, the language center. For example, if you live in the Spanish hall, "you don't have to talk in Spanish all the time, but if you're doing Spanish work there's always someone to help you," a junior explained. Oldenborg's dining hall—one of three at Pomona—offers language tables where students can practice conversing over lunch.

Since meal plans can be used at any of the other Claremont campuses' dining halls, students have a total of eight dining halls to choose from. The different meal plans offer either a set number of meals per week or meals plus "flex dollars," which are accepted at the "Coop Fountain," a student-run snack and smoothie shop and convenience store. For a nicer, sit-down meal, students can visit the Sagehen Café. One of Pomona's most popular dining features is "Snack," a weeknight study break, in which the dining halls reopen at 10:30 p.m. and students can enjoy free snacks. "We come at the end of the day to just kind of run into each other, sum up our days, relax, eat, and talk. It's great because I always get hungry at night," said a junior. In general, students say they are really satisfied with the food.

The meal plan's flex dollars can't be applied off-campus, but Pomona does offer a "Claremont Cash" card, which works like a debit card at campus stores and about half of the stores in "the Village," which is what students call the surrounding town of Claremont. The Village "is a little bit on the small side" and "a little sleepy," with not much nightlife, according to students. About a third of the town's population consists of retirees, and students describe it as "such a safe, nice, quaint little town; we feel completely comfortable walking around, even at night."

Pomoniana and More
Activities outside the classroom aren't just limited to exploring the Village. Pomona students can join clubs not just on their own campus, but also those at any of the other

campuses. One of Pomona's most popular clubs is "On the Loose," which rents out outdoors equipment, sponsors several outdoors trips every week, and trains students to lead trips. Favorite destinations include Death Valley and Joshua Tree.

Also, "it's really easy to get a job if you want a job." Students mentioned jobs at the libraries and other campus facilities, as well as positions as volunteer coordinators and interns in the Pomona College internship program. Under this program, students can take normally unpaid internships in the L.A. area, but still receive wages from Pomona.

> **"The smart and personable people you will meet at Pomona and love for the rest of your life—that's really the best thing about it."**

Although Pomona fields a variety of Division III teams, athletics don't dominate other campus activities. "I wouldn't say our school is the greatest on athletic spirit," said one student. The Pitzer-Pomona Sagehens' biggest rivals are the neighboring Claremont McKenna-Scripps-Harvey Mudd teams, especially in basketball, which can get "pretty heated." Coaches at Pomona understand that students' focus is on academics, so "it's nice for people who want to continue playing sports in college, but not dedicate their lives to sports," said a sophomore.

In keeping with Pomona's sunny, carefree atmosphere, campus traditions are often more quirky and fun than steeped in history and legend. All of the fountains on campus are chlorinated because on students' birthdays, "it's a tradition to dump them into the fountains." Possibly the oddest bit of Pomona lore is the campus' fascination with the number 47. From Pomona's highway exit (47) to the founding date of Claremont McKenna (1947) to the number of students in Pomona's first graduating class (47), the number seems to be everywhere, and one student even wrote a thesis on all the different places 47 occurs in nature. Alum Joe Menosky '79, a writer and co-producer for *Star Trek*, has also inserted the number into episode after episode of the series.

With academic rigor and opportunities comparable to that of any liberal arts college and a relaxed, intimate atmosphere, Pomona is home to happy students, caring faculty, and a sunny "California attitude." As one senior said, "I feel like we are on the one hand selecting bright students, but they're not just smart students who study a lot; we choose people who are really decent. There are so many instances where I've had a conversation with someone and they've surprised me in so many ways and made me realize how good people can be."—*Vivian Yee*

FYI
If you come to Pomona College, you'd better bring "sunblock and sunglasses, innovativeness and inventiveness."
What is the typical weekend schedule? "Get out of class on Friday, do a little work or go into town, play a game of basketball or volleyball, go to a dorm party at one of the 5-Cs, sleep in Saturday, work and hang out, go to events or concerts or lectures, go out to dinner in the village and party again. Sunday, people work."
If I could change one thing about Pomona, I'd "expand the college a little: it's too small."
Three things every student at Pomona should do before graduating are "break into the pool after hours, watch the sun set at Joshua Tree National Park, and leave with a really great group of friends."

Scripps College

Address: 1030 N. Columbia Avenue, Claremont, CA 91711
Phone: 909-621-8149
E-mail address: admission@scrippscollege.edu
Web site URL: www.scrippscollege.edu
Year Founded: 1926
Private or Public: Private
Religious Affiliation: None
Location: Suburban
Number of Applicants: 2,097
Percent Accepted: 39%
Percent Accepted who enroll: 32%
Number Entering: 264
Number of Transfers Accepted each Year: 55
Middle 50% SAT range: M: 630–710, CR: 640–740, Wr: 640–740
Middle 50% ACT range: 28–32

Early admission program EA/ED/None: ED
Percentage accepted through EA or ED: 15%
EA and ED deadline: 1-Nov
Regular Deadline: 1-Jan
Application Fee: $60
Full time Undergraduate enrollment: 937
Total enrollment: 956
Percent Male: 0%
Percent Female: 100%
Total Percent Minority or Unreported: 40%
Percent African-American: 4%
Percent Asian/Pacific Islander: 10%
Percent Hispanic: 10%
Percent Native-American: 1%
Percent International: 4%
Percent in-state/out of state: 45%/55%
Percent from Public HS: 60%

Retention Rate: 96%
Graduation Rate 4-year: 74%
Graduation Rate 6-year: 80%
Percent Undergraduates in On-campus housing: 91%
Number of official organized extracurricular organizations: 200
2 Most popular majors: Fine/Studio Arts, Political Science and Government
Student/Faculty ratio: 10:1
Average Class Size: 19
Percent of students going to grad school: 60%
Tuition and Fees: $41,736
In-State Tuition and Fees if different: No difference
Cost for Room and Board: $12,950
Percent receiving financial aid out of those who apply: 49%
Percent receiving financial aid among all students: 54%

One of the first things that comes to students' minds when describing Scripps College is its intimate community, coupled with a great location outside of Los Angeles. Scripps is the only single-sex school among the Claremont Colleges, offering a highly reputable education to about 950 female students. Although, students are quick to point out that they chose Scripps because of the great education and numerous opportunities it offers, not because of its all-female student body. So if you want to spend four years in a college that has perfect weather, Mediterranean architecture, a proximity to a large city and reputable academics, maybe take a closer look at Scripps.

An All-Female School

One of the advantages of going to an all-female school is its "very warm, friendly atmosphere." According to one student, "A lot of kids here went to high schools with as many or even more people. That's why we didn't feel at the beginning that college life was so overwhelming." Her sentiments are echoed by other members of the student population.

"The small student body makes it a great and really close community," added one.

Despite the small enrollment, however, Scripps is located right next to the other four Claremont Colleges, all of which are coeducational. As a result, being an all-female school does not mean that there is no interaction with male students. In fact, since students often register for classes in the other colleges, there are plenty of opportunities to make friends with people in the other colleges, both male and female. "Scripps is like part of a much larger campus. You get to go to other colleges all the time, so you don't have to worry about Scripps being an all-female college," said a student. One undergrad pointed out that, as a single-sex school, Scripps receives "differing, condescending attitudes from other colleges in the consortium," but most people agree that the consortium system works very well for Scripps' social atmosphere.

The City of Trees and PhDs

As an upscale suburb of Los Angeles, Claremont is also known as the "City of Trees and

PhDs," thanks to a high concentration of professors working in the city's universities. The older neighborhoods of Claremont take pride in their shade-covered streets, making Scripps "a delightful place to live in."

The primary shopping center is at the Village, a collection of small shops and restaurants located at walking distance of the Claremont Colleges. Some students complain about the overpriced shopping, but they generally agree that, "the Village is indispensable for college life." Whenever they crave a little more excitement than the Village, students can jump on a train and visit Los Angeles. Although downtown Los Angeles is still about 30 miles away, it only takes ten minutes for Scripps students to walk to the MetroLink station, a railway system that connects directly to Los Angeles Union Station.

Within the Claremont Colleges, Scripps' own campus is very small. It extends over about three blocks and is only built around one single quad, the Jaqua Quadrangle. Nevertheless, the small campus adds even more to the College's intimacy, and according to the students, "the Mediterranean Revival architecture that dominates the campus feels very welcoming to us."

Sharing Is Fun!
Scripps is generally ranked among the top 30 liberal arts colleges by *U.S. News and World Report*. It is a relatively selective college, accepting less than 50 percent of the applicant pool. "Above all else, people come to Scripps because it has a strong academic program," said a student.

By sharing facilities with the other colleges of the consortium, Scripps, despite its small size, offers its students the level of resources and opportunities of a large university. "The departments here are often interrelated to the same departments of the other colleges," said one junior. "For example, Scripps College has a Joint Science Department with Pitzer and Claremont McKenna." This close relationship between the colleges maximizes the resources of the consortium, letting the students explore a greater number of opportunities.

Just like most other liberal arts colleges, Scripps has an interdisciplinary Core Program, which focuses on critical thinking. The Core is divided into three different courses. Core I teaches the students about the relationship between knowledge and cultures. Core II lets the students choose between different courses that offer in-depth studies of topics introduced in Core I.

Core III focuses on innovation and requires the students to come up with a self-designed project as part of the course. According to a student, "Core I is important. It builds the foundations for future undergraduate work. Core II is not as beneficial, as it is too narrow. My section, at least, did not seem to end up anywhere. Core III is a wonderful experience. It makes one feel potent and encourages applying what you've learned."

In addition, the students are also required to fulfill the general requirements, which include one class each in fine arts, letters, writing, natural science, social science, race and ethnic studies and mathematics. Students also have to take three semesters of a foreign language. These rather extensive requirements enable the students to acquire knowledge and skills in a variety of fields, an important goal of the College.

Scripps' classes are generally small, having less than 20 students, which lets students interact frequently with their professors. Since there are no teaching assistants, the professors devote a significant part of their time to office hours in order to help their students. "I interact a lot with professors outside of class," one undergrad explained. "I go to office hours frequently, have done an internship with one professor, and have gone to conferences with some others."

Kicking it with the Consortium
Scripps provides its students with great dorm rooms. "The average dorm room is spacious, elegantly furnished, and clean." Each dorm also has a browsing room, a small quiet library that forbids male entrance.

> "During Friday and Saturday, there are generally several parties going on in different colleges, but if you just restrict yourself to Scripps, you might not find anything interesting during the weekends."

Scripps athletes participate in competitions with Claremont McKenna and Harvey Mudd as one single team. Scripps does have its own clubs, but many larger organizations draw members from the entire consortium.

The weekend life is similarly conjoined with that of the other colleges. Students usually go to parties in any of the Claremont Colleges, since Scripps' small size usually does not make for extremely exciting parties. According to one student, "During Friday and Saturday, there are generally several parties going on in different colleges, but if you just restrict yourself to Scripps, you might not find anything interesting during the weekends." But lack of social life said, one student still cited the biggest disadvantage of being at Scripps as being that "they make you leave after four years."—*Xiaohang Liu*

FYI
If you come to Scripps, you'd better bring "a stapler!"
What is the typical weekend schedule? "Friday: party. Saturday: party, L.A. Sunday: work, work, and work."
If I could change one thing about Scripps, I'd "have more diversity."
Three things every student at Scripps should do before graduating are "to play glow-in-the-dark Frisbee on the lawn at midnight, attend candlelight dinners, and participate in the Humanities Institute."

Deep Springs College

Address: HC 72, Box 45001, Dyer, NV 89010-9803
Phone: 760-872-2000
E-mail address: apcom@deepsprings.edu
Web site URL: www.deepsprings.edu
Year Founded: 1917
Private or Public: Private
Religious Affiliation: None
Location: Rural
Number of Applicants: 186
Percent Accepted: 7%
Percent Accepted who enroll: 92%
Number Entering: 12
Number of Transfers Accepted each Year: Unreported
Middle 50% SAT range: M: 700–800, Cr: 750–800, Wr: 750–780
Middle 50% ACT range: Unreported
Early admission program EA/ED/None: None

Percentage accepted through EA or ED: NA
EA and ED deadline: NA
Regular Deadline: 15-Nov
Application Fee: $0
Full time Undergraduate enrollment: 26
Total enrollment: 26
Percent Male: 100%
Percent Female: 0%
Total Percent Minority or Unreported: Unreported
Percent African-American: Unreported
Percent Asian/Pacific Islander: Unreported
Percent Hispanic: Unreported
Percent Native-American: Unreported
Percent International: Unreported
Percent in-state/out of state: 20%/80%
Percent from Public HS: 50%
Retention Rate: 100%
Graduation Rate 4-year: Unreported

Graduation Rate 6-year: Unreported
Percent Undergraduates in On-campus housing: Unreported
Number of official organized extracurricular organizations: Unreported
2 Most popular majors: Liberal Arts and Sciences, General Studies and Humanities
Student/Faculty ratio: 4:1
Average Class Size: 9
Percent of students going to grad school: 96%
Tuition and Fees: $0
In-State Tuition and Fees if different: No difference
Cost for Room and Board: $0
Percent receiving financial aid out of those who apply: NA
Percent receiving financial aid among all students: NA

Deep Springs College is absolutely unique. Founded in 1917, this two-year, all-male, tuition-free, 26-student educational institution remains an anachronism in the landscape of higher education. Whether it's because of Deep Springs' precious isolation, its drug and alcohol-free student body, its commitment to training young men for lives of service, or the fact that it's situated on a working farm and cattle ranch, every Deep Springer will agree that there is no college like it. Students at Deep Springs give up the amenities and resources of a normal college campus to live, study, and work hard in an isolated desert valley in Eastern California. While graduates from other universities may reminisce about their time in college, there's a reason why

Deep Springs' alumni always refer back to their "Deep Springs experience."

Don't Let Me Out!

The first thing any visitor to Deep Springs will notice is its isolation. An hour's drive from the closest town (Bishop, CA) and five hours from the closest cities (Las Vegas and Los Angeles), Deep Springs is a little speck of green in the middle of a high desert valley. This isolation is made even more intense by the students' self-imposed "isolation policy" which states that students cannot leave the valley or have visitors while school is in session. It may seem excessive, but this policy does have its benefits. "We never meet new people at Deep Springs, but we meet the same people over and over again, each time with more intensity and understanding," one second-year student commented. The students also uphold a policy against the use of drugs and alcohol during term which, like the isolation policy, is self-imposed and self-regulated. These rules are a part of the Self-Governance process which allows the students to effectively own and run the college while they are enrolled. "Students hold each other accountable for upholding rules, completing all of their tasks, and generally running the college," one recent graduate explained. "Rarely are young people given so much responsibility and so many opportunities."

Each student at Deep Springs sits on a committee (Applications, Curriculum, Communications, or Review and Reinvitation Committee) and each committee is responsible for running a part of the college. Whether they're reading essays and accepting the incoming class, interviewing and hiring faculty, or writing and publishing the college brochure, every student has a hand in making the place run. The student body also gathers every Friday night for a collective meeting where committees give reports, legislation is discussed, and issues are debated. During the winter these meetings are held in the dorm or the boarding house, though in the summer students often drive out to remote spots in the desert to meet around a campfire, under the stars. Meetings often run late into the night, only ending when all the business has been completed, or when the cows need to be milked.

The Self-Governance process is also a way for students to hold positions of responsibility. Some of the positions include: student body president, labor commissioner, secretary, annual giving representative, and committee chair. "You are a political member before you are a social member of this community," one first-year student noted, and most students do hold an elected position in the Self-Governance process before they graduate.

Home On the (Gas) Range

At the same time that students at Deep Springs run the administrative side of the college, they also provide nearly all the labor for the school, farm, and cattle ranch. Though they pay no tuition, students are required to work an average of 20 to 30 hours per week in various jobs. Labor positions are assigned by the student Labor Commissioner and change often, so students get to experience a lot of different kinds of work before they graduate. "One term you might be cooking dinner for the community every night, and the next you're building fences or herding cows." The one job that every Deep Springer is required to do is BH duty, which includes washing dishes, mopping floors, and cleaning up after meals. Other labor positions include butcher, gardener, farm assistant, and dairy boy.

Many students enjoy the labor program because of the practical skills that they learn, like cooking, carpentry, or welding, but even the work they'll probably never do again, like slaughtering or milking cows, has its benefits. "Deep Springs is first and foremost about learning to put the needs of the community and of the farm and ranch on which you live above yourself, and coming to cherish yourself as a piece in the puzzle," said one second-year student. Deep Springers also use the time during work to talk or think about intellectual issues. Four hours of painting a wall or digging post-holes in the desert is a good amount of time to think about an upcoming paper or discuss a reading with another student. Most students come to appreciate the labor program as an important part of their education, and not as a distraction from academics. "With so much physical work to do all the time, academic work begins to seem like a privilege and a kind of relaxation. It really makes you appreciate your education."

Will This Class Ever End?

Classes at Deep Springs are comparable to courses at top level institutions, except that you'll never have to sit in a lecture hall with 300 other students. Most classes have enrollments between four and 10 students, and nearly all of them are seminars. The only two required courses are composition and public speaking, the latter taken every semester. Class discussions can get very intense, since the students all know each other perhaps too well. "Classes here are intense, and students often expect more of each other than professors are able to expect of students in other, more traditional environments," said one second-year student. "At Deep Springs, if a peer doesn't prepare well and class discussion suffers as a result, you have both a right and a responsibility to confront him about it." Though this kind of intensity can be daunting for new students straight out of high school, the general atmosphere in class is one of deep concern and engagement with issues. "Classes at Deep Springs are like a cross between a big family meal and a trial in court: personal, rigorous, intense, and deeply enjoyable."

Since students and their professors live within a few steps of each other, classroom discussions often continue after class is over. It's not uncommon for students to continue debating an issue in the dining hall at lunch and through their afternoon work. "I don't think that 'the way people think' could be more important at another school than Deep Springs," as students are always engaging each other's beliefs and thought processes inside and outside of class. Professors often open their homes to students at night to continue discussions, help edit papers, or just to have coffee. "The most common social activity is talking. Simply talking," and Deep Springers certainly do a lot of it: with their professors, each other, and the families and kids that make up the community.

The majority of the courses at Deep Springs are in the humanities or literary arts, though a number of math and science courses are always offered. To keep the curriculum balanced, Deep Springs employs three long-term professors in Humanities, Social Sciences, and Math and Natural Sciences. Along with these three, the student body hires a handful of visiting professors each semester to teach anything from "Figure Drawing" to "Wittgenstein's *Philosophical Investigations*."

Dance It Off

Whatever diversity Deep Springs may lack in its small and somewhat homogeneous student body, it makes up for in the larger campus community. Though only around 50 people live in the valley, they range in age from very young to very old, and come from all over the country and the world. Professors often bring their spouses and kids along, and everyone takes part in the greater community of Deep Springs. The one obvious thing lacking is female students, though the issue is formally debated every year and is a constant topic of discussion. "Most students' feelings about going to a single-sex school change radically, in all kinds of directions, once they've actually been at Deep Springs," said a recent graduate. But the lack of girls doesn't stop the boys from having their fun. "Of course we dance (boogie)," explained a second-year. "An hour of heavy boogie-ing provides enough exercise and catharsis to last a week or so."

> "Students who are looking for a challenging academic environment should look into Deep Springs."

The valley provides great opportunities for hiking, running and climbing, and even though Deep Springs has no sports program, students will often organize games of soccer or basketball in the free half-hour before dinner. But as any Deep Springer will tell you, free time is hard to come by. Often weekends are filled with extra work projects, slaughters, cattle drives, or music practice. "There isn't much free time, but dance parties, shooting guns, making paintings, and reading groups occupy the little that there is." Often, because of the amount of work and responsibility every student must take on, relaxation feels just like procrastination. But then again, every student signed on to push themselves and take on a challenge. One graduate summed it up nicely: "Attending Deep Springs is like running a marathon. While you're in it you can only think about how hard it is, but once it's over you can look back and see what an amazing thing you just did."—*Jesse Bradford*

FYI

If you come to Deep Springs, you'd better bring "a toothbrush. Almost everything else you need can be found in the bonepile (communal clothing stockpile)."

What is a typical weekend schedule? "Cooking a meal for the community, preparing for a Heidegger reading group, doing committee work, a game of soccer, working on a couple essays, a quick boogie, then a few hours of solid reading."

If I could change one thing about Deep Springs, "I'd add a couple of hours to each day."

Before graduating, every Deep Springer should "cook an elaborate meal without enough help, stay up all night writing a paper then go for a swim in the upper reservoir at dawn, and punch a charging bull in the face."

Mills College

Address: 500 MacArthur Boulevard, Oakland, CA 94613
Phone: 510-430-2135
E-mail address: admission@mills.edu
Web site URL: www.mills.edu
Year Founded: 1852
Private or Public: Private
Religious Affiliation: None
Location: Suburban
Number of Applicants: 2,251
Percent Accepted: 57%
Percent Accepted who enroll: 13%
Number Entering: 168
Number of Transfers Accepted each Year: 189
Middle 50% SAT range: M: 520–620, CR: 530–660, Wr: 520–630
Middle 50% ACT range: 24–29
Early admission program EA/ED/None: EA

Percentage accepted through EA or ED: 67%
EA and ED deadline: 15-Nov
Regular Deadline: 1-Aug
Application Fee: $50
Full time Undergraduate enrollment: 881
Total enrollment: 936
Percent Male: 0%
Percent Female: 100%
Total Percent Minority or Unreported: 58%
Percent African-American: 8%
Percent Asian/Pacific Islander: 10%
Percent Hispanic: 17%
Percent Native-American: 1%
Percent International: 2%
Percent in-state/out of state: 80% /20%
Percent from Public HS: 80%
Retention Rate: 78%

Graduation Rate 4-year: 54%
Graduation Rate 6-year: 60%
Percent Undergraduates in On-campus housing: 55%
Number of official organized extracurricular organizations: 45
2 Most popular majors: English; Ethnic, Cultural Minority, and Gender Studies
Student/Faculty ratio: 11:1
Average Class Size: 15
Percent of students going to grad school: 20%
Tuition and Fees: $38,066
In-State Tuition and Fees if different: No difference
Cost for Room and Board: $11,306
Percent receiving financial aid out of those who apply: 91%
Percent receiving financial aid among all students: 84%

Mills College, an all-female liberal arts college in Oakland, California, has been committed to women's education for over 150 years. In fact, Mills made news in 1990 when the board of trustees voted to admit males to the undergraduate program. Students, outraged, immediately adopted the slogan "Better Dead than Coed." They mounted protests, officially shutting down the campus, and they refused to resume their normal lives until the board of trustees reversed their decision. Eventually, the trustees conceded, and Mills reinforced its position as a school dedicated to women's education. That take-charge spirit is characteristic of Mills students, who remain a group of empowered women committed to making the most of their education.

Blaze Your Own Trail

Historically, Mills has been a school of "firsts": the first women's college to the west of the Rockies, the first women's college to offer a computer science major and a 4+1 MBA degree, and even one of the first liberal arts colleges to offer a modern dance degree. Mills students agree that their academic experience is completely "what you make of it." One student noted that it's possible to "slack" through a semester with easy classes, but said that it is equally possible to have a hard semester by taking classes from hard professors—it's all up to the individual.

The general education requirement at Mills consists of 36 credits in what the school calls three "outcome categories": skills, perspectives, and disciplinary experiences. The skills category includes classes in written communication, quantitative reasoning, and information technology skills. Perspectives courses include women and gender, multicultural, and interdisciplinary studies. Classes in arts criticism, historical perspectives, natural sciences, and human behavior comprise the disciplinary exercises category. Despite the variety of academic requirements at Mills, many students complain about the lack of diversity in the choice of classes, saying they wish there were "more fun and random classes." Fortunately, for those seeking classes outside the box, UC Berkeley and other Bay Area schools welcome Mills students to cross-register in some of their programs.

Some of the most popular Mills majors are English, psychology, and Political, Legal, and Economic Analysis. Several students complained about the school's recent loss of the theater major. "The theater department was dropped because there weren't enough people majoring in it," one student explained. And although there's still a theater club on campus, those looking to major in theater arts may be disappointed. For those Mills women anxious to get a head start on advanced degrees, the school has seven dual degree programs, in which students can get master's degrees in Business Administration, Public Policy, Infant Mental Health, Interdisciplinary Computer Science, Engineering, Mathematics, or they can get a Credential in Teacher Education. Another specialized degree program at Mills is its Nursing Leadership Program, which consists of two years of liberal arts followed by two years of nursing school.

The Hills of Mills

Living at Mills is like, as one student put it, living in a "gorgeous oasis" with "beautiful architecture." The campus has recently completed a significant amount of renovations, such as a new environmentally friendly "green" science building. Mills women agree that their dorms are "very nice." Freshmen live in singles or doubles in two residences

right in the middle of campus, and their housing is not too shabby. "One of our buildings, Orchard Meadow, is considered one of the nicest dorms on campus," one freshman boasted. There are a total of five residence halls at Mills. Upperclass women can choose among on campus apartments, townhouses, or house co-ops.

> "Most Mills women are usually feminists and interested in women's rights—or at least, they become so after four years here!"

The main dining hall at Mills is called Founders Commons, and it is set atop a hill. Students generally agree that the food is "fairly good for a college." The cafeterias are independently owned, and, to the relief of many Californians, "there are always vegetarian and vegan options." In addition to dining halls, Mills has a teashop that serves hot breakfast and "quick meals like hamburgers," along with a popular coffee shop, Café Susie's.

Unfortunately, Oakland has no real "college-town feel." In fact, some students even go so far as to say that, "the area around campus does not feel very safe." Nonetheless, Mills has its own shuttle system and even a bus stop outside its front gate, making it easy to get on and off campus. There are several restaurants and shops off campus that are popular with Mills women, especially the Italian favorite, La Fiesta Pizza. And, for those looking to escape from Oakland entirely, San Francisco and all its distractions are just a car or shuttle ride away.

Friendly Feminists

Outside of the classroom, Mills women are famous for being friendly and sociable. One freshman enthused, "on the first day of college, I sat down at tables at the cafeteria where I didn't know anyone, and was warmly welcomed!" The student body of Mills is notoriously diverse, both ethnically and culturally. One Caucasian woman even went so far as to joke that "sometimes I feel like a minority."

The women of Mills also have their own unique take on age diversity: about a quarter of the undergraduate population is made up of "resumers," or students over the age of 23. Resumers are usually students who have taken time off from their studies to pursue careers or raise families. Resumers have their own apartments on campus that welcome spouses and children. Yet, far from being secluded from the rest of the population, students universally proclaim that there is no real division on campus between resumers and regular undergraduates. Friendships form between women of all ages.

The integration of resumers into the community is just one aspect of Mills' openness and tolerance of differences. These include sexual orientation as well. "There is a lesbian stereotype," one student said, "but although there are many lesbians on campus, it is often hard to tell whose toast is buttered which way." No matter one's sexual preference, "most Mills women are usually feminists and interested in women's rights—or at least, they become so after four years here!"

Partying Without Guys?

Mills women agree that their school is not, by any means, a party school. Most students go out on weekend nights, and because many students don't have classes on Fridays, weekends tend to include Thursdays. There are a few popular campus-wide parties, including the Fetish Ball, which discourages clothing. Alcohol has little presence on campus. One freshman noted that she has seen "very little drinking in the freshman dorms." Even once you hit the age of 21, "even then it has to be done behind closed doors," one student explained. Students do note that drugs, mostly pot, are a lot more prevalent on campus than alcohol.

Be warned, Mills women don't often get a chance to mingle with members of the opposite sex. In fact, most couples around the school are female-female. Mills allows men to stay overnight in the dorms for up to seven nights each month, which is good news for students with boyfriends at other schools. Mills' graduate school, on the other hand, *is* coed, and Berkeley and Stanford are not too far away, so students say that if you're really looking for men, they're not too hard to find if you're willing to make a small trek.

Fun and Games

Athletics are admittedly not Mills' main focus, and, not surprisingly, the school doesn't have a football team. However, as a Division III school, Mills has seven varsity sports: cross country, crew, soccer, swimming, tennis, volleyball, and track and field. Students generally seem happy that more inexperienced athletes are allowed to participate since some of the pressure is off. As one Mills woman put it, "We take pride in what we've got." If varsity sports aren't your thing, you can get a workout by playing club sports, or by taking yoga and swimming classes at the gym.

Off the field, there are a plethora of student clubs and organizations, some favorites of which are the Anime Club, Horror Movie Club, Superhero Club, and the Gay/Lesbian Alliance. Mills women say that there is definitely something for everybody to be involved in, and if not, students are encouraged to start new organizations. Many students also get on-campus jobs, like serving food in the campus cafeteria.

A Tradition of Empowerment

In a school rooted in tradition, Mills students say that one of their favorite rites of passage is Paint Night. Students assign a color to each class, and on Paint Night—which takes place in the spring—seniors storm the campus and paint surfaces the color of their class. This tradition, fun and silly as it is, ties into Mills' continual emphasis on fostering strong women, ready to use their education to make a difference in the world around them. Still stubbornly single-sex, Mills continues to be a place where students and administration both remain believers in the power of all-women's schools.—*Becky Bicks*

FYI
If you come to Mills you'd better bring "an open mind."
What's the typical weekend schedule? "Enjoying weekend brunch, relaxing during free time, and evening on-campus activities."
If I could change one thing about Mills, I'd "make the campus more accessible, offering a shuttle to and from the airport at break time."
Three things every student at Mills should do before graduating are "explore the whole campus, get an on-campus job, eat the dining hall waffles for breakfast."

Occidental College

Address: 1600 Campus Road, Los Angeles, CA 90041
Phone: 800-825-5262
E-mail address: admission@oxy.edu
Web site URL: www.oxy.edu
Year Founded: 1887
Private or Public: Private
Religious Affiliation: None
Location: Urban
Number of Applicants: 5,882
Percent Accepted: 42%
Percent Accepted who enroll: 23%
Number Entering: 573
Number of Transfers Accepted each Year: 60
Middle 50% SAT range: M: 600–690, CR: 600 600, Wr: 610–690
Middle 50% ACT range: 26–30
Early admission program EA/ED/None: ED

Percentage accepted through EA or ED: 11%
EA and ED deadline: 15-Nov
Regular Deadline: 10-Jan
Application Fee: $50
Full time Undergraduate enrollment: 2,079
Total enrollment: 2,089
Percent Male: 43%
Percent Female: 57%
Total Percent Minority or Unreported: 43%
Percent African-American: 6%
Percent Asian/Pacific Islander: 16%
Percent Hispanic: 14%
Percent Native-American: 2%
Percent International: 3%
Percent in-state/out of state: 46%/54%
Percent from Public HS: 58%
Retention Rate: 94%

Graduation Rate 4-year: 82%
Graduation Rate 6-year: 86%
Percent Undergraduates in On-campus housing: 80%
Number of official organized extracurricular organizations: 105
3 Most popular majors: Economics, Diplomacy and World Affairs, English
Student/Faculty ratio: 9:1
Average Class Size: 17
Percent of students going to grad school: Unreported
Tuition and Fees: $41,860
In-State Tuition and Fees if different: No difference
Cost for Room and Board: $11,990
Percent receiving financial aid out of those who apply: 77%
Percent receiving financial aid among all students: 79%

If living close by to one of the country's biggest cultural hubs, sandy beaches, and the rolling purple mountains of southern California sounds like a pretty sweet deal, Occidental College might be the perfect fit for you. Perched on a hilltop in the historic Eagle Rock neighborhood of Los Angeles, this small school boasts a population of just over 2,000 students who are both high-achieving and very laid back, in a climate that can't really be beat. Oxy, as it is known among students, was one of the first schools to include the word "diverse" in its mission statement, and the community lives up to that goal. Although it is a very small school, Oxy provides diversity not only in the student body, but also in the breadth of academic options, the expansive extracurricular opportunities, and the great resources of Los Angeles.

The Core of it All

The school may be small, but the educational requirements certainly are not. The distributional core at Oxy requires all students to take three courses in math and lab sciences, take three culture and fine arts courses across two time periods and three world areas, achieve 102-level proficiency in a foreign language, and complete a fine arts class. Although students are generally expected to have fulfilled these core requirements by the end of their junior year, "that isn't strictly enforced," according to one student.

Oxy lays an emphasis on linking the theoretical to the practical. Students often complete internships in tandem with their classes, and there is even a special program during election years for students who wish to work on political campaigns. A student explains: "Politics students can spend most of fall semester working for a campaign. Then they come back in November and take classes and write a paper about it." Oxy also endeavors to provide students with a first-hand educational experience through its freshman year Cultural Studies Program (CSP), which takes full advantage of the resources Los Angeles has to offer. One freshman said that her CSP took her around to concerts in L.A., which allowed her to get off campus while bonding with members of her class.

The school definitely does not skimp on the academics, and students say that small classes play a large role in the effectiveness of education at Oxy. While one student said that class size "depends on the department and class level," he also noted that his classes one semester "ranged from four to 10 people." Even introductory science courses only have about 20 to 30 students each. The small size provides students with great access to professors, whom one student called "very flexible and accommodating" and another "receptive." A sophomore said that he has "gotten together with professors over lunch, sometimes to discuss class-related issues, and sometimes just to get to know them better." This relaxed relationship between students and professors contributes a great deal to the learning environment at Oxy, and it allows for students to learn not from imposing figures, but from "actual human beings." The small size of classes and student population at Oxy is, however, a blessing and a curse. One student explains that, because of the small class sizes, "It's pretty apparent whether you have or haven't done the work."

Living and Breathing Oxy

The small size applies to the campus as well. Despite the "beastly, steep hill" that divides the campus into upper and lower components, students say that "most of the stuff you need" is fairly conveniently located on the small campus, including two dining halls. One student says, "You can walk from one end of campus to another in less than 10 minutes." A junior considers this intimate scale a mixed bag: "You can't go outside and be a stranger for more than 10 minutes," he explains. "It's hard to feel lonely but it's also hard to feel anonymous."

Because classroom buildings are on lower campus, students do not need to go to upper campus often. In fact, "unless you can fly," the stairs make a trip up there quite the commitment. Still, upper campus houses some of the nicest dorms as well as Keck Theater, where performances are frequently held. Lower campus is still the center of community life, as the two all-freshmen dorms are located there along with two housing upperclassmen. Students agree that most of the dorms are essentially the same, but they disagree about which is the nicest. One freshman mentioned, "Haines has [students of] all four years and a really nice porch," while a sophomore highlighted the newer Rangeview Hall, which is "very fancy. All the rooms have

private bathrooms, there's a weight room, and a bunch of posh lounges. The only problem is that it's pretty far away." Another distinctive dorm is Pauley, which "places a special emphasis on bringing together students of different cultures," although "that could be said of any dorm." Students are required to live on campus for their first three years at Oxy, though juniors can petition to live off campus. "A lot of people actually petition senior year to stay on campus," explains one student, since Oxy's dorms are so livable and since the surrounding area is largely quiet and residential.

The Ins-N-Outs of Oxy Social Life

"People mostly stay on campus during the weekends. If they leave, it's usually just during the day to go to the beach or late night In-N-Out runs or concerts." Given a location that makes it "hard to get off campus without a car," Oxy encourages students to stay on the hill and make the most of the college environment. Some students warn of the dangers of getting stuck in the "Oxy bubble," however. One junior comments: "Being in a student organization and connected to something bigger helps to" break out of the bubble. "Having a car or having a friend who has a car is pretty important," since "not that many people utilize public transportation." There is, fortunately, "a good sushi place within walking distance" as well as other eateries and cafés in Eagle Rock, the neighborhood where Oxy is located.

Students describe the party scene at Oxy as "low key" and "not very organized," especially since there's only a modest Greek presence on campus. Explains one student: "Greek life is not very big," but "those that are involved really like it." Although students admit that the party scene is "mostly centered on drinking," they are quick to point out that "it's unfair to lump all drinkers together. Many people are very reasonable" and do not overdo the partying. Oxy students also have excellent access to concerts and performances, both on campus and in the L.A. area. One student noted that, on the other hand, there is little pressure to go out at all. "There is a little kitchen in the dorm and you can stay in, bake a cake, and watch a movie—it all depends on who you hang out with." Even within such a small community, there are many different options depending on how comfortable the student feels. One student summed it up well: "If partying is your scene, you can definitely find it, but people also spend a lot of time just hanging out with small groups of close friends."

Fun in the Sun

Extracurricular organizations are a large focus for many students, and there are plenty to choose from. One student mentioned "yoga and political groups" as some of the most popular clubs on campus, while another student considered orchestra, *a cappella*, Glee Club, and Dance Production big draws, both for people involved and the students who "show up to their shows in big numbers." Although students may find their niches in different places, one sophomore said, "Oxy's a small enough community that there isn't really one main social scene; they all kind of overlap."

> "If you get tired of blue skies and 80 degrees, then I guess you wouldn't like Oxy."

Besides devoting time to clubs, "lots of people have on-campus jobs." Students emphasize that Oxy is very good at supplying jobs and making them available for anyone. Popular jobs include working at the Cooler, one of the dining halls, driving the Oxy Bus, a campus-wide shuttle, researching, doing grounds work, and helping in the financial aid office.

Oxy-gen Bonds

"The first word that pops into my mind to describe the Oxy community is 'welcoming,'" said one junior. The words "open" and "welcoming" seem to be buzzwords among Oxy students, who say they feel very connected to their tight-knit community. One sophomore explained, "It's a small enough community that even with total strangers you're almost guaranteed to have mutual friends, and there's a lot of overlap in social circles." Although at such a small school students are likely to "see a lot of the same people," they generally appreciate the closeness of the campus and the comfortable environment. "Students are very vocal" and at the same time "very accepting of what other people have to say." In addition to the touted "openness" of the student body, the environment also makes for sunny dispositions. When asked about the climate, one student paused before saying, "well . . . it rained twice. Otherwise, it's sunny." Blessed with sun, access to a great American city, and a small community of open, happy students, "people love Oxy" and it's no wonder why.—*Andrew Koenig*

FYI
If you come to Occidental, you'd better bring "flip-flops!" (for the shower *and* for the sunny outdoors).
What is the typical weekend schedule? "Thursday night is the beginning of the weekend, but most people just stay up late and do some low-key hanging out and sleeping in, then go to Stewie Hall, the party dorm, on Friday and Saturday nights."
Three things all students at Occidental should do before graduating are "take a class with [Professor of Music] Simeon Pillich, get dunked in a fountain midnight on their birthday, and find the Taco Truck at three in the morning."

Pepperdine University

Address: 24255 Pacific Coast Highway, Malibu, CA 90263
Phone: 310-506-4392
E-mail address: admission-seaver@pepperdine.edu
Web site URL: www.pepperdine.edu
Year Founded: 1937
Private or Public: Private
Religious Affiliation: Church of Christ
Location: Suburban
Number of Applicants: 7,949
Percent Accepted: 30%
Percent Accepted who enroll: 26%
Number Entering: 627
Number of Transfers Accepted each Year: Unreported
Middle 50% SAT range: M: 560–680, CR: 550–670, Wr: 560–660
Middle 50% ACT range: 25–30

Early admission program EA/ED/None: None
Percentage accepted through EA or ED: NA
EA and ED deadline: NA
Regular Deadline: 15-Jan
Application Fee: $65
Full time Undergraduate enrollment: 3,021
Total enrollment: 3,447
Percent Male: 46%
Percent Female: 54%
Total Percent Minority or Unreported: 47%
Percent African-American: 7%
Percent Asian/Pacific Islander: 10%
Percent Hispanic: 13%
Percent Native-American: 1%
Percent International: 6%
Percent in-state/out of state: 60%/40%
Percent from Public HS: Unreported
Retention Rate: 89%
Graduation Rate 4-year: 72%

Graduation Rate 6-year: Unreported
Percent Undergraduates in On-campus housing: 58%
Number of official organized extracurricular organizations: 50
2 Most popular majors: Business Administration and Management, Kinesiology and Exercise Science
Student/Faculty ratio: 13:1
Average Class Size: 15
Percent of students going to grad school: 53%
Tuition and Fees: $40,500
In-State Tuition and Fees if different: No difference
Cost for Room and Board: $11,844
Percent receiving financial aid out of those who apply: Unreported
Percent receiving financial aid among all students: 75%

A t a glance, Pepperdine University might look like a party school. Almost every point on its scenic Malibu, California campus has views of the Pacific Ocean, and it is a short drive to Los Angeles. But Pepperdine bills itself as a Christian university committed to the highest standards of academic excellence and Christian values. It seeks to educate students devoted to excellence and motivated by their belief in God. The school tries to accomplish this through its religious devotion, extensive emphasis on international experience, and general education program that all students must complete. Pepperdine seeks to create individuals with a solid grasp of both their duties to the world and their duties to themselves.

Focusing on religion

Pepperdine's spiritual commitment is based on its affiliation with the Church of Christ. George Pepperdine, who founded the university in 1937, was a devout member of the church who was alarmed at the rate at which college students lost their faith. He founded the university that bears his name in order to provide the best education possible while supporting its students' belief. The university accepts students from all faiths, and tries to extend its ideals of religious devotion and tolerance to its students. But the university also asks all students "to open their minds to be introduced to the Christian faith." It carries out that request by requiring three total courses on the Bible and Christianity. Perhaps because of those requirements, religious diversity mostly exists only in terms of different Christian denominations. There were no Jews, Muslims, or Buddhists in the 2010 freshman class. That bothers some students. "There's some diversity, but mostly you'll just meet blonde Republican Christians," said one.

God's people

Pepperdine might not have religious diversity, but it does advertise a student body that has a majority of minorities. Moreover, students agree, the brand of Christianity on campus is progressive and as welcoming as the school's publications advertise. "This is a very accepting campus because it's full of progressive young Christians who are sick of the old school religion they heard from their parents' generation," said a sophomore. That progressiveness means that some students can be more open than might be expected of a Christian school—especially about their sexuality. "It's a problem," said a junior. "The boys are gorgeous and the girls are stunning, but all the cute guys are gay."

The people and location might be gorgeous, but that doesn't translate into Pepperdine being a laid back party school. The campus is dry and there are no residences for the fraternities and sororities that count a third of the student body as members, so one student says, "We don't go to a party school. Here you're going to be learning sober." But not totally sober, argue other students with access to cars. Many of those students have given up the dorms they all praise for off campus housing for precisely that reason, as well as the high cost of the meal plan. "Because Pepperdine has such a strict no tolerance drinking policy and it can hit you even after you turn 21, most students move off campus after freshman year," said a sophomore natural science major.

To live off campus or to access the bulk of social life on campus, those same students say that cars are a necessity. The school's campus may be suburban, but Hollywood and Los Angeles are just a short drive away. "If you're a partier, you'll need to be willing to drive off campus and drink," said a senior. "Nothing happens on campus."

Wait, This is College

Although Pepperdine boasts a beautiful campus, its academic reputation was not heavily praised in previous years. But, that may no longer be the case. In 2005, it had one of its largest applicant pools, with over 7,800 applicants and 837 freshmen and transfer students enrolled. "I think Pepperdine is getting more and more academically ambitious students," one senior said. "Good thing for the reputation, maybe not so much for the people who have to compete with them."

Students can complete their studies in 38 different fields of study to receive their bachelor's degrees. Motivated students can choose to complete a master's degree in one of seven areas. To promote a well-rounded education, Pepperdine encourages students to take courses in new areas, which they have not previously explored or experienced. In accordance with their founder's ambitions, students are required to take three terms of religious classes. "This [mandatory religion courses] is the biggest downside for me as a student because I respect the religion, but would not like to be forced to take those courses," one student said.

Pepperdine has structured their courses in a way that allows a close relationship between the instructor and the student by having small class sizes. "When I was in high school, I hated classes where there were a huge number of people," one student said. "I get a better opportunity to learn, ask questions, and interact with other students in the smaller environment."

However, students are not limited to stay in California all four years. At some point in their academic career at Pepperdine, a student may choose to take one or more semesters abroad in a country such as Germany, England, Italy, and various other countries. It is this educationally diverse opportunity that separates Pepperdine from other Christian universities. Students can either go during the regular semester or over the summer. Studying abroad can also help fulfill the language requirement. "You should never miss out on being able to study abroad," one student said. "It is unlike any other experience because we are so used to how things are in the United States and this puts everything into perspective. I definitely appreciate many things I previously took for granted more now and the people were all really nice."

Blue All Around

Complain about whatever you want, but the picturesque campus is unparalleled and students rarely deride the excellent on campus housing available to all students. "The dorms are unlike anything I have seen at any school I visited and this makes the university even more appealing," one visiting student noted. At no time are students given mediocre housing unlike other universities that typically bestow the less appealing living arrangements to freshmen. However, it should be noted that some students choose to live off campus despite the comfortable living arrangements. "It's about having the space and the freedom to move around," one off campus student said.

The student body disagrees that the only beautiful element of the campus is the majestic blue waters. "We have the best-looking student population of the entire United States," one student boasted. It is not rare to see this self esteem common among students, many of which can be seen wearing bathing suits and tanning on the pristine beaches. When asked why she would like to attend Pepperdine, a female student responded, "Well, the guys are so cute!"

However, a key downside to the serene, beach milieu is the fact that Pepperdine is not a college town. Students will need to have a car to go off campus if the beach is not their primary source of entertainment. The idea of traveling to nearby Santa Monica, Westwood, and Los Angeles is not that easy given the heavy Southern California traffic.

Athletics

The emphasis placed on religion and faith is present in the athletic realm as well as the academic. Pepperdine follows the principles set forth by their founder George Pepperdine: "Therefore, as my contribution to the well-being and happiness of this generation and those that follow, I am endowing this institution to help young men and women prepare themselves for a life of usefulness in this competitive world and to help them build a foundation of Christian character and faith which will survive the storms of life."

"There's some diversity, but mostly you'll just meet blonde Republican Christians."

Despite the small size of the undergraduate class, Pepperdine can boast an unparalleled level of success in national championships. "We are a small school that has had great success and a number of the teams are nationally ranked," the Director of Sports Information added. At the end of the day, Pepperdine places its priority on the Christian faith and much of the athletic mindset stems from being a devout Christian university. According to the Director of Sports Information, "Pepperdine tries to develop student athletes that will be leaders with a service based mindset and become well rounded people."

For students committed to their faith as well as to academics, Pepperdine is the place to be. It would be difficult to convince anyone to leave the stunning campus and palatial dorms, but the school's top-of-the-line study abroad opportunities might just do the trick. So might the absence of a typical college social scene on campus. Students say they're happy and you will be too—this is Malibu we're talking about, after all.

—*Preetam Dutta and Max de la Bruyere*

FYI
Most everyone in the school is Christian.
What can you do if you don't want to go to the beach? Party.
The guys and girls on campus are hot.
People here actually study when they're not at the beach.

St. Mary's College of California

Address: 1928 Saint Mary's Road, Moraga, CA 94556
Phone: 925-631-4224
E-mail address: smcadmit@stmarys-ca.edu
Web site URL: www.stmarys-ca.edu
Year Founded: 1863
Private or Public: Private
Religious Affiliation: Roman Catholic
Location: Suburban
Number of Applicants: 3,730
Percent Accepted: 78%
Percent Accepted who enroll: 24%
Number Entering: 695
Number of Transfers Accepted each Year: 293
Middle 50% SAT range: M: 470–600, CR: 470–600, Wr: Unreported
Middle 50% ACT range: 21–26
Early admission program EA/ED/None: EA

Percentage accepted through EA or ED: Unreported
EA and ED deadline: 15-Nov
Regular Deadline: 1-Feb
Application Fee: $55
Full time Undergraduate enrollment: 2,687
Total enrollment: 2,799
Percent Male: 39%
Percent Female: 61%
Total Percent Minority or Unreported: 53%
Percent African-American: 5%
Percent Asian/Pacific Islander: 10%
Percent Hispanic: 22%
Percent Native-American: 1%
Percent International: 2%
Percent in-state/out of state: 88%/12%
Percent from Public HS: 55%
Retention Rate: Unreported
Graduation Rate 4-year: 53%

Graduation Rate 6-year: 61%
Percent Undergraduates in On-campus housing: 59%
Number of official organized extracurricular organizations: 43
3 Most popular majors: Business Administration, Management and Operations, Communication and Media Studies, Psychology
Student/Faculty ratio: 13:1
Average Class Size: 19
Percent of students going to grad school: 48%
Tuition and Fees: $37,000
In-State Tuition and Fees if different: No difference
Cost for Room and Board: $12,840
Percent receiving financial aid out of those who apply: 94%
Percent receiving financial aid among all students: 84%

A midst the big-city bustle of both San Francisco and Berkeley, St. Mary's College lies nestled in the picturesque town of Moraga, California. The surrounding woody scenery and majestic green hills give the campus a tranquil vibe that one student describes as "beautiful for its small-town-lazy feel." While the campus's location may at times feel isolated and lonely, particularly on the weekends when many students travel to the surrounding large cities in the Bay Area, the school makes sure to provide a variety of activities for students to participate in such as Saturday rock climbing and laser tag adventures. This small private college provides a well-balanced mix of strong academic programs, a solid Christian foundation based on the teachings of the De La Salle brothers, and a formidable athletic program whose basketball team often contends in the NCAA's "March Madness."

Something for Everyone

Students are quick to boast about the variety of unique career specific programs that St. Mary's offers including the nursing program, engineering program, and the "Teachers for Tomorrow" program. The nursing and engineering programs are unique in that the initial undergraduate years are spent at St. Mary's and the final undergraduate years are spent at a partner school. Students in the nursing program spend two years at St. Mary's and then later transfer to Samuel Merritt University in Oakland, California. The engineering program also has a similar system with students spending three years at St. Mary's and then transferring to the University of Southern California to complete the degree in two years. The "Teachers for Tomorrow" program also attracts many students to St. Mary's because it allows them to attain their bachelor's degree and teaching credential in five years. Students also have the option of taking three additional courses in order to also attain a Master of Arts degree in teaching. For those who are understandably unsure of their post-graduation plans, the Integral Program of Liberal Arts offers a solution. The program takes a liberal arts approach to learning and has been described by students as "basically its own college" because of the fact that classes featured in the program can only be taken by Integral students. The program focuses on a broad spectrum of subjects but all are taught in seminar style. The classes are all based on discussion. One student noted that the program was interesting because even in science and math classes, students are still pushed to "talk about what those things mean." Some students joke about those in the program saying, "all they do is talk referring to the Integral system of no tests." A panel of professors presents students with their final grades by evaluating the students as they sit in front of them. The Integral program is also beneficial for anyone interested in entering a career that will require proficient public-speaking skills because students are forced to regularly participate in class as part of their grade. One student noted that this system "forces those who are shy to come out of their shell."

Unique Opportunities

St. Mary's academic calendar is based on the "4-1-4" system in which there are two semesters in which students take four credits, and one month in the middle, dubbed "Jan-term" during which students focus intensively on one class only. The off-kilter classes offered during the month of January include "You Can't Make Me Do This," "Transmission, Translation, and Transformation: Astronomical Ideas in the Islamic World," and "Tool or Trade: Bicycle History." Classes meet for two and a half hours, four days a week. There are no classes on Wednesdays, which gives students a much-appreciated mid-week break for students to unwind. Some students treat the midweek break as a quasi-weekend and an opportunity to make Friday come a little earlier. Students also have the opportunity to go off-campus during Jan-term through study abroad programs in countries such as Brazil and Italy. Students do not have to travel far to have a memorable experience, however. One example of this is the course called "Live Sentence" during which students travel to San Quentin prison to speak with the inmates about their experiences. Despite some classes having heavy reading assignments, for the most part, students regard Jan-term as "a good time to catch up and take a little breather."

Social Scene

While students admit that St. Mary's is "not a party school" and it is not unusual to find students "just hanging out in someone's room watching a movie" on a Saturday night, they also say that there is a party scene present for those who want it. On-campus parties are generally smaller because they are hosted in people's dorm rooms and are also therefore likely to be shut down by Public Safety, the campus police, quickly. Most students agree that the best parties are those hosted off-campus at upperclassmen houses. Although others point out that loud off-campus parties contribute to the strained town-gown relations. "Moraga is mostly old people and families. They don't want to have to deal with rowdy students, so they call the police for noise violations," one student explained. Upperclassmen feel that the best parties to attend are those in the townhouses, the upperclassmen on-campus housing, because it is less likely for those parties to get shut down. "The older you get, the less strict the rules are," one student explained. Aside from drinking, students also state that there is a fairly large marijuana presence on campus, "but not more than any other Northern California school."

> "I love walking to class and being able to run into and say hi to at least ten people."

Housing: The Luck of the Draw

While St. Mary's is known for its small size, in recent years the number of students enrolling as freshmen has increased. The entering freshman class of 2014 was the largest in St. Mary's history to date. Unfortunately for freshmen, this led to forced doubles and triples in rooms that were originally designed to be singles and doubles. Not all complain about their freshman housing, however. Many students are content with their dorms, particularly those that live suite-style. "Basically, it's all about luck. Some freshmen get rooms with in-suite bathrooms. Others get forced triples," one student explained. While some describe the lottery system as fair, others complain about the fact that everyone pays the same amount for housing, despite the fact that some rooms are clearly bigger than others. Housing at St. Mary's improves by year, however, and by the time students become upperclassmen, they get to enjoy the campus townhouses, which are all designed apartment-style with their own living room, kitchen, and bathroom. Not all upperclassmen are guaranteed housing, however, which forces students to live in the neighboring cities of Moraga, Lafayette, and Orinda.

Small Colleges: A Double-Edged Sword

Most St. Mary's students can agree that the college's small size is extremely beneficial in the classroom. The class size, which is generally around twenty students, allows for in-depth discussions and for students to get to know their professors very well. At the same time, some students feel that the size can be a hindrance to the social scene, particularly on weekends when many students go home or off-campus. While one student "can't imagine the classes being any bigger," she also admits that "the school feels almost lonely" on the weekends. Others embrace the size. "I love walking to class and being able to run into and say hi to at least ten people" one student gushed. Most St. Mary's students can agree that the campus's small size and surrounding greenery give it a serene feel; despite its size, there is plenty to do: from going to a basketball game, to taking part in a school-sponsored Saturday trip, to watching a movie in a friend's room. At St. Mary's, students are taught based on both a liberal arts philosophy and the beliefs of the De La Salle Christian brothers, which gives for a very well-balanced community overall.—*Yvette Borja*

FYI

What is the typical weekend schedule? "Friday night: go to an off-campus party, come back to drink in your room or chill with friends and watch a movie. Saturday: go to Walnut Creek to go shopping or go to San Francisco and sight-see. Sunday: get a late lunch with friends, relax, do homework, optional Church service on Sunday nights."

If I could change one thing about St. Mary's I'd "make it so that not as many people went home on the weekends."

Stanford University

Address: 355 Galvez Street, Stanford, CA 94305-6106
Phone: 650-723-2091
E-mail address: admission@stanford.edu
Web site URL: www.stanford.edu
Year Founded: 1885
Private or Public: Private
Religious Affiliation: None
Location: Suburban
Number of Applicants: 32,022
Percent Accepted: 7%
Percent Accepted who enroll: 72%
Number Entering: 1,674
Number of Transfers Accepted each Year: 23
Middle 50% SAT range: M: 690–790, CR: 670–760, Wr: 680–780
Middle 50% ACT range: 31–34
Early admission program EA/ED/None: EA

Percentage accepted through EA or ED: 14%
EA and ED deadline: 1-Nov
Regular Deadline: 1-Jan
Application Fee: $90
Full time Undergraduate enrollment: 6,870
Total enrollment: 6,887
Percent Male: 51%
Percent Female: 49%
Total Percent Minority or Unreported: 68%
Percent African-American: 11%
Percent Asian/Pacific Islander: 20%
Percent Hispanic: 18%
Percent Native-American: 4%
Percent International: 7%
Percent in-state/out of state: 45%/55%
Percent from Public HS: 58%
Retention Rate: 98%

Graduation Rate 4-year: 79%
Graduation Rate 6-year: 93%
Percent Undergraduates in On-campus housing: 91%
Number of official organized extracurricular organizations: 600
3 Most popular majors: Biology/Biological Sciences, Economics, International Relations and Affairs
Student/Faculty ratio: 6:1
Average Class Size: 19
Percent of students going to grad school: 52%
Tuition and Fees: $40,050
In-State Tuition and Fees if different: No difference
Cost for Room and Board: $12,291
Percent receiving financial aid out of those who apply: 80%
Percent receiving financial aid among all students: 80%

Lazy palm trees, gorgeous weather, luscious Spanish-style architecture, happy students—if you're looking for a pre-eminent research institution with the quintessential West Coast vibe, Stanford University is the school for you. Home to some of the nation's most innovative entrepreneurs and brilliant students, especially in the sciences and engineering, Stanford does an excellent job of entwining superlative academics with a diverse array of extracurricular and pre-professional opportunities to satisfy every student's needs, enfolding the experience in a spirit of cooperation and noncompetitiveness that causes its student body to be ranked consistently as one of the happiest in the country.

Studying was Never So Much Fun

Stanford is famous for its seemingly laid-back students and relaxed pace of life, but do not let the easy-going atmosphere deceive you: Stanford academics are no walk in the park. "Most students here are actually quite Type-A"; and the hefty 180 units required for graduation and the unique quarter-system calendar make for a challenging experience. The average course load is 15 to 16 units per quarter, and because of the shorter length of the quarter, this translates into a virtually unremitting series of midterms from the second week to "Dead Week" before exams.

All students are required to fulfill General Education Requirements (GERs), in three categories: "Introduction to the Humanities"— "honestly, it's a waste of time, uselessly time-consuming"; "Disciplinary Breadth"— these are simply courses in each of five major areas of study "that essentially fulfill themselves"; and "Education for Citizenship"— encompassing classes on "really cool topics like gender studies and globalization." Most students praise their academic experience, citing "attentive professors" and "an amazing advising system" as reasons for their contentment. Indeed, although especially freshman introductory classes can become quite large—"my linear algebra class exceeded maybe 300 students," stated one freshman— professors are still extremely accessible and hold "extensive office hours" to motivate students to visit them.

Students are especially enthusiastic about Stanford's myriad interdisciplinary majors: human biology; science, technology, and society; modern thought and literature; and urban studies are only a few examples of the bountiful opportunities the university presents for combining disparate interests. However, biology and economics remain the most popular majors. Prospective humanities majors should expect a slightly easier experience: one student majoring in the sciences averred, "The fuzzier majors have a much easier time garnering an A and maintaining a high GPA than the rest of us." Although a Stanford education is not immediately associated with the humanities, the quality of scholarship in those subjects is by no means inferior. Indeed, another student emphasized, "professors in those departments are even more supportive of and accessible to dedicated students."

Life Beyond the Classroom

From the leather easy chairs in the Lane reading room of the Green Library to the sparkling labs of the Clark Center, students are immersed in a variety of rich learning experiences during the day. The Haas Center for Public Service is particularly popular among students, sporting over 600 volunteer, internship, and research opportunities. "The opportunities are extremely accessible and multifarious—there is something for everyone," one student commented. There are also more than 650 clubs and organizations, and each of these is supported by the Student Activities and Leadership division of Stanford's Student Affairs office. SAL staff and student peer advisers take responsibility for guiding students to the opportunities and organizations that best befit their interests.

> **"The opportunities are extremely accessible and multifarious—there is something for everyone."**

Stanford's support of student's extracurricular intellectual exploration does not end with the school year. Rather than merely relax after a grueling three quarters, the majority of students use their summer quarter to acquire real-world experience through internships, research, or study-abroad programs like the Bing Overseas Program or Summer Research College that Stanford sponsors. Stated one sophomore, "Study abroad, especially in non-English-speaking countries, is a big deal: about 50 percent of students go abroad, and there are many resources to do so. Research is also a huge deal, and students who are interested start as early as their freshman year."

Living at Camp Stanford

Stanford offers one of the most diverse housing systems of any university, sporting the standard dormitories of 60 to 200 people; self-operated houses of 25 to 50 residents; and independent co-ops, which require complete student control over cooking and cleaning. The incredible variety of options, ranging from academic and theme houses to Greek houses to university-owned apartments, inevitably leads to some disappointment and some euphoria, and it is Stanford's lottery system, "The Draw," that seals students' fate. Most students seem to agree on one point, that "the most popular dorms are those either on The Row, where all the frat houses are, or as near The Row as possible, because that's where the social scene is." Yet a small number of freshmen choose to participate in the Program in Structured Liberal Education, an intensive residential community that provides freshmen only with a comprehensive introduction to the liberal arts in an intimate living and learning environment. And although there are 16 fraternities and 12 sororities on campus, less than 15 percent of students feel the need to go Greek. It seems that whether students are blessed with palatial three-room suites accompanied by a masterful chef, or condemned to cramped one-room triples, by and large, they are quite content.

Students' biggest complaint about living at Stanford, besides the "terrible forced doubles," is the mandatory expensive meal plan, in which all students must participate as long as they reside in a dorm. The average yearly cost for the meal plan exceeds $5,000, a considerable fee for standard dining hall fare. "I'm not at all impressed with Stanford Dining; the meal plan should definitely be more flexible," grumbled one student. Those students who do tire of the cafeteria food—"trust me, you won't eat more than 14 meals in a week"—usually go out with friends to one of the myriad restaurants in the area or on campus. The CoHo coffeehouse, Treehouse, Subway, and Peet's Coffee are popular campus eateries, but many students who seek to venture farther bemoan the exorbitant prices of surrounding Palo Alto. Thus, although Palo Alto is elegant and affluent—"a treat to occasionally indulge in"—it is no college town, and this fact tends to foster what some call the "Stanford bubble." However, there is never a lack of things to do: theater performances, a cappella concerts, cultural shows, and Row house parties always keep students busy. And for the entrepreneurially minded, the proximity of Silicon Valley and the slew of venture capital firms on nearby Sand Hill Road create incredible opportunities.

There is a reason students fondly refer to their school as "Camp Stanford:" the sunny skies and grassy fields, Frisbee-throwing students and flip-flop-wearing professors, stellar athletics and powerful sense of school pride all create an exhilarating and richly rewarding experience. One student summed up life on the "Farm" nicely: "Amazing academics, check. Top-notch sustainability report card, check. Diversity, check. Groundbreaking research, check. Successful entrepreneurs, check. The most brilliant students of the world, check. And a superlative record in football, check. I love you, Stanford!"—*Sejal Hathi*

FYI
If you come to Stanford, you'd better bring: "the desire to explore, a Frisbee, a bike, and your workout clothes."
What's the typical weekend schedule? "Chill Friday nights, party Saturdays, hit the books Sunday."
If I could change one thing about Stanford, I'd change: "the meal plan schedule."
Three things every student at Stanford should do before graduating are: "attend an Entrepreneur Thought Leader seminar, go to the Big Game, and hike the Dish."

University of Caliornia System

Students from California undoubtedly will have heard of the University of California, the state's leading public university system for high-achieving high school students. But the UC system stands out not only in California, but across the country, and even the world. A model for public institutions across the United States, eight of its undergraduate campuses rank in the top 100, six in the top 50, and two in the top 25 universities in the country. With more than 230,000 students, 1.6 million living alumni and an overall endowment of $6.7 billion as of 2011, students looking to enter the UC system will be joining good company. Counting 32 Nobel laureates and 254 members of the National Academy of Sciences within their faculty, UC students are able to get a world-class education without the hefty price tag that comes with private colleges.

So Many Choices
The UC system counts nine campuses among its members, along with a tenth school, San Francisco, which is limited to graduate study in the health sciences. As the charter campus, Berkeley is still regarded by some as the system's flagship school, leading the other campuses with its tradition of academic excellence. But the University of California, Los Angeles, and UC San Diego are not far behind. In fact, these three schools rank in the top 15 among public and private universities worldwide. At UC Berkeley, students interviewed consistently remark on its competitiveness, due to the drive that Berkeley students have to live up to the school's rigorous but rewarding demands. UCLA's admissions rate is comparable to Berkeley's—both hover around 20 percent—and UCSD has already made a name for itself both in the U.S. and abroad for its excellence in the sciences. Irvine boasts an ideal campus location in sunny Orange County, just miles from the beach, not to mention its technological and scientific instruction. Davis is a leading university known for its premier agricultural research and environmental friendliness as well as strength in math and sciences. Santa Barbara is quickly proving itself as a rising star in the academic world for its active research, which includes 11 national research centers. Santa Cruz can find pride in its physics, math and astronomy programs, as well as its political science and art departments, not to mention its convenient location right outside beautiful Monterey Bay, just a short trip away from San Francisco and San Jose. Back down south near the greater Los Angeles area, Riverside maintains its reputation for pioneering citrus research and entomology, as well as well-known programs in science fiction and photography. Last but not least is Merced, founded in 2005 as the newest addition to the UC family. Although it is located in a rural area associated with agriculture (it's just miles from Yosemite National Park), it emphasizes cutting edge research in the fields of natural science, math and engineering.

Something for Everyone
While each school handles its admissions separately, students only need to use one application for all the UCs, thereby simplifying the process for students. All eligible students from California are guaranteed a spot in the UC system, though admissions to their top choice of campuses is not necessarily guaranteed. Through statewide admissions, the UC system automatically accepts students among the top eighth of California public school graduates, as well as the top four percent of any given high school. If eligible students are not granted admissions to their top choices, they are then referred to other UC campuses which still have open space. Because several UC campuses have fairly competitive admissions policies, some students will inevitably be disappointed, but even those who end up at their second, third or even fourth choice colleges generally find themselves satisfied with their experience. As one student said about UC Irvine, "The people that come to this school are friendly and the atmosphere is welcoming and comfortable. This was not my first choice school, but when I came here, I grew to like it a lot."

The UC system no longer uses affirmative action policies after the passing in 1996 of California's Proposition 209, which prohibits public institutions such as the UC schools from considering race, sex and ethnicity in their selection processes. As a result, underrepresented minorities and students from underprivileged backgrounds have had a more difficult time enrolling at UC schools, especially those in the proverbial top tier. As such, issues of racial imbalance have arisen, but the UC system has named representing California's diversity in its schools as one of its priorities. Riverside itself can boast of a student body that draws its strength from diversity—the school has topped national rankings in ethnic and socioeconomic diversity, third and fifteenth in the nation, respectively.

All in all, the University of California offers a variety of opportunities among its many campuses and within each campus, the benefits of a huge array of strong academic departments. Students who are looking for a quality education but don't want to graduate with significant debt will certainly be able to find the rewarding experience they seek in the UC system. With so many campuses and a wide range of strengths in research and departments, the UC system is bound to have something for everyone.
—*Catherine Dinh*

University of California / Berkeley

Address: 110 Sproul Hall, #5800, Berkeley, CA 94720-5800
Phone: 510-642-3175
E-mail address: Visit website to submit questions
Web site URL: www.berkeley.edu
Year Founded: 1868
Private or Public: Public
Religious Affiliation: None
Location: Urban
Number of Applicants: 50,393
Percent Accepted: 22%
Percent Accepted who enroll: 37%
Number Entering: 4,109
Number of Transfers Accepted each Year: 3,451
Middle 50% SAT range: M: 630–760, CR: 600–730, Wr: 610–740
Middle 50% ACT range: 26–34
Early admission program EA/ED/None: None

Percentage accepted through EA or ED: NA
EA and ED deadline: NA
Regular Deadline: 30-Nov
Application Fee: $60
Full time Undergraduate enrollment: 24,636
Total enrollment: 35,838
Percent Male: 46%
Percent Female: 54%
Total Percent Minority or Unreported: 72%
Percent African-American: 3%
Percent Asian/Pacific Islander: 40%
Percent Hispanic: 10%
Percent Native-American: 1%
Percent International: 7%
Percent in-state/out of state: 93%/7%
Percent from Public HS: 85%
Retention Rate: 97%
Graduation Rate 4-year: 60%

Graduation Rate 6-year: Unreported
Percent Undergraduates in On-campus housing: 35%
Number of official organized extracurricular organizations: 300
3 Most popular majors: Computer Engineering, English Language and Literature, Political Science and Government
Student/Faculty ratio: 15:1
Average Class Size: 12
Percent of students going to grad school: Unreported
Tuition and Fees: $32,281
In-State Tuition and Fees if different: $9,402
Cost for Room and Board: $15,308
Percent receiving financial aid out of those who apply: Unreported
Percent receiving financial aid among all students: Unreported

Students at the University of California at Berkeley enjoy the University's challenging and stimulating academic environment combined with its constant access to beautiful California Bay Area. Considered the top public university in the nation, UC Berkeley—affectionately known as "Cal"—commands an impressive 1,232 acres of campus and a thriving urban city life, only minutes away from San Francisco.

4.0 GPA: Hard to Get, Harder to Keep

UC Berkeley offers six different colleges for undergraduate students: the College of Letters and Science, College of Environmental Design, College of Chemistry, College of Natural Resources, College of Engineering and the Haas School of Business. Each college has its own graduate requirements although UC Berkeley requires a fulfillment of seven "breadth" courses that cover a wide range of the humanities and sciences. According to one freshman in the College of Chemistry, "As a chemical engineering major, we have few humanities requirements, but a *lot* of technical science and engineering courses that we have to take." Although requirements differ from college to college, all students must take specific requirements in order to receive their Bachelor's degree, including Entry Level Writing, American History and American Institutions. "The curriculum is designed to inspire students to become actively interested and knowledgeable about subjects outside the scope of their particular major," said one freshman in the College of Letters and Sciences. "For example, due to the breadth program, I've taken courses that have discussed ancient Greek philosophical views, a subject that fascinated me and that I wouldn't have otherwise been exposed to if it wasn't for the breadth requirement."

UC Berkeley currently offers more than 100 majors, and among its popular majors are typically Molecular and Cell Biology, Electrical Engineering and Computer Science, Psychology, Business Administration and Economics. Students wishing to enroll in the Haas School of Business must apply for the two-year program during the fall of their sophomore year and, if accepted, begin taking business classes their junior year. Although enrollment in the Haas is limited to 700 students, one aspiring Haas freshman noted, "It's possible for underclassmen who have not yet been admitted to Haas to also take upper division courses."

Average class sizes range from 20 to over 200 students, depending on the structure of the class (discussion-based or lecture) and the material covered; some popular classes, such as Political Science 179, may have as many as 700 students. Berkeley offers a range of different courses, from advanced physics courses to "Physics for Future Presidents," which focuses on the hands-on side of physics instead of mathematical and quantitative aspect. As a large public university, students at Berkeley are often placed on wait-lists for course registration. According to one student, however, "the horror stories about students having to commit more years to finishing their degree are often both over-exaggerated and misunderstood. If a student is diligent and attends his or her classes, he or she is almost always accepted into the class."

While students agree that grading at Berkeley can be tough with terrible curves,

most concede that the system is fair and enjoy the challenging environment. "At Berkeley, it's decently easy to get B's but exponentially difficult, almost impossible, to get A's," said one freshman, who added that she did at least enjoy "the bonding experience over the extremely difficult midterms and finals." According to one sophomore in the College of Engineering, "course grades are curved so that there is a balance distribution of grades, even if the raw scores are abysmal."

Living in an Urban City

Students at Berkeley are guaranteed housing for two years. Prior to arriving on campus, students rank dorm preferences and, if they do not specify a roommate, fill out a housing application to determine a compatible roommate. All but two dorms at Berkeley are co-ed, although most buildings do set aside one floor only for women; Stern Hall is only for women, while Bowles Hall is exclusively for men. Although there are no dorms specifically for freshmen, most upperclassmen tend to move off campus by their sophomore or junior year anyway. Each student has an RA who lives on campus, guides incoming freshmen and enforces dorm rules. According to one sophomore, "RAs are friendly undergraduate students who organize events for their floors, such as Christmas parties or dinner get-togethers." One student added, "My own RA planned frequent excursions to SF, Oakland and the movie theatre for our floor."

Berkeley's architecture ranges from the "old and distasteful to regal and modern." According to one student, "Sproul Hall (the main administrative building) looks like a grand Greek building, while Wurster Hall (the architecture building, ironically enough) is infamous for being rather unattractive—supposedly to inspire architecture students to do much better."

There are four dining halls, known as "dining commons" or "DCs" at Berkeley, each of which are located near or inside a dorm building. Although the food is "decently good," students unsatisfied with DC food may choose to eat out instead. There are also on campus cafes and minimarkets where students can spend meal points in lieu of eating at a dining hall. According to one student, "The dining commons are buffet-styled with many different cuisines available every night with frequent themed nights—the meals leading up to Thanksgiving, for example, all included turkey as a main dish."

Golden Bears and the Golden Gate Bridge

With San Francisco just across the Bay, Berkeley students frequently find their weekend schedules packed with trips to "San Fran," parties at fraternities and sororities, football games, and a cappella performances. On Thursday, Friday and Saturday nights, students enjoy going to apartment parties or clubbing in San Francisco. Because most upperclassmen move off campus by their sophomore or junior year, underclassmen and upperclassmen generally do not mingle over the weekends. Nonetheless, students easily make friends at Berkeley. According to one freshman, "my floor itself is a great community of people that I've bonded very closely with. As a result, I have a wide social net at Berkeley that I can hang out with."

Although alcohol and binge drinking is not a problem on campus, marijuana is a common presence. One student noted that Berkeley is considered the country's "marijuana capital," and students have easy access to pot. While alcohol and drugs are not technically allowed in dorms, "the amount of enforcing really depends on the RA, and even then, alcohol and drugs are not strongly enforced at all outside of dorms."

> "There's such a wide range of people to interact and meet with that one is never short of fun. This turns the size of Berkeley from being one of its detractors to being one of its strong suits."

There is also a variety of social opportunities for students uninterested in alcohol or marijuana, including weekend concerts, musical performances, cheap movies and multiple dining options such as Blondie's Pizza or Crepes-a-Go-Go. Students can also go shopping in one of Berkeley's many thrift shops or discover their musical preferences at Rasputin Records, a large records store in walking distance. Although most students do not own cars because "parking at Berkeley is a nightmare," most commute using the free bus service or the BART transrail, making transportation easy and accessible.

More to Love

Berkeley students are as intense about their extracurricular activities as they are about their academics, and students have the opportunity to join an enormous variety of organizations. "Berkeley is HUGE in all ways," said one freshman. "There are lots of frats, sororities, a cappella teams, great sports teams, many intramural sports, and clubs for basically any interest." Professional fraternities and organizations are especially popular, and clubs such as the Asian Business Association or Circle K (a community service organization) are among the larger clubs on campus. Moreover, Berkeley also offers its fair share of unusual organizations, including a Quidditch team and the Cal Hawaii Club, for students looking for a unique college experience.

Students at Berkeley are intensely proud of being Bears and their shared pride is manifested most strongly during the Big Game, the annual football game between Berkeley and its rival Stanford University. Every evening before the Big Game, students on the Berkeley rally team organize a blazing bonfire rally at the Greek theater to encourage school spirit. Generally, however, students don't need extra encouragement to take pride in their school. According to one freshman, "I had initially expected the worst, but found the best. Once I discovered my own niche in Berkeley, all those cautionary tales against the school because of its size disappeared." Another sophomore agreed, adding, "There have been times when I was treading academic rough waters, but upon hindsight, I think these past semesters have been rather rewarding. Given a second chance, I would choose Berkeley again."—*Caroline Tan*

FYI

If you come to Berkeley, you'd better bring "all your attention, focus, motivation, creativity, brains, and willpower to work your butt off."

If I could change one thing about Berkeley, I'd "change the attitude of people who place so much concentration on getting good grades instead of learning."

The biggest college-wide tradition/event at Berkeley is "the Big Game Day. Everyone dresses up and gets pumped for it."

University of California / Davis

Address: 178 Mrak Hall, One Shields Avenue, Davis, CA 95616

Phone: 530-752-2971

E-mail address: undergraduateadmissions@ucdavis.edu

Web site URL: www.ucdavis.edu

Year Founded: 1905

Private or Public: Public

Religious Affiliation: None

Location: Suburban

Number of Applicants: 43,295

Percent Accepted: 45%

Percent Accepted who enroll: 23%

Number Entering: 4,501

Number of Transfers Accepted each Year: 5,466

Middle 50% SAT range: M: 570–690, CR: 530–650, Wr: 540–660

Middle 50% ACT range: 24–30

Early admission program EA/ED/None: None

Percentage accepted through EA or ED: NA

EA and ED deadline: NA

Regular Deadline: 30-Nov

Application Fee: $60

Full time Undergraduate enrollment: 24,787

Total enrollment: 25,096

Percent Male: 45%

Percent Female: 55%

Total Percent Minority or Unreported: 67%

Percent African-American: 2%

Percent Asian/Pacific Islander: 37%

Percent Hispanic: 16%

Percent Native-American: <1%

Percent International: 3%

Percent in-state/out of state: 98%/2%

Percent from Public HS: 84%

Retention Rate: 93%

Graduation Rate 4-year: 42%

Graduation Rate 6-year: 80%

Percent Undergraduates in On-campus housing: 25%

Number of official organized extracurricular organizations: 364

3 Most popular majors: Biology, Economics, Psychology

Student/Faculty ratio: 16:1

Average Class Size: 25

Percent of students going to grad school: 40%

Tuition and Fees: $34,098

In-State Tuition and Fees if different: $12,794

Cost for Room and Board: $12,697

Percent receiving financial aid out of those who apply: 58%

Percent receiving financial aid among all students: 54%

The largest in the University of California system, UC Davis features a sprawling campus (covering 7,309 acres) while maintaining the atmosphere of a small college town. Nestled in the California Central Valley, Davis offers a variety of environs, from rolling pastures to state-of-the-art athletic and research facilities. For students desirous of the hustle-and-bustle of a major city, Davis is a mere 15 miles away from Sacramento and only an hour away from San Francisco; however, resources on campus abound, with about $800 million devoted to research, over 600 clubs, and 23 varsity sports teams. While a close-knit academic community, students at UC Davis have plenty of room to explore their passions and their surroundings.

Where Science Stands out from the Crowd

UC Davis is comprised of four colleges—Agriculture and Environmental Sciences, Biological Sciences, Engineering, and Letters and Science—to which prospective freshman apply. Within each college, there are "a lot of different choices and opportunities," leading to varying distributional requirements. Students typically take anywhere from 14 to 18 units each quarter. As one student said, a unit roughly correlates to an hour of class time, which corresponds to double the amount of hours of work outside of class.

A sophomore majoring in Community and Regional Development said that the workload is "definitely do-able" with effective time management skills. A freshman Biology major cautioned, however, that the pace and amount of homework assigned is much more intense than in high school. She added, "At Davis, I was rarely assigned any 'due-the-next-class' assignments and spent the majority of my study-time reading the material and self-teaching." Some classes, for instance, assign a "ridiculous" amount of reading.

Class sizes vary, with some introductory classes averaging around 400 to 500 students. Regarding large lectures, a freshman said, "You hardly ever get one-on-one with the professor." Other courses, however, are much smaller, and are taught in the style of seminars. Professors are considered to be accessible. One student remarked that her Calculus professor held office hours every day of the week, stressing that "he was available for you" if more help was necessary. Some professors are better than others, and occasionally, students gripe about "teachers with accents." Teaching assistants—graduate students—are helpful in filling in the gaps.

Science at Davis is perceived to be more difficult, with the humanities as the "easier" route. One student deemed the programs in agriculture and biology to be "incredible," remarking that "this is the place to be if you want to have a career in either field." One student said that the Animal Science major (typically absent from other universities' major offerings) is particularly strong, leading to a variety of different specializations such as Livestock and Dairy, Equine Science, and Companion Animals. The major is particularly hands-on and career-oriented, as one student said that freshmen are expected to witness the slaughter of livestock in the spring semester. "You're going to have to be accustomed to death in any animal profession," she said. That being said, students gain experience quickly in their chosen major, with 41% of undergraduates choosing to partake in research during their college careers.

While engineering is considered to have a significant presence at Davis, some of the most popular majors are Psychology, Economics, and Biology. Courses in the Chemistry department, particularly those that satisfy general education requirements, are "extremely hard." That being said, most students believe that grading is fair and equitable, though it may vary from professor to professor. Some courses that are more difficult, such as general chemistry, are curved. Help is ample should students struggle. One student remarked, "Tutors are everywhere—people are just sitting in the service centers, waiting to help you."

Enrolling in classes is considered to be "competitive." Registration is controlled by Pass Times, intervals in which particular groups of students may enroll in classes. Athletes and honors students are given priority pass times, on the first day of registration. Freshmen are given last preference and are allotted days toward the end of registration week to sign up for classes. Passes are further divided into Pass 1 and Pass 2. In the first, students typically try to get "as many classes as [they] can," while in the latter, registration is open to everyone, and waitlists burgeon.

Students were quick to reassure that the waitlist is not impossible to overcome. One student noted that since professors ultimately hold sway over their class sizes, "they'll probably let you in if you go talk to them." Further, while those with later pass times may have difficulty in obtaining the necessary prerequisites with their desired professor, "AP scores really do help" in allowing students to surpass general requirements. Ultimately, persistent students who "keep refreshing until registration opens and type really fast will get the classes [they] want."

From Pass Times to Pastimes

As seen from preference given to athletics for Pass Times, health and fitness is a large part of campus. A student said, "People bike everywhere on campus, and everyone is really athletic." As such, the Activities and Recreation Center (dubbed the ARC) is quite popular amongst students.

Students' perception of sports teams, however, is mixed. Regarding school spirit, a student said, "I think there's a lot more enthusiasm for the Aggie Pack freebies [distributed at the games] than the sports." Though UC Davis isn't as competitive as some of the other NCAA Division I colleges, a freshman said, "Students still love to support our teams."

That being said, sports—particularly intramurals—are "really celebrated." One student noted, "We have an entire wall in the ARC dedicated to winning IM teams." Soccer and volleyball in particular are quite popular.

When students aren't busy exercising or competing on the field, students are "very committed" to extracurricular activities such as the California Aggie (the school newspaper) and KDVS (Davis's radio station). Students may join sororities and fraternities, or become a part of one of the many Christian fellowships on campus. Unique clubs abound, such as those devoted to League of Legends, Harry Potter, or Draft Horse and Driving. Others engage in research and internships, such as those involved in Wild Campus, a wildlife conservation program.

There are also a plethora of jobs on campus—such as at the Coffee House, the UC Davis Bookstore, or through Unitrans, a student-run transportation system. Obtaining a job is considered to be "easy and convenient," according to a freshman. Ultimately, opportunities to become more involved abound at Davis. As one student said, "You just have to know where to look."

Comfortable, though Pricy Living

Freshmen are guaranteed on-campus housing and are sorted into one of three main residential hall areas—Segundo, Tercero, and Cuarto. Host to about 2,300 students, Segundo is considered to be the largest of the three. While most halls in the Segundo area are typical of a college campus, Primero Grove offers apartment style living. Previously only home to graduates, due to an influx of students, lucky freshmen are allotted their "own kitchen, living area, and bathroom."

Located on the southwest side of central campus (near the dairy farm), Tercero is a newer area. As Cuarto is not located on central campus, it is considered to be the "quietest" of the dorm areas. Cuarto comes outfitted with a pool and Jacuzzi.

Resident Advisors (RAs) "make the transition from home to college a bit easier." Located on every floor of a dorm, RAs "follow the rules" but are also considered to be "fun." One sophomore commented, "I have a friend who is an RA and all her residents adore her."

Each residential hall area comes equipped with a Dining Commons. The food is "very vegan and vegetarian friendly," with pizza, hamburgers, grilled cheese, and a salad bar as old standbys. Mongolian BBQ is also a popular choice. One student griped, "It's cheaper to cook for yourself than pay for a meal plan." Some students have taken to selling their meal swipes in an attempt to remedy the system.

After freshman year, sophomores and upperclassmen typically live in apartments. As UC Davis has "really large sponsored apartment areas," prices are considered to be more affordable than continuing to live in the residential hall areas.

The Social Scene

While a student commented that "Davis is known more for its academics than its social life," she was quick to add that the social scene is still good, just not as prominent as at other colleges. Students are "pretty laid back," effecting a "very welcoming atmosphere." Greek life isn't considered to be the "dominant force" on campus, though it does have a significant presence. Fraternities and sororities are perceived to "have parties all the time." One student noted, "If

you don't join up though, it is still very possible to have a vibrant social life."

Much akin to the average college, drinking is prevalent on campus, though students are "not shunned or judged" if they choose not to partake. Bars in Downtown Davis are a hot spot for students on Thursdays, Fridays, and Saturdays. Downtown Davis is "what you make of it," with one student describing it as having a "theme park" atmosphere. "Made for college students," the downtown area is generally perceived to be affordable, offering "a lot of deals and coupons." Popular attractions include line-dancing at the Davis Graduate and eateries such as Caffé Italia and CREAM.

Down-to-Earth Students

Students consider UC Davis to be "very diverse." One student said, "There are people from the bay area, from SoCal, and a lot of international students as well." A freshman added, "We have people from all walks of life and all with different opinions on how the world should work. You would find a niche here." While life can be a bit "lonely" at times due to the largeness of the campus, students at Davis are "friendly and genuine." Many students regard Davis as the "happiest UC." One freshman observed that "mostly people here are just obsessed with cows"—not necessarily a problem on a campus well known for its agricultural prowess.

> "We have people from all walks of life and all with different opinions on how the world should work. You would find a niche here."

Not Just a "Cow Town"

A freshman said, "I heard that [Davis] was a boring 'cow town,' but after visiting the campus, I fell in love." Though Downtown Davis is "cozy and friendly," central campus has plenty to offer. The Silo, a converted pig barn, is host to a variety of restaurants and—for students craving caffeine—Starbucks. The Silo Patio hosts a Farmer's Market every Wednesday. For those seeking to explore the more "peaceful" environs of Davis, the Arboretum features "a mile-long river" and 100 acres of gardens. The Quad is the heart of the Davis campus—students are "always laying out on the grass, taking naps or throwing Frisbees around."

Campus traditions include the Aggie Ball,

the Undie Run (a celebratory event during finals week), Pajamarino, and the Whole Earth Festival. One student advised "playing sardines [a variation on hide-and-seek] in the Social Sciences building," a space that resembles the "Death Star because of its metal exterior and maze-like layout."

UC Davis offers "woodsy" environs and an atmosphere befitting a small town, while providing an escape to the more bustling metropolises. One student sums up her experience well: "I think UC Davis is beautiful. I absolutely love it. It is such a breath of fresh air compared to the city I came from and I'm glad for the experience."—*Amanda Buckingham*

FYI
If you come to UC Davis, you'd better bring "a bike" and a "fantastic bike lock!"
Three things every student at UC Davis should do before graduating are "ride the double-decker bus," "take pictures with cows," and "explore the library—it's like magic."
What surprised me the most about UC Davis when I arrived was "how quickly I came to consider Davis my second home. The easy-going and welcoming atmosphere made the transition for me really easy and I can already tell how much I will miss it once I graduate."

University of California / Irvine

Address: 204 Aldrich Hall, Irvine, CA 92697-1075
Phone: 949-824-6703
E-mail address: admissions@uci.cdu
Web site URL: www.uci.edu
Year Founded: 1965
Private or Public: Public
Religious Affiliation: None
Location: Suburban
Number of Applicants: 45,742
Percent Accepted: 45%
Percent Accepted who enroll: 21%
Number Entering: 4,405
Number of Transfers Accepted each Year: 5,939
Middle 50% SAT range: M: 570–680, CR: 520–640, Wr: 530–640
Middle 50% ACT range: Unreported
Early admission program EA/ED/None: None

Percentage accepted through EA or ED: NA
EA and ED deadline: NA
Regular Deadline: 30-Nov
Application Fee: $60
Full time Undergraduate enrollment: 21,367
Total enrollment: 21,976
Percent Male: 46%
Percent Female: 54%
Total Percent Minority or Unreported: 78%
Percent African-American: 2%
Percent Asian/Pacific Islander: 51%
Percent Hispanic: 15%
Percent Native-American: <1%
Percent International: 3%
Percent in-state/out of state: 99%/1%
Percent from Public HS: 86%
Retention Rate: Unreported
Graduation Rate 4-year: 57%

Graduation Rate 6-year: 79%
Percent Undergraduates in On-campus housing: 41%
Number of official organized extracurricular organizations: 492
2 Most popular majors: Business/Managerial Economics, Political Science and Government
Student/Faculty ratio: 19:1
Average Class Size: 7
Percent of students going to grad school: 30%
Tuition and Fees: $33,030
In-State Tuition and Fees if different: $10,152
Cost for Room and Board: $11,611
Percent receiving financial aid out of those who apply: Unreported
Percent receiving financial aid among all students: Unreported

Halfway between Los Angeles and San Diego lies the sunny campus of UC Irvine. With beaches, restaurants and shopping destinations within close reach, students at this school can enjoy strong academics without a stressful atmosphere. Taking a peek at this low-key campus will reveal college staples such as supportive freshman dorms, as well as the bonuses of great meal options and a budding hip-hop scene.

Break out those calculators
At UC Irvine, math and science are kings. Students agreed that their school is more math, science and engineering based and stronger in these fields than in the humanities. This is

reflected in some of the popular majors on campus—biology (in which the school has a very strong department), chemistry and engineering; psychology and social sciences are also popular. Despite the science-leaning tendencies of the school, UC Irvine makes sure that its students get a well-rounded education through the Breadth Requirements, which require students to take classes across a variety of academic disciplines including social sciences, humanities and math.

On the whole, classes at UC Irvine tend to be on the large size, though "it depends on your major and the class you're taking," one junior explained. Writing or art classes typically have a max of 20–30 students, while lower-division bio classes can have up to 450 students. A psychology major said, "In the classes I have been in, the average number is about 150 to 200 students." Students said classes begin to get smaller in upper-division courses specifically in the major. To get into classes, students register according to how many units they have completed, so upperclassmen have first dibs. Students said certain classes—writing classes, labs, popular major/minor classes and GE's—are hard to get into because so many are competing for the same spots. However, students in the Campus-Wide Honors Program are one of the first to register for classes regardless of units taken, which is one of the major perks of the program. First-years get accepted into this program while they are still in high school (no additional application necessary), but current and transfer students must apply.

Grading at UC Irvine varies, depending on the professor's choice or the department. The more competitive classes such as biology, chemistry and mathematics are curved down so that a certain amount of A's, B's, C's, D's and F's are set in advance. For other classes such as language courses, they are curved in the sense that the maximum amount of students that can receive A's is 15 percent and the rest receive a B+ and lower. One junior explained, "It is definitely possible to get A's, but there are those teachers that make it hard to get them. The older professors are usually the ones that don't curve in their classes." But despite the occasional competitive curve and difficulty in getting into popular courses, "the academic life is very rewarding due to the prominent and notable professors that teach here," a Social Ecology major said.

Living in Irvine

For incoming freshmen, there are three main housing options—Middle Earth, Mesa Court, and Arroyo Vista. The first two are dorming communities, whereas students who live in Arroyo Vista need to take a shuttle to get to class since it is located off of the main campus. The application for first-year housing is very specific on helping students find the right people to live with, and according to upperclassmen, the freshman dorms are very comfortable and fit the needs of students living away from their parents for the first time. "It's recommended for first-years. You meet a lot of new people and learn a lot about each other," one student said.

The dorm community is composed of a variety of small buildings, each with specific themes that fit the students' interests, though some dorm rooms are nicer than others, depending on which hall you get. The general rule is, "The newer the hall, the bigger your room," as one junior put it. UC Irvine guarantees two years of on-campus housing, and most people move into on-campus apartments their second year after living in dorms as freshmen. In their third year, students move off campus to the many apartments near campus.

Each hall in the dorms has its own RA, but students say that they usually aren't that strict about policies because they are students themselves and thus, more lenient. In addition, a senior commented, "RA's for the dorms are really nice people and they act as mentors, friends, and teachers for freshmen—they help make living on campus fun and easy." Students praised Irvine for its safety, overwhelmingly citing Irvine as "one of the safest cities to live in" and being known as "the safest city in California."

As for food, there is a plethora of options in restaurants, both on- and off-campus. Even among the dining halls, there are distinctions—Mesa Court has one dining hall while Middle Earth has two. Students living in Mesa Court or Middle Earth have three meal plans to choose from, and one junior advised, "People usually never finish their meals so it's better to choose the cheapest one." She added, "The food seems to be getting better every quarter, and you can even choose from organic foods." In addition to dorm dining halls, there is also an on-campus food court which offers a variety of choices, including Chinese food, pasta, Quiznos, and Wendy's. For those who need their caffeine fix, there are two coffee shops on campus—Starbucks and Cyber A Cafe. UC Irvine also has its own pub and three other "restaurants" on different parts of the campus. Meal options include the option of flex dollars, which is money you can use at any of these places. Of course, the Southern California experience wouldn't be complete without In-N-Out, the quintessential California fast-food chain that serves fresh burgers and fries. Students can find one literally on their doorstep, as there is one right across the street from campus at the University Town Center, which also features a Yogurtland. In addition, you can find sandwiches, Mexican food and Japanese food, just to mention a few.

Feel the Beat

UC Irvine offers many clubs that fit specific interests and culture. One student noted, "Clubs are run by very enthusiastic members who are willing to give the time to making the club prosper and letting students feel comfortable." But another student added, "How much a person commits to their club/ organization really depends on the person." Many people are involved in culture clubs such as Chinese Association, Korean-American Student Association, and Tomo No Kai (Japanese Club), to name a few. Due to the school's student population, which students describe as not very diverse, these culture clubs tend to be Asian-American-oriented.

A school in the suburbs of Orange County with a majority of Asian students may not seem like it would have this reputation, but the campus features prominent hip-hop dance teams. "A lot of people know UCI as the 'hip-hop dance' university," a junior said. The school has four hip-hop teams, the most famous of which is Kaba Modern, which was featured on MTV's "America's Best Dance Crew." As a result, "a lot of hip-hoppers want to go to UCI," a student explained.

Students say there are many social scenes on campus, including the aforementioned cultural clubs and dance teams, in addition to academic clubs, a cappella groups and sports teams. But fraternities and sororities are by far the most dominant, students say. During the first two weeks or so of every quarter, the Greek society takes over the campus to promote their fraternities and sororities. One junior described the experience: "At the beginning of the school year, there will be booths set up at the club fair, as well as on Ring Road. You will get bombarded with flyers to rush for their fraternity/ sorority. Panhellenic frats and sororities

have a different rushing process than Asian fraternities and sororities." Thursdays are usually when fraternities and sororities have clubbing events, and conveniently, there are usually buses taking people to the club so they don't have to worry about drinking and driving. Students say that not everybody drinks ("Those who go to parties usually drink; those who don't go to parties don't drink"), but alcohol and pot are popular around campus. Dorm policies are the same as anywhere else—students can't get drunk in the dorms (no alcohol or drugs are allowed), but students can *be* drunk in the dorms. One student added, "I would say that the people who drink the most are those who are involved in sorority and frat events."

On other nights, students say they usually just hang out at each other's apartments or dorm rooms, or attend club events and meetings. Other low-key weekend options include going out to eat and shopping at Fashion Island in Newport Beach or South Coast Plaza and the Irvine Spectrum, which are popular malls nearby. In addition, students said many people have Disneyland passes and sometimes hang out and eat at Downtown Disney or go watch fireworks at night. One student said, "On the weekends, a lot of people stay or go home every other weekend, but usually, on the weekends there isn't really much to do in Irvine." On the whole, though, a junior summed up social life at UC Irvine as "it's what you make of it."

> **"A lot of hip-hoppers want to go to UCI."**

Students who end up at Irvine can expect to dress to impress, even to class. A Film and Media Studies major said, "People at school are definitely into fashion, and our school is good on keeping up with the latest fashion trends." However, he added, "There are also a lot of people who have their own style/attitude. Unlike high school, it's okay to dress the way you want and not be judged for it."

UC Irvine may not be as high-profile as its counterparts in Berkeley or Los Angeles, but the experience can be just as positive. As one senior reflected, "The people that come to this school are friendly and the atmosphere is welcoming and comfortable."
—*Della Fok*

FYI

If you come to UC Irvine, "you'd better bring money and a swimsuit."

What's the typical weekend schedule? "Most SoCal people leave on the weekends, which leaves all the NorCal people alone in Irvine."

If I could change one thing about UC Irvine, "I'd put on-campus apartments within walking distance of class. Why are off-campus apartments closer to classes than on-campus apartments?"

Three things every student at UC Irvine should do before graduating are: "make a lot of friends, join a club, and learn the area because there are so many restaurants around campus!"

University of California / Los Angeles

Address: 1147 Murphy Hall, Box 951436, Los Angeles, CA 90095-1436

Phone: 310-825-3101

E-mail address: ugadm@saonet.ucla.edu

Web site URL: www.ucla.edu

Year Founded: 1919

Private or Public: Public

Religious Affiliation: None

Location: Urban

Number of Applicants: 57,670

Percent Accepted: 33%

Percent Accepted who enroll: 24%

Number Entering: 4,610

Number of Transfers Accepted each Year: 5,330

Middle 50% SAT range: M: 600–740, CR: 570–680, Wr: 580–710

Middle 50% ACT range: 25–31

Early admission program EA/ED/None: None

Percentage accepted through EA or ED: NA

EA and ED deadline: NA

Regular Deadline: 30-Nov

Application Fee: $60

Full time Undergraduate enrollment: 25,416

Total enrollment: 40,675

Percent Male: 45%

Percent Female: 55%

Total Percent Minority or Unreported: 68%

Percent African-American: 4%

Percent Asian/Pacific Islander: 36%

Percent Hispanic: 16%

Percent Native-American: <1%

Percent International: 6%

Percent in-state/out of state: 93%/7%

Percent from Public HS: 76%

Retention Rate: 97%

Graduation Rate 4-year: 64%

Graduation Rate 6-year: 87%

Percent Undergraduates in On-campus housing: 36%

Number of official organized extracurricular organizations: 850

2 Most popular majors: Biology, Political Science and Government

Student/Faculty ratio: 17:1

Average Class Size: 15

Percent of students going to grad school: Unreported

Tuition and Fees: $34,496

In-State Tuition and Fees if different: $11,618

Cost for Room and Board: $13,968

Percent receiving financial aid out of those who apply: 55%

Percent receiving financial aid among all students: 49%

The sky's a powder blue, the grass a perfect green. The sun shines hot and white. Archways and bell towers are brick—buildings bake in the heat while a fountain shoots cool water into a cloudless sky. No, this isn't Tuscany. This is UCLA. James Dean and Jim Morrison walked these paths. Carol Burnett and Reggie Miller sauntered across these lawns. The University of California, Los Angeles is both slice of heaven in Southern California and one of the country's most rigorous colleges.

California Dreamin'

You might ask yourself—how can anyone study when it's eighty degrees out? But students at UCLA study all year round, despite perfect weather and a perfect location. UCLA is one of the country's most well-regarded universities—*U.S. News & World Report* ranks it as the second best public university in the nation. Students enroll in any of the five undergraduate colleges: the College of Letters and Science, the Henry Samueli School of Engineering and Applied Science, the School of the Arts and Architecture, the School of Theater, Film, and Television, or the School of Nursing. Considered the "academic heart of UCLA," the College of Letters and Science is ideal for those interested in the humanities, the social sciences, the life sciences, or the physical sciences. Students in the College of Letters and Science (that is, about 85% of undergraduates) can pick from over 109 majors and a wide variety of classes. The School of Engineering offers similar academic breadth, from civil engineering to bioengineering. And Ethnomusicology and World Arts and Cultures are popular majors in the School of Arts and Architecture. All of the colleges equally offer many minors and specializations, from Naval Science to Chicano studies. The colleges are all prestigious, but one student admitted that "it's easy for you to transfer from engineering," and not the other way around.

While UCLA has only a few entry-level requirements, each undergraduate must complete University requirements, College requirements, and Department requirements to obtain a bachelor's degree. For the most part, students meet the University requirements with AP credits and SAT scores. On the other hand, the College requirements vary and students of the College of Arts and Sciences must fulfill the so-called General Education requirements: three courses in the Foundations of the Arts and Humanities, three courses in the Foundations of Society and Culture, and four courses in the Foundations of Scientific Inquiry. While demanding, these requirements form an educational keystone, revealing "to students the ways that research scholars ... create and evaluate new knowledge" and fostering an "appreciation for the many perspectives and the diverse voices that may be heard in a democratic society." The GE requirements, said one student, "are, unfortunately, busywork." Using lists of classes that fulfill each requirement, students just "try to pick the ones that fit their schedules."

While those majoring in the humanities and social sciences don't have much trouble getting into classes, one student reported that STEM majors find the process "extremely difficult." However, some underclassmen obtain "junior or senior status" with Advanced Placement credits, and these underclassmen get priority at the beginning of the quarter, when picking courses online. Of course, a sophomore said that most "professors are willing to add a few extra students" if the class is already full. And since UCLA has quarters and not semesters, classes go by in a flash, a mere ten weeks. Though some students love this academic calendar, an English major complained that quarters were too short—"right at ten weeks, you're starting to build relationships with professors." Another

student agreed UCLA is "very fast-paced and the quarters take time to get used to" but it definitely "keeps you in check." No matter the hiccups, underclassmen and upperclassmen agree—UCLA's academics are great. A sophomore lauded "the diversity in what we study."

Sun's out, Guns out

But at UCLA, everyone's motto is *work hard, play hard*—students engage in a wide variety of activities outside the classroom. The University boasts of over 800 different clubs and organizations, each one more vibrant than the next. Even extracurriculars get competitive, noted one student, and it's important to feel "like you're actually participating in something important." For some, that something is the Armenian Students Association. For others, that something is UCLA's newspaper, *The Daily Bruin*, or *Prime*, the quarterly magazine. Many campus organizations are big time commitments, and one student compared her work for *The Daily Bruin* to "another class." Despite the strict requirements—staff writers must publish on a bi-weekly basis—that same student added that she loves being "a part of this huge production." As members of various organizations, students meet people and discover new passions. The Pediatric AIDS Coalition, for example, hosts a 24-hour dance marathon every year, bringing the whole campus together. And the University has a thriving a capella scene as well—UCLA's Spring Sing is an exciting mix of concerts and skits, showcasing the student body's musical and theatrical skills.

Of course, athletics are a "huge part of UCLA culture," noted one student. The UCLA Bruins compete in ten men's varsity sports and thirteen women's varsity sports. Part of the NCAA Division I, the Bruins have won 110 NCAA championships. Most recently, the women's soccer team won the 2013 championships. Alumni attend games at the Rose Bowl and the Pauley Pavilion. Most spectators deck themselves out in college paraphernalia or paint their faces True Blue and Gold, UCLA's official colors. The student body has a "huge team spirit," confirmed an undergraduate. And the big game (a football game against the University of Southern California) is really a full weekend of crazy parties and tailgates and bonfires, the yearly climax of a heated rivalry.

But most of the time, "Thursday night is party night," divulged one sophomore. While only thirteen percent of students participate in Greek life, many non-Greek students attend frat parties to unwind after a stressful week. A non-Greek undergraduate noted that Greek life is "relatively big on campus," but certainly not the only option. Students don't feel pressured to drink or go out—many eschew the "play hard" part of "work hard, play hard." But, said one student, "if you want it, you can definitely find it."

Living in the City of Angels

The beautiful, sunny Bruin Walk slices UCLA's campus in half, dividing North Campus from South Campus, the STEM classes from the humanities and social sciences. The farther north you walk, the "artsier it gets," explained one English major. While one student noted that this "creates a little bit of tension and obviously a separation," another added that GE classes bring North Campus and South Campus people together, allowing for diverse and interesting friend groups. One student mentioned that "flyering" is a "little too aggressive" on UCLA's Bruin Walk and so she avoids central campus altogether.

But housing has nothing to do with this divide. Most freshman live in triples that are "awful," according to one student. Sophomores, on the other hand, live in doubles and singles, while juniors and seniors live off-campus, in Westwood apartments. While the "newer dorms are phenomenal," the housing from the eighties is "not so phenomenal," reported one sophomore. "It just gets claustrophobic." However, students agree that their campus is both beautiful and surprisingly safe. While L.A. has relatively high crime

rates, "if you take the right precautions, everything should be fine," noted an on-campus undergraduate.

> "It's not that distracting since everyone's on top of their game. We all know when we need to crack the books."

The upperclassmen's Westwood apartments are quite nice, according to most students, and the surrounding area is lovely, full of shops and restaurants and theaters. Both Santa Monica and the Pacific Ocean are twenty-five minutes away and The Grove, a mall by Beverly Hills, is a welcome distraction. On the weekends, "a lot of people go hiking and a lot go shopping in Santa Monica," said one student. After sunset, many students hit "Hollywood to go clubbing." Yet despite the many temptations, "it's not that distracting since everyone's on top of their game. We all know when we need to crack the books."

In general, UCLA students see very few downsides to college life. The University's food is "excellent," the campus itself an architectural wonder, and the L.A. public transportation both convenient and cheap. "The best part of UCLA is the weather," laughed one sophomore. "You need motivation to keep going," said another. "But it's worth it." A third still couldn't believe her fellow students—"everyone at UCLA is so bright. I love it here."—*Amanda Buckingham*

FYI
If you come to UCLA, you better bring "flip-flops—everyone wears Rainbow flip-flops all the time."
If I could change one thing about UCLA, I'd change "the dorm situation because living in a triple takes its toll."
What differentiates UCLA from other colleges is "the atmosphere—people are genuinely happy and nice and they want to be here."

University of California / Riverside

Address: 1120 Hinderaker Hall, Riverside, CA 92521
Phone: 951-827-3411
E-mail address: discover@ucr.edu
Web site URL: www.ucr.edu
Year Founded: 1954
Private or Public: Public
Religious Affiliation: None
Location: Suburban
Number of Applicants: 26,478
Percent Accepted: 78%
Percent Accepted who enroll: 22%
Number Entering: 4,458
Number of Transfers Accepted each Year: 4,086
Middle 50% SAT range: M: 480–610, CR: 450–560, Wr: 460–570
Middle 50% ACT range: 19–24
Early admission program EA/ED/None: None

Percentage accepted through EA or ED: NA
EA and ED deadline: NA
Regular Deadline: 30-Nov
Application Fee: $60
Full time Undergraduate enrollment: 17,809
Total enrollment: 18,242
Percent Male: 48%
Percent Female: 52%
Total Percent Minority or Unreported: 84%
Percent African-American: 7%
Percent Asian/Pacific Islander: 38%
Percent Hispanic: 31%
Percent Native-American: <1%
Percent International: 1%
Percent in-state/out of state: 99%/1%
Percent from Public HS: 91%
Retention Rate: Unreported

Graduation Rate 4-year: 39%
Graduation Rate 6-year: 63%
Percent Undergraduates in On-campus housing: 32%
Number of official organized extracurricular organizations: 264
3 Most popular majors: Biology, Business, Psychology
Student/Faculty ratio: 19:1
Average Class Size: 27
Percent of students going to grad school: Unreported
Tuition and Fees: $34,652
In-State Tuition and Fees if different: $11,850
Cost for Room and Board: $12,100
Percent receiving financial aid out of those who apply: 77%
Percent receiving financial aid among all students: 74%

The orange groves and botanical gardens lining University of California, Riverside serve as vestiges of its past as the UC Citrus Experiment Station. The university opened in 1954, and because of its proximity to the Box Springs Mountains, commonly called the Highlands, it became known as home of the Highlanders. As an ode to the Highlands of Scotland, UCR's mascot Scotty the bear soon donned a kilt, and an impressive bagpipe team assembled.

U.S. News and World Report recently ranked UCR the fourth most racially diverse campus in the nation. With a student body that is 40 percent Asian, 30 percent Latino, 17 percent Caucasian, and 8 percent African American, UCR offers a cultural learning experience outside of the classroom. A freshman recalled a time when, unable to find a free table in the crowded lunch area, she sat in a random seat and struck up a conversation with two people who happened to be from Britain and Afghanistan. "Whenever a group of students comes out of a lecture hall, I see Asians, Caucasians, African-Americans . . . It makes the UCR community as a whole more open to new ideas and less biased towards others," said one undergrad.

Sibling Rivalry

Let's take a moment to confront the elephant in the room. Every UC has an acronym: there's University of Caucasians Lost among Asians (UCLA), UC Socially Dead (UC San Diego), University of Casual Sex and Beer (UC Santa Barbara), and then there's UC Rejected. UCR has a reputation as a safety school because of its higher admittance rate, 78 percent, compared to that of its older UC sister schools. "I just wish UCR had a better name," noted one freshman who turned down offers from UC Berkeley and UCSD to matriculate at UCR. And UCR certainly deserves more than what its reputation suggests. The university boasts an impressive faculty, keynote speaker events, and a modern, hip campus, qualities that have contributed to its growing number of applicants, and it will not be long before UCR outgrows its nickname.

Students' at UCR characterized the university as having more of a humanities emphasis and noted the university's strong business administration program. For those interested in medicine, a selective UCR/UCLA Thomas Haider Program in Biomedical Science consists of 24 undergrads who are guaranteed admission to UCLA's medical school. Students enrolled in UCR's honors program take extra workshops on top of their regular course load.

Classes fill up quickly, with lectures usually consisting of more than 150 students and discussion sections consisting of 20 to 30. UCR is home to such influential faculty members as Susan Straight, a Riverside native and professor in the creative writing department, who has won numerous awards for her novels. "The faculty keeps us up to date and goes out of their way to help us," said one student, who remembers a time in chemistry lecture when the professor was so inspirational that his class stood up, cheering.

Meet me at the HUB

On-campus housing is clean, albeit cramped. Some freshmen are forced to live in triples meant to be doubles. But the close comfort of the dorms, arranged by floors and halls, provides for late-night bonding. "There will always be people walking around and awake even at 4 a.m.," said a resident of East Lothian, one of the four freshman dorms. True to Highlander spirit, most buildings on campus are named after places in Scotland: Pentland Hills, Aberdeen, Stone Haven, etc. After freshman year, many students ditch their faux-Scottish abodes and move off campus into apartments, making UCR a major commuter school.

The place to be at UCR is the HUB, the Highlander Union Building. The three-story structure houses meeting rooms, lounges, restaurants, the school newspaper, and various administrative facilities. The focal point of the campus is the Bell Tower, which chimes on the hour, signaling the start and end of classes. On some days, a professional carillonneur can be heard, and Wednesdays at noon feature the aptly named "Nooners," small concerts at the tower that liven up the HUB.

R-Side

Located about 50 miles east of Los Angeles, the inland city of Riverside is nicely situated so that weekend excursions to L.A. or the beach are just a quick trip away. It helps to have a car while studying at UCR, although the parking situation is woefully lacking. As a result, parking has become both an art form and an exercise in stealth. "[Students will] follow students back to their cars, inching slowly behind them. Some will even give students a ride back to their car in return for their parking space. Others fail to find parking, skip class, and just head home," said one junior. For the locomotive challenged, the University Village beckons just a 10-minute walk away with theatres, restaurants, and shops. And for an instant getaway, just cross the street to Getaway Café, a sports bar where one senior said she met many of her friends.

Riverside is a nice town, but areas around it in San Bernardino County can be sketchy. "The police keep us too informed," said one student, who has since taken to carrying around pepper spray. Daily reports of all the robberies in nearby areas freak out the student body, making them extra vigilant.

TGIF

According to one junior, at UCR "there is no sign of human life on the weekends." Because so many students are from the SoCal region, the vast majority of the school heads home once class is out. Only a few special occasions keep undergrads on campus for the weekend: Block Party, Heat, and Spring Splash. The Associated Students Program Board (ASPB) coordinates these free concerts that take place during fall, winter, and spring quarter, respectively. Headliners such as Estelle, Common, Taking Back Sunday, Shiny Toy Guns, Far East Movement, Steve Aoki, and Nas have all performed in recent years. But devoid of this star power, students stay on campus only if they need to get work done in the ghost town that UCR provides over the weekend.

That is not to say that UCR doesn't know how to have fun. On Wednesdays, the frats and sororities congregate at the Bell Tower, and the atmosphere is "really social and lively," said one frat pledge. While Greek life plays a major role in the campus party scene, one need not be a member to partake in the revelry. ASPB planned a Homecoming Bonfire featuring fireworks, laser tag, a mechanical bull, and quintessential California cuisine: In-N-Out. But be forewarned—as in most colleges, alcohol is omnipresent. "Every party has alcohol, even a pajama party," said one markedly disappointed freshman who was startled by students' openness about drinking, drugs, and sex.

Here Comes the Sun

Seasonal affective disorder is not an issue at UCR, where the sun shines year round. And when the weather gets sweltering, the clothes come off. The beginning of fall term saw a daily uniform of tank tops, shorts, and sandals. "That was literally the least amount of clothing I could wear without people giving me weird looks, and I was still sweating," said one male undergrad.

> "Whenever a group of students comes out of a lecture hall, I see Asians, Caucasians, African-Americans . . . It makes the UCR community as a whole more open to new ideas and less biased towards others."

The sunshine that bathes UCR reflects the university's generally sunny disposition. It is a young, open, growing campus that offers abundant resources for those who wish to seek them out and an ethnic melting pot that is a learning experience in itself. But be sure to either have a car, friends with cars, or especially loving parents willing to double as chauffeurs, because come Friday, you'll want to be cruising down PCH or heading home for your mom's cooking. While UCR is alive and well five days a week, when it comes to the weekend, it knows there's no place like home.—*Cora Ormseth*

FYI
If I could change one thing about UCR, "I'd add a parking structure for undergrads."
What surprised me most when I arrived at UCR was that "everyone was from SoCal."
If you come to UCR, "you'd better leave your microwave and mini-fridge. They're provided in the dorms."

University of California / San Diego

Address: 9500 Gilman Drive, 0021, La Jolla, CA 92093-0021
Phone: 858-534-4831
E-mail address: admissionsinfo@ucsd.edu
Web site URL: www.ucsd.edu
Year Founded: 1959
Private or Public: Public
Religious Affiliation: None
Location: Suburban
Number of Applicants: 48,093
Percent Accepted: 38%
Percent Accepted who enroll: 22%
Number Entering: 3,947
Number of Transfers Accepted each Year: 6,408
Middle 50% SAT range: M: 610–720, CR: 540–670, Wr: 560–690
Middle 50% ACT range: 25–31
Early admission program EA/ED/None: None

Percentage accepted through EA or ED: NA
EA and ED deadline: NA
Regular Deadline: 30-Nov
Application Fee: $60
Full time Undergraduate enrollment: 23,289
Total enrollment: 23,663
Percent Male: 49%
Percent Female: 51%
Total Percent Minority or Unreported: 76%
Percent African-American: 2%
Percent Asian/Pacific Islander: 44%
Percent Hispanic: 13%
Percent Native-American: <1%
Percent International: 7%
Percent in-state/out of state: 97%/3%
Percent from Public HS: Unreported
Retention Rate: 95%

Graduation Rate 4-year: 55%
Graduation Rate 6-year: 83%
Percent Undergraduates in On-campus housing: 34%
Number of official organized extracurricular organizations: 568
2 Most popular majors: Biology/Biological Sciences, Economics
Student/Faculty ratio: 19:1
Average Class Size: 15
Percent of students going to grad school: 30%
Tuition and Fees: $35,006
In-State Tuition and Fees if different: $12,128
Cost for Room and Board: $11,684
Percent receiving financial aid out of those who apply: 77%
Percent receiving financial aid among all students: 63%

The University of California, San Diego, is one of 10 colleges in the University of California system and is located in La Jolla, California. The school was founded in 1959 as a science and engineering research institution in hopes of becoming the next CalTech. Today, UCSD is ranked one of the top public universities in America, known for excellence not only in scientific research but also in undergraduate academics and student life.

Get the GE out of the way!

The undergraduate program at UCSD is separated into five divisions. These include the Arts and Humanities, Biological Sciences, Physical Sciences, Social Sciences and the Jacobs School of Engineering. Students may take classes from any of these divisions, provided they complete their General Education (GE) Requirements. Depending on the residential college into which you are placed, your GE requirements can vary greatly. Some find the GE requirement a way to explore areas of interests outside of their major, while others find it a nuisance. One junior International Studies major complains, "I'm in Revelle which has the most GE requirements. I've had three quarters of chem, one of bio and physics, while other colleges have less!" There are six of these colleges and on top of designating your GE requirements they also serve as residential halls. Muir College is known to have very loose requirements and the most recently established Sixth College has requirements focusing on culture, art and technology. When applying, each student indicates which colleges they would like to study and live in, and for the most part "you end up where you're supposed to," said one senior.

Classes tend to be larger during freshman and sophomore years—many have up to 500 students in one lecture hall, with alternate times offered during the day. Upper division classes taken during the junior and senior years tend to be smaller and more intellectually stimulating. However, UCSD also offers Freshman Seminars to freshmen who miss the intimacy of high school classrooms. The offerings are unique, from French New Wave Cinema to Psychology of Humor.

Studying is a must and UCSD students make it a major priority. Students say that in general they take academics very seriously and many classes at UCSD are very competitive, in particular the science and engineering courses. "If one does not keep up with their work, they will lag behind for sure,"

said one junior. Another factor that makes academics fast-paced and intense for students is the quarter system. Rather than switching classes in the middle of the year like most colleges, UCSD adopted the unconventional quarter system. Most students claim to enjoy this rapid turnover "because you get to take a variety of subjects during one year."

The Jewel

While school takes up a majority of time for the UCSD kids, they still manage to get involved on campus, partake in festivities and kick back and relax. The name of the city La Jolla comes from the Spanish "la joya" meaning "jewel," and most students would agree that it's a gem of a city. It is primarily a suburban area known for its high-class neighborhoods and expensive rent. One student says of La Jolla, "The area is definitely pretty, the beach is right there, the air is clean, and we're so close to Sea World and the San Diego Zoo." However, the high cost of living and lack of parking space for cars can be a problem for students. But another junior claims, "Despite what others may say, there is a lot to do in La Jolla [without spending money]. My advice is . . . go on random adventures!" A senior in Warren College says, "I love La Jolla because of the climate. You can't beat sunny, high 60, low 50, every day of the year!"

> **"You can't beat sunny, high 60, low 50 every day of the year!"**

During the weekend, when they aren't studying, UCSD students can find a plethora of activities to engage in. The going-out crowd is rather small at UCSD and many of those that go out on the weekends are involved in Greek life. There are 10 fraternities and nine sororities on campus and some are known for throwing "insane" parties. Those who choose not to go Greek still have weekend options. San Diego and La Jolla have nightclubs and the campus is close to other college-populated towns at Mission Beach and Pacific Beach. An experienced senior added, "Also, it's only a 30-minute drive to Mexico where hundreds of underage students go to party."

Campus Traditions

While normal weekends are usually pretty tame, students go crazy during the annual Sun God festival, named for one of a dozen public art pieces on campus which together comprise the Stuart Collection. The Sun God is a winged structure by the artist Niki de Saint Phalle located near the Faculty Club. But the Sun God is also an all-day extravaganza with concerts, games, and "a lot of drinking." Although music aficionados complain that "they don't get very good performers or big names often," the majority agree that "it's great. You get to see all of your friends from all the colleges, enjoy a fun night with a free concert, and then head over to OVT (a late night café) and grab a midnight snack."

Another anticipated campus tradition is the Pumpkin Drop in the fall and the Watermelon Drop during the spring. The Watermelon Drop comes from a physics exam question in 1965 involving the velocity of a dropped object. The event today involves the dropping of a large watermelon from the top floor of Revelle College's Urey Hall and a beauty pageant resulting in a Watermelon King and Queen. One student cites this event as the "weirdest thing I've seen on campus." The Pumpkin Drop is similar but involves a large pumpkin filled with candy instead of a watermelon.

College Spirit?

Student life on campus is defined also by the various extracurricular activities that UCSD crs take part in. Due to the high percentage of Asian-Americans on campus, there are many cultural and political groups for various Asian-American interests such as the Japanese American Student Organization. Also, student-run papers are widely circulated. *The Koala*, a somewhat controversial, satirical humor paper, and the *UCSD Guardian*, the campus newspaper, are both read extensively on campus. Such enthusiasm is not universal, however. Despite UCSD's 23 varsity sports teams, most students agree that there isn't much support for the Tritons. "I wouldn't say UCSD is very school spirited. The lack of a football team probably makes it worse. I myself haven't been to any sports games," said one junior.

The aforementioned residential college system is by far the most significant aspect of student life at UCSD. "I personally like the college system," one junior in Muir College remarked. "It gives you that small campus feel within a larger university. I didn't understand the benefit of it going into school, but now it's one of my favorite features of UCSD. It allows you to meet more people and gives you a much more accessible administrative office and faculty." In fact, the college system is so ingrained into the students that some feel they have more spirit and pride toward their residential college than to the University itself. "I'm from Muir, the best college EVER!" exclaimed one senior.—*Lee Komeda*

FYI

If you come to UCSD, you'd better bring "a surfboard, a bike to get around the huge campus and a willingness to find a club that interests you."

What's the typical weekend schedule? "Usually, I have to put some time away for studying since UCSD is a quarter system and it moves quickly. We usually play a little beer pong, go out to eat, relax from the school week and just meet up with friends and socialize."

If I could change one thing about USCD, I'd "add more parking spaces. Parking on campus SUCKS!"

Three things every student at UCSD should do before graduating are "visit the cliffs of Black's Beach on a full moon, spray paint the stairwell at Mandeville and experience Mexico (the overrated-ness of Tijuana)."

University of California / Santa Barbara

Address: 1210 Cheadle Hall, Santa Barbara, CA 93106-2014
Phone: 805-893-2881
E-mail address: admissions@sa.ucsb.edu
Web site URL: www.ucsb.edu
Year Founded: 1909
Private or Public: Public
Religious Affiliation: None
Location: Suburban
Number of Applicants: 46,671
Percent Accepted: 46%
Percent Accepted who enroll: 17%
Number Entering: 3,700
Number of Transfers Accepted each Year: 5,622
Middle 50% SAT range: M: 560–680, CR: 540–650, Wr: 540–660
Middle 50% ACT range: 25–30
Early admission program EA/ED/None: None

Percentage accepted through EA or ED: NA
EA and ED deadline: NA
Regular Deadline: 30-Nov
Application Fee: $60
Full time Undergraduate enrollment: 18,806
Total enrollment: 19,186
Percent Male: 47%
Percent Female: 53%
Total Percent Minority or Unreported: 61%
Percent African-American: 3%
Percent Asian/Pacific Islander: 14%
Percent Hispanic: 18%
Percent Native-American: 1%
Percent International: 1%
Percent in-state/out of state: 97%/3%
Percent from Public HS: 87%
Retention Rate: 91%

Graduation Rate 4-year: 62%
Graduation Rate 6-year: 81%
Percent Undergraduates in On-campus housing: 33%
Number of official organized extracurricular organizations: 423
3 Most popular majors: Biology, Economics
Student/Faculty ratio: 17:1
Average Class Size: 25
Percent of students going to grad school: Unreported
Tuition and Fees: $36,473
In-State Tuition and Fees if different: $13,595
Cost for Room and Board: $13,345
Percent receiving financial aid out of those who apply: 55%
Percent receiving financial aid among all students: 66%

I magine a warm, sunny Saturday afternoon spent lounging on the beach with your friends and planning for another night out together. If you are a student at the University of California, Santa Barbara, this isn't a dream Spring Break vacation, but is, instead, a typical day of living and learning on the southern California coast.

Life's a Beach, but School is School

The 17,000 undergraduates, called Gauchos, who call UCSB home quite literally live on the beach, something in which most students take great pride. It's no surprise that the presence of their very own beach only adds to the laidback, West Coast culture UCSB embodies. In fact, while the architecture of UCSB is not particularly noteworthy, with a "hodgepodge of buildings that are concrete 60s institutional style, while others are ultramodern," as one student described, students feel that the abundant natural beauty of the campus more than makes up for what is lacking. Students' favorite places on campus were, appropriately, "Campus Point," where the campus meets the sea, and the lagoon walk.

Academics at UCSB, however, are no vacation. The school has a stellar reputation in the sciences and engineering, and the Bren School of Environmental Science is nationally renowned. While such science majors are highly regarded, students admit that "there is a definite lack of respect toward the 'easy' majors," with a zoology major adding, "here it's like, 'Oh, you're a communications major? How is tanning and drinking with no homework?'" Some classes, on the other hand, are appreciated by both science and humanities students as being easy and fun. Several students interviewed said that some of their favorite classes had been theater classes. "I've taken all the theater and film classes I can without having to declare it as a major," explained a sophomore math major.

Some new, state-of-the-art science facilities parallel these departments' strengths. A particular highlight is the Marine Biology building, with one side of the building designed to look like a lighthouse and a room at the top with windows that offer a 360-degree view of the surrounding area, including the Pacific Ocean and the Santa Ynez Mountains. Even more impressive than the facilities are the professors who teach in them: five UCSB faculty members are Nobel Laureates.

A universal complaint about the university's academic atmosphere is the effects of severe budget cuts due to the state government's recent financial crisis. With fewer classes offered and fewer faculty members to teach these classes, it is often difficult for students to enroll in popular or required courses. "It took me two quarters of 'crashing' classes to get into general chemistry!" griped the zoology major. Students "crash" a course when they are unable to enroll during registration and employ various strategies in an attempt to eventually land a spot on the roster. Many UCSB students are all too familiar with this process.

While it may be difficult to secure a spot in these popular introductory courses, the classes are large, sometimes reaching 800 students. This contributes to an "anonymous" type of academic experience, said a biology major. "Our professors don't know us past our student I.D. numbers. Nobody will hold your hand in anything." Many students agreed that it is the responsibility of the student to make personal connections with professors during office hours, through which faculty make themselves "easily accessible," according to a math major. She added that when students do attend office hours, they find that "UCSB's faculty is extremely nice."

I.V., D.P., and UCSB

When the weekend finally rolls around, UCSB proudly lives up to its party school reputation. Every weekend, you'll find the ragers in Isla Vista. The name is simply shortened to "I.V." by Gauchos and Santa Barbara City College students, who live—and party—in the area as well. I.V. is a tight-knit community right off campus, in which 50 percent of the residents are students. Their apartments, packed in next to each other over the span of a few blocks, are also home to some serious revelry at night. "It's pretty wild, pretty crazy," said a

political science major attempting to explain the party scene to an outsider. The craziest, and most popular, of these parties are usually to be found on the beach front street Del Playa (called "D.P.") in student apartments with prime ocean views. The most famous night of debauchery is on Halloween, "a ridiculous, multiday orgy that people from all over California attend." Another revered UCSB party occurs right on the beach, and more specifically in the ocean itself. For Floatopia, held each spring, "everyone brings floaties and booze and then makes giant drinking rafts!" Recently, however, the police have been cracking down on Floatopia, and last year they closed the beaches altogether to prevent the students from celebrating. Students cleverly changed the name of the event that year to "No-topia."

It's Not All Greek to Me

With such a vibrant party scene, it might surprise people to know that Greek Life, while certainly present, does not dominate the social scene as it does at many other large state schools. A freshman member of a sorority explained, "The Greek system is not a large part of UCSB social life," saying that only 2 of her closest friends are also involved. Still, she said, "I love being Greek because it makes such a large school smaller." While the parties in the few weeks after sorority and fraternity rushes "could compete with *Old School* and *Animal House*, they mellow out from then out and consist of parties called TG's (themed gatherings)," says the sorority member. As a non-Greek student explained, "People will sometimes go to frats for parties, but mostly they stay on D.P. Ocean views beat puke filled yards any day!" Prospective students will be happy to know that there is, in fact, no dominant social group at UCSB. As the same non-Greek student described it, "everybody indiscriminately parties regardless group." A freshman added that, when it comes to nightlife, "There is really no single group you could award all the fame to. There are always random people enjoying life and partying large."

Sailing the Not-So-Sober Seas

And when these groups party together, they drink together. While students agree that most people drink, they also say there are students who do not. A Greek member said, "There is a large population of people who sail the sober seas. I personally don't know them that well, but they are there!" That being said, when students are partying in I.V., drinking has a strong presence. When asked if there are problems with binge drinking, a biology major responded, "I like to count the amount of ambulances I hear heading to D.P. on the weekends. Does that answer your question?" Overall, however, most students manage to party responsibly. In terms of drug usage, marijuana is most common. "Marijuana is more popular than cigarettes here," said one student. All students agreed that harder drugs, while they can be found, are not seen very often. Students who choose not to imbibe still have options for having fun on the weekends. State Street is a shopping district in Santa Barbara with movie theaters and restaurants as well, and is a popular hang-out destination for students. Students also insist that the best things to do at UCSB don't even involve drinking. One freshman explained, "There are so many active things to do besides drinking. You can go to the beach, play volleyball, play in the sun, and so on. I believe that is the best way to make friends." Another student added that, while parties are fun, "my best times at UCSB are spent watching the sunset with my closest friends while someone plays the guitar."

Who Are We, Anyways?

Students overwhelmingly enjoy the social scene their school has to offer, but all are quick to point out that their parties do not define UCSB and its student population. "We party a lot, but we study a lot too. People somehow manage to do it all," argues a senior. Another student added that her fellow Gauchos aren't simply party lovers. When describing the student population, she offered, "There's a multitude of democrats, hippies, free spirits, and beach lovers, but all students are intelligent and have motivation and goals. As the school gets harder to get into, I believe UCSB will be characterized with more respect!" Still, one student had a less enthusiastic view of the student population. "Our school is not that diverse. There are a lot of bro surfer dudes and bleach blondes with the occasional Asian." Other students believe that these ideas of "typical" surfer bros and ditzy blondes are just stereotypes. One freshman said, "I was surprised to meet so many genuine, academically driven people. It is not a shallow

environment. It's a beautiful place to learn and make life-long friendships."

Get Involved

What do Gauchos do when they're not studying, partying or at the beach? Plenty. While one student complained that, "people aren't that involved—I feel like they are either busy partying or busy studying," other students had different views, saying their classmates were "very committed" to extracurricular activities. Some students like to cheer on their sports teams, just not the typical ones. One student observed, "Our soccer games get sold out pretty quickly!" That's not surprising, considering the UCSB men's soccer team is very competitive and won the NCAA championship in 2006. It is important to note, however, that UCSB lacks a football team, which some students saw as a negative feature, in that there is not much school spirit on campus. Varsity sports don't have a large presence, but students are often found being active themselves at the gym. The athletic facilities received high marks from students. "They are like a temple for working out! We even have an indoor rock climbing wall," said a sophomore. Other students prefer to stay active in alternative ways, such as through the Excursion Club. The Excursion Club, one of UCSB's best-known student groups, goes on outdoor adventures throughout the year, including hiking, skiing, rock-climbing, and even skydiving! Luckily, with UCSB's location in southern California, all of these activities are possible within relative proximity to the campus.

For students seeking extracurricular involvement through less adrenaline-rushing means, options still abound. The daily campus newspaper, *The Daily Nexus*, is the only entirely student-run daily newspaper in California, and all students interviewed agreed that it is the most popular student publication at UCSB. Still, opinions were mixed. One student said, "It is really only a source of sudoku and crosswords during lecture." That's better than Facebook, at least.

When they're not in class, students can also become involved with the UCSB Student Entrepreneurship Association (SEA). SEA is a group for business-minded students to engage in networking and a resource for transitioning into the job world after graduation. One student interviewed said his friend was a member who, in true Santa Barbara fashion, designs his own surfboards.

Sweet Home Santa Barbara

Students find meeting new people easy at UCSB, and those interviewed said the freshman year dorms are most conducive to making new friends. One student explained, "it is so easy to become close with people you live with and see around often," and all students interviewed said that living in the dorms are an essential—and fun—part of the freshman experience at UCSB. There are seven dorms for freshmen only, one dorm for all classes, and one exclusively for upperclassmen. Most students seem satisfied with on-campus housing, noting that three of the dorms even have ocean views. After freshman year, most students decide to move into apartments in Isla Vista, but the university is currently adding more dorms so that 50 percent of the student population will be able to live on campus. Even upperclassmen in Isla Vista nostalgically think back to their time living on campus as freshmen. "The dorms are very nice and clean, and they are probably the most social places anyone will ever live!" said one sophomore.

> "My best times at UCSB are spent watching the sunset with my closest friends while someone plays the guitar."

It is clear that most students feel at home at their school, whether they are studying in the library, partying in Isla Vista, or enjoying the California sunshine on the beach. While Gauchos may have to deal with budget cuts and large class sizes, they are still able to graduate with a highly respected—and memorable—college education. When asked if she would choose UCSB again if she had to do it all over, one student affirmed, "Yes. We don't have a small-school feel or a football team, but we compromise. UCSB is truly unique."—*McKenna Keyes*

FYI
If you come to UCSB, you'd better bring "a bike lock, a bikini, and maybe a pen."
What's the typical weekend schedule? "Going out at night, going to the beach when it's warm during the day, and reading in the afternoon."
If I could change one thing about UCSB, "I'd make everyone just a bit more studious to increase our reputation. Instead of being 'the party school,' being the school that 'parties and works hard.'"

University of California / Santa Cruz

Address: Cook House, 1156 High Street, Santa Cruz, CA 95064
Phone: 831-459-4008
E-mail address: admissions@ucsc.edu
Web site URL: www.ucsc.edu
Year Founded: 1965
Private or Public: Public
Religious Affiliation: None
Location: Suburban
Number of Applicants: 27,658
Percent Accepted: 65%
Percent Accepted who enroll: 18%
Number Entering: 3,291
Number of Transfers Accepted each Year: 3,374
Middle 50% SAT range: M: 520–640, CR: 500–630, Wr: 510–620
Middle 50% ACT range: 22–27

Early admission program EA/ED/None: None
Percentage accepted through EA or ED: NA
EA and ED deadline: NA
Regular Deadline: 30-Nov
Application Fee: $60
Full time Undergraduate enrollment: 15,411
Total enrollment: 15,668
Percent Male: 47%
Percent Female: 53%
Total Percent Minority or Unreported: 55%
Percent African-American: 3%
Percent Asian/Pacific Islander: 23%
Percent Hispanic: 20%
Percent Native-American: 1%
Percent International: <1%
Percent in-state/out of state: 97%/3%
Percent from Public HS: 87%
Retention Rate: Unreported

Graduation Rate 4-year: 45%
Graduation Rate 6-year: 66%
Percent Undergraduates in On-campus housing: 48%
Number of official organized extracurricular organizations: 151
2 Most popular majors: Art, Business
Student/Faculty ratio: 19:1
Average Class Size: 15
Percent of students going to grad school: Unreported
Tuition and Fees: $36,294
In-State Tuition and Fees if different: $13,416
Cost for Room and Board: $14,727
Percent receiving financial aid out of those who apply: 59%
Percent receiving financial aid among all students: 56%

F amous for once employing the pass/fail grading system and known by many as a "hippie" school, the University of California at Santa Cruz offers an exciting, though somewhat alternative college experience. Located in a redwood forest on the coast of Northern California, UC Santa Cruz provides students with a liberal arts education in a relaxed environment.

Pass/Fail? Not quite.

Although Santa Cruz no longer employs its infamous pass/fail, many students still describe academics at Santa Cruz as laid back and not too intense. Although students seem satisfied with academics, some wish they were more rigorous. "It'd be nice if it were more challenging," said a student. Freshmen usually take large intro lectures, which many students say they do not feel they need to attend. Distribution requirements are easy to fulfill. Students love the mandatory core and writing classes. Based on his or her interests, each student picks a residential college before

arriving at Santa Cruz, and the core classes are smaller seminars with around twenty students that center around the college's theme; for example, Porter College's theme is Arts in a Multicultural Society and one of its core classes is called "Arts Practicum." Even for the larger lectures, students feel professors are accessible and easy to get to know because of the small number of graduate students. "All of my professors and TA's have office hours twice a week," said a student, "so it's easy to get help if you need it."

Although Santa Cruz is known for being less academically prestigious and easier to get into than the other UC's, it is also famous for many of its science departments, including astronomy, engineering, and other sciences. "It's a very science-related school," said a student. "A lot of kids here are majoring in some kind of science." Many students, however, major in the humanities and social sciences, with economics as one of the most popular majors. There are many research opportunities for undergraduate research because of the small number of graduate students.

Where are all the parties?

Santa Cruz provides a unique college experience. Though it exists, Greek life does not have a large presence on campus. There are five fraternities, but they are not housed. Santa Cruz also does not have a lot of school spirit when it comes to sports, and there isn't much turnout for athletic events. Most of the partying takes place off campus because alcohol and drug policing is strict. "The social life is pretty laid back," said a student. For those looking for the traditional college social life, UC Santa Cruz may not be the right place for them. "It doesn't feel like the college experience," said one student. "People are stuck in their dorms a lot." Santa Cruz does, however, provide students with other opportunities to socialize. One of the most popular clubs is the Ski and Snowboard Club. Intramural sports are also popular. Many students also love the communities within their residential colleges. "The RA's plan a lot of events for freshmen in their colleges," said one student. "I made most of my friends in the dorms."

Students love the school's location. The campus is located in a redwood forest about a fifteen-minute bus ride away from the beach. "It feels like you're hiking when you walk to class," said one student. "In a good way. It's beautiful." Students also frequent the downtown Santa Cruz area, which like the campus has an alternative vibe. "They don't like chains in Santa Cruz," said a student, "so there are a lot of little independent shops and restaurants. Really unique stuff." Since Santa Cruz doesn't have a traditional party scene, many students, especially freshmen who are not allowed to have cars, come to the downtown for the weekends for off-campus parties at upperclassmen's houses or just to hang out and watch a movie.

The quality of on-campus housing varies between residential colleges. Freshman dorms can be anything from cramped to comfortable with lots of space. Building types also vary by college; for example, College 8 is like "a Victorian house" but is "crappy inside," while students in Stevenson live in a series of smaller houses. Most sophomores live in on-campus apartments that students describe as being spacious with a kitchen, living room, dining room, and bedrooms upstairs. There is a two-year housing guarantee, so many juniors and seniors move off campus into houses in Santa Cruz, though these houses are "really expensive" because they cater more to the wealthier inhabitants of Santa Cruz than to students. Food also varies between residential colleges, and there are some popular on-campus cafes like Oaks Café and Tacos Moreno, where students can use their meal plan "flexis."

Nudity?

Santa Cruz has a number of quirky traditions that define the UCSC experience. "No one should leave Santa Cruz without doing at least one naked run," said a student.

"The first rain in a year, students run through campus naked." In addition to naked run, "4/20" is an important Santa Cruz tradition when on April 20 students take to a part of campus called East Field and spend the day smoking pot. "It's a total weed school," said one student. Indeed, Santa Cruz has a reputation for being a weed-hippy school, but what is the Santa Cruz student body really like?

The student body is ethnically diverse but not as diverse as other California schools with about 50 percent of students identifying as Caucasian. About 97 percent come from within California, but in terms of the type of people that go to UC Santa Cruz, there seems to be a range. "People can be too laid back," said one student. "So laid back that they don't want to do anything." Still, others say it's impossible to categorize. "Everyone here is so different," said one student. "You really can't call the people as hippy or prep or those kinds of things."

> **"Santa Cruz students are laid back. It's not too intense here."**

For students who want a college experience a bit different from the norm, UC Santa Cruz would be a good prospect. The campus is beautiful, located in a redwood forest next to the beach. Those who are not concerned with Greek life and sports would do well to consider UC Santa Cruz.—*Lia Dun*

FYI
If you come to Santa Cruz, you'd better bring "pot."
If you come to Santa Cruz, you'd better leave "your bike. The hills are devilish."
Three things every student at Santa Cruz should do before graduating are "naked run, 4/20, hike."

University of Redlands

Address: 1200 East Colton Avenue, Redlands, CA 92373-0999
Phone: 909-748-8074
E-mail address: admissions@redlands.edu
Web site URL: www.redlands.edu
Year Founded: 1886
Private or Public: Private
Religious Affiliation: None
Location: Suburban
Number of Applicants: 3,757
Percent Accepted: 67%
Percent Accepted who enroll: 25%
Number Entering: 646
Number of Transfers Accepted each Year: 179
Middle 50% SAT range: M: 520–620, CR: 520–620, Wr: Unreported
Middle 50% ACT range: 22–27
Early admission program EA/ED/None: None

Percentage accepted through EA or ED: NA
EA and ED deadline: NA
Regular Deadline: 1-Apr
Application Fee: $30
Full time Undergraduate enrollment: 3,032
Total enrollment: 4,431
Percent Male: 45%
Percent Female: 55%
Total Percent Minority or Unreported: 46%
Percent African-American: 3%
Percent Asian/Pacific Islander: 4%
Percent Hispanic: 4%
Percent Native-American: <1%
Percent International: 1%
Percent in-state/out of state: 69%/31%
Percent from Public HS: Unreported
Retention Rate: 86%
Graduation Rate 4-year: 54%

Graduation Rate 6-year: 66%
Percent Undergraduates in On-campus housing: 53%
Number of official organized extracurricular organizations: 106
3 Most popular majors: Business/Marketing, Social Sciences, Liberal Arts
Student/Faculty ratio: 15:1
Average Class Size: 19
Percent of students going to grad school: 41%
Tuition and Fees: $37,302
In-State Tuition and Fees if different: No difference
Cost for Room and Board: $11,206
Percent receiving financial aid out of those who apply: 85%
Percent receiving financial aid among all students: 79%

Boasting an enviable location in the midst of Southern California, the Univeristy of Redlands lies at the base of the magnificent San Bernardino Mountains. The desert landscape is indicative of the great weather year-round, but also serves as a reminder that a Redlands experience without a car can quickly turn into a very isolated one. Most students find a way to get around the small city and many say they appreciate the college's small size, citing the student entering class size and the 15:1 student-faculty ratio as proof that they are more than just numbers here. "Coming from a small high school, I feel like Redlands has helped make the transition a very smooth one," said one junior. "Almost all of my professors know my name and I often see them outside of class." With a beautiful campus, small classes, and professors who are interested in teaching, Redlands seems to offer a good deal; that is if you're willing to pick up the tab.

When Nature Calls: Being Aware of Your Surroundings

The Redlands campus has been used as a set for recent films such as *Rules of Attraction* and *Joy Ride*, but even if the college grounds are attractive, it's the surroundings that stand out the most, for they offer great opportunities for students to interact with nature. Students recognize their surroundings as full of opportunities for wildlife observation, rock climbing, hiking, mountain biking, photography or just camping out. To this end, Redlands helps organize "Outdoor Programs" which may last from as short as a weekend afternoon to a month during the summer. "Going out on the hot air balloon was the coolest experience ever!" recalled one student. Other available excursions include bungee jumping, skiing, snowboarding, skydiving and surfing.

For those who wish to take their own initiative, Redlands has everything the casual outdoorsman needs: tents, sleeping bags, backpacks and rain gear are all available to students for free. Although a credit card is required as deposit, students generally agree that the rental shop is very accessible. "As long as you plan a few days in advance, you can usually get what you need."

Unfortunately, while its surroundings may be a paradise for the outward bound, the small city of Redlands (population approximately 75,000) does not have much to offer. The town is a little far from central campus, but almost everyone either owns a car or knows someone who does. The trolley system that operates during the mornings and afternoons doesn't run during the nights, but it's usually easy to catch a ride. Downtown Redlands boasts many of the most popular fast food shops, as well as some fancier Italian restaurants and coffee shops, which students and townspeople frequent. Besides going downtown, students use their cars to "catch a late-night snack or go shopping at the nearby outlet malls." One student agreed that "Redlands will definitely get dull very quickly if you don't get out often." He commented that he and his friends often go into downtown Los Angeles or San Diego. Some upperclassmen also go to Las Vegas—about five hours away.

Making Service a Way of Life

Although students often reveal their concern for the lack of economic diversity at Redlands, one thing that can be said about the kids here is that they know how to get their hands dirty to serve others. Community service is integrated into the curriculum and students must complete a combination of service instruction and outreach requirements. While some students serve at the local high schools, others use their summers or May terms to go as far as Africa. One senior recalled her experience with helping victims of Hurricane Katrina as "one of the most enriching experiences of my entire life." She added, "I felt like I was really making a difference in people's lives and I really want to go back." The same student agreed that Redlands seems to attract a more service-oriented crowd, "but it's not like a huge deal for everyone."

A Bold Academic Experiment

The flagship of the Redlands academic experience is the Johnston Center for Integrative Studies. Requiring a supplemental application, the center admits a limited number of the incoming freshman class. Students in the Johnston Center have unparalleled control over their education. Students may create their own major and choose their own courses. They are also allowed to write contracts for individual courses, leaving it to the students to decide how they will go about meeting their educational needs and which requirements they will fulfill. Quizzes may be substituted for longer tests or papers, and vice-versa. It's also possible to increase or decrease the credits for many courses by contracting to do more or less work.

However, as is true of many things, there's a catch: each contract must be negotiated between the student and the professor, and complete academic freedom is more of an aspiration than a reality. All Redlands students are also expected to graduate with sufficient "depth" and "breadth" in their studies. "The distributional requirements are complex and pretty burdensome," a freshman pointed out. "I think it's a little easier for the Johnston kids because they don't have to take any particular courses, but for those in the LAF [Liberal Arts Foundation], there's not that much freedom because you have to be worrying about your requirements so much."

Unlike large research universities, Redlands is focused on teaching. Students express a lot of respect for their faculty and really like the individualized attention. "My expectations have been surpassed over and over again," said one student. Another student added: "Having such small classes helps me keep motivated. I feel like I know my professors and my professors know me. I also know who I'm working with and that makes me feel much more comfortable. I don't think I'd be as motivated if I were taking larger classes at a bigger school." Most people refer to their peers as "competent" or "smart," but generally agree that the school "does not attract the biggest minds. Most kids care about their classes and study, but their interest rarely goes beyond the classes they're taking. This is not the kind of place where you'll find people discussing philosophy all day, although politics seem to be a common dinner table topic."

One aspect of Redlands that is appreciated by almost everyone in the community is the strong emphasis that is placed on study abroad. Although the focus is often on European countries to the exclusion of other regions of the world, there are ample opportunities for Redlands students to study a semester or a whole year abroad through a university-approved program. The most popular study abroad destination is Salzburg, Austria. Credit and financial aid are easily transferable. Students hoping to spend less time abroad may also opt to take one of the courses during the "May term." The May term refers to one month of intensive study, usually undertaken abroad. Courses during the May term include "Japanese Gardens" and "Economics in Buenos Aires."

Housing for All Tastes

Redlands doesn't approach housing in a "one-size-fits-all" fashion. While all undergraduates are guaranteed a room on-campus, every year, students can choose to live in one of the dozen or so different halls. Each of these housing complexes has its own perks and advantages. Some of them, like East Hall, are for freshmen only, while Cortner Hall and Melrose Hall tend to have more upperclassmen. Melrose, with its extended quiet hours, is also seen as a good fit for the more studious. On the other hand there's North Hall, the closest to the gymnasium and thereby host to many of Redlands' jocks. Some of the halls are same-sex, but most are coed.

"Most people seem to be happy with their living conditions," one junior said. "The most common complaint about housing is that some halls are not air-conditioned and it can get extremely hot during the summer." Students are advised to bring a fan—or several. "It was pretty bad the first few weeks of the fall semester," noted a freshman. "However, for most of the year the weather was just perfect." Still, those who hail from colder weather may often be less excited. SNOW (Students in Need of Winter) is a student group that brings together all those who are interested in following the ski season in the nearby Sierra Nevada.

Besides the regular housing options, students may also elect to live at one of the fraternity or sorority houses. Although there are several Greek organizations around campus, they don't seem to dominate the social scene. "Generally, there are a few guys who are really into it, but Greek life just isn't as big as you would expect." Students estimate that less than 10 percent of their peers have donned Greek letters.

It's Not Just About the Academics

Redlands offers a fairly wide variety of extracurricular activities and student groups. Opportunities for giving back to the community are plentiful through volunteer groups and there are many student-run religious and cultural organizations as well. The University also has an outstanding debate society, often placing among the top in the country. In fact, debate is valued so much at Redlands that the University offers merit scholarships for outstanding debaters.

Everyone has an opportunity to play sports—at some level—at Redlands. "It's fairly easy to be a walk-on at Redlands if you played in high school," said one junior who plays for the basketball team. "Some kids certainly get recruited, but some sports membership may be almost half walk-ons." The most popular club sports include golf, lacrosse, ultimate Frisbee and ice hockey. There is also an equestrian club.

While many find Redlands too small by the end of their four years, most enjoy the tight-knit community it affords. Within that community, some complain of "a total lack of diversity," and one student remarked that the stereotypical Redlands student was "your average intellectual rich white kid from the West Coast." This does seem to be changing, as Redlands has been recruiting more widely and applications have been increasing significantly in recent years. For all its insularity, Redlands seems to be about unexpected surprises. Whether students enjoy uncovering these hidden treasures will dictate whether they survive their four years out in the oasis of the Californian desert.
—*Gerardo Giacoman*

FYI
If you come to Redlands, you'd better bring: "a car or a friend who has one; also, bring a fan, or several in case your housing unit is not air-conditioned."
What's the typical weekend schedule? "Fraternity parties are prevalent during the weekends, but with the recent crackdown on alcohol consumption, weekend nights usually involve hanging out with friends, or getting out of Redlands to find a real party."
If I could change one thing about Redlands, I'd "move it closer to Las Vegas and fight the formation of social cliques."
Three things that every student should do before graduating are: "attend the festival of lights, make a 2 a.m. Del Taco run, drive to Mexico for Spring Break."

University of Southern California

Address: 700 Childs Way, Los Angeles, CA 90089-0911
Phone: 213-740-2311
E-mail address: admitusc@usc.edu
Web site URL: www.usc.edu
Year Founded: 1880
Private or Public: Private
Religious Affiliation: None
Location: Suburban
Number of Applicants: 33,760
Percent Accepted: 24%
Percent Accepted who enroll: 35%
Number Entering: 2,973
Number of Transfers Accepted each Year: 2,558
Middle 50% SAT range: M: 650–750, CR: 620–720, Wr: 640–740
Middle 50% ACT range: 29–33
Early admission program EA/ED/None: None

Percentage accepted through EA or ED: NA
EA and ED deadline: NA
Regular Deadline: 10-Jan
Application Fee: $65
Full time Undergraduate enrollment: 17,380
Total enrollment: 36,896
Percent Male: 45%
Percent Female: 55%
Total Percent Minority or Unreported: 59%
Percent African-American: 6%
Percent Asian/Pacific Islander: 25%
Percent Hispanic: 25%
Percent Native-American: <1%
Percent International: 11%
Percent in-state/out of state: 58%/42%
Percent from Public HS: 55%
Retention Rate: 96%

Graduation Rate 4-year: 68%
Graduation Rate 6-year: 86%
Percent Undergraduates in On-campus housing: 41%
Number of official organized extracurricular organizations: 642
3 Most popular majors: Business/Marketing, Social Sciences, Visual and Performing Arts
Student/Faculty ratio: 9:1
Average Class Size: 15
Percent of students going to grad school: 29%
Tuition and Fees: $42,818
In-State Tuition and Fees if different: No difference
Cost for Room and Board: $12,078
Percent receiving financial aid out of those who apply: 60%
Percent receiving financial aid among all students: 38%

To find a Trojan, you don't have to go back to Greek mythology; in fact, you can find more than 16,000 of them right here in the heart of sunny Southern California. USC students, just like the warriors for which they were named, are filled with pride and tradition. And unlike other schools that may have reputations for being "nerd schools" or "party schools," USC students say their school has the best of both worlds. As one senior said, "USC is becoming more focused on academics, which is reflected in its increasing national and international standings, but the great thing about this campus is that the social atmosphere has not taken a backseat to the greater focus on academics." From the time students step onto the beautiful campus that forms a backdrop for many a Hollywood movie, to the many years students have after graduation, USC students are and will always be Trojans.

Nuts and Bolts of the Classroom

Class sizes at USC vary, and depend on what type and level of classes you're looking for. As one junior explained, "USC boasts about having smaller class sizes, but that's not necessarily true. Just because it's a private school doesn't mean the ratios get any smaller." Average lecture halls can run up to 300 students in one room, but writing classes, which everyone has to take, are usually limited to only 12–15 students. Students say that getting into core classes isn't competitive since there are more available seats than students, but spots for interesting elective classes, such as Ballroom Dancing 101, can fill up pretty fast, especially with juniors and seniors who have priority. Both class sizes and grading usually vary between departments—popular majors on campus are Business, Biological Sciences, and Communications, and majors known for being particularly difficult are Architecture, Engineering, and the sciences in general.

Grading at USC, while not super generous, is fair, students say. "Since I'm a pre-med major, my workload is immense compared to other majors. Being a science major is competitive already, but being a pre-med is even more competitive," said a student majoring in Biological Sciences. Good thing competitive core science classes are curved, then. This system saves a lot of students—students who get B's or B+'s on exams will still probably end up with an A-, or even an A, by the end of the semester. One senior added, "Most classes are curved and there also many professors who don't mind giving A's to everyone who deserves them." Smaller classes like business and language classes usually aren't curved, but the general rule of thumb is that if it's a class with a lot of people, it will be curved.

Professors, however, can be a mixed bag. While most instructors are accessible and easy to talk with during their office hours, others are less open. Professors who are here for research—since USC is a research school—are required to teach as well, so those who would rather bury themselves in work don't try to make themselves accessible to students. Luckily, Trojans have other means of finding academic support in the form of study groups, which students readily form to help each other out. "I like that the atmosphere isn't generally a cutthroat competition. The school really wants us to do well so they make a lot of resources available to students like supplemental instruction and free tutors," a junior said.

Trojans Gone Greek

It's no coincidence that USC has a dominant Greek scene—after all, their Greek nature is practically written in their Trojan name. A freshman noted, "Everyone knows not to make plans with a frat/sorority member on a Monday night because they have to go to Monday night dinners." Greek life is evident all throughout campus, but the core is off-campus on West 28th Street, more commonly known as The Row. With a fifth of the total student population involved with Greek life, and many more involved in service and ethnic Greek communities outside Panhellenic and Interfraternal councils, it's no surprise that much of the partying that goes on at USC happens out on The Row. However, good times are not just limited to frat parties—students often also hit up the 9-0 Bar, a local favorite, and house parties hosted in apartments. And with the City of Angels in their backyard, USC students also have the opportunity to go clubbing in the hot streets of Downtown Los Angeles.

While not everyone at USC drinks, a large majority do—one student guessed that upwards of 80 percent of the students on campus drink. While binge drinking is not so big

a problem that the University needs to address it, students recognize they have peers who regularly drink at unhealthy levels. But beyond drinking and partying, USC also offers many other opportunities to kick back and enjoy the Southern California sun. Students say having a car is nice, but not necessary since it's easy to find other friends who have cars for exploring the area. Even students who live nearby stay on campus over the weekends. It's easy to get into the heart of L.A., and there's always something fun to do. Places to explore range from Little Tokyo and Chinatown to the fashion district, and they're all within a few miles of each other. One junior enthusiastically, and simply, described USC's social life as "Great!" as she went on to explain, "I like USC because the people there are smart, but they still know how to have fun. I guess it's just the atmosphere of being in Southern California and how it's always so chill."

The social scene at USC is a dynamic one. One senior reflected on his experiences at USC and said, "There is a niche for everyone. If you are into the arts scenes, then you can find that. If you are into partying, then you can find that. There is something for everyone. It is up to the student to find the right fit."

Diversity at USC is present, but at the same time, also lacking. Students say that the typical USC student is rich—indeed, "University of Spoiled Children" is a common nickname for the school. There are frat boys and sorority girls who tend to be rich because going Greek requires a fair amount of money, but there are also many students who are on financial aid, so not necessarily everyone is loaded. "A typical USC student is a white trust fund baby, but there are also a lot of students here from a modest background," one student said. Students say there are a lot of preps, jocks, and band geeks like in high school, but that USC is less cliquish. Despite diversity in interests and geography, to name two facets, students said their peers tend to hang out within their own ethnic groups. But at the end of the day, as one junior noted, "I find that USC is really diverse and many 'groups' are just chill, down-to-earth kinds of people."

Pimp My Housing, Please?

To be frank, housing at USC is not great. Underclassmen have priority in on-campus housing, but even then, students usually move out by the time they are sophomores. This is because of USC's rather limited geographical area—the campus is right in the middle of South Central Los Angeles—so there isn't much room for expansion. "Freshmen and sophomores get priority in choosing University housing, so if you're a senior, I would say good luck in trying to find a place to live," a junior said.

Most off-campus apartments are about a block or more away from campus, and the farther away from campus you get, the more dangerous it is. While USC may get a bad reputation for being in the middle of South Central, students say the campus is safe at night, if you stay conscious about it. "They always tell us to walk in groups and not to be alone at night. The dumb students are the ones who walk home alone at 3 a.m. after a party—they're the ones who get robbed," a senior explained. Students say housing at USC needs to be improved, and the school has started what it calls a Master Plan and has already started buying property and building new housing complexes near campus.

> "I felt like I was able to ease into college comfortably because the campus makes a huge effort to get people involved and people really fall in love with USC."

As for meal options, one student described them as "kind of sucky." USC has two cafeterias—EVK and Parkside, the latter of which serves more international foods and is generally regarded as the better dining hall. The Ronald Tutor Campus Center has a food court, a minimarket w/ sandwich shop, a nice cafe, and a fancy restaurant. The center is huge, with a big atrium, ballrooms, and tons of meeting rooms across two buildings. There's also Café 84 which is "alright"; one student summed up USC's dining options as "Most are mediocre." Students can also go out to the 9-0, which is a bar near campus, or stay on campus and go to Traddie's, which is short for Traditions Bar.

Hope You Like Football!
While housing and food may leave students wanting more, USC's extracurricular activity opportunities just might be the thing to fulfill a Trojan's appetite. One aspect of USC that is extremely important is students' dedication to extracurricular activities. With more than 700 student organizations, there is definitely something for everyone. One popular extracurricular is community service.

"Our geographic location near Downtown Los Angeles allows us to become deeply involved in community service. I love that USC encourages community service and the strong sense of family is a strong plus," said one student who is the president of a service fraternity.

The most visible outside-the-classroom activity is one in which only a small fraction of the student population directly participates. But while the number of students on the field as football players and cheerleaders is quite small, many students make it out to the stadium for football games. With pre-games, tailgates, and post-parties, football at USC is everything you've seen on national television and more. "We're practically defined by our football team. If you don't buy a spirit card, which allows you to go to football games and more, you are probably crazy for not doing so," one junior said. Even students who aren't into sports find themselves among the most hardcore of USC football fans. "There's a huge football culture on this campus. There is extreme pride and everyone from students to alumni goes all out. On game days, every single inch of the main campus is filled with people and everyone is wearing red," a senior said.

Join the Family
This dedication to USC football reflects something larger, which is the dedication to the school as a whole. Students say they are part of "the Trojan Family" and that a strong sense of pride and tradition is instilled in them from the first day they step onto campus. "I felt like I was able to ease into college comfortably because the campus makes a huge effort to get people involved and people really fall in love with USC," a junior said. Partly because networking is so important at USC, relationships are strong within the school and outside of it. Alumni come back for career fairs and workshops looking specifically to hire fellow Trojans, and it is these lasting ties that form the core of what it means to go to USC. One student explained, "Whenever I see a fellow Trojan outside of school, even if they are a stranger, there's already a connection because of the school. Sometimes we may exchange a few words or a 'Fight On!' sign while passing by. It sounds kind of cheesy, but it's true."

Reflecting upon her time as a Trojan, one senior said, "I think that a lot of people have a misconception that USC is just a school full of rich kids, and that students basically buy their diploma. I also used to believe this before I entered, but I was surprised that most of the people I've met come from middle-class families, and most wealthy students do not flaunt their wealth." So if you're ready to challenge yourself, and have your preconceptions challenged as well, get ready to immerse yourself in the Trojan family and make friendships and connections that will last a lifetime.—*Della Fok*

FYI

If you come to USC, you'd better bring "an open attitude to different types of people and personalities because you never know who you will end up becoming friends with here at USC."

What's the typical weekend schedule? "Thursday is the big party night because many people don't have classes on Fridays: they call it 'Thirsty Thursday.' People have small parties every night, though, and a lot of people go to Hollywood or Westwood on the weekends."

If I could change one thing about USC, "I'd change its location to an area with more shops and restaurants so there would be more things to do."

Three things every student at USC should do before graduating are "join a club, fraternity or sorority, go to at least one football game, definitely, and eat at Chano's, which is this old Mexican drive-through place that looks dirty, but it's really good Mexican food!"

Whittier College

Address: 13406 Philadelphia Street, Whittier, CA 90608
Phone: 562-97-4238
E-mail address: admission@whittier.edu
Web site URL: www.whittier.edu
Year Founded: 1887
Private or Public: Private
Religious Affiliation: None
Location: Urban
Number of Applicants: 2,196
Percent Accepted: 70%
Percent Accepted who enroll: 19%
Number Entering: 292
Number of Transfers Accepted each Year: unreported
Middle 50% SAT range: M: 460–590, CR: 470–580, Wr: 470–570
Middle 50% ACT range: 19–25
Early admission program EA/ED/None: EA

Percentage accepted through EA or ED: Unreported
EA and ED deadline: 1-Dec
Regular Deadline: Rolling
Application Fee: $50
Full time Undergraduate enrollment: 1,400
Total enrollment: Unreported
Percent Male: Unreported
Percent Female: Unreported
Total Percent Minority or Unreported: 65%
Percent African-American: 7%
Percent Asian/Pacific Islander: 11%
Percent Hispanic: 11%
Percent Native-American: 1%
Percent International: 2%
Percent in-state/out of state: Unreported
Percent from Public HS: Unreported
Retention Rate: 78%
Graduation Rate 4-year: 52%

Graduation Rate 6-year: 52%
Percent Undergraduates in On-campus housing: 63%
Number of official organized extracurricular organizations: 68
3 Most popular majors: Social Sciences, Business/Marketing, Parks and Recreation
Student/Faculty ratio: Unreported
Average Class Size: 15
Percent of students going to grad school: Unreported
Tuition and Fees: $36,992
In-State Tuition and Fees if different: No difference
Cost for Room and Board: $10,598
Percent receiving financial aid out of those who apply: 72%
Percent receiving financial aid among all students: 72%

1,695 undergraduate students attend Whittier College, a small liberal arts school 18 miles southeast of Los Angeles in the city of Whittier, California. Students at Whittier take advantage of the school's small student body and class sizes by forging strong relationships with their classmates and professors.

Fewer Students, More Options

The average class size at Whittier is 17 students, and the school boasts a 13-to-1 student-faculty ratio. Many of the classes are discussion-based seminars that allow plenty of interaction and strong relationships with professors. Class sizes do vary below and above the average, but one student reported that "even the biggest classes are small." Another enthused, "Professors really know who you are and know what your aspirations are. They'll try to get you internships and point you in the direction that you need to be. It's very nurturing."

Whittier offers over 30 majors and about as many minors. According to an upperclassman at the college, two popular majors are those in business and kinesiology, especially among the school's varsity athletes, who make up a significant portion of the school.

One unique aspect of the Whittier education is the January term, or "Jan Term." For one month between the fall and spring semesters, students focus their energy on a single course that can be on essentially any topic. One student took a class on Clint Eastwood films, and another took a trip to Greece after taking a Greek class during the fall.

To accomplish its goal of offering a liberal arts education, Whittier has distributional "Lib Ed" requirements that take up almost half of every student's curriculum. Each student must take three or four courses in each of the "Four C's": community, communication, cultural perspectives (including foreign language classes), and connections.

Every freshman must take a College Writing Seminar, a course in the community category that is connected to another class on any of a number of topics. These two linked classes have the same students to allow the class to bond as a group. One student interviewed took a course on the US-Mexican border, and another had taken a course on Fairytales. The subject of the writing seminar doesn't matter as much as "learning how to write a college paper," one student said. He added that the class significantly helped his writing during his transition to Whittier.

True Community Feel

In order to maintain a close-knit community on Whittier's campus, all students are required to live on campus through their junior year. Freshmen live in one of three freshman dorms that are concentrated in the same area on campus. One freshman said that the physical proximity of the freshmen community made it easier to get to know everyone when he first arrived on campus. Students are allowed to choose their roommates for their freshman year, and many athletes take advantage of this policy by rooming with teammates. Freshman roommates take the same College Writing Seminar in the fall in order to foster an educational bond early in every student's career.

Sophomores and juniors can live in one of six upperclassmen residential halls. A favorite is Harris Hall, which has suites for 12 to 16 people. Seniors often move off campus to apartments and houses, most of which are close by, but some require a drive to and from class. Most sports teams have houses off-campus, and other houses belong to societies, which are Whittier's equivalent to fraternities and sororities. The societies are a small part of Whittier culture, and one student noted that there is a social divide between athletes and society members.

Most students, especially those living on campus, have a meal plan that allows them to eat at the Campus Inn, or CI, the campus dining hall. Student opinion on the food is mixed—one student said that she liked it, and that "they really try to do gourmet food," while another said that it's "standard cafeteria food." Other food options include restaurants in downtown Whittier and The Spot, an on-campus store that serves late-night snacks from sandwiches to Mexican food.

A Nightlife Dominated by Sports

Whittier students are generally active during the weekends, and sports team houses often host parties that are open to all students. Whittier is a dry campus, but one student estimated that well over 60 percent of students drink at off-campus houses. Another said that parties at sports houses are "definitely the dominant social scene," especially because all of the sports teams at the school get along so well together. He estimated that half of non-athletes generally intermix with the athlete crowd on weekends.

Alcohol use is common, and marijuana is "prevalent but not a huge problem," one student said. Another said that a minority of students uses hard drugs, but that they are not at all prevalent among students.

For those seeking a more low-key nightlife, Whittier still has plenty in store. There are often movie screenings and drama productions on campus, which are popular, and The Spot is open until 11 every night including weekends.

And for those with cars, which nearly half of students have on campus, Los Angeles is just 18 miles away. A junior said that bars in L.A. are popular for students who are 21, but most who are underage stay in Whittier on the weekends. Students can also take advantage of the hot California weather in the fall and spring and head to beaches on the coast, which is a half hour drive from the campus.

A Small, Diverse Campus

Many students agreed that Whittier's small student body size is one of the most defining aspects of the college. With fewer than 2,000 students on campus, and about 1,700 undergraduates, it is easy to get to know a large chunk of the student body without much effort. A junior said that at first, the small size was "a shock for me, because it's not really the traditional college experience whatsoever. But looking back on it, I wouldn't be as close to as many people as I would if the school was bigger. You walk into a party and you know everyone there. It's more of a homey community vibe than most colleges."

Because "everyone knows everyone," one student said, random hookups are less common at Whittier than at bigger schools. "There are actually a lot of relationships for a small school," he said.

> **"It's not really the traditional college experience whatsoever."**

Despite the small size, Whittier maintains one of the most diverse campuses in California. About 50 percent of students are students of color, and about a third are Latino. Most students come from the West Coast, but 28 states and 14 countries are represented in total. With such a variety of interests on campus, students have the opportunity to pursue just about any extracurricular club or activity, ranging from the Associated Students of Whittier College Senate, the school's student government, to KPOET Radio, a student-run radio station. More than 60 other clubs are registered with the school, including a live action-role playing club and the Quaker Campus, the school's student-run newspaper that publishes weekly. Intramural sports are also quite popular, especially football in the fall and soccer in the spring.

One of the most popular activities, however, is competing on one of Whittier's 22 varsity sports teams. The Whittier Poets compete in the Southern California Intercollegiate Athletic Conference in NCAA Division III. Some of the most popular sports are soccer and lacrosse, and the men's water polo program is consistently a national contender.

With a community so diverse in demographics and interests, most Poets find what they want in their four years at Whittier. If you're seeking a small, tight-knit school with warm, Los Angeles weather year round, Whittier may be the school for you.—*Greg Cameron*

FYI
One thing that surprised me about Whittier was "how quickly I came to know everyone."
If I could change one thing about Whittier, it'd be "the housing rule. Juniors should be able to live off campus."
One item every Whittier students need to bring with them is "a fan to deal with the California heat."

Colorado

If Colorado College had a mantra it would be something along the lines of to be yourself is to fit in; it's a good thing we can all manage that. And the Block Plan, its heart and soul, is not too shabby itself, especially against the rugged Colorado backdrop. With the school's geographic paradise, structural freedom, and one-of-a-kind student body, your years at Colorado College can be whatever you want them to be.

Block Plan

Colorado College is the Block Plan. An alternative to the classic three-to-four-classes-at-once term, blocks allow students to really zoom in on one subject that especially sparks their fancy. The academic recipe: step one—give a topic your undivided attention for eighteen days; step two—repeat eight times. Note: even if you get tired of whatever it is

that you're learning, remember to pour in your all. While the structure stipulates that students soak in a whole course of information in less than a month, it also allows for more hands-on creative ways of acquiring knowledge that are unlike those of the anonymous lecture. If you don't want to be stuck in a classroom, you don't have to be. Another step in the recipe—sprinkle on some real-world experience. According to one junior, at Colorado College, "geology classes can study geology in the Rocky Mountains [and] Homer's epic poems can be taught in the Mediterranean." The whole experience can be a whirlwind, though; don't expect to have hours and hours of time to yourself. In the face of so much stress, "quirky dressing is a must," one senior says.

The school's statistics themselves are impressive. Classes cannot have more than twenty-five people per instructor, meaning that students learn in smaller groups, a stimulating method channeling cooperation, participation, and preparedness. This also allows for stellar relationships between professors and their students; each teacher is more than happy to sit down with a pupil to discuss whatever it is that may be of interest. This always-present availability of help balances out any difficulties that could arise from all that there is to do. In a survey of favorite professors, the most commonly mentioned was history scholar Dennis Showalter, but so were teachers from most departments; in reality, each member of the faculty has strengths, it just depends on with whom students decide to develop connections. Students describe grading as reasonable; there is no hyper-curving. The most intricate process seems to be that of choosing classes, though it has its good and its bad—one must make the best use of his or her 80 points each year. As one sophomore says, "it just depends on how good of a gambler you are."

Cracking Conventionality

With Colorado College's cozy-sized student body, a cold shoulder is never turned—not in the classroom, and especially not in the community. A categorization of Colorado College students: uncategorizable. There is every kind of person on the campus expressing him or herself in every way. A senior remarked that "the only way of dressing that isn't commonplace is the 'preppy' look." And a group of individuals comes with a guaranteed open-mindedness, at least to a certain extent. The block system makes for a pretty interesting group of people, too; because everyone has chosen to dedicate themselves so wholeheartedly to one subject matter, there is always something to talk about with soon-to-be friends and oh so many different intellectual thirsts. A sophomore assures that she has "learned to look deeper within the meaning of diversity," for while there may be a "lack of ethnic diversity . . . people who seem the same as you by looks are very different."

> "People who seem the same as you by looks are very different."

A junior describes the "variety of annual parties, such as Halloween, XXXmas, Winter Ball, Drag Ball, and Llamapalooza,"

some with musicians, some with activities, and some with both. If anything rules the party scene it is the festivities of the sport teams, not the Greek life that sometimes defeats all other kinds of life; parties are accessible—there really is no sense of the exclusivity that is sometimes integral to college merrymaking. Because students want to party together, if you want to get in somewhere, you can. While athletes are known for hosting fun events, they are in no way unapproachable. The earthen Colorado hills make it difficult to not love being outside; sports-related endeavors are a large part of students' experiences—not in a cliquey sense, per se, but in an appreciating-your-surroundings way. Treks through the wilderness that is Colorado never get old—don't forget your tent!

Daily Details

Students' experiences with the dorms can be sculpted by their specific needs. While, for the most part, freshmen live alongside one another, sophomores, juniors, and seniors are given more of a choice. If you enjoy a certain subject or hope to pursue a certain lifestyle, there may be a specific house to satisfy that need. Seniors can choose to leave the traditional dorm for their own places, however many opt out, preferring to stay close to those with whom they have grown up on campus. Students feel safe going out at night; an alarmingly high rate of crime is certainly not a pertinent problem. If any issue should arise, Resident Advisors' ears are open, without fail. Food is prepared for every eater, always with a healthy swing; the central dining hall, Rastall, is cushioned by smaller eateries, more specialized in their dishes. As for the presence of illegal substances, those most consumed are alcohol and drugs, of which the most popular is marijuana. There is no especially restricting alcohol policy—just don't make an intoxicated fool out of yourself. If you look, you can definitely find harder things, but there is no pressure to use them.

After Class?

Whatever it is that Colorado College students gain through the trials and tribulations of their arduous curriculum without a doubt transfers to other facets of their lives. Sports are a huge part of the lifestyle, especially with such a conducive setting. While hockey and soccer are the most well-known, hype-worthy sports, most students use their free time to play intramurals, whether on campus or around it. These games are huge community builders—multitudes gather at games. Others are involved in whatever their specific interests are—theater, sculpture, music; if you like something you will be encouraged to pursue it. And whatever that is, there is genuine student support—students love to see what their peers have created.

If your search for the perfect school is at least partly shaped by the idea of a place where freedom comes with all of the other classic marks of an A+ institution, you're not going to get much closer. Colorado College is that place, surrounded by organic earthly beauty, intellectually explorative students, and, of course, the Block Plan. It really does never get old.
—*Liliana Cousins*

FYI

Three things every student at Colorado College should do before graduating "are 1) the incline [a grouping steps that seem to go on forever] 2) Bombs and Wings 3) DU-CC Hockey game."
The biggest college-wide event at Colorado College "is Psychedelic Bowling."
If you come to Colorado College, "you'd better leave your high heels behind."

Colorado School of Mines

Address: 1500 Illinois Street, Golden, CO 80401
Phone: 303-273-3200
E-mail address: admit@mines.edu
Web site URL: www.mines.edu
Year Founded: 1874
Private or Public: Public
Religious Affiliation: None
Location: Suburban
Number of Applicants: 9,785
Percent Accepted: 46%
Percent Accepted who enroll: 19%
Number Entering: 875
Number of Transfers Accepted each Year: 128
Middle 50% SAT range: M: 600–690, CR: 540–640, Wr: Unreported
Middle 50% ACT range: 25–30
Early admission program EA/ED/None: None

Percentage accepted through EA or ED: NA
EA and ED deadline: NA
Regular Deadline: 1-Jun
Application Fee: $45
Full time Undergraduate enrollment: 3,456
Total enrollment: 4,488
Percent Male: 79%
Percent Female: 21%
Total Percent Minority or Unreported: 25%
Percent African-American: 2%
Percent Asian/Pacific Islander: 5%
Percent Hispanic: 6%
Percent Native-American: 1%
Percent International: 4%
Percent in-state/out of state: 78%/22%
Percent from Public HS: 90%
Retention Rate: 84%
Graduation Rate 4-year: 27%

Graduation Rate 6-year: 63%
Percent Undergraduates in On-campus housing: 43%
Number of official organized extracurricular organizations: 126
3 Most popular majors: Chemical Engineering, Mathematics, Mechanical Engineering
Student/Faculty ratio: 15:1
Average Class Size: 16
Percent of students going to grad school: 14%
Tuition and Fees: $25,248
In-State Tuition and Fees if different: $11,238
Cost for Room and Board: $7,626
Percent receiving financial aid out of those who apply: 91%
Percent receiving financial aid among all students: Unreported

The name of the University may be slightly misleading. Yes, the Colorado School of Mines does place a great deal of importance on mining, but that is only a small portion of what it does. In fact, the University is considered to be among the best engineering schools in the country. Located in Golden, Colorado, a town originally built to serve miners, the School of Mines was founded in 1873 and even operated its own experimental excavations to teach students about the intricacies of mining. Today, it is home to more than 4,000 students and represents one of the most important research institutions in Colorado and a top destination for engineering students.

Not Just Mining

Given the name of the University, it is obvious that not too many humanities majors attend the school. Of course, CSM does offer some social sciences programs, but they are mostly limited to a bachelor of science in economics or a number of minors in subjects such as humanities and international economy. As a result, the focus of the University is on applied sciences, engineering, and geology, the three main academic divisions of the university. "Our school is obviously an engineering school," said one student. "It is a public school, but we are really prestigious and we receive some of the best technical training you will find anywhere." Furthermore, the school is mostly focused on undergraduate education, as less than one-quarter of the student body are postgraduates.

Given the specialized nature of the University, CSM only has 13 academic departments, ranging from economics to metallurgy. There are less than 30 majors offered at the school, and only one—Economics—is not science and engineering related, although it is important to point out that a bachelor of science in economics also requires a great deal of training in mathematics. For those interested in liberal arts, a select number of minors are also available to broaden the students' knowledge in humanities and social sciences. "We have programs in things like humanities," said one student. "But think about it: when you go to a college called the School of Mines, not too many people are going to take those kinds of classes."

The academics at CSM are vigorous. An example of the demands of the coursework is the long list of required classes at the school. CSM, like most other schools, has a core sequence of classes that must be taken by all students to ensure that everyone has the skills necessary to succeed in college. Unlike other institutions, however, the required classes at CSM are very specific. For example, everyone must take Calculus I, II, and III, Differential Equations, and a number of physics and chemistry classes. While students at many other schools can choose among a variety of classes often vaguely related to numbers to fulfill their requirements in mathematics, students at CSM undergo very intense and specific training. "The core courses are important because you are going to need them anywhere," said one student. Indeed, given that almost everyone is in a field related to engineering, the calculus classes are essential for the rest of their stay at the university.

Given the academic vigor, it is not surprising that students do feel the pressure from the classes. "People say that introductory engineering classes are supposed to overwhelm people who are not fit to major in engineering so that they can go and choose other things," said one student. "I don't think it is that way, but you definitely have to work to keep up with classes." While the classes can be difficult and the professors sometimes very demanding, students also sense that they do have easy access to their instructors. "The school is not that big," said one student. "That's why we do get to meet and talk to professors very often. It's great because you don't get that in many other schools."

> **"The city is not big, but it has everything I need as a college student."**

One other advantage of attending CSM is that it is a research university, thus presenting students the opportunity to experience real-life applications of what they learn in the classrooms. The different engineering labs and institutions provide the more entrepreneurial students with a head start in their future academic pursuit or simply allow them to see what the top scientists and engineers do in their jobs.

The University is ranked among the top 100 national universities by the *U.S. News & World Report*. It accepts 46% of the applicants, but entering the university is no easy task. It has a very selective process. After all, given the academics of the school, it is important for prospective students to have the ability to follow the course load of CSM as well as have the quantitative skills demanded by many of the school's classes.

Not So Fun but Plenty of Beer

Besides the presence of CSM, the city of Golden is perhaps best known for being home to one of the largest breweries in the world, the Coors Brewery, which offers tours and, sometimes, access to an enormous amount of beer at a discounted price. Besides the brewery, the city is relatively small, and the economy greatly dependent on the University. It is located in the foothills of the Rocky Mountains and is only 15 miles away from Denver. Therefore, even though it has a population fewer than 20,000 people, Golden does have easy access to other parts of Colorado, not to mention a great view of the mountains from the University's campus. "The city is not big, but it has everything I need as a college student," said one junior.

No one is required to live on campus. However, the school strongly recommends students live in University residences at least for the duration of freshman year, which is often considered an essential part of college experience. The majority of first-year students do choose to live in dorms. Furthermore, living on campus gives students different benefits, such as tutoring, which can be much more difficult to access when living off campus. "The residence halls are not great," said one student. "But you definitely meet more people, so you should stay on campus during your freshman year. After that, most people find apartments elsewhere." In fact, the majority of upperclassmen choose to live away from CSM's campus. Some people do choose apartments at Mines Parks, which are unfurnished and close to campus, thus allowing students better accessibility to the university's facilities while being able to live off campus.

The party scene at CSM, however, is relatively uninteresting. The Greek life exists but is not particularly vibrant. Students do hold parties during weekends, but it is clear that CSM is not a party school. "You will find some things to do during weekends, but there is not much variety," said one student.

"If you want, you can also go to Denver, which is not that far if you have a car," added another student.

A School for the Future

In recent years, CSM found great success in its athletic programs, which mostly compete in Division II. The football team has received some recognition in the national media for being a very good program, but the most successful athletic program is cycling. In fact, given the location of the University, it is not surprising that the school is a mountain bike powerhouse, finishing in the top three in the nation several times during the last few years.

For students willing to work hard during their college years and looking for a top-notch engineering degree at the price of a public university, look no further than CSM. Of course, Golden is not the busiest city in the world, and the party scene may leave students with some small disappointments. Nevertheless, it is clear that the school offers a very good education, not to mention a great deal of interaction between professors and students. It is a widely recognized institution with a number of research opportunities even for undergraduates. Therefore, do not let the name School of Mines make you believe that it is only a school about digging up coal from mountains. It is much, much more than that.—*Xiaohang Liu*

FYI
If you come to CSM, you'd better bring a "work ethic."
What is the typical weekend schedule? "Some studying and hanging out with friends."

Colorado State University

Address: 1062 Campus Delivery, Fort Collins, CO 80523-8020
Phone: 970-491-6909
E-mail address: admissions@colostate.edu
Web site URL: www.welcome.colostate.edu
Year Founded: 1870
Private or Public: Public
Religious Affiliation: None
Location: Suburban
Number of Applicants: 12,494
Percent Accepted: 86%
Percent Accepted who enroll: 42%
Number Entering: 4,392
Number of Transfers Accepted each Year: 2,012
Middle 50% SAT range: M: 500–620, Cr: 500–600, Wr: 560–660
Middle 50% ACT range: 22–26
Early admission program EA/ED/None: None

Percentage accepted through EA or ED: NA
EA and ED deadline: NA
Regular Deadline: 1-Feb
Application Fee: $50
Full time Undergraduate enrollment: 20,765
Total enrollment: 27,030
Percent Male: 48%
Percent Female: 52%
Total Percent Minority or Unreported: 16%
Percent African-American: 2%
Percent Asian/Pacific Islander: 3%
Percent Hispanic: 6%
Percent Native-American: 2%
Percent International: 1%
Percent in-state/out of state: 79%/21%
Percent from Public HS: Unreported
Retention Rate: 83%
Graduation Rate 4-year: 35%

Graduation Rate 6-year: 65%
Percent Undergraduates in On-campus housing: 25%
Number of official organized extracurricular organizations: 330
3 Most popular majors: Constructing Engineering Technology, Kinesiology and Exercise Science, Psychology
Student/Faculty ratio: 18:1
Average Class Size: 24
Percent of students going to grad school: Unreported
Tuition and Fees: $18,858
In-State Tuition and Fees if different: $5,418
Cost for Room and Board: $7,382
Percent receiving financial aid out of those who apply: 71%
Percent receiving financial aid among all students: 62%

I f location is everything, then Colorado State University has it made. In addition to sitting at the crossroads of the Great Plains and the Rocky Mountains, CSU is also blessed by the calm, relatively crime-free nature of Fort Collins, its host city, and by clement weather that supplies 10 months' worth of sunny days every year. Students at CSU definitely appreciate the opportunities their environment provides them, and "hiking and biking" are among the most popular activities on the outdoors-oriented campus. But students enjoy the opportunities opened to them by the university's 330 extracurricular organizations and rigorous academics as well. Though prices have risen for in-state and out-of-state students alike, CSU is still an excellent bargain.

Though the university offers no early action or early decision programs (all applications are due on February 1), CSU students must choose a large part of their academic path before they arrive on campus. During application, Ram-hopefuls must choose between eight colleges within the larger university: Agricultural Sciences, Applied Human Sciences, Business, Engineering, Liberal Arts, Forestry and Natural Resources, Veterinary Medicine, and Biomedical Sciences. Additionally, students are expected to choose a major before they arrive to campus, which is something that as much as a third of the incoming class chooses to subvert every year by selection of the "open option," a path offered by numerous departments which allows major selection to be postponed. However, even this delayed-selection path only buys students a year—whether they choose to go open option or not, all Rams must choose a major by the beginning of their sophomore year. But for those who are terrified of commitment and still want to enjoy the Colorado air, never fear: a university-wide program allows freshmen to take courses across a wide variety of academic departments before locking into their majors with finality.

Once you've chosen your path, it's time to pick classes. Fortunately, CSU has you covered: the school offers over 150 programs of study with dozens of unique classes within each. Most students try to register for classes online; however, beware of procrastination because delaying online registration can often mean that the class you want is no longer available since popular courses fill up fast. CSU also mandates that students take certain required "core" courses in addition to their electives, but such requirements often get a bad rap from the student body. In particular, CO 150 (Intro to Writing) was called out as the "worst class on campus" by several students due to the lack of passion present in its teaching.

But don't get CSU's academic rigor wrong: sure, the school demands commitment from its students early on, but educators also know how to have fun. "Psychology of Human Sexuality" hosts an annual "porn day," on which the entire class watches a pornographic film and discusses its psychological values and effects, and FTEC 260, "Brewing Science," takes students on a statewide tour of Colorado's world-famous breweries and allows them to brew their own recipes in class, something that is "unique to CSU."

Living the Life

All freshman Rams are required to live in one of the 13 on-campus residence halls during their first year. Most dislike this requirement, but the halls do their best to make the experience of freshman housing as positive as possible by allowing students to submit rooming preferences ahead of time and by giving each hall a specific theme. Whether you go to Academic Village, the honors dorm, Corbett, the party dorm, or any of the other 11 halls, you know what you're getting into in advance. Furthermore, the CSU housing system is currently undergoing a massive renovation project, an effort that most students approve of. "On-campus housing has gotten much better since they began refurbishing it," said one student. "The new dorms are really nice."

After freshman year, most CSU students choose to seek off campus housing, which despite the renovation is generally regarded as much nicer than the dorms. One reason for this is the food: though on-campus dining

is tolerable, the cuisine of surrounding Fort Collins is legendary among foodie Rams. "Off campus food equals amazing," raved one student. Still, for freshmen stuck close to campus and upperclassmen who prefer the dorms, food isn't a problem: CSU offers highly flexible meal plans to all on-campus resident students, including an all-you-can-eat residence hall dining center and access to any of the myriad restaurants housed in the Lory Student Center.

Another draw of off campus life is the bar scene. High-quality in-house brews and themed nights of the week offered by numerous businesses make bar hopping a weekend standard for most upperclassman. Specials are offered daily, though Tuesdays and Thursdays seem to be the preferred nights by the mostly-senior contingents that haunt the bars. For on-campus partying, Greek Row still dominates: rush is one of the most advertised events on the campus, and many Rams devote themselves exclusively to the party scenes offered by frats and sororities.

> **"The people are awesome and the campus is beautiful."**

Most students bring a car with them when they come to campus. Though foot and bike transit is extremely popular, many students still need a vehicle to traverse the lengthy streets of Fort Collins' open city plan. Out of town excursions are popular, too, especially the 65-mile hop to Denver. Cars can even extend the environmental side of campus life—as one student said, "You need to be able to get out and go see the mountains."

From the gridiron to the gridlock

The football team is a major part of school spirit at CSU, and the student body turns out in droves to Hughes Stadium, the ancestral home of Rams football, to watch games in spite of the generally-held feeling that the stadium is dilapidated and in need of better parking for students and guests alike. Nevertheless, student support for the football team—and, indeed, for all CSU athletic programs—is high. There's just one problem, though, which one student sums up nicely: "It would be great to have a better football team."

For those who aren't adroit enough to play for a varsity Division I athletic team,

CSU has large support for intramural sports as well. If students are unable to find their niche sport somewhere in between soccer, ultimate Frisbee, and inner tube water polo, the administration supports students who want to add a new sport to the already highly competitive (and lengthy) list.

Beyond sports, intramural or otherwise, CSU boasts 300+ extracurricular clubs and activities of every make and model. From the Circle K chapter, a collegiate international service organization; to forays into politics courtesy of the Associated Students of Colorado State University, the university's highly-popular student government program; to up-to-the-minute news delivered by a campus newspaper, radio station, and television program, CSU doesn't disappoint those who seek involvement beyond their courses. The arts, too, are in good hands, with multiple yearly exhibits on display for student viewing at the Curfman Gallery and the Lory Student Center. And just as with academics, the university wants to help students see all there is to see before they commit: a bi-annual "Involvement Expo" allows campus organizations the chance to strut their stuff for the student body.

Overall, life as a CSU Ram comes down to taking advantage of opportunities. With 300 days of sun every year, easy access to hiking trails and ski slopes, and a vibrant student body ready to try anything twice, Colorado State University lends itself well to ambitious students who also want to live life in the great outdoors. And with a family of 30,000, there are plenty of friends to hit the trails with. As one CSU senior summed it up, "The people are awesome, and the campus is beautiful."—*Robert Peck*

FYI
If you come to CSU, you'd better bring "jackets, boots, gloves, hats, and a bicycle."
What's the typical weekend schedule? "Sleep in late, work or hike during the day on Saturday, and party into the night. Sunday is study/hangover time."
If I could change one thing about CSU, it would be "more parking. The parking lots need to be fixed really badly!"

United States Air Force Academy

Address: HQ USAF/RRS, 2304 Cadet Drive, Suite 2300, USAF Academy, CO 80840

Phone: 719-333-2520

E-mail address: rr_webmail@usafa.edu

Web site URL: www.usafa.edu

Year Founded: 1954

Private or Public: Public

Religious Affiliation: None

Location: Suburban

Number of Applicants: 11,627

Percent Accepted: 13%

Percent Accepted who enroll: 81%

Number Entering: 1,269

Number of Transfers Accepted each Year: Unreported

Middle 50% SAT range: M: 620–700, CR: 590–680, Wr: 570–650

Middle 50% ACT range: 29–32

Early admission program EA/ED/None: None

Percentage accepted through EA or ED: NA

EA and ED deadline: NA

Regular Deadline: 31-Jan

Application Fee: $0

Full time Undergraduate enrollment: 4,619

Total enrollment: 4,619

Percent Male: Unreported

Percent Female: Unreported

Total Percent Minority or Unreported: 27%

Percent African-American: 6%

Percent Asian/Pacific Islander: 8%

Percent Hispanic: 8%

Percent Native-American: 1%

Percent International: 1%

Percent in-state/out of state: 7%/93%

Percent from Public HS: 79%

Retention Rate: 88%

Graduation Rate 4-year: 70%

Graduation Rate 6-year: 72%

Percent Undergraduates in On-campus housing: 100%

Number of official organized extracurricular organizations: 77

3 Most popular majors: Aerospace, Aeronautical and Astronautical Engineering, Business, Social Studies

Student/Faculty ratio: 8:1

Average Class Size: 16

Percent of students going to grad school: 7%

Tuition and Fees: $0

In-State Tuition and Fees if different: No difference

Cost for Room and Board: $0

Percent receiving financial aid out of those who apply: NA

Percent receiving financial aid among all students: NA

The United States Air Force Academy demands both academic and physical excellence, a challenge that many find difficult to meet. The first challenge one meets in becoming a cadet is being admitted. Subsequently, cadets are constantly tested both in and outside of the classroom with strict rules and harsh reprimands. Although the environment is intense, the benefits of attending such a university are incalculable. Cadets are paid to attend school, become part of a closely knit squad, live in beautiful Colorado and learn how to fly.

Not an Easy Transition

When a new freshman enters the Air Force Academy compound for the very first time, the transition from high school to college takes on a new meaning. Known to the upperclassmen as "doolies," the freshmen have to adjust to many lifestyle changes. The USAFA imposes a strict daily regimen for all cadets, but freshmen experience fewer privileges and less space to live in. The beginning of a freshman's career as a cadet begins with mandatory Basic Cadet Training during the summer. This five-week-long program teaches future cadets basic military skills and serves as a preliminary "weeding out" of prospects. Not everyone is able to endure such an intense lifestyle, even at the beginning.

Cadets are divided randomly into 36 squadrons of 120 each. Each squadron includes students from all four years and determines where a cadet will live. Although everyone lives in the squadrons, the living arrangements differ according to class. Freshmen live in the most crowded rooms with three roommates, while sophomores and juniors live with two, and seniors live with just one roommate. This squadron system provides smaller groups within the academy for cadets to bond.

At USAFA, hierarchy and experience are very highly valued. With each year, cadets are given more freedom and privileges. Only seniors are allowed to have a car at school, and are thus more likely to get the opportunity to party at neighboring colleges such as

Colorado College and Colorado University in Colorado Springs. For freshmen, the Academy institutes strict prohibitions against underage drinking, where getting caught with alcohol can lead to expulsion. The most treasured forms of freedom are leave and phone privileges. As a first-year, cadets may only receive phone calls during the weekends and cannot leave the premises other than when on break. After the first year, cadets may leave the campus and visit local areas. Therefore, it's definitely better to be an upperclassman, but the fact of the matter is that every cadet has to go through freshman year.

The cadet dining facilities are akin to other military schools within the U.S. Mitchell Hall is the largest dining hall where the entire cadet wing assembles to eat family-style breakfast and lunch everyday. This type of dining means preparing and serving 12,000 meals per day. Because of this, specialized dining is very rare and many cadets view the food as "getting old very fast."

Studying Among the Best

The USAFA is ranked as the number one Baccalaureate Program in the West, according to *U.S. News & World Report*'s "America's Best Colleges 2010," making it clear that academics are taken very seriously. The average class size is small, ranging from 15 to 20 students, allowing for a more personalized form of learning. In addition to taking courses that fulfill one's major, all cadets are required to take several military courses. Many find the academic scene highly rigorous and competitive. Once a cadet is admitted, they compete with the other students for grades as everything is graded on a curve.

Cadets usually study about 20 hours a week, usually during the mandated study periods scheduled during the day when not in class. Otherwise, cadets are expected to study in their rooms or in the library during Academic Call to Quarters (ACQ). This highly regulated studying time is implemented to ensure academic success and contributes to the overall goal of efficient use of time.

Students are required to have at least 132 credit hours to graduate, but most end up having far more due to the mixture of military and major courses offered. Most cadets either major in engineering or management and each have their own reputations. One cadet said, "The engineering majors are geeks, the computer science majors don't even bother looking for dates, and the management majors don't bother doing homework

because it is more of a recommendation than a requirement." The engineering major regardless of its specification is considered the hardest, where the management major is considered the easiest and most flexible major available.

Extracurriculars

All cadets are required to participate in the athletic program the Air Force offers, which includes both physical education courses and competitive sports. If a cadet does not participate in a varsity sport, then he or she is expected to participate in at least one intramural sport. These sports range from Ultimate Frisbee to soccer and are very competitive.

> **"There truly is nothing better than to compete for the Academy."**

Varsity sports are prevalent at the academy, with about one fourth of all cadets participating in them. And the teams are known to take a lot of pride in what they do. All athletes are expected to participate in their sport and fulfill all other requirements, an obligation that can prove to be difficult at times. One swimmer remarked, "Being an athlete here at the Air Force is like doubling the military requirements. It literally is like another job. However, all varsity athletes are very respected and there truly is nothing better than to compete for the Academy."

Because of the required involvement in extracurricular activities and the highly enforced regimen, cadets don't have a lot of free time. Luckily, they don't have to worry about making money, for every cadet is paid a salary monthly. A variety of scholarships is also offered to many cadets. Although they are banned from outside employment, the student salary and lack of tuition and rooming and board expenses clearly make up for it. Overall the USAFA is one of the best colleges out there for those who want to make a difference. For many cadets, being able to serve one's country and gain an education is an honor. You learn the skills you need to survive both on the battlefield and in the workplace. The highly accomplished staff, class offerings, emphasis on leadership skills, and the networking opportunities available make the Air Force an incredible experience. However, be warned that this school is not for the weak.—*Taylor Ritzel*

FYI

If you come to the Air Force Academy, you'd better bring "an ability to stick it through freshman year; it gets better from there!"

What's the typical weekend schedule? "Training classes and study hours during the weekend, however most of the time is free time."

If you could change one thing about the Air Force Academy, "I would get rid of noncommissioned officer (NCO) presence here. The AFA is training cadets to be commissioned officers, and NCOs have no part in the training of cadets."

Three things every cadet should do before graduating: "Remain standing and cheering for the football team even though it's the fourth quarter and the team is losing by over three touchdowns, use your uniform to pick up the opposite sex, deploy overseas to see what you are getting into."

The University of Colorado at Boulder

Address: 552 UCB, Boulder, CO 80309-0552

Phone: 303-492-6301

E-mail address: apply@colorado.edu

Web site URL: www.colorado.edu/prospective

Year Founded: 1876

Private or Public: Public

Religious Affiliation: None

Location: Suburban

Number of Applicants: 20,995

Percent Accepted: 83%

Percent Accepted who enroll: 30%

Number Entering: 5,145

Number of Transfers Accepted each Year: 1,973

Middle 50% SAT range: M: 540–660, CR: 530–630, Wr: Unreported

Middle 50% ACT range: 23–28

Early admission program EA/ED/None: EA

Percentage accepted through EA or ED: Unreported

EA and ED deadline: 1-Dec

Regular Deadline: 15-Jan

Application Fee: $50

Full time Undergraduate enrollment: 24,012

Total enrollment: 26,433

Percent Male: 53%

Percent Female: 47%

Total Percent Minority or Unreported: 25%

Percent African-American: 2%

Percent Asian/Pacific Islander: 6%

Percent Hispanic: 7%

Percent Native-American: 1%

Percent International: 2%

Percent in-state/out of state: 67%/33%

Percent from Public HS: Unreported

Retention Rate: 83%

Graduation Rate 4-year: 41%

Graduation Rate 6-year: 65%

Percent Undergraduates in On-campus housing: 24%

Number of official organized extracurricular organizations: 500

3 Most popular majors: International/Global Studies, Physiology, Psychology

Student/Faculty ratio: 18:1

Average Class Size: 16

Percent of students going to grad school: 21%

Tuition and Fees: $29,480

In-State Tuition and Fees if different: $9,152

Cost for Room and Board: $11,278

Percent receiving financial aid out of those who apply: 86%

Percent receiving financial aid among all students: 64%

Founded in 1876, the University of Colorado at Boulder provides students with extensive academic resources, though CU students are just as likely to hit the slopes as they are to hit the books. Students rave about Boulder's cultural opportunities, environmental friendliness, and of course, its striking mountainside location. With many students boasting that CU's campus is the most beautiful in the nation, students are proud to join the ranks of CU alumni, including several Nobel Laureates, astronauts, and the two co-creators of South Park.

In the Classroom and in the Lab

As a large research university, CU has something to offer for any academic interest. Psychology remains by far the most popular major at CU, and one psych major said his undergraduate courses fostered his interest in pursuing a PhD in clinical psychology. Other popular majors include English, international affairs, and environmental studies.

Several students praised the opportunities to work alongside professors in the lab and out the field. One senior explained, "I participated in academic research since my freshman year, which is rare as an undergraduate. In fact, I received a grant for independent research from my school as a junior."

For a university of its size, CU professors and academic advisors are "very effective" when it comes to addressing student needs. An environmental studies and geography double major praised the advising in her departments. She added, "I particularly love that our university's online audits enable you to understand advising and are self-explanatory so that you know exactly what [classes] you've taken and need to take." Another student noted that his advisor helped him into get into a really popular class.

While some students dive head first into their academics, many admitted there is a large range of academic intensity. "A lot of students here are basically ski bums. I sometimes wish people would take academics more seriously," said a senior.

> **"A lot of students here are basically ski bums."**

For students who tire of Colorado living, a number of students take advantage of study abroad opportunities. One student explained that the study abroad office is really helpful. "Even if CU doesn't offer a program in a particular country, they will help you get into other programs."

From WilVill to the Hill
All freshmen are required to live on campus. While dorms are "not the fanciest residences" around town, students agree that living on-campus freshman year allows students to make close friendships and integrate to life at CU "before they whisk off to find apartments of their own as sophomores." While most dorms are relatively similar in terms of layout and style, one student noted that "WilVill" is notoriously the worst freshman dorm.

In terms of partying in the dorms, one student said, "Our no-alcohol policy in the residence halls is strictly adhered to." However, another student explained that he was lucky enough to get a "cool RA" his freshman year

who would often look the other way when students were drinking. Nonetheless, most freshmen know to save the partying for trips to frats and upperclassman residences on the Hill, a neighborhood known as "party central."

All freshmen are required to be on a food plan. The main dining hall on campus is the Center for Community, or "C4C." Here, students get to sample a variety of international cuisine, including stations for sushi, Mexican, Italian, and even Persian dishes. Reflecting Boulder's deep commitment to environmentalism, C4C has received a LEED GOLD certification for sustainability. There are also a few smaller dining halls around campus that serve more traditional American fare. True to its hippie reputation, a large contingent of students on campus is vegetarian and vegan. These students praise CU's dining halls for providing veggie and vegan dishes at every meal. When students get bored of on-campus dining, there are always "tons of health-food stores" around town in Boulder.

One student praised a Boulder city ordinance that stipulates that buildings can't go beyond a certain height, thereby opening much of campus to the striking Flatirons, the rock formations surrounding campus. Many students also love the design of CU's campus. "The main aesthetics are really beautiful," one senior explained. "All the buildings are designed by the same architect, and the staff put a lot of effort into maintaining a variety of vegetation and trees on campus. In the fall, the leaves on many of the trees turn royal purple." Only two main roadways go through campus, leaving a lot of space for students to get around to class by walking or biking.

Eco-Friendly Entertainment
Students call Boulder "the most sustainable and environmentally-friendly city in Colorado," and possibly even in the country. One student raved that you can find "compost bins all over the city." Another student described Boulder as "artsy, outdoorsy, and young."

Reflecting its artsy vibe, Boulder is home to many music halls and venues, such as Fox, which hosts several popular bands. Pearl Street is the main hub of the city, lined with restaurants and shops. One senior explained, "My favorite things to do in Boulder include evening walks down Pearl Street, hiking at the Chautauqua, and exploring the many food and art stores in town." For those who crave a bigger city lifestyle, "Denver is

45 minutes away by bus and much less than that by car."

> "My favorite things to do in Boulder include evening walks down Pearl Street, hiking at the Chautauqua, and exploring the many food and art stores in town."

From Mountaineering to Volunteering

With over 1,000 student groups, CU students can "always find a niche." Popular organizations include the CU Student Government, which is divided into executive, legislative, and judicial branches, a "great opportunity" for students interested in a career in politics. The Hiking Club is the oldest student club on campus, and organizes hikes every weekend throughout the American Southwest. Performance groups, cultural organizations, and campus publications also draw a large number of CU students. Students committed to volunteerism can find a wealth of local volunteer opportunities through the Volunteer Resource Center.

CU's endless extracurricular and recreational opportunities are perfect for students who crave new experiences. As one student describes, "If you are looking for a monotone, boring, and cookie-cutter university, CU is not for you!" However, a few students complain about the homogeneity of the student body. "There's very little diversity. It's a pretty white, upper-middle class school." As would be expected at a state university, a majority of students are from Colorado, but CU's worldwide reputation also attracts a number of out-of-state and international students. One Nigerian student explained, "I'm getting the best of both worlds as an international student at CU. Sure, there are times when I'm the only one in my class with any resemblance to myself, but that doesn't matter because there is beauty in standing out."

420 Ways to Have Fun

CU students certainly live up to their party reputation. "Boulder has some of the best micro-breweries in the country, so there's a lot of beer consumption." Marijuana is another popular drug of choice and has been recently legalized in the state of Colorado. One student mentioned that CU hosts an annual 420 celebration every April 20, when everyone "goes out on the main quad and lights up." He boasted that that in 2012, over 10,000 visitors came to celebrate 420. Students also explained that the dubstep music scene was growing in local Boulder venues. As a result, "ecstasy and other club drugs" are becomingly increasingly common on campus.

Students also love to cheer on their beloved Buffaloes at football games, decking themselves out in gold and black, the school colors. Colorado State University is CU's main football rival, and CU-CSU games are held in the NFL stadium in Denver to fit the tens of thousands of raving fans.

Greek life is another major component of social life on campus. Students claim that rush week is always "really intense" for girls interested in sororities. Frats are not officially a part of CU due to an incident several years ago when they refused to obey school policies, so frats conduct most of their business off-campus. Greek life is primarily centered on the Hill, which gets swarmed on the weekends.

And of course, many students at CU spend their free time hiking, skiing, and snowboarding. With the variety of recreation that the mountains offer, it's no surprise that students describe the ideal CU student as a "lover of the outdoors." Boulder is known as one of the healthiest and most active cities in the country, and CU students take this reputation to heart. From twilight trips up the Flatirons to dance parties at Boulder clubs, CU students are far from sedentary. And with a top-notch academic and research facilities at their disposal, CU students know how to exercise both their body and mind.—*Jessica Blanton*

FYI
If you come to CU, you better bring "snow gear and a sense of adventure."
What's the typical weekend schedule? "On Friday, party on the Hill; Saturday, attend a Buffaloes football game; and Sunday, sleep in or maybe go hiking in the Flatirons."
Three things everyone should do before graduating are: "Go to the Red Rocks Amphitheatre, go skiing or snowboarding, and kiss the buffalo in the Pearl Street Pub when you turn 21."

University of Denver

Address: 2197 S. University Boulevard, Denver, CO 80208
Phone: 303-871-2036
E-mail address: admission@du.edu
Web site URL: www.du.edu
Year Founded: 1864
Private or Public: Private
Religious Affiliation: None
Location: Urban
Number of Applicants: 9,337
Percent Accepted: 72%
Percent Accepted who enroll: 18%
Number Entering: 1,216
Number of Transfers Accepted each Year: 393
Middle 50% SAT range: M: 560–660, CR: 540–650, Wr: 530–640
Middle 50% ACT range: 25–30
Early admission program EA/ED/None: EA

Percentage accepted through EA or ED: 37%
EA and ED deadline: 1-Nov
Regular Deadline: 15-Jan
Application Fee: $50
Full time Undergraduate enrollment: 4,951
Total enrollment: 11,797
Percent Male: 44%
Percent Female: 56%
Total Percent Minority or Unreported: 32%
Percent African-American: 3%
Percent Asian/Pacific Islander: 4%
Percent Hispanic: 8%
Percent Native-American: 1%
Percent International: 7%
Percent in-state/out of state: 52%/48%
Percent from Public HS: Unreported
Retention Rate: 88%
Graduation Rate 4-year: 57%

Graduation Rate 6-year: 73%
Percent Undergraduates in On-campus housing: 43%
Number of official organized extracurricular organizations: 160
3 Most popular majors: Biology, Business Management and Marketing, Business/Commerce
Student/Faculty ratio: 10:1
Average Class Size: 15
Percent of students going to grad school: 16%
Tuition and Fees: $36,936
In-State Tuition and Fees if different: No difference
Cost for Room and Board: $9,093
Percent receiving financial aid out of those who apply: 84%
Percent receiving financial aid among all students: 84%

L ocated a few miles from downtown Denver, the oldest private institution in the Rockies is ideal for political junkies, outdoor enthusiasts, and the academically ambitious. DU students are relentlessly active, whether studying in the classroom, skiing on the slopes, partying on fraternity row, or organizing the first of the 2012 presidential debates.

From Business to Biology

Students agree that pre-frosh activities and the freshmen seminars are some of the best ways to get to know people. Although the difficulty can vary quite a bit, it is generally agreed that freshmen seminars provide a relatively "gentle" introduction into college life. Furthermore, students meet their fellow seminar participants during pre-frosh activities so that they have a group of familiar faces off the bat, and their seminar instructor doubles as their advisor for freshman year.

In addition to the freshmen seminar, students are also required to take at least one foreign language course, as well as courses in math, natural inquiry (natural science or social science), and analytical inquiry (English, literature, philosophy, etc). Beyond these requirements, students can also apply for the competitive Pioneer Leadership Program, which culminates in a minor in leadership, or the Honors program, which allows students to take advanced seminars and culminates in a thesis.

Grading varies by professor, but in general professors are regarded as "pretty fair." Professors are exceptionally willing to make themselves available to students, and there are almost no courses are taught by TAs. Most classes have fewer than 30 students, so "professors know who you are," and even big intro courses are still typically fewer than 100 people. Small classes do have their drawbacks, however, as students complain that classes are often difficult to get into, and are thus forced to take a lot of electives.

The most popular majors are business, international relations, psychology, and biology. The Josef Korbel School of International Studies is especially strong. The school also offers wonderful opportunities for dual enrollment with the business or other professional schools. As far as majors go, engineering and science tend to be the most difficult because of more "rigid" requirements, students say. As one senior noted, "Anyone getting a B.S. probably spends the most time doing homework." International Relations, Business, and the social sciences tend to be the next tier, and humanities are the most flexible in terms of course options. In terms of academic rigor, students say that it is "not easy, but not impossible" to get an A in science courses, while business courses have a reputation for grade inflation. Marketing is seen as easy because it has "lots of group projects," and students agree that introductory courses are "not particularly challenging."

Living, Learning, but not Always Dining

DU students come to know and love DU for its many steeples, copper roofing, and distinctive red-brick buildings. Students observe that "everything is pretty new" due to frequent renovations, the latest of which has been the library. Other recent additions include the newly-constructed Nagel Hall.

All freshmen and sophomores are required to live on campus. Freshmen live in Centennial Halls and Johnson-McFarlane, or J-Mac, while sophomores graduate to Nelson Hall or Nagel Hall. Centennial Towers is shared by freshmen and sophomores. Within these options, students have the opportunity to designate a preference for living in themed floors (Centennial Halls) or wings (J-Mac), called Living Learning Communities, or LLCs, based on exploring common interests like social justice, entrepreneurship, or environmental sustainability. Similar arrangements exist for students in the Honors or Pioneer Leadership programs.

Seventy percent of students study abroad, typically in the fall of junior year, after which they tend to "break away" from on-campus housing. Although only 44% of students live on campus, most upperclassmen choose to live in residential areas near campus, which undergraduates frequent when they want to "get away," so the campus still feels like a close-knit community.

The main dining options are Centennial Halls and Nagel Hall. Students report that food is "not well liked" and one student described it as "fairly repetitive and industrial." Students frequently opt instead for the Jazzman's Café or the Sidelines Pub, both conveniently located in the Driscoll Student Center, or take advantage of one of the many affordable options near campus, which include the original Chipotle.

Not Your Everyday Greek Life

Much of the social scene centers around Greek life, of which more than 20% of students are a part. But Greek life at DU is a far cry from the stuff of Animal House or other movies. In general the community is characterized as more "chill" and the different fraternities and sororities have good relationships with one other. As one sophomore explained, DU has more of a "Greek community" than a "Greek system." Greek organizations are further united by their strong commitment to philanthropy. Nevertheless, students report that Greek life is "not the most diverse place" and that there exists a "very real divide" between those who take part and those who do not. However, the Greek community is taking great strides to reach out to minorities and increase diversity.

While Greek life dominates the social scene, Winter Carnival, which some students cite as the biggest tradition on campus, is a non-Greek alternative that brings students together on the mountain. An upperclassman remarked that while it "attracts a nice mix of students," Winter Carnival definitely appeals more to younger students because of the novelty.

Taking Advantage of Denver's Geography

One major adjustment to life at DU is the conspicuous lack of a football team, and getting used to that can be a "big transition." The major sport on campus is hockey, although lacrosse and basketball are popular as well. One student complained that the administration's "focus on athletic program isn't as strong as it could be" and said school spirit is "kind of weak" compared to that of bigger schools, although others praised the fact that "spirit in university sports has really increased." Part of this increase in spirit could be attributed to the DU Grilling Society, which reportedly has a "large presence," and can be found helping out at tailgates and other sporting events.

> "Everyone's excited about getting into the outdoors."

Students have described DU as an unusually fit and physically "active" community and say that "everyone's excited about getting into the outdoors." Through the Alpine Club, students can take advantage of the local geography, embarking on ski trips and other outdoor excursions that are generously subsidized. Most classes do not meet on Fridays, and the long weekends provide excellent opportunities for physical activity, be it skiiing, kayaking, or snowboarding.

Life at DU and in Denver offers a unique "union of the urban and the natural" that is a particular draw for active minds and active bodies. As one junior observed, when people recognize the opportunities a setting like this provides, "more and more people come here to be in Denver."—*Chris Taylor*

FYI

If you come to University of Denver, you'd better bring "skis, because otherwise you're going to get left out."

If you come to University of Denver, you'd better leave behind "your swim trunks."

Three things that every student should do before graduating from the University of Denver are "go to Red Rocks, go camping or up in the mountains, and go to the original Chipotle."

Connecticut

Connecticut College

Address: 270 Mohegan Avenue, New London, CT 06320
Phone: 860-439-2200
E-mail address: admission@conncoll.edu
Web site URL: www.conncoll.edu
Year Founded: 1911
Private or Public: Private
Religious Affiliation: None
Location: Suburban
Number of Applicants: 4,316
Percent Accepted: 38%
Percent Accepted who enroll: 30%
Number Entering: 492
Number of Transfers Accepted each Year: 65
Middle 50% SAT range: M: 610–700, Cr: 620–720, Wr: 670–720
Middle 50% ACT range: 25–29
Early admission program EA/ED/None: ED

Percentage accepted through EA or ED: Unreported
EA and ED deadline: 15-Nov
Regular Deadline: 1-Jan
Application Fee: $60
Full time Undergraduate enrollment: 1,996
Total enrollment: 2,026
Percent Male: 40%
Percent Female: 60%
Total Percent Minority or Unreported: 27%
Percent African-American: 4%
Percent Asian/Pacific Islander: 4%
Percent Hispanic: 5%
Percent Native-American: 1%
Percent International: 6%
Percent in-state/out of state: 27%/73%
Percent from Public HS: 55%
Retention Rate: 91%

Graduation Rate 4-year: 82%
Graduation Rate 6-year: 86%
Percent Undergraduates in On-campus housing: 99%
Number of official organized extracurricular organizations: 60
3 Most popular majors: English, Political Science, Psychology
Student/Faculty ratio: 10:1
Average Class Size: 15
Percent of students going to grad school: Unreported
Tuition and Fees: $46,675 comprehensive fee
In-State Tuition and Fees if different: No difference
Cost for Room and Board: Included with tuition
Percent receiving financial aid out of those who apply: 77%
Percent receiving financial aid among all students: 41%

C onnecticut College is a liberal arts institution in southeastern Connecticut, overlooking the Thames River and just minutes from the Long Island Sound. With its manageable size and small student body, ConnColl has a cozy and cohesive feel. The school's honor code is an important tradition and source of pride for students, and its effects can be seen in many different aspects of college life.

Academics and Administration

With a student to teacher ratio of just 10:1, the teachers are generally very accessible, and classes are small and intimate learning environments. "One thing I really liked was the advising I received as a freshman," said one sophomore. "If you make the effort to approach them, teachers can really learn a lot about you as a student and make your transition into college that much easier." Students must fulfill general education requirements spanning seven different core areas, but few find these to be limiting. In addition, all incoming students choose from a selection of freshman seminars, giving them an opportunity to experience some of the best available courses in their first year.

The honor code allows students unique levels of comfort with their studies not found at other institutions, in particular when it comes to final exams, which are self-scheduled and not proctored.

Perhaps the most impressive college program is CELS (Career Enhancing Life Skills) through which students complete workshops to receive funding for internships. This is an incredible opportunity for students at a "small school," especially for those who would for financial reasons be less inclined to take unpaid internships in fields they enjoy. One veteran of CELS went so far as calling it "the best-run office on campus. Most who do it say it is the best thing that ever happened to them."

A point of particular interest at ConnColl is campus celebrity Leo Higdon, the College President who took office following the 2005–2006 school year. Young, energetic and student-friendly, the president can often be seen walking around campus and asking students for their input on various campus issues. Not the tallest head administrator around, he has earned such nicknames as "Big Hig" and "Higgie Smalls," according to one student who proudly claims to have a T-shirt with his face on it.

Campus

Students at ConnColl are "a pretty homogeneous group of preppy white kids, most of whom are from 'right outside Boston,'" according to one interviewee. "We're not all totally preppy, though. We've got our fair share of hippies and artsy fartsy kids," said another. The student body is small enough that most faces are familiar by sophomore year, giving the campus a tight, family feeling. This unity is reinforced by campus-wide events such as "Camelympics," an inter-dorm competition organized by students that happens every fall and lasts for 48 fun-filled hours. Events range from midnight volleyball games to scavenger hunts to Scrabble.

> **"My experience has been that, once you find something you like to do, the College opens up a world of opportunities."**

Extracurricular activities are widely available as there are numerous clubs, organizations, volunteering opportunities, and sports teams at the varsity, club, and intramural level. Nearly all campus groups are run by students, allowing a deep level of involvement. According to one student, "My experience has been that, once you find something you like to do, the College opens up a world of opportunities."

The campus is actually comprised of several hundred acres, although "for the part you walk around on a day-to-day basis, it would take you only 10 minutes to go from the tip of south to the tip of north," said one

junior. The rest of campus is an arboretum managed by the College. Another unusual feature of the campus is that soccer and lacrosse games are played on a field situated in the middle of a cluster of dorms known as south campus, making them very convenient locations for socializing.

Some students complain about a lack of variety in the dining halls, particularly when it comes to healthy options, but the dining services work hard to take student feedback into account when preparing their menus. The meal plan is included in the comprehensive tuition, room and board fee, and is unlimited. Students can eat as much as they want and enter any dining hall on campus as many times as they want. Despite this apparent flexibility, some feel that the availability of food is too restricted due to hour constraints and the fact that only one dining hall is open on the weekends.

Housing

The campus is unofficially divided into three areas: north, central and south. South has older dorms and is loud, whereas north is newer and quieter. Central campus is less defined, but conveniently located. There is no Greek life at ConnColl, but south campus picks up the slack as far as parties are concerned. Said one admittedly biased south campus stalwart: "North has A/C and nicer rooms, but it's boring and more anti-social . . . south is way more fun."

There are no RAs at ConnColl, in keeping with the honor code and the amount of trust the administration puts in the students to behave appropriately. Instead, there is one "house fellow" in charge of each dorm, as well as SAs (student advisors) who are generally sophomores and who do not serve a disciplinary function, but rather help ease the transition into college life for freshmen.

"I know zero people who live off campus," said one sophomore. There are options for off campus housing, but 99% of students choose to stay in the dorms, which helps draw the various years together and create a stronger feeling of campus unity. While first-year rooms are typically "nothing to write home about," the housing provided for upperclassmen is a big incentive for staying on campus. Juniors and seniors are guaranteed comfortably sized singles if they want them and many sophomores can get them as well.

New London

According to one sophomore, "It's very important to have a car or a good friend who does, although parking sucks for freshmen, and Campus Safety loves to ticket." The College does, however, have a free bus service that brings students from campus to downtown New London. In addition, the College sponsors monthly trips to New York City for various events, and many students take advantage of these opportunities.

The city itself receives mixed reviews from interviewed students. "Like any city, it has its bad areas; it also has beautiful areas. There are some great restaurants and also good beaches only 15 minutes away by car," said one student. Shopping opportunities are limited, but there are a Target and a Walmart close by for essentials. The average student leaves campus at least once a week to eat out.

Weekend

The weekend scene at ConnColl is quite lively, especially considering the lack of a Greek scene or a true urban downtown close by. Very few students have class on Fridays, so ConnColl weekends start Thursday afternoon. Drinking is definitely the focus of most students' weekends, and there are often keg parties in the south campus dorms. Any keg on campus must be signed for by two students who have taken a one-day class called Keg 101. One sophomore resident of south campus described the weekends as "Loud.

South campus is loud on Saturday because of soccer games, but the night life is just as loud."

Enforcement of drinking laws is not strict, in keeping with the honor code, and Campus Safety is generally lenient with drinking; its first responsibility is making sure students are safe, not getting them into trouble. The lack of a Greek system tends to make for a much more inclusive weekend scene at ConnColl. "I love that. I feel like everyone is equal as far as social life is concerned," one student said.

Aside from drinking, the administration makes a great effort to provide alternative activities on the weekends. FNL (Friday Nights Live) is a weekly concert on campus. In addition there are weekly Thursday Night Events, ranging from dances to comedians to movie nights to tie-dye. These events are typically more popular among freshmen, and one older student described them as "kind of lame, and definitely repetitive after a year or two." New London itself does not provide many nightlife alternatives in terms of cultural enrichment, a cause of complaint for non-drinkers.

Coming to Connecticut College, one will find a quaint, beautiful campus filled with prepsters who know how to have a good time, as well as one of the better liberal arts curricula available.—*David Allen*

FYI
If you come to Connecticut College, you'd better bring "a car, the latest copy of the J. Crew catalog and a Red Sox hat or something else related to Boston."
What is the typical weekend schedule? "Thursdays are parties, Fridays are pretty chill, and Saturdays are parties with lots of kegs in south campus."
If I could change one thing about Connecticut College, I'd "change the 'average' Conn student so it's not hard to fit in if you aren't decked out in Vineyard Vines. Oh, and also I'd get rid of the coed bathrooms. Those freak me out sometimes."
Three things every student at Connecticut College should do before graduating are "participate in Camelympics, live in south campus and ring the gong."

Fairfield University

Address: 1073 N. Benson Rd., Fairfield, CT 06824
Phone: 203-254-4100
E-mail address: admis@mail.fairfield.edu
Web site URL: www.fairfield.edu
Year Founded: 1942
Private or Public: Private
Religious Affiliation: Roman Catholic–Jesuit
Location: Suburban
Number of Applicants: 8,732
Percent Accepted: 59%
Percent Accepted who enroll: 17%
Number Entering: 927
Number of Transfers Accepted each Year: 75
Middle 50% SAT range: M: 540–630, CR: 520–610, Wr: 540–630
Middle 50% ACT range: 23–27

Early admission program EA/ED/None: EA
Percentage accepted through EA or ED: 58%
EA and ED deadline: 15-Nov
Regular Deadline: 15-Jan
Application Fee: $60
Full time Undergraduate enrollment: 3,469
Total enrollment: 5,128
Percent Male: 42%
Percent Female: 58%
Total Percent Minority or Unreported: 15%
Percent African-American: 3%
Percent Asian/Pacific Islander: 3%
Percent Hispanic: 8%
Percent Native-American: <1%
Percent International: Unreported
Percent in-state/out of state: 23%/77%
Percent from Public HS: 55%

Retention Rate: 90%
Graduation Rate 4-year: 74%
Graduation Rate 6-year: 77%
Percent Undergraduates in On-campus housing: 85%
Number of official organized extracurricular organizations: 100
3 Most popular majors: Finance, Marketing, Psychology
Student/Faculty ratio: 13:1
Average Class Size: 24
Percent of students going to grad school: 20%
Tuition and Fees: $36,075
In-State Tuition and Fees if different: No difference
Cost for Room and Board: $10,850
Percent receiving financial aid out of those who apply: 70%
Percent receiving financial aid among all students: 48%

Also known as "J. Crew University" due to its almost homogeneous "preppy" population, Fairfield University is a college in Connecticut characterized by strong academics, a vibrant social scene and a myriad of extracurricular activities. The campus is warm, pretty and inviting. It is also free from the gothic architecture that characterizes some of New England schools and most students find its suburban setting "convenient."

Education for the Mind, Body and Spirit

Fairfield University's Jesuit approach to education sets it apart from other tertiary institutions in that it provides to those enrolled, a holistic college experience that seeks to educate the mind, body and spirit. At the undergraduate level, students choose amongst courses offered by the College of Arts and Sciences, School of Business, School of Nursing, School of Engineering and the College of Continuing Studies. Hence, in addition to a liberal arts education, Fairfield students are provided with a platform on which they can explore their career options and apply in-class education to prospective career pathways.

Furthermore, for academically motivated freshmen and sophomores, there is the option of being a part of the prestigious Honors program. This is a program into which only fifty freshmen are admitted each year. Amongst many other things, it seeks to nurture an ability to question and analyze information as well as to stimulate an insatiable quest for knowledge of Western traditions, heritage, history and culture. Those who have had the privilege of being a part of this program describe it as "culturally enriching" and "insightful."

Fairfield University students never talk about academics without mentioning the enormous amount of support that they receive from faculty members. The small class ratio of 13:1 gives professors enough proximity to identify the academic strengths and weaknesses of their students and to build upon or help mitigate them. The library staff is also famous for its enthusiasm to help; and in addition, there exists a myriad of tutoring programs and special support groups such as the Women in Mathematics, Science, Technology, and Engineering that provide academic assistance to women in science. As a female prospective Chemistry major put it, "I chose Fairfield University because it has a high med-school acceptance rate and there is just the right amount of support for me to excel in my major."

Situated Exactly Where I Want It

"Fairfield is close to everywhere!" one student pointed out excitedly. Fairfield University is an hour from New York, ten minutes from the beach, and five minutes from both the Fairfield train station and the Fairfield public library. In addition, Fairfield is close to Stamford where one can go deal hunting at the mall and is served by numerous restaurants. Some students find this setting particularly advantageous as it allows them easy access to internships and volunteer opportunities in local hospitals, businesses and in organizations where they can gain invaluable work experience.

Fairfield University's generous financial aid package is particularly attractive as it can provide up to full funding throughout the four years of college. Despite the flailing economy (or maybe because of it), Fairfield University increased its financial aid package by 13%. For many students, this was the major factor that they considered when they chose to matriculate at Fairfield.

Diversity, Religious and Otherwise

Fairfield University is a very inclusive place where anyone can easily fit in. "You can be as religious as you want to be, if you want to be religious at all." For the devout, the school goes out of its way to incorporate all religions. In December, the time of Kwanzaa, Hanukah and Christmas, the school runs activities that encourage the inclusion of everyone, such as competitions in which students are required to decorate their rooms according to the three holidays.

However, Fairfield University still has a long way to go in addressing ethnic diversity on its campus. "If I could change anything about Fairfield, I would definitely make it more diverse," one student lamented. Fairfield is a predominantly preppy college (hence the nickname J. Crew University) and a vast majority of its student population is white and comes from the rich New England suburbs.

Life in General

Undergraduates have the option of living in eight residence halls, in townhouses or in beach houses. Each residence hall has an easily accessible kitchen where one can cook up a storm or just make a cup of tea. For many students, this is a plus as it provides a break from the monotony of the food that is offered at the dining hall.

The townhouses and beach houses are generally occupied by upperclassmen and are famous for huge gigs and parties. While many sophomores and freshmen can host parties in their dorm rooms, most of the big parties are held in the townhouses or the beach houses. There is always something going on every night and drinking and hookups are predominant. However, recent developments and conflicts between non-University beach house inhabitants and Fairfield University beach house inhabitants have led to stricter police supervision of the beach area and speculation over whether or not Fairfield University will still hold its position as one of the Top Party Schools on the Princeton Review list.

During the day, Fairfield students engage themselves in the numerous extracurricular activities that the school has to offer. These include musical groups such as the jazz ensemble and the glee club, ethnic societies, writing publications and political organizations. "You can even form your own organization too!"

> **"Fairfield has just the right amount of support for me to excel in my major."**

Fairfield is not dominant on the sports scene and does not have a varsity football team. However, it has a strong men's basketball team that is known and revered throughout the state.

If you are looking for a place to explore spirituality while challenging yourself academically, Fairfield is definitely worth considering. The upbeat social tempo encourages interaction among students and its curriculum has produced graduates who are well equipped both socially and intellectually to enter the world.—*Senzeni Mpofu*

Quinnipiac University

Address: 275 Mount Carmel Avenue, Hamden, CT 06518
Phone: 203-582-8600
E-mail address: joan.isaacmohr@quinnipiac.edu
Web site URL: www.quinnipiac.edu
Year Founded: 1929
Private or Public: Private
Religious Affiliation: None
Location: Suburban
Number of Applicants: 13,847
Percent Accepted: 69%
Percent Accepted who enroll: 17%
Number Entering: 1,587
Number of Transfers Accepted each Year: 540
Middle 50% SAT range: M: 560–630, CR: 540–610, Wr: Unreported
Middle 50% ACT range: 23–27

Early admission program EA/ED/None: None
Percentage accepted through EA or ED: NA
EA and ED deadline: NA
Regular Deadline: Rolling
Application Fee: $45
Full time Undergraduate enrollment: 5,686
Total enrollment: 5,971
Percent Male: 38%
Percent Female: 62%
Total Percent Minority or Unreported: 21%
Percent African-American: 3%
Percent Asian/Pacific Islander: 3%
Percent Hispanic: 5%
Percent Native-American: >1%
Percent International: 1%
Percent in-state/out of state: 30%/70%
Percent from Public HS: 70%

Retention Rate: 86%
Graduation Rate 4-year: 69%
Graduation Rate 6-year: 73%
Percent Undergraduates in On-campus housing: 75%
Number of official organized extracurricular organizations: 90
3 Most popular majors: Business, General Physical Therapy, Psychology
Student/Faculty ratio: 12:1
Average Class Size: 15
Percent of students going to grad school: 37%
Tuition and Fees: $32,850
In-State Tuition and Fees if different: No difference
Cost for Room and Board: $12,555
Percent receiving financial aid out of those who apply: 72%
Percent receiving financial aid among all students: 68%

At only 2 hours from Boston, 90 minutes from New York, and 10 minutes from New Haven, Quinnipiac University in Hamden, CT, is perfectly situated to let its students experience both the excitement of urban nightlife and the comfort of the suburban day. And students don't miss out on either experience—every student interviewed said that a "must-do" for any QU student is a nighttime visit to New Haven. Yet despite their frequent trips to the city, QU students claim that there is little lacking on their 212-acre campus.

This Is Who We Are

Students at Quinnipiac hail largely from Connecticut and the surrounding areas (according to statistics put out by the university, of this year's enrolling freshmen, 1,371 came from Connecticut, Massachusetts, New York, or New Jersey). But QU isn't a commuter school by any means; though one underclassman worried that people would go home on the weekends, she claims that she soon discovered that the opposite is true. Another sophomore explains that "I don't feel like I live 30 minutes away; QU is its own world."

Learning New and Old

For students interested in following a liberal arts curriculum that leads down a less-than-traditional path, QU may be the way to go. Quinnipiac requires all its students to take an intensive core curriculum consisting of 46 credits, including three "University Seminars": "The Individual and the Community," "National Community," and "Global Community."

The reward for completing this rigorous course of study lies in the chance to graduate with a degree in one of 52 diverse majors, ranging from the typical English and Economics degrees to the far less common Diagnostic Imaging and Interactive Digital Design degrees.

Yet students at QU are more interested in their classes than their degrees. Most students claim that professors are dedicated to their students, and that class sizes are small. One public relations major explained that, coming from a small high school, she was concerned about not getting the attention she needed but found that "not only do I have great relationships with my professors, but what's great is that many of them are still working in their field." With a student-to-faculty ratio of 12:1, classes are rarely bigger than 25 students. Even the marketing major who disliked the campus, the food, and the social life praised QU's professors.

One of the most exciting parts of a QU curriculum is its study abroad program. One senior estimates that over 80% of QU students study abroad at some point during their four years. One junior, who is currently studying abroad, praises the program, explaining that it costs no extra money beyond typical Quinnipiac tuition. Though students claim that it is easy to get into a study abroad program, they say that the easiest route to an approved program is to attend QU's sister school in Ireland.

Room and Board

Students at QU are guaranteed three years of housing, and many move off-campus during their junior year to live in apartments in surrounding towns. Housing consists of a mixture of dorms and suites, with, best of all, free wireless. "The dorms are all well maintained; they have a lot of new buildings and they are enjoyable to live in," says one sophomore marketing major. "And wireless Internet is good to have."

Students also enthusiastically talk about the beauty of the campus and its closeness to Sleeping Giant Park, a state park with over 30 miles of hiking trails. "Campus is absolutely beautiful, especially in the fall with all of the foliage and the mountains," says one freshman. Students enjoy the compact size of the campus, although some lament that upperclassman housing is not located on Main Campus and that shuttles are therefore used to get to class. Overall though, most students agree that "the campus is absolutely BEAUTIFUL."

> **"Campus is absolutely beautiful, especially in the fall with all of the foliage and the mountains."**

By contrast, there is distinct lack of enthusiasm for the food. Though one student admits that the grilled cheese is pretty good, this is not exactly a screaming compliment for a campus where one student claims "they give us no money for food, and the quality is awful." QU students are served on an "a la carte" basis, paying per food item, and many students admit that the amount of food on the meal plan is not enough for a hungry student to get by. At least not if that student doesn't want to be hungry anymore.

It's (Not) All Here

For many QU students, Thursday and Saturday nights are spent in New Haven. Though the university attempts to make this commute easier, by offering a shuttle to the nearby city, students complain that the service takes far longer than it should. "It's only twenty minutes away," says one sophomore, "but because it stops in so many different places it takes an hour to get there." A junior majoring in psychology adds, though, that she thinks the shuttle system is important because it keeps students from drinking and driving.

On-campus weekend life is a mixture of school-hosted events, clubs and sports, and parties. "Drinking laws are enforced more than they should be for a university," says a sophomore marketing major. "Security abandons their role of protecting students and decides to police them instead." But not all students are unhappy with the school's policies; one student explains that, even though there is a lot of drinking on campus, no one gets in serious trouble for alcohol violations unless they are causing disruptions. And despite the prevalence of drinking on the QU campus, students claim that you don't need to drink to have fun. "There is a lot of drinking," says one student, "but you don't have to drink to have fun, because there are so many other things to do."

As far as clubs and organizations go, Greek life has been growing, says one member of the class of 2011, though there are only four sororities and three frats on campus and no Greek houses. Students not interested in Greek life can find their niche in any one of the over 70 organizations that QU offers, ranging from "anime club to Irish club," according to one sophomore. Students are also encouraged by the University to form their own clubs if they find that already existing ones don't meet their needs.

The University and its RAs host a number of events every month. One sophomore in the public relations major praises the school for making it so easy to have fun and make friends: "I'm really shy," she explains, "but they had a lot of great programs to help us make friends, and I did the first day. The RAs are also great, and definitely helped make the transition easier."

Finally, sports make up a major part of life at Quinnipiac. With 19 NCAA Division-1 sports teams, Quinnipiac is a school loaded with athletic pride, especially when it comes to hockey. "Since we're a D1 school," says one student, "sports are pretty big, even though you don't get people going to much else other than hockey. Hockey is really big here." Students at hockey games often proudly sport QU gear, creating a sea of "Boomer the Bobcat" sweatshirts.—*Heather Robinson*

FYI

If you come to Quinnipiac, you'd better bring: "LOTS OF MONEY FOR NEW HAVEN! You better bring a lot of Easy Mac also—our café sucks so you need to make sure you have food in the dorms to keep yourself alive."

What's the typical weekend schedule? "People go out hard (to New Haven) on Thursdays, and usually Saturdays. Friday nights are more house parties or dorm parties."

If I could change one thing about Quinnipiac, I'd: "change how big the school is. They let more and more freshmen in each year, and we are going to change from being a 'medium' size school to 'large' pretty quickly."

Three things to do before you graduate: "Go to Toads, attend a Yale vs. Quinnipiac hockey game, and climb Sleeping Giant State Park Mountain."

Sacred Heart University

Address: 5151 Park Avenue, Fairfield, CT 06825-1000
Phone: 203-371-7880
E-mail address: enroll@sacredheart.edu
Web site URL: www.sacredheart.edu
Year Founded: 1963
Private or Public: Private
Religious Affiliation: Catholic
Location: Suburban
Number of Applicants: 7,569
Percent Accepted: 60%
Percent Accepted who enroll: 22%
Number Entering: 1,000
Number of Transfers Accepted each Year: 328
Middle 50% SAT range: M: 490–580, CR: 480–560, Wr: Unreported
Middle 50% ACT range: Unreported
Early admission program EA/ED/None: ED

Percentage accepted through EA or ED: Unreported
EA and ED deadline: 1-Dec
Regular Deadline: Rolling
Application Fee: $50
Full time Undergraduate enrollment: 3,442
Total enrollment: 4,198
Percent Male: 40%
Percent Female: 60%
Total Percent Minority or Unreported: 12%
Percent African-American: 4%
Percent Asian/Pacific Islander: 1%
Percent Hispanic: 6%
Percent Native-American: <1%
Percent International: 1%
Percent in-state/out of state: 32%/68%
Percent from Public HS: Unreported
Retention Rate: 77%

Graduation Rate 4-year: Unreported
Graduation Rate 6-year: Unreported
Percent Undergraduates in On-campus housing: 60%
Number of official organized extracurricular organizations: 80
2 Most popular majors: Business, Finance
Student/Faculty ratio: 13:1
Average Class Size: 22
Percent of students going to grad school: Unreported
Tuition and Fees: $32,474
In-State Tuition and Fees if different: No difference
Cost for Room and Board: $13,070
Percent receiving financial aid out of those who apply: 94%
Percent receiving financial aid among all students: 89%

Sacred Heart University is one of the country's largest Catholic universities, along with Notre Dame and Boston College. Located in suburban Fairfield, Connecticut, the school has a student body numbering about 4,000 with degrees offered in 40 programs of study. This university offers a breadth of study combined with a distinctive Catholic tradition of education. With new majors and programs being continually developed and added, the curriculum at Sacred Heart offers challenging and diverse academics for students. The university campus situated on 67 beautiful acres in the town of Fairfield is in the shadow of big metropolitan areas such as New York and Boston while still maintaining a distinctive suburban atmosphere.

Contemporary Education, Catholic Tradition

Sacred Heart offers a good selection of majors from which to choose while emphasizing a lot on the vocational pathways of its students. Well-known programs include the combined physical therapy and occupational therapy programs where students are able to obtain their bachelor's and professional degrees in less time than usual. Other health professions such as the undergraduate program in nursing and the pre-professional tracks are very popular among students. The College of Health Professions is distinguished with having the best physical therapy program in Connecticut and one of the top five in New England. Students at Sacred Heart can study anything from business economics to religious studies with numerous opportunities to obtain an accelerated master's degree in five years instead of the standard six. "There are a lot of options," says a sophomore. The honors program at Sacred Heart University allows exceptionally prepared students to challenge themselves further with more student-oriented small lectures and presentations as well as more access to resources and academic and social advising. Students in the honors program are required to take more courses and more rigorous courses in addition to standard requirements that culminate in an Honors Portfolio or research presentation in the annual Honors conference.

Students in all programs complete the required core curriculum to be eligible for the bachelor's degree. The core is broken down into three areas of concentration: foundational, common, and elective. The foundational core is fulfilled by classes in the humanities, arts, social science, natural science, religion, and philosophy. This is aimed at developing more socially minded students in a global world. The common core, focusing on The Human Journey, is distinct in a Sacred Heart education that sharpens ethical thinking and moral decision making. "It makes you not only a better student, but a better person," remarks a senior. This part of the core curriculum is grounded in the Catholic traditions of the University with classes including The Human Journey, Literary Expression of the Human Journey, The Human Community, and The Human Community and Science Discovery. This portion of the core is capped off with The Search for Human Truth, Justice, and Common Good. The final portion of the core is completed with elective courses in a chosen major.

> **"[Sacred Heart] makes you not only a better student, but a better person."**

With new programs being added every day, Sacred Heart aims to keep students' educations relevant in the real world. The University itself is split into the College of Arts and Science, John F. Welch College of Business, College of Education and Health Professions, and University College as the four constituent undergraduate schools. University College, owing to the University's aim to maintain relevance, is a unique school catering to adult learners and non-traditional students with evening, weekend, and accelerated classes. Whatever your goal, Sacred Heart has a program that will cater to it.

Campus Life

Life at Sacred Heart is typical of many suburban universities; lush green turf and lots of open space. The main campus itself is located in Fairfield, CT, with satellite campuses in cities around the state including Trumbull, Stamford, and Griswold. The University also maintains international campuses in Luxembourg and Ireland. The majority of students here hail from the New England area with New York, New Jersey, Connecticut, and Massachusetts as the top feeder states.

One thing that many students seem to notice is the lack of diversity on campus. The student body is overwhelmingly white at 85% of the total population. "It seems like everyone here comes from the same background with the same experiences," recounts a freshman. The lack of diversity may be off-set by the plethora of activities available to students on campus and in the surrounding area. Making friends and finding one's niche at Sacred Heart seems to be less of a problem as many people are friendly and welcoming. "People seem to be nice here," says a fresh-man. The lack of diversity does not mean so-cial isolation. From day one, entering freshman have access to special services in adjusting to college life. Additionally, every freshman is provided with a laptop com-puter as part of Sacred Heart's mission to incorporate technology into the classroom.

Residential life has evolved greatly since the school's founding in 1963 as a mainly commuter school. With the inception of resi-dential life and on-campus living in 1991, over 70% of the undergraduate population now live on campus. Freshmen are housed mainly in Seton, Merton, and Roncalli Halls while sophomores are almost exclusively in the Commons. Rooms are generally very nice since most buildings are fairly new, being less than 20 years old. Upperclassmen may also choose to live in off-campus university-owned housing in apartment and townhouse style arrangements. Most residence halls are within close proximity to class buildings and other on-campus amenities with the excep-tion of some off-campus housing. The one University dining hall on campus is not oper-ated by the actual University but a secondary food-service provider. "The food is so-so," says a sophomore. "You definitely need to pick and choose," cautions another student. With residential life relatively new to the uni-versity's history, it's to be expected that some services are not as developed as at other older, more-established universities.

The Spectrum

Social life on campus revolves around the University's focus on service and learning. Each year over 1,200 students and faculty log in over 30,000 hours of community ser-vice on campus and surrounding areas. The Sacred Heart chapter of Habitat for Human-ity, for example, has gained recognition as one of the top 10 chapters in the nation for their work. However, community service is not the only way students get involved around campus. Athletics offer another way for ev-eryone, not just athletes, to get involved. The Pioneers compete with 31 Division I teams and 800 athletes but the school also has a thriving club sports scene with over 500 stu-dents participating in 23 club sports each year. In addition, there are over 85 clubs and organizations to keep students occupied. Anything from the American Chemical Soci-ety chapter of Sacred Heart to cheerleading to ministry clubs can be found on campus. "There's something for everybody here," reminisces a freshman.

The social life doesn't stop there though. Greek life is notable on campus with sorori-ties outnumbering fraternities 2 to 1. The six sororities and three fraternities provide campus with the typical frat party scene seen on most college campuses. Greek life doesn't dominate the scene here, but their presence can be felt. The fraternity and so-rority life here is not as widespread because it doesn't need to be. Students have easy ac-cess to one of the busiest and exciting cities in the world: New York City, a little more than an hour away by train. Students at Sa-cred Heart can inexpensively frolic in the Big Apple, and many do. Boston, the other big metropolitan area, is about 150 miles away and accessible by bus.

Pioneer Life

All in all, Sacred Heart students come here because they want a traditional Catholic edu-cation that can maintain relevance in today's ever changing world. Classes prepare stu-dents not only for a vocation through their professional studies, but also to be lifelong learners and thinkers. Academics are fairly rigid with multiple core curriculums but that's the exact reason why some students choose Sacred Heart: for the core. Social life is not limited but rather is centered around the school's Catholic traditions. The school offers a unique educational experience that will delight those looking for a traditional ed-ucation with Catholic traditions in a modern-day suburban university.—*Hai Pham*

FYI

If you come to Sacred Heart, you should bring: "a car. It will make everything so much easier."
What would you change about Sacred Heart? "More diversity and more dining options."
What should every Sacred Heart student do before they graduate? "Join a community service club, visit NYC, and sit out on the lawn."

Trinity College

Address: 300 Summit Street, Hartford, CT 06016
Phone: 860-297-2180
E-mail address: admissions.office@trincoll.edu
Web site URL: www.trincoll.edu
Year Founded: 1823
Private or Public: Private
Religious Affiliation: None
Location: Urban
Number of Applicants: 4,688
Percent Accepted: 43%
Percent Accepted who enroll: 29%
Number Entering: 591
Number of Transfers Accepted each Year: 24
Middle 50% SAT range: M: 610–690, CR: 590–680, Wr: 610–700
Middle 50% ACT range: 24–29
Early admission program EA/ED/None: ED

Percentage accepted through EA or ED: 68%
EA and ED deadline: 15-Nov
Regular Deadline: 1-Jan
Application Fee: $60
Full time Undergraduate enrollment: 2,211
Total enrollment: 2,331
Percent Male: 49%
Percent Female: 51%
Total Percent Minority or Unreported: 37%
Percent African-American: 7%
Percent Asian/Pacific Islander: 6%
Percent Hispanic: 7%
Percent Native-American: <1%
Percent International: 6%
Percent in-state/out of state: 18%/82%
Percent from Public HS: 40%
Retention Rate: 92%
Graduation Rate 4-year: 81%

Graduation Rate 6-year: 85%
Percent Undergraduates in On-campus housing: 95%
Number of official organized extracurricular organizations: 105
3 Most popular majors: Economics, English Language and Literature, Political Science and Government
Student/Faculty ratio: 10:1
Average Class Size: 16
Percent of students going to grad school: 19%
Tuition and Fees: $41,980
In-State Tuition and Fees if different: No difference
Cost for Room and Board: $11,380
Percent receiving financial aid out of those who apply: 54%
Percent receiving financial aid among all students: 54%

It is no mystery why many argue that Trinity is currently one of the most popular colleges in the nation: the combination of its caring faculty, small class sizes, and supersocial student body justify a nearly 50% jump in applications for the Class of 2015. Even though some students grumble about the preppy feel, frat scene, and tension with the surrounding city of Hartford, applicants clamor for a spot at this "Little Ivy." While roughly half of students play sports on some level, almost all cheer for the varsity teams; none gets more support that the illustrious men's squash team, which holds the nation's longest collegiate varsity winning streak ever.

Great Liberal Arts Education

Regardless of major, students rave about the professors and classroom environment. Trinity boasts a 10:1 student faculty ratio, and students love how engaging their classes are. Thanks to the small class size—between 15 and 20, on average, according to a sophomore—"there is an emphasis on debate and discussion," a senior said. "Classes where the teachers just lecture are few and far between." Even "large" introductory lecture courses rarely have more than 50 students. On top of the extensive in-class interaction with professors, students appreciate how available professors make themselves out of class. "It is very normal for your professor to ask you to meet them over lunch," a sophomore remarked. "They will sacrifice their personal time to make sure that you understand the course material."

As a liberal arts college, Trinity students must take courses across five disciplines: the Arts, Humanities, Natural Sciences, Numerical and Symbolic Reasoning, and Social Sciences, as well as demonstrate proficiency in a foreign language. While one senior lamented that the newly instated language requirement seemed like a waste of time, most students value the required breadth of course study. "It pushes you out of your comfort zone," said a sophomore. "I have never heard of anyone complain about them."

Students must receive 36 course credits

to graduate. Each of the 38 majors requires roughly 12 courses of study; minors require more or less half that total. Approximately 15% of students choose to double major, and one quarter of the study body elects to focus on one of Trinity's signature interdisciplinary majors including neuroscience and public policy and law. The college also boasts a Center for Urban and Global Studies. "Trinity's academic strength is in the humanities," commented a junior; indeed, multiple students said that the strongest and most popular majors are Economics, English and Political Science. Despite the school's focus on the humanities, students added that the Engineering program is renowned.

While freshmen select courses last, they benefit from a first-year program that merges the academic and social. All freshmen, except those enrolled in other guided study programs, must take a first-year seminar, a class of roughly 15 students that engages topics ranging from "Witchcraft in Colonial America" to "Science and the Consumer." Every freshman is placed in dorms near the other students in his or her freshman seminar. Remarked one junior: "I am still really close with the kids in my seminar. You just have a special bond with them." Seminar professors also act as academic advisors until students select a major in the spring of their sophomore year.

Trinity places a special emphasis on its study abroad culture, not surprising as approximately 70% of the students in every class elect to spend a semester or year away from Hartford by the time they graduate. Students choose among a range of options, including spending time in Trinity's own campus in Rome or participating in one of the Trinity Programs in Barcelona, Buenos Aires, Cape Town, Paris, Trinidad or Vienna. The college also has 90 other pre-approved programs across the globe.

Work Hard, Play Hard—At a Frat
After Trinity students spend their week-nights hard at work in the newly renovated library, there is little argument where the place to be is on Thursday, Friday and Saturday nights (for those "ambitious" students, Tuesday too!): the row of frat houses on Vernon Street. While Trinity's president has vowed to lessen the influence of Greek life, for now "the frat life rules the scene," said one sophomore. Not surprisingly, Trinity features an entrenched drinking culture according to a senior, and campus security

rarely does more to underage drinkers than ask them to throw out their drinks.

Even if going to frats three nights a week doesn't hold much appeal, a senior said that the members of the exceedingly social student body find ways to have fun. Kids tend just "to go to dorm common rooms and hang out," said a freshman, and themed houses provide other options, adding that he wished Trinity had an established student center. Despite this lack of a central gathering place, the fact that few students leave campus without a car fosters a strong sense of community. "It's like a family atmosphere in that you are able to see people you know frequently," said a freshman. "It's very easy to make friends that you love being friends with." Most students said there is no getting around the reality of Trinity's image as a haven for wealthy white prepsters from New England boarding schools. Yet students expressed differing opinions on how the lack of racial diversity impacts the feel of the college. Said one sophomore, "The diversity is getting a lot better, but it is still not where it should be. If you are not a rich white kid, you will feel left out—but there are a lot of people working to change that." Another sophomore countered that she doesn't mind the lack of ethnic diversity because everybody brings a diversity of experience and talents that constitute the dynamic campus feel.

> **"It's very easy to make friends that you love being friends with."**

Trinity holds a number of all-campus events through the year to foster campus unity. Multiple students raved about Spring Weekend, a three-day extravaganza including a big-name concert, barbequing and lounging on the quad just after the return from spring break. The fall concert also brings out large crowds of Trinity students.

A Major Emphasis on Athletics
The only campus events that draw equal crowds as the frats are the athletic competitions, and the Division III Bantams are a force to be reckoned with. The men's squash team holds the national record for the longest winning streak in any collegiate sport. Successful football, soccer, and lacrosse teams round out the group of ultra-successful varsity sports in the Trinity athletic program. Trinity students turn out in large numbers

not only to support the varsity squads, but also to compete on the club and intramural levels; roughly 40% of students suit up for a varsity or club team and students enjoy support for more than 15 intramural sports including flag football and yoga.

For those who don't wish to break a sweat outside of class, Trinity features a wide range of nonathletic extracurricular activities. Editors of the weekly student newspaper, *The Trinity Tripod*, said they loved working on the publication. Television and radio broadcasts help Trinity students further hone their skills in communications. According to a sophomore, the five a cappella groups are popular organizations on campus. An Outing Club also sponsors off-campus activities.

The Bubble
Students had very positive things to say about the sprawling 100-acre campus that features multiple grand gothic buildings as well as a towering chapel. Multiple students highlighted the quad as their favorite place to lounge after the long Connecticut winter; in the words of one senior, the Trinity quad is "what you see as a kid dreaming about the collegiate experience."

Trinity students are provided housing for all four years. The college features 26 dorms that are organized into four "neighborhoods" around campus. Most freshmen live in doubles, though some have singles or triples. Housing generally improves with seniority as the school gives preference in the dorm lottery to upperclassmen. Some students choose to live off campus, as well. Students had mixed reviews for the accommodations—in the words of one junior, "There is a range of dorm quality, but none are horrible." Trinity dining options—one buffet style and

two a la carte options—received mixed reviews as well.

One of the reasons some students expressed frustration toward the mediocrity of on-campus dining was because of the challenges of eating out—one of the ramifications of Trinity's location right outside of gritty Hartford, among the most crime-filled cities in America. One freshman said that one of the issues with the socioeconomic troubles of the city is that the school welcomes residents from surrounding neighborhoods onto campus to use some of its facilities. He said that this open-door policy conflicts with the school's interest in safety. Indeed, on-campus burglary is all too common and assault on campus is not unheard of. Many students believe, however, that some Trinity suburbanites bring these incidents on themselves by acting irresponsibly in the urban setting. "A lot of kids don't know how to handle themselves," said a junior. "We are fine as long as people are smart and have common sense—just don't walk by yourself at night!" Those willing to venture into Hartford, the state capital, can take advantage of internship opportunities. Boston and New York City are both two hours away by car.

"Everybody loves it forever"
But beyond the realities of living in Hartford, Trinity students relish their years as Bantams. There is perhaps no better testament to this than spiking numbers of applications in recent years. Trinity students truly value the friendships they form both in and out of the classroom, between faculty and peers alike. In the words of a senior, "If you want a small school where you really get to know your professors and know that your friends are going to be your friends for the rest of your life, then Trinity is a great place."—*Daniel Weiner*

FYI
Best place for food at midnight: "The Cave" [campus café].
Stereotypical Trinity student: "Northeastern boarding school graduate wearing a Patagonia fleece."
If you come to Trinity, you'd better bring: "An open mind in terms of making friends."

United States Coast Guard Academy

Address: 31 Mohegan Avenue, New London, CT 06320-8103

Phone: 860-444-8503

E-mail address: admissions@uscga.edu

Web site URL: www.uscga.edu

Year Founded: 1876

Private or Public: Public

Religious Affiliation: None

Location: Suburban

Number of Applicants: 2,374

Percent Accepted: 16%

Percent Accepted who enroll: 78%

Number Entering: 297

Number of Transfers Accepted each Year: Unreported

Middle 50% SAT range: M: 590–670, CR: 550–640, Wr: 540–630

Middle 50% ACT range: 25–29

Early admission program EA/ED/None: EA

Percentage accepted through EA or ED: 29%

EA and ED deadline: 1-Nov

Regular Deadline: 1-Feb

Application Fee: $0

Full time Undergraduate enrollment: 1,045

Total enrollment: 1,045

Percent Male: 70%

Percent Female: 30%

Total Percent Minority or Unreported: 25%

Percent African-American: 3%

Percent Asian/Pacific Islander: 4%

Percent Hispanic: 10%

Percent Native-American: 1%

Percent International: 2%

Percent in-state/out of state: 4%/96%

Percent from Public HS: 81%

Retention Rate: 89%

Graduation Rate 4-year: 59%

Graduation Rate 6-year: 62%

Percent Undergraduates in On-campus housing: 100%

Number of official organized extracurricular organizations: Unreported

3 Most popular majors: Mechanical Engineering, Oceanography, Political Science

Student/Faculty ratio: 8:1

Average Class Size: 15

Percent of students going to grad school: Unreported

Tuition and Fees: $0

In-State Tuition and Fees if different: No difference

Cost for Room and Board: $0

Percent receiving financial aid out of those who apply: NA

Percent receiving financial aid among all students: NA

Each year graduates of the United States Coast Guard Academy go on to join the oldest life-saving service in the world. While education at the highly competitive academy is free, students are obligated to serve in the U.S. Coast Guard for a minimum of five years (and 85% choose to serve for more time). The school is notable for being among the smallest of the five U.S. federal military academies, as well as the intensity of its academic programs. All cadets leave with a Bachelor of Science and years of physical and mental preparation for the leadership and discipline required of them in the service.

According to students, there are a lot of reasons to want to be at the Coast Guard Academy: top-notch academics, a small student body, and job security post-graduation. One cadet said that the primary attraction for him was "the life-saving aspect" at the core of what it means to be a coast guard. "For me, it was a mission," he said. "For a lot of people it's free education."

Life as a SWAB

Cadets agree that the first year can be particularly trying, but incredibly rewarding in the long run as long as you stick it through. Before entering the Academy their freshman fall, all students are required to go through an extremely intense seven-week-long initiation boot camp.

The challenges don't stop when they arrive on campus, however. Freshmen at service academies typically go through an "indoctrination year," which culminates in the taking of an indoctrination test, after which they are no longer "swabs," as freshmen are commonly known.

First year (or fourth-class) cadets are a very distinctly segregated body, and abide by a separate code of rules, which include greeting everyone they pass in the hallways, and running whenever they are in gym gear, no matter where they're going. They also must be in uniform whenever they go off base. Freshmen are not permitted to maintain Facebook accounts, or to play music out loud in their dorms.

While some first year students expressed frustration with these policies, they noted that it ensures that freshmen bond with other freshmen by all going through these situations together. After the first year, they are free to become friends with upperclassmen, but already have a bond with the members of their own class.

These rules gradually ease up as students pass through the ranks. Older students, who have been out on boats, say that what may seem like stupid rules when you first encounter them as a freshmen—such as always having to know what the next three meals will be, how many days until the next break, or what movies are playing at the local theater—develop skills that allow one to memorize and retain information quickly out in the field.

Freshmen are required to maintain strictly professional relationships with older classmates, to mimic the military chain of command. They cannot, for instance, call older students by their first names, and are not supposed to form friendships with them.

Because of the Academy's incredibly small size—roughly 200 in each class, and 1,000 in the school overall—cadets are forced to look out for one another in a unique way. The mentality is of holding one another accountable to the rules, and upperclassmen are incredibly invested in the success of the freshmen, one said.

Upperclassmen find professional ways to help the first year students out, taking time out of their own schedules to mentor freshmen, from hosting study and tutoring sessions to quizzing them as they prepare for their indoctrination test.

A Day in the Life

During the week students wake up promptly at "0600," and must be ready for morning formation and breakfast 20 minutes later. Military training begins at 0700, and classes at 0800.

Around noon cadets regroup for noon formation and lunch, before returning to class for the rest of the afternoon. The entire school eats together family style for breakfast and lunch. This means cadets sit at tables of 10 at a table, and pass dishes around. USCGA is reputed to have the best-quality food out of all of the service academies. Student opinions on the quality of the food vary, but as one cadet pointed out, the food is free, and if you don't like it, "there's always peanut butter and jelly."

Students have an athletic period from 4 to 6 in the afternoon, and eat dinner between 5 and 7 p.m. Dinner is served in the buffet style that most people think of when envisioning a college cafeteria, with plenty of options and pizza, pasta, salad and fruit always available.

The evening is taken up with activities and studies. Cadets have lots of options when it comes to filling the free time they do have. Many if not most cadets choose to participate in additional sports teams on top of their required athletic credits, and many students interviewed said that sports teams form a core of the social life at the school.

While cadets are required to do a specific number of community service hours, many choose to do more than the requirement. Community service also provides opportunities for more inter-year unity on a smaller scale. One cadet said he marvels at the ability of the student body to get so much done each day.

"Our day is the same length as everybody else's, but we do so much more," he said. "We can't do things like sit around and watch TV or play video games, but we get our work done, and we find ways to have fun."

Since all students live in the same building and don't have a choice about where or who they live with, housing isn't really a contentious issue at USCGA.

Cadets change roommates every semester, rotating through the members of their class. The rationale is that on the fleet there could be people you don't like, and if you're stuck on a boat that's 200 feet long, everyone needs to be able to get along no matter what.

"When you see cadets walking down the hall, you know everyone," one student said. "There's no one you could ask in the class for help who wouldn't give it."

Many students try to get to bed by the time Taps is played at 10 in preparation for the repetition of this exhausting routine the next day. When asked about the one thing they would change about USCGA if they could, student answers were almost universal—to allow them the option of napping during the day.

"Grade Deflation"

Many students say they were surprised at just how much emphasis the Academy places on academics. "When they say that it's challenging, that's real," one cadet warned.

There are only 8 majors to choose from, and 70% of students are engineering majors.

Students said that if anything there is a culture of "grade deflation" at USCGA. One student said that when cadets apply to graduate school, the Academy encloses a disclaimer saying a 2.5 GPA from USCGA is more or less the equivalent of a 3.5 from most other institutions.

"Most people coming to the Academy have never gotten below a B in their life," one cadet said, explaining that students are often shocked to see their first failing grades sometime their sophomore year.

For the first two years students take more or less the same classes, before dividing up into one of eight majors. The majority of students major in a form of engineering, which are known to be the most difficult and harshly graded courses. Others can elect to major in Government or Management, which are supposed to be easier.

Students also expressed enthusiasm for the more specifically Coast Guard–oriented courses built into their schedules, where they learn the nautical science and map technology skills they will soon being applying in the field.

Some yearly social events include the annual homecoming weekend football game, which brings the core of the student body together into one place for the first time in the school year.

The school holds a popular winter ball, which gives the students an unusual opportunity to see each other dressed up. Students try to make time for a personal life, though most accept such maxims as "if she's in blue, she's not for you" or "blue on blue don't mix," and go outside the school—often to the neighboring Connecticut College—to find romance.

USCGA is well known for its Glee Club, which sings and performs all across the country. Students also regularly put on plays and performances on base, with a show going up every month or so. Visual arts have less of a presence on campus, according to one cadet, though students are encouraged to develop creative writing and speaking skills through competitions held every year.

One year, 14 cadets were expelled for the use of a form of synthetic marijuana commonly called "spice." When it comes to illegal drugs, the prevailing attitude among the students is that they're just not worth it, particularly since drug tests do occur. Nevertheless, one cadet said that the incident served as a "wake up call" about just how serious the consequences for any violations could be.

USCGA has a zero-tolerance policy when it comes to drugs and alcohol for those under 21, and the consequences for violating it can be extremely severe. Even for those of legal drinking age, alcohol consumption on base is limited to designated places, or special events where drinking is allowed. That being said, underage drinking does happen.

"At the end of the day, we're still college kids," one cadet said, saying that some are only too willing to take advantage of opportunities to get off campus and drink to decompress.

Life at Sea

Students considering the Coast Guard Academy should be prepared to be challenged academically, physically and emotionally over their four years. There's a lot students at the Academy must give up, but every student interviewed said that they would choose the Coast Guard Academy again. But while the appeal of free tuition, a small school environment and incredible job security after graduation are all draws, students interviewed don't recommend coming to the Coast Guard Academy unless you are truly prepared to be tested, and fully embrace the mission that the Coast Guard represents, at least for the next nine years.

For the student prepared to test themselves, and embrace the mission at the Academy's core, cadets interviewed said each experience at the Coast Guard Academy proves rewarding in the long run, whether or not this is immediately apparent. Students also agreed that the bonds these demanding experiences create among the student body are unparalleled.

"It sounds corny, but you really do become friends with everybody," one student said.

> "Our day is the same length as everybody else's, but we do so much more."

Each summer cadets go on training programs by class that prepare them to apply the skills and discipline they learn during the school year on the open seas. One cadet, echoing the feelings of many, said that this experience made him "realize how much I was capable of—that I didn't think I was."

Time at the Academy may fly by, but the friendships, lessons and skills one takes away from it come to define graduates' experiences for a lifetime, both on the high seas and beyond.—*Anya Grenier*

FYI

If you come to the U.S. Coast Guard Academy, you'd better leave any fake IDs behind, because "if you're caught with it, you're done."

If I could change one thing about U.S. Coast Guard Academy, I'd "let people nap when they want."

What you should know to have fun at the U.S. Coast Guard Academy: "Keep your personality—don't be a robot," and branch out: "Everyone has something that they do to remind them that they're not at the academy, everybody needs a coping mechanism."

University of Connecticut

Address: 2131 Hillside Road, Unit 3088, Storrs, CT 06268-3088
Phone: 860-486-3137
E-mail address: beahusky@uconn.edu
Web site URL: www.uconn.edu
Year Founded: 1881
Private or Public: Public
Religious Affiliation: None
Location: Rural
Number of Applicants: 27,247
Percent Accepted: 47%
Percent Accepted who enroll: 26%
Number Entering: 3,327
Number of Transfers Accepted each Year: 1,107
Middle 50% SAT range: M: 580–670, CR: 550–640, Wr: 550–650
Middle 50% ACT range: 25–29

Early admission program EA/ED/None: EA
Percentage accepted through EA or ED: 72%
EA and ED deadline: 1-Dec
Regular Deadline: 1-Feb
Application Fee: $70
Full time Undergraduate enrollment: 17,063
Total enrollment: 17,815
Percent Male: 51%
Percent Female: 49%
Total Percent Minority or Unreported: 36%
Percent African-American: 6%
Percent Asian/Pacific Islander: 8%
Percent Hispanic: 7%
Percent Native-American: <1%
Percent International: 3%
Percent in-state/out of state: 77%/23%
Percent from Public HS: 87%
Retention Rate: 92%

Graduation Rate 4-year: 56%
Graduation Rate 6-year: 75%
Percent Undergraduates in On-campus housing: 74%
Number of official organized extracurricular organizations: 303
3 Most popular majors: Business, Political Science and Government, Psychology
Student/Faculty ratio: 18:1
Average Class Size: 15
Percent of students going to grad school: 30%
Tuition and Fees: $25,152
In-State Tuition and Fees if different: $8,256
Cost for Room and Board: $11,050
Percent receiving financial aid out of those who apply: 49%
Percent receiving financial aid among all students: 48%

With a history dating back to 1881, University of Connecticut is a large public school with the tradition of more famous private universities, and recent years have seen UConn prove itself to be one of the most academically and athletically prominent public universities in the Northeast.

The University

Four-fifths of UConn's almost 22,000 undergraduates live and study on the main campus in Storrs, Connecticut, and the rest attend one of UConn's five regional campuses located all about the state. Most of the student body hails from the state, but the lack of geographic diversity has little effect on the intellectual diversity.

UConn offers its undergraduates over 100 programs of study for 7 different undergraduate degrees among these different campuses. The academic core of the university is the College of Liberal Arts and Sciences, located on the main Storrs campus, which graduates about half of UConn's baccalaureate students. The College requires students to complete 120 credits worth of classes, each usually worth three credits, including general education requirements for Writing Competency, Quantitative Competency, Second Language Competency, Arts and Humanities, Social Sciences, Science and Technology, and Multiculturalism and Diversity. The classes most commonly used to fulfill these requirements "are usually pretty large, just like any intro class," said one student. UConn offers an honors program for students looking for a greater challenge with smaller class sizes. Of course students are not limited to the College of Liberal Arts and Sciences, but even those who enroll in the College can apply to one of the University's specialized schools—such as the Business School, Pharmacy School, or School of Education—by their junior year.

> **"There's always someone you can make friends with, whether you want to drink or you want to study. There are so many people here that it's unavoidable."**

Some of UConn's more popular majors include Business and Psychology, but even more difficult majors such as "the plentiful forms of Engineering still have quite a large student base among scientifically-minded people," one student said.

Parties and Apartments

Of course, UConn students are always ready to take their well-deserved break from classes each weekend, and while the school alleges its anti-drinking policies are strictly enforced, UConn is popularly seen as a party school where "whether or not you get in trouble depends on whether or not you get written up by the RA, who really couldn't care less," said one freshman, and another student agreed that "people make 'Thirsty Thursday' a very big deal in the residence halls and none of the RAs really care." Most students take the trip to the off-campus Carriage House or to the Celeron Square Apartments to get their partying done on the weekends. Students explain that "the walk is kind of long, but it's definitely safe and can be a bonding experience for fellow travelers." On Saturdays, "everyone tends to go out (and it's especially easy for the girls to get into frat parties all located along Huntington Lodge Rd.)," said one male student, "but if you have connections, you'll be fine." The frat scene at UConn is not very large, but it is always noticeable. "It helps to rush a frat to make friends, but it is in no way necessary," said another student. UConn students see their school as a place where "you can party with literally thousands of people at once during Spring Weekend or sit in your dorm with a few good friends. There's always someone you can make friends with, whether you want to drink or you want to study.

There are so many people here that it's unavoidable."

The Housing Jungle

Freshman moving on to UConn's Storrs campus are guaranteed housing, which is definitely a luxury at a university with such a large number of students and, recently, an unexpectedly high percent of admitted students matriculating. Aside from those who, for example, live in honors housing, live in the EcoHouse, or live with fellow members of the WiMSE (Women in Math, Science & Engineering) Learning Community, most freshmen will move into one of the eleven dorm buildings on North Campus or one of the seven dorms on Northwest Campus when they begin their college career. While those who live on Northwest get a relatively new and nice dorm, "freshmen in North live in 'The Jungle'; it's pretty old and until recently were very loud and crowded party spaces," according to one student who described North's dorm rooms, which usually hold up to three people.

After one or two years on campus, students commonly move into apartments of their own, but students say that these apartments aren't often very close to classes and "they are sometimes as hard to find as it is to find a room in the dorms." Unfortunately, housing has been a struggle for the UConn administration and students for several years now.

The Storrs campus offers its students eight dining halls, which one student said "[range] from 'Gross, they put mayonnaise on our pizza'—disgusting, to 'Holy moly, they got pad thai!'—awesome." These dining halls are spaced throughout the campus, but students recognize that "people living on Northwest get the best freshman housing and also the best dining hall."

Since almost four-fifths of UConn's student body hail from Connecticut, returning home on weekends is rather common. However, one student said that this is not a large problem at all: "Although I originally expected most people to leave on the weekends as a typical state 'suitcase-school,' there's plenty to do on the weekends when others aren't around, and you're never alone."

Huskymania

UConn is well known for its sports teams, and this is totally unsurprising given their perennial success. Both the women's and men's basketball teams have established dominance, as yearly they compete for national championships, with the women's team recently winning a much-publicized 90 games in a row, the longest winning streak of any NCAA men's or women's basketball team. Tickets to watch the Huskies dominate in the on-campus Gampel Pavillion and the XL Center in nearby Hartford are so popular they sometimes become rather scarce, but "if you're lucky you can snag a ticket" and enjoy a really exciting game on a Friday night in the winter.

The football team, playing at home in the 40,000-seat Rentschler Field, also has become quick to rise to fame. The Connecticut Huskies football team became a full-fledged member of Division I-A in the first two years of the millennium, and in the same decade as its membership, has reached a high ranking. Keeping up with this high level of excellence, the soccer teams and field hockey team have proven their mettle, going far in several NCAA tournaments in recent years.

For those who are not varsity quality (a high standard in such an athletically successful university), UConn also offers its students plenty of intramural sports ranging from the standard football and basketball to others such as dodgeball. The IM games are very much for fun, but in a school with such athletic prowess and pride, they also result in "some seriously fierce competition." Students say that this competitive nature is something to be expected, and feel that their Husky pride is well-deserved.
—*Connor Moseley*

FYI

What's the typical weekend schedule? "Basketball game, party, or maybe an intramural football game with some friends, catch up on work and maybe some sleep."

What differentiates UConn the most from other colleges is "the ridiculous amount of school and team spirit."

If I could change one thing about UConn, I'd change "the fact that many people like to leave on the weekends."

Wesleyan University

Address: 70 Wyllys Avenue, Middletown, CT 06459

Phone: 860-685-3000

E-mail address: admission@wesleyan.edu

Web site URL: www.wesleyan.edu

Year Founded: 1831

Private or Public: Private

Religious Affiliation: None

Location: Suburban

Number of Applicants: 8,250

Percent Accepted: 21%

Percent Accepted who enroll: 32%

Number Entering: 748

Number of Transfers Accepted each Year: 140

Middle 50% SAT range: M: 660–740, CR: 640–740, Wr: 650–750

Middle 50% ACT range: 30–33

Early admission program EA/ED/None: ED

Percentage accepted through EA or ED: 43%

EA and ED deadline: 15-Nov

Regular Deadline: 1-Jan

Application Fee: $55

Full time Undergraduate enrollment: 2,854

Total enrollment: 3,215

Percent Male: 45%

Percent Female: 55%

Total Percent Minority or Unreported: 40%

Percent African-American: 7%

Percent Asian/Pacific Islander: 6%

Percent Hispanic: 6%

Percent Native-American: 0%

Percent International: 7%

Percent in-state/out of state: 7%/93%

Percent from Public HS: 57%

Retention Rate: 94%

Graduation Rate 4-year: 84%

Graduation Rate 6-year: 93%

Percent Undergraduates in On-campus housing: 98%

Number of official organized extracurricular organizations: 200

3 Most popular majors: Social Sciences, Area and Ethnic Studies, Psychology

Student/Faculty ratio: 9:1

Average Class Size: 19

Percent of students going to grad school: Unreported

Tuition and Fees: $43,974

In-State Tuition and Fees if different: No difference

Cost for Room and Board: $12,032

Percent receiving financial aid out of those who apply: 84%

Percent receiving financial aid among all students: 47%

Named the "Most Annoying Liberal Arts College" by the gossip blog Gawker in 2007, Wesleyan University has a strong reputation for being an ultra-liberal school where political correctness is not just commendable but necessary. While this image of Wesleyan certainly rings true to many students, the University has seen a gradual shift toward a new identity. Situated in Middletown—nearly halfway between Boston and New York—Wesleyan provides a refined breeding ground for the expression of diverse perspectives for its multifaceted students.

Sincere and Studious Students

The academic atmosphere at Wesleyan can be described as being extremely genuine. Students consider learning to be an intrinsically valuable endeavor, and tend to push themselves to learn as much as they can. Although there are some people who are GPA-conscious—"You have to work hard for an A, but it's not impossible"—students "work hard because they like what they do: they're not all mindless drones." According to one sophomore, there are a good number of "ideologically driven classes with political perspectives," especially within feminine, gender, and sexuality studies, in which "young activists are being taught by the wise, old activists." However, another student mentioned that while there is an abundance of politically motivated courses, standard "objective" classes do exist at Wesleyan. Indeed, Wesleyan's science program is one of the strongest amongst the small liberal arts colleges: it receives the largest amount of National Science Foundation grants and also recently built a science center.

The Wesleyan education focuses on developing in each student "10 essential capabilities"—including writing, speaking, interpretation, intercultural literacy, and effective citizenship. In the liberal arts tradition, students are expected to meet Gen Ed Expectations, although these are somewhat less stringent than at other comparable institutions. There are two special academic programs that Wesleyan students can enter during their sophomore year. The College of Social Studies (CSS) is a rigorous interdisciplinary program that integrates economics, political science, history, and government through colloquia, tutorials, and seminars. CSS has a reputation as being a program "for people who want to run the world." The other alternative is the humanities-oriented College of Letters (COL)—also known as the "College of Love." Both programs involve a number of courses without grades, with written evaluations in their stead. According to one student, admitted students tend to be somewhat insular and host parties on Mondays, since they have group assignments due on Sunday nights. The CSS and COL tend to be in the student body's general consciousness, as everyone knows about the programs, and most people have probably considered applying at one time or another.

Among the academic departments, the Department of Film Studies, led by the renowned film critic Jeanine Basinger, is regarded as particularly strong. The numerous alumni have a very successful track record and have penetrated the ranks of the Hollywood elite through the achievements of the group known as the "Wesleyan mafia," which includes Michael Bay (director of *Transformers*, *Armageddon*, and *The Rock*), Joss Whedon (creator of *Buffy the Vampire Slayer*), and Laurence Mark (producer of *Jerry Maguire*). The Film Studies program attempts to integrate "history and theory with practice" and emphasizes the analysis of film over merely its production. Most of the program takes place in the state-of-the-art Center for Film Studies, which also houses a vast and unique film archive.

The academics at Wesleyan are as intimate as they are sincere. Students find that the small size of the school lends to the ease with which students can interact and eventually befriend their professors. For example, one student noted that apart from a "few arrogant professors" most of his professors had gotten to know him better, typically through relationships beyond the classroom: "Our professor took [our class] to his house and had a BBQ, where we also played croquet in his yard." The ability to get really close to a professor is a distinct benefit at a small liberal arts college such as Wesleyan. In the end, small class size and a passionate, vocal student body allow classes to "get some really great conversations going," where students pay serious attention to each other while furiously scribbling notes.

Lively Liberalism

The political climate at Wesleyan has always been—and continues to be—very liberal. One student, while speculating on the presence of conservative-leaning students on campus, remarked, "Even if there were conservative people, they're probably hiding it." Students on the right of the political spectrum seem to have trouble finding space to express themselves openly and honestly without being ostracized.

Without a doubt, Wesleyan has played a key part in many of the country's most progressive movements. According to one student, Wesleyan was a frontrunner in the civil rights movement. For example, a number of professors traveled down to Mississippi and demonstrated alongside Dr. Martin Luther King. This sort of historical precedent has affected Wesleyan's contemporary political culture. One student mentioned that the countercultural movement's lifeblood in part lies in the "sense of history that exists [at Wesleyan], a sense of Wesleyan as countercultural—even before the sixties—a sense that has extended until now."

On campus, the "social activist" groups maintain a very active presence. For example, according to one junior, the "Transgender/gay/lesbian community [and their associated clubs] host viewings of pornographic films on a regular basis." Beyond the socially aware, the assertive presence of "hipsters"—not to be confused with "hippies," although they also exist on campus—at Wesleyan elicit reactions such as "pretentious wannabes" or "elitist crowd." Without fail, a large portion of Wesleyan students draw on the lifestyle made famous by residents of Williamsburg, Brooklyn. Of all the organizations on campus, the Eclectic Society, a fraternity, provides Wesleyan's social glue: its hipster members host many of the more well-attended parties on campus.

> **"Wesleyan is a very experimental place, which is a fun thing to be as a college—it's fun to have people who aren't afraid of doing something abnormal."**

Although it is clear that Wesleyan's student body represents a broad spectrum of ethnic, geographic, and cultural backgrounds, some students question the extent of interactions that occur between people from different comprehensive worldviews. One student cautioned that one's understanding of the diversity of the student body "depends on what kind of angle you're coming from." While he appreciated the multitude of viewpoints, he pointed out that "There are a bunch of people

who don't branch out and try to meet people with fresh views." Another student mentioned that "There is a pretty clear segregation that sort of naturally happened. You wouldn't want to say that in public though—there's a lot of political correctness." Although it may look as though Wesleyan is an ideal "melting pot" of unique individuals coming together to form the Wesleyan identity, there is certainly a share of the student body that remains skeptical of the tolerance of its peers.

In a nutshell, according to one junior, Wesleyan students can best be characterized as "socially aware and offbeat people with a variety of tastes." The student body is composed of people with a range of personalities and perspectives from all walks of life. Students place a high emphasis on the discovery of one's own identity, and the ability to express and enact such an identity with minimal restraint. The lifestyle of the inhabitants of West College ("WestCo") serves as a testament to this theme. Inhabitants of the so-called "naked dorm" make their own rules on how they should live and behave in their residence. That clothing is optional should be readily apparent; in addition, meetings are planned at odd times such as 9:13 P.M. as a way to break the norm in society that events must occur on the hour or at 10- or 15-minute intervals. WestCo's inhabitants—and, more broadly, Wesleyan students—are constantly pushing their creative abilities to the limit in an attempt to better expose their interests to the world around them: Wesleyan students are not afraid to confidently live their lives as they see fit.

Freedom on Foss Hill

Students find that living at Wesleyan is remarkably easy. This begins with the wide range of campus living options available to students. Freshmen usually begin their Wesleyan experience in freshman dorms, where they are paired up with other new students. As they become upperclassmen, students have the opportunity to live in normal dorms. "Program housing," where small groups of students can live in houses with unique mission statements (e.g. community service house) are available, as well as senior houses, which are semi-off-campus and wood-frame. The sprawl of the campus is very manageable and the campus living situation meets every student's needs.

Another way in which students live easier lives comes from the fact that the administration—intentionally or not—turns a blind eye toward the pervasive drug culture that exists on campus. Students tend to favor marijuana and the psychedelic effects of occasional shroom and acid trips. A number of students confirmed that a majority of the student body smokes weed. In fact, Wes Fest weekend—when accepted high school seniors come visit Wesleyan—is always scheduled to include April 20th (an important day for marijuana lovers), on which day the student body congregates en masse on Foss Hill. One student proudly asserted that Foss Hill was a "legendary place on 4/20, where literally 1,500 people with bongs meet on the Hill." Foss Hill is widely regarded as both the central location and favorite hang-out spot on campus. Students pass by it between classes and agree that "it's a place to go on the nice, sunny days for a nice game of Ultimate Frisbee."

An Experimental Experience
Upon comparing their pre-matriculation expectations to post-matriculation realities, most students seem to agree that Wesleyan does lie on the frontier of political activism. One student said the political atmosphere "surprised me, because I didn't realize just how political the school was." Above all, however, the school is about experimentation, and a number of students agree with this description. One sophomore praised the benefits of testing out new things: "Wesleyan is a very experimental place, which is a fun thing to be as a college—it's fun to have people who aren't afraid of doing something abnormal." But then again, it's okay to be "normal" too, because, at the end of the day, "If you're fine with being normal, you can still find your crowd."—*Wookie Kim*

FYI
If you come to Wesleyan, you'd better bring "weed: you'll make lots of friends."
What is the typical weekend schedule? "Wake up for brunch on Saturday, work a bit, hang out under the sun on Foss Hill, go to a performance event (like Samsara), head to Eclectic or Fountain Street. Work all of Sunday."
If I could change one thing about Wesleyan, I'd "change the repressive remnants of political correctness that actually make people self-censoring and make conversations less interesting."
Three things every student at Wesleyan should do before graduating are "do shrooms in the graveyard, go to an Eclectic party, and see Prometheus (a fire-throwing group) at the base of Foss Hill."

Yale University

Address: PO Box 208234, New Haven, CT 06520-8234
Phone: 203-432-9300
E-mail address: undergraduate.admission@yale.edu
Web site URL: www.yale.edu
Year Founded: 1701
Private or Public: Private
Religious Affiliation: None
Location: Urban
Number of Applicants: 26,003
Percent Accepted: 8%
Percent Accepted who enroll: 69%
Number Entering: 1,343
Number of Transfers Accepted each Year: 34
Middle 50% SAT range: M: 710–790, CR: 700–800, Wr: 710–800
Middle 50% ACT range: 32–35

Early admission program EA/ED/None: EA
Percentage accepted through EA or ED: 14%
EA and ED deadline: 1-Nov
Regular Deadline: 31-Dec
Application Fee: $75
Full time Undergraduate enrollment: 5,310
Total enrollment: 11,701
Percent Male: 48%
Percent Female: 52%
Total Percent Minority or Unreported: 51%
Percent African-American: 7%
Percent Asian/Pacific Islander: 16%
Percent Hispanic: 16%
Percent Native-American: 1%
Percent International: 11%
Percent in-state/out of state: 7%/93%
Percent from Public HS: 55%
Retention Rate: 99%

Graduation Rate 4-year: 97%
Graduation Rate 6-year: 99%
Percent Undergraduates in On-campus housing: 88%
Number of official organized extracurricular organizations: 350
3 Most popular majors: Social Sciences, History, Interdisciplinary Studies
Student/Faculty ratio: 6:1
Average Class Size: 15
Percent of students going to grad school: 23%
Tuition and Fees: $40,500
In-State Tuition and Fees if different: No difference
Cost for Room and Board: $12,200
Percent receiving financial aid out of those who apply: 96%
Percent receiving financial aid among all students: 60%

When Yale's newly renovated Bass Library reopened at midnight in October 2007, the event seemed more like a late-night blowout than the opening of a library. But as students raced through the underground stacks, admiring the new shelves and sampling the café's organic fare, the library extravaganza tied together the aspects of Yale life that its students cherish. With love of learning at the center of the Yale experience, students still find ways to create fun and new traditions in the unlikeliest of ways, all within the context of a university that continues to grow and reshape itself while maintaining centuries of tradition.

A Community of Scholars

Founded in 1701 by Congregationalist ministers, Yale has maintained a commitment to academic excellence ever since. But don't let the world-renowned professors intimidate you—the University is well-known for its strong focus on undergraduate education, which means that faculty members are not so pressured to publish and conduct research that they fail to throw themselves wholeheartedly into teaching their undergraduates. One sophomore said she has found that there is a "robust dialogue between students and faculty." And while entering an academic institution filled with thousands of other motivated high-achievers may seem daunting as well, Yalies—who are known as both Bulldogs and Elis—find that their fellow students provide a supportive rather than cutthroat environment and are usually more than willing to study and brainstorm together.

As part of its liberal arts curriculum, Yale requires students to fulfill 36 credits—as opposed to the 32 mandated by the other Ivy League schools—including courses to fulfill a major and two course credits each in the humanities and arts, the sciences, the social sciences, quantitative reasoning and writing. The additional foreign language requirement may be completed with between one and three courses, depending on previous language study. While these rigorous requirements contribute to an intense academic environment, students said, rather than oppressive, they found the challenge to be more of an opportunity to thrive. One junior remarked that he felt "acceptably overwhelmed."

One reason that many students feel overwhelmed is the 2,000 courses from which to choose. During the first two weeks of each semester, students take advantage of "shopping period" by attending as many classes as they wish—and sometimes as many as they can fit into a day—and deciding whether they like the professor and course material before officially enrolling. And when the time comes to enroll in courses, students report little trouble in gaining access to the ones they want, with the exception of some competitive seminars with caps of 15 to 18 participants, and even then "talking to the professor and making your case usually does the trick." Most courses have between 15 and 30 students, though some introductory lectures host more than 100. Among the most popular majors are history, economics, and political science, and there is a lot of interest in psychology and the premed track, particularly biology. Professors and courses that students highly recommended included Introduction to Psychology with either Paul Bloom or Marvin Chun, History of Modern China with Jonathan Spence, Sex, Evolution, and Human Nature with Laurie Santos, and Constitutional Law with Akhil Amar.

For those looking to fulfill the distributional requirements, there are a variety of gut courses, including Philosophy of Science, and Computers and the Law, although some students warned that while there may be less work, these supposedly easy classes are not guaranteed A's. Humanities-oriented students who take gut classes instead of opting to hike up "Science Hill" early each morning are often ridiculed by the more scientifically inclined, and a mechanical engineering major said he and his friends "do debate the relative difficulty of the sciences and the humanities." Other students said while classrooms in the different disciplines are separated geographically by the Hill, residential life and extracurriculars bring everyone together seamlessly. An English major said she enjoys that Yale's academic life "really helps stimulate interesting conversations outside the classroom. People aren't afraid to admit that they're really passionate about a subject."

The All-Important Sorting Ceremony

Many of these intimate dialogues in dining halls or dorm rooms are fostered by the residential college system, which Yalies across the board identify as one of the most distinctive, rewarding features of life as a Bulldog. Students are randomly sorted into one of the 12 colleges, which serve as a living community, social environment, intramural sports base, and source of unique pride and loyalty. That almost 90 percent of Yale students choose to live on campus for all four years is a testament to the strong bonds that are formed among those that share a college. While the 12 differ architecturally—Jonathan Edwards is Gothic, Davenport is Georgian, and Morse and Stiles are 60s-era Saarinen designs, for example—and they offer different amenities, the random assemblage of students is representative of the University at large. While Yale, with around 5,400 students, is midsized, the colleges help to make the school more personal. A Morse College student described the residential college system as "an amazing opportunity to escape the major college campus. It's a community within a community, with a master and dean and so many resources, like a library and buttery." Along with cheap late-night food from the buttery and the convenience of the nearby library, colleges also offer a variety of facilities, including gyms, movie theaters, performance spaces, and woodworking areas.

Old Campus houses freshmen from 10 of the 12 colleges, allowing members of the same class to get to know each other before moving into their respective colleges. Students in the larger Timothy Dwight and Silliman may live there all four years. The colleges also provide both academic and general support, from the freshman counselors who live on Old Campus to masters and deans, who live in the colleges and are enthusiastic about getting to know students. The University has almost completed the renovation of the 12 colleges, which has transformed suite arrangements, added new facilities, and beautified, all while retaining the traditional architecture and atmosphere. Each year, students in the college being renovated live in "Swing Space," a recently constructed dorm that features long hallways of suites with common rooms, kitchenettes, and private bathrooms. Students said that while Swing is less centrally located than many of the colleges, its living arrangement is a refreshing alternative from the norm, which consists of separate entryways and complex suites of between two and 10 residents, rather than the hallways common at other schools.

With the "Hogwarts-style" Commons, a dining hall in each of the 12 colleges, plus additional eateries in the University's professional and graduate schools, Yalies seem to have a lot of dining options. But some said they feel constrained by the requirement that on-campus students purchase a meal plan, even though they can exchange meals for flex dollars to be used at the convenience store. The benefit of eating in the dining halls, in spite of the sometimes monotonous food, is the knowledge that you will almost always have someone you can sit with, and a strong sense of community develops. The Sustainable Food Project, which brings local-grown and organic food to dining halls, may be "often healthier but not always tastier," although students said they gave the spirit of the project high marks.

Not Too Busy to Have Fun

Even as the residential colleges provide a social foundation, students raved about the many opportunities to "find your scene." Although students said there are definitely some distinct social groups—such as athletes and hipsters—a film major said he has "always felt that one can easily move throughout groups as long as you have the right disposition and outlook." Extracurricular activities are a common method of meeting new people. In terms of drinking, students estimated that about two-thirds of Yale students drink, but it is "perfectly acceptable" for someone to choose not to and still hang out with people who imbibe. Yale's policy towards alcohol consumption is fairly lenient, despite recent Connecticut laws that strengthened adherence to restrictions. A junior commented that "the policy of Yale has always been to give us a lot of respect in that regard, and they're not going to strongly enforce us on drinking . . . but they do take care of us when we over-drink and need help." As for drugs, the junior's perception of on-campus use was that "it's probably mostly just pot and maybe some cocaine, but I don't think too many people do really hardcore drugs."

In any case, students take advantage of campus events as well as parties, ensuring that alcohol does not by any means dominate University socializing. The myriad campus groups devoted to putting on dance, theater, comedy, and musical productions guarantee that there will always be something happening in the evenings, and periodic residential college council-sponsored dance parties and special events add to the fun. Morse and Stiles's Prohibition, previously Casino Night, in November regularly draws more than 2,000 students, there's the Spider Ball in April, and neon-clad students dance the night away to Duran Duran at Silliman's '80s-themed Safety Dance in October. During the day, the residential colleges' "Master's Teas" are well-known for bringing interesting and prominent figures to campus for intimate talks with groups of students—recent visitors include children's folk singer Raffi, the editor of the *Harry Potter* books and the pop group Hanson, while past guests include former Supreme Court Justice Sandra Day O'Connor and author Kurt Vonnegut.

The majority of Yale students are politically liberal, and those that self-identify as moderates tend towards the left as well, but there is a strong contingent of conservative students who do find a voice on campus amongst all the Yale Dems activities. When it comes to clothing, Elis know how to dress well, as befitting the New England private school stereotype, but while it's not uncommon to see guys wearing button-downs and slacks to class, sweatpants are accepted as well. Yalies are perceived as being predominantly middle-class, students said, and approximately 60 percent of the student body receives some form of financial aid. The campus is racially and ethnically diverse, and student organizations dedicated to celebrating unique cultural heritages are prominent fixtures on campus. A sizable 10 percent of the student body hails from outside the United States, but the rest "come from New York or California, and not often in between." The openly gay community at Yale—which is often labeled the "gay Ivy"—is a testament to the high level of acceptance on campus; a gay junior remarked that "you can't really be openly prejudiced or comfortably prejudiced here because you just won't fit in." Moreover, a senior in Branford explained that labels do not have to be all-encompassing: "It's okay to be gay and not to be defined by being gay here."

Out in the Elm City
When they arrive on campus, Yalies immediately face the question of how the University integrates with the surrounding city. While New Haven still retains some of its reputation for crime and racial tension, the city is on the upswing, having undergone major efforts at revitalization over the past two decades. One area near campus that students mentioned as indicative of how the city is changing is Ninth Square, located a few blocks from campus. Formerly a district of abandoned storefronts, Ninth Square has been overhauled by a city commission. Several restaurants, including Indian, French bistro and Malaysian cuisine, have opened in the area. Older standbys near campus include Yorkside, a multitude of Thai restaurants and

"the burrito cart" for meals, while Rudy's, Hot Tomato's, and Viva's are popular nighttime stops.

But even as new businesses multiply close to campus, students still point out the University's problems integrating with the New Haven community. Occasional incidents of crime on campus, usually muggings, have students conscious of taking big-city precautions, such as not walking alone at night. One student remarked, "I think people feel safe but also realize they need to be responsible and aware." Some panhandlers are such fixtures that they have acquired quasi-affectionate monikers, such as the "Flower Lady" and the "Shakespeare Lady." The surrounding area does provide myriad opportunities for community involvement, including tutoring and canvassing for local political candidates. Furthermore, all the excitement of New York City is less than two hours away by train.

Quirky or Cultish? You Decide.
It's hard to go wrong with 350 registered undergraduate organizations. There are the campus favorites, such as political groups, publications, cultural groups, community service organizations, and a cappella groups. And then there are the quirkier niche groups, such as the Society for the Exploration of Campus Secrets, whose members sneak around campus looking for access to hidden Yale locales, and the Anti-Gravity Society, which draws the school's jugglers. The Yale College Council provides opportunity for student government involvement. Some of the organizations, including the Yale Political Union, the *Yale Daily News*, and a cappella groups, have reputations for being "cultish," but students will tell you that most undergraduates are very committed to their extracurricular activities. A good number of students have jobs as well, mostly on campus.

The Yale men's hockey team has recently risen to the top of national rankings and now regularly draws full attendance at Ingalls Rink. Otherwise, except at the epic Harvard–Yale football game every November, school athletic pride doesn't surface very often. Few undergraduates regularly attend other sporting events, even though the rowing and sailing teams are of international caliber. The Bulldogs' home, the Yale Bowl, holds more than 64,000 spectators, and Payne Whitney Gymnasium is the second-largest gym in the world. The Harvard–Yale game is almost better known for its tailgating, alumni reunions and pranks pulled by each school than for the football game itself.

> **"People aren't afraid to admit that they're really passionate about a subject."**

The Harvard–Yale rivalry certainly encompasses athletics, but it also extends into good-natured competition over which student body enjoys better quality of life, which school is ranked higher in a particular year, and other quibbles. While the jury is still out on a scientific conclusion, the emphatic Yale refrain persists: "Harvard sucks!"

And a unique Yale pride does follow students not only through their four "bright college years" in New Haven (as the school song goes), but into their later years as well, through the alumni community. While a junior affirmed, "I think there are more spectacular, friendly, and interesting people here than I thought possible," a sophomore happily pointed out that "students didn't choose Yale to get a 4.0—they chose it because it's a genuinely intellectual place to be." Even as Yale looks to the future—for example, through globalization initiatives that connect the University intimately to China—it manages to retain an atmosphere of tradition, both in academics and fun. Any undergraduate studying grand strategy with the bells of Harkness Tower playing Britney Spears in the background can tell you that.—*Kimberly Chow*

FYI

If you come to Yale, you'd better bring "a coffeemaker and a big mug to go with it!"

What's the typical weekend schedule? "On Thursday night, go to a bar like Rudy's; try to get errands done during the day on Friday, then go out to a play, room party, organization-sponsored dance party, a cappella concert, improv show, or some combination thereof on Friday and Saturday nights; go to a late brunch and cram in as much studying as possible on Sunday, and go to bed too late."

If I could change one thing about Yale, I'd "work on the sometimes tense relationship between Yale and the city of New Haven."

Two things every college student at Yale should do before graduating are "climb Harkness Tower and go to a naked party."

Delaware

University of Delaware

Address: 116 Hullihen Hall, Newark, DE 19716-6210
Phone: 302-831-8123
E-mail address: admissions@udel.edu
Web site URL: www.udel.edu
Year Founded: 1743
Private or Public: Public
Religious Affiliation: None
Location: Suburban
Number of Applicants: 23,510
Percent Accepted: 54%
Percent Accepted who enroll: 26%
Number Entering: 3,365
Number of Transfers Accepted each Year: 802
Middle 50% SAT range: M: 550–660, CR: 540–640, Wr: 540–650
Middle 50% ACT range: 24–29
Early admission program EA/ED/None: None

Percentage accepted through EA or ED: NA
EA and ED deadline: NA
Regular Deadline: 15-Jan
Application Fee: $75
Full time Undergraduate enrollment: 15,146
Total enrollment: 15,887
Percent Male: 40%
Percent Female: 60%
Total Percent Minority or Unreported: 22%
Percent African-American: 5%
Percent Asian/Pacific Islander: 4%
Percent Hispanic: 6%
Percent Native-American: <1%
Percent International: 3%
Percent in-state/out of state: 37%/63%
Percent from Public HS: 80%
Retention Rate: 92%
Graduation Rate 4-year: 67%

Graduation Rate 6-year: 77%
Percent Undergraduates in On-campus housing: 44%
Number of official organized extracurricular organizations: 250
3 Most popular majors: Biology, Nursing/Registered Nurse, Psychology
Student/Faculty ratio: 15:1
Average Class Size: 25
Percent of students going to grad school: 55%
Tuition and Fees: $25,940
In-State Tuition and Fees if different: $9,670
Cost for Room and Board: $10,196
Percent receiving financial aid out of those who apply: 57%
Percent receiving financial aid among all students: 55%

Delaware is a small state, but UDel punches above its weight. Founded in 1734, the school combines a typical big-school party scene with academic rigor that led authors Howard and Matthew Greene to include it in their book *The Public Ivies: America's Flagship Public Universities*. For a student who wants the ideal college experience—a small town, challenging classes, and a top-notch football team—UDel is a must-see.

Classes to Endure, Classes to Enjoy

UDel packs 15,000 undergrads into the town of Newark (pop. 31,000) but gives them room to roam when they enter the classroom. The university offers 128 majors alongside over 100 minors, allowing students to pursue any field they choose, from Fashion Design to Agricultural Economics (UDel's functioning farm is open to all students).

All majors come with requirements; those in the science and engineering programs are the most restrictive, but all students in the College of Arts and Sciences need at least one course in four different (and extremely broad) subject areas. Reactions to required classes range from ambivalent to ecstatic. "My biology lab was a breeze after high school bio," said one sophomore, "but it was very time-consuming." Another student, though, felt transformed by the lab course she "thought (she) would dread" and decided on a natural-science major halfway through the semester. Despite the Breadth Requirements' ability to open students' minds, many expressed relief that advanced high-school credits let them test out of a few mandatory courses.

Outside of required classes, students who leave themselves open to new experiences always find something to love. Undergraduate instruction receives high praise: "Every professor I have is extremely approachable and truly invaluable," one freshman told the Guide. An average class size of 25 guarantees attention outside of the largest lecture courses, and professors hold office hours outside of class that give dedicated students the chance to earn "extra credit or special hints about upcoming exams." Students who want to be even more selective with their schooling can apply to the Dean's Scholar Program to design their own major or retool their requirements. There is also an Honors College, featuring heavy reading, smaller classes and housing in separate dorms near a much-needed library.

Working for the Weekend

UDel is an academic powerhouse in a range of subjects. The school's depth of scholarship is almost unequaled among midsize public universities, and UDel's sciences are especially impressive, with one of the nation's strongest chemical engineering programs and recently established scholarly institutes for alternative energy and biotechnology. Like the Honors College, the sciences discourage complacency—according to one freshman, "engineering students are struggling now because most of them breezed through their senior year of high school." Students in many majors agreed that classes in the college require more work than anything they took before arriving.

And then the weekend arrives. UDel students agree; if you want to find a party, there's always something available. From Friday night to the early hours of Monday morning, Greek and other groups keep the campus community awake and active; more than 50% of males on campus are fraternity members. Says one freshman: "it's impossible not to find a party on the weekend if the frats are being frats." However, it's also very possible to celebrate college life without crowding into the "random, hot, sticky" Greek scene, whether it's a private party in the house of an upperclassman, a cultural event (Wiz Khalifa drew a crowd of thousands in October 2011), or an impromptu "late-night, seven-hour adventure" with a few choice friends.

Despite the university's busy social scene, restrictions on alcohol exceed those set by most public colleges. A "three-strikes-and-you're-out" policy promises suspension for drinking in the dorms, while new businesses on Main Street are not allowed to sell it at all. But off-campus parties go mostly undisturbed, and on-campus dry events are a daily occurrence thanks to the student social committee. Overall, UDel students can choose their own nightlife; "it's all here," said one sophomore.

Fight! Fight! Fightin' Blue Hens!

In the wider United States, UDel might best be known for the strength of its football program. The Blue Hens reached Division I-AA title games in 2007 and 2010, and over 20,000 fans fill Delaware Stadium for an average home game. On game day, "The atmosphere is amazing . . . if you're not screaming in support, then you'll stand out," says one freshman. The volleyball and men's soccer teams also find success within the Colonial Athletic Association, and 19 other varsity sports compete for student attention alongside club sports and intramurals. Even YoUDee, the school mascot, was inducted into the Mascot Hall of Fame in 2006. UDel might not be the starting point for many NFL or NBA careers, but student-athletes and student-fans alike will find a happy home at the university.

Cuisine, Culture, and Clubs

Newark is a small town dominated by the college at its center, but like UDel, it packs a lot into a small space. One student calls Main Street "one of the best in any college town," and delicious restaurants abound, from the usual mix of coffee shops to Main Street Sliders and Grotto's, a Delaware tradition "unlike any other pizza I've eaten, in a good way." For many undergrads, IHOP is unbeatable as a light-night eating destination: "Breakfast is the best meal of the day; why shouldn't I eat it twice?" Clothing stores on Main tend to be expensive, but Delaware's lack of sales tax delights out-of-staters, and any other retail services a student could require thrive in Newark's central thoroughfare.

> **"The atmosphere is amazing . . . if you're not screaming in support, then you'll stand out."**

For culture hounds eager to see the latest indie film or blog-beloved band, Newark may disappoint; the local music and art scenes are growing, but still relatively scarce given

UDel's size. Fortunately, the town is a mere twelve miles from Wilmington, Delaware's urban center, and less than an hour's drive from Philadelphia. Day trips to Philly are common, and the twin University Student Centers, Perkins and Trabant, offer big-screen movies and bus trips to cities, ski resorts, and other destinations. However, beware that the heavy rainy weather—in winter and spring—may prevent excursions outside.

Of course, there is no reason to leave campus for students who want to keep busy. UDel packs hundreds of non-Greek, non-sporting organizations: theater troupes, cultural clubs, a capella, marching band, religious groups, community service organizations, and more. "Everyone finds a niche," multiple students told the Guide verbatim—and the entering classes of close to 5,000 freshmen per year make starting a new niche a very doable task.

Your New Home: Now With Friends Inside!

UDel is not a hotel, but students generally come to enjoy their living spaces in spite of—or perhaps because of—their flaws. Off-campus apartments are available starting in sophomore year, but 90% of undergrads stick with dorms nonetheless. One sophomore explained: "People love their dorms . . . it's a pure, inexplicable affection." Rodney might not be the most comfortable, but one denizen swore that "all us members of the Rodjects come out with newfound survival skills: evolution at its finest." Dickinson's distance from campus ensures that "those who live there become the closest." Most freshmen rooms are not spacious, but first-year students say that just strengthens the social bonds they form with fellow boarders. "We may fight and bicker and yell at each other, especially during the weekend," one freshman said, "but that doesn't take away from us becoming brothers and sisters."

Other than bed and the classroom, the UDel dining areas are the most common place to spend time. The verdict? Answers range from "very decent for campus food" to "bring your own to avoid starvation," but the majority of students fall into the former category, and UDel's breakfasts and vegetarian options win especially high praise. The variety offered in official campus eateries grows thin after a few months, but students can keep their cuisine fresh by purchasing a dining plan that offers credit toward meals at Chik-Fil-A, Dunkin' Donuts, and various a la carte options that prepare everything from sandwiches to sushi. In short, students needn't fear starvation, and for some, college life is "the perfect opportunity to try new foods."

Who Lives Here, Anyway?

UDel takes more than a third of its students from Delaware and most of the rest from other Eastern states, which leaves some students wishing for a more diverse atmosphere. Caucasians are a solid majority, and several students remarked on the similarity of dress, outlook on life, and socioeconomic background. Still, the university grows more diverse every year, with a recent influx of Chinese students for whom UDel is their first taste of the United States. What homogeneity does exist in the student body ironically makes parts of the school more diverse, as cultural and political groups expand by taking in members with different viewpoints or skin tones. While cultural groups remain somewhat isolated in their activities, students noted the "fresh effort" by student organizers to unite a miscellany of clubs with all-encompassing events like the global-themed party that ended the university's International Education Week.

All in all, UDel can be a place for anyone and everyone, be they scholar, athlete, urban or rural. An enormous selection of classes gives students the chance to become whatever they want, while over 300 activities enable them to try anything they've ever wanted to do. The university is a haven for kids of every calling, and even those who haven't yet felt called to do anything will be hard-pressed to resist getting swept into the ocean of opportunities this perfectly placed Eastern location has to offer.—*Aaron Gertler*

FYI

If you come to UDel, you'd better bring . . . "An umbrella and rain boots."

What is the typical weekend schedule? "Party 10pm Friday-2am Saturday, sleep until 11am, try to do homework/attend a game/go to a club event, party 10pm-2am Sunday, sleep until 11am, wake up and do homework. But not necessarily every weekend!"

Three things every student at UDel should do before graduating are "See a football game, jump in the fountain, and eat at every restaurant in Newark."

District of Columbia

Address: 4400 Massachusetts Avenue NW, Washington, D.C. 20016-8001
Phone: 202-885-6000
E-mail address: admissions@american.edu
Web site URL: www.american.edu
Year Founded: 1893
Private or Public: Private
Religious Affiliation: Methodist
Location: Urban
Number of Applicants: 15,847
Percent Accepted: 53%
Percent Accepted who enroll: 15%
Number Entering: 1,284
Number of Transfers Accepted each Year: 910
Middle 50% SAT range: M: 580–670, CR: 590–690, Wr: 580–690
Middle 50% ACT range: 25–30

Early admission program EA/ED/None: ED
Percentage accepted through EA or ED: 55%
EA and ED deadline: 15-Nov
Regular Deadline: 15-Jan
Application Fee: $45
Full time Undergraduate enrollment: 6,042
Total enrollment: 9,967
Percent Male: 37%
Percent Female: 63%
Total Percent Minority or Unreported: 37%
Percent African-American: 5%
Percent Asian/Pacific Islander: 5%
Percent Hispanic: 5%
Percent Native-American: <1%
Percent International: 6%
Percent in-state/out of state: 21%/79%
Percent from Public HS: Unreported

Retention Rate: 86%
Graduation Rate 4-year: 62%
Graduation Rate 6-year: 69%
Percent Undergraduates in On-campus housing: 75%
Number of official organized extracurricular organizations: 180
3 Most popular majors: Business, International Relations, Communications
Student/Faculty ratio: 14:1
Average Class Size: 15
Percent of students going to grad school: Unreported
Tuition and Fees: $33,283
In-State Tuition and Fees if different: No difference
Cost for Room and Board: $12,418
Percent receiving financial aid out of those who apply: 61%
Percent receiving financial aid among all students: 69%

Founded in 1893, American University has since grown and expanded with its Washington D.C. setting to provide unique opportunities to its students. From government internships to special events, students are able to take advantage of the opportunities provided by the university's surroundings, all while enjoying the resources of a prestigious university.

No Curve . . . Just Hard Work

Six different schools are housed within American University: College of Arts and Sciences, Kogod School of Business, School of Communication, School of International Service, School of Public Affairs, and Washington College of Law. Undergraduates are able to attend all the schools except for Washington College of Law. American is well-known for its international studies and business programs, but interaction with professors seems to vary from school to school. A student in the College of Arts and Sciences said her professors were easy to find and to get along with. In addition, she added that a perk of her college was that her professors knew her name, whereas students in other schools said they had to work to get professors to know who they were. Although biochemistry is seen by most people as being the hardest major, one student says it really "depends on the caliber of the person." For instance, while some would consider sciences difficult, some science students view the political science or literature majors as difficult due to the large quantities of reading required for those courses. Even though American University is more well-known for its humanities programs (particularly international studies), one student said that "students in each department pretty much think that the others have it harder. I think biochem is easier than stats or micro. They think vice versa. We're all nice to each other, even if we're in different schools." That said, the classes typically deemed as the hardest are ones in the chemistry and biology departments, as well as microeconomics and macroeconomics. Classes at American are generally worth 3 credits each, but language classes and science classes including labs can be worth up to 4 or 5 credits each. A College of Arts and Sciences student said, "I get mostly A's. A lot of people make the Dean's list for the college. The harder you work, the greater the rewards. I don't think any of my teachers so far curve."

> "We're all nice to each other, even if we're in different schools."

Social Life What You Make of It
As far as a social life goes, the experience seems to vary from person to person. People usually go out on Friday and Saturday. Options include going out to eat, attending frat parties, going to clubs or visiting monuments and museums. Cars are not seen as a necessity, as the Metro station is close to campus and the university provides shuttles for transportation; however, upperclassmen are known to have cars. Both upperclassmen and underclassmen alike attend frat parties, but upperclassmen tend to have more private parties than the younger students. "People party on campus nightly," a student said. The Greek scene was described by a student as "there, but avoidable." Some people don't attend frats, whereas others rush and enjoy the experience. Drinking is a personal choice, as is drug use. American University is a dry

campus, and the rules are enforced when seen, so some students "hide things well," as one student described it.

Hangout Spaces Galore
The living experience, like the social scene, varies from student to student. RA's live on each floor and are supposed to handle disputes and promote floor unity. Some are strict, but others are more lax. Even though dorms get better with seniority, a lot of people tend to move off campus as they get older, and most are living off campus by senior year so that they can do internships. As far as campus hangouts go, The Tavern is a popular dining venue that provides a relaxing atmosphere. At nighttime, a good place to hang is The Perch, a coffeehouse, or the Davenport Lounge. A unique building on campus is the Katzen Arts Center, which houses the American University Museum, the Studio Theatre, a recital hall and the departments of arts and performing arts. The campus is safe at night, as is the surrounding area, which consists of fairly wealthy neighborhoods. "Homeland security is down the street. NBC is too," one student said. The surrounding area has good hangout places as well, such as Chipotle, Z-burger, Starbucks, Robeks, as well as bars and clubs. Metro Center and Dupont are also popular places.

One City, Infinite Opportunities
American University has well over 100 student organizations, but some of the most prominent ones are a capella groups, dance teams, cheer teams, crew and RHA. RHA, or Residence Hall Association, is the student government for each residential hall whose goal is to improve the quality of life for each residential hall as well as build a greater sense of community among American University students. Some members are very committed to their extracurricular activities, particularly members of RHA, but the amount of student involvement in organizations depends on the student. Publications are also a fairly popular form of extracurricular participation, with the AU *Eagle* in particular being popular. Sports don't seem to really have a major presence on campus, but basketball games and volleyball matches are known to draw crowds. "The bleachers are filled, but not everyone goes," one student remarked about these events. Overall, the distinguishing factor of American University seems to be its D.C. location, which gives students access

to opportunities unavailable to those at other universities, such as hearing President Obama speak. No matter what opportunities present themselves, students agree that having downtown Washington D.C. close to campus allows students to use the city's offerings to enrich their college experiences.—*Liliana Varman*

FYI

Three things every student at American should do before graduating are see a play, go to a game, take a class with Professor Patrick Jackson.
What differentiates American the most from other colleges is the ability to do interesting double majors and minors (i.e., biochemistry and theater).
What surprised me the most about American was the beauty of the campus itself.

Catholic University of America

Address: Cardinal Station, Washington, D.C. 20064
Phone: 202-319-5305
E-mail address: cua-admissions@cua.edu
Web site URL: www.cua.edu
Year Founded: 1887
Private or Public: Private
Religious Affiliation: Roman Catholic
Location: Urban
Number of Applicants: 5,180
Percent Accepted: 81%
Percent Accepted who enroll: 22%
Number Entering: 901
Number of Transfers Accepted each Year: 202
Middle 50% SAT range: M: 500–610, CR: 510–610, Wr: Unrepoted
Middle 50% ACT range: 21–27
Early admission program EA/ED/None: EA

Percentage accepted through EA or ED: Unreported
EA and ED deadline: 15-Nov
Regular Deadline: 15-Feb
Application Fee: $55
Full time Undergraduate enrollment: 3,326
Total enrollment: 5,470
Percent Male: 46%
Percent Female: 55%
Total Percent Minority or Unreported: 14%
Percent African-American: 5%
Percent Asian/Pacific Islander: 3%
Percent Hispanic: 7%
Percent Native-American: <1%
Percent International: 3%
Percent in-state/out of state: 1%/99%
Percent from Public HS: Unreported
Retention Rate: 82%

Graduation Rate 4-year: Unreported
Graduation Rate 6-year: Unreported
Percent Undergraduates in On-campus housing: 68%
Number of official organized extracurricular organizations: 100
3 Most popular majors: Architecture, Nursing, Political Science
Student/Faculty ratio: 11:1
Average Class Size: 20
Percent of students going to grad school: Unreported
Tuition and Fees: $30,670
In-State Tuition and Fees if different: No difference
Cost for Room and Board: $11,320
Percent receiving financial aid out of those who apply: 91%
Percent receiving financial aid among all students: 88%

Founded in 1887, The Catholic University of America has come to be known for its tight-knit community whose religious foundation and Washington, D.C. location provide students with a broad spectrum of opportunities to explore during their four years.

Intimate Academic Community

Catholic University students can enter one of the many undergraduate tracks available, including the School of Arts and Sciences, the School of Engineering, and the Benjamin T. Rome School of Music. Three of the most popular majors include Political Science, Drama, and Psychology. Catholic's School of Nursing and School of Architecture and Planning are also very well-respected and popular.

Most majors require five classes per semester, but workload "really depends on your time management," according to one student. In addition to major-specific courses, students at Catholic must take a certain number of religion classes—though this requirement does vary by major.

"Some are more work-intensive than others, but there's no one major that leaves you with no time to do anything else," said an accounting major.

With less than 4,000 undergraduate students on campus, Catholic affords its students smaller class sizes—most classes hold fewer than 20 students. "A benefit of having smaller class sizes at the school is you learn the material more easily, no matter your major, because you have more interaction with your professors," one student explained.

Though classes are generally managed by TAs, professors routinely hold office hours (generally 4–5 per week) for students. It is during this time that students have the chance to develop bonds with their professor and ask any questions they may have.

"The professors make themselves very available. With class sizes of twenty people, they'll have two or three courses, tops. They really get to know you by name, and, from the start, they take care of you."

Historically, students have considered Introduction to Peace Studies, Greek Literature in Translation, and Dynamics of Christian Spirituality as some of the most rewarding classes offered to undergrads at Catholic.

The Catholic-D.C. Scene

Students at Catholic take full advantage of the fact that their college campus is located at the heart of one of the liveliest, most prominent cities in the country. While extra-curriculars and student groups on campus keep students tied to their school community, most of the Catholic University social scene takes place off campus in Washington, D.C.

"A lot of kids, when they're freshmen or even sophomores, usually end up going to [events in the city] on Friday nights, and on Saturday nights might go downtown to the monuments or go out with the kids they met Friday night," a senior said.

Various university-sponsored organizations offer cheap tickets to various D.C. events, including Washington Wizards and Nationals games, midnight movie premiers, and musical/theater performances. One such organization is Catholic's Campus Ministry, which "sells tickets throughout the week—

they're generally $5 and they include transportation most of the time."

Popular attractions in the D.C. area include the national monuments (White House, Lincoln Memorial, Washington Monument, World War II Memorial), museums (Smithsonian Institute, National Gallery of Art), and theaters (Shakespeare Theatre Company, The Studio Theatre, National Theatre). Chinatown is also a popular spot for students looking for a bite to eat or for an exciting cultural experience.

For students uninterested in exploring the touristy route through the nation's capital, Catholic finds itself in close proximity to several major universities including Georgetown University, George Washington University, and American University. "You're always going to know someone at one of those schools, so you'll always get invited to different sports events, etc.," explained another Catholic University senior.

Culture of Shared Faith

Freshmen and sophomores are required to live on campus, but upperclassmen have the right, which many end up exercising, to life off campus. While many students choose nearby apartment complexes or group with friends to rent student houses, another popular option is affiliated apartment-style housing.

> **"There are all kinds of opportunities in the city."**

Though most of the social scene at Catholic University takes place off campus, there remains plenty to do on campus. Greek life is not as prominent at Catholic as it might be on other campuses, but the party scene "is the kind of thing where, if you look for it, it's almost too easy to find." The university's administration does, however, maintain strict policies regarding underage drinking.

Cardinal Athletics

Students agree that there is a decent amount of fan support for the sports events that occur on Catholic's campus. "During our home football games, the stands tend to be filled," said one student. After the fall, men's and women's lacrosse and baseball draw good crowds in the spring. Club sports, such as ice hockey, men's and women's rugby, ultimate frisbee, and intramural sports are available to students not competing on the varsity (Division-III) level. The campus gym, the Du-Four Center, is also available for student use throughout the week.

Beyond Catholic

"There are all kinds of opportunities in the city," said one student in reference to internships and career options at Catholic. There is not an overwhelming sense of pre-professionalism on campus, however Catholic University's Office of Career Services has deep connections to employers in D.C. and elsewhere. One student on the business track noted that many professors at Catholic have work experience at D.C.-area firms. Catholic also maintains strong connections to political and government career opportunities, fields into which many students and graduates enter via an internship or job offer.

Small School in a Big City

Going to college in a city as big as Washington, D.C. can get pretty busy, but students at Catholic seem to agree that they get the best of both worlds: a close, intimate community on campus nestled in a prominent city that is rife with academic, professional, and social opportunities. But don't let the allure of Capitol Hill distract you from the availability of on-campus resources. With small class sizes, plenty of extracurriculars, exciting student activities, and a strong religious presence (for those seeking it), you can find your niche at Catholic. This college truly strikes the balance between intimacy and balance that very few others can claim.—*Marek Ramilo*

FYI

If you come to Catholic, you'd better bring "a passion for politics."
What is the typical weekend schedule? "Friday: go clubbing in D.C.; Saturday: spend time with friends and party at night; Sunday: go to church and study."
Three things every student at Catholic should do before graduating are "spend a late night at Johnny K's, walk around the monuments at night, and go to a protest."

George Washington University

Address: 2121 I Street NW, Suite 201, Washington, D.C. 20052
Phone: 202-994-6040
E-mail address: gwadm@gwu.edu
Web site URL: www.gwu.edu
Year Founded: 1821
Private or Public: Private
Religious Affiliation: None
Location: Urban
Number of Applicants: 19,606
Percent Accepted: 37%
Percent Accepted who enroll: 30%
Number Entering: 2,123
Number of Transfers Accepted each Year: 980
Middle 50% SAT range: M: 600–690, CR: 600–690, Wr: 600–690
Middle 50% ACT range: 26–29
Early admission program EA/ED/None: ED

Percentage accepted through EA or ED: Unreported
EA and ED deadline: 10-Nov
Regular Deadline: 10-Jan
Application Fee: $65
Full time Undergraduate enrollment: 10,701
Total enrollment: 22,710
Percent Male: 45%
Percent Female: 55%
Total Percent Minority or Unreported: 40%
Percent African-American: 7%
Percent Asian/Pacific Islander: 10%
Percent Hispanic: 6%
Percent Native-American: <1%
Percent International: 5%
Percent in-state/out of state: 2%/98%
Percent from Public HS: 70%
Retention Rate: 90%

Graduation Rate 4-year: 72%
Graduation Rate 6-year: 77%
Percent Undergraduates in On-campus housing: 64%
Number of official organized extracurricular organizations: 220
3 Most popular majors: Social Sciences, Business, Psychology
Student/Faculty ratio: 13:1
Average Class Size: 18
Percent of students going to grad school: 20%
Tuition and Fees: $40,437
In-State Tuition and Fees if different: No difference
Cost for Room and Board: $9,920
Percent receiving financial aid out of those who apply: 74%
Percent receiving financial aid among all students: 37%

Going to school in the nation's capital certainly has its advantages. Just a few blocks from the White House, and a mere Metro ride from the National Archives and Capitol Hill, the GW campus is a hub of activity for its students. At GW, lazy afternoons easily turn into historical and political adventures, and even an early morning run has the unique appeal of boasting the Washington Monument and the Jefferson Memorial as backdrops. The Supreme Court is nearby, as is Embassy Row and the Smithsonian Museums. In fact, it's possible to spend four years at GW and not have enough time to explore all of the many options available. Located in the nation's political center and one of the world's most beautiful cities, George Washington University stands out for the opportunities it gives students for learning both inside and beyond the classroom. Whether you're a politics buff or not, it's certainly an exciting place to be.

One Part Academia, One Part Politics

George Washington University is comprised of six individual schools, each with its own requirements, to which aspiring freshmen apply directly: The Columbian College of Arts and Sciences, The School of Media and Public Affairs, The School of Business, The School of Public Health and Health Services, The Elliot School of International Affairs, and the School of Engineering and Applied Science. Although the six schools may seem to have a narrow focus, each student must fulfill general liberal arts requirements, and students are permitted and encouraged to take classes outside of their specific school. (Students warn, however, that it is important to be on top of your own classes and requirements, because it is surprisingly easy to "fall through the cracks" here.) In addition, GW offers a number of specialized programs including an eight-year Integrated Engineering/M.D. program, a seven-year B.A./M.D. program, and an Integrated Engineering and Law Program. The University Honors Program is a smaller, more selective college within the university that allows students a four-year, multidisciplinary, interschool undergraduate experience. Acceptance to the Honors Program is also sweetened with a significant merit-based scholarship.

The GW faculty and classes receive solid reviews, though students are careful to warn that "It really varies based on your school, major, and professor." Most students are "happy with the accessibility of the faculty and the quality of the teaching," though students emphasize the need for their peers to make the effort to engage their professors. The workload is described as "pretty average" by most students, with some emphasizing the rigor of first-year/introductory classes. "They try to weed you out," one senior remarked. Grades are "fairly accurate," and there isn't too much "grading on a curve." Double majoring is fairly common, and not too difficult. Class sizes vary, with introductory lectures being the largest. Other classes are usually smaller, with an average of 18 students. Small discussion groups led by TAs are a popular way to master the material discussed in larger lectures.

Because of GW's central location, academics tend to go hand-in-hand with taking advantage of the opportunities available in Washington, D.C. Many students are able to intern and work during the school year, with government agencies being a popular job option. "Getting an internship or a job in government or politics may be easier during the school year," one student noted, "because fewer students are looking for work than in the summer, when tons of undergrads want to work and live in D.C." Other advantages of GW's location include the fact that professors will frequently bring notable speakers and politicians in to speak to their classes, and field trips to museums and other attractions are often part of course work.

A World of Social Possibilities

"Because we're in a city, people spread out a lot on weekends," said one senior. Many students head to bars or dance clubs in D.C., and while they complain about the cover charges, they generally agree that there's little to do on campus at night. "Sometimes freshmen party on campus," said one sophomore. "But as you get older, I think the bars and clubs are more of a draw. You can't really come to GW without a fake ID." That said, partying on campus can be difficult—there is officially no alcohol allowed in campus housing if you are under 21, and students caught three times with alcohol are forced to relinquish their campus housing. Any student found with an illegal substance must move off campus at the first strike. Community Facilitators (CFs) are GW's answer to residential advisers, and while many students reported "becoming friends with" their CFs, Community Facilitators are more than willing to write up students on alcohol charges when necessary. Despite this, drinking seems to be a large part of social life at GW. Upperclassmen gravitate toward the bars in Adams Morgan, a notoriously fun part of the city, and bars closer to home, like McFadden's on New Hampshire Ave. The meal plan, called GWorld, can be used at certain local restaurants, which students reported to be a nice feature of GW dining. Students generally say that the meal plan is "good, though nothing to brag about," and are likely to dine out on the weekends, noting the restaurants on Georgetown's M Street and in Dupont Circle as particularly good options.

> **"It is often hard to tell if someone you pass is a GW student or a government employee."**

Drinking may be a big part of social life at GW, but fraternities and sororities are not. Greek life is an option for students that are interested, but many GWers think it unnecessary and a hindrance to enjoying all that Washington, D.C., has to offer. While students report that their peers are "pretty friendly," they also acknowledge that "The University isn't particularly helpful in helping people meet each other." Overall, being in such a great city provides a lot of opportunity, but also causes GW to lack a sense of community spirit. Most students meet their friends through their majors or extracurricular activities, even though few people feel defined by these groups. The administration attempts to foster a greater sense of community spirit by hosting events like Fall Fest and Spring Fest, and increasing the number of formal balls.

Students at GW think of themselves as "fit," and most take part in intramurals and take advantage of the beautiful Washington scenery by frequently running around the city. Many athletic teams are in the Atlantic 10 Conference as well as NCAA Division I. Students tend to show their (limited) school spirit by attending basketball games, as basketball is by far "the most popular sport on campus." Extracurricular activities are also popular, and most students get involved in at least one organization. "There are tons of options," said one student, "especially in the realm of political and cultural organizations."

Students take advantage of their surroundings by joining clubs that take them to the National Gallery of Art and the Capitol, among other locales. Students tend not to feel categorized by the clubs they join, and enjoy the fact that "It always seems like you can meet someone new."

Location, Location, Location

The location of the George Washington University is its greatest draw to students, although particular departments are also very attractive. The main Foggy Bottom Campus (there is a smaller campus called Mount Vernon) is composed of four-by-four square city blocks. "It is definitely an urban, city campus," said one student, "and it is often hard to tell if someone you pass is a GW student or a government employee." While students complain about a lack of grassy space, they are always quick to realize how lucky they are to live in such a beautiful and vibrant city. Students generally feel very safe on campus, though "Of course, we're in a major city, so you have to be careful." Security measures have been increased with the threat of terrorism in recent years, and most students seem to feel that the school is doing all it can to protect their well-being.

Freshmen and sophomores are required to live on campus, and freshmen are usually split between Thurston (affectionately called "the tenements" by residents) and about four other dorms. Thurston is the largest freshman dorm on campus, and like all on-campus locations, offers apartment-style or suite living (some have kitchens, some do not). Juniors and seniors are not guaranteed on-campus housing, and may take their chances in a lottery that works on the basis of seniority. Mitchell Hall is one of the most sought after, offering attractive living conditions: all single dorms and a veranda. Many upperclassmen opt for apartments in the city (which are "SO EXPENSIVE!" warns one student) and some choose to live in the suburbs of Maryland or Virginia. For others, sorority and fraternity houses are the way to go.

The Marvin Center—the school's student union—is largely regarded as the center of campus life. The Marvin Center houses the headquarters and offices of student organizations, as well as a few fast-food and chain restaurants. Meals can be eaten in the Marvin Center or in standard dining halls, where food is described as "good but unhealthy." The center is a hub for students, a place where "Lots of kids hang out, do their work, and get meals." The center also houses a grocery store and travel agency. The Marvin Center is considered a great convenience, especially for freshmen who don't yet know their way around the city. "If you need something, chances are you can get it there."

Official school statistics show a geographically and racially diverse student population, but students tend to think the school is too dominated by the wealthy. Students complain that people at GW are ostentatious about their wealth. "People here are well-off, and they let you know it." While there are definitely stereotypes about well-dressed,

BMW-driving students, others claim that it really depends on where you choose to hang out, and with whom. "A stereotype is just that," said one articulate senior, "it underrepresents the variety of student 'types' on campus."

With a prime location in the hub of the political world, George Washington University provides an education in academics, politics, and real-life, city living. With so much to see, do, and learn, students are more than happy with their choice to come here. "I love GW," said one senior, "and I don't know many people who feel otherwise."—*Erica Ross*

FYI

If you come to GW, you'd better bring "a coffee mug for the Starbucks on every corner in D.C.!"
What is the typical weekend schedule? "Wake up late, do some work, go out all night, and wake up late again the next day!"
If I could change one thing about GW, I'd "make the administration more accessible to students."
Three things every student at GW should do before graduating are "go to the monuments at night, get a Manuche dog, and party in Georgetown."

Georgetown University

Address: 37th and O Streets, NW, Washington, D.C. 20057-1270
Phone: 202-687-0100
E-mail address: guadmiss@georgetown.edu
Web site URL: www .georgetown.edu
Year Founded: 1789
Private or Public: Private
Religious Affiliation: Roman Catholic–Jesuit
Location: Urban
Number of Applicants: 16,163
Percent Accepted: 21%
Percent Accepted who enroll: 47%
Number Entering: 1,579
Number of Transfers Accepted each Year: 368
Middle 50% SAT range: M: 650–740, CR: 650–750, Wr: Unreported
Middle 50% ACT range: Unreported
Early admission program EA/ED/None: EA

Percentage accepted through EA or ED: 8%
EA and ED deadline: 1-Nov
Regular Deadline: 15-Dec
Application Fee: $65
Full time Undergraduate enrollment: 7,038
Total enrollment: 11,979
Percent Male: 45%
Percent Female: 55%
Total Percent Minority or Unreported: 30%
Percent African-American: 7%
Percent Asian/Pacific Islander: 11%
Percent Hispanic: 5%
Percent Native-American: <1%
Percent International: 8%
Percent in-state/out of state: 2%/98%
Percent from Public HS: 49%
Retention Rate: 96%
Graduation Rate 4-year: 90%

Graduation Rate 6-year: 92%
Percent Undergraduates in On-campus housing: 71%
Number of official organized extracurricular organizations: 103
3 Most popular majors: English, International Relations, Political Science and Government
Student/Faculty ratio: 11:1
Average Class Size: 26
Percent of students going to grad school: 31%
Tuition and Fees: $37,947
In-State Tuition and Fees if different: No difference
Cost for Room and Board: $12,753
Percent receiving financial aid out of those who apply: 72%
Percent receiving financial aid among all students: 40%

Nestled in a distinct residential neighborhood of Washington, D.C., Georgetown University encompasses the charms of both city and suburban life. Yet, given its tremendous wealth of resources, dynamic population, and sometimes-controversial stances, the political noise generated on this campus makes for a college experience that is by no means pastoral.

Friendly Internal Rivalries

The undergraduate experience at Georgetown is markedly diverse, with four primary schools: Georgetown College, The Edmund A. Walsh School of Foreign Service, The Robert Emmett McDonough Business School, and the School of Nursing and Health Studies. Although students live, work, and play together, prospective Hoyas apply for admission to one of the four colleges, becoming affiliated with that school upon matriculation. Of the internal divisions, students said the differences only manifest themselves during mock competition, and one University tour guide described the practice as "Harry Potter-esque." In a similar vein, students admitted to the presence of some interschool tension, but were quick to add that the tension was not strongly palpable. "We have a lot of University pride, but a lot of school pride too," said one senior.

As always, there are stereotypes about students in each of the schools. One junior explained: "There's the idea that business school kids are only there to make money; that SFS students are arrogant, conceited, naïve, and think they're the most intelligent people on campus; and that the College kids don't know what they want to do with their lives since all 900 of them come in here undeclared. The Nursing kids don't really have a reputation since there are only around 80 of them per year."

The "Georgetown Paradox"

The "Georgetown Paradox" is the understanding that "Everyone wants you for your internship, but you have no way to get to that internship," explained a sophomore. The inaccessibility of Georgetown is the primary gripe among its students. Although the University provides a bus system, many students complain about its irregularity and unreliability. "Things would be better if we had a Metro stop," said one freshman. "But I think it's because Jackie Onassis, who owned four homes in the neighborhood over the course of her lifetime, didn't want Georgetown to be accessible to just anyone." With the Georgetown stamp of approval on their resumes, most students have no problem securing competitive internships throughout the D.C. area. "Anything that I've applied for, I've gotten," said one McDonough student. "It's a matter of deciding between what you've been offered. For example, Ameriprise Financial almost exclusively recruits Georgetown students." It seems that for a Hoya the only real problem is getting there.

A Hoya Halloween

Founded alongside the country, Georgetown stands as America's oldest Catholic and Jesuit university. And with over 200 years of history, it is one with its fair share of unique traditions spanning the traditional and the innovative. Not only do Georgetown students ceremoniously steal the clock handles from Healy Clock Tower and mail them to the Vatican to be blessed by the Pope, they also dance in the Dahlgren Fountain, evoking the opening credits of the television show *Friends*.

Another Georgetown staple is the nightly 11:15 p.m. candlelight Catholic mass, held in the major University chapel, Dahlgren Chapel of the Sacred Heart, and most frequented on Sunday nights. On a Hoya's 21st birthday, it is practically mandated that they celebrate at "The Tombs." And around the holidays, students are known to climb up and sit in the lap of the statue of their founder (Archbishop John Carroll) and tell him what they want for Christmas.

Basketball games are another Hoya institution. As one McDonough student put it, "Attending a Georgetown basketball game will change your life." Students described the scene as a mass of gray-clad Hoyas (the school colors are gray and blue) roaring with applause each time the team scores. "Of course, some people Georgetown it up and wear a popped collar underneath," said one sophomore. The respect for Georgetown basketball extends even to the band. One New Jersey native said, "Our pep band gets more respect than any other pep band in the country." But this immense fan base lacks a football counterpart. Some students said that the football team is so bad that "People pretend we don't have a football team." With basketball characterized by a self-described "cult of followers," it is clear that Hoya pride is expressed most intensely on the court, not on the field.

The biggest campus tradition is undeniably Halloween night. The 1973 William Friedkin film, *The Exorcist*, was filmed almost entirely on Georgetown's campus. This fact adds fuel to the eerie fire driving the renowned Hoya Halloween. Students generally agreed with one senior's conclusion that "Halloween is the biggest thing on campus." That night, students dress up and proceed to the main assembly hall, where they watch the film on a jumbo screen, then go down to the intersection of M Street and Wisconsin to dance in the street. One student bragged that the Hoya holiday tradition was rated among the top towns featuring fun Halloween celebrations.

The Jesuit Influence
Students report that there are a lot of Jesuit professors, but that the Jesuit influence was only very strong around Christmas when "mangers pop up around campus." A freshman who said he was initially apprehensive of attending a Catholic-affiliated school said that his fears of "a Jesuit behind [his] back" were quickly allayed when he found their presence was not overwhelming. "The Jesuit tradition is a very welcoming and open one. There is some restriction, but they're very accommodating and open to hearing things," he said. However, other students pointed to the fact that the pro-choice group on campus is not allowed to table like other campus organizations and that, though they are permitted to distribute flyers, anyone offended by their literature can tear them down. They also noted that none of the on-campus stores can sell condoms, though they admitted there is an unrestricted CVS just four blocks away from campus. Students further explained that Red Square is a free-speech zone, where one can "pretty much say anything" without repercussions.

Not Your Average Greek
Georgetown University does not officially recognize traditional fraternities and sororities. But there are some illegitimate on-campus Greek organizations in addition to recognized professional and service organizations. "It's not your typical college Greek life; it's more of the resume-building than boozing-up kind," explained one junior. On-campus parties are not centered around Greek life, but are popular in the University townhouses, of which there are roughly 70 within a one-block radius of the front gates, populated by upperclassmen. However, recent changes to drinking policies and restrictions on parties have made on-campus fiestas almost extinct. "All it's done is push alcohol use into the surrounding areas," said one senior. Despite the enormous backlash

from students and months of publications devoted to criticizing the new crackdowns, Georgetown's prime social life now exists primarily along the town's bar-lined streets.

What's in the Salad?
Georgetown students consistently commented on the University's widespread culture of looking good. "We're always ranked among the fittest campuses, and I think that's a function of the fact that when Georgetown selects its well-rounded students, a lot of them happen to be varsity athletes and come from a culture of being fit," explained one female freshman. Other students, however, were more skeptical, and sometimes sarcastic, in their justifications of the University's fit reputation. "There's a rumor that they spray carbs on the salad to get the kids to gain weight," stated one junior. "Actually, I think eating disorders are another Georgetown tradition."

> "For the most part, I feel a real sense of community here, but if you want to see a split on Georgetown's campus, come visit around election time."

"There is a lot of competition in terms of who can put on the biggest show of carrying the largest Louis Vuitton bag without breaking a bone," said a male Marketing major. Others elaborated on the student body's fashion choices as conclusively preppy. "We do have a large preppy contingency and that's going to happen at any higher-level school that feeds from higher-level prep schools, but Georgetown does seem to take it to an extreme," commented one freshman male. "I do feel outnumbered as a public school grad." Other students commented on the same phenomenon. "Some of the things you wonder if people do in real life, they happen here. People are playing croquet on the front lawn; kids go quail hunting," said an SFS female. Students described the overall atmosphere as reflecting "the two p's—pearls and polos," and said that the prep level increases when people go out. One senior said, "The preppy look is definitely noticeable, but not universal."

Class, Clinton, Class . . .
Georgetown's capital location ensures proximity to a great deal of political events, an all-star faculty, various specialized courses, and famous speakers. "When people are in

D.C. and want to give a speech, they come to us, we don't go to them," said a female Finance major. Students remembered instances of famous speakers coming to campus and commented on the choice between seeing Bill Clinton speak or going to class. "It was pretty funny that when Bill Clinton came to town, I remember his motorcade was blocking my path, and I actually got annoyed," recalled one senior. "The idea of choice in that situation is ridiculous, but sometimes class wins out."

It comes as no surprise that this choice would be difficult for Georgetown students who are at once notoriously studious and politically active. Hoyas are known to take it to the streets when bothered by, well, anything. Students have even mobilized to protest Walmart representatives speaking on corporate responsibility. Recently, students mobilized against a series of assaults on individuals identified as homosexual, critiquing the University's position on the matter and raising the difficult issue of what a Catholic institution's position should be on such a sensitive topic. Students did, however, note that the mood at Georgetown is typically one of unity. "For the most part, I feel a real sense of community here, but if you want to see a split on Georgetown's campus,

come visit around November," said a junior, referencing election time.

Popular Georgetown majors include English, international relations, political science, and government. The school is noted for rigorous requirements, like "Map of the Modern World." All SFS students must pass this course in order to graduate, and in order to pass this course, they must successfully distinguish and name every country in the world, its capital, population, religion, and political system. Another requirement is "The Problem of God," fulfilled with one of 24 sections that, depending on the professor, can range from getting a comparative religion approach to a psychological one to general theology. On Georgetown's general requirements, a senior said, "You're going to love them or hate them, but the fact that they're requirements means there are a lot of ways to get them done."

Georgetown students appear well-versed in working within established frameworks to accomplish their goals. They succeed at holding down impressive internships while handling full course loads, protesting for gay rights at a Catholic university, demolishing the competition on the basketball court and becoming scholars, while having a great deal of fun.—*Nicholle Manners*

FYI

If you come to Georgetown, you'd better bring "a pastel Polo."

What is the typical weekend schedule? "Friday: go to classes, if you have any, do work for a while in the library, go out to dinner, come back to campus to party or study, depending on the weekend; Saturday: go out to the city during the day, party at night; Sunday: spend the entire day in the library."

If I could change one thing about Georgetown, I'd "overhaul the dining hall food; it's horrendous and every prospective student should be warned."

Three things every student at Georgetown should do before graduating are "go to a basketball game, go to a performance at the Kennedy Center, and protest in Red Square."

Howard University

Address: 2400 Sixth Street, NW, Washington, D.C. 20059
Phone: 202-806-2700
E-mail address: AskEM@howard.edu
Web site URL: www.howard.edu
Year Founded: 1867
Private or Public: Private
Religious Affiliation: None
Location: Urban
Number of Applicants: 7,603
Percent Accepted: 54%
Percent Accepted who enroll: 35%
Number Entering: 1,443
Number of Transfers Accepted each Year: 250
Middle 50% SAT range: M: 440–650, CR: 460–660, Wr: 410–650
Middle 50% ACT range: 20–28
Early admission program EA/ED/None: EA

Percentage accepted through EA or ED: Unreported
EA and ED deadline: 1-Nov
Regular Deadline: 15-Feb
Application Fee: $45
Full time Undergraduate enrollment: 6,988
Total enrollment: 6,988
Percent Male: 33%
Percent Female: 67%
Total Percent Minority or Unreported: 32%
Percent African-American: 67%
Percent Asian/Pacific Islander: 1%
Percent Hispanic: 0%
Percent Native-American: <1%
Percent International: 5%
Percent in-state/out of state: 23%/77%
Percent from Public HS: 80%

Retention Rate: 84%
Graduation Rate 4-year: 43%
Graduation Rate 6-year: 63%
Percent Undergraduates in On-campus housing: 55%
Number of official organized extracurricular organizations: 150
3 Most popular majors: Biology/Biological Sciences, Journalism, Radio and Television
Student/Faculty ratio: 8:1
Average Class Size: 9
Percent of students going to grad school: 60%
Tuition and Fees: $13,215
In-State Tuition and Fees if different: No difference
Cost for Room and Board: $6,976
Percent receiving financial aid out of those who apply: 96%
Percent receiving financial aid among all students: 96%

Washington, D.C., one of the most diverse cities in the United States, is home to one of the oldest historically black colleges, Howard University. A private, federally funded institution, of nearly 7,000 students, Howard University is an up-and-coming research institution. Known as the "Black Harvard," Howard offers degrees through doctoral and professional levels, various extracurricular opportunities, and traditions, making Howard an excellent school in an exciting city.

The Mecca

Self-known as the "Mecca of Black education," Howard University is the richest black educational institution in America, and one of the country's top research schools. Howard has always been synonymous with either medicine or law studies; and, although these areas are still popular and prestigious aspects of the school, many different colleges have grown significantly in the past few years.

Students choose from one of several different colleges to focus on during their time at Howard (Arts and Sciences, Communications, etc.). Though, recently, the University has taken initiatives to "revamp the curriculum" and "reach higher ground" according to former president Sidney A. Ribeau, in order to "maintain the highest standards of academic and administrative excellence." Howard University plans to reduce the number of majors and graduate programs. Among those on the chopping block: classics and African studies, Old World language majors such as Russian, and philosophy. Students will still be able to take courses such as African-American Philosophy and Slavery in the Ancient World. The changes have met criticism but the leadership feels it necessary to formulate a curriculum that will not only challenge its students but also prepare them for a changing world. Ribeau commented, "I feel a tremendous sense of responsibility to those who came before me, and an even greater responsibility to those who come after me. One challenge is to continue to convince our community that if you attend Howard University, your child has a full opportunity to be successful, both in terms of human growth and potential, and professional growth and potential in this society."

In conjunction with one's major, many students take on a subsequent minor and fulfill an undergraduate requirement termed "practical education," manifested in areas such as the required physical education classes. Though some of these classes are large, classes are usually intimate (8:1 teacher ratio). The total undergraduate enrollment is around 7,000 and freshmen enrollment is around 1,500 students. According to one senior, "Because of the small class sizes, teachers develop strong relationships with their students. They are constantly supplying them with opportunities for internships and ways to utilize being in Washington, D.C." It is because of these great teachers that there are certain must-take classes at Howard such as Literature of Love and Pan-Africanism. With readings that vary from Toni Morrison to William Shakespeare, Literature of Love is a class that encourages students to seek to understand human interaction through famous literary works. Well-known professors such as Dr. Gregory Carr and John Davis are integral parts of life at Howard and are constantly seen at functions all around campus.

The Whose Who?

With a thriving social scene, Howard has opportunities for all different types of people to get involved with student activities. HUSA, Howard University Student Association, is one of the biggest groups on campus. Howard students serve on the Board of Trustees and on University-wide committees. They can express their views through student organizations, as well as *The Hilltop* student newspaper—rated "The Best Campus Newspaper" by the *Princeton Review*—and the *Bison Yearbook*. Howard University invites you to visit their newly redesigned Newsroom that helps you stay connected with the University, its students, faculty, staff and alumni. Other students are involved in a wide variety of extracurriculars, including everything from putting on pageants to joining step groups. *The Hilltop* is very highly regarded and has won numerous accolades both nationally and at the yearly Historically Black Colleges & Universities conference. Mock Trial is also highly acclaimed at Howard.

Howard University was the first team to win two national championships in the same year, both the 1997 National Silver Flight Tournament and the 1997 National Championship. In accordance with the international student population, the African Student Association and the Caribbean Student Association are also huge forces on campus. Along with chapters of national organizations such as the NAACP and NSCS (National Society of Collegiate Scholars), Howard boasts a unique system of clubs for each of the fifty states. These clubs are known to host activities and gatherings such as the well-attended yearly party thrown by the Louisiana and Texas Clubs. There are other school-wide activities such as "ResFest" where different dormitories divide into teams and compete against other dorms in competitions such as dance contests and sporting events.

Although there are lots of different social scenes around campus, none is more dominant than Greek life. One student said "Part of the reason the Greek scene here is so prominent is because of its legacy on campus. Greeks have a responsibility that goes beyond partying." Fraternity and sorority members hold positions of power around campus and have a very prominent place at Howard. The groups strive to be more than just social groups, emphasizing both community service and African-American unity.

In addition to evolving living situations and eating habits, the social scene, too, changes, as students get older. The clubbing scene begins to fade and instead of heading out to clubs like H2O, FUR, and Love, as they did as freshman and sophomores, upperclassmen tend to socialize at bars, house parties, and more sophisticated places such as The Diner, which is a coffee-shop-like place to hang out. As the workload increases and the realization dawns that professional life is quickly approaching, many seniors spend weekend time differently than they did their first few years at Howard.

Coming Home to Howard

The annual homecoming is a definite must-see. One student said, "some say it's the vibe, while others say it's the events. Some say it's the people and others say it's the hype. No matter what is said, the fact remains that people have always talked about Howard University's homecoming. With homecoming, students are thinking back to past experiences in anticipation of what's to come." People from all over the world come to gather together and share in special activities and events that last all week long. From the moment that guests arrive on campus on Sunday, they have the option of attending chapel services, talent shows, concerts, and more. One of the most famous events is the step show that takes place at the yard, where each fraternity has its own section from which to observe the events. Although the weekend is technically centered on sports, the hype is more about the gathering of all different people in a single venue. When asked about homecoming, one sophomore said, "The fact that you can meet so many people from so many different regions and backgrounds, all with the same goal in mind, is a beautiful thing." For those who doubt the importance of the event: Homecoming was even mentioned in a Ludacris song. Besides the events that characterize homecoming, alumni and other prominent members of the African-American community who return to Howard are reminded of the time they spent at the gorgeous, hilly campus lined with old, New England–style buildings.

> "We come from diverse backgrounds and circumstances and share a unique heritage, but what we all have in common is that we're HERE, right where we belong, both with something to gain and something to give."

No matter what type of background a person comes from or what activities he or she participates in, Howard is a place where students can build on their potential and grow into future leaders. A student best explained, "We come from diverse backgrounds and circumstances and share a unique heritage, but what we all have in common is that we're HERE, right where we belong, both with something to gain and something to give." Howard has awarded more than 95,000 degrees. In fact, Howard produces more African-American Ph.D.s and MDs than any other university in the world. And with more than 3,000 faculty members, it has the largest concentration of African-American scholars in the world. Notable Howard alumni include Nobel Laureate Toni Morrison, Emmy Award–winning actress Phylicia Rashad, singer Jessye Norman, actress-producer Debbie Allen, Dr. LaSalle Leffall, Jr., Thurgood Marshall, L. Douglas Wilder, and former United Nations Ambassador Andrew Young.

The Capitol

Washington, D.C., is considered to be one of the liveliest metropolitan areas in America and the over 16 colleges in the city definitely have something to do with that. The different colleges have established particular cultures for their surrounding areas.

Howard is often referred to as the mecca, or the center, of every historically black college, or, even, the University of the nation. The unified pride that the students have in the school's history and what it represents is real and substantial. This shared legacy is felt and strongly exuded whether it be in academics, sports, or extracurriculars. Howard University is moving forward, constantly striving to become better and more competitive with each passing year. More importantly, most students understand that *their* legacy will be their contribution to the upward trajectory of their beloved University. For a student who wants legacy, pride, and a voice at an institution, a pilgrimage to the mecca is a clear choice.—*Dashell Laryea*

FYI
Typical weekend schedule? Go to a house party on Friday night, relax outside during the day on Saturday, head to Adams Morgan or a bar on Saturday night, and then recover and relax on Sunday, take a shuttle to church in the morning and catch up on work the rest of the day.
Stay for Homecoming, it's a must.
Take in a free performance at The Kennedy Center's Millennium Stage every evening at 6 pm. Acts include everything from performances by the National Symphony Orchestra to gospel groups to jazz musicians to poetry slams.

Florida

Tallahassee, Florida, is known as a great college town. Since the city has two major universities, students who matriculate at Florida A&M (FAMU) can expect that something is always going on. In addition, as the State University System's only historically black university, FAMU has a long tradition of separating itself from the pack and retaining its individuality.

Structured Study

Undergraduates at FAMU have their pick of 62 majors in 11 different colleges. Much of the educational activity that goes on at FAMU is geared toward professional or pre-professional studies. In particular, the University's strongest programs are reputed to be in the School of Business and Industry, the College of Education, the School of Architecture, and the College of Pharmacy. The College of Engineering, which is shared with Florida State University, is also popular and well respected.

Students sometimes complain that the education they receive is a little too structured. "My academic program is way too narrowly defined," one freshman said. "There is little room for personal exploration." On the whole, however, students say the academics are "reasonable" and "manageable" if, like most FAMU students, one enters the school with a clearly defined notion of one's professional goals.

One aspect of FAMU's pedagogical goals

that distinguishes the University from its State University System peers is its commitment to undergraduates. While FAMU is trying to expand its graduate program enrollment across disciplines, most of the school's energies are geared toward its undergrads. All classes are taught by professors, who as a general rule interact often and individually with their students. TAs are hired only to assist with labs and occasionally to substitute for faculty. This focus on undergraduates has always been a hallmark of the FAMU education.

Chilling at the Set

Housing headaches have long been considered a part of life at FAMU, though this may be changing for the better in the near future. Most students have traditionally lived off campus, but there are residence halls as well. The University requires all freshmen whose families live 35 or more miles away to live in the dorms. In order to create a more tight-knit community, the University has been trying to make its housing options more attractive to all students. To date, those in the dorms tend to be ambivalent about their living conditions. "[It's] fine—nothing great, nothing awful," one student said. Meal plans are required of those who do live in on-campus housing.

For those who choose their own accommodations, Tallahassee offers a wealth of housing options that cater to college students. Apartments are generally available, and local places to shop and grab a bite to eat (including two malls) are abundant. Clubs and restaurants are also popular destinations. FAMU's campus is very near downtown, which offers not only practical and social advantages but also great educational and professional-development opportunities, given Tallahassee's status as the capital of Florida. FAMU has several established internship programs with local institutions, such as the popular program that places journalism majors at the *Tallahassee Democrat*, the local daily newspaper, for a summer or more.

There is plenty to do on campus as well. One popular hangout is "the Set," which is a common area near the Student Union. It contains the post office, the bookstore, a market and a TV room. Such shared spaces give off-campus residents a great excuse to hang out with on-campus friends. "It is great to have the Set so that off-campus people like myself can still stay connected with the rest of the student body," one sophomore said.

Never a Dull Moment

Popular activities among students include the Student Government Association, fraternities and sororities, musical events, pre-professional societies, journalism, theater and sporting events. With so much going on, it goes without saying that FAMU students are an active, spirited group.

One of the challenges of the student government has been to keep off-campus students involved in the larger campus life. According to most accounts, they have succeeded admirably. "They do a terrific job," one student said. One popular annual event is "Be Out Day," which brings the student body out to the athletic fields for a day of food, partying and games. Another SGA-run event that "we all look forward to each year" is Homecoming.

The Greek system is another big draw for students. According to the Office of Student Union and Activities, all of the national historically black fraternities and sororities have chapters at FAMU. In addition to these more traditional college Greek houses, there are also numerous community-service organizations and honor societies.

> "I am going out into the real world with not only solid academic training, but a host of life experiences that I won't soon forget."

Music is also an important part of life at FAMU. The gospel choir is very popular, and the marching band, known as the Marching 100, has achieved an international reputation. The second largest college marching band in the world, the Marching 100 has been featured in a Bastille Day parade in Paris and was suspended after the hazing death of a member in 2012 (since re-instated but...) played at President Clinton's second inauguration. Several predominantly black high-school bands in North Florida and other areas intentionally imitate the flamboyant, showboating style and discipline of the Marching 100.

FAMU Rattler sports are a pretty big deal in Tallahassee, even though they are often in the shadow of the larger and better-known teams of Florida State University. Students show their school spirit by decking themselves in orange and green and attending

NCAA Division I sporting events, especially football, which is in Division I-AA. Intramural sports are also popular and are described as "fierce and fun."

A Close Community

With most schools in the country focusing their recruiting efforts on increasing diversity, FAMU has bucked the trend. The school is very proud of its status as Florida's only public historically black university, and has made the recruitment of high-achieving black students its No. 1 priority. At times, FAMU has performed as well as or better than such universities as Harvard, Yale and Stanford in recruiting National Achievement Scholars.

Students say that although they wish there were more diversity on campus, they do appreciate and enjoy the community they have. "I love this community, but . . . there is much to be desired in terms of creating a more diverse student body," one senior said. "I look outside and everyone is so much like me." Of course, the students do have diversity when it comes to their backgrounds and interests (although around 75 percent are from Florida). There is considerable political diversity, but strikingly uniform is the students' take on homosexuality. The small community of gay students isn't organized, and students say they're "not very open-minded when it comes to that."

FAMU has been a traditional top choice for many black students from Florida because of its respected preprofessional and professional academic programs, its warm environment (in more ways than one), and its commitment to undergraduate education. As one senior put it, "I am going out into the real world with not only solid academic training, but a host of life experiences that I won't soon forget."—*Jay Buchanan*

FYI
If you come to FAMU, you'd better bring "sunglasses."
What is the typical weekend schedule? "Friday, catch up on sleep; Saturday, go out and party; Sunday, do all the work from the previous week."
If I could change one thing about FAMU, "I'd improve the landscape. There are too many bushes around here."
Three things that every student at FAMU should do before graduating are "chill at the Set, volunteer in Tallahassee and attend Homecoming."

Florida Institute of Technology

Address: 150 West University Boulevard, Melbourne, FL 32901-6975
Phone: 321-674-8030
E-mail address: admission@fit.edu
Web site URL: www.fit.edu
Year Founded: 1958
Private or Public: Private
Religious Affiliation: None
Location: Suburban
Number of Applicants: 3,168
Percent Accepted: 82%
Percent Accepted who enroll: 25%
Number Entering: 635
Number of Transfers Accepted each Year: 338
Middle 50% SAT range: M: 540–640, CR: 500–610, Wr: Unreported
Middle 50% ACT range: 22–28
Early admission program EA/ED/None: None
Percentage accepted through EA or ED: NA

EA and ED deadline: NA
Regular Deadline: Rolling
Application Fee: $50
Full time Undergraduate enrollment: 2,594
Total enrollment: 5,118
Percent Male: 61%
Percent Female: 39%
Total Percent Minority or Unreported: 24%
Percent African-American: 8%
Percent Asian/Pacific Islander: 3%
Percent Hispanic: 6%
Percent Native-American: <1%
Percent International: 17%
Percent in-state/out of state: 55%/45%
Percent from Public HS: 56%
Retention Rate: 73%
Graduation Rate 4-year: 42%

Graduation Rate 6-year: 58%
Percent Undergraduates in On-campus housing: 37%
Number of official organized extracurricular organizations: 99
3 Most popular majors: Aerospace/Aeronautical Engineering, Aviation Management, Mechanical Engineering
Student/Faculty ratio: 13:1
Average Class Size: 16
Percent of students going to grad school: 20%
Tuition and Fees: $30,190
In-State Tuition and Fees if different: No difference
Cost for Room and Board: $10,250
Percent receiving financial aid out of those who apply: Unreported
Percent receiving financial aid among all students: Unreported

Nestled in a tropical, lush environment and boasting a challenging curriculum with unique research opportunities, the Florida Institute of Technology stands apart from other technical universities. Indeed, this small technical school, located five minutes from the beach, offers more than just an education: Florida Tech prepares its students for life.

Challenging Courses

Despite the appeal of relaxing on the beach, students at Florida Tech take academics seriously. Many said they find the academics to be difficult, but rewarding. As one student said, "Classes are challenging. They really put you to the test."

Students say that one of the best aspects of academics at Florida Tech is the small size of a typical class. Since many classes enroll less than 20 people, students have the chance to actively engage in classroom discussions and interact with the professor. As one sophomore said, "You're not just a number. Professors get to know your name, and you get to know a lot about them too. It's a really nice relationship, but they keep it very challenging."

On top of their classes, many students take advantage of the excellent hands-on research opportunities available at Florida Tech. From manatee preservation and beach erosion studies to working at NASA or Lockheed Martin, every student can plug into Florida Tech's extensive research program.

Along with the requirements for each major, most students have to complete core classes, which include Physics I and II, Calculus I and II, Civilization I and II, and Differential Equations and Linear Algebra. Students must also complete various communication classes, including Composition and Rhetoric, Writing about Literature, and Science and Technical Communication.

Although Florida Tech offers numerous majors through its Colleges of Engineering, Science, Aeronautics, Business, and Psychology and Liberal Arts, three popular majors are Aerospace / Aeronautical Engineering,

Aviation Management, and Mechanical Engineering.

"Everything Under the Sun"

Student organizations and clubs exist for "everything under the sun," as one sophomore said. Indeed, with many registered student organizations on campus, "There's something here for everyone," and students have little trouble finding organizations that interest them. Popular organizations range from bowling and sport fishing to math and skydiving. Many students also get involved with community service. Florida Tech has its own organization for Habitat for Humanity as well as a program for working with local elementary school students.

Students at Florida Tech participate in 22 intercollegiate sports at the Division II level. While Florida Tech may not be known for its varsity athletics, students said that the soccer and basketball teams have recently been particularly successful. One sophomore commented that "Athletic spirit could be better, although it has improved in the last couple of years." For those not as eager to indulge in athletics at such a high level, Florida Tech also offers many opportunities to get involved with intramural sports.

Social Life

General friendliness seems to abound at Florida Tech. According to one student, "People will bend over backwards to help you." And, because Florida Tech has a small student body, "Everyone really gets a chance to get to know all the students."

> "It wasn't what I was expecting . . . it was a lot better."

On campus, "There's always something going on," as one sophomore said. The student-run Residential Hall Association and the Campus Activities Board set up popular campus events, including comedy shows, concerts and an International Fair, which allows students to explore the traditions of people from different cultures across the world.

Off campus, most students spend their free time hanging out on the beach. While there, people enjoy a range of water activities, including surfing, boating, kayaking or simply relaxing in the sun. Students can also drive less than an hour to get to Disney World.

Greek fraternities and sororities attract a large number of students and are a dominant presence on campus. Some students complain about a lack of on-campus parties, though they acknowledge that parties do take place off campus. Florida Tech tends to have a strict policy against alcohol, although students do not always follow it—"We still drink, of course," one sophomore commented.

Florida Tech's uneven male-female ratio of 65:35 affects social life on campus. Male students joke that, "If you don't find a girlfriend in the first couple of weeks in freshmen year, you won't ever find a girlfriend." However, such sentiment is not pervasive throughout the entire student body. As one male student said, "It doesn't bother me too much. I probably have more female friends on campus than male friends."

Around Campus

Students live in one of six campus residential halls and two apartment complexes. Campbell and Wood Halls offer housing primarily to freshmen, although their convenient locations draw many upperclassmen to share these residencies as well. Roberts Hall is the largest residence facility on campus and houses only freshmen. Women may choose to live in Shaw Hall, a female-only residence. Outside of the residence halls, students love the Columbia Village Suites and Southgate Apartments. The Southgate Apartments, which come with in-suite amenities and an outdoor pool, are so popular that "people wait outside and sleep in tents for a week to get in," said one student. All freshmen are required to live on campus, while about half of the remaining students choose to live off campus.

Residence halls are watched over by student RAs. One sophomore mentioned, "RAs are pretty strict compared to other schools."

Students tend to find the food at Florida Tech to be decent. As one student said, "When I come back from break, I'm excited to eat the food. But after three weeks, I'm kind of tired of it." Students often socialize at "The RAT," an eatery and pub on the lower level of Evans Hall that also features a big-screen TV, game room, and computer cluster. Off campus, students enjoy eating at local restaurants such as Carrabba's Italian Grill, City Tropics Bistro and Outback Steakhouse.

Not Typically Techie

Despite its name, Florida Tech offers much more than an education in technology. From the lush botanical gardens on campus to the beautiful beaches just miles from campus, from scuba diving to watching shuttle launches at Kennedy Space Center, from graphs to Greek life, Florida Tech offers the complete college experience. One student put it best, "I wasn't sure what I was getting into. It just blew me away. It wasn't what I was expecting . . . it was a lot better." —*David Flinner*

FYI
If you come to Florida Tech, you'd better bring "a calculator."
What's the typical weekend schedule? "Friday: Get out of class as early as possible and take a nap; Saturday: hang out at the beach; Sunday: study."
If I could change one thing about Florida Tech, I'd "lower tuition."
Three things every student at Florida Tech should do before graduating are "help out with some community service projects and make many trips to the beach!"

Florida Southern College

Address: 111 Lake Hollingsworth Drive, Lakeland, FL 33801-5698
Phone: 863-680-4131
E-mail address: fscadm@ flsouthern.edu
Web site URL: www.flsouthern.edu
Year Founded: 1883
Private or Public: Private
Religious Affiliation: Methodist
Location: Urban
Number of Applicants: 2,559
Percent Accepted: 58%
Percent Accepted who enroll: 28%
Number Entering: 424
Number of Transfers Accepted each Year: 148
Middle 50% SAT range: M: 470–600, CR: 480–600, Wr: 460–570
Middle 50% ACT range: 20–25
Early admission program EA/ED/None: ED

Percentage accepted through EA or ED: 14%
EA and ED deadline: 1-Dec
Regular Deadline: 1-Mar
Application Fee: $30
Full time Undergraduate enrollment: 1,693
Total enrollment: 1,801
Percent Male: 40%
Percent Female: 60%
Total Percent Minority or Unreported: 20%
Percent African-American: 7%
Percent Asian/Pacific Islander: 1%
Percent Hispanic: 6%
Percent Native-American: <1%
Percent International: 4%
Percent in-state/out of state: 75%/25%
Percent from Public HS: 79%
Retention Rate: 71%
Graduation Rate 4-year: 37%

Graduation Rate 6-year: 52%
Percent Undergraduates in On-campus housing: 74%
Number of official organized extracurricular organizations: 70
3 Most popular majors: Biology, Marketing, Psychology
Student/Faculty ratio: 13:1
Average Class Size: 14
Percent of students going to grad school: 27%
Tuition and Fees: $22,145
In-State Tuition and Fees if different: No difference
Cost for Room and Board: $7,850
Percent receiving financial aid out of those who apply: 82%
Percent receiving financial aid among all students: 62%

Finding a pleasant atmosphere to enjoy the Florida sun is never hard at Florida Southern College. Located in the town of Lakeland, the Moccasins boast a championship-caliber women's golf team, proximity to some of the most beautiful beaches in the world, and by all accounts one of the most hospitable institutions in the South. "I would definitely choose to go here again. There are tons of great people and great professors," said one proud student.

Rockin' the Classroom
Florida Southern is known across the country for its scholastic excellence. It consistently ranks as one of the best academic colleges in the Southeast. Undoubtedly one cause for FSC's educational acumen is its small class sizes. Most classes average

around 15 students, with popular lectures being the only courses where you might get lost in a crowd. One student commented that "It's a nice learning environment because classes are smaller and more intimate. The professors know you by name." Florida Southern also offers a wide variety of courses from guts like Jogging, Waterskiing, and Physical Education, to more challenging fare such as New and Old Testament, Classical and Medieval Philosophy, and Human Genetics. Students also report that being rejected from a class you really want to take is virtually a nonissue. "If you need to get into a certain course, just talk to the professor."

Party like a Mocc-star

During the day, a plethora of leisure activities is available to your average Moccasins. They can enjoy the beautiful Florida weather on the shores of Lake Hollingsworth, hop in the car and take a 35-minute drive down the road to enjoy that same weather at Clearwater Beach, or shop at the new outdoor mall at Lakeside Village, which boasts over 100 stores. When the sun sets, however, Lakeland doesn't really offer too many party options for Florida Southern students. The scene usually starts on Thursday evenings, and begins with a trip to traditional crowd-pleasers like Chili's, Bennigan's, or Applebee's. For students who don't want to go too far, the local club scene is dominated by Kau Kau Korner, a legendary bar just off Florida Southern's campus. Students who don't mind traveling pile into their cars on the weekends to sample the sizzling nightlife of nearby Orlando and Tampa's Ybor City.

For those not into that scene, the Association of Campus Entertainment (ACE) has worked in recent years to make life in Lakeland more exciting. "The school made a concerted effort to plan weekend activities to keep students on campus," said one student. These dogged efforts have paid off. ACE has even managed to lure some comedians that have been prominently featured on networks like Comedy Central.

If you are looking for illegal drugs or a school whose drug policy is pretty lax, then Florida Southern is not the campus for you. One student reported that "the drug rules are pretty strictly enforced, especially for the freshmen." Florida Southern is also a dry campus, but the drinking restrictions are much less strict than those on drugs. Florida Southern does have Resident Assistants, who vary in temperament. "It depends on the person: some are laid-back, some not so much.

Some are more involved than others." Strict RA or not, a Florida Southern senior said that "If you want to find a place to drink, you'll definitely be able to."

Oh Those Generous Greeks!

Greek life is pretty important at Florida Southern. One student estimated the Greek population to be even higher than the official statistics. Frats and sororities are quite vocal and involved on campus. Despite this, "Lakeland does not allow sorority and fraternity houses, so certain dorm rooms are considered fraternity or sorority areas," explained one sorority member. Though these dorms are set aside for Greek use, the connection is informal and no one fraternity lays claim to a whole dormitory. Also, these frats aren't all about partying and debauchery; many students report that Greeks at Florida Southern have to be well-rounded. "We're really big on philanthropy, and are also really involved in student government and other leadership roles on campus," said one fraternity member.

Doin' It Big in Lakeland

There are many students who move off campus into cheaper housing close to school after their freshman year. On the other hand, many Moccasins enjoy staying on campus for the four years they'll be there. "At this small school, if I didn't live on campus, I would really be out of the loop," said one student. Students described their campus as "pretty diverse" with "A lot of students from Florida, but also people from up north and out west. However, there are more East Coast students."

One common complaint among FSC's pupils is the mediocre food in the dining hall. There are also concerns about the limited hours the dining hall is open. Fortunately, beneath the dining hall there is a 24-hour café to satisfy all the late-night hungers from working out, partying, or just hanging with your friends. If you prefer your meals over a good book, then you can head to the cybercafé where Moccasins stay up late nights fueled by Starbucks coffee, typing away furiously on their laptops. In addition, there is also a yogurt stand that serves smoothies for those days when the sun beats down particularly hard.

Get Up, Get Out, and Do Something

Anyone who wants to sit on their duff for their college career had better not apply to

Florida Southern; students usually have their hands in a lot of pots. "We're usually pretty committed to different activities. There are lots of student athletes," explained one Moc. Florida Southern competes in Division II of the NCAA in all of its sports. The Mocs lay claim to 27 national championships. Residing in gorgeous central Florida, it comes as no surprise that FSC is home to some of the best golfers at the college level with 12 men's golf championships and four women's golf championships, including one in 2007.

> **"Our location, history, and the fun stories behind the school differentiate us from other colleges."**

Despite the consistent excellence of the golf team, baseball and softball are by far the most popular sports on campus. The men's baseball team has even played exhibitions with MLB's Detroit Tigers. However, in an effort to increase student participation in the school's other stellar athletics programs, a Sports Management Club has recently been founded. Also, on weekday afternoons the intramural warriors take advantage of the extensive IM fields. Moccasins are just as active off the field, too. Since Florida Southern was originally founded as a Methodist college, theology and church do play a role in the day-to-day activities on the college grounds. "Campus ministry is also a large part of the campus life," reports one student. Other students, however, don't feel pressured into taking part in the various religious activities.

Everything Is All-Wright

Florida Southern's most famous attribute is its bond with one of the most renowned architects of the 20th century. "We have the largest collection of Frank Lloyd Wright architecture in the world on our campus," bragged one student. One of the most popular Wright works are the underground tunnels he built for the Cold War. "Lots of kids try to get in there." There is also the recently reconstructed Water Dome, which was a part of FSC's campus as early as 1948 but has now been built to Wright's original specifications. Consisting of a huge pool surrounded by fountains cascading together at the monument's center, the Water Dome is the crowning piece of a paean to the daring mind and bold spirit that Frank Lloyd Wright represented.

Florida Southern is also a haven for the supernatural. It seems that the residents of a particular freshman dorm have spotted a ghost. "It's [former] President Spivey's son. You'll hear a basketball bouncing, and then you have to say 'No, Allen, I don't want to play,' and he'll go away." Students enjoy the color that comes with living in a place like Lakeland. "Our location, history, and the fun stories behind the school differentiate us from other colleges," said one sophomore.— *JonPaul McBride*

FYI
If you come to Florida Southern you'd better bring "a Frisbee, a car, and an open mind."
What's the typical weekend schedule? "Go see a comedy show, grab dinner at Lakeside Village, run around Lake Hollingsworth, and chill at the beach on Sunday."
If I could change one thing about Florida Southern, I would "change how different our breaks are from other schools, especially spring break."
Three things every student at Florida Southern should do before graduating are "go to Kau Kau Korner, take funny pictures with the statues, and take a religion class."

F l o r i d a   S t a t e   U n i v e r s i t y

Address: PO Box 3062400, Tallahassee, FL 32306

Phone: 850-644-6200

E-mail address: admissions@admin.fsu.edu

Web site URL: www.fsu.edu

Year Founded: 1851

Private or Public: Public

Religious Affiliation: None

Location: Urban

Number of Applicants: 28,313

Percent Accepted: 58%

Percent Accepted who enroll: 37%

Number Entering: 6,145

Number of Transfers Accepted each Year: 3,260

Middle 50% SAT range: M: 560–640, CR: 550–650, Wr: 550–640

Middle 50% ACT range: 23–28

Early admission program EA/ED/None: None

Percentage accepted through EA or ED: NA

EA and ED deadline: NA

Regular Deadline: 18-Jan

Application Fee: $30

Full time Undergraduate enrollment: 28,864

Total enrollment: 41,087

Percent Male: 45%

Percent Female: 55%

Total Percent Minority or Unreported: 31%

Percent African-American: 10%

Percent Asian/Pacific Islander: 4%

Percent Hispanic: 12%

Percent Native-American: 1%

Percent International: 1%

Percent in-state/out of state: 95%/5%

Percent from Public HS: 53%

Retention Rate: 99%

Graduation Rate 4-year: 53%

Graduation Rate 6-year: 73%

Percent Undergraduates in On-campus housing: 15%

Number of official organized extracurricular organizations: 450

3 Most popular majors: Finance, Psychology, Criminology

Student/Faculty ratio: 22:1

Average Class Size: 25-29

Percent of students going to grad school: Unreported

Tuition and Fees: $18,243

In-State Tuition and Fees if different: $3,799

Cost for Room and Board: $5,825

Percent receiving financial aid out of those who apply: 52%

Percent receiving financial aid among all students: 37%

L ocated in the heart of Tallahassee, Florida State University offers its over 40,000 students a beautiful campus, a plethora of extracurricular opportunities, and a variety of fun social venues. With excellent athletic teams and a unique sense of pride in the Seminole community, FSU is known for its students' passionate school spirit. Given its well-rounded liberal arts program and enjoyable campus environment, FSU is certainly worth considering for all those looking for a good education at a large and lively university.

Going North to Get to the South

The vast majority of FSU's students are Floridians. Yet Tallahassee's atmosphere is likely to surprise many of the state's natives. Located in the northern panhandle of Florida, Tallahassee actually seems more like the South to the Floridian freshmen than many of their hometowns. One new student proclaimed her surprise that "Everything about Tallahassee felt completely different from Florida, including the buildings, the people, and even the trees." The weather is

quite different from the rest of the state. A freshman remarked that "As long as it's not August," the weather is "not bad, and high temperatures even dip into the 70s and 60s as early as October." Aside from the temperature differences, students are often pleasantly surprised that Tallahassee has less humidity and rain than the rest of Florida. As one senior said, "The weather here makes the campus feel more like Georgia or Alabama, in a really good way."

FSU's location also makes it an ideal school for both the studious scholars and collegiate socialites. As one freshman put it, "Tallahassee is a great mix between a large college town and a vibrant Southern capital." Within walking distance is the Florida Capitol Building, where students can learn about politics firsthand. For those interested in the social scene, the Strip, a commercial district located right across from FSU, is a good place to enjoy free time. The Strip includes Chubby's and Potbelly's, two infamous Tallahassee hangouts that double as nightclubs, and a good number of shops and restaurants. As one freshman explained, "The unique mix of intellectually stimulating venues and upbeat social centers in this city makes Tallahassee a truly incredible college town."

A True Liberal Arts Experience
Students at Florida State University tout their well-rounded academic programs. Popular majors include finance, psychology, and criminology. "Business administration seems to be the most popular major here," said one sophomore. "But, being in Tallahassee, a lot of students also choose the political science and international studies tracks." However, unlike most other state schools, Seminoles can wait until their junior year to declare a major. Many take advantage of this by trying a variety of courses. One freshman schedule included such courses as "Multicultural Film, Mythology, American Government, and German I," while another included "Chemistry I, Biology I, and General Psychology." Students at FSU find this freedom in selecting classes one of FSU's greatest academic assets.

FSU also has an excellent Honors Program with high scholastic standards and great academic rewards. Students in FSU's Honors Program receive many perks, including "really nice dorms" and "early registration for classes." In addition, FSU Honors students are allowed to live in the Honors building (Landis Hall) for more than a year, take Honors classes throughout their college years, and receive registration benefits, making this program a very desirable option.

FSU students can also choose from several other great programs. Two highly regarded alternatives include creative writing and film studies. Students brag that FSU has one of the best creative writing programs in the country. It offers a great variety of classes and, as one sophomore claimed, "FSU has world-class writing professors." Students can also take film studies as a major, if they are in The College of Motion Picture, Television, and Recording Arts. According to one junior, this is a "phenomenal program" that shows students "how to make their own cinematographic works of art, while also learning to understand other classic and contemporary works."

Though FSU's academic programs are a great fit for many students, some do see important drawbacks. Students have found that the mathematics and engineering programs are quite small, with smaller faculty and facilities. Students admit that many of their classes are lecture-based and place little emphasis on individual attention. One freshman bemoaned the "lack of availability of TAs" and also complained that professors at times were "virtually inaccessible." However, many students found that, with "persistent emailing" and "diligent planning," they were usually able to receive the help they needed. Indeed, despite these drawbacks, for a large public university FSU fosters a great learning environment with which most students are very satisfied.

A Customized, Newly Renovated Campus Life
The majority of freshman at FSU live on campus, and most have found FSU's dorms and facilities to be comfortable, easily accessible, and in great condition. Recent renovations have led the newly renovated dorms such as Wildwood and Degraff to be the dorms of choice. One freshman noted that most dorms are "small but comfortable" and was also very pleased to find that most of FSU's dorms are "conveniently located near the center of campus." Special housing in Landis Hall is also available for Honors students. As one freshman Honors student noted, "Rooming with other Honors students makes the Honors program at FSU that much more enjoyable and gives you a tight-knit group of friends."

College life on campus also offers a variety of fun places for students to hang out with friends or relax. Students cite Landis Green as a major on-campus hangout. "Landis Green is a beautiful courtyard area and is a huge part of what makes FSU the school it is. We play football or Frisbee there, talk with friends, or study, and students can even sunbathe in the Florida heat while doing homework, which is very cool." Westcott Fountain also offers a place for students to cool off, and birthday swims in the Fountain are a major part of FSU tradition. Students also relax at the Suwannee Room, where they can "eat good food and have good conversation with friends." FSU's Oglesby Union Center is also a great place to find fast food: students can choose from a local Chinese food venue, a Hardee's, and a Pollo Tropical, among others. To work off those extra calories, students spend many afternoons at the Leach Center, FSU's three-story on-campus workout facility, and students are also very active in FSU's intramural sports programs.

If students at FSU wish to leave campus most find they are actually within walking distance of a vibrant social scene. Though Seminoles feel that their college is more than just a party school, they are very proud of the notorious party scene that can be found at the many nightclubs of the Strip and the fraternity and sorority houses nearby. Alcohol is "a must-have" for most social events, but students are strictly forbidden to bring alcohol on campus, so most partying takes place in off-campus apartments and dance parties at Chubby's or other nightclubs on the Strip. Hook-ups are also frequent at such events. As one freshman bragged (to the concurrence of several others), "FSU takes great pride in the beauty of its women. FSU girls are by far among the prettiest you will ever see."

Most upperclassmen choose to live off campus. "That is actually for the best," said one freshman, "since FSU's dorms are already crowded, and apartments are actually cheaper." In addition, many freshmen concede that RAs here can be a problem. One freshman noted that her RA was "very unsociable and not very helpful" and that many of her friends also had problems with RAs. Also, parking at FSU, said one freshman, is "Abysmal . . . after the first two weeks I brought my car back home. It was too much of a hassle." FSU students also lament that there is not enough racial diversity on campus. However, despite these concerns, most students enjoy their on-campus living experience.

Seminole Pride and Success in Athletics and Beyond

Though FSU is known for its party scene, it is even better known for its prized football team and fan base. "Football at FSU is a religion. The Florida State Seminoles are its holy ministers, and the fans and alumni are its loyal, devout followers," one sophomore proclaimed. The FSU Seminoles boast a fan base in the hundreds of thousands both in Tallahassee and around the state. The Student Boosters sponsor massive pep rallies such as the Downtown Getdown and huge tailgating events. Tradition is also important for Seminole football games. As one sophomore explained, "Each game starts with the Seminole mascot, the Osceola, galloping onto the field with a flaming spear that is thrown into the center of the field to rile up the fans." Indeed, football at FSU is a significant source of school pride, especially during match-ups with FSU's two major rivals, the University of Florida and the University of Miami.

Though football is the major sport of choice, FSU also has a variety of excellent varsity and intramural sports. College basketball and baseball are very popular at FSU. According to one sophomore, the school has "an awesome baseball team, possibly one of the best in the country." For FSU's more casual athletes, intramural sports are an essential element of life. "FSU has an intramural league for almost every sport you can imagine," explained one freshman. "Flag football actually has over 500 participants this year." In addition, the Leach Center's athletic facilities are state-of-the-art and include two floors of workout equipment, an indoor track, and an Olympic-sized swimming pool. Yoga, spinning, and aerobic exercise classes are also offered there for free, so students of all athletic inclinations can enjoy working out.

> **"Football at FSU is a religion. The Florida State Seminoles are its holy ministers, and the fans and alumni are its loyal, devout followers."**

In addition to athletics, FSU has a strong set of extracurricular activities. Greek life is the predominant activity at FSU. One freshman said, "Almost everyone I know is pledging for a fraternity or sorority." Greek organizations give students leadership opportunities and can be more party-oriented or career-based depending on the chapter. FSU's Student Government Association also hosts a variety of events, including Parents' Weekend festivities and weekly movie nights. Also, students can apply to intern for the Florida State Legislature at the Capitol Building, which, as one senior noted, "is life-changing, if you have the time and the discipline to do it."

Finally, a unique and valuable gem in FSU's treasury of school pride rests in the excellent study-abroad program. One junior said that FSU "has one of the best study-abroad programs in the country." For the program in England, "It's right in the heart of London, and had so many different courses. It gave me so much cultural knowledge, was great for my political science major, and was a blast." FSU also offers programs in other locations, including Panama, Spain, France, China, Australia, Italy, and Costa Rica. Indeed, FSU's study-abroad program is something that truly distinguishes FSU from other universities.

FSU is a well-rounded academic institution that offers students unique academic opportunities and a lively atmosphere of social events. As one student said, "FSU is a place where students party hard, Seminole pride and history is celebrated, valuable lessons are learned, and life-changing opportunities are found."—*Andrew Pearlmutter*

FYI

FYI

If you come to Florida State University, you'd better bring "good walking shoes. You do a lot of walking at FSU."

What is the typical weekend schedule? "Friday nights are spent partying at a friend's apartment or clubbing at the Strip. On Saturdays, most go to the football game after tailgating and then party. Sundays are spent sleeping in and studying."

If I could change one thing about FSU, I'd "add more parking garages and bring a better variety of food to the campus."

Three things every student at FSU should do before graduating are "tour the Florida Capitol Building, study abroad with FSU's amazing study-abroad program, and go to a Florida State Seminoles football game."

New College of Florida

Address: 5800 Bay Shore Road, Sarasota, FL 34243-2109
Phone: 941-487-5000
E-mail address: admissions@ncf.edu
Web site URL: www.ncf.edu
Year Founded: 1964
Private or Public: Public
Religious Affiliation: None
Location: Small city
Number of Applicants: 1,414
Percent Accepted: 53%
Percent Accepted who enroll: 24%
Number Entering: 183
Number of Transfers Accepted each Year: 27
Middle 50% SAT range: M: 580–670, CR: 640–740, Wr: 600–690
Middle 50% ACT range: 27–31
Early admission program EA/ED/None: None

Percentage accepted through EA or ED: NA
EA and ED deadline: NA
Regular Deadline: 15-April
Application Fee: $30
Full time Undergraduate enrollment: 801
Total enrollment: 801
Percent Male: 40%
Percent Female: 60%
Total Percent Minority or Unreported: 24%
Percent African-American: 2%
Percent Asian/Pacific Islander: 3%
Percent Hispanic: 13%
Percent Native-American: 1%
Percent International: <1%
Percent in-state/out of state: 80%/20%
Percent from Public HS: 80%
Retention Rate: 82%

Graduation Rate 4-year: 45%
Graduation Rate 6-year: 63%
Percent Undergraduates in On-campus housing: 76%
Number of official organized extracurricular organizations: 90
3 Most popular majors: Biology, Psychology, Economics
Student/Faculty ratio: 10:1
Average Class Size: 18
Percent of students going to grad school: 17%
Tuition and Fees: $28,949
In-State Tuition and Fees if different: $6,032
Cost for Room and Board: $8,472
Percent receiving financial aid out of those who apply: 100%
Percent receiving financial aid among all students: 89%

Nestled in the spacious kitchens of converted mansions and with classroom notes lit by overhanging chandeliers, New College of Florida is a place where students learn in an intimate, hard-working environment. Built right along scenic Sarasota Bay, New College, a public honors college for the liberal arts, is home to only 800 students and boasts a ten-to-one faculty to student ratio. New College is the only college of its kind in Florida, and unique from the standard undergraduate experience in myriad ways. From receiving one's first narrative evaluation to being able to recognize all of the members of one's graduating class,

New College will go beyond its students' college expectations.

Academics like Yoga—Flexible and Self-Driven

New College identifies four principles that emphasize self-analysis, exploration, real mastery of information, and a joint search for learning between professor and student. It is highly selective, and the application process focuses heavily on students' high school extracurriculars: "It's attracting students that have consistently tried to push their boundaries," said one sophomore. New College offers a flexible curriculum that allows students to carve their path based on their own interests and goals, and there is strong encouragement for undergraduate research and experience outside of the classroom. For example, a junior Art History major explained that she gets credit for her internship at the Ringling Art Museum on campus, and has a system with her advisor to judge and evaluate her performance there. However, while students do have flexibility, they must also fulfill a set of seven Global Arts requirements, which cover a variety of areas, such as humanities, social sciences, and natural sciences. There is not a strict credit system to graduate, but instead there is a system of contracts, where every semester each student says how many "points" (one for each course) he or she will get (in other words, how many classes he or she will pass). Within the contract, if a student said she wanted to take four out of four and only passes three out of four, she would have "failed" that contract and not met requirements.

Courses tend to be writing-intensive and are structured in a very interdisciplinary way. "It's like: these are the topics we are going to be discussing, and this is the lens we'll be looking at them through. There aren't requirements in the typical type of linear way," said a senior. "You get out of it as much as you put in," she added. Students are tossed in at an advanced level, and due to the intimate class sizes, may be asked to lead a lecture or be in charge of managing an entire class discussion. In seminar courses, there are often student facilitators of the material, explained a senior.

The size of the classes at New College is a truly exceptional characteristic of the school. The biggest classes, such as Intro Psych, max out at around 30 to 45 students—but that's an aberration. A junior noted that one of her courses is a six-person seminar, a normal course not marketed as a small seminar. "It's really great because you develop intimate intellectual relationships with your peers and your professors, and get to engage in dialogue with someone who has a doctorate in that area. We're able to start doing that our first year," she said. Popular majors, or "concentrations," are biology, psychology, and economics.

While the student body is very small, there is often competition to get into courses. Professors ask students to write down on an index card why they want to be in the class or bring a three to five-page essay in on the first day. "No one ever gets in a serious pinch, but there is the need to keep the classes small. Professors aren't going to let everyone who wants to be in all the time," said a sophomore.

The evaluation system at New College is also extremely unusual. There are no letter grades; rather, the courses are evaluated in a narrative fashion; you can strongly, marginally, or not satisfy the course (fail). The evaluations are meant to go over a student's entire progress in the course. "I remember when I got my first narrative evaluation, I satisfied the course and did really well, but then I was given other things I could have talked about and improved," shared a current junior. "You're not just praised, but it's a great resource and a great tool." For natural sciences, professors will critique lab write-ups to encourage improvement. The written evaluations are often discussed in meetings with the professor.

When asked about his favorite and least favorite aspects of New College academics, a senior referenced the amount of assigned writing. "It's a giant pain in the neck, but I think that the push to really make your thoughts cogent and in a really academic format is something that is going to benefit me a lot later on in life," he said.

An Intimate Seaside Family

The sunset along Sarasota Bay is said to be phenomenal, and upon wandering to the waterside students can hear the beat of people playing drums and see others idling on the swing set. This is just one scene out of many that exemplifies New College's tight-knit community. All but about 100 students live on campus in one of the main residence halls, including the first-year dormitories designed by world-famous architect I.M. Pei, and many of which are set up in ways that encourage interaction. The campus itself is home to a lot of newer architecture. The cement is reminiscent of barracks, according to one student, but the majority of the academic buildings are repurposed mansions right on the bay. "It's incredible to be able to have a class in there. It's absolutely gorgeous," said a sophomore. And Palm Court, a really beautiful courtyard (also designed by Pei) where the three first-year residential halls are located is fondly called "the center of the universe." From 10 pm till one or two in the morning on Friday and Saturday nights everyone is invited to dance parties there. "We all like to party together," said a sophomore.

The supportive sense of community is seen in the RA system as well. RAs hold a unique role that differs from other schools, acting as peer mediators between residential life and administration. "We definitely define our job as students first, RAs second," said a junior. "We're really a community resource, someone to come talk to; we don't want freshmen to look and think: that person's a narc, they're going to do a room check and see I have 15 handles of vodka. That's not our job description," she said. Instead, they are heavily involved in planning events such as sessions on how to study better, or bringing in puppies from the local shelter. "We want to create a positive and healthy community," she said.

Students work really hard and party really hard. Each year there are a few annual parties, such as a Great Gatsby–themed evening with a jazz band and lots of champagne. Three times a year they hold "PCPs"—Palm Court Parties—which each have a special theme, such as Neverland, Bioluminescence, or Jurassic Park, and with the help of a $1,600 budget for the event, the school undergoes a temporary transformation. But whether or not there is a special event, there are always lots of places to dance—"that's something our school cares a lot about—more than they should, in my opinion," shared one sophomore. Each year there is also a party involving an elaborate survey that goes out to all the students, and residents of one of the upperclassman dorms match people based on their "absurd results." This is followed by a big soiree where people are jokingly matched. "Sometimes it's actually a good match but more than likely you will know the person you get matched with," commented a senior.

A Community of Dance and Service

New College students are notable for their dedication to community service and dance. Many are involved in the student-directed and choreographed dance show that takes place once each semester, while numerous others spend time to tutor at the New College Childcare Center. Students also hold campus jobs or are involved in the creative journal or the school newspaper, *The Catalyst*. "It's definitely a school for people who are overachievers in a sense, because a lot of people are always doing something else [besides classes]," said one senior.

At such a small school, there is not much of a focus on athletics, though the sailing team is quite devoted. The sailing team, however, is only part of a club league, as there are no official sports teams. Don't expect any enormous, rowdy stadiums going crazy over a football game. There are men's and women's soccer teams that play against adult teams within Sarasota, but they don't play in a league against other colleges. Sometimes people play soccer on the tennis courts, said one student. "Each time it's a different theme—drunk soccer, drunk dodgeball. There's a very big cult following for that."

For students who might be a little antsy to see some new scenery, campus is a five-minute drive, or fifteen-minute bike, from the small city of Sarasota. Since Sarasota doesn't have much of a "city" or "downtown," several students expressed that they wouldn't enjoy it if they didn't have their peers there as well. Venturing into downtown doesn't usually happen unless people want to get Thai food or frozen yogurt, and "only one or two bars are nice and not just old, boozy men," according to a junior. The one salsa club is "really hit or miss," and so, as a student explained, the lack of activity in Sarasota spurs the public parties on campus every weekend.

In terms of on-campus dining, students start out with a $1,000 à la carte meal plan. "The dining hall is pretty small, and I don't really like the food there necessarily; however, at every meal they have multiple vegetarian options and at least one vegan option," said a student. The dining system takes care to order organic products and have a lot of microwavable vegan and vegetarian offerings available. There is also a student-run cafe on campus that is all vegetarian and generally more frequented for its higher-quality food.

> "It's great because you develop intimate intellectual relationships with your peers and your professors, and get to engage in dialogue with someone who has a doctorate in that area. We're able to start doing that our first year."

But regardless of the dining or downtown Sarasota's disputable qualities, the community is what students at New College share at the end of the day, and it's a type of community that few college campuses can offer. To imagine the tens of thousands of students at regular Florida state universities just around the bend and to then picture the idyllic Ringling Mansion poised by the lapping waters of the bay is to paint college experiences from two alternate universes. If you are looking for intimacy with your peers and your professors and a place where you will be deeply motivated and closely guided toward improvement, then there hardly seems a better place for you than New College.—*TaoTao Holmes*

FYI

If you come to New College, you'd better bring "a lot of self-motivation or self-drive and a curious mind."

If you come to New College, you'd better leave "your inhibitions" behind.

Three things every student at New College should do before graduating are: "walk down to the bay and see the sunset at least once a week, gain a close relationship with one of your professors, and take advantage of being at such a small school and really push yourself to grow and be a leader."

Rollins College

Address: 1000 Holt Avenue, #1502 Winter Park, FL 32789
Phone: 407-646-2161
E-mail address: admission@rollins.edu
Web site URL: www.rollins.edu
Year Founded: 1885
Private or Public: Private
Religious Affiliation: None
Location: Suburban
Number of Applicants: 4,416
Percent Accepted: 54%
Percent Accepted who enroll: 23%
Number Entering: 555
Number of Transfers Accepted each Year: 97
Middle 50% SAT range: M: 545–640, CR: 550–640, Wr: Unreported
Middle 50% ACT range: 24–28
Early admission program EA/ED/None: ED

Percentage accepted through EA or ED: 41%
EA and ED deadline: 15-Nov
Regular Deadline: 15-Feb
Application Fee: $40
Full time Undergraduate enrollment: 1,818
Total enrollment: 1,818
Percent Male: 41%
Percent Female: 59%
Total Percent Minority or Unreported: 34%
Percent African-American: 4%
Percent Asian/Pacific Islander: 2%
Percent Hispanic: 10%
Percent Native-American: <1%
Percent International: 6%
Percent in-state/out of state: 57%/43%
Percent from Public HS: 53%
Retention Rate: 81%
Graduation Rate 4-year: 59%

Graduation Rate 6-year: 68%
Percent Undergraduates in On-campus housing: 66%
Number of official organized extracurricular organizations: 100
3 Most popular majors: Economics, Business, Psychology
Student/Faculty ratio: 10:1
Average Class Size: 15
Percent of students going to grad school: 41%
Tuition and Fees: $38,400
In-State Tuition and Fees if different: No difference
Cost for Room and Board: $12,000
Percent receiving financial aid out of those who apply: 83%
Percent receiving financial aid among all students: 79%

S ituated on picturesque Lake Virginia in Winter Park, Rollins College, "feels as if you have entered a storybook upon your first walk on campus, and [students] often have to pinch [themselves] that [they] get to call this place home." Yet while students do spend time enjoying the beautiful campus and Florida weather, many students study hard and immerse themselves in the opportunities that Rollins has to offer.

School is what you make of it

Students at Rollins rave about the school's small class sizes. "Class sizes are averaged around 17, but even that is a pretty large class here," said one student. Another added, "This allows you to really connect with your professor and other students." This makes for a very personal experience—don't expect to be able to skip class regularly. And while some students do spend more time on the beach than on their studies, students who apply themselves out of the classroom find themselves in a challenging and stimulating environment. The biggest major at Rollins is Psychology, but Economics, Biology, Music and Theater majors are also prevalent. A number of students also major in International Business, but beware, as it "is commonly-known as the most difficult major" at Rollins. Finally, students love their professors. "Every professor I have had has either been fantastic or at least good," one said.

If You're Bored . . .

When Rollins students aren't in the classroom or on the beach, there's a lot else to do—although not everybody takes advantage of the opportunities. "Rollins offers many extracurricular activities, but not everyone gets involved. It's worth it if you do though," one student said. Rollins boasts both the oldest college newspaper in Florida, a weekly called *The Sandspur*, and the oldest radio station in the state, 91.5 WPRK FM. The Tars compete in the NCAA Division II Sunshine State conference, but "sports are not that big" and "usually not many students attend games." It's not hard to find activities to get involved in on campus. As one student put it, "You can find nearly every organization that comes to mind here, despite our small size. In addition, organizations are very easy to start up here, if you don't find what you want."

> **"Buildings on this campus are gorgeous."**

Students have also found it easy to find friends through extracurricular activities. One counsels, "Don't be afraid to join organizations. At least go to the info sessions! It's at these clubs where you'll probably meet some great friends."

Not a Bad Way to Live

Not only do students enjoy Florida weather year-round, but, "Buildings on this campus are gorgeous." Architecture is Spanish-Mediterreanean, and sidewalks and roads are made with bricks or cobblestone. Rollins's location on Lake Virginia encourages lots of tanning and outdoor activity, as the school has "two beaches, two outdoor pools and free sailboat and canoe rentals."

Students are a little bit less enthusiastic about housing, but still acknowledge it as "relatively nice." While the school requires freshmen to live on campus, upperclassmen are allowed to live off campus—although housing is guaranteed for all four years at Rollins. "All on-campus housing is alcohol free, regardless of whether it is a freshmen dorm or not," which has prompted certain fraternities and sororities to have locations off campus. While Greek life doesn't dominate the social scene, its presence can certainly be felt on campus. Because of recent crackdowns, dorm room parties have become less common and fraternity parties have become more low-key. Still, there's plenty to do in a school located close to Orlando. According to one student, "We tan, we study, we dance (often all at once), we eat, we party, we play board games, we play sports, we go to the many amusement parks of Orlando; there seems to be a new and fun activity every week." Clubs and bars (including gay bars) often attract Rollins students.

Student body diversity doesn't qualify as one of Rollins's calling cards. "I would say the 'stereotypical' Rollins student is preppy, white, and upper-middle-class," said one student. Still, students note that people from all walks of life attend Rollins. Furthermore, Rollins students seem receptive to others. "I have not really come across anyone who is against opening up that group to new people," one said.

Hungry for More?

"The food is relatively good, although pricey," said one Rollins student. Students noted a great bagel bar option in the dining halls, as well as options such as sushi and pizza. One complaint about the dining, however, is that the school does not offer enough variety. If you're hungry late at night, multiple options are available to students, including Dave's Down Under, which serves diner-type food, and The Grille, which serves "light-type food."—*Alexander Eppler*

FYI
The biggest college-wide event at Rollins is "Fox Day, where school is cancelled one random day in Spring! Only the President of Rollins knows the date it will be on for each year."
What surprised me the most about Rollins when I arrived was "how good-looking everyone was!"
If you come to Rollins, you'd better bring "flip flops, a bathing suit, and sunglasses (some designer labels wouldn't hurt either)."

Stetson University

Address: 421 N Woodland Boulevard, DeLand, FL 32723
Phone: 800-688-0101
E-mail address: admissions@stetson.edu
Web site URL: www.stetson.edu
Year Founded: 1883
Private or Public: Private
Religious Affiliation: None
Location: Urban
Number of Applicants: 3,884
Percent Accepted: 51%
Percent Accepted who enroll: 28%
Number Entering: 546
Number of Transfers Accepted each Year: 100
Middle 50% SAT range: M: 480–610, CR: 490–620, Wr: 480–590
Middle 50% ACT range: 21–26

Early admission program EA/ED/None: ED
Percentage accepted through EA or ED: Unreported
EA and ED deadline: 1-Nov
Regular Deadline: 15-Mar
Application Fee: $25
Full time Undergraduate enrollment: 2,070
Total enrollment: 2,134
Percent Male: 43%
Percent Female: 57%
Total Percent Minority or Unreported: 23%
Percent African-American: 6%
Percent Asian/Pacific Islander: 2%
Percent Hispanic: 12%
Percent Native-American: <1%
Percent International: 4%
Percent in-state/out of state: 83%/17%

Percent from Public HS: 78%
Retention Rate: Unreported
Graduation Rate 4-year: 55%
Graduation Rate 6-year: 67%
Percent Undergraduates in On-campus housing: 66%
Number of official organized extracurricular organizations: 125
2 Most popular majors: Business Administration and Management
Student/Faculty ratio: 11:1
Average Class Size: 16
Percent of students going to grad school: 60%
Tuition and Fees: $32,940
In-State Tuition and Fees if different: No difference
Cost for Room and Board: $10,254
Percent receiving financial aid among all students: 97%

It's tough to deny the allure of packing swimsuits and tanning lotion instead of snow pants and boots in preparation for college. But Stetson University, in sunny DeLand, Florida, isn't just any laid-back, rural Florida school. It's known for solid academics—including several well-respected professional programs—and a vibrant campus atmosphere.

Academics

According to *U.S. News & World Report*, Stetson consistently ranks among the best regional schools in the Southeast. There is a lot to choose from when it comes to academics: with over 60 major and minor fields available to undergraduates in the College of Arts and Sciences, the School of Business Administration and the School of Music, students can study anything from digital arts (a collaboration between the departments of Art and Computer Science and the School of Music) to chemistry to business law.

In addition to completing the requirements for a major, undergraduates in the College of Arts and Sciences must fulfill a stringent set of distributional requirements, which encompass the areas of "Foundations" (basic courses such as English, math and foreign language), "Breadth of Knowledge" (natural and social science), "Bases of Ethical Decision Making" (ethics courses), and a nonacademic requirement, "Cultural Attendance," which entails attending approved cultural events every semester. Some academic requirements can be waived with AP scores, but either way, the fact remains that you will get a well-rounded education at Stetson. "All the requirements can be irritating," one junior said. "But . . . if you're an English major, at least you have the experience of having taken some science."

There are also several programs that encourage Stetson's brightest to go beyond the curricular minimum. The Honors Program, for example, gives students the opportunities to take a Junior Honors Seminar and design their own major, as well as encouraging them to study abroad. Although any entering student may apply, most accepted students have had SAT scores in the 50 percent range of 1490 and 1800 and 41 percent have been in the top 10 percent of their high-school class.

As one might expect from a school with such a variety of academic disciplines and such a small student body, classes at Stetson are small, and professors are accessible. With relatively few classes within each division, majors often encompass broad areas of study. Students change their majors often, a process that is apparently neither difficult nor stigmatized. But having small class sizes—even in such traditionally impersonal disciplines as business—can make all the difference for some. "You do tend to bond with your professors, whether you like it or not," said one senior, a marketing major. "I have not been in a class with more than 50 students."

Once students have experienced the ease of getting into their desired classes and the delight of having the professor know their names from day one, there's the actual class work to consider. More difficult subjects are rumored to be biology, chemistry and music. At one point, "Music Theory" had the highest failure rate on campus. Communications and education, according to students, are easier majors.

Dorm Life

Since freshmen, sophomores and juniors are all required to live on campus, "dorm life" at Stetson is often synonymous with "campus life." "The dorms aren't particularly nice," one sophomore said, "but they are amazing places to meet people and really learn how to live on your own." Students praised the location of the dorms—they are all within walking distance of central campus.

Other facilities are certainly not lacking. The college gymnasium and pool received high marks. The gym offers classes during the semester, and the pool is "very spacious and a good place to relax," presumably since most of the year is bathing-suit weather.

The dining halls are also decent. The main eating facility is Commons, which is apparently "fair" in terms of food and seating arrangements. Known as a social place, Commons is an area where "You can just pick up a conversation with anyone really." Stetson's flexible dining plan allows students to cash in unused meals for purchases at other eateries close by, such as the popular grill Hat Rack, Einstein Bros. Bagels, and the nearby smoothie shop.

Campus Life

Though Stetson features a variety of clubs and activities for students, the Greeks, with their six fraternities and five sororities, tend to be the biggest force on campus. They often host large parties and events in their mostly off-campus venues. Most of these events are nonexclusive.

> **"You couldn't ask for a safer place to have a school."**

Two other prominent groups on campus are the Council for Student Activities (CSA) and the Student Government Association (SGA). They have been responsible in the past for bringing in such big-name acts as Less Than Jake and Busta Rhymes. In addition, Stetson hosts a variety of speakers every year. "If you want to hear a speaker every week at Stetson, you definitely can," one senior said. There are, of course, a variety of smaller organizations that cater to more specific groups; these, however, tend to be less active.

Athletics are also a big part of campus life. Although the school lacks the draw of a football team, students report that the other varsity teams' events are well-attended and popular. While the teams themselves "tend to keep together," according to a senior non-athlete, this doesn't keep the rest of the student body from going to games and cheering them on. The basketball and soccer teams receive the most attention. Intramural sports are also popular.

Outside the Bounds of Campus Grounds

The town of DeLand is not generally known as a fun place to hang out, but it has its advocates. This minority says that the town fulfills all "basic needs" with a Walmart and several chain restaurants, that the historic downtown area provides a nice walk, and that "You couldn't ask for a safer place to have a school."

But those who seek a setting that includes more than McDonald's, picturesque promenades and a sense of security flock instead to Daytona or Orlando, each of which is less than an hour away. Popular destinations include malls, clubs, bars, theme parks and anything else the rural town just can't provide. To this end, many students do bring cars to campus, but—as with most colleges—the limitations of on-campus parking can make owning a car more of a burden than anything. Many students use their cars to drive home to other Florida cities on a regular basis.

For those who choose to stay on campus or in DeLand, there is certainly not a dearth of things to do. The most popular parties, thrown by the Greeks, are generally held off campus, but there are large on-campus parties as well. These tend to be contained by Public Safety, Stetson's security detail. Drinking is prevalent at all of these parties, but there are alternatives. Many groups, particularly various Christian ones, host dry events on a regular basis. Drug use does occur at Stetson, but it is easy to avoid and by no means popular. According to students, alternatives to "traditional" college partying include bowling, ice-skating, going to the movies, and listening to live music.

Conclusion

So why choose Stetson? For many, the appeal is that the college is "a small school close to home." Around 80 percent of the students are Floridians; it's tough for any Florida native to consider going anywhere farther north for school. But the year-round sun is not the only draw: Stetson features high-quality academics on a gorgeous campus. Although it is located in a rural town, Orlando and Daytona are close enough that students don't feel stranded. Add to that the small classes, accessible professors, school spirit and general commitment to excellence, and you've got a school that would be hard for anyone to pass up.—*Jay Buchanan*

FYI

If you come to Stetson, you'd better bring "a bathing suit, because we have a nice pool and people take trips to the beach very often."

What is the typical weekend schedule? "Friday, drive to Daytona; Saturday, spend the afternoon in Daytona and hang out with friends; Sunday, relax in DeLand."

If I could change one thing about Stetson, "I would bring a better selection of food during the weekends."

Three things that everyone should do before graduating from Stetson are "go to all the beaches, join a club or Greek organization and get involved, and enjoy it!"

University of Florida

Address: 201 Criser Hall, Box 114000, Gainesville, FL 32611-4000
Phone: 352-392-1365
E-mail address: ourwebrequests@registrar.ufl.edu
Web site URL: www.ufl.edu
Year Founded: 1853
Private or Public: Public
Religious Affiliation: None
Location: Suburban
Number of Applicants: 26,513
Percent Accepted: 43%
Percent Accepted who enroll: 55%
Number Entering: 6,329
Number of Transfers Accepted each Year: 2,150
Middle 50% SAT range: M: 600–690, CR: 570–670, Wr: Unreported
Middle 50% ACT range: 26–30

Early admission program EA/ED/None: None
Percentage accepted through EA or ED: NA
EA and ED deadline: NA
Regular Deadline: 1-Nov
Application Fee: $30
Full time Undergraduate enrollment: 30,475
Total enrollment: 45,701
Percent Male: 45%
Percent Female: 55%
Total Percent Minority or Unreported: 41%
Percent African-American: 10%
Percent Asian/Pacific Islander: 8%
Percent Hispanic: 17%
Percent Native-American: <1%
Percent International: 1%
Percent in-state/out of state: 96%/4%
Percent from Public HS: 82%
Retention Rate: 96%

Graduation Rate 4-year: 82%
Graduation Rate 6-year: Unreported
Percent Undergraduates in On-campus housing: 23%
Number of official organized extracurricular organizations: 86
3 Most popular majors: Biology, Political Science and Government, Psychology
Student/Faculty ratio: 20:1
Average Class Size: 15
Percent of students going to grad school: Unreported
Tuition and Fees: $27,933
In-State Tuition and Fees if different: $5,657
Cost for Room and Board: $8,800
Percent receiving financial aid out of those who apply: 99%
Percent receiving financial aid among all students: 90%

S wish. Gurgle. Gulp. Ahhhh. Refreshing, isn't it? Light, tangy, and just a little salty, Gatorade is cherished as an electrolyte-replenishing elixir for athletes around the world. Where'd this wondrous creation come from? Why, the University of Florida of course! It was the blistering summer of '65 . . . little did UF physicians realize that their secret brew would become the official sports drink of the NFL—a title it holds to this day. One of the most influential schools in the South, UF excels in academics and athletics. With A+ students, UF consistently graduates at the top of its class.

Is It In You?

UF, is, like, *the* school to get into in the state of Florida. Meaning, it gets a mind-boggling, incredible amount of in-state applicants every year. In the state of Florida, the Bright Futures scholarship covers approximately 80% of in-state students' expenses. However, the acceptance rate has been dropping as more and more students clamber for entrance into Gator Land. Acceptances are mailed out in late February, but unlike most private schools, UF lets students fend for themselves in terms of finding a place to stay. With its overwhelming incoming class size, often students prefer to live off campus. Gainesville is overflowing with student apartment complexes that allow students to have the freedom of owning a car and taking care of their own apartment while sharing it with a few friends from high school. However, of course, with luxury come risks. Good luck finding a parking spot during rush hour.

For those that manage to snatch a dorm on campus, there is an Internet system in the late spring where students essentially advertise themselves and hope that their match finds their ad. This pick-your-own-roomie system is risky at times. There are chances that one could find their lifelong best bud, but as another freshman put it, "It can be a nightmare. My roommate and I absolutely did not get along. I wish I'd just chosen someone from my high school to room with me." While not all cases are this extreme, it is recommended that prospective roommates chat a bit, and get to know each other's sleeping habits and such before proceeding.

Take It Off

That's right. Hello, Sunshine State, where the weather's always balmy. Chilly at times, but still better than the climates of other northern schools. This smart school is a mix of all kinds of extracurricular activities. Social life is everywhere. Whether one joins a tennis club, a robotics team, or a horticulture club, people at UF know how to work hard and play hard.

There is no stereotypical UF Gator. One student said that, "We're a super diverse student body who all know how to have a good time." UF has students from all over the world as well. South Africa, Korea, China, Japan, Mexico—and all feel welcomed." With an undergraduate body that spills over 30,000, this comes as no surprise.

> "We're a super diverse student body who all know how to have a good time."

Play the piccolo? The oboe? Don't even know what these instruments look like? No problem! If one is, in any shape or form, a music addict, UF's band program will welcome you with open arms. Marching band students travel to every football game and get perks like precious tickets in the best sections of the stadiums. For the true paintbrush wielding, charcoal stained, turpentine reeking art lover, museums and galleries surround UF's campus. For instance, the Samuel P. Ham Museum of Art has a permanent collection of over 6,000 original pieces that consist of prints, ceramics, photographs, paintings, and sculptures. The artwork displayed there represents areas from all around the globe: the South Pacific, Europe, Africa, and Asia. Best of all? 'Tis free to visit.

Most students also get jobs in their spare time. Locally, a student can pick from a variety of employers. From being a store clerk at the local Gainesville Mall, to volunteering at the local teaching hospital, opportunities abound. The UF Center for Leadership and Service oversees dozens of student organizations. Gator Teen Mentors is a program that pairs UF undergrads with "at-risk" high school students and aims to provide these students with the resources and skills to successfully pursue further education. Another group, called the Women's Leadership Council, is a group of undergraduate women at UF who try to empower women with the skills that prepare them to lead in the diverse and ever-changing settings of the 21st century. It doesn't take too much looking to find a club or organization that will suit one's taste at this school, for sure.

It's Such a Rush, She's Such a Crush

Yep, UF is one in a million. Especially, when the sun goes down. Greek life plays a huge role in the social scene. You've got your Tri-Delt's, your Kappa's, your Sigma-whatever's, the list goes on and on. Drinking is highly prevalent, but mind you—these Floridian reptiles can hold their liquor. If you wanna roll with them, you better start practicing. Don't think that their straight-A grades mean that they can't play a nasty game of beer pong.

Tailgating. Huge deal? Understatement. Hear, Hear! Welcome to the UF-FSU game. At the biggest game of the year Gators size up Florida State Seminoles in an all-out tailgating war. Die-hard Gator fans start drinking at 8 am. No joke. Get ready for some hyped-up screaming, shouting, and yelling about Gator dominance. The stadium vibrates with thousands upon thousands of students painted over in royal blue and zesty orange.

Not so into the prospect of blowing your eardrums? Check out Gator Nights hosted by the Reitz Union! Funded by the Student Government group on campus, it's the leading late night program in the Southeast and takes place every Friday night of fall and spring semesters. It offers free first-run movies, comedians, interactive lectures, improv shows, novelties, cultural events, dances, artists and even video game tournaments. Forget late night coffee, Gator Nights even provide a free midnight breakfast! No matter where you choose to go, the nocturnal creature inside will most definitely be satisfied at the University of Florida.

We Canz Read Good?

Aside from the memorable parties, the great friends, the excitement of athletic games— there is schoolwork. Luckily UF prides itself in holding to a high level of academic excellence. Some of the popular majors are biology, political science and government, and psychology. However, in a school this size, there are indeed challenging courses that force students to reconsider their majors.

Worry not, for UF does provide freshmen with plenty of academic advisors. The great thing about this state school, one freshman pointed out, is that "AP credits are accepted and can really speed you through." If a student truly excelled through high school and took say 10 AP courses, then they can graduate in three years—or less! Though, most students simply take their time and just use the AP credits to waive out of prerequisite courses.

Summer Session is an option that many students also take to get some credits out of the way. This is most common for premeds. Since UF has no strict defined premed major, most students that dream of wearing a white lab coat and responding to the sweet sound of "Doctor (fill in the blank)" feel that taking some courses over the summer can help boost GPA. Summer classes usually have fewer students and give students a chance to focus more on their classes due to an overall smaller course load. A junior once recounted a horror story about his physics class that had a class average of a "D." However, when he retook the class over the summer, he triumphantly returned with a B. Keep that in mind, dear premeds. Swamp dangers lurk in the land of the Gator. Without a doubt, Summer Sessions A, B, and C ensure that the campus stays a bustling place of activity all year round.

One problem with the size of the classes at UF is that some students find it easier to just stay in their dorm and watch the class lectures online. UF's extended open courseware program hopes to remedy the difficulties that students face when going to such a large public institution. A freshman noted that her Intro to Political Science class had "over 700 kids. I even see some kids go to class, struggle to find a seat, turn on their laptops, and watch the lecture online, while in the building! Like, they need binoculars to see the board!" Incredible, isn't it? Nevertheless, if one is not afraid of waves of people, UF could be a perfect fit.

Beer, bros, bands, and books. If one can handle the crowd surfing and is willing to keep up with the university's ambitious academic goals, then UF should be at the top of their college application list. UF is a stronghold in the South—a school filled with Gators that live by the "party-hard, work-hard" philosophy. A plethora of activities exist, and the social scene is both engaging and varied. It's an absolutely stunning campus, dripping with Spanish moss and scattered with ancient oaks. Truly, UF is a vibrant place to be. Go Gators!—*Anna Wang*

FYI

If you come to the University of Florida, you'd better bring: "something orange, something blue, something old, and something new."

If I could change one thing about the University of Florida, I'd "create more on-campus dorms . . . with air-conditioning!"

What's the typical weekend schedule? "Go out and party! And then worry about Monday's physics test . . ."

Three things every UF student should do before graduating are: "Go to the game! Go to the game! Go to the game!"

University of Miami

Address: PO Box 248025, Coral Gables, FL 33124-4616
Phone: 305-284-4323
E-mail address: admission@miami.edu
Web site URL: www.miami.edu
Year Founded: 1925
Private or Public: Private
Religious Affiliation: None
Location: Suburban
Number of Applicants: 25,895
Percent Accepted: 39%
Percent Accepted who enroll: 21%
Number Entering: 2,132
Number of Transfers Accepted each Year: 1,637
Middle 50% SAT range: M: 620–700, CR: 590–680, Wr: 580–680
Middle 50% ACT range: 28–32

Early admission program EA/ED/None: EA and ED
Percentage accepted through EA or ED: EA: 54% ED: 18%
EA and ED deadline: 11/01 and 11/01
Regular Deadline: 15-Jan
Application Fee: $65
Full time Undergraduate enrollment: 10,368
Total enrollment: 15,657
Percent Male: 49%
Percent Female: 51%
Total Percent Minority or Unreported: 48%
Percent African-American: 6%
Percent Asian/Pacific Islander: 6%
Percent Hispanic: 6%
Percent Native-American: <1%
Percent International: 8%
Percent in-state/out of state: 40%/60%
Percent from Public HS: 63%
Retention Rate: 90%

Graduation Rate 4-year: 64%
Graduation Rate 6-year: Unreported
Percent Undergraduates in On-campus housing: 40%
Number of official organized extracurricular organizations: 216
3 Most popular majors: Business/Marketing, Communications/Journalism, Biology
Student/Faculty ratio: 9:1
Average Class Size: 16
Percent of students going to grad school: 32%
Tuition and Fees: $39,654
In-State Tuition and Fees if different: No difference
Cost for Room and Board: $11,528
Percent receiving financial aid out of those who apply: 78%
Percent receiving financial aid among all students: 52%

In the suburbs of Miami, around 10,000 lucky students can do homework while tanning at the pool, cheer on great sports teams and dance all night in world-famous nightclubs. The University of Miami students take learning seriously, but having fun is just as important to them. "The U" offers incredible opportunities to do both.

An Ocean of Academic Offerings
Undergraduates at Miami study at nine different schools: Arts and Sciences, Business, Engineering, Architecture, Nursing, Music, Marine and Atmospheric Sciences, Education and Development, and Communication. Each school has different graduation requirements, but all students must fulfill general education requirements that are designed to prepare students with a wide range of knowledge and skills. Students are required to take the introductory English 105/106 if they do not place out with AP exams. In addition, students must take five other writing-intensive courses to graduate. Mathematics is another

required area of proficiency; a class above Math 101 is needed to graduate. The equivalent of three semesters of a foreign language is also mandatory. Miami requires courses in three "areas of knowledge": six credits each in "Natural World" and "People and Society," and 12 in "Arts and Humanities." The requirements can be demanding, but many can be satisfied with AP credits. They can also lead to taking interesting classes that would otherwise not be considered. Two science majors said their courses on Greek and Roman mythology and the history of photography were among the best they had taken.

Business, Biology, and Communications are the most popular majors at Miami. Neuroscience, Biochemistry, Biomedical Engineering and Architecture are known for being exceptionally difficult. "Introduction to Religion" and communications courses are known for being less strenuous. The Rosentiel School of Marine and Atmospheric Sciences is one of the world's leading centers for research in these subjects, and it offers an array of unique and challenging courses. One junior majoring in marine affairs said that marine science professors are "crazy, in a good way." Marine science labs are fun, hands-on learning experiences, and may include studying dolphins in an aquarium or wading through salt marshes.

Like at most universities, class sizes at Miami vary widely. "On my campus tour they said that the average class had 11 students, but I have yet to experience that. Most classes have around 25 students, except for huge lecture classes," a sophomore said. The top ten percent of each incoming freshman class is invited to Miami's Honors Program, which offers small seminars in all colleges and schools of the university. One student said the Honors International Relations seminar he took freshman year had only six students. "It was really incredible; we worked with professors really closely."

The U of EDM

University of Miami students generally "are outgoing and looking for a good time." Freshmen usually attend house parties, while upperclassmen frequently go to clubs in downtown Miami. The city has become one of the world capitals of EDM (Electronic Dance Music), and this has had a big impact on social life at the university. Seniors will go see famous DJs perform at South Beach on any night of the week, and almost half the student body attends the massive ULTRA Music Festival in the spring. For a more relaxed party atmosphere, upperclassmen go to bars in the Coconut Grove neighborhood near campus. Of course, many students are drawn to the sun, waves, and wild house parties of Florida beaches on weekends. The vast majority of students drink, and while binge drinking does occur, most students feel that it is not any worse than other universities. If students are caught drinking underage, the University will confiscate the alcohol and notify their parents. Adderall is heavily passed around on campus and some obtain illegal drugs in the city of Miami. In the words of a senior, when it comes to alcohol and drugs at Miami, "no one judges you . . . no one cares."

Living in Paradise

The abundance of palm trees and exotic plants can make a stroll through the University of Miami's campus feel like a jungle adventure. "Campus looks like Jurassic Park

sometimes. There are plants that I never even imagined," a sophomore said. Ducks, parrots, cats, manatees, and the occasional snake or alligator can be seen in the campus palm trees and waterways. Lake Osceola's central location and the glider chairs on its banks make it a popular place to study, chat with friends, or simply reflect. "At night they illuminate a fountain in the middle of the lake. It makes you want to think deep thoughts," a student said. The architecture at the University of Miami is predominantly modern concrete, "functional, not beautiful." Students living on campus are assigned to one of Miami's five residential colleges: Eaton, Hecht, Mahoney, Pearson, and Stanford. Pearson and Mahoney house many of the university's student-athletes; Stanford and Hecht are larger dorms designated for freshmen. Each floor of the freshman colleges houses 35 to 40 people and contains a large and frequently cleaned communal bathroom. "You get really close to the people on your floor," a sophomore said. "Those people become your best friends." Each floor also has an RA, a junior or senior who supervises freshmen and eases them into the transition to college. RAs at Miami maintain a safe environment on their floors, but most allow freshmen plenty of freedom. "My RA was fantastic . . . His policy was don't do anything stupid . . . don't do anything dangerous, don't break things," a student recalled. On many floors, freshmen freely store and drink alcohol.

The University of Miami provides many opportunities for freshmen to meet each other and become integrated into campus life. Students from every dorm at Miami compete in an annual competition called Sports-Fest, which is typically dominated by the freshman residential colleges. Individual floors also vie to be the best. "Every floor gets their own shirt; usually they have 'subtly inappropriate' things on the back," a sophomore said. Students compete in games like flag football and dodgeball that "get pretty intense. It's a big deal, and it's really fun." After freshman year, many students move off campus into Coral Gables apartments, the University Village, or Greek houses. Miami also has a large population of commuter students that get involved in campus life through the Association of Commuter Students.

Meals are served to undergraduates at two all-you-can-eat dining halls. One student said she enjoyed the variety of food options and the friendliness of the dining hall staff. The student meal plan also designates several hundred dollars a month as "dining dollars" that can be used at the Hurricane Food Court and other on-campus eateries. Dining dollars are welcome at the Rathskeller, a beloved campus restaurant that serves, burgers, wings, beer, and more classic American fare. Pool tables, dartboards, flat screen TVs, and comfy sofas make "the Rat" a great place to hang out with friends. It also hosts live bands and dance parties.

Big Games and Beach Bodies

The University of Miami football team is no longer dominant, but the games and the tailgating scene are still a central part of student life. Some students get pumped up with energy drinks, while others take advantage of the alcohol that is sold in Sun Life Stadium. At games, "everyone is loud and drunk and having fun," one student said. Freshmen quickly learn all the cheering traditions such as "putting up four fingers at the beginning of the fourth quarter as a sign that we own it, and just generally doing whatever our mascot, Sebastian the Ibis, tells us to do. We love Sebastian!" The University of Miami has a tradition of widespread athletic success. Football draws the biggest crowds, but a varsity swimmer singled out Miami's golf, tennis, volleyball and women's basketball teams as the best at the university. Sports and exercise are part of most students' daily routine. Intramural sports are very popular, and some club sports teams travel around the country for competitions. The university's Wellness Center offers cardio and weight lifting equipment, exercise classes, pools, basketball courts, a juice bar, and much more. Many students work hard to maintain a year-round beach body. "People here wear as little as possible . . . they feel pressured to look good all the time."

> **"Students here want to be outside having fun."**

Salsa, SCUBA and Much More

Along with their rigorous studies and unparalleled nightlife, Miami students devote time to over 200 clubs and organizations. The student government plans many events and outings; in 2012 they bused fifty freshmen to a free Miami Heat game. The Salsa Craze dancing club and the SCUBA diving club, two of the most popular on campus, let students enjoy the cultural and natural resources of Miami. Some organizations, like the campus newspaper *The Hurricane*, have offices in the University Center (UC), which also contains a convenience store, the food court and the Rathskeller. The university eagerly awaits the completion of the new Student Activities Center, a 119,000 square-foot glass and steel building that will offer meeting space for student organizations, new retail stores, and the relocated Rathskeller. Just under 20% of undergraduates are members of the university's 33 fraternities and sororities. Greek houses host plenty of parties but they are far from the *Animal House* stereotype. A sophomore said that his frat has "a lot of smart premed people, and we do a lot of philanthropy." Greek life is growing in popularity at Miami, but it still is not as prevalent as at is many southern universities. Athletes, especially the football team, tend to keep to themselves and some party hard in their rare free time. However, "you don't have to be an athlete or Greek to have a social life."

A Shared 'Cane Spirit

The Miami student body is extremely diverse. Hispanic and Cuban culture is proudly celebrated throughout the year, and on campus "you'll hear Spanish all the time." 2,700 international undergraduates, graduate students, and faculty at Miami represent 115 countries. While some students fit the U of M stereotype of being from wealthy, or even "excessively wealthy" backgrounds, there are many students from middle-class families and nearly half of all students receive financial aid from the university. "There are people of all races and religions. It's great to meet such a grab-bag of people," one student said.

While beautiful weather and palm trees might define its uniquely beautiful campus, the spirit of the University can only be seen in its diligent, adventurous and happy students. "Students here want to be outside having fun. I was expecting to come to a school where having fun was a top priority and [Miami] fulfilled that."—*Josh Mandell*

FYI

Weekend Schedule: "Sleep, tan, party, sleep, tan, work."

3 things to do before graduating: Attend a home football game, go to South Beach, go to Ultra (world's largest Electronic Dance Music [EDM] concert.)

"What surprised me the most about UM when I arrived was was that despite what people might think about it, because of its location, student body, etc., it really is academically rigorous."

University of South Florida

Address: 4202 East Fowler Avenue, Tampa, FL 33620-9951	**Percentage accepted through EA or ED:** NA	**Graduation Rate 6-year:** Unreported
Phone: 813-974-3350	**EA and ED deadline:** NA	**Percent Undergraduates in On-campus housing:** 16%
E-mail address: admissions@usf.edu	**Regular Deadline:** 1-Mar	**Number of official organized extracurricular organizations:** 507
Web site URL: www.usf.edu	**Application Fee:** $30	
Year Founded: 1956	**Full time Undergraduate enrollment:** 29,975	
Private or Public: Public	**Total enrollment:** 40,027	**3 Most popular majors:** Business/Marketing, Social Sciences, Biology
Religious Affiliation: None	**Percent Male:** 43%	
Location: Urban	**Percent Female:** 57%	
Number of Applicants: 27,017	**Total Percent Minority or Unreported:** 44%	**Student/Faculty ratio:** Unreported
Percent Accepted: 38%	**Percent African-American:** 10%	**Average Class Size:** 14
Percent Accepted who enroll: 30%	**Percent Asian/Pacific Islander:** 7%	**Percent of students going to grad school:** Unreported
Number Entering: 3,378	**Percent Hispanic:** 7%	**Tuition and Fees:** $14,994
Number of Transfers Accepted each Year: 5,680	**Percent Native-American:** 1%	**In-State Tuition and Fees if different:** $5,806
Middle 50% SAT range: M: 540–630, CR: 520–620, Wr: 500–600	**Percent International:** 2%	**Cost for Room and Board:** $9,190
	Percent in-state/out of state: 91%/9%	**Percent receiving financial aid out of those who apply:** 80%
Middle 50% ACT range: 23–27	**Percent from Public HS:** 95%	
Early admission program EA/ED/None: None	**Retention Rate:** 81%	**Percent receiving financial aid among all students:** 68%
	Graduation Rate 4-year: Unreported	

I f you are searching for a college with a fun campus environment, a warm, sunny location, and great academic programs in business, engineering, and science, the University of South Florida is a school worth considering. In addition to enjoying USF's excellent sports teams and numerous nearby social scenes, students there take advantage of the many perks associated with being college kids in Tampa, Florida. Indeed, whether it is spending a day at the beach (only half an hour away), visiting one of the two nearby major theme parks, or enjoying exciting Division I football games, USF students always have something fun to do while they receive an excellent education.

Getting the Sunshine State Experience

Located in suburban Tampa, USF presents its students numerous benefits, creating an environment that students at other colleges only experience during spring break. Living in Florida is "a blast," according to one sophomore from out of state, who added, "Winters at USF are fantastic, since they are virtually nonexistent." The weather in Tampa is ideal during the winter and spring months, when high temperatures fall comfortably between 60 and 80 degrees, and low temperatures rarely dip below the mid-30s. Most students find the winter months to be enjoyable, and they can frequently be seen lounging about in the many green areas on campus. However, some students did complain about Florida's heat and humidity in the summer and fall months. If you play outdoor sports, be advised, "It is very, very easy to get dehydrated, especially with the high heat and humidity. The Florida heat in August, September, October, and May can be intense."

Students also find that USF is an ideal location within the city itself. One freshman noted, "Two incredible Florida theme parks, Busch Gardens and Adventure Island, are only about five minutes away from campus." In addition, USF is located "about 10–15 minutes north of downtown Tampa, which has Ybor City and Channelside as two major entertainment districts." Channelside has a variety of entertainment venues, including a movie theatre with an IMAX screen, a state-of-the-art bowling alley, and a great variety of clubs and restaurants. Ybor City not only has numerous nightclubs but also a Gameworks, a movie theatre, a line of shops, and a lot of restaurants. The beach is only a 30-minute drive away; students typically recommend Clearwater Beach as a great, year-round hangout place. The many sports teams in the area are also popular venues for students. They frequent both the Tampa Bay Buccaneers football games and the Lightning hockey games. The New York Yankees also conduct their spring training in Tampa. Furthermore, USF's football team, the Bulls, attracts massive crowds weekly, making the University a virtual mecca for sports enthusiasts. However, one student did advise against watching one specific team. "Even though they practically give away the tickets," one junior noted, "it's just not worth seeing the Devil Rays play baseball."

USF's Academic Trifecta

USF has a strong academic program, especially in the areas of business, engineering, and premed. It also has all the benefits of a large university while placing emphasis on personal attention. Incoming freshmen can take a class called "The University Experience," which helps them get acclimated to college life while instructing them in the research techniques and study habits that they will need to be successful. Students report that USF's business program is very popular on campus. "Most of the people I know are enrolled in at least some type of business-oriented class," one freshman explained,

"and many of my friends have already decided to take business administration as their major."

For students not interested in a business-related major, there are lots of excellent options. USF's premed program is quite reputable. USF's campus includes the Moffitt Cancer Center, which is one of the top cancer research institutions in the nation and a place where many students volunteer. USF's engineering program is also noteworthy for its great faculty. One student bragged that her professor in the robotics department, Ms. Robin Murphy, missed the first day of class to deploy her robotic technology at the Crandall Canyon Mine to search for mining accident victims underground. This happens to be "just one of many examples in which USF faculty members make a difference."

While USF's academics are very strong in many aspects, students admit that it is not an ideal school for those pursuing math or humanities majors. One freshman criticized the mathematics department for having professors and teaching assistants that "do not speak English very well, are hard to understand, and not very able to help the students." The humanities department, many students complain, needs more classes and does not have enough majors from which they can choose. Despite these drawbacks, however, USF has a solid academic record overall that continues to improve each year.

Living the Good Life, On or Off Campus

A sizable number of students at USF are commuters who live nearby. Most of these students, however, cite financial concerns for this choice. One junior noted that it was much cheaper for him to stay in an apartment nearby and that most students who opt to stay off campus do so for similar reasons. Campus living at USF is generally quite enjoyable. "I made most of my friends here by hanging out in dorms and watching movies together," noted one sophomore. "The dorms are tiny but conveniently located, and the University tries to pair you up with people you will be compatible with, so nightmare roommates are rare." Most students cite the Marshall Center as the best hangout location on campus. One freshman boasted that the Marshall Center includes "lots of pool tables, a big-screen TV, video games, a food court, and live bands that play every week." Students report that the food at USF is also quite good. In addition to a cafeteria-style meal plan, students can choose from Burger King, Subway, Einstein's Bagels, and Ben and Jerry's, among others. The library is also a great place to get together for academic and social purposes; it has a Starbucks on the first floor and is centrally located. Students also frequent the school's many courtyards and greeneries, which "have plenty of shade and are great places to study or talk to friends."

If students want to get off campus for some fun but do not have money for a night downtown or a day at Busch Gardens, the Gator Dockside is known as a good place to get together with friends. One student noted that "Gator nuggets and watching sports are a must" at this restaurant. USF students also frequent the nearby University Mall, which has a variety of shops and restaurants less than five minutes away from campus. The numerous athletic events held on campus each week, which students can get into for free, are also popular.

When on campus, students report that safety is not a major issue; in fact, "aside from the occasional bike thief," students feel safe. However, some lament that parking is an issue. While new parking lots are being constructed, "parking is terrible" at USF, and commuters complain at "having to arrive up to an hour early at times" to secure a spot close to class and that they "park really far away, which can be annoying."

A Social Scene with Something for Everyone

USF has a unique combination of athletic, Greek, and service organizations. Athletics (participating in or watching) are at the forefront of such activities. As one student noted, "Club-level and intramural sports are always fun" and are "easy to join and stay active in." By far the most popular sport at USF is football, and two major student organizations hold tailgating parties at every home game. The Student Bulls Club is probably the more universal athletic booster organization, as it is open to all students and sets up events at both home and away games for football, basketball, volleyball, soccer, and other Bulls sports. The Beef Studs is the other major athletic booster organization on campus. One freshman stated, "The Beef Studs are a one-of-a-kind, die-hard group of fans that wear body paint at every event, always keep the crowd pumped, and travel to just about every game. I'm not even sure if they ever remove the body paint, even during the week."

> "The Beef Studs are a one-of-a-kind, die-hard group of fans that wear body paint at every event, always keep the crowd pumped, and travel to just about every game. I'm not even sure if they ever remove the body paint, even during the week."

For those not as enthusiastic about sports, USF has a variety of other organizations. One freshman said, "Joining student government is a great way to become involved." Student government organizes school-wide social events and runs the Campus Activities Board, which oversees the funding and administration of student-run organizations on campus. The 42 fraternities and sororities represent the Greek life that plays a major but not dominant role in USF's social scene. While USF has its fair share of fun parties, students there are proud that drinking and drugs "are not a major problem." As one freshman put it, "No one really feels pressured to drink if they go to parties here."

For the more altruistic students, community service organizations and events are also thriving parts of campus life. Students work with Metropolitan Ministries, Habitat for Humanity, and other local non-profits. USF even hosts the region's Special Olympics competition every March. Indeed, as one student said, "USF has an endless number of activities that continue to grow with the interests of the student body. So even if students can't find something they are interested in, they can easily start it up and get funding from the school."

Mixing Business with Pleasure

Finally, students at USF place unique emphasis on career preparation. Alpha Kappa Psi, one of USF's coed professional business fraternities, prepares its members for successful careers in the corporate world. They frequently hold workshops, coach each other for interviews, host speakers from business-related fields, and visit the offices of major companies in the area. Furthermore, students at USF become involved in fields where they have a personal, lifelong interest. One particularly driven freshman with a keen interest in hockey secured a marketing internship with the Tampa Bay Lightning, an "incredible, life-shaping experience" in which he has been able to combine "a love for hockey with a career interest in marketing and management." For him, this "has opened the door for a whole new world of opportunities." A host of similar career-oriented internships are available through the Moffitt Cancer Center and in the surrounding community. As the same freshman noted, "USF has a well-known career fair each year and is uniquely adept at helping interested students get quality internships in areas that they are really passionate about. USF really values a well-rounded education."

Overall, the University of South Florida is a strong, up-and-coming large state university that allows its students to enjoy their college experience filled with Florida-style fun, lots of school spirit, and numerous academic and career-oriented opportunities. As one student aptly and enthusiastically put it, "USF is a place where great individuals come for a great, fun experience in a great place where there are great academic programs and opportunities."—*Andrew Pearlmutter, special thanks to Steven Marsicano*

FYI

If you come to the University of South Florida, you'd better bring "something green. School spirit is big here."

What is the typical weekend schedule? "Fridays are spent hanging out with friends near campus or at someone's dorm. On Saturday, most go to a football game or some other type of athletic event, and then party or hang out that night. On Sunday, students start studying and preparing for the next week of classes."

If I could change one thing about USF, I'd "add more parking garages."

Three things every student at USF should do before graduating are "visit local landmarks such as Busch Gardens and Clearwater Beach, spend an evening at the Dockside and eat gator nuggets, and go to all the home football games. Go Bulls!"

Georgia

From its origins in 1889 as a seminary for women to its recent renovations featuring a three-story rendering of Agnes Scott's DNA, Agnes Scott College has had an incredible history as a women's college famed for its liberal arts education and its warm atmosphere. Located just outside of Atlanta, the weather provides a welcoming home for students year-round. But above all, strong academics with a focus on leadership and a thriving social life complete the beauty of a hip and enthusiastic women's campus.

Professors and Credits and Homework, Oh My!

Many students have said that the amount of work is "crazy," but all are quick to point out that many professors will "give extensions if you need them and will always work through things with you." Scotties do mention that their professors tend to become notorious with the Classics department taking the cake. One sophomore described how her Roman Civilization teacher came to class and conducted it in the persona of Gaius Sempronius Gracchus. "For a day or so afterward, he signed all his e-mails to us 'GSG.'"

There are few academic requirements—approximately one per discipline, along with two PE classes and several others for a total of 128 credits across 8 semesters. These requirements can be fulfilled through a variety of unique classes; in short, there are enough options that artsy students need not fear the math requirement. One undergrad explained that she was "Immensely grateful that I was so challenged to learn and broaden my horizons."

Students agree that Agnes Scott is difficult. "There are 'marginally less difficult' majors and then there is biochemistry. Our creative writing department is fairly competitive; any of the science majors are challenging," joked one Scottie. However, the atmosphere is collaborative rather than aggressive, so "People won't sabotage you or anything."

Since there are less than 1,000 undergraduates, the atmosphere at Agnes Scott is incredibly cozy. Class sizes range from three or four students to a maximum of 42, but with such a small student body, "They rarely fill to that point." In accordance with the liberal mindset of the school, assignments tend to be fairly innovative. One student recalled designing "a giant kids' book about a scientific experiment done with fear genes" and another professor "gave us our daily quiz one day by asking us to line up appropriately in a phalanx—spears and shields included—and we marched on Agnes Scott." And for those who want a study-abroad experience without having to undergo separation anxiety, Global Connections allows students to take "a 'trip' class and then go on a mini-study abroad trip with that class."

Working Hard, Playing like Crazy

Beyond homework and classes, Agnes Scott students keep busy. School nights tend to be set aside for homework and other extracurriculars, peppered with some trips to neighboring Georgia Tech to meet guys. Sports are very low-key, with calmer fans on the sidelines. However, when asked, a student exclaimed, "Football! We have been undefeated for the last hundred years" and promised to send out shirts to anybody who asked. As at any other college campus, Frisbee is a popular pickup game. Extracurricular groups include WAVE (the feminist group), the Anime Club, the Asian Studies Department (because the academic department does not exist), Latinas Unidas, Classics Club, Witkaze, Arabic Lunch Table, Scottie Social Dance, and many more.

The upperclassmen tend to split between the Mortar Club, which is very conservative and traditional, and the significantly more lax Pestle Club, which "just sets out to be the diametric opposite of Mortar Board." Freshmen tend to mix and mingle at larger and more organized functions, like the Red Light Green Light party, swing dance nights, movie nights and other on-campus events, while upperclassmen tend to gravitate to Georgia Tech for the coed environment. Describing Greek life on campus, a junior joked that "Our Greek system is limited to my Theocritus class. We don't have sororities. We are a sorority."

As part of the feminist environment, people do respect personal preferences. Many students joked that first-years go in believing "Agnes will turn you gay" but in reality, people just become more supportive of the atmosphere around them. The campus is complimented for being very open and diverse. A Caucasian woman from the Midwest rattled off a list of groups with high profiles at Agnes Scott, including "Dems, Republicans, Libs, Pagans, Christians, Jews, Muslims, lesbians, transgenders, straight women, girls who look like men, girls who look very fem, black, brown, Indian, Native American, Hispanic, white and paler than white" before trailing off.

Amazing Atlanta

The campus is very calm, thanks to its scenic location just outside Atlanta. One upperclassman could not stop gushing: "It's very quaint and small and Gothic. The dining hall looks like 'The Great Hall' of Harry Potter." Just a few miles on MARTA, Atlanta's metropolitan rail system, gets you into the city, which offers incredible sports venues, nightlife, zoos, and much more.

> "We don't have sororities. We are a sorority."

The campus residences are extraordinarily varied. The freshmen are put in two dorms, Winship and Walters. Students in each consider the other their rival, although a couple of years of perspective blurs the two. Not many students live off campus, which makes the student body that much closer and intimate. And as such, there are a great number of traditions, as one student listed: "Ringing the bell in the tower when you get a job or are accepted to grad school, getting thrown in the alumnae pond if you're engaged, running around mostly naked at Black Cat, capping the spring of your junior year for Pestle Board, and, of course, the campus ghosts . . ."

Agnes Scott, more than any other women's

college, offers an incredible opportunity for community as well as education. When asked if she would go back to Agnes Scott, a soon-to-graduate student said, "I'd be here in a heartbeat. I've grown up and learned both emotionally and academically. I feel like I could function in the world after being here, as a person rather than a 'woman.'" And, of course, it's just plain beautiful!— *Jeffrey Zuckerman*

FYI

What's the typical weekend schedule? "Chill. And then panic about homework. Some people do more of the homeworking. We party or see movies or watch reruns of Project Runway. LOTS of Project Runway."

If I could change one thing about Agnes Scott, I'd "try to get just a little less homework."

Three things every student at Agnes Scott should do before graduating are "chill at Java Monkey, spend the night in the light lab, and visit the health center with a headache to see how long it takes them to give you a pregnancy test."

Emory University

Address: Boiseuillet Jones Ctr, Atlanta, GA 30322
Phone: 404-727-6036
E-mail address: admiss@learnlink.emory.edu
Web site URL: www.emory.edu
Year Founded: 1836
Private or Public: Private
Religious Affiliation: Methodist
Location: Urban
Number of Applicants: 17,027
Percent Accepted: 26%
Percent Accepted who enroll: 30%
Number Entering: 1,357
Number of Transfers Accepted each Year: 260
Middle 50% SAT range: M: 670–770, CR: 650–740, Wr: 660–750
Middle 50% ACT range: 30–33
Early admission program EA/ED/None: ED

Percentage accepted through EA or ED: 40%
EA and ED deadline: November 1st and January 1st (FD I and ED II)
Regular Deadline: 15-Jan
Application Fee: $50
Full time Undergraduate enrollment: 7,441
Total enrollment: 13,893
Percent Male: 45%
Percent Female: 55%
Total Percent Minority or Unreported: 31%
Percent African-American: 10%
Percent Asian/Pacific Islander: 17%
Percent Hispanic: 4%
Percent Native-American: 1%
Percent International: 13%
Percent in-state/out of state: 16%/84%
Percent from Public HS: 63%
Retention Rate: 96%

Graduation Rate 4-year: 83%
Graduation Rate 6-year: 90%
Percent Undergraduates in On-campus housing: 70%
Number of official organized extracurricular organizations: 250
3 Most popular majors: Business, Economics, and Biology
Student/Faculty ratio: 7:1
Average Class Size: 18
Percent of students going to grad school: 42%
Tuition and Fees: $40,600
In-State Tuition and Fees if different: No difference
Cost for Room and Board: $11,628
Percent receiving financial aid out of those who apply: 87%
Percent receiving financial aid among all students: 65%

With distinguished faculty members such as Former U.S. President Jimmy Carter and His Holiness the XIV Dalai Lama, Emory offers a rigorous curriculum to "enable students to develop individual expertise and values, expressed in service to others." This top 20 research university has a motto of "A wise heart seeks knowledge" and its small classes and high quality of professors reflect their philosophy. Emory encourages its students to pursue their interests and to be inquisitive. Even though it leans toward math and science, its liberal arts college is recognized internationally.

Rigorous Academics Without Competition

Emory offers a diverse and wide selection of courses to its undergraduate students. With 70 majors and more than 55 minors, Emory covers a wide range of subjects. Popular majors on campus include Business, Economics, and Biology. Emory is a known leader in HIV research and has the longest-running program to integrate sustainability into the educational curriculum. Although Emory offers a lot of opportunities to those who are interested in sciences, Emory does not leave the humanities behind. The multitude of courses that Emory has offers an even blend of math, science and humanities classes, and the General Education Requirements (GERs) are more centered on the humanities than math or science.

For undergraduates, Emory offers four schools, each with its own application: Emory College of Arts and Sciences, Oxford College, Goizueta Business School and Nell Hodgson Woodruff School of Nursing.

Students in Emory College must satisfy the recently updated General Education Requirements. This includes one course in First-Year Seminar Classes (FSEM), one course in the First-Year Writing Requirement (FWRT), three courses in Continuing Writing Requirement (WRT), one course in Math & Quantitative Reasoning (MQR), two courses in Science, Nature and Technology (SNT), two courses in History, Society, Cultures (HSC), four courses in Humanities, Arts, Performance (HAP) & (HAL), one one-hour course in Personal Health (HTH), and three one-hour courses in Physical Education and Dance (PED). While this list may look daunting, many of these requirements can be satisfied with a score of four or five on AP tests.

Emory offers two special programs to its undergraduates after their second year. During their sophomore year, students can apply to Goizueta Business School or Nell Hodgson Woodruff School of Nursing. After spending junior and senior year in these schools, they can receive either a bachelor's degree in business administration or a bachelor's of science degree in nursing.

Even though Emory is a prestigious university with high academic standards, the lack of a bell curve in most classes makes Emory a place where students focus on working together and in groups. Students find that there is a lack of competition among students because of the lack of a rigid bell curve. "We don't work against each other. [The classes] focus on study groups and working with other students," says a premed freshman. One exception is the classes in the Goizueta Business School, or the "B-School" as it is more commonly known. The bell curve is applied in business classes and these classes can be extremely rigorous. However, the difficulty and amount of workload do not deter the B-School students.

> "I'm honored to learn from professors who are experts within their fields, and their passion helps to make lectures more engaging."

Class size is definitely one of Emory's many strengths. The average is 18 students. Students praise the "accessibility" and the "high caliber" of professors. One student stated, "They really try their best to be available for students and put their best effort into helping the students." Another exclaimed, "I'm honored to learn from professors who are experts within their fields, and their passion helps to make lectures more engaging." Emory's dedication to its students encourages them to pursue their passions and continue to seek knowledge.

No Football . . . But There's Dooley!

Emory University began with the help of a one million dollar donation from Asa Candler, the founder of The Coca-Cola Company. However, the one rule was that Emory could never have a football team. Over 100 years later, Emory has honored Candler's wishes and doesn't have a football team. However, Emory does have the unofficial mascot Dooley who safeguards Emory's school spirit. Dooley began as a lab skeleton in an 1899 biology lab and started writing his own column, Dooley's Column, in the school newspaper. Now, he shows up around campus wearing a cape surrounded by bodyguards. It is commonly known that secret societies have the obligation of keeping Dooley's identity safe and maintaining the campus tradition every year. One of the biggest traditions on campus is Dooley's Week and Dooley's Ball, the culmination of Dooley's Week. During one week in March, events such as comedy shows, concerts, food samplings and movie screenings are open to students and the community. During this week,

Dooley frequently appears and causes mischief on campus. He can dismiss any class with his water gun and successfully increases school spirit. The week ends with Dooley's Ball, the most-attended social event of the year.

Geeks and Greeks

Social life, especially on the weekend, is centered off campus unless Emory is hosting a major event. However, without the use of a car, many freshmen find the need of public transportation to get into Atlanta a hassle and costly. However, there are many options to socialize on campus. If students are not in the mood to party, Starbucks and Yogli Mogli, the frozen yogurt place near campus, are popular places to hang out that are close by. If students are in the party mood, there are many options on and off campus. The most popular option on campus is the fraternities on "Frat Row." There are 14 fraternities and 12 sororities. The sororities are not allowed to have parties, so many people congregate around the frats, which are not discriminatory. "It's free for everyone—girls and guys, and you can generally get in with or without an invite," one freshman remarked. Frats are also right next to freshmen dorms so they are easy to get to, especially for people without cars. Sports teams also have parties but an invitation is necessary.

Emory is not a party school. "I can probably say that a lot of students stay in their dorms on the weekends, because most of the students are not from the Atlanta area," notes one student. However, "It's pretty common to find students drinking—it's rare that there's nothing to do," one freshman stated. The party scene at Emory benefits from the laid-back attitude of the police. Even though there are police cars stationed on Frat Row, students can walk past them carrying Solo cups full of beer without any reaction or complaint from the police. Students at Emory also have medical amnesty, which serves as a "free pass" for any misdemeanor related to alcohol. If something happens, friends can call 911 and nothing will go on the record on the first offense.

Nerdy, Athletic and Engaged

When questioned about the typical Emory student, many students could not find a label. "We have students who spend most of their free time in the books, students considered preppy, students who are really involved in sports, and students who like to get involved with dancing and the arts," stated a premed student.

However, some students said that most people come into Emory as prospective science majors and there is a "slight division between students of difference focus." Most people at Emory seem to fit into categories of Pre-Business, Pre-Med, or Pre-Law and one of the first questions usually asked is "Well, what's your focus?" However, this slight rift does not completely separate the groups and many students are able to make friends in many different groups. While the Emory student body is diverse in interests, some students felt that the majority of Emory students are nerdy. "There are definitely a lot of nerds but I feel like everyone has a bit of nerd in them at Emory to deal with the rigor," stated a freshman.

But Emory's "nerdiness" does not stop its student body from being athletic. Even though Emory is a Division III school, it does not mean that Emory students are not athletic. In fact, most students participate in intramural sports and clubs.

Other popular clubs on campus are the a cappella groups. One of the traditions in Emory is that all the a cappella groups perform in front of the dining hall the first Friday of every month. Even though many Emory students share their love of music and a cappella, many students say that Emory students have very diverse extracurricular activities and one club is not more popular than the next.

Amazing Accommodations in Atlanta

Even with the large number of clubs and volunteer activities on campus, most students find that the number one way to make friends is getting to know your hall mates. And with hall bonding traditions, such as SongFest where freshmen write and perform songs as a hall, many people find that dorms are a quick and easy way to make friends.

Freshmen and sophomores are required to live on campus and they have beautiful newly renovated dorms to choose from. For freshmen, there are eight air-conditioned dorms with choices of rooms from singles to suite-style. Students can even choose three dorms with themes of Global Cultures, Living Green, and Citizenship. For upperclassmen, there is the opportunity to live in the much-desired Clairmont Tower apartments. All the sophomores try to get dorms in Clairmont and with good reason. Each apartment is air-conditioned, has a kitchen, a bathroom and laundry room. Most of the apartments also have balconies. Coupled with the gorgeous Georgian weather, it's hard to find a student with a campus-related complaint. What's better than getting a degree in a "five-star hotel"?—*Sharon Qian*

FYI

If you come to Emory, you'd better leave "any preconceived notions behind."

The typical weekend schedule: "Thursday night is frat or club night; Friday night is frat or dorm party night; Saturday is homework and frat and any other party night; Sunday is doing the work you put off until then."

If I could change one thing about Emory, I'd "make sports more popular. It'd be fun to have more school spirit and teams to cheer on."

Georgia Institute of Technology

Address: 225 North Avenue NW, Atlanta, GA 30332-0320

Phone: 404-894-4154

E-mail address: admission@gatech.edu

Web site URL: www.gatech.edu

Year Founded: 1885

Private or Public: Public

Religious Affiliation: None

Location: Urban

Number of Applicants: 9,664

Percent Accepted: 63%

Percent Accepted who enroll: 43%

Number Entering: 2,626

Number of Transfers Accepted each Year: 448

Middle 50% SAT range: M: 650–730, CR: 590–690, Wr: 580–670

Middle 50% ACT range: 27–31

Early admission program EA/ED/None: None

Percentage accepted through EA or ED: NA

EA and ED deadline: NA

Regular Deadline: 15-Jan

Application Fee: $50

Full time Undergraduate enrollment: 12,565

Total enrollment: 18,742

Percent Male: 68%

Percent Female: 32%

Total Percent Minority or Unreported: 45%

Percent African-American: 5%

Percent Asian/Pacific Islander: 18%

Percent Hispanic: 5%

Percent Native-American: <1%

Percent International: 5%

Percent in-state/out of state: 70%/30%

Percent from Public HS: Unreported

Retention Rate: 92%

Graduation Rate 4-year: 31%

Graduation Rate 6-year: 76%

Percent Undergraduates in On-campus housing: 59%

Number of official organized extracurricular organizations: 311

3 Most popular majors: Business Administration, Industrial Engineering, Mechanical Engineering

Student/Faculty ratio: 14:1

Average Class Size: 19

Percent of students going to grad school: 41%

Tuition and Fees: $25,182

In-State Tuition and Fees if different: $6,040

Cost for Room and Board: $7,694

Percent receiving financial aid out of those who apply: 44%

Percent receiving financial aid among all students: 32%

Georgia Institute of Technology is a college name with a certain gritty, metallic taste at the end. Images of short circuit wires, helter-skelter reading glasses, and test tubes abound. Often shortened to just GTech, this school embodies your typical "Insert-Letter-Here-Tech" school. But it's got more to offer than a dedication to advanced science and technology. And it's more than a pretty brick campus snuggled away in downtown Atlanta.

We Get It, We're Engineers.

The vast majority of the undergraduate students at GTech major in the sciences. Typically, the word "engineering" appears somewhere in the official name. However, GTech houses six different departments: the Colleges of Architecture, Engineering, Sciences, Computing, Management, and the Ivan Allen College of Liberal Arts. A freshman Yellow Jacket cautioned that "You should expect to work a lot. A lot. It's all about time management."

Students note that classes are usually "challenging," but not impossible in that there are strong support networks available. For Biomeds specifically, BROS will always be there to lend a hand. BROS stands for Biomedical Research and Opportunities Society and it helps students network with upperclassmen and graduates to find tips for success and opportunities for greater involvement.

Georgia Tech is lauded nationally for some of its more specialized engineering majors. Not only is it a blue ribbon winner in prestigious fields such as industrial engineering and biomedical engineering, this school has consistently ranked in the top ten in aerospace, biomedical, nuclear, and radiological engineering over the past couple of years. Rest assured, GTech will continue to be a pack leader for years to come.

Regarding core curriculum, all majors must take at least one introductory calculus class, English Composition I and II, two lab-intensive sciences, and several courses in the humanities, fine arts, and social sciences. Students feel that this core recipe has certain advantages and disadvantages. At the very least, they contribute to a better-rounded student upon graduation.

Normally, classes in the humanities such as English garner a smaller class size when compared to intro-level calc. English classes often only have around 20 students.

One student noted that many intro-level science and math courses serve as "weed-out" classes that cause many students to lose hope in certain subjects. Chemistry I, Physics I, and Calculus II in particular have low pass rates and harsh curves. Rumors of the "Four Horsemen of Calc II" even drift across campus. Success, thus, depends greatly on high school preparation and self-motivation.

Slurp. Fizzy. I Heart CO_2.

Scientific research is the name of the game at GTech. The school has an Undergraduate Research Opportunities Program that provides students with a list of labs for in-school and summer research with professors to gain insight on scientific explorations and discoveries. It also has a Cooperative Education Program that gives undergrads the chance to attend school for five years. During these five years, students would alternate semesters of full-time work with semesters of full-time study. It is one of the largest of its kind in the United States.

Here's where GTech's location in the midst of Atlanta comes into play. Industry leaders such as NASA, Coca-Cola, and General Electric often turn to picking the brains of Georgia's brightest and most dedicated.

I Say Yellow, You Say Jacket!

As a public institution, a majority of the students are Georgia residents. However, there is a very diverse representation of states and countries such as India, South Korea, and Germany. Social life is usually tossed in with red Solo cups, crumbling buildings, and beer-stained floors. Fraternities. The cumbersome and unequal gender distribution within the student body, along with difficult course loads, opens the doors for Greeks to take first place. Approximately one-fourth of the freshman class pledges to one of the 40-plus chapters on campus. The usual menu of mixers, punch pong, and "liquor treating" is heartily served.

However, for those who prefer to avoid self-induced memory loss and value their liver, GTech offers a plethora of student-run and school-sponsored clubs. Activities range from cultural as in the Indian Club to technical such as the Robotics Team. Musicians flock to join the Georgia Tech Band programs. Members of the 300-plus-member marching band travel to every football game and invite students from nearby universities without football programs to participate. It's an amalgam of talented performers from all over Georgia. If you can't toot a horn, but can belt "My Heart Will Go On" with frightening enthusiasm, GTech offers several a cappella groups who will welcome you with open arms. Some of the most popular ones are "Nothin' but Treble" and "Infinite Harmony." There's even an "Under Water Hockey Club," if the daredevil inside isn't satisfied.

The dating scene at the school is easily remedied by the campus's closeness to other North Georgia colleges, including Spelman and Emory. Students thus mingle and gain opportunities to explore the rest of Atlanta and its surrounding suburbs.

Looking to remedy nightmares of last week's physics test? Try soaking in some city sights. MARTA (Metro Atlanta Rapid Transit Authority) has you covered. The Georgia Aquarium, a stone's throw away, is famous for being the only aquarium in the United States to house bus-sized whale sharks. The South African diamond shark,

Nandi, attracts waves of tourists from all over the world with her 13-foot manta ray wingspan. If peaceful giants are not what one is looking for, the Atlanta Symphony Orchestra is another option. Nearby eateries such as Mellow Mushroom, The Varsity, and Chipotle are sure to keep ravenous students well fed.

Buzz Buzz Sting

It's summer, the bees . . . jackets are, well . . . swarming. Regardless, it's luminous and temperate on GTech's sprawling emerald landscapes. Rustling trees tickle students with shade, while shielding them from the concrete jungle meters away from the edge of campus. Nestled snuggly between two major highways, the campus is indeed a southern jewel. Georgian architecture dots dormitory buildings and nearby Greek houses on East campus. West campus is newer and more spread out, inviting long relaxing walks. All one needs is their own picnic basket—a freshman warned against the rather drab dining hall pickings.

There's no doubt that GTech has a passionate student body that isn't so easily clique-ified. Students proudly consider themselves "crazy," but most definitely know how to have a good time. Donning brazen yellow and bold black during school games is second nature to the student body. Screaming school pride comes off as instinct. Nowhere else do "TI-89 wielders" roar alongside "basketball jocks," high-five with "Mac wizards" and bump elbows with "acid-stained lab rats."

Churning out some of the most talented engineering masters in the country, this school has a lot to offer. It should never be thought of as just your typical "Insert-Letter-Here-Tech" school.—*Anna Wang*

FYI
If you come to Georgia Tech, you'd better "leave sleep behind."
If I could change one thing about Georgia Tech, I'd "make out-of-state tuition cheaper!"
What's the typical weekend schedule? "Friday night: something fun (i.e. party); Saturday: club-related activities, sometimes sleeping in and sometimes homework; Sunday: homework and laundry."

Morehouse College

Address: 830 Westview Drive, SW, Atlanta, GA 30314
Phone: 404-215-2632
E-mail address: admissions@morehouse.edu
Web site URL: www.morehouse.edu
Year Founded: 1867
Private or Public: Private
Religious Affiliation: None
Location: Urban
Number of Applicants: 2,277
Percent Accepted: 67%
Percent Accepted who enroll: 46%
Number Entering: 700
Number of Transfers Accepted each Year: 127
Middle 50% SAT range: M: 470–590, CR: 470–580, Wr: Unreported
Middle 50% ACT range: 19–24
Early admission program EA/ED/None: ED

Percentage accepted through EA or ED: Unreported
EA and ED deadline: 15-Oct
Regular Deadline: 15-Feb
Application Fee: $45
Full time Undergraduate enrollment: 2,729
Total enrollment: 2,891
Percent Male: 100%
Percent Female: 0%
Total Percent Minority or Unreported: >99%
Percent African-American: 95%
Percent Asian/Pacific Islander: 0%
Percent Hispanic: <1%
Percent Native-American: <1%
Percent International: 3%
Percent in-state/out of state: 30%/70%
Percent from Public HS: 80%
Retention Rate: 84%
Graduation Rate 4-year: 32%

Graduation Rate 6-year: 49%
Percent Undergraduates in On-campus housing: 40%
Number of official organized extracurricular organizations: 34
3 Most popular majors: Biology, Business/Commerce, Computer and Information Sciences
Student/Faculty ratio: 15:1
Average Class Size: 9
Percent of students going to grad school: 25%
Tuition and Fees: $14,318
In-State Tuition and Fees if different: No difference
Cost for Room and Board: $8,748
Percent receiving financial aid out of those who apply: Unreported
Percent receiving financial aid among all students: Unreported

Nothing illuminates the excellence of the Morehouse College education better than its impressive crop of graduates. Martin Luther King, Jr., Spike Lee, Samuel L. Jackson, countless distinguished professors, lead researchers, CEOs, and Rhodes scholars are examples of the "Morehouse Men" that graduate from this premier, private, historically black liberal arts college for men. Just 10 minutes from downtown Atlanta, Morehouse offers students an array of opportunities that parallels the diversity of talents and interests in its students.

Fashioning a Morehouse Man

Morehouse College, originally founded as the Augusta Institute, was established just two years after the Civil War to prepare students to be educators or enter the ministry. Under the leadership of visionaries, Morehouse became one of the leading Historically Black Colleges and Universities (HBCUs) by expanding its curriculum and acquiring the resources necessary to prepare African-American males for the challenges they face inside and outside of the classroom. Morehouse soon left the bottom of a church's basement for the now 61-acre campus in Atlanta.

Over 140 years later, Morehouse provides a quality liberal arts education with 26 majors from which students may choose. Although some students call the course offerings "standard and conservative," many find the variety of courses interesting, unlike those of many liberal arts colleges, and at nearly half the price. The students also report difficulties dealing with the administration, though they admit the educational opportunities far outweigh any shortcomings.

True to its mission, Morehouse's General Education requirements develop the talents necessary to graduate "empowered, informed, and responsible" men. In accordance with its goal of providing a structured learning environment, Morehouse mandates that freshmen enroll in a yearlong academic and social orientation to college life.

Orientation meets on a weekly basis and is on a "Pass/Fail" system that students said "would require a student to never attend" to fail. Most students find the topics, like safe sex and personal finance, useful and interesting.

The Crown Forum is another favorite among students. Receiving its name from a famous quotation encouraging Morehouse men to grow tall enough to wear their crown, the Crown Forum helps mold students' characters and cultural competency. Students are required to attend a minimum of six events per semester for six semesters, though many say they have attended more. Overall, students are happy with the requirements because they help them "discover unknown interests and talents" that can guide them toward their majors, and say there is flexibility in the timing of scheduling some of the less popular requirements like religion.

Nearly one-third of the students at Morehouse eventually major in Business Administration. Other popular majors are Biology, Business/Commerce, and Computer and Information Sciences. Even though students find Morehouse to be a "supportive and encouraging" environment to grow academically, they acknowledged that "Business general requirement classes can be very competitive, with students contending for Fortune 500 internships." In addition, the Morehouse course load is considered intense for any student majoring in the natural sciences. However, students feel that their advisors are a "great resource," as evidenced by students' successful applications for research internships and medical school. Students reported an average of 9 students per class, which made professors accessible and "genuinely interested in their students' success."

Opportunities to Branch Out

Students searching for a greater challenge than the curriculum provides can enter the Morehouse College Honors Program (HP) during their first year, if they meet certain criteria. The HP provides students with smaller classrooms and more advanced course offerings than the regular courses, and is taught by distinguished professors. Army ROTC is also available to Morehouse students through Georgia Institute of Technology. The college also offers a plethora of internships, on-site learning opportunities, and community service projects in which roughly three-fourths of the student body

participates. Through the Bonner Office of Community Service, which has partnerships with numerous organizations like the NFL YET Boys & Girls Club and Hands on Atlanta, students can easily make substantial contributions to their city. Many students also find additional service and mentoring opportunities on their own.

Morehouse's location and prestige affords its students many opportunities to learn off campus. Since they are a part of many academic consortiums, the men of Morehouse may spend a semester or academic year at universities such as Stanford and New York University, enroll in classes at colleges at Spelman, or participate in the Georgia Institute of Technology's Dual-Degree Engineering Program. These opportunities are highly recommended by students because they help Morehouse men "develop contacts, learn in unique environments, and meet women."

Life in the "A"

The single-sex education and living arrangements allow Morehouse students to "focus when it is time to focus, and party when it is time to party." "The well-known and active students" are usually leaders of popular campus organizations like student government and the NAACP. Since freshmen are required to live on campus, "class unity" quickly develops and most students become active upon their arrival. Many students meet classmates with similar interests while working on projects for science competitions or in organizations like the Morehouse Business Association.

> "Morehouse was a nurturing environment; I fell in love with the College and developed into a responsible and cognizant citizen."

After their first year, many students opt to live in the many affordable off-campus apartments near the college. Many upperclassmen have cars. "House parties and the clubs on Peachtree Street" are where students from all local colleges and universities congregate. Students report a "relatively easy time for Morehouse Men to meet other students, especially girls from other colleges in Atlanta." Greek life also attracts many Morehouse undergraduates, but problems with hazing have kept many of the "Divine Nine" National Pan-Hellenic Conference fraternities officially "off the yard."

Despite the varying interests and talents students from across the world bring to Morehouse, "a true brotherhood develops" with the men recognizing each other's talents and desiring to better not only themselves, but also their surrounding community. As one student aptly summarized his experience, "Morehouse was a nurturing environment; I fell in love with the College and developed into a responsible and cognizant citizen. In other words, I became a man of Morehouse College."—*Ayibatari Owi*

FYI

If you come to Morehouse, you'd better bring "a suit, a nice tie, and a white dress shirt."
What's the typical weekend schedule? "Most students get off work on Friday, then head to happy hour and house parties. Students study during the day on Saturday and go out to the clubs on Saturday night, sleep late, and then start the grind again on Sunday."
If I could change one thing about Morehouse I'd "change the religious foundation requirement."
Three things every student at Morehouse should do before graduating are "join extracurricular groups, mature and grow, and learn the history of the school."

Spelman College

Address: 350 Spelman Lane SW, Atlanta, GA 30314
Phone: 404-270-5193
E-mail address: admiss@spelman.edu
Web site URL: www.spelman.edu
Year Founded: 1881
Private or Public: Private
Religious Affiliation: None
Location: Urban
Number of Applicants: 5,656
Percent Accepted: 33%
Percent Accepted who enroll: 30%
Number Entering: 553
Number of Transfers Accepted each Year: 101
Middle 50% SAT range: M: 490–570, CR: 500–580, Wr: Unreported
Middle 50% ACT range: 21–25
Early admission program EA/ED/None: ED and EA

Percentage accepted through EA or ED: Unreported
EA and ED deadline: 1-Nov, 15-Nov
Regular Deadline: 1-Feb
Application Fee: $35
Full time Undergraduate enrollment: 2,226
Total enrollment: 2,343
Percent Male: 0%
Percent Female: 100%
Total Percent Minority or Unreported: 100%
Percent African-American: 92%
Percent Asian/Pacific Islander: 0%
Percent Hispanic: 0%
Percent Native-American: 0%
Percent International: <1%
Percent in-state/out of state: 31%/69%
Percent from Public HS: 84%
Retention Rate: 88%

Graduation Rate 4-year: 67%
Graduation Rate 6-year: 77%
Percent Undergraduates in On-campus housing: 48%
Number of official organized extracurricular organizations: 17
2 Most popular majors: Political Science and Government, Psychology
Student/Faculty ratio: 12:1
Average Class Size: 14
Percent of students going to grad school: Unreported
Tuition and Fees: $14,470
In-State Tuition and Fees if different: No difference
Cost for Room and Board: $8,750
Percent receiving financial aid out of those who apply: 82%
Percent receiving financial aid among all students: 75%

Spelman College in Atlanta, Georgia, offers the intimacy of a women's college without the seclusion—all-male Morehouse College, which is also a historically black institution, sits directly across the street. Spelman has just over 2,300 women enrolled which, according to students, makes the experience extremely personal.

Interdisciplinary Offerings

Spelman is a liberal arts college, so students are required to take a large variety of classes before graduating. There are requirements in English, math, the humanities, women's studies/international relations, fine art, and physical education. Students say the most popular majors are Political Science and Government and Psychology but things may change with the recent introduction of a new major, African Diaspora in the World. The ADW major is interdisciplinary and focuses on the study of black people and culture throughout the world.

Class sizes are small, with an average of 14 students in each. The workload is also reasonable, as one student said she does about eight hours of studying a week. Spelman boasts many accomplished scholars and professors, including Pearl Cleage, a well-known author, and Dr. Christine King Farris, the only living sibling of Dr. Martin Luther King, Jr. Both women are active professors at the College and teach classes on a regular basis. Some Spelman students expressed concern that the school's close, personal atmosphere leads professors to expect too much and to be too hard on the students, but many seniors said they were grateful for the personal attention they had received throughout the years. One student said, "They feel responsible for your success—that's why they are so hard on us. But I think it's worth it in the end."

Getting Along with the Girls

Like many women's colleges, Spelman students are constantly fighting the myth that there are no opportunities for interaction with the opposite sex. This just isn't true, says one Spelman sophomore: "We do everything with Morehouse—we can cross-register for classes, their football team is essentially our football team, and most social events are jointly organized."

> **"They feel responsible for your success—that's why they are so hard on us. But I think it's worth it in the end."**

Students say social activities at Spelman are strongly dominated by fraternities and sororities. The city of Atlanta offers many options as well—students said their weekend activities are often centered around clubs and events located downtown. Thursdays, Fridays, and Saturdays are the most popular nights to go out, but Spelman is a dry campus, meaning no alcohol can be consumed on school grounds. Consequently, nearly all parties take place off campus. The annual Battle of the Bands contest is one of the biggest parties of the year for Spelman students, attracting students from historically black colleges all over the country.

Atlanta offers decent public transportation, but the majority of upperclassmen still bring cars to campus. Parking is "absolutely horrible," according to one junior. Many students said MARTA, the Metropolitan Atlanta Rapid Transport Authority, is inexpensive and an excellent alternative for getting around in the city.

Spelman students come from all over the country, but in a racial sense the College is not particularly diverse. One sophomore said there are less than five non-black undergraduates enrolled at the school, though this is to be expected considering its reputation as an historically black college.

Southern Comfort

Spelman is not the kind of campus where students live in school housing all four years—most live off campus by junior year. It might have something to do with the dorms themselves. A sophomore student said the dorms "Don't have air-conditioning, they are very small, and the buildings are really old." Despite this, students feel the exteriors of the dorms are aesthetically pleasing and "very pretty." Freshmen are required to live on campus, and freshman dorms are staffed by residential advisors. RAs are not generally strict, according to one freshman, but she said they are very involved in a student's freshman experience.

According to most students, dining at Spelman leaves something to be desired. There are essentially two options for meal-plan dining—Jaguar Underground Grill and Alma Upshaw Dining Hall. Both serve the typical cafeteria fare, though the Underground Grill is arranged food-court style. One junior said the décor of the dining locations is very nice, but the food is simply bad.

To earn extra cash, many Spelman students work in retail—at the mall or in local shopping centers. There are not any particularly prominent student groups on campus, but most students interviewed said most Spelman Jaguars are heavily involved in at least one activity.

Running with the Jaguars

This all-female historically black college (HBC) is all about tradition—freshmen and seniors have celebrated Founders Day for decades. During the event, held every year in April, the freshman and senior classes must wear white dresses and are joined by various alumnae to celebrate Spelman's "birthday." Additionally, the Spelman campus features a grassy area known as "The Oval" which is the location of an arch that students are not allowed to walk under until after graduation.

Students said interactions between the Atlanta community and Spelman are "nonexistent" and occasionally hostile. They said that, when help is offered by the College, the community generally rejects it and all in all Spelman and the local community do not have the "best relationship." While Spelman students say they feel safe on campus, the surrounding area has significant crime rates like any other metropolitan area. One

sophomore offered this advice: "The area outside of campus is definitely not that safe at night; you should always walk with someone else if it's late." Spelman's security force includes state-certified policemen who retain the same powers (arrest, etc.) as any member of the Atlanta Police Department.

So what is it like to go to an all-women's college? A senior student said, "Going to an all-girls school has only enhanced my college experience. I think guys and girls add a different dynamic than all one sex. With just girls, we have a more intimate setting and discussions are more productive."—*Samantha Broussard-Wilson*

FYI
If you come to Spelman, you'd better bring "a skirt."
What's the typical weekend? "Going into the city to shop, eat, and maybe going to a club at night."
If I could change one thing about Spelman, I'd "improve the administration: they are very unorganized and don't generally like students."
Three things every student should do before graduating are "cross-register at Morehouse, take MARTA into the city, and go to a sporting event."

University of Georgia

Address: Terrell Hall, Athens, GA 30602
Phone: 706-542-8776
E-mail address: undergrad@admissions.uga.edu
Web site URL: www.uga.edu
Year Founded: 1785
Private or Public: Public
Religious Affiliation: None
Location: Suburban
Number of Applicants: 17,408
Percent Accepted: 59%
Percent Accepted who enroll: 45%
Number Entering: 4,667
Number of Transfers Accepted each Year: 1,524
Middle 50% SAT range: M: 560–670, CR: 560–660, Wr: 560–660
Middle 50% ACT range: 25–29
Early admission program EA/ED/None: EA

Percentage accepted through EA or ED: Unreported
EA and ED deadline: 15-Oct
Regular Deadline: 15-Jan
Application Fee: $60
Full time Undergraduate enrollment: 24,408
Total enrollment: 25,947
Percent Male: 42%
Percent Female: 58%
Total Percent Minority or Unreported: 23%
Percent African-American: 7%
Percent Asian/Pacific Islander: 7%
Percent Hispanic: 4%
Percent Native-American: <1%
Percent International: 1%
Percent in-state/out of state: 91%/9%
Percent from Public HS: 78%
Retention Rate: Unreported

Graduation Rate 4-year: 51%
Graduation Rate 6-year: 79%
Percent Undergraduates in On-campus housing: 28%
Number of official organized extracurricular organizations: 637
2 Most popular majors: Biology, English Language and Literature
Student/Faculty ratio: 19:1
Average Class Size: 26
Percent of students going to grad school: 22%
Tuition and Fees: $24,411
In-State Tuition and Fees if different: $6,676
Cost for Room and Board: $8,708
Percent receiving financial aid out of those who apply: 48%
Percent receiving financial aid among all students: 43%

A bit over one hundred miles northeast of Atlanta lies Georgia's flagship university—the University of Georgia. Established in 1785, the University has deep ties with the surrounding area of Athens, a city with a vibrant music, restaurant and bar scene. Within the past twenty years, UGA has transformed from a regional school known mainly for its parties to a renowned academic institution.

HOPEing for an "A"

Created as a lure in the early 1990s so that Georgia students stay in-state, the HOPE Scholarship Program provides free tuition to all Georgia residents who maintain a 3.0 GPA throughout high school and college. In doing so, admission to upper-tier state schools, including the University of Georgia, has become much more difficult in recent years because of high-performing Georgian students' decisions to stay in-state. As the Georgia tax base continues to shrink, however, state representatives have called for HOPE to be restricted to a need-based program, a highly divisive move.

The University of Georgia is comprised of sixteen colleges—including a recent satellite campus of the Medical College of Georgia to which incoming freshman may apply. These range from the Franklin College of Arts and Sciences, the general "catch-all" school, to the specialized College of Agriculture and Environmental Sciences. Students typically apply to the highly coveted preprofessional schools, such as the Terry College of Business and the Grady School of Journalism, in the spring of their sophomore year.

Popular majors include Biology, English Language and Literature, and any variety of "pre-anything." Students also note that the Genetics—the only such major available at a public school in the South—and Biochemistry and Molecular Biology majors are increasingly desired by students. Students note grading as a whole to be difficult, with the notion of a curve being virtually nonexistent. Surprisingly, students note that though the Chemistry department is the most difficult by far, the History and Philosophy departments "aren't a piece of cake either," though no department has an easier reputation than the engineering department—since none exists. Led by the current president, efforts have been made to establish an engineering school, but, as for now, that is a realm dominated by academic and sports rival Georgia Tech.

Yet, according to one current freshman, "at times, it can seem like sixty to seventy percent of the student body is preprofessional." However, many students drop their ambitions for medical school after enduring the "weed-out" class in general or organic chemistry. Curriculum requirements vary by both college and major, but all students are required to complete two semesters of English, two of math and one of physical education in order to graduate from the University, in addition to a class on Georgia history.

Though class sizes vary widely for department and course level, the University boasts its fair share of classes numbering more than three hundred. In addition, students can participate in First-Year Seminars, one hour per week, more intimate classes focusing on relatively obscure topics such as "The hobbits: fact or fiction?" or "Bob Dylan." Nonetheless, the faculty is praised for being easily accessible, with mandatory office hours each week and a sincere desire to help students. Notable professors include Darroll Batzer of the entomology department who students note as being "incredibly enthusiastic."

Athens: A Quintessential College Town

Located 1.5 hours away from the metropolitan capital of Atlanta, Athens, the home to the University of Georgia, caters largely to the taste of the University's students. A city of slightly over 100,000, Athens can boast of over one hundred bars, most of which are open to the 18-and-up crowd. As such, a student typically ends up downtown to finish up a night of "going out." With the weekend beginning on Thursday evening, one student commented that he wished that the festivities occurred a bit less frequently.

"I like going out maybe once a week, but three or four times is too much," she said.

On-campus entertainment options also exist, driven mainly by the Greek life system on Thursdays. With over twenty-five percent of the campus participating and 1,500 out of 2,400 freshman girls participating in sorority rush, students admit that the scene is "big, but is far from being dominant." Rush process occurs mainly during the first weeks of fall semester and consumes the entire day. A recent inductee said that the process was "Crazy for sororities. It's five days, going from house to house to house, from 6 AM to 6 or 7 PM." And though the prevalence of a heavy bar and Greek Life scene could signify a lax attitude toward alcohol, the administration strictly enforces a zero-tolerance policy. Even though ranked the number one party school by the Princeton Review, one alcohol-related offense results in probation, an immediate loss of any financial aid (including the HOPE scholarship for Georgia residents) and can end in a transfer to a local university.

The RAs, though widely regarded as kind and chill, particularly concerning administrative issues (e.g., a leaking ceiling), strictly prohibit alcohol in all rooming situations—even for students who are twenty-one—and punishment for storing alcohol is equal to that of drinking.

However, a large percentage of students walk out of the "Uallowed arch" (which, according to University lore, if students pass through before graduation, they will not graduate from the University), a black arch present on North Campus, during the weekends. Some visit home, but some students, particularly freshman, lack cars, citing high fees and hassle for parking spaces. More upperclassmen retreat to their off-campus apartments, becoming less involved in campus life as they gain credit-hours. The vast majority of upperclassmen have a job on campus, and substitute extracurricular activities on campus for extra hours working.

Nevertheless, some students claim that UGA exemplifies the "white, preppy, upper-middle class student" stereotype with little diversity otherwise, but other students attest to the presence of international students as a source of diversity. "It almost doesn't faze me anymore to hear others speaking in another language or wearing the garbs of their native country," a freshman said. And "no one really judges if you go to class dressed to the 9's or in gym shorts and a T-shirt."

Although the high ratio of in-state students, approximately 91 percent, can impede students from forming new friendships, the students report that both the Greek Life system and other extracurriculars function as ways to break out of one's preformed social circle.

Living as a Dawg

All UGA freshmen are required to live on campus, barring extenuating circumstances, and are typically segregated into three "high-rise" dorms, each having nine floors: Russell and Creswell, which are both coed, and Brumby, an all-girls dorm known for its high concentration of future members of sororities. Students apply for dormitories online immediately after they are admitted. Some luckier freshman apply early enough for housing to gain a spot in

the Oglethorpe, or "O-house," which is coveted for its central location on campus and non-communal bathrooms—and its Georgian architectural style, reminiscent of North Campus, and contrasting with the institutionalism of the other dorms.

Students can also choose to reside in a language-immersion community, or an Oxford-like residential college. Those who qualify for the honors program, requiring a separate application process before or during their years at Georgia, can live in the envied Myers dorm, known for its spaciousness.

Upperclassmen also have the opportunity to dorm in East Campus Village, a series of upper-scale quasi-apartment housing which the University leases to students. Freshman varsity athletes also share in that privilege. However, most upperclassmen tend to secure off-campus housing after their freshman year, typically using the large amount of apartment housing that abuts the University. A current sophomore cites the inexpensive relative cost, lack of guaranteed on-campus housing for sophomores and a sense of "freedom" as reasons for moving off campus.

> "It was pretty much what I expected: large amount of students, tons of classes to choose from, and lots of activities to partake in."

A universally adored area of the University is North Campus, featuring grand classical architecture and grassy fields and a plethora of buildings which house most of the humanities departments. Contrastingly, South Campus, playing host to the science buildings, should not be considered whatsoever for its architectural charm, looking like an industrial plant. Other parts include East Campus, which includes the new forty-million-dollar Lamar Dodd School of Art, and West Campus, where the majority of freshmen reside. In addition, the newly renovated Tate Student Center, costing thirty million dollars to reconstruct and LEED certified gold, lies centrally located on campus.

Students rave about UGA's four dining halls, all having their general perks, with some continuously serving breakfast and others being continuously open. Meal plans come in two denominations, a five-day plan and a seven-day plan. Both plans allow unlimited swipes on the days specified by the plan. But all dining halls close at two PM on

Sunday, leaving students left to fend for themselves for dinner. However, some students see this as a distinct advantage.

"It gives you a reason to explore Athens, and learn more about the local eateries," one student said.

In fact, UGA dining is so popular among students that the infinitive "to Snellibrate" is used, a combination of Snellings, a popular dining hall, and to celebrate, after a "rainy day" or a high score on an exam or some other personal victory or defeat, typically late at night.

After "Snellibrating" to the greatest extent possible, taking advantage of the fact that the dining halls are unlimited cafeteria style, a student will head to Ramsey Student Center, a 420,000-square-foot athletic facility, to avoid gaining the "freshman fifteen."

While the most popular student organizations are the philanthropic UGA Hero and Miracle for Life, students assign prestige to the debate societies, including the Desmothian Literary society and the Phi Kappa Literary society.

"They're almost like fraternities," one freshman said. The most well-read student publication is the independent newspaper, with a relatively liberal tilt, *The Red and Black.*

However, virtually all students agree that the biggest extracurricular of the students is tailgating. Though recently barred by the administration from doing so on historic North Campus due to beautification concerns, students sacrifice their sleep deficit so that they can support the "Bulldawgs" in the red and black, the school's colors, on the ball field. For the football games most girls wear a dress on Game Day. And while the football team has suffered a recent lack of playoff success, both the basketball and gymnastics teams have surged in popularity. Sports remain a valued tradition at the University of Georgia. A freshman claims that each time she walks past Sanford Stadium, the football stadium of the University and often called the "Dawghouse": "It's almost as if I now feel like I belong, it's hard to describe."—*John Klement*

FYI
Three things every student at UGA should do before graduating are: "see the Dog Walk" (a series of painted bulldog statues in downtown Athens), "take a picture with Uga," and "ring the chapel bell."
If you come to UGA, you'd better bring "your pair of Chaco sandals."
What differentiates UGA the most from other colleges is "our awesome UGA pride."

Hawaii

University of Hawaii

Address: 2600 Campus Road, Honolulu, HI 96822
Phone: 800-823-9771
E-mail address: uhmanoa.admissions@hawaii.edu
Web site URL: www.hawaii.edu/admrec
Year Founded: 1907
Private or Public: Public
Religious Affiliation: None
Location: Urban
Number of Applicants: 7,196
Percent Accepted: 67%
Percent Accepted who enroll: 39%
Number Entering: 1,879
Number of Transfers Accepted each Year: 2,751
Middle 50% SAT range: M: 510–620, CR: 480–580, Wr: 480-570
Middle 50% ACT range: 21-25
Early admission program EA/ED/None: None

Percentage accepted through EA or ED: NA
EA and ED deadline: NA
Regular Deadline: 1-May
Application Fee: $50
Full time Undergraduate enrollment: 11,360
Total enrollment: 13,952
Percent Male: 46%
Percent Female: 54%
Total Percent Minority or Unreported: 76%
Percent African-American: 1%
Percent Asian/Pacific Islander: 66%
Percent Hispanic: 3%
Percent Native-American: <1%
Percent International: 4%
Percent in-state/out of state: 75%/25%
Percent from Public HS: 66%
Retention Rate: 78%

Graduation Rate 4-year: 15%
Graduation Rate 6-year: 55%
Percent Undergraduates in On-campus housing: 19%
Number of official organized extracurricular organizations: 161
3 Most popular majors: Biology, Art, Hospitality
Student/Faculty ratio: 14:1
Average Class Size: 15
Percent of students going to grad school: Unreported
Tuition and Fees: $21,024
In-State Tuition and Fees if different: $7,584
Cost for Room and Board: $8,493
Percent receiving financial aid out of those who apply: 61%
Percent receiving financial aid among all students: 58%

The benefits of attending the University of Hawaii at Mānoa go far beyond the beautiful nature that makes Hawaii a top destination for tourists from around the world. As the flagship institution of the state's public education system, the University is also the primary research body of Hawaii. Furthermore, UH is not just a college for in-state students. In fact, over 20% of the student body hail from outside of Hawaii, demonstrating that the school offers a good education and a great quality of life that are able to attract students from not only the continental United States, but also foreign countries.

Study of the Pacific

UH is divided into 19 different colleges and schools, including several specialized ones that are pertinent to Hawaii, such as the College of Tropical Agriculture and Human Resources and the School of Hawaiian Knowledge. The University also places strong emphasis on the study of the Pacific region, particularly East Asia. In fact, some of the best programs by UH are in the School of Pacific and Asian Studies. Furthermore, the business school is also known to provide very good undergraduate programs to students. Given the location of the university, the different marine programs are also highly acclaimed.

The University offers nearly 90 undergraduate majors and slightly fewer than 40 minors. The academic programs are notable for the availability of ethnic and regional studies centered on Hawaiian history and culture. Given the large selection of courses, students generally agree that UH has sufficient variety of programs to satisfy almost any types of academic pursuit. "It is a pretty big school," said one student. "We are the biggest university in Hawaii, and we have a really complete set of classes from engineering to liberal arts." In addition, it is worth noting that more than 6,000 graduate students also study at UH, thus giving the more ambitious undergraduates the opportunity to take a graduate class, if only for the experience.

As in most universities, UH has a lengthy list of core requirements, which are classes that must be taken by all students regardless of majors. They are used to ensure that all graduates have the necessary skills in a wide range of professions. The core is divided into two categories: the foundation and the diversification requirements. The classes in foundation are used to give students basic skills in writing, mathematics, and logic. It also has a multicultural component, in which students learn about cross-cultural interactions. The diversification requirements are simply classes in other majors that students must take to be exposed to other academic fields. "You never know," said one student. "You might find out that you really like arts even if you always thought that you wanted to study engineering."

The pressure of academic life at UH is considered easily manageable by most students. "As long as you don't fall behind too much," said one student, "you will not have too much trouble in classes." Of course, the difficulty can vary depending on the topic as well as the professor who teaches the class.

> "I have some professors who really encourage people to go ask questions in their offices."

As is often the case in a large public university, the introductory lectures can be very big and not very interactive. However, for upperclassmen, it is much easier to find smaller classes where students have greater access to professors. "If you like small classes, eventually you will have the chance to be in them," said one student. As to the availability of instructors to answer students' questions and offer advice, most people agree that professors at UH are generally happy to see students outside of classes. "I have some professors who really encourage people to go ask questions in their offices because so few people actually bother to show up," said one student.

Although UH is not considered a particularly selective school during the admissions process, students agree that people on campus are generally talented people. "I feel that most people here have some unique talent or skill," said one student.

Paradise Island

Of course, in the United States, it is difficult to find a school with weather like that of UH. For many people, that is certainly part of the reason to attend the University. "I had a choice to go to New England, but it is just so much more comfortable here," said one student. The University is located in Mānoa, a residential neighborhood of Honolulu and only three miles from the downtown. Surrounding the University are beautiful mountain ranges, since Mānoa is situated in a valley. Nevertheless, one can also spot the high-rises of downtown Honolulu. Some people who have not been to UH may expect to see the Pacific Ocean when they are on campus; unfortunately, the campus is not actually on the seashore. Nevertheless, students still have easy access to the ocean as well as beautiful sandy beaches fewer than two miles south of the campus.

The immediate surroundings of the University are relatively disappointing for students. Since it is located in a residential area, the campus and its surrounding blocks do not have too much to offer in terms of restaurants, bars, and clubs. "You will not find much around the school," said one student. "The good news is that we are so close to downtown Honolulu." Indeed, with the center of Hawaii only a few miles away, students looking for fun weekend activities, shopping, or good eateries can simply go to the city. "I really like Honolulu," said an out-of-state student. "It has this really relaxed, warm atmosphere. It makes you feel you are on vacation all the time."

Since the school is located in a residential neighborhood, housing options outside of the college are widely available, and the majority of students opt to stay off campus. The University certainly has its own residential program, largely divided into two different kinds of living arrangements. The majority of on-campus housing is in the form of traditional residential halls. Most students live in doubles, and each room is furnished. All students in residential halls must also participate in the board program, which includes meal plans. For upperclassmen seeking more independence, several apartment buildings are also available, and each unit contains a kitchen, living room, and bedrooms, all of which are already furnished.

Given the large number of off-campus students, the partying scene within the boundaries of the University can be limited. However, given the proximity to Honolulu and the ocean, students generally travel a few miles to the seashore and enjoy the numerous activities there. As expected, the beaches are certainly one of the most popular spots for the students, not to mention the downtown clubs. "The thing about going away from campus is that you can have a lot of fun," said one student. "But if you want to hang out just with college kids, then you may be disappointed, because in clubs, you find people from everywhere."

A Southern Environment

Since the school is in Hawaii, the majority of students are Asian or Pacific Islanders and multicultural. "The school is mostly Asian or Asian-descent, but you find people of all ethnic groups, and what is special about here is that we are all very tolerant and enjoy the diversity," said one student. Ultimately, UH simply offers a great quality of life. It is friendly, fun, and not too stressful, thus providing a great, memorable college experience.—*Xiaohang Liu*

FYI
If you come to UH, you'd better bring "a swimsuit."
What is the typical weekend schedule? "Some partying and enjoy all the outdoor activities we have."
If I could change one thing about UH, I'd "move it a couple of miles down the road."
Three things every student at UH should do before graduating are "enjoy every minute while you can, go to other islands, and go hiking."

Idaho

University of Idaho

Address: PO Box 444264, Moscow, ID 83844-4264
Phone: 208-885-6326
E-mail address: admissions@uidaho.edu
Web site URL: www.uihome.uidaho.edu/uihome
Year Founded: 1889
Private or Public: Public
Religious Affiliation: None
Location: Rural
Number of Applicants: 8,248
Percent Accepted: 77%
Percent Accepted who enroll: 32%
Number Entering: 1,757
Number of Transfers Accepted each Year: 1,214
Middle 50% SAT range: M: 490–610, CR: 480–600, Wr: 460–570
Middle 50% ACT range: 20–26
Early admission program EA/ED/None: None

Percentage accepted through EA or ED: NA
EA and ED deadline: NA
Regular Deadline: 1-Aug
Application Fee: $50
Full time Undergraduate enrollment: 6,844
Total enrollment: 9,573
Percent Male: 54%
Percent Female: 46%
Total Percent Minority or Unreported: 17%
Percent African-American: 1%
Percent Asian/Pacific Islander: 2%
Percent Hispanic: 2%
Percent Native-American: 1%
Percent International: 1%
Percent in-state/out of state: 66%/34%
Percent from Public HS: 90%
Retention Rate: Unreported

Graduation Rate 4-year: 21%
Graduation Rate 6-year: 54%
Percent Undergraduates in On-campus housing: 33%
Number of official organized extracurricular organizations: 128
3 Most popular majors: Biology, Multi/Interdisciplinary Studies, Psychology
Student/Faculty ratio: 17:1
Average Class Size: 25
Percent of students going to grad school: Unreported
Tuition and Fees: $18,376
In-State Tuition and Fees if different: $5,856
Cost for Room and Board: $7,304
Percent receiving financial aid out of those who apply: 74%
Percent receiving financial aid among all students: 62%

The University of Idaho provides a lot of things promised of a small town in land-locked America, including friendly people and a focus on agriculture. While the U of I is no mainstay of diversity, and a sometimes disconnected administration means that students do a lot of their own degree-planning legwork, students looking for an intimate campus with the social benefits of a large university will find their promised land at the University of Idaho.

Academics

Students say that the academic frontier at the University of Idaho—notable alumni of which include the first-ever female, Republican vice-presidential nominee Sarah Palin and Jack Lemley, construction manager of the Chunnel—can be really hard or really easy—it's all up to them. The University is well-known for the close relationship it has with the Idaho National Laboratory (INL), a governmental science and engineering laboratory that focuses on environmental, energy and nuclear technology. As a result, programs in engineering and the life sciences are well-funded and popular. That being said, students are quick to list engineering and chemistry classes at the University among the most difficult. Agricultural and food sciences programs are also popular choices, and feed graduates into Idaho's flourishing farming and dairy industries. U of I partners with Washington State University in nearby Pullman, Wash., in many of these departments, which contributes to the availability of equipment and talented faculty and graduate students, who often serve as TAs for large lectures. Communications is understood to be the easiest major possible. The school's business department, while generally considered markedly less demanding than anything in the sciences, is a place where many students find common ground—"Everyone has a business minor," notes one.

As is often the case at large universities, lecture classes required early in a student's curriculum tend to be very large and can be weed-out classes, with less-generous grading than upper-level classes. Students in every major are required to take at least one math and one science course, but most have no trouble finding an easy way around their requirements, with classes like Math 123, "Mathematics Applied to the Modern World," and Geography 100, "Physical Geography." Other favorite, unusual classes include Business 103, "Introduction to Professional Golf Management," and Psychology 330, "Human Sexuality," affectionately known as "Dirty 330."

Students note that a department's level of funding has a meaningful effect on the undergraduate experience in that department. Funding is largely a function of donations by graduates, so engineering and business-oriented disciplines are the most cash-flush on campus. One obvious way in which this disparity manifests itself is in the frequency of course offerings, even those required for the major. One French major noted such a required class that is only offered every other year, and only in the fall— it isn't uncommon that students in such situations must extend their time at the University by a semester or a year for the sake of access to that single class. That's to say nothing of what happens when students wait the semester or year, and then can't get into the class because of capped enrollment or registration bottlenecks, a circumstance for which the University administration has little sympathy.

All of which might not be so bad, if the University devoted resources to helping students plan their track to degree completion, but advising is a sore point for many students. While general advising is available for freshmen unsure about their choice of major, "As soon as you get into your department, advising goes downhill fast." The system is very decentralized, students say, with department advisors changing almost every semester and the role often filled by the newest members of the department, who may have less expertise navigating the system than the students

themselves. Appointments with advisors can be hard to make, and many students remember taking classes that could have counted for more than one requirement, or which counted for no requirements at all, despite their advisors' information to the contrary.

Professors, fortunately, are another matter. Students are enthusiastic about the faculty they work with and find them accessible. Smaller departments are most intimate, and students find it possible to develop close relationships with their professors. Some even have favorite members of professors' supporting administration: "The secretary of the history department has probably saved my life multiple times."

To Greek or Not to Greek?

The course of University of Idaho students' social lives is charted early and depends a lot on their decision whether or not to go Greek. Wherever they end up, social life at U of I can be rather segmented. Greek life is prominent on campus, and frat brothers and sorority sisters tend to associate with one another, to the exclusion of students outside the circle. "I really wish there wasn't such a huge delineation between the Greek system and everything else," said one student. "I have friends in the Greek system that I really don't hang out with, and that's lame." The alternative to the Greek system for most freshmen is living in the dorms, where they make the friends they'll have for the rest of college. Even within the dorms, athletes often separate into cliques and move off campus within their first semester, and "the music kids stick together."

U of I students have a bone to pick with their reputation as a party school: "Not everyone is an alcoholic." Moscow is a small town and social life can revolve around the bar scene, but that's true even for students who aren't serious drinkers. Theirs is a nominally dry campus, and the administration makes a proactive attempt to catch offenders and educate students; punishment often centers around classes on drinking responsibly. "They're not necessarily condoning it [alcohol consumption], but they're trying to make sure people are safe." Some fraternities are expressly dry as well. Bars take the legal drinking age seriously, and fake IDs are traditionally unsuccessful, so the social world opens up a lot when students turn 21. Popular bars include John's Alley, The Plantation, The Corner Club, and Garden Lounge; Casa Lopez and The Alehouse are restaurant bars with good drink specials. One student sums up the party scene this way: "You don't have to look too hard to find a party, but it's not like the dorms are going crazy with drunk kids hanging out every door." There is a prominent coffeehouse subculture on the campus, with strongholds at Bucer's, The Sisters' Brew Café and The One World Café, "a bastion of liberal thinking," in one student's words.

Moscow is fairly isolated, so most students stay in the area on weekends. A car isn't a necessity in town, and can sometimes be a hassle, since parking around campus is limited and parking enforcement very stringent. A free bus system runs all over the campus and the town of Moscow, so students without cars have no trouble getting around. That said, many students keep cars, and they're necessary to get away. The nearest big-city experience is in Seattle, about a five-hour trip by car. That opportunity for escape is important to students who struggle with the small-town pace and feel of Moscow. The university system supports the town in many ways, especially the many bars, restaurants and coffeehouses. Moscow hasn't forgotten it, and town-gown relations are symbiotic and pleasant. The town is small, but there is no shortage of things to do for the motivated student—the well-known Lionel Hampton School of Music supports a healthy culture of live performance, especially of jazz; the Arboretum and nearby Moscow Mountain make for nice walking and hiking; the Kenworthy Theater is a historic way to enjoy a movie; and Elizabethan enthusiasts will enjoy the Kiva Theatre, which stages plays regularly and seats in the round.

Campus Living

Two main options exist for University of Idaho freshmen making housing plans: the Greek system, which rushes at the very beginning of the fall semester, and the residence halls. Residence hall living is perfect for the student who enjoys structure, doesn't want to deal with paying bills, and enjoys a social atmosphere, since there are always people around. Some halls are explicitly restricted to first-years; most notable is the Tower, which boasts 11 stories of coed (by floor) housing. Another large residence is Wallace Hall, also coed by floor. Some housing is in the single- or double-bedroom-in-a-long-hallway tradition, and some is suite-style, but whatever the organization, the University administration is very flexible and reasonable about students interested in making changes in their housing

at any time in the year, for any reason. "If things aren't working out with your roommate, or anything else, they ask you to wait it out for two weeks, and if you still want to switch, you can." Different residence halls have different personalities. Examples are a hall for students in agriculture (characterized by flannel outerwear and cowboy boots), an engineering hall, and a hall for students in the education departments. Single-sex housing is also available; Graham Hall is all male, Houston Hall and Hayes Hall are all female. For sophomores who choose not to move off campus or go Greek in their second opportunity to rush, there is the Living and Learning Community, a hall dedicated to second-year students. Most students on the dorm track spend one year in a residence hall before moving off campus. Many cite RAs as a reason to escape dorm living as soon as they have friends with whom they'd like to find an apartment. While some RAs can be cool, they say, dorm living usually feels more like a police state, with strict University alcohol and furnishings policy enforcement: "Unless you get a good RA, you're going to be dealing with someone trying to catch you with an illegal candle."

"Not everyone is an alcoholic."

Dining options on campus are dismal, which may account for the thriving restaurant business in Moscow. The largest, best-known dining halls are Bob's Café and Commons. A fair variety of foods is available, including pasta dishes, a salad bar and ever-present hamburgers, hot dogs and grilled cheese sandwiches, but the menu never changes, and as one student puts it, "You can get tired of pasta." Dining halls also keep odd hours—Commons, for example, closes at 4 p.m.—but students on a meal plan can use their Vandal Card at a variety of smaller coffee-shop venues around campus, so food is always available somewhere. Favorite off-campus dining options include The Pita Pit, with varied Greek offerings, and The Breakfast Club, which does a brisk business in brunch and lunch specials.

The U of I campus is beautiful, and students appreciate it. Composed of mostly brick buildings, it's an ivy-covered haven in the woods of northern Idaho. The campus was designed by Frederick Law Olmsted, the landscape architect responsible for Central Park in New York City, and a favorite location for many is the lawn in front of the administration building. The campus is intimate, and students feel it's a factor that distinguishes their school from other, more commuter campuses in the state.

Extracurriculars

Athletics and the Greek system are major drivers in extracurricular activities at the University of Idaho. Vandal pride is strong, although students are candid about the disappointing performance of their teams. Football and men's basketball are the most popular varsity sports on campus. The former has shown especially weak performance in recent years, but game attendance remains strong and historic moments of domination over rival Boise State University are fresh in the minds of die-hard fans. An aggressive anti-BSU T-shirt campaign takes place every year leading up to the schools' annual football face-off. In addition to varsity sports, intramural activities are going on all the time, and students love the University's recently opened Student Recreation Center. Students of every level of athletic ability have access to the climbing wall—the largest of any university in the United States—massage services and "Every kind of free-weight, cardio machine or court you could ever want."

The Greek system, by design, requires a great deal of community service activity, and philanthropic pursuits are going on all the time on campus. Student government at U of I is good at organizing large events like speaking engagements or campus-wide community service trips, but students say that involvement in the voting and planning process is low. Many students have jobs for 10 to 20 hours a week, either on campus in help-desk or library services or off campus in restaurant work.

Extracurricular activities are an important way for students to experience diversity on campus, which is far from extensive, but is developing. Students characterize the campus as predominantly white and middle- to upper-middle-class, although socioeconomic perceptions are skewed downward by the proximity of Washington State University, recognized in the area as a very wealthy campus. U of I students are primarily natives of Idaho, and those not from Idaho tend to come from other Pacific-Northwestern states. Scholarships offered to multicultural students, especially those from Alaska, are improving the campus's diversity score, and the campus is adapting to broader horizons with recent introductions of multicultural fraternities and sororities. There are also a growing number of groups on campus for gay, lesbian, and transgender students.

Students considering the University of Idaho should, in short, be prepared to be intrepid if they want to be challenged, and will experience four or five years of relative homogeneity in demography and opportunities for socializing. Still, students will find their classmates friendly and willing to try new things, and the community formed at the University of Idaho will likely be a lasting one.—*Elizabeth Woods*

FYI
If you come to the University of Idaho, you'd better bring "your party pants."
What is the typical weekend schedule? "Party Friday and Saturday nights, and spend all day Sunday working; and maybe, depending on the season, do something adventurous during the day on Saturday, like go for a hike or see a football game."
If I could change one thing about the University of Idaho, I would "want a Target somewhere nearby."
Three things every student should do before graduating are "go to a drag show in Pullman, WA, take advantage of the VandalCard by renting an Xbox or a laptop from the University, and sing great karaoke at the otherwise terrible CJ's Nightclub."

Illinois

DePaul University

Address: 1 East Jackson Boulevard, Chicago, IL 60604
Phone: 312-362-8300
E-mail address: admitdpu@depaul.edu
Web site URL: www.depaul.edu
Year Founded: 1898
Private or Public: Private
Religious Affiliation: Roman Catholic
Location: Urban
Number of Applicants: 10,294
Percent Accepted: 70%
Percent Accepted who enroll: 35%
Number Entering: 2,522
Number of Transfers Accepted each Year: 2,512
Middle 50% SAT range: M: 510–620, Cr: 510–630, Wr: 590–670
Middle 50% ACT range: 21–26

Early admission program EA/ED/None: EA and ED
Percentage accepted through EA or ED: 59%
EA and ED deadline: 15-Nov
Regular Deadline: 1-Feb
Application Fee: $40
Full time Undergraduate enrollment: 15,024
Total enrollment: 22,377
Percent Male: 44%
Percent Female: 56%
Total Percent Minority or Unreported: 29%
Percent African-American: 8%
Percent Asian/Pacific Islander: 8%
Percent Hispanic: 11%
Percent Native-American: 1%
Percent International: 1%
Percent in-state/out of state: 84%/16%
Percent from Public HS: 74%
Retention Rate: 85%

Graduation Rate 4-year: 39%
Graduation Rate 6-year: 64%
Percent Undergraduates in On-campus housing: 19%
Number of official organized extracurricular organizations: 170
3 Most popular majors: Accounting, Communications, Finance
Student/Faculty ratio: 14:1
Average Class Size: 26
Percent of students going to grad school: Unreported
Tuition and Fees: $22,365
In-State Tuition and Fees if different: No difference
Cost for Room and Board: $9,801
Percent receiving financial aid out of those who apply: 75%
Percent receiving financial aid among all students: 62%

If you take the Brown Line to the Fullerton Stop on the Chicago El, you'll exit onto a bustling street in the Lincoln Park neighborhood of Chicago. But just hang a left and in a few minutes you'll be in the tree-lined heart of DePaul University. DePaul offers its students the best of both worlds: a school committed to the life and study of its undergraduates and a wealth of opportunities to be involved in the "real world" in Chicago. With about 22,000 students and the whole city open to exploration, few people at the University have a chance to be bored. Although it has been known as a commuter school in the past, DePaul is rapidly attracting students from all over while maintaining its uniquely Midwestern warmth and sense of community both inside the University and within Chicago through service and active learning.

Domains of Learning
DePaul takes its commitment to integrating into the surrounding urban environment very seriously. In fact, the first choice freshmen must make when they are accepted is whether to take the Discover Chicago or Explore Chicago class. In Discover, freshmen arrive at school a week early to participate in weeklong orientation programs that allow students to "totally immerse themselves in one aspect of the city's culture." These programs run the gamut from "Poverty Amidst Plenty," which gives students

the opportunity to visit homeless shelters and participate in community service activities, to "Biking in Chicago," which allows students to go on bike trips that help orient them to the traffic patterns while taking in the sights. Much like Discover, but expanded to cover the entire first quarter, Explore allows students to get a "more in-depth view of the inner workings of Chicago." This includes everything from a class titled Understanding Beauty in Chicago to a quarter devoted to studying the Chicago Cubs.

DePaul does not stop initiating service learning after the first quarter. The University offers many opportunities for "experiential learning," which covers study abroad, internship, and service learning areas. In fact, DePaul's Center for Community-Based Learning focuses on volunteer work and sponsors such popular classes as Peace, Social Justice, Conflict Resolution, and Psychology outreach programs that allow students to work in area clinics and get credit for it. Given the number of outside resources available, it doesn't come as much of a surprise that many students double-major and/or double-minor in applied fields such as Peace Studies and Political Science-International Relations. This interdisciplinary approach to learning permeates the atmosphere of the school, and students say that many people are very politically engaged as a result.

This sense of active engagement also extends to the rest of the academic environment, as students say the "Focus of classes is more on practice than just study." For example, art history classes often come with a studio art component, just as English majors will frequently get a teaching certification in addition to their liberal arts degree. That extends in particular to the School of Commerce, which boasts "a lot of ties to accounting firms," say students, as well as a "business mindset as opposed to a pure learning mindset."

Potential Blue Demons take note: the classroom is front and center in a DePaul education, and prospective students should be prepared for a broad range of requirements that encourage active thinking and participation. The core curriculum, called the Liberal Studies Program, is comprised of a set of "learning domains," which involve completion of arts and literature, philosophical inquiry, religion, scientific inquiry, Self and the Modern World, and Understanding the Past requirements. Each of these broad-based areas allows for a great deal of freedom in choosing the classes that most interest the

student, which "brings a lot more individualism into the program," say students. The Honors Program also works to tailor the broader school requirements to individual students. A member of the Honors Student Government noted that while the required classes are more specific in the honors program, "All honors classes are capped at 20, which means that they might be a little harder to get into, but in the end, it's worth it for the close engagement with the professors." In fact, one student said, "Biggest class had forty-five people in it . . . actually, there are only two or three places on campus that will even hold more than fifty people."

That closeness is also manifested in the love-it or hate-it quarter system that DePaul uses as opposed to the traditional semester. Summers are a little shorter, with school ending in late June, but students enjoy a six-week winter break. Students typically take classes three out of four quarters, as the fourth quarter is summer vacation. Students give the system mixed reviews, mentioning that "You never get bored or feel like you've wasted a semester if you end up taking a class you're not that into." A sophomore agreed, saying, "You can sample things more and experience lots of classes, and you can focus more on each one while you're taking it." And one senior hit upon a very important factor for most students, noting, "One class can't mess up your GPA because you have so many to pad any not-so-great grades."

Students also appreciate the fact that DePaul is not a research university— "Professors are very present in their fields in terms of writing and peer-reviewing, [but] the focus is clearly on teaching and coming up with new ways to present material and get students engaged."

Hit That High(Rise)

One of the hallmarks of DePaul student life is the exodus from on-campus living after freshman and sophomore year. Students are quick to say that prospectives shouldn't be turned off by this: "You stay friends with most of your friends from freshman year, and even though you don't see people congregating to go out as much, the upperclassmen are the ones who have the parties . . . so you'll see people no matter what." One junior noted that freshman year "Feels like a smaller community because you see the same people and develop a real sense of camaraderie, [but] living in an apartment becomes completely natural." Although students readily admit it is a "different lifestyle," one that includes "being independent and paying your own bills," they also say that it is "very freeing" and "exciting to live on your own with your friends." Because of the culture of living in neighborhood apartments, the campus "isn't as hoppin' on the weekends," but students insist that "Lincoln Park is a lively neighborhood, so it never feels like a dead corn town."

And never fear: there's still plenty to do, both off campus and on. When asked about the biggest party day, one junior responded, "Um, every day?" While it's clear that De-Paul students are not shy about letting loose, students say that partying comes down to "less of a woo-hoo, we're in college, let's drink" atmosphere and more of a "hanging out with friends or go to a bar" environment. Students admit that many of their peers have fake IDs and that drinking is fairly prevalent on campus, but they also note that the college has a safety-first policy. DePaul provides a public safety escort from 6 p.m. to 6 a.m. every day.

For students who find that the drinking scene isn't their thing, there are plenty of events on and around campus to keep them busy. One of DePaul's most striking qualities is the diversity of its student body. As a result, there are "tons and tons of different cultural events going on all the time." Everything from the Black Student Union to a Spanish dance group to Hillel holds activities on the weekends. This is true of the diversity of the campus in general as well—as one senior said, "You definitely see people from a lot of different backgrounds."

> "A lot of people here worked really hard to be the first in their family to go to college, and it gives a very diverse perspective in class when there are people with those experiences right there: it's not just a hypothetical."

Although there are admittedly "a lot of people from Illinois and Ohio," students think there is "true diversity" at DePaul in the sense that you can "Come as you are—there is somewhere you'll fit in here." While students note that there is still separation among groups, they laud the school's particular efforts to broaden the scope of diversity by accepting students who are diverse not only in race, but also in socioeconomic status, state and country of origin, ideas,

and belief systems. One junior also noted that there are "many first-generation college students at DePaul. You don't usually think about this in terms of diversity, but it really gives you perspective."

The Windy Campus

With the Chicago skyline serving as the main campus attraction, students at DePaul should never be worried about being stuck behind gates or locked into exclusively meeting people from the 18–22 set. When "the whole city is your campus," students recommend preparing for "interaction with *real people* every day." While Chicago is certainly different from many college towns, students really appreciate the cultural and community-oriented opportunities it provides. In fact, one senior noted that the "community comes into life a lot more than at other places." As an example, she pointed to the relatively large number of people from the community who come in and take classes at DePaul as well as the very large number of students who perform community service, both through DePaul and on their own initiative. On an academic level, "Things don't have to be as abstract as they are in the classroom because you can go out and experience them." This extends to the internship and work opportunities. This is particularly useful for the large number of business majors, as it gives them concentrated networking contacts from which to draw and plenty of alums who are happy to help out a fellow Blue Demon.

However, students do warn prospectives that they should prepare for a very different college experience. "It does take something away from the college experience," admitted one junior, and another student added that the whole perspective on college changes "when you're not walking across a campus to get home." Still, they note that the Student Center, the gym, the coffee shop, and study tables at the Schmidt Academic Center, known by students as SAC, tie the DePaul community together. One sophomore said, "We're definitely not separated completely, and the ways that De-Paul are different are mostly really good, and add another level to the college experience."

The DePaul "Thing"

"It's not really our motto . . . and it's not really a slogan . . ." One student tried hard to describe it, but the best she could think of was "the DePaul Thing." This three-tiered saying perfectly encapsulates DePaul, students say, and it goes something like this. DePaul is: "1) Catholic—in the true root meaning of oneness, 2) Urban—in the commitment to the urban community, 3) Vincentian—in the goal of serving and loving each other." Although it may not have an overarching name, the DePaul credo, of sorts, really brings together the aspects of the school that separate it from other large, urban universities. DePaul's deep commitment to the community that surrounds it permeates every aspect of student life, and this creates a bond between students that keeps them together even in the midst of a busy city. One student captured this sense perfectly when she said: "DePaul feels real. We have all the resources and cultural opportunities of the city, but in the end, Chicago attracts down-to-earth kids from the Midwest. It's real."—*Hannah Jacobson*

FYI

If you come to DePaul, you'd better bring "a fully loaded iPod (kids are really into music here), a bike lock (a bike is really useful for getting around the city)," and "warm boots!"

What is the typical weekend schedule? "Thursday, go out to the bars, meet some new people, and get great drunk food; Friday, sleep in, have a class or a club meeting, go shopping, and go to the beach if it's nice out; Saturday, do some community service, like the AIDS Walk, during the day, then at night go to a bar, go to a party, go see a show, or go to one of the tons of concert venues around Chicago; and Sunday, grab the brunch buffet at the Student Center: it's crucial for curing hangovers!"

If I could change one thing about DePaul, I'd "make it easier to get on-campus housing and streamline the bureaucracy so it would be easier to get answers from the higher-ups."

Three things every student at DePaul should do before graduating are "go on a service immersion trip to experience something outside DePaul and Chicago, get to know the city by visiting neighborhoods that are off the beaten path, and sit in the arms of the Father Egan statue!"

Illinois State University

Address: Admissions, Campus Box 2200, Normal, IL 61790-2200

Phone: 800-366-2478

E-mail address: admissions@ilstu.edu

Web site URL: www.ilstu.edu

Year Founded: 1857

Private or Public: Public

Religious Affiliation: None

Location: Suburban

Number of Applicants: 13,671

Percent Accepted: 67%

Percent Accepted who enroll: 35%

Number Entering: 3,182

Number of Transfers Accepted each Year: Unreported

Middle 50% SAT range: Unreported

Middle 50% ACT range: 22–26

Early admission program EA/ED/None: None

Percentage accepted through EA or ED: NA

EA and ED deadline: NA

Regular Deadline: 15-Nov, 1-Feb

Application Fee: $40

Full time Undergraduate enrollment: 16,959

Total enrollment: 20,799

Percent Male: 43%

Percent Female: 57%

Total Percent Minority or Unreported: 11%

Percent African-American: 5%

Percent Asian/Pacific Islander: 2%

Percent Hispanic: 4%

Percent Native-American: <1%

Percent International: Unreported

Percent in-state/out of state: 99%/1%

Percent from Public HS: 88%

Retention Rate: 83%

Graduation Rate 4-year: 41%

Graduation Rate 6-year: 70%

Percent Undergraduates in On-campus housing: 30%

Number of official organized extracurricular organizations: 250

3 Most popular majors: Elementary Education, Marketing, Criminal Justice Sciences

Student/Faculty ratio: 19:1

Average Class Size: 25

Percent of students going to grad school: Unreported

Tuition and Fees: $16,444

In-State Tuition and Fees if different: $9,814

Cost for Room and Board: $7,458

Percent receiving financial aid out of those who apply: 60%

Percent receiving financial aid among all students: 46%

The oldest public university in Illinois, Illinois State University boasts a diverse student body of under 17,000 undergraduates. Located two hours south of Chicago in Normal, Illinois—yes, the city is really called "Normal"—the school certainly is anything but a normal state school.

Big School, Small Class

Students at Illinois State University have to complete a minimum of 120 credit hours to graduate, about one-third of which are for general education requirements. However, with over 167 fields of study and a 312-page course catalog, there are many ways for students to fulfill those hours. For example, among the University's many courses is one that allows finance majors to manage a $400,000 portfolio their senior year.

Students say that, despite the University's size, class sizes average around 25 students, with almost all classes taught by professors, and students praised the variety of professors at the school and their accessibility. As one student said, "I like how there are many different ways of teaching in one school. You'll be able to find teachers who teach to the way you learn." Grading is straightforward, most said, and tests rarely have to be curved; students who work hard generally earn As and Bs.

ISU was founded as a teaching school, and its teacher education program remains its flagship course of study, ranking among the top 10 teacher education programs in the nation. Students say ISU's strength as a teaching school has pushed the school to be stronger overall in the humanities.

Illinois State University also boasts the oldest laboratory schools in the nation. Thomas Metcalf Laboratory School and University High School, both part of ISU, teach students from nursery school through 12th grade, and education students spend much of their time at the schools. They are required to have 100 hours of work with K-12 students. However, as one senior advised, "Don't be frightened by that number [100 hours]. There are so many things that qualify for the hours; they are very easy to rack up. Personally, I already had my 100 hours by the end of my freshman year."

One of the most striking features of ISU's campus is its new College of Business building. Opened in 2005, the building has drawn more students and faculty to the program, the University claims. Perhaps even more striking than the new building, however, is the Marketing department's dress code. Students are required to wear business casual dress to their marketing classes. The policy change elicited mixed reactions from students and faculty alike. As one junior put it, "I think it's good and bad. I have a struggle every morning with what I'm going to wear . . . but it gives the class a more professional feel."

Life on a Breezeway

Although most upperclassmen live off campus, underclassmen at Illinois State University have a wide variety of residence halls from which to choose—10, to be exact. As one sophomore put it, "The dorms as a whole are a blast to live in because . . . there always seems to be something going on."

At 28 stories, Watterson Towers is the tallest residence hall in the world. It holds 10 "houses," each considered an individual residence hall. Because of Watterson's design, the central elevator only stops at each house, and students take a breezeway from the center elevator to their respective house, from where they take the stairs to their room. Student comments about Watterson, unsurprisingly, focus on the building's size—some like the close proximity to 2,000 other students, while others felt that the bustle made it harder to make friends.

> **"The dorms as a whole are a blast to live in because . . . there always seems to be something going on."**

Athletes generally live in Tri-Towers on the west side of campus due to its proximity to the athletic facilities, though the recently renovated rooms pull even nonathletes from the centrally located dorms. Because of that proximity to the athletic facilities, students say it has a "fun atmosphere on game days for football and basketball." Although they say that athletics haven't been too big a deal on campus, in recent years school spirit has increased largely due to the success of the men's basketball team.

The rest of the residence halls border the campus's east and west sides, and all are scheduled for renovation as part of a 15-year plan.

On-campus students are required to enroll in a meal plan, and each residential complex has a dining hall. The University recently switched from an à la carte to an all-you-care-to-eat system, which has upset some students who were used to picking up small snacks throughout the day. In general, students were very satisfied with the dining options available, which range from fast food to traditional cafeteria fare.

Students say the Resident Advisors are generally relaxed. As one freshman put it, "They are basically just there if you have any questions and to make sure you don't break the rules too much." With the exception of one floor in one residence hall for students of age, alcohol is prohibited in the dorms, and the University's stringent drinking policies mean that underage students caught with alcohol on campus may be fined. However, perhaps worse than the fine is the alcohol education class that underage students caught drinking have to take at 8:00 a.m. on a Saturday morning.

Though the school is not terribly diverse—11 percent of students identify as a minority, a statistic congruous with the demographics of the surrounding area—students say that they feel the school's atmosphere is very inclusive. Additionally, they say that the convergence of rural, suburban and urban (read: Chicago) students adds a unique mix to the student body.

The Normal Life

As one junior put it, "When the weather is nice, the quad is always packed." Whether students are doing homework, playing football, or, occasionally, reassuring their professor that it was, in fact, a good idea to move class outside, student life happens on the quad (which, for fans of foliage, also happens to be a registered arboretum). Most academic buildings are on the main quad, so it is rarely a long walk between classes, and pedestrian over- and underpasses mean that, even when traveling to buildings off the main quad, students rarely have to cross more than one street.

To the east of the University lies uptown Normal, which has a number of local restaurants, bars and stores that cater to students. Many of these businesses are open late at night. The area is currently undergoing a major face-lift that is bringing a new hotel and train/bus terminal to the area. Trains make the two-hour trip between Normal and Chicago many times each day, and tickets cost about $12 each way. Farther east lies Normal's twin city, Bloomington, which offers even more restaurants and shopping.

Because of University policies, most partying occurs off campus. According to one senior, "The Greek scene is pretty dominant; however, there are many other social opportunities, as well." Underclassmen tend to go to organized parties hosted by either fraternities or individual students living off campus, while upperclassmen flock to the bars in nearby uptown Normal and downtown Bloomington. One popular destination is Pub II in uptown Normal, which one junior called "THE ISU bar." Pub II is famous for its food, and finding a parking spot there any time of day is tough. Unfortunately for underclassmen, bars in the area only admit those over 21. As such, some underage students will make the 45-minute trip to the University of Illinois campus in Champaign-Urbana, where the minimum age for bars is 19.

True Midwestern Living

True to its roots in the fields of Illinois, Illinois State University simultaneously offers students Midwestern hospitality and a 21st-century curriculum. Its solid academics, enthusiastic faculty, and central location make for a great environment. As one freshman said, "It has a small-town feel . . . it just has a really friendly atmosphere," as she affirmed her satisfaction with her choice to come to ISU.—*Rustin Fakheri*

FYI

If you come to ISU, you'd better bring "notecards, because you're gonna be doing a lot of studying."

What is the typical weekend schedule? "Wake up at 11, study until about 5, eat dinner at The Rock . . . [then] go out for a couple hours to apartment parties."

If I could change one thing about ISU, "I'd make the meal plan change back to when you chose your items and your meal card was like a debit card and deducted money."

Three things every student at ISU should do before graduating are "sit in the big bowl-shaped fountain outside Stevenson Hall," "go to Pub II, THE ISU bar," and "live in a friendly dorm like Hewett or Tri-Towers to make lots of friends."

Illinois Wesleyan University

Address: PO Box 2900, Bloomington, IL 61702-2900
Phone: 309-556-3031
E-mail address: iwuadmit@iwu.edu
Web site URL: www.iwu.edu
Year Founded: 1850
Private or Public: Private
Religious Affiliation: None
Location: Urban
Number of Applicants: 3,345
Percent Accepted: 60%
Percent Accepted who enroll: 26%
Number Entering: 517
Number of Transfers Accepted each Year: 70
Middle 50% SAT range: M: 580–680, CR: 580–670, Wr: Unreported
Middle 50% ACT range: 26–30
Early admission program EA/ED/None: EA

Percentage accepted through EA or ED: 52
EA and ED deadline: November 15th
Regular Deadline: February 15th (recommended)
Application Fee: $0
Full time Undergraduate enrollment: 2,082
Total enrollment: 2,090
Percent Male: 43%
Percent Female: 57%
Total Percent Minority or Unreported: 16%
Percent African-American: 5%
Percent Asian/Pacific Islander: 5%
Percent Hispanic: 5%
Percent Native-American: <1%
Percent International: 4%
Percent in-state/out of state: 84%/16%
Percent from Public HS: 79%
Retention Rate: 91%
Graduation Rate 4-year: 80%

Graduation Rate 6-year: 81%
Percent Undergraduates in On-campus housing: Percentage of students living in on-campus housing: 75%
Number of official organized extracurricular organizations: 165
3 Most popular majors: Business Administration, Music, Biology
Student/Faculty ratio: 11:1
Average Class Size: 17
Percent of students going to grad school: 33%
Tuition and Fees: $36,602
In-State Tuition and Fees if different: No difference
Cost for Room and Board: $8,476
Percent receiving financial aid out of those who apply: 91%
Percent receiving financial aid among all students: 64%

E verybody here is so nice," one Illinois Wesleyan senior said, and she would probably know. With an enrollment of about 2,100 undergraduates, IWU is smaller than many public high schools, allowing students to quickly form a common identity. Studying in Bloomington, students reap the rewards of the school's unique academic offerings, including the Gateway Colloquium seminars for first-years, an annual student research conference and May Term, which allows undergrads to explore non-traditional learning experiences. And if anything can be gleaned from the school's strong record of alumni giving, it is that IWU's unique programs and tight-knit community make a lasting impact on the students who step through its doors.

Challenging and Welcoming Work

Professors are very accessible to IWU students, who often develop meaningful relationships with faculty outside of class. Because the school is entirely undergraduates, most students are lavished with attention. Classes range from largish lectures (50–100 people) to very intimate seminars (less than 10 people), and come in varying levels of difficulty. "For the most part," said one sophomore, "the classes are as challenging as you make them."

Certain programs are developing a reputation for particular excellence, with the expectations for students in these majors rising accordingly. Biology, Business Administration, and Music are the hot majors, and produce some of the school's top graduates. "A 3.0 in the bio program would translate to a 3.8 almost anywhere else," said one Biology major. Additionally, many science majors cite the value of being able to do research under the guidance of their professors.

The Business program boasts its own unique learning experience. "We have more discussion, more hands-on experience," one Business major said. The Business department has a successful record of placing students in summer internships in Bloomington, Chicago, or elsewhere in the country. Despite the recent prevalence of these two programs, IWU still offers strong liberal arts programs true to its founding in 1850.

Today, most upperclassmen agree that the younger classes are smarter and more interesting every year. "I don't think I would still get in if I had to apply now," noted one senior. First-years who do make the cut benefit from the Gateway Colloquium, a series of small, discussion-oriented classes that focus on writing skills. Students also enjoy the John Wesley Powell Undergraduate Research Conference, a yearly event at which students present their research to the rest of the campus community. "You shouldn't miss it," exhorted a female senior.

Campus Culture and Living Arrangements

If there is a stereotype of IWU students, it centers on their background. "As much as the administration tries to push diversity, everyone comes from the same kind of suburb," said one transfer student. "To some extent, everybody here is a little bit of a nerd," added a physics major.

Stereotypes aside, IWU students are generally hardworking, smart, and from an upper-middle-class economic background. "As such," noted one student from the Chicago suburbs, "the students demand a relatively high level of living."

> **"To some extent, everybody here is a little bit of a nerd."**

Integral to the "high life" at IWU is gaming. Video and computer gaming are popular pastimes in the dorms, especially for the guys, with the majority of rooms linked to facilitate multiplayer tournaments. "College is the ultimate gaming experience," declared one male student. Intramural sports are also an option, but casual sports, such as Frisbee on the quad, are more prevalent. One sophomore, however, disagreed, saying that the political side of university life was more interesting.

Most students applaud the on-campus housing, and though a few live off campus, all are in assigned dorms during freshman year. "I was surprised to have gotten a really cool roommate," one freshman noted. The school has a fairly successful method for putting roommates together and, according to one sophomore, it really "encourages everyone to get to know each other."

A Small Student Body Congregates

The size of the student body doesn't limit its spirit, especially on the few occasions that a large group congregates. All students agree: "Basketball is big." The team is ranked in Division III, and a home basketball game draws more than half of the student body. Other varsity teams are well-regarded, but definitely not as well-supported as basketball. In balancing the athletic experience with his academic load, one varsity swimmer emphasized the accommodation of his professors, "They are very willing to give me makeup tests." An athlete could do much worse than the facilities he will be able to use at IWU. The Shirk Center is the large athletic complex and, according to one student, "Everything is kept up very well."

The Student Senate also gathers large amounts of attention on campus, as it is the primary liaison between the school administration and the students. "The administration is genuinely receptive to student input," noted one student who worked in the admissions office.

Finally, weekend afternoons and early evenings, much of the student body congregates at the student center, which screens films, brings comedians and other live acts to campus, and acts as a simple meeting point for students before the night's activities.

Food and Drink

"The food is really good," exclaimed one excited sophomore. Still, a freshman noted that "A lot of upperclassmen claim it gets old really fast." So, if the students get tired of "Saga," the main dining hall on campus, they can go to a few on-campus alternatives or take their hunger into Bloomington. Nevertheless, "You have not had the full experience," one sophomore explained, "until you are yelled at by this crazy old lady in the dining hall."

After being chewed out by the elderly, students like to party on the weekends. The fraternities and sororities provide a large majority of the options, though there are invariably other parties on many occasions, if not on every night. Additionally, for those with ID, there are a number of bars in Bloomington that become frequent destinations.

Student opinion regarding the Greeks is mixed. Some think that the parties could be better, while others praise the generally strong social scene given the size of the student body. The truth, however, is that "If you are in the mood for a party, you'll definitely be able to find one."

Extra Opportunities

The experience at IWU would not be complete without "the monkey pit." Beneath a bridge next to the science offices, one can often see students lounging in a space that looks similar to a monkey habitat at a zoo, prompting its nickname.

But the final distinguishing element of the IWU educational experience is May Term. Students finish second semester at the end of April, but almost all continue with a three-week term immediately thereafter

called May Term. During May Term, each student takes one class, which meets once a day for a few hours. While it is possible to take normal classes to satisfy major or graduation requirements, most students take advantage of various exciting opportunities.

Students take courses on campus that are offered according to a professor's hobby or special interest. Particularly popular are travel classes. During May term, students can study biology in Costa Rica or Australia, theater in New York City, international politics in the European Union, or classical music in Italy, among other options.

Yet the essence of Illinois Wesleyan remains the opportunities that await students when they leave the school. One senior said, "I feel like I will take the knowledge that I learn here into the real world."—*Peter Johnston*

FYI

If you come to IWU, you'd better bring "Mountain Dew to stay up late."

A typical weekend at Illinois Wesleyan consists of "sleeping late, partying, studying, and playing video games."

If I could change one thing about IWU, I would change "the math department."

Three things every student at IWU should do before graduating are "get yelled at by the crazy old lady at the dining hall, go to a basketball game, and play in the monkey pit."

K n o x   C o l l e g e

Address: Box K-148, Galesburg, IL 61401
Phone: 309-341-7100
E-mail address: admission@knox.edu
Web site URL: www.knox.edu
Year Founded: 1837
Private or Public: Private
Religious Affiliation: None
Location: Suburban
Number of Applicants: 2,419
Percent Accepted: 61%
Percent Accepted who enroll: 21%
Number Entering: 307
Number of Transfers Accepted each Year: 42
Middle 50% SAT range: M: 580–670, CR: 610–710, Wr: 580–670
Middle 50% ACT range: 26–31
Early admission program EA/ED/None: EA

Percentage accepted through EA or ED: Unreported
EA and ED deadline: 1-Dec
Regular Deadline: 1-Feb
Application Fee: $40
Full time Undergraduate enrollment: 1,371
Total enrollment: 1,371
Percent Male: 42%
Percent Female: 58%
Total Percent Minority or Unreported: 9%
Percent African-American: 4%
Percent Asian/Pacific Islander: 6%
Percent Hispanic: 5%
Percent Native-American: <1%
Percent International: 6%
Percent in-state/out of state: 52%/48%
Percent from Public HS: 83%
Retention Rate: 91%

Graduation Rate 4-year: 64%
Graduation Rate 6-year: 74%
Percent Undergraduates in On-campus housing: 94%
Number of official organized extracurricular organizations: 102
3 Most popular majors: Anthropology, Economics, Political Science
Student/Faculty ratio: 12:1
Average Class Size: 13
Percent of students going to grad school: 24%
Tuition and Fees: $30,180
In-State Tuition and Fees if different: No difference
Cost for Room and Board: $6,726
Percent receiving financial aid out of those who apply: 95%
Percent receiving financial aid among all students: 94%

Just a three-hour Amtrak ride from Chicago, Knox College offers a liberal arts education without the distractions of a bustling metropolis. A coed private college in Galesburg, Illinois, Knox is small, with fewer than 1,500 students, all of them undergrads, in total. This cozy student body makes Knox an attractive option for students seeking a close-knit community on campus. A unique academic calendar and Midwestern friendliness help distinguish Knox from its East Coast peers, while Knox's name recognition and up-and-coming status give it an edge over other regional liberal arts schools.

Thinking Outside the Box

Knox takes pride in its progressive legacy. Established in 1837, Knox counts several prominent abolitionists among its founders, and the college served as a stop on the Lincoln-Douglas Debate tour back in 1858. Today, Knox receives accolades of a different sort. Loren Pope featured Knox as one of his 40 *Colleges That Change Lives,* which highlights schools that emphasize undergraduate education and facilitate personal growth. Meanwhile, *Washington Monthly* included Knox in its 2010 College Guide, which ranks schools "based on their contribution to the public good." This academic and community-oriented spirit shapes life at Knox today.

Students describe Knox as a "community of learning" with "hard and rigorous" classes. "You will see students in the library until 1 a.m. if that is necessary," said a premed, who noted that Knox's math and sciences programs are considered the school's hardest majors. When work gets challenging, Knox students have many avenues through which to find support. Students often form study groups, and they describe their professors as helpful and enthusiastic. "Most" professors, students say, "live a few miles away from campus, so they are available whenever you need them."

In their first term at Knox, all students must take a First-Year Preceptorial, a small seminar that introduces students to college-level work and liberal arts methodologies. Topics tend toward the philosophical; past Preceptorials include "War," "Cinematic Visions," and "The Challenges of Sustainability," among others. With 38 majors, Knox offers a fairly wide variety of academic disciplines to explore. Prospective students need not determine their major when applying, and students are encouraged to take courses in a wide variety of fields before

determining an academic focus. Knox's classes are generally small, averaging about thirteen students, though students say introductory courses in popular fields, especially the introductory sciences, can be slightly less intimate with upwards of thirty students per class. For the preprofessionally minded, Knox offers advising for students looking to pursue careers in fields like medicine, engineering, and law. As a testament to its progressive past, Knox also hosts the nation's only program designed to prepare students for the Peace Corps upon graduation.

> "At Knox, people of different looks, lifestyles, and interests come together because they all share a love of learning and an aspiration for a better future."

Knox's academic calendar distinguishes it from its peer institutions. Students at Knox follow a unique "3-3" academic calendar, in which students take three courses during each of the college's three ten-week terms. This schedule gives students the entire month of December free, enabling them to pursue volunteer work, internships or travel—or simply return home to work and catch up on much-needed sleep. As to the school's overall academic culture, students say Knox's schedule and support system helps students achieve a good balance between work and play. "Students are concerned about academics, but make time to do things other than schoolwork," said a student.

Little College on the Prairie

Knox calls Galesburg, Illinois its home. Galesburg is a small city of fewer than 34,000 people, many of whom are affiliated with Knox itself. Students cite the benefits of Galesburg's cozy vibe—including unique small-town features like a "little flea market with festive food and fun trinkets"—yet they also acknowledge the limits of attending a smaller school in a smaller city. "I don't really go into the city itself," said a freshman. "Most of the school's activities happen on campus." For students seeking the excitement of a big city, "Chicago is only a train ride away for people who want a more exciting weekend every once in a while," a student said.

Outside of the classroom and onto the playing field, around 60% of students participate in Knox's varsity, club, or intramural teams. Knox offers 21 NCAA Division III teams. One issue of contention on campus is the divide between students and student-athletes. One varsity athlete interviewed explained that most of her friends are members of the athletic community at Knox, especially from her team. That being said, don't mistake Knox athletes for dumb jocks; members of sports teams "work hard to be excellent student-athletes."

Though social divisions do emerge on Knox's campus, students cite no problems making friends. Students say orientation groups and classes are common ways to meet new people and make new friends; in addition to a campus-wide orientation at the beginning of the term, Knox offers special orientations for international and multicultural students, as well as for athletes. Fraternities and sororities also have a presence on campus; around 20% of students count themselves as members of Greek organizations.

Home on the Range

At night, Knox's social scene resembles that of other smaller colleges, with a decent balance between parties and events like student-group performances. "There is a party scene for people who want it," said a student, but Knox students agree that students rarely, if ever, pressure abstaining peers to drink. Divisions between drinking and non-drinking students don't seem to affect campus social life; everyone is welcome at most parties, which tend to be low-key. "I think that at the end of the day it all depends on your personal choices," said a student. "There isn't a distinct group that I would point out as the drinkers."

Dorm life is also central at Knox, where the vast majority of students choose to live on campus. For freshman, choosing a dorm is simple; students fill out an application detailing their housing preferences, hoping to be placed in dorms corresponding to their wants and needs. Other housing options, geared toward upperclassmen, include apartment-style living, on-campus houses, Greek organizations, and special-interest houses especially for international or multicultural students.

Overall, students cite Knox as a welcoming, diverse community. "The beauty of Knox," said a student, is that "everyone is really nice and friendly." And "At Knox, people of different looks, lifestyles, and interests come together because they all share a love of learning and an aspiration for a better future," said another." Though students acknowledge Knox is not a perfect institution, a prospective student seeking a strong community in a small environment will find an excellent option in Galesburg.—*Marissa Medansky*

FYI
If you come to Knox, you'd better bring your "own sense of identity and culture" and "an open mind."
If I could change one thing about Knox, I'd change "the relationship between students and student-athletes."
What differentiates Knox the most from other colleges is: "the blend of different cultures and people."   .

Lake Forest College

Address: 555 North
Sheridan Road,
Lake Forest, IL 60045
Phone: 847-735-5000
E-mail address:
motzer@lakeforest.edu
Web site URL: www.lakeforest
.edu
Year Founded: 1857
Private or Public: Private
Religious Affiliation: None
Location: Rural
Number of Applicants:
3,198
Percent Accepted:
54%
**Percent Accepted who
enroll:** 24%
Number Entering: 406
**Number of Transfers
Accepted each Year:**
64
Middle 50% SAT range:
M: 530–670, CR: 560–640,
Wr: 550–630
Middle 50% ACT range:
23–28
**Early admission program
EA/ED/None:** EA and ED

**Percentage accepted
through EA or ED:**
Unreported
EA and ED deadline:
1-Dec
Regular Deadline: 15-Feb
Application Fee: $0
**Full time Undergraduate
enrollment:** 1,481
Total enrollment: 1,516
Percent Male: 41%
Percent Female: 59%
**Total Percent Minority or
Unreported:** Unreported
Percent African-American:
6%
**Percent Asian/Pacific
Islander:** <1%
Percent Hispanic:
12%
Percent Native-American:
<1%
Percent International:
16%
**Percent in-state/out of
state:** 53%/47%
Percent from Public HS:
68%
Retention Rate: 84%

Graduation Rate 4-year:
60%
Graduation Rate 6-year:
68%
**Percent Undergraduates
in On-campus housing:**
77%
**Number of official organized
extracurricular
organizations:** 60
3 Most popular majors:
Communication; economics;
psychology
Student/Faculty ratio:
12:1
Average Class Size: 18
**Percent of students going to
grad school:** 30%
Tuition and Fees: $36,920
**In-State Tuition and Fees if
different:** No difference
Cost for Room and Board:
$8,660
**Percent receiving financial
aid out of those who apply:**
92%
**Percent receiving financial
aid among all students:**
24%

Lake Forest College, often referred to as "Chicago's National Liberal Arts College," is a small school located in the quaint suburb of Lake Forest, Illinois, 30 miles north of Chicago. With a diverse, spirited, and enthusiastic student body of approximately 1,400 students representing 47 states and 72 countries, Lake Forest College promotes a liberal arts education within a cohesive student-faculty environment. As one student put it: "[Lake Forest] is a community of interesting, motivated, and most of all FUN people!"

Academics

Academic requirements at Lake Forest are not excessively rigorous. One student explained, "Graduation requires a 2.0 and certain foundational requirements that are typical of small liberal arts schools (two math or science classes, a culturally diverse class, and so on)." This flexibility allows students to explore multiple programs: "General education requirements are light, so it's easy for people to double major and minor." One disillusioned student complained that, although "grading is relatively fair," it is somewhat inflated, and that the academics are not as challenging as some would like. However, another student pointed out that programs have become increasingly rigorous over the past few years: "The workload is getting heavier because LFC is becoming a better school. It's challenging, but doable."

The University offers a variety of popular majors such as communications, psychology, business, art history, economics and politics, as well as some more challenging majors like education, chemistry and other math- and science-oriented subjects. In general, majors in the humanities are considered much easier and more popular, while the science and math departments are more highly accredited and recognized—in particular the economics department. While there is not a large selection of course offerings in these majors, students greatly enjoy the quality of instruction and accessibility of the professors: "I love the fact that the professors who teach at LFC could teach at Northwestern or the University of Chicago as well (lots of them used to actually), but they come here because they like teaching to undergrads in a small environment." One student went so far as to say, "I can call or e-mail professors whenever! They are very concerned with helping you do well." Specific professors mentioned were Robert Baade, Carolyn Tuttle, and Robert Lemke in the Economics Department; Les Dlabay in Business; DeJuran Richardson in the Math Department; and Spanish professor Lois Barr. James Marquardt's "World Politics" was also noted as a "key class."

> **"I can call or e-mail professors whenever! They are very concerned with helping you do well."**

Students who apply to Lake Forest College can also seek acceptance into the Richter Program, a competitive freshman research program. Accepted students remain on campus for the summer to pursue research with a professor.

Social Life

The social life on campus is dominated by sports teams, fraternities, and sororities. Lake Forest College boasts 14 varsity sports teams, in addition to various intramural and club sports. The most popular sports are hockey, football, and rugby. A large portion of the student body is involved in sports in some way. Although the facilities are often described as "inadequate," this doesn't stop the spirited and enthusiastic student body from enjoying them. A student-run organization led by the University's mascot, Boomer, supports the varsity sports teams. For a small fee, a student can join the "Athletic Council," more commonly known as the "Forest Fanatic," and take advantage of a free Fanatic T-shirt, VIP seating at home games, free food at select games, reduced bus fare to away games, e-mail notifications of upcoming events and behind-the-scenes updates and highlights.

As for Greek life, there are seven fraternities and sororities (some of which are international). One member of Delta Kappa Epsilon said, "The sororities are strong and fraternities are lacking numbers. However, I have absolutely no regrets about joining a fraternity at Lake Forest College. It has been an amazing experience for me." A member of Delta Delta Delta described the Greek scene as "relaxed, small, personal, and authentic." Another student pointed out that, while Greeks tend to be the "most involved" at Lake Forest and often secure top positions in student government, "You don't have to be a Greek to be integrated in the school. Non-Greeks are friends with Greeks."

As the surrounding town of Lake Forest isn't exactly thriving, the overall social scene at LCF is largely campus-based. While most upperclassmen have cars, the majority stay in the area. There are a few campus-wide parties, typically hosted by the fraternities, as well as semiformals for various student organizations. The annual "Winter Ball," held in the botanical garden, the "Mr. Casanova Contest," and the "DKE Rampant Lion March Party" are particularly popular. The University has recently tightened up its alcohol policies, but the majority of the campus drinks. As for drugs, one student explained, "They are common but not socially acceptable. They are used behind closed doors (even hidden from other students)." Another stated that drugs are not common at all. As for those who are of drinking age, some venture into the city on the weekends and hit up Chicago's bars. The city of Chicago also offers many alternatives to a typical college social scene such as Navy Pier, museums like the Field Museum, an aquarium and planetarium, two major league baseball teams, a hockey team, an NFL football team and fabulous shopping on Michigan Avenue.

The University takes pride in community service activities. Although Lake Forest itself doesn't offer many opportunities, Chicago, which is only a 45-minute drive or 90-minute train ride away, provides many unique community service opportunities. The Big Brothers/Sisters program of Lake County is one such group. Located in Gurnee, a suburb about 20 minutes north of Lake Forest, this group has been around since 1904. Many Lake Forest College students volunteer for the program, which focuses primarily on mentoring throughout the Chicago community. Other activities include literary groups such as Collage, as well as political organizations including the League for Environmental Awareness, College Democrats and College Republicans. Art and performance groups exist, and the University boasts a number of additional religious, cultural, academic, and business-oriented groups.

Campus Life

Although the social scene is somewhat constrained by the general attitude and environment of the town itself, Lake Forest provides nice, on-campus living arrangements. Freshmen are assigned dorms, while upperclassmen pick through a random lottery system. There are some specialized dorms—an all-girls dorm, an international dorm, four substance-free dorms—while the remainder of the dorms are mixed. Alcohol is allowed in a select number of the dorms and only if the inhabitants of the rooms are 21. Gregory is known as the party dorm.

One girl explained, "A large majority of students live on campus because no one can afford a home in Lake Forest." The town itself is described as "very high-class," "an affluent neighborhood" in a "very safe community—the safest in Illinois." One perk this exclusivity offers is the availability of high paying babysitting jobs. However, one student noted the homogenizing effect of the school's setting: "The campus looks like a country club, the town is one of the richest in the United States, and this environment tends to influence the students; in some ways, I think, the environment 'preppifies' everyone."

There have been a few recent additions to the campus, like the brand-new library and student center. As for on-campus food, one girl described it as "excellent for cafeteria food!" On-campus living includes three meals per day Monday through Friday and two meals per day on the weekend. Miramar, The Lantern, Teddy O's, The Grill and The Wooden Nickel are popular local eateries among students.

In general, this small, somewhat secluded university is able to differentiate itself from other universities through its personable professors and enthusiastic social life. One specific reason not to overlook this university, as one student put it: "It is a small liberal arts school close to a big city; it is not located in the middle of nowhere!"—*Caroline Kaufman*

FYI

If you come to Lake Forest, you'd better bring "a hat and mittens because it gets cold, an empty stomach because the cafeteria food is awesome, and a hardworking, positive attitude."

What's the typical weekend schedule? "After class on Friday, take a nap and then get ready to go out . . . South Campus is where the parties are; sleep in late on Saturday and head to the cafeteria in your PJs, watch movies, and then get ready to go out all over again! Sunday: get your work done . . . Occasionally there are All-Campus Parties that everyone attends . . . they are really fun."

If I could change one thing about Lake Forest, I'd "make the Education Major less difficult! The classes are demanding and tons of work, but it is all worth it in the end because they have a history of 100 percent job placement after graduation."

Three things every student at Lake Forest should do before graduating are "eat at the cafeteria, get involved with on-campus organizations, and study abroad: we have great programs."

Loyola University, Chicago

Address: 820 North Michigan Avenue, Chicago, IL 60611-9810
Phone: 312-915-6500
E-mail address: admission@luc.edu
Web site URL: www.luc.edu
Year Founded: 1870
Private or Public: Private
Religious Affiliation: Roman Catholic-Jesuit
Location: Urban
Number of Applicants: 23,032
Percent Accepted: 55%
Percent Accepted who enroll: 20%
Number Entering: 1,930
Number of Transfers Accepted each Year: 1,611
Middle 50% SAT range: M: 520–640, CR: 540–640, Wr: 510–628
Middle 50% ACT range: 25–29
Early admission program EA/ED/None: None

Percentage accepted through EA or ED: NA
EA and ED deadline: NA
Regular Deadline: Rolling
Application Fee: $0
Full time Undergraduate enrollment: 9,084
Total enrollment: 16,040
Percent Male: 37%
Percent Female: 63%
Total Percent Minority or Unreported: 31%
Percent African-American: 4%
Percent Asian/Pacific Islander: 11%
Percent Hispanic: 12%
Percent Native-American: <1%
Percent International: 2%
Percent in-state/out of state: 65% / 35%
Percent from Public HS: 68%
Retention Rate: 87%

Graduation Rate 4-year: 51%
Graduation Rate 6-year: 69%
Percent Undergraduates in On-campus housing: 38%
Number of official organized extracurricular organizations: 195
3 Most popular majors: Biology, Nursing, Psychology
Student/Faculty ratio: 15:1
Average Class Size: 28
Percent of students going to grad school: Unreported
Tuition and Fees: $33,294
In-State Tuition and Fees if different: No difference
Cost for Room and Board: $11,570
Percent receiving financial aid out of those who apply: Unreported
Percent receiving financial aid among all students: Unreported

The largest Jesuit University in the nation, Loyola University in Chicago aims to provide its nearly 16,000 students with opportunities and experiences that are unique and different from all other leading universities in the nation. Combining core Jesuit values with the diversity that a city like Chicago boasts, Loyola University in Chicago challenges each student, undergraduate and graduate, to expand their minds through service, stimulating classroom settings, and interactions with a variety of interesting people.

Remembering Their Past

Loyola University in Chicago makes a promise to each student who steps on its campus—students will be prepared to "lead extraordinary lives" in the future. Loyola expects its graduates to be the leaders of tomorrow, and it looks to the five core principles of a Jesuit Education to achieve this goal. There must be a commitment to excellence. Loyola students are expected to seek knowledge and bask in the classroom. The Jesuit relationship to God is equally important. Loyola promotes maintaining a strong and well-developed belief system so that one may help others to deepen their own relationships to God. Loyola also stresses a strong commitment to service and global awareness. Loyola students should demonstrate a well-rounded understanding of the world and its people, and then they must use their knowledge and awareness to serve their communities and seek justice for all. The final characteristic of a Jesuit Education ensures a consistent focus on values and justice that create a strong but fair leader in whatever field. One student recognized the value of the Jesuit foundation of Loyola: "The Jesuit mission is *huge.* Service learning is required for graduation. People who come to Loyola want to make a difference and are very driven and passionate."

Hard to the Core?

Loyola University in Chicago, probably more than any of its other characteristics, takes pride in its unique academic system. Students are encouraged to "learn broadly" by choosing from more than 70 undergraduate majors and taking full advantage of the 15:1 student/faculty ratio. Classes are small, unless they are a major lecture, with only 28 students per class. Loyola is well known for its humanities, but there is also a strong pre-med program. Students name biology, nursing, and psychology as other popular majors.

The faculty is kind, and eager to impart some of their vast knowledge to their students. Professors are extremely willing to meet students outside of the classroom to talk about, well, anything! "The teachers that I have had are very agreeable and . . . one of my favorite aspects of the academic life at Loyola," one student said. Even more impressive about Loyola's staff is that professors have almost always worked in their respective fields before coming to the Windy City. "All of my favorite professors have worked for major companies before teaching so they have incredible experience that lends to a very hands-on teaching style. I feel like they have a lot more to offer than simply reciting the textbook," said one sophomore.

> "All of my favorite professors have worked for major companies before teaching so they have incredible experience that lends to a very hands-on teaching style."

Indeed, Loyola focuses on real experience as a valuable and necessary tool for the classroom. Students, in their path to "extraordinary lives," must first possess the real life skills that naturally accompany such futures. Given its incredible location in a major city, Loyola University in Chicago encourages its students to take advantage of the many academic opportunities that Chicago has. There are numerous research and fieldwork opportunities at many of the city's major institutions. Among the long list are the Lincoln Park Zoo, Field Museum, and Adler Planetarium. One student exclaimed, "I'm in an events planning class right now that is amazing! I am a . . . double major, and I have already had a ton of hands-on classes. My advanced advertising class this semester is re-creating an entire ad campaign and presenting it to a firm in Chicago."

But, perhaps one of the most unique aspects about Loyola's academic structure is its strict core curriculum. The Core includes 15 required courses that span 10 knowledge-area learning outcomes. This naturally results in a high number of credits required for the core curriculum. Each student is expected to take one writing seminar, one art course, one quantitative analysis course, and two courses each of history, literature, philosophy, science, social science, and theology. The courses aim to create a unique, well-rounded education that encourages students to further develop and pursue the ultimate goals of leadership and unparalleled intellectual skill in the field of their choice.

Life on the Water and in the Windy City

Loyola University of Chicago's campus has 3 distinct Chicago area campuses: the Maywood Campus, the Water Tower Campus, and the Lake Shore Campus. The Maywood Campus is home to Loyola's medical center, while the other two campuses house most of the undergraduate students. The Lake Shore Campus, as its name suggests, overlooks Lake Michigan from its location right next to the water. The Water Tower Campus is located in the middle of downtown Chicago's most famous shopping strip on Michigan Avenue. Students can easily get from one part of the campus to the other with special passes that provide unlimited access to the University's shuttle service and Chicago's aboveground metro, the El. The student body generally likes the effect of two main campuses. "My favorite part of campus is anything along the water, especially the IC because it is 3 stories of glass windows and absolutely beautiful. I also love having a downtown campus because I can experience the best of both worlds," one student remarked. Another student agreed that the Michigan Avenue campus was equally as important as the scenic Lake Water campus: "I love spending time at the downtown campus because it is in the middle of the city and I can truly grasp the fact that I am living in one [of] the greatest cities in America."

Of course, living in a major urban area has its downsides. Loyola has a commitment to exposing its students to a variety of new experiences and people that go along with a city like Chicago. However, Loyola, even more so, values its students' safety and well-being. "Safety is sometimes an issue in the area surrounding Loyola but the Campus Police has been handling the situation well. We have a transportation system that will drive you anywhere near campus so that you do not have to walk alone at night. Sometimes I feel unsafe at night but mainly it is not a concern of mine," said one sophomore.

Perhaps, this, in part, led to the requirement that undergraduate students live on campus in dorms for the first two years. Living in the dorms for the first couple years allows students to ease into the experience of living in a major city. Freshmen live in freshmen-only dorms, and sophomores live in sophomore-only dorms. Freshmen dorms vary greatly, but sophomores live in apartment-style dorms complete with individual kitchens. All residential buildings are relatively nice (though some, of course, are smaller), but there is a lottery that students enter which decides their actual room assignments. One student looked back on her experience with fondness. "I got a really good one [with] 3 bedrooms, 2 baths, kitchen, living room with 4 other girls. I loved it!" After the first two years, students are given the option of living off campus and most eventually do so. There is always a push to further immerse oneself in Loyola's rich surroundings.

Loyola Knows How to Have Fun!
Although Loyola's social scene is not centered around the same kinds of things and activities as many other schools, the student body certainly has no trouble finding things to do. Sports are not as big at Loyola as they are at other schools. For example, there is no football team so basketball, soccer, and hockey are the most popular sports. There is also, therefore, not a great deal of social energy that centers around athletic events. Greek life is also not as present as at some other schools; one student described the breakdown of student social groups as such: "8.9% Greek, some athletes, the kids who aren't Greek or athletes but hang out with them and then a lot of hipsters."

But this is not to say that Loyola students do not go out. Quite the opposite, in fact! There are two main bars by campus that students frequent because "everyone has a fake." And, once students turn 21, they usually head to Lincoln Park or downtown. Still, it is absolutely not a problem if one does not want to drink. "I think a majority of people drink," said one sophomore, "but not to the excess that is seen on other campuses. A lot of girls on my honors floor last year didn't drink." There are also a number of off-campus and on-campus parties that are somewhat smaller in size but "just as fun as frat parties." One student described a typical weekend at Loyola: "The typical weekend schedule is Thursday Night partying for some and homework for others. Friday night, there is usually a party somewhere or the bars are always a good option. Saturday during the day usually consists of sleep, homework and sometimes exploring the city of Chicago. Saturday night there are more parties and a lot of people usually end up at a bar near campus to end the night."

Popular Extracurriculars
As was stated earlier, Loyola's varsity sport scene is not as popular as it sometimes is on other campuses, but students are still often involved in some kind of athletic or physical activity. Intramural sports are a nice, stress-free alternative to competing at the varsity level in various sports. One student described intramurals as "very relaxed, but also very fun" because "there usually aren't many games, so it doesn't take as much of a commitment."

Really, the amount of time each extracurricular takes is unique to each club. It definitely depends on the extracurricular when judging dedication and commitment. Said one student, "I am in a sorority, and most people are very involved. I am also on the club swim team and there is much less involvement. However, those who are involved really love it. There are so many options that people usually get pretty excited once they find the club that is right for them." There are so many different organizations on campus, like the student said, that it is hard to determine which clubs are generally the most popular. However, it is pretty universally accepted that *The Phoenix*, Loyola's newspaper, has a great staff that successfully "cover all the current events around campus and the changes that happen within the administration of the college." This is also the case for the college's literary magazine, *The Diminuendo*, which is published twice a year and selectively accepts submissions from all students.

Aside from the two main campus publications, students generally agree that employment plays a big role in their lives as students at Loyola. Many students have jobs, both on and off campus, that provide both an interesting pastime and a source of funds. "A lot of people have jobs. Loyola is expensive so many people need to make some extra money to help with tuition. Internships are also a requirement for graduation for many majors," explained one student.

In general, Loyola University in Chicago provides its students with opportunities and experiences that are not easily found on other campuses. For one student, this uniqueness is exemplified by the two campuses, one right on the lake and the other in the heart of the city. "This opens [up] so many opportunities. Somehow though, the campuses are very connected and I never feel alienated or like I'm missing out because we are split up." For another student, the Loyola student's one-of-a-kind experience is a product of the Jesuit traditions upon which the school is founded: "What surprised me the most about Loyola when I arrived was how nice all the students were . . . [and the] focus on helping others and . . . serving the community." Naturally, the things that set this institution apart vary by student but one thing all Loyola students *can* agree on—they are confident that they made the right decision. When asked if she would choose Loyola if she had the chance to change or stay, one student responded wholeheartedly, "If I could do the whole applying to college process again I would definitely pick Loyola without a doubt."—*Edirin Okoloko*

FYI

If you come to Loyola, "you'd better leave your car behind because Chicago traffic can be pretty bad."

What's your classic weekend schedule: "Class, workout, nap, fun activity (downtown or exploring somewhere), pregame with close friends, head to a larger party or the bar, go to bed or post party . . . Sleep in Saturday (unless you have tests/work), lounge with friends or do something fun in the city/campus, repeat Friday night . . . Sleep in Sunday, homework, homework, homework, laundry!"

Three things every student should do at Loyola: "skinny dip in Lake Michigan, sample every Chicago pizza place, and go shopping on Michigan Ave. during Christmas time."

Northwestern University

Address: PO Box 3060, 1801 Hinman Avenue, Evanston, IL 60204-3060	**Early admission program EA/ED/None:** ED	**Retention Rate:** 97%
Phone: 847-491-7271	**Percentage accepted through EA or ED:** Unreported	**Graduation Rate 4-year:** 86%
E-mail address: ugadmission@northwestern.edu	**EA and ED deadline:** 1-Nov	**Graduation Rate 6-year:** Unreported
Web site URL: www.northwestern.edu	**Regular Deadline:** 1-Jan	**Percent Undergraduates in On-campus housing:** 65%
Year Founded: 1851	**Application Fee:** $65	**Number of official organized extracurricular organizations:** 415
Private or Public: Private	**Full time Undergraduate enrollment:** 8,273	**3 Most popular majors:** Economics, Engineering, Journalism
Religious Affiliation: None	**Total enrollment:** 8,476	**Student/Faculty ratio:** 7:1
Location: Suburban	**Percent Male:** 48%	**Average Class Size:** 9
Number of Applicants: 25,013	**Percent Female:** 52%	**Percent of students going to grad school:** 23%
Percent Accepted: 26%	**Total Percent Minority or Unreported:** 43%	**Tuition and Fees:** $38,088
Percent Accepted who enroll: 32%	**Percent African-American:** 5%	**In-State Tuition and Fees if different:** No difference
Number Entering: 2,078	**Percent Asian/Pacific Islander:** 18%	**Cost for Room and Board:** $11,703
Number of Transfers Accepted each Year: Unreported	**Percent Hispanic:** 7%	**Percent receiving financial aid out of those who apply:** 60%
Middle 50% SAT range: M: 690–780, CR: 670–750, Wr: 670–750	**Percent Native-American:** <1%	**Percent receiving financial aid among all students:** 60%
Middle 50% ACT range: 30–33	**Percent International:** 5%	
	Percent in-state/out of state: 25%/75%	
	Percent from Public HS: 65%	

Northwestern University, the only private university of the Big Ten, is a top-tier university located in Evanston, Illinois. Bordering Lake Michigan and only an hour away from Chicago, students there have easy access to both the excitement of the city as well as peacefulness of the suburbs.

Six Colleges, One University

Northwestern students appreciate the academic experience, commenting on the diverse course options and range of requirements, the fast pace of the quarter system, and the ability to find a comfortable workload.

Requirements depend on which college the student is in, and there are six different colleges at Northwestern University. The Weinberg College of Arts and Sciences, the most popular, requires proficiency in a foreign language and two courses in each of the following: natural sciences, the social/behavioral department, quantitative category, ethics and values, and history. While

these requirements seem strict, one freshman said that she welcomes the broad distribution of her course load. "There's just a lot of really interesting courses, and because of the distributional requirements, I don't feel guilty taking courses that don't really relate to my major."

While the broad range of classes in the College of Arts and Sciences is liberating for some, many students speak of an entirely different lifestyle for engineers and math majors. "If you're an engineer here, it's very, very, very difficult," said one freshman girl in the School of Communications.

The dynamic between students in different areas of study is generally one of mutual respect, according to a Weinberg student. "I tell my friend that I have to go read 100 pages of *Anna Karenina*, and he's like 'oh my God!'" At the same time, however, humanities students appreciate the difficulty that engineering students face.

The amount of work also depends largely on your major, and can vary from person to person within a major. "I feel like the engineers and people who are premed tend to be busy, while those in other majors tend to be sporadically busy," said one freshman.

That said, most Northwestern students, regardless of major, remark that the quarter system does not allow time to settle down and get too comfortable. "It feels like you're always studying for midterms," said one student, "but this can be a blessing in disguise. If you're taking a class you don't like, it's over quickly, and over my four years, I'll take eight more classes than the semester student."

Northwestern students also appreciate the lineup of special classes and noteworthy professors at their University. In a class called Human Sexuality, the professor brings in homosexuals, bisexuals, transsexuals, and sexual offenders throughout the semester to speak about their experiences in guest lectures.

Students also laud the faculty at Northwestern, which includes Nobel Prize winners. Despite the accomplishments of the faculty, students find their professors generally accessible, saying that "if you want to meet up with them, just shoot them an e-mail."

Dancing with Wildcats

Northwestern students, known affectionately as "wildcats," say that there are plenty of social opportunities, ranging from annual events like Dance Marathon to the standard Friday night at a fraternity. While the social component is what you make it, students say that most people they know are pretty socially engaged.

Much of the weekend revolves around the Greek scene, but the diverse student body finds equally diverse outlets for activity. One sophomore girl said that the party scene fits most people's interest and comfort level. "If that's what you're into, you won't have a problem finding parties and drinking, but if you don't want to drink, it's easy to find other things to do." Northwestern is an officially dry campus, so the drinking regulations are strict, but this doesn't stifle the partying as much as it shapes people's drinking habits. The dry campus rules "force people who want to drink, especially those underage, away from the public eye." But one freshman says that drinking is "not like a big problem. People are pretty responsible."

The typical going-out schedule consists of Monday night at the Keg of Evanston, Thursday at the Deuce (another bar), and Friday and Saturday mostly at frat parties, though some motivated students organize trips into Chicago with friends.

The Greek scene is a strong presence. Rush is in January, and "boys have Sunday Night Dinners for all of fall quarter, but girls' contact with sororities begins with rush," according to one freshman girl.

The student body is hard to characterize simply; one junior said that "'educated' is the only real defining characteristic that fits." The students are generally friendly, a fact that a sophomore attributed to the school's location. "It is the Midwest, after all." Another student said, "I've been told that you can categorize all of Northwestern as 'closet nerds.'"

Nerdy as they may be, Northwestern students easily make friends. Dorm life, pre-orientation trips, extracurricular activities, and classes provide opportunities to get socially involved. "I know a lot of people who live in my dorm. My floor is like a family now," said one freshman.

While some students describe the population as pretty homogeneous, they acknowledge the presence of diversity as well. "It's pretty white-bread, but they're trying to diversify," said one sophomore. According to one freshman, though, the campus is incredibly diverse. "I just remember walking down Sheridan Road and I heard conversation in four different languages in a ten minute walk. There are people coming from all across the world to this school."

Where Modern Meets Historic

Northwestern's campus is beautiful and quaint, displaying a variety of different architectural styles. Some buildings, such as Deering Library, are "typical ivy-covered Harry Potter-esque," while others "look like prisons." Nonetheless, Northwestern students love their campus and particularly its proximity to both the city and nature. Bordering Lake Michigan and only an hour away from Chicago, students enjoy a combination of both scenic and city life. The Lakefill, a man-made pond by Lake Michigan, is a favorite campus spot for Northwestern students. As described by one junior, "being able to walk to the edge of the water and just sit for a while listening to the waves hit the rocks is a very nice luxury."

Campus dorm options include residential halls, which are generally larger and just a "regular dorm," or residential colleges, which generally "have a theme and a tighter knit community." Residential colleges—assigned based on academic interests, gender, or cultural ethnicity—require interested students to fill out an application, although the process is "not very intense." Incoming freshmen rank their top five housing options in the spring, while upperclassmen are assigned a priority number and choose their rooms on that basis. Dorms generally carry their own stereotypes: Jones attracts theater and performance majors, while Bobb appeals to hardcore partygoers. As one freshman put it, "Bobb is the rage dorm. If you want to come home drunk and throw the trash around, you should live in Bobb." The North-South divide also play into dorm stereotypes. "North campus dorms are more hard-partying, and filled with more athletes. South campus tends to be artsier, with theater and film kids," said one sophomore, who added that housing "is not like living in a luxury hotel, but it's pretty good, and being close to your classes is worth it when it's 10 degrees."

Northwestern has six dining halls which offer the same types of food but on different rotations. Although the food is described as "pretty good," one sophomore admits that it's "not out of this world," instead enjoying his favorite meals outside of campus. According to one freshman, "Evanston has many restaurants, coffee shops, and bars. It's a whole mecca of entertainment on food right outside campus," including Thai food, deep-dish pizza, and the always-popular Burger King.

Work Hard, Play Hard

Students at Northwestern are "involved to a fault" in campus extracurricular activities, ranging from traditional organizations such as Model United Nations and mock trial to more unconventional ones, including the Happiness Club and Dance Marathon Committee, which organizes the University's annual 30-hour dance competition for charity. Campus jobs are similarly popular, and qualifying students are eligible for the Work-Study Program, which guarantees underprivileged students a job on campus. Some of Northwestern's more unique jobs include making calls for the Phone-athon or driving for SafeRide, a shuttle service for students at night.

Organizations on campus advertise events and send messages to the student body by painting "The Rock," a large boulder that sits between University and Harris Hall on Northwestern's campus. Student groups interested in painting the boulder must guard it for 24 hours, from sunrise to early morning the next day. Painting "The Rock" is one of the biggest traditions on campus and, according to one sophomore, "there are even people that propose by painting The Rock." Other traditions include the Primal Scream, an annual event on the Sunday before finals when students "scream as loud[ly] as they can to let out their stress," and the "Wildcat growl," in which students make wildcat claws with their hands during football games and growl at the other team.

Northwestern's many traditions unify the student population and give them an enriching and memorable college experience. According to one sophomore, "I think what makes Northwestern different from other schools is that almost everyone at Northwestern is very smart, trying to save the world, double majoring with a minor, and involved in 30 different activities, but they're pretty down-to-earth about it." One freshman added that if given the chance to choose colleges again, not only would she choose Northwestern again, but she would also "probably apply early."—*Caroline Tan, John Stillman*

FYI
If you come to Northwestern, you'd better bring "a bike, a down comforter, and a purple scarf."
What is the typical weekend schedule? "Dinner at Elder, Party at The Keg, study all day Sunday."
If I could change one thing about Northwestern, I'd change the "library. It's a labyrinth, there are practically no windows, and it's an ugly cement block in the middle of campus. It's an uncomfortable place to study."
Three things every student at Northwestern should do before graduating are "skinny dip in Lake Michigan, get lost in the Technological Institute (one of the biggest academic buildings in the country!), and participate in the Primal Scream."

Principia College

Address: 1 Maybeck Place,
Elsah, IL 62028
Phone: 618-374-5181
E-mail address:
enroll@prin.edu
Web site URL: www.prin.edu
Year Founded: 1898
Private or Public: Private
Religious Affiliation:
Christian Science
Location: Rural
Number of Applicants:
226
Percent Accepted: 56%
**Percent Accepted who
enroll:** 92%
Number Entering: 129
**Number of Transfers
Accepted each Year:**
Unreported
Middle 50% SAT range:
M: 470–610, CR: 470–600,
Wr: 443–610
Middle 50% ACT range:
19–28
**Early admission program
EA/ED/None:** EA

**Percentage accepted
through EA or ED:**
Unreported
EA and ED deadline: 15-Nov
Regular Deadline: 1-Mar
Application Fee: $0
**Full time Undergraduate
enrollment:** 535
Total enrollment: 542
Percent Male: 48%
Percent Female: 52%
**Total Percent Minority or
Unreported:** 19%
Percent African-American:
1%
**Percent Asian/Pacific
Islander:** 1%
Percent Hispanic: 1%
Percent Native-American:
0%
Percent International:
13%
**Percent in-state/out of
state:** 12%/88%
Percent from Public HS:
61%
Retention Rate: 79%

Graduation Rate 4-year:
72%
Graduation Rate 6-year:
Unreported
**Percent Undergraduates in
On-campus housing:** 99%
**Number of official organized
extracurricular
organizations:** 29
3 Most popular majors:
Business, Fine Arts, Mass
Communication
Student/Faculty ratio: 8:1
Average Class Size: 15
**Percent of students going to
grad school:** 27%
Tuition and Fees: $25,200
**In-State Tuition and Fees if
different:** No difference
Cost for Room and Board:
$9,500
**Percent receiving financial
aid out of those who apply:**
87%
**Percent receiving financial
aid among all students:**
79%

A s the only exclusively Christian Scientist college in the world, Principia College attracts followers of its faith from all over the globe. Located high above the bluffs in Elsah, Illinois, over the Mississippi River, the small liberal arts school affectionately known as Prin, is a small, tight-knit community dedicated to both academic excellence and devotion to the Christian Scientist faith.

The Freshman Experience

Since Principia's founding in 1898, its academic mission has evolved, placing an increased emphasis on developing students' analytical thinking, problem solving and communication skills. In order to address the specific academic needs of freshmen, Principia instituted its First Year Experience (FYE) program in 1998. Upon arrival, each freshman enrolls in FYE, which consists of two or three courses to be taken during one's freshman year. Each program of courses has a unique theme and incorporates several classes from different departments, and the

variety of programs allows freshmen to choose a theme that appeals to their personal academic interests. "The FYE program is designed to make sure all freshmen are on the same writing level," one sophomore said. The classes aren't reputed to be the best that the college offers, but students find it to be a great way to make friends when everyone arrives on campus. After FYE, students choose from 32 majors and four minors, or they may design and petition for a special major not already offered by the school.

Principia's freshman schedule is designed to facilitate people getting to know each other right away. All freshmen arrive one week early for orientation, and are then divided into "family groups." When freshmen move into their rooms, they usually have one or two roommates—and in many cases, they've already gotten to know them before school started.

A Commitment to Academics

No matter what they major in, Prin students will have a hard time skipping class or dozing off during lectures. As one junior explained, "Most of the classes are 20 students or less, and attendance is a part of the grade in most classes." The upside is that the small classroom size and campus environment make professors very accessible. "Most of them list their home phone or cell phone numbers on the course syllabus," said one student. This comes in very handy on the weekend—at least half of which, students say, is dedicated to doing homework. Mass communications and studio art are among the most popular majors, and students say the college offers a healthy balance of work-intensive courses and fun classes that are less focused on homework. Even though the college recently faced a faculty reduction, students said they haven't felt limited by their choice of professors. "Given the small size of the school, it's amazing how wide a variety of excellent professors we have," one student remarked.

Live by the Code

Outside the classroom, Principia students are held to an additional standard of integrity known as the honor code. The school's honor code is based on the principles set forth by Mary Baker Eddy, the discoverer and founder of Christian Science, and by Mary Kimball Morgan, who founded Principia. While most secular liberal arts schools have some sort of general honor code loosely regulating the basics—i.e. no plagiarism and no stealing—Principia's code addresses its students' more personal and spiritual activities. It outlines specific requirements for social conduct, academic integrity and performance, financial integrity and spiritual reliance. In following the code, students agree to abstain from alcohol, tobacco, drugs and premarital sex, as well as rely exclusively on Christian Science for healing. Principia's administration finds that following these guidelines is vital in fulfilling Principia's original mission and keeping in line with the Christian Scientist faith. Enforcement of the code is taken very seriously. Students say the code contributes to a strong sense of trust usually absent elsewhere. "It's great to feel trusted as a student," one sophomore said. "During finals, professors feel free to leave the room. And the trust is all around campus—most room doors don't have locks on them, and I leave my laptop around all the time."

College Life In and Out of Prin

Do not be fooled by Principia's claim to be a "small" liberal arts college—its campus spans 2,500 acres. Since the nearest town is 20 minutes away, Prin has its own social committee that "provides a wide range of activities both on and off campus for the students and ways to get to them." Special events include live music courtesy of on- and off-campus bands, weekly movies screened on a large movie screen and regular parties hosted by dorms. When students want to get away from campus, St. Louis is a frequent destination, with its restaurants, sports teams, and a famous zoo. All can be accessed within a 40-minute drive from campus, and many students own cars to give them more options. Campus food, many students say, is not the best and can get rather tiresome. Although students admit that "There is some drinking that goes on, both on campus and off," it's against the code, and undergrads caught drinking can get suspended. "Some people still drink, but it's definitely not a campus-wide thing," another student explained.

Feels Like Home

Nearly all students live on campus in one of 10 houselike residences, many of which were designed by the renowned architect Bernard Maybeck. In fact, Principia was designated a National Historic Landmark to honor Maybeck's exceptional architecture. All new freshmen live on campus in two dorms: Anderson House and Rackham Court. Each freshman dorm houses eight upperclassmen who serve as resident assistants (RAs). And the living ain't shabby. One Principia student even went so far as to say that ". . . Anderson House is enormous and beyond beautiful . . . we are all spoiled. I could not have asked for a better place to live my first year in college." The college is also home to many international students, who come from places like Germany and beyond. Another student explained that the type of the students who choose to come to Principia, along with the community feel of campus, makes the college a really nurturing environment. "The people here are incredible. There's a small student body, but everyone is universally kind and caring. It's a really close-knit community. People always smile, even if they don't know each other."

> "People always smile, even if they don't know each other."

After freshman year, almost all students move to another house where they reside their sophomore, junior and senior years.

Some students, referred to as nontraditional students, or "non-trads" (generally those students older than traditional college age), live in Hitchcock, one of three "cottages" designed by Maybeck, or in off-campus housing. Yet, most Prin students reside on campus and enjoy Maybeck's architecture and the campus's great facilities. All residences are equipped with computer labs, laundry rooms and kitchens—and there are Christian Science and academic study rooms available in each building that are open at all times. Students agreed that houses serve as smaller communities where people make friends and become involved in extracurricular activities. Each house has its own student government and board members who plan social functions, coordinate intramural athletics and lead student orientations. Aside from planning activities within the house, the board members coordinate annual campus-wide activities in each residence. Rackham House kicks off the first weekend of the fall with an annual toga party, and Ferguson has a popular haunted house during Halloween. Later in winter the Sylvester House holds an '80s dance in their rec room. Members of each residence come together each year to throw some fun cohouse parties, and everyone on campus gets to enjoy activities planned by all of the other houses throughout the year, which, as one junior put it, is "not a bad deal!"

Get Involved!
The combination of Principia's small and motivated student body and the college's

vast resources makes it a great place to cultivate leadership roles in extracurricular activities. In terms of sports, Principia is a Division III school and has 10 varsity sports teams for men and women, not to mention a variety of IMs. There are multiple opportunities to get involved in theater and musical groups as well, including the annual winter dance production and the spring play. Prin students can write for the campus newspaper, edit the yearbook, host a radio show on Principia's FM-radio station (WTPC), or even help to coordinate the annual Public Affairs Conference (PAC), which tackles questions like, "Is Democracy the Global Solution?" Extracurriculars often take up much of the time that homework doesn't, students say. Student ambassadors carry the college's mission with them wherever they go. Getting back to basics, the Christian Science Organization (CSO) offers undergraduates a chance to further the study of their common faith. "I love that everyone here is a Christian Scientist," one student said. "It automatically gives us something that we all have in common here, and it creates a really supportive community." About a quarter of the student body goes to chapel services every week. Principia offers both a multitude of activities and opportunities for its students and furthers its mission to instill the values of the Christian Science Church by creating a positive atmosphere of friends for all students to enjoy.—*John Aroutiounian*

FYI
"It can feel pretty isolated sometimes, so a good chunk of time is spent off campus."
What's a typical weekend schedule? "Football, volleyball, or basketball game Saturday afternoon, a movie or trip into town Saturday night, church Sunday morning and homework Sunday afternoon."
Three things everyone should do before graduating Principia are: "travel abroad, be part of a dance or theater production, and go to the City Museum with all your buds!"

Southern Illinois University at Carbondale

Address: Carbondale MC 4710, Carbondale, IL 62901-4512
Phone: 618-536-4405
E-mail address: admrec@siu.edu
Web site URL: www.siuc.edu
Year Founded: 1869
Private or Public: Public
Religious Affiliation: None
Location: Suburban
Number of Applicants: 12,664
Percent Accepted: 59%
Percent Accepted who enroll: 38%
Number Entering: 2,867
Number of Transfers Accepted each Year: 3,727
Middle 50% SAT range: M: 430–560, CR: 430–540, Wr: Unreported
Middle 50% ACT range: 18–24
Early admission program EA/ED/None: None

Percentage accepted through EA or ED: NA
EA and ED deadline: NA
Regular Deadline: Rolling
Application Fee: $30
Full time Undergraduate enrollment: 13,321
Total enrollment: 15,137
Percent Male: 56%
Percent Female: 44%
Total Percent Minority or Unreported: 33%
Percent African-American: 21%
Percent Asian/Pacific Islander: 2%
Percent Hispanic: 5%
Percent Native-American: <1%
Percent International: 2%
Percent in-state/out of state: 88%/12%
Percent from Public HS: Unreported
Retention Rate: 69%
Graduation Rate 4-year: 46%

Graduation Rate 6-year: Unreported
Percent Undergraduates in On-campus housing: 30%
Number of official organized extracurricular organizations: 408
3 Most popular majors: Business Administration and Management, Elementary Education and Teaching, Health/Health Care, Administration/Management
Student/Faculty ratio: 16:1
Average Class Size: 14
Percent of students going to grad school: 58%
Tuition and Fees: $18,225
In-State Tuition and Fees if different: $7,290
Cost for Room and Board: $8,648
Percent receiving financial aid out of those who apply: 78%
Percent receiving financial aid among all students: 81%

Southern Illinois University at Carbondale is a major research university with a small-college feel set in the quaint town of Carbondale, Illinois. One hundred miles from St. Louis and 330 miles from Chicago, SIUC is in the heart of southern Illinois, surrounded by national parks and right next to the beautiful Crab Orchard Lake. When students aren't busy hiking or exploring, they take classes in one of the University's eight smaller colleges: College of Agricultural Sciences, College of Applied Sciences & Arts, College of Business, College of Education & Human Services, College of Engineering, College of Liberal Arts, College of Mass Communication & Media Art and College of Science. Within the eight schools, undergraduates may choose between 200 majors, minors and specializations. Students hail from all 50 states, leading to a diverse student body united behind their enigmatic mascot, the Saluki. As an Illinois State school, though, students from Illinois tend to dominate—88 percent of students hail from somewhere within the state.

Saluki Pride

Few colleges or universities have claims to a more unique mascot than SIUC. The saluki is an Egyptian hunting dog also known as the Royal Dog of Egypt. As one student explained, "If you cut off southern Illinois and flip it over, it kind of looks like Egypt. It's also really fertile land down here and near a number of rivers, so it's a bit like the Fertile Crescent. People started calling it little Egypt, which led to the mascot of the Saluki." But Saluki pride doesn't stop with the interesting backstory. One of the most popular traditions at SIUC is called the Saluki Sprint, which involves the entire freshman class running across the football field at the first home game of the season.

The last seven years have seen dramatic improvements on campus under a project created by then-SIUC chancellor Walter Wendler called the Saluki Way. It has included a new football stadium, a renovated student arena and a number of other campus improvements.

Where Major Research University Meets the Small-College Experience

SIUC students enter a specific college right off the bat, choosing whether they wish to pursue agricultural work or engineering, the liberal arts or mass communication, among other choices. Their enrollment in a college dictates their graduate requirements. As one Saluki explained, "For the College of Mass Communications and Media Art, for example, you need 120 hours, which includes many credits toward your major, but also basic classes like English 101, a basic science class, a basic math class and a foreign language requirement." Students in the Business major typically work towards a particular certificate, such as to become a Public Accountant, which requires 150 hours of coursework before interested students take the certificate exam. One of the best things about the Business major, students said, is the option to take exciting electives—such as Government and Non-Profit Accounting or Risk Management—beyond the required courses. According to SIUC students, the smaller colleges offer opportunities to engage more directly with professors and get to know students within your major. Though students described the school as having more of an emphasis on math and science, they also noted the opportunity to take any number of classes outside of your college or major. History of African Americans in the Media is one particularly popular course, which draws a number of students even outside of the Communications major due to the popularity of the professor, Mr. Novotny Lawrence.

To guide students in their course selection and decision about majors, the University has seven general "Education Academic Advisors," who have "walk-in" hours when students may consult any one of the seven advisors for advice about registration and how best to fulfill degree, University, and state requirements. Each advisor has a different specialty—such as biological sciences, foreign languages, social work or agriculture—so that students may select to speak with an advisor with expertise in their field of study.

Despite the size of the school, students said it is not difficult to get into even the most popular classes. Basic classes, such as 100-level classes, depend almost entirely on scheduling since there are sometimes more than 40 sections of the same introductory-level course. Two hundred- and 300-level classes become slightly more competitive, Salukis noted. These classes tend to fill up quickly; students typically get priority within their major.

With over 15,000 undergraduates on campus, it might seem possible to simply get lost in the crowd. SIUC professors are committed to not letting that happen. "Faculty members are incredibly open to just meeting up and talking," one student said. "Professors will often respond to an email within minutes." Whether it's a question about a homework assignment or guidance about course selection, professors are committed to being a resource to students about academic issues and beyond. Even in large lecture courses, professors make an effort to learn every single student's name, students said.

SIUC prides itself in affording its students the opportunity to take the skills they have learned in the classroom out into the world. Students in the Mass Communications school, for example, said they often spend entire weekends helping out with a TV or radio production. "One time we had a show where local bands came in, and we had to shoot a TV show from it," one Communications major said.

Numerous Social Options

With over 450 registered student organizations (or RSOs), students have no shortage of extracurriculars to choose from. From conservation clubs to Ultimate Frisbee, activities beyond the classroom abound. "I met most of my friends through extracurriculars," one SIUC student mentioned, adding that clubs and student organizations provide the best way to get to know people with common interests on a casual basis. An added plus, students said, is finding activities that are extensions of your academic interests. Students in the Communications major often take part in the broadcast journalism club.

Social opportunities abound at SIUC. Known as one of the Midwest's foremost party schools, SIUC boats a host of opportunities to kick back with friends on the weekend. Popular spots for a drink include Carbondale bars, fraternity and sorority houses and students' off-campus houses. In total, 19 fraternities and 9 sororities exist on campus, many of them targeting specific cultural groups or areas of interest, such as the agriculture fraternity or the black fraternity.

Alcohol is strictly forbidden from dormitories, though students said that Residential Advisers are typically understanding. RAs are upperclassmen who live, one per floor, with students in the dorms. Bars are particularly popular because anyone 19 and over is allowed in, students noted. "And it's really easy to get older kids to buy you drinks," they added. Friday and Saturday are the major party nights on campus, but students also go out on the weekdays depending on special events or specials offered at bars. "Tuesday is a big night because it's dollar night at the bars, which means almost every drink is only a dollar," one student said.

But social activities do not begin or end with drinking, as students made clear. For many Salukis, weekends involve laying low, getting food with friends, seeing bands at local bars or other venues, going up to St. Louis for a day, or going hiking nearby. The University also takes it upon itself to host a number of events throughout the school year, including a major haunted house for Halloween and special events at the dining halls with the University's Chancellor. SIUC's Student Center houses a full bowling alley and is a popular place for students to meet up, grab fast food and even get some homework done beyond the library. Students also enjoy heading out to support their fellow Salukis at sporting events. The Salukis compete in the NCAA Division I Missouri Valley Conference. The women's volleyball team is particularly popular, students said.

Students said that the best recipe for a fun weekend is to make a core group of friends, which is easily made at SIUC. "You meet and talk to so many just by living with all different kinds of people in the dorms," one Saluki said, reminiscing about his freshman year. Living-learning communities are an option for students who wish to live on the same floor or the same building with people in your major. "The school actively creates opportunities for you to make friends," students said, hosting events such as the Southern Social, a barbeque with classically southern food and music.

Home Away from Home

Salukis take pride in their housing options on campus. Most underclassmen live in one of the University's four main undergraduate residence halls, each of which has its own dining hall and common rooms. These are Brush Towers, Thompson Point, University Park and University Hall. The four major residence halls comprise 18 residential buildings in total. SIUC opened apartment-style halls in 2007, called Wall & Grand, which are popular with Seniors and are fully furnished, including washers and dryers. Students over the age of 21 are permitted to live off campus, and most upperclassmen choose to do so. Many students opt for the medium-sized houses that have been in the hands of SIUC students for years. These houses are largely on nearby residential streets, making the commute to classes as simple as walking from a dorm room.

Dining options accommodate all different sorts of diets, and Salukis emphasized the quality of the food in most of the major campus dining halls. Online menus and clear food labels allow students to identify meat-free options and to know the ingredients in their food. A typical breakfast at SIUC might include an omelet, hash browns and fresh fruit. For lunch, students might choose from a turkey burger, cheese ravioli, garden salad and cherry pie for desert. Dinner might bring pork chops (reputed to be a dining hall specialty), flame-roasted corn and red velvet cake. The food, SIUC students made clear, does not disappoint. SIUC also makes a special effort to buy from local producers whenever possible, supporting local Carbondale business and reducing its carbon footprint.

Though one of the most populous regions in southern Illinois, the city of Carbondale boasts a small-town feel with the resources of a much bigger city. The city's business district is home to a number of large shopping malls, which include nationwide chains in addition to locally owned shops and boutiques. All sorts of restaurants dot the area of Carbondale surrounding the SIUC campus. With both fast-food chains and higher-end options, students looking for a bite to eat off campus have no shortage of choices. One particular favorite, students said, is Houlihan's, a bar and grill that serves an array of American, Italian and Pan-Asian cuisine.

On paper, Southern Illinois University at Carbondale might seem daunting, a place where you can't stand out. Yet its diversity of options in all realms—academics, extra-curriculars, and even food—show that there is no need to fear losing your individuality at SIUC.—*Isaac Stanley-Becker*

FYI

If you come to SIUC, you'd better bring: "ramen" and "warm clothes when you plan on sitting through an entire game at Saluki Stadium in the winter"

If you come to SIUC, you'd better leave behind: "your ego and any preconceived notions of who you were in high school" and "bigotry—the students here are unbelievably diverse"

The biggest college-wide tradition at SIUC is: "when people bring actual Salukis to football games"

Three things every student at SIUC should do before graduating are: "go rock climbing at Garden of the Gods, visit the state park and make lifelong friends"

University of Chicago

Address: 1101 E. 58th Street, Rosenwald Hall Suite 105, Chicago, IL 60637
Phone: 773-702-8650
E-mail address: collegeadmissions@uchicago.edu
Web site URL: www.uchicago.edu
Year Founded: 1891
Private or Public: Private
Religious Affiliation: None
Location: Urban
Number of Applicants: 19,340
Percent Accepted: 19%
Percent Accepted who enroll: 38%
Number Entering: 1,387
Number of Transfers Accepted each Year: 54
Middle 50% SAT range: M: 700–780, CR: 700–780, Wr: 690–770
Middle 50% ACT range: 30–34

Early admission program EA/ED/None: EA
Percentage accepted through EA or ED: 30%
EA and ED deadline: 1-Nov
Regular Deadline: 3-Jan
Application Fee: $75
Full time Undergraduate enrollment: 5,184
Total enrollment: 12,316
Percent Male: 51%
Percent Female: 49%
Total Percent Minority or Unreported: 54%
Percent African-American: 5%
Percent Asian/Pacific Islander: 16%
Percent Hispanic: 8%
Percent Native-American: <1%
Percent International: 9%
Percent in-state/out of state: 22%/78%
Percent from Public HS: 64%
Retention Rate: 98%

Graduation Rate 4-year: 85%
Graduation Rate 6-year: 91%
Percent Undergraduates in On-campus housing: 56%
Number of official organized extracurricular organizations: 400
3 Most popular majors: Biology/Biological Sciences, Economics, Political Science and Government
Student/Faculty ratio: 7:1
Average Class Size: 7
Percent of students going to grad school: 20%
Tuition and Fees: $41,853
In-State Tuition and Fees if different: No difference
Cost for Room and Board: $12,633
Percent receiving financial aid out of those who apply: 48%
Percent receiving financial aid among all students: 46%

Its acceptance rate is increasingly Ivy Leaguish, but the University of Chicago and its students retain a "cheerfully masochistic" spirit, the traditional commitment to intellectual rigor, and sincere love for the life of the mind. Don't be scared off by the self-deprecating T-shirts that infamously advertise UChicago as the place "Where Fun Goes to Die." You won't find many football fanatics or frat stars on the leafy Hyde Park campus, but from the world's largest scavenger hunt to $1 milkshakes on Wednesdays to impromptu library dance parties, there's plenty of brainy fun to be had at the University of Chicago.

"It's not Harvard—you have to work for an A"

Making generalizations about UofC students is challenging because they take pride in their individuality, according to one fourth-year majoring in Law, Letters & Society, but it's a safe bet that everyone chose the school because they love learning and are willing to put in a lot of time and energy to do it. Academics at UChicago are characterized by rigor, demanding assignments, and a sometimes-frustrating lack of grade inflation. Because the University operates on the quarter system, with students on campus from late September to December and January to

June, coursework is condensed into 10 weeks, upping the academic ante even further. Although students generally support each other (and sometimes suffer together), the high-pressure environment can lead to stress and intense competition for infrequently granted As. Overall, however, students praise the drive for intellectual achievement—not money, status, or a name-brand education—that marks everyone at UChicago. "People come to the University of Chicago from all walks of life because they're smart," said a first-year who found his first quarter difficult but inspiring. "Not because they think the school's name sounds good. It's a community of people who are here to push themselves to be smarter. Nothing else."

> "People come to the University of Chicago from all walks of life because they're smart. Not because they think the school's name sounds good. It's a community of people who are here to push themselves to be smarter. Nothing else."

Uniquely comprehensive general education requirements, known as the Core, take up about a third of each student's total course load. Testing out is pretty much impossible—everyone must do the Core, designed to "give each student a common vocabulary of ideas and skills," according to the University. Students may take a variety of classes to fulfill the Core, but all complete six quarters of courses in humanities, civilization studies, and the arts; six quarters of natural and mathematical sciences; three quarters of social sciences; and the language requirement, which can be satisfied with IB or AP credit. Humanities, civilization studies, arts, and social science courses are all capped at 20 students, so first-years, who often take mostly Core classes, are immediately exposed to seminar-style learning.

Because core classes often include at least a few students who loathe the subject, they can be hit or miss, said one first-year who spent his first term at college reading Marx, the Iliad, Genesis, and Plato—"so much Plato." Science types tend to dislike the hum and soc requirements, as they're called, and English majors often search for the most basic math sequence (statistics is popular among humanities kids) and civilian-friendly science classes. One fourth-year said core courses can become "a slog to get through," especially if you end up with a weak professor or apathetic classmates. The Core, however, allows students to explore "a little bit of everything," which is particularly helpful to first-years who were good at everything in high school. And for every Core class with a weak teacher, there's another taught by a faculty celebrity, said a fourth-year who was introduced to *The Prince* by one of the country's leading Machiavelli scholars.

While UChicago's general education requirements are unusually significant, majors at the University are less demanding than at many other schools. One fourth-year majoring in Law, Letters & Society said her major required just 12 courses, leaving her free to explore other disciplines. Light course requirements, however, does not mean majors are easy: students agree that every major at the University is academically demanding, and one benefit of the Core is that everyone learns to respect (if sometimes grudgingly) disciplines they'd otherwise ignore. A third-year Economics and Statistics double major who spends upwards of 30 hours on problem sets each week said that when a Philosophy major friend was practicing for a timed essay exam, "All I could think was, 'I'm so glad I don't have to do that.' I think the Core teaches you that every subject can be really rigorous."

After dabbling in just about everything through the Core, the largest number of students become Economics majors. Biological sciences, Political Science, English, History and International Studies are also popular. Additionally, Chicago offers several unique interdisciplinary majors that enable students to craft individualized programs focused on books, the law, human development, or the history of medicine.

No matter which major they choose, most students spend a lot of time in the library. "It gets way harder after the first year," said one third-year. "Although I did not realize that at the time." For the most part, professors are dedicated, accessible and passionate—although that can be a downside when every professor feels entitled to assign mountains of work because "they feel like they have a stake in your entire life." But the work becomes more manageable when all your friends are in the library with you, and procrastinating by going out would be impossible because everyone's too busy with a paper or problem set. Instead, students bring the party to the library: a new campus organization books a study room once a week to host a 15-minute dance party, complete with snacks and electronic music.

At Home in Hyde Park

Since students spend so much time in the libraries, it's no surprise that they are an architectural highlight of the campus. The Law Library is known for its Hogwarts-esque Gothic beauty, while the popular Regenstein is a brutalist hulk. The Mansueto Library's glass dome ceiling makes it a magical place to study during a snowfall. The rest of the campus buildings exhibit similar architectural diversity, with a beautiful Gothic quad at the heart of campus and more contemporary buildings at its periphery. Surrounding the campus is the neighborhood of Hyde Park, offering bars, restaurants, easy access to downtown Chicago and, for most third- and fourth-years, apartment residences.

Before they go off campus, however, most students form close friendships in their dorms through the University's distinctive House system. Prior to arriving on campus, freshmen choose from 12 dorms, ranging from the centrally located 715-resident Max Palevsky to the 79-resident Blackstone Hall ten minutes away from campus. Singles, doubles, suites, and even apartment-style rooms are all available to freshmen. When students are assigned a room, they're also placed into a House. Housemates all live in the same area—Max P. hosts eight houses, divided by floor, and Blackstone hosts just one. Houses have their own unique traditions, compete against each other in intramurals, and go on trips into Chicago and to restaurants in Hyde Park. For first- and second-years, the House system is a major focal point of social life, serving as a cozy microcosm of the university and allowing students to meet people with different interests and backgrounds. After freshman year, students can choose who to live with, but most who stay on campus remain within their dorm and House.

Two Residential Assistants in each house plan study breaks, trips, and special activities. A third-year RA said he takes a pretty lenient attitude toward parties and drinking in the dorm because he sees his role as fostering community, not "saving kids from sin," like the RAs of horror stories he's heard from friends at other schools. The University does not allow alcohol in common spaces, but students over 21 may have it in their rooms. Drug use, the RA said, is generally less tolerated than underage drinking, but in all cases, "They try to keep the actual police out of things as much as possible."

Most students move into off-campus apartments by their third year. "Staying on campus is totally dorky after second-year," said a fourth-year who does indeed live off campus. Rents in Hyde Park are cheap and apartments abound within a 20-minute walk of campus. Living off campus is popular because it allows students to live with their friends and escape the meal plan, generally agreed to be mediocre (although older students say it has improved significantly in the past two years) and inconvenient for students who live far from one of the two dining halls. A free shuttle service helps off-campus students get to and from their residences.

Since students live all over the neighborhood, the University employs its own large private police force—but some feel that this creates tensions between the UofC and the "profoundly impoverished" surrounding communities. Students agree that caution and self-awareness are enough to stay secure around campus, "but if you want to be somewhere idyllic, go somewhere else." The University's police often stop perceived trespassers and, according to a fourth-year, have been known to engage in racial profiling. "I wouldn't want to be a black male student at the University of Chicago," she said.

The practices of the University police have stirred considerable outrage among the campus's small activist community, said a third-year Statistics major. Student activists also promote discussions of diversity and equity on campus. International students comprise 9 percent of the student body and geographic diversity continues to increase, but domestic minorities remain underrepresented. "It's one of the things we talk about the most," said the Statistics major. He added that UofC students seem particularly unafraid to challenge authority, including the University administration, when they have complaints or concerns.

Social Life: Heaven and Hell

UChicago's biggest party of the year is the Heaven & Hell blowout hosted by one of the fraternities, which decorates each floor of its off-campus house according to the descriptions of heaven, purgatory, and hell found in Dante's *Inferno*. Just as they can choose which floor of this party they wander through drunkenly, UofC students can choose whether to make their social lives heaven or hell, argued a fourth-year who considers herself to be much more social than the average student. "Some people are choosing a lifestyle where they are not having fun, but it is clearly their choice," she said of students who spend Friday and Saturday nights at the library. Fraternities host parties throughout the week, older students hold get-togethers in their off-campus apartments, and downtown Chicago frequently offers concerts and shows—if students are willing to break away from their studies for a night or two.

About ten percent of students go Greek, and many first-years have their first partying experiences at frat houses—though this often loses its appeal as the year wears on, and the Greeks are not a dominant force on campus. Social life at the University isn't dominated by any particular group or organization, so it can feel segmented, students said. But it seems to improve with age as students meet more people and move off campus. "Most of the social life ends up being first-years going to parties they don't really like or understand, and upperclassmen having apartment parties and just inviting their friends," said a first-year fraternity pledge. Drinking is definitely common, but a first-year who does not drink said she'd never felt uncomfortable or pressured to imbibe.

While partying may not unite the campus, big traditions like Kuvia (early-morning exercises held in January), the Polar Bear run, the Summer Breeze Festival—featuring bouncy castles, cotton candy, rides, games, and a massive concert in the evening—$1 milkshakes on Wednesdays at the Reynolds Club, and the annual Scav Hunt certainly do. It is these traditions that give the University its distinctive flavor and disprove the self-deprecating slogans; thousands of students working to figure out how to build a nuclear reactor, lead a lion or tiger onto the quad, or obtain a pen that has been used to sign a bill into law are definitely having fun, though it may look different from fun at other universities.

As the University's admissions rate has declined, some students have taken to the op-ed pages of the *Chicago Maroon* to moan about the perceived demise of the quirky, dedicated intellectuals admitted when acceptance rates were in the double-digits. But as long as the traditions, demanding professors, and even self-deprecating T-shirts continue to celebrate hard-core academicism, for better or for worse, the University of Chicago seems poised to retain its distinctive character. —*Isabelle Taft*

FYI
What differentiates UChicago the most from other colleges is "our love of learning, which overpowers our desire to do anything else. And we make fun of ourselves for it."
If you come to UChicago, "you'd better leave your ego behind."
Three things every student at UChicago should do before graduating are "1. Drink alcohol in the Regenstein Library. 2. Help out your House team with Scav. 3. Go to Lake Michigan for a walk and a break from campus."

University of Illinois / Chicago

Address: Box 5220 m/c 018,
Chicago, IL 60680-5220
Phone: 312-996-4350
E-mail address: uicadmit@
uic.edu
Web site URL: www.uic.edu
Year Founded: 1965
Private or Public: Public
Religious Affiliation: None
Location: Urban
Number of Applicants:
14,889
Percent Accepted: 63%
**Percent Accepted who
enroll:** 34%
Number Entering: 3,204
**Number of Transfers
Accepted each Year:** 2,588
Middle 50% SAT range:
M: 510–660, CR: 460–610,
Wr: 480–620
Middle 50% ACT range:
21–26
**Early admission program
EA/ED/None:** None

**Percentage accepted
through EA or ED:** NA
EA and ED deadline: NA
Regular Deadline: 15-Jan
Application Fee: $50
**Full time Undergraduate
enrollment:** 16,806
Total enrollment: 27,850
Percent Male: 46%
Percent Female: 54%
**Total Percent Minority or
Unreported:** 63%
Percent African-American:
9%
**Percent Asian/Pacific
Islander:** 25%
Percent Hispanic: 25%
Percent Native-American:
<1%
Percent International: 2%
**Percent in-state/out of
state:** 98%/2%
Percent from Public HS:
Unreported
Retention Rate: 82%

Graduation Rate 4-year: 20%
Graduation Rate 6-year: 46%
**Percent Undergraduates
in On-campus housing:**
19%
**Number of official organized
extracurricular
organizations:** 370
3 Most popular majors:
Biology, Business, Psychology
Student/Faculty ratio: 19:1
Average Class Size: 15
**Percent of students going to
grad school:** 33%
Tuition and Fees: $25,046
**In-State Tuition and Fees if
different:** $12,656
Cost for Room and Board:
$10,194
**Percent receiving financial
aid out of those who apply:**
78%
**Percent receiving financial
aid among all students:**
70%

University of Illinois in Chicago, the second campus founded under the University of Illinois system, is the largest university in the Chicago area with over 27,000 students. The university is made up of 15 colleges and offers over 74 majors, but its prominence comes from its role in the scientific community. The university houses the largest medical school in the nation and spends over $340 million in research. Located near the Chicago Loop, UIC students take advantage of city life and events during the weekends. Many students even commute or live in off-campus apartments.

Premed: UIC's Got It

UIC's reach is broad—one in ten Chicago residents who graduated from college earned their degree from UIC. Though it offers majors in architecture, education, engineering, liberal arts and social work, the institution's main focus lies in health care.

UIC's College of Medicine is the country's largest medical school, and its presence among the Illinois health-care community is uncanny. One in six Illinois physicians were trained in UIC. Math and Science are the most prevalent subjects in this university and often feature curves when it comes to grading. Organic Chemistry and Symbolic Logic are among some of the most difficult courses offered in UIC. Though students say the humanities at UIC are easier than the sciences, there is no rivalry between the two departments.

Nonsciences: A Thrilling World

Every UIC student must complete 120 credit hours, which are divided between general education classes, electives, college specific classes, and courses specific to a student's major. Classes become more specialized toward a degree as years go by. Gaining admission into a class depends heavily on how many credits a student has already earned. Students with more hours completed receive preference when it comes to registering for courses. In this way, incoming freshmen, who have earned Advanced Placement credits or have placed out of introductory courses with their ACT or SAT scores, can receive better placement into courses than their fellow freshmen. "It is very competitive getting into classes," said one student. "It's first come, first served. You're given a date and time to sign up. Juniors and seniors go first. Then sophomores. Then incoming freshmen last."

Class sizes in UIC vary. Large lectures can hold up to 300 people while discussions house anywhere about 15 students. Smaller classes typically hold around 20 students. Since UIC focuses much of its energy on research, some students say instructors aren't always the most proficient when it comes to educating. "Many of the professors here didn't go to school for teaching, they went to become professionals in their subjects which is why some are very bad teachers," said one sophomore. "They know what they are talking about, but they aren't good at conveying information." That being said, students do agree that professors are always available to offer extra help and office hours.

Besides catering to the research world, UIC allows students the opportunity to explore the liberal arts. The Honors College was founded to offer motivated students and faculty members a place for more academic exploration. Students admitted to the program have access to their own study halls, computer labs and advisors. Students must apply to both the Honors College and a UIC degree granting college. Students are dually enrolled in both. Members of the program are expected to take part in Honor College activities and maintain a 3.4 or higher grade point average.

A Commuter's Heaven

With the beauty of Chicago comes the convenience and affordability of commuting to school. Less than a quarter of undergrads live on campus. The rest commute by train or live in apartments that surround the campus. Upperclassmen and underclassmen alike say the university is "dead" on weekends since those that live in nearby suburbs choose to visit home while others choose to explore Chicago. "If someone is looking for a large amount of people to live on campus, then this college isn't for them," said a sophomore who lives in one of the apartments off campus.

On-Campus Living

For the few who do brave on-campus living, housing gets better with seniority. Incoming freshmen are asked to pick their top three residential halls and fill out survey questions. Campus Housing then sorts them into dorms. Sophomores, juniors, and seniors enter a lottery at the end of each year to choose the dorm they want. Upperclassmen receive better positions in the lottery system, and upperclassman halls try to

cater to students who want singles. UIC students can choose their roommates during any of their years in the university. The dorms are traditional style with community bathrooms and common areas. In the past few years some of the housing has been renovated, but students agree James Stukel Towers, which was built less than five years ago, offers the best housing.

> **"I was surprised by just how friendly everyone actually was when I got here."**

Freshmen have Residential Assistants and Peer Mentors to help them through their first year at UIC. Peer mentors are staff members who guide freshmen academically while Residential Assistants are upperclassman who make sure freshmen abide by Campus Housing policies while helping new students bond in the residential halls. Freshmen say that, for the most part, their Residential Assistants are laid-back and offer the support they need for the first year of college. Residential Assistants, however, have the task of enforcing UIC's alcohol and drug policy. The use of illicit drugs and underage drinking will result in a Conduct Process and in more severe cases, a meeting with the Dean of Students. "We all basically live by the concept, 'If you make smart decisions, you will not get in trouble,'" said a Residential Assitant. "Alcohol is allowed in dorms for those who are 21 and up in limited amounts."

Pennants and Cocktails: UIC Social Scene

Athletics and school pride make up a big part of the social setting in UIC. Since it has no football team, UIC students cheer on their basketball team in the Pavilion. UIC is home to 370 student organizations and clubs.

The social lives of upperclassmen and underclassmen tend to differ. Most freshmen and sophomores interact in dorms or places around school like the Quad or Recreational Facility. Upperclassmen like to take advantage of the bars and clubs around Chicago during their weekends. Students say the campus has a laid-back setting. "I was surprised by just how friendly everyone actually was when I got here," said one student. *U.S. News & World Report* ranked UIC the eleventh most ethnically diverse university.

UIC is a world-class institution that offers students the freedom to explore their interests and challenges them to test their limits. It has students face the realities of the world and encourages them to go outside of the bubble created in college campuses.—*Liz Rodriguez-Florido*

FYI

What is the typical weekend schedule? "Take the subway, walk around the city, get Sprinkles cupcakes, head to the beach, go to a restaurant and then maybe do some homework."

If I could change one thing about UIC, I'd "have it have a football team. You can't fit a football stadium in the middle of Chicago."

If you come to UIC, you'd better leave "any discrimination" behind.

University of Illinois / Urbana-Champaign

Address: 901 West Illinois Street, Urbana, IL 61801
Phone: 217-333-0302
E-mail address: admissions@illinois.edu
Web site URL: www.illinois.edu
Year Founded: 1867
Private or Public: Public
Religious Affiliation: None
Location: Urban
Number of Applicants: 27,291
Percent Accepted: 67%
Percent Accepted who enroll: 38%
Number Entering: 6,929
Number of Transfers Accepted each Year: 1,805
Middle 50% SAT range: M: 680–770, CR: 530–660, Wr: Unreported
Middle 50% ACT range: 26–31
Early admission program EA/ED/None: EA

Percentage accepted through EA or ED: Unreported
EA and ED deadline: 10-Nov
Regular Deadline: 2-Jan
Application Fee: $50
Full time Undergraduate enrollment: 31,540
Total enrollment: 43,862
Percent Male: 56%
Percent Female: 44%
Total Percent Minority or Unreported: 38%
Percent African-American: 7%
Percent Asian/Pacific Islander: 14%
Percent Hispanic: 14%
Percent Native-American: <1%
Percent International: unreported
Percent in-state/out of state: 92%/8%
Percent from Public HS: 75%
Retention Rate: 94%

Graduation Rate 4-year: 62%
Graduation Rate 6-year: 80%
Percent Undergraduates in On-campus housing: 50%
Number of official organized extracurricular organizations: 1000
3 Most popular majors: Engineering, Business/Marketing,Social Sciences
Student/Faculty ratio: 16:1
Average Class Size: 25
Percent of students going to grad school: 26%
Tuition and Fees: $27,980
In-State Tuition and Fees if different: $13,838
Cost for Room and Board: $10,080
Percent receiving financial aid out of those who apply: 65%
Percent receiving financial aid among all students: 46%

L ocated between two small towns in southern Illinois, the University of Illinois at Urbana-Champaign offers the quintessential large university experience. Known for its excellent academics, Illinois is also home to a dominant sports culture, abundant Greek life, and a lively campus atmosphere.

United by a Passion for Learning.

Students at Illinois are divided into different academic colleges from the time of application, each with its own set of graduation requirements. Illinois's engineering programs are world-renowned and not surprisingly, classes in mathematics and the sciences are supposed to be much more demanding. "Humanities is considered easier," one engineering student said. "Students who are in my math and science classes sometimes joke about switching into some random humanities major when it gets really hard." Students also note that few science classes are curved, and those that are sometimes deflate grades rather than ease the coursework. Nonetheless, students at Illinois are motivated about learning and appreciate the opportunities granted by a strong engineering school despite the increased workload. Another engineering student praised the research being conducted by his professors. "The progress being made in engineering, physics, and math is something that really sets Illinois apart," a sophomore engineering major said. Moreover, the enthusiasm that attracts applicants to a competitive school like Illinois leads them to appreciate the passion of their classmates. Students are known for helping each other, often studying in groups and working on homework assignments together. "I love my engineering classes because I've met so many people as interested as I am in studying and learning," said one freshman.

The love of learning unites students at Illinois across the academic schools. Each college selects James Scholars for an honor program based on grades and test scores. Along with several other honors programs that recognize applicants for different sets of academic criteria, this distinction allows students to have an earlier selection of classes and gives them the opportunity to work on special projects or participate in smaller seminars. Illinois also offers "discovery courses," for freshmen, which are really small and feature close interaction with a professor. One freshman said, "I took a course called Science and Pseudoscience. It was surprisingly interesting and the small class size made it a lot easier to get to know the professor." For the most part, however, classes at Illinois are relatively large and impersonal. Several students remarked that the lack of student-teacher interaction was their least favorite discovery about Illinois. One freshman complained, "Sometimes you just feel like a number in your classes." Regardless, Illinois offers classes on both sides of the spectrum, with an outstanding engineering program and numerous and varied opportunities to excel in the humanities and social sciences.

Fighting Illini

Students at the University of Illinois at Urbana-Champaign almost universally agree that varsity athletics have an incredibly notable presence on campus. The teams are competitive, especially the basketball team. "Football and basketball season are huge here," one student said. "Everyone watches or goes to the games, and there is definitely a lot of school pride for our sports teams." School pride organizations are popular, giving devoted fans a channel for organized spirit. Intramurals are also popular. According to one student, "There is a giant intramural sports program that is run through the University. Some, like flag football, are even extremely competitive." Even students not involved in sports have the luxury of incredibly nice athletic facilities, which many take advantage of. "The fitness centers are busy literally all hours of the day," one student remarked. "They offer really cool workout and dance classes too." More whimsical Illini even participate in quasi-athletic activities like "Falling Illini," the skydiving club, and broomball, a sport invented by college students.

> "I've met so many people as interested as I am in studying and learning."

Due to its large size, Illinois offers countless extracurricular activities beyond sports as well. The passion held by students for their pursuits outside the classroom is fervent, and this has led to the large number and prevalence of student organizations. "Everyone I know is really committed to their activities," one student said. "Even if it takes a lot of work it's worth it because people are usually able to find some extracurricular they really care about." Ethnic clubs are popular, as is the campus newspaper, the *Daily Illini*. Generally, Illinois students show the same devotion out of the classroom as they do in their academics, both on and off the field.

Got Greek?

Illinois is known for its dominant fraternity and sorority culture. "It's basically the biggest Greek scene in the country," one junior noted. Weekend social life is filled with frat parties, and many people move off campus to live in the houses of their fraternity or sorority after freshman year. Regardless of participation in frat culture, drinking is commonplace at Illinois. Alcohol is technically not allowed in the dorms, one of the reasons for Greek life's popularity, but students, especially freshmen, still seem to drink in the dorms. The commercial area of town also boasts a variety of bars, which are popular hangouts for students, often with certain bars serving as "haunts" for various social circles. "I love going to bars here because they admit anyone over nineteen even if they can't drink," one underage student said. "I like being able to go dance and chill with my friends without alcohol being an issue."

Though it may not be a popular choice at Illinois, many students still choose to abstain from alcohol. Freshmen have the option of living in Snyder, a substance-free dormitory. While all the dorms at Illinois discourage alcohol usage, students who live in Snyder have a mutual understanding to respect the choices of their peers. "I like having the option to go out and party if I want to, but not having to live with it all the time," one freshman living in Snyder said. "It's nice having the choice."

Snyder is one of many dorms at Illinois that have a theme, explicit or implicit. The "six pack," a group of dorms, is known as the home of partiers, while other dorms are known for embracing foreigners. Engineering students tend to cluster in dorms closer to their academic buildings due to the large size of campus, leading to a somewhat polarized living dynamic. This doesn't last long, however, as most people move off campus sophomore or junior year. "The off-campus housing here is great because it can be just as cheap as the better on-campus housing and you don't have to deal with strict RAs or sticking to the meal plan," said a senior.

At the end of the day, Illinois students have active social lives despite their commitment to academic excellence, lending itself to well-rounded students and a balanced environment. The incredibly strong engineering program, combined with honors options in the humanities, provides students with a world-class education—on the budget of a public university. If you think living in a town with thousands of other college students sounds like a good time and don't mind putting in the hard work, the University of Illinois at Urbana-Champaign may be the place for you to spend your next four years.—*Natasha Thondavadi*

FYI

Before graduating everyone should "go to an Illinois basketball game and take a nap in the student union."
If I could change one thing about Illinois "I'd make it easier to get around campus."
The biggest college tradition at Illinois is "the Oskee Wow Wow song."

Wheaton College

Address: 501 College Avenue, Wheaton, IL 60187
Phone: 800-222-2419
E-mail address: admissons@wheaton.edu
Web site URL: www.wheaton.edu
Year Founded: 1860
Private or Public: Private
Religious Affiliation: Interdenominational Christian
Location: Suburban
Number of Applicants: 2,083
Percent Accepted: 66%
Percent Accepted who enroll: 45%
Number Entering: 602
Number of Transfers Accepted each Year: 86
Middle 50% SAT range: M: 610–700, CR: 600–730, Wr: 590–710
Middle 50% ACT range: 26–32
Early admission program EA/ED/None: EA

Percentage accepted through EA or ED: 62%
EA and ED deadline: 1-Nov
Regular Deadline: 10-Jan
Application Fee: $50
Full time Undergraduate enrollment: 2,434
Total enrollment: 3,026
Percent Male: 48%
Percent Female: 52%
Total Percent Minority or Unreported: 17%
Percent African-American: 2%
Percent Asian/Pacific Islander: 7%
Percent Hispanic: 7%
Percent Native-American: <1%
Percent International: 1%
Percent in-state/out of state: 22%/78%
Percent from Public HS: 61%
Retention Rate: 94%
Graduation Rate 4-year: 77%

Graduation Rate 6-year: 84%
Percent Undergraduates in On-campus housing: 90%
Number of official organized extracurricular organizations: 75
3 Most popular majors: Social Sciences, Business/Marketing, English
Student/Faculty ratio: 12:1
Average Class Size: 15
Percent of students going to grad school: 40%
Tuition and Fees: $28,960
In-State Tuition and Fees if different: No difference
Cost for Room and Board: $8,220
Percent receiving financial aid out of those who apply: 73%
Percent receiving financial aid among all students: 54%

Wheaton College isn't just another small liberal arts college with a picturesque campus, excellent professors and rather unsuccessful sports teams: it is above all a Christian college. Students come to Wheaton hoping for something more than a degree in music or mathematics. They seek knowledge of "how to better serve God." Wheaton students also point to the strong sense of community on campus as something that sets Wheaton apart.

Integrating Faith and Learning

Students say classes at Wheaton are very challenging but manageable. Science majors are known to be particularly difficult, but students say there are challenging classes in almost every department. "There isn't an honors program—I think if there was everyone would be in it," said one freshman. Students say Wheaton seems to attract perfectionists, leading to a somewhat competitive atmosphere at times.

> "There isn't an honors program—I think if there was everyone would be in it."

Like most students at liberal arts colleges, students at Wheaton are required to fulfill general education requirements with courses in subjects such as English literature, history and natural sciences. More unique to Wheaton are the numerous requirements in theological and biblical studies. All students take a course on both the Old and New Testament as well as courses on Christian thought and culture.

Academic standards are high at Wheaton, "but professors are very helpful and focused on teaching," according to one sophomore. Wheaton encourages close relationships with professors through its "Dine with a Mind" program. Students are given five meal cards to pay for a professor's meal in the dining hall. It's a chance to continue a discussion from class, ask for spiritual guidance, or see pictures of their grandkids–or maybe all three. Students say that Wheaton professors are religious as well as academic guides. Wheaton's commitment to Christian education means that every class, not just the ones in the Theology department, is based in a Christian worldview.

Another important component of Wheaton academics is its music program. Calling someone at Wheaton a "Conservie" isn't a comment about their political views—it's a nickname for students in the Conservatory of Music. The Conservatory offers six different majors, including performance, music education and music and ministry. While one Conservatory student said at times it feels like there is "a Conservie bubble," Conservatory students are still integrated with the rest of the college, living in the same housing and mixing with other students in general education classes.

Living by the Covenant

Asked about drugs and drinking on campus, a freshman said that for the most part, "it's just not there." All students sign a Community Covenant, pledging not to use alcohol or drugs while they are at Wheaton and they stick to their word. Most students who choose Wheaton are fully aware that it's far from a party school. For some, it's an attraction. "It's nice not to have the pressure," said one sophomore. Students say there is a very small percentage of students who break the rules, known as the Wheaton Underground, but most students have very little contact with this group unless they try to seek them out.

Wheaties still love to have fun. The College Union organizes various parties, a popular Talent Show, and live music nights. Dorm floors and on-campus houses host theme parties. Ever since a ban on social dancing was lifted in 2003, there have been several college-sponsored dances every year. And for those who feel a little suffocated by the small campus, Chicago is less than an hour away by train. Most students stay on campus during the weekends. Freshmen are not allowed to have cars on campus, though many upperclassman have them.

Most Wheaton students seem satisfied by housing, and nearly all students live on -campus. On-campus housing options include four residence halls, as well as 13 college-owned houses and several college-owned apartment complexes. Freshman will meet many of their first college friends on their floors. Floors are single-sex, but each floor has a brother or sister floor, and "bro-sis" get-togethers are popular. Fischer, a coed dorm for freshmen and sophomores, is considered the most social on campus, while Traber is "the jock dorm," according to one freshman. Upperclassmen tend to try for the campus-owned apartments and avoid Saint and Elliot apartments.

In underclassmen dorms, members of the opposite sex can only visit each other's floors during a few hours two days per week, or during special "open hours." Guys and girls are free to hang out together in dorm lounges and lobbies, and in most dorms students can be found in the lobby at almost any time. "Lobby couples" take advantage of these spaces by spending all their free time there "being obnoxiously couple-y," said one student, but generally lobbies are fun places to socialize or study together. The regulations for upperclassmen are less strict, though overnight visits are still technically forbidden.

These strict regulations on how guys and girls interact, along with a gossipy small campus atmosphere and student attitudes toward dating can make casual dating a little difficult, though students say it improves over time. There are plenty of single people on campus who want to date, but guys are hesitant to ask girls on dates. In a place where seniors worry about having a "ring by spring," an invitation to a movie is seen as the first step toward a marriage proposal. As a result, most relationships at Wheaton are serious relationships, even though many students say they would like to see more casual dating.

Proud to be a Wheatie

Wheaton students have school pride: "you see about 20 Wheaton T-shirts in a row," said one freshman. This pride shows when Wheaties turn out to support football and soccer teams, which do well in Division III competition. Intramural sports are also very popular, with opportunities for fairly intense competition as well as laid-back goofing around with friends. Wheaton students tend to be in good shape. Almost all are active in some way, whether as members of a varsity, club or intramural team or as a dedicated gym goer.

Wheaties admit that campus diversity isn't fantastic, but the school does try to attract a diverse group of students. There is some ethnic diversity and socioeconomic diversity but the average Wheaton student is still a middle- to upper-class white kid. One diverse group that Wheaton attracts are students from missionary families. These bring with them stories of childhoods spent in Zambia or Zimbabwe and unique perspectives developed in their time away from the U.S. There are few to no openly gay students on campus. Politically, Wheaton students lean right but some say they've become less conservative during college. Wheaton students are united by their Christian faith, but the college is interdenominational. Most students identify with some variety of evangelical Protestantism, though not all.

Part of being a Wheatie is taking part in its many school traditions. For example, Wheaton students may adhere faithfully to the Community Covenant as far as drinking goes, but for the sake of a seven-foot-long concrete slab, they've been known to break a law here and there. The slab in question is known as the Bench—erected in the 1920s and placed outside Blanchard Hall for the exclusive use of seniors. The juniors first stole the bench around 1950, and since then juniors and seniors have waged a bitter war for possession of the bench. In 1959, the seniors suspended the bench from a helicopter and flew over the football field during the homecoming game to taunt the junior class. More recently, in 2005, a high-speed car chase for the Bench resulted in several speeding tickets.

Another Wheaton tradition is ringing the tower bell in Blanchard Hall to announce an engagement. Wheaton seems to have more of these to announce than other colleges, though some students say that might be a stereotype: "I feel like Wheaton has a rep for people getting married, but it's exaggerated," said one student.

Attending Wheaton is a unique college experience. While most students who choose Wheaton seem very satisfied with their decision, they also admit that they know their school wouldn't be right for everyone. Some students also worry that four years at Wheaton might leave them unprepared for "the real world," where not everyone will share or understand their beliefs. But for the most part, Wheaton students seem to deeply value the way Wheaton has shaped them intellectually and spiritually. "After my first semester, I know I would definitely choose Wheaton again," said one freshman.—*Sonja Peterson*

FYI
If you come to Wheaton College, you'd better bring "lots of crazy clothes for theme parties."
Three things every student should do before graduating are "explore Chicago, play IMs and have a snowball fight."
What differentiates Wheaton most from other colleges is "the amazing community."

Indiana

DePauw University

Address: 101 E. Seminary, Greencastle, IN 46135

Phone: 765-658-4006

E-mail address: admission@depauw.edu

Web site URL: www.depauw.edu

Year Founded: 1837

Private or Public: Private

Religious Affiliation: Methodist

Location: Suburban

Number of Applicants: 4,439

Percent Accepted: 68%

Percent Accepted who enroll: 22%

Number Entering: 664

Number of Transfers Accepted each Year: 23

Middle 50% SAT range: M: 570–660, Cr: 560–660, Wr: 620–690

Middle 50% ACT range: 25–29

Early admission program EA/ED/None: EA and ED

Percentage accepted through EA or ED: Unreported

EA and ED deadline: 1-Nov

Regular Deadline: 1-Feb

Application Fee: $40

Full time Undergraduate enrollment: 2,276

Total enrollment: 2,276

Percent Male: 44%

Percent Female: 56%

Total Percent Minority or Unreported: 16%

Percent African-American: 6%

Percent Asian/Pacific Islander: 3%

Percent Hispanic: 3%

Percent Native-American: 1%

Percent International: 2%

Percent in-state/out of state: 54%/46%

Percent from Public HS: 83%

Retention Rate: 92%

Graduation Rate 4-year: 79%

Graduation Rate 6-year: 81%

Percent Undergraduates in On-campus housing: 99%

Number of official organized extracurricular organizations: 119

3 Most popular majors: Economics, English, Communications

Student/Faculty ratio: 10:1

Average Class Size: 15

Percent of students going to grad school: 31%

Tuition and Fees: $29,300

In-State Tuition and Fees if different: No difference

Cost for Room and Board: $8,100

Percent receiving financial aid out of those who apply: Unreported

Percent receiving financial aid among all students: Unreported

---

At DePauw University, the students' sense of fun and the college's unique traditions more than compensate for the Midwestern chill. With a flourishing Greek life scene and a tight-knit population of "casual and accepting" students, this small but proud private liberal arts college offers a welcoming atmosphere. Through its distinctive combination of a strong liberal arts education and preprofessional opportunities, DePauw encourages its students to apply their intellects to the working world. As one senior put it, "DePauw really emphasizes putting yourself out there, getting involved, and getting everything out of the time you have in college."

Challenge, Freedom, and Excitement: All in a Day's Work

The classes and academic standards at DePauw "definitely require you to work," but there is plenty of freedom to choose courses, and there are several "exciting" options for learning outside of the classroom, a freshman said. Depending on the type of bachelor's degree being pursued, students need to take either 31 or 33 course credits: 31 for normal Bachelor of Arts, Bachelor of Music, and Bachelor of Musical Arts degrees, and 33 for a Bachelor of Music Education degree at DePauw's well-known music school. All students except those in the music school must take courses that fulfill three skill areas:

expository writing, quantitative reasoning, and oral communication. They also have to take classes in six distributional areas: natural science and mathematics; social and behavioral sciences; literature and the arts; historical and philosophical understanding; foreign language, and self-expression through performance and participation (which can involve physical activity, the arts, or participation in a campus extracurricular activity). Students agree that these requirements hardly restrict their college experiences at all. "It's possible to get out of taking subjects you hated in high school and just take classes you're interested in," a junior said.

Meanwhile, DePauw's unusual academic calendar, which includes a monthlong Winter Term in addition to the traditional fall and spring semesters, gives students the option of having adventurous, flexible learning experiences. Since Winter Term projects are graded on a "satisfactory/unsatisfactory" basis, one senior described them as "a lot of fun and not that stressful." Students can choose among dozens of short, on-campus courses ranging from EMT certification to wildlife management to campanology (the history and practice of bell ringing). They can also study at another college, do research, take an internship to build up their professional experience, or go on special study projects in different countries. One sophomore said she traveled to Morocco on a study trip just to tour the country and learn about its cultural offerings.

Yet another academic opportunity offered by DePauw is the set of five programs of distinction, which allow top students to experience "enhanced study." Students can apply to become Honor Scholars, Management Fellows, Media Fellows, Science Research Fellows or Information Technology Associates. Each program comes with its own set of benefits and hands-on experiences: while Management Fellows can enroll in special seminars and take paid semester-long internships during their junior year, Science Research Fellows are able to receive graduate-level science research opportunities.

Inside the classroom, the learning environment is both intimate and challenging. A sophomore said she had never been in a class larger than 50 people, and average class sizes hover around 15, according to students. Although the intimate, personal setting does ensure that no student slips through the cracks—"I'm afraid of sleeping in class or skipping class because my professor actually knows me," a freshman said—students said they enjoy the personal bonds they develop with professors, who tend to be "dynamic" and liberal-leaning. In addition to high-quality teaching and mentoring, professors at DePauw will also invite students over for dinner or ask students to babysit, students said. All in all, it makes for fairly demanding academic work: classes at DePauw are challenging but not impossible.

DePauw's focus on academics is complemented by its state-of-the-art campus technology; the campus is known for being one of the most "connected" and "wireless" in the country. Professors can hold online office hours and give out exams and homework online, and the campus boasts of a comprehensive wireless Internet. To ensure that students can take advantage of the campus's technology, all freshmen are required to bring laptops to DePauw.

It's (Almost) All Greek to Me

Almost three-quarters of DePauw students are involved in the University's large, active Greek life scene, which dominates DePauw social life and makes for a unique party scene. With 14 fraternities and 11 sororities, including two of the oldest fraternity chapters in the country, it's "rush or be rushed," as one sophomore put it: even the minority of students who decide not to join a fraternity or sorority end up having a large circle of Greek friends and often attend parties in Greek houses. But the Greek scene is far from intimidating. Because so many students rush, "It's really easy to get into a fraternity or sorority if you want to," a senior said, adding that the Greek system is not competitive at all. Instead, it provides many traditions, great housing, and a plentiful, fun party scene. Although Greek parties do involve "a lot of drinking," students say no one is pressured to drink at DePauw.

However, some pressure still exists to join the Greek scene because so many students rush, and "independents," as students who choose not to join fraternities or sororities are called, sometimes feel ostracized. A senior said he had to work harder to meet new people and establish connections at first because he chose not to rush. Several students, both Greek and independent, criticized the Greek party scene, saying parties on campus are "hot, crowded, drunken messes that get old after sophomore year." On-campus parties are limited to the Greek houses, although organizations and the University itself often organize events such as concerts and movie screenings.

Upperclassmen often skip the Greek party scene altogether in favor of Greencastle, the surrounding town, which has several bars that are popular with both townies and college students—favorite haunts include the Duck, Topper's, and Third Degree. One bar, Moore's, even features karaoke. "You can actually hear yourself talk and you don't have to drink that much in bars, but at the frats, everyone drinks a lot," a senior said. Other than the bars, however, Greencastle has little entertainment to offer, students say; it is a small, "pretty dull" rural town. Still, students frequent Marvin's, a classic American diner that stays open later than most other Greencastle restaurants and also employs students. Marvin's special garlic cheeseburger, or "GCB," has even become part of campus culture. Nearby Indianapolis, Indiana's largest city, is a popular destination for short road trips, since many students have cars and "Indy" is only an hour away from Greencastle.

Greencastle may lack the excitement of a big city, but it is certainly safe, and features a small-town atmosphere with typical Midwestern picturesque scenery. A freshman said he felt "completely safe" at DePauw—and added that "Wherever I leave it, my stuff is completely safe too." Students regularly walk around at night and usually leave their doors unlocked. Meanwhile, students take advantage of Greencastle's "peaceful, green, and pretty" Bowman Park to just hang out and relax. The campus itself is full of greenery and attractive, classic brick buildings, such as East College, which is the oldest building at DePauw and is listed on the National Register of Historic Places.

Living on campus is required for all four years, so students live in one of eleven residence halls, with their fraternities or sororities, or in University-owned apartments. As freshmen, students all live in dorms, which usually feature coed floors and communal bathrooms as well as "small but nice and well-kept" rooms. Upperclassmen can continue to live in the dorms, move into Greek "mansions," or enter an apartment lottery for juniors and seniors. The apartments are furnished, cost about the same as living in the residential halls, and do not require their inhabitants to be on the University meal plan. Although a junior said DePauw's campus dining "isn't terrible," students agree that eating in fraternity or sorority houses or off campus in Greencastle offers better quality and more variety.

A Bell Worth Fighting For

DePauw varsity teams compete in NCAA Division III, and its women's golf, softball, and basketball teams have been especially successful in recent years. The women's basketball team has won several conference championships and one Division III national title. Still, DePauw games are not especially well-attended; students say they rarely have enough time in their busy schedules to go to games. But many students participate in intramural sports, which "are fun and keep us fit, but aren't too big of a time commitment," a sophomore said.

> "DePauw really emphasizes putting yourself out there, getting involved, and getting everything out of the time you have in college."

The one reliably popular game at DePauw is the Monon Bell Classic—simply known as "the Game"—in which the DePauw Tigers take on the rival Wabash College in football. One of the nation's oldest college football rivalries, the Game regularly attracts many current students as well as alumni, who will "pay through the nose" to get seats, according to a junior. Since the two schools are only 27 miles apart, many of the players and students on both sides are friends, relatives, or former classmates, making the Game even more heated. The teams battle for the Monon Bell trophy, a 300-pound locomotive bell that was first introduced in 1932—to keep Wabash students from stealing it when DePauw wins the trophy, the University seals the bell in a glass case.

Fun Traditions and an Easygoing Atmosphere Await

Students say DePauw's student body tends to be from the Midwest, especially Indiana, and moderate to conservative-leaning, with few minority students. However, DePauw's atmosphere is anything but dull and homogenous. Not only are the students friendly and outgoing, they also eagerly participate in a rich variety of traditions, from Boulder Run to an annual bike race in late April to a game known as "campus golf." In Boulder Run, students streak from their dorms to the Columbia Boulder, a campus landmark, while in campus golf, students dress in traditional golf attire and use golf clubs to hit tennis balls around campus courses. Although there are no actual holes, students attempt to hit their balls against specific targets while walking around student-designed unofficial golf courses.

Not only are DePauw students active in campus life, they are also generally easygoing and accepting, creating a casual, pleasant atmosphere. At DePauw, a junior said, "Everyone is definitely different, but most people still get along and manage to have a good time and get a good education at the same time."—*Vivian Yee*

FYI

If you come to DePauw, you'd better bring "a car and golf clothes for campus golf!"

What is the typical weekend schedule? "Friday is the day to hang out and go party-hopping at the frat houses or the bars; you still party on Saturday, but it's a little more laid-back. On Sunday, study, do work and hang out."

If I could change one thing about DePauw, I'd "add more minority students and more out-of-state students."

Three things every student at DePauw should do before graduating are "take a road trip to Indianapolis, eat a GCB at Marvin's, and rush a fraternity or sorority."

Earlham College

Address: 801 National Road West, Richmond, IN 47374	**Percentage accepted through EA or ED:** 96%	**Graduation Rate 4-year:** 62%
Phone: 765-983-1600	**EA and ED deadline:** 1-Jan	**Graduation Rate 6-year:** 70%
E-mail address: admission@earlham.edu	**Regular Deadline:** 15-Feb	**Percent Undergraduates in On-campus housing:** 87%
Web site URL: www.earlham.edu	**Application Fee:** $30	**Number of official organized extracurricular organizations:** 70
Year Founded: 1847	**Full time Undergraduate enrollment:** 1,200	**3 Most popular majors:** History, Psychology, Economics
Private or Public: Private	**Total enrollment:** 1,097	
Religious Affiliation: Quaker	**Percent Male:** 43%	
Location: Suburban	**Percent Female:** 57%	**Student/Faculty ratio:** 12:1
Number of Applicants: 6,205	**Total Percent Minority or Unreported:** 11%	**Average Class Size:** 14
Percent Accepted: 69%	**Percent African-American:** 7%	**Percent of students going to grad school:** 22%
Percent Accepted who enroll: 27%	**Percent Asian/Pacific Islander:** 2%	**Tuition and Fees:** $28,600
Number of Transfers Accepted each Year: 43	**Percent Hispanic:** 2%	**In-State Tuition and Fees if different:** No difference
Middle 50% SAT range: M: 540–660, Cr: 570–690, Wr: 560–680	**Percent Native-American:** 1%	**Cost for Room and Board:** $6,200
Middle 50% ACT range: 24–29	**Percent International:** 20%	**Percent receiving financial aid out of those who apply:** 90%
Early admission program EA/ED/None: EA and ED	**Percent in-state/out of state:** 31%/69%	
	Percent from Public HS: 68%	**Percent receiving financial aid among all students:** 56%
	Retention Rate: 82%	

Earlham College, located in Richmond, Indiana, is a more than a college. It is a rich community centered on the Quaker ideals of fairness and equality, stimulating students to grow both as individual learners and as active members of society. As one alumnus noted, "The education here is geared toward individual learning, and if you expect to be spoon-fed a degree and then feel accomplished, you'll be sadly mistaken."

From the General Education Program to the May Term

A liberal arts education to its very core, Earlham provides a well-rounded, but also focused, education in which Earlhamites experience small class discussions and one-on-one work with professors. Starting at the very beginning, with the small Freshman Seminars required of every incoming student, Earlham courses encourage students to challenge themselves and how they think, act, and behave. This year's Fall Semester Seminar, for example, starts with the question "how shall we live?" and ties together both the Quaker philosophy and the Earlham community in a discussion on how to espouse the values that one endorses. Moving on from the Earlham Seminars, students must complete the General Education Program in which they must demonstrate proficiency in four basic categories: the Natural Sciences, the Social Sciences, the Humanities, and the Fine Arts. Whether taking chemistry or an English class, students report that professors are incredibly approachable and are always at hand to answer questions that students may have. In addition to these academic offerings, Earlhamites also have the opportunity to study in what they refer to as May Term—a period of time during which students can take on-campus or off-campus classes taught in an "intense" and "innovative" style. A staple of the Earlham education is its focus on international opportunities as well as the diversity that comes from the large proportion (20%) of international students. With many study abroad options in places as far as Nicaragua, Tanzania, and Japan, Earlhamites take on the globe and learn how to be true global citizens both within the college campus and outside.

From ESG to Dance Alloy

With the rich academic life at Earlham comes also a vibrant experience outside of the classroom—with its NCAA Division III athletics and its high student participation in leadership positions, Earlhamites feel that they truly have control over their own collegiate experience. Students can be a part of the Earlham Student Government, affectionately referred to as ESG, and through this organization make direct connections with the university government and have a profound

effect on the school's administrative policies. With many extracurricular options, Earlhamites can choose to participate in anything ranging from the "Society of Physics Students" to "Dance Alloy," a performance group that mixes together dances from all kinds of backgrounds, to anything in between. In addition to these extracurricular activities, students can also be involved in a large number of cultural, ethnic, and religious groups that are not only student organizations but also student support groups.

Although Earlham is a dry campus, students agree that there are always ways to have fun—whether that involves alcohol or not—through on-campus performances, activities, and festivities. In fact, students report a preference to stay on campus rather than leave for the weekend, citing "campus cohesion" and the "quirky theme parties" as major weekend draws. This idiosyncratic approach to partying and social life represents the adventurous side of the Earlham student body and showcases their creativity for all aspects of their lives.

And, of Course, What You've Really Been Waiting for . . .

Housing! Divided into First Year Residence Halls and Residence Halls, students cite the residential experience as one of the major reasons for the tightly woven community evident in the Earlham student body. As one recent alumnus stated, "As mushy as it is to say, we have a wonderful campus community."

> "As mushy as it is to say, we have a wonderful campus community."

Clearly Earlhamites are part of a closely-knit community based on the Quaker tradition as well as on the challenge to question oneself and grow from this experience. It is no doubt that students are "constantly engaged" and, as one alumnus stated, "I am challenged in my assumptions and beliefs almost everywhere I go."—*Astrid Pacini*

FYI

If you come to Earlham, you'd better bring a "sense of independence and willingness to find things out for yourself."

What is the typical weekend schedule? "A concert, dirt-cheap beer, a theme party, reading, and papers."

Three things every student at Earlham should do before graduating are "go off campus for a semester, take a random class outside of your major and interest area, and serve on Earlham Student Government in some way."

Indiana University / Bloomington

Address: 300 North Jordan Avenue, Bloomington, IN 47405-1106
Phone: 812-855-0661
E-mail address: iuadmit@indiana.edu
Web site URL: www.indiana.edu
Year Founded: 1820
Private or Public: Public
Religious Affiliation: None
Location: Suburban
Number of Applicants: 29,059
Percent Accepted: 70%
Percent Accepted who enroll: 35%
Number Entering: 7,181
Number of Transfers Accepted each Year: 629
Middle 50% SAT range: M: 520–640, CR: 510–620, Wr: Unreported
Middle 50% ACT range: 23–28
Early admission program EA/ED/None: None

Percentage accepted through EA or ED: NA
EA and ED deadline: NA
Regular Deadline: 1-Aprl
Application Fee: $50
Full time Undergraduate enrollment: 30,394
Total enrollment: 31,626
Percent Male: 49%
Percent Female: 51%
Total Percent Minority or Unreported: 8%
Percent African-American: 4%
Percent Asian/Pacific Islander: 4%
Percent Hispanic: 2%
Percent Native-American: <1%
Percent International: 5%
Percent in-state/out of state: 67%/33%
Percent from Public HS: Unreported
Retention Rate: 89%
Graduation Rate 4-year: 50%

Graduation Rate 6-year: 71%
Percent Undergraduates in On-campus housing: 36%
Number of official organized extracurricular organizations: 300
3 Most popular majors: Business/Commerce, Communication, Journalism
Student/Faculty ratio: 18:1
Average Class Size: Unreported
Percent of students going to grad school: Unreported
Tuition and Fees: $12,778
In-State Tuition and Fees if different: $3,196
Cost for Room and Board: $5,714
Percent receiving financial aid out of those who apply: 79%
Percent receiving financial aid among all students: 71%

Bloomington, Indiana, is the quintessential college town. The only unusual thing about it is that the college it surrounds has almost 32,000 total students. IU may seem like the typical big state school, but its students say that it's much more than that. It has a Midwestern warmth that brings the large campus together as a community and, despite the size, IU students are connected in school spirit and true friendliness. With unique academic programs and endless opportunities to get involved, IU is full of motivated students who want to make the most of their college experience inside the classroom and beyond.

Inside IU Academics

If reading about a big state school conjures the image of huge auditoriums seating 5,000 people and professors who probably have no idea who half the students are, fear not, say students. "My first semester was full of interactions with each of my professors on an individual basis, and I had classes ranging from 20 students to 300." The range of class sizes is normal for this University, where flexibility in the educational program is key. One junior said, "The core education differs for every major, which means I never have to take math again!" The ability to take classes that interest students on a personal level is a trademark of the Indiana education. IU encourages students to enter under the "exploratory" option, which allows them to fully experiment with a broad range of classes before settling on a major. One student said, "I think this keeps people loving school; education should be about pursuing your passions, not about a random guess as to what profession you will have at the age of forty." This focus on the individual and the awareness that each student is different sets IU apart.

With the same philosophy of exploration and a broad educational spectrum, IU offers some unique major programs that many students enjoy immensely. LAMP is the Liberal Arts and Management Program, which allows a student to double-major in business and liberal arts. Students say that this program consistently gets rave reviews for its creative seminars and flexible approach to learning. One student explained the appeal of the program in terms of the students themselves: "The business school at IU, Kelley, is very prestigious but often students get frustrated with the thought of giving up liberal arts classes for the sake of a successful future. The clear understanding that students have more than just one interest comes through strongly with this program." Similarly, a minor in LESA, the Leadership, Ethics, and Social Action program, gives students the opportunity to explore a variety of fields while still having some direction.

> "Everyone finds something to do here. People can sit in their rooms and play Halo, but there's also a club for that."

The prestige of the Kelley School of Business, the sociology department, and the Jacob School of Music draw students to IU. But students say that what makes the academic environment truly special is the high caliber and approachability of the professors. One student said, "I think IU is unique because the professors are all well-known scholars with impressive backgrounds, yet they are down to earth and really love to teach." Although students admit that it "takes individual effort" to get to know professors in such a large environment, they also say that "IU across the board makes it easy to get one-on-one attention."

Ancient Greece

With 45 fraternities and sororities to choose from, many students at IU do decide to go through the rush process. Although officially only about 17 percent of students are involved in Greek life, students say that the campus undeniably feels the Greek presence. While one student said, "You're not missing out if you're not in a frat," he also commented that frats "bring the campus together." Because on-campus housing almost exclusively contains freshmen, upperclassmen need other places to go. Students say that there is "good housing around campus," but one student also mentioned that this is one reason to go Greek. Most people who join a fraternity or sorority end up living in the frat or sorority house, which are governed by the school even though they are not technically located on campus.

Saturday Night Fever

Fraternities and sororities clearly preside over partying, but one student asserted that "IU is too large to have a dominant social scene. There is truly a niche for everyone." Still, weekends on campus do revolve around drinking for most students. There are six bars within walking distance of central campus, and upperclassmen tend to center their partying on those. Underclassmen are "less likely to have the means to get into the bars, so they party at the frats or go to dorm and house parties." Regardless of how people decide to let loose, one student pointed out that "People hardly ever leave campus because we all want to be with the family we've formed at school." Cars are allowed, but students agree that they are more of a hassle than anything, since "IU tickets more than the entire city of Cincinnati." With downtown Bloomington only "ten steps away" from campus, students don't need to go far to find entertainment. One student summed up the weekend experience with the statement, "People here really know how to party."

On Campus at IU

"The campus as a whole is very kind and friendly," one junior said, while a freshman agreed, "IU has such a friendly campus!" This extends to the wide range of political views that comes from a fairly equal number of liberals and conservatives on campus. Both parties are "very vocal," students say, and it "makes for great debates in political science classes!" The involvement in politics is only one way in which students can get involved. One student said, "Sports are huge here, especially the basketball team, which has been ranked in the top twenty-five." The same student also said that there are many opportunities for club and intramural sports for those not quite of the varsity caliber. For those more musically inclined, the a cappella scene is prominent, with the all-male Straight No Chaser and the women's group Ladies First. Even if those particular activities don't sound particularly exciting, "Everyone finds something to do here. People can sit in their rooms and play Halo, but there's also a club for that." Another student said, "It's impossible not to get involved." IU recognizes that, just as students have more than one interest in the classroom, their extracurricular passions are varied. As such, the school makes it possible to explore many different areas, from club sports to a cappella and everything in between. "Anything you want to do, there's a way to do it."

IU in Focus

"It's fun here all the time—there's always something to do." This sense that opportunities are limitless comes through in the academics, the extracurriculars, and in the students themselves. The school creates an environment in which students are not only allowed but also positively encouraged to explore a diverse curriculum and take advantage of all the resources of a large university. IU recognizes that every student is different, and as a result the school is set up so that each person has the chance to get what he or she wants and needs out of the college experience. As one student put it, "Investigate IU! There's a lot more beneath the surface."—*Hannah Jacobson*

FYI

If you come to IU, you'd better bring "a fake ID."

What's the typical weekend schedule? "Thursday night: go out, Friday night: go out, Saturday night: go out, and Sunday do homework."

If I could change one thing about IU, I'd "make it warm all year round."

Three things every student at IU should do before graduating are "swim in Showalter Fountain, see an IU basketball game, and go to a Straight No Chaser concert!"

Purdue University

Address: 475 Stadium Mall Drive, West Lafayette, IN 47907

Phone: 765-494-1776

E-mail address: admissions@purdue.edu

Web site URL: www.purdue.edu

Year Founded: 1869

Private or Public: Public

Religious Affiliation: None

Location: Suburban

Number of Applicants: 30,707

Percent Accepted: 65%

Percent Accepted who enroll: 32%

Number Entering: 6,459

Number of Transfers Accepted each Year: Unreported

Middle 50% SAT range: M: 540–680, CR: 500–610, Wr: 490–610

Middle 50% ACT range: 23–29

Early admission program EA/ED/None: None

Percentage accepted through EA or ED: NA

EA and ED deadline: NA

Regular Deadline: 1-Mar

Application Fee: $50

Full time Undergraduate enrollment: 29,429

Total enrollment: 30,836

Percent Male: 58%

Percent Female: 42%

Total Percent Minority or Unreported: 26%

Percent African-American: 3%

Percent Asian/Pacific Islander: 5%

Percent Hispanic: 3%

Percent Native-American: <1%

Percent International: 11%

Percent in-state/out of state: 71%/29%

Percent from Public HS: Unreported

Retention Rate: 89%

Graduation Rate 4-year: 40%

Graduation Rate 6-year: 71%

Percent Undergraduates in On-campus housing: Unreported

Number of official organized extracurricular organizations: 900

3 Most popular majors: Mechanical Engineering, Management, Computer and Mechanical Engineering

Student/Faculty ratio: 13:1

Average Class Size: 25

Percent of students going to grad school: Unreported

Tuition and Fees: $27,061

In-State Tuition and Fees if different: $8,893

Cost for Room and Board: $9,896

Percent receiving financial aid out of those who apply: Unreported

Percent receiving financial aid among all students: 95%

Purdue University is known for being a leading engineering and agriculture school in the U.S. So, it's no surprise that 23 of Purdue's alumni have become (or are in the process of becoming) astronauts. The University is home to a little under 30,000 undergraduates who in addition to their excellent academics, are legacies of a long tradition in athletic dominance.

If You Want to be an Astronaut . . .

Originally founded to instruct men and women to lead productive and utilitarian careers, Purdue University remains true to its roots with its renowned engineering, aerospace and physics departments. However, the University also has strong programs in the pharmaceutical sciences, veterinary medicine and computer science.

Despite Purdue's acclaim in the sciences, the university also has reputable humanity and social science departments. One of the most prominent is the Krannert School of Management, whose undergraduate program was recently ranked #19 by the *U.S. News & World Report*. Regardless of the breadth of educational opportunities, almost a fifth of undergraduates major in engineering.

Students can register in a plethora of subjects. The university offers courses in over 210 major areas of study and students may choose to enroll in the Undergraduate Studies Program which permits undergraduates to try out the options available at Purdue for up to four semesters before selecting a major. Notwithstanding, some of the colleges, such as the College of Engineering, significantly limit the students' ability to explore a variety of different subjects due to vigorous predetermined academic curricula.

The alma mater of 23 astronauts, Purdue has excellent aviation and aerospace departments. As a matter of fact, because of the emphasis on these subjects, the campus has an airport. Used primarily by the aviation technology department, the airport enables aerospace engineering students to test their constructions while at the same time offers them the option of obtaining their own flight licenses.

A unique opportunity offered by the same department is Design/Build/Fly. Admitted students attend to aeronautical projects in teams to construct their own aircraft and enter them in the Design/Build/Fly competition held by the American Institute of Aeronautics and Astronautics. One aeronautical engineering student said of the program, "Purdue gives me the tools needed to create a better future, helping me fulfill not only my dreams but also to encourage others to do so."

Further emphasis on creative approaches on research is instigated by the university's "Discovery Park" which is essentially a multidisciplinary research park that provides students with useful practical work experience.

Purdue's nearly 30,000 undergraduates comprise the second largest student body in Indiana. This fact more or less could dictate large classes. Most students interviewed have said that they are not daunted by this fact, as there is extensive use of technological aids, which span from microphones to effective screen placements in lecture halls. Although lectures are normally larger, class size averages around 24 students and size typically decreases for more advanced and specialized courses.

Although the university uses curves, getting A's can be difficult. According to a freshman, "[grades] depend on the major but C-B are normal." Although all of Purdue's courses are considered challenging, math and science courses are generally considered harder than humanities courses.

Where Greeks Don't Drink

As Purdue is a state school, a significant percentage of the undergraduates are Indiana residents. This statistic significantly influences campus social life as many locals choose to leave campus on weekends to visit their families—which triggers a remarkable decrease of the campus population. This fact also denotes that a notable percentage of students have cars, something that expands the undergrads outing possibilities as it permits them to visit large nearby metropolises such as Indianapolis and Chicago more easily.

Greek life is prominent and influential on campus. Statistics estimate that approximately 5,000 students are members of fraternities or sororities, which amounts to about 17% of the student body. Many Greek organizations provide housing and meal services and involve their members in various ways, from intramural athletic competitions to community service activities. The organizations host various social functions which often enable members to interact with other campus organizations. Most Greeks also abide by Purdue's very strict undergraduate no-alcohol policy, as organizations that refuse to do so are severely penalized by the university.

Different policies have been enforced, and many Greek organizations have been placed on suspension in the past as a result of alcohol abuse. Alcohol abuse is treated as a serious threat to student health and so the university tries to enforce alcohol education throughout the year in order to avoid any unwelcome situations.

On weekends, many students that remain

on campus choose to go out to bars or cafés. Widely attended bars include Harry's Chocolate Café and Where Else? Harry's Chocolate Café, although originally a soda shop, is now a favorite bar. Alternatively, students might choose to casually hang out in dorms.

Popular university-wide events include Homecoming and Halloween. During Homecoming, students can attend the Boilermaker Night Train Parade—which features marching band displays and a march to the stadium for the Homecoming football game. Football is important for what is one of Purdue's most distinct traditions, the "Breakfast Club." While this is not aimed for underclassmen due to the potential for alcohol abuse, participating students dress up in costumes before home games. The students, who wake up at 6 am to attend, go to local bars and drink before going to the game.

X-Tra Sporty

An institution that has three school mascots is bound to have strong school spirit and the athletic merit to match up to it.

Out of the four Purdue mascots, the "Boilermaker Special," a Victorian-era railroad locomotive, is the only official university mascot. The train design symbolizes the strength of the university's engineering programs. There have been various versions of the mascot in the past, the current one being the "Boilermaker Special V." The locomotive is maintained by the student members of the Purdue Reamer Club, and is available for free rides on Fridays and can be rented for private events. A smaller version of the mascot, the Boilermaker Special VI, is affectionately known as the X-Tra Special. This mascot often appears in home games and some indoor functions—places where the Boilermaker Special V cannot go to due to its massive size.

The other two mascots are an example of, albeit fictional, Purdue potential legacies. Purdue Pete, a mascot that first appeared in the '60s, is portrayed to be an ardent Boilermaker that holds a hammer in one hand and always sports a hard hat. His younger brother, Rowdy, aspires that one day he too will become a Boilermaker.

A founding member of the Big Ten Conference, the oldest Division I athletic conference in the U.S., Purdue athletics are first-rate. Currently, the university has 18 Division I/I-A teams and its football and basketball are among the best in the nation. The men's and women's basketball teams have won more Big Ten Championships than any other university and Purdue is traditionally

called the "Cradle of Quarterbacks" as it has produced a large number of NFL stars.

There is a wide variety of sports and this enables students to take part in those that suit them the most. In addition to traditional ones such as tennis, swimming and—of course—football, there are some more unconventional sports students can compete in such as Quidditch and Ultimate Frisbee.

The university owns a wide range of athletic amenities that are at the students' disposal. Currently, Purdue is undertaking a multimillion-dollar renovation and expansion of RSC, the Purdue Student Fitness and Wellness Center. Additionally, there are many intramural sports where students can participate for fun that do not require the skills, experience or commitment that varsity sports do.

Other than the individual gym resources at the RSC like weights and treadmills, the center offers an abundance of group courses. Group Exercise, or "Group X," offers a multitude of programs students can choose from ranging from cardio workouts and aqua aerobics to Zumba— a workout program that fuses Latin and international music and accompanies it with dance. "Learn to Play" is another fitness program offered by the university that fosters progressive learning where classes gradually expand in their complexity and require increasing acquisition of skills. The university also provides the students with the option to hire instructors for classes outside the complex for an additional fee.

Purdue in the Prairie

While at Purdue you get a feeling of vastness and openness. When walking across the Purdue terrain, you are surrounded by a profusion of trees that are inhabited by squirrels and other small arboreal fauna. In the warmer months, you are in the midst of green brilliance and during the cold winters you are encircled by mountains of snow. The campus is decorated with statues and fountains and you cannot fail to admire the consistency of the red brick layout.

The majority of the campus is built in classic red brick. Exceptions to this pattern are observed in Rawls Hall and the Krannert Building which are primarily made out of limestone. Another building with significantly reduced use of red brick in its structure is the Neil Armstrong Hall of Engineering, that is primarily made out of glass although it too uses red brick in parts of the structure. The building was dedicated/completed in 2007 and on the front porch has a statue of the astronaut. It appears that although engineering students love the building, they come to significantly dislike it as soon as they "have an all-nighter in it" said an engineering student. The Hall among other things features a replica of the Apollo 1 command module which hangs from the ceiling of the building's atrium.

Another structure favored by the students is the Steven C. Beering Hall of Liberal Arts and Education which is a preferred place for study of many students across the disciplines, although it primarily houses several departments of Purdue's College of Liberal Arts and Purdue's School of Education.

Many students opt for dorm housing as the prices are "reasonable" said a freshman, although this is mostly the case with underclassmen. Housing prices depend on room size, occupancy and amenities. Some dorms are considered to be better than others; First Street Towers, a hall that first opened in July 2009, is considered to be among the nicest and most expensive ones. Others, as for example Earhart Hall which is favored by engineering students, have their own character and often consist of different "learning communities."

Although the university does not have its own private transit, students can use City-Bus which is operated by the municipality free of charge as it is subsidized by the university. There are specific routes which are designed for the students' use and stop at most of the widely used campus buildings. CityBus is also used by locals.

> **"Purdue gives me the tools needed to create a better future, helping me fulfill not only my dreams but also to encourage others to do so."**

The city of West Lafayette and the university are heavily interdependent. West Lafayette is primarily a university city so most businesses thrive thanks to the university, a fact that leads to citywide Purdue Pride. According to a student, you can see people wearing Purdue apparel in many off-campus locations, even if these people are not officially affiliated with the university.

Diversity Overload

Purdue is dominated by students who succeed in various fields. While it's predominately an agricultural and engineering school, it also has strong programs in the humanities and the social sciences. The university has vast resources for all of its students which range from a brand-new Fitness Center to an airport. The balance of academics, social activities and athletics make Purdue a place where everyone can find something they are passionate about.
—*Katerina Karatzia*

FYI
If you come to Purdue, you'd better bring "Warm gear and boots."
If you come to Purdue, you'd better leave "your Indiana University apparel" behind.
The biggest college-wide tradition/event at Purdue is "becom[e] an astronaut after graduation."

Rose-Hulman Institute of Technology

Address: 5500 Wabash Avenue, Terre Haute, IN 47803
Phone: 812-877-8213
E-mail address: admissions@rose-hulman.edu
Web site URL: www.rose-hulman.edu
Year Founded: 1874
Private or Public: Private
Religious Affiliation: None
Location: Rural
Number of Applicants: 4,298
Percent Accepted: 62%
Percent Accepted who enroll: 19%
Number Entering: 506
Number of Transfers Accepted each Year: 40
Middle 50% SAT range: M: 630–720, CR: 550–670, Wr: 530–640
Middle 50% ACT range: 27–32
Early admission program EA/ED/None: None

Percentage accepted through EA or ED: NA
EA and ED deadline: NA
Regular Deadline: 1-Mar
Application Fee: $40
Full time Undergraduate enrollment: 1,887
Total enrollment: 1,895
Percent Male: 79%
Percent Female: 21%
Total Percent Minority or Unreported: 19%
Percent African-American: 2%
Percent Asian/Pacific Islander: 3%
Percent Hispanic: 3%
Percent Native-American: <1%
Percent International: 6%
Percent in-state/out of state: Unreported
Percent from Public HS: Unreported
Retention Rate: Unreported
Graduation Rate 4-year: 72%

Graduation Rate 6-year: 81%
Percent Undergraduates in On-campus housing: Unreported
Number of official organized extracurricular organizations: 97
3 Most popular majors: Biomedical Engineering, Chemical Engineering, Mechanical Engineering
Student/Faculty ratio: 12:1
Average Class Size: 25
Percent of students going to grad school: 20%
Tuition and Fees: $37,197
In-State Tuition and Fees if different: No difference
Cost for Room and Board: $10,445
Percent receiving financial aid out of those who apply: 98%
Percent receiving financial aid among all students: 98%

I f you are looking for a top-notch science education, a close community of students, and enviable job opportunities post-graduation, Rose-Hulman Institute of Technology may be for you.

All About Engineering

A private college with only 2,000 students, Rose Hulman features a tight-knit atmosphere where everyone knows each other. A junior said the thing she likes most about Rose is that the students are willing to help each other and are friendly. She added that faculty members are especially available to help students, thanks to an open door policy that allows students to come to their office and ask questions any time. Rose-Hulman also ensures that all of its classes are taught by professors with PhDs, resulting in outstanding quality of teaching. "Rose has got a good reputation in the industry," a student said. "It's easy to get a job after graduation."

Although distributional requirements ensure that all students take classes in the humanities, Rose-Hulman is "basically an engineering school"—little surprise given that the *US News and World Report* ranks it the best undergraduate engineering school where a doctorate is not offered. Indeed, 90 percent of students major in an engineering discipline. The curricula are also highly specialized, and a student said that there is a lot of time for classes outside of one's major. Still, students say some of the best courses are in non-engineering fields, and one of the most popular courses is World Geography. Rose-Hulman makes it a point to emphasize the role of the liberal arts in a liberal engineering education.

Not Many Girls, But Lots of Free Food

Though engineering students may have a reputation for heavy workloads and limited social lives, one junior said that they always find opportunities to socialize, though he added that its location in the small city of Terre Haute and the lack of girls limit the social experience. Another student added that girls from other schools like St. Mary of the Woods help "fill the vacuum" and turn up at parties.

Rose-Hulman's various outreach programs and student publications reflect its tilt toward the sciences. The quarterly journal *Cryptologia*, based out of the United States Military Academy and focusing on issues in cryptology, was founded at Rose-Hulman in 1977. Another reputable publication is the Rose-Hulman Undergraduate Mathematics Journal, which invites submissions by undergraduates from all institutions.

> "Rose has got a good reputation in the industry. It's easy to get a job after graduation."

And then there is the food. There is a lot of free food through the year, and one student said it is one of the biggest of perks of coming to Rose-Hulman. Student cooperatives and even academic departments organize cookouts through the year, attracting many undergraduates. As for the normal daily meal plan, the university offers dining services at six locations on campus. The breakfast served at the dining halls, which sometimes includes curly fries and egg burritos, is especially popular among students.

Dear Old Rose
Having been around for 140 years, the institution has come to have a number of traditions associated with it. Many of these are associated with the Fightin'

Engineers—Rose-Hulman's athletics teams. There is Rosie the elephant, the mascot for the Engineers, often seen in the form of a costumed student on the field during games involving the school. Homecoming sees a flurry of activity, especially the homecoming bonfire, put together by the freshmen with some assistance from upperclassmen. And then there's the elusive official Rose-Hulman ring, which can only rest upon the finger of seniors. The school spirit of this institution is perhaps best encapsulated by the first two lines of the school song, Dear Old Rose: "Dear Old Rose, the sweetest flower that grows; here's to your colors rose and white. Here's to the ones who've kept them bright."

The school touts itself as the combination of a rigorous scientific education and a thriving on-campus life. For instance, it boasts of an extensive art collection, including 130 pieces of 19th-century British watercolors. But, on the other hand, the main thrust of the college will always focus on the fact that, as one student pointed out, it ranks among the top 20 colleges in terms of starting salaries of graduates.

Either way, both sound like a good deal for students, prospective and current. Given that science education is being heralded as the "next big thing" for colleges, Rose-Hulman certainly seems to be well poised to attract students with its academic offerings. While students interested in the humanities and social sciences usually won't make it their top choice, those of the slightest scientific persuasion will find its clubs, journals and scientific opportunities appealing.—*Dhruv Chand Aggarwal*

FYI
1. Coming to Rose Hulman, you should leave behind . . . your laziness
2. The most apt adjectives for people at Rose Hulman is . . . smart, hard-working and ambitious
3. The best food that Rose Hulman's dining manages is . . . curly fries and egg burritos in the morning.

Saint Mary's College

Address: Le Mans Hall, Notre Dame, IN 46556

Phone: 574-284-4587

E-mail address: admission@saintmarys.edu

Web site URL: www .saintmarys.edu

Year Founded: 1844

Private or Public: Private

Religious Affiliation: Roman Catholic

Location: Suburban

Number of Applicants: 1,387

Percent Accepted: 61%

Percent Accepted who enroll: 30%

Number Entering: 333

Number of Transfers Accepted each Year: 47

Middle 50% SAT range: M: 500–600 CR: 480–600 Wr: 490–610

Middle 50% ACT range: 22–28

Early admission program EA/ED/None: ED

Percentage accepted through EA or ED: 90%

EA and ED deadline: 15-Nov

Regular Deadline: None/ Priority Application deadline: 1-Mar

Application Fee: Regular fee: $30; Online: No application fee

Full time Undergraduate enrollment: 1,539

Total enrollment: 1,555

Percent Male: 0%

Percent Female: 100%

Total Percent Minority or Unreported: 17%

Percent African-American: 2%

Percent Asian/Pacific Islander: 2%

Percent Hispanic: 8%

Percent Native-American: <1%

Percent International: 1%

Percent in-state/out of state: 29%/71%

Percent from Public HS: 55%

Retention Rate: 85%

Graduation Rate 4-year: 70%

Graduation Rate 6-year: Unreported

Percent Undergraduates in On-campus housing: 84%

Number of official organized extracurricular organizations: 70

3 Most popular majors: Communication Studies/Speech, Communication and Rhetoric, Elementary Education and Teaching

Student/Faculty ratio: 10:1

Average Class Size: 15

Percent of students going to grad school: 30%

Tuition and Fees: $31,300

In-State Tuition and Fees if different: No difference

Cost for Room and Board: $9,800

Percent receiving financial aid out of those who apply: 96%

Percent receiving financial aid among all students: 94%

With its unique curriculum and strong sense of community, Saint Mary's College is a hidden gem nestled in Notre Dame, Indiana. Though some applicants may be intimidated by the all-female environment, the emphasis on individual growth and progress may encourage you to take a second glance at this college. Bound together by school spirit and spirituality, Saint Mary's students continue a strong tradition of scholarship and study abroad.

Sophia Scholars

A tight-knit community, Saint Mary's is known for its intellectually curious "belles" who pursue diverse majors and interests. The Saint Mary's entering Class of 2016 were the first to embrace a new curriculum, the Sophia Program, which helps integrate curriculum requirements with selected majors and minors. Drawn from the Greek word for wisdom, the Sophia program replaces the General Education courses that students were previously required to take. While the General Education program stressed writing and foreign language proficiency, the Sophia Program emphasizes "learning outcomes" (LO), or educational goals in the form of overarching values such as understanding and responsibility.

As the program unfolds, the Class of 2016 take courses related to LO-1, or Knowledge Acquisition and Integration of Learning. The crux of LO-1 is a focus on accepting diversity, "the multifaceted nature of religion and the Catholic tradition," and providing an interdisciplinary understanding of "the ways that people interpret and act in the world," according to the Saint Mary's Bulletin. Over the coming years courses that relate to LO-2, Cognitive and Communicative Skills, and LO-3, Intercultural Competence and Social Responsibility, will be added to the Sophia curriculum.

Freshmen found that the Sophia curriculum added a sense of coherence to their general requirements courses, unifying the disparate subjects under an overarching theme. "Though each class had its own lectures and topics, I felt I had a larger learning goal outside of my classes because of Sophia," said one student. The integration of spiritual and academic goals within the curriculum is indicative of the nurturing environment, which students said inspired them to grow emotionally and intellectually. As an example of the important role that academics play in student life, one student cited the rush to reach the library early during finals week and midterms. Students, who usually study in the Cushwa-Leighton Library, arrive early to get access to printers or prime study spots.

Belles Beyond the Classroom

Saint Mary's Belles also are encouraged to pursue experiences outside of the classroom through the extensive study abroad program. Around 50 percent of Saint Mary's students participate in some form of study abroad program during their time at college. The college is ranked seventh in the U.S. for the number of undergraduate students studying abroad for an academic year, and twentieth in total undergraduate study abroad participation.

Students at Saint Mary's are offered academic year abroad, summer break and semester break study programs that provide stimulating international experiences. Among the school's recent initiatives is a plan to launch a new summer abroad program in Peru, just one of over 20 locations where Saint Mary's students can enroll in associated programs. Students interested in art history, music appreciation, and classical studies can consider a year aboard in Rome, Italy, while others passionate about African literature, history, and ethnic studies can consider a program in Pietermaritzburg, South Africa. Saint Mary's is one of the few Catholic universities partnered with Blackfriars Hall at Oxford University, which allows students to participate in a unique exchange program.

Summer abroad programs offer the opportunity to pursue a combination of service learning and spirituality outside of the classroom. A trip to Greece, for example, offers students the opportunity to learn about the "Greco-Roman world of the first urban Christians converted by Paul the Apostle," according to the program description. Another opportunity, a trip to Honduras, gives students the chance to immerse themselves in Honduran culture through work in villages and orphanages and trips to nearby Maya ruins.

Students stressed the importance of their study abroad experiences in complementing the environment provided by the challenging classes, and preparing them for new experiences. One student said that her summer trip abroad led her to reconsider her career path. Though she was already passionate about education, she said that after volunteering teaching in an orphanage in Africa, she now hopes to work abroad. One French major said an experience during her study abroad in Dijon, France, inspired her to settle on her major. Beyond helping confirm a passion or interest, another student felt her experience helped her "really mature emotionally, intellectually and spiritually."

The importance of a study abroad experience has also received recognition from the President of Saint Mary's, Carol Ann Mooney, who said, "Today's graduates must be prepared to work and compete with colleagues from around the globe and potentially to spend some portion of their careers living outside of the United States."

An All-Woman's College in the Backyard of Notre Dame

Saint Mary's helps foster independent, empowered belles within an all-woman environment. Being in an all-female environment, said one student, led her to reconsider the stereotypes about women's bodies and encourage fellow students to respect their own bodies. This past year, Saint Mary's launched an initiative to raise awareness about eating disorders on campus. The initiative, titled "Celebrate Your Spiritual gifts, Heart, Abilities, Personality and Experience (SHAPE)," offered the community advice from speakers and nutrition specialists. Students could also participate in confidential screenings.

> "It's great to have a small school environment with the close-knit Saint Mary's community, but still have the feel of a much larger school just across the street."

Though students study in an all-female environment, the Belles are only a stone's throw from Notre Dame University. The relationship between the two schools often emerges in a social setting, as the much larger Notre Dame offers a coeducational social environment.

The administrative relationship between the two schools—in terms of resources and responsibilities—was the subject of debate in the student newspaper. Students at both schools ultimately arrived at the conclusion that both were informed by the other's presence. Saint Mary's recently elected to introduce graduate programs that will be open to men. In January of 2013, the college announced it would introduce three graduate programs, of about 120 students total, which would include some males for the first time in the school's history.

Overall, with its emphasis on a strong curriculum and study abroad, Saint Mary's offers a dynamic environment for driven girls to thrive. The tight-knit school provides a spiritual, emotional, and academic home for its students—while not too far away from the bustling campus of Notre Dame.—*Apsara Iyer*

FYI

If you come to Saint Mary's, you'd better bring "a positive, outgoing attitude."
What's the typical weekend schedule? "Cheer on Notre Dame on football Saturdays, hang out in friends' rooms, study or go to the movies."
Three things students should do before graduating: "play on an intramural dodgeball team, visit the Center for Spirituality and cheer on the Belles at a home game!"

University of Notre Dame

Address: 220 Main Building, Notre Dame, IN 46556
Phone: 574-631-7505
E-mail address: admissions@nd.edu
Web site URL: www.nd.edu
Year Founded: 1842
Private or Public: Private
Religious Affiliation: Roman Catholic
Location: Urban
Number of Applicants: 14,503
Percent Accepted: 29%
Percent Accepted who enroll: 56%
Number Entering: 2,068
Number of Transfers Accepted each Year: unreported
Middle 50% SAT range: M: 670–770, CR: 650–740, Wr: 650–740
Middle 50% ACT range: 31–34

Early admission program EA/ED/None: EA
Percentage accepted through EA or ED: 45%
EA and ED deadline: 1-Nov
Regular Deadline: 31-Dec
Application Fee: $65
Full time Undergraduate enrollment: 8,442
Total enrollment: 11,992
Percent Male: 53%
Percent Female: 47%
Total Percent Minority or Unreported: 28%
Percent African-American: 4%
Percent Asian/Pacific Islander: 6%
Percent Hispanic: 6%
Percent Native-American: 0%
Percent International: 4%
Percent in-state/out of state: 7%/93%
Percent from Public HS: 50%
Retention Rate: Unreported
Graduation Rate 4-year: 96%

Graduation Rate 6-year: Unreported
Percent Undergraduates in On-campus housing: 81%
Number of official organized extracurricular organizations: 265
3 Most popular majors: Business/Marketing, Social Sciences, Foreign Lang. & Lit.
Student/Faculty ratio: Unreported
Average Class Size: 15
Percent of students going to grad school: 31%
Tuition and Fees: $41,417
In-State Tuition and Fees if different: No difference
Cost for Room and Board: $11,388
Percent receiving financial aid out of those who apply: Unreported
Percent receiving financial aid among all students: Unreported

Just to the north of unexciting South Bend, Indiana, is the lush campus of the University of Notre Dame. But the campus is not this university's only selling point: academics, athletics and faith are entwined in an energetic suburban setting,

Notre Dame is justifiably regarded highly in the region and around the country. This regard manifests itself locally in the passionate school spirit that suffuses everything; one senior, soon to graduate, said that "if there's one thing I'll miss when I leave it's just how much everyone loves the place." Whether at Mass or in the 80,000-person capacity football stadium, Notre Dame's just-over 8,442 undergraduates know just how lucky they are to be there.

A Right to Choose

Notre Dame's academic spirit incorporates both depth and breadth, preparing students for all manner of future options. All entering Freshman join the First Year of Studies, a program that allows them to not only take a broad range of arts and science courses, but also to take advantage of an academic advisor who can counsel students about prospective majors and suggest courses to take. In addition to all this, Notre Dame offers academic support for writing, reading and basic mathematics, ensuring students get a good foothold when they begin the college journey. One sophomore said of First Year of Studies that she "would not have had it any other way."

At the conclusion of freshman year, students are confronted with a choice between five undergraduate colleges, in which they will spend their next three years. Each of these colleges focuses on a specific curriculum: the college of arts and letters (the most popular), the college of science, the school of architecture, the college of engineering and the Mendoza College of Business. The choice, naturally, is not easy; one sophomore summarized his choice as "trying to find the best out of a lot of good options." Each college has their own requirements that must be fulfilled in the sophomore year before a major can be declared.

Still, once the challenge of choosing classes has been overcome, students at Notre Dame generally enjoy their classes, which typically have fewer than 40 students. While one junior reported taking an introductory science class with over 200 students, she also said her more recent classes, which had as few as eight students, were "intimate chats with wonderful professors." Others agreed about the quality of professors, who by university requirements need to hold at least four office hours a week to engage with students. These hours can be more productive than class time; one student said that "in office hours the professor would run through the problems as if a personal tutor, while in class [the professor] was a machine." Student-faculty interaction is further enhanced by the free access professors have to the dining halls, allowing productive discussion to take place in and out of the classroom.

And the workload? The consensus among interviewed students was decidedly "manageable," though one senior said that in her time at Notre Dame she had faced several periods with homework that "took more hours than [there were] available in a day." Nevertheless, students entering Notre Dame are aware of the demanding course work, and are ultimately free to choose how much of a challenge to make their education.

An Upright Institution

Notre Dame is at heart a Catholic institution, and few prospective students are unaware of the fact. Over 90 percent of students identify as Christian, with around 80 percent of them being Catholic. The high self-reported figures, however, may not necessarily be reflected in reality. One student described the religious feeling on campus as "definitely there, but it's not overwhelming at all." Unsurprisingly, theology is a requirement for all students, though it need not be Catholic theology.

> "Notre Dame is about commitment—to academics, football, and faith."

Students are assigned dorms when they enter Notre Dame, and are generally expected to remain there all four years, though many move off campus in their senior year. Each has its own distinct identity—a senior still living on campus said each dorm has it's own "reputation, a sort of flavor of life"—and combined with structural features like mascots and hall governments, ensures most students identify strongly with where they live. Moreover, in the absence of Greek life, the closest relationships tend to be formed by the dorm system. A sophomore, who said his best friend at the college was his roommate from freshman year, suggested that while roommates are randomly assigned, "chance is on your side" when it comes to being matched with relatable roommates.

Each dorm has a chapel in which Mass is held every day except Saturday. Given the high attendance rate, some students suggest that faith is another unifying factor on campus, strengthening community values and evoking a feeling of extended family among students.

But Notre Dame's Catholic affiliation affects dorm life beyond individual faith. All dorms are officially single sex and the university enforces a visitation policy, known as "parietals," that specify certain times members of the opposite sex are allowed to visit. These are generally unpopular, and at least one student described them as "inconvenient," though none said it ought to be a deterrent to coming to Notre Dame. And better still, to compensate for the stringency of the policy, all residence halls have 24-hour social spaces in which parietals are not enforced, allowing students to socialize.

On and Off the Field

Notre Dame students are busy on and off the field. Partying—whether at local bars including Corby's, the Linebacker, and the Fever, or on campus—routinely takes place from Thursday to Sunday. While enforcement of ID laws has been getting stricter in recent years, according to students alcohol is still accessible and drinking is by no means a prerequisite for having fun. Indeed, hard alcohol is banned on campus and punishments can be severe.

Throughout the fall, weekends feature rambunctious tailgates for football games involving Notre Dame's team, the Fighting Irish. While its performance in recent years has not matched the team's storied past, almost every student buys season tickets and "the shirt," whose color changes each year, making student supporters instantly recognizable. "It's just an amazing show—both by the boys on the field and us in the stands," one student said when asked to describe a home game. Friday night pep rallies are boisterously attended, with bagpipes played around midnight; on Saturday morning, the campus is "electric" with excitement as everyone with any relationship to the university packs into the stadium, according to one student.

And football is not the only sport big on campus—"you'll find people into pretty much all sports here," one student says. He said virtually all students participate in dorm sports, which can get very serious,

and many students take advantage of the university's excellent training facilities.

Of course, a university of Notre Dame's caliber is not without myriad other extracurricular offerings. Clubs and organizations exist to satisfy almost every taste and interest, and one student was quick to point out that "if something doesn't exist, it isn't difficult to start it up." Theater, community service, and music groups are among the most popular extracurricular activities on campus.

A Tradition—And Loving It

A common complaint is the lack of diversity among the student body. One student suggested that the homogeneity of students arose because of "how traditional Notre Dame is," though he was quick to add that he knew many interesting nonwhite and non-Catholic students and counted many as his friends. There is definitely a conservative slant to things on campus, ranging from politics to social life, but progressivism and other liberal ideologies are not absent from the workings of campus, most students report.

The sense of tradition carries over to the city Notre Dame is situated in, South Bend, Indiana, which features all manner of chains near campus, including J.Crew, Urban Outfitters, Burger King, and Starbucks. "It can be hard to find exciting options after a while," one senior commented, but students generally said they were happy with the university's location in the city and more broadly, as cold as the area might get at times.

And why wouldn't they be happy? The opportunity to learn, grow and have fun at a place so steeped in tradition is something "you realize you'll probably never get again," according to one senior. Another student described the university thus: "Notre Dame is about commitment—to academics, football, and faith." The rewards of this commitment make Notre Dame a university thoroughly worth committing to.—*James Lu*

FYI
If you come to Notre Dame, you'd better bring "Fighting Irish apparel."
What is the typical weekend schedule? "Tailgating, tailgating, tailgating. And of course parties, rest, and a little study slotted in somewhere."
If I could change one thing about Notre Dame, I'd "improve integration with the city."

Valparaiso University

Address: 1700 Chapel Drive, Valparaiso, IN 46383
Phone: 219-464-5000
E-mail address: undergrad.admissions@valpo.edu
Web site URL: www.valpo.edu
Year Founded: 1859
Private or Public: Private
Religious Affiliation: Lutheran
Location: Suburban
Number of Applicants: 2,932
Percent Accepted: 85%
Percent Accepted who enroll: 27%
Number Entering: 692
Number of Transfers Accepted each Year: 304
Middle 50% SAT range: M: 510–620, CR: 490–600, Wr: 480–590
Middle 50% ACT range: 23–29
Early admission program EA/ED/None: None

Percentage accepted through EA or ED: NA
EA and ED deadline: NA
Regular Deadline: Rolling
Application Fee: $0
Full time Undergraduate enrollment: 2,872
Total enrollment: 4,056
Percent Male: 48%
Percent Female: 52%
Total Percent Minority or Unreported: 22%
Percent African-American: 7%
Percent Asian/Pacific Islander: 2%
Percent Hispanic: 2%
Percent Native-American: <1%
Percent International: 3%
Percent in-state/out of state: 39%/61%
Percent from Public HS: Unreported
Retention Rate: 85%
Graduation Rate 4-year: 75%

Graduation Rate 6-year: Unreported
Percent Undergraduates in On-campus housing: 67%
Number of official organized extracurricular organizations: Unreported
3 Most popular majors: Business/Marketing, Social Sciences, Health Professions
Student/Faculty ratio: 13:1
Average Class Size: 17
Percent of students going to grad school: 28%
Tuition and Fees: $31,040
In-State Tuition and Fees if different: No difference
Cost for Room and Board: $8,756
Percent receiving financial aid out of those who apply: 87%
Percent receiving financial aid among all students: 79%

Nestled in the small Midwestern town of Valparaiso, slightly over 4,000 students can be found studying, cheering at a basketball game, or organizing the latest charity extravaganza. Maybe a few freshmen are reconnoitering the "haunted" dorm, or lounging in the new student union Harre Union. It's a typical weekday evening at Valparaiso University, a modest Lutheran college where almost 80 percent of the students are affluent, conservative Caucasians, nearly all united in a common faith and a dedication to hard work and social justice. This spirit of integrity and dedication pervades all of campus life, guiding students both in their studies and in their extracurricular activities.

The Valparaiso Core of Success

All freshmen are required to take the Valparaiso Core, a yearlong interdisciplinary course titled "The Human Experience" that is equivalent to general education requirements at other schools. "The Human Experience" is organized into five units, each a discussion of texts on real-life issues: Creation and Birth, Coming of Age and Education, Citizenship and Service, Love, Work and Vocation, and Life and Death. "It's a really great way to meet other students and gain a solid foundation and wide base of knowledge for the rest of a student's academic experience at Valparaiso," one senior noted.

Those students desiring a more challenging academic environment can choose to apply for "Christ College," Valpo's four-year honors college. Study begins with a two-semester course sequence freshman year called "Texts and Contexts: Traditions of Human Thought," which seeks to stimulate critical reading of, persuasive writing about, and focused debate on great works of literature. Christ College is an opportunity for students to amplify their own potential as well as capitalize on the best that Valparaiso academics can offer. "Christ College has probably been the most valuable experience I have had here: I have grown as an individual and together with my class in ways I never could have conceived as a freshman."

Meteorology and Engineering are among the popular areas of study, "so the campus can seem a little nerdy sometimes," a humanities major admitted; but students can take courses in any of Valparaiso's four colleges:

Arts and Sciences, Nursing, Engineering, and Business Administration. The workload, especially for science majors, can exceed 20 to 30 hours per week, "but this is hardly bad," assured one student: "I still had enough time to maintain three part-time jobs." And the professors are always considerate and eager to offer their advice and support to those students who ask for it. Indeed, across the board, students agree that Valpo's greatest strength is the intimate class size, usually 20 to 25 students at most, and the incredible accessibility of all of their professors. One chemistry major shared proudly, "I have the cell phone numbers of all of my professors," while another concurred, "If I need help with anything, I can approach my professors right away and be sure of prompt assistance." No Teaching Assistants lecture or oversee the classes, functioning in more of an auxiliary than a primary role. Additionally, the advising system receives high praise, as students are offered a smorgasbord of mentors, tutors, and counselors, the latter including preprofessional as well as major and minor advisers.

Rules, Religion, and Social Justice

Outside of the classroom, students are engaged in a slew of activities, though the most popular are religious associations, Greek life, and intramural sports. There are several academic clubs—Chemistry Club, the English Society, the Society of Physics Students are just a few—and "almost every club is affiliated with a missionary trip." If students are not attending a club meeting or working in Valpo's solitary Christopher Center Library, they are probably at a party, a social fundraiser, or a basketball game. Basketball is the one sport guaranteed to attract throngs of students, for when there is a game, visitors can expect a campus starkly deserted except for the packed stadium: "Very few clubs even attempt to hold productive meetings on game nights," laughed one student.

Greek life is also prominent on campus, with about a fifth of the student body belonging to a fraternity or a sorority. Such student involvement in Greek life gives fraternities and sororities formidable clout in student government, as a student's probability of winning election and successfully passing legislation can arguably be solely determined by his membership in a Greek organization. Still, one student states, "Greek organizations are incredibly inclusive: there is little separation between Greek students and non-Greek students, and several Greek events are open to the entire campus." And if Greek life doesn't sound appealing, there are myriad other groups to join. For example, social justice groups like the Social Action Leadership Team (SALT) are always looking for passionate underclassmen to organize service events, philanthropic dance parties, or campus-wide humanitarian campaigns.

> "One of the reasons I decided to come to this school was the incredible friendliness of the students. . . . Although people are fairly set in their views, Valpo is very relaxed and welcoming."

Only a small, brazen contingent of students can be found partying hard, however, because Valpo is a dry campus, and freshmen in particular have a separate curfew for the first month. All Valparaiso students are not permitted on opposite-sex floors in the dorms later than 1 a.m. on weekdays and 2 a.m. on weekends, and rules are strictly enforced. One student put it bluntly: "It sucks." Every dorm elects a group of students called the Judicial Board to mete out punishments for noise and curfew violations, alcohol use, and door propping, although the J-Boards are notorious for their leniency. Much more stringent is the Valparaiso University Police Department, which often works collaboratively with the city police to punish students for alcohol and drug use.

Freshmen through juniors are required to live in dorms on campus, unless they belong to a fraternity or sorority. There is a reason for this rule, for "the best part of living in the dorms is the openness of community, especially freshman year." Most of the nine residence halls have double rooms and community bathrooms, and the University's two upperclassmen apartments offer suite-style living with private bedrooms, a common room, and a shared bathroom. And the University is planning to renovate the dorms even further and build larger and plusher residences for upperclassmen. Despite the fairly comfortable accommodations, 30 percent of undergraduates choose to eschew the strict campus life by living on their own.

Pushing Boundaries

But even then, there is only so much more they can do in the immediate area. Valparaiso is a small Midwestern town, usually dormant, but intermittently stirred to a tepid liveliness for the annual Popcorn Festival and the county fair. Most students don't patronize bars, although the few that do mention Brewski's and Northside Tap as favorites. The town's redeeming point seems to be its proximity to other, more enticing locales. One student explained, "The best thing about Valpo is that you can always hop onto one of the free buses the University provides and travel to the beach 30 minutes away, or to Chicago just an hour away." Most students will take advantage of this opportunity a few times a month, although sometimes, of course, their studies can keep them busy for weeks.

Overall, students praise their Valparaiso experience as all that they could ask for. "You get from it as much as you invest in it: if you utilize all of the University's resources, you're set for a rewarding four years in college." Another student shares, "One of the reasons I decided to come to this school was the incredible friendliness of the students. I would be walking around as a prefrosh and people would just stop and hold the door open for me. Although people are fairly set in their views, Valpo is very relaxed and welcoming." Thus, if you are searching for a friendly peer group, accessible professors, and a small-town atmosphere, Valparaiso may be just the place for you.—*Sejal Hathi*

FYI

If you come to Valparaiso, you'd better bring: "rain boots, a Frisbee, a beach towel to go to the Dunes, and expectations for a small room."

What's the typical weekend schedule? "Sleeping in, waking up late, doing homework, hanging out with friends, and indulging Sunday."

If I could change one thing about Valparaiso, "I'd get rid of the 'dry school' rule and place air-conditioning in the freshman dorms."

Three things every student at Valparaiso should do before graduating are "running down the hill behind Guild-Memorial Hall; attending at least one Midnight Madness event, the first basketball practice of the season; and eating at El Amigo, a late-night Mexican restaurant."

Wabash College

Address: 301 W. Wabash Avenue, Crawfordsville, IN 47933
Phone: 765-361-6225
E-mail address: admissions@wabash.edu
Web site URL: www.wabash.edu
Year Founded: 1832
Private or Public: Private
Religious Affiliation: None
Location: Suburban
Number of Applicants: 1,419
Percent Accepted: 56%
Percent Accepted who enroll: 37%
Number Entering: 247
Number of Transfers Accepted each Year: 6
Middle 50% SAT range: M: 540–660, CR 510–620, Wr: 490–610
Middle 50% ACT range: 22–28
Early admission program EA/ED/None: EA and ED

Percentage accepted through EA or ED: Unreported/88%
EA and ED deadline: 1-Dec & 15-Nov
Regular Deadline: Rolling
Application Fee: $40
Full time Undergraduate enrollment: 872
Total enrollment: unreported
Percent Male: 100%
Percent Female: 0%
Total Percent Minority or Unreported: 25%
Percent African-American: 5%
Percent Asian/Pacific Islander: 2%
Percent Hispanic: 2%
Percent Native-American: 0%
Percent International: 6%
Percent in-state/out of state: 68%/32%
Percent from Public HS: 91%
Retention Rate: 88%

Graduation Rate 4-year: 64%
Graduation Rate 6-year: 64%
Percent Undergraduates in On-campus housing: 84%
Number of official organized extracurricular organizations: 64
3 Most popular majors: Social Sciences, Philosophy & Related Studies, English
Student/Faculty ratio: 11:1
Average Class Size: 15
Percent of students going to grad school: 29%
Tuition and Fees: $32,450
In-State Tuition and Fees if different: No difference
Cost for Room and Board: $8,500
Percent receiving financial aid out of those who apply: 89%
Percent receiving financial aid among all students: 85%

In Crawfordsville, rural Indiana, 900 students make their way across the idyllic campus of one of America's last three remaining all men's liberal arts colleges. This is Wabash College, a place where students know their professors, and professors know their students. With its small student body and an average class size of 15, Wabash offers motivated young men a top-notch liberal arts education within a supportive network of dedicated students, professors and alumni.

Small classes, top academics

Students at Wabash benefit from small class sizes and have the opportunity to forge close relationships with professors. "You're hard pressed to find a class with more than 25 students," one senior noted. "Upper-level classes are especially small." Emphasis is heavily placed on student-professor relationships, with students praising across the board professors whose interest is in teaching, not their own research. "The doors are always open, and professors are willing to help." The College splits its majors into three different divisions. Division I contains the sciences; Division II the humanities; and Division III the social sciences. Chemistry, Biology and Political Science are particularly popular majors and in addition the College attracts many prelaw and premed oriented students, despite not having an official major in those areas. The acceptance rate into law and medical school is markedly high compared to other competing institutions, with many students choosing to follow this path. As well as offering these more traditional courses, Wabash professors take pride in sharing any unusual interests. "Unusual classes run the gamut. You'll find psychology professors whose research interests span from fatherhood to the impact of cocaine on the reward centers of brains in rats."

In order to be introduced to reading and writing at the college level, freshmen are required to take part in the freshman tutorial program. Courses are based on faculty interests and currently include topics ranging from "Men in Tights: Genders and Superheroes" to "Winning World War II: Winston Churchill." Alumni play an important role in life at Wabash, with its endowment currently standing as one of the highest per student in the nation. Students are offered many opportunities to benefit from alumni connections and internships,

often as early as their freshman year. As part of a tutorial on the Industrial Revolution, several freshmen got the opportunity to take a weeklong trip to northern England in their first semester. "That's not something my friends at state schools were doing as freshmen," one happy student said.

Where's Wally? Socializing at Wabash

Though students praise Wabash's beautiful campus, many are disappointed in the lack of a college town. "There is nothing of great excitement on the weekends in Crawfordsville, In.," one freshman noted, and as a result many students spend the weekend "writing papers and studying for the week's upcoming exams." Other students take the opportunity to attend on-campus games (cheered on by Wally, the school mascot) or visit friends at nearby schools, with Purdue, IU and DePauw University being popular weekend destinations. Though the student government is working on adding more campus-wide events to the calendar, students remain disappointed with the lack of off-campus hangout spots. At night, the only places open in Crawfordsville are fast-food restaurants. "I wish we had the luxury of late night food carts and better local restaurant hangouts for students," one upperclassman said.

The result is that social life is campus-centered and revolves largely around Greek life. Much of the student body is Greek, with up to 60% of students actively involved in fraternities. Rushing for freshmen takes place in the first semester, and brothers will live in their fraternities for all 4 years. Frat houses offer the best accommodation, as the college recently completed a ten-year project to rebuild and renovate the chapter houses. Students say dorms for independents "aren't bad" and "have plenty of space," but extensive renovations and a new student center are next on the college's list of building projects.

For those not involved in Greek life, socializing at Wabash can be a bit "all over the place." Most of the social life centers on work during the week, as everyone is "pretty focused," with students seeing people in the library or "getting together over lunch or dinner just to chat." The relatively small size of the college bolsters the "strong camaraderie of the student body" and means the majority of faces seen around campus are familiar ones. Despite the lack of firm hangout spots, life at Wabash is "interesting and fun," with one senior adding that "some of the best memories you'll have happen at the seemingly most banal, spontaneous times."

> At Wabash, you're not doing something right if you don't know the names of roughly three-quarters of the people you pass as you travel through campus.

Taco Bell, Monon Bell

While Taco Bell may be one of the few late night eateries open for students, the annual Monon Bell Classic is the biggest event of the year. Hailed "the longest continuous rivalry west of the Alleghenies," the 119-year-old football game sees Wabash take on nearby DePauw University. The winner receives college-wide accolades and an old train bell from a locomotive on the Monon Railroad, which goes through both campuses. Wabash currently leads the series, with one satisfied student affirming "this year's seniors managed to keep the Bell for all four of their years here." No pressure, prefrosh.

Athletics at Wabash are excellent, with the college boasting one of the best-ranked athletics facilities in the nation. The Little Giants compete in the NCAA Division III and bat well above their comparatively small size. Ten varsity sports are on offer, with football, swimming and cross-country being the most popular. Sport is a plus, but most men at Wabash speak with unreserved praise for the outstanding academics and social camaraderie on campus. "As clichéd as it sounds, we truly are as men of Wabash a fraternity of brothers," one proud freshman said. Whether cheered on by Wally or not, such school spirit continues well beyond Wabash. Just check out its endowment.—*Jasmine Horsey*

FYI

One thing you wish you would've known before coming to Wabash: "I wish I would've known that the town isn't much of a college town. By that, I mean that there aren't many places for students off campus."

What surprised me the most about Wabash when I arrived was "how much our alumni care about their alma mater."

What's the typical weekend schedule? "If there's a game on campus, most go to it. If not, many leave for the weekend to visit friends. Others stay on campus and catch up on work."

Iowa

Cornell College

Address: 600 1st St. SW, Mt. Vernon, IA 52314

Phone: 319-895-4000

E-mail address: communications@cc.edu

Web site URL: www.cornellcollege.edu

Year Founded: 1853

Private or Public: Private

Religious Affiliation: Methodist

Location: Suburban

Number of Applicants: 3,791

Percent Accepted: 39%

Percent Accepted who enroll: 24%

Number Entering: 354

Number of Transfers Accepted each Year: 39

Middle 50% SAT range: M: 540–670, Cr: 560–670, Wr: 620–710

Middle 50% ACT range: 24–29

Early admission program EA/ED/None: EA and ED

Percentage accepted through EA or ED: 25%

EA and ED deadline: 1-Nov

Regular Deadline: 1-Mar

Application Fee: $30

Full time Undergraduate enrollment: 1,115

Total enrollment: 1,115

Percent Male: 47%

Percent Female: 53%

Total Percent Minority or Unreported: 16%

Percent African-American: 3%

Percent Asian/Pacific Islander: 1%

Percent Hispanic: 3%

Percent Native-American: 1%

Percent International: 3%

Percent in-state/out of state: 30%/70%

Percent from Public HS: 85%

Retention Rate: 85%

Graduation Rate 4-year: 60%

Graduation Rate 6-year: 66%

Percent Undergraduates in On-campus housing: 87%

Number of official organized extracurricular organizations: 76

3 Most popular majors: Economics, English, Psychology

Student/Faculty ratio: 11:1

Average Class Size: 14

Percent of students going to grad school: Unreported

Tuition and Fees: $26,100

In-State Tuition and Fees if different: No difference

Cost for Room and Board: $6,970

Percent receiving financial aid out of those who apply: 79%

Percent receiving financial aid among all students: 68%

No, Cornell College is not an Ivy League university in Ithaca. Despite its small size and rural setting, however, it does attract some top talent from across the country—and it was founded 12 years earlier than that other Cornell in upstate New York. At Cornell College in Mount Vernon, Iowa, students have the opportunity to enroll in only one course at a time, join "social groups" and participate in one of the country's few college steel drum ensembles.

One-Course-At-A-Time

For students who prefer concentrating on only one subject as opposed to juggling four or five per semester, Cornell's unique One-Course-At-A-Time, or OCAAT, scheduling system is a big attraction. All courses are scheduled in blocks, with each year consisting of nine, three-and-a-half week blocks. Most courses meet for morning and afternoon sessions every day of the week, with courses requiring labs often running longer sessions than other courses. Overall students tend to give OCAAT very positive reviews. As one student described, "It allows students to focus and also to be more intense."

Additionally, students said they appreciate OCAAT for the strong student-faculty relationships it fosters as well as for the flexibility it provides. Because professors, too, have only one course at a time to focus on, they can devote all their energy and resources to the students of that particular course. Students described their professors as "awesome" and "totally dedicated" to teaching and advising. And, since so many professors live right in the small town of Mount Vernon, casual meetings outside of the classroom are very common.

Furthermore, class sizes tend to be fairly small, since all are capped at 25 students (some are even capped at 18), including introductory-level courses. The combination of small classes and block scheduling thus gives students more opportunities to attend field trips, take advantage of their own classrooms—which are not shared during the block period, and get one-on-one attention from professors.

Of course, as any student will tell you, OCAAT has its drawbacks, too—aside from the fact that taking an uninteresting course will only be that much worse when one has to go to it every day for a month. Students also acknowledged that while OCAAT works well for most classes, it can be problematic for certain areas of study. For example, it might be difficult to cram certain technical or memorization-intensive courses, such as an introductory language course or mathematics class, into such a short period of time. But students also said Cornell is in the process of trying to adjust OCAAT slightly to better accommodate these differences. Possibilities include combining harder courses into two-block courses, or grouping some classes for interdisciplinary purposes.

Cornell also allows for a decent amount of academic flexibility. Students said they appreciated OCAAT because it allows them to take a "vacation block" if they so desire. During that time, they might decide to go on a trip, do some community service, relax, or get an early start on a summer internship. The college also makes it relatively easy for students to double-major, or to add a minor to their major. One student, who had planned on majoring in biomedical engineering before coming to Cornell, said she decided to take advantage of the school's flexibility and create her own tailor-made biophysics major. "There's a big emphasis on independence," she explained.

Not Just Another Cornfield in Iowa

Due in part to Cornell's unique academic offerings, students said the school is surprisingly not as homogenous as one would expect. "For being a small school in the middle of a cornfield in Iowa, it's really diverse," noted one junior. Although racial diversity is perhaps not as strong as in some other colleges—"it's predominantly white middle-class"—Cornell's 1,100 students do hail

from all over the country, with only about 20 percent coming from Iowa. Students also said that while the campus is often described as "very liberal," voices from a broad political spectrum are heard as well. "We lean to the left, but there's room for discussion and there's a lot of it that goes on," remarked one student.

In addition to OCAAT, Cornell's diverse base of students might also be attracted to the school for its beautiful campus and lively atmosphere. "I know a lot of people who made their decision to come here solely based on the campus—we're located on a hill, one of the few in Iowa," one student joked. The architecture, too, is noteworthy. Mt. Vernon, a town of just over 4,000, boasts three National Historic Districts. "The campus is often described as a 'slice of New England hilltop in the Midwest,'" noted one student, "and I think it's kind of corny but also kind of true." Though many of the buildings on and around campus do tend to be old, they are also well-preserved and often newly renovated.

The 91 percent of students who live on campus also tend to live in older buildings, although one newly built senior dorm features a more modern suite-style setup. While the dorms may not be "as lavish as some other places," they do the trick and suit students "just fine."

Unfortunately, the quality of the food is not quite as impressive as the campus scenery and architecture. Students are required to purchase meal plans, with either 14 or 20 meals per week, and even students living off campus must still purchase a partial meal plan of seven meals a week. Although students said the quality of the food and the setup of the college's single cafeteria were "improving," they also said having a meal plan can get tiresome. "We're a 'Tier II' school when it comes to food," noted one senior. "There's even worse and I can't imagine what that would be."

Getting Involved

Cornell students also take advantage of the many extracurricular organizations available. About 90 different student organizations exist, but if there's not a group that strikes a student's fancy, he or she is easily able to start one independently. The Student Senate is in charge of doling out funds to the various organizations, which range from the Medieval Renaissance Club to the Union of Progressive Students to *The Cornellian*, the college newspaper. One of the more popular activities at Cornell is Pandemonium, a steel drums ensemble comprised of about 20 people performing a wide variety of traditional and contemporary music on four different kinds of drums.

> **"Because we're so small and isolated, it really pulls our campus together."**

Athletics are also very popular at Cornell, with several intramural activities offered during each block period. Though traditional sports, like basketball and volleyball, tend to be the most popular, students also participate in intramural watermelon seed-spitting contests, indoor whiffleball games, and dodgeball tournaments. While many also participate in varsity sports, students noted that there's definitely an athletic and nonathletic crowd on campus. Interest in athletics is "not campus wide," but games for football, as well as for basketball and volleyball, tend to get "pretty decent" turnouts, particularly for such a small college. Wrestling also tends to be popular, as Cornell is in one of the toughest Division III wrestling conferences in the country.

Going Social
Unlike at larger institutions, much of the social interaction at Cornell tends to take place on a smaller scale—a characteristic many students said they appreciated. "It's a small town so it's a much smaller scene, but I'm the type of person who's okay with that," explained one senior. Another noted that "because we're so small and isolated, it really pulls our campus together." The Performing Arts and Activities Council at Cornell also hosts a number of popular activities, bringing popular comedians, bands, or speakers to campus for all to enjoy on the weekends.

However, Cornell students are still able to enjoy large campus-wide parties, with "social groups" frequently hosting some of the larger off-campus gatherings. Social groups act similarly to fraternities and sororities elsewhere—but while they have Greek names, they are not nationally-affiliated and so are unique to Cornell. Some of the groups are service-based, like the Taus and Rhozes, and others are more "party-oriented," like the Delts, Owls and Phi-Os. About half of all students are members of a social group, but parties are often open to the entire University. Although events including the Delts' St. Patty's Day party and the Gamma's pig roast are popular, the social groups also host formals and semiformals every year, too.

If the pub scene is more fitting to a party-goer's interest, there are several bars within Mount Vernon, "each of which usually has a different crowd on a given weekend night." For a wider array of entertainment options, a lot of students also travel to Cedar Rapids or Iowa City (where the University of Iowa is located), both of which are a mere 20-minute car ride away. Students said that while alcohol is popular and easily accessible, there is "no more or less of a problem than at any other college."

Testing the Waters
Students suggested that potential Cornell applicants might consider spending a night or going to classes for a day or two to feel out the One-Course-At-A-Time schedule. "You either love it or hate it," remarked one student, adding that a fair number of students realize upon entering Cornell that one course at a time may not suit them as well as they thought. Regardless, incoming freshman should look forward to taking advantage of small class sizes and professor accessibility. "Professors are here because they like to teach, and the interactions we can have with them are just priceless." And, of course, they might also want to check out Cornell's social groups, scenery, and historic landmarks. One student said, "If you're looking for a good time here, you'll find it."—*Kendra Locke*

FYI
If you come to Cornell College, you'd better bring "a lot of warm clothing, because it gets pretty windy here."
What is the typical weekend schedule? "Go to social group parties, bars, or Iowa City or Cedar Rapids on Friday and Saturday nights, and relax with friends or study on Sunday."
If I could change one thing about Cornell College, I'd "put it somewhere warmer, maybe by a beach somewhere."
Three things every student should do before graduating are: "Go sledding down Pres Hill in downtown, go camping at Palisades-Kepler State Park, and take a block off and spend it however you want."

Grinnell College

Address: 1103 Park Street, Grinnell, IA 50112

Phone: 641-269-3600

E-mail address: askgrin@grinnell.edu

Web site URL: www.grinnell.edu/admission

Year Founded: 1846

Private or Public: Private

Religious Affiliation: None

Location: Rural

Number of Applicants: 3,217

Percent Accepted: 43%

Percent Accepted who enroll: 34%

Number Entering: 468

Number of Transfers Accepted each Year: 25

Middle 50% SAT range: M: 620–710, CR: 610–740, Wr: Unreported

Middle 50% ACT range: 28–32

Early admission program EA/ED/None: ED

Percentage accepted through EA or ED: 69%

EA and ED deadline: 15-Nov

Regular Deadline: 2-Jan

Application Fee: $30

Full time Undergraduate enrollment: 1,678

Total enrollment: 1,678

Percent Male: 47%

Percent Female: 53%

Total Percent Minority or Unreported: 19%

Percent African-American: 5%

Percent Asian/Pacific Islander: 8%

Percent Hispanic: 6%

Percent Native-American: <1%

Percent International: 11%

Percent in-state/out of state: 12%/88%

Percent from Public HS: 65%

Retention Rate: 94%

Graduation Rate 4-year: 84%

Graduation Rate 6-year: 86%

Percent Undergraduates in On-campus housing: 87%

Number of official organized extracurricular organizations: 300

3 Most popular majors: Political Science, Psychology, Economics

Student/Faculty ratio: 9:1

Average Class Size: 18

Percent of students going to grad school: Unreported

Tuition and Fees: $35,428

In-State Tuition and Fees if different: No difference

Cost for Room and Board: $8,272

Percent receiving financial aid out of those who apply: 81%

Percent receiving financial aid among all students: Unreported

Grinnell College is a small school in a small town, but size hasn't stopped it and, in many ways, has defined its tightly knit intellectual and social community. Founded in 1846, Grinnell has since become a top choice for students thanks to its challenging academic program, quirky student body, and numerous—though often unconventional—extracurricular opportunities. Named the "Best All-Around College" in *Newsweek*'s "Hot Schools of 2004" list and ranked eighteenth on the *U.S. News & World Report*'s list of best liberal arts colleges for 2011, Grinnell, though located "basically in the middle of a cornfield," is a renowned institution that will provide students with an excellent education and a unique social experience.

Small Classes, Large Workload

Classes at Grinnell are small. Even popular introductory classes remain at under 30 students, which allows for close interactions with professors starting on the first day of class in freshman year. On the downside, it also means that it is difficult to slack off or blend in.

A new system of course selection has eliminated competition for most popular classes, and students get into their top choices without a fight. "I got all my first-choice classes, even as a freshman," boasted one student.

Sociology is generally considered the easiest major on campus, and the sciences are thought to be the hardest. Weekdays "are pretty much exclusively for studying" due to a large workload with significant amounts of reading. Grinnell students, though, don't mind. Course work is usually interesting. "We read primary documents, not textbooks about those documents. It is not about memorizing facts and regurgitating them, it is about analyzing everything yourself," said one student. "Your teachers want you to challenge them. You're not supposed to accept what is given," said another. This, in combination with small class sizes, allows students to develop close relationships with professors.

The only academic requirement at Grinnell is the first-year tutorial, in which groups of 12 students develop their writing skills on a wide range of topics, ranging from serious classes on "Russia in Revolution" to amusing courses like "The Onion, Sarah Silverman, and Flatulence: Why Are Funny Things Funny?"

Grinnell also offers students the chance to create their own courses via the Mentored Advanced Project program (MAP). It allows students to work with a member of the faculty on "scholarly research or the creation of a work of art." Another option is to take ExCo, or Experimental College, which is a number of informal, often student-taught classes on a range of topics that interest students, townspeople, and staff alike.

Sound Body, Sound Mind
To study, students retreat to the Burling Library or either of the two student centers, Harris Center and Joe Rosenfield Center. Students rave about the library's study gym, which is essentially "a playscape for studying. You can climb ladders to get to where you want to work," said one student. Traditional seating, of course, is also available. The recently renovated Harris and the brand-new JRC boast not only places to study but also an assortment of recreational facilities such as game rooms and a concert hall. Many students also choose to spend time in the lounges of their dorms.

Grinnell's new gym is popular, as are the newer dorms on East Campus, which boast air-conditioning and new furniture. Students live in East, South, or North Campus. East Campus is the quietest, North Campus has many athletes, and South Campus has the most parties. Though off-campus housing is often more affordable than on-campus housing, most students choose to live on campus.

Dining at Grinnell is "pretty good," with enough selection for a student to claim that "there's definitely something for everybody." A pastry chef on staff makes "absolutely amazing" desserts. However, there are many popular dining options off campus, including AJ's Steakhouse, La Cabana, and Pizza Hut.

Not a Bunch of Dirty Hippies
Grinnell students boast about their self-governance policy, which is a variation of the honor code for everyday living to hold students accountable. In practice, this means the administration "lets you do what you want, as long as you're not dumb about it.

It's pretty sensible," said one student. There are also Student Advisors, volunteers who live with undergraduates. They do not function as police or traditional residential advisors, but rather as community builders who are under no obligation to report illicit activities, such as substance abuse.

> ". . . a bunch of dirty hippies. [P]eople here will always shower once a month, whether they need it or not."

Partying includes weekly dance parties, with themes like '80s, Fetish and Cross Dress. The small campus and student body allow different cliques to socialize on the weekends and on Wednesdays, which is "a big party night, if you don't have a ton of work to get done," said one student. For nondrinkers, there is no pressure to imbibe. However, for the most part, students drink, and a large number smoke pot, which can "really overwhelm the campus social scene sometimes." The presence of marijuana on campus is what leads some students to characterize themselves self-deprecatingly as "a bunch of dirty hippies," but as one student explained, "We are aware of it, and it's not really true. We joke that people here will always shower once a month, whether they need it or not."

In their free time, students also explore the town of Grinnell, which is "the stereotypical Midwestern town with stereotypical Midwestern chain stores," commented one student. Town-gown relations are peaceful, perhaps because "there really isn't much" in Grinnell. Wal-Mart is a frequented resource, and "if you don't like Wal-Mart, you're screwed," said one student.

Work-study programs are also popular. Most participants are assigned to Dining Services, which "can be a drag," but there are other options. "I was able to find a job playing with babies in the child-care center," one freshman said.

United by Procrastination
There are "way too many different things to do" at Grinnell. No experience is needed to join extracurricular activities, which include a theater program that freshmen can "actually get into." Also bountiful are community service opportunities, publications, and singing groups. A large number of famous people, bands and speakers also travel to

Grinnell. "Even though it is in Iowa, Ashton and Demi were here a while back, and I could see them from my dorm window," one student said.

Sports do not draw large crowds at Grinnell. "We're good in our division, I think," said one student. Another believed that if Ultimate Frisbee were a sport, Grinnell would be ranked first in the nation "for enthusiasm at least." Some gripe about the students lacking athletic spirit, instead dedicating themselves to nontraditional sports like the Quidditch team rather than more traditional athletics.

What students love about Grinnell athletics, however, is that "the jocks here are smart." Indeed, "everyone defies stereotypes here." One student recalled how the quiet football player in her psychology class turned out to be a "huge fan of Japanese and Chinese culture and wanted to study there in the future." Another explained, "You can't make any assumptions about anyone. Every single person is enormously different." A common trait for all students is said to be "the ability to procrastinate. We're all really good at it, and it's probably one of the things that link us all together."

Most students also love the idea of going to a small school. There "is such a sense of community," and "everyone wants you to be here." Grinnell's large endowment means not only good financial aid but also good quality of life. "Everything you could possibly want is here at Grinnell," said one student. The rigorous academic experience in combination with an eclectic community of intellectuals makes life at Grinnell College truly a "one-of-a-kind experience." —*Erica Rothmam*

FYI
What is the typical weekend schedule? "Go to a free Grinnell-sponsored event during the day, watch a movie with some friends, hit a few dorm parties, and wake up the next morning to go to the library."
If I could change one thing about Grinnell, I'd "move it out of Iowa."
Three things every student at Grinnell should do before graduating are "get to know a professor well, play a game of Ultimate Frisbee, and climb on the study gym."

Iowa State University

Address: 100 Alumni Hall, Ames, IA 50011-2011
Phone: 515-294-5836
E-mail address: admissions@iastate.edu
Web site URL: www.iastate.edu
Year Founded: 1858
Private or Public: Public
Religious Affiliation: None
Location: Suburban
Number of Applicants: 11,058
Percent Accepted: 89%
Percent Accepted who enroll: 44%
Number Entering: 4,335
Number of Transfers Accepted each Year: 1,527
Middle 50% SAT range: M: 530–680, CR: 510–640, Wr: Unreported
Middle 50% ACT range: 22–27
Early admission program EA/ED/None: None
Percentage accepted through EA or ED: NA

EA and ED deadline: NA
Regular Deadline: 1-Jul
Application Fee: $30
Full time Undergraduate enrollment: 21,004
Total enrollment: 25,668
Percent Male: 57%
Percent Female: 43%
Total Percent Minority or Unreported: 7%
Percent African-American: 3%
Percent Asian/Pacific Islander: 3%
Percent Hispanic: 3%
Percent Native-American: <1%
Percent International: 4%
Percent in-state/out of state: 79%/21%
Percent from Public HS: 93%
Retention Rate: 85%
Graduation Rate 4-year: 33%
Graduation Rate 6-year: 65%

Percent Undergraduates in On-campus housing: 39%
Number of official organized extracurricular organizations: 699
3 Most popular majors: Management Science, Marketing/Marketing Management, Mechanical Engineering
Student/Faculty ratio: 16:1
Average Class Size: 25
Percent of students going to grad school: 17%
Tuition and Fees: $16,514
In-State Tuition and Fees if different: $231 per Credit-Hour
Cost for Room and Board: $6,715
Percent receiving financial aid out of those who apply: 87%
Percent receiving financial aid among all students: 79%

Lying between rolling fields of corn and the small city of Ames, Iowa, the campus of Iowa State University is known as one of the most beautiful in America. A vast twenty-acre central lawn includes a fountain sculpted by Dutch artist Christian Petersen, Lake LaVerne (home to resident swans Sir Lancelot and Elaine) and the Reiman Gardens. While both a major research university and a member of the Big 12 Conference, the school prides itself on creating a supportive atmosphere and a small-community feel.

A relaxed, friendly Midwestern attitude characterizes the student body, which a freshman described as "really laid-back and down-to-earth." She went on to marvel, "My first day here, I was wandering around, looking lost, and a number of people just walked up to me and offered to help me out!" Most students tend to wear jeans and a sweatshirt, often featuring Cy the Cyclone, voted "Most Dominant College Mascot on Earth" by CBS sports fans in 2007. "You see cyclone stuff everywhere," noted one student. Although much of the student body may fit the white, farm-kid stereotype, a growing number of minority students, especially Asian students, are bringing increased diversity to campus. "For Iowa, it's diverse," a freshman declared.

Hitting the Books

Iowa State offers more than 100 majors and preprofessional programs, which are organized among the seven colleges of the University: Agriculture and Life Sciences, Business, Design, Engineering, Human Sciences, Liberal Arts and Sciences, and Veterinary Medicine. Students enter one of these colleges sorted according to their major. Undecided students are automatically placed in the College of Liberal Arts and Sciences, where they take a range of classes to help them decide what to study. While graduation requirements depend on major, Engineering and Veterinary Medicine are known for being especially rigorous programs. "Engineering is really tough," one student affirmed, perhaps unsurprising for a school that was the home of the world's first computer. Agricultural programs are also well regarded.

Some students complained about large class sizes, especially in introductory courses, but added that classes get much smaller once students get more advanced in their majors. Professors were unanimously described as helpful and open. "It's just up to the student to take the initiative," said one freshman. "If you just go to their office hours or ask to speak with them before or after class, they're usually really happy to talk with you." While the classes were described as "challenging," students commended the school for its academic support network, saying that ISU "does a good job of helping students." All freshmen are assigned faculty advisors, and supplementary instruction is offered for general education classes. Learning communities, small groups of students who take a few classes together and may also live on the same floor in their dorms, also help students with academics.

Where to Call Home
While students are not required to live on campus, the vast majority of incoming freshmen choose to live in the dorms. "It's a great way to meet people," said one recently arrived freshman. "People generally leave their doors open and you can say hi just walking down the hall." Resident advisors create a sense of community by holding weekly floor meetings and often scheduling special activities. There are a number of different residential buildings on campus, which vary in size, age, and amenities. Although some dorm rooms were described as "kind of small," many have been recently renovated and feature such comforts as wall-to-wall carpeting and air-conditioning. Two gyms near the dorms were also praised as "state-of-the-art." Several major dining centers as well as retail locations accepting Dining Dollars, food money saved on students' ID cards, ensure that students stay well fed.

Upperclassmen often take advantage of the new University-owned apartments, which were described as "really new and modern." Others choose to take advantage of apartments in surrounding Ames, although the longer walk to classes in chilly Iowa winter weather deters some. Fraternities and

sororities also serve as housing for upperclassmen.

Boring Cornfields? No Way!
Although Iowa may not be known as a mecca of activity and cosmopolitan flavor, students say that "there's plenty going on, you just have to go find it." Comedians, lectures, and concerts abound on campus, and Student Union Board (SUB) films are popular events on Friday nights. Nearby Campustown features several convenience stores, bars, and restaurants. Those in search of more action tend to go into Ames or Des Moines. Although many students have cars, the bus system, known as CyRide, offers an easy and free option for getting around. "The bus system is great," gushed one freshman. "It takes you close or right next to every class, and it always runs on schedule." On weekend evenings, the Moonlight Express (or, as it's nicknamed, "the drunk bus") ensures students a safe journey home from a night on the town.

> "I love walking around the campus here—it's so beautiful!"

Greek life also serves as a popular form of social activity, although it is described as "not dominant." "While most people on campus do drink," said one student, "there are things going on if you don't want to." Fraternities and sororities also pride themselves on philanthropic involvement, and often perform community service in Ames. Those looking for a lower-key weekend often take advantage of offerings at the Memorial Union, which includes art exhibits, a food court, and bookstore. On a lower level there is even a bowling alley, billiards, and arcade. Beware, though—legend dictates that if you step on the zodiac symbols on the floor near the entrance, you'll fail your next test!

From Campaniling to VEISHEA
Campaniling, one of Iowa State's oldest and best-loved traditions, is a classic rite of passage for Iowa State students. On the Friday night of homecoming, hundreds or even thousands of students gather under the old clock tower on central campus to kiss their significant other at the stroke of midnight. Those particularly enamored might even walk around Lake LaVerne three times without talking, which supposedly destines them

to be together forever. Homecoming week also features barbeques, fireworks, concerts, a pep rally, and tailgating.

The other major event of the year is VEISHEA, an entirely student run event held each spring. The initials represent the five original colleges of Iowa State: veterinary medicine, engineering, industrial science, home economics, and agriculture. Events include a huge parade with floats built by student groups, a talent show, concerts, and booths and open houses open to the community. Ames families and parents mingle with ISU students while browsing the hundreds of activities and displays. "VEISHEA is one of the most fun events of the year," one student excitedly proclaimed.

All About Cy

For a school whose football team was described as "pretty average this year," Iowa

State students are a spirited bunch. School sports games, especially wrestling, basketball, volleyball—and, of course, football—all receive good showings. Intramurals are also "incredibly popular," with tournaments every week, sometimes featuring competitions between dormitory floors or teams. Options include such traditional sports as ice hockey and softball, as well as more unusual options like broomball, dodgeball, and even card games.

Other popular extracurricular activities include volunteer programs, cultural groups, and clubs. Many organizations are centered around students' majors, such as the Advertising Club or the Agricultural Business Club. No matter what their activity, ISU students are characterized as spending a lot of time on extracurriculars. "I would say that most people do four to five clubs," one student asserted. "People enjoy being involved."—*Elizabeth Chrystal*

FYI

If you come to ISU, you'd better bring "a camera to take a picture of the beautiful campus, and an umbrella for getting across it when it's wet!"

What's the typical weekend schedule? "Some people leave on Friday afternoon to go home for the weekend. People staying on campus usually catch a film or go out with friends. Saturday, study or go to the football game if there is one and tailgate, party all night. Sunday, catch up on work and maybe go to club meetings in the evening."

If I could change one thing about ISU, I'd "make the walk to classes shorter in the winter and in the rain. The campus is nice, but it's a pain when the weather's bad!"

Three things every student at ISU should do before graduating are "go to VEISHEA, share a kiss under the Campanile (the bell tower on campus), and attend a home football game."

University of Iowa

Address: 107 Calvin Hall,
Iowa City, IA 52242
Phone: 319-335-3847
E-mail address:
admissions@uiowa.edu
Web site URL:
www.uiowa.edu
Year Founded: 1847
Private or Public: Public
Religious Affiliation: None
Location: Urban
Number of Applicants:
18,939
Percent Accepted: 84%
**Percent Accepted who
enroll:** 29%
Number Entering: 4,557
**Number of Transfers
Accepted each Year:** 2,082
Middle 50% SAT range:
M: 560–705, CR:460–640,
Wr: Unreported
Middle 50% ACT range:
23–28
**Early admission program
EA/ED/None:** None

**Percentage accepted
through EA or ED:** NA
EA and ED deadline: NA
Regular Deadline: 1-Apr
Application Fee: $40
**Full time Undergraduate
enrollment:** 21,176
Total enrollment: 29,518
Percent Male: 46%
Percent Female: 54%
**Total Percent Minority or
Unreported:** 25%
Percent African-American:
2%
**Percent Asian/Pacific
Islander:** 3%
Percent Hispanic: 3%
Percent Native-American:
<1%
Percent International: 9%
**Percent in-state/out of
state:** 51%/49%
Percent from Public HS:
90%
Retention Rate: 86%
Graduation Rate 4-year: 40%

Graduation Rate 6-year:
63%
**Percent Undergraduates
in On-campus housing:**
29%
**Number of official organized
extracurricular
organizations:** 467
3 Most popular majors:
Business, Communications/
Journalism, Liberal Arts
Student/Faculty ratio: 16:1
Average Class Size: 15
**Percent of students going to
grad school:** Unreported
Tuition and Fees: $25,099
**In-State Tuition and Fees if
different:** $7,765
Cost for Room and Board:
$8,750
**Percent receiving financial
aid out of those who apply:**
61%
**Percent receiving financial
aid among all students:**
46%

Settled in the middle of vibrant Iowa City and split by a river running through campus, the University of Iowa offers a small-town community feel at a large Big Ten school. In a town where people bleed black and gold, Iowa students find their home a "gorgeous, fun, and homey location," as an enthusiastic sophomore noted. With newly renovated athletic facilities, hundreds of student organizations, and classes such as the World of the Beatles, the University of Iowa leaves little room for complaints. Students agree: the Hawkeye spirit is unmatched, the academics are challenging and the social scene will not disappoint.

Wide Variety, Extensive Requirements

With the University of Iowa's General Education Program, most students spend their first two years completing requirements in distributional areas such as rhetoric, foreign language, interpretation of literature, historical perspectives, natural sciences, quantitative or formal reasoning, social sciences and distributed general education. If

reading that list leaves you exhausted, you're not alone. Iowa students agree that the requirements are excessive. Though most students apply to another college within the University, such as Iowa's business or education schools, after two years, the requirements provide a wide base with eclectic classes.

Iowa offers fun freshman seminars that liven such a requirement-centric schedule with choices like The Age of Dinosaurs, Elementary Psychology, and Stars, Galaxies, and the Universe. Students agree that physical education options such as pilates, yoga and weight training provide a welcoming break to the monotony, though they fill up quickly. After freshman year, popular majors include communications and business; while more challenging—or "unusually hard," as one savvy junior warned—tracks include engineering, nursing, and dentistry. In addition, Iowa boasts an impressive Creative Writing department, with alumni such as Kurt Vonnegut.

With an enrollment of over 20,000 undergraduate students, majors and departments vary in both degree of difficulty and number of required courses. Despite being a large school, students insist that professors make themselves accessible and possess a genuine interest in students' experiences. As a senior explained, "I feel we have a diverse staff and that there is really a professor out there that will touch each and every student who comes through the University." Students rave about professors eager to reach out, regardless of the lecture size. With larger lecture classes, however, comes students' control over the heaviness of their workload. Each department looks to interest students by moving them out of the classroom, and students generally appreciate the faculty's effort to instill a passion in students to pursue their interests both in school and the community.

Whether studying business management or the era marked by John Lennon and Paul McCartney's catchy lyrics, Iowa students guarantee that everyone will meet passionate professors who truly enjoy teaching. From nationally recognized writing programs to competitive nursing schools, the Iowa curriculum provides students with enough choices within requirements and chosen areas of study to form a well-rounded education.

From the Dirty Burge to the Palatial Pentacrest

Split by the scenic Iowa River, the University's campus offers a range of architecture from the east to the west side of the river. Dorms are located on either side of the river, brewing pride and a covert rivalry between those who live on either side. While one side facilitates sleeping in and the pajamas-to-class look by being closer to all the classroom buildings, the other allows a welcome break from school and the academic environment. On the west side of the river students may live in the Mayflower or Parklawn dorm, while the east side offers dorms such as Currier and the so-called "Dirty Burge." With underclassmen comprising an overwhelming majority of on-campus inhabitants, some dorms earn themselves reputations, such as the notorious "Dirty Burge," a dorm recognized in *Playboy* magazine as one of the top 10 places to get lucky. Some reputations, however, are less sexy—everyone knows Hillcrest is for athletes and Daum is for the "smart kids," as a sophomore noted.

Regardless of living on the east or west side, in the athletic or honors dorm, all students love the community feeling on-campus housing provides to underclassmen. Specific floors, in some cases, are even designated for fields like "Women in Science and Engineering" or "Writers' Communities." Each floor also has its own RA who fosters and develops dorm communities as well as enforces dorm regulations. Though RAs must monitor their respective floors, most students enjoy their relationship with a neighboring upperclassman.

After sophomore year, the majority of students live off campus in apartments that are all within a mile of campus. Parking spots are limited around campus, but the University offers a bus from residential areas to the center of campus. Without dorms to conveniently hang out with friends, students often stop by the Iowa Memorial Union (IMU) between classes and relax in the Hawk Lounge. On warmer days, students socialize on Hubbard Park's grassy fields or enjoy the beautiful surroundings of the historic Pentacrest buildings. The five oldest buildings sit in the center of campus, most noticeably the old capitol building that can be easily recognized by its gold dome. New and renovated facilities, such as the business school's state-of-the-art Pappajohn building, join Iowa's historic Pentacrest buildings to form a mix of architecture marked by both tradition and innovation.

The meal plan elicits few complaints, offering three options for the number of meals per week and a dining hall on the east and west side of campus. The food is served buffet style, with as much food as you want for each card swipe. Overall, Iowa's campus features a strong community, a variety of architectural styles and numerous food options under the meal plan. As one junior explained about having such a close-knit campus in a city, "The residents of Iowa City have as much pride in the University as the students, making the institution and the town seemingly one."

The Greeks and Athletes

Starting with freshman year's on-campus housing, meeting people at the University of Iowa is the least of students' worries. Students love being a Hawkeye and different social groups don't stifle the overriding pride of attending Iowa. Athletics, the Greek system, and downtown Iowa City dominate the social scene, but at Iowa, "people are friends with people from different groups. The cliques disappear at this school. Everyone is supportive of others," claimed a Hawkeye senior.

The University prohibits alcohol in dorms, but the Greek scene, consisting of 19 fraternities and 18 sororities, compensates with popular parties. Vitos, an Iowa City bar, is a popular Thursday night destination, while outgoing freshmen are found at Summit. Luckily, bars admit students who are 19 or over, leaving little divide between the underclassmen's and upperclassmen's social spheres. Though the University may have a strong reputation for drinking—as one student bragged, "Iowa is definitely a huge party school"—drinking is optional and only one part of Iowa's social scene. The school's numerous student clubs and organizations plan annual events that are well attended. Students within specific disciplines, such as engineering, enjoy close relationships with peers they lived with or recognize from class. Athletic events and celebrations, fraternity parties and local bars earn high marks from students, but by no means exclusively make up the social scene.

Midwestern Charm

Behind each student's praise of the University of Iowa and the beautiful campus lies the backbone of Iowa's Midwestern charm. Though about 51 percent of the student body is from Iowa, students agree that the University strives to admit a diverse group of students from those regions. Once students reach Iowa City, they immediately fall in love with the welcoming, vibrant community with its Midwestern charm trademark. As a nostalgic senior reminisced, "Iowa is a large school that feels small: the campus is compact, the people are friendly, and the school spirit is like no other—that I will truly miss. The residents are extremely supportive of the Hawkeyes and the students of the University."

The Iowa River, a University of Iowa staple, also adds to the University's unique environments. As one west side native described, "I enjoy the west side because you have a separation of school and home. Walking across the river every day gives me a chance to clear my head and get some thinking done." Few American campuses can offer such stunning scenery in the heart of their campus, and Iowa students do not take that for granted.

Harkey's Nest

Everyone loves the school's mascot Harkey the Hawkeye and students live for Iowa football. Regardless of a winning season or playing in a bowl game, every game day the Iowa City streets are a sea of black and gold. Football, basketball and Iowa's acclaimed wrestling program draw the largest crowds, but everyone on Iowa's campus is somehow involved in promoting the college and representing its student body.

> "Iowa is a large school that feels small: the campus is compact, the people are friendly, and the school spirit is like no other."

Athletes enjoy perks such as the newly renovated Kinnick Stadium and their own private building for studying, but intramurals, clubs and volunteer organizations also receive campus funding with very high participation levels. Intramurals provide a great outlet to meet new people and can become very competitive. Popular intramurals include basketball, flag football, sand volleyball, rock climbing and Texas Hold'em. The University has 500 student organizations and clubs such as the 24-hour Dance Marathon, the largest organization on campus that raises money for children with cancer, and the 10,000 Hour Show, where students receive a concert ticket for every 10 hours of volunteering completed.

An experienced junior said it best: "I thought Hawkeye pride was about athletics; it's about so much more than that." From day-long dance marathons to Thursday nights at Vitos and a sold-out game at Kinnick Stadium, the University of Iowa is anything but boring. Iowa graduates leave college with a cemented love for the Midwest and unrelenting Hawkeye pride.—*Cara Dermody*

FYI

If you come to the University of Iowa, you'd better bring "a good pair of walking shoes, your Iowa apparel, and a 19-year-old ID for Iowa City bars."

What is the typical weekend schedule? "Attend a football or basketball game on Saturday, drink with friends that night, and spend Sunday hanging out at the Coralville mall or finishing up some work."

If I could change one thing about the University of Iowa, I'd "flatten the hills on campus."

Three things every student at the University of Iowa should do before graduating are "participate in the dance marathon, go for a run along the Iowa River, and go to a Hawkeye football game!"

Kansas

Address: 119 Anderson Hall, Manhattan, KS 66506

Phone: 785-532-6011

E-mail address: k-state@k-state.edu

Web site URL: www.k-state.edu

Year Founded: 1863

Private or Public: Public

Religious Affiliation: None

Location: Rural

Number of Applicants: 6,658

Percent Accepted: 95%

Percent Accepted who enroll: 50%

Number Entering: 3,128

Number of Transfers Accepted each Year: 1,017

Middle 50% SAT range: Unreported

Middle 50% ACT range: 27–31

Early admission program EA/ED/None: None

Percentage accepted through EA or ED: NA

EA and ED deadline: NA

Regular Deadline: Rolling

Application Fee: $30

Full time Undergraduate enrollment: 18,545

Total enrollment: 23,081

Percent Male: 52%

Percent Female: 48%

Total Percent Minority or Unreported: 20%

Percent African-American: 4%

Percent Asian/Pacific Islander: 2%

Percent Hispanic: 4%

Percent Native-American: <1%

Percent International: 7%

Percent in-state/out of state: 86%/14%

Percent from Public HS: 81%

Retention Rate: 79%

Graduation Rate 4-year: 24%

Graduation Rate 6-year: Unreported

Percent Undergraduates in On-campus housing: 37%

Number of official organized extracurricular organizations: 594

3 Most popular majors: "Economics & Business, Biology, Psychology"

Student/Faculty ratio: 14:1

Average Class Size: 15

Percent of students going to grad school: 18%

Tuition and Fees: $15,360

In-State Tuition and Fees if different: $5,625

Cost for Room and Board: $6,084

Percent receiving financial aid out of those who apply: 53%

Percent receiving financial aid among all students: 80%

As one of the nation's first land-grant schools, Kansas State University has always been known for its top-notch agriculture programs. However, it also boasts several of the leading academic departments in the nation. Four of its nine colleges are ranked in the top ten in the United States: the College of Agriculture, College of Human Ecology, College of Architecture and College of Veterinary Medicine. Among the state's high school seniors and community college transfers, K-State is ranked as the No. 1 choice of university.

Real-World Preparation

Students have the opportunity to begin taking courses in their college of choice as early as freshman year. As the backbone of the University, the College of Arts and Sciences has the largest student enrollment, with about 7,000 undergraduates. But with more than 250 majors available and 50 minors to choose from, many students tend to mix degree programs to match their specific interests. For example, K-State has the largest Leadership Studies program in the country, with over 1,200 students earning a minor in that program.

Each department has its own general education requirements that students must meet before graduation. The requirements vary from college to college, but they can include English, math, foreign language and even public speaking courses. Though some students complain that requirements are a nuisance, others recognize that such courses help provide a "broad, well-rounded education," even though they may not be related at all to one's major.

Each student is assigned a faculty member

who serves as their academic adviser at the beginning of freshman year. Students said advisors have been known to be helpful not only for providing academic assistance, but for providing "real-world" guidance as well, such as finding part-time jobs or internships in a student's field of interest. According to one student, the K-State faculty is committed to "instructing students so that we walk away with the traits needed to be successful."

Students noted that the relationship between students and professors at K-State is "pretty good," and that professors on the whole are perhaps more receptive and dedicated to the undergraduate's education than at other similarly large research universities. One sophomore remarked that the faculty has "been good as far as making undergraduates feel like they're important." He said the majority of professors are interested in interacting with their students, and receptive to speaking with anyone during designated visiting hours. While introductory classes tend to be quite large—often enrolling several hundred students at a time—upper-level courses tend to be much smaller, sometimes with as few as 10 students in the more advanced ones.

K-State also provides its students with a good learning environment. All of the University's general classrooms are currently being renovated to serve state-of-the-art technology, and the campus is completely wireless. Students described their buildings as "very beautiful," with fairly uniform architecture throughout, accented by limestone and ivy.

An At-Home Atmosphere

Despite the fact that K-State boasts more than 23,000 undergraduates, it "has the sort of atmosphere that makes everyone feel comfortable." In fact, many students enjoy studying at K-State because it has "such a friendly campus." One student noted that the administration "bends over backward to help you out," adding that such guidance was one of the main reasons she decided to attend the University in the first place. While the majority of students are from Kansas, the quality of academic programs and the school's out-of-state affordability also make it an attractive place for students from all over. All 50 states are represented in the student population, but most out-of-staters come from Missouri, Nebraska, Texas and Colorado.

Students agreed that most people feel very comfortable on campus, no matter what their background is. Others, however, noted that Kansas is a conservative state and characterized the University, too, as somewhat of a "closed and conservative place." One foreign student remarked that even though the majority of people on campus and in the surrounding town are "very nice to outsiders," sometimes he got the sense that many are "just not used to dealing with people from different cultures." Still, students at K-State tend to be more moderate in their political views than one might expect, and overall the campus is "very receptive" to different opinions and backgrounds.

The Little Apple

One hundred and twenty-five miles west of Kansas City and populated by just over 50,000 residents, Manhattan, Kansas, is definitely known as a college town. Yet it is also home to Fort Riley, a large military base, so its residents are accustomed and welcoming to large amounts of people moving in and out of town.

> "[K-State] has the sort of atmosphere that makes everyone feel comfortable."

Students agreed that the University's relationship with Manhattan is a very good one—the community is involved in University activities, and students are also involved in the community. For example, the student government sends liaisons to attend all city commission meetings and some have even been elected to the city commission, so that a line of communication is maintained between the city and the student body, while the town's residents often attend many of the athletic and cultural events held on campus. Students said that residents are "generally really supportive" of the University, beyond the standard occasional complaints about things like parking, traffic congestion and noise during large events.

Some K-State students complain of a lack of activity and shopping options in Manhattan, since it's primarily a college town. However, they also noted that it is an extremely affordable place to live, and in the words of one student, "you can concentrate here pretty well." Furthermore, residents on the whole are very "nice and kind" to students who are new to the area. Some even noted that Manhattan is experiencing quite a bit of growth, and that several new retail and housing opportunities are being developed as well.

Housing provided by the University is separated from the city, but most students do decide to live off campus. While freshmen are not required to live on campus, it is highly encouraged and about 90 percent choose to do so. By sophomore year, students begin moving into apartment buildings, townhomes or houses, and by junior year the majority of students choose to live away from campus. The University is currently in the process of completing a $100 million housing project to be completed in 2015 that will include more town houses and apartments to supplement the existing suites and residence halls.

Kicking Back in Aggieville

Despite its location in the "Little Apple," K-State campus and surrounding area provide plenty of options for students looking to have a good time. Aggieville, an approximately four-block district of bars, cafés, restaurants and nightclubs within walking distance of campus, is a popular place for crowds to gather both during the week and on the weekends. While it may not be filled with tons of "trendy, hip lounges" for students to hang out in, students said the bar scene is "great," and that there are plenty of fun places to meet up with friends.

With a fairly sizable portion of the student body deciding to join fraternities or sororities, some students considered K-State to be a "huge Greek school." As one student noted, "If you decide to go to the Greek system, your life pretty much revolves around that stuff." Though drinking is a big part of the social scene, particularly for students in the Greek system, "there's still a lot of stuff to do if you don't drink." And for students not involved in fraternity or sorority life, there's also a fairly sizable house party system.

One student described the social scene at K-State as an "at-home atmosphere that's really laid-back and accented by great nightlife." Yet for those not as interested in the bar or frat scene, there are plenty of other options as well. A union programming council coordinates activities several nights each week, while other student groups sponsor their own events. The student union, for example, puts on concerts, free movies and poker nights, among other programs.

Rooting for the Wildcats

As a member of the Big 12 Athletic Conference, K-State boasts championship football and basketball teams. Football games in the fall are an extremely popular activity with students and the Manhattan community alike, who also enjoy attending away games every once in a while. The school has big rivalries with the state's other big public school, the University of Kansas, but also competes heavily with Nebraska and Oklahoma. The Homecoming game is a fairly strong tradition at K-State, during which fraternities, sororities and other student groups create giant floats and parade around town with the marching band.

Beyond the Wildcats, students have the opportunity to participate in almost 600 student clubs and organizations on campus encompassing a broad range of interests, including academics, politics and religion. Groups like the Future Financial Planners, Entrepreneurs Club and Pre-Veterinary Medicine Club also emphasize career interests. Club sports are popular as well, and include water polo, lacrosse, softball and even skydiving teams. Students said campus involvement is a strong tradition at K-State, and one added that the University does a "pretty good job of getting students interested and active in student organizations."

Students recommended that incoming freshmen get involved in some sort of student organization when they arrive on campus. Many agreed that they developed a strong sense of camaraderie working with their peers in various organizations, and that they tended also to interact socially with their groups on the weekends as well. Athletics, in particular, are a good way for students to get to know the University a little better—whether it is joining a club team, playing an intramural sport or just cheering on the Wildcats at a football game. The large number of clubs is also conducive to helping students develop leadership skills, which is something that K-State emphasizes heavily. As one student commented, "The University really empowers students to do great things if they come with an open mind and a positive attitude."—*Kendra Locke*

FYI
If you come to K-State, you'd better bring "school spirit and a love of football!"
What's the typical weekend schedule? "The bar scene is big on Thursday nights, students go out
   with friends on Fridays and Saturdays, and relax around town or study in the library on Sundays."
If I could change one thing about K-State, I'd "improve the transportation situation by adding some
   parking garages and developing a mass-transit system."
Three things every student should do before graduation are "go to an away football game, spend a
   summer in Manhattan to get to know the town a little better when there aren't so many students
   around, and check out the outdoor opportunities in the Konza Prairie Preserve, which is owned by
   the University."

University of Kansas

Address: 1502 Iowas Street, Lawrence, KS 66045
Phone: 785-864-3911
E-mail address: adm@ku.edu
Web site URL: www.ku.edu
Year Founded: 1866
Private or Public: Public
Religious Affiliation: None
Location: Urban
Number of Applicants: 10,157
Percent Accepted: 93%
Percent Accepted who enroll: 36%
Number Entering: 3,702
Number of Transfers Accepted each Year: 2,305
Middle 50% SAT range: Unreported
Middle 50% ACT range: 22–28
Early admission program EA/ED/None: None

Percentage accepted through EA or ED: NA
EA and ED deadline: NA
Regular Deadline: 1-Apr
Application Fee: $30
Full time Undergraduate enrollment: 19,852
Total enrollment: 26,266
Percent Male: 51%
Percent Female: 49%
Total Percent Minority or Unreported: 23%
Percent African-American: 4%
Percent Asian/Pacific Islander: 4%
Percent Hispanic: 4%
Percent Native-American: <1%
Percent International: 6%
Percent in-state/out of state: 74%/26%
Percent from Public HS: Unreported
Retention Rate: 79%

Graduation Rate 4-year: 34%
Graduation Rate 6-year: 58%
Percent Undergraduates in On-campus housing: 22%
Number of official organized extracurricular organizations: 588
3 Most popular majors: Business/Marketing, Journalism, Social Sciences
Student/Faculty ratio: 20:1
Average Class Size: 25
Percent of students going to grad school: 28%
Tuition and Fees: $22,608
In-State Tuition and Fees if different: $9,222
Cost for Room and Board: $7,080
Percent receiving financial aid out of those who apply: 53%
Percent receiving financial aid among all students: 43%

With three campuses in Lawrence, Kansas City, and Overland Park, the University of Kansas is considered the flagship institution of higher learning in the state. Founded in 1866, KU is a comprehensive research university that serves more than 20,000 undergraduates. More than three quarters of the student body comes from within the state, in large part due to the relatively low tuition for Kansans. Nevertheless, given that thousands of students from other states as well as foreign countries also come to KU for their undergraduate education, it is clear that the University certainly has a number of qualities that would attract out-of-state students. Indeed, KU has a strong academic tradition with a large selection of majors and a commitment to improve student life, making the University an attractive place to spend four years of undergraduate study.

In the Classrooms
Prospective students must choose a specific undergraduate school when they submit an application to KU. There are 12 schools, and all except the Medical School are open to undergraduate enrollment. However, only four units within the University are open to freshmen. The others have significant prerequisites

that must be completed before admissions. First-year students have access to the College of Liberal Arts and Sciences, Engineering, Music, and Architecture. Upperclassmen can eventually enroll in other parts of the University such as Business, Journalism, and Pharmacy. Overall, the undergraduate program is very complete, satisfying the pursuits of those who are interested in liberal arts studies and those who are more focused on career preparation.

The University offers more than 190 majors. While there are the traditional chemistry, economics, and history, KU also has much more specialized fields of study, such as cytotechnology, which is the examination and detection of cancer cells. "What is great about KU is that you can be as specific as you want in your major or as broad as you want," said one student.

> **"What is great about KU is that you can be as specific as you want in your major or as broad as you want."**

The University offers an honors program that offers smaller classes oriented toward discussions and research. Honor students also have better access to faculty support and priority enrollment to courses that may otherwise be filled up during the regular sign-up periods. Both incoming and current students can apply to the honors program, but an application is required. For admission into honors, students must have good standardized test scores and strong performances in high school in both receiving high grades and taking challenging classes. "The Honors Program is really useful when you want to get into the classes you want," said one student.

The general education requirements, which are obligatory classes for all students, vary from school to school. After all, people in the engineering school should generally have much better mathematics training than those studying history; therefore, it would be foolish to require the mathematics classes for both engineers and historians. In the College of Liberal Arts and Sciences, students must complete a long list of courses in English, foreign language, western and non-western cultures, sciences, and mathematics. Most of the classes are finished within the first two years of study because they can help pinpoint students into the specific majors as well as provide

the necessary general skills in all high-level classes. "The requirements can sometimes get complicated, but I like them because you are exposed to a variety of topics instead of just your major," said one student.

As to the classes, they are generally manageable. "There are a few professors who are out there to get you," said one student. "But I think most of them are pretty lenient." The class sizes vary from a dozen students to several hundred. For freshmen, it tends to be difficult to get into many of the oversubscribed courses, particularly smaller ones. "It can be frustrating when you are a freshman," said one student. "However, you will eventually get your chance as you get more seniority." Ultimately, for a school considered one of the top 50 public universities in the country by different rankings, the overall assessment of KU academics is quite positive.

Mount Oread

The KU main campus rests on Mount Oread of Lawrence, Kansas, though the name "mount" may be a little misleading. After all, the hill on which KU is located is only 200 feet above the city. Lawrence is the sixth largest metropolitan area in Kansas, which translates into a population of fewer than 100,000. It is mostly considered a college town, and much of the city's activities evolve around KU. However, students do not find Lawrence particularly exciting. "It is a nice, pretty town, but there is just not much to do here," said one student. "The biggest attraction in town is KU, so there is nothing exciting outside of the campus."

The University offers two female-only residences and six coed dorm buildings. The accommodations are quite nice compared to many other universities. The furnishing is simple but sufficient. Like most state universities, on-campus housing is mostly catered to freshmen and sophomores. Juniors and seniors often get a group together and find either apartments or houses in nearby areas. Going off campus is, for many students, a sign of growth and maturity, not to mention the fact that careful budgeting can save students money by moving off campus.

The dining services are responsible for over 20 locations spread across campus. However, there are only three residential dining halls. Others are different cafés, convenience stores, or small retails. Students are mostly happy with the dining options, at least for a short amount of time. After all, most people do not eat on campus for all four years, since off-campus students often have meals elsewhere.

The party scene often revolves around Greek life. As in most universities, no one feels extremely pressured to join a fraternity or sorority, but they certainly represent good socializing opportunities. Most events by Greek houses are open to everyone. In addition, off-campus students also host parties in different locations. "You will find nice parties to have fun every weekend, but they can get repetitive, and then you might want to find other things to do, like going to some on-campus shows or just trying to find something interesting in Lawrence," said one student.

Basketball and the Rest

For all those interested in sports, KU must be one of the most heard-of universities on television, in large part due to its highly successful basketball program. Historically, KU men's basketball ranks third among all collegiate teams and is tied fourth for the total number of national championships. KU is not only one of the most storied teams in the sport. Its first head coach, James Naismith, was in fact the inventor of basketball. The team also once featured all-time greats in professional basketball, such as Wilt Chamberlain and Larry Brown. Due to all these reasons, KU basketball games are not only packed, sometimes the tickets can be extremely difficult to find. "I think we have really strong school spirit because our basketball program dominates almost every year," said one student. KU's location may leave some wanting more, but its solid academics and an ardent school spirit make it a good choice.—*Xiaohang Liu and Paul Treadgold*

FYI
If you come to KU, you'd better bring "a bike. It can be really useful."
What is the typical weekend schedule? "You have to go to basketball games and party the rest of the weekend."
If I could change one thing about KU, I'd "make it easier to sign up for classes."

Kentucky

Centre College

Address: 600 West Walnut Street, Danville, KY, 40422
Phone: 859-238-5350
E-mail address: admission@centre.edu
Web site URL: www.centre.edu
Year Founded: 1819
Private or Public: Private
Religious Affiliation: Presbyterian
Location: Rural
Number of Applicants: 2,176
Percent Accepted: 63%
Percent Accepted who enroll: 25%
Number Entering: 345
Number of Transfers Accepted each Year: 25
Middle 50% SAT range: M: 570–670, CR: 560–700, Wr: 550–680
Middle 50% ACT range: 26–30

Early admission program EA/ED/None: EA
Percentage accepted through EA or ED: 40%
EA and ED deadline: 1-Dec
Regular Deadline: 1-Feb
Application Fee: $40
Full time Undergraduate enrollment: 1,236
Total enrollment: 1,241
Percent Male: 45%
Percent Female: 55%
Total Percent Minority or Unreported: 9%
Percent African-American: 3%
Percent Asian/Pacific Islander: 2%
Percent Hispanic: 2%
Percent Native-American: 1%
Percent International: Unreported
Percent in-state/out of state: 60%/40%
Percent from Public HS: 70%
Retention Rate: 94%

Graduation Rate 4-year: 84%
Graduation Rate 6-year: Unreported
Percent Undergraduates in On-campus housing: 98%
Number of official organized extracurricular organizations: Unreported
3 Most popular majors: Social Sciences, English, Biology
Student/Faculty ratio: 11:1
Average Class Size: 18
Percent of students going to grad school: 40%
Tuition and Fees: $29,600
In-State Tuition and Fees if different: No difference
Cost for Room and Board: $7,400
Percent receiving financial aid out of those who apply: 60%
Percent receiving financial aid among all students: 60%

Situated in the middle of the Bluegrass State, Danville, Kentucky, is the home to Centre College, a top-50 liberal arts college of around 1,200 students. Founded in 1819, Danville is an hour or two away from big-city attractions while maintaining a small-town feel with Southern charm. Centre provides its students an education that is rich in depth and width while offering an intimate environment suitable for social and personal growth.

Harvard of the South

Centre has been called the Harvard of the South, and students there agree with the sentiment behind the moniker. "But since Centre has more Rhodes scholars per capita than Harvard, we really think that Harvard should be referred to as the 'Centre of the North.'" The pride is not unfounded. The average student to teacher ratio is 11:1 and 97% of the professors have earned their doctoral degrees. One student called academics at Centre "well-rounded," adding that the intense workload and strict grading is backed up by an opportunity for growth and a diverse array of options.

Undergraduate students must fulfill Basic Skills Requirements in three areas deemed essential: expository writing, foreign language, and mathematics. In addition to that, students must also earn a total of 12 convocation credits every year for a grade of A on their transcripts. Convocation credits can be fulfilled by attending events ("convos") that are designed to help students become more cultured; students choose from around 40 theater shows, academic talks, music shows, and art exhibitions, among others. In the realm of regular classes, Centre offers a huge variety. There is everything from organic chemistry—which is considered one of the harder classes in the college—and Classics of Ethnography to Glass Blowing, Basketball as a Religion, and The Crusades. The Crusades is a class students can take during "Centre Term" which is a short January term that lasts about three weeks between the fall and spring semesters. In the class, students must make a 45 minute documentary on the Crusades, complete with advertisements and jokes. Students dress up and pillage all around campus, armed with fake swords and a video camera.

Taking advantage of Centre's variety is a cinch. Students report no real difficulties in getting into classes, noting that the college has a very streamlined process of registering kids. One student said that despite her major in the sciences, she is able to take upper-level dramatic and visual-arts classes. And teaching these captivating classes are great professors and an average class size of 18. One student calls professors "the life of academics at Centre" and it is undeniable that Centre professors are particularly dedicated, available, and friendly, in addition to being excellent scholars. "I am really going to miss the many conversations I've had with professors about so many different topics," one student said. "They have not only been my teachers, but also good friends, parental figures, and great mentors for my own personal success." In line with the spirit of the professors, Centre offers students "The Centre Commitment"—if a student meets academic and social requirements, they are guaranteed an internship, a study abroad experience, and graduation in four years. If Centre fails to meet these requirements, the student gets an additional, tuition-free year.

Frat Row and Diversity

Danville is no big city, and that is no secret. Its population is around 15,000 and social options off campus are limited. Campus life and festivities, however, offer a traditional Southern school social life coupled with a diverse array of new and exciting options. Greek life is a prominent figure in social life at Centre, where rushing is a big deal, and frat parties are the center of party life. But one member of a sorority at Centre explained that it is in no way exclusive or demanding. "I've never felt that being in a sorority has affected my reputation or inhibited my friend group in any way," she said.

Party nights are Wednesday, Friday, and Saturday. Wednesday is for the "hardcore partiers," while Friday is suitable for freshmen and Saturday is the biggest party night of the week. The frats are known for throwing annual parties like Phi Kappa Tau's "Air Guitar," a huge deal on campus which includes a dance competition. Sigma Alpha Epsilon's "Paddy Murphy" and Sigma Chi's "Derby Days" are other big parties. If a student is not too immersed in Greek life, there are other options: there are parties in dorms and apartments, homecoming, and Carnival, a one-day festival and party hosted by the Student Activities Council, featuring astro-jumps, rock-climbing walls, and bands. And because of Centre's liberal alcohol policy, drinking is a common (but certainly not universal) activity on campus. "Strawberry Andre champagne, Kentucky bourbon, Natty Lights," one student remarked, "are the most popular on campus." While alcohol is prevalent, there is no pressure to drink and many can choose not to because a variety of campus parties are designated as dry. Centre's strict drug policy, however, prevents a drug scene from forming. "I feel like if drugs are used, no one knows about it," one student said.

> "Centre is different because its number one priority is its students. Everything is personalized."

As for the diversity of the student body, Centre does pretty well despite its location in a small, rural town in Kentucky. Students explain that while Centre is not divided into clear cliques, there is evidence of segregation. There are the athletes, the artsy kids, the nerds, the World of Warcraft kids, "the J.Crew and Brooks Brothers crowd," and the "Lilly Pulitzer hoard." In the past, Centre has received applications from 48 states, but 60% of the students enrolled come from Kentucky. Socioeconomic diversity is not something that Centre talks about extensively, but one student is assured that it exists, despite preconceived notions. "There is no such thing as the rich, white stereotype at Centre—there is the fun, outgoing, helpful stereotype." It is important to note, nonetheless, that the student body is mostly white, Southern, and upper-middle class.

Campus Strolls

Centre's campus is a beautiful one, filled with buildings that are modern and old, and with trees and greens to satisfy a need for refreshment. Old Centre is a "historic and beautiful" building on campus that students like to pride themselves on. The Greek Revival structure stands on a slight hill, and a tree with a rope for swinging attracts students on lazy afternoons. Campus Centre is a favorite hangout spot. It features the dining hall, Everyday Cafe, which offers an alternative to traditional dining halls, with fireplaces, and a game room upstairs, complete with billiards, ping-pong, foosball, and multiple video gaming systems.

Dormitories are, apparently, nothing special. Freshmen dorms are known to promote cross-class and cross-gender bonding and often define a student's group of friends. Because of Centre's Dorm, conditions tend to improve with seniority; Pearl Hall is Centre's newest and hottest housing option and has been certified LEED GOLD for its environmentally friendly design. There are very few themed housing options at Centre, and most dorms are randomly assigned freshman year and beyond. But every year, the administration assigns a residence hall to the "artsy, international, nerdy" types who are into art, theater, or dance. There is also a substance-free hall for those who request it, and RAs to make sure things are in order in every residence hall on campus. "The RAs exist, but they don't make a huge difference,"

one student said. "You either don't care about them, or you're their friend."

Two prominent landmarks on campus serve as the center of two Centre traditions. The college seal, which is set in the sidewalk in front of Old Centre, is the home to a romantic myth. Legend has it that if two students kiss on top of the seal, they will end up married (which isn't too big of a stretch—a large number of Centre alums are married to each other). Another is a statue called "The Flame" which was originally donated by an alumnus. The tradition is called "running the flame" and can be witnessed during Rush Week or after big athletic victories. One student explained that "it involves stripping naked in your dorm, running to The Flame, circling it three times and returning, often chased by the Department of Public Safety, also known as campus police."

Like most other colleges in the South, Centre is home to frats, sororities, preps, and Natty Lights. But both the administration and student body are working toward creating an environment that is more open, more international, and more cultured. And so far, it has been working. A wide diversity of students will feel at home there. Socially and academically, Centre offers a rich experience.—*Margaret Lee*

FYI
If you come to Centre, you'd better bring boat shoes.
If I could change one thing about Centre, I'd get better restaurants in town.
What surprised me the most about Centre when I arrived was how frickin' awesome it was.

University of Kentucky

Address: 100 Funkhouser Building, Lexington, KY 40506
Phone: 859-257-2000
E-mail address: admissions@uky.edu
Web site URL: www.uky.edu
Year Founded: 1865
Private or Public: Public
Religious Affiliation: None
Location: Urban
Number of Applicants: 13,537
Percent Accepted: 69%
Percent Accepted who enroll: 46%
Number Entering: 4,328
Number of Transfers Accepted each Year: 1644
Middle 50% SAT range: M: 500–630, CR: 490–610, Wr: 470–600
Middle 50% ACT range: 22–28
Early admission program EA/ED/None: None

Percentage accepted through EA or ED: NA
EA and ED deadline: NA
Regular Deadline: 15-Feb
Application Fee: $50
Full time Undergraduate enrollment: 19,927
Total enrollment: 27,108
Percent Male: 49%
Percent Female: 51%
Total Percent Minority or Unreported: 21%
Percent African-American: 8%
Percent Asian/Pacific Islander: 3%
Percent Hispanic: 3%
Percent Native-American: <1%
Percent International: 1%
Percent in-state/out of state: 76%/24%
Percent from Public HS: Unreported
Retention Rate: Unreported
Graduation Rate 4-year: 29%

Graduation Rate 6-year: 57%
Percent Undergraduates in On-campus housing: 27%
Number of official organized extracurricular organizations: 348
3 Most popular majors: Business/Marketing, Communications/Journalism, Education
Student/Faculty ratio: 18:1
Average Class Size: 25
Percent of students going to grad school: Unreported
Tuition and Fees: $18,740
In-State Tuition and Fees if different: $9,128
Cost for Room and Board: $9,974
Percent receiving financial aid out of those who apply: 69%
Percent receiving financial aid among all students: 51%

A school with more than 19,000 undergraduates, the University of Kentucky boasts a wide variety of courses and majors, accessible faculty, and a basketball team with the "most ridiculous and hardcore fan base ever."

Book Learnin'

Students appreciate the wide variety of majors and courses offered, but they cringe when it comes time to register for classes; one senior Spanish major lamented that "unless you have early registration benefits, it can sometimes be very difficult to get into classes that you want" and said that some of the classes are too big. The problem is especially salient for science majors in popular departments like biology and chemistry; indeed, another student estimated that the average class size for a science course was around 200 students. Still, one senior says, "Many students start off being premed but quit later on."

At such a large school, students say that they initially expected professors to be inaccessible but were pleasantly surprised to discover the opposite was true. While one senior sociology major advises that "it's up to students to forge ties with professors," students agree that professors are very approachable and willing to help students if asked. Several students recommend courses taught by Kim Woodrum, UK's director of General Chemistry, and Dr. Alan DeSantis, a popular communications professor. Nevertheless, one student who switched her major from biology to Spanish reveals, "I've found that my English and Spanish professors are much more approachable than when I was a Biology major and tried to visit those professors' office hours."

This divide between the sciences and the humanities extends beyond their faculties; students feel strongly that studies in the humanities are considered far easier than studies in math and sciences. Still, the University offers a variety of courses and majors in both areas. In the humanities, students rave about Human Sexuality courses and unique minor programs, like Folklore and

Mythology, Indian Culture, and Appalachian Studies. On the flip side, UK's engineering programs are lauded by students, and the school's medical center offers plenty of opportunities for research.

For many, the financial benefits for in-state students outweigh the disadvantages of attending such a large university. Indeed, many students cite scholarships as their primary reason for coming to UK; the University offers many awards to incoming freshmen ranging from the full-ride Otis A. Singletary Scholarship to the Flagship Scholarship, which automatically awards $1,500 to freshmen who score a 26–27 on the ACT and maintain a 3.30 unweighted GPA.

For advanced students, UK also offers an Honors Program that grants them advanced registration privileges and small seminar courses in the Program. Honors students must take four interdisciplinary colloquia that each concentrate on an era in the history of the Western world. Students are also required to complete an independent project either with a member of the Honors faculty or in the department of the student's major.

"It was one of the best academic experiences I had at UK. The faculty is engaging, and some of the students are very motivated to learn," says a sophomore Sustainable Agriculture major of the Honors Program. "All of my honors classes were fascinating." As a bonus, the colloquia courses also satisfy UK's distributional requirements, which include classes in humanities, sciences, writing, mathematics, foreign languages, and non-Western cultures.

Another unique program that the University offers is the Discovery Seminar Program for freshmen. These courses are small seminars with fewer than 25 students that often satisfy University requirements and focus on topics like comparative geology and ecocentrism.

Off Campus, On the Ball

Students coming to the University of Kentucky don't expect to stay there for long. At least, not in the dorms.

"Mainly freshmen live in dorms," says one junior. For this reason, many students say that housing does not improve with seniority because it doesn't really matter. "Sophomores, juniors, and seniors live in off-campus apartments or Greek housing," says one senior. Students say that one reason that people move off campus so soon is that it is more cost-effective. Meal plans are a particular area that needs improvement

according to many students, who complain that they are not flexible enough and over-priced. Popular on-campus spots include Ovid's Café and Blazer Café, but students are more excited about Lexington's off-campus restaurants and bars. Students also feel safe in Lexington, which one sophomore described as a "bikeable city," which also contributes to the high number of students who move off campus. In addition, students highly recommend experiencing Keeneland, a Thoroughbred horse racetrack.

Another reason for such a large off-campus population? The campus maintains a very strict policy on alcohol; the entire campus is dry, and if caught with alcohol, students face UK's three-strike policy, in which punishments increase with each infraction until the student is eventually expelled. However, one freshman says, "These policies aren't enforced equally around campus. It depends on where you live and who catches you."

Go Wildcats!

But the dry policy melts on game day. Renowned for its winning basketball team, the University of Kentucky takes pride in the Wildcats, who hold the record for the most all-time victories in the history of college basketball. Students and alumni alike get seriously pumped for games, and according to one junior, "Basketball is like a religion at UK." Another student says, "I have never, ever seen people that into any sports team."

> **"Basketball is like a religion at UK."**

With such a large fan base, it's natural that athletics take up a lot of room in students' social activities. Only slightly less important to the student body? Greek life.

Making up nearly 20% of the student population, those students involved in Greek life praise it gratuitously, but students on the outside say "it is a very exclusive group whose events and parties are not open to everyone." Although one Tri-Delta sorority member claims that there exists no hatred between sororities and that "everyone hangs out," one senior not in a fraternity or sorority says of the social scene at UK, "If you are not in a frat or a sorority, you are left to fend for yourself."

One advantage students believe that Greek life has is that the very formal rush week that takes place before classes begin in the fall gives participants a chance to "meet new people and get involved before school even starts!"

Still, for students not interested in either of these pursuits adjusting to UK might be difficult. Although another favored activity among the student body is involvement in religious organizations, those students who join religious organizations are often the same ones who participate in Greek life and regularly attend athletic events. "Sometimes I feel like I'm the only one in the world without season tickets and Greek letters," says one freshman anthropology major.

Home Is Where the Heart Is

The students who do love the University of Kentucky love it without hesitation. Students say that the atmosphere is friendly and supportive—not what you'd expect from a large research university. Despite its shortcomings, the University of Kentucky has that special something for many students, whether it's a community of die-hard basketball fans or the Sustainable Agriculture program. Says one sophomore biology major, "I decided to go to UK because as soon as I set foot on campus, it felt like home."—*Lauren Oyler*

FYI

If you come to the University of Kentucky, you'd better bring "your drinking shoes and a healthy obsession with UK athletics."

What's the typical weekend schedule? "Go out with your fraternity or sorority on Friday, sleep in until it's time for tailgating on Saturday, go out with your fraternity or sorority again on Saturday, and do homework all day on Sunday."

If I could change one thing about UK, I'd "make cooking facilities more available for all students."

Three things every student at UK should do before graduating are "experience Keeneland, go to a basketball game, and try to get into the 18th floor of the Patterson Office Tower."

Louisiana

Address: 1146 Pleasant Hall, Baton Rouge, LA 70803
Phone: 225-578-1175
E-mail address: admissions@lsu.edu
Web site URL: www.lsu.edu
Year Founded: 1860
Private or Public: Public
Religious Affiliation: None
Location: Urban
Number of Applicants: 15,093
Percent Accepted: 73%
Percent Accepted who enroll: 46%
Number Entering: 5,135
Number of Transfers Accepted each Year: 1,205
Middle 50% SAT range: M: 550–650, CR: 520–630, Wr: 490–600
Middle 50% ACT range: 23–28
Early admission program EA/ED/None: None

Percentage accepted through EA or ED: NA
EA and ED deadline: NA
Regular Deadline: 15-Aprl
Application Fee: $40
Full time Undergraduate enrollment: 23,396
Total enrollment: 27,824
Percent Male: 49%
Percent Female: 51%
Total Percent Minority or Unreported: 21%
Percent African-American: 9%
Percent Asian/Pacific Islander: 3%
Percent Hispanic: 3%
Percent Native-American: <1%
Percent International: 1%
Percent in-state/out of state: 85%/15%
Percent from Public HS: 57%
Retention Rate: 85%

Graduation Rate 4-year: 27%
Graduation Rate 6-year: 59%
Percent Undergraduates in On-campus housing: 25%
Number of official organized extracurricular organizations: 300
3 Most popular majors: Biology, Psychology, Business
Student/Faculty ratio: 21:1
Average Class Size: 24
Percent of students going to grad school: Unreported
Tuition and Fees: $13,800
In-State Tuition and Fees if different: $5,086
Cost for Room and Board: $7,238
Percent receiving financial aid out of those who apply: 57%
Percent receiving financial aid among all students: 76%

As the largest institution of higher learning in the state, Louisiana State University is also the flagship school for Louisiana. Located in Baton Rouge, LSU may be best known among sports fans as the home of the Tigers, a college football powerhouse. Nevertheless, in the academic world, the University is also well known for its top-notch graduate programs and research projects. Home to more than 20,000 undergraduates, LSU offers a large variety of opportunities to students in both academics and research. Opened as an institution focused on military training, LSU now ranks among the nation's top-tier universities and attracts students from around the world.

Plenty of Choices

LSU is a large university. In fact, it is composed of 17 different schools and colleges, ranging from the traditional College of Arts and Sciences to the School of Library and Information Science. However, the present scheme of academic organization is under review. The University is working to make the system work more efficiently. "It does not make much difference which school you are in," said one student. "Besides your major, you probably will end up taking classes outside of your school anyway because there are extra requirements that you have to fulfill."

LSU has majors in over 70 fields of study. Students can also choose from a large selection of concentrations from within each major. For example, students majoring in Chemistry can choose to focus on chemical, physics, polymers, secondary education, or any other fields related to the topic. "In terms of majors, you have a lot of options," said one student. Furthermore, a great number of students at LSU are also preprofessional, focusing their studies to prepare for graduate school in medicine, engineering, and a variety of academic fields. "A lot of people know exactly what to study. That is why we have so many pre-somethings at LSU," said one student. "It is also a good thing to know your major before you come here because then you don't spend too much time on unrelated classes."

The class size at LSU can be slightly overwhelming for some incoming freshmen. Some lectures can have several hundred people, and students are often sitting in places where they can barely spot the instructor. Of course, those are mostly introductory classes. Smaller seminars that encourage student participation are also available, especially for upperclassmen. Some majors, like those in humanities, can sometimes have much smaller classes earlier in the students' academic years. People in majors that require a long list of introductory classes, such as biology, can expect to have many large lectures before finding smaller classes.

Registration for classes can also be difficult, especially for smaller classes. "It can be really frustrating," said one student. "Sometimes, you just get unlucky and cannot be in the classes you like." For all those wishing to have an easier time with registration and better access to smaller classes, the University does have an honors program, which allows students to enroll in relatively small classes that focus on discussions. Furthermore, honors students at LSU must complete more extensive independent projects and theses.

According to most students, the classes are manageable at LSU. "You just have to make sure that you are not taking five really hard classes all at once," said one student. Professors are generally helpful and open to students' suggestions. However, it is certainly much easier to know professors for all those in smaller classes. It is more difficult for students in large lectures to approach their instructor. Of course, the teaching assistants from those lectures can be valuable resources, at least for the most part. "Some of the teaching assistants really try to help us," said one student. "You should definitely take advantage of this opportunity. Sometimes, they can be much more helpful than professors." Different tutoring and counseling facilities are also widely available to those needing help in topics such as mathematics and writing.

Most students are certainly satisfied with their academic experience and believe that not only do they learn a great deal in classrooms, but they can also acquire a lot of knowledge from one another. "You will find a lot of intelligent people who are going to blow you away with their knowledge," said one student. "We have people of diverse interests, and you can learn so much from them just by having a conversation with them."

Baton Rouge

As the second largest city of Louisiana, Baton Rouge is home to more than 200,000 people. It is also one of the most important ports on the Mississippi River. The city has also been one of the fastest-growing metropolitan areas of the United States. In addition, southern Louisiana is well known for its culture. After all, there is still a strong French influence in that part of the country, which is certainly reflected by Baton Rouge and its celebration of Mardi Gras. "Baton Rouge is the capital of Louisiana and probably the most important city after New Orleans," said one student. "So we have a lot of things to do here. But many people just don't take the time to explore the city." Indeed, a number of students have indicated that they spend much of their time within the University's campus and rarely venture outside, thus missing out on many of the activities provided by Baton Rouge.

> "LSU is great. We have a little bit of everything."

The majority of students live off campus. "You can find a lot of housing at a pretty decent price around campus. Also, you will probably have rooms bigger than what you find in dorms," said one student. However, most people agree that freshmen should live on campus. "Dorm life is part of a college experience," said one student. It is much easier to meet new people and adjust to college life without worrying about finding, paying for, and maintaining off-campus housing. According to students, the dorm rooms are well kept, but very small.

The University operates two residential dining locations, as well as a large number of retail eateries. The meal plans consist of meals, served at one of the two dining halls, and paw points, which are dining dollars that can be used at any of the retail locations, which range from McDonald's to small coffee shops. "The food here is fine," said one student. "And if you don't like dining halls, there are a lot of really good eateries around campus."

Greek life is a major part of the social scene at LSU. The fraternities and sororities host some of the biggest parties on weekends. For those not interested in Greek life, there are many bars and clubs around LSU. At the same time, the city of Baton Rouge certainly presents many nightlife activities for students. The school maintains a relatively strict alcohol policy, but, as long as the parties are approved beforehand, students generally encounter no problem with the campus authorities.

Geaux Tigers

It is almost impossible to talk about LSU without mentioning football. The team has the 12th most victories in NCAA history, three national championships, and 13 conference titles. Playing in a stadium that seats more than 90,000 people, the Tigers provide one of the most important weekend activities for LSU students. Starting with tailgates early in the morning, almost the entirety of Saturdays is reserved for football games. As a result, the University has a very strong school spirit with cheers of "Geaux Tigers" instead of "Go Tigers" to emphasize the Cajun history of Louisiana.

"LSU is great. We have a little bit of everything," said one student. That pretty much sums up student experience at LSU. There are plenty of academic and social opportunities. Although some parts of college life, such as big lectures and on-campus housing, are not as great, most students are happy with their college choice and the education that they receive.—*Xiaohang Liu and Paul Treadgold*

FYI
What is the typical weekend schedule? "Football."
If I could change one thing about LSU, I'd "build more parking spaces."
Three things every student at LSU should do before graduating are "explore Baton Rouge, attend a football game, and go to a Mardi Gras parade."

Loyola University

Address: 6363 St. Charles Avenue, Campus Box 18, New Orleans, LA 70118-6195

Phone: 504-865-3240

E-mail address: admit@loyno.edu

Web site URL: www.loyno.edu

Year Founded: 1912

Private or Public: Private

Religious Affiliation: Roman Catholic

Location: Suburban

Number of Applicants: 5,399

Percent Accepted: 57%

Percent Accepted who enroll: 25%

Number Entering: 773

Number of Transfers Accepted each Year: 231

Middle 50% SAT range: M: 540–650, CR: 570–670, Wr: 550–660

Middle 50% ACT range: 24–29

Early admission program EA/ED/None: None

Percentage accepted through EA or ED: NA

EA and ED deadline: NA

Regular Deadline: None/ Priority Application deadline: 12/1

Application Fee: $20

Full time Undergraduate enrollment: 2,859

Total enrollment: 4,772

Percent Male: 41%

Percent Female: 59%

Total Percent Minority or Unreported: 45%

Percent African-American: 17%

Percent Asian/Pacific Islander: 4%

Percent Hispanic: 13%

Percent Native-American: 1%

Percent International: 2%

Percent in-state/out of state: 42%/58%

Percent from Public HS: Unreported

Retention Rate: 82%

Graduation Rate 4-year: Unreported

Graduation Rate 6-year: Unreported

Percent Undergraduates in On-campus housing: 49%

Number of official organized extracurricular organizations: 90

3 Most popular majors: Marketing, Communication Studies, Psychology

Student/Faculty ratio: 10:1

Average Class Size: Unreported

Percent of students going to grad school: 64%

Tuition and Fees: $33,302

In-State Tuition and Fees if different: No difference

Cost for Room and Board: $10,900

Percent receiving financial aid out of those who apply: 85%

Percent receiving financial aid among all students: 99%

Imagine the quintessential college experience: arriving for the first day of freshman year with suitcases in hand, feeling lightweight as your body fills with anticipation as you face the school you will spend the next four years attending. At Loyola University of New Orleans, a sprawling luxurious green front lawn in front of the century old Marquette Hall, which faces New Orleans's stunning Audubon Park, makes the first-impression experience truly memorable.

Small University in the Big Easy

Loyola is a Jesuit university situated in uptown New Orleans, directly in front of the historic St. Charles Avenue streetcar line. The Loyola campus is very centralized with most buildings and student dormitories within half a mile of each other. "It is easy to get to class on time," one student said. "You can just roll out of bed and get to class in three to five minutes. It is great to have such a small campus."

Although Loyola is religiously affiliated, students do not feel the weight of the school's Catholic ties on a day-to-day basis. "Professors will sometimes mention the Jesuit ideals that the university is built upon, but there is not a feeling of Catholicism everywhere you go," said one student. Another student noted that the only time he is reminded of the University's religious ties is when he walks by the Holy Name of Jesus Church to the left of Marquette Hall and witnesses newlywed couples emerge. "This happens a lot," he said, especially during the spring.

Many students noted that they enjoyed the year-round subtropical climate in New Orleans, which although may be sweltering in the summer never becomes too chilly in the winter. New Orleans' Audubon Park, a block off campus, is especially vibrant with floral colors in the spring.

New Orleans itself is an exciting city that students love to become involved in: through community service, culinary touring or nightlife. New Orleans boasts many cultural festivals, ranging from Po-Boy fest, which celebrates the traditional French bread sandwich, to the Jazz and Heritage Festival, which draws artists such as Simon and Garfunkle and Pearl Jam. One student said the most popular festival with Loyola students is the Voodoo Experience, a festival, held in October. "Voodoo Fest," as students call it, features popular music like Eminem and Ozzy Osbourne.

The city may be so enticing that people who grow up in New Orleans never want to leave. One student said, "I feel that Loyola is maybe 66 percent local (New Orleanian), and 33 percent out-of-city. Or maybe 75 percent to 25 percent."

> **"It is easy to get to class on time. You can just roll out of bed."**

Loyola's Web site reports that 58 percent of students come from out of state, with 48 states represented. However, some students feel that classmates originally from New Orleans may be more prominent on campus.

And All that Jazz
Students say that Mass Communications and Music are the two strong and popular areas of study for undergraduates. In fact, Loyola offers four derivations on the Mass Communications major: Advertising, Journalism, Media Studies and Public Relations. Loyola offers fourteen different majors involving music, ranging from Music Composition to Vocal Performance to Music Industry Studies to Music Therapy, and it boasts successful music graduates including New Orleans natives Harry Connick Jr. and Ellis Marsalis. Although the plethora of music classes may seem a haven for a music enthusiast, one student said, "I have heard that music industries and music are pretty hard." Music students are faced with "a lot of work," the student said, "but they enjoy it as far as I can tell." And all students enjoy the benefits of having a strong music program. "The free student jazz performances are wonderful," one student said.

For other majors, like the sciences and social studies, one student commented that the workload for these courses was not too bad, but not too easy. The student said, "For every lecture period, maybe about 1.5 or 2 hours is put into studying and reviewing material covered that day." Students have a lot of help though in covering and understanding their coursework. A student said, "Faculty members are indeed very accessible and very friendly. The fact that Loyola is so small means that the teachers develop a closer relationship with their students than perhaps a bigger university would."

Southern Comfortable
In terms of social life on campus, many students noted that everyone at Loyola was reasonably friendly. "Everybody's relatively nice," one student said. "It's pretty easy to make friends." The student added, "New Orleans is just a friendly city." The student population is very diverse. One student commented that there is not one dominant social scene, that there is a generally even mix of different kinds of people. "It seems to be an even mixture of your typical preps and hipsters," a student said.

Many students drink, one student said, but binge drinking "is not a big problem." Loyola's policy on alcohol, the student explained is, "If you have alcohol in your room and you're not 21 and [the Loyola police] catch you, you get a fine. If they catch you with drugs in your room you get arrested, not necessarily expelled." New Orleans' drinking laws are fairly lenient; people over 21 can publicly carry open plastic containers containing alcohol. The open container law is very rare in other cities.

Greek life is not big at Loyola, although the university does have sororities and fraternities. One student compared Greek life at Loyola to other universities in the state: "It's nothing like Louisiana State University or Tulane University. It's just not super important to be in a frat or sorority here."

Another student mentioned how close the ties are between Loyola and Tulane University, situated directly next to Loyola and often overlapping in student life. One student said, "I have a whole lot more friends at Tulane than here at Loyola, and I hang out with those Tulane friends in most of my free time."

Student life within Loyola usually stays on campus, save for local festivals or concerts. The most popular social venues include the just off-campus Friar Tucks and Club Ampersand and the Howling Wolf in downtown New Orleans.

Sweet Home Louisiana
Loyola's beautiful campus and happy student body would make anyone feel at home. Although Loyola has a large proportion of

students from Louisiana, nonlocals revel in local festivities and Southern culture. Loyola students like the tight-knit nature of a small school on a small campus within a large, vibrant city.—*Susannah Albert-Chandhok*

FYI

If you come to Loyola, you'd better bring "a friendly attitude."

If you come to Loyola, you'd better leave "a heavy coat."

Every student should, before graduating, attend the Voodoo Experience, a festival that is "life changing."

Tulane University

Address: 6823 St. Charles Avenue, New Orleans, LA 70118

Phone: 504-865-5731

E-mail address: undergrad.admission@tulane.edu

Web site URL: www.tulane.edu

Year Founded: 1834

Private or Public: Private

Religious Affiliation: None

Location: Urban

Number of Applicants: 43,815

Percent Accepted: 26%

Percent Accepted who enroll: 14%

Number Entering: 1,625

Number of Transfers Accepted each Year: 425

Middle 50% SAT range: M: 620–700, CR: 610–700, Wr: 620–710

Middle 50% ACT range: 29–32

Early admission program EA/ED/None: EA

Percentage accepted through EA or ED: Unreported

EA and ED deadline: 15-Nov

Regular Deadline: 15-Jan

Application Fee: $0

Full time Undergraduate enrollment: 5,993

Total enrollment: 7,803

Percent Male: 43%

Percent Female: 57%

Total Percent Minority or Unreported: 33%

Percent African-American: 8%

Percent Asian/Pacific Islander: 5%

Percent Hispanic: 5%

Percent Native-American: 1%

Percent International: 3%

Percent in-state/out of state: 31%/69%

Percent from Public HS: Unreported

Retention Rate: 91%

Graduation Rate 4-year: 74%

Graduation Rate 6-year: Unreported

Percent Undergraduates in On-campus housing: 44%

Number of official organized extracurricular organizations: 250

3 Most popular majors: Business, Health Services, Psychology

Student/Faculty ratio: 8:1

Average Class Size: 15

Percent of students going to grad school: Unreported

Tuition and Fees: $41,884

In-State Tuition and Fees if different: No difference

Cost for Room and Board: $9,824

Percent receiving financial aid out of those who apply: 73%

Percent receiving financial aid among all students: 92%

Tulane University is a school of many dualities. It is an international research university with over 35 different countries represented; yet it is described as an intimate community of students and faculty. There is both a strong pride in "The Green Wave" and, perhaps, an even greater pride in its city, New Orleans. Students enjoy the strong campus culture with relaxed Greek life and local dives, but also venture downtown to listen to live jazz and taste classic Southern fare. Students take business classes alongside glassblowing courses, eat cheese fries and dance on the tables of campus bars, and engage in community service throughout New Orleans—NOLA, to adopt the campus lingo. "There are so many different types of people," said one sophomore, "I love that there isn't just one type of Tulane student."

Rigorous, yet relaxed

Tulane has different academic requirements depending on the degree, which range from traditional disciplines such as business, law, and liberal arts, to programs distinct to Tulane such as its renowned Public Health and Tropical Medicine degree. All students in the School of Liberal Arts must fulfill a set of distributional requirements that include courses in the humanities, social sciences, mathematics, and foreign language. One junior noted that she did not feel particularly stressed or overwhelmed in fulfilling these expectations.

"There are so many different types of people," said one sophomore, "I love that there isn't just one type of Tulane student."

One element that distinguishes a Tulane education is its first year TIDES Program (Tulane Interdisciplinary Experience Seminar), which aims to provide "meaningful connections with a small group of students." The two freshmen interviewed expressed an appreciation for the New Orleans-centric content of over 70 available courses. The program seems to embody the broader Tulane educational philosophy: learning material highly flavored with the culture of its surroundings.

Tulane also offers select admission to its Honors Program, which provides an enhanced learning environment to students with competitive high school records and strong standardized test scores. One sophomore, who is currently in the honor program, said that she chose Tulane Honors because, unlike other schools' equivalent programs, "the Tulane honors program is much more integrated into the rest of campus."

Students reported that one's workload varies depending on which major and department an individual is pursuing. One freshman said that since she was taking pre-requisites for the business school, she had a more exam heavy schedule, while her roommate had more writing assignments. Certain majors on campus are noted for being particularly difficult, including Biomedical and Chemical Engineering, Architecture, Cell and Molecular Biology, Legal Studies, Neuroscience, Chemistry, and Physics. In contrast, two students reported that the Jewish Studies classes and Western Tradition classes, including "The Art of Listening," and drama courses such as "The Fundamentals of Acting" were known to be

easier. The most popular majors include Business, Social Sciences, and Biology, which represent the wide array of interests that can be found throughout the student body.

Student criticism of academics at Tulane stem from some of the organizational structures and logistics associated with classes. Registration for courses was reported to be difficult since the small class size often cannot accommodate the large amount of student interest. Although the process has reportedly been improved in the last couple of years, one junior went so far as to describe registration as "stressful" and a "nightmare." As well, two underclassmen expressed opposition to Tulane's policy of giving priority course access to students with "more credit," which disadvantages freshmen and sophomores by enrolling them last. One freshman reported how a certain economics course even had a waiting list of nearly 40 students. However, the frustration that accompanies the period of selecting classes often has an upside in the average size and scale of Tulane courses. While certain lectures may have more than 100 students, students enjoyed that many of their courses had less than 30 students, which allows for an "intimate" environment of learning.

Tulane draws from a diverse group of academics to form its faculty, with its most famous professors including Melissa Harris-Perry, James Carville, and Dr. Eamon Kelly. As a whole, both underclassmen and upperclassmen said that professors were highly accessible and host office hours around three times a week. One sophomore said that not only did many of her professors bring a passion to their teaching, but are also available outside of the classroom to help with internships and grants. While the difficulty of grading differs from teacher to teacher, as a whole, one freshman felt that teachers were very understanding and flexible with issuing grades. "I feel as if professors really want to help and make sure their students are able to get the grade they deserve," she said.

A "jazzy" social scene
Tulane is a highly social campus, consistently ranking as one of the most active party schools in the country. Although less than 40% of students participate in Greek life, it certainly has a strong presence on campus, according to all students interviewed. Still, one junior said that unlike

other schools, opting to join or not join a fraternity or sorority does not affect a student's social life. Often, frat parties are open to the entire campus and if not, alternate parties and plans are nearly always available. "What I love is that there are so many different social scenes to participate in," said one sophomore. "No matter what you're into, there is a good place to be with people who share your interests."

No discussion of Tulane is complete without reference to all that New Orleans has to offer. "New Orleans is the dominant social scene, " said one student. "It's an adventure every night." Many students expressed similar sentiments, stating that they enjoy exploring the nightlife downtown, listening to jazz on Frenchmen Street, shopping on Magazine Street, or hanging out at Audubon Park. Despite popular belief, going to the famous Bourbon Street in The French Quarter of New Orleans is a less common occurrence among students, aside from formals and Mardi Gras. One student said she only went as a "bucket-list type thing" and that students tend to prefer the bars around campus. Most popular are The Boot, which offers 50 cent shots on Tuesday nights, The Bulldog on Wednesday nights, F&M's on Thursday nights, which is known for their cheese fries, and The Palms on Friday nights. As a whole, the underclassmen and upperclassmen social experience is not too different, however upperclassmen tend to attend more informal house parties, while bar organized events tend to attract a younger crowd. Some of the more notable campus parties include, AEPi's rave every Halloween and during Mardi Gras, an American themed party hosted by SAE in the beginning of the year, and Cowboy Christmas near the end of the first semester. And, of course, nearly all students celebrate with the New Orleans residents in February for Mardi Gras and Fat Tuesday festivities.

Similar to many of its peer institutions, Tulane faces substance abuse on campus. Three students interviewed noted the prominence of drugs on campus, with marijuana and alcohol being the most typical items found at parties and in dorms. One freshman noted that there is no overt pressure to participate in the drinking or drug culture, however if one wishes to use "upper drugs" including cocaine and acid, "there is easy access to it behind closed doors." Punishment for possession of different substances differs, with marijuana being punished more harshly than alcohol. One upperclassman

noted that it is often the freshmen that are most likely to binge drink and get sent to the hospital, yet they often are able to learn their tolerance over the course of their four years. In addition, there are RAs on every floor who often ensure the drinking policy inside the dorm, however one freshman said, "if you play by the rules and are respectful, you won't have any issues with them."

Since Tulane is located in an urban environment, safety is something many students are aware of when walking through the streets late at night. Although the surrounding neighborhood of Tulane is one of the wealthier areas in New Orleans and is relatively safer, armed robberies are not uncommon within a few miles of the school. Tulane also offers blue light security, which will contact a police escorts for students in danger, and Safe Rides, a bus services that will pick students up within a mile radius of campus. The general consensus among students is that if one approaches New Orleans as one would any metropolitan area, students will be well protected and safe.

A mosaic of interests

Although students at Tulane come from all fifty states and from 35 different countries, some students interviewed felt that the campus did not feel particularly diverse. One junior noted that she felt a majority of the students were from the Northeast or California, were predominantly Caucasian, and were either Christian or Jewish. One Jewish freshman even went so far as to jokingly refer to the school as "Jewlane," due to the prominence of the religion on campus. Another student noted that even if appearances may seem similar on the surface, "people come from all different backgrounds." While there may be a large number of students from the coasts, Tulane also has a large number of students from the New Orleans area and from the South, both of which contribute to the overall geographic diversity of the campus. Many students said it would be hard to categorize a specific look on campus since there is "not one type of student," but most agreed that people dressed casually with some preppy flair.

The general style of buildings on campus is Neo-Romanesque, while dorms tend to be more modern. Gibson Hall, the first structure on the present Tulane campus, is described as being one of the most distinctive buildings of the University. Dinwiddie,

Richardson Memorial, Newcomb Hall, and Norman Mayer are also notable buildings on campus. However, one junior noted that her favorite part of campus were the majestic oak trees. "They are absolutely beautiful, and provide the perfect amount of shade from the hot New Orleans sun," she said.

Dorms at Tulane each carry their own distinct personality. Certain freshmen dorms, Sharp and Monroe, tend to attract a more social crowd; Butler is known as the "nerdier" dorm since it is for honors students; and Wall is for students that are "very involved," since it requires an essay to be housed there. Similarly, the sophomore dorms, Phelps and Irby tend to be more party-oriented and SoHo (sophomore honors) tends to be more studious. Most students interviewed said that while housing gets better with seniority, many students choose to move off campus during junior and senior year.

Students at Tulane enjoy becoming involved in the hundreds of student groups that exist on campus. From student government to Greek life, Community Action Council of Tulane University Students (CACTUS) to VOX: Voices for Planned Parenthood, and a Quidditch team to a cheese club, students have ample choices to fulfill their area of interest. Two students noted that the campus newspaper, *Tulane Hullabaloo*, is not too popular, with some students opting for online content such as articles posted on *HerCampus.com*. On-campus jobs, such as being a desk attendant, are popular, as are job opportunities within New Orleans, including babysitting, waitressing, and working for small businesses. "There is something for everyone," said one sophomore. "It is easy to get involved."

While school spirit is common on campus for both the school and for the city, some students said that athletic spirit could be improved. While the non-athletes facilities have been described as "state of the art," complete with indoor and outdoor pools, spinning studio, and basketball courts, the new football stadium is still currently under construction. One freshman noted that he was optimistic about the completion of the new stadium and its impact on school spirit since the games held at the Superdome can often be inconvenient. Still, one student noted that whenever anyone is at the football game they are often decked out in school colors, olive and blue, and can be counted on to cheer on The Green Wave.
—*Larry Milstein*

FYI
If I could change one thing about Tulane, "I'd make the food on campus better."
Three things every student at Tulane should do before graduating are "go to Bourbon Street, try a belgnet at Café du Monde, and listen to live jazz."
The biggest college-wide tradition/event at Tulane is "Mardi Gras."
What surprised me the most about Tulane when I arrived was "how hot the weather was."

Maine

Bates College

Address: 2 Andrews Road, Lewiston, ME 04240
Phone: 207-786-6000
E-mail address: admissions@bates.edu
Web site URL: www.bates.edu
Year Founded: 1855
Private or Public: Private
Religious Affiliation: None
Location: Urban
Number of Applicants: 4,434
Percent Accepted: 30%
Percent Accepted who enroll: 34%
Number Entering: 445
Number of Transfers Accepted each Year: 217
Middle 50% SAT range: M: 630–700, CR: 635–710, Wr: Unreported
Middle 50% ACT range: Unreported
Early admission program EA/ED/None: ED

Percentage accepted through EA or ED: Unreported
EA and ED deadline: 15-Nov
Regular Deadline: 1-Jan
Application Fee: $60
Full time Undergraduate enrollment: 1,660
Total enrollment: 1,660
Percent Male: 49%
Percent Female: 51%
Total Percent Minority or Unreported: 19%
Percent African-American: 3%
Percent Asian/Pacific Islander: 6%
Percent Hispanic: 2%
Percent Native-American: <1%
Percent International: 5%
Percent in-state/out of state: 11%/89%
Percent from Public HS: 56%
Retention Rate: 93%

Graduation Rate 4-year: 83%
Graduation Rate 6-year: 88%
Percent Undergraduates in On-campus housing: 92%
Number of official organized extracurricular organizations: 112
3 Most popular majors: Economics, Political Science, Psychology
Student/Faculty ratio: 10:1
Average Class Size: 15
Percent of students going to grad school: Unreported
Tuition and Fees: $46,800
In-State Tuition and Fees if different: No difference
Cost for Room and Board: Included with tuition
Percent receiving financial aid out of those who apply: 94%
Percent receiving financial aid among all students: 40%

B ates College, a small liberal arts school generally grouped with other Maine colleges such as Bowdoin and Colby, is located in Lewiston, Maine, a town whose claim to fame, as one student pointed out, is that "Mohammed Ali fought here." However, this middle-of-nowhere school proudly boasts such a fun-loving, tight-knit college community that students overwhelmingly proclaim that they could not imagine themselves elsewhere.

An Academic Stronghold
There is no doubt that Bates offers a first-class education for its students; national surveys consistently rank Bates among the top liberal arts colleges in the nation. Though small liberal arts colleges often do not have the resources to offer the wide array of subject areas and depth of study that universities can provide, students at Bates almost universally cite the small class size as something that sets Bates apart from other colleges. According to one freshman, "The great thing about Bates is that the classes are pretty small. You are not merely considered a number in the classroom, but instead you become an active participant whom the professor really gets to know." The average class size at Bates is only 20 people, and each student works individually with a faculty member on their senior thesis. Professors are also generally thought of among students to be easily approachable outside the classroom and extremely receptive to student interest. "In my experience, professors are very happy to talk outside of class about their research, any problems

you may be having in the class, concerns, or just life in general. I've also realized that professors are happy to talk to students who aren't in their classes if they show an interest in the professor's field," said one Bates student.

> "The great thing about Bates is that the classes are pretty small. You are not merely considered a number in the classroom, but instead you become an active participant whom the professor really gets to know."

Although Bates students generally agree that its academics are some of the best offered in the country for its size, the college's approach to academics isn't perfect. In order to ensure the diversity integral to a liberal arts education, Bates has distributional requirements, including a three-science-class requirement that "for nonscience people is just too much!" The workload has also been described as very demanding, one student adding that there is "a LOT of reading." However, another freshman commented that "the workload can be intense when midterms and finals come around, but normally it is manageable if you learn how to organize your time." Students also observe that there is very little competition both in and out of the classroom, even in the face of heavy workloads.

How Batesies Get Down

The tiny town Lewiston, Maine, keeps students close to campus, resulting in a phenomenon that students may either love or hate known as the "Bates Bubble." However, most Batesies seem to love it, saying that that there are enough parties, events and activities on campus to keep most students from either needing or wanting to leave. According to one student, "Because of our isolation and lack of nightlife in Lewiston and lack of Greek Life, it's not your typical college scene. That said, Frye street, our campus houses, is alive and loud Thursday-Saturday, as are many of the dorms, and parties are incredibly inclusive to everyone. If partying's not your scene, there are always concerts, shows, and other activities put on by the school, as well as plenty of students who prefer to stay in at night." The small nature of the school is conducive to creating a cohesive community,

and students are generally extremely happy with their on-campus social life. "Students generally don't want to leave campus because there's too much going on and they don't want to miss it. I can't imagine missing a weekend here!" commented one student.

There are no fraternities or sororities at Bates; however, this is generally considered an advantage rather than a disadvantage. According to one freshman, "The social scene is much more open because of the lack of a Greek system." The students make up for this with huge annual parties, such as the '80s dance, Halloween dance, and foam dance, which according to one student, "are the place to be, these ain't your high school homecomings!"

In terms of drinking, the school has a relatively strict hard-liquor policy: students are subject to a three-strike rule applying to hard liquor that lasts all four years. The three-strike rule requires anyone seen in a room with hard liquor to be given a strike; students with three strikes must meet with the dean. However, this rule applies only to hard liquor and drugs; the school is much more lenient in regards to wine and beer. According to students, "A lot of students do drink, but it is definitely not something you need to do to have fun here, and I know a lot of people who go out each weekend and never drink."

For those few students who have cars and want to get off campus, Lewiston is located relatively close to Freeport, a shopping hub, and Portland, which boasts great restaurants, a bustling city life, and a wide array of ski slopes. However, the center of Bates is clearly the campus itself, and students see this as one of Bates's major attractions. Another student commented, "Every once in a while people will drive out to dinner on the weekends, or those who have cars will drive to ski resorts, but most of the time students stay on campus."

Bates also offers a wide array of extracurricular activities which most students are involved in. Athletics are popular, and students can participate on the varsity, club, or intramural level. While many students do participate in athletics, students seem to only flock to the bleachers for big rivalry games. In addition, there are four competitive a cappella groups that are extremely popular. One student exclaimed, "The Deansmen and the Manic Optimists are all-male groups, the Merimanders are all women, and the Crosstones are coed. They are all amazing! They have concerts every once in a while and they are always packed!"

A Home Away from Home

Students overwhelmingly describe the Bates population as extremely friendly, welcoming, and accepting. One student proclaimed, "If there's one reason to come to Bates, it's the people." Several students explained that, possibly due to the fact that there are two all-freshman dorms to foster a sense of family among the members of the class, their best friends have generally been people they lived with freshman year. In addition, preorientation programs are offered to give freshmen additional chances to make friends and become comfortable in an environment away from home.

Students describe the Bates campus as extremely welcoming, in part due to its small size. One student commented, "It is very easy to meet people because on the weekends you go out with friends from your floor and you end up meeting people from different dorms and classes. The students at Bates are so friendly!" Another student agreed: "It's incredibly easy to meet people because the campus is so small, and everyone's looking for new friends."

While the school has been making efforts to diversify, some students complain of the lack of campus diversity, both in terms of race and socio-economics standing. However, as one student commented, "When walking around campus, you wouldn't necessarily know that the students come from families with money—students really don't flaunt it. The 'dress-code' is very laid-back, which is great. People wear sweatpants everywhere, and that's completely accepted. While some people do get more dressed up on the weekends, it's certainly not fancy at all; I wore heels one night and felt completely out of place." While Bates may not be as diverse as some of its peer institu-

tions, this does not seem to cause any measure of discontentment among students.

Facilities Galore

At Bates, the relatively small campus is designed to foster a sense of community among the students. Most freshmen are placed in one of three freshman dorms: Smith, Clason, and Milliken. Upperclassmen often move off campus to nearby houses or, according to one student, "an area called the village, which is made up of apartment-like buildings with suites inside."

One unique thing about Bates is that there is only one dining hall, which was created in response to a request from the students to create an even more close-knit community. Commons, the dining hall, is "the hot spot on campus." The students describe the food as "surprisingly good" and describe Commons as the perfect place to hang out, chat, and people-watch. Commons seems to be the main source of meals for students; most students interviewed described the local food offerings as both few and less-than-desirable.

In terms of favorite hangouts, there is also Pgill (full name: Pettengill Hall), a building open 24 hours a day that contains classrooms, lounges, professors' offices, and "really comfortable couches." Pgill is described by one freshman as "a much more relaxed study space than the library, and it's nice to have another place to go to work. It also has a wall of windows that overlooks the pond, so it's absolutely gorgeous."

Bates is known for being in the middle of nowhere, and it does not shy away from this reputation. However, this feature may be one of the reasons that it hosts such a tightly knit community—an aspect praised as almost everyone's favorite thing about Bates. In the midst of impressive academics and a beautiful landscape, this home away from home hosts some of the happiest students around.—*Lillian Childress*

FYIs:
If you come to Bates, you'd better bring "a big winter coat and slippers from L.L.Bean."
What's the typical weekend schedule? "Go out on Friday night, sports or homework on Saturdays and then out, work on Sundays. Weekend mornings are usually dedicated to long brunches at Commons."
If I could change one thing about Bates, "I'd create an underground tunnel for students to get to Commons and other buildings without having to freeze!"
Three things every student at Bates should do before graduating are "do the puddle jump (jump in the pond in the middle of January as part of Winter Carnival), go to Commons drunk, and spend a full night in Pgill.

Bowdoin College

Address: 5000 College Station, Brunswick, ME 04011-8441
Phone: 207-725-3100
E-mail address: admissions@bowdoin.edu
Web site URL: www.bowdoin.edu/admissions
Year Founded: 1794
Private or Public: Private
Religious Affiliation: None
Location: Suburban
Number of Applicants: 6,033
Percent Accepted: 19%
Percent Accepted who enroll: 44%
Number Entering: 491
Number of Transfers Accepted each Year: 6
Middle 50% SAT range: M: 650–750, CR: 650–760, Wr: 660–750
Middle 50% ACT range: 29–33

Early admission program EA/ED/None: ED
Percentage accepted through EA or ED: 18%
EA and ED deadline: 1-Nov
Regular Deadline: 1-Jan
Application Fee: $60
Full time Undergraduate enrollment: 1,751
Total enrollment: 1,762
Percent Male: 49%
Percent Female: 51%
Total Percent Minority or Unreported: 27%
Percent African-American: 6%
Percent Asian/Pacific Islander: 11%
Percent Hispanic: 9%
Percent Native-American: 1%
Percent International: Unreported
Percent in-state/out of state: 12%/88%
Percent from Public HS: 55%
Retention Rate: 98%

Graduation Rate 4-year: 86%
Graduation Rate 6-year: 91%
Percent Undergraduates in On-campus housing: 94%
Number of official organized extracurricular organizations: 109
3 Most popular majors: Government, Economics, English
Student/Faculty ratio: 10:1
Average Class Size: 16
Percent of students going to grad school: 80%
Tuition and Fees: $38,190
In-State Tuition and Fees if different: No difference
Cost for Room and Board: $10,380
Percent receiving financial aid out of those who apply: 74%
Percent receiving financial aid among all students: 41%

B owdoin is one of those unique colleges that appears genuinely loved by all its students, and the intensity of this ardor expands well beyond the unmatched quality of the dining scene and cuisine—though the focus on time spent eating together, in a way, does exemplify values held by this highly selective, extremely intimate liberal arts college tucked up in Brunswick, Maine, where all members of the campus seem to share a particular drive for a broader perspective beyond what they're studying, devoting a lot of their time to activities and pursuits outside of the classroom.

Professors in the Know

Bowdoin fosters an incredibly supportive learning environment, and students seldom talk about their grades. The biggest lecture very rarely spills over 50 students, while the rest of the courses range from 15 to 30, depending on the department. "Though Bowdoin has a lot fewer options than some other schools, generally you can take what you want. At bigger schools people are talking about some great class with some great professor but it's impossible to get into—here, there aren't as many class offerings but you can actually do the things that are advertised," said a senior.

Among the top majors are Government, Biology, English, and Economics, and while students all have something they know they want to take, they are eager to apply their knowledge more broadly. The workload is difficult to generalize and dependent on a person's schedule, but according to a student, "I feel like if you want to get an A, it's totally achievable." For anyone having trouble in a course, he or she can talk to the professor and connect with a tutor at the Center for Learning and Teaching, free of charge.

The classroom exudes an academic vitality, where "everyone sort of carves their own path," said a student. With a ten-to-one faculty to student ratio, professors are unbelievably accessible, almost universally responsive, and understanding about deadlines and extensions. "My Constitutional law professor has been at Bowdoin for 50 years, went to Bowdoin, and has no phone or email but is constantly having office hours. I've never had a professor not know who I am," said a senior. What is exceptional about Bowdoin professors is that they don't limit their advice to what they teach in the classroom, but often push students toward people or clubs they think they will do well in. "They have a grasp of the social scene and will help you bond with other students," said a junior.

A Foodie's Paradise: Fine Dining and Good Living

The two dining halls are a crux of campus life, and for good reason. "It's the number one reason I decided to go here—no one will ever shut up about how great the food is. The size of the school facilitates this feeling you want to be in the dining hall because that's where you see everyone. I'll sit there for two hours at dinner while people come and go. I feel like that's what college is all about," said a senior. There's even a challenge known as "kill the night," the object being to linger the longest in the dining hall at every meal for one day. In terms of the two dining halls, one is bigger and more open and the second a little cozier, but there is no kind of social split between the two as might be found at another college; rather, there is a strong sense of social cohesion. There are a lot of specialty dishes and locally sourced food, customizable meals, plus themed nights multiple times a month. For a taste: lobster on the first day of school, and sometimes blow-torched crème brûlée.

The freshmen are on a weekly 19-meal plan while upperclassmen have more choice, and if hungry outside of mealtimes there is the café in the student union and "Super Snack" on Thursday, Friday and Saturday nights from 11 p.m. to 1:30 a.m. The student union is also a central hang-out spot where people can play pool, collect mail, or study.

The campus is mostly red brick buildings with white trim around the windows, but there is also some variation in the architecture. "All the buildings built before the 1960s are absolutely beautiful, especially in the winter," said a student, who also praised the Walker Art Building by the prominent architects McKim, Meade and White. The science buildings are more modern while the Chapel lends a touch of Gothic feel.

Most people live on campus the first three years, though housing is said to get worse after freshman year. There are nine freshman dorms, two of which are filled with doubles and the rest consisting of quads or quints with rooms connected by a common

room and sharing hall bathrooms. Each dorm has an RA and each hall a proctor, who are focused on safety rather than getting kids in trouble. These dorms have all been recently redone and are located in the center of campus with 60 students in each. Proctors are on duty during weekends with food and movies, and serve as a friend and ally for their freshmen. "You get the talk but it's just to scare you—they're just looking out for your best interests. They see how important it is to have that support," said a freshman.

After freshman year, students can move into upperclassman dorms or one of the eight social houses, converted frats which now organize school social events. Each freshman dorm is affiliated with a social house to give new students an even more inclusive social environment, and members of the houses are matched with freshman buddies. The social houses have nice accommodations but generally come with party-planning responsibilities, and though the administration is trying to change this, they are currently occupied with mostly sophomores. "It's a little sad because each social house has no institutional history and it's so regulated by the school who gets to live in each one of them, so there's no thread between years. They're so PC about it with even ratios and the right kind of people who are going to program events," complained a senior. For sophomores not inclined to live in a social house, there are apartments a quarter mile away from campus which count as on-campus housing. After freshman year, the dorms are bigger, each with a few hundred students.

> "I've never had a professor not know who I am."

The Tower, where a lot of seniors live, has divided reviews; one student described it as "a visual eyesore inside and out." Luckily, there are tons of houses (less so apartments) off-campus that you can split with friends for relatively cheap. A large number of students have jobs as part of work-study or are just looking to make some extra money, and there are plenty of opportunities, whether in the café, dining halls, bookstore, art museum, or elsewhere.

With such a prominent number of athletes, Bowdoin has a heavy sports culture, but besides that, there's no dominating sort of vibe. "It's pretty well-rounded in terms of the kind of people who go here, from the Outing Club to the art department. It's a very balanced place," said one student. Over the past ten years, the school has tried hard to diversify in terms of both racial makeup and geographic distribution—as one student phrased it, "to transform Bowdoin from a bastion of rich, white male students to a place where you can be surrounded by diversity." There are lots of New Englanders moseying around in sweatpants who will work in finance after graduation, plenty of students from the South very involved in religious activities, and a number of people from scattered parts of the country. "Everyone is pretty laid-back but at the same time motivated and interesting," said a student. There is a paucity of international students, and internationals don't receive financial aid. However, for all others, Bowdoin continues to be need-blind with a no loans policy, meaning that it meets the full calculated financial need of all enrolled and entering first-year students—one of the few schools to stay so through the financial crisis.

Pursuits and Places Outside the Classroom

There are a slew of clubs and organizations on campus, and people are constantly motivated to start their own. The Outing Club, a cappella groups, and the weekly newspaper, *The Orient*, all have large memberships, and clubs involved with gender and sexual violence have recently received a lot of attention. "Everyone at Bowdoin is passionate about at least one or two extracurricular activities. They're heavily involved, not just preprofessional; it's one thing that binds us all together," remarked a student.

For a change of pace, students can also meander around town. Compared to almost all small towns in which elite small colleges are located, "Brunswick is by far the best," according to a senior. The town doesn't revolve around the college but is proud to have it there, and relations between the school and residents are very smooth. "There's a misconception about Maine that it's the middle of nowhere and there's nothing. But you have everything you need within five or ten minutes," said a student. Downtown has small, family-owned shops and restaurants, while a five-minute drive away (either by Zipcar or taxi) is a shopping

complex with anything you're missing: Wal-Mart, Best Buy, and the usual. There's a farmer's market on the town green on Fridays and a converted mill at the end of town overlooking the river that now holds a café and gallery. Outside of Brunswick there's also Portland, a great city within half an hour's drive and soon to be accessible by a new train line.

Party Hard or Lay Low

Frats were scrapped 15 years ago and turned into the social houses which Bowdoin has today. Social houses put together campus-wide parties, with usually two every weekend. As can be the case, "if you don't drink alcohol, it can be very difficult at first to adjust," a student admitted. The houses are the dominant social scene for first and second-years, while juniors and seniors tend to have more private parties in their own off-campus houses. "I've heard there is a party every night of the week but most people only go out weekends. It depends on your schedule," said a student. Everything is usually over by one or two, but not because of security; campus security is best represented by one of the security staff who is loved to death by students. Similar to proctors, "he makes it extremely apparent his mission is our safety and not getting us in trouble," said a student.

For a freshman partied out after a crazy few months or someone who prefers low-key weekend activities, there are movies, dance showcases, music recitals and singing concerts to see as well. Sometimes bands or other performers are brought in from outside campus. "Ivies" is a huge and eagerly anticipated event in the spring hosting a bunch of bands, concerts, and parties.

Though drinking is big, drugs are not at all prevalent, and there is also the chemical-free social house and freshman dorm for those who don't want to be involved in either.

Bowdoin has an incredibly active student body—both physically and intellectually. Students don't have a single-minded academic focus, but realize the importance of outside pursuits. There will always be a sports game to watch, a discussion to take part in, or a group of students engaged in conversation late into the evening in one of the dining halls, a delicious meal sitting pleasantly in their stomachs.—*Tao Tao Holmes*

FYI

If you come to Bowdoin, you'd better bring "your favorite recipes, because the dining hall will cook them."

If I could change one thing about Bowdoin, "I wish we had more international students, and sports weren't such a centerpiece."

"What surprised me the most about Bowdoin when I arrived was that all the staff are incredibly kind people who are really committed to making the experience for students as good as it can be. There's a really strong bond between students and staff."

Colby College

Address: 4000 Mayflower Hill, Waterville, ME 04901-8848

Phone: 207-859-4828

E-mail address: admissions@colby.edu

Web site URL: www.colby.edu

Year Founded: 1813

Private or Public: Private

Religious Affiliation: None

Location: Rural

Number of Applicants: 4,835

Percent Accepted: 31%

Percent Accepted who enroll: 32%

Number Entering: 482

Number of Transfers Accepted each Year: 9

Middle 50% SAT range: M: 640–710, CR: 640–720, Wr: 630–710

Middle 50% ACT range: 28–31

Early admission program EA/ED/None: ED

Percentage accepted through EA or ED: 43%

EA and ED deadline: 1-Jan

Regular Deadline: 1-Jan

Application Fee: $65

Full time Undergraduate enrollment: 1,846

Total enrollment: 1,846

Percent Male: 46%

Percent Female: 54%

Total Percent Minority or Unreported: 14%

Percent African-American: 2%

Percent Asian/Pacific Islander: 8%

Percent Hispanic: 3%

Percent Native-American: <1%

Percent International: 5%

Percent in-state/out of state: 10%/90%

Percent from Public HS: Unreported

Retention Rate: 96%

Graduation Rate 4-year: 83%

Graduation Rate 6-year: 88%

Percent Undergraduates in On-campus housing: 94%

Number of official organized extracurricular organizations: 98

3 Most popular majors: Biology, Economics, Political Science

Student/Faculty ratio: 10:1

Average Class Size: 12

Percent of students going to grad school: Unreported

Tuition and Fees: $48,520

In-State Tuition and Fees if different: No difference

Cost for Room and Board: Included with tuition

Percent receiving financial aid out of those who apply: 73%

Percent receiving financial aid among all students: 43%

Tucked away on Mayflower Hill in the tiny town of Waterville, Maine, Colby College offers top-notch academic programs, a friendly student community, and some of the best dining hall food in the country. The campus itself plays a huge role in Colby's student life, even though downtown Waterville is just around the corner. With lots of volunteer and study-abroad options and a wide spectrum of political and social opportunities, Colby students may be right in believing they have it all.

Campus on a Hill

Colby's setting atop Mayflower Hill, though perfectly picturesque in any season of the year, isolates the school from the town. The fact that "a lot of people are from New England and are white," as one student put it, probably doesn't help. "They call it the Colby bubble," said a sophomore of the school's insularity. "If you get involved with the community," she added, "[people on campus] call it 'bursting the bubble.'"

The steps of Miller Library have served as a popular site for drunken revelry for decades, according to a 1970 graduate and current students. The long-time tradition known as Champagne Steps, when seniors celebrated their last day of classes by drinking on the library's steps, was abolished after 20 students were hospitalized for alcohol poisoning during the 2008 event. But Mules continue to occupy the steps every year for Dog Head, the weekend closest to St. Patrick's Day. "People start drinking themselves into oblivion on Friday and don't stop until Sunday. Everybody is on the steps to watch the sunrise," said one student.

This school's drinking culture has some serious history: Colby is widely credited with having invented the drinking game Beer Die in the 1970s. The game, which is similar to beer pong but uses a die, was allegedly invented by some brothers in Colby's chapter of the frat Lambda Chi Alpha. Today, players of Beer Die can be found on college campuses nationwide. Though the game is still played, Colby frats and sororities were banned in 1984.

Cracking the Books
Colby prides itself on "project-based learning" and learning by doing, and students are generally pretty satisfied with the school's academic offerings. There are some standard requirements (a freshman English course and credits in science, lab science, literature, social science, and language through the 127 level), but Colby has a "diversity requirement" for graduation as well. This means taking two courses that deal with diversity issues in the U.S. and in other countries.

Colby has another unique offering: "Jan Plan," the monthlong winter term when students have the opportunity to take on intensive projects outside of their major. "If you're a physics major, you can explore your interest in photography," said one student.

People cited biology, economics, languages, English, government, political science, and international relations as popular majors. "Generally when you tell someone you are a humanities major they will almost inevitably roll their eyes," wrote one student. "Economics/Government majors think they are God's gift to the earth and will undoubtedly tell you that their major is the hardest major," she added.

> "[Colby is] surprisingly vibrant for such a small school."

As for Colby's easiest majors, geology came to many people's lips. "It's known as rocks for jocks," said a sophomore. Another student wrote that if you're a geology major

at Colby, "you probably smoke a lot of weed." And Colby students say they don't have to devote too much energy to getting into classes, with possible exceptions being Jan Plan courses and certain special programs like the dual-degree engineering program with Dartmouth College.

Relatively small classes (students estimate the biggest lectures to be around 40 students), approachable professors, and a hefty but manageable workload are a few of the things students appreciate about Colby. However, it's safe to say that students find time in their week to unwind as well.

Mule Pride
From sports to student government to community service, Colby offers a lot to do outside of the classroom. "People at Colby are generally very involved, usually in many diverse extracurricular activities," wrote one student. Colby's Student Government Association is a popular campus activity. It sets campus policies and handles student funding proposals.

Sports are huge on campus: one sophomore called the annual Colby-Bowdoin hockey game the single biggest campus event of the year. The school has a "disproportionate number of athletes" for its small size, the same student remarked. Less than fifty miles from Sugarloaf Mountain and with an average annual snowfall of 60 inches, Colby has a strong ski team and an active Outing Club. The Outing Club owns its own cabin and organizes hiking trips on the weekend. Varsity games are well-attended, students say, but intramurals are popular too.

Social Scene
While a sheltered environment sometimes goes hand in hand with a monotonous social scene, Colby proves quite the contrary—it is "surprisingly vibrant for such a small school," intimates a freshman. Waterville truly is the ideal balance of city life and calm. The beautifully cozy ambiance provides small-town tranquility, a limitless array of outdoor activities, both on land and in water, a college bar, and campus-wide events like Loudness Weekends, fun festivals that allow students a breather. Meanwhile, the campus's accessibility to the large town of Freeport and the city of Boston by school transportation caters to students' more material needs—shopping galore. A car can come in very handy. The absence of Greek life on campus only ups the standard

of dorm-life liveliness—there is no shortage of fun. It only makes sense that Colby claims the game of Beer Die as its own. As with many colleges, drinking is an inevitable part of the culture. Colby, however, has taken the initiative to prohibit hard liquor, though one sophomore says—unless you are caught red-handed, in which case you must face the consequences—a simple: "Security Guard: Were you drinking hard alcohol? Student: No. Security Guard: Ok" will do. While drinking is especially predominant here, perhaps due to the lack of big-city attractions, students can always opt out. In fact, substance-free housing encourages just this, giving those who wish to stay sober a safe haven. While marijuana and cocaine are used in certain crowds, drugs are not a dominant recreational activity. A portrait of the typical student? That of a well-to-do Caucasian jock from somewhere on the East Coast (a generalization, of course, but not all false). But don't get the wrong idea—Colby has recently pushed to greatly diversify its admits, implementing recruiting programs and the like.

Campus Life

While dorms are said to improve with seniority, where you live depends mainly on your luck in the draw—once you have completed your first year, the lottery system kicks in. The mixing of freshmen, sophomores, juniors, and seniors allows everyone to get to know each other, regardless of year. Some residences deliberately appeal to certain kinds of people, such as the artistically inclined. Others do so less intentionally, such as the famed Dana—characteristically wild—and its substance-free opposite, Foss. Senior year some choose to leave the dorms for places in the city. Campus Advisors living alongside students can help with any qualms or questions that may arise. Students can always switch things up meal-wise. Where to eat is a choice between dining halls—Roberts, Dana, and Foss—among which cooking styles vary greatly. Students are open to meeting new people—the campus's friendly air creates an inherent sense of safety.

Colby College really does have a little bit, or should I say a lot, of everything. With the "Jan Plan," you can get creative; with the wide offering of sports, you can be athletic; you can also challenge yourself with the small-class curriculum, get to know teachers, and just enjoy the East Coast landscape minus the city smog.—*Charlotte McDonald and Liliana Cousins*

FYI
If you come to Colby, "You'd better bring a sweater. And a coat. And a scarf, and gloves, and a hat."
If you come to Colby, you'd better leave behind "Bowdoin paraphernalia."
Three things every student at Colby should do before graduating are "climb up to the top of the Clock Tower," and go to "Big G's (sandwich shop) and Dog Head . . . the party weekend closest to St. Patrick's Day."

College of the Atlantic

Address: 105 Eden Street, Bar Harbor, ME 04609
Phone: 207-288-5015
E-mail address: inquiry@coa.edu
Web site URL: www.coa.edu
Year Founded: 1969
Private or Public: Private
Religious Affiliation: None
Location: Rural
Number of Applicants: 314
Percent Accepted: 69%
Percent Accepted who enroll: 32%
Number Entering: 70
Number of Transfers Accepted each Year: 18
Middle 50% SAT range: M: 500–650, CR: 600–690 Wr: 550–680
Middle 50% ACT range: 25–29
Early admission program EA/ED/None: ED

Percentage accepted through EA or ED: 44%
EA and ED deadline: 1-Dec
Regular Deadline: 15-Feb
Application Fee: $45
Full time Undergraduate enrollment: 353
Total enrollment: 370
Percent Male: 36%
Percent Female: 64%
Total Percent Minority or Unreported: 2%
Percent African-American: 0%
Percent Asian/Pacific Islander: 1%
Percent Hispanic: 1%
Percent Native-American: 0%
Percent International: 14%
Percent in-state/out of state: 20%/80%
Percent from Public HS: Unreported
Retention Rate: 82%

Graduation Rate 4-year: 45%
Graduation Rate 6-year: 61%
Percent Undergraduates in On-campus housing: 43%
Number of official organized extracurricular organizations: Unreported
3 Most popular majors: Biology, Ecology, Education
Student/Faculty ratio: 11:1
Average Class Size: 12
Percent of students going to grad school: 55%
Tuition and Fees: $31,470
In-State Tuition and Fees if different: No difference
Cost for Room and Board: $8,490
Percent receiving financial aid out of those who apply: 95%
Percent receiving financial aid among all students: 82%

In 1969 a bunch of Harvard grads got together and decided that people would benefit by learning to understand the importance of how humans interact with their social and natural environments. The interdisciplinary approach they drew up boiled everything down to what they called Human Ecology. They chose the picturesque little seaside town of Bar Harbor, Maine, as the site for their project. Soon enough, they had created a small school of extraordinary opportunities that challenged students to rethink their roles in the world.

And the Meaning of Life Is . . .

Before graduation, every College of the Atlantic (COA) student is required to produce a thesis that answers the question "What is human ecology?" Human Ecology, the sole major at COA, introduces students to an interdisciplinary approach to defining the relationship between humans and the natural environment. Yes, it's a big topic to tackle, but when you are taking classes like "Landscapes of Power," "The Aesthetics of Violence," and "Use and Abuse of our Public Lands," somehow the answer tends to work itself out.

The degree requirements are extensive, but reveal COA's unique learning philosophy. To graduate, students must engage in community service, pursue an internship of at least one term, create a final project, and write a Human Ecology essay discussing their development as a human ecologist.

Although some struggle to find their area of focus, most say that COA "doesn't box you in with a major." Students can switch their focuses within the Human Ecology major. One senior reported that she had switched her focus from environmental law to Latin American studies to a preveterinary school track. However, with a student body of approximately 360 and faculty of approximately 40, COA is a "hard place to specialize when there are two professors who are the math department and another two who are the philosophy department," according to one third-year student. The 80 classes offered per trimester also quickly fill up to their average limit of 18. Some students find it frustrating that the small school may not offer classes within their particular interest.

In turn, COA encourages students to pursue independent studies. One student explained, "If you're motivated, good, if not, you might have a hard time here. For example, most of my work in the last year and a half has been independent, outside of class. I did an internship, then a group study, followed by a residency (the equivalent of three interconnected independent studies), and when I get back from Yucatan I'm going to do my senior project." Graduation requirements also call for students to take time off from campus to do an internship.

On average, students take three classes per trimester—"four can be a lot." The workload focuses on class presentations and "intense" papers, as opposed to exams. An 11:1 student-faculty ratio means that students get individual attention and know their professors well—everyone is on a first-name basis!

Classes also make use of research resources that include Mt. Desert Rock and Great Duck Island Lighthouse, Mt. Desert Island Biological Laboratory, Jackson Laboratory, a weather station, and a Global Monitoring System. "We may, for example, dissect whales or seals found on the coast and determine the cause of death," explains one student.

Housing: Converted Mansions, but Limited Space

COA guarantees housing, usually singles, for first-years only. The three-level horseshoe-shaped Blair-Tyson dorm houses about 40 students. Around six to eight students share a kitchen and a bathroom, which features recycled toilet paper and no stalls! Seafox, a converted mansion, is "supposedly" substance-free, but really just a more quiet dorm of 12 students with spectacular views of the ocean. RAs are pretty easygoing about marijuana and alcohol and even bring their first-years to off-campus parties to bond with upperclassmen. One RA admitted, "I'm pretty loose about it. Although if someone is having a problem, I'd certainly confront him about it."

Most upperclassmen envy the first-years who get to stay on campus. "I had a blast!" claimed a former Blair-Tyson dweller. "But there's not enough room for us, which is a bummer." Upperclassmen find apartments in town about five minutes away or in more remote locations reached by bike or car.

The Grub: A Vegan's Paradise

The environmentally conscious student body enjoys top-ranked cooking at its sole dining hall Take-a-Break, or TAB in local lingo. PETA (People for the Ethical Treatment of Animals) has consistently ranked TAB one of the best college dining halls for its vegetarian and vegan fare and once gave it the privileged title of "Veggie Valedictorian" in 2002. "The worst thing about the dining hall is its dining hours: dinner between 5:30 and 6:30 is kind of ridiculous," complained one student. Also, no meals are served on the weekends, so students make use of the many on-campus kitchens.

The food is all organic and mostly from local farms, including the COA's own Beech Hill Farm where students can participate in the work-study program or volunteer. All waste is disposed of in the school's compost garden. Being on the ocean, TAB features a lot of fresh seafood. "Basically, it's not McDonald's, so don't come looking for it," affirmed one senior.

The Weekend Chill

The illegal substance of choice is reportedly marijuana, "unsurprising" for the "chill" school that enrolls many "hippied-out" students. As opposed to hard liquor, beer is the choice beverage. "My buddies and I might throw back a couple of beers, but we don't often get rip-roaring drunk," reported a third-year student. Another student warned, "There are no crazy discos or mad party places, so if that's what you're looking for you might have a hard time here. It is Maine, after all." Students claim that hard drugs are pretty rare.

Because there are no Wednesday classes (due to Student Government meetings), "there are two weekends, Tuesday nights and Friday and Saturday nights." The scene starts, according to one student, "ridiculously early! Things get started around 8:00 and end by 11:30 or 12:00." Parties are held mainly at upperclassmen residences. The Thirsty Whale, Little Anthony's, and Nakorn Thai are popular town bars. "Only really good IDs work," complained one student about the strict drinking policy.

As for the dating scene, news travels fast. One senior lamented her days as a first-year, when she "may have made one too many 'mistakes' that I couldn't escape. I saw them around nearly every day." Some students admit COA is a hard place to date because there are not a lot of new people to meet around. But the small size "makes random hookups a lot less random." COA is also very tolerant and accepting of homosexual relationships. Reportedly, "lesbians are usually more open than gay males."

Students Take Charge

The Student Government at COA is a remarkably powerful body. It has significant say in all major decisions of the school. Students even attend Trustee meetings. Classes do not meet on Wednesdays to accommodate Student Government committee meetings in which most students participate. Additionally, at 1 p.m. every Wednesday an All College Meeting to which all student organizations and committees report takes place. One student complains, however, "It's always the same people that show up and, for the most part, say the same things, so reaching common decisions has less to do with compromise and more with tiring your opponent."

"I would not come here if I were a Republican."

The Student Activities Committee, a branch of the Student Government, brings about two or three bands per term to perform in TAB. The committee also sponsors coffeehouses, weekly Open Mike nights, the Winter Carnival and Earth Day.

For the Outdoorsman in You

COA sports teams are completely nonexistent. But students are serious about outdoor activities, rain or shine. First-years pile all the essentials—boots, bikes, backpacks, cross-country skis, you name it—into the family car when they first arrive. With Acadia National Park in COA's backyard, students can be found scaling the island's mountains (at least ten!) on weekends and have often tackled them all by graduation. Students have free passes to the local YMCA, can explore the miles of bike trails, catch a free whale-watching ride with the Allied Whale (a program for sea-mammal study and saving), or sit on the dock with their toes in the water and watch the sailboats float by.

Winter term is known as the trimester for hard work because subzero temperatures supposedly keep people inside. This hibernation is overstated, claimed one student. Even when Bar Harbor shuts down at the end of tourist season, COA students are still recreating outdoors with cross-country skiing, snowshoeing, broomball and even midnight dips in the ocean. With all these activities, TV is reportedly "*not* a big pastime." At COA, something like the campus tree swing is a big attraction.

Who You'll Meet

Students at COA report that Earth Day is "the only day that we actually get off." Naturally a place like this is going to attract a certain kind of student. One student described the typical student as "someone who smells like tea-tree oil, has dreadlocks, wears Birkenstocks and is environmentally aware, politically conscious, outdoorsy, pretty athletic and earthy." Oh, and liberal. "There are maybe three Republicans here," warned one student. "I would not come here if I were a Republican." Although the school is often stereotyped, many students admit surprise at the diversity of opinion. One third-year student remarks, "I wasn't expecting anyone to challenge me." Another student determined the "dirty hippie" population to be less than a quarter of the school.

Students are generally from an upper-middle class socioeconomic background, and though a portion of the student body hails from Maine, students come from all over the United States. For such a small school, COA boasts a significant number of international students who are attracted by the special full-scholarship package as well as the uniqueness of the school. In one student's words, "COA students usually have really strong beliefs about a lot of things, and like to voice them. I guess another way to look at it is that if you took the staple 'weird kids' from any high school, most of them would fit in just fine at COA."—*Baily Blair*

FYI
If you come to COA you'd better bring "a Nalgene, a backpack and long johns."
What is a typical weekend schedule? "Go for a hike, do some reading, chill with friends and lay low."
If I could change one thing about COA, I'd "move it to the tropics or a big city."
Three things every student should do before graduating are "join the Yucatan Program, go for a swim at Sand Beach on a night in January and summit all the mountains on the island."

University of Maine / Orono

Address: 5713 Chadbourne Hall, Orono, ME 04469-5713
Phone: 207-581-1561
E-mail address: um-admit@maine.edu
Web site URL: www.umaine.edu
Year Founded: 1865
Private or Public: Public
Religious Affiliation: None
Location: Rural
Number of Applicants: 7,247
Percent Accepted: 78%
Percent Accepted who enroll: 31%
Number Entering: 1,754
Number of Transfers Accepted each Year: 679
Middle 50% SAT range: M: 480–600, CR: 480–590, Wr: 470–580
Middle 50% ACT range: 21–27
Early admission program EA/ED/None: EA

Percentage accepted through EA or ED: Unreported
EA and ED deadline: 15-Dec
Regular Deadline: Rolling
Application Fee: $40
Full time Undergraduate enrollment: 9,183
Total enrollment: 11,501
Percent Male: 52%
Percent Female: 48%
Total Percent Minority or Unreported: 15%
Percent African-American: 2%
Percent Asian/Pacific Islander: 1%
Percent Hispanic: 1%
Percent Native-American: 1%
Percent International: 2%
Percent in-state/out of state: 81%/19%
Percent from Public HS: Unreported
Retention Rate: 79%

Graduation Rate 4-year: 33%
Graduation Rate 6-year: 58%
Percent Undergraduates in On-campus housing: 40%
Number of official organized extracurricular organizations: 224
3 Most popular majors: Business/Marketing, Education, Engineering
Student/Faculty ratio: 15:1
Average Class Size: 15
Percent of students going to grad school: 25%
Tuition and Fees: $26,308
In-State Tuition and Fees if different: $10,588
Cost for Room and Board: $8,944
Percent receiving financial aid out of those who apply: Unreported
Percent receiving financial aid among all students: Unreported

A big state school in the middle of the woods, with a cold climate to boot, might seem daunting at first. But as students at the University of Maine will tell you, there are many reasons to brave the freezing temperatures and take advantage of this vibrant community. The University that once had a live black bear as its official mascot and was known for being a legendary party school has since evolved into a respected national research university, but the students are still just as supportive of their UMaine Black Bears. From the cheering crowds at the Alfond Arena to the picnickers taking advantage of the first day of spring, it's clear that the University of Maine provides a unique opportunity for both in- and out-of-staters to make the most of the Pine Tree State.

Bear-ing All with Bananas

Founded in 1865, the UMaine campus in Orono is the largest in the University of Maine system. As a public state school, it's not surprising that 84 percent of its student body hails from Maine itself. But the 16 percent remaining call 47 states and numerous countries home, making for a campus that is surprisingly diverse for a state that one student called "one of the whitest states, if not the whitest." She continued, "The University of Maine is probably the place to go if you're looking for some ethnic and religious diversity because there is a lot of it on this campus, all things considered being in Maine." The minority students, who make up 6 percent of undergraduates, have the opportunity to participate in a number of ethnic and cultural organizations, including the Asian Student Association and the Black Student Union.

Most of the student population, generally either "Mainers" or New Englanders, sport a preppy style, usually American Eagle or Abercrombie, students said. Others said the campus has its fair share of rebels, both in terms of fashion and lifestyle. One girl confessed, "We're all kind of hicks." But she was quick to point out that "There are those guys who wear flannel, but they're not roaming around hunting things."

There are a few things that do unite just

about all UMaine students, and one of them is supporting their Black Bears. Legend has it that the University's original mascot was a live black bear cub that lived in one of the fraternity's basements when not appearing at sporting events. Today's incarnation, Bananas the Bear, may do a better job of pumping up the crowds; the original cub was fired after attacking the University of Connecticut husky at a basketball game.

The hockey team is universally cited as the biggest draw for sports spectators. The school pep band always makes an appearance, and the roaring crowds of both UMaine students and Maine locals are a constant fixture at the Alfond Arena, usually lining up outside for tickets far in advance. The men's ice hockey team, two-time NCAA Division I national champions, in 1993 and 1999, is a great source of pride for the entire state. "People go crazy and wear jerseys and paint their faces," a junior described.

> **"We're all kind of hicks."**

The other athletics teams, which also engage in Division I competition, may not have as much star power, but their games also attract many fans. Football is also very popular, and the basketball team's rivalry with the New Hampshire Wildcats, at 105 seasons in a row, is the longest continuous basketball rivalry between any two non–Ivy League schools.

Making a Large University Small
Black Bears can carry their determination into the classroom, too, with plenty of opportunities available at UMaine for academic excellence. The general education requirements, or "Gen Eds," are designed to produce "broadly educated persons who can appreciate the achievements of civilization, understand the tensions within it, and contribute to resolving them." Each student must take a certain number of credits in the following areas: science, human values and social context, mathematics, writing, and ethics. Every student, regardless of major, must also complete a "capstone experience," usually during the senior year, which is the culmination of his or her specific course of study. All Gen Eds must be taken for a letter grade in order to satisfy the requirement. "I'm on a one-track [course of study]," a music education major said. "The Gen Eds require me to get out of that box

for a minute and open my mind to other subject areas. There's probably a little bit of groaning, but it's one of those things that gets done, often freshman year."

The most popular majors are business/marketing, education, and engineering, with the latter generally cited as one of the most challenging offered at the University, as well as one of the most famous departments. The sciences in general, especially the nursing and biology programs, are well known for their rigor and progressiveness. The marine biology department is also lauded.

When students are accepted into the University of Maine, they gain entrance to specific programs based on the strength of their applications. If they do not meet the requirements for a program or are unsure of what they want to concentrate in, first-years enroll in the Exploration Program, which allows them to transition to college life and settle on an academic area, even to bolster their qualifications for a certain program. Some of the benefits of this option include an academic advisor with whom they meet on a regular basis and the opportunity to take a first-year seminar. Students looking for a more personalized education throughout their four years at the University can opt to enroll in the Honors College if they make the cut. Honors students enjoy smaller classes and close working relationships with faculty members. They also have the option of designated honors housing.

As can be expected of a large state school, students often encounter difficulties in gaining entrance to certain high-demand classes, but "teachers sometimes make exceptions." Class sizes range from around 25 in the smaller lectures to 200 to 300 in the largest survey courses, but one girl said she has a class with only three people. Classes are usually offered once a year, if not each semester, so the most common reason that students enroll for a fifth year is that they were undecided about their major, not that they could not get into core classes.

A junior cited the school's size as one of the biggest academic attractions: "I think there's something for everyone. Because we are a university, the biggest university in the state, and we have a lot of students, there's pretty much going to be a major for you."

Raising the Steins
"A lot of people have the perception that UMaine is a huge party school because at one point it was, and I don't think it necessarily is anymore," a sophomore said.

Indeed, the University has recently been taking steps to curb out-of-control partying, with both reputation and students' safety in mind. "The University's known as being a party school, so it's really important to [the administration] that we crack down, and that we don't allow freshmen to be drunk all the time," a junior explained. The RAs in each dorm, where drinking is prohibited, are known for being fairly strict. The repercussions for breaking the rules include attending alcohol education meetings, and repeat offenders can be kicked out of the dorms. "Does that mean [drinking] never happens?" one student asked rhetorically. "No, but it is punishable."

Since it's fairly difficult to party in on-campus housing, much of the party scene takes place in the frats and the off-campus apartments. While one girl said she was surprised that Greek life was so present on campus, she said the presence of the frats and sororities has not been a negative part of her experience. The frats hold many of the parties, and Friday and Saturday nights are known as the big nights to go out. Pot is pretty commonplace, as it is on most college campuses, and binge drinking is not a major problem, perhaps in part because of the 2001 founding of Maine's Higher Education Alcohol Prevention Project. The initiative aimed to address the problem of binge drinking as it worsened on college campuses. However, the celebrated college fight song, the Maine Stein Song, is still proudly shouted at athletic events. As undergraduates sing "Fill the steins to dear old Maine," they had better have their IDs on them.

The off-campus bar scene in Orono is not too exciting; there are a couple in town, along with a dance club that a good number of people frequent. There isn't much to do overall in Orono. Besides the legendary Pat's Pizza and a number of other coffee shops and restaurants, it is a quiet town with residents that generally have good relations with the University. In fact, many of them are affiliated with UMaine. For more bars and restaurants, as well as a grocery store, some students take the 10-minute drive to nearby Bangor, the third-largest city in the state.

Indoors and Outdoors

There's a lot to occupy students' time on campus, though. They can even get fed reasonably well. York, Hilltop, and Wells Commons offer all-you-care-to-eat dining. The latter two were recently renovated and offer a variety of standard and multiethnic cuisines. Students cited the Maine Marketplace in the Memorial Union as the most popular dining option, though. Here, students can use their meal plans to purchase a wide range of à la carte meals, including pizza, sandwiches, burgers, sushi, Chinese and Mexican food. They can either use one meal swipe and receive an entrée and snacks, or they can pay by the item. A number of meal plans are available, comprising both meal swipes and dining funds.

The 19 residence halls are generally considered to be acceptable, students say. Freshmen participate in the First Year Residence Experience (FYRE) and are assigned to one of the following dorms: Androscoggin, Cumberland, Gannett, Knox, Oxford, Somerset, Balentine, Penobscot, and Colvin. The latter three are designated for honors students. These are traditional undergraduate residence halls, usually with two students to a room, while upperclassmen have this option as well as the choice of living in suites. "Some of the dorms are on the older side, but I think overall they're not too awful," a sophomore concluded. As part of the FYRE, freshmen are grouped together in one part of campus and have the opportunity to make friends with many of their classmates through this close-knit community.

Theme housing includes a substance-free dorm and an "outdoorsy" dorm, the latter of which organizes trips to the mountains and the surrounding area to ski, bike, hike, and participate in all manner of recreational activities. A junior pointed out that none of the dorms, and indeed none of the buildings on the UMaine campus, are taller than four stories. She said she thinks it is because the University is built on an island in a marsh, and that buildings cannot be taller than they are because the campus will sink into the water, but she admitted that it could be just a rumor.

Many students have cars, even freshmen, and parking can be a difficult issue. The significant number of commuter students contributes to the congestion. Permits cost $50 for the year, with decals designating cars as faculty, resident or commuter, with corresponding lots. Those who trespass into other lots "are lucky if they aren't ticketed." But students point out that cars are useful for going home or just into town. While the campus is considered to be "pretty safe," students interviewed did say they wish it were better lit, both because it would make them feel more secure at night and because it is difficult for drivers to see pedestrians.

The architecture on campus is mostly brick, with many trees and green spaces adding life. In the winter, snow coats everything, but it is "still aesthetically pleasing." One student said her favorite thing to do is to sit on the Mall, an open space in the middle of campus, at the beginning of spring when "the campus is buzzing and everyone is happy." With a number of construction projects recently completed and others in progress, the UMaine campus seems to always be an exciting place. The Collins Center for the Arts was recently renovated, as was the gym.

Most UMaine students do their best to take advantage of their surroundings, often going on trips to Acadia National Park or other natural areas. But whether you're a flannel-wearing mountain man or someone who prefers to stay indoors during inclement weather, there are plenty of opportunities to do both at the University of Maine. One student said she had gotten used to the school's size, saying, "It's kind of nice having a lot more students—more things get contributed to the campus, and there are more ideas floating around." Another added, "I have plenty of time in my life to move away and see the world, but I'm glad I stayed in Maine for college."—*Kimberly Chow*

FYI

If you come to the University of Maine, you'd better bring "a pair of winter boots: it was negative 20 degrees at one point."

What's the typical weekend schedule? "On Friday, go to a hockey game, then hang out with your friends at Pat's Pizza; sleep in on Saturday, maybe go to another athletic event, then hit up the frats; Sunday, catch up on work."

If I could change one thing about the University of Maine, "I would make the weather warmer!"

Three things every student at the University of Maine should do before graduating are "go to a hockey game, sit on the Mall in the spring, and eat at Pat's Pizza."

Maryland

Address: 1021 Dulaney Valley Road, Baltimore, MD 21204-2753
Phone: 410-337-6100
E-mail address: admissions@goucher.edu
Web site URL: www.goucher.edu
Year Founded: 1885
Private or Public: Private
Religious Affiliation: None
Location: Suburban
Number of Applicants: 3,563
Percent Accepted: 73%
Percent Accepted who enroll: 17%
Number Entering: 399
Number of Transfers Accepted each Year: 118
Middle 50% SAT range: M: 510–620, CR: 540–670, Wr: 540–650
Middle 50% ACT range: Unreported
Early admission program EA/ED/None: EA

Percentage accepted through EA or ED: 43%
EA and ED deadline: 1-Dec
Regular Deadline: 1-Feb
Application Fee: $40
Full time Undergraduate enrollment: 1,472
Total enrollment: 2,362
Percent Male: 31%
Percent Female: 69%
Total Percent Minority or Unreported: 25%
Percent African-American: 6%
Percent Asian/Pacific Islander: 3%
Percent Hispanic: 4%
Percent Native-American: <1%
Percent International: 1%
Percent in-state/out of state: 23%/77%
Percent from Public HS: 67%
Retention Rate: 78%

Graduation Rate 4-year: 57%
Graduation Rate 6-year: 62%
Percent Undergraduates in On-campus housing: 80%
Number of official organized extracurricular organizations: 60
3 Most popular majors: English, Communications, Psychology
Student/Faculty ratio: 9:1
Average Class Size: 15
Percent of students going to grad school: Unreported
Tuition and Fees: $32,636
In-State Tuition and Fees if different: No difference
Cost for Room and Board: $10,104
Percent receiving financial aid out of those who apply: 81%
Percent receiving financial aid among all students: 59%

Goucher College, located just eight miles outside of Baltimore in the town of Towson, is a small liberal arts college that focuses on big issues. Although the school enrolls nearly 1,500 undergraduates, their resources for students go far beyond the 287 acres of Goucher property. With new study-abroad requirements, for which students are granted at least $1,200 to cover travel costs, interinstitutional programs with Johns Hopkins University and with Baltimore Hebrew University, and many opportunities for work and study in Baltimore and Washington D.C., Goucher's small community has become a college recognized for expanding knowledge outside of the small liberal arts college bubble.

Education Without Boundaries

With a motto like "Education without Boundaries," Goucher offers students plenty of opportunities in and out of the classroom. With thirty-one majors and six interdisciplinary areas, a five-year BA/BS program in Science and Engineering with Johns Hopkins, and numerous study-abroad programs available during the optional January term, Goucher makes it easy for students to pursue any interest they may have. Many students agree that although there are relatively few of them, their academic interests vary widely. Psychology is the most popular major on campus, and the visual and performing arts have become more popular over the years, especially with Goucher's renowned dance major. But if students still feel confined by the majors, Goucher allows them to create their own.

Goucher's general education requirements (also known as Gen Ed) include proficiency in a language, English composition, and computer technology along with a distribution of courses in the arts, natural sciences, humanities, social sciences, and mathematics. Most nonscience majors who are looking to fill their natural sciences "Gen Ed" requirement take the largest course—up to around one hundred students—at Goucher, "Introduction to Psychology," taught by the beloved Dr. Ann McKim. Dr. McKim is a "very memorable and very enthusiastic" professor who is known for keeping her students—all one hundred of them—interested and entertained.

Freshmen are also required to take two classes. One is a freshman seminar and the other is a Connections class, where freshmen meet with their upperclassmen peer mediators and talk about important issues regarding college life. However, some freshmen say the class is only effective if the peer mediator is actually dedicated to the class, which is not always the case. Overall, many freshman agree that assimilating into Goucher is easy from the beginning, and the required freshman classes can be a "great way" to meet new people and learn about a topic they would "not usually be interested in." Still, students say that freshman year can lead to some serious culture shock, as new students adjust—and even conform—to the very liberal atmosphere of the small campus.

In terms of academic difficulty, Goucher gets mixed reviews, but one senior said "that is only because some majors are more difficult than others." The English and Natural Science majors get reviews of being more difficult, while Psychology and Communications are known for being more "lenient with grading." Overall, most students agree that "you only get out of classes what you put into them" and "if you really want an A, and if you work hard enough, it is attainable." One of the reasons many students can succeed in their classes is because of the accessibility of professors. Goucher has a 9:1 student to teacher ratio and an average class size of 15, which translates into having professors "almost always able to meet when you want to schedule a meeting." Some students even said they have become friendly with professors who they've never even had "because Goucher tries to make professors and students on a more equal level; we call most teachers by their first names."

A Unique Social Experience

Even before freshman year, each class of Goucher students has the opportunity to meet people with all different interests through preorientation programs. Students agree that while the diversity—cultural, geographic, and socioeconomic—at Goucher is not very great, it improves each year. For a small liberal arts school, some students were "surprised by how many lacrosse 'bros' and athletes there are." But overall the "stereotypical" Goucher student is "very hippyish and free from a middle-class family on the East Coast." Overall, students are "really friendly" and "people will always be waving to you on the Van Meter Highway" (Goucher's walkway between the academic and residential quads).

"Right now, my main group of friends are the people on my floor and the people I do [activities] with," says one freshman. Seniors and freshmen both agree that the friends they have are the ones they live with and the ones with whom they participate in extracurricular activities. Usually "the athletes hang out together," but athletes agree that they "don't feel limited, even by age. Most parties have people of every age." While there is not a strong divide between students, "there are definitely different groups." One student on the women's lacrosse team said that "parties are mostly small groups of friends . . . our school is too small and parties would be broken up if they were over thirty people." With no Greek system at Goucher, parties are generally confined to students' rooms.

> "We're a very liberal school . . . it kind of comes with the territory."

While parties are small, that does not stop Goucher students from partying as hard as at any other college. Many students agree that alcohol is very common on campus, and marijuana is as well because "we're a very liberal school . . . it kind of comes with the territory." Students who are less interested in partying say that it can be "difficult to find alternatives—you have to try." While alcohol and marijuana can be found, the rules are "definitely enforced," especially by Community Assistants (CAs)—upperclassmen who oversee dorm life—who get reviews between being "really relaxed" and "pretty strict." The CAs are not just in charge of making sure parties don't get out of control, but they also deal with issues between roommates and with technical problems, and they can advise students on anything from classes to clubs.

Goucher social life at night does not consist only of small parties in dorm rooms. Students also hang out in the Gopher Hole, a coffeehouse on campus that's open late, often has live music on weekends, and serves food like quesadillas and "really good" smoothies. In the middle of the fall semester, students gear up for "Humans vs. Zombies," a weekend-long game that involves many pumped-up members of the student body, Nerf guns, and mild "implications of violence." Another big social event is Get into Goucher Day (GIG), when all classes are canceled on a surprise day and the campus is converted into an amusement park. Many students call it "the best day of the year." The "formal" event of the year is Gala, a night of dancing and good food. However, not every student can go to Gala, as the limited number of tickets is distributed based on seniority, starting with the seniors and "trickling down" to a few lucky freshmen.

Outside of the usual weekend events, many Gophers, as Goucher students are commonly called, are involved in volunteering, jobs, and internships. By senior year, about 70 percent of Goucher students will have had an internship. Many students find job opportunities on campus, but with Baltimore nearby and a mall in the neighborhood, many students work off campus. The Goucher student body is also involved in helping the community, through on- and off-campus organizations. Goucher also features some "unique" clubs such as the Goucher Pirate Alliance, which is known for having bake sales where the members dress up in pirate garb. Otherwise, there are over sixty other options for students, ranging from student government to the campus radio station to student publications, such as the newspaper *The Quindecim (The Q)*.

With seventeen NCAA Division III teams at Goucher, athletes have a big presence on campus. However, many students admit that sports at Goucher are "mostly athletes going to athletes' games." Despite the fact that sports do not get too much nonathlete spirit, students agree "we have a lot of school spirit, just not in the traditional way of going to sports games." The athletic program at Goucher is ever expanding, with brand-new fields and a new cardio center and weight room. All facilities are open for nonathletic use, and Gophers are excited about the renovations.

Going Green at Goucher

Goucher's new initiative to "go green" has been extremely effective and gets high marks from students. Over recent years, Goucher has expanded its "green" program by building environmentally friendly buildings, selecting a "green supplier" to cater the dining halls, selling "eco-friendly" items at the bookstore, and holding many events for students to learn about sustainability. Ground broke in 2007 for the Athenaeum, Goucher's new "green building," which now holds the library, performance space, an art gallery, a computer lab, a restaurant, and many more facilities. Students can enjoy the quadlike outdoor terrace, which is on the roof of the building and carpeted with grass. While Goucher is calling the Athenaeum its "Crowning Jewel," students say that the campus "is [already] really beautiful" and is laid out "really well."

For students who live in dorms, there are a few buildings that students can pick based on a lottery system. Most dorms have students of all ages, but some are more "luxurious" than others.

Sophomores, juniors, and seniors can also live off campus in apartments, many of which are owned by Goucher. When students want to go into Baltimore or Washington, D.C. (an hour away from campus), "about half of students have cars," but there is also a shuttle that goes between Goucher and the other universities in Baltimore, ending at the Harbor in Baltimore. "Zipcars are also an option for students who don't have cars but want to rent one."

When Goucher students get hungry, they have a lot of different options both on and around campus. Ranging from Stimson, the largest dining hall, to the Cheesecake Factory that recently opened, Goucher students have a myriad of options when it comes to eating. Students are "pretty satisfied" with the food on campus. In Heubeck Dining Hall, students have different stations to choose from, including a deli station and the sustainable Global Green Exhibition station.

Overall, Goucher students are proud of their campus and of what Goucher has to offer them. Goucher students are quick to point out the interesting facts that make their school unique. Gophers tell legends about the twenty-four-mile-per-hour speed limit sign, the nuclear fallout shelter, the mummy that Johns Hopkins allegedly "stole" from their school, and the beautiful trails located right off campus. Students agree that in the end, it's the school's "quirky self-expression that is inherent in most students" that makes Goucher different from any other school.—*Willi Rechler*

FYI

If you come to Goucher you better bring "plenty of warm layers for the winter," "a Nerf gun for Humans vs. Zombies," "a blanket for outside lounging," and "lots of Expo markers for your white board."

A typical weekend at Goucher is "everyone goes out Friday to the harbor or an off-campus party, then to the Gopher Hole or game room," and Saturdays consist of "brunch in the morning, then repeat Friday night" with Sunday "a full day in the library."

If I could change one thing about Goucher I'd "make us have more school spirit."

Three things every student at Goucher should do before graduating are "Go to the Gopher Hole events, get their own radio show, and attend a Goucher party."

Johns Hopkins University

Address: 3400 North Charles Street Mason Hall, Baltimore, MD 21218
Phone: 410-516-8171
E-mail address: apphelp@jhu.edu
Web site URL: www.jhu.edu
Year Founded: 1876
Private or Public: Private
Religious Affiliation: None
Location: Urban
Number of Applicants: 14,848
Percent Accepted: 24%
Percent Accepted who enroll: 33%
Number Entering: 1,206
Number of Transfers Accepted each Year: 26
Middle 50% SAT range: M: 660–770, CR: 630–730, Wr: 630–730
Middle 50% ACT range: 28–33
Early admission program EA/ED/None: ED

Percentage accepted through EA or ED: Unreported
EA and ED deadline: 1-Nov
Regular Deadline: 1-Jan
Application Fee: $70
Full time Undergraduate enrollment: 4,591
Total enrollment: 6,437
Percent Male: 53%
Percent Female: 47%
Total Percent Minority or Unreported: 44%
Percent African-American: 4%
Percent Asian/Pacific Islander: 19%
Percent Hispanic: 8%
Percent Native-American: <1%
Percent International: 8%
Percent in-state/out of state: 13%/87%
Percent from Public HS: 69%
Retention Rate: 97%
Graduation Rate 4-year: 81%

Graduation Rate 6-year: 89%
Percent Undergraduates in On-campus housing: 60%
Number of official organized extracurricular organizations: 250
3 Most popular majors: Biomedical/Medical Engineering, Economics, International Relations and Affairs
Student/Faculty ratio: Unreported
Average Class Size: 14
Percent of students going to grad school: 38%
Tuition and Fees: $37,700
In-State Tuition and Fees if different: No difference
Cost for Room and Board: $11,578
Percent receiving financial aid out of those who apply: 47%
Percent receiving financial aid among all students: 46%

There are two things bound to bother most students at Johns Hopkins University. The first is leaving the "s" off of Johns when speaking the name of this prestigious Baltimore institution. Founded in 1876 as the nation's first research university, Johns Hopkins was named for its first benefactor whose given name was actually Johns, his mother's maiden name. The second "no-no" is the assumption that all Hopkins students are either premeds or hard-core science majors. Although celebrated for its medical school and for providing an unsurpassed premedical education, Johns Hopkins is also extremely strong in the humanities, social sciences, and engineering. Its International Relations program is considered perhaps the finest in the nation, and its writing and art history majors are top ranked. In fact, only about 30 percent of entering freshmen at Hopkins profess an interest in medicine, a number that diminishes over time.

Homewood Bound

Although the Johns Hopkins Medical Institutions are world-renowned, the heart of the university can be found at its Homewood campus, a beautifully manicured 140-acre parklike setting adorned with redbrick Georgian Federalist-style buildings. Brick, granite, and marble walkways wend their way through lush green lawns, sculpture gardens, and beds of blue and white flowers. "The beach," an expanse of lawn that extends out from the Milton S. Eisenhower Library, is a magnet for students who want to relax, sunbathe, or socialize. All freshmen and sophomores live in or adjacent to Homewood. Freshmen live in the Alumni Memorial Residences (AMRs), or enjoy the air-conditioning in Buildings A and B. While air-conditioning in Baltimore has its advantages, many freshmen prefer the AMR setup. "I made so many friends in AMR I," one sophomore said. "It was a great place to live and a great way to meet a lot of people." Some freshmen and many sophomores live in Wolman and McCoy, which have kitchenettes and large common areas. In the past, upperclassmen have had to live off campus in apartments that abut Homewood. With the completion of Charles Commons in 2006, more students have opted to remain in university-operated facilities. Charles Commons, an extremely attractive and functional new building, houses more than 600 undergraduates as well as the 29,000-square-foot Barnes and Noble campus bookstore. Situated across Charles Street, a main thoroughfare that borders the main campus, it is a convenient and desirable residence. "Charles Commons is impressive," said one junior. "The suites are really well appointed and the opportunities for socializing in the dining facility and the common spaces really make this a fantastic place to live. It is a major addition to campus life." In addition, the University has taken over several existing apartment buildings adjacent to the new facility, performing

some renovations and instituting better security.

The level of security and the degree of safety on campus in view of Baltimore's urban problems and crime rate (which is falling) are important concerns voiced by prospective students. The university has invested a great deal of time and money in assuring that there are plenty of "Hop Cops" to patrol the campus at all times, security guards at the entrances to all of the dormitories and affiliated apartments, and 24/7 walking escorts and vans available to students. "The campus is safe as long as you are aware of your surroundings," said a junior. "It's like any urban school."

Several other building projects are being pursued concurrently to both expand the campus and substantially renovate existing classroom facilities. The Decker Quadrangle venture, completed in November 2007, created a new public entrance to the campus, a new visitors and admissions center, a building to house the computational sciences departments, and a substantial underground parking facility. In addition, Gilman Hall, the heart of the Homewood, is in the process of undergoing a complete renovation, the plans of which call for the creation of a movie theater and glass-enclosed atrium.

Dining options have expanded greatly on campus and many of the dining areas and food courts have been renovated. Vegetarian and kosher foods are available at all times in certain venues. Freshmen are required to participate in the meal plan, while upperclassmen generally choose to prepare their own meals.

Academics: Hold the Stereotypes, Please

The student body at Johns Hopkins is ethnically diverse and a significant international population is represented on campus. The academic curriculum is rigorous, and students quickly come to realize that the "grade inflation" found at most other top colleges and universities is not characteristic of classes here. Many courses are graded on a curve. Contrary to the common stereotype that Hopkins undergraduates, particularly premeds, are intensely competitive and will work to the detriment of their fellow classmates, stealing reading materials and sabotaging lab projects, most students find their peers to be helpful and more internally motivated than externally driven by grades. "The Hopkins stereotype is ridiculous," said one senior premed. "I have never heard of a single instance of such nonsense. In fact, sophomore year my chemistry lab partner once stayed up with me all night to try to help me figure out why my data did not work out."

Perhaps to diminish the stress of grades and to promote an easier transition to the academic rigor of the Hopkins's curriculum, first-semester grades are "covered," which means they are never seen by graduate schools and are not factored into calculations of a student's GPA. First-semester grades are simply designated on the transcript as Satisfactory or Unsatisfactory. This policy has been uniformly applauded by Hopkins students, who consider covered first-semester grades to be a factor encouraging them to be more eclectic in their choice of courses and less concerned about not doing well during the period of their first exposure to the demands of academic, social, and extracurricular life at Hopkins.

> "I very quickly learned that the best person to answer a question that I might have had was the professor herself."

Students are affiliated with one of two undergraduate divisions of Johns Hopkins, the Zanvyl Krieger School of Arts and Sciences, and the G. W. C. Whiting School of Engineering. The former is the core institution at Hopkins and enrolls approximately 63 percent of the student body, the remainder being part of the Whiting School. Most students find the professors to be extremely approachable and committed, especially in the upper-level classes, which are small. "I very quickly learned that the best person to answer a question that I might have had was the professor herself," one student said. Teachers generally do not just go through the motions at review sessions. "One evening, my biochemistry professor ran a study group until midnight and did not leave until every question was answered!" Students in Arts and Sciences choose from over 60 established undergraduate majors and minors. Many of these programs are ranked among the best in the country. In addition, students may design an interdisciplinary major with the assistance of a faculty adviser.

Distribution requirements for Arts and Science undergraduates are far from onerous and there is a loose core curriculum. A minimum of 30 credits out of the 120 required for the B.A. degree must be obtained in areas outside of the major. For majors in the humanities or social sciences, 12 of the 30 are required to fall within the disciplines of science or mathematics. Natural or quantitative science majors must earn at least 18–21 credits in the humanities or social sciences. In addition, Arts and Science students must take at least 4 courses that are designated writing-intensive.

Students in the G. W. C. Whiting School of Engineering pursue majors in nine distinct areas of study, including Mathematics and Statistics, Biomedical Engineering, Chemical Engineering, and Computer Science. The Department of Biomedical Engineering was ranked the best in the country by *U.S. News & World Report* and the Department of Geography and Environmental Engineering in the top five nationally. Generally between 120 and 130 credits are required for a B.S. or B.A. degree from the Whiting school.

Between semesters, Hopkins undergraduates are given a unique, voluntary opportunity to receive up to two Pass/Fail "enrichment" credits in one of four areas, including Academic Enrichment, Personal Enrichment, Experiential Learning, and Study Abroad. Academic Enrichment courses are free. Every January during Intersession, many students avail themselves of the chance to take an interesting class while enjoying part of their winter break on campus.

Taking Learning Beyond the Classroom

Research at Johns Hopkins is particularly encouraged, and there are enormous opportunities for students to become involved in projects with renowned faculty members, especially in the natural, social, and behavioral sciences. It is estimated that nearly 80 percent of Hopkins undergraduates engage in some sort of research outside of the classroom. The dedication of Johns Hopkins to research is reflected in the fact that the university ranks number one in the receipt of federal funds for research and development in science, medicine, and engineering. One female junior commented that she has "been involved in three different research projects since coming to Hopkins, both in my major (Psychology) and at the Medical School. The experience has been amazing and my advisor is always available to talk about our work."

Up to 70 percent of Hopkins students get involved in volunteer work in the community and frequently tutor inner-city elementary school students in a variety of subjects. In addition, there are 250 undergraduate clubs to attract students including a variety of publications and singing groups. "There is something for everybody's interest," said one male freshman. "I am still deciding about which of the many different school publications I want to join." The *Johns Hopkins News-Letter*, founded in 1896, is the oldest continuously published newspaper in the country and one of the most popular extracurricular venues.

Work Hard, Play Hard

No one would deny that Johns Hopkins students take their academic responsibilities very seriously. During finals period, the main library's doors are open all night, and the facility is generally full to the rafters at that time. Nevertheless, Hopkins students take their socializing seriously as well. Most students feel that the social life on campus has been steadily improving. During freshman year, the main party venues are the fraternity houses, which are situated off campus. About 1,000 undergraduates belong to one of eleven fraternities and seven sororities. Freshmen especially find frat parties an excellent way to meet classmates, albeit hot and noisy. Upperclassmen, however, generally choose "house parties" in student apartments instead of the frat scene. "Underclassmen are easy to please because they don't know any better," chuckled one male senior. "By junior year, you just don't want to chug frat Jell-O shots." Near campus, in the surrounding Charles Village, PJs and Charles Village Pub (CVP) are popular watering holes. Off campus, a short cab ride away, the Inner Harbor is a draw for students on the weekends, especially in the area called Power Plant. In addition, many undergraduates go to Fells Point, where there are several clubs. Excellent shopping and restaurants can be found in neighboring Towson.

Lacrosse! Lacrosse! Lacrosse!

Hopkins fields teams in all major collegiate sports, but lacrosse is unquestionably the preeminent Blue Jay sport on campus, and the source of a great deal of school spirit. In fact, Johns Hopkins lacrosse is Division I, while all other sports teams compete in Division III. Lacrosse players are actively recruited at Hopkins, and such efforts have resulted in 44 national titles for the men's team, including nine NCAA Division I titles, the most recent being awarded in 2007. Women's lacrosse too has become extremely competitive.

Hopkins has fielded top Division III teams in baseball, basketball, fencing, swimming, and water polo. For students who prefer just keeping in shape, Hopkins opened a 60,000-square-foot recreation center in 2001 that includes a climbing wall in addition to the usual cardiovascular conditioning machines.

No one would argue that Johns Hopkins is a party school. Its curriculum is intense but rewarding and the opportunities for research unsurpassed. If you are a serious student who is looking for an ethnically diverse and academically superlative school in an urban setting, and you appreciate opportunities for research, then Hopkins may just be the place for you. Loving lacrosse wouldn't hurt either!—*Jonathan Berken*

FYI
If you come to Johns Hopkins, you'd better bring "an 'I love Lacrosse' T-shirt."
What is a typical weekend schedule? "Go out Friday night, study Saturday morning, go to a lacrosse match or other sporting event in the afternoon, go to a frat or house party Saturday night, wake up late and study all day Sunday."
If I could change one thing about Johns Hopkins, I'd "get rid of bell-curve grading in classes."
Three things that every student at Johns Hopkins should do before graduating are "go to Pete's Grill, go to Fell's Point for Halloween, and cheer on the Blue Jays."

St. John's College

Address: PO Box 2800, Annapolis, MD 21404
Phone: 410-626-2522
E-mail address: admissions@sjca.edu
Web site URL: www.stjohnscollege.edu
Year Founded: 1696
Private or Public: Private
Religious Affiliation: None
Location: Urban
Number of Applicants: 357
Percent Accepted: 80%
Percent Accepted who enroll: 47%
Number Entering: 136
Number of Transfers Accepted each Year: 20
Middle 50% SAT range: M: 590–680, CR: 640–740, Wr: Unreported
Middle 50% ACT range: 27–30
Early admission program EA/ED/None: None
Percentage accepted through EA or ED: NA

EA and ED deadline: NA
Regular Deadline: None/ Priority Application deadline: March 1
Application Fee: $0
Full time Undergraduate enrollment: 460
Total enrollment: 463
Percent Male: 54%
Percent Female: 46%
Total Percent Minority or Unreported: 21%
Percent African-American: 1%
Percent Asian/Pacific Islander: 1%
Percent Hispanic: 4%
Percent Native-American: 1%
Percent International: 7%
Percent in-state/out of state: 21%/79%
Percent from Public HS: 60%
Retention Rate: 82%
Graduation Rate 4-year: 55%

Graduation Rate 6-year: 70%
Percent Undergraduates in On-campus housing: 70%
Number of official organized extracurricular organizations: 64
3 Most popular majors: Liberal Arts and Sciences, General Studies and Humanities
Student/Faculty ratio: 8:1
Average Class Size: 15
Percent of students going to grad school: 10%
Tuition and Fees: $43,256
In-State Tuition and Fees if different: No difference
Cost for Room and Board: $10,334
Percent receiving financial aid out of those who apply: 76%
Percent receiving financial aid among all students: 73%

For anyone who has dreamed of sitting around a beautiful campus in one of America's oldest towns, reading the great works of the Western Canon like Aristotle, Ptolemy, and Kant, and discussing them with a tight-knit community of thoughtful students, St. John's College is a dream.

A True Liberal Arts School

Perhaps the truest liberal arts college in the United States, the St. John's education, or "The Program" as they call it, is unique. Students spend four years learning math (calculus, astronomy, and geometry) and seminar (literature, philosophy, and classics), three years of science (biology, chemistry, physics), one year of music, and four years of language (French and Greek), using only primary source materials; students never use textbooks, instead, Euclid guides students through geometry, Plato through philosophy, and Newton through physics.

The college believes that there is no greater teacher than the books themselves. Thus, professors at St. John's are called "tutors" and their job is not to lecture but to guide a discussion that will lead students, or "Johnnies" to the heart of the books. "Everyone is interested in reading and discussing, and it always amazes me how willing people are to talk about anything and everything," one student notes. Students agree that the academic experience is extraordinary and the best part of St. John's. "If academics are not the reason why you want to go to St. John's then you should not apply," a student commented.

Grades Don't Matter

St. John's encourages students to learn for themselves, not for the sake of a grade. According to one student, "We're encouraged to learn for the sake of learning, not for the sake of a little number on a piece of paper." There are no exams or formal grading given during the semester, and although grades are given at the end of each course (primarily so students can apply to graduate school) students can choose not to look at them. Although most students appreciate the independence the school gives them by deemphasizing grades, some students complain that because of the lack of formal assessments, the grades given can seem arbitrary because the grading standards are left entirely up to each tutor. "While in one class, you might get an A with a certain type of performance, in another class you might get a B or a C with the same type of performance, and you never know which one it is until the semester is over," a senior described.

A Quaint and Historic Town

Annapolis is a quaint colonial town set on the Chesapeake Bay that for a few years served as the capital of the United States under George Washington's presidency. Today, the town is host to both St. John's and the US Naval Academy. Despite its quaint historic charm and the presence of several colleges, the town gets mixed reviews from students. While one student describes its history and architecture as "an absolute gem" she also notes that it lacks in entertainment options. The one-of-a-kind shops and sailing culture tend to appeal to an older crowd, and although there are a few good restaurants, only a small number of pubs are open late. Students also find that though the campus is well situated close to the historic district of Annapolis, the public transportation system is unreliable and can make going to the mall or the movies or anywhere that is not within walking distance quite difficult. Nevertheless, students note that with the rigors of the academic program, they have limited time to leave campus anyway. A second campus in Santa Fe, New Mexico, is also quickly becoming a liberal arts educational powerhouse in the southwest region. This second satellite campus follows the traditions and mission of the original Annapolis campus, giving students a comparable educational experience across both campuses.

When Not Reading or Sleeping . . .

Outside of attending classes and lots of studying, on-campus life revolves around extracurricular activities and "hanging out." Popular extracurricular activities include the King William Players which puts

on a play each semester, The Gadfly, the student newspaper, and an active intramural sports scene. One student notes that though there are a number of experienced athletes, "The environment is surprisingly open to people who have never played sports before." Less popular clubs tend to have a high turnover rate; "There are a lot of clubs on campus, but around half of them disappear by the end of the semester or the year."

The campus coffee shop, located right at the heart of campus, serves as a central social center because of its quaint, comfortable atmosphere and "the best food on-campus, although that isn't saying much." Other Johnnies, referred to as "room-Johnnies," tend to stay in their rooms occasionally socializing with their neighbors but rarely leaving the building except to go to class and the dining hall. "Quad-Johnnies," a subset mostly composed of social freshmen, tend to hang out on the quad socializing and drinking. Be warned, however, that the administration can be particularly strict about underage drinking. Although everyone agrees that underage drinking is prevalent, every once in a while the college cracks down. "My year, they kicked out four sophomores for underage drinking," a student notes.

A Tight-Knit Community

With only 400 to 500 students, St. John's is a very small community; by the end of freshman year everyone at least recognizes everybody. While some students like the tight community others are bothered by the fact that "everyone on the campus knows your business."

> "Everyone is interested in reading and discussing, and it always amazes me how willing people are to talk about anything and everything."

Additionally, many students complain about the lack of diversity on campus although in some ways this is improving. "Most people come from upper-class well-educated families while there are a minority of students from middle-class backgrounds." Ethnic and racial diversity is also limited. "The school has tried to recruit more ethnic and racial minorities but they've been very unsuccessful." According to one student, the biggest problem is economics. "The school is really expensive, and does not offer a traditional education which would provide the graduating students with a specific field or career." Furthermore, while the school offers need-based financial aid, it can still be very expensive for students from disadvantaged backgrounds. "The first year, the college offered me a fairly generous aid package, but after that it decreased significantly; I'm graduating with $65,000 in loans," a senior says. He also notes that some of the most interesting students have had to leave because of financial difficulties. Yet despite the lack of ethnic and socioeconomic diversity, in recent years, the international student body has increased and the college is making a noticeable recruiting effort in non-traditional locations. At the very least, students say that there is tons of "intellectual diversity" and for a school that is all about ideas, that is the most important thing.

Leaving the Cave

A given week at St. John's includes reading the great works of western literature and discussing them with classmates hours into the night. On Mondays and Thursdays the whole campus attends their seminars at the same time. On Wednesdays, quad-Johnnies gather in the quad to celebrate the weekly New Year, because "Johnnies learn more in a week than most college students do in a year," and on Fridays, many students attend the campus lecture which occasionally brings in notable speakers such as Elie Wiesel and Andrew Young. On weekends, students hang out at Annapolis bars, talk at the coffee shop or go to campus parties ranging from the occasional waltz party, a St. John's tradition, to more standard college parties at off-campus houses. Between all of this, they are reading constantly. More than anything else, St. John's College is the ultimate college of the mind and "everything else is secondary."—*Sage Snider*

FYI

If you come to St. John's, you'd better bring: a thick skin because it can be difficult academically and socially.

What's the typical weekend schedule? Friday night lecture, the movie club shows a classic movie on Saturday nights, off-campus parties (usually one or two), and lots and lots of philosophical conversations.

Three things every student at St. John's should do before graduating are: Get a Hodson Trust Internship, take out all your tutors to lunch, and go to Croquet Weekend where St. John's beats the Naval Academy at Croquet!

St. Mary's College of Maryland

Address: 18952 East Fisher Road, St. Mary's City, MD 20686-3001

Phone: 240-895-5000

E-mail address: admissions@smcm.edu

Web site URL: www.smcm.edu

Year Founded: 1840

Private or Public: Public

Religious Affiliation: None

Location: Rural

Number of Applicants: 2,133

Percent Accepted: 65%

Percent Accepted who enroll: 32%

Number Entering: 443

Number of Transfers Accepted each Year: 99

Middle 50% SAT range: M: 550–650, CR: 568–680, Wr: 558–660

Middle 50% ACT range: 24–29

Early admission program EA/ED/None: ED

Percentage accepted through EA or ED: 47%

EA and ED deadline: 1-Nov

Regular Deadline: 1-Jan

Application Fee: $40

Full time Undergraduate enrollment: 1,902

Total enrollment: 1,982

Percent Male: 41%

Percent Female: 59%

Total Percent Minority or Unreported: 23%

Percent African-American: 8%

Percent Asian/Pacific Islander: 3%

Percent Hispanic: 3%

Percent Native-American: <1%

Percent International: 2%

Percent in-state/out of state: 85%/15%

Percent from Public HS: 70%

Retention Rate: 87%

Graduation Rate 4-year: 67%

Graduation Rate 6-year: 74%

Percent Undergraduates in On-campus housing: 86%

Number of official organized extracurricular organizations: 82

2 Most popular majors: Biology, English Language and Literature

Student/Faculty ratio: 12:1

Average Class Size: 13

Percent of students going to grad school: 34%

Tuition and Fees: $24,082

In-State Tuition and Fees if different: $12,005

Cost for Room and Board: $10,915

Percent receiving financial aid out of those who apply: 59%

Percent receiving financial aid among all students: 61%

A public university that traces its origin to the 1840s, St. Mary's College is the public honors college of Maryland. Located about 40 miles from Washington, D.C. on the western shore of the Chesapeake Bay, St. Mary's College is a highly regarded liberal arts institution. Although it does offer a Master's program in teaching, the college's primary focus is definitely undergraduate education. As most people who attend state schools crowd into large lecture halls of universities that enroll tens of thousands of both undergraduate and graduate students, St. Mary's College provides schooling with individual attention at the cost of a public university.

State, Yet not State

In accordance with most state governments, Maryland has its own charter system that incorporates all public institutions of higher learning. For years, St. Mary's College was part of the system but opted out in 1992 during a fiscal crisis and was subsequently named the public honors college of Maryland. The concept is that everyone at St. Mary's College is an honor student. At the outset, it may seem strange. After all, what difference does it make to bestow the title honors college when everyone at the school is at the same level? Compared to the rest of the University System of Maryland, however, St. Mary's College is supposed to represent the top institution that offers the best intellectual environment. In fact, according to *U.S. News & World Report*, the college is ranked number one among all public liberal arts colleges.

St. Mary's College is a small school. With approximately 2,000 students, it is smaller than many high schools around the country. The advantage of the small size is that it ensures personal attention by the faculty to the students. "Because the school is so small, it is much easier to get to know professors," said one student. "By graduation, I feel that I know most people who are on campus, both professors and students." To enhance the intimacy of St. Mary's learning environment, the classes are mostly seminars where students learn through discussions and debates. "I sat through a couple of classes that have fewer than 10 people," said one student. "It is great because then you have more time to present about your own views."

One disadvantage of St. Mary's College is the number of academic programs. In fact, the school only has 22 majors, and one of them is the student-designed program of study, in which one can come up with his or her own curriculum based on the courses offered by the college. Of course, any program made by a student is subject to approval by the school administration. The 21 other majors are the more traditional liberal arts programs, such as biology, history, and economics. "It is true that we don't have many choices," said one student. "But we are a liberal arts college, so you need to understand that people who come here are looking for a general type of education, not something specific like electrical engineering." Although most students do consider the number of majors a downside of St. Mary's College, most of them do not feel affected because they enjoy having a liberal arts education. "Studying at St. Mary's is not about knowing all the facts about a field. It is all about developing the skills you need to succeed," said one student.

> "By graduation, I feel that I know most people who are on campus, both professors and students."

Since everyone is an honors student, the workload is certainly heavy, and students are relatively competitive. "There are a lot of smart people who really want to do well in school," said one student. "And sometimes, it is hard to keep up with them." According to students, it is important to remain well organized. After all, students who are poor planners tend to be easily overwhelmed by schoolwork. "You have to make sure that you do not fall behind," said one student. "It can be really difficult to keep up with classes afterward." Despite the intensity of some of the classes, it is important to point out that the majority of students are able to manage their schedules with relative ease and have plenty of time

to participate in different extracurricular activities. "You have to work hard, but since we are an honors college, most people who came here are definitely ready for this type of pressure," said one student.

As one of the top 100 liberal arts colleges in the country, the admissions process is very competitive. Only approximately 65 percent of the applicants are accepted. "Students at St. Mary's are very smart," said one student. "But don't be intimidated by other people. If you get in, that means you are smart too."

The Beginning of America
One of the most important facets of the college advertised by promotional materials of St. Mary's College is its location. At the outset, for a college student, perhaps there is nothing special about St. Mary's City, where the college is located. In fact, many people may think that the location is a disadvantage. After all, the so-called city is more similar to a village. What is special about St. Mary's City, however, is that it is the fourth-oldest British settlement in the United States. Large portions of the city are now considered National Historic Landmarks. "The historical importance of St. Mary's City cannot be overlooked," said one student. "There is not much to do here, but at least we live in a historic place with a beautiful campus of nice, old buildings."

The great majority of students live on campus. After all, it is a small school in a rather removed part of Maryland, thus the sense of community provided by college residences can be very helpful to many students. Freshman housing is generally closely monitored by staff members and has many more features that provide advice and support to students. "Getting to know people who live around you is the first step to making friends in college," said one student. "That is why living on campus during freshman year is so important." After the first year, upperclassmen can enjoy greater freedom and independence in one of the town houses or apartment-style residences. The quality of the dorms is generally considered adequate by the students. "I definitely would love to have big rooms, but, having been to other schools' dorms, I think we are actually pretty decent," said one student.

The main dining hall is called the Great Room, which can seat about 400 students and serves as an all-you-can-eat facility. Beyond the Great Room, there are also a few sandwich and coffee places around campus. Students can choose from eight different meal plans, though there are limitations based on the year. For example, freshmen only have access to three different plans, all of which focus on eating at the dining hall instead of using flex dollars at different restaurants around campus. For upperclassmen, obviously there are more options, since some students are by then living off campus.

Many parties happen on campus because that is where the majority of students are located. However, most people do feel that St. Mary's City is not very interesting with very few activities for students, especially during weekends, a time when people finally find some time to relax. Many do choose to go to Washington D.C. or even Baltimore during weekends to enjoy a more vibrant city atmosphere.

An Honors Experience

St. Mary's College may not be very different from any other small liberal arts schools. After all, it is located in a rather removed part of the state. It has only 2,000 students and offers few majors. However, what distinguishes St. Mary's College is that it is a public college providing a great education. Whenever a school offers strong academics at a discounted price, it certainly becomes a college choice worthy of consideration. —*Xiaohang Liu*

FYI

If you come to St. Mary's College, you'd better bring "a car."

What is the typical weekend schedule? "Work during the day, party at night."

If I could change one thing about St. Mary's College, "I'd add more majors."

Three things every student at St. Mary's College should do before graduating are "take a trip to Washington, D.C., tour the history of St. Mary's City, and remember to have fun."

United States Naval Academy

Address: 117 Decatur Road, Annapolis, MD 21402

Phone: 410-293-1914

E-mail address: webmail@usna.edu

Web site URL: www.usna.edu

Year Founded: 1845

Private or Public: Public

Religious Affiliation: None

Location: Urban

Number of Applicants: 17,419

Percent Accepted: 8%

Percent Accepted who enroll: 85%

Number Entering: 1,245

Number of Transfers Accepted each Year: Unreported

Middle 50% SAT range: M: 590–690, CR: 550–670, Wr: Unreported

Middle 50% ACT range: 25–31

Early admission program EA/ED/None: None

Percentage accepted through EA or ED: NA

EA and ED deadline: NA

Regular Deadline: 31-Jan

Application Fee: $0

Full time Undergraduate enrollment: 4,603

Total enrollment: 4,603

Percent Male: 80%

Percent Female: 20%

Total Percent Minority or Unreported: 32%

Percent African-American: 6%

Percent Asian/Pacific Islander: 4%

Percent Hispanic: 12%

Percent Native-American: <1%

Percent International: 1%

Percent in-state/out of state: 4%/96%

Percent from Public HS: 60%

Retention Rate: 97%

Graduation Rate 4-year: 84%

Graduation Rate 6-year: 84%

Percent Undergraduates in On-campus housing: 100%

Number of official organized extracurricular organizations: 100

3 Most popular majors: Economics, Political Science, History

Student/Faculty ratio: 8:1

Average Class Size: 16

Percent of students going to grad school: 2%

Tuition and Fees: $0

In-State Tuition and Fees if different: No difference

Cost for Room and Board: $0

Percent receiving financial aid out of those who apply: NA

Percent receiving financial aid among all students: NA

Since Secretary of the Navy George Bancroft founded the school in 1845, the United States Naval Academy has been one of the most prestigious military institutions in the country. Located in picturesque Annapolis, Maryland, the Naval Academy prides itself on training a generation of future military officers. The application process is rigorous, requiring a congressional appointment and a high score on a physical aptitude test; once a student has been accepted, the school covers all tuition expenses in return for a five-year post-graduation military commitment. Though life at the Academy is strictly regimented and the extended hazing process can become disheartening, the sense of camaraderie among the midshipmen by graduation remains unsurpassed by any other college. Despite the hazing and hardship, students praise their school for the dedication of the faculty to students' success and the sense of community amongst peers.

What a Plebe

First-year students at the Naval Academy are disparagingly referred to by the upperclassmen as "plebes," short for plebeians, the lowest class in the ancient Roman social hierarchy. The life of a plebe begins before the official start of the school year during what's known as "Plebe Summer." The Academy defines the goal of plebe summer as "to turn civilians into midshipmen." Heads shaved and civilian clothes discarded, the plebes are thrust directly into the whole new world of the Naval Academy. "You're very disoriented, especially in the beginning," said one midshipman. "However all of the yelling and pressure forces you to learn very fast." Each day starts with intense physical exercise, followed by activities and indoctrination training. Forget cell phones and computers, plebes are completely isolated from the outside world with the exception of snail-mail. Training itself is very difficult both physically and mentally. "You find yourself doing things you never thought possible, like memorizing long paragraphs word for word or telling the time of day from the position of the sun because you aren't allowed watches." Although certain amenities like cell phones are returned to the plebes upon completion of summer training, freshman year is still rough; approximately sixteen percent of the students will drop out before sophomore year.

Even after the summer, plebes occupy the lowest rung on the Naval Academy hierarchy. "We always have to be jogging in the hallways," said one freshman. "We have to greet every upperclassman as sir, and when we're outside, we always have to walk on the longest walkways." And forget distractions: television, DVDs, and music are all prohibited for freshmen. Not to mention the fact that upperclassmen can quiz you at any time. "You have to memorize everything," said one plebe, "including the menu and the days until the next break." Though intense and at times exhausting, this period is intended to test the plebe class's dedication to the academy, and things get much better each year. "It gets a lot better after freshman year," one student said, "the bad stuff makes you a lot closer."

Sound Mind in a Sound Body

Although prospective students would expect the Academy's emphasis on physical fitness, academics are considered to be just as important. "The workload is ridiculous," one student said. Students are required to take at least 15 credit hours a semester, but most take more. One student said that it was common for students to take as many as 23 credit hours a semester and play a varsity sport.

> "You can go up to any graduate anywhere in the world and have an understanding because you shared this experience."

But that's not the only studying midshipmen have to do. At the end of every week, one plebe explained, every plebe is required to take a "professional knowledge exam," which tests knowledge about various naval topics including weapons and the history of the navy. "It's basically like taking an extra class," one student explained. "If you don't pass, you don't get privileges over the weekend."

But fear not, although the classes are tough, Academy professors go out of their way to offer assistance. "The average class size is around 20, no more than 30," said one midshipman. "It's like a high school class." Professors offer their students the opportunity for extra instruction, taking into account the hectic schedule of a midshipman and will even come in late at night to meet with eager students. "The professors are everything," said one midshipman. "If you're going in and you go talk to the professor, they can give you whatever grade they want; they take effort into account and really want us to succeed." Another way that students are able to get extra assistance on their homework is through junior and senior peer tutors. "I go every week," one student said. "It's hard to do it on your own, but the older kids really help you through it; they've been there before and they know what you're going through."

Go Navy, Beat Army!

One of the campus's oldest traditions is Army Week, the week of the Army-Navy football game. Though attendance at all football games is mandatory for the midshipmen, there is nothing quite like the Army game. "People go absolutely nuts," said one student. "Throughout the week before the big game, pranks proliferate on campus. There are printers flying out windows, mattresses everywhere, shaving cream bombs, and plenty of pies," an upperclassman described. The regular rules for plebes are suspended, and the entire campus bonds through a series of elaborate pranks. "The idea is to show spirit, and somehow that manifests in a bunch of crazy pranks." The regular decorum of the Academy disintegrates into spirit missions, peanut butter on door handles, and food-fights. The mayhem suffuses the entire school with an incredible amount of energy. "Going into the game you're really pumped up," said one student. "You feel really close to your classmates."

We are Family

Despite it all, or perhaps because of it all, students at the Naval Academy are bonded like nowhere else. "You can go up to any graduate anywhere in the world and have an understanding because you shared this experience," one midshipman said. All meals are served family-style, with students passing dishes to each other instead of impersonally shuffling cafeteria trays. The 30 companies, each containing approximately 140 midshipmen, into which each student is randomly assigned become "like even tighter fraternities." Members of the same company live together, eat together, and train together. From I-Day (the first day at the academy), students are put in their companies and they stay together for all four years. Through the good times and bad times, the company is there; in the words of one upperclassman, "The stress and pain of the Academy brings us together because we go through it together and help each other out any way we can."—*Jane Menton*

FYI
If you come to the USNA, you'd better bring "something to look forward to; when things get tough, it's nice to have that one thing you know will be there when you get finished."
Would you do it again? "Yeah, I would. It's a tough place to go to, but there isn't a better place to be from."

University of Maryland / College Park

Address: Mitchell Building, College Park, MD 20742-5235
Phone: 301-314-8385
E-mail address: um-admit@uga.umd.edu
Web site URL: www.umd.edu
Year Founded: 1856
Private or Public: Public
Religious Affiliation: None
Location: Urban
Number of Applicants: 26,310
Percent Accepted: 44%
Percent Accepted who enroll: 34%
Number Entering: 3,929
Number of Transfers Accepted each Year: 3,359
Middle 50% SAT range: M: 610–710, CR: 580–680, Wr: Unreported
Middle 50% ACT range: Unreported
Early admission program EA/ED/None: EA

Percentage accepted through EA or ED: Unreported
EA and ED deadline: 1-Nov
Regular Deadline: 20-Jan
Application Fee: $55
Full time Undergraduate enrollment: 26,876
Total enrollment: 37,595
Percent Male: 53%
Percent Female: 47%
Total Percent Minority or Unreported: 45%
Percent African-American: 13%
Percent Asian/Pacific Islander: 14%
Percent Hispanic: 14%
Percent Native-American: <1%
Percent International: 2%
Percent in-state/out of state: 68%/32%
Percent from Public HS: Unreported
Retention Rate: 95%

Graduation Rate 4-year: 63%
Graduation Rate 6-year: 81%
Percent Undergraduates in On-campus housing: 44%
Number of official organized extracurricular organizations: 574
3 Most popular majors: Social Sciences, Business/Marketing, Biology
Student/Faculty ratio: 18:1
Average Class Size: 25
Percent of students going to grad school: Unreported
Tuition and Fees: $26,026
In-State Tuition and Fees if different: $8,655
Cost for Room and Board: $9,942
Percent receiving financial aid out of those who apply: 50%
Percent receiving financial aid among all students: 38%

Less then fifteen miles from the nation's capital, the University of Maryland sits on more than a thousand acres of green, suburban grass. Home of the Terrapins, Maryland is well known as a prestigious research university with Division I athletics and a strong sense of school pride. The school's numerous academic, extracurricular, and athletic options provide plenty of opportunities for its 25,000 students, so it's no surprise that wherever one goes on campus, shouts of "Go Terps!" are sure to be heard.

Options for Everyone

With over a hundred academic majors and eleven colleges and schools, the University of Maryland offers every student the chance to study what they love. Applicants select one of the eleven schools on their UMD application, and while many students choose the more traditional College of Arts and Humanities, a great deal apply to the Robert H. Smith School of Business, the Philip Merrill College of Journalism, the College of Education, and other schools.

All Maryland students need to complete 120 course credits in order to graduate, with a minimum of 12 credits per semester to be considered a "full-time student." The school has a CORE program, which consists of nine course credits in the humanities, ten in math and science, nine in social sciences and history, and three in emerging issues. There are a few more specific English and math requirements. Maryland also requires each student to get six credits at the advanced level in one or more fields outside their major, but many students choose to take a few more classes and use those six credits toward a certificate. Most Maryland students don't feel too daunted by the requirements, and note that "it's pretty easy to fulfill them without really trying," because there are so many interesting classes to take.

The university also has a variety of special academic programs, including the College Park Scholars program and the Honors

College. The College Park Scholars program, which is divided into a variety of academic fields ranging from Media, Self, and Society to Global Public Health, allows students the opportunity to live in a unique residential community, take exclusive courses, and interact with professors in smaller class settings. The prestigious Honors College offers students access to many interdisciplinary courses and multiyear programs, such as the Gemstone research program. Overall, students are very impressed with Maryland's academic program, and some even argue that the school "doesn't get all the credit it deserves."

The one downside to Maryland's academics, according to some students, is the grading system. At UMD, there's no difference between an A– and an A+; with both grades, students are awarded a 4.0 grade point average. However, the same holds true for grades in the B range—and anything in the B range earns the student a 3.0. While this can be seen as "an advantage for A– students," some students feel discouraged knowing that their B+ is worth the same amount as their classmate's B–.

The "Horseshoe" and the "Graham Cracker," Just Minutes from the White House

One way that many students make Maryland's large campus feel smaller is by getting involved with the popular Greek system. With dozens of fraternities and sororities to choose from, any student who wants to "go Greek" can easily find his or her niche. Fraternity housing can be found on "Frat Row," also known as the "Horseshoe" because of the shape the fraternity houses make. Right next to the Horseshoe is the "Graham Cracker," another complex of fraternity and sorority houses. Frat parties are a common occurrence, with multiple parties happening each weekend. Other perks of being involved in the Frat system include special events during Homecoming and Greek Week.

However, the frat party scene does not completely dominate social life at Maryland. Frat Row sits on one side of Route 1, the main street in College Park, which is also home to a variety of restaurants and bars popular with UMD undergrads. Because Route 1 is so close to campus, it's a popular location for any Maryland student looking for a night out. Many students also choose to take the Metro (a four-dollar ticket and thirty-minute ride) to Washington, D.C., where they can enjoy the restaurants, bars, and clubs. Maryland

students love having a "movie-esque" campus so close to a big city, because "there's always something to do," and whenever they "don't feel like spending money to go out in D.C., there's always a frat party or a bar close to campus where you'll have a good time."

> **"Maryland is like a more down-to-earth version of lots of bigger state schools."**

Although drugs and alcohol are prohibited by the school, most students don't feel threatened by the administration. RAs are pretty lenient, and students say that it's unlikely someone will be punished unless they're "being ridiculous." Although some students smoke pot, most agree that alcohol is much more prevalent on campus.

Overall, Maryland students feel as if there is a good balance between studying and partying. "Maryland studies very hard and parties very hard," one student said, while another pointed out that there were never weeks devoted solely to studying or solely to partying. One student described Maryland as "a more down-to-earth version of lots of bigger state schools." Then again, UMD has gotten billed as one of the Top 20 Party Schools for the last few years.

Learning, Laughing, and Laying Out on the "Mall"

With 36 residence halls and a variety of off-campus housing options, every student can find something comfortable at Maryland. Students can apply for housing and request specific dorms, such as Cecil, an all-girls hall, or Elkton, the notorious party dorm. With such a huge campus, many students have to walk pretty far to get to class, but most students ignore distance when choosing their residence halls. One of the best ways to make friends at Maryland is by getting to know the people on your floor, and most students credit their housing arrangements with making them feel at home.

About 76% of UMD students are Maryland natives, and many others are from the nearby New Jersey, Pennsylvania, and New York areas. However, the student body still feels very diverse. "Any type of person can go [to Maryland]," and "there's always somewhere to fit in." One of the most popular campus locations is the "Mall," a large, shallow reflecting pool modeled after the pool in front of the Lincoln Memorial in Washington, D.C. When weather permits, Maryland students love to lie out, study, or play games of football—and, on occasion, Quidditch—on the beautiful green grass surrounding the Mall. Students also frequent the Stamp Student Union, the student activities center that's home to the University Book Center, the Hoff Theater, and numerous dining options.

Although Terps love their campus, most agree that the city of College Park is pretty "sketchy." Students are advised not to walk alone at night, and some cautious girls even carry pepper spray when they go out. Another common complaint is the quality of the dining hall food. However, the dining halls "always have chicken fingers and fries," and are also vegan-friendly, with salad bars and vegan options readily available. For freshmen who want to avoid the dining halls, the meal plan also includes "TerpBucks," meal dollars that can be used at the Union Shop and popular chain restaurants like Starbucks.

A Toast to Testudo

When Maryland students aren't studying or partying, chances are they're involved with one or more of the school's numerous extracurricular programs. Freshmen get to know all of the university's extracurricular opportunities by attending the First Look Fair, during which all of the organizations line up on the Mall and try to recruit new members. "Everyone reads the *Diamondback*," Maryland's main college paper, and other on-campus publications are also popular. With numerous a cappella, comedy, and service groups, there's something for everyone.

Maryland is well known for its Division I athletics teams, and many students flock to the football and basketball games every year. Student attendance is high even when the teams have losing seasons, partly because students can get free tickets to the games. Their mascot, Testudo—a diamondback terrapin always clad in UMD red—is one of the most famous mascots in college sports.

However, Testudo is more than just a mascot—he's also the center of one of the most famous campus superstitions. Maryland students say that "rubbing Testudo's nose"—that is, the nose of a statue of the beloved tortoise—will bring good luck. The legend goes on to say that the one year the main statue of Testudo was under renovation, the overall campus GPA dropped significantly.

One thing that stands out about UMD is the amount of school spirit and the unity among the student body. Although the students are "very diverse" and come from all socioeconomic, ethnic, and religious backgrounds, they all have one thing in common: Terrapin pride. Walking along the lush, green grass toward many of the freshman dorms, it's impossible to miss the welcoming sign painted on the football stadium: Home of the Maryland Terrapins. For UMD students, home is where Testudo is.—*Iva Velickovic*

FYI
If I could change one thing about Maryland, it would be the neighborhood. It's pretty sketchy, and I feel unsafe walking around at night.
One thing I wish I knew before I came to Maryland was that freshmen are allowed to bring cars. You do have to pay a fee, but it's totally worth it because it gives you the opportunity to explore Bethesda, DC, and other places nearby.

Massachusetts

Amherst College

Address: PO Box 5000, Amherst, MA 01002
Phone: 413-542-2328
E-mail address: admissions@amherst.edu
Web site URL: www.amherst.edu
Year Founded: 1821
Private or Public: Private
Religious Affiliation: None
Location: Rural
Number of Applicants: 7,745
Percent Accepted: 15%
Percent Accepted who enroll: 38%
Number Entering: 452
Number of Transfers Accepted each Year: 14
Middle 50% SAT range: M: 660–760, CR: 670–770, Wr: 670–760
Middle 50% ACT range: 31
Early admission program EA/ED/None: ED
Percentage accepted through EA or ED: 34%

EA and ED deadline: 15-Nov
Regular Deadline: 1-Jan
Application Fee: $60
Full time Undergraduate enrollment: 1,683
Total enrollment: 1,683
Percent Male: 50%
Percent Female: 50%
Total Percent Minority or Unreported: 38%
Percent African-American: 11%
Percent Asian/Pacific Islander: 11%
Percent Hispanic: 11%
Percent Native-American: <1%
Percent International: 7%
Percent in-state/out of state: 10%/90%
Percent from Public HS: 58%
Retention Rate: 97%
Graduation Rate 4-year: 96%

Graduation Rate 6-year: 98%
Percent Undergraduates in On-campus housing: 98%
Number of official organized extracurricular organizations: 100
3 Most popular majors: Political Science, Psychology, Economics
Student/Faculty ratio: 8:1
Average Class Size: 17
Percent of students going to grad school: 75%
Tuition and Fees: $36,970
In-State Tuition and Fees if different: No difference
Cost for Room and Board: $9,790
Percent receiving financial aid out of those who apply: 80%
Percent receiving financial aid among all students: 52%

G iven their many, varied interests, you might be surprised to find that the overwhelming majority of students at Amherst College at least agree about one thing: "the 'h' in the name is not pronounced." Yet, regardless of this phonetic unity, Amherstians pride themselves on their school's diversity, be it academic, social or extracurricular. With 36 available majors and 100 student organizations to choose from, it's no wonder that Amherst's 1,700 undergraduates feel that they can do almost anything at a place which—despite its intimate size—offers some of the most wide-ranging options anywhere.

Open Curriculum, Open Minds
Multiple students note that the first thing that comes to mind when thinking about academics at Amherst is the school's distinctive lack of a core curriculum. With the exception of a required seminar in freshman year, Amherst allows its students the freedom to design their own course of study, which gives them full responsibility over their educational choices.

On the whole, Amherstians are content with these First-Year Seminars, which focus on subjects ranging from happiness to history to physics to philosophy. "The seminars are there just to ensure that you can think, write and analyze a text cogently before you settle on a particular major," said one freshman at the end of his first semester. "Besides, the fact that there are around 30 of them means that there's something available for everyone, whatever their interests." Students praise the discussion-based nature of these seminars, which lets them bounce their ideas off of one another and their professors in a collaborative setting.

Nor do Amherstians object to having to declare a major by the end of their second year and having to complete 32 credits in order to graduate. Majors typically span from eight to ten courses, but can be tailored to any given student's personal preferences. The great thing about having no distributional requirements, students say, is that the curriculum's structure lies at the individual's discretion. "Since there are no core requirements," one senior double-majoring in English and Russian noted, "I've been able to take classes in 11 or 12 different departments already, no problem." During his junior year, the same student also tried his hand at jazz guitar, in lessons which were wholly funded by the school, and took a cognitive spirituality class with the head of the physics department, Arthur Zajonc, who was the personal physics tutor to the Dalai Lama for a year. Hence, as a sophomore majoring in psychology pointed out, one of Amherst's biggest selling points is that "the incentive for students to take a certain class is entirely their own desire to be in that class; unlike at other colleges, it's not about climbing the distributional ladder."

> **"Great professors in small departments with lots of money means that you can do almost anything you want."**

Some students, however, are frustrated by the difficulties of registering for courses taught by Amherst's "celebrity professors"— such as Arthur Zajonc in physics, Hadley Arkes in philosophy and Austin Sarat in political science—because class sizes are limited. "Upperclassmen and people who have settled on a major typically get preference," said one sophomore. "But, the trade-off is that if you get into one of these classes, the experience is that much more intimate." Indeed, Amherstians praise the small size of both seminars and lectures, which, according to one junior, typically average about 17 and 40 people respectively. This allows for students to develop more personal relationships with their peers and their teachers within and outside of the classroom. Dinners at professors' houses are not unheard of. Meanwhile, students at Amherst praise the wide availability of educational resources, whatever their own individual pursuits entail. As one senior put it, "great professors in small departments with lots of money means that you can do almost anything you want."

Small classes at the college incentivize students to come prepared and ready to participate. "Silence from one side of the discussion table is much more noticeable in a tiny classroom setting," one freshman said. Yet, Amherst students of all years find that the intimacy of their academic experience creates an atmosphere of friendly cooperation rather than fierce competition. Cliché though it may be, students are convinced that they work hard—and play hard—together. "Amherst is by far the most relaxed place I've been," one sophomore claimed. "People here just want to pursue their interests and breathe; it's totally chill."

But if they happen to get tired of its small classrooms and need a change of pace, Amherst also offers its students the opportunity to take courses at four other nearby institutions through its membership in the Five College Consortium. The consortium is an unusual cooperative arrangement among Amherst, Smith, Mount Holyoke, and Hampshire Colleges and the University of Massachusetts-Amherst, where all five campuses are linked by a free bus system. "By their fourth year here," one senior noted, "I'd say about 75% of people have taken at least one course somewhere else, since some courses just aren't available at Amherst," such as certain language classes, or those that relate more specifically to job skills.

Amherst: Where Only the "h" is Silent

Passion for learning aside, students at Amherst are convinced that they know how to have a good time. Amherstians, they report, orchestrate a careful balancing act between their studies and their social lives every week. Though one sophomore noted that some students can seem like "academic zombies from Sunday through Wednesday," he went on to say that "everybody seems to forget their work from Thursday night until Sunday morning."

So what do students at Amherst do to keep themselves busy during weekends? Well, as with so many other aspects of their school, Amherstians have options. Even though there are no official fraternities on campus, students can "almost always find typical college beer-fest parties in 'the Socials,'" a quad surrounded by dorms with suites. "The

Social Quad has wonderful dorms," one junior stated, "but on weekends, they smell like alcohol and are pretty much on a nonstop rave." Luckily for those who choose not to party, the Social Quad is all the way at the bottom of a hill, "so you can't really hear the music," and substance-free housing is available to freshmen upon request. "But there's absolutely no pressure to drink if you don't want to," one freshman noted.

Given this, students still seem to agree that Amherst's administration has a somewhat lax policy when it comes to dealing with drinking on campus. In line with the school's mission to respect its members' diversity of lifestyle, Amherst rarely invades upon its students' personal lives, unless their behavior becomes disruptive or dangerous. "They basically spend the first three months telling us how to drink safely, since we're not supposed to be doing it in the first place," one freshman said. "But they're only going to bust a party if things really get out of hand." Amherst also hosts a special TAP ("The Amherst Party") once a month, which, according to one student, are "really safe, really fun, and really big . . . and not just in the drinking or bump-and-grind sense." Traditional themes include an '80s dance party, a Halloween costume party, and a tropical Luau.

In addition to extra courses, the Five College Consortium offers Amherst students the opportunity to go off campus and meet other people if they ever feel caught in "the Amherst bubble." In the words of one senior who gives tours at Amherst, "it actually does make a difference having 35,000 people your age within a 10 mile radius. It means that you can pretty much always find a new crowd if you want, but also that there's just generally lots of fun stuff going on in the area." He pointed out the fact that Amherst is located in the Pioneer Valley, the second largest booking venue in all of New England, which means that there are "concerts, clubs, bars, all kinds of ridiculous festivals, readings by traveling writers, academic symposia every month."

Besides standard partying, students say that there are always on-campus events like movie showings in the campus center, comedy club performances, and free concerts in the recital hall. One student, for example, mentioned the fact that "theatre majors are actually required to write or direct a play, so there are about three or four plays here every two weeks or so." At Amherst, students claim, "there will never be a night where you don't have something to do."

Purple Pride and Decent Dorms

Other than how they pronounce the name of their college, Amherst students also agree that athletes have a noticeable presence on campus. By one junior football player's estimates, for instance, about a third of the school plays a varsity sport. The integration of athletes and their non-athletic counterparts in the same dorms, moreover, appears to lead to a lot of school spirit, since "basically everybody knows someone on one sports team or another." "We support our athletes a lot," one sophomore said. "They're basically our heroes." This is especially true in games against Amherst's longtime rivals—such as Williams, Middlebury, and Wesleyan—for which almost everybody comes out wearing purple and white. And though athletes at Amherst get all the glory when they triumph on weekends, students concur that there is not a 'jock or not' divide at their college. "Most athletes here are pretty nice," another sophomore noted. "They're not your stereotypical jocks. A lot of them actually have the impulse to be socially active and do community service work."

Dorms, as one senior put it, "are sort of a mixed bag." While most Amherstians praise the spacious living arrangements in buildings like Appleton, Valentine, James, and Sterns, some lament having to live in "trailer-like arrangements," which one freshman attributed to "Amherst over-accepting students this year." On the other hand, the majority of students are content with regular dorms that consist of "one bathroom, one RC per floor, and anywhere from 15 to 20 people per floor." And though living arrangements for first semester freshmen are about the same—singles or doubles, but no personal bathrooms—upperclassmen get the choice of having suites or multiple bathrooms. One junior also mentioned special subsidy- and language-housing on campus, which centers around a common language, culture or sometimes a religious belief.

Regardless of the housing situation, Amherstians agree that their campus is very safe with very few problems. "Whenever there's a police incident in the Five College area, we get a police notification via email," one freshman said. "Security presence is noticeable, but by no means overbearing." So, students at Amherst are largely free to enjoy their college's idyllic setting and the beautiful New England feel of the entire place without any safety concerns.

Ultimately, students at Amherst say that they can pursue their interests because they live amid conditions which are conducive to their drive and enthusiasm across a wide range of academic, social and extracurricular lifestyles. With a student body the size of most American public high schools, it's no wonder that Amherstians left and right praise the "intimate atmosphere" that their school fosters. "Everyone here is looking out for one another," one senior said proudly. "It's as simple as that."—*Andrew Giambrone and Danielle Trubow*

FYI

If you come to Amherst, make sure to bring "the preppiest winter clothes you can find in a 10 mile radius; we have a reputation to uphold with the other colleges in the consortium, you know?"

Three things you have to do before you graduate are: "take a class with Austin Sarat, attend Hampshire Halloween, and sled down Memorial Hill."

What surprised me most about Amherst when I arrived was "the prevalence of athletes and their influence on social life."

Babson College

Address: 231 Forest Street, Babson Park, MA 02457
Phone: 800-488-3696
E-mail address: ugradadmission@babson.edu
Web site URL: www.babson.edu
Year Founded: 1919
Private or Public: Private
Religious Affiliation: None
Location: Suburban
Number of Applicants: 3,530
Percent Accepted: 35%
Percent Accepted who enroll: 34%
Number Entering: 453
Number of Transfers Accepted each Year: 83
Middle 50% SAT range: M: 590–680, CR: 560–640, Wr: 570–650
Middle 50% ACT range: 25–29
Early admission program EA/ED/None: EA and ED

Percentage accepted through EA or ED: Unreported
EA and ED deadline: 1-Nov
Regular Deadline: 15-Jan
Application Fee: $65
Full time Undergraduate enrollment: 1,851
Total enrollment: 3,439
Percent Male: 60%
Percent Female: 40%
Total Percent Minority or Unreported: 44%
Percent African-American: 6%
Percent Asian/Pacific Islander: 14%
Percent Hispanic: 10%
Percent Native-American: <1%
Percent International: 22%
Percent in-state/out of state: 54%/46%
Percent from Public HS: 50%
Retention Rate: 93%

Graduation Rate 4-year: 84%
Graduation Rate 6-year: 87%
Percent Undergraduates in On-campus housing: 86%
Number of official organized extracurricular organizations: 60
3 Most popular majors: Accounting, Business Operations, Finance
Student/Faculty ratio: 16:1
Average Class Size: 35
Percent of students going to grad school: Unreported
Tuition and Fees: $36,096
In-State Tuition and Fees if different: No difference
Cost for Room and Board: $12,020
Percent receiving financial aid out of those who apply: Unreported
Percent receiving financial aid among all students: 42%

Babson College, located in the Babson Park section of Wellesley, Massachusetts, is a school that strives to create the next business leaders of the world. This undergraduate program combines liberal arts and business in order to teach its students the values of a "practical business education." From the beginning of freshman year, students create their own business, immediately reinforcing the concept of experience instead of only in-class learning. Although Babson features a relatively wealthy student body, Babsonians are still ambitious to learn how to succeed in the business world.

Hands-on Preparation for the Real World

Babson students are required to start their own business—the first of many—in a freshman-year class called Foundations of Management and Entrepreneurship (FME). In this program, a team of students learns how to create and run a business, which at the end of the course is liquidated and the profits donated to charity. The course teaches students that becoming a CEO requires teamwork, plenty of effort, and true dedication.

But it is not all business at Babson. Freshmen take three additional classes that are mostly chosen for them. Two of the classes are in the liberal arts, and students say that the majority of liberal arts classes try to connect to business "every once in a while," although that does not mean that the teachers work together to distribute workloads. One sophomore said although he didn't expect professors from different departments to work together, "There have been plenty of times when I have 60 pages of reading and a test to study for on the same day. It can be overbearing at times." When students reach their junior and senior years, there is much more flexibility in their schedules.

Although Babson students are not required to pick a concentration outside of business, most do. Babson's concentrations provide ways for students to focus on the part of business that they love. Concentrations range from American studies to statistics to the literary and visual arts. The most common concentrations are Entrepreneurship and Finance. Whether a student chooses a concentration or not, everyone graduates with a BA in Business.

Babson has about 1,800 enrolled undergraduates, which translates to small classes. According to one senior, "The biggest class at Babson is FME, which has about sixty students. After that, you'll never have more than forty in a class." Most liberal arts classes are even smaller, including a few ten-person classes. The size of all classes at Babson gives students an opportunity to be in contact with some of the most influential business leaders of today. Rather than just hiring teachers who have studied business and have followed business trends, Babson also hires CEOs, CFOs, and other executives of major businesses, such as the popular professor Leonard Green, CEO of the Green Group. Although the teachers have high-powered jobs and often busy lives, Babson students give rave reviews to teacher-student relations. Professors at Babson have a reputation for helping outside of the classroom with not only class work, but in the workforce. Some teachers

help students find jobs, and that provides opportunities that are "huge when you hit senior year."

Grading at Babson is notoriously difficult, but students say an "A" is attainable when enough effort is put in. One senior said that participation is a component in grading, so interaction with other students and professors "is important, and can make a little bit of a difference in your grade." Some students are convinced that there is grade "deflation" for many classes, although teachers and many students insist that it does not exist. The real difficulty, one student said, is that "teachers have very high expectations for Babson students."

The Business Mentality

Babson's focus on business means that students are generally very driven toward their specific interests. Due to the nature of this attitude, some students say that the social environment is an even mix between collaborative and competitive. Babson fosters the idea of group work, which means that there are always people to help you. However, many point out that when they leave Babson, everyone is going into the same industry, which can create "some tension between students, because you know that you'll eventually be competing with your best friends for the same job." Many students agree that the balance between working together and working against each other is another way that Babson mimics the business world.

> "Upperclassmen pay attention and look out for underclassmen with similar interests. Everyone wants to help freshmen because they are always looking for new people to start a business with."

The business mentality of Babson really helps the freshmen assimilate into the student body. "Upperclassmen pay attention and look out for underclassmen with similar interests. Everyone wants to help freshmen because they are always looking for new people to start a business with," one freshman remarked. The freshmen do not only get support from upperclassmen, but First Year Seminar (FYS) also provides busy freshmen with weekly information on time management along with help with classes through a peer mentor, their FYS professor, and a faculty advisor. One freshman said that it could even get "overwhelming at how many people are checking up on you."

Babson Doesn't Just Work Hard . . .

As hard as students work at Babson, a combination of three-day weekends (there are rarely classes on Fridays), monthly "Knight" dance parties in the Knight auditorium, and the on-campus Pub create an environment where students can balance work and play. Students generally agree that a vast majority of students drink. Other "hard drugs" are not too common, except many students admit to using Adderall on school nights to focus. The policy on alcohol is not completely loose, but partygoers are given several warnings by RAs before the Babson Police (affectionately called Babo) are called in to break up the party. The jobs of the RAs are to look out for the students, not get them in trouble. The new honor code states that students have an obligation to help, not to report students who get sick from alcohol.

Outside of the dorm room parties, one sophomore club athlete said "you will always find a party on campus." The pub on campus, Roger's Pub, is open to all students, and those over 21 wear wristbands so they can purchase drinks. Once the pub closes at midnight, everyone disperses from the pub to either frat parties or parties in suites where a bunch of friends—often varsity athletes—live together. With all of the events on campus, commuting to Boston is not too common among students. The students who usually travel to Boston at night are often international students who have apartments there. On campus, there are many events not based around alcohol that are widely attended by students. The Campus Activities Board plans around 50 events a year, including "Knight parties." Many campus-sponsored events attract all kinds of people, and often incorporate international culture. For example, the South Asian club throws a Bhangra dance on campus that attracts many students, especially because of the "intrigue of free food."

Any time a student wants to plan a campus-wide event, Babson can subsidize the party or gathering.

Who Are The Future Business Leaders of the World?

The "stereotypical" Babson student is a "white, wealthy, preppy workaholic who is very self-involved." However, diversity on campus is growing, and with every year, the numbers of international students and women increase. According to a senior girl, "The difference in numbers between men and women is not obvious at all. The only times we think about it is when people are making jokes about it." In the case of international students, who make up about 20 percent of the population, the stereotype is that they are "rich" and often "royalty from some country." Most of the people who live off campus are international students, students say, and the perception is that many international students are known for having "multiple expensive cars." Overall, students agree that many Babsonians can be a "little flashy." "There are some kids who have more than one car with them," one freshman noted. But despite the stereotypes, the truth is that there are students from all socioeconomic backgrounds, and there are many students on financial aid and scholarship, with students receiving a total of about $25 million in financial aid, in addition to Babson grants, each year. Babson offers many scholarships to students that are based on all different criteria to accommodate people from all backgrounds.

When living on campus, the dorm situation "gets better with seniority," and varies depending on where you live. Few people complain about housing, as most dorms are described as being "better than those at the other colleges I've visited." Babson also gets high marks when it comes to roommate pairing. Freshmen agree that Babson "really takes your rooming form into consideration." Overall, the care that Babson puts into its social life allows students to enjoy their experience as a businessperson and a scholar.—*Willi Rechler*

FYI

If I could change one thing about Babson, "I'd move it out of the middle of dry-town Wellesley and put the same campus in the middle of Boston!"

If you come to Babson, you'd better bring: "your BlackBerry, a suit, a Northface . . . and a whole bunch of business ideas before FME starts."

Three things every student at Babson should do before graduating are: 1) "Get a 100 on an exam," 2) "Take a class with Len Green," and 3) "Stay at a Knight Party until 2 a.m."

What is the typical weekend schedule? "Weekends start on Thursday night and everyone's at pub. Friday night is a lighter night, but people go out or go to Boston, and Saturday is a big campus party night. On Sunday, everything shuts down and everyone does work."

Boston College

Address: 140 Commonwealth Avenue, Chestnut Hill, MA 02467
Phone: 800-360-2522
E-mail address: NA
Web site URL: www.bc.edu
Year Founded: 1863
Private or Public: Private
Religious Affiliation: Roman Catholic
Location: Suburban
Number of Applicants: 30,845
Percent Accepted: 26%
Percent Accepted who enroll: 27%
Number Entering: 2,167
Number of Transfers Accepted each Year: 166
Middle 50% SAT range: M: 640–730, CR: 610–700, Wr: 620–710
Middle 50% ACT range: 28–32
Early admission program EA/ED/None: EA

Percentage accepted through EA or ED: 36%
EA and ED deadline: 1-Nov
Regular Deadline: 1-Jan
Application Fee: $70
Full time Undergraduate enrollment: 9,060
Total enrollment: 13,087
Percent Male: 49%
Percent Female: 51%
Total Percent Minority or Unreported: 29%
Percent African-American: 6%
Percent Asian/Pacific Islander: 9%
Percent Hispanic: 8%
Percent Native-American: <1%
Percent International: 3%
Percent in-state/out of state: 29%/71%
Percent from Public HS: 53%
Retention Rate: 96%
Graduation Rate 4-year: Unreported

Graduation Rate 6-year: Unreported
Percent Undergraduates in On-campus housing: 82%
Number of official organized extracurricular organizations: 223
3 Most popular majors: Communication, English, Finance
Student/Faculty ratio: 13:1
Average Class Size: 15
Percent of students going to grad school: 25%
Tuition and Fees: $37,950
In-State Tuition and Fees if different: No difference
Cost for Room and Board: $11,610
Percent receiving financial aid out of those who apply: 77%
Percent receiving financial aid among all students: 70%

The location is superb: the village of Chestnut Hill is just a short train ride away from the exciting city of Boston. The academics are excellent; the high standards and diverse curriculum ensure quality education. To top it off, whether you prefer parties or tailgates or a cappella shows, you don't have to choose because you can attend all three in just one day. BC boasts impressive credentials on many fronts.

Attention: Get to Work!

Being a liberal arts school, BC ensures that each of its students receives a broad education encompassing many disciplines. The college is made up of four schools: the College of Arts and Sciences, Lynch School of Education, Carroll School of Management, and the Connell School of Nursing. Each school has its own set of specific requirements. However, classes in literature, modern history, philosophy, theology, the natural sciences, the social sciences, the arts, cultural diversity, and writing are common to all. But the requirements are rarely a point of complaint since they are fairly easy to fulfill. As one junior pointed out, "While you have the required math class you dread, and a language requirement, I appreciate the core for letting me explore my options."

With options, each student can make what he or she wants out of his college experience. To make their schedules more interesting, students can take classes such as sign language, dance, or the anticonsumerist "Shop till you drop." Students recommend taking a class with Professor Seth Jacobs, who teaches history and is an expert on the Vietnam War. Class sizes vary from 12-person seminars where personal attention abounds to 200-person lectures for those who like the anonymity. Moreover, the workload, while generally manageable, can certainly be adjusted. The communication major is known for its lighter workload and higher GPAs, while the sciences are collectively acknowledged to be difficult. As one student put it, "If you want an A, you have to work for it." The professors are known to be accessible and hold regular office hours for those willing to make the effort to talk to them.

Change on the Horizon
The students are guaranteed housing for three years at BC. This means that about half of the junior class moves off campus each year. For those who do remain on campus, the choices vary by year. Dorms are assigned through a lottery. The freshmen are divided between Upper and Newton campuses, the latter being more secluded from the general population of the college while providing a close-knit sense of community. Since housing improves with seniority, the seniors get to choose from among four-to-six-person suites in apartment-style housing, featuring private bathrooms and kitchens. For the more outgoing, there is also the option of living in the senior-only mods, which are known for their spacious backyards and party-friendly atmosphere.

There are six dining halls on campus, and the food gets thumbs up from the students, although the meal plans are considered overpriced. A popular option is Lyons dining hall, affectionately named "The Rat," which features plenty of fried options. McElroy and Corcoran Commons are praised for their long hours; some days they stay open till two a.m. As an alternative, students often venture out to Cleveland Circle, where there are a large variety of restaurants ranging from sushi places to an Applebee's. Of course, there is always the option of checking out the multitude of restaurants in Boston: "Take the train in and you have the world at your fingertips," one junior points out.

There are no central hanging-out areas on campus, but the cafeterias serve as worthy substitutes. The green areas around campus also provide good spots to relax in the afternoons, and the students enjoy the beautiful flowers planted throughout. As one senior said, while the overall look of BC is very pretty, "The campus is confused." The architecture ranges from gothic to modern, and there are some in-between. Currently, BC is working on a 10-year plan to renovate the campus by updating outdated dorms and academic buildings. As one student said, "Change is on the horizon."

Party Like It's Your Job
When the weekend comes around, BC students take the opportunity to exercise their right to play hard. For seniors, the definition of a weekend is rather flexible, and the fun starts as early as Wednesday. As one student claimed, "The school is a lot more social than I'd expected." Bars such as Mary Ann's and Roggie's Brew & Grille on Cleveland Circle (a center of shopping and social activity) are cited as local favorites for hanging out. Those of legal drinking age (read: with good fake IDs) take the opportunity to travel into the nearby Boston area, with its vibrant bar and club scene.

Most of the students, however, simply seek fun locally; while there are no frats, students take advantage of the plentiful parties at the senior mods or at the apartments of students who live off campus. The mods are also a regular tailgating site before sporting events. Another popular event on campus is the exclusive Middlemarch dance, which requires participation in a scavenger hunt to obtain tickets.

Drinking is a regular activity on campus in spite of the official dry campus rules. RAs are present in every dorm and, while most are pretty lenient, they are known to be stricter on the underclassmen. Students advise "be smart," as there are ways to get around the watchful eyes of administration.

The atmosphere is generally friendly, and people meet friends through classes or dorms. Unfortunately, students often complain that the school lacks diversity in terms of ethnicity and economic background. The stereotypical BC student looks like he or she "stepped out of a J. Crew catalog with a hangover." To battle the stereotypes, groups like AHANA (African-American, Hispanic, Asian, and Native American) work on campus to increase diversity.

Super Involved
An important part of BC is its abundant school spirit. Each class has its own motto printed on the iconic gold "Superfan" T-shirt which is adorned by an eagle, the school mascot. Students proudly wear it during all sporting events. Football, basketball, and hockey have the highest attendance rates. Those who don't want the strenuous commitment of a varsity sport get involved in the popular intramural teams around campus, soccer and basketball being the most widespread.

Outside of sports, regular extracurricular involvement is at a high level. Among the most popular organizations are student government, College Republicans and Democrats, and dance teams of all sorts. *The Heights* is the student-run newspaper.

The Jesuit background of the college is most felt in the level of student involvement on campus. The tradition emphasizes volunteer work on campus, and the Appalachia Volunteers program, which does work in the Appalachian region for organizations such as Habitat for Humanity, boasts a membership of over 600 students. Many students also hold jobs as part of the work-study program; the dining hall employs the most students.

"You get here and even though it might not have been your first choice, you see all the upperclassmen say they love it," one senior said. "You learn to love it as much as they do." At BC you work hard, play often, and explore plenty. A great college experience is guaranteed.—*Dorota Poplawska*

FYI

If you come to BC, you'd better bring "money and a popped collar."

What is the typical weekend schedule? "Sleep till noon, go to a football game on Saturday, and party at night."

If I could change one thing about BC, I'd "make it more diverse."

Three things every student should do before graduating from BC are "spend the night at Bapst Library, participate in Marathon Monday [the Boston Marathon], and attend a football game at Alumni Stadium."

Boston University

Address: 121 Bay State Road, Boston, MA 02215
Phone: 617-353-2300
E-mail address: admissions@bu.edu
Web site URL: www.bu.edu
Year Founded: 1839
Private or Public: Private
Religious Affiliation: None
Location: Urban
Number of Applicants: 33,390
Percent Accepted: 59%
Percent Accepted who enroll: 22%
Number Entering: 4,163
Number of Transfers Accepted each Year: 752
Middle 50% SAT range: M: 590–690, CR: 580–680, Wr: 590–670
Middle 50% ACT range: 25–30
Early admission program EA/ED/None: ED

Percentage accepted through EA or ED: 37%
EA and ED deadline: 1-Nov
Regular Deadline: 1-Jan
Application Fee: $75
Full time Undergraduate enrollment: 18,733
Total enrollment: 19,951
Percent Male: 41%
Percent Female: 59%
Total Percent Minority or Unreported: 48%
Percent African-American: 3%
Percent Asian/Pacific Islander: 12%
Percent Hispanic: 6%
Percent Native-American: <1%
Percent International: 9%
Percent in-state/out of state: 23%/77%
Percent from Public HS: 74%
Retention Rate: 91%

Graduation Rate 4-year: 75%
Graduation Rate 6-year: 80%
Percent Undergraduates in On-campus housing: 65%
Number of official organized extracurricular organizations: 400
3 Most popular majors: Business, International Relations, Psychology
Student/Faculty ratio: 14:1
Average Class Size: 15
Percent of students going to grad school: 29%
Tuition and Fees: $37,050
In-State Tuition and Fees if different: No difference
Cost for Room and Board: $11,418
Percent receiving financial aid out of those who apply: 80%
Percent receiving financial aid among all students: 44%

Located conveniently in the heart of Boston, Boston University presents its students with solid academics, friendly people, and a famous hockey team. And, if you're looking for off-campus adventures, the Boston T will take you anywhere you like in one of the most exciting and historic cities in the country.

What Do You Make of It?

Among BU's 17 graduate and undergraduate schools and 250 degree programs, there is plenty of room to maneuver. Still, as one sophomore commented, "It seems like everyone is either a premed or pre-law." Other popular majors include international relations, psychology, and management. The university curriculum also offers a challenging honors program for ambitious freshmen and sophomores. Like most universities, BU holds large lectures for most introductory courses with smaller discussion sections attached. Upper-level classes shrink significantly to as low as 10 or even five students. Surprisingly, competition for those classes is not really a problem, and an undergrad's chances only improve with seniority. And if lady luck is not on your side, "there are so many options, you can always find something else you will enjoy," like a class taught by Elie Wiesel, Nobel Peace Prize–winner and one of the most popular professors at BU.

Rumors about grade deflation at BU are universally acknowledged to be based on "a misconception," according to one sophomore, "no one has ever been able to prove its existence." At BU, students praise their professors for being accessible; as one student stated, the experience is "what you make of it."

No ID, No Way

Despite the strictly enforced policies against drinking, alcohol still finds its way into the lives of most BU students. Student social life is diverse in terms of locale; many undergraduates center their weekends around parties at off-campus apartments or the few off-campus frats (not funded or recognized by the university). The nearby colleges such as MIT and Harvard also offer viable party options. One student said that the Boston scene "opens up many social lives for those over 21 (or those with a really good fake ID)," and upperclassmen flock to the numerous bars and clubs in the area, such as Jillian's and The Dugout. Without an ID, students are out of luck, as Boston recently passed a law prohibiting any underage clubs, causing many undergrads to simply take their chances in the RA–monitored dorms (although some say that that is a riskier option). BU weekends typically start on Thursday for those resourceful enough to avoid the Friday classes. If you prefer your weekends dry, never fear—there are still vibrant options for a social life outside of drinking activities, many of which take place in Boston, a city that provides endless restaurants, theaters, and shopping along Newbury Street.

From Jail to Hotel

The dorms at BU vary from great apartment-style dorms to small closetlike rooms. Competition is stiff for the recently built student village apartments, as well as two other residences that were former hotels on Commonwealth Avenue. Yet getting a good dorm is a matter of luck of the draw. One student warned that some of the dorms "have been designed by an architect who used to design jails." Warren Towers, the freshman dorm, has some of the least desirable rooms; however it makes up for it by having its own vibrant and close-knit social community. Students describe the campus, which is divided into East and West, as "long and skinny." The West campus is the more lively side, since it tends to house more athletes and parties. Moreover, many students move off campus after their sophomore years. The primary complaints from all students concerned BU's old-fashioned guest policy: coed sleepovers were prohibited. And although students realize that the policy is meant to ensure safety on campus, it is commonly referred to as "outdated." Recently the student governing body at Boston University, the Student Union, worked with the administration to change the guest policy to give students more freedom as well as more responsibility.

> "There are so many options, you can always find something else you will enjoy."

Fortunately, food rates pretty well at BU. There are five dining halls on campus and endless restaurants, some favorites of which include T. Anthony's pizza restaurant or anything in the North End. For those on the run, there are fallback options such as the George Sherman Union and numerous small convenience stores along the campus.

BU students generally do not bring cars to campus, and as anyone who has ever driven in Boston will tell you, it is not a good idea to have a car. Besides the nightmarish parking, students agree that Boston's one-way streets will significantly impede even the most experienced of navigators. The extensive subway system known as the T, however, more than makes up for the lack of personal transportation.

East Coast Style

This ultimate East Coast university has a generally friendly atmosphere. Students say that it is easiest to meet people through dorms and extracurriculars, although sometimes smaller classes foster friendships too. Students claim that BU could be more diverse, but there are actually students from all 50 states and over 100 countries. Every race and ethnicity is represented, usually to a far greater degree than is the case at state universities.

Some of the most popular clubs at Boston University are student governments and the programming council. The campus is also home to many cultural clubs like the Indian Club, which is one of the biggest organizations on campus. Students report that many, if not most, of their peers have jobs. Many work on campus in dining halls through work-study programs. Others find that Boston has plentiful job opportunities, including waiting tables or working as cashiers.

Skates Are Required

Yearly balls and dances as well as weekly parties bring tradition to BU. "We also have an up-and-coming basketball program and a very popular, very involved new student spirit group nicknamed 'the Dog Pound,'" said a student representative. And, since the school does not have a football team, what spirit exists is entirely poured into the hockey team; hockey games are some of the most crowded and energetic events at BU, with the pep rallies against BU rival, Boston College, widely attended. In fact, the BU versus BC hockey game is one of the most entertaining and well-attended events on campus.

For those who have no interest in hockey, Boston provides more than enough sports teams for which to root, including the Celtics, the Red Sox, and the New England Patriots. For those hoping for an active life of their own, the university has many popular intramural teams, as well as a three-floor fitness and recreation center.

Boston University may not have the packed football stadiums of other schools, but BU students have pride in their school. And with Boston as the students' backyard playground, who could say no to that?
—*Dorota Poplawska*

FYI
If you come to BU, you'd better bring "money."
What is the typical weekend schedule? "Wake up late, gym, dinner and desserts at North End, party."
If I could change one thing about BU, I'd "improve the guest policy to something less strict."
Three things every student at BU should do before graduating are "Go to a baseball game at Fenway Park, attend a BU versus BC hockey game, and attend an Elie Wiesel lecture."

Brandeis University

Address: 415 South St., MS003, Waltham, MA 02454-9110
Phone: 781-736-3500
E-mail address: admissions@brandeis.edu
Web site URL: www.brandeis.edu
Year Founded: 1948
Private or Public: Private
Religious Affiliation: None
Location: Suburban
Number of Applicants: 7,724
Percent Accepted: 33%
Percent Accepted who enroll: 30%
Number Entering: 759
Number of Transfers Accepted each Year: 102
Middle 50% SAT range: M: 650–730, CR: 640–720, Wr: 540–730
Middle 50% ACT range: 29–32
Early admission program EA/ED/None: ED

Percentage accepted through EA or ED: 32%
EA and ED deadline: 15-Nov
Regular Deadline: 15-Jan
Application Fee: $55
Full time Undergraduate enrollment: 3,216
Total enrollment: 5,327
Percent Male: 44%
Percent Female: 56%
Total Percent Minority or Unreported: 19%
Percent African-American: 4%
Percent Asian/Pacific Islander: 10%
Percent Hispanic: 5%
Percent Native-American: <1%
Percent International: 8%
Percent in-state/out of state: 26%/74%
Percent from Public HS: Unreported
Retention Rate: 93%

Graduation Rate 4-year: 86%
Graduation Rate 6-year: 88%
Percent Undergraduates in On-campus housing: 77%
Number of official organized extracurricular organizations: 253
3 Most popular majors: Biology, Economics, Psychology
Student/Faculty ratio: 8:1
Average Class Size: 15
Percent of students going to grad school: Unreported
Tuition and Fees: $37,294
In-State Tuition and Fees if different: No difference
Cost for Room and Board: $10,354
Percent receiving financial aid out of those who apply: 53%
Percent receiving financial aid among all students: 48%

What do an Olympic fencer, the author of *Tuesdays With Morrie* and *The Five People You Meet in Heaven*, and Bill Schneider have in common? The answer's a no-brainer: they're all alumni of Brandeis University, one of the youngest and most renowned private research universities in America.

Located in Waltham, Massachusetts, Brandeis is just nine miles west from Boston, simultaneously offering students easy access to the exciting city life and the comforts of a suburban campus. Besides its academic prowess (*U.S. News and World Report* has ranked it among the top 35 national universities every year since its inception), Brandeis is famous for its emphasis on community service and its extraordinarily high percentage of Jewish students, for which the reason can be traced back to its unusual founding as the nation's only nonsectarian Jewish-sponsored college.

Academics: Intense but Intimate

Brandeis boasts a rigorous liberal arts education that "combines the faculty and resources of a world-class research institution with the intimacy and personal attention of a small liberal arts college"—and they're perfectly entitled to their bragging rights. Not only does Brandeis count among its faculty "six members of the National Academies, four Howard Hughes Medical Institute investigators, three Pulitzer Prize winners and two MacArthur Foundation 'genius grant' recipients," but it's also not uncommon for a freshman to be learning from these academic giants in an intimate setting. According to one freshman, "Last term I was one of about three freshmen in a 30-person writing Intensive journalism class with Professor Eileen McNamara, the Pulitzer Prize winner. I was intimidated at first since the professor was so well known and I was obviously young (it was an entirely discussion based class), but I spoke with her on the first day and she said it was fine for me to be in that class—she was very open to her students' ideas, although she made her opinions known too, and I soon became comfortable."

The existence of University Seminars also makes distinguished faculty easily accessible to students. A hallmark of the Brandeis curriculum, University Seminars are designed specifically for freshmen and emphasize the importance of interdisciplinary studies. It is a course requirement for freshmen, along with the other requirements of Science, Social Science, Humanities, Creative Art, Quantitative Reasoning, Writing, Foreign Language, Oral Communication, Non-Western and Comparative Studies, and Physical Education. Students can fulfill the last requirement with anything from intense self-designed work-out classes in the gym to Dance Dance Revolution and yoga.

The wide range of distributional requirements and the diversity of Brandeis itself have made Ethnic Studies and International and Global Studies two popular majors, along with Psychology and Biology (a common major for premed students). Other popular yet not-so-commonplace majors and minors include Peace, Conflict, and Coexistence; the Near-Eastern Judaic Studies; HSSP (Health: Science, Society and Policy Program); and Social Justice and Social Policy.

> **"A lot of classes can count for many different things, so it's really easy to double major and pick up a minor on top of that."**

This may seem like a lot to ask, but Brandeis students are up on the game. "A lot of classes can count for many different things, so it's really easy to double major and pick up a minor on top of that," noted one Anthropology/Social Science major. "And they leave you room for fun classes, too." Of course, students don't mean "fun" in the sense of an easy class—the typical Brandeis student is eager to get as much as they can out of any class. And it's easy to find your niche in the wide range of classes they offer at the school. You might be interested in the English class "Witchcraft and Magic in the Renaissance," or a section of an introductory Global Studies class that teaches you everything you would ever want to know about Bollywood movies, or something totally unrelated.

"I love that there are very few set tracks or prerequisites for the humanities classes," said one International and Global Studies major. "A lot of people come here thinking they'll be premed and end up changing their minds because of a really cool seminar they initially took just to fulfill a requirement."

Because Brandeis is fairly small (a little over 3,000 undergrads), almost all classes are taught by teachers, with TAs only grading papers or leading discussions. And although some professors are more popular than others, "they do a really good job having us sign up for classes—they arrange it in time blocks, and popular classes are often changed to earlier time slots. Upperclassmen do get higher priority, but if you're dedicated enough to wake up for an 8 AM class, you'll almost always get in. It's really fair."

"Party school" Recognition by *Playboy*?

"Brandeis isn't a party school," the interviewed students of Brandeis said unanimously. There are a fair amount of people who are very much into the party scene, but they are definitely not the majority; as one freshman described, "If you walk around campus on a Friday night, you're not going to see a lot of parties."

This is in part due to the proximity of Boston, for many students use the campus shuttles (coined Bran Vans) to gain access to the bars and restaurants of Harvard Square or Newbury Street in downtown Boston. "The Bran Vans are really convenient. They go everywhere and most come every 15 minutes and run till 2 AM," said one student. "With them and the city buses, you really don't need cars unless you want to go to the mall or something. And parking's such a hassle."

Alcohol and pot are easy to come by at Brandeis, where people are more open to drugs than most nearby colleges—"You smell it everywhere, so you eventually get used to it," quipped one freshman. It's very rare that a student will feel pressured to do something he or she is not inclined to do. Normally, Brandeis students see themselves as members of a "geeky but extremely friendly campus": "Most people are pretty geeky about wanting A's," noted one girl.

But when Brandeis students go out, they go *out*: in *Playboy*'s 2010 list of top party schools of the nation, the school's Liquid Latex Body Art Show was listed as Best College-Supported Art Project. "Apparently the performers wear thongs and body paint, and that's it," said one freshman about the notorious performance. "It's supposed to be amazing, though Pachanga (a school-sponsored dance) was pretty wild too—there was a line of ambulances waiting at the door because so many people go to the hospital for alcohol poisoning every time the party's hosted. It really didn't seem like Brandeis at all."

Castle on a Hill

At 905 acres, the Brandeis campus is fairly small, making it very convenient for the students to walk from class to class. One student boasted that although she had two successive classes on opposite sides of the campus, she was able to cross campus in a record 10 minutes. "But it's close to impossible to bike in most places because this is the hilliest school I have ever seen. It's great for sledding, though; when you're studying in the library during the winter, you can hear people screaming as they sled downhill."

Although there are no theme dorms at Brandeis, there are special community service–intensive areas within residential halls to which interested students apply. There is also a picturesque castle, complete with staircases and hallways that lead nowhere, random sinks, and a rumor of secret passages—it's no surprise that it's the most popular residential hall of all.

With outstanding academics, tons of interaction between faculty and students, and a cozy campus close to a big city without being in it, it's not hard to see why the majority of students said they would choose Brandeis again if they had the choice.—*Lahn Matsumoto*

FYI

If you come to Brandeis, you'd better bring "snow boots, a cheery disposition, and a sled for the library hill."

If you come to Brandeis, you'd better leave "your bathing suit (there isn't an on-campus pool—yet) and Kosher food (it's taken care of!)" behind.

What is the typical weekend schedule? "Fridays we go to a few classes, 'comprehend' the weekend's homework, watch a free showing of a newly released movie, hang out with friends until late, and maybe go to a party. Saturdays we brunch at Usdan, go sledding, hang out, or go to some student events shindig, begin homework, and stay up late. Sundays we sleep in, brunch at Usdan again, and do homework at the library with friends."

If I could change one thing about Brandeis, "I'd make dining hall hours more regular (weekends are really annoying and things close by 7 pm) and/or have more flexible meal plans that are less expensive."

The biggest college-wide tradition/event at Brandeis is "the Liquid Latex Dance Show and the Pachanga dance."

Clark University

Address: 950 Main Street, Worcester, MA 01610-1477	**EA and ED deadline:** NA	**Graduation Rate 6-year:** 76%
Phone: 508-793-7431	**Regular Deadline:** 15-Jan	**Percent Undergraduates in On-campus housing:** 74%
E-mail address: admissions@clarku.edu	**Application Fee:** $55	
Web site URL: www.clarku.edu/admissions	**Full time Undergraduate enrollment:** 2,222	**Number of official organized extracurricular organizations:** 94
Year Founded: 1887	**Total enrollment:** 3,330	
Private or Public: Private	**Percent Male:** 40%	**3 Most popular majors:** Psychology, Government, Biology/Biochemistry
Religious Affiliation: None	**Percent Female:** 60%	
Location: Urban	**Total Percent Minority or Unreported:** 12%	
Number of Applicants: 5,299	**Percent African-American:** 2%	**Student/Faculty ratio:** 10:1
Percent Accepted: 56%		**Average Class Size:** 21
Percent Accepted who enroll: 20%	**Percent Asian/Pacific Islander:** 6%	**Percent of students going to grad school:** 36%
Number Entering: 650	**Percent Hispanic:** 4%	**Tuition and Fees:** $34,220
Number of Transfers Accepted each Year: 166	**Percent Native-American:** 1%	**In-State Tuition and Fees if different:** No difference
Middle 50% SAT range: M: 540–650, CR: 550–660, Wr: 550–660	**Percent International:** Unreported	**Cost for Room and Board:** $6,650
Middle 50% ACT range: 24–28	**Percent in-state/out of state:** 34%/66%	**Percent receiving financial aid out of those who apply:** 74%
Early admission program EA/ED/None: ED	**Percent from Public HS:** 74%	
Percentage accepted through EA or ED: 76%	**Retention Rate:** 91%	**Percent receiving financial aid among all students:** 52%
	Graduation Rate 4-year: 73%	

F ounded in 1887, Clark University is a college with a rich history. Originally founded as an all-graduate university, it is one of three institutions that helped establish the Association of American Universities. Quietly existing in the city of Worcester, Massachusetts, Clark still retains its prestige not only as a graduate institution, but also as a place where undergraduates can grow in a learning environment. Fittingly, their motto is, "Challenge convention, Change our world."

Not Just Psych

Clark is widely known for its psychology department. As one student said, "Almost everyone here is a psych major." Clark's prominent connection with psychology dates back to its first president, G. Stanley Hall, founder of the American Psychological Association and the first person to earn a PhD in psychology from Harvard. Psychoanalysis was first brought to the United States through Sigmund Freud's "Clark Lectures" at the university. Two statues commemorate Freud's visits and one student commented that "Freud is our unofficial mascot."

Although psychology is the most popular major at Clark, Government and International Relations, Biology, Business Management, and Communication and Culture are close behind. In general, Clarkies find their classes "laid-back" and "uncompetitive." One student commented that Clark has "a lot of active and outspoken people who are passionate about what they believe in but I don't feel like people are stepping all over each other to outdo one another." The average class size at Clark is 21, and students tend to enjoy the intimate environment and the close relationships that fosters. It is in this intimate classroom setting where students take unique and thought-provoking classes such as "Political Science Fiction."

The Price Is Right: Five for Four

Clark has 32 majors and 30 minors for students to choose from, and it is the only institution that offers Holocaust and Genocide Studies as an undergraduate concentration.

If those options aren't good enough for you, you can create your own major through the self-designed major program. This multi-discipline major allows students to combine over three departments to pursue research and knowledge in the field of their dreams. For more ambitious students, Clark recommends the Accelerated B.A./Master's Program, also known as the "Fifth-Year-Free" Program. Every year, 20 percent of the graduating class stays behind at Clark for a fifth year, free of charge, to pursue a Master's Degree in one of 12 areas including management, history, chemistry, geographic information sciences, and education. Established in 1994, this program has received national attention for its admirable aim to have students "deepen their knowledge of a particular field and enhance their credentials for the job market."

Home Is Where Themes, RAs, and Cheese Steaks Are

During their four years at Clark, 76 percent of students live on campus. Due to the plethora of on-campus housing options, many students have no regrets about staying there. Freshmen live in one of three first-year halls: Bullock, Wright, and Sanford. Although most of these rooms are singles, doubles, or triples, some lucky denizens of Sanford Hall enjoy spacious suites with a common living space and a private bathroom.

> "We have a lot of active and outspoken people who are passionate about what they believe in, but I don't feel like people are stepping all over each other to outdo one another."

In order to address the needs of gay, lesbian, and transgender students, Clark has adopted a gender-blind/neutral housing policy where students can opt to share a room with other students regardless of sex. For those concerned with awkward 3 a.m. bathroom encounters, Dodd Hall offers single-sex housing for women. Juniors and seniors mainly live in Maywood Street Hall where four-, five-, or six-person suites provide students with apartment-like comfort and privacy.

In addition, the Theme House Program at Clark creates an opportunity for students to merge their personal and academic interests. A member of Clark's faculty is assigned

to each house and, along with the Group Leader, organizes social events and educational programs to foster a sense of community on campus. Some of these Theme Houses include the Body and Soul House, the Just Yell Fire self-defense house, the Sexual Wellness and Awareness House, and Everyday is a Holiday House, a humble abode dedicated to celebrating lesser-known holidays around the world.

Unlike some schools, the presence of Residential Advisors significantly impacts the residential experience of each hall. Each year there are typically 35 RAs, of which 20 are First Year Experience RAs who specialize in the needs of freshmen. One student notes, "If you get a cool RA, you get cool activities!" RAs shape students' daily lives by throwing social functions, as well as by writing up rambunctious partiers for violating campus alcohol policies. Although RAs come in all shapes, sizes, and degrees of leniency, most agree that RAs, in general, are "chill" and "super-friendly."

Food at Clark brings a less enthusiastic response. "Boring and not really edible," commented one sophomore. After a new food distributor was brought into Clark, reactions were not favorable. "The best thing they have is probably the Philly cheese steak," said one student. No wonder vegans and vegetarians often find the food in "The Caf" unsuitable for their needs. However, there are alternatives for the ravenous Clarkie—the Bistro is an on-campus café that offers students savory sandwiches and eggs cooked every way possible. Also, the city of Worcester offers restaurants within walking distance of central campus for students looking to satiate their culinary cravings.

Out on the "Woo-town"

The city of Worcester (pronounced by locals as "WOO-stah") is 40 miles from Boston and the second largest city in Massachusetts. One student finds Woo-town "not a particularly busy city—but there are plenty of grocery stores and huge theaters where we get some great bands like Marilyn Manson and Gym Class Heroes." Although most activities off campus are hard to get to without a car, there is a Student Council Van that conveniently transports students to the mall on the weekends and the "Woo Bus" makes various parts of Worcester accessible.

Some students are concerned about the safety of Worcester, particular in Main South, the neighborhood where Clark is located. "Never walk alone," says one student.

Dorm rooms are generally safe, but off-campus students should make sure to lock up properly. However, one veteran Clarkie says, "There are cop checkposts everywhere and, if you are responsible, you'll be fine. Nowhere in the world is it safe to walk around with a laptop at 3 a.m."

Hookahs and Drinking Sprees

On the weekends, some Clarkies take the train into Boston to barhop while most stay on campus for the partying. "Clark is not a dry campus," but students say it is "essential" to have an ID for the occasional "State Liquor run." Smoking culture, especially hookah smoking, is very popular at Clark. The University recently loosened their smoking policy and now students can be found puffing away on the green without being bothered.

Several times a year, campus-wide events take center stage in the social scene at Clark. One of the most beloved is "Spree Day," during the spring semester. Tradition holds that the date be kept secret, but students always seem to know when it will take place. On this most-anticipated day, classes are canceled, a carnival and concert are held on the green, livers are destroyed by 10 a.m., and hangovers nursed by 4 p.m. Though Spree Day only comes once a year, students agree that Clark is a great place to spend four wonderful years of their lives.—*Lee Komeda*

FYI

If you come to Clark, you'd better bring "a hookah."

What is the typical weekend schedule? "Friday, take the free buses during the day to go to malls and Boston. Saturday, attend a few parties and smoke a hookah. Sundays are reserved for studying."

If I could change one thing about Clark, I'd "change its size. Sometimes it's too small and gossipy."

Three things every student at Clark should do before graduating are "get involved with a student group, get to know President Bassett, and go to a foam party."

Emerson College

Address: 10 Boylston Street, Boston, MA 02116
Phone: 617-824-8600
E-mail address: admission@emerson.edu
Web site URL: www.emerson.edu
Year Founded: 1880
Private or Public: Private
Religious Affiliation: None
Location: Urban
Number of Applicants: 6,944
Percent Accepted: 37%
Percent Accepted who enroll: 30%
Number Entering: 774
Number of Transfers Accepted each Year: 423
Middle 50% SAT range:
M: 550–640, Cr: 580–670, Wr: 640–700
Middle 50% ACT range: 24–29
Early admission program EA/ED/None: EA

Percentage accepted through EA or ED: 59%
EA and ED deadline: 1-Nov
Regular Deadline: 5-Jan
Application Fee: $60
Full time Undergraduate enrollment: 3,293
Total enrollment: 4,197
Percent Male: 44%
Percent Female: 56%
Total Percent Minority or Unreported: 24%
Percent African-American: 3%
Percent Asian/Pacific Islander: 4%
Percent Hispanic: 6%
Percent Native-American: 1%
Percent International: 10%
Percent in-state/out of state: 20%/80%
Percent from Public HS: 72%
Retention Rate: 88%

Graduation Rate 4-year: 72%
Graduation Rate 6-year: 72%
Percent Undergraduates in On-campus housing: 42%
Number of official organized extracurricular organizations: 60
3 Most popular majors: Cinematograph, Writing, Arts
Student/Faculty ratio: 14:1
Average Class Size: 14
Percent of students going to grad school: 13%
Tuition and Fees: $26,880
In-State Tuition and Fees if different: No difference
Cost for Room and Board: $11,376
Percent receiving financial aid out of those who apply: Unreported
Percent receiving financial aid among all students: 54%

Nestled in the heart of the Boston theater district, Emerson balances an expertise in the arts and communications with a focus on a liberal arts education. Emerson students come to school driven to succeed, passionate about their intended path, and cognizant of their individual strengths and weaknesses. Involving themselves passionately in their extracurriculars, Emersonians create strong connections with fellow students that make their four years at college fun and prepare them well for the world outside of Emerson.

Come Prepared

Nearly every Emerson student selects his or her major before stepping foot on campus. Although it is possible to come in undeclared, Emerson boasts such specialized programs that choosing a department on one's college application is now almost a given. Most students cite their ability to "jump right in" the world of their major starting their freshman year as an advantage rather than a source of stress.

Emerson is primarily known as an arts school, and many students spend their college careers in the VMA (Visual and Media Arts) department studying sound, cinematography, and film. There is incredible room for specialization; after learning the fundamentals freshman year, students have the opportunity to concentrate in anything from documentary production to lighting. Emerson's "elite" performing arts department produced TV legends Jay Leno and Henry Winkler, though Emersonians are equally proud of people who work behind-the-scenes to design last year's Oscars.

In the School of Communication, students get hands-on experience in marketing, journalism, and a host of other specific majors and concentrations. One senior marveled that her classes were consistently "taught by people still active in the professional world or who spent a lifetime in the field," citing a particular professor who ran his own agency for years and "consults on the side." Students enjoy the vast number of options they have academically, both in and outside the classroom. One sophomore journalism major is currently covering Boston news for a class on beat reporting, but plans to take a class specifically focusing on music journalism, her intended career.

Emerson prides itself on its devotion to communication and the arts in a liberal arts context. Students face a set of "Gen Ed" requirements under the umbrella of exposure to a wide variety of subjects. Leave your protractor at home, though, because Emerson offers a grand total of three math classes. Though double majoring can be challenging, since "every major is so demanding and has such specific classes to take," many Emersonians pursue one or two of over 25 minors, ranging from Business Studies to Music Appreciation. For the most part, students are content in their classes and majors, though one student "frequently wishes they were more serious and more of a challenge."

With an undergraduate population of around 3,500, students rarely find themselves in classes with over 20 people–the biggest lecture has around 70. "Teachers really want you to succeed," said one student, who mentioned that she has emailed papers to her professors to get feedback before the due date. Getting good grades is not too difficult if one puts in the proper time and effort. "Teachers don't want to give out bad grades and students don't want to get them," said one student. "It's graded on a pretty fair scale and curved upwards."

Not Just a "Stoner College"

Weekends at Emerson are widely acknowledged to start Thursday nights. Parties and social events range throughout the weekend "and Monday and Tuesday and Wednesday, with less frequency, but I'm not saying it hasn't happened," said one student. Most "giant and sweaty" parties occur off campus, in less expensive Boston neighborhoods like Allston where many upperclassmen live. Those wishing to stay on campus can attend smaller get-togethers with friends or head over to nearby Gypsy Bar. Though everyone makes fun of it, every Emerson student secretly aspires to go there on his or her 21st birthday.

"Emerson is fondly referred to as a stoner college," one student said, referencing the fact that "mostly anyone you ask smokes weed." One senior joked, "It's the creative types—that's what they do." Many students drink and do drugs, but Emerson "doesn't want to get you in trouble if you're not messy." For example, Emerson grants students medical amnesty, meaning that if a student seeks medical help, the college will not persecute him or her for underage drinking.

Emerson students describe themselves as "creative, eccentric, and forward thinking." Depending on the major, students range from "the weird kids from high school" or "pretentious kids who come to class in heels." Emerson boasts solid populations of hipsters, materialism, and skinny jeans. According to one sophomore, "This year, we had a large influx of bros. When I see them, I'm kind of confused. Welcome to Emerson College, now complete with bros and gays." Emersonians are proud of their very own internet meme, Emerson Kid Lion, a lion donning a beanie and cigarette on a purple and gold background.

Diversity

There is an Emerson saying, "Gay by May," which reflects the large number of homosexual students who "come out" their freshman year. Emerson overwhelmingly supports its diverse population and is known as one of the most gay-friendly schools across the nation. When members of the Westboro Baptist Church planned a protest in 2010, the Emerson students gathered for a "Love is Louder" rally. A drag show, called "Dragtoberfest" is school-sponsored.

Ethnic diversity is less impressive, though Emerson's new president, M. Lee Pelton, is taking big strides to address this. Pelton, the college's first African American president, has striven to tackle the racial bias in tenure allotment, and last year's freshman class was statistically less white than the previous year. "Right now we're at a turning point," one junior said. "We've grown at a steroid-like pace in the last decade. Suddenly we have name-recognition, and now we have a leader to nurture the community."

Real-world Experience and Fictional Sports

Students say that Emerson truly shines outside of the classroom in the world of its extracurriculars. "You have a lot of kids who are really driven and passionate, so everything that comes out of Emerson is really polished," one student said. "In that atmosphere, everyone wants to show off." Another added that "everyone is hyper-involved in extracurricular activities." With the specifics of the classroom environment, most Emersonians have some sort of plan or life goal, and they use extracurriculars as a means to that end.

For the budding journalist, the Berkeley Beacon is Emerson's chief undergraduate paper. Coming out once a week, "the paper flies off the racks Thursday morning and most on-campus students can be seen with it," one journalist said. Many marketing majors join EMcomm, a student-run marketing firm

serving real clients in the Boston area. Students say that they learn things much earlier through their mini-internships than they do in the classroom. Emerson also boasts a TV and radio station, scores of magazines and journals, and a multitude of student-run productions throughout the year.

The only negative of the extracurricular scene is the lack of space Emerson has to host them. One student described Emerson as a "vertical campus." The campus resides in the middle of one of the most urban parts of Boston, and while the administration is hoping to gain new spaces and re-appropriate existing ones, the basic fact is that "there are so many organizations for such a small school," one student said.

> "You have a lot of kids who are really driven and passionate, so everything that comes out of Emerson is really polished. In that atmosphere, everyone wants to show off."

While Emerson has some solid sports teams, including the women's soccer team, it is an acknowledged fact on campus that the quidditch team is by far the most popular. Based on the sport in the *Harry Potter* novels, quidditch has grown in popularity throughout the northeast liberal arts colleges over the last few years, and Emerson is no exception. The squad made it to the quarterfinals in the 2011 Quidditch World Cup and has been practicing hard to top that this year. "We have real sports teams, I swear we do, but they get angry that quidditch is the most popular," said one sophomore.

Yes, They Have a Castle

Emerson owns a 14th century restored castle, complete with two moats, in the Netherlands around 2 hours away from Amsterdam. Every semester, around 80 students are selected by lottery to study abroad and live inside Kasteel Well. Classes are Monday to Thursday, leaving students with a three-day weekend. According to one student, "[The administration] wants you to go off campus and explore Europe." Students who go cite the experience as one of the best parts of their Emerson careers.

For those less inclined to drafty castles, Emerson offers two other popular "study abroad" options: spending a semester in Emerson's Los Angeles campus and participating in Emerson's Prague Summer Film Program. The former offers classes amongst the majors and is set to grow with the completion of the Hollywood Center, expected 2012. The latter is geared toward juniors and seniors interested in the Czech film scene.

At Emerson, the room selection process can be unpleasant as there is no priority by class. Students choose housing groups and suite styles; then complete an online housing request and wait for a confirmation or rejection notification. Emerson offers a large array of housing—from Colonial to Little Building suites. Since Emerson has no official housing allocation period, students may have to knock on doors of current suite-owners to preview and choose among Emerson's many options, a process referred by a student publication as "ding-dong-dorm hunting."

Beantown

Making full use of Emerson's location in the center of Boston, Emersonians treat Boston as their campus. Students use public transportation to get to off campus parties and interact with the Boston sports scene. One sophomore, who lived in Boston her whole life, said that coming to Emerson gave her "a new perspective on what living in Boston is like."

Boston Common, a large park home to the Boston Public Garden and a host of fountains and ponds, is located across the street from most Emerson buildings. "I live in it," one student said. "If it's a nice day, you will see every kid out there, reading a book, eating lunch, or having a picnic." Students say they feel safe in the Common at night, and large groups can often be found there over the weekends, hanging out and climbing trees.

The Emerson Mafia

No, this isn't a scene from *The Departed*. Students see the Emerson mafia, a network of Emerson alumni helping Emerson students make their way into society, as a draw to the school. Emerson boasts connections to various industries throughout the country, and students are glad to have people helping them "in the real world."

For the most part, Emersonians are very happy in their four years at school, and few would consider going anywhere else. Though one student said, "The joke is that nobody here ever sleeps or has free time—everyone has jobs, internships, extracurriculars, and classes," students are passionate about what they do and wouldn't have it any other way. Emerson students are proud of their unique school culture and leave Emerson after four years feeling prepared academically and ready to face the real world creatively and with the passion that defined them at Emerson.—*Mason Kroll*

FYI
If you come to Emerson, you'd better bring "fashion sense in winter wear."
If I could change one thing about Emerson, it would be "priority in dorm allocation."
Three things every student at Emerson should do before graduating are "help someone make a movie, go to a party in Allston [town just minutes from downtown Boston], and take a stroll down the Esplanade [3-mile stretch on the Charles River]."

College of the Holy Cross

Address: 1 College Street, Worcester, MA 01610-2395

Phone: 508-793-2443

E-mail address: admissions@holycross.edu

Web site URL: www.holycross.edu

Year Founded: 1843

Private or Public: Private

Religious Affiliation: Roman Catholic

Location: Urban

Number of Applicants: 7,353

Percent Accepted: 33%

Percent Accepted who enroll: 31%

Number Entering: 751

Number of Transfers Accepted each Year: 49

Middle 50% SAT range: M: 610–690, CR: 600–690, Wr: 600–700

Middle 50% ACT range: 27–31

Early admission program EA/ED/None: ED

Percentage accepted through EA or ED: Unreported

EA and ED deadline: 15-Dec

Regular Deadline: 15-Jan

Application Fee: $60

Full time Undergraduate enrollment: 2,782

Total enrollment: 2,905

Percent Male: 47%

Percent Female: 53%

Total Percent Minority or Unreported: 34%

Percent African-American: 5%

Percent Asian/Pacific Islander: 5%

Percent Hispanic: 10%

Percent Native-American: <1%

Percent International: 2%

Percent in-state/out of state: 37%/63%

Percent from Public HS: 52%

Retention Rate: 95%

Graduation Rate 4-year: 92%

Graduation Rate 6-year: 92%

Percent Undergraduates in On-campus housing: 90%

Number of official organized extracurricular organizations: 102

3 Most popular majors: Economics, English Language and Literature, Political Science and Government

Student/Faculty ratio: 10:1

Average Class Size: 14

Percent of students going to grad school: 23%

Tuition and Fees: $40,910

In-State Tuition and Fees if different: No difference

Cost for Room and Board: $11,270

Percent receiving financial aid out of those who apply: 65%

Percent receiving financial aid among all students: 61%

Nestled in the city of Worcester, Massachusetts, is the College of the Holy Cross, America's oldest Roman Catholic College. Initially founded in 1843 as a Jesuit school for boys, today the school prides itself in the diversity of experiences that students have, the rigor of the academic programs, and the tight-knit community formed around the city.

Optional: SATs

Holy Cross is exclusively an undergraduate institution; therefore students receive the undivided attention of faculty and administration. When asked why she chose Holy Cross over other colleges, a senior replied, "Because I knew that I would be in an environment that prioritized academics above everything." In choosing its students, Holy Cross prioritizes a candidate's interests, activities, recommendations, and high school transcript over standardized tests scores. In fact, while they are suggested, the SAT and ACT are not required for applying to Holy Cross.

A Bachelor of Arts degree is awarded to all that complete 32 semester-long courses, with requirements in arts, literature, religion, philosophy, history, and cross-cultural studies. Twenty-seven majors are offered and students can also select concentrations as well. Like many liberal arts colleges, pre-professional track programs such as pre-business, pre-medicine, and pre-dental are offered as well. Holy Cross is particularly noted for its economics, chemistry, political science, and English departments. Also worthy of mention is its classics department, which is one of the largest in America. Uniquely, the department integrates Greek and Latin Studies with advanced information technology and archaeology.

Academic learning outside of the classroom is also highly valued at Holy Cross, which is why they encourage students to participate in "Experiential Learning" programs. Students can take a semester or a year abroad or participate in the Semester Away Program which allows students to pursue academic interests at other institutions that are not available at Holy Cross, but many complained that the semester-long options were limited. The summer internship programs are offered to certain sophomores and juniors as an opportunity to gain professional experiences related to a student's career related goals. These internships, developed through a network of parents, alumni, and friends of Holy Cross, have been extremely popular.

Holy Cross boasts a faculty to student ratio of ten to one. However, don't expect classes to be easy because they are small. "Classes were very challenging and the professors definitely expected a lot," one recent alumna stated. But have no fear, you'll have plenty of support. "The professors always knew who you were and were great about being there for you, whether it be holding review sessions or extending office hours."

Easy Street and the "Woorats"

Residential life at Holy Cross is divided into three different areas of campus comprising 10 residence halls. As freshmen, you will be placed in one of the residence halls located at the northern end of campus known as Easy Street. While the option of moving off campus is available for second, third, and fourth year students, most Holy Cross students stay in campus housing for their entire four years. Upperclassmen mainly live in the lower part of campus, in the halls of Alumni, Carlin, Loyola, and Williams. The most coveted of them all are the apartments in Williams Hall. After construction was completed in 2003, upperclassmen fought at the annual lottery for these apartments equipped with separate showers, kitchens, living rooms, and individual bedrooms.

For food, Holy Cross students have a wide variety of options. In addition to the main dining room, there is the food court, the lunch-through-late-night Crossroads, or Cool Beans and CB2, both coffee shops. Most students have no complaints about the dining services at Holy Cross. "I really like the food at Holy Cross!" gushed one student. "They have specialty nights in the dining hall like Thanksgiving dinner and Birthday Cake night!" For those with special dietary needs, the dining services have Weight Watcher meals, heart-healthy selections, and vegetarian entrees.

While campus is generally a good place to live, Worcester (pronounced Wooster) has its ups and downs. "Town-gown" relationships have gotten better in the past few years, but there is a divide between the "Woorats" and the Holy Cross Crusaders. "The locals are usually pretty nice to students as long as you

don't go out of your way to offend them," said one student. Holy Cross shares Worcester with Worcester Polytechnic Institute and Clark University and is in a "consortium" with them, encouraging interaction between the students.

Bleeding Purple

Holy Cross's athletic teams are known as the Crusaders, and the official school color is the royal purple used by Emperor Constantine the Great. Holy Cross is one of the founding members of the Patriot League, which also includes American University, United States Military Academy, Bucknell University, Colgate University, Lafayette College, Lehigh University, and the United States Naval Academy. Athletic support and school spirit are very high at Holy Cross. "Holy Cross has a ton of school pride. We bleed purple! When the basketball championships were held here, everyone was painted in purple and you had to stand diagonally to fit into the gym!" gushed one track and field runner.

> "Holy Cross has a ton of school pride. We bleed purple!"

School pride is also sustained by the large number of campus-wide events and traditions held annually. Some of these events are organized by the Purple Key Society, a service honor society dedicated to increasing school spirit and community building. One of them is the 100 Days Dance, held when 100 days are left for the graduating class. This includes a dinner followed by a dance where each attendee makes a list of seniors that they try to kiss before the night is over. PKS also organizes the Purple Pride Day, when the entire school is covered in royal purple, and purple T-shirts, cookies, balloons, and stickers are given out to foster enthusiasm for the school. Another tradition is Skirt Day, which is considered the first day of spring and girls (who make up 53 percent of the student population) wear skirts for the first time in the year.

The social scene at Holy Cross is regarded with much enthusiasm as well. While there are no fraternities or sororities on campus, residence halls serve their function as smaller social communities within the campus. In particular, Wheeler Hall is known as the rowdiest hall. "It was great, everyone knew your name, and we were the only dorm [for underclassmen] not off Easy Street," says one ex-Wheeler resident. Wheeler Hall is also the birthplace of the popular campus sport Stickball, which started in the 1940s. You can have a great time even if you aren't in Wheeler too. On Tuesdays, upperclassmen, mainly seniors, congregate at the Pub in the Hogan Campus Center. For those underage, Tuesdays mean going to the "10 spot," an open mic night for bands and performances held at Crossroads, one of the food courts. Worcester also has plenty to offer for social activities. Students often frequent the malls at Solomon Pond and the restaurants on Shrewsbury Street.

Achieving a good balance of academics, athletics, and socializing seems to be the modus operandi of these students. All three aspects of college life are met with enthusiasm and open-mindedness at Holy Cross. If this sounds like your cup of tea, "going purple" may be a good idea for next year.—*Lee Komeda*

FYI

If you come to Holy Cross, you'd better bring "purple face paint!"

What's the typical weekend schedule? "Go to a sports game, study, go to the movies or a restaurant on Shrewsbury Street, hang out in friends' rooms, and study, study, study on Sunday!"

If I could change one thing about Holy Cross, it would offer "more semester-long abroad programs. It is tough to go away for a whole year."

Three things students should do before graduating: "Participate in the Appalachia Service Project, go on the Silent Retreat, and enjoy Cape Week."

Hampshire College

Address: 893 West Street, Amherst, MA 01002

Phone: 877-937-4267

E-mail address: admissions@hampshire.edu

Web site URL: www.hampshire.edu

Year Founded: 1970

Private or Public: Private

Religious Affiliation: None

Location: Suburban

Number of Applicants: 2,842

Percent Accepted: 61%

Percent Accepted who enroll: 27%

Number Entering: 437

Number of Transfers Accepted each Year: 33

Middle 50% SAT range: M: 540–660, CR: 610–700, Wr: 590–700

Middle 50% ACT range: 26–29

Early admission program EA/ED/None: EA and ED

Percentage accepted through EA or ED: 25%

EA and ED deadline: 15-Nov

Regular Deadline: 15-Jan

Application Fee: $55

Full time Undergraduate enrollment: 1,428

Total enrollment: 1,428

Percent Male: 42%

Percent Female: 58%

Total Percent Minority or Unreported: 16%

Percent African-American: 5%

Percent Asian/Pacific Islander: 4%

Percent Hispanic: 6%

Percent Native-American: 1%

Percent International: Unreported

Percent in-state/out of state: 18%/82%

Percent from Public HS: 48%

Retention Rate: 79%

Graduation Rate 4-year: 52%

Graduation Rate 6-year: 65%

Percent Undergraduates in On-campus housing: 90%

Number of official organized extracurricular organizations: 94

3 Most popular majors: Film/Video and Photography, English, Fine arts

Student/Faculty ratio: 11:1

Average Class Size: 16

Percent of students going to grad school: 50%

Tuition and Fees: $37,789

In-State Tuition and Fees if different: No difference

Cost for Room and Board: $10,080

Percent receiving financial aid out of those who apply: 88%

Percent receiving financial aid among all students: 55%

A small, liberal arts college in Western Massachusetts, Hampshire may sound like it would provide the traditional New England undergraduate experience. Hampshire, though, provides an anything but traditional eight semesters for its 1,500 students. There are no grades. There are no "majors." There are, however, students devoted to learning, and faculty members committed to guiding their otherwise self-directed pupils along their intellectual journeys. Hampshire is also a member of the Five College Consortium, along with Amherst College, Mount Holyoke College, Smith College, and University of Massachusetts Amherst, which gives more breadth and depth to its resources. A student sums up Hampshire by saying, "Hampshire is a sanctuary where you come to find and hone the craft you choose."

Hampshire's Roots

The idea for Hampshire germinated in 1958, when the presidents of the other four Consortium colleges decided to re-evaluate the idea of a liberal arts education. They outlined their conclusions in a document called "The New College Plan," and many of these same ideas echo in Hampshire's founding curriculum. Hampshire then physically sprouted from purchased orchards and farmland, admitted its first students in 1970, and grew into the "experimental" college it is known as today.

The Individual Experience: Academics

Instead of "majors," Hampshire students craft an interdisciplinary course of study made up of three Divisions over the course of their time at Hampshire. In Division I: Basic Studies, students choose one class offered by each of the five schools of Cognitive Science; Humanities, Arts, and Cultural Studies; Interdisciplinary Arts; Natural Science; and Social Science, in addition to three more classes of their own choosing. In Division II: The Concentration, students narrow their academic focus and might choose to pursue an internship, international exchange program, or delve into a different kind of field study. Division III: Advanced Study, serves as the culminating project for Hampshire students. With the freedom of the academic curriculum, though, comes the responsibility of constructing it. One student said, "The Div System allows you to build exactly the kind of academic experience you're interested in and is a big reason why I wanted to come to Hampshire. I didn't want to be checking off boxes for requirements. It's a lot more responsibility because classes are your choice so you have to make those classes worthwhile." The written evaluations students receive from professors at the end of a class, though (instead of grades) help guide this unique learning process. A student said that the written evaluations "are an amazing sign of respect because the teacher has to know who you are. They help create a really special, productive student-teacher relationship and I feel better giving a graduate school a written evaluation from my teachers instead of just letter grades because I feel like they say so much more." Once a student's academic requirements have been filled, he or she is declared "Div-free" and loudly rings the bell by the library in celebration.

The Div III projects year to year not only showcase the uniqueness of the academic interests of the Hampshire student body, but also the uniqueness of its student personalities in general. There is no "cookie cutter" Hampshire student, despite the "earthy" or "hippie" stereotype. The typical student, though, is "somebody who's passionate about something and has decided to live their life by practicing that something. A Hampshire student is someone who's interested in looking at themselves and what they want to do through as many lenses as possible." If you walked into SAGA (which appears to be a capitalized acronym but is not, just another amusing example of Hampshire bending the boundaries), the main dining hall, a student says you would most likely hear a conversation about, "anything from gender to Israel v. Palestine to a new yo-yo trick to *Anna Karenina* and everybody talks about quality of food, but especially talks about classes. We don't switch off when we get to the dining hall. I see lots of kids eating with books and I think that's wonderful. Discussions are opened by classes, not closed when they end."

The Green Experience: Eco-friendly Environment

Hampshire is incredibly and undeniably "green"—and not just because of its eight hundred acres of woods or nearby mountain range. Students, faculty, and staff at Hampshire remain dedicated to reducing their carbon footprint. Most recently, the college has installed an innovative Solar Canopy at the Chuck and Polly Longsworth Arts Center, made up of 2,880 square feet of photovoltaic modules. Hampshire has also recently acquired environmentally friendly self-service cars with ZipCar, Inc., that are available across campus to any member of the Hampshire community. The college also boasts a free, private bus system that runs between the Five Colleges; the Hampshire College Farm, a working farm that promotes sustainable agricultural practices; a campus-wide composting program, and many more "green" initiatives.

Besides conserving the environment, Hampshire students love to play in it. ORPA, the Outdoors Program/Recreational Athletics group, gives students the opportunity to backpack, hike, even rock climb, and students can rent cross-country skis, sleeping bags, tents, and other outdoor equipment whenever the spirit moves them. Mixed Nuts, a student run food market started in the 1970s, serves as another example of Hampshire's verdant streaks. The dining hall also offers numerous vegetarian and vegan options, for the "green" at heart (or stomach).

The Living and Social Environment

Most first year Hampshire students live in single dorms, but second, third and fourth year students live in "mods," a defining feature of the college. "Mods" are apartment-style dorms that can house between four and ten students and are equipped with a kitchen, a common room area, and at least one or two (sometimes three) bathrooms. It is within this living environment that the Hampshire social scene flourishes. A Hampshire student described dorm life like this: "My hall is like a really tight-knit family. We're all cool with each other. I practice music with an amazing violinist who lives next to me and usually go to the lounge a lot to hang out with people. My new favorite thing is just to eat goat cheese on bread in my room with my friends and talk about interesting things. There's a different smell on every floor, though. The bottom floor might smell like weed, the second floor like incense, the third like throw-up, and the fourth like fruit. Dorm life is also interesting because it's all these different personalities stuck in one space and nobody wants to go outside because it's so cold so just because of our geography we are made to love each other."

Though the college does have a reputation for drug use, many students resent this claim and say that overall, the social scene is much more diverse because the people are so multi-faceted and multi-dimensional.

One student says, "Hampshire kids have really weird talents. Kids ride around on unicycles and are professional yo-yo-ers and hypnotists. We're a very eclectic crowd and we're really weird. We make everything into a question which can be obnoxious but is always really interesting." Special speakers, local bands, and the social life at the other Consortium schools are available to students, which broadens the variety of available activities.

Even if Hampshire is not "traditional" in the traditional sense, there are still long-standing customs that define Hampshire's social year. One is Hampshire Halloween, which used to be called "Trip or Treat" in its early heyday. Now, the campus-wide party has scaled back a bit and is "invite only," meaning Hampshire students receive a limited number of tickets to dole out to non-Hampshire students. Despite these efforts to contain the party, Hampshire students still say proudly that, "it's a lot of fun. Mostly people just get really drunk and really super out of it but the best part is checking out all the amazing costumes. It's a wild time. There are huge fireworks and people are going wild and it feels totally surreal." Another treasured Hampshire holiday is the Keg Hunt, which takes place on Easter. What replaces the eggs goes without saying, and students, Solo cups in hand, enjoy the search and usually frolic in the grass with a Frisbee after the kegs have been found and enjoyed. The annual Drag Ball also occurs in the spring. Students attend this dance dressed as members of the opposite gender.

An Individual's Overall Experience

Hampshire has been called the "graduate school for undergraduates" because of its strong emphasis on independent course study. A student at Hampshire can explore, focus, and come to define his or her academic passions in a way not many other colleges can offer, but only if the student expends the effort to do so. A student explains, "Here you're put in the driver's seat and I really love that about Hampshire but it's also very scary."—*Madeline Duff*

FYI
A Hampshire student needs "a cause, self-discipline, the will to exercise, and a pencil to write down all the interesting things that happen in a given day."
Hampshire's greatest weakness is "that since it's so individual it can sometimes be isolating and hard to connect with a large group of people. Sometimes we get so caught up in individualizing our projects that we lose sight of the collective group around us."

Harvard University

Address: 86 Brattle Street, Cambridge, MA 02138
Phone: 617-495-1551
E-mail address: college@fas.harvard.edu
Web site URL: www.harvard.edu
Year Founded: 1636
Private or Public: Private
Religious Affiliation: None
Location: Urban
Number of Applicants: 27,642
Percent Accepted: 8%
Percent Accepted who enroll: 76%
Number Entering: 1,658
Number of Transfers Accepted each Year: Unreported
Middle 50% SAT range: M: 700–780, CR: 690–800, Wr: 690–790
Middle 50% ACT range: 31–35
Early admission program EA/ED/None: None

Percentage accepted through EA or ED: NA
EA and ED deadline: NA
Regular Deadline: 1-Jan
Application Fee: $65
Full time Undergraduate enrollment: 6,651
Total enrollment: 20,263
Percent Male: 50%
Percent Female: 50%
Total Percent Minority or Unreported: 33%
Percent African-American: 8%
Percent Asian/Pacific Islander: 17%
Percent Hispanic: 7%
Percent Native-American: 1%
Percent International: 10%
Percent in-state/out of state: 16%/84%
Percent from Public HS: 66%
Retention Rate: 97%
Graduation Rate 4-year: 97%

Graduation Rate 6-year: 98%
Percent Undergraduates in On-campus housing: Unreported
Number of official organized extracurricular organizations: 400
3 Most popular majors: Economics, Government, Psychology
Student/Faculty ratio: Unreported
Average Class Size: <20
Percent of students going to grad school: Unreported
Tuition and Fees: $36,173
In-State Tuition and Fees if different: No difference
Cost for Room and Board: $11,042
Percent receiving financial aid out of those who apply: 88%
Percent receiving financial aid among all students: 60%

Founded in 1636, Harvard University is the oldest college in the United States and often considered one of the top universities in the world. Students, known affectionately as "Cantabs," enjoy easy access to world-renowned professors, high-achieving classmates, and city life in Boston. With 44 Nobel Laureates as former and current faculty, there is little doubt that Harvard has a wealth of resources and opportunities to offer both its students as well as graduates.

Aiming for A's

Harvard undoubtedly commands international recognition for its outstanding academics and highly intelligent student population. Although students generally graduate in four years, some choose to undergo Advanced Standing, a program which allows students to graduate in three years before obtaining a Master's degree. At Harvard, majors are known as concentrations, and some of the most popular ones include Economics, Mathematics, and Government.

Core classes tend to have up to 400 to 500 students, although seminars, which are non-core classes, are typically much smaller. According to one freshman, "The classes are competitive in the sense that everyone strives to do well, but people don't think of other students as competition. We enjoy having other help." While engineering, math, or science classes are known for their extra difficulty, Cantabs do not mind the added challenge. One student remarked, "You gotta take what you gotta take." Despite the reputed difficulty of science classes, however, Harvard students looking for a hands-on learning experience can take "Cooking for Science," cooking in class while learning the scientific principles behind each delicious meal.

In general, grading at Harvard is relatively laid-back. According to one freshman, "grading tends to be very forgiving at Harvard. There is definitely a sense of grade inflation on campus, as most classes are typically curved to a B+, although professors do have full control over their own grading styles." Another student added, "Getting a B+ or A– is very doable, although getting an A will take a bit of work." Yet, it isn't the inflated grading policy that characterizes Harvard's academic atmosphere. "I like the flexibility that we have in choosing classes, and I like that there are lots of introductory classes in very different subjects, which makes exploring possible," said one student. "I really appreciate the caliber of our professors and how it can really contribute to the quality of classes." If students do feel stressed out, they can participate in Primal Scream, a campus tradition in which students collectively scream as loudly as they can the night before finals, before resuming their studies.

While most appreciate Harvard's academic excellence, some criticize the lack of academic advising available to students. According to one sophomore, "Students are given three advisers during their freshman year, but these advisers usually have little impact on a freshman's academic life because organized contact is typically rare." Others cite inconsistencies among different course sections for a particular class; nonetheless, Harvard students are overall content with their academic experience and appreciate everything that their university has to offer.

Partyin' It Up, Crimson Style
Those interested in partying can find parties hosted by student groups in dining halls or student dorms. Alcohol is prevalent, although students are not generally pressured to drink. According to one student, "There is a distinct drinking culture at Harvard, but there are enough students that do not drink so that they are not particularly disadvantaged socially if they choose not to drink." Harvard also has its fair share of substance abuse, although neither drugs nor binge drinking is a major problem on campus. According to one freshman, "You can pretty much get away with alcohol and drugs as long as you don't do it so excessively that you go to the hospital or start to disturb the public."

> "People from the outside describe us as being cocky, but I don't really see much of that inside Harvard."

Alcohol and partying aside, students interested in a different social experience are definitely not left out in the cold, thanks largely to Boston's various shops and restaurants, including a nearby Chipotle franchise that remains a favorite among students. Others choose to spend their weekends on campus, enjoying free time with their friends or catching up on homework in Lamont Library.

Not Your Typical House
Before arriving on campus as freshmen, Harvard students fill out a housing application form in order to find a compatible roommate. Freshmen are randomly assigned to one of the 17 freshman dormitories and live in the same room for one year. In March of freshmen year, however, Harvard students receive their "House" affiliations through a randomized process known as "sorting," which designates their intra-Harvard identity. Each House contains dorm rooms for undergraduates, resident tutors, its own dining hall, library, administrative officials, as well as other student facilities. Students are assigned to one of 12 Harvard houses with up to seven of their friends, creating a "blocking group."

Students typically live on campus for all four years and, for the most part, dorm life has remained fairly consistent. Students entering the Harvard Class of 2015, however, should be aware of recent renovations that are slated to begin in 2012. According to one student, "Harvard has voted in recent weeks to allocate nearly $1 billion in funds to renovating the Upperclass Houses, meaning that current high school students entering Harvard in the coming years should be able to experience a more enhanced House experience."

Unsurprisingly, campus architecture is "old . . . really old" and campus scenery is characterized by red brick and grassy lawns. Tourists at the Crimson Ivy often visit the Science Center, which houses five lecture halls and numerous academic departments, and nearby Annenberg Hall, the centrally located freshman dining hall that still remains a favorite among tourists.

The Whole Package
Harvard students are as serious about their academics as they are about their extracurricular activities. Some prominent organizations on campus include the International Relations Council, *The Lampoon*, *The Crimson*, and Women in Business (which

has over 400 members). Not everything about Harvard is always serious, though. Students in Hasty Pudding Theatricals come together every year to award the Hasty Pudding Man and Woman of the Year, reflecting a fun side of Harvard students that doesn't take away from their passion. According to one freshman, "something unique about Harvard is really the commitment people have to their extracurriculars. People do a million things—and stay active in all of them."

Outside of campus clubs and organizations, Crimson students are also extremely active in the job market. One of the biggest employers is Harvard Student Agencies, Inc., an organization comprised of many subsidiary agencies that employ students all over campus. While some student employees work at HAS cleaners offering laundry plans, others sell Harvard apparel at The Harvard Shop; some even take advantage of alcohol on campus, working as bartenders for HSA Bartending. Others take more traditional roles as student workers in campus libraries or research assistants for Harvard professors.

Unlike club activities, however, sports are not a major presence on campus. As one student aptly said, "Games are free for a reason." Another student added that "While there is a bit of pride associated with Harvard athletics, attending athletic events is usually not the thing to do." This doesn't mean, however, that Harvard students are completely sports illiterate. During the annual Harvard-Yale football game, Cantabs eagerly don Crimson scarves and sweaters, proudly showing their collegiate loyalty and support for the Harvard football team. According to one sophomore, "There is a big athletic presence on campus, and student athletes are definitely a big part of the Harvard community, so it's very common for students to go to athletic events to see their friends in action."

Overall, Harvard is an excellent school for students seeking a first-class academic experience and the company of some of the world's brightest minds. Unlike contemporary portrayals of the University, Cantabs are generally down-to-earth and can successfully strike a balance between studying hard and playing hard.—*Caroline Tan*

FYI

If you come to Harvard, you'd better bring "tourist repellant, a lot of warm clothes, and your own toilet paper."

Three things every student at Harvard should do are "hook up with someone in the stacks of Widener Library, run Primal Scream, and pee on the John Harvard statue."

What surprised me the most about Harvard is that "it's better than you could ever imagine. Seriously."

Massachusetts Institute of Technology

Address: 77 Massachusetts Avenue, Cambridge, MA 02139-4307

Phone: 617-253-1000

E-mail address: admissions@mit.edu

Web site URL: www.mit.edu

Year Founded: 1861

Private or Public: Private

Religious Affiliation: None

Location: Urban

Number of Applicants: 12,445

Percent Accepted: 12%

Percent Accepted who enroll: 69%

Number Entering: 1,067

Number of Transfers Accepted each Year: 17

Middle 50% SAT range: M: 720–800, CR: 660–760, Wr: 660–750

Middle 50% ACT range: 31–34

Early admission program EA/ED/None: EA

Percentage accepted through EA or ED: 30%

EA and ED deadline: 1-Nov

Regular Deadline: 1-Jan

Application Fee: $65

Full time Undergraduate enrollment: 4,172

Total enrollment: 10,220

Percent Male: 54%

Percent Female: 46%

Total Percent Minority or Unreported: 60%

Percent African-American: 9%

Percent Asian/Pacific Islander: 26%

Percent Hispanic: 12%

Percent Native-American: 1%

Percent International: 8%

Percent in-state/out of state: 10%/90%

Percent from Public HS: 70%

Retention Rate: 98%

Graduation Rate 4-year: 83%

Graduation Rate 6-year: 91%

Percent Undergraduates in On-campus housing: 90%

Number of official organized extracurricular organizations: 415

3 Most popular majors: Engineering, Computer Science, Physical Science

Student/Faculty ratio: 6:1

Average Class Size: 9

Percent of students going to grad school: 50%

Tuition and Fees: $36,390

In-State Tuition and Fees if different: No difference

Cost for Room and Board: $10,860

Percent receiving financial aid out of those who apply: 82%

Percent receiving financial aid among all students: 64%

Nestled in the quintessential college town of Cambridge is one of the nation's most prestigious and intellectually demanding universities, the Massachusetts Institute of Technology. Famous worldwide for producing brilliant engineers and scientists, MIT nevertheless offers a richly diverse community of scholars all united by a passion for learning. Distinguished equally for its undergraduate research opportunities, its humanities program, and its legendary hacking tradition, MIT promises an unforgettably rewarding experience for those students ready to meet the challenge.

Not for Everyone

MIT students will admit that the school's ponderous, often overwhelming workload and academic rigor is not for everyone, yet the students who feed off and thrive in the intense environment never stop savoring its fruits. "MIT opens up an entire world of possibilities," gushed one student. "It's a lot of work," another student admitted, "but it's so, so worth it by the time you're done." Students state that with their first class, their entire thinking process is transformed, for professors don't seek simply to recite and impart facts and formulas: they try to change how students assimilate and apply information by teaching them how to think, rather than what to think. It is that principle of organic problem-solving that sets MIT apart as an extraordinary institution of undergraduate learning.

MIT requires every student to take 17 General Institute Requirements before graduation: nine in math, science, and technology, and eight in the humanities, arts, and social sciences. Those students who desire a more intimate learning environment to support them in satisfying these requirements can join one of four Freshman Learning Communities, small and cohesive groups that foster close interaction between faculty and students. And to ease all freshmen into the system, MIT offers a pass/no record grading scale the first semester, in which an A, B, or C appears uniformly as a pass grade while a D or F is completely erased from the student's permanent transcript. The second semester, freshmen are graded on an A/B/C/ no record basis. "The pass/no record grading has really given me a chance to explore my interests outside of academics and discover all the opportunities MIT has to offer," shared one freshman. And students definitely need that transition period. Yet, ultimately, one student reflected, "People here tend to be pretty apathetic with regards to GPA. There's no such thing as Latin honors here, and people do tend to be pretty idealistic (sadistic?) with regards to classes, taking tons and tons at a time, putting learning before grades."

> **"It's a lot of work, but it's so, so worth it by the time you're done."**

The typical MIT workload is four to five classes requiring a total time commitment of 50 to 60 hours each week: "You're pretty much working all the time—it's like community bonding happens over working nonstop." And although classes often contract to as few as 10 students for higher-level courses, freshman year can congest up to 400 students into a lecture hall, especially in introductory classes. Yet professors are accessible if you take the initiative to talk to them—that means being persistent at packed office hours—and students study collaboratively rather than competitively: "The professors write the problem sets in such a way that it is absolutely indispensable that you work in groups in order to finish."

From A Cappella to Video Games: Giving the Brain a Break

As heavy as is the workload, however, MIT students still find the time to invest in sundry extracurricular activities. Featuring everything from the Underwater Hockey Group and the Laboratory of Chocolate Science to Engineers Without Borders and the Black Students Association, MIT's 415 student organizations offer an outlet for all students. And if you have a passion that has not yet been provided for, you can easily create a club of your own, no matter how outlandish the purpose. "The cool thing about MIT is that everybody is really passionate about something, usually random things, so you can voice crazy ideas and people won't look at you strangely," explained one student.

Noted for its large number of a cappella and choral groups, as well as for its tremendous Undergraduate Research Opportunities Program (UROP), in which 80 percent of students participate, MIT offers students several ways to get involved. One of the best times to explore nascent interests is Independent Activities Period (IAP), a month-long session in January, after Winter Break, during which students can stay on campus or go abroad to pursue personal projects or take different types of classes.

MIT is also one of the few top-ten research universities characterized by an incredibly vibrant Greek life. Fifty percent of undergraduate men, and 27 percent of undergraduate women, belong to one of the 27 fraternities or 6 sororities on campus, but these are not the students who would normally join the Greek system. Rather than the bacchanalian party scene dominant at other colleges, Greek life at MIT is an "academic support system" of students all motivating and encouraging one another to persist in a fiercely challenging intellectual environment. Thus, although Greek life does figure prominently in the MIT social scene, it is not the center of attention: hundreds of students take advantage of the weekend frat parties, sometimes even inviting their friends from other Boston universities, but many more—particularly upperclassmen—choose to patronize one of the several local bars for their taste of nightlife. Avalon, Embassy, and Crossroads Irish Pub are all favorites.

Those students desiring some fun without alcohol can partake in Cambridge's many theater, arts, and shopping options. Popular are CambridgeSide Galleria, a mall that offers a free shuttle service to MIT's Kendall Square, and Central Square, the center of the music scene. Students also occasionally frequent the Museum of Science and the Museum of Fine Arts, to both of which they are given free daily admission. Or, if students have too much work and just need a short brain break, especially on weeknights, dorms are always prime locations for spontaneous fun. At any one time, a visitor can observe students relaxing by playing with foam weapons, competing in video games, or participating in hypothetical scenarios involving spaceships or engineering technologies. "These seemingly silly activities can be a huge stress relief when you've spent the last several hours doing problem sets in your room," shared one student.

They also reflect students' willingness and eagerness to explore new things, regardless of the consequences. "There's a lot of eccentric expression here—for example, the dorms are laced with murals of internet memes and other generally humorous images, which form a part of student expression. Also, there is a lot of secretive stuff going on around campus—for example, an explosion can go off at all random hours of the night and produce a mushroom cloud several hundred feet

high—and those sorts of random things become pretty commonplace."

Perhaps the best description of the MIT experience is the school motto the students have created for themselves: I.H.T.F.P., which represents both "I hate this f-ing place" and "I have truly found paradise." These constantly busy, perpetually sleep-deprived students have still learned how to uncover and savor the fun in every activity, whether it's an onerous problem set or the latest scandalous prank. Therefore, despite the challenges and the expressed duality of the MIT experience, "it's a relationship still full more of love than of hate: a lot of love, and a few hard nights."—*Sejal Hathi*

FYI

If you come to MIT, you'd better bring: energy drinks, a bike, cooking utensils, a nerf gun, and an oscilloscope.

What's the typical weekend schedule? Sleep in, work nonstop until you can let loose at a party.

If I could change one thing about MIT, I'd: make the advising more standardized.

Three things every student at MIT should do before graduating are: participate in Mystery Hunt, go on an Orange Tour, and take linguistics with Norvin Richards.

Mount Holyoke College

Address: 50 College Street, South Hadley, MA 01075
Phone: 413-538-2023
E-mail address: admission@mtholyoke.edu
Web site URL: www.mtholyoke.edu
Year Founded: 1837
Private or Public: Private
Religious Affiliation: None
Location: Suburban
Number of Applicants: 3,359
Percent Accepted: 52%
Percent Accepted who enroll: 31%
Number Entering: 542
Number of Transfers Accepted each Year: 102
Middle 50% SAT range: M: 580–690, CR: 510–700, Wr: 620–710
Middle 50% ACT range: 27–31
Early admission program EA/ED/None: ED

Percentage accepted through EA or ED: Unreported
EA and ED deadline: 15-Nov
Regular Deadline: 15-Jan
Application Fee: $60; online application is free
Full time Undergraduate enrollment: 2,286
Total enrollment: 2,333
Percent Male: 0%
Percent Female: 100%
Total Percent Minority or Unreported: 52%
Percent African-American: 4%
Percent Asian/Pacific Islander: 6%
Percent Hispanic: 7%
Percent Native-American: <1%
Percent International: 22%
Percent in-state/out of state: 26%/74%
Percent from Public HS: 62%
Retention Rate: 91%

Graduation Rate 4-year: 78%
Graduation Rate 6-year: 81%
Percent Undergraduates in On-campus housing: 94%
Number of official organized extracurricular organizations: 111
2 Most popular majors: English Language and Literature, International Relations and Affairs
Student/Faculty ratio: 9:1
Average Class Size: 16
Percent of students going to grad school: 20%
Tuition and Fees: $41,270
In-State Tuition and Fees if different: No difference
Cost for Room and Board: $12,140
Percent receiving financial aid out of those who apply: 86%
Percent receiving financial aid among all students: 79%

Located in the calm hamlet of South Hadley, Massachusetts, Mount Holyoke College is a women's college known for both its homey feel and high-powered academics. The campus is known as one of the most beautiful in the country, and helps to foster close bonds among the tight-knit community. As a member of the Five College Consortium, Mount Holyoke students are able to take classes and interact with students at Smith College, University of Massachusetts at Amherst, Amherst College, and Hampshire College. Caring professors and individualized support help students take advantage of a myriad of academic and social opportunities.

Vigorous Academics

Academics at Mount Holyoke can be described as "very rigorous." Students are required to fulfill a variety of distributional requirements that include three courses in the humanities, two courses in science and math, and two courses in the social sciences. They must also fulfill a foreign language requirement, a multicultural perspectives course, and six units of physical education. Although such requirements may seem daunting, most describe them as "not hard to meet at all" and note that "you can fit your interests within the requirements." Students are also required to choose a minor, second major, or a certificate program through one of the Five Colleges. In addition, Mount Holyoke offers dual-degree engineering programs through MIT, California Institute of Technology, and the Thayer School of Engineering at Dartmouth. Some of the more popular majors include biology, English, and international relations. Smaller but very well-regarded departments include astronomy and gender studies. The popular first-year seminar program, which includes such courses as "Gods and Monsters" and "African Cinema," allows freshmen to get to know their professors and fellow students during their first semester on campus. Although professors are known for assigning a demanding workload—"every professor thinks that his class is your top priority," noted one student—they are universally praised for being accessible, engaging, and genuinely interested in their students. Courses such as dance, scuba diving, and horseback riding provide a break from academic life and take advantage of the college's beautiful natural surroundings.

Mount Holyoke is also unique in that it offers an optional January term, or J-term, a month when students can take advantage of workshops or study abroad. Students are able to cross-register at any of the members of the Five College Consortium, which are all serviced by a free busing system among the different campuses. The system allows students to take courses in subjects not offered at Mount Holyoke and meet students at nearby schools.

Lakes and Waterfalls

With a campus designed by Olmstead and Sons, the developers of Central Park, it's not hard to see why Mount Holyoke's surroundings are unequivocally described as "beautiful." Featuring two lakes and seven waterfalls, the campus is dotted with benches for studying and talking. Although the closest town, South Hadley, is considered small and sleepy, students can easily travel to Amherst or Northampton using the college's busing system when they feel the need to get away.

The dorms, which house approximately 93 percent of students, are praised for fostering close relations among the student body. Most dorms house students from all four classes, allowing students the chance to get to know upperclassmen. Freshmen are assigned housing based on extensive surveys and usually live in doubles or triples. By their senior year, most students live in singles. Dorms vary in size and age, ranging from modern brick buildings to ivy-covered halls with a view of one of the college's lakes. All dorms are governed by a Hall President, or HP, and three to six Student Advisors, or SAs. These students host study breaks, help with acclimation to college life, and ensure enforcement of rules. Although Public Safety maintains a presence on campus and open alcohol isn't technically allowed in hallways, students say they find few problems with the school's regulations. "They just want to make sure that we're safe," said a junior.

The quality of the food is widely praised, with one student even describing it as "delicious!" Every dorm features a dining hall, and cafés in the campus center and the library relieve hunger pangs between meals or at night. Vegetarian, vegan, kosher, and halal options are offered at every meal. Students can also load money onto their meal cards to use off campus.

Activities for All

Extracurricular life at Mount Holyoke is characterized by variety and passion. Sports, which consist of 14 varsity teams and various club sports, are very popular among students, particularly crew, rugby, hockey, and Ultimate Frisbee. Even if they don't join a team, many girls enthusiastically cheer on their classmates on the field. The newly refurbished athletic center, which features TV-equipped cardio machines and is open to all students, garners glowing reviews. Music and dance also play an important part of life on campus, with the college boasting many a cappella groups, performing ensembles, and outside concerts. SGA, the Student Government Association, is another popular way for students to get involved. Other student groups discussing issues of diversity and sexual identity feature prominently in campus life.

Socially, students remark that although people with similar interests tend to stick together, Mount Holyoke is an overwhelmingly friendly place. "This is not a party school," a sophomore asserted. Although many students drink, options abound for those who choose not to imbibe. On-campus social activities include dorm parties, movies, and a cappella jams. Las Vegas Night, Mount Holyoke's biggest party of the year, features dancing and gambling. Other popular on-campus events include the "Drag Ball" in early February and Spring Carnival Weekend, which attracts dance and musical performers to the college. During the weekends, many students use the bus system to meet members of the opposite sex at Amherst or UMass. "Although Mount Holyoke is a women's college, you are not abandoned to a corner of the earth were there are no men," joked one senior.

Atypical Experience

While Mount Holyoke, as a women's college, may not offer the typical college experience, students are overwhelmingly happy with the school. "Although I never saw myself at a women's college, I wouldn't trade a minute of my time here for anything," declared one senior. Students believe that the benefits of an all-female environment more than make up for the extra trouble they have to go to to meet members of the opposite sex. Openness and acceptance characterize the campus, and Mount Holyokers are known for being open-minded, down-to-earth, and intelligent. The student body is incredibly diverse, with an exceptionally high number of international students. The school is also accepting of students of all sexual orientations and relationships.

Although Mount Holyoke is not for everyone, the majority of students who attend the college are extremely happy with it. "Mount Holyoke provides such a great balance of academics with a well-rounded life," says one senior. "I couldn't imagine myself anywhere else."—*Elizabeth Chrystal*

FYI
If you come to Mount Holyoke, you'd better bring "a box full of costumes—you've never seen so many theme parties in your life!"
What's the typical weekend schedule? "Hang out on Friday with friends; relax, shop, or go to a sports game on Saturday, go out to a party on-campus or by taking a bus off-campus; have brunch and do homework on Sunday."
If I could change one thing about Mount Holyoke, I'd "make South Hadley a little more exciting. It's very quaint, but it seems a bit isolated after four years."
Three things every student at Mount Holyoke should do before graduating are "climb Mount Holyoke on Mountain Day, go to an a cappella jam, and enjoy crepes at Sunday brunch."

Northeastern University

Address: 360 Huntington Avenue, Boston, MA 02115

Phone: 617-373-2200

E-mail address: admissions@neu.edu

Web site URL: www.northeastern.edu

Year Founded: 1898

Private or Public: Private

Religious Affiliation: None

Location: Urban

Number of Applicants: 37,688

Percent Accepted: 38%

Percent Accepted who enroll: 20%

Number Entering: 2,836

Number of Transfers Accepted each Year: 1,287

Middle 50% SAT range: M: 630–710, CR: 600–680, Wr: 590–680

Middle 50% ACT range: 28–31

Early admission program EA/ED/None: EA

Percentage accepted through EA or ED: Unreported

EA and ED deadline: 1-Nov

Regular Deadline: 15-Jan

Application Fee: $70

Full time Undergraduate enrollment: 15,905

Total enrollment: 15,905

Percent Male: 49%

Percent Female: 51%

Total Percent Minority or Unreported: 48%

Percent African-American: 4%

Percent Asian/Pacific Islander: 8%

Percent Hispanic: 5%

Percent Native-American: <1%

Percent International: 10%

Percent in-state/out of state: 38%/62%

Percent from Public HS: Unreported

Retention Rate: 93%

Graduation Rate 4-year: Unreported

Graduation Rate 6-year: 75%

Percent Undergraduates in On-campus housing: 53%

Number of official organized extracurricular organizations: 250

3 Most popular majors: Business/Marketing, Engineering, Health Professions and related sciences

Student/Faculty ratio: 13:1

Average Class Size: 15

Percent of students going to grad school: 18%

Tuition and Fees: $37,840

In-State Tuition and Fees if different: No difference

Cost for Room and Board: $13,220

Percent receiving financial aid out of those who apply: Unreported

Percent receiving financial aid among all students: 59%

S etting itself apart from the Boston area's assortment of colleges and universities, Northeastern University places a great emphasis on training professionals as well as educating college students. While maintaining its focus on educating its students, Northeastern places undergraduates with different internship positions at different companies during their college years. In the classroom and in the workplace, Northeastern students are given many chances to learn, and they take advantage of their opportunities.

Studying in the Co-op

The most prominent feature of undergraduate studies at Northeastern University is its innovative cooperative education program. Almost the entirety of students at Northeastern go to school for five years (while paying the tuition for four) because of the structure of the co-op. Students alternate between six-month periods of traditional academic study and six-month periods of paid professional work experience.

Because of this unique schedule, students gain not only academic knowledge, but also insight into what their future careers will be, experience on the job, and more generally experience in the professional world. Northeastern seniors have already built up a strong resume and learned important interview skills. On top of that, students with the opportunity to work in the industries of their interest have the ability to network and make contacts with professionals and professors in their field. This of course can lead to better employment prospects after graduation, or to even more opportunities and flexibility while an undergraduate. One student studying business said, "many professors obviously have connections with other professionals within their field and I know of several students who have received assistance from professors in creating their own cooperative education position."

Students of the co-op, many of whom enter the program their freshman year, take orientation classes that focus on professional skills such as resume writing and interviewing. And when these students begin work the following year, they begin to get a better sense of what their career field ought to be, and if their current job is the right fit for them. Of course, the money that students earn while on the job is a welcome motivator, and it is not uncommon for students to graduate from Northeastern and move straight into employment, sometimes with the firms that employed them during their undergraduate study. One student described her feelings about the co-op program: "I would absolutely say that the integration of the cooperative education program within the academic curriculum is by far my favorite part about Northeastern's academic life. We gain invaluable experiences through these positions and are able to truly apply what we learn in the classroom to real-world scenarios."

While not at work in the co-op, students must complete the requirements for graduation, including Northeastern's First-Year Learning Communities; four classes in the arts and humanities, social sciences, and science/technology; four writing-intensive courses; a Comparative Study of Cultures class; two Mathematical/Analytical Thinking classes; one Integrated Experiential Learning course; and a Capstone course. Additionally, students must fulfill the specific class/credit requirements for their major.

The typical workload of a Northeastern student completing these requirements during the academic session can be "pretty intense" due to the nature of the cooperative education program built into the curriculum. Students are typically researching job positions and companies they seek to work for and scheduling interviews, as well as balancing their classwork with extracurricular involvement. "It can be difficult to juggle all of these things at once considering the fact that many of the cooperative education positions are very competitive," one student explained.

Living and Learning at Northeastern

Upon their arrival to Northeastern, freshmen move into "very normal" freshman residence halls—described by one student as "providing the bare essentials"—most of them with separate gender by floor or hallway, with a community bathroom. Honors freshmen get nicer housing in the newer International Village, which has semi-private singles (connected by a bathroom) as well as doubles connected by a bathroom. Freshmen are generally assigned their dorm based on their preference for a particular Living Learning Community, which houses people with similar interests or majors together. After freshman year, students are granted a lottery number, which usually gets better with seniority. Along with the better lottery numbers, upperclassmen housing on the whole is said to be "much nicer," as sophomores, juniors, and seniors can choose to live in on-campus apartment-style housing, singles in International Village, or off campus. Many of the upperclassmen living on campus are housed in the West Village halls, which are described as "AH-MAZ-ING"; however, one student warned that the luxury of West Village may come with a price tag that may not be worth it. It is important to know that if students take co-op positions at locations outside of Boston, they will have to find their own means of housing and transportation. Of course this could be a welcome change of scenery for some. But a student who takes a position in Boston has the option to remain living in Northeastern housing.

> "We gain invaluable experiences through the integration of the cooperative education program within the academic curriculum and are able to truly apply what we learn in the classroom to real-world scenarios."

Students on campus have plenty of options when it comes to mealtimes. There are three dining halls on campus, each with its own set of specialties: "Stetson East has great burgers, Stetson West has amazing stir-fry, and International Village is our 'green' dining hall and the newest—it has many more options as far as international cuisine, like Indian food, Sushi, Italian, etc." Students looking for meals outside of the dining halls can find satiation at one of the many off-campus restaurants that accept either meal plans or meal money. These include Qdoba, Starbucks, Dunkin' Donuts, Subway, Pizza Hut, Taco Bell, Wendy's, and Jamba Juice as well as local favorites.

After Work . . .

At the same time, students at Northeastern are not simply all work, but many do choose to spend their free time making money. According to one student, "Some people, me included, continue working at their co-op jobs part-time after their six-month period ends." Many others, however, that choose to continue to work do so in on-campus work-study positions.

Students who want to spend some of their time outside of class not working have plenty of options for extracurricular fun. One student had this to say about extracurricular activities at Northeastern: "There is a huge amount of options and something for everyone who wants to try or wants to really do a sport but can't commit to a team sport. And there are tons and tons of clubs so that everyone can find what they want, and if somehow there isn't one, you can create a new one." Referring to the intramural sports scene, "Some of the most popular are Broomball and Frisbee." Some of the prominent organizations on campus include the various a cappella groups, as well as the Resident Student Association, Tastemakers Magazine (a music magazine), and *The Huntington News* (the popular student newspaper), and some more examples of the groups found on campus include NUHOC (an outdoors club that takes students on various camping, skiing, and other outdoor trips), Northeastern's Chapter of the American Chemistry Society, NEURONS (NU's Neuroscience club), as well as the College Republicans and the College Democrats.

. . . Time to Play

On the weekends at Northeastern, many students try to take their break from their busy lives as the social scene flourishes. Underage drinking is common, but a significant percentage of the undergraduate population does not drink. Those that do so on campus are leading slightly more risky lives, since the university has a harsh policy on drinking. "Melvin Hall is a popular place to party because it's next to The Fens (a park that's nice in the day and super sketchy at night) and on the very edge on campus," but generally off-campus parties or parties at other schools are more popular. The surrounding city of Boston means there is always something to do off-campus, as older students can go to bars or clubs, and plenty of students will party at the other universities nearby. Since many students do not have classes Friday, "Thursday nights some people go out but the main nights are Friday and Saturday nights and if they want to party usually people go to Mission Hill (a fifteen-minute walk), BU (a five-minute walk), or MIT (a fifteen-minute train ride)."

All in all, students at Northeastern have a wonderfully rounded experience. While they get pre-professional training, industry contacts and a killer resume from the co-op, they don't have to miss out on the experience of higher education and campus living and learning. Instead, they have a new experience entirely, one that can teach them better than any class.—*Connor Moseley*

FYI

If you come to Northeastern, you'd better bring "heavy coats, an umbrella, and comfy shoes because you'll be walking in the rain a lot."

What differentiates Northeastern the most from other colleges is "the co-op, which absolutely sets Northeastern apart from traditional schools."

What surprised me the most about Northeastern when I arrived was "how close it is to everything in the city, but still gives you that closed off feeling of a campus."

Simmons College

Address: 300 The Fenway, Boston, MA 02115
Phone: 617-521-2051
E-mail address: ugadm@simmons.edu
Web site URL: www.simmons.edu
Year Founded: 1899
Private or Public: Private
Religious Affiliation: None
Location: Urban
Number of Applicants: 3,522
Percent Accepted: 57%
Percent Accepted who enroll: 17%
Number Entering: 354
Number of Transfers Accepted each Year: 158
Middle 50% SAT range: M: 500–590, CR:490–600, Wr: 510–610
Middle 50% ACT range: 22–26
Early admission program EA/ED/None: EA

Percentage accepted through EA or ED: 57%
EA and ED deadline: 1-Dec
Regular Deadline: 1-Feb
Application Fee: $55
Full time Undergraduate enrollment: 1,752
Total enrollment: 1,969
Percent Male: 0%
Percent Female: 100%
Total Percent Minority or Unreported: 32%
Percent African-American: 6%
Percent Asian/Pacific Islander: 7%
Percent Hispanic: 4%
Percent Native-American: <1%
Percent International: 3%
Percent in-state/out of state: 61%/39%
Percent from Public HS: Unreported
Retention Rate: 75%

Graduation Rate 4-year: 62%
Graduation Rate 6-year: 72%
Percent Undergraduates in On-campus housing: 48%
Number of official organized extracurricular organizations: 91
2 Most popular majors: Nursing/Registered Nurse, Psychology
Student/Faculty ratio: 13:1
Average Class Size: 16
Percent of students going to grad school: Unreported
Tuition and Fees: $31,280
In-State Tuition and Fees if different: No difference
Cost for Room and Board: $12,470
Percent receiving financial aid out of those who apply: 94%
Percent receiving financial aid among all students: 85%

Nestled in the bustling city of Boston rests the tranquil oasis of Simmons College. Roughly 2,000 young women attend Simmons for its liberal arts with a special focus on science. Students rave about the close-knit student body and excellent, approachable professors, which combine to form a welcoming and laid-back atmosphere.

Science Anyone?

Simmons College offers a liberal arts education with special career preparation opportunities. The nursing program feeds student internships in the city, while the physical therapy major has a six-year doctorate program. Science at Simmons is especially strong. Nursing, biology, and chemistry are considered the most difficult majors, while communications and psychology are "not as demanding, but still difficult," according to one student. Class size is small, making it easy to enroll in most classes and enabling students to take a more active role in the classroom. Students rave about their professors.

One student explained, "[The professors] give you their e-mail, cell phone number, home number, office number, and office hours. They want you to come and talk to them. They are interested in helping their students."

Students must fulfill academic distributional requirements in six "modes of inquiry": Creative and Performing Arts; Language, Literature and Culture; Quantitative Analysis and Reasoning; Scientific Inquiry; Social and Historical Perspectives; and Psychological and Ethical Development. In the process, students become more well-rounded and prepared for life after college. The requirements are surprisingly unrestrictive, though, and one student commented, "I found that I was able to experiment more during my freshman year than my friends at other schools."

An Escape from Beantown

The Simmons campus receives high marks from its students. Its peaceful green quadrangle in the middle of a busy Boston neighborhood serves as a quiet haven. One student exclaimed, "Our campus is beautiful. Most people come onto campus and forget they are in a city. When you walk through the gates, it feels very much unlike a city and a lot more like home." The campus is divided into an academic portion and a residential portion separated by one city block. The residential campus consists of a picturesque quadrangle bounded by the College's residence halls and Bartol Dining Hall. Also located on the residential campus is the Holmes Sports Center, boasting an eight-lane swimming pool, suspended track, weight room, sauna, basketball court, dance studio, and squash courts. Next door is the Simmons Health Center, which offers its comprehensive services to students.

> "[The professors] give you their e-mail, cell phone number, home number, office number, and office hours. They want you to come and talk to them. They are interested in helping their students."

Approximately a five-minute walk from the residential campus is the main campus. Here the College's main classrooms are located in the Main College Building (affectionately referred to as the "MCB") and the Park Science Building, where all science courses are taught. The main campus also hosts the Beatley Library and the newly constructed and unusually named One Palace Road Building. One Palace Road provides a number of student resources such as career services and counseling, as well as two graduate school departments.

Standard of Living at Simmons

The quality of dorm rooms differs at Simmons depending on renovations and specific buildings. Most freshmen live in doubles in Mesick, Morse, or Simmons Hall, but there are a few triples. There is an RA on every floor, and one student said, "They're just there to help out, and are not too strict." Students are very pleased with their living situation. Recently renovated Evans Hall and Arnold Hall are "really nice and the only ones with elevators on campus," one student reported. Praise is not as free-flowing, though, when students are asked about the food at Simmons. Bartol Dining Hall is Simmons' main dining hall and students label

the food as "fair." Luckily for hungry Simmons students, the best of Boston's restaurants, with its first-class seafood and ethnic fare, lie just outside the College's gates. Other dining options available to students on campus include the Quadside Café, serving as a snack bar and grocery, The Fens, with a deli and grill, and Java City (Simmons' Coffee Kiosk), which doles out coffee and snacks.

Livin' It Up in Beantown

One student put it best by saying, "Basically, Boston becomes your campus." For this group of young women, the possibilities of the city are boundless. Students are able to take advantage of the city's many fabulous restaurants, go shopping on Newbury Street, attend a Boston Red Sox game, and go to a concert at the Orpheum Theater. Boston offers anything and everything under the sun . . . and under the moon as well, as Simmons girls take advantage of the city's exciting nightlife.

Simmons is a dry campus, and because of alcohol and noise restrictions students often go out to Boston clubs or to frat parties at BU and MIT for a more festive atmosphere. One student comments that because of this situation, "Simmons girls have a lot of random hookups because they really don't know when the next chance will be." These meetings often develop into something more substantial, however, and students note that many of their peers are involved in serious relationships—both heterosexual and homosexual.

From Tea to Tennis

Students describe the student body as "intelligent" and "friendly." The small class size promotes unity and school spirit. According to one student, a tradition that has been going on for a few years now is the Friday Hall Teas, where all the girls from each hall come together to "have tea or snack on goodies and just hang out and have fun."

Many Simmons students take part in sports and other extracurricular activities. The campus is described by one "as very active and involved." Simmons is home to eight Division III varsity sports, and one student described Simmons sports as "not awful"—basketball and soccer seemed to be the most popular sports among students. Other student organizations such as Simmons College Outreach, a student-run community service organization, and the Student Government Organization are just two of the many student activities and clubs in which students take part.

When John Simmons founded this college in 1899, his mission was to allow women to earn the "livelihood" they deserved and to create a new generation of well-educated women. Today his mission continues to be realized, as Simmons produces well-prepared, independent women ready to enter the world.—*Kieran Locke*

FYI
If you come to Simmons College, you'd better bring a "Boston Red Sox hat."
What's the typical weekend schedule? "Hanging out, shopping, and eating in Harvard Square or on Newbury Street and going to an occasional party at a fraternity from a neighboring college."
If I could change one thing about Simmons, "I would change the dining-hall food."
Three things every student at Simmons should do before graduating are "visit the Isabella Stewart Gardner Museum, eat Ankara Frozen Yogurt, and go on the Swan Boats in Boston Commons."

Smith College

Address: 7 College Lane, Northampton, MA 01063
Phone: 413-585-2500
E-mail address: admission@ smith.edu
Web site URL: www.smith.edu
Year Founded: 1871
Private or Public: Private
Religious Affiliation: None
Location: Suburban
Number of Applicants: 4,015
Percent Accepted: 47%
Percent Accepted who enroll: 34%
Number Entering: 631
Number of Transfers Accepted each Year: 119
Middle 50% SAT range: M: 590–690, CR: 600–730, Wr: 620–720
Middle 50% ACT range: 26–31
Early admission program EA/ED/None: ED
Percentage accepted through EA or ED: 9%

EA and ED deadline: 15-Nov
Regular Deadline: 15-Jan
Application Fee: $60
Full time Undergraduate enrollment: 2,588
Total enrollment: 2,588
Percent Male: 0%
Percent Female: 100%
Total Percent Minority or Unreported: 57%
Percent African-American: 5%
Percent Asian/Pacific Islander: 12%
Percent Hispanic: 7%
Percent Native-American: <1%
Percent International: 9%
Percent in-state/out of state: 22%/78%
Percent from Public HS: Unreported
Retention Rate: 90%
Graduation Rate 4-year: 83%

Graduation Rate 6-year: 88%
Percent Undergraduates in On-campus housing: 95%
Number of official organized extracurricular organizations: 100
3 Most popular majors: Economics, Political Science, Psychology
Student/Faculty ratio: 9:1
Average Class Size: 12
Percent of students going to grad school: Unreported
Tuition and Fees: $39,800
In-State Tuition and Fees if different: No difference
Cost for Room and Board: $13,390
Percent receiving financial aid out of those who apply: 70%
Percent receiving financial aid among all students: 71%

Nestled in the bright, still beauty of New England, Smith College is a women's liberal arts college full of tradition and brimming with life. Founded in 1871, it is one of the Seven Sister colleges, and a member of the Five Colleges consortium. It is among the largest women's colleges in the United States with around 2,600 undergraduates enrolled at any given time. With a strong academic standing and a vibrant residential life, Smith is a good choice for any intelligent and highly-motivated woman seeking a college education.

Academics
Smith's academic rigor is well-documented, both in liberal arts and in the sciences. Among other things, it is the only women's

college in the United States with its own accredited undergraduate engineering degree, and boasts a formidable list of 37 departmental majors, 10 interdepartmental majors, and various minors, as well as the possibility for a student to design her own major. These majors range from the commonplace such as Chemistry and Sociology down to the unique and downright weird, such as Landscape Studies. However, according to Smith official tallies, their most popular majors remain Political Science, Psychology, Art, English, Economics and Biology.

In keeping with this wide range of disciplines offered, Smith's curriculum is decidedly open-ended, with no particular mandatory classes, and indeed no requirements to take classes in any particular field. The exception to this almost complete freedom in course selection is if the student wishes to be eligible for Latin Honors or a Liberal Arts Commendation. In that case, she must have had at least one course in the seven fields of literature, history, social science, natural science, mathematics/philosophy, arts, and foreign language.

Despite being a large liberal arts college, Smith is still small in comparison with most universities. One freshman was impressed with the intimacy of classes, saying that all her small classes—generally around fifteen people—were taught by professors. "TAs are for drop-in questions," she says. However, she acknowledges that "some classes are challenging," especially those involving a great deal of reading and essay-writing. Another student concurs that "overall academics are tough, though it does vary per class."

Smith Traditions

Imagine: you wake up in the morning, groggy and grumpy, remembering you have a class in fifteen minutes. Then, you hear the bells ringing out all across campus. You throw open the curtains, and look out at a beautiful autumn day. It's Mountain Day at Smith, where all classes are cancelled in favor of enjoying the fall, and the surrounding farms are open for apple and pumpkin picking. Students appreciate the tradition and the breath of fresh air: a freshman observes that "it is a great chance to get to know your friends and housemates in a completely stress-free environment. It is just so much fun."

Mountain Day isn't the only tradition at Smith. Other events occur throughout the school year, such as the Convocation party, which is a celebration of the beginning of the fall semester and a welcoming-home party

rolled all in one, where students walk around in bizarre and creative themed attire.

Other annual traditions include Illumination night, held the weekend before commencement, where the campus is lit by candles and lanterns, and seniors are serenaded on the steps of the library before being ceremoniously pushed off the stairs, symbolizing their sudden, flailing entry into the "real world." There is very much a sense in which Smith's time-honored traditions, carried on year by year, bring living and breathing history into the course of the year.

Lifelong Friends

When asked about life at Smith, one student commented, "Social life here is pretty diverse. There are people partying and people who study all the time." Another student adds that "The typical weekly schedule is school during the day and homework at night," while "the typical weekend schedule is parties at night and homework, especially on Sundays, during the day." If anything, social life at Smith seems to be centered around the "houses," which are renovated mansions serving as self-contained dormitories. Freshmen are assigned randomly to a house, though there is the possibility to move to another house. There are various housing options, including substance-free housing, a French house, and an in-house dining co-op house.

> "[Smith] makes me more confident about myself being a woman."

Indeed, Smith's housing is exceptionally nice. Although the average single measures around 9' × 10', while the average double is 12' × 14', individual rooms vary, and there are many more singles than doubles in most houses, meaning that students will have singles for at least two years out of their four at Smith. Most houses have their own dining halls, parlors, kitchens and laundry rooms. In addition, many of the houses overlook the scenic Paradise Pond, which sports a waterfall and is hemmed with trees and spacious green lawns.

While room draws, house transfer requests and sometimes roommate assignment are handled through school administration, administration does not usually have a direct presence in the houses. Instead, two senior students, the head resident and the house coordinator, are responsible for the day-to-day running of the house, giving it an intimacy that is not usually found in large dormitories. "Every house is like a family," enthuses one student. "The house system enables us to be very close and be life-long friends."

Feminism and awareness

Smith is a women's college, and it shows. A quick glance through Smith's largest publication, *The Sophian*, reveals a sharp awareness of gender issues, as well as a rare and refreshing openness of discourse about issues such as lesbianism and transsexuality. "Public Safety's new self-defense course aims to empower women," says an article, while another opines that "transgender tolerance [. . .] can be explained just as carefully now as civil unions were back then." One current freshman feels that Smith being a women's college shapes life at Smith. When asked what Smith offers that another college couldn't, she replied, "It makes me more confident about myself being a woman."

Indeed, the same confidence lies in Smith itself, which brims with all the beloved traditions of a venerable old institution, while at the same time possessing a bold modernity in its ideas. I have roots in the past, it seems to proclaim, but my eyes are very much on the future. For the similarly bold, motivated and intelligent, Smith may well be the perfect choice.—*Sijia Song*

FYI

If you come to Smith, what should you definitely bring? "An open mind."

What is the typical weekend schedule? "Parties at night and homework, especially on Sundays, during the day."

If there's one thing you could change about Smith, what would it be? "I would not change anything. It would not be Smith if something changed."

Tufts University

Address: Bendetson Hall, 2 The Green, Medford, MA 02155

Phone: 617-627-3170

E-mail address: admissions.inquiry@ase.tufts.edu

Web site URL: www.tufts.edu

Year Founded: 1852

Private or Public: Private

Religious Affiliation: None

Location: Suburban

Number of Applicants: 15,433

Percent Accepted: 24%

Percent Accepted who enroll: 35%

Number Entering: 1,316

Number of Transfers Accepted each Year: 148

Middle 50% SAT range: M: 680–760, CR: 670–740, Wr: 680–760

Middle 50% ACT range: 30–33

Early admission program EA/ED/None: ED

Percentage accepted through EA or ED: Unreported

EA and ED deadline: 1-Nov

Regular Deadline: 1-Jan

Application Fee: $70

Full time Undergraduate enrollment: 5,150

Total enrollment: 10,026

Percent Male: 49%

Percent Female: 51%

Total Percent Minority or Unreported: 43%

Percent African-American: 5%

Percent Asian/Pacific Islander: 11%

Percent Hispanic: 6%

Percent Native-American: <1%

Percent International: 6%

Percent in-state/out of state: 33%/67%

Percent from Public HS: 59%

Retention Rate: 97%

Graduation Rate 4-year: 92%

Graduation Rate 6-year: 92%

Percent Undergraduates in On-campus housing: 62%

Number of official organized extracurricular organizations: 160

3 Most popular majors: Economics, English Language and Literature, International Relations and Affairs

Student/Faculty ratio: 9:1

Average Class Size: 15

Percent of students going to grad school: Unreported

Tuition and Fees: $41,998

In-State Tuition and Fees if different: No difference

Cost for Room and Board: $6,162

Percent receiving financial aid out of those who apply: Unreported

Percent receiving financial aid among all students: 50%

The geographical region between the cities of Somerville and Cambridge boasts some of the brightest and most talented young students in the world. Called the "Brainpower Triangle," its borders are delineated by the location of three of the top institutions in America—Harvard University, Massachusetts Institute of Technology, and Tufts University. Tufts, a private institution, is renowned for its internationalism, study abroad programs, and of course, its giant elephant mascot. Tufts is located on Walnut Hill in Medford, where diligent Jumbos trek up every morning, rain or shine (or sleet, snow, hail).

An Experimental College

Tufts is divided into 10 schools, two of which are devoted to undergraduate studies: the School of Arts and Sciences and the School of Engineering. Tufts boasts a rigorous undergraduate program focusing on interdisciplinary studies. It's no surprise then, that International Relations, which combines history, politics, humanities, and economics, is the most popular major. "I loved being an IR major—I got to learn everything I was interested in," one recent graduate said. The IR program is a department on its own, but it also "borrows" faculty from 16 other departments. But don't be fooled by the breadth of the major, because it's definitely not lacking in depth. While most majors only require six semesters of foreign languages, IR requires eight semesters.

IR is not the only area in which Tufts undergraduates excel. In addition to other programs that are typical of other liberal arts colleges, Tufts has a unique program called The Experimental College. "The oldest organization of its kind in the United States," the Ex College offers over 100 courses that explore issues of current importance and interdisciplinary courses that are not offered in the more orthodox departments. This includes the peer-taught first-year seminar programs called Explorations and Perspectives. Seniors and juniors teach these classes and are awarded graduation credit for their leadership. Some past favorites include "Beyond BeBop: Miles and Coltrane," and "Adolescent Fiction."

This involvement of the students in teaching is indicative of the Tufts academic experience as a whole. Tufts has a student-faculty ratio of seven to one, and classes rarely exceed 100 students. Most of the classes are discussion style and teaching assistants are rarely needed. "During my junior year I got to know my professors really well. They're very approachable and I've gone out to drink with one of them once!" exclaimed one senior. The caliber of professors that work at Tufts is top-notch and something that the students consider themselves lucky to have access to. Notable faculty include a former American Psychological Association president and many Nobel Prize recipients.

The Pen Is Mightier Than the Jumbo

Tufts claims the honor of the first American football game between two American colleges. Although Tufts was victorious against Harvard in 1875, athletics have been somewhat lacking in recent years. Tufts is a member of the NCAA Division III in sports and is also a member of the New England Small College Athletic Conference. While the mighty Jumbos excel in particular games such as squash and sailing, athletics is not their forte. This might be attributed either to the fact that Tufts does not offer scholarships for athletes, or "because our mascot is a gigantic elephant," one student speculated. While varsity athletics may lack in school spirit, have no fear if you are a sports buff. Tufts has a 70,000 square-foot indoor sports center which includes four tennis courts, a state-of-the-art fitness center, and a six-lane indoor pool and a sauna—everything you need to stay in shape.

> **"[A cappella] is everywhere. You can't escape it."**

If you think that trekking up the hill every morning is enough exercise for you, there are plenty of other organizations to be involved in at Tufts. If you're a singer, you can join one of Tufts's six a cappella groups. "It's everywhere," said one nonsinger. "You can't escape it." Many of these groups are award-winning and go on national tours over breaks. For instance, the Beelzebubs, or Bubs, as they are commonly called, had the esteemed a cappella honor of opening for the renowned Rockapella group this winter at their concert in downtown Boston.

If singing's not your thing, perhaps you can find your niche in one of the numerous on-campus publications. The *Tufts Daily* is where most Jumbos get their news from, and writers for the *Daily* have gone on after Tufts to be writers for the *New York Times* and the *Boston Herald*. Those looking to do journalism on the side can opt to write for the *Tufts Observer*, a weekly magazine. "The amount of work and commitment I have for the *Observer* is great—it doesn't take over my life, but it's enough for me to take it seriously," one writer said. One of the most anticipated publications on campus is *The Zamboni*, "Tufts' only intentionally funny magazine." This 16-page tabloid is issued six times during the year, and while reviews of it are mixed among the student population ("THEY seem to think it's funny"), it is your survival guide to the ins and outs of the Tufts social scene.

Fakes, Frats, and Forests

While many students may cite the school's proximity to Boston as one of the reasons why they chose to go to Tufts, in reality, most of the partying takes place on campus. Boston "sucks for underage kids" due to its strict ID-ing policy and underclassmen do not enjoy the same level of leniency with underage drinking that one may find in other big cities like New York. "Having a good fake is essential," one sophomore said. Once they are 21, Tufts kids often frequent the bars in the Medford area—the Somerville Theater is good for musical groups, and there are a few 19+ clubs that are good for a night of dancing. If you do make it to Boston for a night of fun, most of the places to go are on Lansdowne Street, where many clubs and bars are lined up for convenient "hopping around." "Avalon is the best one," said one Lansdowne Street enthusiast. "On Thursday and Friday it is 19 plus and they play really good music!"

There's plenty of partying to do on campus as well. Most of them are "keggers" thrown by frats. Tufts is very Greek-friendly, housing 11 fraternities and five sororities. While the sororities seldom throw wild, crazy parties, the frat scene is very prominent on campus as they organize large theme parties throughout the year. The Tufts administration has been "chill" about the underage drinking and partying that goes on at these frats and sees Greek life as an opportunity for Tufts students to form a community of their own and to exemplify leadership. However, students have noted that recently they have been stricter about alcohol violations than in the past.

Unfortunately, doing kegstands and going to clubs can get a little old after four years. So Tufts students take the opportunity to use the Loj, a retreat destination that is owned by Tufts and open to all of the Tufts community. Located in Woodstock, New Hampshire, the Loj offers opportunities to go skiing, hiking, apple picking, rock climbing, and swimming. To get involved in maintaining and running trips to the Loj, one can join the Tufts Mountain Club, an outdoor club dedicated to "exploring the great outdoors, physically exerting yourself," says a recent alum. So whether you have the study hard, party harder mentality of a frat brother or if you like to muse about philosophy over a fire and a glass of wine, Tufts has a little bit of something for everyone.—*Lee Komeda*

FYI

If you come to Tufts, you better bring "about 10 foldable umbrellas because chances are, you'll lose half of them and your roommate will steal the other half."

If I could change one thing about Tufts, I would change "the school color and mascot: Jumbo is just weird."

What's the typical weekend schedule? "On any given weekend you can probably find people going out to the local pubs on Thursday and Fridays. Saturday you might hit up a concert or a play and then head over to a frat house for a themed party. Sunday, if you can manage to get yourself out of bed, STUDY!"

Three things every student should do before graduating from Tufts are "take a special someone to the Library roof, have Sunday lunch at Dewick, and go to Spring Fling."

University of Massachusetts/ Amherst

Address: 37 Mather Drive, Amherst, MA 01003-9291
Phone: 413-545-0222
E-mail address: mail@admissions.umass.edu
Web site URL: www.umass.edu
Year Founded: 1863
Private or Public: Public
Religious Affiliation: None
Location: Suburban
Number of Applicants: 29,452
Percent Accepted: 68%
Percent Accepted who enroll: 21%
Number Entering: 4,563
Number of Transfers Accepted each Year: 1,991
Middle 50% SAT range: M: 540–640, CR: 520–620, Wr: Unreported
Middle 50% ACT range: 23–28

Early admission program EA/ED/None: EA
Percentage accepted through EA or ED: 75%
EA and ED deadline: 1-Nov
Regular Deadline: 15-Jan
Application Fee: $70
Full time Undergraduate enrollment: 21,373
Total enrollment: 27,569
Percent Male: 49%
Percent Female: 51%
Total Percent Minority or Unreported: 35%
Percent African-American: 3%
Percent Asian/Pacific Islander: 7%
Percent Hispanic: 7%
Percent Native-American: <1%
Percent International: 1%
Percent in-state/out of state: 74%/26%
Percent from Public HS: Unreported

Retention Rate: Unreported
Graduation Rate 4-year: 51%
Graduation Rate 6-year: 68%
Percent Undergraduates in On-campus housing: 60%
Number of official organized extracurricular organizations: 276
3 Most popular majors: Business/Marketing, Social Sciences, Psychology
Student/Faculty ratio: 19:1
Average Class Size: 25
Percent of students going to grad school: 18%
Tuition and Fees: $25,585
In-State Tuition and Fees if different: $12,797
Cost for Room and Board: $10,310
Percent receiving financial aid out of those who apply: 62%
Percent receiving financial aid among all students: 56%

Located in the largest community of Hampshire County, UMass Amherst welcomes every year more than 4,000 freshmen. The campus is located in the small town of Amherst, MA, which is 90 miles from Boston and 175 miles from New York City. UMass Amherst is part of the five public university system of the Commonwealth of Massachusetts, which includes UMass Boston, UMass Dartmouth, and UMass Lowell. While being a large research university with more than 20,000 undergraduates, students seem to agree that there is a place for everyone at UMass.

Party School! or Party School?

Although for a long time UMass Amherst has maintained the reputation of a large "party school," students say it is a matter of choice and relativity. Students note that while there are parties every night in different dorms, at off-campus houses, and especially at fraternities, and some people start their weekend early, there is no pressure to do so. People party as much as they want and as much as they can afford. "Social life in college is all up to the individual. There are plenty of opportunities to be social but people don't have to be," comments a freshman. One student points out that UMass Amherst might seem like a party school because it is bigger in size, and therefore able to host more parties, but that in comparison to smaller schools, the ratio is the same.

Speaking of parties and weekend fun, the Greek scene is very popular at UMass Amherst. Parties organized at fraternities and sororities often have long waiting lines and there is an admission fee for most of them, a student noted. A considerable amount of the student population participates, since there are ten fraternities and sororities on campus. And if you are worried about the hazing to mark your initiation in the Greek life, don't be. There is no hazing allowed for fraternities or sororities at UMass Amherst.

That's right, it is against school policy to make freshmen haze for acceptance; it is also against state law.

Yet, while fraternities and athletics cover a large part of the social scene, students report enjoying the size of the school, as it does not allow for a dominant group, or specific cliques to be formed, since there are so many different people. Also, the number of students makes it easy to meet new people, and feel like you are in a new place every day, a freshman commented.

If you are worried of walking around the campus at night while coming back from a party, students said that there is no need. Apart from intoxicated students coming back, students report feeling safe and able to walk at night. One student commented, "It is a safe place, you just need to look out for drunk kids doing stupid stuff."

If parties on campus are not to your liking, you can always leave the campus and explore Amherst. While students noted that Amherst's scenery is certainly not urban, many love it! Students agreed that there are a lot of good pizza places to eat around town, and great coffee shops. However, students complain that there aren't enough shops close to their residences. One freshman noted, "It is a hassle to take the bus everywhere to go shopping." And while some upperclassmen have cars, students said that it is uncommon for freshmen.

Five at the Price of One

One unique aspect of the academic experience at UMass Amherst is the ability to attend five schools at the same time, students comment. Through the Five College Consortium, which is a partnership between five schools which include Smith, Mount Holyoke, Amherst, and Hampshire Colleges, UMass Amherst students, upon the completion of their first semester, can take classes for credit at the other four colleges. Students comment that in doing so they have the chance to broaden the range of people they know and friends they meet. What's more, students can have their meals, and use resources such as libraries, and borrowing books at all colleges.

"The only way to get a desired result in class is to go to every class, pay attention, do homework, and study hard," one freshman says. Students report that studying and homework take up most of their time. They agree that the party scene is present, but mostly on weekends. Most students have class every day, from Monday to Friday, and

they study during the day on weekends, and party later.

Almost 90 majors are offered to students, as well as the possibility to minor in distinct fields of study. If students feel that none of the majors fully encompasses all their interests and future career paths, they can construct their own program of study, through the Bachelor's Degree with Individual Concentration, which allows students to design their own majors.

Most people, though, report finding something they love at UMass Amherst and even enjoying the general requirements they have to fulfill in order to get their degree. These requirements include one class in writing, basic math skills, analytical reasoning, biological and physical world, social world, interdisciplinary courses, social and cultural diversity. However, students report finding it easy to fulfill these requirements, even though only one of the courses taken in their major department counts towards their requirements, and they add that they can even take many classes that interest them. They do however express unhappiness at finding that there is a great focus on the research aspect of the school, and not as much undergraduate focus as they expected. One freshman comments, "I was surprised that Teacher's Assistants teach my discussion sections."

Minutemen Cribs

UMass Amherst students are diverse in their personalities and interests, and so are their places of residence. A freshman commented that there are distinct personalities and characteristics associated with each dorm, such as "the athletes'" dorm, "the blonde-girl" dorm, the "party" dorm, the "geek" dorm. Many students are assigned to specific dorms on the basis of interest and major for students who declare their major upon matriculation through the Talent Advancement Programs. TAP is designed to group students with similar interests, so that it is easier for the RAs to organize activities and trips specifically oriented towards the students' interests. Many students reported this to be something they would change about their school, because it disables them from befriending people of different interests. For freshmen that matriculate with an undeclared major, residences are assigned through a lottery system, where students rank where they want to live on campus by building during orientation. There are five living areas at UMass Amherst from which students can choose to live in, Southwest, Central, Orchard Hill, North East, and Sylvan. They all vary in architecture and organization. Each of them has its pros and cons, a student commented. While freshmen don't complain about their residences, they agreed that most of the upperclassmen do not live on campus, since the area around offers an accessible residential situation.

In the midst of these five residential areas, UMass students can choose between a variety of housing options ranging from gender free and same-sex housing, co-ed suites, alcohol-free twenty-four hour quiet floors, as well as the Thatcher Language program, which is targeted towards students seeking to achieve proficiency in a foreign language. And for students who don't want to live in a dorm anymore but still want to remain on campus, the university offers the North Apartment program which enables students to rent an apartment right on campus. Groups of students, co-ed or same-sex can get together and apply for housing in these apartments.

> "Everyone can fit in somewhere at UMass. Go Minutemen!"

Most students are content with the food served in the dining halls. There are four dining halls on the campus, and all students can have their meals at either of them, or at any of the other colleges' dining halls. Students have the choice of having an unlimited meal plan or a more restricted one. Students highly recommended the unlimited one. One freshman noted, "The dining hall has incredible food and a lot of diversity among the meals. There is sushi, stir fry, a sandwich line, a grill station, a salad bar, a vegetarian section and a main meal line that changes throughout the day. Something for everyone." And if you get tired of cafeteria food, you can always use your flex swipe at the on-campus stores and restaurants, though the swipes don't work in the local businesses.

The University has implemented many reconstructions of residences and academic buildings, in their dedication to emphasize the academic aspect of the university, and subdue the rumors of its party-oriented nature, a student suggested. Southwest, one of the residences, is in the process of being renovated and should be finished by next year, a student commented.

As far as substance abuse goes, drugs and alcohol are strictly prohibited by school rules in all the dormitories, but students say that it depends on their RA's policies; some are more lenient than others. And while laws and restrictions apply, a lot of people drink but certainly not everyone. Students commented that while most parties are thrown by upperclassmen that have an easier access to alcohol, it is fairly easy for freshmen and sophomores to have access to alcohol as well.

If you are used to warm and predictable weather, you might want to reconsider your wardrobe. New England weather can be harsh, so bring your jacket, scarf and gloves! As one freshman comments, "If I could change one thing about UMass Amherst I'd put it in a warm climate, it is damn cold and windy." Yet, while the weather might be challenging, many students love their experience. As a freshman stated, "The atmosphere in Amherst is great. Everyone is very friendly and happy to be at UMass. There is a lot of diversity and clubs. Everyone can fit in somewhere at UMass. Go Minutemen!"—*Iva Popa*

FYI
If you come to UMass Amherst you better bring "snacks, laptop, and an alarm clock."
One thing I would change about my school is "adding more stores on campus."
Three things every student should do before graduating from UMass Amherst: "Meet with a professor, go to athletic events, and meet as many people as possible.

Wellesley College

Address: 106 Central Street, Wellesley, MA 02481-8203
Phone: 781-283-2270
E-mail address: admission@wellesley.edu
Web site URL: www.wellesley.edu
Year Founded: 1870
Private or Public: Private
Religious Affiliation: None
Location: Suburban
Number of Applicants: 4,001
Percent Accepted: 31%
Percent Accepted who enroll: 41%
Number Entering: 573
Number of Transfers Accepted each Year: 20
Middle 50% SAT range: M: 640–750, CR: 650–740, Wr: 660–750
Middle 50% ACT range: 29–32
Early admission program EA/ED/None: ED

Percentage accepted through EA or ED: 45%
EA and ED deadline: 1-Nov
Regular Deadline: 15-Jan
Application Fee: $50/free online
Full time Undergraduate enrollment: 2,502
Total enrollment: unreported
Percent Male: 0%
Percent Female: 100%
Total Percent Minority or Unreported: 58%
Percent African-American: 6%
Percent Asian/Pacific Islander: 23%
Percent Hispanic: 23%
Percent Native-American: 0%
Percent International: 12%
Percent in-state/out of state: 14%/86%
Percent from Public HS: 64%
Retention Rate: 96%

Graduation Rate 4-year: 85%
Graduation Rate 6-year: 91%
Percent Undergraduates in On-campus housing: 93%
Number of official organized extracurricular organizations: 160
3 Most popular majors: Social Sciences, Area and Ethnic Std., Biology
Student/Faculty ratio: 8:1
Average Class Size: 15
Percent of students going to grad school: Unreported
Tuition and Fees: $40,660
In-State Tuition and Fees if different: No difference
Cost for Room and Board: $12,590
Percent receiving financial aid out of those who apply: 81%
Percent receiving financial aid among all students: 56%

I n 1870, Henry and Pauline Durant founded Wellesley to give young women a college education as rigorous as that of their male peers. Since then, Wellesley has graduated a large number of famous alumnae, including former Secretary of State Madeleine Albright and Secretary of State Hillary Clinton. Although the college's cachet may have diminished a little after the spread of coeducation, the passion, drive, and college pride of Wellesley students is as strong as ever.

Bankers and Bluestockings

Schoolwork is king—or should we say, queen. Its liberal arts curriculum expects students to fulfill writing, quantitative reasoning, and foreign language requirements, and take classes in eight of nine distribution areas. In addition, they need to meet the multicultural requirement, studying one unit's worth of non-Western culture. Despite the breadth of the curriculum, students say that the variety of classes makes fulfilling requirements both easy and enjoyable. As one first-year said,

"Even if you're not interested in a certain field, you can find something you enjoy." A junior who had completed her requirements sophomore year concurred: "It's really not difficult to fulfill anything."

With 30 departmental and 21 interdepartmental majors, Wellesley offers over 1,000 courses in a diverse selection of academic fields—and Wellesley women love the intellectual buffet. Students were enthusiastic about a wide variety of classes, including seminars on environmentalism, the History of Western Music, and "1968," a course devoted entirely to—you guessed it—the year 1968. One first-year student said she had met people doubling majors like "biology and political science [or] Latin American studies and music." Students agree, however, that the economics department is a big presence on campus. According to data released by the Wellesley College Office for Public Affairs, 15 percent of the Wellesley class of 2009 majored in economics and nearly 30 percent went to work in business after graduation. "A lot of Econ people are trying to go into banking and finance," a junior explained. Other popular majors include political science and psychology. Although students may not declare majors in math and hard sciences in droves, one science major praised the all-female environment for cultivating interest in physics, chemistry, and math, fields that are traditionally underrepresented among women.

Students also praised the professors, who "really want students to talk to them and come to them with any problems," as one junior said. With a 9:1 student-faculty ratio, classes tend toward the intimate. This same junior named the small class sizes as her favorite thing about Wellesley's academics: "I think it makes you a lot more into your work, wanting to participate and be a part of the class." In addition, Wellesley professors tend to be both highly knowledgeable and able to transmit their knowledge to their students. Some have even written the textbooks for the classes they teach. This marriage of availability and fluency in their subject matter makes the professors one of the college's greatest assets.

> **"I've met nerdy music people and nerdy politics people . . . Everyone here is nerdy about something."**

The Wellesley workload is no joke. Academics take priority over socializing and extracurricular activities, and it shows. "During the week it's just silent, because everyone here is studying," a first-year said. Still, challenging classes don't translate into C's across the board. In 100- and 200-level classes with ten or more students, professors are required to create a curve with a B+ average. (In 300-level classes or higher, or in classes with fewer than ten students, no curve exists.) This works to students' advantage in math and science classes, while the humanities and social science departments tend to "scale down" the averages because their students usually receive higher grades. As one psychology major described, straight-A students are "either incredibly energetic and brilliant—or they study constantly, don't really socialize, and are otherwise psychotic."

Better get crazy!

Suburban Riches, Boston Fun

Wellesley is a small, affluent town outside of Boston. Students say there's not too much interaction between students and residents; and as one student put it, "I think the extent of our relationship with the town is walking into town to CVS and to the bank." Two problems keep the college from embracing its town. First, the average college student doesn't have the money for the expensive restaurants and boutiques that the town of Wellesley offers. Second, the town is, in the words of a junior, "not a real town." Simply put, Wellesley's just not big enough to support the pizza places, concert halls, and dance clubs that would draw student interest.

But while students may consider the rich suburban-family demographics of Wellesley a drawback, the town does have some perks. Students are able to find well-paying jobs easily. Babysitting is especially popular— "The people in town are so rich, they pay really well," a junior said.

But despite living in the suburbs, students still have the city just a short ride away. Wellesley's proximity to Boston keeps students connected to urban living. The city is "very accessible" from Wellesley, and it offers good entertainment to young women about town. As one student said, "Boston always has concerts, shopping, whatever you want to do." Trips to Boston aren't exclusive to upperclasswomen. All students flock to Boston for weekend entertainment.

Wellesley Women, Cutting Loose

While an all-female student body may sound like a drag to some, Wellesley women know that single-sex education doesn't lack fun. The Wellesley Senate bus runs a route from Wellesley to the Boston-Cambridge area and back every hour. While MIT frat parties are the most popular destination, a number of colleges in the Boston area host good parties, and students choose which to attend based on the people they know at a given school. The bus goes both ways as well: "We have parties here, and guys will come from Harvard, MIT, Babson, BU, BC, Tufts . . ."

While some Wellesley students celebrate the wealth of parties in the Boston area as an opportunity to meet new people, form a larger community, and meet guys, others dislike the artificiality such party-based interactions promote. One sophomore said, "Personally, only seeing men in a frat-party atmosphere tends to reinforce negative stereotypes about them—that is, they're usually trying to hook up with girls" rather than anything more. Because of the lack of male-female interaction in a more day-to-day casual environment, "it takes a very determined individual to go out and make male friends" as opposed to just hooking up. A first-year commented that her good male friends were the boyfriends of girls on campus.

Of course, one doesn't need men to have friends, or even to date. The lesbian and bisexual community is visible and active on campus. The largest annual party at Wellesley is the Dyke Ball, which began as a prom for students who were unable to attend their high school proms due to their sexual orientation. The Ball is now a campus-wide bash to which all Wellesley students can come and cut loose.

Wellesley students definitely don't need to make the trek to find close friends. Wellesley students will sometimes say that they don't need sororities "because we're all one big sorority." One first-year said she decided to matriculate at Wellesley because of how nice the students were: "Everyone is friendly. Upperclassmen will give you directions, help you with your homework." In addition, the sisterly atmosphere creates a level of freedom in intellectual and social self-expression that many students did not have in high school: "I've met nerdy music people and nerdy politics people . . . Everyone here is nerdy about something. That might be our defining feature. Even the cool kids—there's something like, 'Oh my God, I love physics!' or 'Astronomy is the coolest thing ever!'"

Diversity at Wellesley is more than intellectual. In race, socioeconomic status, political affiliation, and sexual orientation, Wellesley students represent a wide range of experiences. One student remarked, "There've been a ton of times, in a party or in a room, where I've realized I'm the only white person there." Another mentioned, "I have friends who are really rich and really poor." And while the political climate does tend toward the liberal, there is a conservative presence on campus. One first-year student said, "One of my roommates is a Ron Paul supporter, so that was interesting, what with the four pictures of Hillary Clinton on my wall."

Four Flavors at Every Meal

In a Wellesley student's first year, she is assigned a dorm. Each floor has a Resident Assistant, who is a student, and a Resident Director, an adult who usually lives in the dorm with her family. The strictness of dorm policy varies, depending on the RA and RD. After the first year, a lottery system determines what order students get to choose their rooms. Seniors get the first group of random numbers, then juniors, and then sophomores. Students said juniors and seniors are pretty much guaranteed singles. Dorms don't have official themes, but each have their own characteristics. Some dorms are considered party dorms, while another is known for being more reclusive, and still another is the "lesbian social scene" dorm. Students said the new dorms by the science center have larger rooms and quieter surroundings, but not as much character as the older buildings.

While students at many other colleges complain of monotonous meals and poorly cooked food, Wellesley women are positive about their dining halls. Wellesley students are on one of the most flexible meal plans possible—they can eat at any dining hall, at any time, as many times a day as they want. And nearly every dorm, as well as the student center, features a dining hall. Although each hall is supposed to have a theme, some are "hard to decipher." As one first-year student explained, "One of them is supposed to be comfort food, but they serve basically the same food my dorm serves, which is supposed to be eclectic cuisine." Despite the sameness, a student said, "I think that in comparison to other schools, the food is quite good, and the management does a good job of listening to student suggestions."

Apparently, one alumna thought that the dining halls lacked something, so she donated money so that every hall would have four different flavors of ice cream every day, at every meal. Do you need another reason to apply to Wellesley?—*Finola Prendergast*

FYI

If you come to Wellesley, you'd better bring "a nice dress, because there are a lot of times where you need to wear a dress."

What's the typical weekend schedule? "If you're one of those people who's into partying, you'd probably go off campus to Harvard or MIT Friday or Saturday night, and study Sunday. Or go to Boston and shop and eat out."

If I could change one thing about Wellesley, I'd have "more on-campus social life instead of stuff in Boston."

Three things every student at Wellesley should do before graduating are "see the campus from the top of Galen-Stone Tower, skinny dip in Lake Waban, and swing next to the Chapel."

Wheaton College

Address: 26 East Main Street, Norton, MA 02766
Phone: 508-286-8251
E-mail address: admission@wheatoncollege.edu
Web site URL: www.wheatoncollege.edu
Year Founded: 1834
Private or Public: Private
Religious Affiliation: None
Location: Rural
Number of Applicants: 3,833
Percent Accepted: 60%
Percent Accepted who enroll: 30%
Number Entering: 437
Number of Transfers Accepted each Year: 57
Middle 50% SAT range: M: 580–660, CR: 580–680, Wr: Unreported
Middle 50% ACT range: 26–30
Early admission program EA/ED/None: ED

Percentage accepted through EA or ED: 84%
EA and ED deadline: 15-Nov
Regular Deadline: 15-Jan
Application Fee: $55
Full time Undergraduate enrollment: 1,622
Total enrollment: unreported
Percent Male: 36%
Percent Female: 64%
Total Percent Minority or Unreported: 32%
Percent African-American: 5%
Percent Asian/Pacific Islander: 3%
Percent Hispanic: 3%
Percent Native-American: 0%
Percent International: 11%
Percent in-state/out of state: 32%/68%
Percent from Public HS: 63%
Retention Rate: 88%

Graduation Rate 4-year: 79%
Graduation Rate 6-year: 79%
Percent Undergraduates in On-campus housing: 95%
Number of official organized extracurricular organizations: 60
3 Most popular majors: Social Sciences, Psychology, Visual and Performing Arts
Student/Faculty ratio: 11:1
Average Class Size: 15
Percent of students going to grad school: 43%
Tuition and Fees: $41,894
In-State Tuition and Fees if different: No difference
Cost for Room and Board: $10,670
Percent receiving financial aid out of those who apply: unreported
Percent receiving financial aid among all students: unreported

Wheaton is a small liberal arts school located in the sleepy town of Norton, Massachusetts. It boasts a challenging and varied academic program where students can take classes in everything from dreams to globalization. The Wheaton community is a close-knit group where even the RAs just want to be your friend. Wheaton students have a thriving extracurricular and social scene that is greatly benefited by the campus's location between Providence and Boston, two cities just begging to be explored by car-owning and train-hopping Wheaties.

The Right Balance

Most Wheaton students are very happy with the academic environment of their campus. "The academics are just right," said one freshman. "I'm not overstressed, but I'm being challenged. And here we have the ability to do well in school and be involved in other activities, too." Popular majors include English and education. Education, along with the natural sciences, is said to be one of the hardest majors because the program involves student teaching and requires that students double major. Wheaton is thought of as more of a humanities school, but the administration is beginning an increased focus on science. They have implemented a plan to rebuild all the science buildings on campus by 2014 and are seen as being very encouraging of students pursuing science majors.

Classes are small, usually 10 to 19 students, except in some introductory lectures. Students say that professors are very committed to getting to know them and being a part of their intellectual growth. "One of my professors gave us extra credit just for coming to her office hours so she could get to know us," said one Wheatie. There are no TAs at Wheaton, further enhancing the personalized touch. Though the professors are friendly and helpful, they are tough. Students don't think there is much grade inflation at all at Wheaton and also report relatively few curves. They stress that one must work hard to do well.

Wheaton students say their distribution requirements, called "foundation courses," are reasonable and they have an interesting array of classes in which to fill them. Foundation courses include a first-year seminar, English 101, a math course, two semesters of a foreign language, and one semester of "Beyond the West," i.e., a class that deals with a culture outside of Western society. In first-year seminars, groups of 20 freshmen become acclimated to Wheaton academic life in a laid-back atmosphere while studying topics that vary from "Surgeons and Shamans" to "The Rituals of Dinner." Wheaton also has a program called Connections, where students are able to choose a set of related courses that interest them. Examples of Connections include "Human Biology and Movement," "Modern Italy," and "Music: the Medium and the Message." Students say the Connections courses are an interesting way to fulfill requirements. Wheaties also take advantage of the fact that their college is a part of the 12-college consortium that includes, among others, Amherst, Bowdoin, Wellesley, and Dartmouth. Wheaton students can attend a college in the consortium for a semester or a year. Wheaton also offers numerous and very popular opportunities for study abroad.

A Perfect New England Family

Nearly every student has high praises for the sense of community at Wheaton. "One of the things I noticed at accepted students' day that I didn't notice at other schools was how friendly everyone was," one freshman said. Wheaton upperclassmen are especially enthusiastic about making sure new students feel welcome and are aware of the importance of not making novice Wheatie mistakes. During freshman orientation, upperclassmen herd confused freshmen into the chapel where they begin to chant the incoming class's graduation year. After the chanting, an upperclassman runs through the chapel and squirts water on an unsuspecting frosh who automatically inherits this illustrious job. Besides being simply funny, this tradition emphasizes Wheaton's fun and family-like atmosphere. The fact that Wheaton's student body numbers fewer than 1,600 seems to be an important reason for this. "I like that it is a small school because I can get to know a lot of people well, but still see a few new faces every day," reported one girl. Additionally, "the importance of acceptance and friendship are stressed at Wheaton," says one Wheatie.

In a testament to their widespread acceptance of difference, students are quick to say that there is no "typical" Wheaton student. When pressed, they will admit that most students are middle- or upper-class and from Massachusetts, Maine, Connecticut, and surprisingly, California. "For some reason, lots of people in California know about Wheaton. I guess they like small liberal arts schools," explained one Wheatie. Another trait that bonds Wheaton students together is being physically fit. A large segment of students is involved in athletic endeavors that vary from varsity sports to the equestrian team to intramurals. There are no sororities and fraternities at Wheaton, and many say that the *a cappella* groups function as a more positive version of the Greek system. *A cappella* is very popular at Wheaton, as are a wide range of other extracurricular activities, especially community service groups. "Wheaton has a lot to offer—there's always something to join," explains one Wheatie.

Though they don't like to be typecast, Wheaton students as a whole can be summed up as both studious and typical preppy New England kids. They seem particularly fond of The North Face fleeces, colorful rain boots, and for the female students, designer purses. Wheaton students admit that their campus is not incredibly diverse, though the administration is working hard to change that. Wheaton boasts a thriving cultural center, the Marshall Center for Intercultural Learning, and is involved in a scholarship program called the Posse Foundation. New York City minority students receive scholarships to Wheaton in groups called posses, which helps them feel less isolated while increasing Wheaton's racial diversity.

Road Trippers

On any given weekend, a large contingent of the Wheaton student body can be found in Boston, which is 40 minutes away, or Providence, about 20. Transportation couldn't be easier since many students have cars and the school offers a shuttle that runs every 30 minutes to a nearby train station. Wheaties love hitting the restaurants, theaters, and club scenes of these two New England cities. The administration encourages their students to take advantage of what their excellent location has to offer. Through the Boston and Providence Connections programs, students pay just five dollars for dinner and a concert or play on select nights. A premium outlet mall is very close to campus, giving Wheaton fashionistas yet another attractive weekend option.

Wheaton students' obvious devotion to Boston and Providence trips shouldn't be seen as a sign that there is nothing to do at Wheaton. Some students admitted that some weekends on campus are a little slow, but there are usually a wide variety of on-campus activities to choose from. The Balfour-Hood Campus Center hosts well-attended theme parties in its large lobby, called the Atrium. Wheaton often hosts concerts as well. Recently, students were surprised when a subsidized concert by a Persian pop star, which they wrote off as random and amusing, was packed with outsiders who happily shelled out $40 a ticket.

> "I know that this might seem pretty lame, but Wheaton really would not function in the same way without the common bond and sense of belonging that the students and professors share."

Wheaton has a campus bar, the Loft, where students can get burgers, pizza, and alcohol "if you're over 21 or have an ID that says you are." Wheaton's 11 theme houses also throw popular parties. The Lyon's Den is the campus coffee shop, and serves as a popular hangout and a more laid-back alternative to the Loft. Though many social events seem to revolve around alcohol, students report not feeling much pressure either way. The administration is fairly lax on students who do drink, and Wheaties are very accepting of students who don't.

Endless Food, and Not Just Wheaties

Most students have good things to say about Wheaton's dining system. They have unlimited access to the two dining halls, one of which stays open until midnight. Pizza and ice cream seem to be available at all times, though there are more nutritious family style options available as well. Unlimited access makes some students grow weary of the selection. "I like the food, but sometimes I get tired of it," said one girl. When this happens, students head to the nearby town of Mansfield to eat at chains like Subway.

The campus is pretty, secluded, and very Ivy League-esque with ivy-covered brick and a quaint pond that surrounds the Chase Dining Hall. The campus is not very big, which adds to the community atmosphere and also helps Wheaties easily get where they need to go. Students like their dorms when there are a proper number of people living in them. Some freshmen find themselves in forced triples on Lower Campus. Upperclassmen, on the other hand, often live on Upper Campus in newly renovated dorms that "are like hotels," said one envious freshman.

Wheaton students are overwhelmingly very pleased with their college. "I know that this might seem pretty lame, but Wheaton really would not function in the same way without the common bond and sense of belonging that the students and professors share," said one Wheatie. The combination of Wheaton's strong sense of community, challenging but manageable academics, and prime location make it a great place to spend four years.
—*Keneisha Sinclair*

FYI

If you come to Wheaton, you'd better bring "rain boots and a DVD player because there's no cable."

What is the typical weekend schedule? "Napping after last class on Friday, trips to Boston and Providence, dances at the theme houses and concerts at the Loft, playing in or going to see a game, and lots of homework on Sunday."

If I could change one thing about Wheaton, I'd "make Norton more exciting."

Three things every student at Wheaton should do before graduating are "jump in the pond, study abroad or do a college exchange, and get really involved in a Wheaton extracurricular activity."

Williams College

Address: 33 Stetson Court, Williamstown, MA 01267
Phone: 413-597-2211
E-mail address: admission@williams.edu
Web site URL: www.williams.edu
Year Founded: 1793
Private or Public: Private
Religious Affiliation: None
Location: Rural
Number of Applicants: 6,478
Percent Accepted: 19%
Percent Accepted who enroll: 45%
Number Entering: 548
Number of Transfers Accepted each Year: 12
Middle 50% SAT range: M: 650–760, CR: 660–770, Wr: Unreported
Middle 50% ACT range: 29–34
Early admission program EA/ED/None: ED

Percentage accepted through EA or ED: 40%
EA and ED deadline: 10-Nov
Regular Deadline: 1-Jan
Application Fee: $60
Full time Undergraduate enrollment: 2,029
Total enrollment: 2,083
Percent Male: 47%
Percent Female: 53%
Total Percent Minority or Unreported: 41%
Percent African-American: 8%
Percent Asian/Pacific Islander: 11%
Percent Hispanic: 11%
Percent Native-American: <1%
Percent International: 7%
Percent in-state/out of state: 13%/87%
Percent from Public HS: 58%
Retention Rate: 97%

Graduation Rate 4-year: 91%
Graduation Rate 6-year: 91%
Percent Undergraduates in On-campus housing: 93%
Number of official organized extracurricular organizations: 110
3 Most popular majors: Social Sciences, Visual and Performing Arts, Biology
Student/Faculty ratio: 7:1
Average Class Size: 9
Percent of students going to grad school: Unreported
Tuition and Fees: $43,190
In-State Tuition and Fees if different: No difference
Cost for Room and Board: $11,370
Percent receiving financial aid out of those who apply: 82%
Percent receiving financial aid among all students: 53%

Founded in 1793 thanks to funds bequeathed by Colonel Ephraim Williams, Williams is a small liberal arts school known for its rigorous academics and picturesque setting. The college is nestled among the Berkshire Mountains in the northwest corner of Massachusetts, a peaceful location about 135 miles from Boston and 165 miles from New York City. Williams boasts an extremely close-knit community that abounds with extracurricular and athletic opportunities.

No Rest for the Weary

One sophomore summed up academics at Williams by stating that "it's very hard to get an A." Academics are known for their rigor, and students generally spend a large part of their days reading and studying. According to another student, "everyone agrees that we work a lot more here than our friends at other schools," and another added that many people "get up early or stay up late to finish their work."

However, students are quick to add that the academic environment is not competitive, but instead "all about collaboration."

The school offers several centers where students can seek help on homework, have a tutor edit a paper, or improve their study skills. Students often work together on problem sets or help friends study for tests. One student declared, "I've been astounded by how willing people are to help."

Students are also pleased with the small class sizes and "personal" feel of academic life. With a student-faculty ratio of seven to one, many classes tend to be around 25 students or fewer. Professors are almost always willing to meet with students outside of class, and occasionally join students for coffee or invite them to dinner. One student proclaimed, "You're not a number. The professors know your name. That's one of the things that first drew me to Williams, and it's definitely true!"

"You're not a number. The professors know your name."

This intimate classroom environment is epitomized by the school's unique tutorial system. Modeled after the tutorial systems of Oxford and Cambridge, the tutorial system spans many disciplines, including the math and science departments. Topics range from a physics tutorial about electromagnetic theory to an economics department course on higher education. Every week, two students meet with one professor to discuss a topic and debate their weekly papers (or, in math and science tutorials, problem sets). Students praise the tutorials for "the opportunity to really learn about a topic in depth," despite the heavy workload. More than half of Williams students graduate having taken one, and some even take two or three.

Williams requires students to take three courses in each of three divisions: Languages and the Arts, Social Studies, and Science and Mathematics. In addition, students must take one course that fulfills the "Exploring Diversity Initiative" requirement, a course that involves quantitative reasoning, and two writing-intensive courses. Finally, students must complete four quarters of physical education, which can be fulfilled by playing a team sport or by taking classes ranging from rock climbing to golf. Most students say that they don't have a problem completing the requirements, since such a broad range of courses are offered that fulfill each distribution. In fact, one sophomore even proclaimed, "I like the requirements!" because it encourages students to dabble in subjects they might otherwise never have tried.

Students also love the freedom offered by Williams' 4-1-4 schedule: four-month fall and spring semesters, with a one-month Winter Study term in January. During Winter Study, students study a variety of unusual topics outside the normal curriculum. Past courses have included "Inside Jury Deliberations" and "Contemporary American Songwriting." Students can also submit their own proposal for a Winter Study project. Many students take advantage of the break to study abroad and take travel classes in locations as varied as Egypt, Vietnam, and Nicaragua. Those who choose to stay on campus take advantage of the lighter academic load—most classes only meet for about 10 hours a week—to meet new people, go skiing, or party.

Popular majors include psychology, economics, biology, history, English, and political science. The art history department is also "world-renowned," with several art museums a short walk away from campus. One student insisted that "everyone should take an art history course while they're here. You can read about an artist for class and then go see one of his paintings a block away!" Study abroad options abound, including the unique Williams-Exeter at Oxford University, in which Williams students become full members of Oxford and gain access to all of its resources. Other opportunities include the Williams-Mystic Program for maritime studies in Mystic, Connecticut, and the new Williams in Africa program.

Williams offers a wide range of academic opportunities, and students are eager to rise to the occasion. As one student put it, "The intelligence of everyone here just blows my mind! Not every conversation here revolves around intellectual ideas, but when you talk to people, it's clear they're really smart."

Purple Mountains and Purple Cows

"Although Williams is a small school, you'd be surprised by how diverse the student body is," one student asserted. "We're not a J. Crew commercial." The campus is "increasingly diverse" geographically and economically, with growing numbers of international students. A sophomore said, "People always surprise me here. Although there are preppy kids, lacrosse guys, and hippie types, no one is one-dimensional." In general, students were characterized as being friendly, outgoing, and athletic. Another student added, "People here do a good job of meeting people outside of their usual 'groups.' Athletes participate in theater. You end up making friends with people from all over."

The vast majority of Williams students, or "Ephs," are involved in one or more extracurricular activities. As one sophomore commented, "Sleep is a very precious commodity. Everyone here is so busy!" Popular activities include a capella groups, dance, and theater, including Cap and Bells—the oldest continuously running student-run college theater group in the country. The Williams Outing Club, which organizes trips and rents equipment for hiking, rock climbing, and winter sports, is also big. Other activities include the student newspaper, the student radio station, and a wide variety of religious organizations. Many students also hold jobs, whether working as tour guides, tutors, or at the library.

About half of all students participate in intercollegiate sports, whether on one of the varsity level or JV teams, or through the club and intramural programs. Williams is consistently ranked as the top Division III school. Popular sports include football, basketball, and crew. In the winter, many people take advantage of Williams' proximity to the mountains to go skiing and snowboarding. The school's athletic complex boasts a pool, squash courts, an ice rink, and a golf course. One sophomore said, "I would have never considered myself an athlete before coming to Williams, but I've really enjoyed participating in sports since I got here."

Even non-athletes enjoy attending games, especially those against rival Amherst. As one junior emphasized, "Even if sports aren't your thing, Williams has a ton of things to do. One of the things I love about Williams is how supportive everyone is of each other—people will cheer on their friends whether they're on the field, on the stage, or just taking a test. School spirit is really strong. Our school color, purple, and the purple cow mascot are everywhere!"

From Entryways to JAs

The freshman housing system was unanimously praised. Incoming freshmen are divided into groups of around 20 students, or "entries," who live in the same vertical or horizontal section of a freshman dorm. Each entry has two Junior Advisors (JAs), who host study breaks during exams, organize trips to see plays or concerts, and occasionally throw parties. JAs are there to make sure that freshmen stay safe and have fun, and do not police students' behavior. Applying to become a JA is an extremely competitive process.

"I became really good friends with the people in my entryway," said one student. "We went to dinner together, we played sports together, and I ended up really getting to know people that I probably wouldn't have met if we hadn't been living in the same entryway." Many freshmen have singles, and while upperclassmen have the option of a double, they are "pretty much guaranteed a single," according to several students.

Upperclassmen live in four clusters, or "neighborhoods," as part of a recent effort by the college to help foster a sense of community similar to that provided by residential houses at other universities. One senior quipped, "It's supposed to be like Harry Potter." Neighborhoods get money to host events, such as barbeques, movies, and dance parties, which students say helps add to the number and variety of events available. The vast majority of students live on-campus all four years, although some seniors choose to live off campus or in Williams-owned "co-ops."

With three dining halls and several snack shops to choose from, students enjoy a wide variety of food, which they describe as "pretty good." That's important, because Williamstown (although very charming) is tiny. One student summed it up: "It's pretty. It's also in the middle of nowhere." Spring Street, the town's main thoroughfare, consists of a few shops, a bar, a bank, and a smattering of ethnic restaurants. Although some students say that the town's small size can feel stifling, one student proclaimed, "Actually, my favorite thing about Williams is that it's rural. The lack of nightlife means that everything people do happens on campus, and promotes more passion for extracurriculars." The college helps compensate for the town's remoteness by funding lots of student activities, and bringing plays, speakers, and DJs to campus. Since there are no fraternities or sororities, parties typically take place in dorm rooms or off-campus houses. All-Campus Entertainment (ACE) also hosts several well-attended theme parties, such as Winter Carnival and Spring Fling. Although a good proportion of students drink, there are plenty of options for those who choose not to imbibe. The student center even hosts a weekly "Stressbusters" event, where students can get free massages and hot drinks.

Students appreciate the college's effort to bring the outside world to campus, raving, "there's always something going on. There is so much more to do than we have time for!" That said, most students say that they appreciate their friends and fellow students most of all. "Some of my best days at Williams have been spent just hanging out with my friends and talking late into the night," one junior said. "This is a great place. There's a real sense that we're all in this together."
—*Elizabeth Chrystal*

FYI

If you come to Williams, you'd better bring "a sense of humor for outrageous jokes, including but not limited to people streaking!"

What's the typical weekend schedule? "Go to a sporting event, take advantage of DJs, plays, and dance shows on campus, party in a friend's dorm. Sunday—work!"

If I could change one thing about Williams, I'd "cut down on the workload a bit to be able to take advantage of more of the extracurricular opportunities."

Worcester Polytechnic Institute

Address: 100 Institute Road, Worcester, MA 01609
Phone: 508-831-5286
E-mail address: admissions@wpi.edu
Web site URL: www.wpi.edu
Year Founded: 1865
Private or Public: Private
Religious Affiliation: None
Location: Suburban
Number of Applicants: 5,698
Percent Accepted: 57%
Percent Accepted who enroll: 22%
Number Entering: 1,005
Number of Transfers Accepted each Year: 65
Middle 50% SAT range: M: 640–730, CR 560–670, Wr: 560–660
Middle 50% ACT range: 27–31
Early admission program EA/ED/None: EA
Percentage accepted through EA or ED: 67%

EA and ED deadline: 10-Nov
Regular Deadline: 1-Feb
Application Fee: $60
Full time Undergraduate enrollment: 3,849
Total enrollment: 5,778
Percent Male: 70%
Percent Female: 30%
Total Percent Minority or Unreported: 36%
Percent African-American: 2%
Percent Asian/Pacific Islander: 5%
Percent Hispanic: 5%
Percent Native-American: <1%
Percent International: 14%
Percent in-state/out of state: 42%/58%
Percent from Public HS: 66%
Retention Rate: 94%
Graduation Rate 4-year: 63%

Graduation Rate 6-year: 64%
Percent Undergraduates in On-campus housing: 50%
Number of official organized extracurricular organizations: 200
3 Most popular majors: Engineering, Biology, Computer Sci.
Student/Faculty ratio: 14:1
Average Class Size: 9
Percent of students going to grad school: 28%
Tuition and Fees: $41,234
In-State Tuition and Fees if different: No difference
Cost for Room and Board: $12,292
Percent receiving financial aid out of those who apply: 86%
Percent receiving financial aid among all students: 75%

WPI is a small polytechnic institute located in Worcester, the heart of Massachusetts. This engineering haven follows a mission of educating its students on practical and theoretical levels and providing a well-rounded academic program that is sure to make future employers take notice.

Study, Study, Study!

The school operates on a system that is different from most. Instead of semesters, there are four seven-week terms, two in the fall and two in the spring. Each term students take three courses. In addition to their major requirements, every student is expected to complete nine credits or units worth of projects: a sufficiency project requiring five related courses and a project or seminar in the humanities area; a social entrepreneurship project requiring a project relating to solving a need in society via technology and science; and finally a major-qualifying project, which is a team-based project in your own major field of study. While students claim that the projects are not difficult to finish and are enjoyable hands-on experiences, they also say that it is a good idea to get the projects not in your major out of the way early on. Electrical and computer engineering, computer science, and mechanical engineering are the most popular majors on campus. The students also mentioned Interactive Media and Games Development as one of the unique majors— one student explained, "It's basically majoring in video games." As fun as that sounds, students warn that when you come to WPI, you'd better be prepared to put in the work, no matter what you major in. The terms go by quickly and it's important to keep up with each of your classes so as not to get overwhelmed. Also be prepared to spend many hours at the lab. The Chemical Engineering major has a reputation for an overwhelming workload, and "Chemistry of Thermodynamics" and "Calculus 3" also have reputations for being difficult classes. But don't let the difficulty scare you. WPI has a student-friendly grading system with grades being A, B, C, and NR (No Record). This means if you get below a C, the class does not count toward your overall GPA and it's as if you never took it.

> "The unique thing [about WPI] is that the professors are extremely, extremely helpful; they will know you by your first name."

Classes are generally small with two to nine being the most frequent class size, exceptions being of course the survey courses, which can have over 50 people in a lecture. Despite their small size, the competition for a spot in a class is not a problem, and if you want to get into a class you can always turn to the professor who is likely to sign a permission sheet letting you into the class. The professors get equal praise with the classes; one senior enthused, "The unique thing [about WPI] is that the professors are extremely, extremely helpful; they will know you by your first name."

Students generally praise the academics at WPI, citing the hands-on experiences involved in projects as the best sources of learning. Classes can also be fun and hands-on, such as the Food Engineering class which teaches you all about food structure and preparation. The final project is to make something and bring it in, and students get pretty creative—some make their own chocolate from scratch or even brew their own beer. The school's focus is on technology and science, which is great for those who are sure that they want to pursue those fields. However, one student who decided that he was into humanities late in his college career complained that it was impossible for him to pursue it at WPI since the departments are small and not up to par.

Party: Calculators Optional

Students unanimously proclaim that Greek life is the hub of social life on campus. About 28 percent of males and 30 percent of females join either a fraternity or a sorority, but students commented that it can feel like much more of the student body is involved in the Greek community. While most people drink on campus there is no pressure to do so. One student explained that "There are a lot of people who are not involved in the whole party scene at all and they have their own social views," citing the game developers club and science fiction society as examples of groups that prefer to have their own gatherings. The school itself also provides

entertainment options with venues such as the on-campus pub The Goat's Head and Gompei's Gutters, an on-campus bowling alley. Those few who wish to wander off campus and explore the Worcester party scene have the option of clubs and bars near Main Street such as Irish Times and Club Red. Students warn, however, that there is very little to do in Worcester.

There is a stereotype that is associated with technical schools. As one student explained, "People tend to associate the students with the geeky look, with the thick glasses and a part on the side, but [at WPI] it's not a majority at all." But another confessed, "We're a little bit geeky," citing frequent math and science jokes that one hears on campus. Still, there are a diverse variety of students on campus, including a relatively generous community of international students that makes up a little over 7 percent of the student body. It is important to note that women are a minority at the school, making up only 30 percent of the student body. A senior girl, however, described it as not a major problem. "When you're a freshman it's a little bit awkward," she said, and while it takes some getting used to, in the end she reported, "It's not a big deal at all. We're all engineers." Another unifying characteristic is that all students are very friendly and in the freshman year the residence halls and classes offer plenty of opportunities to make good friends.

Is There Room for Me?

For the 59 percent of the student body who lives on campus the options are pretty standard. There are seven dorms in addition to an apartment complex and four smaller houses of 10 to 20 residents. Among these, East Hall is the newest dorm on campus and it's also the most coveted residence for upperclassmen. Due to space restrictions it can be pretty difficult to get into a dorm via the school's lottery system, which is based on seniority.

While the campus is considered safe, the general area outside of campus can be quite sketchy, even dangerous. This can lead to a college bubble feel on campus. At the same time, students don't mind much as they proudly proclaim that WPI is the most beautiful campus among Worcester's numerous colleges. Many like to hang out at the student center, the central hangout spot featuring pool tables, foosball tables, and a food court. When hunger strikes, Morgan Commons serves as the main dining hall. It is rated above average but has a tendency to get monotonous. Other options include a Dunkin' Donuts on campus, a convenience store, and Goat's Head, which doubles as a restaurant. For off-campus options, students recommend Highland Street, which offers many restaurants such as Sahara and Sole Proprietor and several coffee shops such as the Bean Counter.

WPI Spirit

Outside of class there is no lack of activities for the students of WPI. Among the 200 registered student organizations, there is a wide range of options including drama, a robotic team, and *The Towers*, the school newspaper that is beginning to grow in popularity.

Athletics also have a great following on campus. One senior explained that there is "wicked lots of school spirit" and "almost fanatical support" for the sports teams, basketball and football being the most popular. For the less athletically gifted there is the option of joining intramural sport teams, which are not as popular but still claim a presence on campus.

With small classes, great professors, and a pretty campus, students generally report being happy with their choice of WPI. The projects focusing on hands-on work further the school's goal of preparing its students for real world jobs. One student assured, "It's an engineer's dream."—*Dorota Poplawska*

FYI
If you come to WPI, you'd better bring "a calculator."
What is the typical weekend schedule? "Homework, homework and more homework, going out to party and hanging out with friends."
If I could change one thing about WPI, I'd "improve the male-to-female ratio."
Three things every student at WPI should do before graduating are "see the gold head trophy which makes rare appearances, jump through the fountain, and go abroad or away for a project."

Michigan

Albion College

Address: 611 East Porter Street, Albion, MI 49224
Phone: 517-629-0321
E-mail address: admissions@albion.edu
Web site URL: www.albion.edu
Year Founded: 1835
Private or Public: Private
Religious Affiliation: Methodist
Location: Suburban
Number of Applicants: 1,958
Percent Accepted: 81%
Percent Accepted who enroll: 30%
Number Entering: 484
Number of Transfers Accepted each Year: 63
Middle 50% SAT range: M: 500–650, CR: 560–630, Wr: 500–630
Middle 50% ACT range: 23–27
Early admission program EA/ED/None: EA

Percentage accepted through EA or ED: Unreported
EA and ED deadline: 1-Dec
Regular Deadline: 1-May
Application Fee: $20
Full time Undergraduate enrollment: 1,860
Total enrollment: 1,860
Percent Male: 48%
Percent Female: 52%
Total Percent Minority or Unreported: 13%
Percent African-American: 3%
Percent Asian/Pacific Islander: 2%
Percent Hispanic: 1%
Percent Native-American: <1%
Percent International: 1%
Percent in-state/out of state: 91%/9%
Percent from Public HS: 75%
Retention Rate: 86%

Graduation Rate 4-year: 63%
Graduation Rate 6-year: 71%
Percent Undergraduates in On-campus housing: 88%
Number of official organized extracurricular organizations: 110
3 Most popular majors: Biology, Economics, Psychology
Student/Faculty ratio: 14:1
Average Class Size: 15
Percent of students going to grad school: 38%
Tuition and Fees: $28,880
In-State Tuition and Fees if different: No difference
Cost for Room and Board: $8,190
Percent receiving financial aid out of those who apply: 85%
Percent receiving financial aid among all students: 94%

Envision approximately 1,800 students crammed into beautiful, but overpopulated, gothic buildings. Everything is surrounded by large trees. This is Albion College, set within the small city of Albion, Michigan. With its newly renovated science complex, a comprehensive First-Year Experience Program, and a place on *Forbes* magazine's list of "America's Best College Buys," this midwestern school provides students a strong liberal arts education with all the benefits of a small college.

No-Nonsense Academics

One student boldly remarked, "Albion is a no-nonsense school." Most students stick to standard majors such as economics, psychology, pre-med, and chemistry. The majority of the atypical classes are religious, one of the more popular of which is called "Death and Dying." The classes are also competitive, in particular the math and science classes; to do well in physical or organic chemistry, you should expect at least 25 hours of studying a week.

In the Albion system, you need 32 credits to graduate, including major and more general liberal arts requirements. Instead of simply creating distributional requirements, each class at Albion is assigned a "mode" and a "category." "Modes"—or the approach to the subject—include Artistic Creation and Analysis, Historical and Cultural Analysis, and Textual Analysis. "Categories"—or the actual subject the class falls under—include Environmental Studies, Gender Studies, and Global Studies. In addition, all freshmen participate in the First-Year Experience, designed to ease students' academic and social transition into college. The program includes Orientation, Common Reading Experience, as well as a set of seminars on topics ranging from "Art in the Environment" to "Vietnam: Then and Now."

Albion also has a few more specific academic programs. One of the best known programs at Albion, the Carl A. Gerstacker Institute for Professional Management, is an honors business program that involves 10 semesters in four years—seven semesters of on-campus study, one summer term after sophomore year, and two internships during the fall term of junior year and the summer after junior year. Many choices for these internships are located in Europe. For students interested in political science, education, law, or community service, Albion also offers the Gerald R. Ford Institute for Public Policy and Service. Founded by the former president, the institute allows students to pursue a major of their choice while taking classes in fields such as ethics, public policy, and government.

Fight for Your Right to Party

Historically, Albion has been known for a large party scene. But Albion officials have cracked down on the party scene in the college, doling out $500 fines to underage drinkers. There have been problems of overdrinking in the past mainly because a small group of students overdo it and, as one Albion student said, "screwed it up for the rest of us." With its isolated location, life at Albion can get monotonous, leading to occasional problems with drug use. Sometimes, though, the isolation can pay off: during the annual "Senior Week" event at the end of the year, Albion students compete in a drinking Olympics in a barn out of town—not your typical end-of-year venue.

"Albion is a no-nonsense school."

Other than the occasional novel event, one of the drawbacks of the remote campus is that many students have a difficult time finding interesting activities. But with the city of Jackson nearby and Ann Arbor less than an hour away, there are plenty of options for the many students who decide to keep cars on campus.

Fraternity parties epitomize the social scene at Albion. Since the student population is generally friendly and outgoing, the frat scene is more open than at other schools, including allowing everyone at the parties. However, the Greek life at Albion has felt the impact of the crackdown on parties, with some students and officials citing the fraternities and sororities as a major source of drinking. But other students are reluctant to call for the elimination of fraternities because many age-old traditions unique to Albion are connected to the Greek system. At least one student expressed a fear about the effect on social life in general, saying that the party scene revolves around the fraternity houses.

Living in Style

Living arrangements are standard for all four years at Albion, with most students living in the dormitories the whole time. The dorm rooms are assigned by seniority, though juniors and seniors sometimes move off campus into neighboring apartments. Freshmen are housed in either Wesley Hall or Seaton Hall; RAs live in all dormitories, and alcohol is prohibited to those who are underage. It depends, however, on how strict the RA is—some supervisors have been known to be lax about the rules.

The dorms are definitely not the only buildings that will catch your eye at Albion. The multimillion-dollar science complex, finished in 2006, is an impressive addition to the campus. Another more noticeable feature of Albion is the quad; located between all the class buildings, the quad is a great place to hang around during the warmer months. The Nature Center is also worth noting for its beautiful landscape. Thought to be the most beautiful spot on campus by many of the students, it is an "unspoiled habitat."

The dining halls are famed for their relatively good cuisine and easily managed meal plans allowing students to pick how many meals they want per week. But be warned that you will have to maintain regular eating patterns, with limited hours. Since the school is relatively small, the only times the dining halls stay open late is during finals. Also, one unique rule is that off-campus residents are not allowed in the dining halls, but with many good restaurants in the town, students have other options when they want to eat out. However, when students do venture off campus, they usually try to be back before dark since the surrounding area is not particularly safe.

Extra Awesome Extracurricular

Albion College hosts extracurricular fun for everyone in many forms. Although it is a

Division III school, sports are very popular—one student estimated that "half of the campus plays a sport." Basketball and football are the most popular spectator events, but students are known for being fickle fans: at times, they rally in full force for Albion, while other times they skip homecoming games entirely to watch other local rivalries such as the University of Michigan versus Michigan State football game. Intramural sports, including soccer, basketball, volleyball, dodgeball, hockey, and tennis, are a must at this school. The IM fields are given great care and the games are known to get very competitive.

There are also some nonathletic clubs that are very popular. The most recognized are "Break the Silence" (the Gay and Lesbian Awareness Group) and the Medieval Club, which puts on mock sword fights and archery competitions.

Overall, Albion is a small school filled with friendly students. Despite the school's isolation, the campus is a beautiful and safe place where students easily become very personal with their professors and are well prepared for life outside of college. Ultimately, Albion is a great place for students who want to have fun, but at the same time are willing to work hard.—*Benjamin Dzialo*

FYI

If you come to Albion, you'd better bring "a friendly, outgoing attitude."

What's the typical weekend schedule? "Friday: No class, or class finishes early. Work out, nap, or do nothing with your friends until you start drinking, which will last all night (or you study). Saturday: Maybe get some work done, typically don't do anything; partying at night. Sunday: Cram day. Wake up late, study all day if need be."

If I could change one thing about Albion, I'd "fix the town: people wouldn't drink so much if the town wasn't falling apart, and there was more to do."

Three things every student at Albion should do before graduating are "attend a talk by at least one of the great speakers Albion brings in, walk in the Whitehouse Nature Center in the winter, and talk with a professor outside of class."

Alma College

Address: 614 West Superior Street, Alma, MI 48801-1599
Phone: 989-463-7139
E-mail address: admissions@alma.edu
Web site URL: www.alma.edu
Year Founded: 1886
Private or Public: Private
Religious Affiliation: Presbyterian
Location: Suburban
Number of Applicants: 1,745
Percent Accepted: 75%
Percent Accepted who enroll: 28%
Number Entering: 362
Number of Transfers Accepted each Year: 559
Middle 50% SAT range: M: 540–640, CR: 530–660, Wr: 520–640
Middle 50% ACT range: 23–29
Early admission program EA/ED/None: ED

Percentage accepted through EA or ED: 48%
EA and ED deadline: 15-Nov
Regular Deadline: 15-Feb
Application Fee: $35
Full time Undergraduate enrollment: 2,086
Total enrollment: 2,123
Percent Male: 47%
Percent Female: 53%
Total Percent Minority or Unreported: 14%
Percent African-American: 4%
Percent Asian/Pacific Islander: 3%
Percent Hispanic: 5%
Percent Native-American: <1%
Percent International: 3%
Percent in-state/out of state: 96%/4%
Percent from Public HS: 91%
Retention Rate: 76%

Graduation Rate 4-year: 60%
Graduation Rate 6-year: 68%
Percent Undergraduates in On-campus housing: 88%
Number of official organized extracurricular organizations: 75
3 Most popular majors: Biology, Business, Kinesiology
Student/Faculty ratio: 13:1
Average Class Size: 15
Percent of students going to grad school: Unreported
Tuition and Fees: $34,586
In-State Tuition and Fees if different: No difference
Cost for Room and Board: $8,120
Percent receiving financial aid out of those who apply: 83%
Percent receiving financial aid among all students: 99%

A college smaller than many high schools, Alma College is located almost exactly in the center of Michigan, away from large cities. The removed location can be considered a drawback; however, Alma provides an excellent liberal arts education, while creating a small community of close-knit students. Therefore, for all those looking to receive a good education in a quiet, small town, Alma can be a very good college choice.

Liberal Arts with a Touch

At the majority of liberal arts colleges, the majors are along the lines of political science, biology, history, and economics. These fields include a wide selection of course content and generally do not indicate a specific professional path. Alma, however, despite being known as a liberal arts institution, offers a number of programs not often found in similar schools. For example, Alma offers majors in business administration and athletic training, two topics that are more pre-professional preparations than liberal arts. Nevertheless, in general, the school remains very much a liberal arts institution, providing only about 40 majors and minors. For all those looking for a challenge, students can design their own multidisciplinary concentration with the help of a faculty member in a process called Program of Emphasis. By carefully choosing and linking different sets of classes, students can create their own major. "I think we have a lot of independence in what we can study here," said one student. "It is a liberal arts school, but we also have classes in more practical areas."

Despite the small size of the college, Alma does have an honors program, which includes special seminars, as well as a senior capstone project. The idea is to help the more ambitious students to create their own portfolio of different independent projects. "Being able to complete something outside of class without too much guidance is an important part of academics here at Alma. It teaches you to be independent," said one student.

As a liberal arts college, it is important for students to be well rounded. Therefore, Alma has a relatively lengthy list of required courses. Like most universities, Alma's requirements start with composition and computation, the two most important skills to college success. In addition, students must take classes in foreign awareness, social sciences, humanities, and natural sciences. "I think it is really important to take a variety of classes," said one student. "At the end of the day, that is what you should be expected to do because you go to a liberal arts college."

Classes are small at Alma, and they encourage discussions. Interactions with professors are plentiful and highly encouraged. "I think what surprised me the most is how closely involved professors are in the education of each student," said one junior. "Some of them really put a lot of energy into each student." In addition, it is very easy to see professors outside of the class setting. "Alma is a small town with a small college, so you are bound to see your professors all the time around campus. Most of them are always happy to chat with you about anything," said one student.

> **"We have a very accepting environment."**

Students have no complaint about the workload. "No one is trying to overwhelm you with work," said one student. "But you also have to realize that you go to college, which means more than just showing up to classes." In fact, weekdays are very busy times for Alma students to finish academic work. "If you don't plan ahead, you will be in trouble," said one student.

The college also aims to create a better sense of global perspectives among students. Alma is home to the Posey Global Leadership Program, which offers scholarships to students to travel anywhere in the world to accomplish a self-designed project. The projects over the years have ranged from attending conferences to research projects to international internships. The goal is to expose students to the realities of other countries instead of confining students to simply reading books about foreign lands.

In a Place Far Away

Alma is granted the title of city, but it has fewer than 10,000 people and certainly does not give the college much of an urban atmosphere. "We live in a small town," said one student. "And there really is nothing to do here. All we have in Alma is Alma College." To make the matter worse, no major city is close to Alma. In fact, Grand Rapids is more than 50 miles away, and Detroit is even farther. Therefore, most students remain restricted to the confines of Alma even during weekends. Occasionally, however, some students do choose to venture to Mt. Pleasant, home of the Central Michigan State University, which means a few more restaurants, activities, and many more students. Since many students have cars, it is relatively easy to access Mt. Pleasant, which is about 15 miles away.

The upside of a small college in a small city is that everyone gets to know each other very well. "You just have three hundred people in your class," said one student. "After four years, you become really familiar with them." Greek life exists at Alma, and it provide venues for weekend parties. Besides a few parties around campus, however, weekends tend to be very quiet at Alma. "You have to be satisfied with a little bit of repetitiveness in terms of weekend activities," joked one student.

The great majority of students live on campus. After all, Alma prides itself as a residential liberal arts college. There are six main residences provided by the college. The students are generally satisfied with their living arrangements. "The dorms are definitely better for upperclassmen," said one student. "Overall, I think Alma has pretty good dorms compared to other schools. The rooms are large enough and well maintained."

Unlike larger universities with dozens of dining locations, Alma has only three eateries. In fact, only one can be considered a dining hall. Then again, for a school of fewer than 1,500 students, that is more than enough. The main location is Hamilton Commons, serving breakfast, lunch, and dinner. There is also a quick lunch alternative and a coffee shop that offers sandwiches and burgers late into the night. "Meals are not bad," said one student. "And I think the hours are flexible enough to meet our needs."

You Must Be from Michigan

The great majority of students at Alma are from Michigan. Therefore, someone who is not from the state may feel slightly out of place, at least during the first couple of months. However, as students point out, Alma is a very friendly college, open to people of all backgrounds. "We don't have much diversity," said one student. "But that is because we are in the middle of nowhere. We have a very accepting environment. In fact, I would love to see more people from outside of Michigan."

The remote location can also be a great benefit to people who do not enjoy the bright lights of a metropolis. "I love it here because it is so small and intimate," said one student. After all, Alma creates a friendly community of students while providing a great education. For all those willing to sacrifice a few conveniences of big cities for a quiet residential college life, Alma may be the right choice for you.—*Xiaohang Liu*

FYI
If you come to Alma, you'd better bring "a car."
What is the typical weekend schedule? "Party at night and work during the day."
If I could change one thing about Alma, I'd "move it a few miles closer to Grand Rapids."

Hope College

Address: 69 East 10th, Holland, MI 49422 to 9000
Phone: 616-395-7850
E-mail address: admissions@hope.edu
Web site URL: www.hope.edu
Year Founded: 1862
Private or Public: Private
Religious Affiliation: Reformed Church
Location: Suburban
Number of Applicants: 2,748
Percent Accepted: 83%
Percent Accepted who enroll: 35%
Number Entering: 799
Number of Transfers Accepted each Year: 57
Middle 50% SAT range: M: 540–660, CR: 530–660, Wr: Unreported
Middle 50% ACT range: 23–29

Early admission program EA/ED/None: None
Percentage accepted through EA or ED: NA
EA and ED deadline: NA
Regular Deadline: Rolling
Application Fee: $35
Full time Undergraduate enrollment: 3,226
Total enrollment: 6,391
Percent Male: 41%
Percent Female: 59%
Total Percent Minority or Unreported: 2%
Percent African-American: 2%
Percent Asian/Pacific Islander: 2%
Percent Hispanic: 3%
Percent Native-American: <1%
Percent International: 1%
Percent in-state/out of state: 70%/30%
Percent from Public HS: 88%
Retention Rate: 88%

Graduation Rate 4-year: 62%
Graduation Rate 6-year: 71%
Percent Undergraduates in On-campus housing: 78%
Number of official organized extracurricular organizations: 67
3 Most popular majors: Business/Commerce, General English and Literature, General Psychology
Student/Faculty ratio: 12:1
Average Class Size: 18
Percent of students going to grad school: 29%
Tuition and Fees: $24,780
In-State Tuition and Fees if different: No difference
Cost for Room and Board: $7,650
Percent receiving financial aid out of those who apply: 97%
Percent receiving financial aid among all students: 88%

H ope College, located near the scenic stretches of Lake Michigan's beaches, is a mid-sized liberal arts school with a strong sense of community grounded in Christian values. Chartered in 1866 by Rev. A. C. Van Raalte of the Reform Church of America, the campus is only a few blocks from downtown Holland, Mich., a small city about 30 miles south of Grand Rapids. While opportunities for a rich Christian religious life abound on campus, students said Hope is accepting of all faith traditions. Academics boast strong programs in the arts and sciences led by professors who like to get to know their students on an individual basis, and there are plenty of extracurricular options to satisfy every interest, from Quidditch to jazz music. Hope students are generally friendly and full of school pride, particularly when it comes to cheering on their blue and orange mascot, the Flying Dutchman, during sporting events.

Getting Your God On

Historically affiliated with the Reform Church of America, Hope places huge importance on faith and morality, fostering an environment for spiritual growth. But while most people on campus are religious, students said their nonreligious peers are "equally welcome." One student who grew up agnostic said he decided to attend one of the college's religious services called "The Gathering"—which occurs every Monday, Wednesday, Friday, and Sunday—and felt that it "opened his heart," later causing him to convert to Christianity. A large portion of the student body is united during The Gathering, as the chapel can barely seat all of the attendees. Students said the tone of religious life on campus is not exclusive or alienating. "You're not going to be indoctrinated," one junior said. "There is no sort of intense discrepancy between [religious and nonreligious students]."

Campus ministry is an important part of

life at Hope, but many of the opportunities for religious involvement stem from student-led efforts, such as group Bible studies. Resident assistants often serve as more than simple dorm disciplinarians: they are willing to advise fellow students on matters of faith. Professors also frequently facilitate conversations about faith and morality in class, and many students take theology courses.

> **"A friendly, family-oriented community"**

Students said that Hope's focus on Christian values results in a "friendly, family-oriented community" that cares for its own, as well as a serious commitment to community service. Opportunities for community service are available through campus organizations such as Casa, which runs a tutoring program for young ESOL students from underprivileged backgrounds. Students can also go on summer service trips, including a yearly one to Cameroon during which students bring clean water to remote villages.

Hitting the Books
Hope is a small campus in which students enjoy manageable class sizes that rarely exceed 30 students. "Professors care about you and take the time to know you not just as a student, but as a human being," one student said. "That personal connection goes a long way in the classroom." Double majors are common, and popular majors include psychology, education, communications, and political science, though the college provides strong programs in the sciences, as well. Students take 16 credit hours per semester, and the workload varies per major, but the sciences are generally more rigorous than humanities. "Organic chemistry is renowned for being an extremely difficult class," said one junior whose pre-med friend is taking it for a second time. A nursing candidate who has had to take many prerequisite courses said he was "rather jealous" of friends of his who had taken classes such as fencing and tae kwon do, as well as "Introduction to World Religions."

Hope also has many study-abroad opportunities that include May, June, and July terms, in addition to the fall and spring semesters. Students said popular destinations include Vienna, Seville, Argentina, Chile, Tokyo, Australia, and New Zealand.

Food and Shelter
Students of all years are housed in the dorms, so freshmen can live down the hall from upperclassmen. Freshman are assigned to dorms and roommates based on information cards they fill out about their habits and preferences. Usually, freshmen will get doubles, which is the most common dorm configuration. Dorms are generally quite nice, especially since Hope has been renovating some of its older buildings recently. Students said the best freshmen dorms are Wyckoff and Phelps because they "offer a nice mix between being able to study in peace and having an active social life." Students in those dorms are "typically very sociable" and "enjoy having a good time," but are also "respectful of others." There are also some known party dorms such as the male-only Durfee, which one student described as a site of "nakedness and anything associated with testosterone." Kollen is similar to Durfee and is known to house athletes who rush fraternities in the spring.

After freshman year, students can opt to enter a lottery system to live in on-campus, single-gendered cottages owned by the college, which are equipped with basic furniture, such as a bed, desk, refrigerator, and kitchen. Some of the cottages are designated for language immersion, in which all residents speak in a foreign language while inside. Seniors can opt to live off campus in downtown Holland, but freshmen, sophomores, and juniors are required to live on campus. Hope's campus is small, and all campus facilities are within 15-minute walking distance of each other.

There are eight fraternities and eight sororities on campus. Members comprise about 10 percent of the student body, but there is "no pressure to join" or engage in their activities. Hope is officially a dry campus, which is strongly enforced among the resident assistants in the dorms, but fraternities throw what one student described as "shady basement parties" in their on-campus cottages where alcohol is served before police on patrol almost always break them up. But most students do not discuss alcohol or drug use because there is a large segment of the study body that does not engage in the partying at all.

All freshmen dine in Phelps Hall, which always has "lots of options," including healthy foods to help students avoid gaining the Freshmen Fifteen. Students in higher years can go to Cook Hall, which students said has more high-end, classy food. Besides the usual suspects—hamburgers, hot dogs, pizza, and French fries—they both have salad bars and sandwich stands, and students can opt for a dining plan that allows them to grab meals on the go. All in all, students are satisfied with their meal options.

Hip Hangouts

There is a vibrant social landscape outside of the party scene. Though most students do not leave Holland on the weekends, there are plenty of activities available on campus in the form of Student Activity Committee–sponsored movie screenings, concerts, comedians, hypnotists, improv troupes, and more. Some popular hangouts around campus include the five-floor library, home to a basement café called Klepz where students socialize, snack, and work on group projects. In downtown Holland a few blocks away, students frequent Lemonjello's Coffee, which one junior described as a "laid-back hipster spot," and JP's Coffee House. While most stores close after 5 p.m., one of students' favorite late-night eateries is Good Time Donuts, where the owner is known to make donuts in front of customers in his boxers—"He's a legend," one student said. Many students also love to knock down some pins at a nearby bowling alley on the weekends. There is no shortage of fun places for students to hang out.

And when you're sick of the library . . .

Students said prominent on-campus extracurriculars include Greek life, an improvisational comedy group called Vanderprov, and Hope Way 2.0, which sponsors social events and "affects culture on campus by promoting bonding among men, as well as spiritual bonding." Hope has several student publications and media, such as the literary magazine *OPUS*, student newspaper *The Anchor*, and the student radio station WTHS. There are many opportunities for on-campus employment, the most popular of which is the college's dining services, followed by grounds keeping. The college also has a variety of clubs, such as swing dancing and Potterheads, a Harry Potter enthusiast group.

Hope does not offer athletic scholarships, but sports are a significant part of school culture. Popular sports include the men's basketball team, soccer team, and women's volleyball team, as well as a proliferation of intramural sports. Hope has a rivalry with Calvin College located in nearby Grand Rapids, and students turn out in spades to cheer on their own at games.

Diversity? Still a Work in Progress

Students have mixed reactions to the concept of diversity at Hope. While all aspects of the political, racial, socioeconomic, and religious spectrum are represented in the student body at Hope, most agree that the majority of students conform to a white, Christian, wealthy demographic. Students are generally friendly, caring, and willing to facilitate discussion among different viewpoints. One student said that there is "definitely a stratification" among conservative and liberal thinkers, and students are hesitant to be candid about their beliefs, which can be a "really uncomfortable subject."

Homosexuality is a particularly thorny topic, since the college has an official policy of "condemning homosexual acts" while giving gays "fair and kind" treatment. Though professors often encourage students to discuss homosexuality inside and outside of the classroom, students agree that the conservative environment stifles the voice of gays on campus, many of whom keep their sexual orientation secret because they are "not quite sure what kind of reaction they will receive." One student cited the existence of a "Gay Cottage," which is regarded as a haven for gays on campus who do not need to fear being judged within its walls. Another said that he could not "morally recommend someone who is homosexual to come to Hope" because such a student might just "find more and more reasons to be silent."

Whether taking part in a Bible study, taking part in a class discussion, or participating in one of Hope College's many clubs, students at Hope stay busy. The college's open, caring spirit makes students feel at home, while the school's dedicated professors ensure that they meet their academic goals. With an active extracurricular life, a vibrant social scene, and a tradition of community service, it's no wonder that students are willing to brave the cold and spend their college years at Hope.—*Nicole Narea*

FYI
If you come to Hope College, you'd better leave hatred of the snow and cold weather behind.
Three things every student at Hope College should do before graduating are exploring a hidden
   sand dune called "The Bowl," making a donut run, and attending a chapel service.
One thing you wish you would've known before coming to Hope: "You can't plan everything;
   sometimes you have to sit back and put it in God's hands."

Kalamazoo College

Address: 1200 Academy Street, Kalamazoo, MI 49006
Phone: 269-337-7166
E-mail address: admiss@kzoo.edu
Web site URL: www.kzoo.edu
Year Founded: 1833
Private or Public: Private
Religious Affiliation: None
Location: Urban
Number of Applicants: 1,979
Percent Accepted: 73%
Percent Accepted who enroll: 27%
Number Entering: 390
Number of Transfers Accepted each Year: 11
Middle 50% SAT range: M: 560–660, CR: 570–670, Wr: 540–650
Middle 50% ACT range: 26–29
Early admission program EA/ED/None: ED, EA
Percentage accepted through EA or ED: 0.62

EA and ED deadline: 20-Nov
Regular Deadline: 1-Feb
Application Fee: $40
Full time Undergraduate enrollment: 1,387
Total enrollment: 1,403
Percent Male: 43%
Percent Female: 57%
Total Percent Minority or Unreported: 17%
Percent African-American: 4%
Percent Asian/Pacific Islander: 4%
Percent Hispanic: 7%
Percent Native-American: <1%
Percent International: 8%
Percent in-state/out of state: 65%/35%
Percent from Public HS: 73%
Retention Rate: 90%
Graduation Rate 4-year: 79%

Graduation Rate 6-year: 83%
Percent Undergraduates in On-campus housing: 75%
Number of official organized extracurricular organizations: 62
3 Most popular majors: Economics, English Language and Literature, Psychology
Student/Faculty ratio: 13:1
Average Class Size: 17
Percent of students going to grad school: 27%
Tuition and Fees: $35,508
In-State Tuition and Fees if different: No difference
Cost for Room and Board: $8,079
Percent receiving financial aid out of those who apply: 87%
Percent receiving financial aid among all students: 87%

You go *where*? Students at Kalamazoo College are used to hearing this when they tell people where they go to school. First, there is the hurdle of realizing that Kalamazoo is in fact a real place, not an exotic landscape imagined by Dr. Seuss. Next, people add, "Oh, you mean you go to Western." Kalamazoo College, right in the heart of the bustling and very real city of Kalamazoo, Michigan, is not, in fact, connected to Western Michigan University, a large state school. K-Zoo, as students affectionately refer to it, is actually a small haven in the midst of a busy city, a community of only 1,340 scholars committed to knowing every face and every name. Despite, or perhaps because of, Kalamazoo's relative obscurity and small size, the school creates an environment where students are encouraged to try everything and stretch beyond the limits of what they think they can do.

The K-Zoo K-Plan
Catchy name aside, this academic program is renowned for its broad spectrum of classes and its emphasis on experimentation. The K-Plan encompasses, but is not limited to, classes chosen from such disparate fields as

physical education, foreign language, math, world religion, and a first-quarter freshman literature seminar. Although the task of completing these requirements may seem Herculean, one freshman reassured prospective students that "the K-Plan is not strenuous to fulfill." In fact, she said, "I feel like I'm getting a broad education—I know they don't want me to limit myself." Along with the importance placed on taking a wide variety of classes comes the out-of-the-ordinary schedule. "Kalamazoo is on the quarter system. We start later, in mid-September, and we end in early June," one student explained. The fact that classes only last for 10 weeks, as opposed to the typical college schedule of 15, makes the experience "really intense," said one student. However, students appreciate the fact that they can "really dive into a subject" since they take a course load of about three classes rather than the four or five one might find at a college with the standard schedule. Because of the shorter, more compressed plan, students find that they get to know their classmates and professors very well. Students reported no classes larger than around 25–30 people, which significantly contributes to the sense of having "personal relationships with professors." One student specifically commended the foreign language department on a French class of only nine people. She remarked that the small class size made it easy to "converse and not get lost in the crowd."

The foreign language department goes beyond small class sizes at Kalamazoo. It is such a large and well-established department that more than 80 percent of students study abroad during their time at K-Zoo. This staggering number is a nod not only to foreign languages themselves, but also to other very popular majors such as economics and international business and relations. Students say that the Center for International Programs is a widely used resource on campus and note that the staff is very helpful with transferring financial aid. The experimentation inherent in the classes students are required to take is mirrored in the popularity of studying abroad, and students appreciate the "balance" between the familiar and the new to which they are exposed at K-Zoo.

Going to the Zoo . . .

. . . really requires a car. The so-called "K-bubble" of the college is comforting in its very small spread, but when students want to get out into town, they say it can be difficult to find transportation. While The Rave, a theater that sells $5 movie tickets, is within walking distance, students recommend the Hot Spot Shuttle to get to the mall. The school itself is "pretty self-contained, which is kind of a drag," lamented one student. Still, students appreciate the school's attempts to reach out into the urban community with programs such as "Farms to K" and tutoring at local inner-city elementary schools. The "Farms to K" program encourages everyone in the city to eat locally and practice conservation. One student said that despite the somewhat isolated campus, the students "reach out to greater Kalamazoo— K-Zoo is a very community-oriented place."

Animal House . . . or Not

It may be hard to get into the city, but the campus itself is conveniently small and compact. The hilly campus has two dorms at the top of the mound, and classroom buildings and the rest of the dorms are scattered right at the bottom. Although the hillside dorms are a bit farther away, one student said, "When I say 'out of the way' I mean about a minute out of the way. The walk across campus is five minutes tops." The two freshman dorms are very different, but students say that each has its good qualities. The largest dorm on campus houses 200 students and has movable furniture, whereas the other has two rooms connected by a bathroom. Upperclassmen have the option of living in suites in their dorms, and the housing process relies on seniority for first picks. All the dorms are coed, although students note that they have single-sex halls. The fact that "most people live on campus until senior year" really contributes to a sense of community on the K-Zoo campus. One student remarked, "I was surprised by how much I mixed. There's not a big difference between classes—friends come from all years."

The lack of fraternities and sororities on campus does not mean that there are no other living options. Off-campus housing is just minutes away on foot and students call it very convenient. There are also four theme houses chosen every year. Sophomores fill out applications for a theme in a group and must agree to sponsor one event per quarter. Students are allowed to rush fraternities and sororities at Western Michigan University, but "hardly anyone does," according to one student. That's also where students go for the big parties—"it's pretty low-key on our campus."

> **"It's nice to walk around campus and see people you know. It feels like a community."**

As far as the campus itself goes, one student said, "It looks very East Coast." With its brick buildings, red brick road, and grassy quad, K-Zoo offers very much the archetypal college setting. The Capital, a big building in the middle of the quad, serves as the center for everything. While Kalamazoo is currently redoing its student center, the new glass-paned expansion of the library overlooking the campus makes up for it in spaces for students. K-Zoo students are proud of the library, redone in 2006. One student boasted, "We've increased the space by 30 percent but increased energy use by only 10 percent. We're very ecologically aware." In addition, the brand-new cafeteria boasts a wooden pizza oven. However, one student said, "I've had worse . . . but they do serve a lot of tofu."

What to Do in the Zoo
Despite the small size of the community, students assure prospective students, or "prospies" as they're known at K-Zoo, that "clubs are filled in." One student said, "I go to a school with a bunch of overachievers, and they want to do everything." As such, students describe a campus with flyers everywhere and event centerpieces on the lunch tables. "Kalamazoo is good about bringing speakers in and providing activities," and the students get "really into what they do." Although students say that the campus "is not sports-oriented whatsoever," they agree that "a lot of people are athletes." The football team may be terrible, but students proudly express their prowess in tennis: "It's what we're known for." Other activities, such as the Frelon Dance Company and the LGBT drag show, Kaleidoscope, provide a wide range of things to do on campus. One student said that "the school allows for you to try more than one thing—you can sing in five different choirs or be as overactive as you want."

The K-Zoo Experience
"People who know about Kalamazoo only have wonderful things to say about it," said one student as she admitted in the same breath that few people fall into this category. But the hidden gem with the "weird name" lives up to its reputation as a school that is challenging while being community-oriented. One student explained, "They want you to try new things and experiment. They expect you'll do great sometimes, and other times you won't do so well." That attitude of exploration and desire to grow beyond the student that arrived on campus permeates every aspect of life. One student summed up the K-Zoo experience when she said, "It's nice to walk around campus and see people you know. It feels like a community."—*Hannah Jacobson*

FYI
If you come to Kalamazoo, you'd better bring "a warm coat!"
What is the typical weekend schedule? "40-minute Fridays make all Friday classes only 40 minutes, and then we party on Friday and Saturday night, followed by everyone going to brunch on Sunday."
If I could change one thing about Kalamazoo, I'd "make it not snow so much: we get all the lake effect!"
Three things every student at Kalamazoo should do before graduating are "study abroad, do an externship, and mudslide on the hill."

Michigan State University

Address: 250 Hannah Administration Bldg, East Lansing, MI 48824-0590	Percentage accepted through EA or ED: NA	Graduation Rate 4-year: 73%

Address: 250 Hannah
Administration Bldg, East
Lansing, MI 48824-0590
Phone: 517-355-8332
E-mail address:
admis@msu.edu
Web site URL: www.msu.edu
Year Founded: 1855
Private or Public: Public
Religious Affiliation: None
Location: Small city
Number of Applicants:
25,500
Percent Accepted: 68%
Percent Accepted who
enroll: 41%
Number Entering: 7,378
Number of Transfers
Accepted each Year: 2,500
Middle 50% SAT range:
M: 540–660, CR:480–620,
Wr: 480–610
Middle 50% ACT range:
23–27
Early admission program
EA/ED/None: None

Percentage accepted
through EA or ED: NA
EA and ED deadline: NA
Regular Deadline: Rolling
Application Fee: $35
domestic; $50 international
Full time Undergraduate
enrollment: 36,337
Total enrollment: 46,648
Percent Male: 46%
Percent Female: 54%
Total Percent Minority or
Unreported: 16%
Percent African-American:
7%
Percent Asian/Pacific
Islander: 5%
Percent Hispanic: 3%
Percent Native-American:
1%
Percent International: 8%
Percent in-state/out of
state: 79%/21%
Percent from Public HS:
Unreported
Retention Rate: 91%

Graduation Rate 4-year:
73%
Graduation Rate 6-year: 74%
Percent Undergraduates in
On-campus housing: 43%
Number of official organized
extracurricular
organizations: 600
3 Most popular majors:
Advertising, Finance,
Education
Student/Faculty ratio: 17:1
Average Class Size: 29
Percent of students going to
grad school: Unreported
Tuition and Fees: $25,722
In-State Tuition and Fees if
different: $10,264
Cost for Room and Board:
$7,076
Percent receiving financial
aid out of those who apply:
64%
Percent receiving financial
aid among all students:
45%

The best test of how long a student has been at Michigan State University is to ask him or her where in Michigan he or she goes to school. The freshest of the freshmen will just say, "East Lansing." The ones who are true MSU Spartans, though, will point to a little spot on their palms near the thumb and say, "right here!" In the Mitten State, you'll find that this is how the real Michiganders show off their home allegiance, and students at Michigan State are happy to become part of it—despite the many feet of snow they're likely to brave during the winter. And there will be lots of them around to ask: with over 36,000 undergrads and 10,000 more in the grad school, MSU has a broad population of students who are joined by an atmosphere of midwestern friendliness, a curriculum as wide as the student body itself, and a deep love of Spartan football.

Not (Just) Another Big State School

Although it can be daunting to try to pick classes at a school that offers over 200 programs of study, students say that it is precisely that broad spectrum of educational opportunities that they appreciate about MSU. Although many choose to navigate this sea of classes in the main college, MSU offers an honors program for those who want the experience of a smaller community within the school as a whole, and three specialized residential colleges with their own unique programs of study. These residential colleges offer focused curricula ranging from the sciences in Lyman Briggs RC to politics and international relations in James Madison to liberal arts and humanities in the newest residential college, the Arts and Humanities RC. Students used many words to describe these colleges, among them "prestigious," "pompous," "reputable," "great," and "worthwhile," and they note that each college attracts students who are "really interested in the subject matter covered." All three of these colleges offer regular as well as honors programs, and require an application process. Although students say classes in the RCs are known for being "amazingly hard," they all agreed that the smaller class sizes—capped at 25—and access to the "incredible professors" make the experience well worth the extra work.

But special programs are not just for RC students. MSU offers "one of the best study-abroad programs in the country—just pick a place, and you can go there," one sophomore explained. A freshman added that the study-abroad program offers opportunities "on all seven continents—yes, seven!" Students say that MSU makes it very easy to go abroad, and in fact, James Madison programs have a mandatory internship or semester abroad built in. Students really like the fact that MSU fosters an expectation of going abroad, because "at other schools, it seems like students are afraid to leave campus. Here, it's the norm." In addition, over half the students who study abroad receive some form of financial aid, which "makes a huge difference."

> "It is really easy to find small groups to hang out with, and the largeness of the school enables students to have the maximum number of opportunities to pursue whatever they might be into."

This is not to say that students who stay on campus have a chance to get bored—far from it! When asked about popular majors, students came up with everything from kinesiology to business to education to veterinary prep to the renowned agriculture program that was part of Michigan State's original land grant. One graduating senior offered, "With such a big school, the classes offered are endless—I wish I had more time to take all the ones I've been interested in."

Spartans Gone Wild

Warriors inside the classroom, these Spartans also know how to leave the books behind and have fun. Students agree that there is "a large drinking scene" at MSU, but they are quick to say that there are plenty of ways to cut loose without breaking out the alcohol. "The Union and the Student Activities Board also have a lot of events and programs that occur on those nights for those that don't want to have the typical drunken party experience," one student pointed out. Activities ranging from bowling to free movies to student talent shows such as Spartan Idol (singing) and Last Spartan Standing

(stand-up comedy) provide great weekend entertainment that does not revolve around frats. That said, the "beer pong tournaments and special theme nights at clubs" are the more dominant social scenes at MSU, both of which make for an extremely lively campus on the weekends.

But weekends won't be the only time off, and the "Sparticipation" extravaganza at the beginning of the year will help funnel new freshmen into extracurriculars and clubs. This activities bazaar places freshmen in the middle of representatives from all the extracurricular groups, which "can be overwhelming," said one, who quickly added that it "ended up being the best way to just dive in and figure out what I wanted to do." A seasoned sophomore coming at it from the other side also noted, "You get a lot of free stuff and it is the best way to figure out what you might want to be involved in because everyone is in the same place at the same time." Popular extracurriculars include the clearly dominant frat scene, but beyond that, the "huge athletics program" provides a draw, in addition to language clubs, Student Activities Board, poetry and creative writing organizations, and even martial arts. A sophomore said, "there is a lot of pride for the sports teams, and the students are very into supporting the school through sports." This takes the form of cheering on the basketball team from the student section, called the "Izzone," gearing up for football Saturdays, or playing sports on any level from casual dorm wars to more intense club athletics. Students say that the great thing about going to such a large school is that "there is pretty much any and every extracurricular you could ever want—there is something for everyone!"

This Is Sparta!

It may be a little less ancient, but the ivy-covered brick of the older buildings on the northern campus of MSU show off the school's picturesque environment. One student raved, "The Red Cedar River runs right through the center of campus and has some really awesome walking paths around it. The botanical gardens are also a must-see." While the dorms themselves are fairly standard, students say they enjoy their time living on campus. "A lot of juniors and seniors move off campus, but dorm locations do get better as you get older, so there's something to be said for that, too," one junior noted. A sophomore added that living in a dorm "has been a great way to meet people and get to know the campus."

As far as going off campus is concerned, students say that upperclassmen are much more likely to do so if only because freshmen are not allowed to have cars on campus. Still, they say the campus is easy to get around on foot or by bus, and that East Lansing itself is "very pleasant."

Scream 4: Spartan Style

Instead of masked killers, this "scream" is an MSU tradition that takes place every finals week. One student explained, "At exactly midnight, everyone sticks their heads outside whatever room they might be studying in and screams at the top of their lungs." This de-stressing ritual serves as a good reminder that even a big school like MSU allows students to form strong bonds both to each other and to the institution. The fear of large universities is not lost on students,

and one shared, "I was really worried that the campus would be too big and that I might get 'lost' with so many people. The great thing is, it is really easy to find small groups to hang out with, and the largeness of the school enables students to have the maximum number of opportunities to pursue whatever they might be into." While one student noted a current lack of diversity on campus, she was quick to say that it seems that "the school is doing its best to change that." Other students mentioned the fact that "MSU draws so many different kinds of people" also helps everyone find a place to fit in despite the size. The traditions and incredible school spirit that pervade the campus of MSU give this fiery student body a lot of common ground and a huge number of opportunities to express it, both inside the classroom and out.—*Hannah Jacobson*

FYI

If you come to MSU, you'd better bring "something green for school spirit!"

What's the typical weekend schedule? "Wake up, grab lunch/breakfast, go to work/practice, hang out in the dorm, chill out with the floor mates (usually playing RockBand), go for early dinner, study, party, go to bed."

If I could change one thing about MSU, I'd "make the campus smaller."

Three things every student at MSU should do before graduating are, "have a picture with Sparty the Statue, paint the rock with a group of friends or an organization you are involved in, and take advantage of the study-abroad program!"

Michigan Technological University

Address: 1400 Townsend Drive, Houghton, MI 49931
Phone: 888-688-1885
E-mail address: mtu4u@mtu.edu
Web site URL: www.admissions.mtu.edu
Year Founded: 1885
Private or Public: Public
Religious Affiliation: None
Location: Rural
Number of Applicants: 4,573
Percent Accepted: 75%
Percent Accepted who enroll: 34%
Number Entering: 1,161
Number of Transfers Accepted each Year: 401
Middle 50% SAT range: M: 580–690, CR: 550–680, Wr: 520–620
Middle 50% ACT range: 24–29
Early admission program EA/ED/None: None
Percentage accepted through EA or ED: NA

EA and ED deadline: NA
Regular Deadline: Rolling with priority consideration by Jan. 15
Application Fee: $0
Full time Undergraduate enrollment: 5,591
Total enrollment: 7,034
Percent Male: 75%
Percent Female: 25%
Total Percent Minority or Unreported: 6%
Percent African-American: 2%
Percent Asian/Pacific Islander: 1%
Percent Hispanic: 2%
Percent Native-American: 1%
Percent International: 7%
Percent in-state/out of state: 20%/80%
Percent from Public HS: Unreported
Retention Rate: 84%
Graduation Rate 4-year: 27%

Graduation Rate 6-year: 65%
Percent Undergraduates in On-campus housing: 44%
Number of official organized extracurricular organizations: 220
3 Most popular majors: Engineering, Computing, Natural & Physical Sciences
Student/Faculty ratio: 11:1
Average Class Size: 30
Percent of students going to grad school: 20%
Tuition and Fees: $22,522
In-State Tuition and Fees if different: $10,762
Cost for Room and Board: $7,738
Percent receiving financial aid out of those who apply: 72%
Percent receiving financial aid among all students: 58%

Originally established in 1885 to train mining engineers, Michigan Tech has evolved into a widely renowned institution with a vast array of opportunities for engineers and nonengineers alike. Located in the upper region of Michigan in the town of Houghton, this midsized college boasts a beautiful campus surrounded by snow-covered mountains, woods, and trails. But don't be fooled by the calm and quiet surroundings—Michigan Tech is one of the busiest places to spend one's college years.

Not Just for Engineers

Michigan Tech prides itself on its abundant research opportunities, especially its prized Enterprise Program. The program provides hands-on work with outfits like NASA, DaimlerChrysler, SBC Ameritech, and the EPA. Teams of 20 to 30 students solve real-world engineering and manufacturing problems submitted by Michigan Tech's industry, business, and corporate partners. The field

of research for each group varies, including, but not limited to, aerospace, alternative fuels, robotic systems, and wireless communication.

Whether you're doing engineering research or not, chances are you'll be working hard at Michigan Tech. As one student said, "Most people here are very into their schooling, so I am able to keep on track as well." The school's atmosphere is intensely pre-professional; undergraduates are often taking career goals into account as they work. One student explained, "Classes are very tough, but our job placement is very high. For pre-med majors, there is an 80 percent for med school, while the national average is 40 percent." This type of education guarantees that Michigan Tech students are prepared for the real world.

Small Town Snow Sports

Houghton, Michigan, is a very cold place, so you better bring some snow boots. The campus is covered with snow, water, woods, and trails, and the university even owns its own ski and snowboarding mountains with discounted season passes for students. The powder-covered mountains and serene hills create a calm, safe campus environment—so safe, in fact, that many people claim Houghton to be the safest town in Michigan.

> **"The people here are very laid-back. . . . I like the whole 'small town' feel."**

But safe definitely doesn't mean boring. With about 180 student groups on campus, there is certainly no shortage of things to do. "[There is] almost too much to do, there are many things I want to do that I just don't have time for . . . and most people think there is nothing to do up here because we're in the middle of nowhere," one student noted. With about 5,300 undergraduates, Michigan Tech is large enough that each activity attracts a substantial group of students. Yet, it is small enough that students can hold leadership positions without feeling too stressed out about their extracurriculars. As one student explained, "The people here are very laid-back. . . . I like the whole 'small town' feel."

Life In the Winter Wonderland

In terms of housing, all freshmen are required to live in one of three fully equipped residential halls, encouraging class bonding and facilitating the integration of the "frosh" into the campus scene. After that, students can choose whether or not to stay on campus for their next three years. To keep themselves entertained, Michigan Tech students take advantage of the many concerts and performances staged around campus; performers have included Mary Chapin Carpenter and Tap Dogs Rebooted. Greek life, in spite of its small numbers, has a substantial influence on the campus's social scene. Greeks coordinate several parties every semester for everyone's enjoyment. One of the biggest events of the year is the annual Winter Carnival held in February. Human dogsled races, ice bowling, snow volleyball, and fireworks are all part of the extravaganza that is Winter Carnival. Groups on campus spend weeks preparing and creating statues and snow sculptures and teams to compete in the various races. The event is so popular that it attracts tourists from all over Michigan.

Diversity is a bit lacking at Michigan Tech: the school is about 85–90 percent Caucasian. Yet, students said that there is a growing international and minority presence, and all undergraduates have the option of participating in exchange programs or study abroad. The gender ratio is also unbalanced. Like most tech schools, the male majority leaves the lucky ladies with ample choices. "The dating scene is more competitive here . . . and the women tend to use that to their advantage," one student explained. Overall, students agreed that Michigan Tech "is very accepting" of all types and is working to improve its reputation and racial and gender diversity.

Hockey, Skiing, and . . . Broomball?

With a Division I Men's Hockey team, a dozen DII teams and many intramural teams, it is no surprise that many students choose to stay active. In fact, nearly 90 percent of students partake in intramurals. "A lot of people like to get involved with sports up here. . . . It is a great way to stay in shape and meet a lot of people," one intramural athlete noted. The cold weather encourages sports unique to snow and ice. Aside from the usual skiing and ice hockey, students use the icy conditions to play a school favorite: broomball. One student explained the glories of their prized sport: "Broomball is huge up here. It is like hockey played on ice but you wear street shoes and use brooms as hockey sticks. . . . You have to wear kneepads, though, or else you will get very bruised. . . . Everybody gets really into it. Everybody!" Students can be found playing broomball whenever possible—during intramural games, pickup games, and, of course, during Winter Carnival.

It is this mix of academic seriousness and fun-loving athletic spirit that continues to draw students to Michigan Tech year after year. And if you are excited by its combination of intellectual and athletic rigor, it just might be the place for you. Just don't forget your kneepads.—*Suzanne Salgado*

FYI
If you come to MTU, you'd better bring "snow shoes and a shovel."
What's the typical weekend schedule? "Days are spent at meetings or in the library, nights are for going out with friends, and Sundays especially are for homework."
If I could change one thing about MTU it would be "to have more parking: I have to get up early to get a good parking spot."
Three things every student at MTU should do before graduating are: "Go cliff jumping, explore the copper country, and learn to ski/snowboard (and if you know how to ski or snowboard, go to Mt. Bohemia)."

University of Michigan

Address: 1220 Student Activities Building, Ann Arbor, MI 48109-1316
Phone: 734-764-7433
E-mail address: ugadmiss@umich.edu
Web site URL: www.umich.edu
Year Founded: 1817
Private or Public: Public
Religious Affiliation: None
Location: Urban
Number of Applicants: 31,613
Percent Accepted: 51%
Percent Accepted who enroll: 40%
Number Entering: 6,481
Number of Transfers Accepted each Year: 1,347
Middle 50% SAT range: M: 640–750, CR: 590–690, Wr: 610–710
Middle 50% ACT range: 27–31
Early admission program EA/ED/None: EA

Percentage accepted through EA or ED: Unreported
EA and ED deadline: 31-Oct
Regular Deadline: 31-Jan
Application Fee: $65
Full time Undergraduate enrollment: 27,027
Total enrollment: 41,924
Percent Male: 50%
Percent Female: 50%
Total Percent Minority or Unreported: 30%
Percent African-American: 4%
Percent Asian/Pacific Islander: 14%
Percent Hispanic: 14%
Percent Native-American: <1%
Percent International: 4%
Percent in-state/out of state: 62%/38%
Percent from Public HS: Unreported
Retention Rate: 96%

Graduation Rate 4-year: 88%
Graduation Rate 6-year: Unreported
Percent Undergraduates in On-campus housing: 37%
Number of official organized extracurricular organizations: 1,000
3 Most popular majors: Social Sciences, Engineering, Psychology
Student/Faculty ratio: 15:1
Average Class Size: 15
Percent of students going to grad school: 4%
Tuition and Fees: $37,782
In-State Tuition and Fees if different: $12,634
Cost for Room and Board: $10,258
Percent receiving financial aid out of those who apply: 76%
Percent receiving financial aid among all students: 51%

H ome to one of the nation's most celebrated college football teams and the lab where Jonas Salk's team first invented the cure for polio, the University of Michigan is every bit as diverse as its rich history. Located in Ann Arbor, UMich has a student body of over 25,000 and academic and extracurricular opportunities for all of its students. Although the university is recognized nationally for its prestigious academic programs, UMich is best known for students' enormous pride—after all, students say, it's absolutely true that "It's Great! To Be! A Michigan Wolverine!"

Academics in Ann Arbor

To accommodate the large student body, UMich is divided into 11 undergraduate schools and colleges, between which there are over 200 academic departments. Applicants apply directly to one of the eleven, and while most choose the interdisciplinary College of Literature, Arts, and Sciences (LAS), other popular choices include the College of Engineering and the School of Art and Design. Within the LAS, UMich also offers a Residential College (RC) program. As part of this four-year interdisciplinary liberal arts program, 900 students are given the opportunity to live with over fifty professors in a "living-learning community" in East Quadrangle Residence Hall. Students hail the program as a "great way to get to know your peers, especially in a school so big."

Another great academic option is the University's Honors College. Select students are offered admission into the program, which features unique advising and research programs, special courses that are often unavailable to the general undergraduate population, and its own housing option. There are also specific residential programs based on disciplines such as art, engineering, writing, and more. For those interested in performing research, University of Michigan's Undergraduate Research Opportunity Program (UROP) provides many opportunities to get involved in professors' research, even as a freshman or sophomore. One common complaint is that although the opportunities are available, it can often be daunting to seek them out as a freshman in a university quite as large as UMich—but "if you're proactive about it, you can do anything."

Requirements at UMich are diverse, but not too daunting. All students have to take classes in the natural sciences, humanities, social sciences, and language over their four years at the university. Most students complete the majority of their requirements freshman year, before declaring their majors. This leaves them with plenty of time to explore the various courses offered by the university, which stretch from typical science and humanities courses to unique lectures and seminars crafted by well-known professors, such as the Law and Public Policy course taught by University of Michigan's general counsel, who once argued in front of the Supreme Court.

The engineering program is certainly the most competitive of University of Michigan's many undergraduate programs, although pre-med, architecture, and business students are competitive to a certain extent. Overall, however, the students praise the university's academic environment as one of cooperation—at a school as big as UMich, it's very easy to find friends to study with and helpful TAs.

Wild Wild Wolverines

There's always something to do at UMich, and most students say that weekends truly stretch over four or five nights every week. And by no means is the social scene limited to nightlife—Saturdays in the fall are full of tailgates throughout the day. Greek life plays a large role on campus, with over three dozen fraternities and sororities on campus. Many freshmen rush "as a way to make friends," with 16% of guys and about 20% of girls choosing to join a fraternity or sorority. Frat parties make up a considerable amount of the nightlife on Friday and Saturday nights, and are particularly popular with freshmen.

However, the Greek system is by no means the only option for going out at UMich—Ann Arbor has dozens of bars and nightclubs that are extremely popular with the student body. The bar scene doesn't really pick up until junior year, but plays an active role for many upperclassmen. Upperclassmen also have the luxury of having larger parties at off-campus apartments or on-campus co-ops.

> "I've never felt more at home than when I'm sitting in the Big House."

Alcohol is the "poison of choice" on campus, and most University of Michigan students say that social events often center on drinking. Although the administration has made attempts to strengthen drinking codes, students say it's easy to avoid trouble. "There's beer everywhere you go," students say, insisting that it's difficult to graduate from UMich without an appreciation for Keystone. There are rumors of an increase in cocaine use on campus in recent years, largely among wealthy students from the east and west coasts. Yet, drugs other than alcohol and, on occasion, marijuana, are few and far between.

Great to Be an Ann Arbor Wolverine

The University of Michigan and Ann Arbor have a very close relationship—students say that they live in "the perfect college town" and brag that oftentimes, it's hard to tell where UMich ends and Ann Arbor begins. The town also offers many interesting things to do, including art museums, jazz clubs, and plenty of nice restaurants. Most of all, students praise Ann Arbor's midwestern hospitality, which makes the midsized suburban town very welcoming.

UMich freshmen live on campus and, although some dorms can be far from classes, find their living situations very comfortable. One of the most popular areas for freshmen to live is the Hill, a complex of five dorms—Stockwell, Lloyd Hall, Couzens, Mosher-Jordan (MoJo), and Mary Markley—that each have their own distinct personality. Most students move off campus after their first or second year, although because the campus is so large, their off-campus apartments sometimes end up being closer to academic buildings than the dorms. It also often keeps them far from one of the University of Michigan's biggest campus superstitions—students say that if you walk on the large brass M in the Diag (a large open space in the middle of Central Campus) before your first blue-book exam, you're sure to fail it.

If there's one thing all students at University of Michigan can agree upon, it's that the university has immense amounts of school pride. Part of the Big Ten conference, UMich has many nationally recognized sports teams that always draw huge crowds, even if it isn't a winning season. Football in particular dominates campus life during fall semester—students spend every Saturday at "The Big House," Michigan's famous stadium that seats over 100,000. Tailgating is also extremely popular among students, who routinely get up earlier on Saturdays than some weekdays to "start the day right." Students, alumni, Ann Arbor residents, and fans from all over flock to the stadium dressed in blue and maize, as if "the whole community had football fever."

That's really what the University of Michigan is all about—even with such a large student body, sports and school pride truly bring the students at the university together in one giant Wolverine family. And with such a big family, it's certain that students can find exactly what they're looking for, be it academic, extracurricular, or social opportunities. The university's academic offerings are widely respected and certainly can't be overlooked, but it's school pride that really stands out at University of Michigan—from dorms to classrooms to the Big House, UMich students are always eager to show off their maize and blue.—*Iva Velickovic*

FYI

If you come to University of Michigan, you'd better bring "a parka—we get tons of snow every winter!"

The number one thing that surprised me most when I came to UMich was "how easy it was to find a community in such a big school, especially within the Greek system."

A typical weekend at University of Michigan includes going out Thursday and Friday, spending most of Saturday tailgating, going out hard on Saturday night, and then finally catching up on work on Sunday.

Minnesota

Carleton College

Address: 100 South College Street, Northfield, MN 55057
Phone: 507-222-4190
E-mail address: admissions@carleton.edu
Web site URL: www.carleton.edu
Year Founded: 1866
Private or Public: Private
Religious Affiliation: None
Location: Rural
Number of Applicants: 4,840
Percent Accepted: 30%
Percent Accepted who enroll: 35%
Number Entering: 509
Number of Transfers Accepted each Year: 22
Middle 50% SAT range: M: 660–740, CR: 650–750, Wr: 650–730
Middle 50% ACT range: 29–33
Early admission program EA/ED/None: ED

Percentage accepted through EA or ED: 36%
EA and ED deadline: 15-Nov
Regular Deadline: 15-Jan
Application Fee: $30
Full time Undergraduate enrollment: 2,005
Total enrollment: 3,991
Percent Male: 48%
Percent Female: 53%
Total Percent Minority or Unreported: 21%
Percent African-American: 5%
Percent Asian/Pacific Islander: 10%
Percent Hispanic: 6%
Percent Native-American: 1%
Percent International: 6%
Percent in-state/out of state: 26%/74%
Percent from Public HS: Unreported
Retention Rate: 98%

Graduation Rate 4-year: 89%
Graduation Rate 6-year: 91%
Percent Undergraduates in On-campus housing: 89%
Number of official organized extracurricular organizations: 132
3 Most popular majors: Biology, Economics, Political Science
Student/Faculty ratio: 9:1
Average Class Size: 18
Percent of students going to grad school: Unreported
Tuition and Fees: $38,046
In-State Tuition and Fees if different: No difference
Cost for Room and Board: $9,993
Percent receiving financial aid out of those who apply: 50%
Percent receiving financial aid among all students: 54%

W hile students searching for the ideal liberal arts college may turn their sights toward New England or the west coast, they would be remiss if they did not consider Carleton College, a small college located in the quaint town of Northfield, Minnesota, widely hailed as one of the top liberal arts colleges in the country. Students interested in Carleton should prepare for a highly rigorous academic curriculum, not to mention one of the coldest winters found in the continental United States. But any Carleton student will cheerfully declare that he or she is happy to overlook the sub-zero temperatures because of the college's friendly student body, approachable professors, and beautiful campus.

A Workload Heavier Than the Snowfall

Known for its academic rigor, Carleton prides itself on providing its students with a well-rounded education. While students pronounced the math and physical science majors to be especially arduous, many agreed that there is no way to get through Carleton without doing one's fair share of work. Students praised Carleton's trimester system for allowing them to dedicate more time to fewer classes, since they are only required to take three at a time. But students also said the fast pace of classes can make each trimester seem like a blur. "If I think about what I learned in the last couple weeks, it feels like it all happened yesterday," said one freshman.

Students added that the trimester system has other drawbacks, pointing to a short reading period and the early onset of midterms.

Still, midterms may seem like a small concern in comparison to the myriad distribution requirements each Carleton student must fulfill. Before graduating, each Carleton student must take two arts and literature classes, two humanities classes, three social science classes, and three math or natural science classes. Among Carleton's most distinctive requirements is the writing portfolio students must submit after their sophomore year. Said one English major: "I had a positive experience putting together my portfolio, but if you don't look at the writing portfolio as a way to reflect on yourself, then it's mostly just a hassle and waste of time." Students also have a language requirement, physical education requirement, and one final requirement known as RAD: Recognition and Affirmation of Difference. One senior said of RAD: "It was created as a requirement to improve diversity education, but it's become a little lackluster. It's kind of a useless requirement that no one really thinks about." Still, other students said they appreciated the function of the distribution requirements—including RAD—arguing that the requirements bring variety to the curriculum and provide exposure to a number of interesting topics.

But regardless of the varied opinions on campus toward Carleton's distribution requirements, students voiced unanimous approval of the school's professors and their involvement on campus. Given Carleton's small size, students work closely with their professors and form close relationships over time. "You can talk to professors about everything," one senior said. "People interact closely at Carleton. If I ever write an article for a publication, I can bank on a professor e-mailing me about it and telling me they liked it." Fortunately, small classes abound at Carleton, offering more opportunities for students to get to know their professors. Students said they found little difficulty getting into the courses they desired, noting that in the unlikely event of getting wait listed, a student can often squeeze his or her way into the class.

But Enough About School . . .
While Carleton's coursework is tough, it is far from the only thing on students' minds. Although Minnesota's harsh winters may seem like a deterrent from social events,

students said it only emboldens them to be more outgoing. "We're in the tundra, so we have to find something to do," one student said. On weekends, that "something" usually includes parties in dorms, as well as on-campus and off-campus houses. Students described Carleton's stance on alcohol to be relatively relaxed, noting that the school's main concern is that students remain safe. Beyond alcohol, students said there is very little substance use, with the exception of marijuana, which students said is used no more or less than at other colleges. Still, students said there is no pressure to use alcohol or drugs, and there are many substance-free events on campus, including dance parties occurring about every week.

> **"I've been hit by a Frisbee four times at Carleton. . . . It's one of the biggest things about spring."**

Yet Carleton students know how to have fun all the time—not just during late weekend nights. Extracurricular opportunities abound on campus, from the newspaper to community service to dance groups. Among the most popular student groups is a dance group called Ebony, which has upward of 100 members. The group requires no previous training to join and has one dance each term, which is usually very well attended. Beyond dance, students find ways to stay in shape. A large majority of Carleton students participate in intramural sports. Still, trumping intramurals and varsity athletics is one sport that permeates every facet of Carleton life: Frisbee. "I've been hit by a Frisbee four times at Carleton," said one upperclassman. "Everyone plays it. It's one of the biggest things about spring." But while students are waiting for spring to arrive, they can be found playing broomball on a flooded rink in the large, open expanse called the Bald Spot.

Living by the Bald Spot
The Bald Spot marks the center of Carleton's picturesque—albeit architecturally eclectic—campus, which is flanked on all sides by Carleton's many academic, recreational, and dormitory buildings. Freshmen are assigned to various dorms with multiple upperclassmen Resident Advisors per floor. RAs at Carleton get to know their freshmen well, as one freshman noted, saying: "I was shocked that these RAs actually cared. They

organize weekly study breaks and meet with us regularly." When students become upperclassmen, they have their pick of a variety of housing, including dorms or on-campus houses. Two new dorms opened during the 2009–2010 school year. Since the college restricts the number of upperclassmen living off campus, only one in 10 Carleton students currently live off campus.

Not only do students at Carleton praise the housing, but they also give positive reviews to the food. There are two dining halls on campus, one on the west side of campus, the other on the east side of campus. Still, students wishing to get away from dining hall food can always venture into Northfield, where a variety of cafés and eateries abound. Northfield garnered praise from students for its safe environment and quaint shops, and as one sophomore noted, "Northfield is a good college town. It's always crawling with Carleton students, and restaurants are always open late to suit your needs." But after four years spent at Carleton, Northfield can start to feel a bit confining, said one senior. "There are a million little antique stores that are way overpriced, and that's pretty much it," he said. Students needing a break from Northfield can always take a 40-minute drive up to the nearby Twin Cities, although students said almost everyone stays on campus during the weekends.

Uniquely Carleton

When asked what makes Carleton different from other colleges, students quickly point to their peers. Carleton places a high priority on diversity in its student body, and students said they are constantly impressed with the seemingly boundless knowledge and affability of their classmates. Still, students said the majority of their classmates come from upper-middle-class backgrounds, although all agreed that everyone comes to Carleton with an open mind and unique perspective. Carleton's LGBT community is small, said one gay student, but the campus is very accepting, and straight students at Carleton seek to be good allies to their queer peers.

But beyond the friendly student body and top-quality education, there are many other facets of Carleton that make it unique. Consider, for example, "Rotblatt," a campus-wide softball game played annually with as many innings as the age of the college (which has climbed above 100). Another famous facet of Carleton life is the Dacie Moses House, a residence left to the school by alumna Dacie Moses, who stipulated in her donation that the house must always have supplies inside for students to bake cookies. Yet Carleton students could not boast about surviving Minnesota without a few winter traditions. One favorite among students is to go sledding down a mammoth hill behind Evans dorm on dining hall trays.

While any Carleton student will name a different tradition as their favorite, many look on their time at the college with affection, noting how difficult they know it will be to leave it after graduation. From late-night hangouts on the top floor of the library to lively discussions in small classes, Carleton students have myriad opportunities to learn from "the best people you'll ever meet," as one student described her classmates.
—*Raymond Carlson*

FYI
If you come to Carleton, you'd better bring "long underwear and a real Frisbee."
What is the typical weekend schedule? "Friday is usually just party hopping, Saturday there's always a dance, Sunday go to brunch and start working on your paper."
If I could change one thing about Carleton, I'd "move Carleton to Minneapolis. The town is a little isolated sometimes."
Three things every student at Carleton should do before graduating are "explore the underground tunnels, even though they're off limits, participate in an intercultural retreat, and go to the Carleton football game against our major rival, St. Olaf."

Gustavus Adolphus College

Address: 800 West College Avenue, St. Peter, MN 56082
Phone: 507-933-7676
E-mail address: admission@gustavus.edu
Web site URL: www.gustavus.edu
Year Founded: 1862
Private or Public: Private
Religious Affiliation: Lutheran
Location: Rural
Number of Applicants: 3,279
Percent Accepted: 71%
Percent Accepted who enroll: 29%
Number Entering: 675
Number of Transfers Accepted each Year: 79
Middle 50% SAT range: Unreported
Middle 50% ACT range: 24–29
Early admission program EA/ED/None: EA

Percentage accepted through EA or ED: 28%
EA and ED deadline: 1-Nov
Regular Deadline: 1-Apr
Application Fee: $0
Full time Undergraduate enrollment: 2,628
Total enrollment: 2,628
Percent Male: 43%
Percent Female: 57%
Total Percent Minority or Unreported: 12%
Percent African-American: 2%
Percent Asian/Pacific Islander: 5%
Percent Hispanic: 2%
Percent Native-American: <1%
Percent International: 2%
Percent in-state/out of state: 80%/20%
Percent from Public HS: 92%
Retention Rate: Unreported
Graduation Rate 4-year: 83%

Graduation Rate 6-year: Unreported
Percent Undergraduates in On-campus housing: 77%
Number of official organized extracurricular organizations: 120
3 Most popular majors: Business, Psychology, Business
Student/Faculty ratio: 13:1
Average Class Size: 16
Percent of students going to grad school: 34%
Tuition and Fees: $30,420
In-State Tuition and Fees if different: No difference
Cost for Room and Board: $7,460
Percent receiving financial aid out of those who apply: 81%
Percent receiving financial aid among all students: 66%

Gustavus Adolphus is not unique among liberal arts colleges in trumpeting its small classes and strong sense of community. But no other college can boast that it brings Nobel laureates to campus for a two-day conference each year (and cancels all classes so students can attend lectures), that its students use cold Minnesota winters as a chance to turn cafeteria trays into sleds, and that it occasionally hosts the king and queen of Sweden—just one modern manifestation of GA's Swedish, Lutheran heritage.

Small Is (Mostly) Beautiful

"Gusties" say they can't imagine taking the big lecture courses common at other schools, because small classes taught by full professors are so intrinsic to the Gustavus experience. With an average class size of 15, and TAs' duties limited to grading assignments, it's easy for students to get to know their professors. A freshman art history major recalled a two-hour chat with an American history professor "that started off with the Civil War and moved on to life in

general," while a junior biology major noted that her professors were eager to invite students to serve as research assistants and to mentor them outside of the classroom. Accessibility and personal attention characterize academics at Gustavus Adolphus, regardless of which of the 64 majors or 15 pre-professional programs a student pursues.

Graduating from GA requires the completion of 32 courses and two January "interim experiences," which each major taking about a third of a student's total course load, with general education requirements taking another third. Students can use their elective course to pursue another major or up to two minors. Most students fulfill general education requirements through the Liberal Arts Perspective curriculum, which requires at least one course in each of nine areas ranging from Mathematical and Logical Reasoning to Biblical and Theological Studies to Fitness. Sixty students each year choose instead the 3 Crowns program, a series of eight complementary courses in history, literature and philosophy that culminate in a senior seminar. One freshman in 3 Crowns described it as "sort of like an honors program," with rigorous classes and motivated participants, though all students are eligible.

Other unique features of Gustavus Adolphus's curriculum are the first-term seminars—small classes taken by all freshmen—and the requirement of three writing classes, with at least one in a department outside the major. The first-term seminar professors also serve as their students' adviser until they choose a major.

Students say the science departments are among the college's best—and most challenging. A senior communications major acknowledged that the physics, chemistry and biology classes, which have weekly lab components, are generally more time-consuming and difficult than courses in the social sciences and the humanities, leading some science and math geeks to proclaim their superiority to English and History nerds. But a junior biology major with a minor in religion noted that all upper-level courses are fairly rigorous, with only general education courses widely considered easy.

While GA's small size makes for an unusually personal academic experience, some students find it has a major drawback: course offerings are relatively limited. In order to complete pre-med requirements, a junior had to cross-enroll at Minnesota State University, Mankato, 15 minutes away. "It does get frustrating to feel you don't have as many options as friends at other schools," she said. One freshman is considering transferring to a larger university because he wants access to a broader array of classes.

Minnesota Nice, Big City Busy

Gustavus students, 77 percent of whom hail from the North Star State, live up to the old adage about Minnesotans: they're nice. They're also seriously involved in sports, community service, the arts, Greek life, and student government—not to mention going out a few times a week. "We've got a lot of great student organizations and students feel a lot of pressure to be involved and sometimes that leads to stress," said a senior. "But students feel like this is a place where they can really connect to other people."

Although 85 percent of students live on campus due to the college's requirement that students apply for special permission to in the town of St. Peter, off-campus houses and apartments are at the center of Gustavus Adolphus social life. A typical Friday or Saturday night is spent at a house party, often followed by a few hours at one of St. Peter's bars, which students appreciate for their local color and laid-back atmosphere. A bus enables students to safely return to their dorms at the end of the night, illustrating the college's "safety first attitude" when it comes to alcohol, according to a senior. The drinking culture is prevalent but not predominant, though one of the most cherished Gustavus traditions is Case Day, when each student attempts to drink a case of beer over the course of the day. "Alumni will come back and talk about Case Day," said a sophomore. "It's always been a big deal."

> "We've got a lot of great student organizations and students feel a lot of pressure to be involved and sometimes that leads to stress," said a senior. "But students feel like this is a place where they can really connect to other people."

Greek organizations at Gustavus were banned from 1988 to 1993 and are now heavily regulated by the university in order to prevent the hazing that was common in the past. Students must have attended Gustavus for at least two semesters before they can pledge, and the pledging period is restricted to three weeks for most chapters. A fraternity member who was involved in the Inter-Greek Senate, which oversees all Greek life at the college, said most chapters are heavily involved in community service and don't have official houses, limiting their visibility and influence on the broader campus social scene.

When it comes to socializing on the campus itself, Gustavus offers plenty of options. "Students rarely leave for the weekend," according to a senior. Performances and shows are well-attended, and though most parties happen off-campus, the Campus Activities Office sponsors dances every Friday night in a space called The Dive. One freshman said the dances are a popular option for underclassmen in particular, because they're easily accessible and reliably fun.

Sports events are also extremely popular, in part because all athletic venues are just a few minutes' walk from most dorms. This being Minnesota, Gusties are particularly rabid fans of their ice hockey team. When not cheering on their varsity athletes (who are often also their roommates, classmates or friends), many students participate in intramurals. A senior on the football team estimated 80 percent of Gusties participate in varsity, club, or intramural athletics.

Students say social life at Gustavus is generally harmonious, but one explanation for that may be the homogeneity of the student body: 87 percent of Gusties are white. A senior who has been involved in the campus Diversity Center said the college provides additional resources and support for minority students and has been working to attract students from underrepresented groups. One junior believes diversity at the college is increasing. "I think the school is pushing that and I'm glad because I definitely think diversity makes class discussions richer," he said.

The campus a tornado built

Gustavus Adolphus today looks much different from the one-building school founded by Swedish Lutherans in 1862. And time, unfortunately, has not been the only change agent: a tornado in 1998 caused $50 million in damages and toppled over 2,000 trees. Today, well-manicured grounds and a popular arboretum betray little sign of the disaster. Old Main, the college's first building, survived the tornado and still hosts classes, while the newest building, Beck Hall, has become a popular place for students to study and socialize between classes. Students say the campus, situated on a hill with Christ Chapel at the center, is conveniently sized yet not too compact, offering several wide-open spaces that are popular places for chatting or informal sports. And the semi-rural location of the campus confers a hidden benefit: there's plenty of space for parking, so anyone who wants to can bring his or her car.

The dorms surround the classroom buildings and are considered fairly standard—not bad, but not great. Freshmen are housed in three dorms—Norelius Hall, Pittman Hall, and Sohre Hall—that are comprised of doubles on single-gender halls. Many students said they met their closest friends on their residence halls, and common areas of freshman dorms are frequently filled with people chatting or studying. Resident assistants are most prominent in the freshman dorms, where they organize activities, host study breaks and ensure students follow the rules. But one freshman said he was pleased to find the RAs are generally fairly lenient and never conduct room searches for illicit substances, though he added he had heard a few "horror stories." After leaving Norelius,

Pittman or Sohre, sophomores all live in a single dorm. "It's really convenient and fun because you live with all your friends, but it still kind of sucks living in a dorm," said a sophomore. Juniors and seniors can live in the more expensive but nicer town-homes and apartments—though a good number elect to leave campus.

Many students expressed frustration with Gustavus's requirement that all students live on-campus. Though most senior applicants who apply to live off-campus are able to do so, some requests are rejected and junior applicants are rarely successful. "I find it pretty frustrating, to be honest, because living off-campus could be a great way to start practicing for the real world," said a junior whose off-campus housing request was denied. But students also acknowledged that having nearly everyone on campus builds a strong sense of community.

While some are unhappy with Gustavus's housing policies, nearly everyone loves the college's food. Many students who live off-campus elect to remain on one of the three meal plans. All items are self-serve and individually priced. Options include a rotisserie grill, pizza, custom-made sandwiches and wraps, a vegetarian station, and a dessert bar. "After a while the choices do begin to get repetitive, but the food itself is very good," said a sophomore. The cafeteria, known as the Marketplace, also serves as a social hub and daytime study spot. It's also the site of one of students' favorite traditions: Midnight Express, when professors serve free soft pretzels, ice cream, soda, wings and other snacks on the night before exams.

Kiss me, I'm Swedish (sort of)

Though the college is no longer majority Swedish, students with Scandinavian ancestry are well-represented at Gustavus Adolphus, and anyone who wants to get in touch with their inner Nordic should be particularly happy here. The college offers a Scandinavian Studies major, popular Swedish classes, and a Swedish House where residents speak Swedish. Reflecting Lutheran traditions, Christmas in Christ Chapel is a major event held before students leave for winter break, featuring student choruses, orchestras and bands performing together as a show tells the story of the nativity, with a new theme each year. In 2012, the king and queen of Sweden visited the school and were honored with a parade.

But nods to Scandinavian culture don't

define the college—one student pointed out that the Marketplace doesn't serve Swedish food and many religions are represented at Gustavus. Ultimately, students agree that

Gusties are united by a drive to get involved, and though the campus is small, it offers plenty of opportunities to do just that.—*Isabelle Taft*

FYI:
Three things every student at Gustavus Adolphus should do before graduating are 1. "Paint the rock" to show pride for your sports team, extracurricular activity, or Greek organization. 2. Network with the great group of alumni. 3. Streak through the arboretum.
The biggest college-wide tradition is Christmas in Christ Chapel.
If I could change one thing about Gustavus Adolophus, I'd change the four-year residential policy. I really do enjoy living off campus and wish I could have done it earlier.

Macalester College

Address: 1600 Grand Avenue, St. Paul, MN 55105
Phone: 651-696-6357
E-mail address: admissions@macalester.edu
Web site URL: www.macalester.edu
Year Founded: 1874
Private or Public: Private
Religious Affiliation: None
Location: Urban
Number of Applicants: 4,565
Percent Accepted: 46%
Percent Accepted who enroll: 27%
Number Entering: 565
Number of Transfers Accepted each Year: Unreported
Middle 50% SAT range: M: 640–730, CR: 670–760, Wr: 660–750
Middle 50% ACT range: 27–32
Early admission program EA/ED/None: ED I, ED II

Percentage accepted through EA or ED: 53%
EA and ED deadline: 15-Nov, 2-Jan
Regular Deadline: 15-Jan
Application Fee: $40
Full time Undergraduate enrollment: 1,958
Total enrollment: 1,996
Percent Male: 42%
Percent Female: 58%
Total Percent Minority or Unreported: 19%
Percent African-American: 4%
Percent Asian/Pacific Islander: 9%
Percent Hispanic: 4%
Percent Native-American: 1%
Percent International: 12%
Percent in-state/out of state: 19%/81%
Percent from Public HS: 59%
Retention Rate: 94%

Graduation Rate 4-year: 87%
Graduation Rate 6-year: 94%
Percent Undergraduates in On-campus housing: 66%
Number of official organized extracurricular organizations: 80
3 Most popular majors: Economics, Political Science, Psychology
Student/Faculty ratio: 11:1
Average Class Size: 18
Percent of students going to grad school: Unreported
Tuition and Fees: $39,974
In-State Tuition and Fees if different: No difference
Cost for Room and Board: $8,768
Percent receiving financial aid out of those who apply: 88%
Percent receiving financial aid among all students: 70%

Macalester is a top-notch liberal arts college. Such a description may immediately create an image of a tiny, perhaps elitist, school covered in ivy and far removed from civilization, but it could not be further from the truth. Surely, Macalester does share some features of a stereotypical liberal arts institution. It has a small enrollment of slightly less than 2,000 students and is located in a quiet residential neighborhood. Yet beyond the school's enclave is also one of the largest urban centers in the United States, the Twin Cities, which offers Macalester the unique sense of both bustling city atmosphere and serene small-town tranquility. Furthermore, despite its location in the Midwest, Macalester has a highly diverse population, with more than 10 percent of its student body coming from overseas.

A Friendly Faculty

With a highly selective admissions process that only accepts 46 percent of applicants, Macalester brings together talented students from around the world. The school ranks 24th on the *U.S. News & World Report*'s list of Best National Liberal Arts Colleges, and *The Princeton Review* grades its quality of life at number three in the nation, showing that it offers a vigorous academic experience coupled with an enjoyable social environment. "The coursework is hard and competitive, as it should be," said one junior. "But I am enjoying every minute of life here."

Macalester offers more than 40 majors, and the most popular ones are political science, biology, economics, English, and psychology. For graduation, students must complete a relatively lengthy set of requirements, designed to ensure their breadth of knowledge. These requirements are similar to those of comparable institutions and include courses on social science, natural science, humanities, writing, foreign language, and quantitative reasoning, which is a euphemism for mathematics-related classes. Unique to Macalester and true to its aspiration to become a truly global university, courses on internationalism and multiculturalism are also listed as requirements.

Another important part of the academic experience is the first-year seminar, taken by every freshman in the fall semester. These classes are small, allow close interactions between professors and students, and place a strong emphasis on writing, an essential skill for anyone who would like to succeed in college. The strong point of this program is that the students can choose from a variety of 30 different seminars, ranging from theater to cellular biology. The professor also serves as faculty advisor for students in the class.

Although the requirements sometimes help students in discovering subjects that they would not have touched otherwise, a few students are ambivalent about taking classes in which they have no interest. "I understand that we need to know different subjects, but it is really hard to find a class that interests me and fulfills the requirements at the same time," commented one student.

As a relatively small college focused solely on undergraduate education, Macalester certainly offers an engaging faculty that gives a high level of attention to the students, unlike many larger research universities, where professors are rarely seen outside of the bi-weekly lectures. "If you try, you can get to know some professors really well and be really good friends with them," remarked one senior.

> "St. Paul is great. It is not New York, but it is still an important city with all kinds of cultural activities and work opportunities."

The tradeoff of receiving such personal attention, however, is that the school lacks the scale and infrastructure of larger institutions. Opportunities can be limited for students seeking laboratory or in-depth research experiences. Nevertheless, the college does have state-of-the-art facilities and tries to remedy some of its disadvantages by offering summer research grants. Studying abroad at a major university can also be helpful. However, as one student said, "if you come here, understand that there are limitations to small colleges."

The Twin Cities

Macalester occupies 53 acres of a historic residential quarter. The campus is approximately a mile away from the gorgeous Mississippi River that separates St. Paul and Minneapolis. Such location allows students to take advantage of city living while enjoying the tranquility of a quiet neighborhood. "St. Paul is great," said one student. "It is not New York, but it is still an important city with all kinds of cultural activities and work opportunities."

On the downside, Minnesota doesn't exactly have San Diego weather. The winters can be very cold. In fact, it has one of the lowest average temperatures of any major metropolitan area in the United States. As one student mentioned, "The winters here are brutal, especially for those from warm places who are not used to this weather." For snow and ice aficionados, however, the Twin Cities certainly receive plenty of precipitation, both during winter—in the form of snow, hail, and sleet—and summer—in the form of thunderstorms.

The Time of Our Lives

Students are required to live on campus for the first two years. Freshmen live in one of the three residential halls specifically reserved for first-year students. Most of them are assigned to doubles, which, as noted by one freshman, "are reasonably well-kept." Lounges are also available for students to meet and socialize. Those interested in gastronomy can take advantage of the kitchens in each residential hall. The upperclassmen generally have rooms that are more spacious and apartment-like. Since Macalester is in a major city, a significant portion of juniors and seniors—about half of them—prefer living off campus. The process of finding a nice home at a low price can be burdensome, but the college does provide rental listings to help its students. In addition to these options, there are also theme houses, including six language houses, the Hebrew House, EcoHouse, the Cultural House, and the Veggie Co-op, available to all after one semester of study.

Despite its small size, a large number of activities can be found on campus during weekends. While some students are drawn by the attractions of the Twin Cities and drift away from the campus during weekends, the majority of students do stay within Macalester, attending different parties or simply hanging out with friends. Given the size of its student body, Macalester has neither fraternities nor sororities. Therefore, most parties happen in dorm rooms. Alcohol, as in most colleges, abounds. Those who wish to remain dry are occasionally pressured to drink, but most of them do not feel out of place by staying sober during parties. "Drinking is widespread," said one student. "But people won't look down on you if you don't drink."

The sports teams compete in Minnesota Intercollegiate Athletic Conference, which belongs to NCAA Division III. "We are a small school," said one junior. "We are not USC or Michigan State, and that shows with our football team." On the other hand, the soccer teams at Macalester are both popular and relatively successful, having achieved consecutive winning seasons. At the same time, a number of students participate in intramural and club sports. "A lot of people enjoy playing sports even though Mac is not a big sports school," said one student.

Good Old Liberals

Macalester has long been considered one of the most liberal colleges in the United States. Therefore, Republicans can feel slightly out of place if they participate in the political scene on campus. "It is rare to find a Republican on campus these days," said one student. "I don't think people would hate someone who is an activist Republican, but I think that person would feel really uncomfortable in political discussions because he or she will be against everyone else." Nevertheless, most students agree that Macalester is generally tolerant of other people's ideas and serves as a good forum for discussions and debates.

Another unique aspect of Macalester is its large population of foreign students for a relatively small liberal arts college. The school has strongly advocated an internationalization of the campus, and the students are particularly proud of this ethnic and cultural diversity. "I think this is one of the most important parts of Mac," mentioned one student. "Seeing people from everywhere around the world is just wonderful and really helps you learn more about the world."

"I think Macalester deserves more recognition and should be a highly sought-after college," said one student. Indeed, given its academic excellence, Macalester is perhaps not as well known as a few other liberal arts institutions. The location in Minnesota and the harsh winter certainly contribute to it. There are also complaints about the small size and thus the lack of different opportunities. Nonetheless, the students are generally happy and glad that they chose to attend Macalester. Ultimately, that is what is important.—*Xiaohang Liu*

FYI
If you come to Macalester, you'd better bring "something warm to keep you warm."
What is the typical weekend schedule? "It depends. It is different every weekend. There is so much to offer in the Twin Cities during day and night. But sadly, not everyone takes advantage of it."
If I could change one thing about Macalester, I'd "move this whole place to a lower latitude."
Three things every student at Macalester should do before graduating are "visit the city during the night, live in a theme house, and start a snowball fight."

St. John's University / College of St. Benedict

Address: PO Box 7155, Collegeville, MN 56321-7155

Phone: 320-363-2196

E-mail address: admissions@csbsju.edu

Web site URL: www.csbsju.edu

Year Founded: 1857

Private or Public: Private

Religious Affiliation: Roman Catholic

Location: Rural

Number of Applicants: 3,221

Percent Accepted: 81%

Percent Accepted who enroll: 40%

Number Entering: 1,039

Number of Transfers Accepted each Year: 51

Middle 50% SAT range: M: 525–655 CR: 488–625, Wr: 484–622

Middle 50% ACT range: 23–29

Early admission program EA/ED/None: EA

Percentage accepted through EA or ED: Unreported

EA and ED deadline: 15-Dec

Regular Deadline: None/Priority Application deadline: Nov 15

Application Fee: $0

Full time Undergraduate enrollment: 3,933

Total enrollment: 4,014

Percent Male: 48%

Percent Female: 52%

Total Percent Minority or Unreported: 15%

Percent African-American: 1%

Percent Asian/Pacific Islander: 3%

Percent Hispanic: 3%

Percent Native-American: 1%

Percent International: 6%

Percent in-state/out of state: 86%/14%

Percent from Public HS: 70%

Retention Rate: 91%

Graduation Rate 4-year: 73%

Graduation Rate 6-year: Unreported

Percent Undergraduates in On-campus housing: 82%

Number of official organized extracurricular organizations: 85

3 Most popular majors: Biology/Biological Sciences, General Business Administration and Management, General Speech and Rhetorical Studies

Student/Faculty ratio: 12:1

Average Class Size: 19

Percent of students going to grad school: 14%

Tuition and Fees: $33,240

In-State Tuition and Fees if different: No difference

Cost for Room and Board: $8,650

Percent receiving financial aid out of those who apply: 97%

Percent receiving financial aid among all students: 94%

The "Bennies" and "Johnnies" of College of St. Benedict/St. John's University know they attend a unique institution. Forget for a moment the on-campus abbey and monastery, which house some of the schools' professors. CSB/SJU, one of the top Catholic liberal arts schools in the country, is actually two schools in one: College of St. Benedict, an all-women's school, and St. John's University, an all-men's school. Each boasts its own administration, athletic program, library, bookstore, and dining halls. Yet at the same time, students from both schools interact with one another on a daily basis, both in and out of the classroom. Only late at night, when everyone is (theoretically) asleep, are the two campuses single-sex.

Not only do CSB/SJU students know their campus is unique, they also know it is gorgeous. The campus is surrounded by woods and filled with trails that offer tons of opportunities for exploration and recreation. Some students, for example, enjoy the "chapel walk," a trail that leads to the Stella Maris Chapel on the SJU campus. Legend has it that if two people walk it together, they will get married.

Two of Everything

Because the institution is really two different schools, students benefit from access to facilities on both the St. Ben's and St. John's campuses. When it comes time to study, they may head to either one of two libraries. According to students, the CSB library often turns into "a social gathering" but also features a café where students can grab some caffeine to fuel late-night studying. Meanwhile, the SJU library offers a quieter atmosphere. While its basement, nicknamed "The Dungeon," is "creepy" for some students, it offers others the silence they need. One junior summed up the difference by stating that he studies "in St. John's library when I want to get things done and St. Ben's library when I don't."

Classrooms are also split between the two campuses. But the half hour between classes gives students plenty of time to commute from one side to the other by taking "The Link," a free shuttle bus service. The Link operates day and night to allow students to travel between St. John's and St. Ben's not only for academic purposes but also to visit friends and participate in extracurricular activities.

Throughout their four years on campus, CSB/SJU students have the opportunity to develop strong relationships with their professors. Even at the introductory level, students may work closely with their professors because class sizes are so small. Additionally, all first-year students participate in a symposium, a seminar capped at 18 students. The professor of the symposium class serves as the academic adviser for his or her students, and students say everyone gets to know each other extremely well. And while they do take academics seriously, students say they still maintain a deep sense of community on campus. "People get really competitive, but in a good way," one freshman observed. "It is not like they are ready to kill each other, but they really give their best to be on top."

Bennies and Johnnies have many opportunities to explore their academic options. "I switched majors more times than I can count," admitted a current double major in communications and Spanish, "and I was even able to study abroad for seven months." The sheer diversity of classes offered and opportunities extended to students is also impressive. In particular, study abroad is a very popular option for students on both campuses. One Bennie pointed out, "You ask your friends 'where are you going to study abroad,' not 'are you going to study abroad.'" CSB/SJU offers 17 different semester-long programs in several countries. In many of these programs, students participate with other Bennies and Johnnies and are taught by local professors. Academic advisers are "very helpful" in working with students to include study-abroad credits in their academic schedule while still completing required classes and the requirements of their major(s).

Eating and Sleeping

Students are more than satisfied with the housing at both St. Ben's and St. John's,

especially with the apartment-style residences available for juniors and seniors. Luetmer, an on-campus apartment complex for CSB seniors, offers each resident her own bedroom and includes a washer and dryer within every apartment. Either a community adviser (CA) in upperclassmen apartments or a resident adviser (RA) in the residence halls will act "as a program planner, conflict solver, therapist, rule enforcer, etc." Furthermore, in accordance with the Benedictine Values, students at SJU adhere to a tradition of keeping the doors to their rooms open when they are in the room. "This allows other students the opportunity to stop in, say hi, and meet new people," pointed out a current sophomore.

Students give campus food mixed reviews. While one student asserted that "it's not that good and it's overpriced," another felt "the food is really good on both campuses." Regardless of how they feel about the food itself, however, students do appreciate the variety of options offered. A popular eating destination is the Refectory, or "the Reef," the dining hall at St. John's.

St. John's and St. Ben's prohibit underage students from drinking on campus, a policy that is strictly enforced. However, on weekends, one freshman observed, "everybody or almost everybody is drinking." A junior added, "If people choose not to drink, they are questioned as to why they made that decision—it seems abnormal." But another student countered, "I get [pressured to drink] more at home with my friends there. I like to have a good time and am pretty crazy without the alcohol, so I seem to fit in just fine." Students over 21 can obtain permits to have parties in their rooms on campus, and St. John's University has its own on-campus pub. Otherwise, students may head to St. Joseph, the town in which College of St. Benedict is located. The small town boasts numerous "party houses" with names such as "Chubbie," "Dingleberry," and "The Chicken Shack."

But weekends at CSB/SJU are about more than just partying. There are frequent opportunities to see movies on campus, attend cultural events such as the Festival of Cultures and the Asian New Year, or even venture into nearby St. Cloud for shopping, dining, or just hanging out. Of course, students also have the option of participating in one of the many extracurricular activities at CSB/SJU. Community service is "a huge thing on campus," and additional opportunities range from writing for the school newspaper to participating in Companions on a

Journey, a faith group, or campus ministry. And of course, there are the football games.

Alumni Gone Wild

Football games are some of the most important student events of the year. "People go crazy!" exclaimed one Bennie. Alumni turn out for the home games with "their spouses, kids, grandkids . . . you name it, they are there." One CSB senior bragged that "there is a lot of pride in being a 'Bennie' or a 'Johnnie.'" As a social event and as a display of school spirit, football games are "definitely a big deal," boasting the "highest attendance for football games among Division III sports." And with a 2007 NCAA Division III national championship under their belts as well as consistently successful seasons in subsequent years, the football games' popularity is well deserved. Students also pointed to hockey and Bennie basketball as other popular sports to attend.

Of course, students have ample opportunities to participate in sports as well. A former varsity swimmer cited his athletic experience on campus as a positive one, stressing that "my coaches were really understanding that my academics come first." Student athletes, who also enjoy a large banquet and dance at the end of the year, note that sports are a great opportunity to meet others. But if the time commitment of a varsity sport is too demanding, participation in intramural sports is always an option. "There is simply no question that the best intramural sport on campus is softball," asserted one Johnnie, who added that large

numbers of Bennies and Johnnies turn out every year for the sport.

Feeling Comfortable on Campus

Campus traditions are numerous. Many rave, for example, about the CSB/SJU Thanksgiving dinner. "Students are dressed formal and served as a table. Somebody from the table has to get up and carve the turkey, and then all the food is served family style," one senior said, adding, "It's really fun." Other traditions range from a large snowball fight on the first snowfall of every year to Pinestock, an annual event in which a "big-name band" comes to campus to put on a day-long music festival. "So many students look forward to April!" one Johnnie explained.

> **"Both campuses are very welcoming, and the students are very friendly."**

Time and again, Bennies and Johnnies point out the feeling of community that truly defines their college experience. "Both campuses are very welcoming, and the students are very friendly," noted one junior. Another pointed to the role of Benedictine Values, a set of 12 Christian guidelines practiced in everyday campus life. Although students may not know them by heart, they nevertheless "play a pretty big role here. . . . Students are helpful and very respectful of one another." Remarked one Johnnie, "I wouldn't change my college for all the money in the world." —*Stephanie Brockman*

FYI
If you come to CSB/SJU, you'd better bring "a smile . . . fitting in means being friendly!"
What is the typical weekend schedule? "Finish classes, have some fun, do a little homework, have some fun, finish the homework you didn't do yet, go to church (time permitting)."
If I could change one thing about CSB/SJU, I'd "have more diversity on campus."
Three things that every student at CSB/SJU should do before graduating are "take the Chapel Walk, study abroad, and go to the annual Thanksgiving dinner."

St. Olaf College

Address: 1520 St. Olaf Avenue, Northfield, MN 55057
Phone: 507-786-3025
E-mail address: admissions@stolaf.edu
Web site URL: www.stolaf.edu
Year Founded: 1874
Private or Public: Private
Religious Affiliation: Lutheran
Location: Rural
Number of Applicants: 4,024
Percent Accepted: 57%
Percent Accepted who enroll: 37%
Number Entering: 844
Number of Transfers Accepted each Year: 48
Middle 50% SAT range: M: 600–710, CR: 600–720, Wr: 580–700
Middle 50% ACT range: 26–31
Early admission program EA/ED/None: ED

Percentage accepted through EA or ED: Unreported
EA and ED deadline: 15-Nov
Regular Deadline: 15-Jan
Application Fee: $0
Full time Undergraduate enrollment: 3,092
Total enrollment: 3,156
Percent Male: 45%
Percent Female: 55%
Total Percent Minority or Unreported: 16%
Percent African-American: 2%
Percent Asian/Pacific Islander: 5%
Percent Hispanic: 2%
Percent Native-American: <1%
Percent International: 3%
Percent in-state/out of state: 52%/48%
Percent from Public HS: 82%
Retention Rate: 93%

Graduation Rate 4-year: 82%
Graduation Rate 6-year: 84%
Percent Undergraduates in On-campus housing: 92%
Number of official organized extracurricular organizations: 189
3 Most popular majors: Biology/Biological Sciences, Economics, Mathematics
Student/Faculty ratio: 12:1
Average Class Size: 19
Percent of students going to grad school: 22%
Tuition and Fees: $38,150
In-State Tuition and Fees if different: No difference
Cost for Room and Board: $8,800
Percent receiving financial aid out of those who apply: 86%
Percent receiving financial aid among all students: 86%

St. Olaf College, located in the small but picturesque town of Northfield, Minnesota, is known for building a solid sense of community. With close to the entire student body living on campus and on its gourmet meal plan, the entire collegiate experience is designed to foster a tight-knit and welcoming community. This Lutheran-affiliated college has almost everything a student could want, from a rock climbing wall to a movie theater.

A Solid Liberal Arts Education

St. Olaf is at its core a liberal arts institution and it has general education requirements that every student must complete in order to graduate. These requirements include several writing courses, two religion courses, a science lab, and even an ethics requirement. Students find the requirements relatively easy to fit into the 35 classes that are required to graduate, although it can be harder for some majors, such as music, for which the general education requirements and the major requirements do not really overlap. There are a few classes that are considered "laid-back" that can help a student complete his core requirements. One example is a class that combines physical education with the teaching of ethics.

Perhaps due to the rigorous general education requirements, the requirements for the majors are thought to be less demanding and it is not uncommon for a student to double or even triple major. The most popular option is to have one major as well as a concentration in that major. St. Olaf has 39 graduating majors including 15 teaching certification courses, 20 concentrations, and 17 pre-professional fields. The most popular majors in order are English, biology, mathematics, economics, and psychology.

St. Olaf operates on a 4-1-4 academic schedule. This means that students have two full semesters of four classes or more and an interim period, also called J-Term, during the month of January immediately following winter vacation. Students must register for their J-Term class the preceding spring, and have a wide variety of classes to choose from. The compact schedule allows for "a truly unique class format," as one student said. These classes are entirely designed by the professor and can include a study-abroad component.

At a school with a self-proclaimed "global perspective," students are encouraged to study abroad. One student said that, out of his house of 10, all 10 had studied abroad, and he estimated that nearly 90 percent of the student population will study abroad at some point during their career at St. Olaf. The J-Term is different than the semester options in that it is much more affordable and it is directly under the supervision of St. Olaf professors. One class recently went to Peru to investigate the Peruvian medical experience and to learn about medicine. Another class, studying the evolution of Christianity, visited Martin Luther's hometown in Germany and the Vatican.

> "When I walk around campus and say hello to my professors, they know my name, even if I only took one class with them three years ago."

Due to the small class size, the students and professors really get to know each other, and professors are happy to help students outside of class, take meals with students, and generally be available. One student said, "When I walk around campus and say hello to my professors, they know my name, even if I only took one class with them three years ago." Another student commented on how her professors offered to help her work on her interviewing skills when they knew she was applying for grants. The faculty goes above and beyond its academic calling to help students develop and hone their intellectual curiosity.

An Environmentalist's Haven

At St. Olaf, the environment is a part of everyday life. Surrounded by nature, the student body has an appreciation for conservation not experienced at many other schools. Students regularly talk about things the school is doing to reduce its energy usage and, despite the fact that the school recently acquired a windmill to provide a significant amount of the campus's electricity, students still feel there is more the administration could be doing.

Environmentalism and conservation are a part of the fabric of life at St. Olaf. In the month of February the entire school gets caught up in "Campus Energy Wars." As one student observed, "People get really into it in the dorms. They'll even turn off the hallway lights at night, which caused some tension because people kept on knocking into things." Another student remarked on the willingness of students to call each other out on environmental issues, exclaiming, "You get reamed if you throw a can in the trash!" This spirit of environmentalism extends to the classroom. One of the most popular classes at St. Olaf is "Campus Ecology," a class with a big environmental focus that teaches students to apply environmental analyses to the St. Olaf campus and is co-taught by a senior or junior student.

Students' appreciation of the great outdoors is expressed in more leisure-oriented ways as well. The campus abounds with hiking and running trails that students take full advantage of. One student observed, "Most of the school year at St. Olaf is pretty chilly and the winter is downright frigid, but you will often see people out cross-country skiing or sledding or playing a pick-up game of broomball on frozen ponds close to campus." Students even sometimes illegally camp in the nearby "natural lands," the better to appreciate the beautiful landscape that surrounds them.

A Campus of Values

St. Olaf College was founded in 1874 by a group of Norwegian-American immigrant pastors and farmers—which, incidentally, explains the prominence of St. Olaf's Norwegian-language department. The college began and continues as a Lutheran institution. There is a chapel located on campus at which many students attend the Sunday service. St. Olaf students are self-described as "homey, family- and value-oriented." While religion is not pressed upon any student and there is an active Muslim community, Protestant Christians and Lutherans in particular are the dominant religious group. There are a number of extracurricular activities that are centered on religion, including Bible studies and Christian fellowships, the largest being the Fellowship of Christian Athletes. Most teams say a prayer before starting their game and it is not uncommon to see heads bowed in brief prayer before a meal in the dining hall.

However, students who are not particularly religious are not uncomfortable on campus, nor do they feel judged. One student, when asked about the presence of religion on campus, said that "it can be a little surprising," but went on to explain that people only really talk about religion in religion class as part of the core requirement. Students can find a religion class on almost all major world religions and teachers are careful to allow students to form their own opinions. Some students express their religion by abstaining from sex until marriage or not drinking. One student remarked, "Students have religious views and they follow them."

Social Life

As one student said, "you make it what you want it to be." In general, students are satisfied with the social life at St. Olaf. One student describes it as "good, although it can be a little slow." In line with its Lutheran values, the campus is dry, meaning that alcohol is not allowed anywhere on campus. All students are in agreement that this does not inhibit the consumption of alcohol. One student even commented that the prohibition of alcohol leads to binge drinking behavior: "People drink stupidly because they need to pregame faster so they don't get caught." Another student, however, felt that the dry campus "was not really enforced. Usually resident life is semilenient, so students drink as much or as little as other college students." This student praised the school for the number of non-alcoholic activities that it organizes in order to support its dry status. Such activities include showings of recent movies every weekend night, dances, different bands and musical groups, and dance performers. Buntrock Commons, the student center, is the home of the Pause, a completely student-run hangout that features pool tables, movies, concerts, and dances.

Due to the dry campus rule, keggers are a nonentity at St. Olaf; closed-door room parties are more the norm. Students also take advantage of the few bars in the town of Northfield. The Rueb 'N' Stein is a campus favorite and has a big Wednesday showing. Froggy Bottom's is another popular bar with a big Thursday night following. For a more chill vibe with live music and imported beers, students go to The Contented Cow, which has more of a pub feel and is a good place for conversation. The dry campus rule also forces students to be somewhat enterprising if they want to throw a big party. Students will sometimes rent a space in the town of Northfield, usually at the Legion, and will host a party there. Such parties are announced via Facebook and generally charge $5 at the door.

Minneapolis and St. Paul are only 45 minutes from the St. Olaf campus, but trips to the Twin Cities are rare, according to students. Seniors are more likely to make the trek to the cities to watch a play or go to a jazz club. In order to get there, students need a car, something the school allows but which few students take advantage of. One student remarked that "having a car gives you more freedom." It can be hard to get out of Northfield and sometimes, students said, they felt a bit isolated. Other students valued the atmosphere that the campus fosters and believe it helps to foster the sense of community that is so strong at St. Olaf.

When asked about the dating scene at St. Olaf, one student replied with some sarcasm, "I wouldn't say it's huge." Another student, when asked, responded with laughter and went on to explain that the gender gap at St. Olaf, which is 55 percent women and 45 percent men, seems even bigger. St. Olaf students are more likely to still be in a relationship with a high school boyfriend or girlfriend than to casually date in college. Of course, the usual casual college hook-ups do occur here, although less frequently than at other schools due to the religious beliefs and values of many students. The tight-knit community feel of the campus also impedes casual dating, as most students know each other and news travels fast.

St. Olaf is a beautiful college where students smile and greet each other whether they know each other or not. Students are friendly, welcoming, and open-minded despite the homogeneity of the student body. The rural setting of the campus encourages the tight-knit sense of community that pervades the campus and makes students feel they are taken care of and part of a larger St. Olaf family. St. Olaf seeks to create whole people who are intellectually curious with solid values. "You're not just getting together for class; you're in the same buildings, living together, learning together, and growing together."—*Tara Singh*

FYI

If you come to St. Olaf, you'd better bring "winter sports gear."

What is the typical weekend schedule? "Friday everyone relaxes during the day, then goes to a house party or something on campus. Saturday people nap, then at night they go to a sporting event or into town. Sundays are a relaxed day to do homework or watch movies."

If I could change one thing about St. Olaf, I'd "not make it a dry campus, more for safety reasons."

Three things every student at St. Olaf should do before graduating are "go to Christmas fest, climb the rock-climbing wall, and spend one night out in the natural lands."

University of Minnesota

Address: 231 Pillsbury Drive SE, Minneapolis, MN 55455-0213

Phone: 612-625-2008

E-mail address: admissions@umn.edu

Web site URL: www.umn.edu

Year Founded: 1851

Private or Public: Public

Religious Affiliation: None

Location: Urban

Number of Applicants: 36,853

Percent Accepted: 48%

Percent Accepted who enroll: 30%

Number Entering: 5,323

Number of Transfers Accepted each Year: 3,383

Middle 50% SAT range: M: 600–720, CR: 530–690, Wr: 550–670

Middle 50% ACT range: 25–30

Early admission program EA/ED/None: None

Percentage accepted through EA or ED: NA

EA and ED deadline: NA

Regular Deadline: Rolling

Application Fee: $45

Full time Undergraduate enrollment: 33,607

Total enrollment: 51,181

Percent Male: 47%

Percent Female: 53%

Total Percent Minority or Unreported: 23%

Percent African-American: 4%

Percent Asian/Pacific Islander: 9%

Percent Hispanic: 9%

Percent Native-American: <1%

Percent International: 5%

Percent in-state/out of state: 68%/32%

Percent from Public HS: Unreported

Retention Rate: 89%

Graduation Rate 4-year: 66%

Graduation Rate 6-year: Unreported

Percent Undergraduates in On-campus housing: 21%

Number of official organized extracurricular organizations: 600

3 Most popular majors: Social Sciences, Engineering, Biology

Student/Faculty ratio: 21:1

Average Class Size: 25

Percent of students going to grad school: Unreported

Tuition and Fees: $18,022

In-State Tuition and Fees if different: $13,022

Cost for Room and Board: $7,932

Percent receiving financial aid out of those who apply: 69%

Percent receiving financial aid among all students: 57%

Nestled at the heart of a metropolis dubbed "the Twin Cities," the University of Minnesota's largest campus has twin sections as well. The Twin Cities campus acts as the center of the University of Minnesota's four-campus system, but branches of the large state university extend to Duluth, Crookston, and Morris.

"A Common Bond for All"

The University's motto says it all. The University of Minnesota, affectionately known as the "U," embraces four locations in five cities and has something to offer all its students. The Twin Cities campus boasts an enrollment of about 50,000 students, both undergraduate and graduate, far more than the remaining three in the system.

But the flagship embraces its twin city roots and is divided into a St. Paul location, which focuses on agriculture, and the Minneapolis campus. The Minneapolis half of the U is further split into the East Campus and West Campus by the Mississippi River and connected by the iconic Washington Avenue Bridge. Adding to the U's sprawling identity, the campus has a few notable "neighborhoods"—Knoll area, Mall area, Health area, Athletic area, and Gateway area. Getting around the large campus can be tricky, especially with the Mighty Mississippi in the way, so signs that make up "the Gopher Way" help students find their way.

The most notable buildings are the Weisman Art Gallery, designed by Frank Gehry, and the historic Greek row located centrally on campus on the Northrup Mall. The U offers eight residence halls and three apartment buildings and guarantees housing to all freshmen. "Living on campus is convenient," but many students commute from their homes near campus, making parking a challenge. Most students live in the "superblock" complex—a four-block area across from the athletics center. Freshmen can live in any of the university's seven dormitories, only two of which are explicitly designated for freshmen. Freshmen are assigned their own Community Advisers, of which there are usually two per floor in each dorm. As one student noted, much of a freshman's social life is centered around their dorm, while upperclassman life is concentrated beyond the campus.

Any students concerned about living in the heart of Minneapolis should be unduly worried; the U's president has put a significant focus on safety, and students praised the array of different resources designed to keep them safe, including security guards who walk pathways at night, security staff in all the dorms, emergency phone hubs located throughout campus, and driving services.

The campus also boasts an impressive student center called Coffman Memorial Union. Not only does the building feature a bowling alley, video games, and billiards, but it also screens movies every weekend that are free to students, faculty, and their relatives. Said one student: "Coffman is a huge component in fostering community."

Go-pher the Gopher

The U boasts a storied athletics tradition centered on the basketball, football, and ice hockey teams. The Golden Gophers participate in a long-standing rivalry game with the University of Wisconsin. "A lot of people go to games and watch them on campus," one student said. Another added, "There is a lot of school pride for sports teams." Dating back to legendary hockey coach Herb Brooks, who later coached the 1980 U.S. men's hockey team to an Olympic gold medal in the "Miracle on Ice," the U's men's ice hockey team has five national championships under its belt. Out-of-staters beware: most hockey recruits hail from Minnesota—all but two members of the current 26-man team are from the Land of 10,000 Lakes.

Athletics, though, are just one piece of the thriving campus atmosphere. Students cited Greek life, the Black Student Association, and other student organizations as prevalent on campus. "People are usually very committed to extracurricular activities," a student said. "I think they are a good way to meet people and relieve yourself from schoolwork." Still, while Greek life is popular on campus, it does not dominate social life for students at the U. The university's more than 600 student groups offer a wide array of opportunities to get involved in campus life—from the student newspaper to religious organizations. "Whatever you're into, you'll find it at the U, and probably there'll be quite a lot of people with you," one student said.

Choices, Choices, Choices

On such a large campus, academic options are hugely varied—from the agricultural programs offered in St. Paul to the College of Design. "The U of M offers very challenging courses but it also offers many fun courses such as dance, sports, and horseback riding classes," a student said. Some popular majors are political science, psychology, business, and the sciences. "U of M has so many majors to choose from," a student marveled.

> "The U of M offers very challenging courses but it also offers many fun courses such as dance, sports, and horseback riding classes."

Academic advising at the U tends to work well, one student explained, given that there is full-time staff with the specific role of advising students on their academic work. Students are advised by someone within their field of study, and while one student said getting a good adviser can be "pretty hit or miss," it helps to have a full-time staff member available to help when needed.

Like any large university, class sizes reach about 100 students for introductory courses, slimming down to about 50 for specialized classes, making it relatively easy for students to get a place in a course.

The workload can get pretty heavy, with an average of two to three papers and exams per class in addition to reading. But a very descriptive course catalog helps narrow down the options. Teachers try to embrace the diversity and variety offered at the U. "I like how teachers are very open minded and teach from many perspectives," a student said. Discussions on the diverse campus are a high point for some students: "What I like most is the different people you meet and the ranges in their experience in what is being taught. The discussion that goes on in class is really exciting."

One student mentioned the ease with which many people at the University of Minnesota make friends: "Many people meet through classes and become friends as well. People often work and study in groups. People also hang out at the U just for fun." Ultimately, the U is a place where not only hockey-playing Minnesotans but Gophers from over 130 countries around the world can live, learn, and make the most of their college years.— *Brittany Golob and Raymond Carlson*

FYI

If you come to the University of Minnesota, you'd better bring "a planner."

What's the typical weekend schedule? "Friday afternoon you're either going to be out running or be at the Rec before the weekend starts, in the evening you'll most likely be at some social event in the dorms or frat row. Saturday you'll go to a sporting event or concert, Saturday night is a mirror image of Friday, and on Sunday you sleep in, maybe watch football, and then get to work."

If I could change one thing about the University of Minnesota, "I'd make the class sizes smaller."

Three things every student at the University of Minnesota should do before graduating are "study abroad, participate in an extracurricular activity, and go have a burger in the Shake & 80s malt shop."

Mississippi

Millsaps College

Address: 1701 North State Street, Jackson, MS 39210
Phone: 601-974-1050
E-mail address: admissions@millsaps.edu
Web site URL: www.millsaps.edu
Year Founded: 1890
Private or Public: Private
Religious Affiliation: Methodist
Location: Suburban
Number of Applicants: 1,186
Percent Accepted: 77%
Percent Accepted who enroll: 24%
Number Entering: 214
Number of Transfers Accepted each Year: 64
Middle 50% SAT range: M: 540–650, CR: 520–640, Wr: Unreported
Middle 50% ACT range: 24–29
Early admission program EA/ED/None: EA and ED

Percentage accepted through EA or ED: Unreported
EA and ED deadline: EA: 1-Dec, ED: 15-Nov
Regular Deadline: Rolling
Application Fee: $0
Full time Undergraduate enrollment: 945
Total enrollment: 965
Percent Male: 49%
Percent Female: 51%
Total Percent Minority or Unreported: 24%
Percent African-American: 9%
Percent Asian/Pacific Islander: 5%
Percent Hispanic: 3%
Percent Native-American: 1%
Percent International: 3%
Percent in-state/out of state: 46%/54%
Percent from Public HS: 62%
Retention Rate: 79%

Graduation Rate 4-year: 62%
Graduation Rate 6-year: 66%
Percent Undergraduates in On-campus housing: 86%
Number of official organized extracurricular organizations: 85
3 Most popular majors: Biology, Business, English
Student/Faculty ratio: 9:1
Average Class Size: 15
Percent of students going to grad school: 48%
Tuition and Fees: $27,650
In-State Tuition and Fees if different: No difference
Cost for Room and Board: $10,312
Percent receiving financial aid out of those who apply: 100%
Percent receiving financial aid among all students: 96%

Though largely unknown outside of Mississippi, Millsaps College is highly respected throughout the area as a school that offers a well-rounded liberal arts education at a competitive price. Though Millsaps Majors may seem to have lackluster school spirit when it comes to supporting their athletic teams, most students enjoy life at Millsaps.

Work Hard

Millsaps was the first school in Mississippi to have a chapter of the academic honor society Phi Beta Kappa, and the school generally ranks high both for its academics and for its relatively low tuition. Millsaps offers 35 majors, and though the requirements vary by major, each student must complete 10 core courses, offered in topics ranging from history to science to mathematics.

A major selling point for many students is the small size of the classes at Millsaps. The average class size is 15 people, and the student/faculty ratio is 9:1. This class size fosters open discussion as well as close relationships between professors and students. According to one student, "The classes are very engaging, very discussion-oriented." Students say that their professors "really do care about their students," and several admitted that they considered the relationships formed with their professors the most valuable part of their college experiences. "I consider some of these professors my friends." While students definitely note that the academic life is very "strenuous," most say they were fulfilled in their academic lives. "I feel like I learn so much."

Party Hard

The social life at Millsaps revolves pretty much exclusively around the Greek system. There are six fraternities and six sororities governed by the Panhellenic Council and the Interfraternity Council. While students say that it is not essential to be in a fraternity or sorority—"It's not like if you aren't Greek you're going to have an awful time"—it seems pretty hard to escape the fact that the Greek scene is *the* scene at Millsaps. This is highlighted in particular by the fact that non-Greeks are referred to as "independents." Though it is perfectly acceptable to be an independent, an independent who won't set foot in a fraternity house might have a hard time finding a party, particularly during freshman and sophomore years. As students get older, however, "they tend to drift off campus more." Many upperclassmen enjoy local spots Hal & Mal's or Schimmels for drinks, music, or just hanging out with their friends. According to one student, "A lot of times you can find your professors at Fenian's."

> "I consider some of these professors my friends."

Drinking rules on campus are pretty sensible. Though rowdy behavior in the dormitories is prohibited, students appreciated the fact that "the RAs treat us like adults." The two large campus-wide events every year are the homecoming football game in the fall and Major Madness in the spring. At Major Madness, students gather on "The Bowl"—the large, grassy area in the middle of campus—and play games, eat, drink, and listen to music. Though the musicians are rarely big-name stars—bands have included Better Than Ezra, Stroke Nine, and the North Mississippi All Stars—"it's definitely stuff you can dance to, sing to, and drink to."

With the exception of the homecoming game, Millsaps students in general don't get extremely excited about sports. "It's definitely not like an SEC school, so if people come to Millsaps expecting that, then they're not going to get it." Instead, supporting athletic teams is more of a matter of supporting your friends who happen to be on those teams than a statement of school pride.

On Campus: Where It's At

Approximately 81 percent of Millsaps students live on campus. Most choose to live in the dormitories for all four years, though some upperclassmen move off campus. The housing is divided up by the North Side and the South Side. Freshman year, everyone lives on the North Side. After freshman year, students pick their rooms based on a room draw, which functions on a point system. Each student entering the room draw receives points based on his or her class year and GPA. Students then combine with their roommates and vie for the best dorms. The residence hall rooms are all double-occupancy, and the halls feature traditional double rooms, apartment-style and suite-style rooms. Though the students admit that the dormitories aren't by any means luxurious, "they do their best to make it pleasant. My friends who are from other colleges always talk about how nice our dorms are here."

For most students, more important than the dorms themselves is the fact that the dorms provide a social outlet as well. "It's really cool when all your friends live on campus." This social atmosphere is also extended to the main cafeteria, also known as "The Caf." The Caf is one of two dining options on campus, the other being the Kava House, which provides quick meals to go. At The Caf, students select from a menu of salads, soups, sandwiches, and daily hot meals. Students generally seem to be quite pleased with the quality of the food, though opinions differ about the variety of food choices. While one senior said that she was "really going to miss [the food] next year," another complained that the food choices were repetitive.

The Center of the State

Students seem to have mixed feelings about being in the city of Jackson itself. In one 2008 ranking, Jackson was ranked the nation's 11th most dangerous city. For this reason, students say they must exercise caution while out on campus, but they don't feel that the crime level in Jackson is detrimental to their college experience. Students are very well aware that "Jackson isn't the safest of cities." While one student said that she generally feels "safe on campus," she was sure to note that she "wouldn't walk around alone in the dark."

One advantage of being in the city of Jackson—which has a population of just under 180,000 people—is the city's position as the capital of the state, and thus the center of state politics. Particularly for students with an interest in politics or government, Millsaps is a good place to get a taste of the political arena. Students say it is very easy to get internships in the state or local government, and state officials will sometimes teach classes at Millsaps as adjunct professors.

Though the city of Jackson is very much a political city, students say that campus life is "not too hardcore politically" and that the student body as a whole does not lean very heavily left or right. Both "the Millsaps Young Democrats and the Republicans are very well represented and well spoken-for." Students say that Millsaps is a place for political expression but that there are also many students who abstain from political discussion altogether.

Diversity?

Students new to Millsaps may be surprised by the lack of geographic and racial diversity. Slightly less than 50 percent of the students are from the state of Mississippi, and the freshman class at Millsaps is generally comprised of approximately 15 to 20 percent minority students. While some students lamented that fact—"I'd like it to be more diverse than it is"—students across the board were impressed by the openness of students to new ideas and to different types of people. "Millsaps is very diverse if you look at the big picture, not just at race." Another noted, "What makes up for [the lack of racial diversity] is the diversity of ideas and of opinions." Though there is little racial diversity on campus, student organizations like the Black Student Association provide minority students with a sense of community.

For many students, the mere size of Millsaps contributes to this openness for different types of students. With just over a thousand undergraduates, "I feel like I've met everyone on campus one way or another," one senior said. Another student chalked up the open-minded atmosphere at Millsaps to the philosophy of education at the school. "They really teach you to be warm-hearted and open to everything and not closed-minded at all."—*Susanna Moore*

FYI

If you come to Millsaps, you'd better bring "a willingness to work hard and party hard."

What is the typical weekend schedule? "Friday: go to dinner and to the fraternity houses; Saturday: watch football all day or go to the football game, eat dinner, preparty, and go to the fraternity houses; Sunday: wake up late and do your homework."

If I could change one thing about Millsaps, I'd "make it farther from home."

Three things every student at Millsaps should do before graduating are "swim in the fountains, Bowl-sit, really get to know a professor."

Mississippi State University

Address: P.O. Box 6334, Mississippi State, MS 39762
Phone: 662-325-2224
E-mail address: admit@msstate.edu
Web site URL: www.msstate.edu
Year Founded: 1878
Private or Public: Public
Religious Affiliation: None
Location: Suburban
Number of Applicants: 9,300
Percent Accepted: 66%
Percent Accepted who enroll: 44%
Number Entering: 2,701
Number of Transfers Accepted each Year: 1,806
Middle 50% SAT range: M: 490–630, CR: 470–610, Wr: Unreported
Middle 50% ACT range: 20–26
Early admission program EA/ED/None: None
Percentage accepted through EA or ED: NA

EA and ED deadline: NA
Regular Deadline: Rolling
Application Fee: $40
Full time Undergraduate enrollment: 14,079
Total enrollment: 15,543
Percent Male: 52%
Percent Female: 48%
Total Percent Minority or Unreported: 29%
Percent African-American: 22%
Percent Asian/Pacific Islander: 1%
Percent Hispanic: 2%
Percent Native-American: <1%
Percent International: 2%
Percent in-state/out of state: 80%/20%
Percent from Public HS: Unreported
Retention Rate: 82%
Graduation Rate 4-year: 60%
Graduation Rate 6-year: Unreported

Percent Undergraduates in On-campus housing: 26%
Number of official organized extracurricular organizations: 326
3 Most popular majors: Business Administration, Elementary Education, Physical Education Teaching & Coaching
Student/Faculty ratio: 20:1
Average Class Size: 25
Percent of students going to grad school: Unreported
Tuition and Fees: $14,670
In-State Tuition and Fees if different: $5,808
Cost for Room and Board: $8,162
Percent receiving financial aid out of those who apply: 56%
Percent receiving financial aid among all students: 54%

Located far away from the noises of big cities, Mississippi State University is a large state university. With an enrollment of more than 15,000 students, both graduate and undergraduate, the public university represents one of the most important institutions in the State of Mississippi. Furthermore, although most students come from within the state, nearly a quarter of undergraduates hail from places outside of Mississippi. Not to be confused with the big rival University of Mississippi—better known as Ole Miss—Mississippi State offers a large selection of opportunities to students while allowing them to enjoy college education far away from bustling metropolitan areas in the quiet and beautiful town of Starkville.

Eight Schools

Despite being the largest public university in Mississippi, the college admissions process remains rigorous. In fact, the school accepts only about two-thirds of all applicants. There is generally a large number of applications in part due to the reputation of the university as a top bargain institution, which provides good education and strong prospects for graduates while being relatively affordable. "I really think that the education I get here is useful," said one student. "For instate students, it is especially worth it."

What is remarkable for Mississippi State is the wide range of academic opportunities that are available to the students. There are eleven schools on campus, ranging from the traditional College of Arts and Sciences to the School of Veterinarian Medicine. It is certainly possible for students to find the program that will satisfy their academic pursuits. "It is a big school, so we have more than one hundred majors and certifications," said one student. "As long as you put in the energy to find the right school and major for you, I think you will really enjoy the school in terms of academics," added another.

An important characteristic of the academic program is the availability of professional training, such as poultry science, wildlife, fisheries and aquaculture, and real estate. All types of curriculum allows students with a clear vision of what they want to do as a professional to directly pursue their future career. "There are a couple of problems with the curriculum here and there," said one student. "But I think the professional preparation is pretty good here."

The number of students per class varies greatly depending on the major and the specific type of course. "There are big lectures, and you may have to try not to fall asleep," said one student. On the other hand, some do like the larger classes because "you can meet more people and really feel like a college student sitting in a big lecture hall."

> "As long as you put in the energy to find the right school and major for you, I think you will really enjoy the school in terms of academics."

Given the large selection of classes, it is very difficult to list all the academic requirements. Nevertheless, all students from Mississippi State must complete the general education requirements, which include English, mathematics, natural sciences, humanities, and social sciences. Like in most institutions of higher learning, these requirements are very important in ensuring that all students, regardless of major or future aspirations, will be exposed to a variety of subjects, thus ensuring the breadth of education that is considered an important part of the college experience.

As to the most difficult majors, students seem to believe that the College of Architecture, which is an important part of the university's academic program, can provide some late-night assignments. Furthermore, just like in many other schools, engineering is also a difficult program. "I guess college is about what you put into it," said one student. "If you try, you can have a lot of challenges even in those easy majors." In the end, however, the student does believe that "engineering is a lot harder than other programs."

The closeness between instructors and students also varies greatly. "It is a big place, so it is not like a tiny school of a couple hundred people where everyone knows each other," said one senior. However, he does confirm that some professors "do try to get to know students." More importantly and unsurprisingly, students who take the initiative to talk to and engage their professors tend to get more out of their classes and have better academic experiences.

Starkville

Anyone who looks to live in a big metropolis should probably look elsewhere for college. In fact, Jackson, the capital of Mississippi and the largest city in the state, is more than 100 miles away. The city of Columbus is only about 20 miles east of the campus, and with less than 30,000 inhabitants, it hardly represents a major metropolitan area. This, however, does not mean that all those who enjoy city life will be disappointed by Starkville, where the university is located. "I thought I wanted to go to school in a big city, but it turns out that I really like it here," confided one student.

Starkville has its own charms. It is truly a university town. The majority of the activities in Starkville are invariably linked to Mississippi State. "It feels like home," said one student. A number of festivals on visual arts are conducted every year, and the student body generally plays a big role in attending and supporting those events.

The campus is very large, and many students believe that cars are essential. "You will obviously find ways to get around campus without a car. The school will help, but it is so much easier just to have a car," said one student.

The dorms are generally fine. A few newer buildings have been added in recent years, and they have received much better reviews than the older ones. As in many large state universities, the majority of upperclassmen live off campus. "I think you should try both on-campus and off-campus housing," said one student. "Living in dorms is part of the college experience, but you should also try to do everything on your own once you get older. That's why you live off campus when you are a junior or senior."

The Bulldogs

It goes without saying that football is important at Mississippi State. The biggest day of the year is probably the Egg Bowl, when the two in-state rivals, University of Mississippi and Mississippi State, take on each other as part of a regular season game. "This is what the football season is all about," said one student. "As long as we beat Ole Miss, then we are happy with our football team," said another. One tradition is for students to ring cowbells at the game, which supposedly brings good luck. After more than 100 head-to-head games, Ole Miss holds a better record, but it has not stopped the fervent fans of the Mississippi State Bulldogs from showing their support en masse during the games.

In addition to sports, Greek life is also important. The sororities and fraternities are the main venues for parties. And while drinking is part of the night life at Mississippi State, students generally agree that people tend to be careful and do not put too much pressure on others to consume alcohol. "We don't have much of a town around here, but at least we have lots of people in the university, so the weekends can be fun."

A Southern Environment

Students at Mississippi State are generally satisfied with their college experience. It has a distinct southern character, being situated in the middle of rural Mississippi. The university really stands out as a solid academic institution that prepares students for their future endeavors. At the same time, the rural environment creates a strong sense of community in Starkville. Combining all these factors, Mississippi State is certainly a top destination for those interested in a good, affordable education.—*Xiaohang Liu*

FYI

If you come to Mississippi State, you'd better bring "a car."
What is the typical weekend schedule? "Go to a football game. What else?"
If I could change one thing about Mississippi State, I'd "add a few more thousand people and stores to Starkville."
Three things every student at Mississippi State should do before graduating are "Egg Bowl, travel around the state, and take an architecture class."

University of Mississippi

Address: 145 Martindale, University, MS 38677
Phone: 662-915-7226
E-mail address: admissions@olemiss.edu
Web site URL: www.olemiss.edu
Year Founded: 1844
Private or Public: Public
Religious Affiliation: None
Location: Rural
Number of Applicants: 10,909
Percent Accepted: 78%
Percent Accepted who enroll: 36%
Number Entering: 3,095
Number of Transfers Accepted each Year: 1,982
Middle 50% SAT range: M: 470–600, CR: 470–590, Wr: Unreported
Middle 50% ACT range: 20–29
Early admission program EA/ED/None: None

Percentage accepted through EA or ED: NA
EA and ED deadline: NA
Regular Deadline: 20-Jul
Application Fee: $30
Full time Undergraduate enrollment: 14,159
Total enrollment: 17,085
Percent Male: 49%
Percent Female: 51%
Total Percent Minority or Unreported: 26%
Percent African-American: 17%
Percent Asian/Pacific Islander: 2%
Percent Hispanic: 2%
Percent Native-American: <1%
Percent International: 1%
Percent in-state/out of state: 52%/48%
Percent from Public HS: Unreported
Retention Rate: 83%
Graduation Rate 4-year: 56%

Graduation Rate 6-year: Unreported
Percent Undergraduates in On-campus housing: 33%
Number of official organized extracurricular organizations: 250
3 Most popular majors: Business/Marketing, Education, Social Sciences
Student/Faculty ratio: 18:1
Average Class Size: 15
Percent of students going to grad school: Unreported
Tuition and Fees: $14,797
In-State Tuition and Fees if different: $5,792
Cost for Room and Board: $6,550
Percent receiving financial aid out of those who apply: 63%
Percent receiving financial aid among all students: 45%

The historic institution nestled in the town of Oxford, just 70 miles south of Memphis, is formally known as the University of Mississippi—but to those in the know, it's Ole Miss. First coined in 1897 as the title of the university's yearbook, Ole Miss is more than a mere nickname. It reflects the institution's deeply-rooted traditions, Southern heritage, and welcoming atmosphere. Above all, the name reflects the affection students and alumni feel for their university, with its scenic campus, close-knit feel, and growing international prestige.

An Intimate Public University

Among public universities, Ole Miss has a strong academic reputation—one that has steadily improved in recent years. With seven undergraduate schools—the College of Liberal Arts and the Schools of Accountancy, Applied Sciences, Business Administration, Education, Engineering, and Pharmacy—the university has a program to offer every student, no matter where their academic interests lie. Among the various schools, the College of Liberal Arts and the School of Business Administration boast the highest undergraduate enrollments.

Over the past few years, Ole Miss has garnered a high national rank among public colleges. Students think the university's growing prestige is deserved. "Academic life at Ole Miss is great," said one student. "Most classes aren't too big, and all the professors I have come across are more than willing to help their students in any way possible."

Ole Miss's relatively small undergraduate population gives students easy access to professors and administrators. The administration has an open-door policy, encouraging students to bring concerns or suggestions straight to the top. Professors, likewise, are eager to meet with students. "Because we're not that big, the student-faculty ratio is pretty good," remarked one senior. Most students agree that class size is not overwhelming, especially compared to other public universities. Upper-level courses generally range from 20–30 students, and one upperclassman noted that many professors require participation. Introductory "core" courses, however, can hold over 150 students.

To give underclassmen the opportunity to take smaller, more specialized classes, the university offers several unique programs. Each year, the McDonnell Barksdale Honors College admits around 120 freshmen with exemplary academic records. "A lot of money has been invested in the honors college, and it offers students great resources," said one student. The Croft Institute, Ole Miss's renowned international studies program, is even more selective, accepting only 40 students a year. But these specialized programs are not for the faint of heart. As one senior noted, "Honors College and Croft classes are more difficult than most."

For the first few months of their college careers, all Ole Miss freshmen must take an hour-a-week course called University Studies. Designed to ease the transition into college life, University Studies gives freshmen a chance to learn more about Ole Miss and to meet classmates.

Southern-Style Living

Students give the university's dorms mixed reviews. "They're pretty nice," said one student. Another called them "outdated." Still another insisted that "the ladies' dorms are nicer than the men's." Whatever their opinion, freshmen are required to live on campus. All university housing is gender-segregated by building. The two main freshman dorms are Martin for women and Stockard for men. Visitation hours are relatively strict; guests must leave by 11 p.m. on weeknights and 1 a.m. on weekends, unless a dormitory's students vote in the first week of the semester to extend these hours. Men's and women's dorms are close together, and most students claim not to mind single-sex housing.

Responding to students' complaints about university housing, the administration has begun extensive renovations. Currently under construction is a massive residential college, where students can live all four years. "The residential college will have a computer lab, a gym, a cafeteria, an auditorium, and more," explained one senior. "If I could go back to my freshman year, I would definitely want to live there!"

Although many students think mandatory on-campus housing for freshmen is a good idea—as one student said, "it forces you to get to know campus and your classmates"—almost all upperclassmen live in Greek houses or off campus. Nearby apartments, while slightly less convenient than dorms, give students more freedom and flexibility. Plus, most Ole Miss students own cars, which facilitate trips to class, the grocery store, and even to Memphis (just over an hour away) to shop or go out on weekends.

Rebel Revelry

When it comes to social life, students agree: Ole Miss knows how to party. "We're not ranked the number two party school for nothing," laughed one senior.

The social scene at Ole Miss is extensive and varied. Greek life is popular on campus—35 percent of undergraduates belong to a fraternity or sorority—and rarely does a weekend go by without a fraternity party taking place. In the spring, each fraternity hosts a no-holds-barred blowout, such as SAE's "Patty Murphy" or ATO's "Gator Bash." Often these parties last an entire weekend, culminating in crawfish cookouts or barbeques with live bands. Fraternity parties are often open to non-Greeks, although students note that women have an easier time getting in than men.

While fraternity and sorority events are a big part of campus life, students agree that non-Greeks won't want for things to do on weekends. "Greek life is a great way to get to know people early on, and fraternity parties are big for freshmen," explained one student. "But as you get older, you find the social scene gears away from fraternity parties—people are over that scene."

The Oxford town square, which students described as "one of a kind," offers plenty of alternatives to the Greek party scene, particularly for the 21-plus crowd. Popular weekend hangouts include Rooster's, a blues and barbeque joint owned by actor Morgan Freeman; Proud Larry's, a more laid-back bar with live music; and the Library, where students 18 and up can come to dance and watch sports games. Rebel Ride, a free transportation service, drives students home when the bars close at 1 a.m. Said one junior: "Oxford is a small town, but there never seems to be a shortage of things going on."

Grooving at the Grove

In the fall, no Ole Miss weekend would be complete without a Saturday afternoon trip to the Grove. Most days of the year, the 10-acre grassy knoll known as the Grove looks like a simple lawn with the occasional magnolia tree. But on game days, it transforms into what one junior calls a "huge party"—an elaborate tailgating event that is rivaled nowhere. In fact, tailgating is somewhat of a misnomer for Ole Miss's version, which doesn't involve cars, trucks, or parking lots. Rather, tailgaters at the Grove reserve open-air tents of red, white, or blue. Students and families bring grills, nice food, silverware,

candles, and occasionally even chandeliers into their tents, and spend the day eating, drinking, and socializing. "Adults and students are chatting, kids are running around—it's very family-oriented," explained one student. Ever the Southern ladies and gentlemen, many students dress up to tailgate at the Grove; girls wear sundresses and guys wear collared shirts with khakis.

School spirit abounds at Ole Miss, and football games are an integral part of the campus experience. After the Grove, students move to the stadium in their semiformal attire to cheer on the Rebels. One student notes that "tailgating used to be bigger than the football game itself," but in recent years, as the team has improved, games have become increasingly popular. In fact, many students center dates on football games, attending the game and its pre- and postparties with their date. Reflecting on the game day experience, one junior said: "There honestly isn't anything like football season at Ole Miss."

Rebelling Against Racism

The shadow of slavery, segregation, and racism has long lingered over Ole Miss, much as its administration and students have attempted to distance the university from the darker aspects of its past. Founded in 1848, the university closed briefly during the Civil War after its students left to fight as "University Grays" in the Confederate army. After the war, the university remained segregated until 1962, when James Meredith became the first black student to walk the halls of Ole Miss, flanked by federal marshals. Race riots and other violence plagued the campus throughout the Civil Rights Movement.

> **"There honestly isn't anything like football season at Ole Miss."**

While most students agree that racism is a problem of the past, controversy has erupted within the past decade over the university mascot, Colonel Rebel. In 2003, Colonel Rebel—who, according to some, looks like an antebellum plantation owner—was banned from the sidelines of football games, but he remains the university's official mascot. While some students would prefer a less controversial mascot, many students, according to one senior, "just don't think about it."

The mascot controversy aside, Ole Miss has made great strides toward diversity and tolerance in the past decades. Today, 19 percent of its undergraduates are minorities, and most students feel that the university's atmosphere is inclusive. Diversity-oriented undergraduate organizations, such as the group One Mississippi, have been created to address racial issues on campus. "We've had such issues with discrimination in the past that we've really had to face these issues head on," explained one senior. Another student agreed, claiming: "We deal with this issue every day; we talk about it in every single class. We've come a really long way."

Ole Miss is an institution steeped in tradition, from its controversial mascot, to its game days at the Grove, to its beautiful and historic grounds. Throughout the past decades, the university has been filtering the good traditions from the bad, enhancing its academics, its facilities, and its diversity. Yet when asked what sets Ole Miss apart, most students didn't cite its academic excellence or picturesque campus. Rather, students believe that Ole Miss's close-knit, community atmosphere—rare among public universities—is what puts the university in a league of its own. As one student stated simply, "At Ole Miss, you just feel at home."—*Elizabeth Bewley*

FYI

If you come to Ole Miss, you better bring "your tent for the Grove. If you don't, you will miss out on one of the best experiences of your life."

What is the typical weekend schedule? "Head to the bars Library or Rooster's on Thursday night, hit up a fraternity party on Friday, tailgate at the Grove and go to the football game on Saturday."

If I could change one thing about Ole Miss, I'd change "the stereotype of Ole Miss being stuck in Civil War times and still being racist."

The three things that every student at Ole Miss should do before graduating are "go to a football game and tailgate at the Grove, get to know Oxford, and eat catfish at Taylor Grocery just outside of town."

Missouri

University of Missouri / Columbia

Address: 230 Jesse Hall, Columbia, MO 65211
Phone: 573-882-7786
E-mail address: MU4U@missouri.edu
Web site URL: www.admissions.missouri.edu
Year Founded: 1839
Private or Public: Public
Religious Affiliation: None
Location: Suburban
Number of Applicants: 17,465
Percent Accepted: 84%
Percent Accepted who enroll: 41%
Number Entering: 6,089
Number of Transfers Accepted each Year: 2,122
Middle 50% SAT range: M: 530–650, CR: 540–650, Wr: Unreported
Middle 50% ACT range: 23–28
Early admission program EA/ED/None: None

Percentage accepted through EA or ED: NA
EA and ED deadline: NA
Regular Deadline: Rolling
Application Fee: $50
Full time Undergraduate enrollment: 24,901
Total enrollment: 32,415
Percent Male: 47%
Percent Female: 53%
Total Percent Minority or Unreported: 18%
Percent African-American: 9%
Percent Asian/Pacific Islander: 2%
Percent Hispanic: 2%
Percent Native-American: <1%
Percent International: 1%
Percent in-state/out of state: 72%/28%
Percent from Public HS: Unreported
Retention Rate: 84%
Graduation Rate 4-year: 69%

Graduation Rate 6-year: Unreported
Percent Undergraduates in On-campus housing: 28%
Number of official organized extracurricular organizations: 600
3 Most popular majors: Business/Marketing, Journalism, Engineering
Student/Faculty ratio: 20:1
Average Class Size: 15
Percent of students going to grad school: Unreported
Tuition and Fees: $21,784
In-State Tuition and Fees if different: $8,989
Cost for Room and Board: $8,643
Percent receiving financial aid out of those who apply: 67%
Percent receiving financial aid among all students: 52%

Walking around the Quad, the most striking features are the Columns, monuments from Mizzou's earliest days. Tradition has each year's freshmen walk through the Columns toward Jesse Hall to show their entrance into Mizzou. Graduating seniors walk through the Columns away from Jesse, signifying their exit from college into the real world. In between are four years at the University of Missouri at Columbia, the largest school in the University of Missouri system and, as its Tigers will tell you, the best. It is home to a striking array of students. Greek life predominates on campus, with rambunctious students holding parties regularly, and there is a wide spectrum of non-Greeks, ranging from artsy people, goths, anti-stereotypes, engineering students, and many others. Just about everybody, however, comes together on weekends for football and basketball games, and Mizzou pride is never as strong as when the fans scream from the stands, "MIZ-ZOU!!!"

Hard at Work

As Missouri's flagship state school, Mizzou caters to a large number of students, and so class sizes vary from 15 to 200. The largest and most popular lecture courses, such as Biology 1010 or Psychology 1010, can be daunting, so smaller classes such as "History of the 1960s" or "American Film History,

1945–Present" offer a more intimate atmosphere for students. Most students consider the workload manageable, although perennial: "I always had something to read or there'd be an online quiz or two that I had to take every day," commented a theater major.

Some students say that the most difficult courses at Mizzou are pre-med and engineering courses, including biochemistry, chemical engineering, and electrical engineering, but a band member pointed out that "all majors have intensely difficult aspects to them. Business students have to struggle through Accounting 1 and 2 and macro- and microeconomics." Another student added that "a lot of majors require intensive writing courses, which are never easy, and the workload increases as you advance into your major." A few special programs help to make sense of Mizzou's large range of academic offerings—there are Freshman Interest Groups for first-year students, Sponsored Learning Communities, and academically oriented organizations on campus.

The standard distributional requirements for a Mizzou degree include college algebra and another math course, English Exposition and Argumentation, a writing-intensive course, American history or government, and a certain number of credits each from sciences, social sciences, and humanities. Many courses can be fulfilled through high school coursework. One student remarked, "I often complained that it was unnecessary for me to take math and science classes . . . but now I understand why. The administration at Mizzou wanted us to be well-rounded. I'm very glad I took biology and algebra and geology, because it really opened my eyes to the world, and helped me understand current events."

Greektown or Not?

Greek life is rampant on campus, with nearly a quarter of the students participating in 52 fraternities and sororities. Opinion on this lifestyle among the remaining students is divided: a large number are very supportive of the community, from Greektown (where most of the houses are located) to the parties they provide from Wednesday through Saturday nights. The remainder complain that "if you don't belong to a Greek group, you might want to avoid living in a dorm that's located so close to Greektown, or it will drive you crazy." For them, there are many other dorms, which all tend to be fairly comfortable. Certain dorms have become more well known for housing large

populations of math and science students or artsy types; the FARC (Fine Arts Residential Community), for example, houses many music students. After freshman or sophomore year, many students will move off campus into apartments or even houses; Columbia, being a small city, offers many inexpensive housing options that are within walking distance of the rest of campus.

With so many students from so many parts of the country, Mizzou has a niche for nearly every student. The school is in the Midwest, so the stereotypical student is a "white, male, Christian Republican who belongs to a frat. Fortunately, that's usually not the case . . . the student body is very racially, ethnically, socially, and politically diverse." Campus security is present, but safety is never a concern. Multiple students said they felt very safe on campus at all hours. One student living in an all-girls dorm said, "We actually are informed of any alerts through e-mail as soon as possible," which is a useful system for such a large state school.

Food is a big deal: all entering freshmen get the famous Tiger-striped ice cream, and all the dining halls have been rated as "tasty." One junior did note, though, that "you have to pay attention to dining hall hours when picking your meal plan." For late-night cravings, the most popular destination is Gumby's. Shakespeare's is also a favorite destination, claiming to have the best pizza in the Midwest.

> "Painted tiger-ears headbands, tiger tails, and black and gold just shower the campus."

Most students are involved with multiple extracurricular groups. The ones with the largest memberships include College Democrats and College Republicans, the Asian American Student Assocation, Black Student Organization, Hillel, and the Muslim Student Organization. Many students remain involved with faith-based organizations. "There are many churches, synagogues, and mosques within walking distance of the campus where students can attend a service," said a business major. The biggest extracurricular is sports, though. "A LOT of students tend to wear Mizzou jerseys on days of competition," said a fan. "MU sports are pretty big in central, rural, and southern Missouri. I can tell ya that, 'cause a lot of people from small towns from all over Missouri would drive up to Columbia to go to football or basketball games—it is something fun for them to do." A clarinet player for the band noted the crazy colors on game days: "Painted tiger-ears headbands (I have one), tiger tails (have one of those too), and black and gold just shower the campus from tots to alums, students to parents." Another student said it straight out: "The one thing that sets us aside from other schools is the spirit; everyone is proud to be a Tiger. MIZ-ZOU!"

The Quad and Beyond

The campus itself stands out as one of the most beautiful areas in Columbia. One upperclassman gushed that "there is an Ivy League feel to the place. And the Quad is just amazing in the spring—people will be playing Frisbee and hanging out by the Columns even at five in the morning!" A fencer said she loves the inner architecture of Ellis, the largest of Mizzou's libraries, as well as the Art Museum. A sophomore pointed out that Mizzou has an amazing athletics center, including a "huge workout center, many basketball courts, lazy river, saunas, pools, the list keeps going!" With so many varsity sports, the athletic center is almost a given.

When students were asked, they said that they would definitely choose to go to Mizzou again. "I had fun, I learned a lot of good stuff, I met so many cool people from all over who made me open my eyes, I made some lasting wonderful friends, and I didn't expect that I'd have such a great time here!" And the Mizzou Pride lasts the rest of your life!—*Jeffrey Zuckerman*

FYI

If you come to Mizzou, you'd better bring "a cell phone, so that you can always catch up with your pals between classes."

What is the typical weekend schedule? "Friday, go out to a party or club, hang out with your friends and go to Shakespeare's Pizza or order from Gumby's. Saturday, relax in the afternoon, take a walk in the park or go to a football game. In the evening, let loose. Sunday, study and do homework."

If I could change one thing about Mizzou, I'd "complete all the construction so our campus can be its most beautiful."

Three things that every student at Mizzou should do before graduating are "jump in the Brady Fountain, ride the Mizzou Tiger, and take a class about a subject you have no clue about."

University of Missouri / Kansas City

Address: 5100 Rockhill Road 101AC, Kansas City, MO 64114
Phone: 816-235-1111
E-mail address: admit@umkc.edu
Web site URL: www.umkc.edu
Year Founded: 1929
Private or Public: Public
Religious Affiliation: None
Location: Urban
Number of Applicants: 4,206
Percent Accepted: 33%
Percent Accepted who enroll: 80%
Number Entering: 1,112
Number of Transfers Accepted each Year: 1,557
Middle 50% SAT range: M: 500–680, CR: 500 640, Wr: Unreported
Middle 50% ACT range: 21–27
Early admission program EA/ED/None: None

Percentage accepted through EA or ED: NA
EA and ED deadline: NA
Regular Deadline: Rolling
Application Fee: $45
Full time Undergraduate enrollment: 9,863
Total enrollment: 15,277
Percent Male: 39%
Percent Female: 61%
Total Percent Minority or Unreported: 42%
Percent African-American: 17%
Percent Asian/Pacific Islander: 8%
Percent Hispanic: 8%
Percent Native-American: <1%
Percent International: 3%
Percent in-state/out of state: 80%/20%
Percent from Public HS: Unreported
Retention Rate: 74%
Graduation Rate 4-year: 44%

Graduation Rate 6-year: Unreported
Percent Undergraduates in On-campus housing: 11%
Number of official organized extracurricular organizations: 220
3 Most popular majors: Liberal Arts, Business/ Marketing, Health Professions
Student/Faculty ratio: 13:1
Average Class Size: 15
Percent of students going to grad school: Unreported
Tuition and Fees: $21,197
In-State Tuition and Fees if different: $9,029
Cost for Room and Board: $8,965
Percent receiving financial aid out of those who apply: 83%
Percent receiving financial aid among all students: 68%

At University of Missouri–Kansas City, it is common for even freshmen to find themselves in a class with fewer than 20 students. With professors who "care deeply" about their students, the school captures the intimacy of a small liberal arts environment combined with the benefits of a medium-sized state university. Though only 10 percent of students live on campus, they still enjoy a vast array of opportunities and express great pride in their alma mater, eager to show their school spirit by supporting the UMKC Kangaroos at soccer games. With increasing enrollment and strong support for research, the university caters to a wide array of academic and extracurricular interests.

Bring Initiative, Find All You Need

UMKC students can obtain a bachelor's degree in over 50 concentrations. One particularly popular track of study at the School of Medicine allows students to spend six years obtaining both a Bachelor of Arts and a Doctor of Medicine degree.

Though UMKC students say competition can make it difficult to get into the best classes, most are ultimately excited by the wide variety of academic opportunities offered. Those interested in pursuing academic endeavors outside of the classroom can take advantage of the university's heavy focus on research. The School of Medicine—especially the Truman Medical Center—has abundant research opportunities, and undergraduates can visit the Office of Research Opportunities to be matched with mentors and financial support. One student praised UMKC for its excellent research and quality of teaching, but did say that students need to be self-motivated to utilize all of the resources available to them at the university.

The class sizes at UMKC are typically small, particularly in courses required for specific majors, allowing students to form close relationships with their professors. "The professors are willing to help you if you need it," said a UMKC junior. "I have found that they are particularly passionate about seeing their students succeed." The faculty-student ratio is impressively high given the university's size. A senior studying theater studies praised UMKC professors for their friendliness, saying, "If they see students in their classes around campus, they'll say 'hi' and ask how the student is doing. It's nice to know they care."

Many students find themselves in classes alongside older classmates and graduate students, making for rigorous academic standards. Some find the academic rigor overwhelming—one current student said that many of the courses have excessively heavy workloads and too few resources available for academic support.

The UMKC has a range of academic divisions, a number of which are well known in the region. Students at the university's School of Law are proud to share that it is one of only seven American law schools that have educated both a U.S. president (Harry Truman) and a Supreme Court Justice (Charles Whittaker). The Conservatory of Music is one of the top conservatories in the country, and students also praise the School of Education for requiring that participants spend time as assistant teachers in the college.

Dorms: Pleasant, but for the Few

UMKC has three residential facilities that have a total living capacity of 1,300. Johnson Hall is the newest residential facility, completed in 2009. While it can only house 328 students, it does boast a number of amenities including suite-style rooms, computer labs, music practice spaces, and a sand volleyball court. The dorms are also within walking distance from all classrooms and dining halls. The dorms are coed, though each has wings divided by gender. The residential facilities primarily offer four-person suites, though they do have a number of singles available each year.

Ninety percent of the student body chooses to live off campus—renting houses near campus tends to be more affordable, and many students say that they enjoy spending time with friends around Kansas City rather than on campus. However, dorms are a popular option for out-of-state students looking to get to know their classmates

quickly in a close-knit environment. School administrators encourage students to spend at least one year living in on-campus housing, noting that it is shown to boost GPAs and foster close friendships.

UMKC's location in Kansas City has been described as "fantastic," with one recent graduate noting that "right outside of campus you have so many fun things available." UMKC students take advantage of the many malls and bars downtown.

> "Right outside of campus you have so many fun things available."

Most students not on the school's meal plan tend not to spend much time in the dining halls, and several are critical of the university's food. One student criticized the food as "nothing special" but noted that there are alternatives to cafeteria food on campus, including Chick-fil-A, Baja Fresh, Subconnection, Einstein's, and Pickleman's. These locations are especially popular because they allow students to use their university swipe cards. One student noted that it is common to see classmates eating their lunches outside on the quad, enjoying the sunshine and the lawns.

Beyond the Classroom

Because so many UMKC students live off campus, they usually socialize in the surrounding city, but there are many opportunities for involvement in university-sponsored activities. The university has 175 officially registered student organizations, with ethnic organizations and academic-focused groups noted as particularly popular. The school boasts a particularly well-known literary magazine called *New Letters*, a nationally recognized public radio program, and several theater organizations with excellent reputations.

Regardless of their passions, all students can find a niche at UMKC. UMKC even boasts such unique groups as a Clarinet Ensemble and a Dental Student Council among its registered student organizations!

UMKC is not considered a "party school," upperclassmen say. Though the university does have several fraternities and sororities, Greek life is not a large component of the social scene. Despite the fact that UMKC has NCAA Division I athletics, sports games are not particularly well attended. One senior noted that the school does not have a football team, though students say that many people do enjoy the soccer and basketball games. One current student said that many enjoy spending time at the Student Union, which has a coffee shop, pool tables, TVs and university-sponsored activities.

UMKC is an entirely dry campus, a policy that is strictly enforced. One female student said, "It's stupid to try to party on campus in the residential halls because the police department is literally right across the street." However, she added that the campus is surrounded by residential neighborhoods where students live and host parties of their own, and drinking is common.

A large school with a diverse student body, UMKC offers myriad opportunities—particularly to those students who take personal initiative, seeking out individual meetings with professors and making full use of academic resources. The school's urban setting shifts student life off campus, but also enriches the school with Kansas City culture. Ultimately, students are appreciative of the opportunities and friendly community they find at UMKC.—*Emma Goldberg*

FYI
If I could change one thing about UMKC, "I'd change the meal plan price."
At UMKC students love to hang out at "the Student Union or even the Miller Nicols Library."
One of the best things about UMKC is that "the professors are really accommodating of my needs."

Washington University in St. Louis

Address: One Brookings Drive, St. Louis, MO 63139-4988
Phone: 314-935-6000
E-mail address: admissions@wustl.edu
Web site URL: www.wustl.edu
Year Founded: 1853
Private or Public: Private
Religious Affiliation: None
Location: Urban
Number of Applicants: 22,428
Percent Accepted: 21%
Percent Accepted who enroll: 34%
Number Entering: 1,632
Number of Transfers Accepted each Year: 119
Middle 50% SAT range: M: 710–790, CR: 680–750, Wr: Unreported
Middle 50% ACT range: 32–34
Early admission program EA/ED/None: ED

Percentage accepted through EA or ED: Unreported
EA and ED deadline: 15-Nov
Regular Deadline: 15-Jan
Application Fee: $55
Full time Undergraduate enrollment: 7,138
Total enrollment: 13,820
Percent Male: 52%
Percent Female: 48%
Total Percent Minority or Unreported: 43%
Percent African-American: 6%
Percent Asian/Pacific Islander: 18%
Percent Hispanic: 18%
Percent Native-American: <1%
Percent International: 7%
Percent in-state/out of state: 7%/93%
Percent from Public HS: 63%
Retention Rate: 97%
Graduation Rate 4-year: 94%

Graduation Rate 6-year: Unreported
Percent Undergraduates in On-campus housing: 79%
Number of official organized extracurricular organizations: 200
3 Most popular majors: Social Sciences, Business/ Marketing, Engineering
Student/Faculty ratio: 7:1
Average Class Size: 18
Percent of students going to grad school: Unreported
Tuition and Fees: $41,992
In-State Tuition and Fees if different: No difference
Cost for Room and Board: $13,119
Percent receiving financial aid out of those who apply: 57%
Percent receiving financial aid among all students: 37%

With a mission to "discover and disseminate knowledge, and protect the freedom of inquiry through research, teaching and learning" Washington University in St. Louis is regarded as the "ivy of the Midwest." As one of the nation's top 15 colleges, Wash U (as it is less formally known) has been known to rival other top institutions in scholarship and nurture to its student body. Located in St. Louis, close to the Loop and Forest Park, students are attracted to St. Louis notables including the arch and the zoo. A visit to campus highlights some of the best aspects of studying and living in the Midwest.

"Let's Be Honest, I'm Here to Get Into Medical School"

The joke amongst many undergrads is that if you do not start out pre-med, then you are not doing Wash U right. This has culminated as something the university is known for because it is notorious for being rigorous and tough when it comes to the hard sciences. "What makes it tough is the amount of classes you have to take," said one recent graduate.

Many of the students interviewed said that majoring in the sciences at Wash U is probably the toughest paths of education that one can choose to go on there. One current sophomore said, "biochemical engineering is probably the most difficult major one can take on at Wash U," because according to him, "as an engineering student you can't just take random classes."

That being said it is important to note that Wash U is not just a math and sciences strong university. In actuality, most of the institution's recognition comes from the fact that it does the liberal arts education so well. Students are well rounded and exposed to a wide range of courses due partly because of graduation requirements ensuring that all Wash U students leave with a truly liberal arts education.

Many of the students interviewed said that it is not hard to complete 120 units of credit as is called for on graduation day: there is a writing intensive requirement, a quantitative reasoning requirement, and one course in Cultural Diversity as well as Social Differentiation. Along with these, Wash U students are expected to take two to three classes in each of four academic subjects: natural science and mathematics, social sciences, textual and historical studies, and language and the arts. There is only one class that every Wash U student is required to take, and that

is Writing I. Despite these requirements, most students find majoring in multiple areas manageable due to the flexibility in which courses satisfy the many requirements. For example, to satisfy their natural science requirement one student might take general chemistry while another might take Human Evolution. "The academic requirements tend to support the concept of multiple majors," said one sophomore who is double majoring in finance and engineering. "A lot of people pick up a major in the B school," said one senior. She explained that it is pretty common because doing an extra major in the B school is not as tough as taking one on in something like a hard science or mathematics course. This is not to say that the work load is not intense. Regarding the difference between humanities and sciences, one student exclaimed, "Neither is easier than the other! Wash U has great, vigorous programs in both the sciences and humanities. I don't think any student feels a disadvantage—or feels inferior to others—based on their majors. I think everyone has a deep respect for each other here, because we all understand how rigorous every academic program is here. Wash U students are ones that put in a great deal of effort and are continuously challenged in whichever subject area they choose to pursue a major in."

> I think everyone has a deep respect for each other here, because we all understand how rigorous every academic program is here

You Can Walk in and Lay Down, Among Other Things

Students are happy with the social life at Wash U. Whether one is interested in taking part in greek life or would rather stay away from the party scene there is a place for every type of socializer. Each year Wash U hosts a festival that is lovingly referred to as WILD (Walk In, Lay Down). WILD is known to host well known artists. This past year they invited Chance the Rapper and students come to expect big headliners to visit campus whenever WILD is going on. Another schoolwide event each year is carnival or students known as Thurtene. The fraternities host most of the on campus parties, and parties are usually open. "They have their closed events," explained a recent grad, "but for the most part fraternity parties are open to everyone on campus." Juniors and Seniors find it easier to travel off campus once they are of age to go to bars and clubs in the city and so in that regard the social life for upperclassmen differs from that of underclassmen, who tend to stay on-campus during the weekends. Students have also said that it is common at Wash U to have friends in all different years. "As an underclassman, I hang out with upperclassmen all the time and I think there's no distinction in social activities between underclassmen and upperclassmen. I think there's a good mixing between people of different grades in social activities," explained a sophomore.

Alcohol is dealt with as a health incident rather than penalization. The university chooses to avoid dealing with alcohol-related incidents unless they are deemed dangerous. "You find all types of parties here," explained one sophomore. "There is always a fair amount of people who don't drink, at any college. At WashU, I have never even felt pressured by other people to drink alcohol. While there definitely is an alcohol culture, I don't find that it is ever overbearing."

There are always different types of activities students can take part in on campus whether they are sponsored by the university or not. It is not uncommon to find someone going to see a guest speaker one night and then attend a frat party the next.

Living On Campus

The consensus for Wash U students seems to be that housing is great. One senior who is now living off campus went as far as to say that it is "unbelievably amazing [because] you can choose between a "modern" or "traditional" dorm on campus, and they're both great types of dorms in their own rights. The housing system works as a lottery, with each person randomly assigned a lottery number. It's a relatively even system, I think. My one grievance is that it's much harder to obtain housing by yourself, compared to obtaining housing as a group of people.

The campus alone is thought to be very unique. Having had the privilege of hosting presidential debates since 1992, students are often set up with political internships. Almost each student polled mentioned "the Bunny," a sculpture, which tells you nothing about Wash U except for the fact that you will not find anything similar elsewhere. Each of the students polled said that Wash U has proven to be more than they could ask for. For this reason alone, they could not imagine college life spent anywhere else.

Every student polled said that, if they had a choice, they would definitely choose Wash U again, and that they wouldn't give up all the options the school affords—study abroad, internships, classes, and social events—for any other college. One student said that what made Washington University truly unique in comparison with Ivy League schools was the opportunity for individual choice: "The Wash U experience is what you make of it, and you're never limited by the preexisting system. I think that's really embodied in something that Dean McLeod, the Dean of Students, says about Wash U. As diverse as Wash U is, he says, the one thing that unites everyone on campus is that 'they want to be active participants in their own education.'"
—*Zunaira Arshad*

FYI
The biggest college-wide event: WILD (walk in, lay down), a huge free concert/party put on by the school that is held in Brookings quad. They have free food and drinks.
One thing I wish I would have known before coming to WashU: doing a pre-orientation program can be extremely nice because you already know some people during orientation week which makes everything significantly less scary and awkward. And they're supposed to be really fun.
What surprised me the most about WashU: the amount of freedom in the dorms, and everywhere for that matter. WashU is very lax . . . There are very few policies. Students can pretty much do whatever they want.

Montana

University of Montana

Address: Lommasson Center 103, Missoula, MT 59812
Phone: 406-243-6266
E-mail address: admiss@umontana.edu
Web site URL: www.umontana.edu
Year Founded: 1893
Private or Public: Public
Religious Affiliation: None
Location: Urban
Number of Applicants: 4,756
Percent Accepted: 94%
Percent Accepted who enroll: 44%
Number Entering: 1,967
Number of Transfers Accepted each Year: Unreported
Middle 50% SAT range: M: 480–600, CR: 490–610, Wr: 470–590
Middle 50% ACT range: 21–26
Early admission program EA/ED/None: None

Percentage accepted through EA or ED: NA
EA and ED deadline: NA
Regular Deadline: Rolling
Application Fee: $30
Full time Undergraduate enrollment: 15,642
Total enrollment: Unreported
Percent Male: 47%
Percent Female: 53%
Total Percent Minority or Unreported: 20%
Percent African-American: 1%
Percent Asian/Pacific Islander: 1%
Percent Hispanic: 1%
Percent Native-American: 4%
Percent International: 1%
Percent in-state/out of state: 73%/27%
Percent from Public HS: 44%
Retention Rate: 72%
Graduation Rate 4-year: 41%

Graduation Rate 6-year: Unreported
Percent Undergraduates in On-campus housing: 20%
Number of official organized extracurricular organizations: 150
3 Most popular majors: Unreported
Student/Faculty ratio: 19:1
Average Class Size: 14
Percent of students going to grad school: 33%
Tuition and Fees: $20,099
In-State Tuition and Fees if different: $5,722
Cost for Room and Board: $7,060
Percent receiving financial aid out of those who apply: Unreported
Percent receiving financial aid among all students: Unreported

Situated at the foot of Mt. Sentinel with the Clark Fork River flowing through its campus, the University of Montana is the ideal place for the adventurous college student. "We're the only university that actually owns a mountain," said an alumnus who graduated in 2012. "We have the Rockies to the west of us and the Great Plains to the east. You're never more than fifteen miles away from a hiking trail." Combined with the small-city charm of Missoula, MT—nicknamed "Zoo Town" for its similar-sounding name and wild party scene—the university is a prime location for undergraduate Grizzlies to prowl. "I love the atmosphere, the Missoula community, and the Montana mountains," one freshman raved—and with stellar science programs, a "beautiful and user-friendly campus," and a variety of social and extra-curricular options, the University of Montana really does provide students with "many options to do cool things."

More than a General Education

Divided into nine undergraduate-inclusive schools and colleges, the University of Montana covers everything from a standard arts and sciences curriculum to specializations in education, forestry and conservation, bio-medical sciences, vocational programs, visual and performance art, and business administration. Among these colleges, undergraduates can choose from 61 minors and 61 majors in their field of interest. But before declaring their majors, students must fulfill 28 to 49 credits under their general education requirements, which include a writing course, two semesters of language, and a science class with a lab, as well as eight other categories that each require a minimum of three credits. Depending on graduation year, disability status, or involvement in a sport, students are assigned specific timeslots for online class registration, and general education and prerequisite courses tend to "get taken up very fast." Although one senior recalled the general education requirements as the "least favorite" part of his college experience, many freshmen enjoy the general education courses because they "meet a lot of different people." Students also like the "variety" of general education classes offered. "What's really nice is that there are eleven requirements you'd have to fulfill, but there would be 40 to 50 different classes under each requirement that you can choose from," said an alumna from the class of 2012. "It helps you get a broader spectrum of knowledge."

To graduate, a Grizzly would typically need a minimum of 120 total credits, although students in education, pharmacy, physical therapy, and applied science programs would need much more. The minimum GPA required to graduate is 2.00, while the minimum GPA required to graduate with honors is 3.40. In addition to their general education requirements, students also have to complete a minimum of 30 credits per major and 18 credits per minor, with at least 3 credits assigned to each course.

With a campus that is "close to a lot of natural resources" and known for its "diversity of wildlife," it comes as no surprise that the School of Forestry is one of the University of Montana's "best," largest, and "most popular" departments. Its strong wildlife biology program has been "ranked in the top five nationally," only surpassed by the University of North Dakota. In addition to forestry and environmental studies, the university also boasts strong pharmacy, science, and health care courses, as well as a "very large Native American Studies program."

Psychology, anthropology, and other social science majors are some of the most popular concentrations, described by a senior anthropology major as "pretty simple" and "one of the easiest degrees on campus." Students can also choose from a range of "cool" and interesting classes, from "Fly-fishing for Women" and "African Dance" to a climate-change science course taught by Forestry and Conservation Professor Steve Running, who received the Nobel Peace Prize in 2007 for his work on the Intergovernmental Panel on Climate Change.

For voracious Grizzlies with a larger appetite for learning, the University of Montana serves a variety of programs more challenging than their social science counterparts, which are known for having an "easier workload" and fewer major requirements. Freshmen can opt to join the Davidson Honors College, in which 700 students of any major take honors-designated classes and work with a professor to create and eventually present their senior honors research project. As a school that has a "stronger science aspect," the university also offers chemistry, microbiology, physics, and pre-pharmacy programs that many students call "rigorous." While most classes at the University of Montana are graded on an A to F scale or on a credit/no credit basis, many science courses curve grades based on the top student's score, making it "much harder to get A's." Grizzlies majoring in the sciences need more credits to fulfill their major requirements, and only have limited exposure to students in other academic fields. "[Science majors] don't have the opportunity to take classes outside their major because they need to fulfill so many requirements," said one senior. "Once they're high up in the department, they're taking classes that other people wouldn't take."

The University of Montana's academic departments "aren't too big," which most students agree is "a good thing to have in an academic setting." Students can often interact one-on-one with faculty members, who provide "a lot of good individual attention." "The faculty is incredible, and they actually care if you graduate or not," said one 2012 alumna. "They've taught around the world and would sit there and help you until you understand something." Professors and tutors also hold weekly "study jams"—informal events during which they answer student questions and local musicians perform in the background.

A freshman or sophomore general education course would typically be a lecture class with 300 to 400 students, while juniors and seniors enjoy smaller 5- to 30-student classrooms. The atmosphere is "not too competitive"—the Grizzly, a ferocious animal in the wild, is typically "laid back" in a classroom setting.

Campus: Cultural Fun

University of Montana Grizzlies thrive on 220 acres of "green luscious grass and colonial-looking brick buildings." The campus is home to "architecture of every style"—modern, old brick, cinderblock, and a new 19,900-square-foot Native American Center—as well as "tons of different trees that don't exist elsewhere in Montana." A non-native magnolia tree towers above a geyser behind the Main Hall, which, with its "giant clock tower," is considered by many students to be "the most distinctive building on campus." The Main Hall lies "right at the head of the Oval," a grassy social hub at the center of campus, and, rising above the Oval and the topmost spire of the Main Hall, Mount Sentinel and its whitewashed concrete "M" overlook the university. "Hiking the M" is a Grizzly tradition, and on Mother's Day, students "hike up to the M and spray-paint 'I love Mom' on the grass," adding an "o" and an "m" to the concrete "M" embedded in the hillside.

Besides the Oval, the University Center is another popular social hub on campus. With a game room, a movie theater, a coffee shop, and a "big terrarium where people study," the University Center is a Grizzly's den with a "greenhouse feel," complete with a food court serving Chinese food, Greek cuisine, burgers, pizza, and smoothies. Students can also eat at the Cascade Country Store or the Food Zoo, the main dining area on the opposite side of campus. Accommodating vegans, Jewish and Muslim students, and people allergic to gluten, the Food Zoo "has options for everybody," and has been distributing more local, farm-grown food with the Farm to College Program. Students living on campus can choose from two meal plans: the cheaper Lommasson Center Meal Plan, which limits their dining options to the Food Zoo and the Country Store, or the All-Campus Meal Plan, which places $65 on students' Griz Cards every week and allows them to eat anywhere on campus.

The dorm, which all students must tolerate during their freshman year, is "good because you get to socialize [with other freshmen], but it's a pretty controlled setting." Before they enroll, freshmen choose their top three preferences online, selecting dormitories in Aber Hall, Craig Hall, Jesse Hall, Elrod Hall, Duniway Hall, Knowles Hall, Miller Hall, Turner Hall, or Pantzer Hall. "You should sign up within the first week, because it's first come, first serve," one freshman advised. The dorm-selection process is highly competitive, with sophomores, juniors, and seniors choosing their rooms before freshmen. However, due to a shortage

of available suites, "most students move off campus after freshman year."

Grizzlies give their freshman dorms mediocre ratings, describing them as "not big, but not bad," "nice, but not amazing," and "small and crowded, but livable." The standard dorm room is equipped with desks, a dresser, a closet, a chair, a bookshelf, a wastebasket, and two or three twin-sized beds, while suites in Pantzer Hall and Miller Hall have the added luxuries of refrigerators and microwaves. "Bigger" and more expensive than doubles, obtaining single-person rooms is a more "competitive" process, and the majority of freshmen live with "one to two other roommates."

Most residence halls are coeducational, with different genders separated by floor. However, students may request to live in an all-male or all-female residence hall, nicknamed "the Virgin Vault" by their peers in coeducational housing. Another specialized residence hall, the honors dorm, offers guaranteed living arrangements for members of the Davidson Honors College.

Two RAs are assigned to each floor, and one floor of each residence hall is reserved for students who don't engage in alcohol and drug consumption. However, although the University of Montana is a "smoke-free campus," this regulation is not well enforced. Since Montana is a state in which medical marijuana has been legalized, "a lot of kids smoke weed," and students report a "higher than average marijuana usage" than in most colleges. "There's not a whole lot of authority on campus," one senior remarked. "A lot of people do things that aren't allowed." The university is also a "dry campus," though, unlike the "smoke-free" rules, the enforcement of regulations prohibiting alcohol has increased in recent years. "People don't really drink on campus," said a senior, "but they do at football games, off campus, or in downtown bars."

Commuter Social Scene

For the most part, Grizzlies describe themselves as "really understanding," "fun-loving," and "laid-back" individuals. A school composed of "outdoorsy hipster types" and bluegrass fans, the University of Montana connects students from contrasting cliques and backgrounds and creates unlikely friendships. "I've seen a cowboy hanging out with a hipster kid," one freshman observed. "[Because of] the huge international program, I've met people from all over the world."

With 70 percent of the school's population hailing from Montana, the school is "not very diverse," one student calling it "a homogeneous group of white people." However, as the university's international programs continue to grow, the majority of students have noticed that the college's diversity is on the rise. "There's a huge Muslim population, a gay population, and people from every nation from Russia to Japan," said an education major who graduated in 2012.

The university's party scene has mixed reviews. Some students claim that the college is "not a huge party school" and that Greek life is "not popular," while others report "bras hanging from trees" and "beer boxes on top of light posts" after wild nights on campus. "There's a really wide range of interests," one senior explained. "It can be a party school if you want it to be." One of the biggest events of the year is the Forester's Ball, an annual dance organized by students in the College of Forestry and Conservation. The Adams Center gym is converted into an Old Western logging town, complete with saloons, a slide, and places where couples can "get hitched." But with recent restrictions the school has placed on on-campus drinking, students often spend their weekends elsewhere. A hardcore-partying minority flies to Las Vegas at least once a month on Allegiant Air, while most students spend their nights in Missoula's lively downtown area. Known for its "big nightlife scene," the city's excitement doesn't wane with the daytime—it is the home of Saturday morning farmer's markets, parades, art fairs, state fairs, and "a lot of cultural festivals," including German Fest, Hemp Fest, and a Day of the Dead Festival held every Halloween. Hungry Grizzlies flock to the Depot and the Press Box, restaurants known for their steaks and excellent bar food. And when they're thirsty, the Grizzly population migrates to the Badlander—a popular bar with "a lot of cheap drinks and sleazy dancing." Blasting club music all through the night, the Badlander is a destination people go to "when they're really trying to party." For relaxed, casual drinking, athletes hang out at Stockman's Bar, while the rest of the hipster-heavy campus go to the Top Hat, the Rhino, or microbreweries oriented around the Clark Fork River. "People in Missoula are very big on the types of beer they drink," said one 2012 alumnus. However, going to downtown bars is "more of an upperclassman thing," since "most kids [on campus] aren't old enough to go to bars." The "crackdown on fake IDs" has increased in recent years, and according to one senior, getting a fake is "a harder thing [for freshmen] to pull off nowadays." Instead, underclassmen do most of their drinking in off-campus house parties. RAs, who live in underclassman dorms and prohibit their alcohol consumption, also organize a series of social events for freshmen such as formal dances during spring and Thanksgiving breaks, and "Go Day," in which different residence halls don team colors and compete in summer camp games.

Whether you're a drinker or not, there's always something going on in Zoo Town.

The campus is in such a prime place," a freshman raved. "You can go hiking or skiing, and there are a lot of activities to do outside of campus. You're very rarely bored." Local and touring bands pop in and out of the city, playing in venues like the Adams Center, the Wilma Theater, and downtown bars like the Top Hat, which boasts a large stage area. While rock, indie, and lesser-known hip-hop artists have been known to perform in Missoula, "the biggest draw is folk and bluegrass bands." Skiing is also "a big deal right now," and many students spend their time at the Snowbowl, a ski resort twelve miles northwest of Missoula. Mountain biking, exploring the woods, and camping in the surrounding Bitterroot Valley are also common pastimes, especially during the warmer fall months.

Community Spectacles

Forester's Ball and Day of the Dead festivals aside, the homecoming and Griz-Cat football games are, among Grizzlies, the must-see social events of the year. Before the recent (and tragic) demise of Hostess, Grizzly fans would "freeze Twinkies and throw them at the opposing team"—their longtime rival, the Montana State Bobcats. Both the Griz-Cat game and the homecoming game mark "really belligerent nights in town," during which students throw a number of house and on-campus parties.

The excitement of the homecoming game isn't limited to the campus alone. "The whole city gets consumed with the Griz—you go to the mall and all you see is maroon and silver," said a 2012 alumna. In fact, the surrounding Missoula community organizes many events in celebration of Grizzly pride, including a "big homecoming parade" consisting of Boy Scouts, horseback riders, notable alumni, and college organizations. A homecoming tradition, students, faculty, and members of the community paint multilingual ways of saying "hello" on a Missoula sidewalk, nicknamed the "Hello Walk" for obvious reasons. Griz blood drives are held to see "who can give the most blood," and terminally ill children from low-income Missoula families are offered a chance to attend the game. With such avid involvement in the community, it's no wonder that, as one freshman states, "the Griz is supported by everyone—not only the school, but Missoula and all of western Montana."

> **"The whole city gets consumed with the Griz—you go to the mall and all you see is maroon and silver."**

Sports, especially football, have a huge presence on campus. While many programs are more competitive, such as football, basketball, club lacrosse, and soccer, intramural sports are more "relaxed," consisting of both conventional activities like hockey and less traditional teams like "water pong"—a variation of beer pong in which water is a substitute for alcohol. "There's a lot of intramural sports year round, from basketball and soccer to ultimate Frisbee, Quidditch, and an inner-tube water polo team," a freshman raved. For students who just want to stay in shape, the University of Montana offers a variety of "not brand-new, but very well-kept" athletic facilities, including the Schreiber Gym, the Grizzly Pool, and the Dornblaser and Riverbowl Fields.

With over 150 student organizations, the university provides a number of extracurricular options for undergraduate Grizzlies. "I think the biggest thing our school has to offer is a really diverse range of interests on campus. No matter how weird your hobbies are, you can find your niche." Aspiring writers can join *The Kaimin*, the main campus publication, while other students may try paragliding or reenacting medieval battles through live-action role playing. "Try everything," advises an economics major who graduated in 2012. "There's rock-climbing, music, and something for everyone, regardless of what you're doing."

Mountains and schools aren't your typical geographic combination, making the University of Montana not your typical college. From general education that's not generic at all to a fast-growing and fast-moving social scene, U of Montana is a college that can make mountains out of molehills.
—*Rosa Nguyen*

FYI
If you come to University of Montana, you'd better bring "a pair of hiking shoes."
If I could change one thing about the University of Montana, I'd "make all the buildings closer together. If you have classes on different sides of the campus, it's hard to make it in time."
Three things every student at the University of Montana should do before graduating are "float the Clark Fork River on an inner tube, hike the M, and go to the hot springs around Missoula."

Nebraska

Creighton University

Address: 2500 California Plaza, Omaha, NE 68178
Phone: 402-280-2703
E-mail address: admissions@creighton.edu
Web site URL: www.creighton.edu
Year Founded: 1878
Private or Public: Private
Religious Affiliation: Roman Catholic
Location: Urban
Number of Applicants: 3,336
Percent Accepted: 89%
Percent Accepted who enroll: 32%
Number Entering: 950
Number of Transfers Accepted each Year: 165
Middle 50% SAT range: M: 540–650, Cr: 520–630, Wr: 590–690
Middle 50% ACT range: 24–29
Early admission program EA/ED/None: None

Percentage accepted through EA or ED: NA
EA and ED deadline: NA
Regular Deadline: 15-Feb
Application Fee: $40
Full time Undergraduate enrollment: 4,104
Total enrollment: 4,647
Percent Male: 40%
Percent Female: 60%
Total Percent Minority or Unreported: 21%
Percent African-American: 3%
Percent Asian/Pacific Islander: 8%
Percent Hispanic: 3%
Percent Native-American: 1%
Percent International: 1%
Percent in-state/out of state: 37%/63%
Percent from Public HS: 55%
Retention Rate: 86%

Graduation Rate 4-year: 61%
Graduation Rate 6-year: 74%
Percent Undergraduates in On-campus housing: 62%
Number of official organized extracurricular organizations: 182
3 Most popular majors: Business, Health, Psychology
Student/Faculty ratio: 12:1
Average Class Size: 22
Percent of students going to grad school: 70%
Tuition and Fees: $25,262
In-State Tuition and Fees If different: No difference
Cost for Room and Board: $8,180
Percent receiving financial aid out of those who apply: 78%
Percent receiving financial aid among all students: 60%

Founded in 1878 as a private Jesuit university in Omaha, Nebraska, Creighton University has become one of the best institutions of higher learning in the United States. The university's location in Nebraska may turn away many students outside of the Midwest region; however, Creighton provides students with a very good education, notable for the close interactions between students and professors.

The Curriculum

Creighton is a relatively small university. Nevertheless, the school is divided into nine colleges and twelve research centers. In fact, the school has the components of major research institutions with the presence of medical, law, and business schools. "We really are a comprehensive university," said one student. "I met people who think that Creighton is just a small college, but we have all the graduate schools."

The small number of undergraduate students and the large scale of the university indicate that students can have close interactions with professors. In fact, classes tend to be relatively small, often under 30 students. As a result, students can have easier access to their instructors, who also have more time for individual students. "I got to know a lot of professors really well at Creighton," said one student. "I think that is something that sets Creighton apart." The accessibility of professors can be highly beneficial for the students in both having a better understanding of the course materials and obtaining help for future endeavors.

The undergraduate program offers about 50 majors in three of the colleges, Arts and Sciences, Business Administration, and Nursing. While the majority of majors are the traditional liberal arts programs of study, such as biology, history, and economics, Creighton also lists a number of more specialized curriculums for students who are more interested in professional preparation. Some of these majors include photo journalism, applied meteorology, and studio art. At the same time, the school also provides strong preparatory classes for graduate schools, since a large number of students are pre-medical, pre-dental, and pre-law. The presence of the professional schools on campus certainly helps those students a great deal in experiencing graduate-level classes and even engaging in more sophisticated research projects. "Creighton is proud of its academics," said one student. The different research centers that are spread across campus also allow the more ambitious undergraduates to have more in-depth investigations of topics that interest them.

> **"There are a lot of really smart people here. You get to learn a lot from them."**

Creighton also provides a number of honors and leadership programs for students who wish to go beyond the basic required curriculums. In the Arts and Sciences Honors Program, students attend more discussion-based classes where people can learn from each other by exchanging ideas. Those in the program will also live together in the same freshman dorm. The College of Business Administration offers a leadership program for students to learn through extracurricular activities.

Students believe that the workload is mostly manageable. Although some science classes can be surprisingly difficult for inexperienced freshmen, most people believe that, after one semester at Creighton, students are generally used to the pace and demands of academics. Of course, it is important for prospective students to be ready to work once they arrive and expect to find many people of great talent on campus. "There are a lot of really smart people here," said one student. "You get to learn a lot from them."

According to *U.S. News & World Report*, the university is ranked first among all midwestern universities where the highest degree offered is the master's degree. It is certainly a very prestigious distinction for the school. The admissions rate is over 80%, but prospective students should definitely expect a competitive selection process, given the relatively high academic standards of the school as well as the quality of applicants.

Gateway to the West

Omaha is the metropolis of Nebraska. It is the county seat and the largest city in the state. For a city known as the Gateway to the West, Omaha's atmosphere falls somewhere between the prairie Midwest and the more fast-paced West Coast. Nevertheless, the city is not exactly a major urban center, and many students believe that it does not offer much to the students. There are a few restaurants, bars, and clubs, features that are expected around a major university. Therefore, most students stay close to campus during much of the school year and do not venture far into the rest of the city. Of course, for students who are interested in outdoor activities, Nebraska certainly provides plenty of opportunities for hiking and boating in the surrounding parks.

Freshmen and sophomores stay on campus at Creighton, and the reviews for housing demonstrate that students are generally fine with their dorms. "The rooms are pretty nice, but they are small," said one student. "As long as you and your roommate get along with the small space, you will like your room." Some of the dorms look like apartment buildings where individual rooms open into one long hallway. Others are arranged in suites, where two bedrooms are connected to a small living room. The majority of juniors and seniors, however, prefer to find housing off campus.

The dining services provide two main dining halls, as well as a number of small shops and stores where students use their meal plans. The plans can be as much as 19 meals per week to 60 meals for an entire semester. As to the quality of food, it generally receives reasonably good reviews, at least for college dining halls. "I go to restaurants once in a while when I am tired of the dining halls," said one student. "But overall, I would say that they do a pretty good job with the food."

Creighton is home to five fraternities and seven sororities, which represent an important part of the social scene. Greek life is certainly critical in organizing large parties during the weekends. "A lot of people join frats, but you don't have to," said one student. "The school is big enough to find your unique group of friends." Another venue for weekend festivities is in the off-campus housing.

Undiscovered Gem

One important part of Creighton University is its Jesuit heritage. While 60% of the students are Roman Catholic, the school welcomes a diverse student body and is happy to embrace

people of all faiths, and approximately 20% of the students are considered minorities.

Creighton is considered one of the top universities in the western part of the country and it certainly has the features of an impressive educational institution. The students receive personal attention from the professors, and it has been widely recognized by a number of college reviews as one of the top universities in the nation, thus making it a very good choice for prospective students. —*Xiaohang Liu*

FYI

If you come to Creighton, you'd better bring "warm clothing."

What is the typical weekend schedule? "Parties on Friday and Saturday. Sunday is for work."

If I could change one thing about Creighton, I'd "build more dining halls."

Three things every student at Creighton should do before graduating are "find a good extracurricular organization, go hiking, and make sure you enjoy your four years."

University of Nebraska / Lincoln

Address: 1410 Q Street, Lincoln, NE 68588-0256
Phone: 402-472-2023
E-mail address: admissions@unl.edu
Web site URL: www.unl.edu
Year Founded: 1869
Private or Public: Public
Religious Affiliation: None
Location: Urban
Number of Applicants: 9,598
Percent Accepted: 62%
Percent Accepted who enroll: 71%
Number Entering: 4,075
Number of Transfers Accepted each Year: 1,350
Middle 50% SAT range: M: 530–670, CR: 510–650, Wr: Unreported
Middle 50% ACT range: 22–28
Early admission program EA/ED/None: None

Percentage accepted through EA or ED: NA
EA and ED deadline: NA
Regular Deadline: 1-May
Application Fee: $45
Full time Undergraduate enrollment: 19,383
Total enrollment: 24,610
Percent Male: 53%
Percent Female: 47%
Total Percent Minority or Unreported: 23%
Percent African-American: 3%
Percent Asian/Pacific Islander: 2%
Percent Hispanic: 2%
Percent Native-American: <1%
Percent International: 2%
Percent in-state/out of state: 82%/18%
Percent from Public HS: Unreported
Retention Rate: 83%

Graduation Rate 4-year: 22%
Graduation Rate 6-year: 42%
Percent Undergraduates in On-campus housing: 40%
Number of official organized extracurricular organizations: 335
3 Most popular majors: Business/Marketing, Education, Engineering
Student/Faculty ratio: 20:1
Average Class Size: 23
Percent of students going to grad school: Unreported
Tuition and Fees: $19,848
In-State Tuition and Fees if different: $7,563
Cost for Room and Board: $8,647
Percent receiving financial aid out of those who apply: 67%
Percent receiving financial aid among all students: 50%

The Big Red. Almost without fail, people across the nation know the Big Red for one thing: their football. With five National Championships under the University of Nebraska's belt, Cornhusker spirit runs deep, especially since Memorial Stadium ranks as the third-largest-populated area of Nebraska after Omaha and Lincoln on game day. To all native Nebraskans and students at the university, there is no messing around when it comes to football.

Making the Grade

Although students may not be as obsessed with academia as they are with UNL football, the university does a lot to accommodate a wide range of interests. By offering over 150 majors and 9 academic colleges intended for those looking to specialize in their given field, students can find what's necessary for a thorough education. For those seeking an accelerated education, the honors program at Nebraska offers an avenue. Requiring a cumulative 3.5 GPA to participate, those in the honors program are provided with special housing, smaller class sizes, and close interaction opportunities with faculty and fellow high-achieving students. Students say that the most academically grueling majors include philosophy, any type of engineering, and organic chemistry. Not all classes are so demanding; UNL provides unique courses such as Introduction to Wine Tasting, Personal Defense, and Ballroom Dancing. One student emphasizes that the "liberal arts environment really encourages students to think freely and pursue individual interests, because it's all offered."

The size of most classes at the University of Nebraska echo the usual class size found at state universities, ranging from 10 to 500 students depending on the type of course, with some classes averaging about 150. The general perception about the undergraduate professors is positive. "Professors are friendly and willing to work with individual students' schedules for out-of-class meetings," one sophomore noted. The TAs are a different story, however. Depending on the major, TAs can either be really helpful or hard to understand, as they may not be able to speak English very well.

Lincoln Living

During their freshman year at the University of Nebraska, students are required to live on campus. Most upperclassmen either move into on-campus apartment-style housing or move off campus entirely. Cather and Pound are two upperclassmen dorms, offering laundry facilities and computer clusters on every floor. Although many end up off campus, the majority of students seem to appreciate their freshman living experience. "You meet a lot of people that you might otherwise never get to know, some of whom become your best friends." All of the housing options offered by the university are fully air-conditioned, although those buildings not recently renovated are of noticeably lower quality.

Almost all the freshman dorms are doubles, with two beds, desks, closets, and high-speed wireless Internet. RAs (Residential Advisors) are upperclassmen whose job it is to keep the freshman dorms free of alcohol and running smoothly. Those who choose to live off campus are able to take advantage of relatively low midwestern housing prices. If a student at UNL does not reside on campus or in an apartment outside of the university's provided housing, he/she most likely lives in a fraternity or sorority. There are a total of 37 Greek houses at Nebraska-Lincoln: 14 sororities and 23 fraternities. Those involved in Greek life seem to "hold more leadership positions on campus" according to one senior. Furthermore, those brothers and sisters in Greek houses on campus have statistically higher GPAs than the overall average GPA of students at the university.

As far as food goes, the dining hall situation leaves everyone with a different taste in their mouths. Always noted as clean and not too crowded, the food's quality is recognized as anywhere from "decent but bland" to "everything one would look for in a college dining hall." However, the Training Table, a dining hall where only UNL athletes are allowed to eat, provides the best food. "They offer prime rib, a more diversified menu, and a nutritionist is on staff in order to make sure athletes are getting the nutritional requirements they need," one junior explained.

The Union

When asked what the central hangout on campus is, students emphatically answer, "the Union!" Known to non-Cornhuskers as the Nebraska Union, the Union is unquestionably the most popular campus social center. Home to the University Bookstore, a convenience store, auditorium, copy shop, game room, food court, and big-screen television lounge, the Union has it all. "If anyone ever needs to study with a group or catch up with some friends, the Union is the place to meet," declared one sophomore. Other than the Union, many Cornhuskers cite Memorial Stadium as the most prized location on campus. Renovated in 1999, the Stadium is now equipped with $40 million worth of new skyboxes.

It's All in Lincoln

If students aren't attending individual parties, team parties, or frat parties, "Haymarket is definitely the place to go," a junior explained. Located in downtown Lincoln, the Haymarket is full of restaurants and shops and is most commonly cited as the place to go for a date or to check out the bar scene on a Saturday night. Because Lincoln caters to college life and is the only real city for miles, many students will stay on campus for the better part of the year. "You really have to stay in the city because there really isn't anywhere else to go," a student said.

> "There is a pride in being a Cornhusker that blows me away."

Aside from holding the highest grades on campus, the Greek houses are infamous for throwing some of the best parties annually. Hosting parties with themes anywhere from "Doctors and Nurses" to "Hollywood," "the frats are definitely where it's at," one student declared. Partying usually starts on Thursday night and lasts until Saturday night. However, most Saturday nights in the fall are spent recovering from a full day at the Cornhusker tailgate rooting on the Big Red.

Outside of academics and athletics, there are a wide range of other possibilities offered through the university and separate student organizations. Students are heavily involved in everything from community outreach volunteer programs to on-campus publications like the *Daily Nebraskan*. Cornhuskers are very satisfied overall with the extracurricular life on campus.

It's All About Football

While football most definitely pulls the biggest crowds, all athletic teams really bring a lot to Cornhusker spirit. Even when teams aren't as successful, they are still able to bring out a crowd. There are a great number of successful teams, including the men's gymnastics team, who have eight national titles under their belts, the women's indoor track and field team with three, and the women's volleyball team with three. For those athletes who aren't quite at the D-1 level, Nebraska offers a very competitive intramural sports program. Being the most popular extracurricular activity, intramural sports serve as a great way to "meet new people." For those students just looking to get a workout in, there's the Lee Sapp Recreational Center, which boasts two indoor tracks, a climbing wall, a weight room, and basketball and racquetball courts. With facilities that nice, there's no excuse not to hit the gym.

For most state universities it's tricky to pinpoint one unifying factor that really seems to bring the campus together. But for Nebraska-Lincoln, it's quite obvious and goes beyond the football field. When asked what the one factor is that differentiates UNL from any other university, one sophomore noted it was "the school spirit absolutely without question. There is a pride in being a Cornhusker that blows me away." UNL is the pride of all of Nebraska and regular Nebraskans, students, and faculty aren't afraid to show it. For Nebraskans far and wide, including those who live and study on UNL's campus or are just there for the game, it really is all about football.
—*Taylor Ritzel*

FYI

If you come to the U of Nebraska, you'd better bring "a warm winter coat. You usually have to walk a little ways to class and it can get very cold."

What's the typical weekend schedule? "Go to a frat party on Thursday and Friday nights, prime before the football game on Saturday, get pizza in Haymarket after, wake up late on Sunday and do homework in the afternoon."

If I could change one thing about the U of Nebraska, "I'd get rid of the train tracks that run through campus. You have to wait on your way to class while trains pass."

Three things every student should do at the U of Nebraska before graduating are "swim in the fountain in front of the Union, pass library class, and go to a football game."

Nevada

University of Nevada / Reno

Address: Mail Stop 120, Reno, NV 89557
Phone: 775-784-4700
E-mail address: asknevada@unr.edu
Web site URL: www.unr.edu
Year Founded: 1864
Private or Public: Public
Religious Affiliation: None
Location: Urban
Number of Applicants: 4,024
Percent Accepted: 88%
Percent Accepted who enroll: 58%
Number Entering: 2,047
Number of Transfers Accepted each Year: 2,030
Middle 50% SAT range: M: 470–590, CR: 460–570, Wr: 440–550
Middle 50% ACT range: 20–26
Early admission program EA/ED/None: None

Percentage accepted through EA or ED: NA
EA and ED deadline: NA
Regular Deadline: Rolling
Application Fee: $60
Full time Undergraduate enrollment: 14,185
Total enrollment: 17,679
Percent Male: 47%
Percent Female: 53%
Total Percent Minority or Unreported: 34%
Percent African-American: 4%
Percent Asian/Pacific Islander: 8%
Percent Hispanic: 8%
Percent Native-American: 1%
Percent International: 1%
Percent in-state/out of state: 79%/21%
Percent from Public HS: Unreported
Retention Rate: 76%

Graduation Rate 4-year: 14%
Graduation Rate 6-year: 46%
Percent Undergraduates in On-campus housing: 16%
Number of official organized extracurricular organizations: Unreported
3 Most popular majors: Business/Marketing, Health Professions, Social Sciences
Student/Faculty ratio: 27:1
Average Class Size: 26
Percent of students going to grad school: Unreported
Tuition and Fees: $19,771
In-State Tuition and Fees if different: $6,176
Cost for Room and Board: $10,868
Percent receiving financial aid out of those who apply: 62%
Percent receiving financial aid among all students: 45%

I n the "Biggest Little City in the World," University of Nevada, Reno is the state's flagship public university. More than 10,000 undergraduates attend the institution, along with nearly 5,000 graduate students. Therefore, UNR certainly offers a wide array of academic opportunities for students. As one-half of the University of Nevada system, which also has a location in Las Vegas, UNR has a long tradition of providing good academic programs to students from around the country and even the world. Sure, it is a state-run public university, drawing most of the student body from Nevada, but many people from out of state do come to UNR to enjoy a relatively affordable education of good quality.

A School of Pulitzers

The history of UNR traces back to the 1800s, but its transformation into today's modern university began in the 1960s when it opened its first medical school. From that point, the school continued to expand in the breadth of academic programs, resulting in a dozen schools and colleges that would satisfy any type of academic pursuit. There are the traditional liberal arts, business, and engineering programs. In addition, UNR also offers degrees in community health sciences, social work, and, of course, journalism. In fact, the Reynolds School of Journalism has produced seven Pulitzer Prize winners. It is therefore not surprising that it has an enrollment of over 500 undergraduates pursuing either majors or minors in journalism. "Reynolds is really prestigious in journalism," said one student. "I think that is why it is a pretty popular major."

One other point of interest is the Mackay School of Earth Sciences and Engineering, which teaches topics such as geology, hydrogeology, and mining. "I don't think you will find too many earth science schools like Mackay," said one student. The combination of engineering and geology makes students' experience particularly rewarding. The university is also home to a major seismology laboratory that operates a series of measuring stations across Nevada to evaluate earthquake risks in the region. Therefore, UNR certainly offers academic opportunities that go beyond the traditional form of classroom teaching.

For those interested in the more traditional fields, UNR presents students with over 80 undergraduate programs, not to mention the presence of graduate classes and students, which means even more opportunities for students. For those who would like to leave Nevada and experience the world, the foreign exchange program, University Studies Abroad Consortium, largely led by UNR, allows students to study in one of 25 countries for the summer, the semester, or even the whole school year. UNR prides itself in its involvement with the program as well as the great study-abroad experience it provides for students. "I really like our study-abroad program," said one student. "It's good to be able to see the world for a semester, and the school makes the application process pretty easy."

Although UNR does have a selective admissions process, nearly 90% of applicants are accepted to enter the freshman class every year. "We are not going to pride ourselves as a selective school, but I think we still have a fairly high academic standard," said one student. "The graduation rate is not that high, but it all depends on the individual," added another. At the end of the day, a large selection of academic opportunities certainly exists and is widely available at UNR, and whether a student succeeds is certainly contingent on the efforts put forth by the person. It must also be pointed out that the education is relatively affordable, especially given today's prices of private college tuition. Therefore, even for out-of-state students, a degree at UNR can be much cheaper and provide much greater value than at other institutions.

Consistent with the mission to educate not only for a career but to broaden each student's worldview, a program called Core Curriculum must be completed by all undergraduates. It means that some students will have to take classes that they do not particularly enjoy. However, depending on the students, these courses can be extremely valuable, especially in making students aware of fields in which they have very little knowledge. "I did not like sciences," said a student. "But the classes I took to fulfill the requirements are actually pretty good and taught me a lot of useful knowledge." Students must receive a minimum of 33 credits in the Core Curriculum, which includes the traditional requirements of mathematics, natural sciences, English, art, social sciences, and humanities. In addition, students must also complete the Capstone Courses, which take an interdisciplinary approach to education, as well as Diversity Courses, which aim to teach students about cultures outside of the Western tradition.

> "We are not Vegas, but we can have pretty good nightlife here, too."

Students generally agree that they are not overworked and do have the time to enjoy pursuits other than academics, such as engaging in academic activities or having a good time during the weekends. "It all depends on the classes you take," said one student. "Overall, the work is not that bad."

The Biggest Little City

Reno is not Las Vegas, but the differences are smaller than one would expect. Just like its much more famous gambling counterpart, Reno is home to a number of casinos and resorts. Fifty years ago, the city was the heart of the gambling world. However, with the rise of Las Vegas, some of the larger casinos have disappeared, replaced by smaller ones. In recent years, different revitalization projects have restored some of the city's former glory. Despite stiff competition from Las Vegas, Reno remains a popular spot for tourists, thus creating a vibrant nightlife. Even though the city is not particularly large, it certainly provides students at UNR plenty of options for the weekends.

Located at the foot of the Sierra Nevada Mountains, Reno is also close to a number of state parks and national forests, thus it's a great place for students interested in outdoor activities. "It is a city with lots of tourists," said one student. "We are not in Las Vegas, but we can have pretty good nightlife here, too. Plus, I am not sure that I want to go to college in Vegas. It is too big and noisy for me."

As in most parts of Nevada, the best form of transportation is by car, especially given the large number of students living off campus. The residence halls, however, are not terrible. "I don't know why there are so few people living on campus. It is not that bad here and more convenient because you don't have to take care of everything yourself." Argenta Hall, the newest addition to the dorms, is especially desirable because of the availability of bathrooms in every room, as well as newer furniture. There are also a number of dining options ranging from one meal per week to lunch-only options for commuters.

The Wolf Packs

UNR does have a strong football tradition, exemplified by a stadium that can accommodate 30,000 spectators and having a highly competitive team in Division I. The most important rivalry is obviously in-state foe University of Nevada, Las Vegas. The winner of the annual contest receives the Fremont Cannon, a trophy replicating an actual Howitzer cannon and representing the heaviest and the most expensive award in college football.

Students generally agree that UNR is a very good college choice. It combines affordability, academic opportunities, and a great supporting staff. For those who would like to take advantage of a large and resourceful state university, UNR is certainly a good destination for prospective students.
—*Xiaohang Liu*

FYI
If you come to UNR, you'd better bring "some gambling skills if you want to frequent the casinos."
What is the typical weekend schedule? "Lots of parties and a little bit of work."
If I could change one thing about UNR, I'd "make public transportation better."
Three things every student at UNR should do before graduating are "see UNR beat UNLV, go to casinos, and take advantage of nightlife at Reno."

New Hampshire

Dartmouth College

Address: 6016 McNutt Hall, Hanover, NH 03755

Phone: 603-646-2875

E-mail address: admissions.office @dartmouth.edu

Web site URL: www.dartmouth.edu

Year Founded: 1769

Private or Public: Private

Religious Affiliation: None

Location: Suburban

Number of Applicants: 13,712

Percent Accepted: 16%

Percent Accepted who enroll: 49%

Number Entering: 1,075

Number of Transfers Accepted each Year: 43

Middle 50% SAT range: M: 680–780, Cr: 670–770, Wr: 700–770

Middle 50% ACT range: 28–34

Early admission program EA/ED/None: ED

Percentage accepted through EA or ED: 37%

EA and ED deadline: 1-Nov

Regular Deadline: 1-Jan

Application Fee: $70

Full time Undergraduate enrollment: 4,085

Total enrollment: 5,437

Percent Male: 49%

Percent Female: 51%

Total Percent Minority or Unreported: 42%

Percent African-American: 7%

Percent Asian/Pacific Islander: 14%

Percent Hispanic: 6%

Percent Native-American: 4%

Percent International: 5%

Percent in-state/out of state: 4%/96%

Percent from Public HS: 61%

Retention Rate: 98%

Graduation Rate 4-year: 86%

Graduation Rate 6-year: 94%

Percent Undergraduates in On-campus housing: 85%

Number of official organized extracurricular organizations: 330

3 Most popular majors: Economics, Psychology, Sociology

Student/Faculty ratio: 8:1

Average Class Size: 13

Percent of students going to grad school: Unreported

Tuition and Fees: $33,297

In-State Tuition and Fees if different: No difference

Cost for Room and Board: $9,840

Percent receiving financial aid out of those who apply: 81%

Percent receiving financial aid among all students: 49%

Located in the pristine wilderness of western New Hampshire, Dartmouth College is the smallest Ivy League college. Its roughly 4,000 students enjoy a rewarding Ivy League education filled with academic opportunities. Dartmouth students also enjoy the benefit of a secluded northern New England campus, as well as an active student community that boasts a diverse array of activities. Indeed, Dartmouth students are very much satisfied with their college experience, exemplified by the university's strong academic programs, exciting campus environment, and numerous extracurricular opportunities.

Seduced by Seclusion

Located in Hanover, New Hampshire, Dartmouth boasts a beautiful natural environment that, according to one freshman, includes "hiking and biking trails amidst beautiful nature scenes, and the bliss of not having any major cities nearby." During the fall and spring months, this environment allows students to enjoy a variety of outdoor activities. One of them is the Dartmouth Outing Club's (or DOC's) freshman trip, in which students take a camping trip throughout northern New England before their fall term. Taking this trip and seeing New England's beautiful streams, rivers, forests, hills, and valleys gives these students a great way to bond and explore. During the winter, according to one sophomore, "when Dartmouth gets a thousand inches of snow and the temperature rarely climbs above freezing, students have frequent midnight snowball fights, take skiing trips, and even sled together on the nearby golf course. The experience is unfathomably fun." To some students, the winter can be a bit much, however. One freshman complained, "By the time December came I had to wear three layers of clothing just to go outside." However, most find that Dartmouth's natural environment and cooler climate shapes the college experience in a positive way.

Dartmouth students enjoy the benefits of small-town life as residents of Hanover, which has a population of about 11,000. As one freshman explained, "Hanover is that quaint little town that everyone sees as part of the American Dream: it has one small street called Main Street lined with mom-and-pop stores, and everyone is really friendly." Students frequently go to Main Street to eat at small restaurants such as Mali's or shop at the Gap, the town's only major clothing store. Nevertheless, to many Dartmouth students, Hanover can at times be very dull. As one junior complained, "Hanover has almost nothing to do. It has one street with a couple of shops and restaurants and nothing else." However, most Dartmouth students generally do enjoy living in Hanover.

A New and Unique Spin on Ivy League Academics

Dartmouth's academic year is split up into quarterly terms, allowing students to take more classes and to schedule an "off" term during which they have no classes and can use their time for other pursuits, such as internships. Students also have a set of distributional requirements including, among others, a first-year seminar, a quantitative reasoning class, a literature class, and three physical education classes. Though some students find this program too regimented, most appreciate it. As one freshman said, "The best part about Dartmouth's academics is that you have to try new things. For example, at a different college, I might not have been able to take a class on Slavic folklore to meet a college requirement. Having these requirements lets me get the best of all academic areas. That's what makes Dartmouth stand out."

An important component of Dartmouth academic life is the accessibility of its professors. As one sophomore said, "Professors have a strong presence, and at times even seem more like older students than faculty members." To ensure that students can have personal interactions with their professors, Dartmouth even has a "Take a Professor to Lunch" program, in which Dartmouth students schedule a lunch meeting with their professors that Dartmouth pays for. As one junior said, "This program is great because it lets me establish a personal relationship with my professors, who really seem to care." Dartmouth's uniquely amiable and accessible faculty is truly one of the best parts of its academic life. In addition, the overall scholastic program is very strong. "No matter what your major is," said one junior, "you will be able to find plenty of excellent classes and a top-notch faculty here."

> "Even during the winter months when Dartmouth gets a thousand inches of snow, students make the most of their environment. The experience is unfathomably fun."

Despite Dartmouth's great academic reputation, however, it still has a few shortcomings. Many students think that Dartmouth is not the humanities school it should be. "There aren't many history majors, language majors, or women's studies majors," said one freshman. "Also, planning to take certain classes can get complicated, since students generally need to take one term off each year to pursue internship opportunities or to relax."

Simplicity with Sophistication: Campus Life at Dartmouth

The vast majority of students at Dartmouth live on campus, and most are quite satisfied with campus life. Due to Dartmouth's relatively small campus, most dorms are not very far from class. Such a setting allows students to bond quickly and have a positive experience. "The average dorm floor has 16 people, give or take," one freshman said. "Each floor has several bathrooms, and each building has its own kitchen and hangout areas, so crowding is not really an issue." Undergraduate Advisors, who supervise the dorms, are also quite friendly and helpful. As one freshman put it, UGAs "are great with helping freshmen and getting them acclimated to life at Dartmouth through advice and hosting dorm parties and events."

Most of the dorms have ample accommodations. By far the most coveted dorm, however, is the Wheelock building, to which the students apply separately for housing. One freshman said that his dorm "had three rooms for two people, and was huge." Wheelock students also enjoy a variety of interesting discussion groups. "Living in Wheelock feels like living in an intellectual community within an intellectual community," one student said. Though other dorms are decent, students caution prospective freshmen to be wary of the River, which is considered the worst building. One freshman complained that her room was so small that she "could only fit furniture in by squeezing it in at awkward angles," while another student complained that the kitchen at the River "is really old, and has a pipe sticking out of the wall." However, on balance, dorm life at Dartmouth is a fun experience.

Though students think that Hanover can be dull, they also believe that Dartmouth's campus life can be both entertaining and enriching. Most students cite their quad area, known as "the Green," as one of their favorite hangouts. Events at the Green include a campus-wide snowball fight and a massive student bonfire. Dining service is also great. The 11 different eateries provide plenty of options for students. The Hopkins Center for the Performing Arts is also a student hub. The Hopkins Center hosts plays, classical and rock concerts, and movie nights. As one student put it, "The Hopkins Center is Dartmouth's house of entertainment." Overall, Dartmouth students have an enjoyable campus life and are rarely without something fun to do.

The Three Ps: Partying, Politics, and Philanthropy

Best known by many as a premier party school from the movie *Animal House*, Dartmouth has a reputation for a particularly vibrant Greek scene. As one freshman noted, "Greek life on campus is prevalent with a capital P. Socially speaking, you might almost feel restricted in your weekend options if you don't join." However, though *Animal House* does speak truth to the prevalence of Greek life on campus, most students feel it is not completely accurate. As one student noted, "Greek life here is not that intense. People party, sure, but they do so responsibly. Dartmouth also has a lot of other on-campus activities." As one sophomore put it, "Greek life is a big part of the Dartmouth social scene, but it is not coercive, and the parties are not that extreme. Even if you don't drink, Greek events can be a blast, and they really create a strong sense of community here. Sometimes movies like *Animal House* only tell part of the truth."

Students also see community service as an integral part of Dartmouth's extracurricular offerings. The Tucker Foundation, Dartmouth's umbrella service organization, encourages student involvement with organizations such as Big Brothers Big Sisters of America, the American Cancer Society, and with projects such as AIDS Global Health Day. The Tucker Foundation also sponsors student service trips, including recovery work trips to New Orleans and service trips to Latin America. Studying abroad is also an activity in which almost all Dartmouth students participate. As one student put it, "Dartmouth has a great study-abroad program with opportunities almost anywhere."

Another salient part of Dartmouth life is politics, especially during the start of every presidential election. Since Dartmouth is located in New Hampshire, which has the earliest presidential primary election in the nation, political life at Dartmouth can be quite intense. This past year, Dartmouth hosted a nationally televised debate for the Democratic Party's presidential candidates. One freshman vividly recalls the experience: "There was so much excitement on campus. Watch parties were thrown, and the auditorium was packed. I got to meet all the candidates, and the discussions with friends afterwards were incredible. One friend even told me that President Barack Obama went to one of his watch parties after the debate." In addition to presidential elections, many students find that politics affects them in other ways: students join advocacy groups, become involved in state politics, and enjoy political discussions. Overall, one of Dartmouth's best-kept secrets is its political atmosphere. Though many of its own students do not see Dartmouth as a political college, the environment is great for all those who are interested in politics.

Dartmouth is a prestigious Ivy League college that provides students with a strong academic program, an entertaining campus, and a lively social scene. As one student best put it, "Dartmouth is a place of incredible opportunity and intellectualism, where ambitious students go to challenge others, be challenged, and continue the lifelong process of enriching themselves through learning."—*Andrew Pearlmutter*

FYI

If you come to Dartmouth, you'd better bring "a warm winter coat."

What is the typical weekend schedule? "Friday nights are spent hanging out at a friend's dorm or going to a show or movie at the Hopkins Center. On Saturdays, do something athletic or do some other extracurricular activity and then go to a frat party at night. On Sundays, most students sleep in, and then study all day."

If I could change one thing about Dartmouth, I'd "renovate the River dorm building and make its rooms bigger."

Three things every student at Dartmouth should do before graduating are "go on a Dartmouth Outing Club trip, participate in the annual bonfires and snowball fights on the Green, and go to a frat party."

University of New Hampshire

Address: 4 Garrison Avenue, Durham, NH 03824
Phone: 603-862-1360
E-mail address: admissions@unh.edu
Web site URL: www.unh.edu
Year Founded: 1866
Private or Public: Public
Religious Affiliation: None
Location: Rural
Number of Applicants: 14,382
Percent Accepted: 73%
Percent Accepted who enroll: 31%
Number Entering: 2,850
Number of Transfers Accepted each Year: 1,013
Middle 50% SAT range: M: 520–620, CR: 500–600, Wr: 530–630
Middle 50% ACT range: 23–27
Early admission program EA/ED/None: EA

Percentage accepted through EA or ED: Unreported
EA and ED deadline: 15-Nov
Regular Deadline: 1-Feb
Application Fee: $50
Full time Undergraduate enrollment: 12,485
Total enrollment: 15,155
Percent Male: 44%
Percent Female: 56%
Total Percent Minority or Unreported: 25%
Percent African-American: 1%
Percent Asian/Pacific Islander: 2%
Percent Hispanic: 2%
Percent Native-American: <1%
Percent International: 1%
Percent in-state/out of state: 56%/44%
Percent from Public HS: 84%
Retention Rate: 87%

Graduation Rate 4-year: 51%
Graduation Rate 6-year: 71%
Percent Undergraduates in On-campus housing: 59%
Number of official organized extracurricular organizations: 200
3 Most popular majors: Business/Marketing, Agriculture, Engineering Technologies
Student/Faculty ratio: 18:1
Average Class Size: 15
Percent of students going to grad school: Unreported
Tuition and Fees: $28,570
In-State Tuition and Fees if different: $15,250
Cost for Room and Board: $10,252
Percent receiving financial aid out of those who apply: 74%
Percent receiving financial aid among all students: 64%

Situated in rural Durham, yet only an hour from Boston, the University of New Hampshire is a model of contrasts. A land-grant, sea-grant, and space-grant institution, UNH cultivates cutting-edge research on par with that of most large universities. At the same time, its idyllic location and relatively small size allow students to foster close relationships with professors and a feeling of community often lacking at many of those same large institutions.

Opportunities abound for the UNH student, and an excellent system of support ensures that those students who want to gain a lot from their experience will certainly do so.

Making the Grade

With seven schools and colleges, and over 100 majors, UNH's academic scene is as lively as its social one. While popular majors include psychology, mechanical engineering, business administration, nursing, and hospitality management, students can also choose to concentrate in fields like entrepreneurial venture creation or soil science.

Graduation requirements are heavy, including 10 general education requirements and four intensive writing courses, and although there are dozens of options to choose from to satisfy each requirement, the most popular gen ed courses, such as "Making Babies," "Elements of Weather," and "Germs," are often difficult to get into. "Still," added one student, "professors often try to help students who really want to take a particular class by making room where they can." Another explained, "The professors are amazing. They are really approachable, which I don't think often happens in academia."

While class sizes can be as large as 500 students in a lecture, most students get more personal attention with average class sizes much smaller for beginner-level and upper-level courses.

The effort it takes to earn a UNH degree depends on the major and courses that you choose. Engineering, medical sciences, nursing, and social work majors are all considered difficult, and "Business Statistics" and "Organic Chemistry" rank at the top of students' "Most Difficult Classes" lists.

While most professors claim that two hours a night dedicated to a course can earn students their desired grade, students add the qualification that that number really depends on the course. But no matter what courses you are taking, "mid-semester can be super crazy, when papers, presentations, and exams creep up on you."

While some students claim that the university's status as a public school has its disadvantages, others appreciate that its large size allow it greater funding and resources in the sciences. UNH offers its students Undergraduate Research Awards (URA) worth up to $1,600, Summer Undergraduate Research Funding (SURF) worth $3,500, and International Summer Research Opportunities Program (IROP) funding, which averaged $6,300 per person in 2007. One student, who studied the sociocultural effects of architectural change in Sri Lanka with an award, claimed that through UNH she received "an opportunity that not many undergrads get."

Another, whose project involved solar neutron detection in Scotland, described the IROP as "the single best program that any university can hope to offer." UNH is also one of only nine universities in the nation that has been distinguished as a land-grant, sea-grant, and space-grant institution.

Tonight's Gonna Be a Good, Good Night . . .

. . . if you can avoid being busted. Though one student explains that "UNH provides a lot of alternative programming on weekends to discourage students' need to drink," drug and alcohol violations are the most commonly punished student offenses on the campus. A 2007 study examining land-grant colleges in New England showed that UNH had the highest number of on-campus arrests for violations of liquor laws, with a total of 264 arrests in 2007.

Nevertheless, students claim that, despite their wild reputation, drinking is not the only way to have fun on campus and that many students drink little, if at all. "It is just as easy to find students who don't drink on weekends as it is to find those who do," said one student. Another added, "I'm not into the drinking scene at all, so I was wondering if I would feel a lot of pressure to drink here, but there is a niche for everyone. Drinking is certainly there, and I'm aware of it, but they do a good job of enforcing the rules."

To help keep students amused sans alcohol, the university hosts frequent events, ranging from Casino Nights to Stress-Relief Nights to twice-weekly movie nights. And beyond the typical weekend parties, UNH hosts several larger events throughout the year. Its most popular, Spring Climax, is a music festival that has featured acts like Snoop Dogg, Ludacris, Lupe Fiasco, Demetri Martin, and Bob Saget.

For students who want to go off campus, the university offers a free weekend shuttle to the coastal town of Portsmouth, seven miles from the UNH campus. In addition, Residential Assistants (RAs) keep their residents amused with tie-dye socials, game nights, and dance (or Dance Dance Revolution) parties.

Of course, social life doesn't just happen on the weekends; with over 180 student organizations, UNH offers something to fulfill every interest. If you've thought of it, UNH likely has it. From the Dairy Club ("increasing student awareness of career opportunities in dairy and related agricultural industries"), to Greek Intervarsity ("a movement of Greeks to experience God and change the world"), UNH offers a host of bizarrely themed clubs, alongside numerous more typical college organizations, such as Habitat for Humanity and French Club.

Fraternities and sororities are frequented by about 10% of the undergraduate population. With approximately 15,000 students, one senior explains, "Joining campus sports and organizations is the best way to make this campus seem smaller." Another said, "The social life at UNH is very active. There is something for everyone. In fact, you often have to ensure that you are not overextending yourself, as it is very easy to let your social life overtake your academic work."

The Double Hockey Sticks

Ask most any UNH student and you'll find that one of the most important parts of the UNH social life, whether you're a player or a spectator, is hockey. The Wildcats lay claim to having trained several NHL players, including Ty Conklin of the St. Louis Blues, Dan Winnik of the Phoenix Coyotes, and James Van Riemsdyk of the Philadephia Flyers. "The men's hockey games are some of the biggest events on campus," said one student.

But playing UNH sports is not just for future professional athletes. UNH offers varsity, club, and intramural teams designed to accommodate every skill level. Varsity athletes are either recruited or endure an intense try-out process, club sports are less rigorous but still compete against other schools, and intramurals are played only between teams of UNH students.

She's a Brick House

UNH's housing, a mishmash of old and new buildings, has something to offer for all students. According to one student, "There are traditional dorms (singles, doubles, triples, forced-triples . . .), suites, and on-campus apartments. They range from as old as the early 1900s to as new as 2008. Some buildings are newly renovated, while others need renovation badly."

Two freshman dorms are located next to what is widely considered one of the best dining halls on campus and are "a great place to be," explained one senior. Students are generally divided by academic major during their freshman year, and a third building, Alexander Hall, has been designated for those freshmen who enter as undeclared liberal arts majors. Students are particularly impressed by the activities organized for freshman dorm members, including trips to Boston and the beach.

For upperclassmen, housing is more varied: athletes tend to fill Congreve, Lord, or McLaughlin Halls, while honors students cluster in Hubbard. For many juniors and

seniors, the lure of adult life leads them to live off campus in apartments in Durham, Dover, Newmarket, or Portsmouth.

The Freshman 15

"While it's not your mother's home cooking, it's still one of the best college dining halls I've ever visited," said one student of UNH's food offerings. Students at the university can choose between three different dining halls, each with its own atmosphere and flavors. In addition to unlimited meals (except on the commuter meal plan), students on any of the UNH meal plans receive either Dining Dollars or "Cat's Cache," which can be spent around campus or at many locations in Durham, and are often accompanied by useful discounts. Students claim that the pricing is reasonable, but that sometimes the food gets boring, as "it's served on a loop," said one student. "You have to get creative."

Saving the Rainforest

Students who spent large chunks of their childhood watching *Captain Planet* may want to attend a college where they can help save the earth just by going. If that's the case, UNH is a good place to start. In 2009, the university was awarded the National Campus Sustainability Leadership Award. In 2010, it was given the highest grade of any school by the Sustainable Endowments Initiative.

> **"I really think your college experience is what you make of it, but also that UNH had exceptional opportunities."**

Students are constantly reminded of their commitment to the environment through energy-saving competitions, clotheslines in some of the dorms, and an annual music festival dedicated to sustainable living called Solarfest. UNH has also recently sought to increase the sustainability of its dining practices by purchasing more organic food and buying more food from local farmers.

Most students feel that both the university and its students do a good job maintaining their commitment to sustainability. According to one environmental science major, "Environmental clubs have a strong presence on campus, and many of those clubs are activist groups."

Famous Last Words

"I really think your college experience is what you make of it, but also that UNH had

exceptional opportunities," explained a member of the class of 2005 who is now attending Harvard Divinity School. A current UNH student added, "Being involved on campus is really important. . . . There are so many things to try here that can really make a big difference to your undergraduate experience." UNH, with its large student body, ample resources, and beautiful campus, offers students the chance at a full undergraduate experience, but that experience only comes to those who are willing to take the responsibility for their own happiness.
—*Heather Robinson*

FYI

If you come to UNH, you'd better bring "rain boots. I didn't expect it to be so wet here!"

What's the typical weekend schedule? "Meals are crucial on weekends. That's when you meet up with your friends and decide what you're doing for the night. A lot of times there will be parties and sports events on the weekend, which are a blast. The nightlife usually starts around seven or eight."

If I could change one thing about UNH, I'd "definitely look into finding ways to lower tuition. If you're an in-state student, it is pretty expensive to go here, even though it is supposed to be more affordable."

Three things every student at UNH should do before graduating are "go to a UNH hockey game, play broomball, and, obviously, take the class 'Making Babies.'"

New Jersey

College of New Jersey, The

Address: PO Box 7718, Ewing, NJ 08628
Phone: 609-771-1855
E-mail address: admiss@tcnj.edu
Web site URL: www.tcnj.edu
Year Founded: 1855
Private or Public: Public
Religious Affiliation: None
Location: Suburban
Number of Applicants: 9,956
Percent Accepted: 47%
Percent Accepted who enroll: 30%
Number Entering: 1,421
Number of Transfers Accepted each Year: 463
Middle 50% SAT range: M: 590–680, CR: 560–670, Wr: 560–670
Middle 50% ACT range: Unreported
Early admission program EA/ED/None: ED

Percentage accepted through EA or ED: 42%
EA and ED deadline: 15-Nov
Regular Deadline: 15-Jan
Application Fee: $75
Full time Undergraduate enrollment: 6,295
Total enrollment: 6,460
Percent Male: 43%
Percent Female: 57%
Total Percent Minority or Unreported: 34%
Percent African-American: 6%
Percent Asian/Pacific Islander: 6%
Percent Hispanic: 9%
Percent Native-American: <1%
Percent International: 1%
Percent in-state/out of state: 94%/6%
Percent from Public HS: Unreported
Retention Rate: 94%
Graduation Rate 4-year: 67%

Graduation Rate 6-year: 69%
Percent Undergraduates in On-campus housing: 62%
Number of official organized extracurricular organizations: 205
3 Most popular majors: Biology/Biological Sciences, General Business Administration and Management, Psychology
Student/Faculty ratio: 13:1
Average Class Size: 24
Percent of students going to grad school: 27%
Tuition and Fees: $19,569
In-State Tuition and Fees if different: $9,760
Cost for Room and Board: $10,677
Percent receiving financial aid out of those who apply: 80%
Percent receiving financial aid among all students: 70%

As one of New Jersey's premier institutions of higher education, TCNJ embodies both the academic experience of a top-notch institution and the price tag of a state school. Therefore, each year, students from every corner of the United States flock to this highly regarded university to learn with each other and from each other.

An Academic Smorgasbord

Students at TCNJ are ready to work. With seven schools spanning fifty disciplines in liberal arts, it has something for everyone. The newly adopted four-credit system, along with a revamped core curriculum, challenges students to engage in rigorous academic training without wearing out. All entering freshmen participate in the "First Year Experience," a wide array of freshman-specific seminars that include anything from "Forensic Science" to "Harry Potter Literature."

The chemistry major offered at TCNJ is one of the most intensive in the nation. According to students, it is in fact more intensive than the engineering program. The chemistry major requires sixteen courses—more than the usual twelve courses per major—in a tight-knit environment where students receive direct individual attention from faculty advisers. The one drawback, as a current chemistry major noted, is that the "course schedule is pretty much fixed for all four years" due to the strenuous nature of the program.

For the medically inclined, TCNJ offers a combined seven-year B.S./M.D. program with the University of Medicine and Dentistry of New Jersey. Admission to this medical-scholar program is highly selective, but it offers a fast track to those who are set on a career in medicine.

Education is one of the most popular majors, stemming from TCNJ's original establishment as a teacher's training school. Communications, biology, accounting, and nursing/exercise science are also popular. Whatever the course of study, students can expect to get very individualized care. Introductory courses, however, can be a little tougher with large lectures of upwards of one hundred students. Faculty advisors generally work hard to find resources for students, said one freshman. If there are still any lingering academic yearnings that have not been satisfied, the global study-abroad program offers students the opportunities to experience the world.

The Lion's Den

Housing on campus can be a bit confusing for some students. TCNJ guarantees housing for all freshmen and sophomores. The proportion of freshmen who live on campus is 95 percent, which decreases to 50 percent for juniors and seniors. The overall on-campus housing rate is about 60 percent. Freshmen are housed in Traverse, Cromwell, or Wolfe Halls, while upperclassmen are scattered in the other dorms and the many townhouses rented by TCNJ. Upperclassmen also have the options of private apartments in the city of Ewing specifically priced for college students, as well as fraternity or sorority houses on and off campus.

TCNJ is in the midst of expanding its housing availability to include juniors and seniors with construction of new apartment suites, located a little farther from central campus, which opened in 2009. The rooms may be small, but many say they offer a feel of coziness. Campus living also contributes to the "tight bonds and camaraderie" among floor mates, noted one freshman. Most residences are centrally located with all buildings and facilities accessible within a ten-minute walk.

Campus safety is an important issue for TCNJ. The college has its very own campus police force that patrols at night in addition to the seventy safety posts located around campus that the students can access in case of emergency. They can also use the safety posts to ask for police escorts during the night. Resident Advisors in the dorms are also in place to ensure a safe learning environment, but they are more focused on

fostering a sense of family. "You can walk into their rooms just to chat or get advice" and they will often "throw floor-wide birthday parties" to bring people together, said one junior. RAs are looked on less as authority figures and more as friends.

> "From martial arts to campus religion to community service, there's always something to do. I'm never bored."

Dining options at TCNJ receive mixed reviews. One trend is that students definitely need to be selective about what they do or do not eat. The food is served buffet-style in the main dining hall. There is a good selection of dishes, but they must be chosen wisely, according to a senior. Options for vegans and vegetarians are scarce. They will have the salad bar as their main staple in addition to a very limited menu of vegetarian dishes. Current students would also like to see the dining halls open a little later since the main dining hall, Eicke, closes promptly at 8 p.m., but there are also other campus-run cafés and eateries. Off-campus dining, on the other hand, might prove more satiating to the gourmet connoisseurs. The city of Ewing is very well aware of TCNJ's presence, and the students have a selection of restaurants that are moderately priced and of exceptional quality.

The Life of a Lion

Prospective students should not be fooled by the small college atmosphere of TCNJ. The party scene thrives there. Thanks to the four-credit schedule system, most students do not have classes on Wednesday, which makes Tuesday a prime time for parties. Friday, of course, is the other main party night. Options include fraternity/sorority parties, private dorms, clubs, bars, and private off-campus parties. There are also many school-sponsored events, parties, and dances, beginning with Homecoming. One complaint is that students should not expect any hot clubs or anchored social spots in Ewing. Those dissatisfied with entertainment options choose to venture into nearby metropolitan areas such as New York or Philadelphia. Downtown Trenton is also a bus ride away with popular student hangouts, eateries, bars, and clubs. Overall, however, the off-campus social scene is a bit lacking, as much of the action takes place within the TCNJ bubble.

Aside from the party scene, there are also a number of activities on campus so that it is almost impossible to be bored. "From martial arts to campus religion to community service, there's always something to do. I'm never bored," said one student. Indeed, anyone can find his or her niche at TCNJ, which boasts over 180 student organizations to suit every taste. It even has a Medieval Knight Club, which is one of the more interesting favorites of students.

The Bottom Line

Many students are very happy to be a part of the TCNJ family and often show their school pride by wearing their TCNJ apparel. Sports are also major contributors to school spirit. People at TCNJ are prone to be the "athletic type," noted one freshman. People "love to exercise" and make great use of the jogging and biking trails that surround campus.

Students are generally happy with their TCNJ experience and point to the astounding hominess that they feel once arriving on campus. They are part of a community rather than a face in the crowd. This feature of TCNJ makes the freshman experience particularly enjoyable and helps their transition to college life. "No one feels alone or segregated," explained one sophomore. Although the consensus seems to point toward a general contentedness, there are also some things students would like to see improve. For one, the location of TCNJ limits nightlife off campus. Students who wish to be closer to metropolitan areas can find New York and Philadelphia to be quite a commute. However, location is the only big complaint students have about TCNJ. The mix of academics, sports, extracurricular activities, and the sense of community makes TCNJ a fulfilling place to embark on the journey of higher education.—*Hai Pham*

FYI
If you come to TCNJ, you'd better bring "a fan."
What is the typical weekend schedule? "Sleep in late, hang out with friends, hit up downtown Trenton, party with friends, and recuperate for the next week."
If you could change one thing about TCNJ, what would it be? "I'd like to change the location to a more urban, metropolitan area where more entertainment options are available on the weekends."
Three things every student should do before graduating are "swim in the water fountain of the science department, eat in downtown Trenton, and go to a Lion football game."

Drew University

Address: 36 Madison Avenue, Madison, NJ 07940	**Percentage accepted through EA or ED:** 77%	**Graduation Rate 4-year:** 69%
Phone: 973-408-3739	**EA and ED deadline:** 1-Dec	**Graduation Rate 6-year:** 76%
E-mail address: cadm@drew.edu	**Regular Deadline:** 15-Feb	**Percent Undergraduates in On-campus housing:** 87%
Web site URL: www.drew.edu	**Application Fee:** $50	**Number of official organized extracurricular organizations:** 80
Year Founded: 1868	**Full time Undergraduate enrollment:** 1,608	
Private or Public: Private	**Total enrollment:** 2,411	**3 Most popular majors:** Economics, Political Science, Psychology
Religious Affiliation: Methodist	**Percent Male:** 40%	
Location: Suburban	**Percent Female:** 60%	
Number of Applicants: 4,191	**Total Percent Minority or Unreported:** 34%	**Student/Faculty ratio:** 11:1
Percent Accepted: 64%	**Percent African-American:** 5%	**Average Class Size:** 19
Percent Accepted who enroll: 17%	**Percent Asian/Pacific Islander:** 6%	**Percent of students going to grad school:** 33%
Number Entering: 456	**Percent Hispanic:** 6%	**Tuition and Fees:** $34,230
Number of Transfers Accepted each Year: 108	**Percent Native-American:** 1%	**In-State Tuition and Fees if different:** No difference
Middle 50% SAT range: M: 530–630, Cr: 530–650, Wr: 610–690	**Percent International:** 1%	**Cost for Room and Board:** $9,476
Middle 50% ACT range: 24–28	**Percent in-state/out of state:** 57%/43%	**Percent receiving financial aid out of those who apply:** Unreported
Early admission program EA/ED/None: ED	**Percent from Public HS:** 61%	**Percent receiving financial aid among all students:** 51%
	Retention Rate: 83%	

Drew University, founded in 1868 on a beautiful green wood in northern New Jersey, forms a very close community with a student body of fewer than 1,800 undergraduates. Despite the urban and suburban surroundings, the campus maintains its loveliness. From recent technological updates in classrooms to the construction of an environmentally-friendly dormitory, Drew looks to the future and focuses on the well-being and education of its students by providing the smaller community with the resources of a much larger university.

A Close Family

Drew University is a liberal arts school that ensures its students have a breadth of studies by requiring that they complete a major and a minor. Drew offers over 50 programs of study for students, and also allows students to propose their own chosen topics for a major. Subjects like English and political science are incredibly popular. However, one student said, "while political science is huge, there is a pretty even split between the arts and humanities and some of the sciences,

like biology. Drew is arguably stronger in the sciences than the humanities."

Many students at Drew also complete pre-medical and pre-law programs, and some enroll in the special dual-degree programs in medicine and in engineering and applied science.

The small size of the school is a huge point of pride for the students and professors at Drew. The small classes at Drew let professors really get to know their students, and students have plenty of access to their professors. One student said the largest class he ever took was "fewer than 30 people. It is smaller than high school, and everyone is way closer with each other and their teachers." One of his classmates agreed, and was excited to say that when students approach professors for help outside of class, "they are more than willing to help."

Almost all classes are taught by professors, except for required freshman writing classes, which are taught by teaching assistants but are still as small as seven people per class. This writing course is required, as well as "Common Hour, a discussion-based symposium for freshmen." After completing these courses, students must also meet credit requirements for arts and literature, humanities, social sciences, science, and math.

Students have the option of graduating with honors in their disciplines by writing an honors thesis. Also, Drew very recently introduced the Baldwin Honors program, which identifies incoming freshmen, places them in honors courses, and focuses them on a community initiative in their junior year—a service learning project dealing with citizenship, social change, or community education—which culminates in a final capstone project in senior year.

Life in the Suites

Madison, New Jersey, is the rather wealthy town that surrounds Drew, and housing there is very expensive and scarce. Most students spend their four years on Drew's campus with their classmates. This leads to a very tight-knit community. One student said, "It's incredible how quickly you can make friends here."

On campus, freshmen are sorted into one of four freshman dorms, and upperclassmen are housed by lottery. The dorms run from singles to doubles and to suites, and residents can opt for coed floors. Each floor is divided between two residential advisers, who are overseen by each dorm building's residential director. According to one freshman, "RAs are generally nice people and aren't out to get you, but they are there to uphold the rules, so don't cross them." Another student said that "you just need to be smart about things, and you won't get into trouble."

Drew University has only one central dining hall, Commons, which is located near most of the living spaces. According to one student, "the food is good, and with the meal plan you can choose points for the café and snack bar in the main classroom buildings." A snack bar in the University Center is "more expensive, but has better food."

Fun in the Suites

Most students stay at Drew during the weekends. Madison, New Jersey, "is not a town that offers a whole lot to college students," according to one Drew student, "but New York City is just an hour away." Parties are a popular weekend activity in student dorms. "Upperclassmen athletes usually have large parties," one student said. These take place in the Suites, which is a dorm for upperclassmen. Special annual events include the Holiday Ball, a winter formal open to everyone, and Junior-Senior, a dance specifically for upperclassmen.

> "It is smaller than high school, and everyone is way closer with each other and their teachers."

Drinking is very common on campus, but students who choose not to partake are still welcome at parties and can find things to do on the weekends, including many social events with various clubs and student groups, and plenty of student performances throughout the year. One senior said, "Most people drink, but some don't. There are nights where it is fun and nights when nothing really goes on. I'm not a huge drinker and I still have fun, so it works for me."

Always Something Going On

Drew students are active in very many extracurricular activities on campus, including writing for the campus newspaper *The Acorn*, community service organizations, and year-round performances with the consistently nationally-ranked theater department. "Student productions in the theater usually have bigger audiences than the sports team," said one student, and according to one senior, most people "are very passionate about their work and their fun in their activities. There is always something going on."

Drew doesn't have a football team, so "varsity soccer and team rugby are probably the biggest sports here." Drew is a member of Division III and has fifteen varsity teams, and also has club teams and intramurals for those looking for fun and socializing without much commitment. Still, intramurals participants "have lots of fun, but tend to be cutthroat at times actually." Students also have the opportunity to keep in shape when they visit Simon Forum and Athletic Center, which houses state-of-the-art gym facilities and an indoor track.

Even though the small school attracts most of its students from New Jersey and the surrounding area, there still exists a "good amount of diversity in the student body" at Drew. One freshman shared, "The people here are pretty friendly in general, and I love the school for its open-mindedness." This love also extends to the wonderful faculty and facilities that the university provides for its students.—*Connor Moseley*

FYI

If you come to Drew, you'd better bring "a bike to get from the dorms to class."

What is the typical weekend schedule? "Crazy parties in the Suites, free movies, and catching up on homework."

Three things every student at Drew should do before graduating are "go to the Shakespeare Theatre, attend Holiday Ball, and go mudsliding and take a swim in Tipple Pond in the rain."

What surprised me most about Drew when I arrived was "how many squirrels and deer can live on one campus."

Princeton University

Address: PO Box 430, Princeton, NJ 08544-0430
Phone: 609-258-3060
E-mail address: uaoffice@princeton.edu
Web site URL: www.princeton.edu
Year Founded: 1746
Private or Public: Private
Religious Affiliation: None
Location: Suburban
Number of Applicants: 26,247
Percent Accepted: 9%
Percent Accepted who enroll: 57%
Number Entering: 1,312
Number of Transfers Accepted each Year: Unreported
Middle 50% SAT range: M: 710–790, CR: 690–790, Wr: 700–790
Middle 50% ACT range: 31–35
Early admission program EA/ED/None: EA

Percentage accepted through EA or ED: NA
EA and ED deadline: 1-Nov
Regular Deadline: 1-Jan
Application Fee: $65
Full time Undergraduate enrollment: 5,149
Total enrollment: 5,220
Percent Male: 51%
Percent Female: 49%
Total Percent Minority or Unreported: 51%
Percent African-American: 7%
Percent Asian/Pacific Islander: 17%
Percent Hispanic: 8%
Percent Native-American: <1%
Percent International: 10%
Percent in-state/out of state: 16%/84%
Percent from Public HS: 58%
Retention Rate: 98%
Graduation Rate 4-year: 90%

Graduation Rate 6-year: Unreported
Percent Undergraduates in On-campus housing: 97%
Number of official organized extracurricular organizations: 250
3 Most popular majors: Economics, History, Political Science
Student/Faculty ratio: 6:1
Average Class Size: 15
Percent of students going to grad school: Unreported
Tuition and Fees: $37,000
In-State Tuition and Fees if different: No difference
Cost for Room and Board: $12,069
Percent receiving financial aid out of those who apply: 59%
Percent receiving financial aid among all students: 58%

There's no doubt about it—Princeton is a hard school. It's one that's hard to get into, and maybe even harder to do well in. But to be fair, most students at Princeton enjoy their experience, despite the incredible effort they put into their studies, because of the tremendous rewards that await them upon graduation. Consistently ranked first or second every year from 2001 to 2013 by *U.S. News & World Report*, it's no coincidence that Princeton offers its students an unparalleled experience in undergraduate education, something that's sure to be widely respected after graduation. Although students spend a lot of time on work,

they also have a good time partaking in Princeton's many traditions, which makes their undergraduate experience particularly unique and enriching.

Work Hard and Play Hard. Really, Really Hard.

One student said, "Most people would probably agree with the following description: Princeton is a great place to be from, but not particularly great to be at." Students said that the value and prestige of receiving a Princeton diploma makes the hard work worth it, but in between the hard work, there is also a lot that can be gained through

Princeton's unparalleled undergraduate experience. "The attention that we get as undergraduates from most professors is unique. Princeton focuses much more heavily on its undergraduates than its graduate students," one sophomore explained. He also added that Princeton's senior thesis, a comprehensive research project in one's major required of nearly all seniors to graduate, is something else that makes the Princeton experience especially valuable.

> "If you strike the right balance between studying and partying, it doesn't feel like school is taking over your life. I came in expecting to work with no rest whatsoever and that hasn't been the case."

But prospective students need not fear *too* much about the hard work. One freshman said, "I guess the most important thing has been to work hard and play hard. If you strike the right balance between studying and partying, it doesn't feel like school is taking over your life. I came in expecting to work with no rest whatsoever and that hasn't been the case." Students say that there is definitely a spectrum of students, ranging from those who take very easy classes and go out four to five days a week, to those who spend a large majority of their time on their studies. But students warn pre-frosh to mentally prepare themselves for the curriculum ahead of them. One sophomore said, "I definitely did not expect to be so unprepared for the difficult coursework, and in general I didn't expect the workload to be so heavy." But students can find solace in the fact that they're not facing this alone. "The best thing about Princeton is the academic environment. You might be working your butt off but it's nice knowing other people are doing the same thing," one freshman said.

Deflated Spirits

While Princeton offers an unparalleled experience in an excellent undergraduate instruction, the university also has a policy of "grade deflation," which is a real and genuine concern for students on campus. Students said that Princeton began a grade deflation policy a few years ago by which approximately only 35 percent of students in a department are allowed to receive A's. Students say that the official reason is that Princeton wants to hold its students to the highest standard by fighting grade inflation and only giving A's to work that deserves the highest grades. This hasn't been happily received by the student population, and some say that it negatively affects the learning atmosphere. "The existence of a hard quota makes it seem like students not only have to do well in classes, but they have to do it better than the other 65 percent of students to get an A, so this fosters competition instead of cooperation," one student said.

In addition, students feel that institutions of similar caliber, notably Harvard and Yale, have grade inflation, which disadvantages Princeton students upon graduation as they try to apply for graduate school and professional programs, or enter the workforce. One freshman noted, "Apparently, Princeton sends out a letter explaining grade deflation to grad schools and companies, but no one knows if they actually bother reading those letters, so I, among many others, worry about that."

It's Not About the Food, It's About the Name

While Princeton does have a residential college system, there isn't intense rivalry between the colleges as is usually the case at similar schools. For the first two years, students can't transfer to be with their friends at other colleges, but by junior year students move to upperclassmen dorms and living arrangements become more flexible. There are three four-year and three two-year residential colleges, so as upperclassmen students can live in university housing on campus with college affiliation, but do not need to live in the college itself. While there are organized activities within colleges such as study breaks, trips, and intramurals, Princeton's social life entirely revolves around the eating clubs, a culture that is unique to Princeton.

In a sense, eating clubs are exactly what they sound like—places to eat. Upperclassmen have the option to either go independent or to join an eating club as their "meal plan" of sorts. There are two types of eating clubs: bicker and sign-in. For bicker clubs students must go through an application process—or bickering, as Princetonians call it—and be selected by the committees of each of these clubs. These clubs are large mansions all located along Prospect Avenue, which is conveniently called the Street by Princeton students.

Ironically, the prestige of each eating club is not about the food at all, but about its name. Bicker clubs are obviously more exclusive than sign-in clubs, but some bicker clubs have such a high reputation that membership is incredibly competitive. For example, students say that Ivy consists of the wealthy, the connected, and the athletic, while Tower has mostly students from the selective Woodrow Wilson School of Public Affairs. In addition, members of certain fraternities and certain sports teams are unofficially "set" for certain eating clubs, so getting into extremely selective eating clubs is very hard, although students say that knowing "the right people" definitely helps with the process. Regarding the selectivity and prestige of the eating clubs, one student said, "The bickering process is definitely stressful and it can be very frustrating when you know there's just nothing you can do to get in because of your background. For example, Ivy costs something like $15,000 a year, so that automatically excludes the poor."

Eating Clubs or Drinking Clubs?

While eating clubs obviously serve their purpose of providing food for students, they also provide something else: drinks, drinks, drinks. Eating clubs double as party places, and although only club members can eat at the eating clubs, the clubs usually allow everyone to party, so students frequently hit up the Street on weekends. "Everyone goes to the Street, period. It's the center of Princeton's party life in the truest sense of 'party' since there aren't really any other options," one student said. He explained that free beer and music draw people to the Street on Thursday and, while most people go to dorm parties on Friday, the Street picks up again on Saturday.

Students say that the parties are usually pretty good. "There are 10 eating clubs, so you're bound to find a good one." Although it's technically illegal, it's an accepted fact that all the eating clubs serve alcohol to minors. Three eating clubs were recently closed for serving alcohol to minors, and students say that when things like that happen, eating clubs usually tighten alcohol policy, but that it usually doesn't last very long. "Princeton doesn't directly own the eating clubs so they can't really do anything about it," one student explained. Students say that administrators are in discussions about having public safety officers patrolling halls to bust parties, but before this the alcohol policy was pretty loose. Students said that they can only get in trouble for serving alcohol to minors or drinking outside, and

that officers only check if students are serving alcohol to minors when parties get really loud and are reported to public safety. "Very few people get into trouble and they're usually only put on probation, but one of the few things Princeton is very anal about is that there are absolutely no drinking games."

Outside the Classroom, Inside the Bubble

Princeton is not much of a college town. Students describe it as a "rich suburb" that doesn't offer much for its college students. "Princeton feels like a tight-knit community because it's kind of isolated and everything is within walking distance. You barely ever set foot outside of campus." Students admit that this creates a "bubble culture," but one said that most people don't seem to mind, and may even really like it. "It's like a castle in the middle of nowhere, as we usually say. I like the relative isolation and peace, and having everything I need close by." However, many students still complain that the town doesn't really have things for college students to do, like bars, clubs, or shopping areas.

But the lack of opportunities in the town may be good in at least one aspect—it makes Princeton students look to their own campus for activities outside the classroom. Students say that extracurricular involvement varies from person to person. Some people are heavily involved, while others might have other time commitments, such as sports, that prevent them from devoting lots of time to other activities. Some of the more prominent clubs include the Black Men's Awareness Group (BMAG), Student Volunteer Council (SVC), and the Asian American Student Association (AASA), while a cappella and dance groups are also very popular on campus. "Most people are committed to one thing, and I get the feeling that the majority of the students are involved in some sort of activity. There are so many things here that you're bound to find something you like, whether that's music, intramurals, or theater stuff."

Out on the fields, Princeton boasts one of the strongest athletic programs in the Ivy League. Princeton has consistently been ranked at the top of *Time* magazine's "Strongest College Sports Teams" lists, and *Sports Illustrated* has ranked Princeton as a top 10 school for athletics. Princeton is particularly well known for its men's and women's crews, which have won several NCAA and Eastern Sprints titles in recent years. In addition, Princeton's men's lacrosse team is widely recognized as a perennial powerhouse in the Division I ranks. Other successful Princeton athletic programs include women's soccer and field hockey, which has won every field hockey conference title since 1994. Princeton athletics is a powerhouse in the Ivy League, which is a definite plus for those who are looking for a prestigious academic experience in addition to a strong athletic experience.

Keeping It Old School

While students agree that Princeton has moved away from its stereotyped image as an elitist school for stuck-up, old-money prep-school kids, the school still has strong roots and values in traditions, as the eating clubs suggest. One of Princeton's traditions is the bonfire held on Cannon Green behind Nassau Hall, which happens when Princeton beats both its rivals—Harvard and Yale—at football in the same season. "It's pretty special, since it doesn't happen that often. Everyone congregates and screams," one sophomore said. Like many other Ivy League universities, Princeton has a myth regarding exiting particular gates as an undergraduate. At the end of Princeton's graduation ceremony, the new graduates proceed out through FitzRandolph Gate as a symbol of leaving college and entering the real world. But according to tradition, anyone who leaves campus through this gate before their own graduation date will not graduate, so students use side exits instead.

Students warn that the old-school tradition of Princeton may also attract a certain type of student, namely those from "old money." While most students are generally pleasant, students warn that those who have not been thoroughly exposed to the East Coast prep-school culture may be in for an initial shock. One student who came from a city public school said he was surprised by the "jock-ish" and "elitist" atmosphere at Princeton. "There are a lot more affluent and wealthy kids here—some really do flaunt it and most don't hide it. I don't have a problem with rich people, and I've certainly met people who are rich and nice, but it's just that they sometimes come across as being obnoxious in the way they act." But another student said that this attitude is not necessarily entirely related to social class, and may have a lot to do with the competitive nature of Princeton's atmosphere. "Of course, there are many rich and snobby people who dress very preppy-ish, but other people are just jerks when it comes to schoolwork, being unhelpful and arrogant. Unless you're lucky, you really have to look around for nice and helpful students."

All in all, Princeton students tend to be happy with their educational experience, even if it means that they're working incredibly hard for the four years they're at school. But between the hard work to get those coveted A's, Princeton students still find the time to pursue passions and party hard, and many keep going by keeping their eyes on the end goal: the prestige that comes with their diploma. The quality of education that Princeton students get is arguably the best on an undergraduate level, and the Princeton name will undoubtedly help students as they leave the bubble and venture off into the world. As one alumni noted, "People know that Princeton graduates will know how to solve anything if you give them enough time to figure out a way."—*Della Fok*

FYI

If you come to Princeton, you'd better bring "obnoxiously preppy clothes for lawn parties, which is when the eating clubs invite bands to come play. It starts Sunday afternoon so everyone's hungover by nine. It happens once each semester, but it's huge."

What is the typical weekend schedule? "If you're a slacker, jock, or something of that nature, you start partying on Thursday nights. If you're a nerd, you probably have 98,234 problem sets due on Friday, so you stay inside to do those. On Friday nights usually only one eating club is open, basically for the sake of the nerds, but for the rest of campus, Friday is usually pretty relaxed: the evenings are often filled with events like dance shows and concerts. Saturday is pretty dead until nighttime, which is hardcore partying, of course, and then Sunday is homework day for everyone."

If I could change one thing about Princeton, I'd "change the grading policy. Enough said."

Rutgers / The State University of New Jersey

Address: 65 Davidson Road, Piscataway, NJ 08854-8097
Phone: 732-932-4636
E-mail address: admissions@ugadm.rutgers.edu
Web site URL: www.rutgers.edu
Year Founded: 1766
Private or Public: Public
Religious Affiliation: None
Location: Suburban
Number of Applicants: 29,532
Percent Accepted: 59%
Percent Accepted who enroll: 35%
Number Entering: 6,031
Number of Transfers Accepted each Year: 2,906
Middle 50% SAT range: M: 560–680, CR: 530–630, Wr: 540–640
Middle 50% ACT range: Unreported

Early admission program EA/ED/None: None
Percentage accepted through EA or ED: NA
EA and ED deadline: NA
Regular Deadline: Rolling
Application Fee: $65
Full time Undergraduate enrollment: 28,903
Total enrollment: 30,351
Percent Male: 51%
Percent Female: 49%
Total Percent Minority or Unreported: 50%
Percent African-American: 8%
Percent Asian/Pacific Islander: 24%
Percent Hispanic: 11%
Percent Native-American: <1%
Percent International: 2%
Percent in-state/out of state: 93%/7%
Percent from Public HS: Unreported
Retention Rate: 92%

Graduation Rate 4-year: 58%
Graduation Rate 6-year: Unreported
Percent Undergraduates in On-campus housing: Unreported
Number of official organized extracurricular organizations: 400
3 Most popular majors: Biology, Engineering, Business
Student/Faculty ratio: 14:1
Average Class Size: 27
Percent of students going to grad school: Unreported
Tuition and Fees: $21,388
In-State Tuition and Fees if different: $12,754
Cost for Room and Board: $11,216
Percent receiving financial aid out of those who apply: 67%
Percent receiving financial aid among all students: 69%

Named most diverse national university for the 13th consecutive year in *U.S. News & World Report,* Rutgers University is a public research university that boasts a wealth of academic programs, resources, and opportunities both in and out of the classroom. With campuses in three distinct Garden State locales, Rutgers, the only university to reject an invitation to the Ivy League, is a serious academic institution rooted in a deep commitment to public education.

A Three-for-One Deal

Rutgers comprises three campuses, the largest and oldest of which is located in the central New Jersey cities of New Brunswick and Piscataway. The smaller southern campus at Camden and northern location at Newark flank the center, forming a university that literally spans the state. Each of the three campuses is distinct in its academic offerings, extracurricular activities, and social life. One thing's for sure—the Rutgers experience is diverse.

New Brunswick students estimate that the ratio of students who live on campus versus those who live off campus is about even, while Newark students said that far more students live off campus. "Most people are dying to get off campus after their second year," revealed one New Brunswick junior resident. Because Rutgers is a public university, it is known to adhere to stringent underage drinking restrictions; students cited this fact as motivation for the move off campus. Douglass Residential College of the New Brunswick campus is an all-female housing option, though in any given year the building may include coed dorms.

All of the campuses boast a wealth of extracurricular activities and clubs, with intramural sports the most popular. Rutgers students point to the variety of options open to those looking for fun: movie theaters, the mall, restaurants, and parties. The consensus among students is that their weekend parties are top-notch. "Come Friday and Saturday night, Rutgers is the place to be," bragged one sophomore. However, since many students have jobs, the weekend is not all about partying. Greek life is not very expansive, with active life primarily at its College Avenue and Livingston locations on the New Brunswick campus. The Livingston locations feature minority and ethnic fraternities and sororities.

In terms of the population's diversity, Rutgers students agree that the university hits the mark and makes continual efforts to maintain its inclusiveness. But they do criticize the disjointed nature of campus life and fault the inefficiency of the transportation system. "Even though nextbus.com reduces the wait, Route 18 construction makes traffic a constant issue," one junior said. Beyond the system of buses that attempts to connect the Rutgers experience on a practical level, the university attempts to create social spaces that foster diversity. The formation of new residential colleges (the first of which is the aforementioned Douglass) represents such an administrative attempt to foster exchange in living communities.

Rutgersfest, the annual campus-wide blowout before final exams, brings three performing artists or groups to the stage to celebrate the closing of the academic year. Even in this endeavor, students cite the diversity of acts as reflecting the diversity of those in the crowd. "Some people come to Rutgers and have an utter culture shock," said one New Yorker. However, students are quick to explain that the diversity of Rutgers is healthy and productive, and when asked about resultant tensions, dispelled the idea. "I have never encountered a problem with it," said one junior. "The people who come here with no experience with difference don't react with prejudice; they tend to be happy to get a taste of the real world."

An End to the "Rutgers Screw"

With the freshman class of 2007, the previous staples of the New Brunswick campus—Douglas, Livingston, Rutgers, and University Colleges—were combined into one undergraduate liberal arts college: the School of Arts and Sciences. This advanced conglomerate offers an expanded set of over 100 majors spanning the humanities, biological sciences, mathematics, and more.

The change was simply one component of the "undergraduate transformation" recently undergone by Rutgers's largest campus. And while most students have praised the effort for making their educational experience much less complicated, others have criticized it for doing the exact opposite. "It

was a good idea in theory, but we weren't ready for it," remarked one junior resident adviser. She lamented that her residents "had no idea what they were doing" and that the academic advising that accompanied the new system needs work. "Academically and residence-wise, things are still in transition," she said.

Despite these administrative hassles, students generally praised the changes. A major benefit of this system is its ability to bring an end to the notorious "Rutgers Screw." Defined by students as a buzzword for the popular notion that, by the time you reach senior status, some unknown requirement or misinformation will keep you from graduating, the "Rutgers Screw" now faces extinction under the transformation's streamlined requirements and staff. Rather than being restricted by college, students can now seek advisers under the unified college to avoid the common pitfall.

> **"My freshman year at Rutgers was the most amazing experience I've ever had; I love Rutgers and I wouldn't pick another school."**

Students also hailed the changes for bringing them together. Previously, each campus had its own traditions, but now Rutgers students are working to forge a single community. "Cap and Skull," a Rutgers College secret society based on leadership and academics prowess, now extends membership invitations to the entire university. According to one exercise and sports science major, "Whatever people have to say about the transformation, it has increased campus unity."

A Warm Welcome

Freshman classes have the advantage of walking into this heightened spirit of cohesion. Upperclassmen characterized their freshman orientations as mediocre, but lauded the newest orientation efforts and the improvement of the football team as ways of bringing the class together. "This year's orientation was amazing, with all these events. We even had a throw-down where we could win prizes," a freshman New Jersey native said. One sophomore commented that the orientation "built them more into a community than [his] first year." Yet even before these changes, students remembered the Rutgers freshman experience fondly. One junior exclaimed, "My freshman year at Rutgers was the most amazing experience I've ever had; I love Rutgers and I wouldn't pick another school."

Incoming classes will also be welcomed by various new, albeit uniform, academic requirements. In place of the previous "non-Western" requirement are the more expansive categories of "Diversity" and "Global Awareness." Those new to Rutgers will still have to pass "Expository Writing," a Rutgers staple known to students as "Expos," to graduate. This infamous RU requirement brought a series of groans from students across the spectrum in terms of major, interests, and origin. The sole comfort students offered regarding the course was that those taking it are by no means alone. "Everyone goes through it; the beauty of it is that you have four years to knock it out," advised one senior. For those weary of getting lost in a sea of numbers, but valuing the resources of a research university, the transformation also ensures that freshmen have the opportunity to engage in new first-year seminars—classes capped at 20 and taught by distinguished Rutgers faculty, aimed at engaging students in serious, speculative dialogue.

Spectacle Sports

Rutgers played Princeton University in the first ever game of intercollegiate football in 1869 (where the present-day Rutgers gymnasium now stands) and won. So it comes as no surprise that a strong tradition of university athletics continues to this day.

The Scarlet Knights have a dedicated and spirited fan base, drawing huge crowds from across the lecture hall aisle. At Rutgers, football dominates the athletic scene. Students cite the team's improvement in recent years for a surge in school spirit. "All I wear is Rutgers clothing," one senior said. Last year, the Scarlet Knights performed well enough to reach the International Bowl in Toronto, Canada, with their star player, Brian Leonard. Leonard was recently drafted into the NFL to play for the St. Louis Rams. According to students, the team has continued to improve as new stars have risen in his wake. Knights say that RU football has become a huge campus event and school spirit has risen alongside the stats. "I have never seen so many Rutgers sweatshirts," commented one senior.

Football is not the only sport that draws crowds at Rutgers. The women's basketball team is renowned for its prowess on the court and has become the media darling of college sports. The team and the school have not let the recent Don Imus controversy derail their efforts. "It really affected us when it happened, but now everything's been smoothed over," said one junior. She went on to explain how the proliferation of Facebook groups and spread of support further unified the school in the face of the media flurry. "School spirit translated into solidarity."—*Nicholle Manners*

FYI

If you come to Rutgers, you'd better bring "a Rutgers T-shirt because you'd better not be wearing another college's shirt."

What is the typical weekend schedule? "Friday: go to the dining hall, go to work, do your homework, go out; Saturday: sleep in late, go to a football game and go out; Sunday: sleep in late and do your homework."

If I could change one thing about Rutgers, I'd "change the bus system and make morning classes later."

Three things every student at Rutgers should do before graduating are "go to a football game, eat a fat sandwich at the Grease Trucks, and go to the Zimmerlie Art Museum."

Seton Hall University

Address: Seton Hall University, South Orange, NJ 07079
Phone: 973-761-9332
E-mail address: thehall@shu.edu
Web site URL: www.shu.edu
Year Founded: 1856
Private or Public: Private
Religious Affiliation: Roman Catholic
Location: Rural
Number of Applicants: 10,851
Percent Accepted: 79%
Percent Accepted who enroll: 13%
Number Entering: 1,135
Number of Transfers Accepted each Year: 444
Middle 50% SAT range: M: 470–580, CR:470–570, Wr: 480–580
Middle 50% ACT range: 20–25
Early admission program EA/ED/None: EA

Percentage accepted through EA or ED: NA
EA and ED deadline: 15-Nov
Regular Deadline: Rolling
Application Fee: $55
Full time Undergraduate enrollment: 4,640
Total enrollment: 5,213
Percent Male: 42%
Percent Female: 58%
Total Percent Minority or Unreported: 49%
Percent African-American: 13%
Percent Asian/Pacific Islander: 7%
Percent Hispanic: 11%
Percent Native-American: <1%
Percent International: 3%
Percent in-state/out of state: 75%/25%
Percent from Public HS: 70%
Retention Rate: 82%
Graduation Rate 4-year: 41%
Graduation Rate 6-year: 56%

Percent Undergraduates in On-campus housing: 43%
Number of official organized extracurricular organizations: 100
3 Most popular majors: Communication Studies/Speech, Communication and Rhetoric; Criminal Justice/Safety Studies; Nursing/Registered Nurse
Student/Faculty ratio: 14:1
Average Class Size: 19
Percent of students going to grad school: 30%
Tuition and Fees: $29,940
In-State Tuition and Fees if different: No difference
Cost for Room and Board: $12,050
Percent receiving financial aid out of those who apply: 91%
Percent receiving financial aid among all students: 86%

Seton Hall University is a private Roman Catholic university tucked away in suburban South Orange, New Jersey, yet surrounded by one of the largest metropolitan areas in the world. The school is steeped in its long-standing Catholic tradition, as the most prominent Catholic university in New Jersey, while being surrounded by the immense diversity and culture in nearby Newark and New York City. The school is most known for its business and diplomacy programs as well as nursing and education. With a mix of old school traditions, new school cosmopolitanism, and focused academics, Seton Hall University offers a place for those who wish to pursue a worldly education in the safety of a tucked-away suburb.

Getting Down to Business

Business seems to be the focus of the undergraduate academic atmosphere at Seton Hall University. "The Stillman School of Business is our most visible and well-known program," remarks a sophomore. Indeed, the undergraduate business program is highly regarded across the Northeast and currently holds the top spot in the state of New Jersey. The Diplomacy program comes in second with regards to presence and prestige. All incoming freshmen are enrolled in one of the six undergraduate schools of the university: Business, Education and Human Services, Nursing, Theology, Diplomacy and International Relations, and the College of Arts and Sciences—Seton Hall's largest undergraduate school. The Nursing and Education programs round out the most popular majors for undergraduates.

The breadth and depth of study at Seton Hall, a liberal arts focused university, depends mainly on the program of study. Math, science, engineering, and nursing programs are markedly more challenging and rigorous than humanities majors, as students point out. The Nursing program is one of the hardest majors at Seton Hall owing to the intensive field and clinical work on which students are graded. Business writing is another notoriously difficult class that all Seton Hall business majors must take. Notoriously easy classes include University Life and Journey of Transformation. These are courses required by the school taken generally in the first year. University Life is simply a course that teaches students how to survive college in regards to study habits, dorm life, etc. Journey of Transformation is a religion course in which students read different religious pieces and then discuss them openly in class. This course is basically an opinion course and "as long as you do the readings you'll get a good grade," says a sophomore.

Regardless of major and class choices, all students at Seton Hall must complete a set of core courses in the Seton Hall curriculum in order to be eligible for the bachelor's degree. The hallmark of the 16-credit core is anchored by classes such as Journey of Transformation, Christianity and Culture in Dialogue, and Engaging the World. These classes in addition to University Life and Core English courses provide students with a uniquely Seton education steeped in the Catholic tradition. In addition to the hallmark courses, students must complete proficiency-infused courses in reading and writing, oral communication, information fluency, numeracy, and critical thinking. "It can be a pain sometimes," reminisced a senior. "Having to fulfill all those requirements in addition to a major; it kind of limits you to the amount of 'just for fun' classes you can take." Still, others praise the core curriculum for opening up their education to courses they would never have taken otherwise.

Perhaps one of Seton's biggest assets is the faculty on hand to help students learn and grow as individuals. Professors tend to be very accessible and "down to earth," remarked a junior. In fact, many classes are taught by professors with very little being taught by TAs. This creates an intimate, small-group learning environment where many students study. It's also a reason for capped classes that may be an annoyance. Some well-known and well-liked professors include Professor Kwame of the Political Science department, Professor Madrazo of the English and Business departments, Professor Athens of the Criminal Justice department, and Professor Rubino in the School of Nursing. However, some students do complain that some professors let their personal beliefs and biases permeate through their teaching. All in all though, professors are generally accessible and well-liked.

Dorm Life

Incoming freshmen are all randomly assigned to one of two dorms: Aquinas Hall and Boland Hall. Roommates are matched according to an online profile created on the housing website. Both buildings are far from central campus with rooms being "not that nice, but tolerable," according to a freshman. Suites of four to five share a common space with a suite bathroom. However, dorm picks do get better with seniority. After freshman year, students get to choose where and with whom they'd like to live. The rooming draw operates on a priority points system where points are earned by attending campus events and activities. Those with the most points get priority pick in the room draw. Upperclassmen dorm rooms come carpeted and often with a sink and mirror in each room. Resident Assistants, or RAs, live in student dorms. Their job is basically just to monitor noise levels, swipe students in at the front desk, and regulate guest policies. They are somewhat strict when it comes to noise levels during quiet hours, but aside from that you "hardly notice them," says a sophomore.

> **"Seton Hall harbors a variety of different people, with some of the nicest yet some of the rudest people."**

The architecture at Seton Hall is very institutional-looking. "It's not that exciting to look at, honestly," remarked a freshman. Popular hangout spots include the Green where students congregate and play sports. Aside from that, other popular hangouts include the Walsh Library and other buildings. Campus eateries are also a place of congregation and socialization with the main dining hall, "inner-caf," serving buffet-style meals and other fast-grab "outer-caf" eateries catering to students on-the-go. Students on meal plans have a certain number of meal swipes per semester and a certain amount of "pirate bucks" that are redeemable at the outer-caf eateries. These include a pizzeria, Nathan's sandwich shop, and the Express, which has snacks and drinks.

Seton Hall Social Club

Seton Hall tends to be a cliquey school with different groups mostly keeping to themselves. Since the school does have a lot of commuter students, the campus tends to empty out on the weekends; that and the close proximity to NYC. Students do generally go out on the weekends, but the options are a little limited in South Orange. However, the excitement of New York City is just a train ride away. Just as the student population is very diverse, the personalities you'll find here tend to encompass a very wide scope. "Seton Hall harbors a variety of different people, with some of the nicest yet some of the rudest people," warns a sophomore. The different mix of student backgrounds, commuters, and personality types make for a mishmash of experiences and social scenes.

Although Seton Hall is a dry campus, drinking seems to be a dominant force in the social life of students. Alcohol is only allowed in upperclassmen dorms contingent upon checking in an amount suitable for "personal consumption." But "everyone seems to drink here," says a senior. Still, those who choose not to drink find their own group and their own scene.

Aside from partying, Seton Hall students are very committed to extracurricular and service activities. The most prominent clubs on campus are the Student Activities Board, WSOU student-run radio station, Black Student Union, and the campus publications *The Setonian* and *The Stillman Exchange*. *The Setonian* is the general campus newspaper while the rival *Stillman Exchange* is written specifically by Stillman Business School

students. Extracurriculars aside, sports and athletic pride play a huge role in organizing undergraduate life. Though Seton Hall does not have a football team, the basketball team is wildly popular with basketball season almost always selling out. The track team was also very popular until it was cut from the budget in the spring of 2010. Overall, "While there are a number of great programs at Seton Hall, there could always be more. For the ones we do offer, I feel they are great. I still wish there were more though," says a sophomore.

The Seton Hall Experience

In general, life at Seton Hall tends to be good. Students are happy to be immersed in such cultural and academic diversity on a manageable campus. The Catholic tradition of education may be new for some, but no one doubts that it permeates through all facets of life at Seton Hall. "You can't walk down the street without seeing a priest or minister waving to students somewhere," noted a sophomore. Seton Hall takes great pride in its Catholic community and has become very well known for it. Some students who come here love it while others don't. It comes down to a matter of preference and taste for what kind of education experience one is looking to have for the next four years.—*Hai Pham*

FYI

If you come to Seton Hall, you should bring "a train pass to go out on the weekends, go home, or visit college friends."

What's the typical weekend schedule like? "Party Friday and Saturday nights. Attend a sporting event Saturday or hop a bus to New York City or the mall and study on Sunday."

If you could change one thing about Seton Hall, what would it be? "I'd make the buildings a little more exciting to look at and have students a little less cliquey and more social all around."

Stevens Institute of Technology

Address: One Castle Point on Hudson, Hoboken, NJ 07030
Phone: 201-216-5194
E-mail address: admissions@stevens.edu
Web site URL: www.stevens.edu
Year Founded: 1870
Private or Public: Private
Religious Affiliation: None
Location: Suburban
Number of Applicants: 3,239
Percent Accepted: 47%
Percent Accepted who enroll: 36%
Number Entering: 551
Number of Transfers Accepted each Year: 83
Middle 50% SAT range: M: 620–700, CR: 560–640, Wr: 550–650
Middle 50% ACT range: 25–30
Early admission program EA/ED/None: ED

Percentage accepted through EA or ED: 78%
EA and ED deadline: 15-Nov
Regular Deadline: 1-Feb
Application Fee: $55
Full time Undergraduate enrollment: 2,362
Total enrollment: 2,369
Percent Male: 73%
Percent Female: 27%
Total Percent Minority or Unreported: 44%
Percent African-American: 3%
Percent Asian/Pacific Islander: 11%
Percent Hispanic: 9%
Percent Native-American: <1%
Percent International: 5%
Percent in-state/out of state: 60%/40%
Percent from Public HS: 72%
Retention Rate: 90%
Graduation Rate 4-year: 38%

Graduation Rate 6-year: 74%
Percent Undergraduates in On-campus housing: 85%
Number of official organized extracurricular organizations: 120
3 Most popular majors: Biomedical/Medical Engineering, Civil Engineering, Mechanical Engineering
Student/Faculty ratio: 7:1
Average Class Size: 26
Percent of students going to grad school: 18%
Tuition and Fees: $38,400
In-State Tuition and Fees if different: No difference
Cost for Room and Board: $12,390
Percent receiving financial aid out of those who apply: 82%
Percent receiving financial aid among all students: 75%

As the name of the school implies, Stevens focuses on the sciences. Though students are hard workers and want to do well, they also try to have fun and take advantage of Hoboken, New Jersey, where the school is located, and New York, which is just across the river. The juxtaposition of the small school and the two larger cities, in addition to the concentration on the sciences, makes for what students term an "atypical" college experience.

No Room for Slackers

At the start of freshman year, students choose their major and take the specific set of courses their chosen track dictates. This system means that the same group of students often has the same classes together for the entire day. "It feels a little bit like middle school," remarked a sophomore.

Students praise the fact that incoming freshmen get their own laptops for free and say that they put their computers to good use during class time. Students must take 19 to 21 credit hours a semester, which is "a

pretty obscene number." The large number of classes and the substantial amount of work given in each course mean that students work very hard much of the time. "You have to be self-motivated to get the work done here," said one junior. "Nobody is holding your hand. Nobody is checking up on you. It is a good thing to have that sort of academic freedom, but you have to make sure you are cut out for this kind of system."

Those looking for guidance from professors or teaching assistants (TAs) can run into trouble. "Professors can be a little hard to connect to sometimes. They are brilliant, but sometimes this doesn't translate into being able to teach." The quality of TAs varies. Some can be helpful, whereas others can be limited by their poor command of the English language.

Engineering, the most popular major, is also cited as one of the most difficult. Though "there are no easy majors here," business technology has the least amount of work, with a relatively easy core. Students can opt to lighten their academic load by spreading it over five years instead of four through the Reduced Load program. The fifth year is tuition-free.

Several other special academic programs exist at Stevens. There are seven-year doctorate, medical, and dentistry programs, as well as a co-op program in which students attend Stevens for five years but work for three semesters at a company instead of going to class. Recruiting companies in the past have included Merck and Johnson & Johnson. Co-op experiences vary. Though some students report that they worked as "personal gofers," others say they have a rewarding educational experience that can only come from "being out in the real world and seeing what it is like, without the pressure of actually having to earn your living because you are still in school."

Greeks and Athletes

Greek organizations are an important part of student life. Besides holding their own events, it often feels like "frats and sororities run everything on campus." The presence of a Greek system makes the student body segment into cliques. "It ends up that the Greeks stay with the Greeks, the athletes with the athletes, the nerds with the nerds," explained one student. However, these cliques do not stop all types of students from participating in extracurricular activities. Most people are involved with at least one group. Many students are also part of the campus work-study program.

Students tend to care little about athletics unless they are in them. Though Stevens has good lacrosse and soccer teams, the fans cheering on the sidelines at games are often exclusively composed of other athletes. Athletes seem not to mind, though, saying that the tightly-knit athletic community lends a lot of support, something that is desperately needed in order to balance athletics and a demanding academic schedule.

Students who are not involved in varsity sports can use the recently renovated Charles V. Schaefer Jr. Athletic Center, which offers squash, tennis, and basketball courts as well as a gym and pool. Intramural sports are also popular.

Weekends at Stevens

There has been a recent crackdown on underage drinking on campus, which particularly affected fraternities. Any Greek organization found serving alcohol to students under 21 was forced to shut down. Much of the drinking culture was driven off

campus into Hoboken and New York City. Fraternities do remain popular, sponsoring Halloween and Christmas parties, among others. The male-female ratio on campus—approximately three to one—means that girls are "rare and really have their choice of guys."

Students who look to imbibe in Hoboken are not short of places to go. Rumor says that Hoboken has more bars per square mile than any other city in the world. Being underage is sometimes a problem, but a freshman explained, "We know how to get around the age restriction." Students also frequent New York City, which offers a wealth of opportunities and nightlife right across the Hudson River.

> **"People think that we spend all our time in front of our computer monitors, but we really do go out."**

There are also weekend activities on campus. A lecture hall in the Buchard Building moonlights as a movie theater. Jacobus Hall has a student lounge with a climbing wall, large television, and pool table.

During the weekends, it often feels like the student population thins. Many students at Stevens are from other areas of New Jersey, and a good portion of the student body goes home on the weekends. Though many dislike the feeling of going to a "suitcase school," one freshman said that being able to go home on the weekends made his transition to college life less stressful.

The Stevens Stereotype

Campus housing is generally considered adequate. Freshmen are guaranteed housing. After the first year, upperclassmen fight for rooms in one of the five dorms. Students like that their rooms are close to their classes, especially during the winter, when the campus turns into a "wind tunnel." Despite the windiness, students like their campus, which has sweeping lawns and views of the New York City skyline.

One student explained that dining at Stevens simply "is not good." However, the dining service is working to improve the quality of the food, and there is now more variety as well as tastier offerings. There are also many eateries in Hoboken, and, of course, there is always New York City.

Students enjoy going into both Hoboken and New York City and insist that, contrary

to the "Stevens stereotype," they do go there to party. "People think that we spend all our time in front of our computer monitors, but we really do go out. Stevens in many ways is an atypical college experience, but we do do normal college things." If you have the motivation and the focus to handle the academics and the independence to handle the social scene, Stevens Institute of Technology can provide an educational and enjoyable, though "atypical," college experience.
—Erica Rothman

FYI

If you come to Stevens, you'd better bring "your calculator."

What is the typical weekend schedule? "Hang out on campus Friday, head into the city on Saturday, and spend all of Sunday into Monday doing schoolwork."

If I could change one thing about Stevens, I would "make it less of a suitcase school."

Three things every student at Stevens should do before graduating are "hang out at a Hoboken bar, throw a Frisbee on the lawn looking out on the city skyline, and spend lots of time complaining about all the work you have to do."

New Mexico

Address: Box 30001, MSC 3A, Las Cruces, NM 88003-8001
Phone: 575-646-3121
E-mail address: admissions@nmsu.edu
Web site URL: www.nmsu.edu
Year Founded: 1888
Private or Public: Public
Religious Affiliation: None
Location: Urban
Number of Applicants: 5,942
Percent Accepted: 95%
Percent Accepted who enroll: 45%
Number Entering: 2,552
Number of Transfers Accepted each Year: 887
Middle 50% SAT range: M: 420–530, CR: 410–530, Wr: 400–520
Middle 50% ACT range: 17–23
Early admission program EA/ED/None: None

Percentage accepted through EA or ED: NA
EA and ED deadline: NA
Regular Deadline: Rolling
Application Fee: $20
Full time Undergraduate enrollment: 12,610
Total enrollment: 14,799
Percent Male: 45%
Percent Female: 55%
Total Percent Minority or Unreported: 66%
Percent African-American: 3%
Percent Asian/Pacific Islander: 2%
Percent Hispanic: 48%
Percent Native-American: 3%
Percent International: 3%
Percent in-state/out of state: 78%/22%
Percent from Public HS: Unreported
Retention Rate: Unreported
Graduation Rate 4-year: 12%

Graduation Rate 6-year: 42%
Percent Undergraduates in On-campus housing: Unreported
Number of official organized extracurricular organizations: 263
3 Most popular majors: Business/Commerce, Curriculum and Instruction, Electronics
Student/Faculty ratio: 20:1
Average Class Size: 16
Percent of students going to grad school: Unreported
Tuition and Fees: $18,268
In-State Tuition and Fees if different: $5,827
Cost for Room and Board: $6,620
Percent receiving financial aid out of those who apply: 76%
Percent receiving financial aid among all students: 54%

Surrounded by desert, New Mexico State University is home to almost 15,000 undergraduates and more than 3,000 graduate students. The college town of Las Cruces serves as the main campus for the university, but several of its many institutes, research centers, and academic programs are spread throughout the rest of New Mexico. A highly diverse campus, the university is known to provide a wide range of academic programs at an affordable price. In fact, NMSU awards degrees ranging from associate to doctorate and has extensive research facilities for those interested in going beyond classes and obtaining opportunities to become involved in the more sophisticated academic projects.

A Research Institution

The university is divided into nine different colleges, including the College of Honors, providing more in-depth education in smaller classes, and the Graduate School. The other parts of NMSU are the Colleges of Agricultural, Consumer, and Environmental Sciences, Arts and Sciences, Business, Education, Engineering, Health and Social Services, and Extended Learning. "You can find all the majors you want here," said one student. "I have friends going to small schools, and I heard that they just have a small number of majors and minors. Here, we have everything."

The undergraduate program boasts more than 80 majors, including rather ingenious programs such as Turfgrass Science and

Management, Rangeland Resources, and Horticulture. The large number of specialized majors in agriculture is due to the institution's original purpose. After all, first opened in New Mexico during the late 1800s, the university originally aimed to educate people about farming and pasturing. Today, of course, NMSU has expanded into a prominent research institution. Nevertheless, it maintained significant resources programs related to agriculture and environmental sciences. "It should not be a surprise that there is so much emphasis on agriculture," said one student. "It is a really important field in New Mexico."

NMSU is very proud that it is among the 100 top institutions in federal research expenditures. The government spends millions every year on the university to conduct experiments and carry out projects. Among the most impressive federal expenditure is the NASA Space Grant, used to ensure the continuation of aerospace research in the United States. The position of the university as a Hispanic-serving institution—awarded for its large student population of Hispanics, which is just below one-half of the entire student body—also ensures that the school remains considerate of the importance of diversity and provides opportunities to all students.

> "You should come here and expect to work."

Given the university's mission of being accessible to students from all backgrounds, the admissions process is not particularly selective. In fact, more than 80% of applicants are accepted every year. At the same time, there are more than 3,000 part-time students, since the school aims to offer as much flexibility as possible to everyone who wishes to receive a good education. However, it does not mean that the school is not strong academically. "You should come here and expect to work," said one student. "Going to NMSU is not an easy walk in the park."

As in most universities, undergraduates are required to take a series of general education courses in addition to those in their majors. The goal is to ensure that everyone receives at least a broad overview of the topics that are present in academia. This should broaden the students' horizons and perhaps interest them in subjects that they never heard of previously. The core requirements are classified in five categories: communications, mathematics, laboratory sciences, social sciences, and humanities. Furthermore, NMSU has a special program entitled "Viewing a Wider World." They are two upper-level courses outside students' own departments so that they can have an in-depth academic experience in a new subject. "It is a fun program," said one student. "You get to experience new things in 'Viewing a Wider World.'"

It must also be pointed out that students at NMSU tend to be happy with the interactions with professors. Of course, much of the accessibility of instructors depends on the personalities of the professors as well as the initiatives taken by students. Nevertheless, overall, students are happy with their instructors' willingness to talk to them about classes or even issues outside of academia, such as careers and student life.

Not Just Las Cruces

Although the university is mostly located in Las Cruces, the second largest city in New Mexico, it also has 33 extensions and 10 research centers spread across the state. Therefore, students can be spread out, especially if they would like to take advantage of one of the research facilities in another part of the state. Nevertheless, the majority of students enjoy their stay in Las Cruces. The weather, of course, can be slightly difficult for people from out of state to acclimate to, given the desert environment. It can be very dry during large portions of the year, combined with large fluctuations in temperature. However, as pointed out by one student, "You don't really think too much about the weather when you are a student. Having a good quality of life on campus is much more important than better weather."

Given its status as a college town, Las Cruces does offer a number of local nightclubs and weekend activities that are catered for students. "It is not New York City," said one student. "But I have no complaints about the nightlife here." Greek life does exist and provides on-campus parties, but it remains only a small part of the college community.

Because of the large number of in-state students and commuters, many students do choose to live off campus. Nevertheless, students are generally fine with the housing options offered by the university. "The rooms are small, but that is how it works with college housing anywhere," said one student. The school also offers an array of dining options to accommodate both those who eat in dining halls every day and those who simply pick up lunch near classes before heading back to their off-campus housing.

Diverse Campus

One of the strengths of NMSU is the diversity of its student body. The school boasts students from all 50 states and 71 countries. "We have people from everywhere," said one student. "I know that people think this is a mostly Hispanic school, but it is actually very diverse and you get to meet people from all over the world."

The NMSU sports teams are called the Aggies, in honor of the school's agricultural heritage. As with most state universities, the biggest rival is the other part of New Mexico's public institution of higher learning, University of New Mexico. The rivalry is so intense that it has been transformed into a formal point system based on head-to-head competition of all sports teams. At the end of the year, a trophy is presented to the winning school. Unfortunately for the Aggies, in the brief history of the competition, University of New Mexico has so far dominated the contest.

Ultimately, students come to NMSU for academic opportunities. Given the affordability of the school, especially for those from New Mexico, it provides an excellent education, as long as the students do their best to enjoy all the facilities and programs that are widely available on campus.—*Xiaohang Liu*

FYI
If you come to NMSU, you'd better bring "sunscreen."
What is the typical weekend schedule? "Get on a trip to El Paso."
If I could change one thing about NMSU, I'd "make the campus smaller and tighter."
Three things every student at NMSU should do before graduating are "go to El Paso, visit other parts of the university besides Las Cruces, and join a club."

University of New Mexico

Address: PO Box 4895, Albuquerque, NM 87131-00001
Phone: 505-277-2466
E-mail address: apply@unm.edu
Web site URL: www.unm.edu
Year Founded: 1889
Private or Public: Public
Religious Affiliation: None
Location: Urban
Number of Applicants: 11,410
Percent Accepted: 64%
Percent Accepted who enroll: 45%
Number Entering: 3,267
Number of Transfers Accepted each Year: 2,227
Middle 50% SAT range: M: 480–620, CR: 480–620, Wr: Unreported
Middle 50% ACT range: 19–25
Early admission program EA/ED/None: EA

Percentage accepted through EA or ED: Unreported
EA and ED deadline: 15-June
Regular Deadline: Rolling
Application Fee: $20
Full time Undergraduate enrollment: 20,655
Total enrollment: Unreported
Percent Male: Unreported
Percent Female: Unreported
Total Percent Minority or Unreported: 62%
Percent African-American: 4%
Percent Asian/Pacific Islander: 4%
Percent Hispanic: 4%
Percent Native-American: 5%
Percent International: 0%
Percent in-state/out of state: 87%/13%
Percent from Public HS: Unreported
Retention Rate: Unreported
Graduation Rate 4-year: 44%

Graduation Rate 6-year: Unreported
Percent Undergraduates in On-campus housing: 10%
Number of official organized extracurricular organizations: 315
3 Most popular majors: Business/Marketing, Education, Health Professions
Student/Faculty ratio: Unreported
Average Class Size: 24
Percent of students going to grad school: Unreported
Tuition and Fees: $19,999
In-State Tuition and Fees if different: $5,809
Cost for Room and Board: $8,068
Percent receiving financial aid out of those who apply: Unreported
Percent receiving financial aid among all students: Unreported

In Albuquerque—one of the fastest-growing cities in the United States—is found the University of New Mexico, a large institution of higher learning well known for its Pueblo Revival architecture and large campus. More than 27,000 students, including over 20,000 undergraduates, study in one of UNM's four campuses. Although it looks like a standard state institution of higher learning, many features of the university, such as the large array of opportunities and the diversity of the student body, can certainly make college experience at UNM particularly enjoyable.

Going Professional

There are twelve different schools and colleges within UNM, demonstrating the scope of the university and the wide range of academic programs. Every school within the university offers undergraduate degrees, except the Schools of Law, Medicine, Public Administration, and Pharmacy, which only provide training to those seeking master's or higher degrees. Even the School of Management has an undergraduate business degree for undergraduates, making students interested in business particularly grateful. "It is really great to have a business program for college students, especially in the School of Management itself," said one student. "You get to learn more and even mingle with people studying Masters of Business Administration, so it is a wonderful program here."

The university offers more than 200 programs, including more than 90 majors for undergraduates. In addition, there are also a number of certificate curricula, which can enrich students' academic experience and provide them with solid training for future employment. At the same time, it is important to point out that the school also has very good liberal arts degrees in the College of Arts and Sciences, which give students both the depth and breadth of skills and knowledge that they need to succeed in careers.

A large percentage of students at UNM, on the other hand, do consider their education mostly as preparation for specific professions. In this aspect, given the large number of programs in engineering, health, and education, the university certainly offers the curricula that can satisfy almost anyone. "I think a lot of people have a job in mind when they come here," said one student. "And we have tons of weird majors so I think everyone will end up finding a suitable major."

The difficulties of the classes depend on the professor and the major. The science and engineering courses, as in most universities around the country, can pose headaches for students. "There are always a lot of freshmen who want to do engineering, but then they realize how hard it is because of the introductory classes and choose something else," said one student. This does not mean that those majors are too difficult for most people. It just implies that some curricula demand slightly more effort and dedication. "You have to come here and expect to work. The classes are not that difficult if you actually plan ahead and stick to your schedule," said one student.

The College of Fine Arts is outstanding, and it includes one of the better-known programs in photography in the country. Furthermore, the Schools of Nursing and Medicine also boast a number of nationally recognized specialties that have placed UNM as a major institution of both teaching and research.

The classes at UNM tend to be relatively large, with lectures that can go up to several hundred people. The experience with the accessibility of professors, on the other hand, can vary from student to student. Some people do stumble upon classes where instructors are very open to interact with students. Others meet professors that are simply unavailable outside of class. The consensus, however, is that the students should make the effort to reach out to faculty members. This can greatly enrich the academic experience.

> "You have to come here and expect to work. The classes are not that difficult if you actually plan ahead and stick to your schedule."

UNM is a state university dedicated to provide opportunities to the public at large. Therefore, the admissions process is not particularly selective, though only about 65% of the applicants are accepted. "You will find very intelligent people here," said one student. "And a lot of them have very different experiences than you, so you can learn a lot from them."

As in most universities and despite the pre-professional tracks of many UNM students, all undergraduates must complete a series of core requirements before graduation. These courses are classified under seven different categories, notably writing, mathematics, natural sciences, social sciences, humanities, foreign languages, and fine arts. While the completion of some requirements can appear cumbersome, they are not designed to overwhelm students. Instead, they attempt to expand everyone's horizon and knowledge in different areas.

Pueblo Revival

The 600-acre Albuquerque campus is well known for its architecture, under the name of Pueblo Revival. It is characterized by adobe constructions, highly prevalent throughout New Mexico. "I really enjoy the southwestern architecture here," said one student. In addition, the university has spent a great deal of resources in renovations and constructions, resulting in a number of large, state-of-the-art facilities, notably the Schools of Architecture and Engineering.

Although Albuquerque is also home to several other institutions of higher learning, UNM certainly stands as its most important university and one of the vital parts of the city's economy. At the same time, Albuquerque is also rapidly growing, as the population of the United States shifts toward the Southwest. "The city will be very big in a few more years," said one student. "There will be a lot of job opportunities just here in Albuquerque."

The urban location of UNM means that students will be able to enjoy the benefits of city living. Restaurants, bars, and other hangout places abound in the city. Furthermore, students will be able to enjoy not only the numerous activities organized on campus by the university and the student body, but they will also have the opportunities to attend different shows and events that are held around Albuquerque.

Given the diversity of students—undergraduate, graduate, and people pursuing continuing education—the sense of college community can be somewhat lost on such a large campus. "It is not hard to meet people," said one student. "But it is not like we are a tight-knit community like those small colleges in rural places." Indeed, there are a large number of commuters attending the university, and that can certainly have some adverse effects on the social scene. Nevertheless, the social life on campus certainly exists, with parties and different festivities. In addition, as one student pointed out, "there are so many people here, so you will definitely find plenty of friends."

Life on Campus

In 2009, UNM decided to renovate a number of residential facilities to make them more appealing to the students. The enhancement of the dorms may increase the satisfaction of dorm life and thus bring more people to live on campus.

Given the university's size and scope, academic opportunities abound at UNM. At the same time, life at Albuquerque can certainly be very enjoyable. That is why UNM attracts thousands of students every year from not only New Mexico but also around the world.—*Xiaohang Liu*

FYI
If you come to UNM, you'd better bring a "readiness for dryness."
If I could change one thing about UNM, I'd "make some classes smaller."
Three things every student at UNM should do before graduating are "visit other places in New Mexico, join a club, and take a class at the School of Fine Arts."

New York

Adelphi University

Address: 1 South Avenue, Garden City, NY 11530
Phone: 516-877-3050
E-mail address: admissions@adelphi.edu
Web site URL: www.adelphi.edu
Year Founded: 1896
Private or Public: Private
Religious Affiliation: None
Location: Suburban
Number of Applicants: 6,865
Percent Accepted: 69%
Percent Accepted who enroll: 21%
Number Entering: 944
Number of Transfers Accepted each Year: 956
Middle 50% SAT range:
M: 500–590, CR: 470–580, Wr: 470–580
Middle 50% ACT range: 20–26
Early admission program EA/ED/None: EA

Percentage accepted through EA or ED: 84%
EA and ED deadline: 1-Dec
Regular Deadline: Rolling
Application Fee: $35
Full time Undergraduate enrollment: 5,137
Total enrollment: 8,354
Percent Male: 30%
Percent Female: 70%
Total Percent Minority or Unreported: 49%
Percent African-American: 13%
Percent Asian/Pacific Islander: 7%
Percent Hispanic: 6%
Percent Native-American: <1%
Percent International: 3%
Percent in-state/out of state: 92%/8%
Percent from Public HS: Unreported
Retention Rate: 81%

Graduation Rate 4-year: 56%
Graduation Rate 6-year: 63%
Percent Undergraduates in On-campus housing: 23%
Number of official organized extracurricular organizations: 80
3 Most popular majors: Business, Education, Nursing
Student/Faculty ratio: 9:1
Average Class Size: 25
Percent of students going to grad school: 38%
Tuition and Fees: $25,240
In-State Tuition and Fees if different: No difference
Cost for Room and Board: $10,000
Percent receiving financial aid out of those who apply: 93%
Percent receiving financial aid among all students: 88%

Tucked away in the middle of an affluent Long Island residential district, the Adelphi campus setting attracts students who reside in nearby communities. If you live on Long Island and are considering commuting to college, you'll find yourself among friends at Adelphi. Although the student body may be comprised of a large commuter population, the university successfully creates an intimate college experience both socially and academically. Adelphi not only provides students with a solid base in academics, it also offers students pre-professional tracks so they may immediately pursue their passions. If you are a student looking to branch out of your home community without really leaving it, Adelphi can offer the best of both worlds. While one student cautions, "Adelphi isn't for everyone—the commuter-school aspect sets it apart," its tradition of strong programs and commitment to developing career opportunities make it worth a closer look.

A Variety of Options

Students interested in Adelphi have the option of applying to the College of Arts and Sciences, the Derner Institute of Advanced Psychological Studies, the Honors College, the School of Business, the School of Education, the School of Nursing, or the School of Social Work. The schools each have different requirements, but students in the popular College of Arts and Sciences must take general education courses that, while "fairly numerous," are "pretty easy as long as you show up." These courses include a freshman orientation experience, an English composition seminar, a freshman seminar, and at least six credits in each of four areas: arts, humanities and languages, natural sciences and math, and the social sciences. One student complained that of those courses there were "a handful I haven't liked." Freshmen also say the required seminar and orientation course is "a necessary annoyance."

Students cite the nursing and business programs as particularly strong. One student raved, "My experiences working in a hospital a few times a week really prepared me for a career in nursing." However, the quality of the experience is very dependent on the teacher you get, a problem that students in various programs and majors mentioned. A communications major said that his professors' personalities had ranged from very enthusiastic about the subject to simply uninspired and "big assigners of busy work."

Many qualified students choose to enroll in the Honors Program, especially because of the generous scholarships Adelphi offers. Honors students live, attend classes, and study together in this exclusive academic and living arrangement, which is "almost its own separate community." However, "you should visit the campus before you just accept the scholarship," warns one student, "because it is a pretty different college experience." For the rest of the population, one of the most common grievances is the difficulty in enrolling in classes. One student complains, "I've been trying to get into this one class for two years and haven't been able to." But once you get into courses, the atmosphere is "very tight-knit, with a close student-faculty relationship," because of the school's small size. Students even mention going into the city for performances and then to bars with their professors.

Adelphi's humanities courses are "much better and more popular" than its math and science offerings, and students "wouldn't recommend the school for pre-med." But many professors "make you think outside the box." Overall, students classified their schoolwork at Adelphi as "definitely not too hard" and found that "grading is fair and lenient."

Seeking Out the Scene

Adelphi's status as largely a commuter school situated in a wealthy Long Island suburb is one of the main obstacles to a really active social life. So many students go home on the weekends that "the campus can be pretty dead by Thursday night," and surrounding Garden City is such a sheltered community that there isn't much night life nearby. In fact, when the campus hosted a Roots concert, it was shut down early because neighbors complained of the noise. The school hosts many other events in the University Center.

Those students who live on or near campus find a reasonable social scene at a few local bars and clubs, where Adelphi's 11 fraternities and sororities often host gatherings for the student body. There are "quite a few" students in Greek organizations, and some "really make themselves known through advertising and recruiting," but because of the Garden City rule that "classifies more than six unrelated girls in a house as a brothel," the sororities don't have their own housing.

Students called Adelphi "more of a drinking school," saying that most people drink in their rooms before heading out to bars and clubs, but since the dorms are dry, "it's hard to tell how many people drink because they have to keep it pretty quiet." Overall, it's very self-controlled, and drugs "can be hard to find," although "pot is available if you want it" and "a lot of people smoke."

One student said that if you want to get socially involved at Adelphi, "you have to actively seek out the scene," whether by attending weekly comedy shows, sampling the popular theater program, or heading out to New York City. The train station is on the edge of campus, just a few blocks away, and the trip takes about 45 minutes. Students really feel that the city is the redeeming factor in the otherwise quiet environment of Garden City—there are just so many opportunities for entertainment, from plays and museums to well-attended bars and clubs.

Most people meet their friends based on their living situations, whether in the dorms or off campus, but the small class sizes make it easy to meet people who share your academic interests. Students characterize the stereotypical Adelphi students as "very Long Islandish: girls get really dressed up to go to class, and boys can be very fashionable and wealthy too." However, others say that there is a lot of diversity at Adelphi, particularly because it attracts many international students. One senior explained, "There is more diversity of culture than of race, because within the largely white population, many nations are represented."

One student said that one of the most

surprising aspects of Adelphi is that its student population is predominantly female. "There are a lot of hookups because guys who are hot and straight are usually taken, and you have to be quick," she admitted. The school does have an overall accepting attitude toward the gay population, which is sizable—in fact, a senior estimated that "half the males are probably gay." In the spring, the Lesbian-Gay-Bisexual-Transgender-Queer (LGBTQ) organization puts on mock "weddings" just to show the community's support for gay couples.

People Do Live Here

Adelphi's campus is described as "truly beautiful," and students estimate that the university spends a sizable amount of money just on landscaping. The effect is a picturesque campus with spacious lawns and well-kept foliage. While many Adelphi students choose to live at home and commute to school, there is a lot of competition for housing on or near campus. Students who live in the dorms have the choice of air conditioning, which is more expensive, but students say that "it's pretty cool in Garden City, so the lack of A/C isn't a big deal." If you want housing and are new to the school, you are entered in a lottery to try to get a room in the full dorms, but if you have already been living there a semester, you have "squatter's rights" and can keep your room. One student explained, "You'll most likely get housing if you want it, but you have to be on top of the deadlines." All of the rooms are doubles and triples, and some doubles used to be triples, so "they're pretty big." The honors dorms have suites, which include a living room and two doubles.

There is an RA on each floor and a residential health director in each building, and while they do enforce the strict no-alcohol policy of the dorms, they are usually "nice and will work with you in other areas." However, "you will get in trouble and your alcohol will be confiscated if you're going to be dumb about it." New Hall is the newest dorm and is thought to be the nicest, while Earle Hall is known for housing a lot of theater majors.

Off-campus housing is apparently more difficult to find, since there are "few apartments for college students" due to the rich residential neighborhood around the campus. When they do find housing, it is usually pretty expensive as well. Students say that pricey off-campus housing is the reason why so many choose to live at home.

Downtown Garden City, a mile away, offers some shopping, including a popular mall, movies, and the nearest grocery store. A shuttle bus takes students to and from the downtown district, but "it can be unreliable or not frequent enough." It's a good idea to bring a car so you can get out of the area, but "the traffic gets pretty bad" and "one of the biggest problems on campus right now is the lack of parking available." However, the university is working to construct a new parking facility.

Students who live on campus are required to purchase a meal plan. However, many do so unwillingly. The food is reportedly "absolutely terrible," but there are other on-campus options, like at Post Hall, which houses a Sbarro, the Panther Grill, and a convenience store, where students can use their meal cards like credit cards. Overall, though, there "isn't much variety and the food is of dubious quality" in the two dining halls. Students say they order takeout from local restaurants a couple times a week and sometimes go out to eat on the weekends. The nearby Chinese and Italian restaurants are "especially good," but "if you drive you can find a lot more options."

Getting Involved

One problem that many students pointed out about student involvement on campus is that it seems very low and apathetic. A senior said that she feels like "people just want to sit around and complain about how there's nothing to do instead of taking advantage of campus events." However, Adelphi does boast a number of organizations that attract loyal followings, such as the Theater Club, the NAACP, Circle K, and its student newspaper, *The Delphian*. Many students also get involved in the Student Government Association, which allows them to voice their opinions about the Adelphi community and lobby for change.

> "You won't get lost in the crowd at Adelphi."

Adelphi is the home of Division I men's soccer and women's bowling teams, though all its other teams are Division II. Students say that "it's not a big athletic school, but a lot of people are interested in going to the games and supporting the Panthers." In fact, one of Adelphi's most fun annual traditions is Midnight Madness, when the men and women's basketball teams are announced at midnight at the beginning of the season, and the school's hip-hop team performs. One guy said, "It's one of the few events that almost everyone goes to and shows their school pride." For those who want to get more involved, intramural sports "always have flyers up" and can even get "intensely competitive."

Many students have jobs, whether working for the school on campus or in the surrounding community. One popular off-campus option is working in the downtown mall. However, a particularly exciting aspect of attending Adelphi is the opportunity to participate in internships in New York City. Many students take advantage of this unique privilege and spend time learning more about their fields of interest.

While Adelphi may not be the typical college experience, it offers a variety of opportunities, from the excitement and internationalism of nearby New York City to renowned professional programs truly dedicated to preparing students for careers. While the school is ideal for many who are looking for a good school close to home, others may want to consider the additional advantages it holds. Even with the lack of an on-campus community, life at Adelphi is close-knit and friendly. As one student put it, "You won't get lost in the crowd at Adelphi."—*Kimberly Chow*

FYI

If you come to Adelphi, you'd better bring "a willingness to involve yourself in campus activities, because the school needs more participation."

What's the typical weekend schedule? "Hanging out with friends and having dinner on Friday, going to the City on Saturday, going to bars and clubs at night, or just going home for the weekend."

If I could change one thing about Adelphi, "I would increase communication between the administration and students, because sometimes I feel like I'm on my own when planning my studies."

Three things every student at Adelphi should do before graduating are "attend the Erotic Student Film Festival, participate in the Student Government Association, and sneak onto the roof of the science building for the great view."

Alfred University

Address: One Saxon Drive, Alfred, NY 14802-1205
Phone: 607-871-2115
E-mail address: admissions@alfred.edu
Web site URL: www.alfred.edu
Year Founded: 1836
Private or Public: Private
Religious Affiliation: None
Location: Rural
Number of Applicants: 3,025
Percent Accepted: 72%
Percent Accepted who enroll: 28%
Number Entering: 560
Number of Transfers Accepted each Year: 131
Middle 50% SAT range: M: 500–620, CR: 480–580, Wr: not used in admission decision
Middle 50% ACT range: 21–26
Early admission program EA/ED/None: ED

Percentage accepted through EA or ED: Unreported
EA and ED deadline: 1-Dec
Regular Deadline: 1-Feb
Application Fee: $50
Full time Undergraduate enrollment: 1,895
Total enrollment: 2,393
Percent Male: 51%
Percent Female: 49%
Total Percent Minority or Unreported: 16%
Percent African-American: 7%
Percent Asian/Pacific Islander: 2%
Percent Hispanic: 6%
Percent Native-American: <1%
Percent International: 2%
Percent in-state/out of state: 76%/24%
Percent from Public HS: Unreported
Retention Rate: 76%

Graduation Rate 4-year: 44%
Graduation Rate 6-year: 60%
Percent Undergraduates in On-campus housing: 76%
Number of official organized extracurricular organizations: 90
3 Most popular majors: Art & Design, Psychology, Mechanical Engineering
Student/Faculty ratio: 12:1
Average Class Size: 15
Percent of students going to grad school: 29%
Tuition and Fees: $25,974
In-State Tuition and Fees if different: No difference
Cost for Room and Board: $10,796
Percent receiving financial aid out of those who apply: 85%
Percent receiving financial aid among all students: 90%

Far from the frenetic pulse of Manhattan lies Alfred University, a small school in a rustic setting that has something to offer everyone. With a world-class art school, a one-of-a-kind program in ceramic engineering, and ample opportunities in business, Alfred academically accommodates a diverse and fascinating student body. When class lets out, the extracurricular options are equally unique, giving the school's students an opportunity to pursue almost any interest imaginable. These elements come together to make Alfred a place of social, artistic, and intellectual growth for all its students.

An Academic Buffet

Incoming freshmen can apply to one of five schools: the College of Business, the School of Engineering, the School of Art and Design, the College of Professional Studies, or the College of Liberal Arts and Sciences. For those interested in entering the College of Business, Alfred offers degrees in accounting, business administration, finance, and marketing. While all the schools are considered challenging, the School of Engineering is particularly work-intensive. The School of Art and Design, a school one student called "top-ten," offers a rigorous workload that is "about problem solving and trying to get you to think about nontraditional styles of art." In the academic realm, Alfred is perhaps best known for its School of Ceramic Engineering. Boasting an international reputation, this school is the only center in the United States that offers a Ph.D. program in the field.

For students with a firm idea of what path they want to follow, the College of Professional Studies, created in the Fall of 2012, offers a number of pre-professional programs. The college includes majors in athletic training, education, accounting, business administration, finance, and marketing and focuses on practical knowledge in each of these fields. These programs stress hands-on experiences as a way to hone your skills and help decide if a career path is right for you.

Those seeking a more generalized course of study can enroll in the College of Liberal Arts and Sciences, which includes a First-Year Experience (FYE) Program. FYE aims to expand students' horizons by exploring issues of race, ethnicity, and gender. The general education requirements also ensure that liberal arts students are exposed to a variety of topics. The requirements are divided into three "basic competencies": writing, foreign language, and quantitative reasoning, as well as six "areas of knowledge": literature, philosophy or religion, the arts, historical studies, natural sciences, and social sciences.

Students who want to study the arts while still enjoying the breadth of a liberal arts education can participate in BAFA, a unique program that allows fine arts scholars to gain a Bachelor of Arts degree. Unlike those seeking entrance to the School of Art and Design, BAFA applicants do not need to submit a portfolio. However, the program does require that students meet all general education requirements.

Alfred also has an honors program, which currently enrolls about 120 students. The program is known for offering seminars on unusual and intriguing topics. Recent course titles include "The Films of Joel and Ethan Coen," "Drinking Up: The Science and History of Alcohol," and "Science and Psychology of Harry Potter." In addition to enjoying classes on offbeat topics, program participants benefit from mentorship and thesis funding.

One benefit of attending a small university such as Alfred is small class size—most courses enroll fewer than 20 students, and even large lectures remain below 100. Intimate class settings are a key attribute of the Alfred academic experience: "I definitely feel like I get a better learning experience. I really get to know my professors and work one-on-one."

The Daily Grind

Incoming students are housed in one of the many all-freshmen dorms, which are corridor-style and coed. Four of these halls are newly renovated, bringing changes that create "a homier environment." Freshman accommodations are generally well regarded by incoming Saxons. "People are happy with the freshman buildings especially because the rooms are pretty large," said one student. Openhym, one of the largest halls, includes large lounges on each floor and a late-night study area. The over 150 first-year students who live in Openhym also have the opportunity to participate in a program called Drawn to Diversity. The program, also known as D2D, offers freshmen the opportunity to "[fight] injustice through creative problem solving" by having faculty members present local or global issues for the consideration of Openhym residents.

This year, Alfred gave its food preparation

a makeover and many students are enthusiastic about the results. However, one student warned that "the food is tolerable, but I've never once gone to the dining hall excited." The facelifts given to dining facilities have received more universal acclaim. Since expanded seating and student lounges were added to its ground floor over the summer, Ade Hall, the largest dining facility on campus, has turned into a popular place for students to do homework and watch TV. Students also enjoy getting together off campus. The Terra Cotta Coffee House is one particularly popular destination, where students go to grab a bite to eat, perform at open mike night, or listen to poetry readings. Other off-campus hangouts include Old West; Nana's Japanese Café; and Café Za, a restaurant and bar.

Getting around Alfred by foot is not always easy. The campus is hilly, and hiking to class during the winter months can be less than pleasant. Although the student body is small, the campus is deceptively large. "You'll be walking a lot," one student said. No matter what the hour, however, you never have to fear for your safety. The university's public safety officers patrol campus day and night and the school has a safe escort service. "The police are wonderful here," one student said. "They're some of the nicest people on campus."

Seeking a Scene
The broad range of academic programs and club offerings available at Alfred result in a diverse student body. One student remarked that although "there are your typical sports team cliques that occur," groups of friends tend to be pretty mixed with respect to majors, hobbies and personalities.

> "One thing that Alfred prides itself in is diversity, whether through race or ethnicity or sexual orientation."

This is in great thanks to the wide variety of clubs. Several students suggested clubs as an excellent way of meeting new people, and for those unsure of what they want to join, there is a wide range of options. Popular groups include the Student Activities Board, Alfred University Television, WALF, the school's campus radio station, and Pirate Theater, a comedy and theater group.

Although Alfred may be known more as a destination for the arts, the athletics scene has attracted more attention in recent years. The football team is consistently among the best squads in the nation in Division III and, according to one student, "everybody really enjoys the environment and loves to cheer for Alfred," mostly at football and basketball games. For those who want to stay active, Alfred has "a club for just about every sport." Intramural sports are popular as well, and the newly renovated gym boasts a complete fitness center and nightly open swim.

Given Alfred's diverse student body and unique academic programs, it's no surprise that nightlife options aren't your typical university fare. Alfred abolished Greek organizations in 2002, following the fraternity-related death of a student. For those still yearning for the traditional frat party, the "sport houses" are a sufficient substitute. These houses, which are rented out by varsity teammates, host frequent parties where the alcohol is free-flowing. According to one student, these parties tend to have a mellower, more social atmosphere than a typical frat house basement rager. Another remarked that, because of the small size of the school, you "see the same people over and over again."

If you grow tired of the sport house routine, there are other weekend options. For those nights when students are seeking a dance party, a club called GJ's in town is a popular option. For a more alternative crowd, houses owned by art students tend to have a different vibe. Neon and strobe lights, along with the creative use of projectors, create a unique space for dancing and socializing.

The Student Activities Board also brings musicians and comedians to campus on a regular basis for those looking for dry options. Popular annual events include the Winter Blues Bash, Glam Slam, and Hot Dog Day, a weekend of activities held in conjunction with Alfred State to raise money for charities. Last year's edition of Hot Dog Day featured live performances from O.A.R. and Gym Class Heroes, and every year there is a parade through town, street vendors selling hand-made pottery, and the mud Olympics.

An Eye-Opening Education
For those looking to study art, ceramic engineering, business, or the liberal arts, Alfred University offers stellar academic

programs in a quaint, picturesque village. The small-town surroundings and tight-knit campus make it easy for students to form fast friendships. But what students emphasize above all else are the sense of community and the diversity of the student body which, for most students, leads to a fulfilling four years.—*Kevin Kucharski*

FYI
If you come to Alfred, you'd better bring "earplugs. It can get loud."
If I could change one thing about Alfred, "I would move it closer to a city. It's literally in the middle of nowhere."
If you want to have fun at Alfred, you should know "that having fun doesn't just mean partying. There are a lot of other fun options on campus."

Bard College

Address: PO Box 5000, Annandale-on-Hudson, NY 12504
Phone: 845-758-7472
E-mail address: admissions@bard.edu
Web site URL: www.bard.edu
Year Founded: 1860
Private or Public: Private
Religious Affiliation: None
Location: Rural
Number of Applicants: 5,459
Percent Accepted: 25%
Percent Accepted who enroll: 38%
Number Entering: 517
Number of Transfers Accepted each Year: 79
Middle 50% SAT range: M: 650–690, CR: 680–740, Wr: Unreported
Middle 50% ACT range: Unreported
Early admission program EA/ED/None: EA

Percentage accepted through EA or ED: 65%
EA and ED deadline: 1-Nov
Regular Deadline: 15-Jan
Application Fee: $50
Full time Undergraduate enrollment: 1,873
Total enrollment: 2,148
Percent Male: 43%
Percent Female: 57%
Total Percent Minority or Unreported: 30%
Percent African-American: 2%
Percent Asian/Pacific Islander: 3%
Percent Hispanic: 3%
Percent Native-American: <1%
Percent International: 10%
Percent in-state/out of state: 24%/76%
Percent from Public HS: 64%
Retention Rate: 83%

Graduation Rate 4-year: 68%
Graduation Rate 6-year: 75%
Percent Undergraduates in On-campus housing: 75%
Number of official organized extracurricular organizations: 120
3 Most popular majors: English, Social Sciences, Visual and Performing Arts
Student/Faculty ratio: 9:1
Average Class Size: 15
Percent of students going to grad school: Unreported
Tuition and Fees: $38,374
In-State Tuition and Fees if different: No difference
Cost for Room and Board: $10,866
Percent receiving financial aid out of those who apply: 100%
Percent receiving financial aid among all students: 62%

Small classes, no core curriculum, and clubs like the "Surrealist Circus"—all of these are typical of Bard College. Located in upstate New York, Bard provides interested students with a unique type of liberal arts education and the opportunity to explore all kinds of enjoyable activities during their four years—even if they involve juggling.

Academics of Choice
At Bard, students are required to design their own course of study based on what admissions materials term a "series of active choices." This decidedly active role in shaping one's own curriculum allows students to focus in on the area they most want to explore. But this doesn't mean there are no distributional requirements. Although the

requirements include, for example, a laboratory science course, such classes can thankfully be fulfilled by the likes of "Acoustics"—though one junior claimed he had to remain on a "wait list for two or three semesters before getting a chance to take it." Despite the fact that at first glance, the requirements seem to be easy, they can often be neglected by students in favor of a more major-intensive curriculum. "My advisers are brilliant professors, but maybe not as helpful as they could have been," explained one student who realized in the middle of his junior year that he was missing five distributional requirements. He also emphasized, however, that professors are "very accessible . . . and give a lot of individualized attention," even personal comments on student transcripts.

One of the features that sets Bard apart is that there are no actual "majors"; instead, students go through an intensive process known as "moderation" in which they present papers and sit before a board of professors in the department they want to study in. "You can either be accepted into your major or deferred, in which case you have to re-moderate. In very few of the majors you can be rejected, such as photography or film, which are the more competitive departments," explained a member of the radio group. Bard has also started a five-year business program.

That said, the most popular "majors" at Bard include film and music, which are also extremely competitive. "There is a cold-calloused filtering system. . . . Professors in the film department won't take you seriously until you actually declare that you're a film major," one student warned. Other difficult majors include economics and political science. Students claim that the least popular major at Bard is "probably Business Skills . . . considering the strong distaste for capitalism here."

A Change of Party Scenery

Bard was once known as one of the biggest party schools in the U.S. In recent years, however, there has been a "massive fragmentation" of the traditional party scene at Bard, forcing students to find other options for the building known as the "Old Gym," which once housed famous events such as "drag races." At present, several years after the Old Gym's closure to social events, no good candidates for a new location have been found. "There's some controversy over the newer options," one student explained.

And although many mourn the drastic change in the party scene at Bard, others say it is still "not as bad as other schools . . . we still live up to [our reputation], though it's much tamer than we used to be."

Political Un-Diversity

Bard is notorious for being one of the most liberal schools in America. "Politically, Bard is not diverse at all," one student explained. "Ethnically there's some diversity, but mostly the student body is composed of wealthy, white Americans." The students, however, are known to be extremely friendly and open-minded and, as one student put it, there is "no place where it's cooler to be gay than Bard." Putnam County, where Bard is located, is a well-known right-wing stronghold, but students claim there is no tension between the community and the college.

Tranquil, Beautiful, Isolated

Bard is located next to the Hudson River and has some remarkable views of the Catskill Mountains. The natural surroundings, however, aren't all that Bard has to offer. Its architecture is greatly varied and noteworthy, too. The Blithewood Manor, home to the Levy Economics Institute, is frequented by students in warmer weather to hang out in the gardens. "We'll go and watch the sunset . . . the views are really beautiful." Also, the Richard B. Fisher Center for the Performing Arts, designed by Frank Gehry, is extremely popular with both tourists and students.

> **"I fell in love with this place and have no desire to leave."**

As for dorms, there exists a fair amount of variety. Students can choose from a vegan co-op, the hotel-like Robbins house, or the ecologically sound Village Dorms (among many others). The Upper College Village Dorms, designed in conjunction with Bard students, are constructed from non-virgin timber sources, and are heated through a geothermal heat exchange system. About half of the dorms have singles, and most of them are coed. Students who live on campus are required to have a meal plan, which caters to vegans, vegetarians, and non-vegetarians. The food is in general pretty good, but one student warned, "The fish and pork should definitely be avoided."

Clubs and Circuses

There are approximately 100 student organizations at Bard. One of the most well-known clubs on campus is the Surrealist Circus, made up of some of the "most creative and boldest people here, in a place where there are many creative and bold people." Bard also boasts several model student civic groups, such as the Bard New Orleans Project, which sent 150 student-volunteers to help repair some of the flood damage incurred by Hurricane Katrina. There is a general lack of enthusiasm for sports at Bard, but that doesn't mean that there aren't any. Soccer is probably the most popular sport on campus, due in part to the lavish facilities donated by an heir to the Ferrari fortune. There are several varsity and club sports for those who wish to get their athleticism on.

Although the Bard College experience requires dedication and foresight on behalf of the students, studying at Bard is incredibly rewarding. As one student put it, "On my first visit to Bard I thought it was a wondrous institution, and so far I have not been proven wrong. I fell in love with this place and have no desire to leave."—*Melissa-Victoria King*

FYI

If you come to Bard, you'd better bring "a bike."

What's a typical weekend schedule? "There is no typical anything here. There are many exceptions to week rules."

If I could change one thing about Bard, I'd "give athletes the ability to pre-register for morning classes, so they don't interfere with practice and games."

Three things every student at Bard should do before graduating are "attend an American Symphony Orchestra performance or theatrical production at the Fisher Center, see the Surrealist Circus perform in the spring, and attend one of the infamous *Moderator* magazine release parties."

Barnard College

Address: 3009 Broadway, New York, NY 10027

Phone: 212-854-2014

E-mail address: admissions@barnard.edu

Web site URL: www.barnard.edu

Year Founded: 1889

Private or Public: Private

Religious Affiliation: None

Location: Urban

Number of Applicants: 4,274

Percent Accepted: 28%

Percent Accepted who enroll: 47%

Number Entering: 574

Number of Transfers Accepted each Year: 135

Middle 50% SAT range: M: 610–700, CR: 640–740, Wr: 650–750

Middle 50% ACT range: 28–31

Early admission program EA/ED/None: ED

Percentage accepted through EA or ED: 48%

EA and ED deadline: 15-Nov

Regular Deadline: 1-Jan

Application Fee: $55

Full time Undergraduate enrollment: 2,356

Total enrollment: 2,356

Percent Male: 0%

Percent Female: 100%

Total Percent Minority or Unreported: 33%

Percent African-American: 5%

Percent Asian/Pacific Islander: 16%

Percent Hispanic: 9%

Percent Native-American: 1%

Percent International: Unreported

Percent in-state/out of state: 31%/69%

Percent from Public HS: 53%

Retention Rate: 95%

Graduation Rate 4-year: 82%

Graduation Rate 6-year: 89%

Percent Undergraduates in On-campus housing: 91%

Number of official organized extracurricular organizations: 100

3 Most popular majors: English, Psychology, Economics

Student/Faculty ratio: 10:1

Average Class Size: 20

Percent of students going to grad school: 22%

Tuition and Fees: $37,528

In-State Tuition and Fees if different: No difference

Cost for Room and Board: $11,926

Percent receiving financial aid out of those who apply: Unreported

Percent receiving financial aid among all students: 42%

Barnard is an all-women liberal arts college. This fact might turn away many female high school students searching for colleges, but a closer look at Barnard shows that it is very different from the stereotype often assigned to single-sex schools. Indeed, this top-notch university located in the middle of Manhattan offers its students not only a great education but also an exciting social life outside the classroom.

A Unique Partnership

Although it is an independent entity with its own faculty, budget, and administration, Barnard is actually an all-women undergraduate institution within Columbia University, meaning that the students have access to all the facilities, classes, and resources that characterize large research institutions. Barnard students can take classes at both their own college and Columbia. As one student noted, "The level of education at Barnard is not very different from that of Columbia because we are in the same classes." One of the interesting results of this rather special partnership is that students are selected by Barnard's own admissions office but receive Columbia degrees. But this is not to say that applying to Barnard is a much easier way of becoming a Columbia student. In fact, only 26.5% of applicants were accepted by Barnard in 2010.

Following the Way of Reason

As a top-ranked liberal arts college, Barnard certainly offers a very strong academic program. True to its motto, "Following the Way of Reason," Barnard insists on providing its students with extensive training in analytical skills, both in depth and in breadth. In order to graduate, each student must have completed 122 points' worth of coursework, including two points' worth of physical education. The number of points assigned to each class varies, but it is generally around three to five.

All freshmen have to take an English class, given the importance of writing at Barnard, and a seminar offering students a chance to challenge themselves intellectually with small group discussions. In addition, all students have to fulfill the general education requirements in nine different subject areas, also known as the Nine Ways of Knowing, ranging from laboratory science to visual and performing arts. The student reactions to these rather extensive requirements are mixed. Some believe that "the requirements are cumbersome and unproductive." Others, however, claim that "these classes can broaden the students' horizons."

Barnard is also a highly competitive school. According to one junior, "The classes here are no joke. Most people work very hard to get good grades." At the same time, classes offered by Barnard are generally small and free of teaching assistants. One student noted, "We interact with professors, not TAs, unlike my friends at other, bigger colleges." This certainly demonstrates one of the major benefits of studying at Barnard: the combination of a small college atmosphere with the colossal resources of an Ivy League university.

Location, Location, Location

Barnard is situated in the Morningside Heights neighborhood of Manhattan. It is only two blocks away from the Hudson River and a short walk from Central Park. Its convenient location in the middle of New York City is one of the main reasons people decide to come to Barnard. In the words of one student, "I wanted to go to a liberal arts school in a big city, and Barnard fit perfectly." Despite being in the Big Apple, Barnard is actually surrounded by several other academic institutions such as the Manhattan School of Music, Jewish Theological Seminary, and, most importantly, Columbia University, which is right across the street.

> "The classes here are no joke. Most people work very hard to get good grades."

These surroundings not only contribute to an educational atmosphere but also offer a much more exciting social life. One student remarked, "Barnard is an all-women school, but we get to meet with guys all the time around campus and in the City." Given the cross-registration of classes, as well as an exchange program with The Juilliard School, it is not at all difficult to meet people from other colleges, both male and female, by simply staying on campus. In addition, New York City itself presents a great social environment. During the weekends, bars and clubs across the city are top choices for Barnard students, who can then meet people from practically everywhere. This lively city life, however, also has downsides. As one student pointed out, "People like to go off campus on weekends, so the campus is depleted of people. If you like to stay on campus and do things with people from your own college, then it is sometimes difficult."

Living on Campus

First-year students must live in the Quad and can only choose between a double and a triple. This has led to many complaints from students about the lack of space. Nevertheless, one student mentioned that colleges in metropolitan areas "all have cramped dorms. We live in New York City, so people can't expect to have huge singles." Residential advisers help first-year students make the transition to college life. They are trained to help in a variety of issues and generally try to be friends and not supervisors. As one student commented, "RAs are friendly, and they can be very helpful if you take the initiative to ask them for advice."

After freshman year, students can choose to live in Barnard dorms, Columbia dorms, or one of the eight off-campus buildings. They can also find off-campus apartments themselves. Despite this opportunity of living independently in one of the busiest cities in the world, however, the cost of renting off-campus is quite prohibitive, and a great majority of Barnard students stays on campus. In addition, Barnard and Columbia offer an educational atmosphere with quads and greens, quite different from the city high-rises, which, as admitted by many students, "can be intimidating at times."

Dining in the City

First-year students must choose Barnard's "unlimited meals per term" meal plan, although there are three other meal plans available after freshman year. Food at Barnard can be summarized, in the opinion of one student, as "acceptable." The college offers a great variety of food options, but there are only two dining locations on campus. Many residences are equipped with kitchens, allowing students to cook their own meals. Cooking, however, can be time-consuming. According to one student, "The kitchens can be very convenient, but don't count on having the time to cook meals everyday." With countless restaurants and cafés nearby, dining out is thus a very popular, though expensive, option for students.

Barnard Bear or Columbia Lions

Although Barnard has the Bear as its mascot, athletes can compete in varsity sports only through Columbia teams—the Lions, which do not incite much interest among Barnard students. "We really don't have that much school spirit," explained one student. "We don't know how much we should identify ourselves with Columbia." Nevertheless, the association with a prominent Ivy League school, which can be overshadowing at times, also offers many benefits that outweigh its disadvantages. Given the quality of education it provides, Barnard stands as a top choice for female students searching for first-class education in an exciting urban environment.—*Xiaohang Liu*

FYI

If you come to Barnard, you'd better bring "clothes suitable for clubs."

What is the typical weekend schedule? "Friday tends to be comparatively quiet. Saturday is when you go downtown and have lots of fun. Sunday is for homework."

If I could change one thing about Barnard, I'd "build better dorms."

Three things every student at Barnard should do before graduating are "go to Midnight Breakfast, travel to every corner of New York City, and have fun on Barnard Spirit Day."

City University of New York Systems

New York City is unique. Known for its skyscrapers and disorderly traffic, the Big Apple is also home to over half a million students. It even has its own university system. In fact, the City University of New York, most often abbreviated as CUNY, is the largest urban public university and the third largest university system in the country, ranked after the public universities of New York State and California. It encompasses 23 schools, including 11 four-year colleges, six community colleges, and six graduate and professional schools. The number of students is also stunning. CUNY enrolls approximately 260,000 university-level students, not to mention a similar number of individuals in adult, continuing, and professional education. A unique arrangement, CUNY is independent of New York State's own public university system, although it does receive funding from both the state and city governments.

Anything for Anyone
The sheer number of institutions and academic programs means a variety of options available to students. There are in fact more than 200 majors for undergraduates, thus providing the opportunity to receive training in either the traditional liberal arts or in career-oriented programs, such as Legal Assistant Studies, available at New York City College of Technology, or Television and Radio, offered by Brooklyn College. "There are all kinds of options for students, and the degrees are very practical and will help us immensely in finding jobs and doing well in them," one student said.

Given the number of options for students, CUNY has divided specialties among its schools. For example, City College is best known for its engineering program. Hunter College, on the other hand, has a large number of students enrolled in its highly acclaimed nursing school. Baruch College offers an undergraduate program within its Zicklin School, known as the largest collegiate business school in the country.

At the same time, the size of CUNY also implies a highly bureaucratic methodology of dealing with students. Surely, studying in New York City is very different from attending a small, rural college, where the school by itself represents a distinct community. The students attending any of the CUNY institutions find that they have to be independent and discover their own options rather than relying on advising from the school faculty and administrators, from whom it is sometimes difficult to obtain valuable guidance. Registering for classes can be frustrating, especially for freshmen and sophomores who are looking for relatively small classes. Nevertheless, this lack of personal attention is not unique at CUNY. In fact, students in most large universities have difficulties in navigating through the complex institutional bureaucracy. "I would like to have more individual attention. Everybody does," said one student. "But my friends in other state schools are also experiencing the same thing. And at least CUNY is now working on new programs to give us a little more personal attention."

Diverse Environment
New York City often boasts its diversity as a major strength, and the same can be said about CUNY. The location invariably means that the student body hails from all imaginable backgrounds. Indeed, more than 30 percent of undergraduates were born outside of the United States, and nearly 40 percent have a native language other than English. More than 150 countries are represented within the CUNY system. "It is a very international school. If you try, you will learn a lot about other cultures," one student explained.

Life in the Big Apple
As its name indicates, CUNY mostly serves students from New York City. Approximately 70 percent of undergraduates have attended public high schools within the City. This means that most people know about the Big Apple fairly well even before enrollment. Financially, it also makes sense for New York students to attend the school. After all, they do not have to pay the hefty charges of room and board. Many live with their families and have part-time jobs off campus.

One major drawback of CUNY is the lack of a collegiate atmosphere. Most students live off campus, and many schools do not even offer dormitories. This is because CUNY is a commuter school. Students go to classes during the day and often have jobs at nights and during weekends. Therefore, many people take more than the traditional four years to graduate, and nearly 30 percent of undergraduates are at least 25 years old. "This is not your normal liberal arts experience," one student said. "People here are practical and have many other things going on besides school."

CUNY makes people independent. The students have to learn to take initiative and find their own opportunities. CUNY does not provide the highly protective and perhaps even insular environment of a traditional four-year college. Instead, it provides a good—and often very practical—education, and the students are on their own for other aspects of collegiate life, such as finding their own social circles and living arrangements. In the end, CUNY is for those who are looking for a good education in a diverse environment without placing too much emphasis on a traditional campus life.—*Xiaohang Liu*

City University of New York / City College

Address: 160 Convent Avenue, New York, NY 10031
Phone: 212-650-6977
E-mail address: admissions@ccny.cuny.edu
Web site URL: www.ccny.cuny.edu
Year Founded: 1847
Private or Public: Public
Religious Affiliation: None
Location: Urban
Number of Applicants: 17,816
Percent Accepted: 45%
Percent Accepted who enroll: 25%
Number Entering: 1,768
Number of Transfers Accepted each Year: 1,578
Middle 50% SAT range: M: 460–590, CR: 430–550, Wr: Unreported
Middle 50% ACT range: Unreported
Early admission program EA/ED/None: None

Percentage accepted through EA or ED: NA
EA and ED deadline: NA
Regular Deadline: None/ Priority Applicaton deadline: 15-Mar
Application Fee: $65
Full time Undergraduate enrollment: 8,145
Total enrollment: 11,310
Percent Male: 47%
Percent Female: 53%
Total Percent Minority or Unreported: 71%
Percent African-American: 21%
Percent Asian/Pacific Islander: 25%
Percent Hispanic: 34%
Percent Native-American: <1%
Percent International: 12%
Percent in-state/out of state: 98%/2%
Percent from Public HS: 85%
Retention Rate: Unreported

Graduation Rate 4-year: 50%
Graduation Rate 6-year: 65%
Percent Undergraduates in On-campus housing: 0%
Number of official organized extracurricular organizations: 145
3 Most popular majors: Engineering, Liberal Arts, Psychology
Student/Faculty ratio: 13:1
Average Class Size: 25
Percent of students going to grad school: Unreported
Tuition and Fees: $11,129
In-State Tuition and Fees if different: $4,329
Cost for Room and Board: $9,900 Room Only
Percent receiving financial aid out of those who apply: 96%
Percent receiving financial aid among all students: 85%

Located in the heart of Harlem, City College is one of the quiet academic gems of New York, producing alumni such as Colin Powell and former New York Mayor Ed Koch, and with faculty such as the co-founder of the String Theory of physics, Michio Kaku. While students at CCNY come from all sorts of backgrounds and living situations, most are from New York City itself. At CCNY, students must balance the rigorous amount of studying required to truly learn with very full personal lives.

An Immovable Foundation

Students at City College are required to maintain a 2.0 GPA or higher throughout the course of their college careers in order to graduate. At the same time, students in the Macaulay Honors College must graduate in four years, and are required to take six liberal arts courses, four of them focusing on New York City—its art, peoples, science and technology, and its future. For students in the Sophie Davis Biomedical program, which provides students with a bachelor's degree as well as the first two years of medical school in the course of five years, every student must get a B or better in every class. Each major has its own requirements. When it comes to grading, there isn't much of a curve, but each professor makes up his or her own rubric, and so it can be kind of surprising. Stated one sophomore, "Don't come in assuming just because City's a CUNY it will be easy. I started with that notion, but my classes have changed my opinion pretty quickly."

Students all agree that the work required at CCNY is more demanding than expected, but is also quite rewarding. "For a lot of students, it's been quite some time since they were last in school, but now they are back, and are willing to work really hard to understand the material," one biology major said. In order to address the needs of a wide variety of students, the school is divided into the social sciences, the humanities, the "hard" sciences, a school of education, a school of engineering, and a school of architecture. Students major in every aspect of these programs, but everyone agrees that Engineering, the first public engineering program of its kind, and Architecture, the only public architecture program in the city, are the most popular.

As far as faculty goes, students feel that City College professors are among the most quirky and unique around. One student recalled, "I had one Earth Science professor who was also a poet. For a lecture on tornadoes, he explained it in a sort of sexual poem. I won't go into explicit detail, but I now know that tornadoes form from the friction between little tiny air molecules, that there's a building-up phase and then once all the liquid is gone . . . you know." Other students agree that the professors make the material more interesting, and insert a lot of their own personality. Furthermore, they are all very accessible to students who are willing to visit them during office hours, and are usually happy to have students assist them in research. Also, students in the honors program and at Sophie Davis are assigned advisers who help them with everything from finding scholarships to making sure the students are on top of their classes.

Classes run a wide range of sizes from introductory psychology lectures of about 400 people to labs with just around 15. Students feel that even though the work is very rigorous, everyone is really supportive of one another: "At Sophie, you'd expect us all to be kind of cutthroat about grades and stuff, but since we all have a seat guaranteed at med school, it's actually designed for everyone to help one another out. It's like that at the rest of the college as well."

Overall, students feel that the education they get at CCNY offers them opportunities that would otherwise not be there. "There's an openness to atypical students here, students who have kids or jobs, that I haven't heard of anywhere else," one student said. "There's a lot of support for everyone, and I think much of that comes from our diverse backgrounds and areas of study." At the same time, there is little communication between those areas of study, and students sometimes are frustrated by taking classes outside of their major.

A Commuter School Where People Know Your Name

CCNY's location at the top of a very windy hill makes it somewhat of a unique site, one that its students must trek to every day. "The 1 Train, the A Train, the D Train, the C, the B, they all come here, but then *you* have to climb up the hill!" one student summed up. "To tell you the truth though, taking the train is a good time to do work, to catch up with friends, and to make new ones." Unfortunately, since it is a commuter school, it can be hard for the average student to meet new people, unless they share a common class or club, or are in the same program. "Most people come to campus, go to class, and then go home, unless they have a club or something," one student said.

At the same time, students tend to be very friendly, and very, very diverse: "It's a good atmosphere. A lot of people are here to get a college degree after not having the chance to for a while, so there's camaraderie between everyone, because everyone is focused on learning and graduating." Upperclassmen tend to help out underclassmen, and there are several programs through which students can get tutoring from one another.

Students do come together for events every couple of months, such as for Relay for Life, Go Green Carnivale, a joint event between the Green Society and the Caribbean Students Club, and the "Fifth Year Blowout," an event at Sophie Davis where the graduating class puts on a massive talent show. Fraternities are present, and do occasionally throw parties, perform community service, and have events on campus, although some students feel that they aren't a major scene.

Every Thursday, students have "club hours," where the organizations meet, discuss plans, and do whatever they are designed to do. Ranging from Intramural Volleyball to the Baskerville Chemical Society, clubs are designed to fulfill every student interest. "There are about a million clubs," exaggerated one student, "and if there isn't one for something you're interested in, you can start a club really easily." CCNY competes against other CUNY schools in a variety of varsity sports, but support is somewhat lacking: "Most people aren't very involved. They don't even know our mascot (it's the beaver)!" one freshman lamented.

On the weekends, students tend to do their own thing. "Most kids go home, study, and chill with their friends and family," reported one student who lives on campus. "Some of the upperclassmen go out to bars because they're legal, but underclassmen tend not to drink." Some drinking does go on in the dormitories, but the school has a zero-tolerance policy toward alcohol and drugs on campus.

Study, Eat, Breathe, Sleep: In Harlem

Most students live off campus, either at home or in apartments near the campus, in order to cut down on travel time. The school does offer housing for students a few blocks away from campus, in a building known as "The Towers," but rent is very high, with some rooms going for $1,000 a month. The rooms themselves are functional and new, but many feel that the Towers are not worth the price. Also, the dorms are open to students from all over the city.

As for location, many students are big fans of the surrounding area. "There are a lot of great places to eat around here," one student said. There is some controversy amongst the students regarding safety in the area. "There's a lot of hype about, you know, 'Ohhh it's Harlem, it's not safe,'" complained a female student, "but my last lab ends at 7:50, and I feel perfectly safe." "After it gets dark, you should travel in groups," countered another. Still, there is consensus that around the campus itself, there are no major problems.

> "There's a lot of support for everyone, and I think much of that comes from our diverse backgrounds and areas of study."

Many students like to avoid the cafeteria, which tends to be expensive and doesn't offer many choices. "It's fuel, but it's not great," an engineering student said. Instead, many buy food in the delis and restaurants in the neighborhood, while others bring food from home and eat it on the Quad. "The Quad is a great place in the spring and summer when the weather's nice. Otherwise, it's too cold and windy," explained a student from Brooklyn. Students also like to eat in the stairways in the North Academic Center, and to hang out in the castle-like Shepherd Hall.

At CCNY, you can find a diverse group of students coming together with one common goal and interest: learning. Students are often surprised by the challenging curriculum they deal with, but are supported by a caring and dense network of professors and friends. "When I went through the college admissions process, it wasn't until the very end that I decided to come to City," explained an Honors College student, "but it really surprised me. The tuition is lower than almost anywhere else, but what really got me was how generous the people were. There are things that you can go through, but still bounce back. City College has taught me that. I would definitely pick it again."—*Simon Warren*

FYI
If you come to CCNY, you'd better bring "a MetroCard."
What is the typical weekend schedule? "It depends on the weekend. If you have a test coming up, it could be study, eat, sleep, repeat, or if it's a more relaxed week, it could be go home, relax, maybe go to a party, and study on Sunday."
If I could change one thing about CCNY, I'd "make the dorms cheaper. A lot cheaper."
Three things every student at City College should do before graduating are "go to a concert at the Apollo, rub Lincoln's nose, and play pool in the student lounge."

City University of New York / Hunter College

Address: 695 Park Ave, Room N203, New York, NY 10065
Phone: 212-772-4490
E-mail address: admissions@hunter.cuny.edu
Web site URL: www.hunter.cuny.edu
Year Founded: 1950
Private or Public: Public
Religious Affiliation: None
Location: Urban
Number of Applicants: 24,701
Percent Accepted: 30%
Percent Accepted who enroll: 25%
Number Entering: 1,854
Number of Transfers Accepted each Year: Unreported
Middle 50% SAT range: M: 500–600, CR: 480–580, Wr: Unreported
Middle 50% ACT range: Unreported

Early admission program EA/ED/None: None
Percentage accepted through EA or ED: NA
EA and ED deadline: NA
Regular Deadline: 15-Mar
Application Fee: $65
Full time Undergraduate enrollment: 15,718
Total enrollment: 21,278
Percent Male: 32%
Percent Female: 68%
Total Percent Minority or Unreported: 59%
Percent African-American: 12%
Percent Asian/Pacific Islander: 18%
Percent Hispanic: 19%
Percent Native-American: <1%
Percent International: 10%
Percent in-state/out of state: 96%/4%
Percent from Public HS: 70%
Retention Rate: 82%

Graduation Rate 4-year: 17%
Graduation Rate 6-year: 40%
Percent Undergraduates in On-campus housing: 4%
Number of official organized extracurricular organizations: 150
3 Most popular majors: Social Sciences, English, Psychology
Student/Faculty ratio: 15:1
Average Class Size: 25
Percent of students going to grad school: Unreported
Tuition and Fees: $10,800
In-State Tuition and Fees if different: $4,000
Cost for Room and Board: $7,958
Percent receiving financial aid out of those who apply: 55%
Percent receiving financial aid among all students: Unreported

With its well-rounded core requirements, CUNY Hunter provides students with a solid education in the middle of New York City, even if the living arrangements sometimes leave a little to be desired. Hunter draws some of the most independent students in New York City and is able to give them a good training in almost every discipline. At Hunter, students are motivated to study and maintain separate lives outside the classroom.

Well-Rounded in the Big Apple

Hunter puts a heavy emphasis on a well-rounded curriculum. All students must take classes in math, U.S. history, English, foreign language, writing, natural science, arts, social sciences, and pluralism and diversity, which deal with, for instance, non-European history and women's studies. For students in Hunter's Honors Program, they also have to take four seminars about New York City over the course of their four years in the school.

Many students are pre-med, which is known for being very challenging. Other popular majors are literature, psychology, and social science. Hunter's education and nursing programs are also outstanding. For those on the pre-med track, many of the classes, such as freshman biology, are designed to "weed out" people who are not committed to becoming doctors. Still, students find that the level of difficulty allows them to appreciate the curriculum. According to one student, "Organic Chemistry tries to teach you the psychology of the carbon atom by making it personal. Don't go in expecting an easy A or B. Expect to learn."

Other classes are more varied in terms of difficulty, as well as class size. While science and honors classes fill up quickly, humanities tends to have small classes, with a maximum of 20 students. Despite the extensive general requirements, the school tries to offer very specific classes, such as "Dante's *Divine Comedy*," "Understanding the Sixties," and "The Psychology of Human Sexuality." These courses are very popular.

Students also greatly enjoy the classes in the Honors Program. "I try to take at least one Honors class a semester," said one sophomore. "The classes are smaller, and the professors are more interested in what they are teaching and whom they are teaching." In addition to these classes, Honors students also get priority when picking classes, not to mention a free laptop, free tuition, and guaranteed free housing. There is also a program called the Opportunity Fund, which provides $75,000 for study abroad, internship, projects, or other activities for each Honors student. "It's a pretty good deal. The Honors Program is the only reason I'm going to Hunter," said one student.

Every student has an adviser over the course of four years who offers guidance when needed. Professors are generally reachable and helpful. While "some professors don't expect much out of students and are boring and not challenging," many are "easy to get along with and very helpful if you are serious about getting help." Students feel that advisers are excellent resources and that it is a very good idea to take the time to get their advice.

As for grading, it is varied. "In general, it is not too tough," said one student. "Depending on the class and the professor, it can be harder. Frosh bio and literature are tough, but usually classes are not too harsh, just about right."

Hunter offers its students a well-rounded education with specific classes that excite and engage students, even though the required curriculum is sometimes cumbersome. One student summed up the attitude toward the requirements: "What I like most about studying at Hunter is that as hard as it is to complete the general education requirements, you see why they exist and appreciate them. Hunter exposes you to everything. But the general education requirements are also my least favorite part. People don't like them because they are required and feel that there is no time to fulfill everything."

Close to Home

Most students at Hunter do not live on campus. Hunter is unique among the CUNYs in that it guarantees housing to all of its Honors students. Students not in the Honors Program can also apply to live on campus through a very competitive online process. Every room is a single, and students get to keep the same room all four years, if they wish.

According to campus legend, Hunter's one dorm, Brookdale, was at one point an asylum for the insane. Now, instead of rooms for electroshock therapy on the first floor and a morgue in the basement, it houses a very popular game room and a swimming pool. Students love the fact that they have private rooms and that all the rooms are identical, although half of them face a courtyard and are slightly more coveted. Living at Hunter is arranged by floor, with an RA and a CA (Community Assistant), both undergraduates, on every floor. There are monthly floor meetings, where students can find out what is happening on their floor and settle issues. Floors can also be all-female or 24-hour quiet.

Students find that the school buildings are quite impressive. "There is a subway stop that gets off right into the school, so it is really convenient," said one student. Everyone takes public transportation to get to and from the school. In addition, the architecture makes it stand out. One of four buildings that make up the school's campus, the Thomas Hunter Building, looks like a castle but has bridges on the third floor, which cross over Lexington Avenue. There is also a recently renovated swimming pool, a new chemistry laboratory, and an athletic facility for all students.

As for food, the cafeteria is not well used. It closes before dinner so that students have to go out, order food, make something, or heat up leftovers. Luckily, the options around the neighborhood are plentiful. Each floor in the dorm has a kitchen, and many students are able to go home during the weekend for home-cooked meals.

The neighborhood surrounding Hunter is mostly safe, and the school is well incorporated into the community. Since the campus is open at night, people come and go freely, but to get into the buildings, particularly Brookdale, they are required to have several ID checks.

Hunting for Friends

When it comes to social life, Hunter is unlike many others. Since most students live elsewhere in the City, many people go home or work after class and don't stay on campus. One student explained, "We're a commuter school, so there isn't much of a sense of community here. There is not an area where students can come together and relax." On the other hand, students living in Brookdale do have the opportunity to get to know their neighbors, and students can hang out between classes at an Honors lounge.

On the weekends, many students go home, although there are house parties. Many students also go out to eat or hang out with friends. Since the school is located on Manhattan's Upper East Side, there are many excellent choices when it comes to restaurants, and some students go to bars as well. However, there is no tolerance for underage drinking. "The security guards at the dorm are very strict," explained one student. "If you come back drunk, they will call an ambulance to take you one block, and you have to pay the fee." There are harsher penalties for those caught drinking in the dorm itself. However, most students reported that binge drinking is not much of a problem at all, and that almost everything happens behind closed doors.

Most friendships are made in classes, clubs, and dorms. Those in the Honors Program have an easier time of meeting new people because "you are kind of forced to, or at least you have a greater chance of meeting people. Most students come in, then go home, and don't really have a chance to sit down and get to know their classmates." Still, the consensus is that almost everyone is friendly and that the student body is one of the most diverse. "I wouldn't be surprised if every single country and nationality were represented," said one student. "You see every type of dress. You have rich people and less fortunate people. On a gradient, I would say it is completely diverse." Other students point out that people of all ages attend the school.

Hunter students also take advantage of the school's location, and get to spend time in some of New York's coolest locations. One sophomore recounted, "I once went to celebrate my friend's birthday on the Brooklyn Bridge." Every year, a big event is the Relay for Life, when Hunter and Baruch combine to form the CUNY Manhattan team. The Undergraduate Student Government also organizes events occasionally.

Big-Hearted Hawks

Hunter offers many extracurricular activities, particularly community service groups and cultural organizations. Many people have jobs or internships, and most people are highly committed to their chosen activities. Fraternities and sororities exist on Hunter's campus, but rather than being communities of people who live and drink together, Hunter's Greek life is focused almost entirely on community service. Campus publications are popular, including the newspaper, called the *Hunter Envoy*, and the literary publication, the *Olive Branch*. Groups like the Socialist Club also put out newsletters.

> "What I like most about studying at Hunter is that hard as it is to complete the general education requirements, you see why they exist and appreciate them. Hunter exposes you to everything."

When it comes to sports, the athletes themselves take their sports very seriously. However, most students feel that there is little school pride. "We may not have a football team," said one, "but I am not sure." The athletic facilities are more widely used for relaxation and fun. There are basketball courts, a gym, a pool, and a small bowling alley.

Hunter students come from everywhere. It is a fantastic place to get a solid—and for Honors students, free—education from one of the top public universities in the United States. While it is easy to feel somewhat disconnected and without a community, students do find friendships and social lives. Academically, Hunter gives students a firm background, although some students would prefer to have more freedom when it comes to choosing classes. As one student put it, "If I had to pick schools again, I think I would choose the Honors College at Hunter again. You get to be independent and don't have to rely on your parents for tuition. There are great professors and advisers who help you find internships. Overall, it is a good deal."—*Simon Warren*

FYI
If you come to Hunter, you'd better bring "sneakers."
What is the typical weekend schedule? "Go home or stay in the dorm, study or hang out. Some people volunteer or work."
If I could change one thing about Hunter, I'd "change the food plan. There is none."
Three things every student at Hunter should do before graduating are "walk from Hunter to Central Park, see the swimming pool, and get used to crowded hallways."

City University of New York
Queens College

Address: 65-30 Kissena Boulevard, Flushing, NY 11367
Phone: 718-997-5600
E-mail address: vincent.angrisani@qc.cuny.edu
Web site URL: www.qc.cuny.edu
Year Founded: 1937
Private or Public: Public
Religious Affiliation: None
Location: Urban
Number of Applicants: 18,453
Percent Accepted: 30%
Percent Accepted who enroll: 27%
Number Entering: 1,495
Number of Transfers Accepted each Year: 2,977
Middle 50% SAT range: M: 480–580, CR: 450–550, Wr: 490–550
Middle 50% ACT range: Unreported

Early admission program EA/ED/None: None
Percentage accepted through EA or ED: NA
EA and ED deadline: NA
Regular Deadline: Rolling
Application Fee: $65
Full time Undergraduate enrollment: 14,618
Total enrollment: 18,928
Percent Male: 39%
Percent Female: 61%
Total Percent Minority or Unreported: 56%
Percent African-American: 7%
Percent Asian/Pacific Islander: 25%
Percent Hispanic: 17%
Percent Native-American: <1%
Percent International: 6%
Percent in-state/out of state: 99%/1%
Percent from Public HS: Unreported

Retention Rate: 84%
Graduation Rate 4-year: 26%
Graduation Rate 6-year: 31%
Percent Undergraduates in On-campus housing: 0%
Number of official organized extracurricular organizations: 114
3 Most popular majors: Accounting, Psychology, General Sociology
Student/Faculty ratio: 17:1
Average Class Size: 25
Percent of students going to grad school: 17%
Tuition and Fees: $9,017
In-State Tuition and Fees if different: $4,377
Cost for Room and Board: $11,125
Percent receiving financial aid out of those who apply: 55%
Percent receiving financial aid among all students: 58%

P riding itself on its reputation as "the jewel of the CUNY system," Queens College offers a diverse education to a diverse student body. With its low yearly tuition—roughly $5,000 for New York State residents—Queens is an affordable option for many students, providing a "good education for a good price." Although the school is a commuter college, even students who live off campus describe it as "an easy place to call home."

"A Broad Education"
Students describe academic life as challenging but manageable. While one transfer student in her junior year stated that her courses were tougher than those at her former school, most students say that grading is fair. A senior commented, "I definitely wouldn't say grading is easy but, if you study and pay attention in class, then you should be fine."

Students also hold their professors in high regard. A junior said, "The professors for the most part are warm, welcoming, accessible, and ready to help when needed. They are available both during their office hours and by email and they are very patient and helpful, as well."

A senior added, "My first semester ever in college, I remember me and a couple of my friends couldn't attend class for a religious holiday. The teacher ran over to us and offered to reteach that lesson, on her own spare time, for the few of us that had missed it. It was just so thoughtful and TOTALLY unnecessary, but she did it anyway— something I'll never forget."

In 2009, Queens College introduced new curriculum requirements. First and foremost, all students must take a minimum of 120 credits, which translates to roughly 40 courses. Students must follow a writing sequence that begins with an introductory course and continues with three additional "writing-intensive" courses. Likewise, students must take an introductory math course and fulfill a foreign language requirement.

Finally, students must complete requirements in Perspectives on the Liberal Arts & Sciences (PLAS), which includes eight courses in Core Areas of Knowledge and Inquiry (such as Reading Literature, Natural Science, etc.) and four courses in Global Contexts (such as United States, World Cultures, etc.). Students do not find the requirements constraining; rather, they provide "a taste of different areas of study" and are conducive to a "broad education."

Queens College offers roughly 75 majors (ranging from psychology to business administration to media studies), three preprofessional programs (pre-engineering, pre-health, and pre-law), and BA, MA, BBA, BFA, BS, and BMUS degrees. Students are required to declare a major by the conclusion of sophomore year and may also pursue a second major or a minor. The Academic Advising Center helps students select courses and choose majors.

For the most part, classes have around 15 to 25 students; however, some of the science courses like chemistry, physics, and biology can have more than 100 students. English courses tend to be very popular. Specifically, many students take Introduction to Poetry (English 165W) to satisfy the Reading Lit (RL) requirement. A sophomore also added that science courses tend to be more difficult than humanities courses.

Queens College offers many special academic programs and experiences, which students widely view as enjoyable opportunities to make new friends and to focus on subjects of interest. Specifically, students speak highly of the Freshman Year Initiative program, which, for many, helped create a smooth transition from high school to college. In the program, students select a "learning community" of interest, which includes a topic-based English course and another course on the same topic. For example, students interested in psychology could choose "Psychology 101+ English 110: Memory" while students interested in computer science could choose "Computer Science 100+ English 110: Digital Revolutions." A student explained that since the same 20 freshmen are in the same classes, it's easy to befriend students who share similar interests.

Queens College's study-abroad program organizes trips to Canada, France, Italy, and Japan as well as trips within the United States. There are also scholarships, grants, and financial aid packages available to subsidize cost.

Finally, the school offers honors programs, such as the Freshman Honors Program, the Honors in the Humanities, and Honors in the Mathematical and Social Sciences. Moreover, the school also participates in the Macaulay Honors College. A senior said, "The teachers really know what they're talking about and plan out curriculums that are fascinating and on topics that I would never dream of exploring. And the teaching styles were always eccentric. There was one history class where we were assigned different roles in specific eras, and actually reenacted a scenario from that time. I've played a Pope during the trials of Galileo, a moderate during the time of the French Revolution, and served as the Congress Leader of Bengal in India circa 1945."

Mixed Thoughts from a Mixed Student Body

As of 2009, Queens College has provided student housing in its first residence hall, The Summit. The building consists of five floors of student suites, each of which has a kitchen area with a microwave, table, and refrigerator; a living room area with a cabinet, chair, and couch; and two bathrooms. The building also has heating, air conditioning, and wireless Internet. Although all suites have four occupants, some have four single bedrooms (which cost $6,900 per person per semester) while others have two shared bedrooms (which cost $4,975 per person per semester). Students also can choose to have a kosher room and/or a coed room.

According to a student, the main benefit of living in The Summit is the convenience. By living on campus, students don't need to commute. Additionally, The Summit has study rooms and is located near classroom buildings, supermarkets, and pharmacies. Finally, the building has laundry facilities, vending machines, music practice rooms, a common area, and a fitness center.

On the other hand, social life is strictly regulated in The Summit. Each floor has two RAs, and drugs and alcohol are firmly prohibited. According to a student, when a room is caught in violation of these rules, disciplinary action will be taken by the school. Additionally, at night only two guests per person are allowed to be signed in.

A sophomore remarked, "I enjoy living in The Summit, but I feel as if their rules are frustrating sometimes. The RAs are there to ensure you have a good year. They are not so effective, but that is not always their fault. Many people in the dorms resent feeling as if they have babysitters."

Several students emphasized QC's "ethnically and religiously diverse student body made up of students with many different interests of study." They stated that the variety of cultures, ethnicities, backgrounds, and opinions differentiate the college from other schools.

Although there is no meal plan for students, students can receive discounts when buying meals in the café. Nonetheless, the café isn't open past around 6:00 or 6:30. A student said that although there are plenty of places to dine, the food is only alright. Students feel that the best food is served in the Student Union, which houses the Agora Café, the SA (Student Association) Diner, and the SA Coffee House (Starbucks). In addition to the on-campus locations, there are also several restaurants and eateries nearby, including Subway, Dunkin' Donuts, a few pizzerias, a wok restaurant, and a café.

Students cited the new science building, the Student Union, the library, and the quad as their favorite parts of campus. A senior explained, "The whole campus is built around the quad and it's huge and gorgeous. The grass is always green and there's tons of space to chill with friends in the nice fresh air, and lots of shade, and trees, flowers, and a grand fountain. The library also has this big clock tower that you can see and hear from anywhere on campus. And everyone always gets lost in the science building— that's a classic."

Students are ambivalent about the school's location. Although the campus is generally located close to students' homes and is very close to New York City, it is also located down the block from the always busy Long Island Expressway.

Current students recommend that other students take advantage of the college's proximity to New York City and that they explore the campus in its entirety. Conversely, they caution other students about the frequent unavailability of printers and the lack of free printing. Students also said that the campus was unexpectedly large and that parking is difficult to find.

While many students have jobs, often working in retail, neither sports nor extracurricular activities play a big role in campus life. A senior explained, "The only pride in the sports teams are within the players themselves. I don't see that many people caring about the sports."

Likewise, the majority of students are "uninvolved" in extracurricular activities. Although some students are deeply committed to extracurricular activities, many commuting students are unable to reach the same level of involvement. A senior said that some students just "don't see the point" in extracurricular activities.

A junior echoed a similar sentiment, saying, "People will join the clubs, the fraternities and the sororities, but only for a name on their resume. Most members don't look to be active."

Nonetheless, there are many clubs for students looking to become involved, ranging from honor societies to publications to cultural/ethnic clubs to religious clubs to academic clubs. Clubs host meetings in the Student Union. The school's student coordinating council, The College Union Programming Board, and the school's newspaper, *The Knight News*, are two of the most prominent clubs. Clubs represent a great opportunity to meet new students and to make new friends. A junior involved with several clubs, including Model Congress and the Political Science Club, said she met many of her friends through the classes she enrolled in and the clubs she joined.

Finally, QC's athletics facilities are open to all students. The Fitzgerald Gymnasium contains a fitness center and an aquatic center, and there is also a tennis center. Moreover, QC offers an intramural sports program, including sports like dodgeball, soccer, and flag football. Nonetheless, few students seem to participate.

The Commuter Complication

Queens College is a commuter college, and, as a junior explained, many commuting students "do not get involved in clubs or student activities because they can just come to school, take their classes, and go home."

Some students who live off campus feel that they miss out on school events. A senior said that he attends events that he's interested in "every now and then"; however, sometimes he's unable to go because it's too inconvenient.

A junior who lives off campus echoed the same sentiment, saying that she feels as if she's "slightly missing out."

On the other hand, some students feel that the commuter culture neither divides the student body nor detracts from campus life. One commuting student says she doesn't feel left out at all, stating, "I'm one of those people who likes to interact with other students and stays on campus to hang out with friends and study."

A junior added, "The school really advertises the events that are held for both residents and commuters." She also believes that time after school and free hour provide opportunities for students to hang out.

Free hour is held on Mondays and Wednesdays from 12:15 to 1:15. During free hour, no classes take place, making it a convenient time to hold club meetings and hang out with other students. Furthermore, about once a month during free hour, there's an event on the quad with a DJ, food, rides, and games.

In addition to free hour, many students go out after classes, especially on Friday nights. A junior said that a typical Friday night can range from going to "a bar in Flushing, to hanging out at a friend's dorm, apartment, or house." Fraternities and sororities also host social events.

Drinking and drugs are "uncommon." A student explained, "Queens College is strict enough that if anyone is caught with those substances, good luck not getting expelled." A sophomore added, "Since most people live off campus, it is not a large issue in the college. In The Summit, people drink and do drugs, but not to a crazy extent. QC is not considered a party school."

Students said the student body as a whole is very cohesive and that it's not difficult to make friends. They also feel that there is no divisible divide between upperclassmen and underclassmen. A junior explained, "You kind of just meet people without really knowing where they stand." Nonetheless, another student conceded that it could be hard to meet new people if you don't participate in clubs and other events.

> "The teachers really know what they're talking about and plan out curriculums that are fascinating and on topics that I would never dream of exploring."

Ultimately, in the words of a senior, Queens College is a school with "a very homey feeling with ample places to study, breathtaking (and meticulous) grounds, and teachers that are patient and willing to give students their time even outside classroom hours." She continued, "I chose Queens because I liked the feel of the campus. They also offered me the opportunity to join an honors program, which I hadn't even applied for—it just showed me that they really pay attention to their students and know who exactly they're catering to."—*Joshua Rosenfeld*

FYI:
Three things every student at Queens should do before graduating are "sit on the quad and breathe, sit in one of those cool ball sculptures outside the art building, and study by a window in the library that has a view of NYC."

One thing I wish I'd known before coming was "you're not going to make any friends unless you join a club or program."

What differentiates Queens from most other colleges is "the beautiful quad area and how awesome it looks and feels in the summer and fall."

Clarkson University

Address: Holcroft House, PO Box 5605, Potsdam, NY 13699
Phone: 315-268-6480
E-mail address: admission@clarkson.edu
Web site URL: www.clarkson.edu
Year Founded: 1896
Private or Public: Private
Religious Affiliation: None
Location: Rural
Number of Applicants: 3,204
Percent Accepted: 79%
Percent Accepted who enroll: 29%
Number Entering: 735
Number of Transfers Accepted each Year: 151
Middle 50% SAT range: M: 610–660, CR: 500–560, Wr: 480–590
Middle 50% ACT range: 24–28
Early admission program EA/ED/None: ED

Percentage accepted through EA or ED: 14%
EA and ED deadline: 1-Dec
Regular Deadline: 15-Jan
Application Fee: $50
Full time Undergraduate enrollment: 2,593
Total enrollment: 2,994
Percent Male: 73%
Percent Female: 27%
Total Percent Minority or Unreported: 9%
Percent African-American: 3%
Percent Asian/Pacific Islander: 3%
Percent Hispanic: 3%
Percent Native-American: <1%
Percent International: 4%
Percent in-state/out of state: 73%/27%
Percent from Public HS: Unreported
Retention Rate: 83%
Graduation Rate 4-year: 58%

Graduation Rate 6-year: 71%
Percent Undergraduates in On-campus housing: 82%
Number of official organized extracurricular organizations: 56
3 Most popular majors: Biology, Business, Engineering
Student/Faculty ratio: 15:1
Average Class Size: 18
Percent of students going to grad school: Unreported
Tuition and Fees: $32,220
In-State Tuition and Fees if different: No difference
Cost for Room and Board: $11,118
Percent receiving financial aid out of those who apply: 100%
Percent receiving financial aid among all students: 98%

Located far away from the bustling noises of cities, Clarkson University is a small community of mostly undergraduates in the northern Adirondack Mountains. Nevertheless, despite its relatively small enrollment of 3,000 students, Clarkson is certainly not a small, liberal college. Not only does it have graduate programs, it is also a prominent research institution. Therefore, Clarkson is one of the rare schools that offer not only the closeness of a small village, but also the facilities of a well-recognized research university.

Small Classes, Big Dreams

Most universities similar to the scale of Clarkson generally only offer one single school, such as the College of Arts and Sciences. Clarkson, on the other hand, is divided into three different institutions: the Wallace H. Coulter School of Engineering, the School of Business, and the School of Arts and Sciences. "We are not a big school," said one student. "But we have all the components that you find at really large schools."

Indeed, despite being in the village of Potsdam, which has a population of only 10,000 people, Clarkson certainly offers the types of programs that are only available at major research institutions.

The school offers more than 50 academic programs, and a large portion of them are in science and engineering. Therefore, it is without surprise that a significant number of students at Clarkson are engineering majors. The academic programs in the field include the traditional curricula of chemical, mechanical, and electrical engineering. At the same time, Clarkson also provides a number of unique and highly specialized programs of study, such as biomedical and rehabilitation engineering and aeronautical engineering. "If you are interested in becoming an engineer, you should definitely consider Clarkson," said one student.

The business program at Clarkson is also considered top-notch. "There are a lot of kids in business too," said one student. "Maybe that's because we have some unique programs in business." Given the university's reputation as a very technical institution, the School of Business also offers very specific coursework to ensure that the students will have a set of practical skills once they leave college. Unlike the generalized business administration programs at most universities, Clarkson has majors such as Financial Information and Analysis and Global Supply Chain Management so that students will acquire knowledge that can be directly transferred to their future professions.

> **"If you are interested in becoming an engineer, you should definitely consider Clarkson."**

Furthermore, there is also an interdisciplinary engineering and management program, which combines the two strengths of the university. It is especially valuable for students who would like to be business managers in fields related to technology, because then they would have knowledge and skills in both areas. Of course, in addition to the engineering and business programs, the School of Arts and Sciences also offers curricula in liberal arts for all those who do not wish to have such specialized education in college.

Of course, it is also important to point out that given the emphasis on technical skills, students are given a relatively heavy workload. "You have to work hard," said one student. "This is not a place where you can slack off and expect to get by," said one student. Although the coursework is not overwhelming, it is certainly important for prospective students to realize that expectations are high at Clarkson. "We are not the most famous college out there, but the professors expect you to do all the work and be really well prepared for classes," said one student. The *U.S. News & World Report* ranks Clarkson among the 120 top national universities in the United States. Therefore, admission to the college can be selective, though more than 70 percent of applicants are accepted every year.

The advantage of being at a small college with emphasis on research is that the professors are quite knowledgeable in their fields and provide access to students. "I was a little surprised at how some professors really want to get to know us," said one student. "I used to be under the impression that

professors just lecture and do not care, but I was wrong. They actually want to know about what ideas we have."

Those interested in more in-depth study can also stay on campus, given the presence of a number of research centers, including the Center for Advanced Materials Processing and the Center for Rehabilitation Engineering, Science, and Technology, which demonstrate how Clarkson is a prominent leader in both materials science and biomedical engineering.

Potsdam and Upstate New York

Clarkson is located on several hundred wooden acres of one of the most rural areas of New York State. Despite being a very small town, Potsdam is also an educational center. Besides Clarkson, the State University of New York, Potsdam, is also located in the area, not to mention SUNY Canton and Saint Lawrence University. Therefore, the small town does provide the different amenities that are well suited for college students, such as a number of bars, restaurants, and other hangout places. "It is not as bad as it sounds," said one student. "Sure, Potsdam is a little boring because it is so small. Yet if you go out and see it for yourself, you will find things to do. Also, the school does organize activities on campus."

The weather, of course, can be cold and uninviting, particularly during the winter, but students certainly do not think that is unbearable. "A lot of people here are used to it, because they are from the state," said one student. "Even if you are not from the region, you will get used to it."

Since Potsdam is small, most students live on campus. Freshmen live in doubles, and upperclassmen have more options, which include apartments and suites. College residences have residential advisers, who act both as enforcers of rules and as counselors to students. The school also offers themed housing in which people of similar interests enjoy their stay on campus together. Some of the themes include entrepreneurs, art, and outdoor activities. The idea is to ensure that students can learn from one another and perhaps organize events together. Of course, a small number of students—roughly 15 percent—choose to live off campus or in one of the Greek houses.

Clarkson offers six dining locations. There are also a variety of dining plans, ranging from 75 meals per semester to 21 meals per week. As in most universities, the reviews for college food are mixed. Most people point out that they do grow tired of the dining halls eventually and often seek different restaurants and eateries to satiate their hunger. "The food is not that bad," said one student. "But after eating all those meals here, you just get tired of them."

Hockey and Party

There are a number of fraternities and sororities at Clarkson, and they offer a good deal of parties during the weekends as well as some community service work for Potsdam. One particular drawback at Clarkson is the small population of female students. Nearly three-quarters of students are male. However, as pointed out by one student,

"There are enough people here. Even though there are a lot more male students than female students, I don't think it has that large an impact on anyone's social life."

Despite the small size of Clarkson, it is also a Division I hockey powerhouse. The Golden Knights, which have been very successful, generally draw major crowds.

Clarkson is certainly special. Most universities similar to Clarkson in size and location tend to emphasize liberal arts. Clarkson, on the other hand, provides top-notch technical training to students. Therefore, if you can brave the cold of Upstate New York to enjoy education at a quality institution, you should definitely take a good look at Clarkson.—*Xiaohang Liu*

FYI

If you come to Clarkson, you'd better bring "clothes to keep you warm."

What is the typical weekend schedule? "Do some work, go to hockey games if you can, and make up for all the lost sleep during the week."

If I could change one thing about Clarkson, I'd "move it to some place just a little warmer."

Three things every student at Clarkson should do before graduating are "go to a Golden Knights game, make sure you get to know Potsdam, and go to Canada just because it is so close."

Colgate University

Address: 13 Oak Drive, Hamilton, NY 13346

Phone: 315-228-7401

E-mail address: admission@mail.colgate.edu

Web site URL: www.colgate.edu

Year Founded: 1819

Private or Public: Private

Religious Affiliation: None

Location: Rural

Number of Applicants: 9,416

Percent Accepted: 24%

Percent Accepted who enroll: 33%

Number Entering: 738

Number of Transfers Accepted each Year: 20

Middle 50% SAT range: M: 640–730, CR: 630–730, Wr: Unreported

Middle 50% ACT range: 29–32

Early admission program EA/ED/None: ED

Percentage accepted through EA or ED: Unreported

EA and ED deadline: 15-Nov

Regular Deadline: 15-Jan

Application Fee: $55

Full time Undergraduate enrollment: 2,868

Total enrollment: 2,903

Percent Male: 49%

Percent Female: 51%

Total Percent Minority or Unreported: 19%

Percent African-American: 6%

Percent Asian/Pacific Islander: 6%

Percent Hispanic: 6%

Percent Native-American: <1%

Percent International: 5%

Percent in-state/out of state: 28%/72%

Percent from Public HS: Unreported

Retention Rate: 93%

Graduation Rate 4-year: 91%

Graduation Rate 6-year: 91%

Percent Undergraduates in On-campus housing: 92%

Number of official organized extracurricular organizations: 186

3 Most popular majors: Biology, English, Psychology

Student/Faculty ratio: 10:1

Average Class Size: 18

Percent of students going to grad school: 20%

Tuition and Fees: $39,545

In-State Tuition and Fees if different: No difference

Cost for Room and Board: $9,625

Percent receiving financial aid out of those who apply: 81%

Percent receiving financial aid among all students: 32%

Thirteen dollars, 13 prayers, and 13 articles. That was the beginning of Colgate University. In 1817, 13 men met in Hamilton, New York, and founded the Baptist Education Society. Almost two centuries later, Colgate University is considered one of the country's top liberal arts universities. With a student population of about 2,800, Colgate seemingly combines the best of both worlds—the intimacy of a liberal arts college and the strong athletics program of a big university.

Nuts for Nature!

Like many of its peers in the world of liberal arts universities, Colgate is located in a small, serene location. Hamilton, a village of around 3,500 people, is nestled right in the middle of New York State, about an hour's drive from Syracuse. It is also two hours away from Cornell University, Colgate's biggest rival in sports.

Quaint Hamilton Village is almost the same size of Colgate, which leads to good town-gown relationships. Even though it celebrated its bicentennial in 1995, the village, originally called "Payne's Settlement," has changed very little. Some students do feel that Colgate's location is a significant shortcoming of the university, given the fact that "there is really not much to do outside of the campus." "Everything in Hamilton revolves around Colgate," added another student. "There is really nothing for entertainment around here."

Nevertheless, students agree that the campus is beautiful. Gorgeous architecture is an important aspect of the university, especially Memorial Chapel's golden steeple, the most recognizable feature on campus. Its pristine location in Upstate New York is also a prime attraction for nature lovers. "Colgate is perfect for people who enjoy the beauty of nature," one student said. Taylor Lake and Payne Creek both sit inside Colgate's campus and provide a relaxing backdrop to an otherwise hectic campus. To make use of all of its surroundings, Colgate's outdoor education program provides a fully equipped Base Camp right on campus, so students can take out rentals for snowshoeing, skiing, backpacking, and even camping. Colgate even maintains a camp in Upper Saranac Lake in the Adirondacks for the exclusive use of its faculty and students.

Despite any perceived shortcomings of the town, Colgate maintains a good relationship with Hamilton, where most of the Colgate faculty and staff live. In fact, about 85 percent of the faculty lives within 10 minutes of the university. Another contributor to the goodwill between Hamilton and Colgate? As one student pointed out, "Most locals go on vacation over Spring Party Weekend."

The Colgate Core

Colgate's admission process might not be as competitive as the Ivies, but it remains a highly selective school with an admissions rate of about 30 percent. The average combined math and critical reading score on the SAT was 1397, and nearly 80 percent of its students are in the top 10 percent of their high schools. The average GPA for the class of 2015 was 3.75. "Given the admission standards," said a student, "the people here are generally smart and willing to work hard."

> "As one student pointed out, 'Most locals go on vacation over Spring Party Weekend.'"

Colgate is a challenging school. Students need to work hard to get good grades, and several introductory classes are particularly difficult. As one student pointed out, "The intro classes are designed to cull the weak." Nevertheless, most students are happy with their classes, which are generally very small, giving students the opportunity to closely interact with their professors.

Undergrads can choose between 52 different majors. There is a core requirement that expects students to take four special classes by the end of their sophomore year. Two of these courses teach students about Western civilization and their contemporary challenges. The other courses are designed to give students a better understanding of a specific culture in the non-Western world and the effects of science and technology.

Colgaters have to take a minimum of 32 classes to graduate, including six classes for distributional requirements in humanities, social sciences, mathematics, and natural sciences, and two physical education credits, a specialty of Colgate. Most students are fine with the requirements. According to a student, "the required core classes are easy but usually involve a lot of reading." The gym classes, however, have mixed reviews. While some love the idea of going outdoors to learn about hiking and survival skills, many others do not think that they should be part of the college curriculum. "I appreciate the goals of the gym classes, but I just don't think that they should still be here at the college level," said a student. "We have so many intramural sports anyway, and half of the students participate in them."

Weekends That Never End

People work hard at Colgate because of the vigorous academic standards, but they also party hard. Undergrads agree that most Colgate students have a solid sense of self-discipline that allows them to do well academically, while enjoying the nightlife.

Since a great majority of Colgate students stay on campus, there is no shortage of things to do. There are always parties going on throughout the week, not just during the weekends. Fraternity parties are probably the most prominent social scene on campus, although the sports teams are also frequent fiesta hosts. Teams often have townhouses or apartments where students go for partying and dancing. For those who grow tired of the Greek system, the Jug is the most frequented bar for Colgate students, who generally agree that everyone should go there before graduating.

With all the partying, most students drink significant amounts of alcohol. But, as many students point out, drinking is not a particular problem on campus. Nevertheless, although there are also social opportunities for those who stay away from the parties, students agree that these are generally limited. Given the number of parties available, it becomes hard for students not to take advantage of them. Plus, since dating is "not the norm" at Colgate, parties seem to facilitate the more prominent random hook-up scene.

Dorms and Diversity

Students at Colgate are generally happy with their freshmen housing, which is fortunate because 92 percent of all Colgate students live in residence halls and university-owned houses. Freshmen are required to live in residence halls, but as they move up, they are free to choose between a wide array of options, including townhouses, apartments, and suites. Another way in which Colgate differs from most colleges is that fraternities and sororities must live in university-owned houses. But most students see no problems with on-campus living. "The residences are great," said a student. "There are nice theme houses for upperclassmen."

Colgate is often seen as a relatively rich, upper-class school, but 29 percent of admitted students are from less privileged backgrounds. Nonetheless, the school tries to attract a more diverse student body, both ethnically and financially. "Colgate is filled with rich, upper-class kids," one student admitted. "But it definitely isn't as preppy as it is made out to be. People are generally laid-back and looking for a good time."

And who wouldn't be laid-back with the serene backdrop of upstate New York and a motivated and fun-loving student body? As one student said, "Colgate is one of those schools that find the right balance between partying and studying. That's why it is so great." When the men of the Baptist Education Society met in 1819, who knew that they would make 13 such a lucky number for 2,800 undergraduates?—*Xiaohang Liu*

FYI
If you come to Colgate, you'd better bring "a worn-in hoodie."
What is the typical weekend schedule? "Friday: happy that it's Friday. Saturday: party time. Sunday: freak out at the amount of work and spend the whole day in the library."
If I could change one thing about Colgate, I'd "move campus to a warmer climate."
Three things every student at Colgate should do before graduating are "go to the Jug, sled around the campus, and hit some balls at the driving range overlooking campus."

Columbia University

Address: 1130 Amsterdam Avenue, New York, NY 10027
Phone: 212-854-2522
E-mail address: ugrad-ask@columbia.edu
Web site URL: www.studentaffairs.columbia.edu/admissions
Year Founded: 1754
Private or Public: Private
Religious Affiliation: None
Location: Urban
Number of Applicants: 22,584
Percent Accepted: 10%
Percent Accepted who enroll: 58%
Number Entering: 1,431
Number of Transfers Accepted each Year: 109
Middle 50% SAT range: M: 670–780, Cr 660–760, Wr: 650–760
Middle 50% ACT range: 29–34

Early admission program EA/ED/None: ED
Percentage accepted through EA or ED: 25%
EA and ED deadline: 1-Nov
Regular Deadline: 2-Jan
Application Fee: $70
Full time Undergraduate enrollment: 5,678
Total enrollment: 28,518
Percent Male: 53%
Percent Female: 47%
Total Percent Minority or Unreported: 51%
Percent African-American: 11%
Percent Asian/Pacific Islander: 23%
Percent Hispanic: 12%
Percent Native-American: 1%
Percent International: 10%
Percent in-state/out of state: 25%/75%
Percent from Public HS: 57%
Retention Rate: 98%

Graduation Rate 4-year: 85%
Graduation Rate 6-year: 94%
Percent Undergraduates in On-campus housing: 95%
Number of official organized extracurricular organizations: 450
3 Most popular majors: History, Political Science, Engineering
Student/Faculty ratio: 6:1
Average Class Size: 15
Percent of students going to grad school: Unreported
Tuition and Fees: $39,806
In-State Tuition and Fees if different: No difference
Cost for Room and Board: $9,980
Percent receiving financial aid out of those who apply: 79%
Percent receiving financial aid among all students: 50%

E stablished in lower Manhattan in 1754 as King's College by King George II of England, Columbia University has lived up to its original charge of providing an education that would "enlarge the mind, improve the understanding, and polish the whole man." First housed in a schoolhouse adjacent to Trinity Church on lower Broadway, the school moved to its present 36-acre site at the turn of the twentieth century. This relocation from a relatively uniform upper-class neighborhood to a far more diverse community, Morningside Heights between the Upper West Side and Harlem, is symbolic of Columbia's metamorphosis from an Anglican colonial college to a vibrant and diverse Ivy League university where free speech, student activism, and community involvement are among its most outstanding attributes.

E Pluribus Unum

Although Columbia College has always been the heart and soul of the university, it was not until the end of the nineteenth century that the various schools that make up the undergraduate and graduate parts of the school were incorporated under a central administration. It was at this time that the "mining school" established in 1864—that would later evolve into the Fu Foundation School of Engineering and Applied Science—and Barnard College for women came formally under the aegis of the university. At the same time, Columbia Teachers College, the Columbia University School of Law, and the Columbia University School of Medicine were officially integrated into the university system. Finally, in 1897, the newly reorganized entity moved to a new campus at 116th Street and Broadway designed by the celebrated architectural firm of McKim, Mead & White. Today, these magnificent examples of turn-of-the-century urban design, crowned by the Low Memorial Library and the huge plaza that it looks out upon, have been complemented by some rather inharmonious modern buildings, the most controversial of which is the Lerner Hall Student Center. Completed in 1999, the design of the 225,000-square-foot edifice, with its glass walls and escalating ramps, has been nearly universally panned by critics and students alike. "It looks like a huge ant farm," complained one student. "And it is rather hard to socialize on an incline."

Cutting to the Core and Going Swimming

It is impossible to talk about Columbia's academics without immediately referring to what is known as the Core Curriculum, a series of seminar-sized required courses in literature, philosophy, history, music, art, and science that are considered to provide the essentials of a liberal education. While some latitude is afforded in the choice of science classes, courses entitled Contemporary Civilization, Literature Humanities, Art Humanities, Music Humanities, and Frontiers in Science are compulsory. While the Core Curriculum is not for everyone, most agree that it provides an excellent foundation for a liberal arts education. Literature Humanities, a year-long course in Western literature that spans Homer to Virginia Woolf, is a particularly popular class, as is Contemporary Civilization, a course that exposes students to many of the seminal texts dealing with Western philosophy.

"The Core Curriculum is one of the reasons I came to Columbia," states a freshman. "The Core exposes you to so many different things you otherwise wouldn't have the chance to study. Every college student should learn from these writers and thinkers." Students find that, to some degree, the Core experience depends on the professors that you get for a particular subject. Opined one coed, "There is some luck involved in fulfilling the Core requirements, since you can't choose your profs for most courses."

In addition to the required courses in literature, philosophy, art, and music, the Core also demands the equivalent of two years of language at the college level and two courses in the Global Core, classes that deal with issues of multiculturalism, race, and gender. This requirement, in fact, is a relatively recent addition to the Core Curriculum, added by the college's Committee on the Core, in reaction to student criticism about the paucity of works by women and non-white, non-Western writers.

A rarity among colleges today, the Core Curriculum mandates that students take a minimum of two courses in physical education. "There are so many offerings," says one sophomore, "that it is always possible to find classes that suit even the most dedicated 'couch potato.'" In addition to the required gym classes, students must be able to swim seventy-five yards in the Uris Pool without resting. Although a seemingly unusual graduation prerequisite, Columbia College is not the only Ivy concerned with whether its undergraduates sink or swim. Cornell and Dartmouth also demand competence in the water.

Students must declare a "major" or a "concentration" (a less extensive version of the major that requires fewer courses) by the end of their sophomore year. Undergraduates may also "double major" or may fulfill the requirements of a major and concentration at the same time. Beyond the Core and the major or concentration, students choose from a wide variety of electives in any department in order to complete the minimum of 124 "points" necessary to graduate.

Location! Location! Location!

Columbia's location in New York, one of the world's greatest cities, is truly one of its most appealing calling cards, and it is not an overstatement to say that New York City can be viewed as an extension of the classroom. Opportunities abound to explore Manhattan's renowned museums (which are free for Columbia students) and to attend the finest theatrical and musical productions. "There are very few classes that meet on Fridays, so weekends start early," states one senior. "Many of us spend Saturday and Sunday afternoons exploring the city." In addition, the culinary diversity of New York lies at the doorstep of the university, as well as nightlife and shopping.

The Living Is Easy

The vast majority of Columbia undergraduates (99 percent of freshmen and 94 percent of upperclassmen) live on campus in university residence halls, and housing is guaranteed to all students throughout their four years. Freshmen choose to live in singles, doubles, or suites in one of five buildings located on the perimeter of South Field, the university's main quadrangle. The suite dorm is considered the most "social," while students looking for a "quieter dorm life" prefer the two mixed-suite dorms. One freshman said, "The dorms are pretty nice and having freshmen housing located in one portion of the campus is really conducive to making a lot of friends right away. My floor is very close and my floor mates are my best friends. The all-freshmen dorms are very social." Upperclassmen are housed by lottery. Single students share apartments or live in dormitory-style accommodations or studios, while couples generally live in studios and one-bedroom units. Families with dependent children live in "family units."

The area around Columbia University is considered very safe. "The campus is fairly small and very secure," notes a senior. "There is a security guard 24/7 at the entrance to all dorms."

Mealtime
Dining options vary from "meals" served in the John Jay dining hall Monday through Saturday, to "Columbia points" which are redeemable for à la carte selections at twelve locations on campus. While all freshmen are required to enroll in the meal plan, it is optional for upperclassmen. After the first year, students may enroll in "dining dollars" or "flex accounts," both of which have dollar balance accounts accessed through the Columbia Card, the university's ID. Kosher food can be found at the John Jay dining hall and at Barnard College for women, the Columbia affiliate located just across the street from the main campus.

Women at Columbia: the College and Barnard
Columbia College first admitted women in 1983 after merger negotiations with Barnard, an all-female college located across Broadway from Columbia, fell apart. While the university has remained closely affiliated with Barnard and students from Columbia's "sister" school can cross-register with Columbia students and freely participate in extracurricular activities, including athletics, some Columbia women do not always look at their Barnard counterparts as full equals. "Since the admissions criteria are more competitive for women at the College than they are for Barnard women, some classmates of mine consider Barnard students as being not as smart or diverse as Columbia women," said one junior. "Personally, I disagree. I have made many friends at Barnard and they are intelligent and interesting."

Outside of the Classroom
Like all outstanding colleges, the extracurricular life at Columbia is extremely diverse.

There are a wide variety of publications including the *Columbia Daily Spectator*, the nation's second-oldest college newspaper, and the *Columbia Review*, the oldest student literary magazine. The Philolexian Society is one of the oldest collegiate literary societies in America. Columbia also fields teams in Mock Trial, Model United Nations, and debate.

There are a dozen a cappella groups and numerous musical groups, including the Columbia University Orchestra, the oldest continually performing university orchestra in the nation. Opportunities for theater performance and comedy abound, including Fruit Paunch, Columbia's improv comedy group.

Where the Lions Roar
There are 31 men's and women's sports teams representing the Lions of Columbia. Barnard students participate on the Columbia women's squads. Although the football teams have not fared well in recent years, many other sports teams have. In 2007, the Men's Track Team won the 4x800 Penn Relay, the first time that an Ivy League track team was victorious in this event in over three decades. Many of Columbia's athletic facilities can be found at the Baker Athletics Complex, located north of the main campus. This campus includes the football field as well as facilities for baseball, soccer, field hockey, crew, tennis, and track. "Having the football field distant from the main campus is a negative," argues one freshman. "I think that is a big reason why a lot of students do not attend the games. My friends and I would rather hang around campus or go downtown on Saturdays rather than going all the way uptown to see our team lose."

The Social Scene
With the Big Apple at their doorstep, most Columbia students avail themselves of the tremendous cultural and culinary opportunities on the weekends, although social life is usually a blend of on- and off-campus activities. "Most people go out on Thursday nights to relax, because there are only a few classes that meet on Fridays," reports one junior. "We usually sleep in on Fridays and get a head start on work and spend Saturday and Sunday afternoons exploring the city. Most people go off campus to one of the many neighborhood restaurants and bars." Students generally divide their weekend time between the Columbia neighborhood, which is full of nightlife, and downtown Manhattan. "Columbia doesn't have a big

party atmosphere," notes a senior. "But students love hanging out together. On the weekends, if the weather is nice, we like relaxing in the floor lounge, hanging out on the steps of Low Library, and having lunch at one of the many on-campus dining locations."

While there are over 20 fraternities and sororities at Columbia, only about 10 percent of undergrads participate in Greek life. "Frat life is definitely present on campus, but it is far from dominant," reports one sophomore. "You can choose to be very involved in it, or you can get through four years without ever going to a frat party."

A Tradition of Activism

Student activism has long characterized the student body. In 1968, students occupied several campus buildings in protest over the university's participation in the Institute for Defense Analyses, a weapons research agency tied to the Pentagon, and what was perceived as a lack of sensitivity toward the African-American population in neighboring Harlem. In the 1970s and 1980s, there were protests and strikes over the university's investments in companies supporting apartheid in South Africa. In 1996, student protests resulted in the addition of Ethnic Studies to the Core Curriculum. In late 2007, some students went on a hunger strike in protest over Columbia's planned large-scale expansion into Manhattanville, a neighborhood north of the main campus.

Free speech is alive and well at Columbia, regardless of the degree to which such speech goes against the grain. This was evidenced in late 2007 by the visit of Iranian President Mahmoud Ahmadinejad to the campus, a demagogic leader whose anti-American policies are well known. In fall of 2008 alone, Columbia University hosted visits from Barack Obama, John McCain, and Hillary Clinton.

Columbia University is, overall, a superb academic institution that prides itself on its emphasis on the well-rounded education of its students. Its Core Curriculum is prime evidence of this, and it is essentially impossible to graduate from Columbia without having developed a broad appreciation for classical academic values. If you love learning, crave the excitement of the Big Apple, and know how to swim, Columbia may be just the school for you.—*Jonathan Berken*

FYI

If you come to Columbia, you'd better bring "a subway map."

What is a typical weekend schedule? "Sleep in on Fridays and get some work done. Explore the city Saturday and Sunday afternoons and hang out with friends on Saturday night."

If I could change one thing about Columbia, I'd "improve the advising system."

Three things that every student at Columbia should do before graduating are "get lost in the city with friends at two in the morning, eat a gigantic slice of Koronet's pizza, and hang out on the steps of Low Library."

The Cooper Union for the Advancement of Science and Art

Address: 30 Cooper Square, New York, NY 10003

Phone: 212-353-4120

E-mail address: admissions@cooper.edu

Web site URL: www.cooper.edu

Year Founded: 1859

Private or Public: Private

Religious Affiliation: None

Location: Urban

Number of Applicants: 3,354

Percent Accepted: 8%

Percent Accepted who enroll: 76%

Number Entering: 214

Number of Transfers Accepted each Year: 40

Middle 50% SAT range: M: 610–780, CR: 610–730, Wr: 620–640

Middle 50% ACT range: 29–33

Early admission program EA/ED/None: ED

Percentage accepted through EA or ED: 16%

EA and ED deadline: 1-Dec

Regular Deadline: 1-Jan

Application Fee: $65

Full time Undergraduate enrollment: 903

Total enrollment: 910

Percent Male: 61%

Percent Female: 39%

Total Percent Minority or Unreported: 63%

Percent African-American: 6%

Percent Asian/Pacific Islander: 17%

Percent Hispanic: 9%

Percent Native-American: <1%

Percent International: 17%

Percent in-state/out of state: 60%/40%

Percent from Public HS: 65%

Retention Rate: 94%

Graduation Rate 4-year: 67%

Graduation Rate 6-year: 70%

Percent Undergraduates in On-campus housing: 20%

Number of official organized extracurricular organizations: 90

3 Most popular majors: Electrical, Electronics and Communications Engineering, Fine Arts and Art Studies, Mechanical Engineering

Student/Faculty ratio: 8:1

Average Class Size: 14

Percent of students going to grad school: 60%

Tuition and Fees: $37,500

In-State Tuition and Fees if different: No difference

Cost for Room and Board: $13,700

Percent receiving financial aid out of those who apply: 100%

Percent receiving financial aid among all students: 100%

Also known as The Cooper Union, or "Cooper," this small university of about 900 undergraduate students occupies five buildings in the East Village neighborhood of Manhattan. Cooper is prominent for its high selectivity, rigorous programs, and especially motivated and focused student body. Over 200 new undergraduates matriculate each year as students of engineering, architecture, or fine arts. Because of the school's urban location and specialized approach to learning, many students believe that studying at Cooper is "not a typical college experience," but one that will prepare them for successful careers in the real world.

Three Schools in One

Prospective Cooper students apply and gain acceptance to three different schools: the Irwin S. Chanin School of Architecture, the School of Art, and the Albert Nerken School of Engineering. With about 550 students, the engineering school is the largest, and it offers majors in mechanical, chemical, civil, and electrical engineering. The art and architecture programs are smaller, with about 200 students each. All of Cooper's programs are highly ranked and selective. Aside from submitting test scores and transcripts, applicants to the art and architecture schools must complete "home tests" meant to gauge their talent through conceptual problems and art projects. In addition, they prepare extensive portfolios of their work, which may be presented to members of the selection committee at several portfolio review days and open houses that take place throughout the year. One artist believes that this long, multi-part process is designed to find people who are truly passionate about their work. "Stay true to yourself, and Cooper is such a great institution, they will be able to recognize your own talent," she said.

For underclassmen at Cooper, core requirements and major-specific prerequisites fill up much of the course schedule. Four semesters of general humanities seminars must be taken by students of all majors. Engineers generally find that these classes are a good way to balance their otherwise heavily quantitative course loads. An engineering student commented that the humanities courses are designed to be less arduous than courses within the majors. Students who enjoy the topics presented to them in these courses may choose to take electives in psychology, sociology, creative writing, economics, international relations, and other fields when they have more free scheduling space in their junior and senior years. Should a student find Cooper's moderate selection of humanities and social science courses insufficient, he or she is permitted to take classes at NYU or The New School.

No One Holds Your Hand
The consensus among students is that Cooper is tough. Engineers should be prepared to do a substantial amount of self-studying. "For me, the hardest part in adjusting to academics [during my freshman year] was having to deal with not having teachers so much as professors," said a chemical engineering student. "A lot of these professors are so smart so they explain it straight out of the book like how you'd explain it to a Ph.D., but they don't know that we don't necessarily think like that yet." Grading is described as "harsh but fair." A civil engineer still remembers the despair he felt throughout his freshman year when he would spend hours on an assignment only to receive a C or low B grade.

Artists and architects are said to "always be in the studio." Studio work is taken very seriously. One artist stated that the major is mostly self-driven and that students independently design and execute projects with the light-handed guidance of instructors. "It's not really about the grade. Most of the students here don't really care about the grading process," she said.

When it comes to academic and career advising, students also have to be especially proactive. "It's really hard to be here if no one is holding your hand," said one student. "It's up to you to network." An architecture major said that she has found professors to offer extremely helpful advice on difficult assignments and general concerns if you seek them out. "But they won't give you the answers," she added. "You learn the process of learning from your own work."

Meanwhile, several students emphasized that Cooper's students are generally supportive of one another. "We all know it's hard. It's not that we're stupid, it's just hard," said an engineering student. "I haven't really felt like anyone's cutthroat. Everyone works really hard, and we're all around to help each other out. No one's out there to do better than anyone else."

> "Stay true to yourself, and Cooper is such a great institution, they will be able to recognize your own talent."

Most students at Cooper are driven by a strong sense of purpose, and the student body has been described as overall "down to earth and practical." "I don't think you would go to Cooper if you weren't at least somewhat certain of what you wanted to do," said a sophomore engineer. It is rare for students to change disciplines during their time at Cooper, and most strive to establish themselves career-wise by joining professional societies of engineers or securing internships and jobs both on and off campus. Alumni connections are strong and the counseling office helps students to secure valuable opportunities in the city. Even with such strong backgrounds in their particular disciplines, however, a significant number of students graduate to pursue medical school, law school, or business school after their time at Cooper.

Freedom Is a Two-Edged Sword
Cooper students are not guaranteed housing after their freshman year. The dorms are "apartment-style" and include a bathroom, kitchen, common room, and one or two bedrooms. There is no dining hall, so students frequently eat out. In some cases, even freshmen will be denied housing due to lack of space in the dormitories. Upperclassmen and those denied housing will need to search for and rent apartments either near school or in the other boroughs of New York City. A significant number of students commute to school daily, which some say detracts from Cooper's social scene.

While some students find the process of searching for an apartment to be a major obstacle, others enjoy the independence of living off campus. "It's kind of nice being on your own because it's the taste of real life," said one student. "East Village is in the middle of everything, so there is a lot of really good food."

Indeed, students have a range of options within walking distance, from cheap falafel, one-dollar pizza, and baked snacks to Thai food, fresh groceries, and high-end restaurants.

Many students cite off-campus housing along with packed schedules to be the primary hindrances to social interaction between students. There are virtually no common "hangout spots," and because most people meet friends through taking the same classes, it is rare for students to make friends in disciplines other than their own. Nevertheless, core requirement classes, sports teams, clubs, and mixed freshman dormitories enable students to bridge the gap between disciplines to some extent.

Partying is rare on any night of the week, especially when the workload is heavy. Late at night during finals week for instance, it will be normal to see that groups of students have taken over classrooms to study, talk, eat, and perhaps watch movies—"just chilling" in each other's company. Rarely able to find free time, artists also relax while working in the studio by snacking, chatting, and sometimes playing movies on their computers. Cooper students are not ashamed to acknowledge that this might seem "very nerdy." In fact, many recognize it and take pride in it as part of their school culture. "Everyone is busy all the time," said a sophomore artist. "I basically live in my studio, but I live there with the 30 other kids in my class." A senior civil engineer echoed that statement. "[Your classmates] are the people you essentially go to war with—war against the classes," he said. "What we have is like a brotherhood."—*Justine Yan*

FYI
If you come to Cooper, you'd better bring "something to keep you going, give you inspiration, [or] something you take solace in, like a teddy bear."
If I could change one thing about Cooper, "The schools would interact more. [Currently] the artists and engineers are complete opposite and barely socialize ever."
Three things every student at Cooper should do before graduating are "explore New York City, try to go to art openings every Tuesday, where students in school get to display their own work, and go on a ski trip in January."

Cornell University

Address: 410 Thurston
Avenue, Ithaca, NY 14850
Phone: 607-255-5241
E-mail address:
admissions@cornell.edu
Web site URL:
www.cornell.edu
Year Founded: 1865
Private or Public: Private
Religious Affiliation: None
Location: Suburban
Number of Applicants:
25,617
Percent Accepted: 25%
**Percent Accepted who
enroll:** 47%
Number Entering: 3,010
**Number of Transfers
Accepted each Year:**
768
Middle 50% SAT range:
M: 660–760, Cr: 620–730,
Wr: 670–740
Middle 50% ACT range:
28–32

**Early admission program
EA/ED/None:** ED
**Percentage accepted
through EA or ED:** 37%
EA and ED deadline: 1-Nov
Regular Deadline: 1-Jan
Application Fee: $65
**Full time Undergraduate
enrollment:** 13,523
Total enrollment: 18,885
Percent Male: 51%
Percent Female: 49%
**Total Percent Minority or
Unreported:** 58%
Percent African-American: 5%
**Percent Asian/Pacific
Islander:** 16%
Percent Hispanic: 6%
Percent Native-American: 1%
Percent International: 8%
**Percent in-state/out of
state:** 38%/62%
Percent from Public HS:
Unreported
Retention Rate: 96%

Graduation Rate 4-year: 84%
Graduation Rate 6-year: 92%
**Percent Undergraduates in
On-campus housing:** 46%
**Number of official organized
extracurricular
organizations:** 823
3 Most popular majors:
Business, Engineering,
Biology
Student/Faculty ratio: 9:1
Average Class Size: 26
**Percent of students going to
grad school:** 71%
Tuition and Fees: $34,600
**In-State Tuition and Fees if
different:** No difference
Cost for Room and Board:
$11,190
**Percent receiving financial
aid out of those who apply:**
88%
**Percent receiving financial
aid among all students:**
40%

The youngest of the eight Ivy League institutions, Cornell University is well known both domestically and internationally as one of the premier educational establishments in the world. It boasts an immense array of resources and opportunities for its nearly 14,000 undergraduates. In addition, its location at the southern tip of the beautiful Finger Lakes gives the prestigious university a lovely learning environment—to the delight of all who enjoy the quiet, intimate atmosphere of small college towns and the chagrin of those who prefer the lively ambiance of big cities. If you would like to study in a large, top-notch institution and do not mind a rather removed location, Cornell ought to be among your top college choices.

Enjoyment of Nature

"The beautiful campus is the reason I came to Cornell," said one student. Indeed, for all those who enjoy nature, Cornell is certainly the place to be. It is located at the southern end of Cayuga Lake in the Finger Lakes region of upstate New York. The university takes pride in its two beautiful gorges, which offer the students small areas of wildlife right in the middle of campus. Many students take the gorge trails on their way to classes to enjoy the sight of the numerous waterfalls that dot the creeks. The school's location in the valley of Cayuga Lake also means that there are a lot of hills. In fact, Cornell is situated on the East Hill, which overlooks the city of Ithaca. This poses considerable inconveniences to the students. As one sophomore pointed out, "The hilly roads sometimes just make you not want to go to classes, especially during the winter."

Ithaca is a stereotypical college town, and Cornell is certainly its dominant institution. In fact, there are only about 30,000 people living in the city, a small figure considering that over 20,000 students are enrolled at Cornell. Ithaca Commons is the most important downtown business hub. However, Collegetown, the southern part of the campus, also has some commercial areas and is much more accessible to students.

Despite the natural beauty, Cornell is

certainly remote and hardly accessible to any major cities. "We don't even have a highway around," said one student. "You have to drive around hill after hill to get to Cornell." The location issue is certainly one of the major complaints and an important factor to consider for prospective students. "Cornell is in the middle of nowhere," remarked one student. "So if you like to leave campus for the weekend once in a while, it might not be a good idea to come here."

Private and Public

Cornell is unique among Ivy League schools for its distinct status as both a private and a public institution. The schools of Agriculture and Life Sciences, Human Ecology, and Industrial and Labor Relations are public schools. New York residents can pay about $15,000 less tuition when attending those three colleges. Other than that, "there is really no difference between the public and private parts of Cornell," said one student. "The quality of teaching is the same for all of them."

The seven colleges at Cornell include some highly specialized ones, such as Industrial and Labor Relations and Hotel Management, and broader ones, such as the College of Arts and Sciences, which is also the largest with more than 4,000 students. Also popular are the College of Agriculture and the College of Engineering, which attract most of those who are interested in science and engineering. High school students apply to one of the specific schools during the admission process, which is highly competitive for every school, as the admission rate is about 20%.

The rural environment of Cornell might turn away some students, but the academics for such a large and resourceful university can be tailored to satisfy almost any kind of learner. "In terms of academics, we have something for everyone," said one student. The school offers about 80 majors, including several unusual ones such as Fiber Science and Apparel Design. Since the Finger Lakes region is also the second largest producer of wine in the United States, Cornell is well known for offering several classes in wine tasting, which are very popular.

The class size at Cornell varies widely. For freshmen, the introductory lectures are quite large, many with hundreds of students. "Some big lecture classes can have 500 people, and the personal attention that students often get at smaller schools is almost nonexistent here," said one student. Indeed, for those classes, the students almost exclusively deal with teaching assistants, not professors. For upperclassmen, the choices of classes broaden, and students can enjoy a huge selection of both large lectures and small seminars. "We have so many different opportunities," said one student. "So it is very important for the students to take advantage of them."

The coursework at Cornell is very challenging. "All incoming students should expect a lot of work," said one sophomore. The different colleges at Cornell have separate guidelines for graduation requirements, which tend to be extensive. One student said, "The required courses are sometimes good, but most of them are simply not useful." In addition, Cornell University mandates that all students take two semesters of physical education or an equivalent such as joining a sports team or even the marching band. In addition, everyone is required to pass a swim test.

Best Food

Cornell offers a variety of housing options. Most freshmen choose the traditional dorm buildings, but they also have the opportunity of living in Balch Hall, which is for first-year women only; the Townhouse Community; or one of the nine Program Houses, which are themed buildings that gather students of similar interests. Freshmen live in North Campus so that they get to know each other during their first year. The students are generally satisfied with their housing assignments, and there are generally plenty of singles available. One student pointed out, "Compared to dorms in most other colleges, Cornell offers more choices, which is generally a good thing." Upperclassmen have even more options, and many of them live off campus.

> "In terms of academics, we have something for everyone."

Cornell is known to have one of the nation's best dining services. There are 31 dining locations on campus, ranging from all-you-can-eat dining halls to à la carte cafés. In addition, there are three convenience stores to serve all those looking for snacks or daily necessities. Nevertheless, despite these excellent campus services, some upperclassmen do point out that "because of Cornell's reputation, many students' expectations of dining halls are too high when they first come here."

Fraternities

There are more than 60 fraternities and sororities at Cornell, and they boast 30% of the student population. These numbers mean that Greek life is an important part of Cornell's social scene. Freshmen especially tend to frequent the numerous frat parties during weekends. Drinking is, of course, one of the main activities there, but those who do not drink are not left out of the social scene. "If you don't drink, there are certainly a lot of activities that you are missing out on, but it's a big school. You can find many people who don't drink and still have fun," said one student.

The life of a student at Cornell can be summarized in one word: choices. Whether it is dining, classes, housing, or weekend parties, the university offers its students a great number of options and a tremendous array of opportunities to explore. Despite its removed location and the lack of personal attention often associated with large institutions, Cornell, with the resources and reputation of a world-class university, is still a top choice for those looking for an exciting and challenging college experience. —*Xiaohang Liu*

FYI

If you come to Cornell, you'd better bring "a bicycle to ride around campus."
What is the typical weekend schedule? "Just like most universities: parties Friday and Saturday nights, and recovering from the parties the rest of the time."
If I could change one thing about Cornell, I'd "move it next to New York City."
Three things every student at Cornell should do before graduating are "travel to every part of the campus—there is always something to discover, go to every single dining hall, and go swimming in the gorge, if you dare."

Eastman School of Music

Address: 26 Gibbs Street, Rochester, NY 14604
Phone: 716-274-1060
E-mail address: admissions@esm.rochester.edu
Web site URL: www.rochester.edu/eastman
Year Founded: 1921
Private or Public: Private
Religious Affiliation: None
Location: Urban
Number of Applicants: 917
Percent Accepted: 29%
Percent Accepted who enroll: 47%
Number Entering: 125
Number of Transfers Accepted each Year: 20
Middle 50% SAT range: Unreported
Middle 50% ACT range: 22–28
Early admission program EA/ED/None: None

Percentage accepted through EA or ED: NA
EA and ED deadline: NA
Regular Deadline: Rolling
Application Fee: $100
Full time Undergraduate enrollment: 500
Total enrollment: 900
Percent Male: 45%
Percent Female: 55%
Total Percent Minority or Unreported: 11%
Percent African-American: 3%
Percent Asian/Pacific Islander: 6%
Percent Hispanic: 2%
Percent Native-American: 1%
Percent International: Unreported
Percent in-state/out of state: 17%/83%
Percent from Public HS: 80%
Retention Rate: 89%

Graduation Rate 4-year: 72%
Graduation Rate 6-year: 86%
Percent Undergraduates in On-campus housing: 73%
Number of official organized extracurricular organizations: 8
3 Most popular majors: Performance, Music Education, Music Composition
Student/Faculty ratio: 4:1
Average Class Size: 5
Percent of students going to grad school: 79%
Tuition and Fees: $20,320
In-State Tuition and Fees if different: No difference
Cost for Room and Board: $7,152
Percent receiving financial aid out of those who apply: Unreported
Percent receiving financial aid among all students: 70%

The Eastman School of Music, located in Rochester, New York, is home to stunning concert halls, a record-breaking library, and 500 of the most talented undergraduate musicians in the country. Eastman is a music conservatory affiliated with the University of Rochester. The school offers a rigorous curriculum in performance, theory, and humanities, as well as access to all facilities and classes at the University of Rochester. With such a holistic approach to music education, as one student said, "If you love music and you're planning on performing, this is definitely the school for you."

Knowing the Notes

Eastman has a top-tier music curriculum. All Eastman students must take music lessons, a freshman writing seminar, theory, and aural musicianship classes, perform in an ensemble, and take one humanities credit per semester. Lessons are often regarded as the most important aspect of education at Eastman. As one student said, "The most important thing is your relationship with your private teacher." During private lessons, young musicians have a chance to hone their skills with accomplished professionals. This faculty-student relationship is frequently a substantial factor in the decision to matriculate at Eastman.

Although most students praise their lesson opportunities, not all are as enamored by the theory requirement. Performance majors are required to take five semesters of theory and aural skills. Due to these requirements, students nickname their school the Eastman School of Music Theory.

> "This seems to be Eastman's common theme. Everyone knows everyone, and everyone loves music."

Aside from lessons and theory homework, students spend their time practicing and rehearsing. Eastman students spend about 2 to 3 hours in rehearsal every day. Most musicians spend an additional 2 to 4 hours practicing outside of scheduled rehearsal time. Practice time varies based upon specialty. Vocalists spend only about an hour practicing, while piano performance majors practice about 6 to 8 hours each day.

The most popular major at Eastman is Performance, although some students choose to major in Music Education or Composition. Eastman is one of the only top-ranking conservatories in the country to offer a degree in music education. A dual degree program is also an option. The program allows students to complete a major at Eastman and one at the University of Rochester. With that said, due to the difficulty of fulfilling the requirements of both majors, few students actually complete the program. It is typical for students to begin the program as freshmen and drop it by the time they are seniors.

Eastman is different from other conservatories because it requires students to take one humanities, math, or science course each semester. Classes in language, political science, creative writing, and history fulfill this requirement. Another typical way to tackle humanities is to explore the classes offered at the University of Rochester. Some find humanities are a necessary part of their education and a break from "doing music all the time." Others find the workload strenuous, and bemoan the fact that they are forced to take classes outside of their educational focus. One sophomore said, "Sometimes the work can be a little crazy when you just want to practice music."

Despite Eastman's hefty requirements, students are complimentary about the academic experience as a whole. "Everyone fits in really well," said a sophomore. "The level is extremely high, but playing with such good people makes you better."

Beyond Beethoven

Eastman is a small, tight-knit community. There is only one main dorm complex on campus. All freshmen and sophomores are required to live in this complex. Freshman dorms are typical doubles with lofted beds. All sophomores are guaranteed singles. Juniors and seniors typically try to move off campus. The dorm complex has a courtyard, common rooms, a game room, a kitchen, laundry room, and two cafeterias. The cafeteria food is "edible," but students sometimes choose to take the bus to the University of Rochester to eat.

Music facilities at Eastman are top-notch. Its concert halls are famous for being "gorgeous"; Kodak Hall, the main performance hall on Eastman's campus, is where the Rochester Philharmonic Orchestra performs. Even though its facilities are state-of-the-art, Eastman continues to increase performance space. It recently built a new concert hall called Hatch Hall. Sibley library is the largest academic music library in

North America, which is useful for musical academic projects. "I have yet to not be able to find what I need there," said a student. Still, even with all of those facilities, practice rooms are in high demand at Eastman and musicians sometimes complain that they have to wait to get one. Once they're inside they are often small and "too hot or too cold."

With top-ranked facilities and some of the most talented young musicians in the country, Eastman's small size makes it a place where "everyone knows almost everyone." Most students believe this makes the college experience more intimate. One student said, "I don't have to walk across campus to see anyone, I can just take the elevator." But the size of Eastman has its drawbacks, and sometimes students look to get out of the Eastman "bubble."

No Treble Finding Fun

Although Eastman students spend countless hours practicing and focusing on academics, there are options for those who want to explore the world outside of Eastman.

Performances are an important part of the conservatory's culture. Eastman constantly hosts all types of concerts, from operas to orchestras. Attending concerts is an important aspect of the Eastman experience. Eastman students can attend recitals, operas, musicals, or chamber concerts. They can also attend professional concerts such as the Rochester Philharmonic Orchestra's. As one student said, "On any given

day you can probably go find something amazing."

Eastman is located in an area of the city of Rochester some described as "dismal" or "sketchy." Others pointed to the off-campus attractions. Java's, a coffee shop right off campus, is a popular destination for students. There is a YMCA within walking distance of the campus. Jazz students go to "jam" in a number of bars in the surrounding area. Students can also venture to restaurants, museums, and parks in Rochester.

Not surprisingly, extracurricular activities often center on music. Students form small instrumental groups. Through a "gig website" they find places to play such as weddings or churches. Also, the Rochester Institute of Technology produces movies and asks Eastman composition majors to write the movie music. Vocal majors participate in operas and a cappella groups. Music-less extracurricular activities are not a dominant part of the Eastman culture. However, students willing to take the 20-minute bus ride have access to all extracurricular activities offered at the University of Rochester.

The neighborhood behind Eastman is where most off-campus apartments are. These apartments throw the parties on the weekends. Students estimate that a little under half of the students go out on weekend nights. Although some go to the University of Rochester to party, most prefer to stay near Eastman. As one student explained, it's better because "you walk in and you know everyone."—*Monica Disare*

FYI
If you come to Eastman, you'd better bring "a warm winter coat and a music stand."
Three things every student at Eastman should do before graduating are "go to an RPO (Rochester Philharmonic Orchestra) concert, visit the library, and put on as many concerts as you can."
The biggest college-wide event at Eastman: "Every couple years Eastman holds a barn dance during orientation. It sounds really lame but it's actually really fun. Freshmen go to a barn in the middle of nowhere, and do a square dancing–type dance."

Eugene Lang College of the New School University

Address: 65 W. 11th Street, Rm. 353, New York, NY 10011
Phone: 212-229-5665
E-mail address: langadmission@newschool.edu
Web site URL: www.newschool.edu/lang
Year Founded: 1978
Private or Public: Private
Religious Affiliation: None
Location: Urban
Number of Applicants: 1,670
Percent Accepted: 63%
Percent Accepted who enroll: 30%
Number Entering: 321
Number of Transfers Accepted each Year: 239
Middle 50% SAT range: M: 490–610, CR: 555–665, Wr: 560–660
Middle 50% ACT range: 23–28
Early admission program EA/ED/None: ED

Percentage accepted through EA or ED: Unreported
EA and ED deadline: 15-Nov
Regular Deadline: 1-Feb
Application Fee: $50
Full time Undergraduate enrollment: 1,294
Total enrollment: 1,294
Percent Male: 31%
Percent Female: 69%
Total Percent Minority or Unreported: 39%
Percent African-American: 4%
Percent Asian/Pacific Islander: 5%
Percent Hispanic: 6%
Percent Native-American: <1%
Percent International: 4%
Percent in-state/out of state: 32%/68%
Percent from Public HS: Unreported
Retention Rate: 73%

Graduation Rate 4-year: 35%
Graduation Rate 6-year: 47%
Percent Undergraduates in On-campus housing: 27%
Number of official organized extracurricular organizations: 34
3 Most popular majors: Unreported
Student/Faculty ratio: 15:1
Average Class Size: 16
Percent of students going to grad school: Unreported
Tuition and Fees: $33,060
In-State Tuition and Fees if different: No difference
Cost for Room and Board: $12,390
Percent receiving financial aid out of those who apply: 71%
Percent receiving financial aid among all students: 51%

Students at Eugene Lang agree that their college lives up to its progressive, liberal reputation. "Our campus is basically New York City," one student said. "The city is at your disposal." Also known as The New School for the Liberal Arts, Eugene Lang College is one of the eight divisions that comprise The New School, a university located mostly in the Greenwich Village area of New York City. Students at Eugene Lang choose from a wide range of courses such as "Queering Activism: Making Creative Resistance," "Consumer Culture," and "Social Justice in Food System," exploring their passions within a broad range of liberal arts fields. Eugene Lang encourages students to immerse themselves in the bustle of New York City, while the school's intimate learning setup enables students to develop close relationships with other students and professors.

Thinking for Yourself

Students characterized Eugene Lang's academic philosophy as one in which the students learn to think for themselves instead of just learning facts. Though students can take large lectures at the university level, classes within Eugene Lang are small and conducted as seminars rather than lectures. "It encourages discussion, and it's not based on test-taking. I've actually never taken a test since going here," one student said. Academics at Eugene Lang are largely focused on the humanities. "The one science major we have is interdisciplinary science," said one student, "but I don't know of anyone who takes it." Course work emphasizes writing assignments and discussions, so students said it is obvious when someone is not prepared for class. The workload is fairly heavy because of the amount of reading required, but students who do the work and attend class regularly tend to achieve good grades. "In a lot of classes, if you miss two classes, you get bumped down a grade," one student said. "You really have to be in the classroom in order to get the benefits."

Members of the faculty at Eugene Lang are highly engaged and often approach class time like a moderator would approach a debate. Professors and students treat each other as colleagues, conversing on a first-name basis, a format that encourages a warm atmosphere inside and outside the classroom. One student said he has not only been to professors' houses for gatherings but also kept in touch with some professors while he was studying abroad one semester. "The professors are really invested in their students," one student said. "You develop more than just a relationship based on grades."

> "You can learn in an intimate context within a large city."

Students also benefit from Eugene Lang's connection to The New School because they can take courses within other divisions of the university. "Because of the university structure, in general we have huge access to classes outside of Eugene Lang," one student said. "But you probably won't meet the prerequisites to take an art class at Parsons." But students said they were surprised by how bureaucratic Eugene Lang has become. "It has this history of being an experiment in education and it still has a lot of those values and image, but it's different now, more bureaucratic," said one student. "They're sort of figuring out how to market themselves still."

No Central Campus

Students described Eugene Lang's campus as a collection of buildings "scattered" around the Lower West Side of Manhattan. "We don't actually have a campus per se," said one student. "There's not a very strong sense of tightly knit community." The University Center, a 16-story building on 14th Street that opened fall 2013, has been designed to serve as more of a focal point for campus, students said. The Center includes dorm rooms, classrooms, and a library. Freshmen at Eugene Lang are guaranteed housing, and most students choose to live in the dorms freshman year. "A lot of my friends are people I met in the dorms," one

student said. Meal plans are available, though students said the dining locations on campus are expensive and do not serve the best food. Eugene Lang dorms, many of which are suite-style with kitchens, are some of the most expensive college dorms in the country, and students said this is one of the reasons that most students move off campus after their first year. "Lang students particularly are very independent from the get-go, and they prefer living on their own," one student said, adding that popular living areas include Brooklyn and Queens, from which many students commute. "A lot of those areas are starting to become very college student–dominated," one student said. "There's a trendy thing about living in Brooklyn at the moment." Nevertheless, students said they were attracted by Eugene Lang's great location, which is within walking distance of many of Manhattan's best centers for art and culture, including most of the West and East Village and Chinatown. "There's a ton of places to eat, it's a really cool area, and it's safe," one student said.

Hipster Domain

Students at Eugene Lang are diverse in many ways, but they are less politically diverse than one would think. "I've met one conservative person here," one student said. "And even they were a libertarian, not even a republican." Still, these liberal-leaning students hail from a wide variety of ethnic and socioeconomic backgrounds, and Eugene Lang attracts students with very different personalities. "There are some people that don't take school seriously, some that take school very seriously, some artsy and trendy, and others who are very academic," one student said. Students said they have made great friends at Eugene Lang, mostly from their time in the freshman dorms and in seminar-style classes. But students said they wished there were more opportunities and locations for students to spend time together and get to know each other outside the classroom. Eugene Lang students in general are less involved in extracurricular activities than students are at other schools. Eugene Lang does not have Greek life or varsity sports teams, and other activities are limited to a small number of active clubs and publications. Eugene Lang's unique version of school spirit showed itself most clearly in 2012 when students voted for the new school mascot to be a narwhal. When they are not studying, most students have part-time jobs or internships and spend their free time at off-campus apartments or bars. There is less of a drinking culture at Lang than at most colleges, because "people don't have binge-drinking, frat-style parties." While drug use is likely as common at Eugene Lang as it is at other schools, students said the Eugene Lang community talks about drug use more than the average college. "Students are more honest about it and more open in general about who they are holistically," one student said.

Eugene Lang may not offer a traditional college experience, but students said they would choose Eugene Lang again if they had the choice because of the intimate experience it provides against the backdrop of a big city. "You're in a great place once you go out into New York City to have a career because you become close to your professors who are active in their fields and industries. They are your mentors, and they get to know you on a deep level," said one student. "That's what makes Lang, Lang."—*Sophie Gould*

FYI
If you come to Eugene Lang, you'd better leave "your Bible" and "your car" behind.
What's the typical weekend schedule? "Wake up at noon, read until 8 p.m., go to the bar, get back at two or three in the morning, sleep, then the schedule starts over again the next day."
If you could change one thing about Eugene Lang, "I'd make it more financially accessible to more people."
What differentiates Eugene Lang the most from other colleges is "the conversation. Whether it's philosophical or even practical, more laid back or cerebral."

Fordham University

Address: 441 East Fordham Road, New York, NY 100458
Phone: 718-817-4000
E-mail address: enroll@fordham.edu
Web site URL: www.fordham.edu
Year Founded: 1841
Private or Public: Private
Religious Affiliation: Roman Catholic-Jesuit
Location: Urban
Number of Applicants: 31,792
Percent Accepted: 47%
Percent Accepted who enroll: 15%
Number Entering: 1,962
Number of Transfers Accepted each Year: Unreported
Middle 50% SAT range: M: 570–670, CR: 580–670, Wr: 570–680
Middle 50% ACT range: 26–30

Early admission program EA/ED/None: EA
Percentage accepted through EA or ED: Unreported
EA and ED deadline: 1-Nov
Regular Deadline: 15-Jan
Application Fee: $70
Full time Undergraduate enrollment: 7,812
Total enrollment: 15,189
Percent Male: 48%
Percent Female: 52%
Total Percent Minority or Unreported: 30%
Percent African-American: 5%
Percent Asian/Pacific Islander: 8%
Percent Hispanic: 14%
Percent Native-American: <1%
Percent International: 6%
Percent in-state/out of state: 52%/48%
Percent from Public HS: Unreported

Retention Rate: 90%
Graduation Rate 4-year: 76%
Graduation Rate 6-year: 80%
Percent Undergraduates in On-campus housing: 76%
Number of official organized extracurricular organizations: 140
3 Most popular majors: Business, Communication, Social Sciences
Student/Faculty ratio: 13:1
Average Class Size: 17
Percent of students going to grad school: 19%
Tuition and Fees: $39,235
In-State Tuition and Fees if different: No difference
Cost for Room and Board: $14,926
Percent receiving financial aid out of those who apply: 74%
Percent receiving financial aid among all students: 67%

Combining the best of both worlds, Fordham is a small school in a big city. Featuring main campuses in Manhattan (Lincoln Center) the Bronx (Rose Hill), and most recently, Westchester, the school fosters an intimate environment while offering all the opportunities of New York City. One sophomore said, "The school is small enough that I always know at least two people who I am going out with, but it's also big enough so that I am meeting new people every day."

Up Close and Personal

The small school environment is something that Fordham students cannot praise enough. One junior gushed about how pleasant it was "to be more than just a name on the roster." The average class size is 22 and lectures hold about 40 students. The very few large lectures that the college offers hold about 100 people and are broken up into smaller discussion sections. There is also an atmosphere of intimacy with the professors, all of whom carry the reputation of being very accessible and keen to form long-term academic relationships with students.

The Fordham curriculum features an extensive list of requirements that dominate freshman and sophomore schedules. In the spirit of a true liberal arts education, the core strives to expose students to everything from math and English to theology, fine arts, and foreign languages. One junior complained that because of the core, "it's frustrating when the time comes to pick a major because you don't get into those classes until junior year." The wide variety of programs offered at Fordham does not make it easier to choose—the school's College of Business Administration, honors program, dance program, and the superb theater program are just a few of the many programs that stand out.

When it comes to academics, Fordham prides itself on rejecting grade inflation; students bemoan the grading curve as rather harsh and are used to working hard both inside and outside the classroom to earn their good grades. The introductory accounting class is especially notorious for its level of difficulty. However, to compensate there are Music History and Life on Planet Earth, which are both known to be gut courses.

Work Hard, Play in New York City

The absence of Greek life on campus escapes the notice of most Fordham students. This is no surprise, however, as the students have New York City as their playground. The freshmen are known to frequent The Jolly Tinker, also known as Tinkers, a local bar. One sophomore explained, "As an upperclassman, you become more independent

and Tinkers gets old." The students from the Rose Hill campus center their social life mainly on what is known as the tri-bar area: Ziggy's, Mugzy's, and Howl at the Moon Inc (or Howl for short). Meanwhile, the more centrally located students of Lincoln Center go out to various Manhattan hotspots. The technically dry campus and presence of RAs discourages dorm parties; however, it is not unusual to hear of a house party at the apartment of one of the many upperclassmen who live off campus.

> "Coming to New York City, I expected it to be less personal, but Fordham really surprised me in its friendly atmosphere."

One junior described the social scene as revolving around the "work hard, play hard" mentality. People are very social and go out every weekend, and since the majority of students are able to avoid Wednesday classes, Tuesday night is also a popular choice for a fun night out. Fordham is a dry campus, meaning that students cannot have alcohol unless everyone in the room is 21. Despite the restrictions, drinking is a prominent feature on campus, and drugs, while more subdued, are not uncommon. The school, however, does make an effort to provide fun events such as Homecoming, President's Ball, and Spring Weekend. The Lincoln Center campus also features endless theater and other fine arts performances, which are popular among the students.

While the school is "definitely a clique school" as one junior described it, people are generally friendly and easy to meet. Friends are made mostly through classes, but also through dorms and extracurricular activities. A typical student of the Rose Hill campus is described as "well-outfitted with designer labels and likely to be from New Jersey, Connecticut, or Long Island." The more colorful and diverse Lincoln Center campus is composed of mostly international and artsy crowds. Lack of diversity is a common complaint about the university, although the various cultural groups, such as the Philippine-American Club and the Hispanic club El Grito de Lares, are prominent on campus and organize a variety of cultural events.

The Fordham Bubble

Despite the urban location, the picturesque campus is a bubble into which students can escape. Gothic architecture, well-kept grassy areas, and the occasional good ghost story (the campus has been featured as one of the most haunted places in the U.S.) are welcoming to students. On warm days walking past Edward's Parade, which students simply refer to as "Eddie's," "the field is covered with people—students lying in the sun, playing soccer, Frisbee."

Fordham may be considered a commuter school. Most students move off campus after their sophomore year or even earlier. The scarce housing is not guaranteed for everyone, and the dorms are nothing out of the ordinary. The coveted Walsh and O'Hare apartment-style residence halls are usually reserved for upperclassmen. Housing is assigned by lottery, so students rely on accumulated "credit hours" and strokes of luck for better housing options. The administration does get a lot of credit though for its above-average efforts to honor roommate requests. Freshman housing options include Alumni Court North and South, and Hughes Hall. Queen's Court is also a popular choice for freshmen, but they must first write a letter to the nun who is the head of the house to convince her why they belong there.

The Bronx location of Rose Hill, while not ideal, is not much of a problem. The campus is unanimously hailed as very safe, complete with tall gates separating it from the neighborhood and guards who scrutinize the ID of everyone who passes through. Students are always traveling into and around the city and visiting spots such as Fordham Road, which features great alternative shopping, or Arthur Avenue, which offers excellent dining and entertainment venues. The NYC public transportation system precludes the need for a car, so parking is also not a problem.

"Food, I'd give it 60 out of 100," a sophomore assessed. While the Marketplace is a pretty dining hall, it tends to disappoint in both quality and variety. The alternative options, however, offer a welcome counterbalance. Flex dollars work at the more popular spots such as the Grill, the student deli, and Dagger John's University Restaurant. One thing students cannot complain about is lack of options for dining out—restaurants are plentiful and diverse, and the Bronx version of Little Italy offers excellent choices right in Fordham's backyard.

Get Active!

Students described school pride as "up and coming." This means that currently, while there is enough support for the sports teams (basketball games sell out, so get your tickets early!), the teams don't have the most successful records. But sports on campus do have a large presence in the form of intramurals, where teams such as the Flying Jesuits Ultimate Frisbee team are quite popular. The student newspaper, *The Ram*, is a weekly publication and many students also enjoy the controversial quips of *The Paper*, an alternative news source akin to *The Onion*.

Fordham students are active and committed to their extracurricular activities. Performance groups such as Mimes and Mummers and Experimental Theatre are very popular. Fashion for Philanthropy is a well-liked option, and many also take advantage of the volunteer opportunities in the shelters and other social justice organizations of the Bronx. Many students also choose to take advantage of New York City, and many work in internships in various businesses around the city.

Opportunities are definitely not lacking at Fordham. "Coming to New York City, I expected it to be less personal, but Fordham really surprised me in its friendly atmosphere," one junior said. Whether you want a sense of close community or a big city to seek adventure, Fordham has it all.—*Dorota Poplawska*

FYI
If you come to Fordham, you'd better bring "your designer shades."
What is the typical weekend schedule? "Hit the tri-bar area on Friday, Saturday sleep in, enjoy a day in the city shopping, and at night it's bars again."
If I could change one thing about Fordham, I'd "make it more diverse."
Three things every student at Fordham should do before graduating are "eat out on Arthur Ave., go streaking across Eddie's Parade, and ride the Ram statue."

Hamilton College

Address: 198 College Hill
Road, Clinton, NY 13323
Phone: 315-859-4421
E-mail address:
admission@hamilton.edu
Web site URL:
www.hamilton.edu
Year Founded: 1812
Private or Public: Private
Religious Affiliation: None
Location: Rural
Number of Applicants:
4,962
Percent Accepted: 28%
Percent Accepted who
enroll: 34%
Number Entering: 472
Number of Transfers
Accepted each Year: 37
Middle 50% SAT range:
M: 640–720, CR: 640–740,
Wr: Unreported
Middle 50% ACT range:
Unreported
Early admission program
EA/ED/None: ED

Percentage accepted
through EA or ED: 47%
EA and ED deadline: 15-Nov
Regular Deadline: 1-Jan
Application Fee: $75
Full time Undergraduate
enrollment: 1,842
Total enrollment: 1,842
Percent Male: 48%
Percent Female: 52%
Total Percent Minority or
Unreported: 34%
Percent African-American:
4%
Percent Asian/Pacific
Islander: 8%
Percent Hispanic: 6%
Percent Native-American: 1%
Percent International: 5%
Percent in-state/out of
state: 30%/70%
Percent from Public HS:
60%
Retention Rate: 96%
Graduation Rate 4-year:
85%

Graduation Rate 6-year:
90%
Percent Undergraduates
in On-campus housing:
98%
Number of official organized
extracurricular
organizations: 80
3 Most popular majors:
Economics, Mathematics,
Politics and Government
Student/Faculty ratio: 10:1
Average Class Size: 14
Percent of students going to
grad school: 40%
Tuition and Fees: $38,600
In-State Tuition and Fees if
different: No difference
Cost for Room and Board:
$9,810
Percent receiving financial
aid out of those who apply:
78%
Percent receiving financial
aid among all students:
41%

For a small school, it's a big deal. A reputation as a writer's college, an idyllic location in upstate New York, and constant inclusion on "Little Ivies" lists have made Hamilton College a well-known destination for students across the USA. Add into the mix quirks like no distributional requirements and a campus that melds the new and the old, and you have a reputable, unique liberal arts college.

Build-an-Education

With the "open" curriculum, students are able to achieve the 32 credits they need to graduate in any number of ways. One freshman noted that she "never feel[s] forced into a class [she doesn't] want to take" while an upperclassman raved about the option to create one's own major. The only restriction is the writing requirement: each student must take 3 writing-intensive courses. Yet these too are "offered in almost all . . . subjects," a pre-med student explained, which means that even the science-minded can easily attain the credits they need. This

is possibly one of the reasons why strong majors range from mathematics (though this department's popularity must be helped by its sushi-themed information sessions) to creative writing, neuroscience to history. The same student may thus be taking classes with both a visiting neuroscience expert and a women's studies professor publishing her third book.

Yet academic life is not all fun and games. "Registering for classes is hell," one international student bluntly stated. With most classes comprising 15 to 20 people and few having more than 35, this is believable. A Hamilton education is not for the fainthearted: even a 200-level class might have homework due every 2 days. Balance, therefore, is key—most students interviewed emphasized this, mentioning that they purposely take classes with varying testing schedules. As they state that grading is difficult and A's are rare, this is probably a good strategic choice. "Weekdays means sitting and studying," a freshman clarified with a sigh. This can pay off: those with GPAs above 90% are placed on the Dean's List. For those who need external help, the world-class writing center and friendly math tutors supplement class time.

Amidst all this, professors and peers seem to play a crucial, calming role. The former are easy to get in touch with, often build close relationships with students, and are popular among those they teach, with some, like Professors Nancy and Peter Rebinowitz, becoming almost campus celebrities. Even better: they are honest. One freshman said she was very glad her teachers told her "about the workload upfront—no bad surprises." And then there's the latter. Some variant of "every student is just as passionate as I am" was one of the first things out of interviewees' mouths. Fortunately, Hamilton seems to escape an issue that plagues many top colleges: overcompetitiveness. This is just one manifestation of the sense of community permeating the school.

A Divided Campus, Social Spaces, and Occasional Hay

You might want to sit down for this one: Hamilton College actually used to be two colleges, Hamilton for men and Kirkland for women. Today, the two are known as the "Light Side" and the "Dark Side," with a feigned rivalry and moaning about the 7-minute walk between them defining their playful relationship. It is the former, with its classic architecture, that students see as a haven for lax-bros and the prep-school brigade, while the modern, "funky concrete" Dark Side is viewed as housing "the hipsters and hippies, who are always sitting in the coffee shop listening to Phoenix on the big couches," said a student athlete. Freshmen are randomly assigned to dorms, and are placed via housing draw come sophomore year. Options abound for the selective, though, with some buildings designated as substance-free, for instance.

Off-campus living, on the other hand, is highly uncommon. Yet many argue that cars are integral to get anywhere. The town of Clinton seems to not satisfy Hamilton students—some visit regularly but many share the attitude of one freshman, who isn't sure if going into what her peers call "the village" is "worth the walk back up the Hill." It does, however, offer varied dining options for those tired of Hamilton Dining, featuring Indian, Mexican, and Chinese cuisine alongside fast food staples.

But being sick of the food seems to be less likely these days. "The dining halls have stepped up their game," an international student explained. The three halls are also flexible with repeat meal swipes—"you can always go and get a snack."

Going out to party is a big part of life at Hamilton, as at any other college. Options vary: the majority of students drink, but the college helps sponsor non-alcoholic events as well. While one freshman said she was "unsure about how much fun [teetotalers] have," there does not seem to be any stigma attached to their decision.

College-sanctioned parties are hosted in the 4 "social spaces" that various organizations, from the eclectic a capella groups to cultural ones, can book. While large and raucous, such parties have a strict code that one student shared with us: "If the campus police arrive, put your drink down . . . just don't be drunk at the party." The administration is very strict about hard liquor, though its policies about beer are lax.

> "Strong majors range from mathematics (though this department's popularity must be helped by its sushi-themed information sessions) to creative writing, neuroscience to history"

Frat parties are another option. Greek events are open to all, and though many students do end up rushing, this is not seen as essential. Students flock to these events, as well as dorm parties and the occasional annual affair, such as the Farm Party, a bonanza of flannel and hay.

"A Nice Mix"

One aspect of Hamilton that every student commented on was its mix. Home to what a freshman called "liberal arts college hipsters, preppy lax-bros and athletes, and outdoorsy granola eaters," it seems this college has no dearth of subcultures for one to slot into. Respondents spoke of making friends via the cozy classes, chance library encounters, or drunken nights out. Classic college behavior is clearly alive and well here.

Close-knit athletic teams, from women's rugby to football, and popular organizations like the Outdoors Club and service organization HAVOC also play key roles in bringing students together. Shared interests make for relationships that last and mean something to the individuals in them.

Adding to this sense of community is an institutional commitment to diversity. Hamilton participates in the national POSSE program, which brings student leaders from oft-neglected public high schools to top colleges across the States, while also running its own Hamilton Educational Opportunity Program for economically disadvantaged students in New York state. Together, these two keep the College on the Hill grounded, accessible and far from snooty.

A liberal arts college with the money to garner university-style resources, Hamilton is a popular and well-liked destination. "Hell yeah" was one girl's sentiment when asked whether she'd enroll there again, and no respondents were unhappy with their experience. Offering an education in diverse subjects, and very generous financial aid packages, it breaks out of the "remote, humanities-obsessed" liberal arts college stereotype. Few other schools are home to such a reputable, accessible milieu.—*Akbar S. Ahmed*

FYI
If you come to Hamilton, you'd better bring "a good hangover remedy."
Three things every Hamilton student has to do before graduating are "hug the statue of Alexander Hamilton naked, hook up in the Kirner-Johnson building, and eat a panini at Opus, the campus coffee shop."
What differentiates Hamilton: the open curriculum, student-faculty closeness, and the streaking team.

Hobart and William Smith Colleges

Address: 629 South Main Street, Geneva, NY 14456
Phone: 315-781-3622
E-mail address: admissions@hws.edu
Web site URL: www.hws.edu
Year Founded: 1822
Private or Public: Private
Religious Affiliation: None
Location: Rural
Number of Applicants: 3,410
Percent Accepted: 65%
Percent Accepted who enroll: 25%
Number Entering: 545
Number of Transfers Accepted each Year: 27
Middle 50% SAT range: M: 540–630, CR: 530–640, Wr: Unreported
Middle 50% ACT range: 24–27
Early admission program EA/ED/None: ED

Percentage accepted through EA or ED: Unreported
EA and ED deadline: 15-Nov
Regular Deadline: 1-Feb
Application Fee: $45
Full time Undergraduate enrollment: 1,868
Total enrollment: 2,069
Percent Male: 46%
Percent Female: 54%
Total Percent Minority or Unreported: 4%
Percent African-American: 3%
Percent Asian/Pacific Islander: 2%
Percent Hispanic: 4%
Percent Native-American: <1%
Percent International: 2%
Percent in-state/out of state: 45%/55%
Percent from Public HS: 65%
Retention Rate: 85%
Graduation Rate 4-year: Unreported

Graduation Rate 6-year: Unreported
Percent Undergraduates in On-campus housing: 90%
Number of official organized extracurricular organizations: 77
3 Most popular majors: Economics, General English Language and Literature, General History
Student/Faculty ratio: 11:1
Average Class Size: 18
Percent of students going to grad school: 30%
Tuition and Fees: $31,850
In-State Tuition and Fees if different: No difference
Cost for Room and Board: $8,386
Percent receiving financial aid out of those who apply: 74%
Percent receiving financial aid among all students: 64%

Set atop a hill, adjacent to the majestic Seneca Lake, sits the campus of Hobart and William Smith Colleges. HWS is actually two schools with separate deans, admissions officers, student governments, and athletic departments. Women apply to William Smith and men apply to Hobart, but all students attend the same classes and share the same beautiful campus. Due largely to its small student body of around 2,000 undergraduates, HWS is the perfect school for college applicants looking for an intimate community and a chance to build strong relationships with professors.

A Liberal Arts Education

Hobart's academics are in very much the typical liberal arts style. Following a semester schedule, students are expected to take four classes each term. It's required for students to take classes in each of the basic disciplinary areas including art and civic engagement. The art credit can be satisfied by a semester of music lessons and a credit for civic engagement, for example, can be earned by volunteering for America Reads. Depending on the subject and professor, class sizes can vary but on average are about 20 students. With 45 majors ranging from English to Studio Art and 20 minors from Child Advocacy to Peace Studies, students are also still given the choice to design their own major. "It's a liberal arts education: strong across the board," one student affirmed. The worst academic characteristic at HWS, according to one student, is that "some of the students in the classes don't appreciate where they are. You can find peers who challenge you, but sometimes they can be entirely uninspiring." Similarly uninspiring are gut classes like "Rocks for Jocks" also known as Geology 101, and "Shakespeare for Non-majors." Pat McGuire, an economics professor characterized by his sweater vests, and Craig Rimmerman, a political science and public policy professor, are both passionate and invested educators to look out for when searching for an extra class. Despite the inevitable hard professor, students consistently praise the teaching staff for their passion, accessibility, and personal investment in their students.

"Because class size and the HWS community are small, you can get a lot of one-on-one time with the professors who are passionate about their subject and about teaching," a student explained. "If you stand out, you can benefit enormously from them."

With an intimate academic setting and thoroughly invested faculty, it is easy to get individual help and to form strong connections with professors, but there are always international opportunities if HWS gets too small. Taking advantage of the well-developed opportunities abroad for students, many take a break from HWS and venture off to other countries for a semester or year abroad.

Luck of the Draw

Housing, much like other college campuses, is often the luck of the draw. Freshmen are placed in a dorm before arriving on campus. Some are placed in "Dirty Durfee," though according to one student, it may not be all that dirty anymore, or in the new dorms recently constructed on the hill. As for upperclassmen, they enter a lottery with their future roommates. Choices for living range from an all-girls dorm, an all-guys dorm, coed housing, fraternities, or theme housing. Students are allowed to create their own theme house by petitioning the dean and getting a group of people together. Some recent theme houses have been the Political Activism House, the Honors House, and the Outdoor Recreation House. Senior-year students can live in O'Dell's Village, a group of condominiums on the far side of campus equipped with a bathroom and kitchen. Seniors can also live off campus if they choose. "Housing is where you meet most of your friends," a student said.

Saga is the main dining hall on campus. With its 3-tiered construction, Saga has the feel of a gymnasium, and the all-you-can-eat menu can be a physical challenge for your digestive system. Saga is part of the newly renovated campus center, and students enjoy hanging out there and socializing. If Saga doesn't hit the spot, there is a café that is à la carte and a pub that serves food and beer if you are of age. Oftentimes during the warmer months, students will take lunch out on the quad and lie out in the sun or walk up the hill to the lake.

Around the World . . . or Not

Campus social life seems to be characterized by hanging out on the quad during warmer months, dormitory socializing, hitting up Parker's or whichever bar hasn't been shut down by the local police, and the occasional frat party (no sororities, sorry, girls!). Students typically stagger into the Water Street Café or Bagels and Cakes the "morning after" for a rejuvenating breakfast.

With only six fraternities, Greek life isn't a big presence on campus and there is no pressure to join. One campus party to look forward to is the spontaneous "Around the World" party, which happens a few times a year in O'Dell's Village. Typically, a resident of one unit will decide on a whim that it's time for a night of "Around the World." Each unit chooses a different drink from some place in the world and students walk around the village trying each drink.

> **"Because class size and the HWS community are small, you can get a lot of one-on-one time with the professors who are passionate about their subject and about teaching."**

Although they have parties with diverse drinks, the attendees, for the most part, are not. The majority of the student body at HWS are white middle-class Americans, many of whom are from upstate New York or Massachusetts. The cultural clubs are strong, close-knit organizations as a result of their small numbers and provide a welcoming community within HWS for its minority students. What HWS lacks in student diversity, it makes up for in diversity of opportunities. HWS has everything from an NCAA Division I national championship–winning sailing team to a coed "drinking team with a softball problem," and students have the freedom to start their own clubs. Students are deeply dedicated to their extracurricular activities and find it easy to be "a big fish in a little pond." On Seneca Lake in beautiful Geneva, New York, with a plethora of academic and extracurricular opportunities, many students have found that they are happy where they are. One recent graduate said that HWS was the best place for him because "it gave me the opportunity to pursue any extracurricular or academic goal I wanted. The small community really offers the opportunity for leadership."—*Hayden Mulligan*

FYI

If you come to HWS, you'd better bring "a windbreaker because campus gets cold from the breeze off the lake."

What's the typical weekend schedule? "Saturdays are brunch at Saga, studying, head to Parker's, back to the frats for late-night fun, and Sundays are devoted to studying."

If I could change one thing about HWS, "I'd enhance the theater and fine arts departments."

Three things every student should do before graduating are "swim in Seneca Lake, go on a Finger Lakes wine tour, and eat a meal with their favorite professor."

H o f s t r a   U n i v e r s i t y

Address: 100 Hofstra University Bernon Hall, Hempstead, NY 11549
Phone: 516-463-6700
E-mail address: admissions@hofstra.edu
Web site URL: www.hofstra.edu
Year Founded: 1932
Private or Public: Private
Religious Affiliation: None
Location: Urban
Number of Applicants: 18,471
Percent Accepted: 54%
Percent Accepted who enroll: 17%
Number Entering: 1,730
Number of Transfers Accepted each Year: 641
Middle 50% SAT range: M: 550–630, CR: 540–630, Wr: Unreported
Middle 50% ACT range: 23–26
Early admission program EA/ED/None: EA

Percentage accepted through EA or ED: 36%
EA and ED deadline: 15-Dec
Regular Deadline: Rolling
Application Fee: $50
Full time Undergraduate enrollment: 8,444
Total enrollment: 11,187
Percent Male: 46%
Percent Female: 54%
Total Percent Minority or Unreported: 17%
Percent African-American: 9%
Percent Asian/Pacific Islander: 5%
Percent Hispanic: 7%
Percent Native-American: <1%
Percent International: 1%
Percent in-state/out of state: 50%/50%
Percent from Public HS: Unreported
Retention Rate: 79%
Graduation Rate 4-year: 34%

Graduation Rate 6-year: 53%
Percent Undergraduates in On-campus housing: 80%
Number of official organized extracurricular organizations: 124
3 Most popular majors: Accounting, Marketing/ Marketing Management, General Psychology
Student/Faculty ratio: 14:1
Average Class Size: 16
Percent of students going to grad school: 29%
Tuition and Fees: $25,700
In-State Tuition and Fees if different: No difference
Cost for Room and Board: $10,300
Percent receiving financial aid out of those who apply: 90%
Percent receiving financial aid among all students: 84%

Formerly an extension of New York University, Hofstra University is now an independent institution of higher learning to nearly 12,000 undergraduates and postgraduates. Located on Long Island away from the noises of New York, yet close enough for students to have easy access to all the amenities of the Big Apple, Hofstra offers a large number of opportunities in academics and research, allowing students to have a meaningful and fulfilling college education. Furthermore, the university is well known for its dedication to education in public service, including serving as the host of one of the 2008 presidential debates. With its great location and strong academics, Hofstra is an intriguing college choice for prospective students.

Nine Schools

The university is divided into nine different units, offering close to 150 undergraduate majors. "We have a big selection of majors. As long as you know what interests you, Hofstra has something for you," said one student. In fact, the majors range from the usual liberal arts degrees to some unique ones rarely found in other universities, such as Exercise Specialist and Urban Ecology. "I think what is great here is that you can have broad majors like Economics or more specific majors like Business Economics," said one student. "That type of flexibility makes sure that you can receive the kind of education that you want."

The one shortcoming, however, is the lack of options in engineering and science. "I think we are so much more focused on social sciences than things like physics and mechanical engineering," said one student. Nevertheless, the university is certainly attempting to strengthen its science departments, starting with the establishment of a medical school in 2011. The idea is that it will raise the profile of the university in the scientific community and enlarge the number of opportunities in the field for both undergraduate and graduate students. It also means greater research opportunities for the more entrepreneurial students.

The university also offers an honors program, available through first-year application. Students who achieve high scores during their time at Hofstra are also invited to join the Honors College. During the first year, honors students enroll in a program called Culture and Expression, which consists of two courses per semester that are often used to introduce students to the art of small class discussions. The idea is that students learn from professors and from each other through debate and discussions, not just through lectures. In addition, students can also enroll in Honors Housing, creating an intellectually stimulating community both inside and outside of the classrooms.

Similar to most universities, Hofstra has a lengthy list of distributional requirements, which are courses that students must take before graduation. They are designed to expose students to a variety of academic fields. These courses include humanities, natural science, social science, and cross-culture, very similar to the undergraduate requirements in other colleges. What is unique about Hofstra is the need to complete classes in interdisciplinary studies, meaning courses that combine contents from different fields of study. "I know some people think it is a pain to complete all the required classes," said one student. "I think they can be tedious, but you still have some flexibility; you are likely to find a few classes that you enjoy."

The classes at Hofstra are relatively small, compared to other universities of similar size. As to the difficulties of classes, they tend to vary. "If you do not want to have too much work, talk to people who have taken the classes with the same professor before to learn about the work load before you take the class," said one student. "It is all about researching about your classes before enrolling in them." Many professors can be very helpful, as long as the student reaches out to them. "Professors are friendly, but it is not like they are going to approach you if you don't understand anything. You need to be proactive," said one student. Overall, students believe that they have access to a very good undergraduate education.

Hofstra does have a competitive admissions process. In fact, less than 60 percent of students are accepted every year. According to students, the university boasts people of great talent and abilities. "You'll find some really intelligent people here," said one student. "And a lot of people have unique talents in music or art. It is really amazing."

Hempstead and New York

Hempstead, where Hofstra is situated, is on Long Island. For students, activities around the immediate area are limited. Of course, given the large student population, there are plenty of parties happening around campus. However, overall, the village does not offer much beyond a small collection of bars and restaurants. The good news is that New York City is only half an hour away by train. "I go to the city all the time," said one student. "Even if you are on Long Island, the public transportation is very convenient in getting you to the city." Once students are in Manhattan, of course, there are plenty of things to do, from concerts to shopping to the great nightlife of New York City.

> **"You'll find some really intelligent people here."**

Over 4,000 students live in Hofstra's residential halls, which range from the traditional dorms to apartments. The university offers residences in six different locations, all of which are conveniently located with easy access to classrooms. Despite the large number of options, the quality of living arrangement is very similar, and students are mostly satisfied, though not overly enthusiastic. "The dorms are what you would expect for college: small but adequate," said one student. While university residences are highly recommended for freshmen so that they can meet more people and become used to the college environment, many upperclassmen move off campus into the surrounding apartments and houses. "I think it is important that people learn to live completely independently. I think you are still sheltered when you live in dorms," said one student.

There are more than 20 dining halls, cafés, and restaurants on the campus of Hofstra. The school runs more than a dozen of those facilities, thus offering a large number of choices. However, as students point out, the variety of options does not mean that the food is great. "I have to go off campus for dining a few times a week," said one student. "The food is fine, but it gets boring and repetitive after a while."

Greek life is an important part of social life at Hofstra as there are a large number of fraternities and sororities on campus. Nevertheless, students who are not interested in them can find plenty of other social opportunities with different clubs, organizations, or simply people they meet in classes or around campus.

Urban and Suburban

The fact that Hofstra falls between an urban and a suburban university is a great selling point. Students are able to enjoy the relative quietness of a Long Island village while being less than an hour away from one of the busiest cities in the world. As a major university with a large number of research centers, academic opportunities abound for students, making Hofstra an excellent choice to spend four years of your life.
—*Xiaohang Liu*

FYI

If you come to Hofstra, you'd better bring "school spirit."
What is the typical weekend schedule? "Go to NYC."
If I could change one thing about Hofstra, I'd "change the distributional requirements."
Three things every student at Hofstra should do before graduating are "go to Dutch Festival, go to NYC often, and visit the rest of Long Island, too."

Ithaca College

Address: 100 Job Hall, Ithaca, NY 14850-7020
Phone: 607-274-3124
E-mail address: admission@ithaca.edu
Web site URL: www.ithaca.edu
Year Founded: 1892
Private or Public: Private
Religious Affiliation: None
Location: Suburban
Number of Applicants: 11,235
Percent Accepted: 74%
Percent Accepted who enroll: 22%
Number Entering: 1,797
Number of Transfers Accepted each Year: 143
Middle 50% SAT range: M: 540–630, CR: 530–630, Wr: Unreported
Middle 50% ACT range: Unreported
Early admission program EA/ED/None: None

Percentage accepted through EA or ED: NA
EA and ED deadline: NA
Regular Deadline: 1-Feb
Application Fee: $60
Full time Undergraduate enrollment: 6,260
Total enrollment: 11,999
Percent Male: 45%
Percent Female: 55%
Total Percent Minority or Unreported: 11%
Percent African-American: 3%
Percent Asian/Pacific Islander: 4%
Percent Hispanic: 4%
Percent Native-American: <1%
Percent International: 2%
Percent in-state/out of state: 46%/54%
Percent from Public HS: 75%
Retention Rate: 84%
Graduation Rate 4-year: 71%

Graduation Rate 6-year: 76%
Percent Undergraduates in On-campus housing: 70%
Number of official organized extracurricular organizations: 172
3 Most popular majors: Communication Studies, Visual and Performing Arts, Business/Marketing
Student/Faculty ratio: 12:1
Average Class Size: 16
Percent of students going to grad school: 40%
Tuition and Fees: $30,606
In-State Tuition and Fees if different: No difference
Cost for Room and Board: $11,162
Percent receiving financial aid out of those who apply: 90%
Percent receiving financial aid among all students: 85%

Originally a music conservatory, Ithaca College now boasts five schools that offer its 6,324 undergraduates a comprehensive education in a number of fields, from communications to health sciences. Although the campus in scenic Upstate New York is small, students find that its size cultivates a friendly atmosphere. Through a number of organizations and campus-wide events, Ithaca encourages students to support local businesses and engage in outdoor activities.

Communication Is Key

Ithaca's most popular majors lie in communication, journalism, and similar programs. Its communications school is known internationally, offering its students a choice of eight undergraduate programs and seven different minors. A sophomore in the journalism program said, "I'm always surprised by the alumni connections," claiming that it is not uncommon for famous alums like CEO of Disney Bob Iger to return to Ithaca to give talks. "For being the size we are, I'm always impressed by how far the people who have come here have gone," he added.

Although it has branched out to offer many programs, IC has stayed true to its musical roots. Many students have noted that the music school has the most rigorous program, adding that the music education program is especially challenging because it requires students to learn multiple instruments. "Those kids always seem to be running around," one student observed. The demands of the music school means that IC's practice rooms are usually booked, making it difficult for others to use them.

Even though it's a small liberal arts school, students do not find the science department lacking. One junior noted, "The science department is good. The equipment is up to scale and the professors are always willing to help with open lab," adding that funding seemed to be high for premeds and those studying physical therapy and biochemistry. An environmental science major said that while she was initially concerned that the liberal arts school might be short of funding for science majors, she has found that it isn't underfunded or lacking resources. Ithaca also offers many ways for students to get more involved in the sciences, she said, explaining that "There are tons of internships and environmental jobs around town that [seek] Ithaca environmental science students."

Occupy Wall Street 101

Starting in fall 2013, Ithaca has instituted the Integrative Core Curriculum (ICC), which requires all incoming students to pick one of six themes—Identities; Inquiry, Imagination, and Innovation; Mind, Body, Spirit; The Quest for a Sustainable Future; A World of Systems; and Power and Injustice—which they will take classes in throughout their time in college. To complete their first year's ICC requirements, freshmen took seminars on a number of unusual topics. One freshman said that he enjoyed his seminar, "The Indie and the Improvised," in which students learned about the corporate system and its role in creating a sustainable future. According to him, many of the ICC seminars stress social awareness. "It's very Occupy Wall Street."

Gorges View

When they aren't studying, IC students enjoy participating in the many clubs and activities that promote outdoor living. A lot of people enjoy visiting the gorges and admiring the waterfalls and some student groups like Outdoor Adventure Learning Community organize trips that go hiking, kayaking, and camping. The trails in the IC Natural Lands provide the perfect place for runners to enjoy a scenic, albeit hilly, jog. It's easy to explore the trails for hours, one student remarked.

Food, Glorious Food

Ithaca has three dining halls: Towers, which students describe as a typical college dining hall; Terraces, which has a more "home-cooked" feeling; and Campus Center, which most students agree has the worst food and atmosphere. One student said that when he eats in Campus Center, he feels like "a senior in an old people's home."

> **"It's very Occupy Wall Street."**

In addition to meal swipes for the dining halls, students on the meal plan are also eligible for Bonus Bucks, which are redeemable in campus stores and dining halls. However, spend wisely! Some students have found that their Bonus Bucks run out quickly because the food is expensive.

Ithaca has more restaurants per capita than New York City, so there are plenty of options to choose from when dining hall food doesn't hit the spot. Most students grab food in IC's college town, Commons, which is home to lots of small businesses, local craftsmen, and chain stores. Across the way from Commons is Cornell's College-town, which also has a number of eateries geared towards college students.

The Performing Arts

Ithaca's students are big on performing arts. In addition to performances done by the music school students, there are weekly open mic nights and open improv nights, comedy club performances, and theater productions and concerts daily. One student highly recommends taking a break from partying to catch a show. "If you decide one weekend to go see [a performance] instead of going out, it's totally worth it."

A cappella is especially popular amongst students, the most well-known group being Ithacapella. This all-male group has four shows each year, which always sell out. Students who are lucky enough to get a seat at an Ithacappella show can enter into a raffle, and the group personally serenades the winner.

Getting Involved

Besides the Cortaca Jug, the wildly popular annual football game between the IC Bombers and the SUNY-Cortland Red Dragons, sports don't play a large role in campus life. However, that doesn't mean sports are non-existent. Students who don't play on any of IC's Division III teams can get involved in either club or intramural sports. Some students say that the competition on the intramural teams, although friendly, can get fierce. "Intramurals are like the team that's trying too hard in gym class."

In addition to a wide variety of pre-professional clubs, students also get very involved in the campus media such as IC's weekly newspaper, the *Ithacan*, the college radio station, and student TV shows. One student observed, "There are always people running around with cameras." Many of Ithaca's clubs promote environmental awareness. One student noted that it seemed like the majority of campus is really committed to going green and staying green. The Gardening Club gives students the opportunity to grow produce in a community-supported garden, and alternate spring break trips are offered which include environmental service.

The Weekend

The weekends see many students leave campus. Those with cars, mostly juniors and seniors, take advantage of the weekend to explore Ithaca and its surrounding areas. Because parking for freshmen is very expensive and inconvenient, they usually stay on or near campus, relying on public transportation to travel any farther. Since Ithaca has no Greek life, those who want to go to frat parties usually crash Cornell parties.

Although alcohol and marijuana definitely have a presence on campus, it is very easy for students not to participate. In addition to watching student performances, many students choose to visit The Pub, a popular place to buy food, do homework, and hang out. IC After Dark also provides alternatives on Friday and Saturday night parties.

Apples Everywhere

Of all the events aimed to encourage students to support local businesses, perhaps one of the most popular is the Apple Fest. Each fall, local farmers come to Commons and bring their apples to a large farmer's market. In addition to eating everything from apple cider to apple pie, students can also enjoy the work of local artists. A junior said that every year, "an obscene amount of people comes." Similar to the annual Apple Fest, but not quite as popular amongst students are the Ithaca Chili Cook-Off and the Winter Festival, which features a chowder cook-off.

Straight Out of an L.L. Bean Catalogue

Ithaca is not known for its diversity. Some students characterize the primarily white student body as very hipster and artsy. "The dress here is definitely Upstate New York. You see a lot of L.L. Bean boots and Patagonia. Everyone is very trendy." However, while the campus lacks ethnic diversity, most students agree that it is full of very open-minded people with diversity in creative interests. Speaking to the accepting nature of Ithaca, a student said, "We're a very accepting, go with the flow kind of campus." Most students can agree that the friendly culture unifies everyone at Ithaca.—*Sarah Bruley*

FYI

Three things every student at Ithaca should do before graduating are "jump in the gorges, go to Apple Fest and get serenaded at an Ithacapella concert."
If you come to Ithaca, you better bring "an umbrella and some rain boots."
What differentiates Ithaca the most from other colleges is "its awesome music scene and passionate students."

The Juilliard School

Address: 60 Lincoln Center Plaza, New York, NY 10023-6588	**Early admission program EA/ED/None:** None	**Graduation Rate 4-year:** 80%
Phone: 212-799-2000 ext.223	**Percentage accepted through EA or ED:** NA	**Graduation Rate 6-year:** 83%
E-mail address: publications@juilliard.edu	**EA and ED deadline:** NA	**Percent Undergraduates in On-campus housing:** 56%
Web site URL: www.juilliard.edu	**Regular Deadline:** 1-Dec	**Number of official organized extracurricular organizations:** 5
Year Founded: 1905	**Application Fee:** $100	
Private or Public: Private	**Full time Undergraduate enrollment:** 510	**3 Most popular majors:** Piano and Organ, Stringed Instruments, Voice and Opera
Religious Affiliation: None	**Total enrollment:** 649	
Location: Urban	**Percent Male:** 53%	
Number of Applicants: 2,416	**Percent Female:** 47%	**Student/Faculty ratio:** 5:1
Percent Accepted: 8%	**Total Percent Minority or Unreported:** 63%	**Average Class Size:** 6
Percent Accepted who enroll: 71%	**Percent African-American:** 4%	**Percent of students going to grad school:** Unreported
Number Entering: 130	**Percent Asian/Pacific Islander:** 11%	**Tuition and Fees:** $32,180
Number of Transfers Accepted each Year: Unreported	**Percent Hispanic:** 4%	**In-State Tuition and Fees if different:** No difference
	Percent Native-American: <1%	**Cost for Room and Board:** $12,280
Middle 50% SAT range: Not Considered	**Percent International:** 17%	**Percent receiving financial aid out of those who apply:** 85%
	Percent in-state/out of state: 89%/11%	
Middle 50% ACT range: Not Considered	**Percent from Public HS:** Unreported	**Percent receiving financial aid among all students:** Unreported
	Retention Rate: Unreported	

The Juilliard School, located at Lincoln Center in New York City, is a conservatory style post-secondary institution founded in 1905 that trains undergraduate and graduate students in dance, music, and drama. Juilliard has an 8% acceptance rate of students who apply and undergo a rigorous audition process to ensure that Juilliard hones the best talent in the performing arts. It is not a surprise, therefore, that Juilliard is one of the top-performing arts conservatories in the world.

Huge Talent in a Tiny Campus

Located in the performing arts capital of the world, The Juilliard School has produced hundreds of top-notch artists from its two-building campus in New York City. Distinguished alumni include world-class violinist Itzhak Perlman, groundbreaking choreographer Paul Taylor, and award-winning actor Robin Williams. Juilliard, a conservatory school of about 1,000 students, is located in Manhattan's Upper West Side at Lincoln Center, home to New York Philharmonic, the Metropolitan Opera, and New York City Ballet. The conservatory's close proximity to renowned performance companies provides Juilliard students with valuable connections and work-study opportunities. While Juilliard's music division is the largest program, the dance and drama programs are much smaller yet equally reputable.

Preparing for the Professional Path . . . and Also Going to College

Entering Juilliard is extremely competitive as auditions are the determining factor and the school has only an 8% acceptance rate. Upon entering the school, the students are immersed in their art, spending up to 14 hours in class and rehearsals before starting their academic work. Juilliard's academic program differs substantially from that of liberal arts colleges because most classes Juilliard students take are related to their artistic division and rarely if ever do they take math or sciences courses. All Juilliard students complete a core humanities class, which most students describe as an English class. Students are subsequently required to take one academic course a year that is not related to their division, courses that are considered electives. There are a few opportunities to take classes at Columbia or Barnard, but most students do not have the time. A music student said, "Humanities courses are very intense and I think some of the teachers forget we're there for music. Finally [you] finish your work and you have to go practice." Finding a balance among academic coursework with technique classes, rehearsals, private lessons, and individual practice is extremely hard according to students. Juilliard academic courses are small, around 15 students. Several students noted that the academic coursework is very rigorous. One student said, "[The] top-notch professors, most of them went to Ivy League schools and expect Ivy League work."

As a result of the rigorous workloads, Juilliard's social life varies among the divisions. Music majors have to spend their weekend days practicing according to one student: "It's usually practicing during the day. . . . Not everyone does or can go out at night." Some students said that while some students do opt to go out on the weekends, others spend their Saturday nights practicing and rehearsing. The dance and drama majors are perceived to have a more flexible weekend schedule. A dance student said, "The dancers are kind of the crazy ones, going out, dressing up and having fun. A lot of musicians don't really go out on the weekends." She added that many students go to upperclassmen off-campus apartments for house parties or see performances downtown, for which they can get free or discounted tickets. A drama student said that "It's hard to be at Juilliard and not be social—at least for the drama students." Yet he also said that students are very balanced when it comes to drinking because there is no time to recover from a couple of nights out in a row and this would take a toll on one's schoolwork. A music student stated that students have fun but "[they] never let partying get in the way of their goals."

Juilliard's campus consists of two connected buildings, the main building where classes meet and the dormitory building. All freshmen are required to live in the dormitories and each is paired with a roommate of a different division to promote social interactions among the different divisions that can end up polarized. Some upperclassmen remain in the dorms but most usually move off campus to Upper West Side apartments. Students generally feel safe on campus, and they feel safe to practice until late at night because they can enter the dorm building without having to go outside.

The Music Men (and Women)
The Music division is the largest division in the school, consisting of about 600 students and incorporating vocal/opera and jazz studies in addition to traditional orchestral instrumental study. At the audition final round students perform in front of the faculty, and each student is chosen by a faculty member to pursue private instruction. The music student's relationship with his private instructor is very important as it helps foster individual improvement and collaboration with the teacher. The relationship provides the student with opportunities for further music study outside of school. As one student described, "[Students] go where the teacher teaches in the summer to continue studying all year," although another option is participating in summer music festivals. During the school year, however, many students form extracurricular small chamber music ensembles and can obtain work experience through job opportunities offered through Juilliard's career office to play at weddings or other events. Another popular work-study job available at Juilliard is ushering at local theaters.

One student said that the general perception of music study at Juilliard is that students "hop around the hallway and play instruments" yet she also emphasizes the difficulty of her field of study. Required classes include private lessons, piano class, music theory (which also involves musical composition), ear training, and music history. Students participate in an orchestra, which allows students of different grades to collaborate and interact. A first-year student remarked, "Upperclassmen were very welcoming; since this school is so small there is more socializing among all the classes." Apart from the orchestral and music ensembles, however, the music division does not have a division-wide community as the division is relatively large and comprised of many sub-divisions based on instrument type. Nevertheless, most of the students interviewed agreed that Juilliard students display a lot of pride in their school.

Home Is Where the Barre Is

The Dance division is the most physically demanding discipline offered at Juilliard, and the exertion only complicates the balance between academic work and dance classes with only 15-minute breaks between classes. Entering the Juilliard dance department is physically trying—right from the three- to four-hour audition, where students take a ballet and modern dance class before the first cut, and those who qualify perform a choreographed solo. Students who pass the second cut then experience a rehearsal-setting class where they display their skills in partnering and learning new choreography before the final round, which is an interview. The extremely selective dance department admits about 25 students a year. One student said that the auditions were "nerve-wracking in that they make cuts."

As a result, class sizes are very small, with an entire grade participating in the same modern class for example. Dance students have to take a number of required courses apart from ballet and modern technique classes, including anatomy, dance history, and literature in music (a music theory course taught by a composer rather than a musician). Rehearsals, which can last late into the night, and performances also factor into students' grades. Students at the end of the day are exhausted; on weekends many students sleep in and try to go out on weekends, although they find it difficult.

As is common in the performing arts world, many of the dance students in a class already know each other from prior dance schools and summer dance intensives. Nevertheless the small group of dancers creates an intimate community that allows freshmen to interact with sophomore and seniors alike. Freshmen start to interact with seniors through Freshmen Initiation in which freshmen are paired with a senior and find out who the senior is only after completing a series of (usually embarrassing) tasks. Another tradition is that seniors celebrate the last Wednesday of their college career by running around the dance studios naked.

All Their World Is a Stage

The Drama division is the smallest division in the school, and it also includes a playwright subdivision that accepts only three students a year. A short personal statement determines if a student is granted an audition that includes a recitation of two Shakespearean and two contemporary monologues; the total audition lasts the entire day for some students between callbacks and waiting periods. Once accepted, drama students enter a close-knit group where drama traditions and stories are kept secret, although a dance student mentioned that drama first-year students visit Times Square and "do some ridiculous acts."

While a drama class consists of under 20 students, the class is divided into four groups and different groups of four to five students take classes together. Drama students take a wide variety of classes including improvisation, miming, clowning with masks, stage combat, and diction. A surprising requirement is three 90-minute sessions of strenuous physical workout, which include tai chi and yoga. Concerning the workouts a drama student said, "[It] makes a massive difference when you're in classes 14 hours a day. You can endure longer." Not only do drama students endure long weekdays, they also have Saturday rehearsals, which last up to six hours. There may be less pressure for rehearsals when there are no performances taking place, but the professors increase the workload with more poems to learn or vocal skills to practice. "We're never taking it easy," says one drama student.

"Once you're in . . . you don't have to outdo each other. We already know you're one of the best."

Students may have endured a grueling audition, but they do not audition for shows while in college. Instead, drama professors select students for specific roles in performances based on a student's fit in a role or a student's need to be challenged. The teachers' close relationship has provided students with surprising benefits. One student said, "[I was surprised at] how successfully the teachers have brought out qualities and useful tools that I already have. They drag things out that nobody could have expected I have."

Attributes Across the Artistic Arenas

Contrary to popular belief, students from all divisions agree that there is little competition among students. One student said that if there is any competition present, it is mostly internal competition to improve one's skills. Another student added that "Once you're in [Juilliard] . . . you don't have to outdo each other. We already know you're one of the best."Juilliard also has a collaborative attitude among the divisions. The school hosts a ChoreoComp where third-year composers create music that dance majors use for choreography.

The school holds auditions across the country, but there are many international students at Juilliard as well, showing the school's commitment to recruiting the best artists to go on to bright futures in the arts. Juilliard students are focused on their career from the start, cognizant of the heavy work involved. Students recommend others to see as many in-school performances as possible because of the high caliber of talent. Yet they also make sure to take advantage of New York City to reap the benefits of living at the heart of a vibrating arts culture

that is even more accessible through Juilliard's resources.

Encore Remarks

The Juilliard School is extremely selective because they are creating the next generation of top-notch artists. Juilliard students undergo an intense liberal arts program in addition to their artistic specialties. The students' coursework is integral to professional development as they hone their skills and artistry. As rising professional artists, Juilliard students are extraordinarily dedicated to their crafts. Some students succeed in balancing work and play, but for many students their work is also their play because their desire to reach their potential is the ultimate game to win.—*Clarissa Marzán*

FYI

If you come to Juilliard you'd better bring "ear plugs (the musicians practice all the time)."
If you come to Juilliard you'd better leave behind "your math and science textbooks."
If there was one thing I could change about Julliard it would be to "make the music division smaller."

Manhattanville College

Address: 2900 Purchase Street, Purchase, NY 10577	**Percentage accepted through EA or ED:** Unreported	**Graduation Rate 4-year:** 51%
Phone: 914-323-5464	**EA and ED deadline:** 1-Dec	**Graduation Rate 6-year:** 57%
E-mail address: admissions@mville.edu	**Regular Deadline:** 1-Mar	**Percent Undergraduates in On-campus housing:** 76%
Web site URL: www.manhattanville.edu	**Application Fee:** $65	**Number of official organized extracurricular organizations:** 48
Year Founded: 1841	**Full time Undergraduate enrollment:** 1,845	
Private or Public: Private	**Total enrollment:** 3,022	**3 Most popular majors:**
Religious Affiliation: None	**Percent Male:** 33%	Business, Psychology, Visual & Performing Arts
Location: Urban	**Percent Female:** 67%	**Student/Faculty ratio:** 11:1
Number of Applicants: 3,927	**Total Percent Minority or Unreported:** 47%	**Average Class Size:** 14
Percent Accepted: 50%	**Percent African-American:** 7%	**Percent of students going to grad school:** Unreported
Percent Accepted who enroll: 27%	**Percent Asian/Pacific Islander:** 2%	**Tuition and Fees:** $31,620
Number Entering: 535	**Percent Hispanic:** 15%	**In-State Tuition and Fees if different:** No difference
Number of Transfers Accepted each Year: Unreported	**Percent Native-American:** <1%	**Cost for Room and Board:** $13,040
Middle 50% SAT range: M: 500–610, CR: 500–620, Wr: Unreported	**Percent International:** 8%	**Percent receiving financial aid out of those who apply:** 94%
Middle 50% ACT range: 20–25	**Percent in-state/out of state:** 64%/36%	**Percent receiving financial aid among all students:** 68%
Early admission program EA/ED/None: ED	**Percent from Public HS:** Unreported **Retention Rate:** 74%	

With its 100-acre campus located in Purchase, New York, a small town thirty minutes from New York City, Manhattanville College offers its students the intimate academic environment of a small college while encouraging them to explore the diversity, resources, and opportunities of the nearby city. Manhattanville students receive a distinctively personal and well-rounded liberal arts education and do not need to worry about a lack of activities to keep them busy—even if they have to travel the thirty minutes to find them.

All Planned Out: Preceptorial and Portfolio

Although Manhattanville is a small school with only 1,800 full-time undergrads, it offers over fifty majors and minors, as well as the option to design your own. As one student studying dance and business noted, "I looked at all the schools in the tri-state area. Manhattanville was the only one that said I could major in Irish Step Dancing." All students are required to have a minor in addition to a major. Some students said the choice gained in the number of majors is lost in the limitations imposed by many distributional requirements. Students must take six credits from four of five areas: mathematics and science, social sciences, humanities, languages, and fine arts. But an upperclassman offered advice, saying that these involved requirements can actually make a course load "less intimidating when your semester is not entirely consumed by classes specific to your major."

> "I looked at all the schools in the tri-state area. Manhattanville was the only one that said I could major in Irish Step Dancing."

Apart from the distributional requirements, all freshmen take the Preceptorial, a yearlong seminar that functions to help students develop college-level thinking, reading, and writing skills, introduce them to important topics in various fields, and guide them in their studies at Manhattanville. Students may choose among Preceptorials covering a diverse array of issues in current events. The instructor of a Preceptorial is also the students' freshman-year academic advisor who will be one of the many faculty members who "really cares about the education of each individual student"

throughout college. Manhattanville students really do gush about the degree of personal attention given to them: "I have gotten to know all of my professors personally, and I can go to them whenever I need help or mentoring."

Another distinctive feature of the Manhattanville education is the Portfolio System. Each student meets with a faculty advisor to plot his or her academic path at the beginning of freshman year. In the spring of each following year, students meet again with their advisors to assess their progress, adjust their plans, and put their best work into a portfolio. At the end of senior year, faculty members evaluate the students' portfolios before allowing them to graduate. Students find that the portfolio actually helps them greatly during their studies because it forces them to plan ahead, as well as after graduation, because they have already gathered and reflected upon their best work and are therefore prepared for graduate school or a job search.

Outside the Classroom

While Manhattanville's academic program and small size create a great sense of academic closeness, the campus, in terms of social life, is not very close-knit. This is due in part to the proximity and appeal of the city, but also because many of the students at Manhattanville are from the tri-state area and either commute daily or go home often on the weekends. As a result, the campus is not as lively as many other colleges on the weekends.

There are, however, a number of major activities throughout each year that attract most of the student body, including Fall Fest, a carnival-like music festival, and its spring counterpart, Quad Jam. Reid Hall—better known as "the Castle"—is the site of the "Castle parties," formals in the winter and spring. The Castle parties bring students together, as an upperclassman reflected: "Most students go to the formals, and they all have different themes, which makes each one special." In addition, there are over thirty clubs and organizations ranging across broad interests, from the Latin Dance Club to the History Club to the Punk Rock Appreciation Club. Students said one of the most popular activities is writing for *The Touchstone*, the Manhattanville newspaper. The student government acts as a liaison between the students and the administration, often planning activities to try to keep the campus lively on the weekends for the students who remain on campus.

But the outward migration of students on the weekends is not to say that the facilities and dorms are lacking. Students have a number of housing options, as there are four dorms, all of which are coed and said to be comfortable. Spellman, a "dry hall," is the freshmen dormitory. Upperclassmen can choose from Founders, Damman, and Tenney, the latter two of which offer various suite-style living options. Students can choose between different-size suites, with the option of both singles and doubles that share a bathroom and common room. Students have a choice between meal plans that vary in the number of meals taken in Benziger Dining Hall and "meal points" redeemable at local cafés and a pub. Dorms also have communal kitchens that students can use if they get tired of dining hall fare.

Manhattanville to Manhattan

Manhattanville is unique in the extent to which it encourages its students to drift from the quiet serenity of Purchase once in a while. The college sponsors trips to New York City that are often integrated into academic coursework. These trips also give students a chance to decide if they truly want to experience life in the city, in which case Manhattanville offers a Semester in New York City program. Participants who are fortunate enough to make the cut live in the city, taking classes taught by Manhattanville professors and gaining work experience in internship positions at major companies located in the Big Apple.

There are also trips whose sole purpose is simply to give students a chance to explore the fun side of New York City, through events like a cruise around Manhattan, visits to the Metropolitan Museum of Art, and ice-skating in Central Park. The Office of Student Activities subsidizes some of the trips, allowing students to see shows like *The Lion King* on Broadway and the Radio City Christmas Spectacular for affordable prices. Students often also visit New York City on their own, taking in the sights and just enjoying themselves on the weekends, a possibility thanks to the Metro-North train connecting Purchase to the city.

Manhattanville is ideal for students who seek personal attention, opportunities in a nearby dynamic city, and a serene campus to return to after an exciting weekend. As one student put it, "The best thing to do is just walk around [New York City]. It's so exciting. Then I get to come back up to Manhattanville where I feel so safe."—*Michelle Yu*

FYI

If you come to Manhattanville, you'd better bring "a lot of Tupperware, mac 'n' cheese, and ramen noodles."

What is the typical weekend schedule? "Going out to the city, staying in the dorm and drifting from room to room with friends, or going to the pub to eat and watch TV."

If I could change one thing about Manhattanville, I'd "[improve] the lack of events on campus."

Three things every student at Manhattanville should do before graduating are "go to all the Castle parties and sports events, go to the White Plains Diner at 3 a.m., and camp out on the quad."

New York University

Address: 22 Washington Square North, New York, NY 10011
Phone: 212-998-4500
E-mail address: admission@nyu.edu
Web site URL: www.nyu.edu
Year Founded: 1831
Private or Public: Private
Religious Affiliation: None
Location: Urban
Number of Applicants: 37,245
Percent Accepted: 32%
Percent Accepted who enroll: 39%
Number Entering: 4,648
Number of Transfers Accepted each Year: Unreported
Middle 50% SAT range: M: 630–720, CR: 620–720, Wr: 620–720
Middle 50% ACT range: 28–31

Early admission program EA/ED/None: ED
Percentage accepted through EA or ED: 33%
EA and ED deadline: 1-Nov
Regular Deadline: 13-Jul
Application Fee: $65
Full time Undergraduate enrollment: 19,482
Total enrollment: 20,965
Percent Male: 40%
Percent Female: 60%
Total Percent Minority or Unreported: 53%
Percent African-American: 4%
Percent Asian/Pacific Islander: 19%
Percent Hispanic: 8%
Percent Native-American: 0%
Percent International: 6%
Percent in-state/out of state: 64%/36%
Percent from Public HS: 65%

Retention Rate: 92%
Graduation Rate 4-year: 77%
Graduation Rate 6-year: Unreported
Percent Undergraduates in On-campus housing: 52%
Number of official organized extracurricular organizations: 350
3 Most popular majors: Drama, Finance, Liberal Arts
Student/Faculty ratio: 12:1
Average Class Size: 15
Percent of students going to grad school: 24%
Tuition and Fees: $37,372
In-State Tuition and Fees if different: No difference
Cost for Room and Board: $12,810
Percent receiving financial aid out of those who apply: 80%
Percent receiving financial aid among all students: 53%

New York University was founded in 1831 by Albert Gallatin with a goal to establish "in this immense and fast-growing city . . . a system of rational and practical education fitting for all and graciously open to all." Today's NYU students agree that this goal has been met. "NYU has a variety of different schools that provide different types of education and skills," said one freshman. "It truly has something for everyone."

Fourteen Schools, Fourteen Stereotypes

The university comprises 18 different schools, colleges, and divisions that specialize in everything from the arts to business to nothing in particular. "Tisch kids work on film and production; the College kids are into liberal arts; Gallatin kids don't know what they want to do and are pretty much free to make it up as they go along," summarized one junior. The university's roughly 20,000 undergraduates are distributed amongst the schools—but not evenly. The majority of undergraduates enroll in the College of Arts and Sciences (CAS).

When asked to explain the typical NYU student, one Tisch student said the task was impossible. "I can't define a typical NYU student without splitting the stereotype into schools," he explained.

Despite the clear breakdown of these conceptions, students praised the university for fostering interaction between students, regardless of school. "We live together. We don't get separated. The lack of separation spreads into our social lives," said one sophomore. Others agreed. "There are a lot of misconceptions, but NYU is really just one school."

Size Isn't Everything

At a university this large, you might assume students are disjointed and separated. But at NYU, even without a central campus, there is something about these "Violets" that keeps everyone together.

"NYU is not too big," concluded one Stern student. "It's very possible to know a lot of people and be very involved, and by being involved, to get to know a lot more people. It's definitely what you make of it." Other students agreed, stressing that students have to be proactive to take full advantage of all that the university has to offer. "As long as you stand up and get involved it's very possible to know people high up and get your face recognized," said one senior.

> "There's not really a sport that brings us together, but NYU kids love NYU. There's a lot of school spirit here."

Despite the size of its population, students say NYU never fails to cater to its students' diverse and eclectic appetites. "We're one of the top schools in the country for providing vegan and vegetarian options at all our dining halls, and kosher options as well," said one junior. "They observe Shabbat in one of the dining halls every week." In addition to more traditional dining hall experiences, students can eat at places like Chick-fil-A, Quiznos, Dunkin' Donuts, and Starbucks. Overall, students praised the university for providing, if not gourmet food, at least a wealth of options. "You can't complain for the most part."

The City That Never Sleeps . . . and the Students That Don't Either

To say that NYU doesn't offer your typical college experience is an understatement. With the heart of the university located in hip, bustling Greenwich Village, students have the luxury of spending four years with New York City as their workplace and playground. And since the university has seriously improved its transportation system in recent years, students at NYU freely engage in the wealth of opportunities in and around their sprawling campus.

"The social life is great, though it's not your normal college scene," explained one senior. Although NYU features some Greek life, there is not much of a formalized network of fraternal organizations on campus. Students described its members as the "few and the proud," saying that they are often indistinguishable from the general population. The university nightlife is primarily focused on the city's various offerings. "There aren't any house parties or frat parties, but you go bar and club hopping."

Some students complained that the social life is overly centered on the city itself. "You go to clubs and a lot of them are big student spots, but unless it's a 'college night,' a lot of times, I'm not even sure who my peers are," said one freshman. "It's really strange that way. The nightlife culture almost forces you to arrive with a fake ID in hand." However, she was quick to add—"Of course, it's fun. Unlike my friends at other colleges, I'm guaranteed a party come Friday or Saturday night . . . or even Tuesday night."

Sports fans might not be as fond of the fun offered up by NYU. Without a football team, the university lacks what some might consider an intrinsic element of any college experience. Though host to spectacle-drawing varsity sports teams like volleyball, basketball, fencing, and soccer, NYU students consistently fail to flock to the stands. "Attendance at sports events is, well, there really isn't attendance at sports events," said one junior. Yet despite lackluster athletic support, NYU students are by no means lacking in school spirit or university pride. "There's not really a sport that brings us together, but NYU kids love NYU. There's a lot of school spirit here."

But We Work Too!

NYU maintains much of its popular academic reputation courtesy of the Leonard N. Stern School of Business and Tisch School of the Arts. But students say the university's excellence reaches far beyond the likely targets. Many cited the economics department as an undiscovered NYU jewel. "We've been the Number One Dream School for a few years now," said one sophomore. "You don't get that way by focusing only on a small group of specialized students," she continued. "Obviously, the university is offering something for us all."

Other students were quick to explain deficiencies in the overall system. "I wish I had smaller classes," said one freshman. "As much as NYU tells you you're not just another number, with some professors it just seems that way." Many courses include lectures and smaller, weekly sessions led by teaching assistants (TAs). One CAS junior succinctly declared, "TAs are pretty much a regular thing here."

Gallatin is often cited as offering more opportunities for small seminars than CAS, but as students advance in their majors, they are given preference to enter seminars in CAS, each generally including roughly 20 students. "It's a university. Lectures are part of the definition of that term. It's just part of the deal, but as you get older, you have more opportunities to take intimate classes," explained one sophomore.

Shanghai? Ghana? Don't You Wanna?

Whether or not NYU offers the most opportunities for small classes, it is certainly the ideal school for a student looking to study abroad. The university offers study-abroad programs in over 25 countries—if you can bear to separate yourself from the bright city lights. Students from other colleges and universities are routinely offered opportunities to study abroad as part of NYU's expansive program. "Where else could you spend the semester in Shanghai or Ghana?" asked an enthusiastic junior. "It's just the best place to be for people who want to learn firsthand about other cultures."

NYU is famous (and infamous) for both its nightlife and its internships. Those looking to capitalize on a variety of resources, work on their dance moves, and master the Big Apple during their college years will find such a choice quite appealing.—*Nicholle Manners*

FYI

If you come to NYU, you'd better bring "a sense of openness because it's a very diverse school."

What's the typical weekend schedule? "Work during the day, party at night all through the weekend starting Thursday night."

If I could change one thing about NYU, I'd "improve financial aid and alumni support: excluding Stern."

Three things every student at NYU should do before graduating are "explore the city, study abroad, and meet lots of new people."

Parsons School of Design

Address: 65 Fifth Avenue, New York, NY 10011

Phone: 212-229-8910

E-mail address: parsadm@newschool.edu

Web site URL: www.parsons.edu

Year Founded: 1896

Private or Public: Private

Religious Affiliation: None

Location: Urban

Number of Applicants: 2,866

Percent Accepted: 63%

Percent Accepted who enroll: 82%

Number Entering: 1,473

Number of Transfers Accepted each Year: Unreported

Middle 50% SAT range: M: 490–620, CR: 480–600, Wr: 490–600

Middle 50% ACT range: 21–26

Early admission program EA/ED/None: None

Percentage accepted through EA or ED: NA

EA and ED deadline: NA

Regular Deadline: 1-Mar

Application Fee: $50

Full time Undergraduate enrollment: 3,745

Total enrollment: 4,191

Percent Male: 21%

Percent Female: 79%

Total Percent Minority or Unreported: 56%

Percent African-American: 6%

Percent Asian/Pacific Islander: 24%

Percent Hispanic: 13%

Percent Native-American: <1%

Percent International: 34%

Percent in-state/out of state: 27%/73%

Percent from Public HS: Unreported

Retention Rate: 83%

Graduation Rate 4-year: 51%

Graduation Rate 6-year: 71%

Percent Undergraduates in On-campus housing: 23%

Number of official organized extracurricular organizations: 25

3 Most popular majors: Visual and Performing Arts, Architecture, Business/Marketing

Student/Faculty ratio: 9:1

Average Class Size: 15

Percent of students going to grad school: Unreported

Tuition and Fees: $39,350

In-State Tuition and Fees if different: No difference

Cost for Room and Board: $15,260

Percent receiving financial aid out of those who apply: 91%

Percent receiving financial aid among all students: 51%

Do you ever dream about your name featured on white tents in Bryant Park during Fashion Week? Do you know you want to spend a life creating and designing but don't quite know how to do it? Do you watch *Project Runway* religiously? If you answered "YES!" to any of these questions, perhaps Parsons School of Design is the right place for you. Founded in 1896 as an art school, Parsons has a rich history of having the first undergraduate programs in disciplines like graphics design, interior design, and advertising. It is now part of The New School, a university network in New York City known for its avant-garde teaching style and unique philosophy. Parsons students enjoy the energy of New York City, the mentorship of notable faculty, and learn the necessary skills to enter the art world after graduation.

The Foundations and Beyond

Undergraduates at Parsons can graduate in four years and obtain either a Bachelor of Fine Arts or a Bachelor of Business Administration. Those who are particularly ambitious and desire a more varied education experience can opt for the five-year joint BFA and BA program, called the BAFA program. This program is hosted in conjunction with Eugene Lang College. Students are often overwhelmed by the changes that college brings and by the stimuli that a new environment provides. Parsons tackles this problem by having every freshman take "Foundation" courses. "They're mandatory for the BFA program. . . . Some of the stuff seems repetitive and dull, but it just made the classes that I took my sophomore year so much more rewarding and interesting," one junior said. The program ensures that students have the necessary technical and methodological understanding of art to succeed in future classes. These classes are broad enough to be applicable to whatever majors the students choose in the end, along with being designed to enhance visual thinking.

Some of the more popular majors at Parsons are Illustration, Design and Visual Communications, and Fashion Apparel Design. The Fashion Design department at Parsons is perhaps the most renowned—its graduates include fashion designers Donna Karan and Tom Ford, plus Tim Gunn, mentor to the designers on *Project Runway* and the former dean of this department. Students in this major are known to be "very cutthroat" and a sense of intense competition is omnipresent in these classrooms. "People are not only very secretive about what they're designing but are constantly trying to outdo each other," one Fashion Design major said. However, she added, "But some people are genuinely helpful and will give you ideas. I guess you just have to find the right crowd."

> **"You become a pro at finding free things to do. But otherwise you will be spending a lot of money on the weekends."**

Another program for students who are particularly driven and motivated is the Chase Scholars Program. Named for William Merritt Chase, the Impressionist painter who founded the art school that eventually became Parsons, Chase Scholars have a "strong interest in design, high academic achievement, and well-developed critical thinking skills but limited studio experience." Special scholarships are also given to those who get into the program.

Jet-Setting

If you start to feel a little overwhelmed by the competition at Parsons, you may want to consider going abroad. "Many juniors take a semester or the whole year to go abroad. I was in Paris the first semester this year. It was wonderful to be studying in a different culture!" one junior raved. Paris is a popular destination for juniors not only because "it's the only city that holds a candle to New York in terms of it being a fashion and art mecca," but because Parsons has a campus in Paris. Some areas of study in which Parsons Paris excels are Communication Design, Fashion Design, and Photography and Fine Arts. Other exchange programs that are available include the Chelsea College of Art and Design in London, Sydney College of the Arts in Australia, and Bezalel Academy of Art and Design in Jerusalem, Israel.

If you can't bear to leave New York for a semester but still want to go abroad, Parsons has an excellent international summer program. These Summer Intensive Studies are open to both Parsons students and non-Parsons students, and are typically five weeks long. Classes try to mesh the subject matter with the culture and history of the host country. For instance, the Summer Intensive Studies in Paris offered "Architecture and

Interiors of Paris: A Drawing Investigation and Photography in Paris."

"A Mini Version of New York"

Even if you don't go abroad, you will be exposed to different ways of thinking, and different cultures and backgrounds due to the diversity of people at Parsons. While there will be many resident New Yorkers in your classes, many students are from out of state and abroad. Parsons recognizes the importance of having a diverse learning environment and is particularly international-student-friendly. The summer before freshman year, international students attend the Summer Orientation Program for International Students (SOPIS). This is an opportunity for international students to get settled in a little early but also a chance to take English as a Foreign Language (ESL) classes and to learn about the city and how the American university system works. "Parsons is like a mini version of the city itself. There are so many people here from other places in the world—we're all learning and inspiring each other every day," one New York native said.

The Big Apple

Not uncommon for schools in large metropolises, Parsons lacks a central campus with greens and dorms. The main campus is in Greenwich Village and the other campus is in the Garment District—fittingly, the David M. Schwartz Fashion Education Center is located there. Parsons has a few residence halls for its students. The Marlton House is most famous for housing Beat poets in the 1960s. The most popular dorm is the Union Square Residence, where students have Union Square Park and its concerts, farmers markets, and shopping right at their doorstep. Freshmen primarily live in Loeb Hall and the 13th Street Residence. Meal plans are available and there are many options in terms of eating venues that Parsons students share with students from The New School.

While the residence halls save students the hassle of finding an apartment in Manhattan, many students choose to live off campus. "Moving off was the best thing for me; I live with someone who goes to NYU and it's been awesome. I'm more independent and I've learned how to cook!" one senior said. Because so many students move off campus, the social scene at Parsons is very fragmented and school spirit is a little weak. However, most students don't seem to mind this, for "there's always something to do in New York."

On or off campus, all students agree that New York is an expensive city to live in: "You become a pro at finding free things to do. But otherwise you will be spending a lot of money on the weekends." But New York serves as an inspiration and playground for all Parsons students. Endless galleries and museums, concerts and music, good places to eat, and the eclectic bar and clubbing scene are all taken advantage of. The fact that there are very few social opportunities on campus does not hinder these students from finding their own niche in the city. The power and the liveliness of New York City is integral to the Parsons experience—so if you think you can thrive in a bustling city life and manage the workload, Parsons may be the school for you!
—*Lee Komeda*

FYI
If you come to Parsons, you'd better bring "a good winter jacket, a fake ID, and a need for creative outlet!"
What's the typical weekend schedule? "Drink and smoke at a friend's apartment and go out to hit up a few bars. Or, alternatively, I could be in the studio working non-stop."
If I could change one thing about Parsons: "A central hangout spot would be great . . . also if the two campuses were closer together."
Three things you should do before graduating are "meet as many people and network for the future, participate in the fashion show, go to as many museums as possible."

Rensselaer Polytechnic Institute

Address: 110 Eighth Street, Troy, NY 12180-3590
Phone: 518-276-6216
E-mail address: admissions@rpi.edu
Web site URL: www.rpi.edu
Year Founded: 1824
Private or Public: Private
Religious Affiliation: None
Location: Suburban
Number of Applicants: 13,465
Percent Accepted: 40%
Percent Accepted who enroll: 21%
Number Entering: 1,154
Number of Transfers Accepted each Year: 199
Middle 50% SAT range: M: 670–750, CR: 610–700, Wr: 580–685
Middle 50% ACT range: 26–30
Early admission program EA/ED/None: ED
Percentage accepted through EA or ED: 47%

EA and ED deadline: 1-Nov
Regular Deadline: 15-Jan
Application Fee: $70
Full time Undergraduate enrollment: 5,407
Total enrollment: 5,431
Percent Male: 71%
Percent Female: 29%
Total Percent Minority or Unreported: 28%
Percent African-American: 3%
Percent Asian/Pacific Islander: 10%
Percent Hispanic: 5%
Percent Native-American: <1%
Percent International: 3%
Percent in-state/out of state: 38%/62%
Percent from Public HS: 74%
Retention Rate: 91%
Graduation Rate 4-year: 64%
Graduation Rate 6-year: 82%

Percent Undergraduates in On-campus housing: 63%
Number of official organized extracurricular organizations: 185
3 Most popular majors: Business, Computer Engineering, Electrical, Electronics and Communications Engineering
Student/Faculty ratio: 16:1
Average Class Size: Unreported
Percent of students going to grad school: 24%
Tuition and Fees: $41,600
In-State Tuition and Fees if different: No difference
Cost for Room and Board: $11,975
Percent receiving financial aid out of those who apply: 96%
Percent receiving financial aid among all students: 97%

O n the bank of the Hudson River sits Troy, NY, home to the Rensselaer Polytechnic Institute. A research university founded in 1824, RPI is widely considered one of the best engineering schools in the nation, and has been called a "new Ivy," thanks to its immense reputation. Trying to make sure its students (of engineering and other disciplines) leave RPI as well-rounded, intelligent individuals, the university certainly puts its students to work, and for them, it is definitely worth it.

A (Metric) Ton of Work

When asked why he chose RPI, one student simply said: "It sets you apart in the engineering world." RPI's stellar reputation and top-notch academic programs make it an appealing option for students interested in engineering and a host of other fields. Students can apply to one of five schools within the university: Science, Architecture, Engineering, Humanities and Social Sciences, or Management and Technology. The architecture program is praised for its professors and its small size—while the university enrolls over 5,000 undergraduates, the prestigious architecture school enrolls 60–70 freshmen per year. Those who make the cut gain access to RPI's lighting research center, one of the best in the country. While RPI is predominantly known as an engineering school, the school is working to further develop its programs in other areas. For instance, the new EMPAC (Experimental Media Performing Arts Center) will mix cutting-edge technology with the arts, a reflection of the growing diversification of academic options, and the Sustainability Studies program, once a possible minor at Rensselaer, is now a full-blown major that "humanities students can soon be a part of."

Slackers beware: RPI academics are intense. As one engineering student said: "It's definitely a lot harder than I thought it'd be.

They say it's hard, but it really is. They're not lying." It's common knowledge that students must spend at least 30 hours a week outside of class just to keep up with the basic material. Most people devote much more time than that, setting aside an entire day (9 a.m. to midnight) each week to catch up on work. At least the professors believe in curving. Though students' final grades are determined by how well they perform in comparison to their peers, competition is not cutthroat. While it does exist, some say "It's us against the teacher more than us against ourselves." Furthermore, the combination of a rigorous program and RPI's good name means that graduates are well prepared for the working world. Students praise the career center and the university as a whole for its focus on landing students enviable jobs after graduation.

The size of classes at RPI varies hugely depending on the nature of the class, "from small groups in recitation to 300 people in the intro chem lecture." All students in the engineering program must take a set of core classes, usually during their first three or four semesters. While students say that the relevance between these core classes and their specific major can seem doubtful at first, professors aim to make the courses applicable to all programs. "You might not know what it relates to when you take it, but longer down the road you get it," said one junior.

With rigorous programs and a large student body, RPI undergrads are encouraged to take a proactive stance in their education. "If you don't put out the effort, you're a number," said one student. Extensive class preparation is required, and students must learn a number of things on their own from the textbook. Students say it "goes both ways" in terms of professor accessibility—some are always available while others are constantly traveling the world. The university is known for offering undergraduates an abundance of research opportunities, and besides their specific fields of study, students happily note that "RPI definitely values that its engineers are pretty well-rounded people and scholars, for a tech school."

Bricks & Bread

Campus buildings boast the best of both worlds: on the outside, the gothic structures have a "traditional, collegiate look," while on the inside they offer cutting-edge technology. Most of the campus is wireless, and every classroom is set up so that students can plug in their laptops. The university even provides incoming freshmen with a personal laptop and wireless card.

The Quad, RPI's largest residence area, sits on the main campus. It houses upperclassmen in single, double, or triple rooms. There are also 10 residence halls, including five freshmen dorms, on Freshman Hill and Sophomore Hill, surrounding the Commons Dining Hall right next to Academic Campus. Upperclassmen looking to escape traditional dorm life can live in the recently renovated apartments, which are complete with a kitchen and dining area. While only first-year students are promised on-campus housing, upperclassmen say they don't have any difficulty finding residences to their liking.

The dining halls' quality receives cautious praise—"It's dorm food, what can you expect? But I've always been excited to eat where I live," one content diner living in BARH (a residence hall home to its own dining hall) reported. There are six styles of food to choose from each night, so "you never go hungry or have nothing that you want to eat at dinner," and one vegetarian student was happy that "there are always options that make it easy for me to eat more than just finding a salad." Students are generally pleased with the flexible meal plans, which allow students "to spend their meals allotted per week pretty much when they want."

Most upperclassmen don't have meal plans, so they cook their own food or purchase meals at the student union. The student-run Rensselaer Union, which incorporates campus-wide technology, is a popular student hangout. It features two floors of food courts, including a Starbucks and a café. The U-shaped quad is another destination for those seeking a place to chill, and the Student Center "convinced a Moe's to open a few minutes from campus"—an additional place to spend some flex points from the dining plan. But the academic rigors don't leave many stretches of time for ambitious RPI students to just lie low. "Honestly, you're going to find most people in the student union center or on their computers," said one student.

A Social Scavenger Hunt

Students generally agree that "you have to look for a good party," thanks to the very busy and demanding academic lives of students. "There are usually a few parties going on each weekend, but never anything crazy," according to one student. Besides some parties at athletic teams' houses, fraternities and sororities have a noticeable presence on campus, with about a quarter of the university involved, and current students encourage incoming freshmen to consider rushing. However, perhaps as a response to pressures from the local town of Troy, the RPI administration has been tightening the reins on underage drinking in recent years, making fraternities hesitant to throw full-scale parties, and leaving the nightlife-starved student body even hungrier for a full social calendar. But of course, students at RPI make it clear that being part of a fraternity or sorority is "totally up to you, and no one looks down on you for being Greek or for not." Outside of the Greek system, popular annual parties include the Big Red Freak-Out or the Black Friday Black-Out, to support the hockey team, and Grand Marshal week, when the elections for student representatives take place. GM week is full of games and "some crazy hats," and students enjoy time off from classes. In general, students point to the academic intensity as the reason behind the tame party scene, like one freshman who said "you only have any time to party, or even do laundry, on the weekend."

While some students still refer to the surrounding town of Troy as, to put it bluntly, "the Troilet," as well as a bit unsafe, others indicate the recent renewal effort that the city has been experiencing. The relationship between RPI and the town, which used to be "not the greatest" due to perceptions of the Greek scene in particular, is "on the mend," according to one member of a sorority. For those so inclined, students of drinking age point out worthwhile destinations like Club Lime, a rugby bar called The Ruck, and O'Learys for food. Troy and Albany also host occasional concerts. While many upperclassmen have a car on campus, few venture outside of the Troy area on a regular basis, instead "walking down a lot of stairs or taking the shuttle" to make their way down into the town for a day. And if students don't want to make a very far trek at all, right next to the very nearby Moe's is Pizza Bella (which actually changed its name to Big Apple Pizza, but "nobody even knows what Big Apple Pizza is unless you say Pizza Bella"), home to the always-popular buffalo chicken pizza as well as "so, so many crazy kinds of pizza."

RPI students are known for their book smarts, but some confess that their peers' social skills could use a little fine-tuning. "Most people at RPI are really pretty geeky guys," admitted one student, echoing a common view on campus that most students are pretty intense computer nerds. One student painted the caricature of an RPI student as someone who "walks around in a black trench coat, doesn't speak any English, and stays in his room to play video games or download porn." Indeed, the high-tech atmosphere can have a downside: plenty of students are said to spend their free time on the Internet or playing video games instead of going out to meet friends or make new ones on weekends. However, many other RPI students are fun, outgoing, and have a great sense of humor; they assure others that the caricature is not the norm and that "there is plenty of social interaction on campus." Overall, undergrads are described as friendly and relaxed people who are "at least a little better at making friends than I worried they would be."

There are conflicting degrees of complaints about the diversity at RPI—the strong academic programs draw students from across the world, and so "there is a large population of international students here," but among students from the U.S., while there are "maybe more Californians than you'd expect," the average Rensselaer student is a well-to-do white male from New England "or at least from the Northeast," according to one freshman who is used to a less homogeneous society in her urban hometown. But students tend to be even less enthusiastic about the gender ratio and dating prospects. While plenty of students "try not to notice it unless they want to notice it," the skewed male-female ratio of 3:1 causes plenty of problems for guys and girls alike. As one Greek brother said: "There are maybe something like 27 fraternities and 5 sororities—just by that fact you can kind of figure it out." Maybe as a result, random hookups and less serious encounters are less popular than more long-term relationships, once they are initiated. Guys sometimes complain of RIBS ("ratio-induced bitch syndrome") among the minority sex, as "girls get to be way pickier since there are so many more guys." But of course, this ratio does cause female students plenty of their own troubles. While some students did say they were pleasantly surprised to see that guys "are a lot less awkward and creepy than the stereotypes would make you think," others lament that "the guys always complain about the fact that there are no girls, but a lot of the guys are the ones who sit in the rooms and play video games," one female explained.

Puck Pros

Hockey is huge at RPI. "Going to a hockey game is like going to a professional game," explained one student. In fact, some players do head straight from RPI to the NHL, including such notable alumni as Joe Juneau and Adam Oates, and one student did say "the main reason I even know about RPI is hockey—my favorite player went here." Men's and women's hockey are the only Division I sports at the university, but football also attracts large crowds. RPI has recently opened the new East Campus Athletic Village, known as ECAV, the "pride and joy" of RPI athletics, which includes a new football field, gym, 50-meter pool, and tennis courts. Whether it's on the varsity, club, or recreational level, many students participate in some sort of athletic activity off campus on the new fields or on the open fields in the area that are shared among less intense teams. Undergrads can often be found skateboard- ing, riding bikes, or in the midst of a snow- ball fight.

Making the Most of It

While the stereotype of the RPI computer nerd seems to have some truth behind it, students have a sense of humor about it and prove that social interaction doesn't have to be limited to study sessions and video game marathons. Facing a massive workload and large introductory classes, students are urged to shape their own paths at RPI, and to make time for fun. "You're going to go crazy if you don't take control of what you're doing," said one student. Another RPI undergrad offered this piece of advice to incoming freshmen: "Bring a willingness to do everything you can. The work is going to be really hard, but you're not going to be able to make it without friends."—*Connor Moseley*

"RPI definitely values that its engineers are pretty well-rounded people and scholars, for a tech school."

FYI

If you come to RPI, you'd better bring "some focus and a whiteboard."

If I could change one thing about RPI, I'd "make the humanities programs a little more developed. The biggest program in the humanities here is Game Design, which I don't think is called 'humanities' anywhere else."

Three things every student should do before graduating are "look into joining Greek life; go to a hockey game: preferably the big game against Clarkson in February; and plan your own schedule: make sure that your senior year you can take one semester that's not crazy."

Rochester Institute of Technology

Address: 60 Lomb Memorial
  Drive, Rochester,
  NY 14623-5604
Phone: 585-475-6631
E-mail address:
  admissions@rit.edu
Web site URL: www.rit.edu
Year Founded: 1829
Private or Public: Private
Religious Affiliation:
  None
Location: Suburban
Number of Applicants:
  14,097
Percent Accepted: 60%
Percent Accepted who
  enroll: 31%
Number Entering: 2,601
Number of Transfers
  Accepted each Year:
  1,203
Middle 50% SAT range:
  M: 560–670, CR: 530–640,
  Wr: 520–640
Middle 50% ACT range:
  25–30
Early admission program
  EA/ED/None: ED

Percentage accepted
  through EA or ED: 66%
EA and ED deadline: 1-Dec
Regular Deadline: 1-Feb
Application Fee: $50
Full time Undergraduate
  enrollment: 13,582
Total enrollment: 16,
  199
Percent Male: 67%
Percent Female: 33%
Total Percent Minority or
  Unreported: 38%
Percent African-American:
  5%
Percent Asian/Pacific
  Islander: 5%
Percent Hispanic: 5%
Percent Native-American:
  <1%
Percent International: 4%
Percent in-state/out of
  state: 50%/50%
Percent from Public HS:
  85%
Retention Rate: Unreported
Graduation Rate 4-year:
  62%

Graduation Rate 6-year:
  Unreported
Percent Undergraduates
  in On-campus housing:
  60%
Number of official organized
  extracurricular
  organizations: 205
3 Most popular majors:
  Mechanical Engineering,
  Information Technology,
  Photography
Student/Faculty ratio:
  13:1
Average Class Size: 15
Percent of students going to
  grad school: 15%
Tuition and Fees: $31,584
In-State Tuition and Fees if
  different: No difference
Cost for Room and Board:
  $10,413
Percent receiving financial
  aid out of those who apply:
  88%
Percent receiving financial
  aid among all students:
  77%

L ocated in the industrial city of Rochester in upstate New York, Rochester Institute of Technology has been providing career-oriented education for more than 125 years. With a driven student body of nearly 17,000 students, eight colleges across different academic disciplines, and a hallmark co-op program, RIT offers an enriching academic experience while students are at the college in order to prepare the students for the abundance of opportunities at their disposal for life after college.

A Kaleidoscopic Assortment of Courses

RIT has something for everyone. Within its network of eight colleges, which covers academic disciplines in the liberal arts, to computer sciences in B. Thomas Golisano College of Computing and Information Sciences, to E. Philip Saunders College of Business and everything in between, RIT offers

90 programs of study. There is also an honor's program that grants students access to special courses as well as extra research or study-abroad advising. Beyond the wide array of academic options, RIT also provides specificity so that students can delve into fields as particular as New Media Development, Bioinformatics, and Photojournalism. "I like the specialization that RIT provides," said one student. "It lets me study exactly what I want."

In terms of classes, RIT operates on a quarter system. This means that four 10-week terms make up an academic year. However, the school year is also divided into fall and spring semesters, each ranging from 15–17 weeks. As a result, there are semester courses as well as quarter courses.

Despite the emphasis on a career-oriented education in a technology-related field, there is no shortage of unique courses that spice up the academic inventory. Classes such as "Big Bang and Black Holes" or "Busting Myths" are interesting but usually not too hard to get into. On the other hand, students fight for extremely popular courses such as "Foods of the World."

Beyond the Classroom

Lucky for RIT students, the enriching assortment of academic courses is only the beginning of what RIT has to offer. The university takes much pride in its Cooperative Education program, which has become increasingly popular among students. Affectionately called Co-op, the program allows students to start accumulating professional work experience related to their specific field of study after completing the first two years of coursework in their academic program. The co-op program allows students to gain first-hand experience in the professional world and earn a reasonable salary while learning. "The co-op program was the biggest draw for me," said an undergraduate student. "In a newly recovered and highly competitive economy, co-oping means that you study for your first and second years, then spend four quarters working in the real workplace. This guarantees you contacts in at least one company, and you'll have a better idea of what you want to focus on. RIT also has really good placement at large tech companies such as Apple, Microsoft, and Google," said one student. According to another student, the co-op program is just one way in which "RIT treats its students like students and not like numbers."

Behind the Bricks

RIT is known for having over 15 million bricks among the walls of buildings and pathways on campus. These bricks house a myriad of dorms of all shapes and formations along with the accompaniment of state-of-the-art facilities. All the freshmen live in dorms with two resident assistants on each floor. After the first year, most students move into on-campus apartments, which vary in size and condition. To cater to its students' diverse interests, there is also specialized housing. According to one student, "There are standard residential dorms with special interest hours for art, photography, engineering, computer science, foreign language, etc." With such an assortment of housing options, RIT is continuously expanding, with the recent completion of "Global Village." In order to improve the quality of students' lives, RIT also has excellent gyms in locations such as the Student Life Center.

The pools not only offer plenty of space for lap swimming but also a hot tub for relaxation.

> **"RIT treats its students like students and not like numbers."**

Besides dormitories, academic buildings, and student centers, there are five main dining halls along with smaller eateries and food stores sprinkled all across the campus. "Gracie's" or, as one student nicknamed it, "Greasie's" is frequented by freshmen as their required meal plan provides for a certain number of meals at Gracie's every week and a certain dollar amount of "food debit" that allows them to buy food at other dining halls or stores. Upperclassmen often opt for a plan of only food debit, which grants them more freedom. Consequently, they frequent other dining halls such as Commons, which is not only close to student dorms but, like Gracie's, can also be reached without going outside during the brutal winters. Brick City is another popular dining hall that not only offers great food but also plenty of space to relax. Other student favorites include Salsarita's at Global Village for its Mexican food and Java Wally's for a good cup of joe.

A Unique Melting Pot

While RIT has students from all of the fifty states and ninety-five countries, its demographic is unlike any other college. To start off, its male to female ratio is 2:1. Moreover, the National Technical Institute of the Deaf also contributes to the uniqueness of RIT's student demographic. In general, the student body is perceived to be predominately Caucasian with a significant percentage of the population consisting of students from New York.

Campus Festivities

Don't let all the pre-professional talk fool you. Outside the classroom, RIT students are a spirited bunch. Here, hockey dominates the sports scene, even more so than football. Last year, RIT men's hockey went to the NCAA Frozen four championship and this year RIT women's hockey is ranked #1 in the nation. As a result, hockey games often bring out students' school pride and the ice rink is packed with cheering students.

On a less conventional side of things, two

annual traditions bring together the student body. In the beginning of the school year, there is "Mud Tug." As part of a classic autumn tradition, students spray down a field to make it muddy, and have a tug of war tournament while raising money for a charity. In the winter, there is a seasonal festival known as Freezefest. Then, in the spring, students gear up for a massive game of Humans versus Zombies, played with Nerf guns, socks, and green bandanas. "If you're okay devoting three-plus weeks to constant paranoia and looking like a bit of a fool, it's lots of fun and really well-run. Otherwise, it can be just as fun watching others play," said an undergraduate

Overall, RIT's diverse array of courses and spectrum of themed housing offers an exciting collegiate environment. Moreover, for students who have a clear sense of their future careers and want to develop themselves in a classroom as well as a workplace setting, RIT's famed "co-op" offers a slew of opportunities to bridge the gap between school and the real world.—*Jenny Dai & Sharon Yin*

FYI
If you come to RIT, leave your football at home. Bring a hockey stick or a Frisbee instead.
What differentiates RIT from other colleges is "between all the buildings, pathways, and so on, there are over 15 million bricks on campus."
The biggest rivalry on campus is the rivalry between the computer science majors and the software engineering majors.

Sarah Lawrence College

Address: 1 Mead Way, Bronxville, NY 10708-5999	**Percentage accepted through EA or ED:** 24%	**Graduation Rate 4-year:** 67%
Phone: 914-395-2510	**EA and ED deadline:** 11-Nov	**Graduation Rate 6-year:** 72%
E-mail address: slcadmit@sarahlawrence.edu	**Regular Deadline:** 1-Jan	**Percent Undergraduates in On-campus housing:** 84%
Web site URL: www.sarahlawrence.edu	**Application Fee:** $60	**Number of official organized extracurricular organizations:** 70
Year Founded: 1926	**Full time Undergraduate enrollment:** 1,288	
Private or Public: Private	**Total enrollment:** 1,328	**3 Most popular majors:** Unreported
Religious Affiliation: None	**Percent Male:** 28%	
Location: Urban	**Percent Female:** 72%	**Student/Faculty ratio:** 9:1
Number of Applicants: 1,927	**Total Percent Minority or Unreported:** 33%	**Average Class Size:** 19
Percent Accepted: 62%	**Percent African-American:** 3%	**Percent of students going to grad school:** Unreported
Percent Accepted who enroll: 28%	**Percent Asian/Pacific Islander:** 5%	**Tuition and Fees:** $44,220
Number Entering: 331	**Percent Hispanic:** 8%	**In-State Tuition and Fees if different:** No difference
Number of Transfers Accepted each Year: 97	**Percent Native-American:** <1%	**Cost for Room and Board:** $13,504
Middle 50% SAT range: Does Not Require	**Percent International:** 5%	**Percent receiving financial aid out of those who apply:** 65%
Middle 50% ACT range: Does Not Require	**Percent in-state/out of state:** 27%/73%	
Early admission program EA/ED/None: ED	**Percent from Public HS:** 51%	**Percent receiving financial aid among all students:** 58%
	Retention Rate: 86%	

Twenty minutes outside of Manhattan by bus, in the hills of suburban New York, lies one of the nation's most highly respected liberal arts institutions, Sarah Lawrence College. Initially founded as a women's college in 1926, the college opened its doors to men in 1968 and continues to maintain a small size and stellar student-to-faculty ratio. With unique academic offerings and a plethora of on-campus activities, Sarah Lawrence effortlessly blends all of the perks of a small school with the resources of a much larger artistic community.

Making the Grade, Where None Are Given

Sarah Lawrence doesn't have "arbitrary" academic requirements; instead, students follow guidelines that call for one course in three out of four academic disciplines: social sciences and history, creative and performing arts, humanities, and natural sciences and math. Every class at Sarah Lawrence "is full of people who want to be there," and most are discussion-based seminars that are capped at fifteen students. There are no TAs at Sarah Lawrence, and the students benefit from the "extremely accessible faculty." The college gives students the opportunity to explore various fields and enhance their creativity, even if it takes them in unexpected directions—a perfect example is famous fashion designer and Sarah Lawrence alum Vera Wang, who came to the college as a pre-med and ended up focusing on theater and art history.

SLC also gives students a unique opportunity to get to know their professors through the conference system. Instead of cramming for finals, the conference system allows students to meet with professors outside of class to develop a long-term project—anything from a long-term paper to performance art—that will incorporate what they've learned in the course. Registration at Sarah Lawrence involves interviewing professors to see if the coursework is compatible with a student's interests and how the student thinks the course and final project will factor in to his or her academic career. Sarah Lawrence students agree that independence and determination are key to success at the college, but also praise the academic advising system as a way to help students figure out what they want from their academic experience. Each student at Sarah Lawrence is assigned a "don," an academic adviser in their field who will help them select classes and provide support for any and all scholastic issues.

Rather than focus on grading, professors at Sarah Lawrence write detailed, candid evaluations of a student's work at the end of the semester. Students are aware that professors can—and will—come down hard on them if they aren't prepared for class, and

most praise the evaluation system as "much more valuable than a letter grade."

Because of the college's small class sizes and close-knit campus, many Sarah Lawrence juniors decide to expand their horizons beyond their college bubble and study abroad for a semester or two. Sarah Lawrence students agree that "going abroad spring semester junior year is a must," and the college offers numerous exciting programs in Florence, Paris, and even Cuba. For actors, there's also the prestigious London Theater Program, which gives students the opportunity to work with leading British directors and actors.

> "Fun at Sarah Lawrence is artsy or in New York."

Yet, no matter where Sarah Lawrence students roam, be it to Italy or nearby New York for class trips to museums, they all agree that the academic environment is one of the college's greatest assets. Students talk about academics "even on weekends" and find that the discussion format they're so used to in classes often finds its way to dining hall dinner tables or the school's beautiful quads. A Sarah Lawrence education is "really about pushing boundaries and learning for the sake of learning."

Small School, Big City

Students' creativity permeates throughout life at Sarah Lawrence, and makes itself particularly noticeable on weekends. There's "always a lot to do on campus," including numerous plays, dance recitals, concerts, poetry readings, and art exhibits. The theater department organizes more than thirty performances each year, ensuring that students always have numerous opportunities to support their theatrically-inclined friends. Students also say that there's "every type of drinker" at Sarah Lawrence, from those who choose to stay sober to "the heavyweight drunks who stumble home every Thursday, Friday, and Saturday."

One thing that Sarah Lawrence doesn't have is Greek life—there are no fraternities or sororities at the college, but most students say that they aren't missed. Instead of "crowded parties with kegs," Sarah Lawrence students prefer to go to off-campus parties or take a 20-minute bus ride into New York City on Saturday nights. Trips into New York are certainly one of the most popular options for going out at Sarah Lawrence, "which can be pretty disappointing for freshmen who aren't used to having to travel to have fun." Although most weekends at SLC can be low-key, students do try to organize the occasional large-scale party, such as Bacchanalia and the well-known Coming Out Dance, which has been prevented in recent years because of problems with drinking.

Liberal, Artsy Living

With an undergraduate population of just under 1,300, Sarah Lawrence is the epitome of a small liberal arts institution. Students love the "tight-knit" community the college's small size creates, and praise the fact that "you see people you know everywhere, so you always feel at home." Most students are creative and passionate about the arts, but support for athletic teams is lacking. However, that's not to say that Sarah Lawrence doesn't have plenty of school pride—as one of the most prestigious liberal arts institutions, Sarah Lawrence has a very strong sense of tradition and students are proud of their rich history.

One of the biggest complaints about the college is its overall lack of diversity, in numerous aspects. Although students come from all over the U.S. and numerous international countries, only 68% are on financial aid, a testament to the college's lack of socio-economic diversity. Most Sarah Lawrence students are "flaming liberals," and

"the far-and-few conservatives have a pretty quiet voice on campus." However, despite the lack of diversity, SLC boasts a very accepting environment, where "everything, from sexuality to religion to whatever, is accepted." Initially founded as a women's college, Sarah Lawrence does have its fair share of "die-hard feminists" and "plenty of gay men," but students do say that everyone on campus has diverse interests and goals.

The campus is fairly self-contained, particularly for freshmen and sophomores. Freshmen say that dorms can be comfortable depending on where you live, with Andrews Court and Gilbert being two of the more popular dorms. In addition to dorms, the college has on-campus houses, which come with kitchens, single bedrooms, and spacious common rooms. Housing is decided by lottery, but it's "fairly easy to get a single after sophomore year, if you want one." Some seniors choose to live in off-campus apartments in nearby Yonkers because of their affordability, and cars are popular among upperclassmen.

For numerous reasons, the students at Sarah Lawrence are enamored with their small college's liberal arts focus and distinct community. Dedicated to both intellectual discovery and artistic ventures, Sarah Lawrence offers a unique academic environment and a living community sure to make students find their niche and feel at home.—*Iva Velickovic*

FYI

Sarah Lawrence is different from most other colleges because of "its unlimited commitment to its students, evidenced by the unique conference system."

What surprised me most about Sarah Lawrence was "how hard it was to put anyone in a box. Sure, we're all pretty artsy, but SLC students have interests that range from astrophysics to sports, too."

If I could change one thing about Sarah Lawrence, "it'd be that most upperclassmen leave campus on weekends."

Skidmore College

Address: 815 North Broadway, Saratoga Springs, NY 12866-1632
Phone: 518-580-5570
E-mail address: admissions@skidmore.edu
Web site URL: www.skidmore.edu
Year Founded: 1903
Private or Public: Private
Religious Affiliation: None
Location: Suburban
Number of Applicants: 6,011
Percent Accepted: 47%
Percent Accepted who enroll: 27%
Number Entering: 768
Number of Transfers Accepted each Year: 86
Middle 50% SAT range:
M: 570–660, CR: 570–680, Wr: 580–690
Middle 50% ACT range:
26–30
Early admission program EA/ED/None: ED

Percentage accepted through EA or ED: 43%
EA and ED deadline: 15-Nov
Regular Deadline: 15-Jan
Application Fee: $60
Full time Undergraduate enrollment: 2,679
Total enrollment: 2,734
Percent Male: 38%
Percent Female: 62%
Total Percent Minority or Unreported: 33%
Percent African-American: 3%
Percent Asian/Pacific Islander: 6%
Percent Hispanic: 7%
Percent Native-American: <1%
Percent International: 3%
Percent in-state/out of state: 33%/67%
Percent from Public HS: 60%
Retention Rate: Unreported
Graduation Rate 4-year: 78%

Graduation Rate 6-year: 80%
Percent Undergraduates in On-campus housing: 83%
Number of official organized extracurricular organizations: 80
3 Most popular majors: Business, English, Psychology
Student/Faculty ratio: 9:1
Average Class Size: 15
Percent of students going to grad school: 19%
Tuition and Fees: $41,520
In-State Tuition and Fees if different: No difference
Cost for Room and Board: $11,304
Percent receiving financial aid out of those who apply: 49%
Percent receiving financial aid among all students: 50%

Tucked away in the affluent horse racing town of Saratoga Springs, NY, Skidmore College's close-knit student body offers a welcoming social atmosphere, both during the week and on the weekends. The relatively young liberal arts college boasts small class sizes, accessible faculty, and plenty to keep students busy, though look elsewhere for spirited crowds at riotous athletic events. For those unfazed by the winter cold and seeking a comfortable balance between studies and parties, the Skidmore Thoroughbreds make a solid bet.

Intimate Academia, In and Out of the Classroom

Freshman are eagerly welcomed into the Skidmore community with a supportive system intertwining the classroom and dorm. All freshmen take a freshman seminar that doubles as their adviser group, the teacher filling the role of adviser and the seminars often focusing on less traditional topics such as food and cooking. Skidmore also tries to house students of these seminars together to further strengthen friendships among peers.

Don't let Skidmore's small size, with classes on average 15 students and sometimes as few as 8, give the impression that its academics are limited. It offers degrees in over 60 areas of study, the popular majors tending to be business, English, and psychology. An attractive aspect for many is the ready-made interdepartmental double majors, such as sociology and anthropology, and business and spanish. There are also strong studio art, dance, and music programs.

"I couldn't ask for more opportunities to study what I love with no boundaries. I am a double major with a minor, and no one ever told me I couldn't do it. I was only encouraged by the faculty who worked with me to make it all possible," said a senior. An exercise science major also praised her experience, lauding the excellent resources and facilities available to her.

The biggest intro class is a tidy 30 or so people. Getting into the smaller, more sought-after classes can be tough as an underclassman, due to a lottery system favoring the upperclassmen. There are a set of general requirements that cover the academic spectrum as at other liberal arts institutions. "I think a lot of them are necessary and give good breadth, but they can sometimes be a little too strict for what classes they count toward," said a senior. Another complaint about the administrative side of academics was that "it's not always clear exactly what your requirements are or what you should do to fulfill them—what's the best course of action before you get in your major."

Teachers are always around and have plenty of office hours, and there are no TAs in sight. If you make the effort to connect, then teachers will too. "The teachers are great—they're always open to making time outside of class to talk," said a sophomore. Well-known profs include Stephen Millhauser, who has written for *The New Yorker*, and Sheldon Solomon, professor of the challenging but popular Intro to Psych course.

Students agree that the workload is moderate if time is managed well. "There are no infinitely or notoriously hard classes. If you work hard you'll get an A. It's not like I'm struggling to pass," said a student. For those who want a challenge, there is the Honors Forum track, which involves a selection process. Grading varies between teachers but is very fair. Some classes will curve so you have the chance to do better. Some have an optional final, and others have several tests throughout with the lowest grade dropped. In addition, department heads are available to discuss any problems that may arise with certain courses or teachers.

Divided but Inclusive

The social scene at Skidmore is slightly divided, a fact apparent upon walking into the dining hall. "On the blue side, the athletes, on the red side, the more artsy kids," said a student. Despite this general trend, which, of course, does not include everyone, meeting new people and mixing among social groups is common and easy to do. "There's a strong sense of community. The school is small enough that you feel like you know everyone, but I'm somehow still meeting new, awesome people every weekend," remarked a senior. According to another, "No one is really discriminating towards who they hang out with. People have, usually, various friend groups. I never felt awkward in a group just because I didn't have a lot of the same interests or wasn't a member of a certain club or whatever." The student body isn't terribly diverse, and among minorities there can be some self-segregation. Most students fall under the umbrella of white, middle- and upper-middle class, fairly liberal kids from the Northeast and some from the West Coast.

Since students living in dorms have a mandatory meal plan, a lot of hanging out goes on in the dining hall, known fondly as the D-Hall. The one dining hall, which was redone in the past five years, is open from 7 a.m. to 11 p.m. and meal plans are quite flexible; while all freshmen have unlimited meals, upperclassmen can put money on their cards and refill when it runs out. The food is generally good, and even "awesome," according to one student, who also liked being able to see the staff prepare and cook the food.

The dorms are not bad, and the apartments off campus are well-praised. Freshmen have one roommate, possibly two (increasingly likely with growing class sizes) and space is generous as college rooms go. Most of the dorms are suites, so several rooms will all share a bathroom, a relief for those fearing big, grungy hall bathrooms. Juniors either move off campus or live in Scribner Village, an apartment complex on the edge of the main campus. Seniors generally live in Northwoods, a complex built five years ago with three or four students to a suite with a kitchen and bathroom, though Scribner and Northwoods are not grade-exclusive. Other new buildings on campus include the Zankel Music Center, featuring a beautiful concert hall, and the Tang Teaching Museum and Art Gallery.

Freshman dorms all have RAs who vary in strictness. "You have to enforce rules, but you're left a lot of personal discretion. If it's not out of control, I just ask students to stop. Some RAs write people up, but there's leeway," said one RA, a senior.

One complaint of Skidmore students is the lack of school spirit for sports teams. At a small D3 school, varsity sports aren't the main focus. People sometimes come out and support when teams are doing well—basketball and field hockey recently earned high attendance—but in general there isn't a huge sports following. The hockey team is trying to increase fans by providing buses to games, since the rink isn't on campus, but it still tends to draw the same small crowd.

Fun Day and Other Fun

There's plenty stirring up outside the classroom to keep students at Skidmore from growing bored. A number of clubs and organizations have a solid membership and are fairly active, though not students' first priority. While the *Skidmore News*, the weekly newspaper, is "not that great," the school's radio station is popular and there is a TV station, SkidTV, for anyone interested. The Equestrian program and Outdoors Club draw in a large group, while those less active may opt for art or even knitting clubs. Intramurals are offered in all the standard sports and pull a decent crowd.

Students can look forward to a number of annual, schoolwide events. Fun Day, at the end of April or early May, is the most highly anticipated; there are bounce castles and bands on the green, and everyone tends to get pretty tipsy. There is also Moorbid, the big Halloween dance; Beatlemania, a fall concert showcasing lots of different performances of Beatles songs; Junior Ring, a semiformal; and the Hunt, a huge, underground scavenger hunt requiring participants to complete ridiculous tasks. Every year, two concerts featuring bands brought in from outside also offer entertainment.

A lot of students keep busy with jobs, either on campus in the dining hall, library, gym, or academic services, or in Saratoga. Students with cars can take the occasional road trip to places like Montreal or Lake George, but for the most part people stay on campus.

Let the (Weekend) Races Begin!

Saratoga is a great town "if you do your research and utilize what's there," according to a local student. Besides the famous horse track, there are cross-country running and skiing races, a state park down the road, and a mall nearby. Saratoga's tourist-driven downtown and Broadway Street offer a range of restaurants and bars, all within walking distance of campus; if not inclined to walk, there are buses running from all over town, including one to and from Skidmore every half-hour. Relations with the town are neither great nor terrible; Saratoga leans to the right while Skidmore tends toward the left.

"Weekends at Skidmore are kind of touch and go. Some weekends are awesome, with tons of parties and places to go, and others are better spent with a few friends," said a senior. There's a good bar scene in Saratoga for upperclassmen or underclassmen with fakes, and school-funded activities on campus for those underage. There's almost always something to do, but it does sometimes quiet down, especially during exam time.

As for Greek life, "there are no frats, which is great. Sometimes athlete houses sort of take the form of mini-frats, but not really, and they certainly don't dominate the social life at all," said a senior. Athletic teams and other groups, such as the Outing Club, host parties at their off-campus houses, and "depending on the house you sort of know what to expect from the parties. The sports teams' houses are sometimes exclusive but other parties not really. It really depends on the size," said a student. All of the biggest parties are at off-campus houses and are a bread-and-butter destination for freshmen, who also tend to spend a lot of time hanging out in large groups in the dorm. The weekend is Thursday through Saturday night, with Friday the most lowkey. Upperclassmen often leave parties and delve into the Saratoga nightlife after midnight.

> "The school is small enough that you feel like you know everyone, but I'm somehow still meeting new, awesome people every weekend."

Skidmore is technically a dry campus, but security is generally pretty tolerant. "It's inevitable that drinking will be going on, so what they do is make sure it's as safe as possible. They're realistic about it," said a student. The policies are not too strict; "If you get caught drinking when you're underage there is a fine and you have to call your parents (it's 50 dollars or something, depending). It's not a zero tolerance policy, but it could be worse. People get in minor trouble a lot—get caught drinking in their dorm room. There are very few instances of serious trouble," said another. Drinking certainly isn't a requisite, and some students refrain, though the vast majority does drink, and drugs are also quite prevalent.

Overall, Skidmore students find little fault with their school. Despite some separation among social groups, everyone still gets along. Though the horse racing season dies away in September, the start of Skidmore's school year is when Saratoga Springs truly comes alive.—*TaoTao Holmes*

FYI

If you come to Skidmore, you'd better bring "really good snow boots (Uggs won't cut it), a desire to drink huge amounts of coffee, and a corkscrew."

If I could change one thing about Skidmore, I'd "have a little more school spirit."

Three things every student at Skidmore should do before graduating are "lie out on the green all day on the first nice day of spring (50 degrees out constitutes a nice day), go to Compton's Diner when it opens at 3 a.m., because you were downtown anyway so why not?, and have one doughboy (a hot cheese and chicken hot pocket) delivered to campus from Esporanto's, they are SO worth it."

St. Lawrence University

Address: 23 Romoda Drive, Canton, NY 13617

Phone: 800-285-1856

E-mail address: admissions@stlawu.edu

Web site URL: www.stlawu.edu

Year Founded: 1856

Private or Public: Private

Religious Affiliation: None

Location: Rural

Number of Applicants: 4,900

Percent Accepted: 39%

Percent Accepted who enroll: 32%

Number Entering: 609

Number of Transfers Accepted each Year: 40

Middle 50% SAT range: M: 570–660, CR: 560–660, Wr: 550–660

Middle 50% ACT range: 25–29

Early admission program EA/ED/None: ED

Percentage accepted through EA or ED: Unreported

EA and ED deadline: 1-Nov

Regular Deadline: 1-Feb

Application Fee: $60

Full time Undergraduate enrollment: 2,303

Total enrollment: 2,327

Percent Male: 45%

Percent Female: 55%

Total Percent Minority or Unreported: 18%

Percent African-American: 3%

Percent Asian/Pacific Islander: 1%

Percent Hispanic: 4%

Percent Native-American: <1%

Percent International: 6%

Percent in-state/out of state: 43%/57%

Percent from Public HS: 68%

Retention Rate: Unreported

Graduation Rate 4-year: 78%

Graduation Rate 6-year: 80%

Percent Undergraduates in On-campus housing: 97%

Number of official organized extracurricular organizations: 117

3 Most popular majors: Economics, Political Science, and Government

Student/Faculty ratio: 12:1

Average Class Size: 16

Percent of students going to grad school: 20%

Tuition and Fees: $42,420

In-State Tuition and Fees if different: No difference

Cost for Room and Board: $11,005

Percent receiving financial aid out of those who apply: 89%

Percent receiving financial aid among all students: 85%

Nestled among the Adirondack Mountains in the small town of Canton, New York, St. Lawrence prides itself on the spectacular natural beauty of its campus and its tightly-knit academic community. The relatively small number of students encourages close relationships, both within the student body and between the students and faculty. St. Lawrence's rural location, while admittedly far from major cities, also affords students a plethora of opportunities for outdoor activities and provides a stunning backdrop for daily walks to class. Although many students complain about the large piles of snow that accumulate

during the cold winter months, most agree that the lively on-campus atmosphere and picturesque surroundings more than make up for the chilly weather.

Studying at SLU

Students at St. Lawrence describe academics as "demanding" and say that "everyone spends a lot of time doing work during the week." However, as one freshman noted, "there's still time to unwind and have fun on the weekends; classes are as hard as you want them to be." Popular majors include economics, political science, and government. Perhaps unsurprisingly given its location in the heart of the Adirondacks, environmental science is also quite common. Thanks to the small size of SLU, students say they are able to get into small classes and enjoy close contact with professors right from the start of their freshman year. Professors are readily available to answer students' questions and problems—some even provide their home phone numbers.

Virtually all classes enroll fewer than fifty students, with the majority of courses capped at twenty. Despite the small class sizes, students say that they are rarely shut out of classes they want to take. Registration takes place online in conjunction with the support of the academic advising program.

St. Lawrence is well known for its innovative First-Year Program (FYP) for freshmen, which is designed to help students adjust to college social and academic life. In the fall of their freshman year, all students live in one of eighteen dorms with the other students in their FYP course. In the spring, students are enrolled in First-Year Seminars, or FYS, which cover a range of subjects. Overall, students give positive reviews of FYP, reporting that they often become close friends with the other students in their dorm and end up spending a lot of free time together. "FYP helps you make friends instantly—it's a good way of getting to know a small group of people," one sophomore said.

St. Lawrence also requires students to complete a set of distribution requirements, which include one course in "Arts/Expression," one humanities class, one social science, and a math or a foreign language course. They must also fulfill a science requirement, which includes a lab, and a diversity requirement. Opinions of these requirements range from "a pain" to "an interesting way to try new things, and not at all hard to do if you map it out." Offbeat courses include offerings such as "The Religious Life of India" and "Economics for Environmentalists."

When it's time to hit the books, many students head for the Owen D. Young library, the main library on campus. Students cite the "treehouse" study areas and group study classrooms as especially popular spots. In fact, some say that the library has become such a social space that it's hard to get work done there!

Dorms and Dining

The vast majority of St. Lawrence students are required to live on campus. Housing choices include traditional dorms, mainly singles and doubles, as well as theme houses, Greek houses, and "lifestyle floors." Greek houses lie just at the edge of campus. One senior living in her sorority house said she liked "always having people around; it's full of girls talking and laughing." Theme housing options include "The Greenhouse" (for environmentally-conscious students) and "The Hub" (a technology-themed house). Groups of seniors are able to live in on-campus apartments or townhouses that often include kitchens and living rooms. Housing is decided via a lottery system, with seniors getting first pick, then juniors, and finally sophomores.

While certain dorms are considered more "luxurious" than others, students say all the dorms are in good condition, and the senior townhouses get rave reviews. Skyes, the largest residence hall, is known as one of the best. However, students reported that all dorms, regardless of whether they are in a good or bad location, have a lively community spirit. As one junior stated, "Almost everyone becomes good friends with the people in their building." Student Community Assistants (CAs) help keep tabs on each floor and host study breaks from time to time.

SLU meal plans and dining options garner high marks. On campus, students can choose from three different eateries: the Dana Dining Center (a traditional all-you-can-eat cafeteria), the Northstar Café (known around campus as "the Pub"), and the Time Out Café in the Newell Field House. The cafés offer a variety of sandwiches, wraps, and salads, and the food there is considered the best on campus. They are also popular meeting spots for groups of friends. Dana often plays host to athletic teams, who eat there after practice, and is known for its delicious brunch on weekends. SLU students can choose from two meal plans: the 21-meal plan, which is only accepted at Dana, and a "Full-Flex Plan," which is accepted at all three on-campus locations. While students enjoy the freedom of the flex plan, most agree that it is impossible not to run out of money before the end of the semester. As one sophomore complained, "when you're eating at the Pub, it can get expensive really fast."

The town of Canton, while small, offers several dining options when students tire of on-campus food. Students often visit the farmer's market to load up on organic fruits, pastries, and cheeses. Other restaurants in Canton include the Blackbird Café, a charming organic eatery; Sergi's, a pizzeria; and

A-1 Oriental Kitchen, a popular delivery choice. The nearby town of Potsdam is home to the Cactus Grill, a Mexican restaurant also frequented by many St. Lawrence students.

From Peaks to Parties
Students at St. Lawrence are known for spending a lot of time on extracurricular activities; as one junior said, "Everyone here does something." The university is home to more than 100 clubs and student organizations, including a number of political organizations, an ultimate Frisbee club, and a Quidditch club. The outing club, the second oldest in the nation after Dartmouth, is one of the most active student organizations. Every year, the club sends hundreds of students to climb the peaks of the Adirondacks as part of "Peak Weekend," as well as on skiing, hiking, and rafting excursions. Many students also spend their time working on *The Hill News*, St. Lawrence's main student newspaper.

> "Canton is VERY rural."

Sports play an important part in campus life, both in terms of student participation and attendance at games. The school's Division I hockey team has strong support among the student body, and the stadium is always filled for their games. The game against Clarkson, the school's main rival, fills the campus with school spirit. Students say that tickets always sell out at least a week in advance. Lacrosse is another big sport, although some students complain about the "lax bro" atmosphere that surrounds the team. For those who don't want to join a varsity team but still want to work up a sweat from time to time, there are plenty of options. St. Lawrence offers a number of club sports or intramural sports such as broomball. One junior said, "Besides being fun, sports are a great way to meet people you might not otherwise come across. I found a lot of my best friends through my team."

Athletic facilities are highly praised. In addition to the fitness center, swimming pool, and basketball courts, St. Lawrence also offers a climbing wall, equestrian arena, and 18-hole golf course. Students reported that facilities are well-maintained and available to everyone.

While the school offers many activities for students to do on the weekends, students say that SLU's remote location can inhibit social life. As one junior said, "Weekend activities are often limited to partying, going into Canton, or going out hiking." On campus, students often host parties in their rooms or go to the Java Barn to see a band. Many students reported that alcohol plays a major role in student life, and one sophomore complained that "St. Lawrence needs to have more activities for students that don't drink." When they want to get off campus, students who have cars often travel to Syracuse and Ottawa, the capital of Canada. Both are a few hours' drive away.

Although the university has initiated new measures to try to increase the amount of diversity on campus, the student body remains overwhelmingly white. As one sophomore stated, "The stereotypical St. Lawrence student is blond, preppy, and from New England." One junior remarked, "I know a few people from Seattle, two from California, and everyone else is from the East Coast." Prevailing political views were described as moderate to liberal, and most students reported the campus climate as tolerant and accepting.

Overall, students described St. Lawrence as a warm and friendly community. One senior summed it up by saying, "It's the kind of place where people check to see if someone is coming behind them to hold the door. That's just how everyone is." The school's caring faculty and small student body foster close relationships. Although the school's distance from major cities might be a drawback for some, many say that the school's stunning natural backdrop and many outdoor opportunities more than make up for the excitement of a big city. As a sophomore said, "This is a great community. People are happy to be here!"—*Elizabeth Chrystal*

FYI

If you come to St. Lawrence, you'd better bring "a flannel shirt and wool socks—musts for walking across the campus on cold days!"

Three things every student at St. Lawrence should do before graduating are "attend a hockey game, attend Peak Weekend (a hiking weekend in the Adirondacks for all SLU students), and indulge in Sergi's pizza."

If I could change one thing about St. Lawrence "it would be the location—Canton is VERY rural. It's at least a two-hour drive to get to anything."

State University of New York System

As one of the largest university systems in the nation, the State University of New York system covers immense geographic and academic areas. With 64 campuses comprising large research universities, smaller colleges, and community colleges, the SUNY system is the most comprehensive and far-reaching state higher education system in the nation. Students may take advantage of the wide array of educational offerings such as vocational, technical, associate, baccalaureate, graduate, and post-graduate programs.

Well-known campuses include Albany, Binghamton, Buffalo, New Paltz, Potsdam, and Stony Brook among many others. With over 386,000 undergraduates and roughly 465,000 in total including gradute and professional students, the State University of New York system has one of the most diverse student populations in any state system. With so many campuses and options, the application process for the SUNY system is streamlined using the Common Application for the majority of the campuses.

As with many state university systems, the majority of students hail from the state of New York. Although there are some out-of-state students, they make up less than one-sixth of the population. That is because in-state students are offered tremendous reductions in tuition and fees. In fact, average SUNY costs for in-state residents are often one-third of tuition and fees of other state university systems. This combination of value and opportunities attracts a very large number of students to the SUNY system each year.

However, with large numbers also come some downfalls. The immense student populations of SUNY campuses and the SUNY system itself make it hard for students to receive individualized attention if they do not seek it. It is easy to get lost in a huge lecture hall of students unless a concerted effort is made to reach out to faculty members. However, once students learn to become self-sufficient and be proactive in their education, the opportunities abound. The sheer size of the SUNY system allows for amazing intrasystem and intersystem networking for research, academics, and social life.

Still, with all pros and cons presented, the affordability, value, and opportunities that the SUNY system offers continue to attract many bright students each year. With so many options from which to choose, students are free to make a place for themselves in the many campuses, specialties, and academic choices. Such is only made available by the large yet encompassing nature of the SUNY system.—*Hai Pham*

State University of New York / Albany

Address: 1400 Washington Avenue, Albany, NY 12222
Phone: 518-442-5435
E-mail address: ugadmissions@albany.edu
Web site URL: www.albany.edu
Year Founded: 1844
Private or Public: Public
Religious Affiliation: None
Location: Suburban
Number of Applicants: 22,188
Percent Accepted: 47%
Percent Accepted who enroll: 22%
Number Entering: 2,325
Number of Transfers Accepted each Year: 2,351
Middle 50% SAT range: M: 530–620, CR: 500–590, Wr: Unreported
Middle 50% ACT range: 22–26
Early admission program EA/ED/None: EA

Percentage accepted through EA or ED: Unreported
EA and ED deadline: 15-Nov
Regular Deadline: 1-Mar
Application Fee: $50
Full time Undergraduate enrollment: 12,327
Total enrollment: 13,114
Percent Male: 52%
Percent Female: 48%
Total Percent Minority or Unreported: 43%
Percent African-American: 10%
Percent Asian/Pacific Islander: 6%
Percent Hispanic: 9%
Percent Native-American: <1%
Percent International: 3%
Percent in-state/out of state: 95%/5%
Percent from Public HS: Unreported
Retention Rate: 85%
Graduation Rate 4-year: 61%

Graduation Rate 6-year: Unreported
Percent Undergraduates in On-campus housing: 57%
Number of official organized extracurricular organizations: 200
3 Most popular majors: Business/Commerce, General English Language and Literature, General Psychology
Student/Faculty ratio: 19:1
Average Class Size: 25
Percent of students going to grad school: 50%
Tuition and Fees: $13,380
In-State Tuition and Fees if different: $5,270
Cost for Room and Board: $10,633
Percent receiving financial aid out of those who apply: 64%
Percent receiving financial aid among all students: 62%

Established in 1844 in the heart of New York's state capital, the State University of New York at Albany is one of the key university centers in the SUNY system. SUNY Albany offers its students the resources of a private research university at the more reasonable prices of a state school. With nine smaller schools of academic discipline to choose from and an honors college that attracts some of New York's top minds, SUNY Albany presents a competitive edge within the SUNY system.

Hitting the Books

SUNY Albany is known as one of New York's largest state schools, but it is also known as one of the most academic. As one of the main university centers, it has more resources and esteemed faculty than many of the other SUNY schools, and it shows. Students say the English, economics, and psychology majors are especially popular, and the school's honors college offers an extra degree of rigor for those who seek it.

Regardless of one's academic inclination, students must complete curricular requirements, known as the General Education program. The Gen Ed program is intended to be completed over four years, and is designed to give students a broad base of knowledge applicable to any future career. Required areas of study include the humanities, a foreign language, natural science, and math or statistics, as well as a number of other fields. Students agree that the Gen Ed requirements are not a burden to complete, but careful schedule planning is necessary in order to secure a seat in those classes.

Of note is SUNY Albany's trimming of departments in response to the current economic downturn. The SUNY system as a whole is experiencing financial difficulties, a shortcoming that, students lament, negatively affects their educations. "It's frustrating," a current junior said, "that next year we won't have a theater, an Italian, or a French program, but we will be getting new apartments. It's just that the money for housing is specifically allocated to building new things, so we can't use that money for programming and classes."

Students say the workload at SUNY Albany is pretty standard and evenly spaced. One student noted, "Like anywhere, you have people who are going to be overachievers and try to be involved in every activity, but then you also have people who are just there for their schoolwork. It all depends on the person."

Dorms, Dining, and Decompressing

Current students agree that SUNY Albany is a social campus. Friendly interaction is fostered strongly by the housing system, which primarily divides students into quadrangles: State, Indian, Dutch, and Colonial Quads. Students also have the option of living in highrise apartment buildings, the Freedom and Empire Commons dorms. According to current students, the vast majority of rooms at SUNY Albany are in a suite format, with bedrooms off of a shared common area. Bathrooms are generally in-suite and are cleaned by college staff.

> "There's a big sense of community. . . . [Living on a freshman quad] really is a good opportunity to meet new people."

While Indian Quad is exclusively for freshmen and upperclassmen are scattered throughout the other quads, students don't feel that division by class is necessarily a bad thing. One student said of Indian Quad, "There's a big sense of community because freshmen are clinging to each other. It really is a good opportunity for them to meet new people." Although students said that "it is extremely popular for upperclassmen to move off campus around junior year," this is mainly due to the quality of the dorms themselves, which are described as anywhere from "very nice" to "average."

As far as the food on campus goes, every quad has a dining hall, and the Campus Center offers meal transfers at popular chain restaurants such as Wendy's and Au Bon Pain. According to students, "Indian Quad has the best food on campus," but the food overall is "generic." One student said of the food, "It's not good or bad . . . but it gets the job done."

Outside of eating and sleeping, students can choose from a variety of extracurricular activities to occupy their time. Most of the clubs and groups are standard, and include musical and theatrical performance groups, cultural interest associations, and student publications. Greek life is neither pervasive nor absent on campus; students say that while fraternities and sororities are popular, they do not dominate social life by any means. Students agree that school spirit runs high, but that spirit is not based on athletics. One student noted that "nobody really goes to athletic events," but people are generally proud to go to SUNY Albany and are happy with their choice. Even the dreary winter weather does not diminish students' pride. While it "gets gray," an expansive network of underground tunnels links the campus's main buildings for easy access. "The tunnels are our primary way of getting around," one student said, "but they're so boring. I've always kind of wanted to paint them."

A Social Affair

The social scene at SUNY Albany is vibrant, but is primarily based off campus. Although students say there isn't a pressure to drink at SUNY Albany, much of the reason social life centers on Albany's downtown area is the school's relatively strict rules regarding alcohol. "State and Indian Quad are dry quads," a current student explained, and in other dorms, "you can only have either 12 cans of beer or a liter of wine or liquor." Another student agreed, "There are no parties on campus unless it's in the apartments, but then it's not really a party, it's a hangout." One RA elaborated on SUNY Albany's alcohol policy: "RAs try to be as lenient as they can, but if it is right in front of them, we have to call the students out on it." Despite these restrictions, students are adamant that Albany's downtown area is a social hotspot—many students go to downtown clubs, bars, and restaurants every weekend, especially on Saturday nights.

Although students agree that "Albany has its problems just like any other city," the student body feels safe venturing off campus. The public bus system is free for students going downtown, and one student stated that she has "never had a problem going down-town." On campus, students feel very secure. "We do have a blue light system and an on-campus police system," a student clarified.

All in all, SUNY Albany is a solid college with slightly above-average academics where the majority of students are very sat-isfied with the quality of life. In fact, one stu-dent summarized, "I love it here."—*Alyssa Hasbrouck*

FYI

If you come to SUNY Albany, "leave high school at home."

What is the typical weekend schedule? "Friday night starts my weekend. Generally I will go to the campus center and get some food there, and if I don't stay in then I will get ready to go downtown. Saturday, I will wake up at about 1 and go to the gym with my friends, and then I will watch TV all day. I go out on Saturday nights, definitely. Sundays are really reserved for homework."

If I could change one thing about SUNY Albany, I'd "paint the tunnels. They're just so dreary and plain."

Three things everyone should do before graduating are "go to the wilderness retreat Dippikill, join a club, and go to Kegs and Eggs."

State University of New York / Binghamton

Address: PO Box 6000, Binghamton, NY 13902-6000	**Percentage accepted through EA or ED:** 53%	**Graduation Rate 4-year:** 66%
Phone: 607-777-2171	**EA and ED deadline:** 15-Nov	**Graduation Rate 6-year:** Unreported
E-mail address: admit@binghamton .edu	**Regular Deadline:** None/ Priority Applicaton deadline: 1-Dec	**Percent Undergraduates in On-campus housing:** 59%
Web site URL: www.binghamton.edu	**Application Fee:** $50	**Number of official organized extracurricular organizations:** 200
Year Founded: 1946	**Full time Undergraduate enrollment:** 11,433	**3 Most popular majors:**
Private or Public: Public	**Total enrollment:** 11,787	Biology/Biological Sciences,
Religious Affiliation: None	**Percent Male:** 53%	Business Administration and
Location: Suburban	**Percent Female:** 47%	Management, Engineering
Number of Applicants: 27,248	**Total Percent Minority or Unreported:** 52%	**Student/Faculty ratio:** 21:1
Percent Accepted: 40%	**Percent African-American:** 5%	**Average Class Size:** 15
Percent Accepted who enroll: 20%	**Percent Asian/Pacific Islander:** 12%	**Percent of students going to grad school:** 45%
Number Entering: 2,228	**Percent Hispanic:** 8%	**Tuition and Fees:** $13,380
Number of Transfers Accepted each Year: 1,787	**Percent Native-American:** <1%	**In-State Tuition and Fees if different:** $5,270
Middle 50% SAT range: M: 620–700, CR: 580–670, Wr: 570–660	**Percent International:** 10%	**Cost for Room and Board:** $11,810
Middle 50% ACT range: 26–30	**Percent in-state/out of state:** 89%/11%	**Percent receiving financial aid out of those who apply:** 78%
Early admission program EA/ED/None: EA	**Percent from Public HS:** 94%	**Percent receiving financial aid among all students:** 69%
	Retention Rate: 91%	

Binghamton encompasses the best characteristics of all types of colleges. All of the benefits of an Ivy League school come at the affordable price of a larger state university. The safety of a small suburban college town combined with the possibilities of life in a city. Enjoying school with the attitude of "work hard, play hard," the students of Binghamton are celebrated for their immense intelligence and down-to-earth, accepting attitudes.

Bang for Your Buck (Or should we say Bing?)

Renowned as one of the "Public Ivies," Binghamton is celebrated for having amazing education at an affordable price. On move-in-day of fall semester 2013, President Obama visited Binghamton's campus to deliver a speech on the importance of affordability of higher education, commending BU's recognition as a premier public university and "best buy" for education. The school boasts of acceptance rates about 10 percent and 13 percent higher than the national average to law and medical schools respectively. Priding itself as a research institute, the school always offers possibilities for undergrads to work next to acclaimed, award-winning scholars. One senior and even a recent transfer bragged of the new research jobs they acquired in the coming semester. One freshman quoted the work as "challenging, but manageable as long as you kept up with it." Binghamton is divided into six schools including Harpur College of Arts and Sciences, Thomas J. Watson School of Engineering and Applied Science, Decker School of Nursing, College of Community and Public Affairs, School of Management, and the Graduate School of Education. Undergraduates must fulfill certain general education requirements; however, certain AP credits can help advance students and push them into a more powerful position when registering for classes.

Transfer Friendly

Binghamton has one of the highest retention rates for colleges in the entire country. In fact, the school is so adored that many end up transferring to BU. They have such a transfer friendly program that consists of a special transfer orientation, a unique transfer mentor program, and special transfer floors for living arrangements.

Community Living

In order to foster a greater sense of unity, the dorms at BU are set up as residential communities. Each community provides the students with the safe feeling of a home-away-from-home while offering a distinguishable identity for the students in the greater Binghamton community. The students really believe that each college has a personality that makes it an exciting and enjoyable place to live and connect with other students. The six communities are College-in-the-Woods (CIW), Dickinson College, Hinman College, Newing College, Mountainview College, and the Apartment Communities. Freshmen have the possibility to rank which colleges they would like to live in and possibility to move locations throughout their career at Binghamton. The living situations among the colleges range from corridor style living to suites of six or more people to single rooms. Newing and Dickinson are the most recently constructed with Dickinson opening in 2011 and Newing in the fall of 2013. Multiple students say their living situations feel like they are "living in resorts" because of how new and clean these dorms are. Some have said that CIW's location near the nature preserve tends to create a "hipster, environmentally friendly and peaceful attitude" among the residents. Hinman's claim to fame is their creation of the Co-Rec football competitions among the colleges. In addition, Hinman is commended for their record of community service and strong student body representation. Mountainview is home to the majority of athletes and international students because the residency is open during many of the shorter breaks. However, the college is also known to be a far walk from the center of campus and up a large hill although "the scenery from up above the normal line of vision is beautiful." The Apartment Communities are open only to upperclassmen with possible family style living and singles. Most upperclassmen end up living off campus their junior and senior years but fondly recall living in the communities. One transfer junior said the communities are perfect to "meet people across all perspectives and they are a great opportunity for networking and learning from peers."

Bearcat Pride and Extracurriculars

Binghamton is a D1 school for athletics however does not have a football team. Since academics are the pride of BU, athletics are often an afterthought in the minds of the students. "You don't see as much school pride for sports as you may see at other state schools" said one Freshmen Lacrosse player. Although you may not see school merchandise plastered to the bodies of the undergraduates, this does not mean they don't have Bearcat pride; they just seem to dress "more professionally" as one freshman said. The basketball games do inspire a big turn-out and often incite the surrounding city community to attend.

Perhaps, sports aren't the biggest concern at Binghamton because the student body is involved in so many other diverse and extraordinary activities. There are so many opportunities, bragged one senior, "I get so many e-mails from so many different clubs across campus, it's hard not to get involved." There are over 10 Accapella groups including The Binghamton Crosbys, Treble Makers, The Rhythm Method, and No Strings Attached that incorporate specific genres and eras of music into their style. Additionally, Explorchestra is an orchestra at BU that composes and performs completely original songs. There are music groups, intramural sports, political groups, newspapers, cultural groups, community service projects and so much more to be a part of on campus and in the greater Binghamton area!

Connectivity

The Career Development Center or CDC is a prominent fixture that makes Binghamton so successful at providing students with quality jobs after graduation. They set up fairs throughout the year and special sessions for teaching students how to create and bolster their resumes, learn special interviewing skills, and possibilities for shadowing alumni. The School of Management has great ties with the accounting industry. Ranked in the top 25 of the country, the school of management has an amazing success rate for providing students with jobs after graduation. One junior management major praised, "SOM career services is one of the best parts about being in the school of management. They always have cool and helpful stuff and alumni and/or recruiters coming." Furthermore, BU has extensive study abroad possibilities for the student body with two fairs to display all of the opportunities presented for students.

The Party Scene and Fun Events

Along with the "work hard, play hard" attitude, Binghamton's weekend unofficially starts on Thursday nights. Much of the partying consists of Frats or Bars in downtown Binghamton. However, the Frat life at Binghamton is not overwhelming and "no one feels pressure to be in a frat." The bars are rather lenient with underage drinking as long as people produce some sort of identification. Students have been known to pass off fakes in order to participate in the bar scene. In order to get to downtown, students have to take some sort of transportation whether this consists of buses or cab rides that are readily available. Parents and students agree "the school and nearby city are safe with ample security." However, the party life is not all there is to do on the weekends. Often, an acapella group will be performing or the school will sponsor special concerts or movies on campus. Spring Fling is an exciting carnival/concert that takes place toward the end of the spring semester and has featured such artists as Drake in past years. One of the biggest events in Binghamton is Parade Day which takes place about a week before St. Patrick's Day. Students will flood the downtown streets to see the festivities and Fireman on their drive to the St. Patrick's Day parade in NYC. Whether you're chilling, hitting up the frat scene, attending a fun concert, or going downtown, there's always an abundance of activities to let loose or relax at Binghamton.

> What surprised me the most about Binghamton when I arrived was "how big it is, and yet, everyone knows somebody through somebody."

Down to Earth and Diverse

The resounding feeling from all students was that Binghamton is a great place to be because of the people. One new student rejoiced, "Everyone is open to talk and there are no real cliques." Another senior said, "The people are so incredible and yet so grounded and down-to-earth." There seems to be an opportunity for everyone to thrive. Although it is a state school, there are many international students and a culturally diverse student population. There is a feeling of acceptance across campus. One student praised, "It is great how LGBTQ friendly Binghamton is. We have rainbow pride and equality programs with civil rights and participate in national events such as day of silence." Overall, the students can't stop praising just how friendly Binghamton is.
—*Stephanie Rogers*

FYI
If you come to Binghamton, you'd better bring "a fake ID (Nightlife is only fun if you're "21" but any ID will do, Binghamton is not strict about IDs at all), a warm jacket, boots, and earmuffs."
If you come to Binghamton, you'd better leave "your bad attitude, bed risers (they are not allowed), bathing suits, sunglasses, and shorts" behind.
If I could change one thing about Binghamton, I'd make the sun shine more than once a semester.

State University of New York / Buffalo

Address: 17 Capen Hall, Buffalo, NY 14260-1660
Phone: 716-645-6900
E-mail address: ub-admissions@buffalo.edu
Web site URL: www.admissions.buffalo.edu
Year Founded: 1846
Private or Public: Public
Religious Affiliation: None
Location: Urban
Number of Applicants: 21,985
Percent Accepted: 51%
Percent Accepted who enroll: 28%
Number Entering: 3,147
Number of Transfers Accepted each Year: 3,442
Middle 50% SAT range: M: 550–650, CR: 500–610, Wr: Unreported
Middle 50% ACT range: 23–28
Early admission program EA/ED/None: ED

Percentage accepted through EA or ED: 70%
EA and ED deadline: 1-Nov
Regular Deadline: None/ Priority Application Deadline: 1-Nov
Application Fee: $40
Full time Undergraduate enrollment: 18,037
Total enrollment: 19,395
Percent Male: 54%
Percent Female: 46%
Total Percent Minority or Unreported: 43%
Percent African-American: 7%
Percent Asian/Pacific Islander: 10%
Percent Hispanic: 4%
Percent Native-American: <1%
Percent International: 15%
Percent in-state/out of state: 96%/4%
Percent from Public HS: Unreported
Retention Rate: 88%

Graduation Rate 4-year: 40%
Graduation Rate 6-year: 65%
Percent Undergraduates in On-campus housing: 34%
Number of official organized extracurricular organizations: 215
3 Most popular majors: Business/Commerce, Engineering, Social Sciences
Student/Faculty ratio: 16:1
Average Class Size: 24
Percent of students going to grad school: 36%
Tuition and Fees: $14,720
In-State Tuition and Fees if different: $5,270
Cost for Room and Board: $10,728
Percent receiving financial aid out of those who apply: 50%
Percent receiving financial aid among all students: 52%

S UNY Buffalo, known as UB to students, is the largest of the 64 State Universities of New York. Established in 1846, UB is one of the most versatile public schools on the East Coast. Most students at UB are from the state of New York, but there are also quite a few students from all around the nation. Since UB is one of the larger public schools on the East Coast, UB students may find themselves getting lost in the crowd, but those who find their niche at the school can take full advantage of the many options available to them.

Diversity in Study

Students at UB are a diverse bunch and have academic options to match up. UB offers 84 undergraduate majors that students can combine in double majors and minors. A junior, who has taken advantage of the many subjects available, remarked, "I am majoring in social science and doing a minor in sociology." In addition, there are special major programs in which individuals can devise their own programs of study. For those who are creative in designing their own majors, UB offers this option. For the ambitious, UB also offers combined-degree programs for some majors where driven students can obtain both their bachelor's and master's degrees in five years. "You can basically study anything you want at UB. A lot of students double-major or -minor or design their own majors," one student said.

UB encourages high achievement from its students. Every year, UB picks 250 incoming freshmen who have demonstrated academic prowess to join the University Honors College, which allows students to receive merit-based scholarships for their four years at UB. In addition, UB has the Distinguished Honors Program, which provides a free, all-expenses-paid undergraduate education. This opportunity is given to as many as 20 lucky students a year.

While many students are pre-pharmacy, pre-business, pre-med, or pre-law at UB, architecture is surprisingly one of the most popular majors at UB. Students agree that UB is a big science and engineering school and these classes are usually harder and heavier in workload. One UB student remarked, "My workload usually depends on what classes I choose to take even if they're not science classes." To graduate, students must have completed 120 credits as well as taken all the required classes for their respective majors or minors. Freshmen also have to take a combination of core classes that usually are outside of their major. Although many students dislike these classes of 300 to 400, some freshmen find what they want to study through their core courses.

> "You can basically study anything you want at UB. A lot of students double-major or -minor or design their own majors."

Students agree that being at a public school means that it is harder to get into classes. "People that have more credits get to register for classes first, so if you are a junior or senior you would get the classes that you need while the rest of the students who have fewer credits might not be able to get in," said a junior at UB. But a freshman noted, "If I really need a class for my major, I can speak to my academic counselor and have him 'force register' me into a class, which they usually will do." UB students study hard and they have the largest library system of all of the State Universities of New York, with one of the biggest collections. Libraries are usually crowded before finals and midterms.

Dorms Become Like Second Homes

Dorm life is big on campus and students and RAs alike try to make dorms and living spaces as homey as possible. A student said, "My RA is pretty cool; she's nice and comes up with events for our floor to do every month and she decorates all our halls." Students at UB participate in dorm activities sponsored by their RAs and often build great fellowships with those they live with.

One UB student who lived on campus said, "Dorms in UB are pretty okay compared to some that I've seen from other schools. The rooms are an okay size, not too small, but not too big either." For a public school, UB dorms seem to satisfy its students. Dorm life at UB is fairly typical: students learn to live with floor mates and roommates in harmony. A junior remarked, "Dorm life can get very noisy. People sometimes come back from parties at four in the morning."

UB has three different campuses. North Campus is the busy, lively part of the university, which is located in suburban Amherst. It has more than 100 buildings and is currently under construction for new student housing. The dorms share a public bathroom and kitchen on every floor so students tend to mingle and know those who live on the same floor. South Campus is located in Buffalo. The architecture is classified as more historic, with a bell tower completing the look. South campus dorms are suite-style; students share a bathroom with their suite rather than their floor. Downtown Campus, the newest addition to the UB campus, is located in downtown Buffalo. It is known for its new buildings and state-of-the-art life sciences buildings.

Victor E. and Victoria S.

The Bulls, Victor E. and Victoria S., are UB's official mascots, and they have certainly brought a lot of victory to the school. The football, baseball, softball, volleyball, basketball, wrestling, swimming, tennis, cross country, soccer, rowing, and track and field teams are all represented in the NCAA Division I. UB athletes have their school to thank in pushing them on to victory; football is a big deal at UB and students will often go to their school's football teams to cheer for their school. A junior at UB said that of all her experiences so far at UB, "sports are a big thing at UB and football is the most popular." The UB Stadium seats 29,013 people, which adds to the exhilarating athletic experience for students and athletes alike. In addition, UB basketball players receive a lot of school pride from students; the Alumni Arena is the second-largest on-campus basketball complex in the state. UB students also participate in intramural sports with other students on campus, where they can hang out with friends and catch a game of Frisbee or just jog around campus before the heavy snows set in for the winter.

The Proof Is in the Numbers

Because UB is such a large school, there are tons of things to do and people to meet.

Looking back on his years at UB, a senior said, "I ended up finding the right group of people at UB who have become my best friends. . . . There are so many different people at UB that you're bound to find the right group." The diverse group of students is offered seemingly endless opportunities to get involved in clubs and activities outside the classroom, and students are very active in their extracurricular activities. One student was thankful for her work-study job at the architecture and planning library, where she can contribute to her tuition. UB offers work-study to many students on campus and quite a few students work during their undergraduate years.

The biggest social events of the year at UB are Fall Fest and Spring Fest, which are held on UB's North Campus. In 2007, Spring Fest was held on Earth Day and musicians such as Jason Mraz and the band Juxtaposse performed for enthusiastic UB students.

Other social events at UB usually happen within dorms, where suite mates or roommates may throw a party for their floor and invite friends.

Although only around 10 percent of the UB student body is involved in Greek life at UB, fraternities and sororities play a big part in the school's social scene. A student in an Asian-interest sorority at UB said, "Greek life is not as popular as it was in the past, but it's still pretty big at UB. It's pretty competitive to rush and it definitely has a dominant presence." Although Greek organizations are competitive in looking for potentials, they also support each other when throwing social or community-wide events on campus.

SUNY Buffalo offers a wide range of academic and extracurricular options to its many students. Students come to accept and even enjoy the city of Buffalo and learn to find their true niche.—*Emily Chen*

FYI

If you come to UB, you'd better bring "snow clothes, because it snows A LOT!"

What is the typical weekend schedule like? "Friday classes and parties at night, sleep in on Saturday, go off campus with some friends to the mall and eat out and spend the night watching a movie with friends, Sunday sleep in and finish up homework for the rest of the week."

If I could change one thing about UB, I'd "add more social places near the school for students to go when they just want to have fun."

Three things every student at UB should do before graduating are "take advantage of internships and international opportunities, go to the annual Welcome Back Party hosted by the Lambdas, and go to a football game."

State University of New York / Stony Brook

Address: 118 Administration Building, Stony Brook, NY 11794-1901
Phone: 631-632-6868
E-mail address: enroll@stonybrook.edu
Web site URL: www.stonybrook.edu
Year Founded: 1957
Private or Public: Public
Religious Affiliation: None
Location: Suburban
Number of Applicants: 27,822
Percent Accepted: 41%
Percent Accepted who enroll: 24%
Number Entering: 2,734
Number of Transfers Accepted each Year: 3,200
Middle 50% SAT range: M: 580–680, CR: 530–630, Wr: 520–630
Middle 50% ACT range: 25–29
Early admission program EA/ED/None: EA

Percentage accepted through EA or ED: 44%
EA and ED deadline: 15-Nov
Regular Deadline: Rolling December 1 recommended
Application Fee: $50
Full time Undergraduate enrollment: 15,034
Total enrollment: 16,342
Percent Male: 52%
Percent Female: 48%
Total Percent Minority or Unreported: 62%
Percent African-American: 6%
Percent Asian/Pacific Islander: 23%
Percent Hispanic: 9%
Percent Native-American: <1%
Percent International: 8%
Percent in-state/out of state: 93%/7%
Percent from Public HS: 90%
Retention Rate: 88%

Graduation Rate 4-year: 44%
Graduation Rate 6-year: 59%
Percent Undergraduates in On-campus housing: 59%
Number of official organized extracurricular organizations: 333
3 Most popular majors: Biology, Psychology, Business Management
Student/Faculty ratio: 19:1
Average Class Size: 26
Percent of students going to grad school: 34%
Tuition and Fees: $13,380
In-State Tuition and Fees if different: $5,270
Cost for Room and Board: $10,574
Percent receiving financial aid out of those who apply: 75%
Percent receiving financial aid among all students: 66%

When its doors opened in 1957, the first version of SUNY Stony Brook had only 100 students. Today, the university enrolls more than 14,000 undergraduates and possesses a campus of more than 1,300 acres. It is a major research institution of New York's public university system and operates some of the nation's premier science laboratories. Although the location of Stony Brook on Long Island seems to suggest proximity to New York City, it actually takes a long ride by train to Manhattan, given the size of Long Island. Nevertheless, the suburban university certainly has its own appeal and presents an interesting experience for all students.

The Best of Both Worlds

Stony Brook has a great reputation as a school that combines research with education. It is considered one of the top 100 national universities by *U.S. News & World Report* for its undergraduate education. At the same time, it is a member of the Association of American Universities, a group of the top 62 research institutions. "I know that we have had a lot of Nobel Prize winners over the years," said one student. "So it is really cool to know that you go to a school with some really respected professors."

The university is divided into eleven schools. Most students are enrolled in the College of Arts and Sciences. The College of Engineering and Applied Sciences is often considered one of the prominent institutions within the university because of the significant presence of research activities in the field. The C. N. Yang Institute for Theoretical Physics, named for a former Nobel Prize winner, is one of the most important research centers in the field and has had successes in many areas since its creation in the 1960s. Furthermore, Stony Brook is also one of the operators of Brookhaven National Laboratory, originally dedicated to nuclear technology research during the Cold War and now expanded into other areas of physics, chemistry, and biology. Despite the research being conducted at Stony Brook, some people do not believe that it adds much to the student experience. "I think the research centers are the high points of the university," said one student. "It shows how many great things the school has accomplished. On the flip side, they don't really help the college students that much because they are so far apart from the undergraduate programs."

For a college as large as Stony Brook, the number of majors is relatively small. In fact, the school offers 65 majors and 77 minors, certainly not a small number, but many schools of comparable size have close to 200 programs. Nevertheless, the students think that the academic options are sufficient. "I know that other schools have really specialized majors," said one student. "But you want to learn a little bit of everything as an undergraduate, so I would prefer a more general program like what we have here." The most popular majors include the usual suspects, such as psychology and political science. However, a significant portion of the student body is also engaged in applied mathematics and statistics, demonstrating the school's commitment to science and engineering.

The series of required classes at Stony Brook has a big name: Diversified Education Curriculum, which is essentially the same as the core requirements of other universities. Students are expected to refine the basic skills in writing, mathematics, and logic. In addition, they must take classes in different academic fields, such as science and humanities, and acquire some global understanding by enrolling in courses about non-Western cultures. "I like the idea of the requirements, but when they are put into practice, they can be really annoying because I am not into what some of the classes teach," said one student.

In general, students find the course load manageable. One drawback is the number of large lectures and the lack of accessibility to smaller classes that encourage discussions. Of course, there are plenty of small seminars. Nevertheless, most classes revolve around the professors spitting out information about a topic, and students scramble to take down what is being said and try to remember and apply that information. "It is a big school, so there is not that much individual attention," said one student. On the other hand, other students think that individual attention can be had. It just requires a little extra effort. "You have to take the initiative to talk to professors after class or at their offices," said one student. "Most people just never bother to do it."

Central Long Island

Stony Brook is a nice, residential hamlet of slightly over 10,000 people. There are not many commercial activities, thus offering the university a relatively quiet atmosphere. Many students come from Long Island and thus are very familiar with the area. Nevertheless, given that it is located in a residential area, Stony Brook is not particularly interesting. To find better nightlife and more diverse weekend activities, students can go to Manhattan, which is about 50 miles away, most easily accessible by local railways. Some people not familiar with the area may mistakenly believe that Long Island is very close to New York City, but it is certainly not the case for much of the island, which stretches nearly 100 miles away from the Big Apple. "Manhattan is close, but you have to plan ahead if you want to go there, or you may end up getting back here really late at night," said one student.

> "You have to take the initiative to talk to professors after class or at their offices."

No one is required to live on campus, though over 80 percent of the freshman class does. After all, it is convenient and a good way to meet people. Those who do not live on campus during their first year often live within the area and can easily commute from home. More than 8,000 undergraduates total live in residences provided by the university, which consist of 28 residence halls and 23 apartment buildings. The dorms are arranged into six different quads, each of which contains three to five dorm buildings. The idea is to create smaller, more intimate communities within a large university. "The rooms are not that bad, and they provide most of the services you need, like wireless Internet," said one student. "That is why I think it is a better option to live in the school dorms than off campus, where the rent can be actually pretty expensive, and you don't have all the amenities you get in the school."

Dining at Stony Brook may not be healthy, as many of the better options consist of fast food, but the university certainly provides a great variety of choices. The food is a combination of dining-hall-style buffet, sit-down restaurants, and fast-food chains, thus a large number of eateries and convenience stores.

Greek life is an important part of the social life. There are 31 fraternities and sororities recognized by the university. Since it is a large campus, people can always find parties on campus during weekends, though it is important to know that many people do choose to go to New York City for a more exciting nightlife or simply go home, if their home is close to campus.

An Experience to Remember

Students at Stony Brook come from all types of backgrounds, creating a diverse campus. Although the great majority of students are New Yorkers who take advantage of the low tuition, there are plenty of out-of-state students, not to mention people coming from overseas. "It is fun to know people of all interests," said one student. "I think that, when you graduate, you will definitely leave here with a great education and some great memories."—*Xiaohang Liu and Paul Treadgold*

FYI

What is the typical weekend schedule? "You should spend one of the days in NYC, and there are some clubs you can go to there."
If I could change one thing about Stony Brook, I'd "make classes smaller."
Three things every student at Stony Brook should do before graduating are "go to a sporting event, go to NYC, and live off campus for a year."

Syracuse University

Address: 900 South Crouse Avenue, Syracuse, NY 13244-2130
Phone: 315-443-3611
E-mail address: orange@syr.edu
Web site URL: www.syr.edu
Year Founded: 1870
Private or Public: Private
Religious Affiliation: None
Location: Urban
Number of Applicants: 22,935
Percent Accepted: 60%
Percent Accepted who enroll: 25%
Number Entering: 3,458
Number of Transfers Accepted each Year: 305
Middle 50% SAT range: M: 540–650, CR: 520–620, Wr: 520–630
Middle 50% ACT range: 23–28
Early admission program EA/ED/None: ED

Percentage accepted through EA or ED: 77%
EA and ED deadline: 15-Nov
Regular Deadline: 1-Jan
Application Fee: $70
Full time Undergraduate enrollment: 13,490
Total enrollment: 14,201
Percent Male: 44%
Percent Female: 56%
Total Percent Minority or Unreported: 44%
Percent African-American: 8%
Percent Asian/Pacific Islander: 9%
Percent Hispanic: 8%
Percent Native-American: 1%
Percent International: 6%
Percent in-state/out of state: 47%/53%
Percent from Public HS: 71%
Retention Rate: Unreported
Graduation Rate 4-year: 71%

Graduation Rate 6-year: 82%
Percent Undergraduates in On-campus housing: 75%
Number of official organized extracurricular organizations: 367
3 Most popular majors: Commercial and Advertising Art, Psychology, Radio and Television
Student/Faculty ratio: 16:1
Average Class Size: 15
Percent of students going to grad school: 16%
Tuition and Fees: $36,300
In-State Tuition and Fees if different: No difference
Cost for Room and Board: $13,254
Percent receiving financial aid out of those who apply: 80%
Percent receiving financial aid among all students: 80%

Perhaps best known to outsiders as the home of the Orange, a successful athletic program of the Big East Conference, Syracuse University is an outstanding institution of higher learning for nearly 20,000 undergraduate and graduate students. Located on a hill southeast of downtown Syracuse, the university is also a leading research institution in upstate New York. Although the bitter, snowy winters are a concern for many prospective students, Syracuse presents a large array of academic opportunities and a very fulfilling social life, thus making it a great college choice for students from around the world.

Having a Plan

The undergraduate program at Syracuse can be pursued in one of the nine colleges: Architecture, Arts and Sciences, Education, Engineering and Computer Sciences, Human Ecology, Information Studies, Management, Public Communications, and Visual and Performing Arts. When a high school senior applies to Syracuse, he or she must make a choice among these colleges. There is also the option of dual enrollment, if the applicant has an interest in two different fields. However, it is clear that the university wants students to make a choice before they enter the university. Of course, it does not mean that the student's academic options are limited once they arrive on campus. After all, the College of Arts and Sciences has a large selection of different majors.

> "Newhouse is definitely the best-known school at Syracuse. A lot of the events held there get a lot of attention from the press."

Although each college has its own strengths and weaknesses, most students agree that the most prestigious one is the S.I. Newhouse School of Public Communications, which is considered one of the best journalism schools in the United States. It has produced a large number of well-known journalists and broadcasters, such as Bob Costas and Steve Kroft. "Newhouse is definitely the best-known school at Syracuse," said one student. "A lot of the events held there get a lot of attention from the press."

The School of Architecture is also recognized as one of the best in the country. It is the fourth oldest in the country, tracing its origin to the 1870s. "If you want to go into architecture, you might want to take a close look at Syracuse. It has a strong faculty and a lot of bright students," said one senior.

A large university, Syracuse offers more than 200 undergraduate majors, including several that are rarely found in other colleges, such as Printmaking and Ceramics. "We definitely have a lot of majors and minors as

well," said one student. "You are a little constrained because they are in a specific college and can only choose majors in that college, but it is always possible to take classes in other disciplines, which is fun."

Classes at Syracuse vary in difficulty, depending on the professors. Careful research at the beginning of the semester will go a long way in helping students obtain the optimal workload. "You should look into the course content before you take a class so that you are not surprised at how much you have to work or how your grade ends up," said one student. The class size, on the other hand, is reasonable. Although popular introductory classes can have more than 200 students, upperclassmen have the opportunity to enroll in seminars of 10 to 20 people, thus having more time for class discussions and debates.

Syracuse also has an Honors Program available to students in any of the colleges. It is designed to enrich curriculums in whatever fields of study the students choose. There are a number of required courses for Honors students so that everyone has a breadth of experiences as well as strong global awareness and civic engagement. Another special program is Syracuse University in Florence, often considered one of the best study-abroad initiatives in the country. In this program established in 1959, students live with host families and study in a small Syracuse campus only ten minutes away from the city of Florence. In addition, the university also offers Discovery Florence, available only to first-semester freshmen entering the College of Arts and Sciences. Unlike most study-abroad programs that are available to juniors and seniors, Syracuse freshmen receive the opportunity to go overseas and experience life in a historic European city.

As one of the top 60 national universities ranked by *U.S. News & World Report*, Syracuse has a selective admissions process. At the same time, it also means a student body that is both talented and focused on academics.

Central New York

Syracuse is the heart of Central New York. Its metropolitan area is comprised of more than 600,000 people. All the usual amenities of a big city are present in Syracuse, ranging from sports complexes to convention centers to a number of colleges and universities. Nevertheless, it is important to point out that Syracuse, despite being the fifth most populous city in New York, is not a booming metropolis. The relative decline of the region over the last few decades resulted in a lackluster appeal of the city to students. "We don't go to downtown often," said one student. "I don't feel that there is much to do here outside of the campus." Indeed, much of the recent development in the city has centered on the university, which plays an important role in Syracuse's economy.

Areas immediately north of the main campus area are good hangout places, especially the few blocks around Marshall Street, which feature a number of bars and restaurants mostly catering to students. Of course, given its proximity to the campus, it is generally filled with students, especially during weekends. Furthermore, Greek life is an important part of social life. With over 40 fraternities and sororities, parties are not hard to find, starting on Thursdays. It is also useful to note that many Greek houses are located very close to the center of the campus. "Restaurants, bars, clubs, and frats are all conveniently located," said one student. "That is one of the best parts of being at Syracuse."

The majority of students at Syracuse live on campus. It is a convenient way to meet people, not to mention easier access to classrooms and different university facilities. The drawback, however, is the freedom from more intense monitoring of student behavior and alcohol use by the university. The quality of the rooms is considered average for most universities, and there are options of learning communities and interest houses, where people of similar lifestyles or interests live together. Starting from junior year, many students do choose to leave dorm rooms and settle in one of the many houses or apartment buildings in nearby areas.

The dining services operate five main dining centers with all-you-can-eat meals, and all of them have options that accommodate vegetarians and vegans. In addition, there are eateries within campus buildings, including a food court that features different fast-food chains.

Syracuse Orange

One of the best-known parts of Syracuse is the men's basketball team, which has appeared three times in the national title game. However, the most successful team must be men's lacrosse, which won the 2009 national championship. Playing in a dome that accommodates up to 49,000 people, the Syracuse Orange is an important force in NCAA Division I sports.

Ultimately, Syracuse, though located in the blustery cold of upstate New York, provides a good education, fun social life, and ardent school spirit. What is there not to like?—*Xiaohang Liu*

FYI

If you come to Syracuse, you'd better bring "something orange."

What is the typical weekend schedule? "Sometimes I feel like I spend the entire weekend on Marshall Street."

If I could change one thing about Syracuse, I'd "make the city a little more fun."

Three things every student at Syracuse should do before graduating are "go to a lacrosse game, snow fight, and take a class at Newhouse."

Union College

Address: 807 Union Street, Schenectady, NY 12308
Phone: 518-388-6112
E-mail address: admissions@union.edu
Web site URL: www.union.edu
Year Founded: 1795
Private or Public: Private
Religious Affiliation: None
Location: Urban
Number of Applicants: 4,946
Percent Accepted: 42%
Percent Accepted who enroll: 26%
Number Entering: 554
Number of Transfers Accepted each Year: 43
Middle 50% SAT range: M: 610–700, CR: 580–670, Wr: 580–680
Middle 50% ACT range: 27–30
Early admission program EA/ED/None: ED

Percentage accepted through EA or ED: 77%
EA and ED deadline: 15-Nov
Regular Deadline: 15-Jan
Application Fee: $50
Full time Undergraduate enrollment: 2,170
Total enrollment: 2,197
Percent Male: 51%
Percent Female: 49%
Total Percent Minority or Unreported: 24%
Percent African-American: 5%
Percent Asian/Pacific Islander: 6%
Percent Hispanic: 5%
Percent Native-American: <1%
Percent International: 4%
Percent in-state/out of state: 43%/57%
Percent from Public HS: 65%
Retention Rate: 93%

Graduation Rate 4-year: 76%
Graduation Rate 6-year: 83%
Percent Undergraduates in On-campus housing: 85%
Number of official organized extracurricular organizations: 105
3 Most popular majors: Economics, Political Science, and Government
Student/Faculty ratio: 10:1
Average Class Size: 16
Percent of students going to grad school: 35%
Tuition and Fees: $54,273
In-State Tuition and Fees if different: No difference
Cost for Room and Board: Included with tuition
Percent receiving financial aid out of those who apply: 72%
Percent receiving financial aid among all students: 71%

The name "Union College" reflects the founders' belief in creating one of the country's first nondenominational colleges where there is "a sense of community devoted to unity rather than sectarianism." Located in downtown Schenectady, New York, Union College is a small liberal arts school dedicated to "broadly educating future citizens of the world." With its unique architecture, such as the 16-sided Nott Memorial built in 1813, and its long history, Union College provides its students with an experience different from any other liberal arts college.

An Education for the "Life of the Mind"

Union College is what one student calls an "engineering liberal arts college." Although engineering majors are required to take 40 courses over their four years as opposed to the liberal arts majors' 36 courses, all students are required to fulfill the General Education curriculum requirements. The General Education requirements include a distribution of courses in the humanities, social sciences, natural sciences, and mathematics. Freshmen are required to take a First-Year Preceptorial class, which hones writing skills; sophomores are required to take a Sophomore Research Seminar; and seniors must complete a thesis. The requirements may sound demanding, but many students agree that they are "rather easy to accomplish" because there are "so many options for classes." In addition to the majors and minors, Union offers several accelerated programs that provide students with the chance to earn two degrees. For example, the Leadership in Medicine eight-year program offers a combination of a bachelor's, master's, and doctoral degree for students in consortium with Albany Medical College. In the Law and Public Policy program, Union and Albany Law School select up to 10 incoming Union students to complete BA and JD degrees in six years.

For students on the Union bachelor's degree track, bioengineering and economics are two of the more popular majors. No matter what the major, class sizes are almost always below 25 and get smaller as the level of the class increases. "Even the lectures are small compared to most colleges," one junior said. Small class sizes also allow student-teacher relationships to be "great." One senior noted, "I never had a professor I couldn't go to for help." Some professors even take students out to dinner if the class is small enough. A first-year Union student laughed and said, "You know that the teachers are dedicated once your teacher asks you why you missed class the next time they see you." One of the most renowned professors on campus is Professor Stephen Berk, whose Holocaust class is extremely popular with students.

Union follows the trimester system, as opposed to the semester calendar of most other colleges. Union begins two weeks later than most schools in the fall and has a winter break of six weeks, which some students say is "too long." During that break, a student can take a three-week mini term abroad to one of ten possible country options. While most schools end in May, the end of the third trimester is in the middle of June. With the trimester system, students have the advantage of taking only three to four classes per trimester. But classes that would be 15 weeks at another school are condensed to 10 weeks at Union.

A focus of the Union experience is studying abroad, which is recommended to every student, and which about 50 percent of students actually do. The Terms Abroad Programs are offered on nearly every continent. Each academic department has its own programs, which are offered for trimester periods, sometimes even for nonmajors. In the Marine Studies program in the spring, students travel to conduct research from Cape Cod to Bermuda to Canada. For those who want to study abroad, conduct research, or find an interesting job, Union offers many fellowships and scholarships for students of every year.

The First Greeks

Known as the Mother of Fraternities, Union College was where the first three Greek societies were created. Greek life on campus is "pretty big," with about 50 percent of sophomores, juniors, and seniors in one of the twelve fraternities and five sororities on campus. But for those not interested in joining, "you will not be ostracized," and almost all parties are open to the entire student body. In response to the social focus on Greek life, in 2004 the college created the Minerva Houses, a residential program made of seven houses to which incoming students are randomly assigned. Each house has its own council and holds its own events, ranging from lunches with professors to all-night dance parties. The houses provide another social outlet for students if Greek life is too much. But some students resent the houses for "trying to define our social lives."

Party nights at Union are usually on Wednesdays, Fridays, and Saturdays because most classes meet on Mondays, Wednesdays, and Fridays. Many parties, especially the frat parties, feature an abundance of alcohol, and many students agree that "binge drinking is a problem, but other drugs are not too visible on campus although they are there." Students also deal with a strongly enforced alcohol and drug policy on campus. If a student acquires five points—for being found drinking or doing drugs on campus several times—they are required to talk to the dean, and with eight points, a student is kicked out.

> **"It looks like a North Face factory exploded just off campus and showered everyone with fleeces and jackets."**

Students at Union have the opportunity to get to know many of their fellow students because of the small community that Union creates. Many students agree that because Union is so small, everyone is very friendly. Although the interests of students are diverse, most students are from the "Northeast and white," and are from "upper-middle-class families." "Most people here are pretty well-off," one student said. The "stereotypical Union kid" is often "preppy" and come winter, it "looks like a North Face factory exploded just off campus and showered everyone with fleeces and jackets."

Life in Schenectady

Union is notorious for its poor relations with the surrounding city. Most students agree that Schenectady is not the best city for a college campus, and while not too many students go into Schenectady, Union takes precautionary steps to make sure every student is safe. Almost all students live on campus, which helps foster Union's community sense. Freshmen have the choice between four different dorms, and by sophomore year, students live in suites that have two bedrooms and a common room. Upperclassmen have the option of living in the

Minerva House—an option not available to freshmen—or some apartments on or off campus, as housing is guaranteed until junior year. Some of the dorms include College Park Hall, once a Ramada Inn, which includes air-conditioning and individual bathrooms. Union also has theme houses where students can live, such as the Iris House, which raises LGBTQ awareness, and the Ozone House, which promotes environmental awareness.

One thing many students agree on is the beauty of Union. In addition to the majestic Nott Memorial building at the center of the campus, other architectural features include the "modern" Olin Center, a sciences building, and the "Greek-like architecture" of Old Chapel. Union makes it very clear that its architecture is unique as is its campus plan, which was the first unified college campus plan in the United States. Another distinctive part of campus is the Reamer Campus Center, which is "always bustling with activity" and there are always "at least a dozen people you know in there at a given time." The first floor of the Campus Center is the central hangout place for students, and at the Campus Center, students can get "better" food than offered in the dining halls.

Most students on campus have meal plans, including upperclassmen, because of the limited dining options off campus. The West Dining Hall and the Upper Dining Hall are the main dining halls for students. Around campus, there are other options such as Starbucks, a convenience store, and the sit-down Café Ozone, where students can use their student cards to get lunch on Fridays. Off-campus food options are five to ten minutes away and require a car. Getting to one of the off-campus food destinations is not a problem for the many upperclassmen who keep a car on campus. Although Schenectady does not have a good reputation among most students, some would say that during the day, Schenectady is a "quaint" and "pleasant town" to go to for a crepe, to see a movie, or to go rock-climbing.

Where Hockey Rules

With student clubs abundant and ranging from politics to cultural activities to social action to sports, every Union student has the opportunity to take part in a group that they are interested in. If they can't find one, all it takes is an online form and 20 signatures to make a new student group. Some of the more prominent clubs are Colleges Against Cancer, which hosts the annual Relay for Life to raise cancer awareness; *Concordiensis*, the weekly school newspaper; men and women's club rugby; and Springfest, the club that organizes the annual Springfest Concert. Recent performers include Pat McGee and Rahzel.

The sport with the largest presence on campus is the men's hockey team, Union's only NCAA Division I sport. Hockey games are known for having a "full student section" with "screaming fans that heckle the other team." Other sports that have big turnouts include football and many games where Union is playing rival Rennselaer Polytechnic Institute. For nonathletes, the fitness center at the Alumni Gymnasium has been updated over the past five years and provides students with new equipment to help them to stay in shape. Another option for nonvarsity athletes is intramural sports, which are "very competitive" on campus. Intramurals include soccer, basketball, and the ever-popular broomball.

Between its "seven traditions" that students insist everyone must take part in before graduating (such as a "naked Nott run" around the Memorial) to its unique academic opportunities, Union provides its students with a community that cannot be replicated anywhere else. One freshman noted that the campus is "very united and everyone learns everyone else's face. It's like a big high school, but better."—*Willi Rechler*

FYI
If you come to Union, you'd better bring "a HUGE winter jacket."
What is the typical weekend schedule? "Go out on Wednesday for a mostly bar night, house or frat party on Friday and Saturday," and "wake up late Sunday, have brunch at West dining hall, and go back to sleep."
If I could change one thing about Union, I'd "get in better touch with Schenectady. The Union bubble needs to pop."
Three things every student at Union should do before graduating are "paint the Idol, do a naked Nott run, and complete the other five traditions that you will learn when you're here!"

United States Military Academy

Address: 646 Swift Road, West Point, NY 10996-1905
Phone: 845-938-4041
E-mail address: admissions@usma.edu
Web site URL: www.usma.edu
Year Founded: 1802
Private or Public: Public
Religious Affiliation: None
Location: Rural
Number of Applicants: 12,264
Percent Accepted: 13%
Percent Accepted who enroll: 82%
Number Entering: 1,312
Number of Transfers Accepted each Year: Unreported
Middle 50% SAT range: M: 580–680, CR: 570–670, Wr: 540–650
Middle 50% ACT range: 25–30
Early admission program EA/ED/None: None

Percentage accepted through EA or ED: NA
EA and ED deadline: NA
Regular Deadline: 28-Feb
Application Fee: $0
Full time Undergraduate enrollment: 4,686
Total enrollment: 4,686
Percent Male: Unreported
Percent Female: Unreported
Total Percent Minority or Unreported: 28%
Percent African-American: 6%
Percent Asian/Pacific Islander: 5%
Percent Hispanic: 9%
Percent Native-American: 1%
Percent International: 1%
Percent in-state/out of state: 7%/93%
Percent from Public HS: 87%
Retention Rate: 95%

Graduation Rate 4-year: 76%
Graduation Rate 6-year: 78%
Percent Undergraduates in On-campus housing: 100%
Number of official organized extracurricular organizations: 116
3 Most popular majors: Business, Economics, Engineering
Student/Faculty ratio: 8:1
Average Class Size: 14
Percent of students going to grad school: 100%
Tuition and Fees: $0
In-State Tuition and Fees if different: No difference
Cost for Room and Board: $0
Percent receiving financial aid out of those who apply: NA
Percent receiving financial aid among all students: NA

L ocated along the scenic Hudson River in upstate New York, the United States Military Academy, or West Point, has provided officer training to the United States Army since 1802. Founded by Thomas Jefferson, the academy endeavors to produce soldiers, scholars, and leaders.

Before the official start of the academic year, cadets must complete a "basic training" curriculum during the summer. During this intensive training, a large part consists of physical exercises such as "ruck marching"—or "marching with a load on your back" in addition to such basic skills like shooting a rifle, properly wearing the uniform, and field-based first aid, including inserting an IV into a fellow cadet. But the cadets tend to learn quickly—or they face "learning from mistakes with corrective PT (physical training)."

Military Academics

During their first two years at West Point, cadets are required to fill a "core curriculum," completing basic requirements in Military History, Chemistry, Leadership, Computer Science, Economics, English, History, International Relations, Law, Literature, Mathematics, Philosophy, Physical Geography, Physics, Political Science, and Terrain Analysis. After completing the requirements, cadets choose one of more than forty majors, including nuclear engineering. Popular majors include "anything engineering," with systems engineering being one of the most coveted. Current cadets report that pure sciences, such as chemistry and physics, have the reputation of being the most demanding, while systems management is one of the easiest majors. Students also laud the faculty of the engineering departments, claiming that the Army experience of the vast majority of instructors (over ninety percent) allows them to show students the real-world applicability of their studies.

With all classes capped at 18 students and a student-teacher ratio of eight to one, students enjoy the attention given by the faculty. Though academics are a critical part of the overall GPA, a cadet's grading average also comprises the military and physical portions of their education. While the physical portion derives from the cadet's performances in sports and the Army Physical Fitness test, composed of pushups, sit-ups, and a two-mile run, the military portion is dependent on "how well you take care of those under you" and performance in basic and summer training.

However, academics still retains the central focus—since 1923, more than 80 students at the Academy have been named Rhodes Scholars.

The "Lowest of the Low"
Students are required to live on campus for their four years at the Academy, with a daily 11:30 p.m. curfew. The dorms, called "barracks," vary widely in form and quality—with some having four rooms per floor and sharing one communal bathroom to others with twenty to thirty rooms and two communal baths—but virtually all rooms house two to three cadets. Students are assigned to their particular barracks on the basis of their platoon, a subdivision in the military structure present at West Point. The entire student body divides into a grouping of four regiments, which are then subdivided into two battalions, both of which are comprised of eight companies with four platoons each.

Instead of a traditional RA system, cadets are subjected to a rigorous hierarchy with freshmen, nicknamed plebes, required to obey virtually any command given by an upperclassman. However, platoon leaders, who are upperclassmen, reside with the freshmen, providing them with leaders to give guidance. "We're the lowest of the low," one current plebe said.

As plebes rise through the ranks, the quality of the rooms typically improves, making the chances of having only one roommate, instead of two, the norm for "plebe" year, decrease.

Recent construction projects on campus include Jefferson Hall–USMA Library and Learning Center, a multimillion-dollar, 141,000-square-foot new facility . . . and a science center.

Diversity in the Army
Cadets claim that diversity is present throughout the Academy, though males make up the vast majority of the class. Females make up only a small percent of the academy, with a relatively high drop-out rate. While the initial ratio of females to males is five to one, by senior year, the ratio drops to ten to one. One female cadet claims that she commonly is "the only girl" or "one of three" girls in her classes. Students cite the struggle of being a student-athlete, with virtually all students involved in some form of athletics, and the increasing amount of responsibility as one moves up the ranks, for the high departure rate for females. In addition, one cadet claims that, due to the relatively higher proportion of females being recruited athletes, and experiencing the associated stresses, they tend to be "the first to go"—part of the relatively large amount of students: twenty-two percent—who fail to graduate.

In sophomore year, students are responsible for one "plebe," and, in junior or senior year, this sense of ownership expands to a squad or company, and then a battalion or regiment—"so it doesn't get any easier," creating higher drop-out rates.

> "Everywhere we go we are constantly reminded that we represent not only West Point but the U.S. Army."

Though West Point can boast of "international cadets," and students from every state are represented at the Academy, cadets from both California and Florida can seem over-represented, claim the students. However, every demographic category seems well-represented, they said.

A "Relaxed" Weekend
Though freshmen say most weekends "you can hang out here and do homework," cadets receive one pass per semester, which they typically use to travel to New York, a trip of a bit more than an hour. In addition, unless a cadet is on "restriction"—a form of probation—they are allowed "walking privileges" around the town, where activities traditionally consist of going into the town of West Point to eat or just hang out.

Alcohol is strictly forbidden in the barracks and cadets attest that "it is not as prevalent as it is at most colleges," but "we have it here." If a cadet is caught with alcohol, they are served an "alcohol board" which consists of an inquisition by the "brigade chain of command" and typically results in "walking hours" where a cadet must walk with a rifle for a period of five hours in a central area of campus.

Cadets enjoy the vibrant extracurricular environment, with some noting the language clubs as being particularly popular for their "trip sections" in which the Portuguese club travels to Brazil over spring break, while the French club travels to

Paris, or French-speaking African countries. Other activities include *Pointer View*, the official newspaper of the school, and even a Close Combat (paintball) club.

And this extracurricular vitality translates into a drive to succeed characteristic of the Academy. "Everywhere we go we are constantly reminded that we represent not only West Point but the U.S. Army," a cadet said. —*John Klement*

FYI
If you come to West Point, you'd better bring: "You don't necessarily need anything because they issue you everything when you get here."
If I could change one thing about West Point, it would be "nearly impossible to answer because a lot of what we do is based on tradition."
What's the typical weekend schedule? "If it's a football game weekend and if your regiment is doing the parade you get up a little earlier on Saturday to form up for that or guard and usher detail; Sunday: Recall formation at seven o'clock, then evening study period until taps at eleven-thirty."

University of Rochester

Address: 300 Wilson Boulevard, Rochester, NY 14627
Phone: 888-822-2256
E-mail address: admit@admissions.rochester.edu
Web site URL: www.enrollment.rochester.edu/admissions
Year Founded: 1850
Private or Public: Public
Religious Affiliation: None
Location: Suburban
Number of Applicants: 12,111
Percent Accepted: 38%
Percent Accepted who enroll: 23%
Number Entering: 1,308
Number of Transfers Accepted each Year: Unreported
Middle 50% SAT range: M: 630–730, CR: 600–690, Wr: 600–700
Middle 50% ACT range: 29–32

Early admission program EA/ED/None: ED
Percentage accepted through EA or ED: 48%
EA and ED deadline: 1-Nov
Regular Deadline: 1-Jan
Application Fee: $60
Full time Undergraduate enrollment: 5,601
Total enrollment: 10,111
Percent Male: 51%
Percent Female: 49%
Total Percent Minority or Unreported: 41%
Percent African-American: 4%
Percent Asian/Pacific Islander: 11%
Percent Hispanic: 11%
Percent Native-American: <1%
Percent International: 13%
Percent in-state/out of state: 53%/47%
Percent from Public HS: 75%
Retention Rate: 96%

Graduation Rate 4-year: 74%
Graduation Rate 6-year: 85%
Percent Undergraduates in On-campus housing: 83%
Number of official organized extracurricular organizations: 220
3 Most popular majors: Social Sciences, Biology, Psychology
Student/Faculty ratio: 10:1
Average Class Size: 29
Percent of students going to grad school: 53%
Tuition and Fees: $41,802
In-State Tuition and Fees if different: No difference
Cost for Room and Board: $12,120
Percent receiving financial aid out of those who apply: Unreported
Percent receiving financial aid among all students: Unreported

Nationally recognized for its focus on the sciences, the University of Rochester is one of New York's most popular research universities. Home to some five thousand undergrads with interests ranging from optics to Indian dance, Rochester has world-class facilities, comfortable housing options, and an open curriculum that encourages its students to explore their interests. Rochester students are not only "independent and capable, but also extremely friendly," and are always eager to expand their horizons, be it by studying abroad or making friends by sledding on dining hall trays.

A Scientific Focus

Founded in 1850, Rochester has been known as one of the nation's top research institutions for decades. Hailed as one of the 25 "New Ivies," Rochester boasts particularly strong science programs, including the nation's oldest optics program. "Science and social science seem more dominant" than humanities majors, but the university also offers "super popular" economics and political science majors that are also nationally recognized. Other offerings for non-science types include a respected film program and degrees offered through the prestigious Eastman School of Music. In addition, the school offers numerous scholar programs, including REBS (Rochester Early Business Scholars) and REMS (Rochester Early Medical Scholars), which give students guaranteed admission to the business or medical school upon matriculation as a freshman.

Rochester students praise their academic environment as "stimulating," noting that although classes can be difficult, the quality of the professors makes them worth the effort. Although some classes are graded on a curve, students would say that "there's basically no grade inflation." "The general attitude at Rochester is that if you put in the effort, you'll do well." Rochester students are also quick to praise their graduation requirements—or rather, the lack thereof. There's only one class that all Rochester students are required to take: a freshman writing seminar. Rochester students across the board list the lax requirements as one of their favorite things about the school; they know they can "take whatever [they] want, without having to worry about getting math or foreign language credits." However, many Rochester students do take numerous classes outside of their major. There's a "general consensus" among science majors that one can't leave Rochester without taking popular international relations or humanities courses; "you'd have to search pretty hard to find a science major at Rochester who didn't have some intellectual interest outside of his field." These interests are nourished by the school's cluster system, by which students have to take a cluster of courses from two fields other than their major. The "clusters" consist of three related courses that can be completed over a student's four years, and "are really easy to do."

Although "intro classes can be pretty big," with around one hundred students per class, students say that the student-faculty ratio improves as one gets older. Seniors in advanced seminars sometimes have as few as five people in their classes, and even freshmen and sophomores note that there are numerous opportunities to take small seminars.

> "If you put in the effort, you'll do well."

For those looking for a break from New York winters, study abroad is a popular option. Although the school is eager to help students "go basically wherever they want to," a particularly popular destination is Arezzo, Italy, where UR has its own specific program to cater to students' needs. The school encourages students to "learn outside of their comfort zone," and even offers a special Take Five Program, which allows students to study a field different from their major for a fifth year after graduation, tuition-free.

Social

"At any school where students study as hard as Rochester, you're definitely going to find kids partying hard, too." For students who want to go out, on-campus frat parties and off-campus bars are popular options, although upperclassmen tend to "stick to parties at off-campus apartments and the like." This is partly due to the dorm's "strict" alcohol policy, which students say can be a pain to avoid even though "the penalties aren't too bad." Frat parties are more typical "freshman fare," and Greek life doesn't play a central role on campus—in fact, "it's easy to go all four years at Rochester without ever setting foot in a frat house." For those who want quiet weekends, it's easy to find relaxing ways to spend a Friday and Saturday night.

Music, dance, and a capella groups are big on campus, and most offer a wide range of options on weekends, ranging from shows to parties. "Every girl at Roch is obsessed with the Midnight Ramblers," campus's most famous a capella group. The Midnight Ramblers are known for their talent and their extremely popular social events, and most Rochester students are quick to tell outsiders that "they were picked by Ben Folds to be on his CD, so you know they're pretty awesome."

One famous Rochester event is Meliora

Weekend, "a combination of homecoming, parents' weekend, and a giant class reunion" that brings thousands of Rochester students, parents, and alums together for a weekend of "awesome parties" and an "overall great time." The weekend's festivities also include a keynote speaker, and the university has drawn some pretty notable ones in the past, including Colin Powell, Anderson Cooper, and Stephen Colbert. Rochester also celebrates "Dandelion Day" each spring with a vast array of outdoor activities, including campus-wide games and a "fairly famous" band.

"Sports? What Sports?"

Located on the banks of the Genessee River, Rochester's campus is known for its scenic views and sled-worthy hills. Freshman dorms tend to be small, but "everyone's a little too focused on their classes to complain about housing." Sophomores and juniors have a wider variety of housing options, including larger singles and comfortable suites. Seniors often choose to live in university housing off campus, such as spacious apartments "perfect for lower-key parties."

School pride at athletic events "could use work," but is never listed as a complaint among the Rochester student body. All Rochester students "like what they're doing, they just don't show it in an in-your-face sports kind of way." Although there are plenty of athletes on campus, the school's sports teams aren't particularly popular. Students do participate in a wide variety of extracurriculars, however, from nationally ranked Indian dance groups such as Raas to numerous volunteer organizations.

School pride is manifested in the "general feeling of community" one gets from the small class sizes and close-knit living quarters, as well as during campus traditions such as Meliora Weekend or Nick Tahoe's run, a competition organized by frats that involves a mad dash and the quick consumption of a "garbage plate." (The dish is another Rochester tradition, a "huge and delicious" plate at a local restaurant that "you'll enjoy, but only want to eat once.")

Although Rochester is most widely known for its stellar science programs, students say there's "an art to being a Rochester student." Students need a particular combination of academic interest, determination, and independence to succeed at UR—"If you know what you want to do, whether it's something extracurricular or related to going out on a weekend, Rochester has all the opportunities you'll ever need. If you don't . . . figure it out."—*Iva Velickovic*

FYI
The number-one thing I wish I'd known before I came to Rochester was "how cold it is—bring your snow boots!"
I chose Rochester because "the only thing that impressed me more than the academic programs was the school's comprehensive financial aid offerings."
Three things every Rochester student has to do before graduation are "climb to the top of Rush Rhees (the library), sled down the back of Sue B (the Susan B. Anthony residence hall for freshman) on dining hall trays, and eat a garbage plate."

Vassar College

Address: 124 Raymond Avenue, Poughkeepsie, NY 12604
Phone: 845-437-7000
E-mail address: admissions@vassar.edu
Web site URL: www.vassar.edu
Year Founded: 1861
Private or Public: Private
Religious Affiliation: None
Location: Suburban
Number of Applicants: 7,361
Percent Accepted: 23%
Percent Accepted who enroll: 35%
Number Entering: 670
Number of Transfers Accepted each Year: 30
Middle 50% SAT range: M: 650–730, CR: 670–740, Wr: 660 750
Middle 50% ACT range: 30–33
Early admission program EA/ED/None: ED

Percentage accepted through EA or ED: 38%
EA and ED deadline: 15-Nov
Regular Deadline: 1-Jan
Application Fee: $60
Full time Undergraduate enrollment: 2,386
Total enrollment: unreported
Percent Male: 45%
Percent Female: 55%
Total Percent Minority or Unreported: 39%
Percent African-American: 6%
Percent Asian/Pacific Islander: 9%
Percent Hispanic: 9%
Percent Native-American: 0%
Percent International: 7%
Percent in-state/out of state: 26%/74%
Percent from Public HS: 65%
Retention Rate: 96%
Graduation Rate 4-year: 87%

Graduation Rate 6-year: Unreported
Percent Undergraduates in On-campus housing: 95%
Number of official organized extracurricular organizations: 105
3 Most popular majors: Social Sciences, Visual and Performing Arts, English
Student/Faculty ratio: 8:1
Average Class Size: 15
Percent of students going to grad school: 35%
Tuition and Fees: $44,705
In-State Tuition and Fees if different: No difference
Cost for Room and Board: $10,430
Percent receiving financial aid out of those who apply: 85%
Percent receiving financial aid among all students: 61%

Tucked away in Poughkeepsie, New York, Vassar College is a small liberal arts college known for its gorgeous campus and small-school feel. Consistently ranked among the top universities in the country, Vassar is highly selective. Originally a women's college and the first of the Seven Sisters colleges, Vassar turned co-educational in 1969 and has a female-male ratio of about 55:45.

A Liberal Arts Education

Vassar's graduation requirements are not particularly demanding: students need only take a freshman writing seminar, demonstrate proficiency in a foreign language (students can test out of this requirement), take at least one quantitative analysis course, and take 34 credits of classes.

Of over 50 majors, the most popular ones are political science, psychology, English, and economics. Vassar also offers many interdisciplinary majors, such as science, technology, and society. Students must have at least 25% of their coursework outside of their major.

Grading policies vary from professor to professor, though in the English department, papers receive only comments and no grades. Students get a grade only at the end of the semester in these classes. Most professors do not curve grades, though some economics and mathematics classes are graded on a curve. One student noted, "People aren't competitive at all and everyone here is just really, really chill."

Students said they never had any trouble talking to Vassar faculty, who are often available during long office hours and are generally very flexible with students' workload. Professors are not afraid to assign long readings and papers, but are generally cooperative about deadlines. Professors are also eager to get to know students personally: one senior said that her co-op house often invites professors over for dinner, and that some of her professors have invited their classes to their houses.

Getting into restrictive classes can sometimes pose difficulties. Like the housing system, the pre-registration system for classes relies on a draw, with each student picking a draw number. Certain seminars and labs fill up quickly, but in general, students can get into most classes with persistence. However, Vassar tries to make it more fair by giving each student a variety of draw numbers over their semesters; someone with a really bad draw number first semester will have a much better one for second semester.

> **"People aren't competitive at all and everyone here is just really, really chill."**

Among the more difficult classes are some of the sciences, especially organic chemistry, as well as an interesting but challenging freshman seminar, Professor Kiese Laymon's Hip Hop and Critical Citizenship. Among the easy gut classes are a number of 6-week classes that can be taken for half a credit, as well as the Art of Film. Some of the more fun and interesting classes offered are the Chemistry and Culture of Cuisine and Yoga in the West.

Though Vassar has a reputation for being particularly strong in the humanities, students said that the sciences are actually just as strong and that there is an increasing focus on supporting the sciences. Currently, Vassar is building a large science center that will be constructed in the next few years. One senior who reflected upon her academic experience said that what she most appreciated about the academic approach at Vassar was its belief that students should explore beyond their major. Denied the ability to take two biology classes her first semester of freshman year, she said branching out ultimately helped her and was a good decision she wouldn't have made on her own.

The Vassar Bubble
Vassar has no Greek life, and instead of being centered around fraternity and sorority houses, Vassar's party scene is ultimately rooted in senior housing and individual dorms. Because seniors don't live in dormitories, they have fewer difficulties with security breaking up their parties, explaining why most parties happen in senior Town Houses.

A majority of students drink alcohol, and the Vassar administration has a Good Samaritan policy towards alcohol. If students call for help for either themselves or their friend, there is no disciplinary action taken. However, security patrols the campus at night and will break up parties that are being particularly loud and disruptive, especially if noise complaints are filed. Students who go to the hospital for alcohol consumption sometimes have to take mandatory classes educating them about the effects of drinking; other students get kicked out of their dorms and moved to a different one if caught excessively drinking. Students described the rules' strictness as "medium."

Despite the presence of drinking on campus, there is no overbearing pressure to drink, as there are events every night for those who opt out of parties. Thursday nights are jazz nights at The Mug, Vassar's local bar, and a steady crowd dances there weekly. Almost every night, there's an a cappella, drama, or music performance going on somewhere on or around campus, and there is plenty for all crowds to enjoy.

Vassar is close enough to New York City (a little more than two hours away on the Metro-North train) that some students choose to visit the city over the weekend, though most students choose to stay on campus. Not too many students have cars, though some upperclassmen use cars to go grocery shopping or take trips outside of Vassar. Among those who do use cars, Zipcars are a popular way of getting around.

Tight Communities Centered Around Dormitories
The dormitory system, comprised of nine different dormitories home to between 170 and 350 students, allows close-knit communities to form. Each dormitory has its own unique reputation, but these reputations change from year to year: From the very start, freshmen are put in groups of ten with a student fellow, a sophomore who is meant to be a guide with no disciplinary role. Each dormitory also has a professor who lives there with his/her family. Girls can request on housing forms to be placed in Strong House, an all-female dorm. Some years, girls will be put in Strong House even if they have not indicated a strong preference.

Freshmen are assigned housing and all live in either doubles or triples. Sophomores and juniors have more choice and have draw numbers to choose their housing arrangements, and many students who ask for singles are granted their requests. Some buildings are particularly old, meaning that not all the rooms are in the best shape, but most students say the housing is not a huge issue, especially given that Vassar is trying to renovate the dormitories.

Dormitories house freshmen through juniors; seniors then move out of dorms and have three options of apartments: the Town Houses (where most of the partying on campus happens), Terrace Apartments (which are closer to the center of campus), and South Commons (which are a little farther out on campus). Vassar also has the unique option of cooperative houses, in which students of all grades live together and make their own food.

Students described Vassar as very diverse in all senses: after changing to a need-blind system in 2007, current seniors said there was a noticeable increase and diversity and now has students of all economic and ethnic backgrounds; 10% of students are from 50 different nations.

A Distinct Campus
The Vassar library resembles a "Victorian castle," and is one of the most distinctive buildings on campus. Vassar has varied architecture, varying from modern, new buildings designed by more recent architects to older brick buildings. The Center for Drama and Film was recently built.

The main dining center, the All-Campus Dining Center, could have better food. Many students opt for other places, such as the UPC Cafe and The Retreat. The surrounding town of Arlington also has many nearby restaurants. Bacio's has pizza until 4 a.m. on Saturdays and the Acropolis Diner is open 24/7; Babycakes, Thai Spice, and Twisted Soul (American fusion food) are also options.

However, the Poughkeepsie area is generally considered unsafe by Vassar students, who generally stay on campus. Though one senior said that based on her experience, this is more of a myth than the actual truth, all students noticed that relations between Poughkeepsie and Vassar are somewhat strained, with one person saying that Vassar is a "bubble" seemingly separate from Poughkeepsie. Many individual organizations on campus work with Poughkeepsie, setting up programs in public schools and doing other outreach work, but it has yet to become the norm.

In terms of extra-curricular activities, Vassar has pretty much everything there is to offer. *The Miscellany News*, Vassar's weekly paper, is popular and widely read on campus. The numerous a cappella groups, like the Vassar Devils, are also a huge part of campus life, in addition to a variety of drama and music performance groups. The Barefoot Monkeys are a circus group that practice around campus and the quad and are a visible part of campus life. VICE, Vassar College Entertainment, is the student's entertainment group that brings outside performers and acts to campus.

Vassar lacks school spirit when it comes to its sports teams: there's no tailgating, and while some of its teams are strong compared to other schools in its division, most students don't follow sports closely. However, Frisbee is a big sport on campus, and people can often be seen throwing a disc around on the quad.

An Established School with Old Traditions
Vassar is rich in traditions, with the biggest annual party being Founder's Day. A carnival with music and free beer for seniors, some students use Founder's Day in the spring as an occasion to try harder drugs. Serenading is an event at the beginning of the year, when the freshmen of different dorms create and sing songs for seniors, who spray them with water guns as part of a bigger water fight. And Vassar students let out the stress from their academics with Primal Scream, which happens at the beginning of finals week each semester: students gather in the quad and scream as loud as they can before retreating to study.

With classes that have no grades, an eclectic array of architecture, proximity to NYC, and screaming as a group relaxation activity, Vassar stands out among colleges simply as a fun place to get a great education.—*Diana Li*

FYI
If you come to Vassar, you'd better leave behind "your tailgating supplies and expectations of Greek life."
Three things every student at Vassar should do before graduating are "go to Bacio's at 2 a.m., take a women's studies class, and see a Barefoot Monkeys fire show."
What surprised me the most about Vassar is that "everyone hangs out with everyone: the athletes, the nerds, and the hipsters all hang out together."

Wells College

Address: 170 Main Street, Aurora, NY 13026
Phone: 315-364-3264
E-mail address: admissions@wells.edu
Web site URL: www.wells.edu
Year Founded: 1868
Private or Public: Private
Religious Affiliation: None
Location: Rural
Number of Applicants: 1,148
Percent Accepted: 71%
Percent Accepted who enroll: 24%
Number Entering: 164
Number of Transfers Accepted each Year: 67
Middle 50% SAT range: M: 460–570, CR: 480–590, Wr: 470–580
Middle 50% ACT range: 21–26
Early admission program EA/ED/None: EA/ED

Percentage accepted through EA or ED: 79%/ Unreported
EA and ED deadline: 15-Dec
Regular Deadline: 1-Mar
Application Fee: $40
Full time Undergraduate enrollment: 559
Total enrollment: Unreported
Percent Male: 28%
Percent Female: 72%
Total Percent Minority or Unreported: 38%
Percent African-American: 14%
Percent Asian/Pacific Islander: 3%
Percent Hispanic: 3%
Percent Native-American: 1%
Percent International: 0%
Percent in-state/out of state: 69%/31%
Percent from Public HS: 88%
Retention Rate: 76%

Graduation Rate 4-year: 47%
Graduation Rate 6-year: 48%
Percent Undergraduates in On-campus housing: 84%
Number of official organized extracurricular organizations: 35
3 Most popular majors: Psychology, Social Sciences, Visual and Performing Arts
Student/Faculty ratio: 10:1
Average Class Size: 15
Percent of students going to grad school: Unreported
Tuition and Fees: $32,180
In-State Tuition and Fees if different: No difference
Cost for Room and Board: $11,000
Percent receiving financial aid out of those who apply: 98%
Percent receiving financial aid among all students: 93%

Pick a tradition, any tradition. Wells has more than enough to go around. Yet despite their overwhelming popularity amongst students, one of the school's most significant traditions has recently been broken. Wells, formerly an all-girls school, admitted its first coed class in the fall of 2005. The close community spirit engendered by such a small campus, however, ensured a smooth change. "For the most part I have had no problems at all," remarked one male freshman. "I feel very at home and the people here are very nice." Indeed, at Wells, community and tradition blend to create the "relaxed and laid-back campus" students value.

One-on-One

Within the framework of a small student body, students have considerable access to their professors. "The one-on-one time that students at Wells get is priceless," remarked one public affairs major. The quality of Wells professors makes this accessibility especially appealing. "Many of my professors are literally brilliant," one freshman exclaimed. And while the grading may be tough, "you learn quite a bit."

One of the more interesting courses offered at Wells is Book Arts, in which students study the processes of book binding and book restoration, and even learn how to use a printing press. "It's really neat," one junior remarked. He also commented on the uniqueness of the college's Book Arts center. Wells also has much to offer to those interested in education. An elementary school, Peachtown, is located on campus and Wells students are greatly involved in its activities.

Science and math majors are a minority. One math major did complain about the lack of incentive to enter her field. "To give copious awards for sports or writing doesn't really encourage others to major in math," she noted. Still, she praised the department itself. "I enjoy it and find it challenging, especially the upper-level courses, which is what I wanted when I came here."

Breathtaking Beauty

Most students are content living on campus. "The campus is absolutely breathtaking. I mean it is really, really beautiful," one freshman explained. However, the process of determining where to live on campus can be slightly more involved. Weld "has the best kitchen and individual bathrooms" while Glenn Park, the former home of Wells's founder, boasts spiral staircases and numerous lounges. Main, the biggest residence hall, also hosts the dining hall and is effectively the center of campus. In addition, the fourth floor serves as the Healthy Lifestyles floor, which offers a living environment in which "people don't get drunk or create havoc." While Leach "is crazy," students tend to avoid Dodge because "the style is a bit . . . retro" and it is farther than the other dorms from academic buildings.

No matter where students end up, the natural beauty of Wells's campus is available for everyone to enjoy. Students have access to the nearby lake for everything from science classes to skinny dipping, and many enjoy spending time on the docks. "There are trees everywhere—I came here because of the trees," one student asserted, adding that "the town of Aurora is also incredibly picturesque."

Just as students agree on the beauty of campus, they also agree on the quality of the food. Unfortunately, the consensus is not a positive one. "The dining hall is awful," complained one junior. "It's so bad," explained a sophomore, "that I *lost* 15 pounds freshman year." Still, there are a few who have good things to say about the food served on campus, so not all is lost. One senior praised "Dean Green's macaroni and cheese at soul food/home cooking night," explaining that "the administration actually comes and serves food sometimes." Furthermore, each residence hall has its own kitchen, so students always have the option of cooking for themselves.

On and Off Campus

The close relationship between the administration and students is not limited simply to the dining hall. "Wells has a ton of committees where students go right to the administration," said one performing arts major. "We have committees for everything from the dining hall to student diversity that meet with the senior staff on a regular basis." Aside from such committees, students have a wide range of opportunities for involvement on campus. Since Wells is strictly an undergraduate institution, Wells women and men have the opportunity to work as TAs in different subjects. Others spend their time in activities ranging from choirs, to the Japanese Culture Club, to groups such as Q&A (Queers and Allies).

Despite the abundance of extracurricular activities on campus, Wells students usually head to nearby Cornell or Ithaca College for parties. And while drinking on campus does exist, "it is usually pretty discreet in dorms. People are fairly mellow." As one junior explained, "People come to Wells to study . . . not party." Still, many students enjoy the social activities centered at Wells. One senior pointed to Sex Collective and the Women's Resource Center as one of her favorites, crediting them with "The Erotic Ball" and "The BDP" (Big Dyke Party).

Whether or not they choose to party in Ithaca, Wells women and men tend to agree that having a car on campus is very convenient. Though Wells offers shuttle van services to a variety of locations, one sophomore points out that they "don't go to too many places and the times at which you're allowed to take the van are set by the Transportation Department." Cars offer students the freedom of movement that shuttles simply cannot provide.

Above All, Tradition

Students love the great variety of traditions on campus, citing them as a large part of what makes Wells unique. The role of traditions is deeply ingrained in campus life, and begins every year with the Senior Champagne Breakfast and Opening Convocations. "We [the entire school] all make a huge circle in front of Macmillian and . . . light candles," a current freshman reported. After convocation, seniors jump into the lake wearing their lingerie.

> **"People come to Wells to study . . . not party."**

"Moving Up Day" is also a monumental event at Wells, officially marking the transition as students move from one year to the next or from student to alum. "The fire alarms are pulled around 6 or 7 a.m. and everyone gathers in front of Main building," one student recounted. "We 'circle up' and do the classes song. . . . After singing, the seniors race to get in line to kiss the feet of the statue of Minerva." Traditions marking the end of the school year include dancing around the sycamore tree on the last day of classes.

No matter which tradition they choose as their favorite, students are enthusiastic about the atmosphere such customs create. "I think it's special; I've never heard of these traditions anywhere else," noted one sophomore.

Wells has much to offer its undergraduates, and students find that their experiences more than exceed expectations. As one senior reflected, "The minute I stepped on campus I fell in love with it. It's exactly the place I knew I had to be and there has never been a moment . . . that I second guessed my decision." She added, "It has helped me grow as a person and challenged me in ways that I'm not sure I would have been at other schools. I love Wells and everything it has done for me."—*Stephanie Brockman*

FYI
If you come to Wells, you'd better bring "a car."
What is the typical weekend schedule? "Sleep, study, then head to Cornell."
If I could change one thing about Wells, I'd "move it closer to a city."
Three things that every student at Wells should do before graduating are "participate in all the traditions they can, skinny dip in the lake, be in a theater or dance production."

Yeshiva University

Address: 500 West 185th Street, New York, NY 10033
Phone: 212-960-5277
E-mail address: yuadmit@yu.edu
Web site URL: www.yu.edu
Year Founded: 1886
Private or Public: Private
Religious Affiliation: Jewish
Location: Urban
Number of Applicants: Unreported
Percent Accepted: 69%
Percent Accepted who enroll: Unreported
Number Entering: 769
Number of Transfers Accepted each Year: Unreported
Middle 50% SAT range: M: 570–680, CR: 550–670, Wr: Unreported
Middle 50% ACT range: Unreported
Early admission program EA/ED/None: None

Percentage accepted through EA or ED: NA
EA and ED deadline: NA
Regular Deadline: 15-Feb
Application Fee: $65
Full time Undergraduate enrollment: 3,076
Total enrollment: 3,076
Percent Male: 52%
Percent Female: 48%
Total Percent Minority or Unreported: 7%
Percent African-American: 2%
Percent Asian/Pacific Islander: 3%
Percent Hispanic: 3%
Percent Native-American: 0%
Percent International: Unreported
Percent in-state/out of state: Unreported
Percent from Public HS: Unreported
Retention Rate: 88%
Graduation Rate 4-year: Unreported

Graduation Rate 6-year: Unreported
Percent Undergraduates in On-campus housing: Unreported
Number of official organized extracurricular organizations: Unreported
3 Most popular majors: Judaic Studies, Political Science, Psychology
Student/Faculty ratio: Unreported
Average Class Size: Unreported
Percent of students going to grad school: Unreported
Tuition and Fees: $31,594
In-State Tuition and Fees if different: No difference
Cost for Room and Board: $9,880
Percent receiving financial aid out of those who apply: Unreported
Percent receiving financial aid among all students: Unreported

Yeshiva University, a prominent Jewish university with six campuses in New York and one in Israel, offers its students the unique opportunity to spend their freshman year on the other side of the Atlantic. With 45 yeshivas and institutions located throughout Israel to choose from, YU students can earn a year's worth of credits and enter YU with sophomore standing. All credits earned are transferable from Israel to YU in New York.

Small Classes, Down-to-Earth Professors

Students at Yeshiva University can undertake both secular and religious studies.

Undergraduates are offered a curriculum that includes typical college classes such as biology and psychology—which are popular on campus, because much of the student body is pre-med—but also includes religious classes such as Halacha (Jewish law), the Bible, and the Talmud. Yeshiva University offers small classes of around 5 to 20 students, except for large lectures such as biology or chemistry that are popular for pre-meds. Within the university, students are separated into schools by gender—Yeshiva College for men and Stern College for women. Students can also enroll in special schools, such as the Belz School of Music and the Sy Symns School of Business. One student described the professors at Yeshiva University as very accessible and down-to-earth. Another student said that most classes at YU are very major-based, in that there are "not so many eclectic classes" that can be found at larger universities; rather, the majority of classes are related to specific popular majors. Some students said that students from individual schools, such as the business school, have "their own clique" on campus. Because the school is located in New York City, guest speakers are frequently brought in to lectures and sometimes are very popular. The only downside to YU's academic life is that the humanities are sometimes looked down upon by students who pursue studies in science or math, because the humanities programs at YU are not as well-known or popular as science programs. The university offers over 30 majors, in addition to a group of joint-degree programs. The school also has an honors program for both Stern College and Yeshiva College.

Varied Housing Arrangements

According to some students, housing at YU is enjoyable because the dorms are nice and it is convenient to not deal with monthly billings and shared cleaning situations. However, other students said that they opted to live off-campus in apartments, specifically because the two dorms separate women and men, and do not allow the opposite sex in dorm rooms. Since the school is divided into essentially two campuses that are more than 100 blocks apart, traveling back and forth between dorms to visit students of the opposite sex can be difficult. The majority of YU students live within a three-block radius of campus, and most upperclassmen move into apartments after living in the dorms. There are three main dorms—Rubin Dorm, on top of a cafeteria and athletic center; MUSS Dorm, considered to be the nicest and situated

above the main Beit Midrash; and Morge, the largest dorm located at the center of campus. Each floor is set up in the style of a hallway with dorm rooms branching off, with a lounge on each floor and an RA who is usually friendly and not strict. The Wilf campus, where the Yeshiva College for men is located, is within easy walking distance of the housing options. The Stern College for women, which is located at the Beren campus in Midtown Manhattan, offers independent housing in addition to three residence halls.

Classroom Outside of the Classroom

Because YU is located in New York City, one of its greatest assets is its location. The school boasts one of the largest Jewish populations outside of Israel, because it is a Jewish university situated in the "Western capital of the Jewish world." Students at YU enjoy the easy access to kosher dining and synagogues. Additionally, students appreciate that they can get on the subway from their campus and travel conveniently throughout New York City. Girls at Stern College, located in Midtown, are very close to Times Square. Students generally do not have cars on campus because of the urban location, so the average YU student uses New York's public transportation system to get around. The school is located very close to several restaurants that are popular among students, particularly a few pizza places and a well-frequented Mediterranean restaurant that serves, according to one student, food that "is probably cancerous but is the best food ever." There is no prominent Greek scene at YU, although the national Jewish fraternity AEPi started a chapter at YU several years ago and men can choose to pledge the fraternity by contacting fraternity brothers for more information. As for the party scene, students at YU have easy access to alcohol by living around many liquor stores that do not typically require ID verification, and some students travel to Midtown for birthday celebrations. However, ultimately, the amount of partying and drinking that can go on at YU depends on "which crowd you're running with."

Spectrum of Religious Involvement

The amount of religious involvement from students at YU varies greatly. Some students are deeply religious and adhere to religious rules strictly, choosing to keep interactions with the opposite sex down to a minimum and staying on campus every weekend for religious observances such as the Sabbath. However, other students see themselves as moderately religious, and a small minority of students identify as non-religious. Because YU is a Jewish institution, there is very little religious diversity on campus—however, many Jewish students come from outside the United States. The university has students from France, Canada, and Israel, among other places. Generally, students tend to know each other from the same neighborhoods, high schools, or yeshivas in Israel. YU is a unique school because of its focus on religious involvement, offering events such as a Hanukkah celebration and a Purim celebration that many students look forward to for months each year. As one student put it, "There are no real traditions at YU, except for the Torah."

Familiar Faces, Communities

Students at YU are friendly with one another, and several students said they recognize the majority of faces around campus. Because underclassmen are often in the same classes as upperclassmen, the university fosters a good sense of community. Friends are easy to make from classes and extracurricular events, in addition to religious events or campus-wide activities. As for extracurricular groups, students usually find their niche in a group such as athletics or the arts, and events for the Sabbath every weekend offer the opportunity to have large meals with a lot of people and join in some communal singing or prayers. Additionally, the university is located in an area that is generally considered very safe by many students. One student said that he feels completely safe walking around the area at 3 a.m., especially because security call phones are stationed around campus.

Yeshiva University is a Jewish university in the heart of New York City with a friendly community and an intimate academic setting. Though the social scene tends to lean toward the "tame," according to several students, people still have fun attending university events or religious celebrations, and there's always the larger city outside of the university's campus if students want to get away for the weekend. Extracurricular groups exist in any field, from athletics to a capella. Overall, the university fosters a strong community of individuals who share the same faith, although the division of the campus into male and female sectors may be a drawback for some students.—*Amy Wang*

FYI
If students could change one thing about Yeshiva, "I would merge the male and female campuses to create one main co-ed campus, making the student life more lively and diminishing the cost of running two campuses."
The biggest college-wide events or traditions at Yeshiva are "religious celebrations, including a celebration of the Jewish holiday Purim."
Before graduating, every Yeshiva student should do the following three things: "take Rabbi Angel's Bible class, spend a Shabbat on campus, and participate in the school's theater scene by acting in a play."

North Carolina

Address: PO Box 7156, Davidson, NC 28035
Phone: 704-894-2230
E-mail address: admission@davidson.edu
Web site URL: www.davidson.edu
Year Founded: 1837
Private or Public: Private
Religious Affiliation: Presbyterian
Location: Suburban
Number of Applicants: 3,940
Percent Accepted: 30%
Percent Accepted who enroll: 39%
Number Entering: 461
Number of Transfers Accepted each Year: Unreported
Middle 50% SAT range: M: 630–720, Cr: 620–720, Wr: 680–740
Middle 50% ACT range: 27–31
Early admission program EA/ED/None: ED

Percentage accepted through EA or ED: 41%
EA and ED deadline: 15-Nov
Regular Deadline: 2-Jan
Application Fee: $50
Full time Undergraduate enrollment: 1,660
Total enrollment: 1,660
Percent Male: 50%
Percent Female: 50%
Total Percent Minority or Unreported: 24%
Percent African-American: 7%
Percent Asian/Pacific Islander: 3%
Percent Hispanic: 5%
Percent Native American: 1%
Percent International: 3%
Percent in-state/out of state: 19%/81%
Percent from Public HS: 48%
Retention Rate: 95%

Graduation Rate 4-year: 89%
Graduation Rate 6-year: 91%
Percent Undergraduates in On-campus housing: 91%
Number of official organized extracurricular organizations: 151
3 Most popular majors: English, History, Economics
Student/Faculty ratio: 10:1
Average Class Size: 18
Percent of students going to grad school: 25%
Tuition and Fees: $30,662
In-State Tuition and Fees if different: No difference
Cost for Room and Board: $9,020
Percent receiving financial aid out of those who apply: 64%
Percent receiving financial aid among all students: 32%

In the quaint, small Southern town of Davidson, North Carolina, you will discover quintessential Southern hospitality—and not just from the townspeople, but from the students that call Davidson College their home for four years. Despite intense academics, it is this supportive and caring atmosphere, combined with a mutual love of learning, that captures the Davidson experience.

Close and extraordinarily tight-knit, it's the community of people that students cite as what separates their school from others. Students interviewed all commented on the friendliness of Davidson students. "Everyone wants to get to know you, more than just who you are. They want to know where you come from, what makes you you, what excites you. They really want to get to know you at a different level," one student said. One student described the culture as "egalitarian," explaining that "everything's an open playing field, in classes and in social life and just using the facilities. Everyone's just willing to share."

Academics Built on Trust and Friendship

Davidson's egalitarian atmosphere stems in part from the seriousness with which the students regard the Honor Code, which prohibits cheating, stealing, and lying. This is not a throwaway piece of paper one struggles to write out in cursive and signs, never to be seen again. It forms the cornerstone of the Davidson community. All students live by it—the Honor Council is student run and members of the student body elect its members. "I'm never afraid to not lock my door. I always trust all of my friends to not steal my stuff. They're free to borrow things. I can leave my computer in the library overnight and know that it's going to be there when I get back. It just creates an amazing community of respect here on campus," said one student.

The Honor Code allows students to trust their professors and vice versa. Davidson's Honor Code means that tests and exams are usually un-proctored and self-scheduled or take-home—"to make sure you're in the most optimal conditions when you're taking an exam," said one student. It works because students at Davidson embrace the liberal arts philosophy of learning for the sake of learning. They're driven and passionate, working extraordinarily hard. "Davidson is full of type A personalities that really like to get their work done and like to do the best they can in everything they possibly do. I think the purpose of Davidson is to prove that you cannot do everything academically," said one student. Several students praised the depth and diversity of intellectual discourse in and outside of class amongst Davidson students. "Some of the people I admire most on this campus are people I disagree with most, either politically or religiously. I love that we can share so much love for each other while having such different views, knowing that that's not what's most important."

The community includes all corners of the college faculty and staff. When one student was to receive an award at the fall convocation, her family, living in California, was unable to attend. She created a makeshift family that included a laundry center staff member who "acts like a mother for me and was so excited too." Another student, describing a popular sandwich shop on campus, noted that the staff would "pretty much know your name and order after the third time you've been there."

The highest levels of administration are no different. The president has "talkbacks" and town halls for discussion with students on topics as important as how to spend new endowment dollars. She has gone out for ice cream with students and invites members of the senior class to dinner. One sophomore recalled an encounter in which the President postponed a trustees meeting in order to comfort her and give her a pep talk, as she was having a breakdown at the time.

"I told her I liked her suit and that's all I meant to say, but she stopped to ask me 'How are you?' I told her I had just come out from a meeting with a professor and she was asking me 'What professor?' My voice cracked and I thought 'Oh my gosh this is the worst thing, I'm about to cry in front of the president,' but it was the best thing that could have happened to me, because she just stopped time for me; for me, a freshman that didn't matter at all."

Perhaps most important in terms of academics, however, is the personal touch of the professors, which makes the academic rigor of the curriculum more manageable, and there's no question that Davidson academics are tough. "I did IB in high school, so I understood 'heavy workload.' But then going to Davidson, it was really a wake up call. I realized that a paper that would get me 100 in high school would get me like a B- or a C in Davidson." Students are expected to visit office hours frequently. "For the last poli-sci paper, I went into a professor's office either three or four times at different points in my paper writing process, and I still might be in trouble after showing up so many times," one student said.

Yet, all students point out professors' genuine desire to help their students learn. "I had an econ teacher who wrote on my test to come see him and I was initially very worried. What he did was to explain every concept I did not understand, sat down with me with a sheet of paper and did it. I was in his office for three hours going over concepts," recalled one student. Another student, who was having trouble speaking Spanish in class, was able to talk to his professor and work out a solution where he could speak to her in private after class every week. Professors are highly accessible outside class and quick to respond to emails, and take time to develop personal relationships with their students. Conversations can be about anything, even subjects unrelated to class. "We just have chats sometimes in our seminar where the professor will just check in and see how life is going," one student said.

Enthusiastic Participation

Davidson passion transfers just as easily to involvement in various extracurricular activities. Civic engagement and community service is highly popular, and all students interviewed were involved in some sort of community service, ranging from political to religious and environmental, as well as helping local high school students to develop civic engagement and nonprofit skills.

Davidson has a Center for Civic Engagement that provides grants and funding for student projects. "I did community service in high school, but nothing like this, and I think being in an environment at Davidson where so may people are involved with the community has helped pushed me there," said one student. Many students are Bonner Scholars, a scholarship program where students must complete 280 hours of community service a year for all four years.

Intramural and club sports are also common activities. Many students who have never participated in sports before enjoy such activities. In terms of varsity sports, basketball is where one can find traditional rah-rah school spirit, while other spirit for other sports is generally less prevalent. A substantial number of students are involved with religious groups and Bible studies. There are standard college activities, including four a cappella groups, a student newspaper and literary magazine, and student government, as well as clubs for more obscure interests such as beekeeping. "If you are interested in something, any random field, there's probably a group for it," said one student, and for those who genuinely cannot find a group for their interests, it is easy to start new clubs.

Divided and Diverse Social Scene

While driven devotion to extracurriculars and academics take up the majority of time at Davidson, students still party heavily on the weekends. "Weekends are reserved for all the type A personalities to blow off a ton of steam," said one student. Social life takes place "down the hill," where senior apartments, fraternities, and eating houses (Davidson's version of sororities) are located. Many students belong to fraternities and eating houses, but Davidson's Greek system is different from most schools. Members do not live in their fraternity houses or eating houses; they are merely buildings for social events and eating. In keeping with Davidson's hospitality, social functions are open to all. There are no gender ratios, cover fees, class limits, or memberships necessary to take part in parties.

"[A friend] and I showed up to a party where we were wearing overalls and Keds and pigtails and looking ridiculous for this childhood themed party. The theme for [the other party] was 'grown and sexy,' and everyone was supposed to be wearing dresses and high heels, and here we were anyway.

Nobody stopped us from going in," recalled one student.

Some dissatisfaction was expressed with the work hard, play hard culture. "It just feels kind of weird to work so hard and be really good students for five days, and then Friday night and Saturday night go crazy. The school has tried to do more for people who do more normal things, and we're close to Charlotte, but it's kind of weird. If you look for it, you can find it," said one student.

Other students disagreed, one student noting that she initially debated about whether to live in a sub-free hall, dorms where the policy and culture against alcohol and drug usage is extremely strict. Ultimately, she decided against it, ending up living in a party hall and feeling comfortable. Another student noted that one does not necessarily need to drink to enjoy the social scene down the hill, adding that he did not drink for the entirety of his first semester and still attended many parties. Davidson's Union Board hosts activities for those "up the hill," such as cupcake and cookie decorating, movie screenings, student performances, capture the flag, and assassins games. Students also have the option of escaping into the city of Charlotte, twenty minutes away. Borrowing cars from friends to do so, with the Honor Code, is easy.

While students agree that there is not much to do in the immediate surrounding area of Davidson, "a classic Norman Rockwell kind of small town in the south," many expressed affection for the generous townspeople, who bake cookies during finals for the students and participate in many school activities such as pumpkin carving. They also bake cakes for the traditional freshmen cake race, in which freshmen participate in a race and win their pick of the cakes in the order that they finish. "Many of them will invite the college students to go for lunch at their house after [Church], and they'll tell us we can study at their house any time we want to," said one student.

> "I was convinced I would never go to a southern school and the feel of the campus is really what pulled me in."

Classic and Comfortable Campus

Of the physical campus, Davidson boasts gorgeous Georgian architecture—"very colonial and Southern and classic and red brick." Another student called it "the idyllic southern school campus," adding that "I was convinced I would never go to a southern school and the feel of the campus is really what pulled me in." Davidson also offers Lake Campus, which sits on the waterfront of Lake Norman, where water sports teams practice, and where students can go to swim and have cookouts. Dorm facilities were recently renovated, including a newly dubbed "sophomore palace" building. There are single and double style rooms, as well as suite style. Seniors live in apartment style housing with balconies and high ceilings. One unique aspect to Davidson housing is its method of organizing freshmen. All freshmen complete a Myers-Brigg personality test over the summer, along with the typical roommate survey. Roommates are then selected by personality type compatibility, and freshmen halls are organized to compose a well-rounded group of personalities.

It's just another example of the way in which Davidson College fosters their strong sense of community, visible in all aspects of student life, even in the smallest details: "Just seeing Davidson students walking around, Davidson students always seem to be walking places together and talking. It seems like just a community that is just so open and close."—*Claire Zhang*

FYI

If you come to Davidson, you'd better bring "hiking shoes, so you can make use of the Davidson Outdoors trips."

If you come to Davidson you'd better leave "your laundry detergent, they do your laundry for you!"

One thing every student at Davidson should do before graduating are: "get into/climb the steeple of Davidson College Presbyterian church."

Duke University

Address: 2138 Campus Drive, Durham, NC 27708
Phone: 919-684-3214
E-mail address: admissions@duke.edu
Web site URL: www.duke.edu
Year Founded: 1838
Private or Public: Private
Religious Affiliation: Methodist
Location: Urban
Number of Applicants: 18,638
Percent Accepted: 21%
Percent Accepted who enroll: 43%
Number Entering: 1,683
Number of Transfers Accepted each Year: 41
Middle 50% SAT range: M: 680–790, Cr: 660–750, Wr: 680–780
Middle 50% ACT range: 29–34
Early admission program EA/ED/None: ED

Percentage accepted through EA or ED: 31%
EA and ED deadline: 1-Nov
Regular Deadline: 2-Jan
Application Fee: $75
Full time Undergraduate enrollment: 6,259
Total enrollment: 11,680
Percent Male: 52%
Percent Female: 48%
Total Percent Minority or Unreported: 32%
Percent African-American: 11%
Percent Asian/Pacific Islander: 14%
Percent Hispanic: 7%
Percent Native American: 1%
Percent International: 7%
Percent in-state/out of state: 15%/85%
Percent from Public HS: 65%
Retention Rate: 96%
Graduation Rate 4-year: 86%

Graduation Rate 6-year: 92%
Percent Undergraduates in On-campus housing: 82%
Number of official organized extracurricular organizations: 200
3 Most popular majors: Economics, Psychology, Public Policy
Student/Faculty ratio: 11:1
Average Class Size: 14
Percent of students going to grad school: 62%
Tuition and Fees: $31,420
In-State Tuition and Fees if different: No difference
Cost for Room and Board: $8,950
Percent receiving financial aid out of those who apply: Unreported
Percent receiving financial aid among all students: 39%

Perhaps best known among sports fans for its successful basketball team, Duke University is also recognized as one of the most prestigious establishments of higher learning in the United States. An urban school in Durham, North Carolina, Duke has a distinct Southern atmosphere as well as an intellectually stimulating environment. Given the university's athletic excellence, school spirit is, by no doubt, very strong and an important part of campus life. This unique combination of sports powerhouse and outstanding research institution offers a unique college experience, much cherished by Duke's students.

Three Schools

Duke is composed of ten schools, two of which—Trinity College of Arts and Sciences, and the Pratt School of Engineering—offer degrees to undergraduate students. There are more than 40 majors available, as well as about 20 certificate programs, which are the equivalent of minors. Duke also has a distinct option at Trinity College called Program II, which allows students to design their own interdisciplinary curriculum. According to one student, "Program II is definitely something worth exploring because it can be made to accommodate personal interests."

To graduate, students must complete 34 semester courses. Trinity College has a lengthy set of general requirements so that each student is exposed to a broad range of subjects. Everyone must take classes in what are called Five Areas of Knowledge and Six Modes of Inquiry, which range from arts and literature to science and technology. These requirements attract mixed reviews. Some students are glad they are learning a variety of topics; others are frustrated by the fact that they have to take classes they are not interested in. The Pratt School requires, in addition to classes in math, science, and engineering, one credit in writing and five credits in the humanities and social sciences.

The coursework at Duke is certainly challenging, although it always depends on the specific classes and majors. As one student pointed out, "if you choose your classes wisely, you can make it as easy or as hard as you want." In addition, the difficulty also depends on majors. The economics department is quite strict with grading, while some students find some humanities departments prone to grade inflation. This is not always the case, however, as most students agree that grading varies greatly from class to class.

Gothic and Georgian

Duke's campus is an interesting combination of Georgian architecture in the East Campus and Gothic revivalism in the West. This results in a beautiful campus as well as a great intellectual atmosphere. "The Gothic buildings here are a joy to walk by every day," said one student.

Duke owns more than 8,000 acres of land, including a 7,000-acre forest just west of the campus, a stunning botanical garden, a golf course, and a marine lab on the Atlantic Coast, more than 150 miles from the main campus. "Duke has lots of resources," said one student. "You can find a lot of great facilities here that you would not find anywhere else."

> "Duke has lots of resources. You can find a lot of great facilities here that you would not find anywhere else."

Freshmen reside in the East Campus, the oldest section of the university, where there are 14 residential halls. Nine of them are conveniently built around a central quad, which also includes a science building, the Lilly Library, Baldwin Auditorium, which is one of Duke's major landmarks, and East Union, which has two dining halls, a convenience store, and other services. The other five residences for freshmen are not part of the quad but have the benefits of close proximity to Brodie Gym and air-conditioning in several buildings, which is very important considering that North Carolina can be very hot during the first and last months of the school year. For upperclassmen, there are other housing options available in both the West and Central Campuses. Only seniors are allowed to live off-campus, and the university has a community housing program that helps students find rentals in the Durham area.

All freshmen must enroll in a full meal plan. Upperclassmen, however, have a variety of options available. In addition, meal plans include dining points, which can be used for pizza deliveries, groceries, and restaurants. According to one student, this point system "is really flexible and allows students to explore different dining places around the area." As for the school's own dining service, most students agree that it is "good but nothing to rave about."

Weekends

Fraternities are the most important element of the party scene at Duke. About 34 percent of the student population is associated with one of Duke's 37 Greek organizations. Drinking, of course, is a dominant, though not essential, part of social life. The school is also trying to find ways to engage students in campus weekend activities, given several incidents at off-campus fraternities during recent years and complaints from Durham residents. Nevertheless, Greek life remains an indispensable part of the party nights, which are scattered throughout the week, including on some weekdays.

Although Duke has the reputation of being a "preppy" college, many students there believe that it is a misconception. "Everyone here is very friendly," said one student. "Surely there are some preppy kids just like everywhere else, but overall I think we have a great social environment."

The interactions between Durham and Duke, however, are rather limited. Durham is the fourth largest city in North Carolina and has many points of interest outside of Duke University, including bars and restaurants. Nevertheless, safety is always a concern, and most students do not venture far beyond the boundaries of the campus. "Students generally think of themselves as part of the Duke community," said one student. "There is not much feeling of being a member of the Durham community."

Blue Devils

Duke has a long history of athletic excellence. The varsity sports teams are known as Blue Devils and are part of the Atlantic Coast Conference. The men's basketball team, headed by Coach Mike Krzyzewski, is known as one of the most successful teams in the history of college sports. According to one student, "basketball is by far the most important sport, and everyone cares about how the team is doing." Both the men's and women's lacrosse teams have also been immensely successful in the last few years, despite the recent issues surrounding the men's team that grabbed national headlines. The best team on campus, however, is probably the women's golf team, which has won five national championships, including three consecutively from 2005 to 2007.

All the sports trophies result in the importance of athletics in the social scene at Duke and a fervent school spirit that some students describe as almost "maniacal," especially when Duke is playing against its most notable rival, University of North Carolina, Chapel Hill, which is only about 10 miles away. Out of the rivalry was created the famous tradition of Krzyzewskiville, where students live outdoors next to the Cameron Stadium in tents for weeks prior to the UNC-Duke game. "It is a great experience," said one student. "It shows how dedicated we are to school spirit."

Clearly, Duke can claim a spot among the colleges with the most ardent sports fans. In addition to this strong school spirit, however, Duke also offers a top-notch facility and faculty. With its commitment to both athletics and academics, Duke stands as one of the top college choices for students around the world.—*Xiaohang Liu*

FYI

If you come to Duke, you'd better bring "a tent to camp outside Cameron."

What is the typical weekend schedule? "School work during the day, and fun time during the night."

If I could change one thing about Duke, I'd "reduce the so-called General Education Requirements."

Three things every student at Duke should do before graduating are: "tent outside Cameron, go to as many basketball games as possible, and go to the Marine Lab."

Elon University

Address: 700 Campus Box, Elon, NC 27244
Phone: 336-278-3566
E-mail address: admissions@elon.edu
Web site URL: www.elon.edu
Year Founded: 1889
Private or Public: Private
Religious Affiliation: United Church of Christ
Location: Suburban
Number of Applicants: 9,505
Percent Accepted: 41%
Percent Accepted who enroll: 33%
Number Entering: 1,286
Number of Transfers Accepted each Year: 190
Middle 50% SAT range: M: 570–660, Cr: 560–650, Wr: 570–660
Middle 50% ACT range: 23–28
Early admission program EA/ED/None: EA and ED

Percentage accepted through EA or ED: 60%
EA and ED deadline: 1-Nov
Regular Deadline: 10-Jan
Application Fee: $50
Full time Undergraduate enrollment: 4,950
Total enrollment: 5,300
Percent Male: 40%
Percent Female: 60%
Total Percent Minority or Unreported: 13%
Percent African-American: 5%
Percent Asian/Pacific Islander: 2%
Percent Hispanic: 1%
Percent Native American: 0%
Percent International: Unreported
Percent in-state/out of state: 30%/70%
Percent from Public HS: Unreported
Retention Rate: 90%
Graduation Rate 4-year: 74%

Graduation Rate 6-year: Unreported
Percent Undergraduates in On-campus housing: 60%
Number of official organized extracurricular organizations: 150
3 Most popular majors: Business, Communications, Education
Student/Faculty ratio: 14:1
Average Class Size: Unreported
Percent of students going to grad school: Unreported
Tuition and Fees: $22,166
In-State Tuition and Fees if different: No difference
Cost for Room and Board: $7,296
Percent receiving financial aid out of those who apply: 58%
Percent receiving financial aid among all students: 31%

Elon University, founded in 1889, is located in sunny Elon, North Carolina, halfway between Greensboro and the Research Triangle of Raleigh, Durham, and Chapel Hill. It is a friendly, intimate Southern campus, one of the most beautiful in the country, and it aims to provide students with a well-rounded education as well as opportunities to explore their interests outside the classroom. The friendliness of students and faculty, the beauty of the campus, and many important annual traditions bring everyone together to make Elon a unified and lively college community.

Learning In and Out of the Classroom

Whether Elon students are studying abroad for a summer, taking classes in the spring and fall terms, or learning about a unique subject during winter term, the University prides itself on offering students the chance to have close relationships with their professors and plenty of academic support. Most

students agree that one of Elon's strengths is this accessibility of the faculty. "It's so obvious they want to help you . . . They want to make sure you do well," one freshman said. All professors are required to have office hours each week, and some even give out home phone numbers to students. "I like the teachers and the fact that I am able to get to know them on a more personal level because the class sizes are so small," a junior said. In fact, large lecture halls filled with 500 students or more simply do not exist at Elon. The largest class size is 33 students, but the average class size is just 21. Students agree that this gives Elon, a school with 5,300 undergraduates, a small and intimate feel.

Elon University is comprised of five colleges: Elon College of Arts and Sciences, the Love School of Business, the School of Communications, the School of Education, and the School of Law. These five colleges offer more than 50 majors and employ 358 full-time faculty. Perhaps one of Elon's most distinctive academic features is its 4-1-4 calendar. Elon students have two four-month semesters in the fall and spring, buffeted by a four-week winter term in between. It is during winter term that students have the opportunity to participate in a diverse array of activities and classes. Each student takes one class that meets for three hours a day, and the classes offered range from yoga and quilting to the Business of NASCAR and Local Government Simulation. Some of these classes even take trips to sites that are relevant to the material they are covering. For instance, this year's Business of NASCAR class took a trip to the Daytona International Speedway.

Although Elon does offer a wide variety of unique classes during its winter term, one freshman said that she wished the regular terms offered "more weird, obscure, cool classes. I feel like we have a lot of the basics but not as many of those cool classes." The winter term is also a good time for students to study abroad, and many do take advantage of Elon's study abroad opportunities. Seventy percent of Elon students choose to study abroad at some point during their college careers.

Elon also offers seven Fellows programs, which allow students who have directed interests coming into college, such as business, education, or teaching, to take classes that suit their career goals early on and to make connections that may help them with their pursuits later in life. The Fellows in each program take classes together and some even go on trips together during the winter term. For instance, one freshman in the Business Fellows program this year took a class called Business and Sustainability for her winter term and traveled to Mexico for a week. She visited family-owned companies and small businesses to learn how isolated villages sustain themselves. Experiences such as this one are not uncommon at Elon, especially since business and communications are generally considered Elon's two strongest and most popular fields of study.

Just as Elon students are committed to excellence in their academic endeavors, so too are they committed to involvement in their extracurricular activities. From Phoenix 14, the television broadcasting club, to *The Pendulum*, Elon's student newspaper and its most popular campus publication, the University offers students a wide variety of ways to pursue their interests outside the classroom. There are clubs for almost everything—even a Hide-and-Go-Seek Club. No matter what the activity, one freshman

noted that "everyone is involved in a lot of different things and it's really easy to get involved in a lot of things." Jobs are also fairly easy to come by if students take the initiative to look around. Shops in the city employ many students and there are also plenty of available jobs on campus.

Elon boasts 16 men's and women's varsity NCAA Division I sports teams and offers 20 intramural and 25 club sports. Although most students would not say that athletics form a dominant presence on campus, one senior said, "People go to the games frequently, but there is not a huge expectation for excellence or winning championships. It is more of a school spirit thing." Intramurals, on the other hand, spark fierce competition amongst Elon students. Flag football, soccer, and basketball are particularly competitive, according to one junior.

Living the Greek Life

From frat parties to movies in nearby Burlington to nights out at one of the three bars on campus, Elon offers just about all types of social life. Although most students would agree that Greek life is a dominant force on campus (about 40 percent of girls join sororities and about 20 percent of boys join fraternities), it is not the only option. "Even if you're not involved in Greek life, you're still included," one freshman said. Another freshman agreed that "Greek life can be as big a part of Elon as you make it. Either you can become super involved, or not so involved. It is up to the individual student." In general, Elon can be a party school for those students who are looking for that atmosphere, but it can also be a very calm place for students who are not.

In this respect, alcohol can play a large role in students' social lives or it can play a very minimal role. "There is alcohol if you want to find it, but not everyone drinks," said one freshman. In fact, some organizations are completely sober and will not serve any alcohol at their events. Elon's alcohol policy is fairly strict. If students are caught with alcohol, they must write an essay and take an online health course. The University is most concerned with students' health and safety, but it also views alcohol possession and drinking as a disciplinary issue. If students are caught with alcohol three times, they run the risk of suspension, and since drinking games are illegal in the state of North Carolina, students caught playing these games may face harsher punishments.

Most weekends, the typical Elon student

will go out starting on Thursday night, usually to a bar on campus. Friday and Saturday nights are comprised of frat parties or bars again. Other students with cars may visit Burlington or Raleigh nearby to get dinner or see a movie. The town of Elon itself is small, but it does have some good restaurants, a mall, a Target, and a movie theater that students visit on the weekends. However, for the most part, students enjoy staying on campus. "I like staying on campus and having that community feeling," one freshman said.

One way that Elon creates this community feeling is through several annual parties and events that bring all students together. There is an 80s party, Festivus (a day-long mud party), a Glow-in-the-Dark Dance, the Elon-a-Thon (a 24-hour dance marathon put on for charity in April that the entire school participates in), and the Polar Bear Plunge (a fundraiser in which students jump into Elon's frigid lake). These traditions keep Elon students feeling connected to the university and help them to develop friendships that will last a lifetime.

> **"Everyone's really, really outgoing. It's kind of amazing actually."**

Elon students say that everyone on campus is pretty friendly. "Everyone is just smiling and happy all the time and says hi to everyone even if they don't know them," one freshman said. It is easy to meet people in classes, Fellows programs, sororities and fraternities, clubs, and especially through living residences. One of the reasons it's fairly easy to make friends, according to one senior, is that "everyone's really, really outgoing. It's kind of amazing actually."

Although Elon students hail from all across the United States as well as from 50 countries, it is lacking slightly in diversity. There are plenty of people from the Northern and Western United States who are surprised to be referred to as "sir" and "ma'am" when they get to Elon, but 30 percent of the student body does come from North Carolina. The university is working on increasing its diversity, but for the most part, students classify Elon as a preppy school with a hint of Southern flavor.

What it Means to be a Phoenix
Although Elon provides students with a multitude of on-campus housing options, most students choose to move off-campus by junior year. Freshmen are required to live on campus in dorms comprised of suites or halls, some of which are coed. Dorms are assigned on a first come, first served basis beginning when a student accepts his or her offer of admission to Elon. Many sophomores, juniors, and seniors try to move into The Oaks or Danieley Apartments, two on-campus apartment-style housing options that are very popular.

However, it is hard for many students to give up living on a campus that is so gorgeous. Elon's campus is considered to be one of the most beautiful in the country, complete with all the amenities necessary for comfortable student life in traditional red-brick, white-column Southern architecture. The campus itself is a botanical garden and is filled with beautiful walkways, fountains, and even a lake.

A central gathering place on campus is the Moseley Center, which contains the admissions office, the campus store, the information desk, a coffee shop, a few large rooms used for receptions, hangout places, the mail room, Octagon (a student grocery store), and much more. When the weather is nice, "you can always see students playing Frisbee in the grass, suntanning, or just doing homework" outside of Moseley, according to one freshman.

In terms of campus security, most students would agree that Elon, North Carolina, provides a fairly safe environment for the University. The town is very supportive of the University and its inhabitants are similar socioeconomically to the students. One senior said that "Elon is really safe and small and tucked-away. It's pretty quiet." The University even offers "Safe Rides," a service that can be called to deliver students wherever they need to go on campus at night if they do not feel safe walking alone.

Students at Elon have mixed feelings about their dining options. They can be on a 10-, 15-, or 19-meal plan that also includes meal dollars available for use at some local restaurants or for snacks in between meals. Dining halls are open all day and there are many to choose from, so it is hard to get bored with the options on campus. Most students agree that dining hall food is fairly good, but it can get old after a while. One senior rated the food around an A– or a B+. But if the dining halls don't live up to students' expectations, the city of Elon has numerous restaurants that students can go to and use "Phoenix cash" to buy food.

Although Elon is a comparatively young school, it is grounded in strong traditions that unite the entire community. For instance, every Tuesday, Elon students gather outside for College Coffee, a chance to talk with professors and fellow students in an informal setting over bagels, donuts, muffins, and coffee. Another tradition important to Elon students centers around Convocation and Graduation. During Convocation in the fall, new students are welcomed with an acorn to symbolize their potential for growth in their four years of college to come. At Graduation, they are each awarded a sapling to show how they have developed as a result of their time at Elon.

And at the end of those four years, Elon students generally feel that their time in college was a rewarding, fulfilling experience and that they would choose Elon over again if they had the opportunity. One freshman said, "We have such a strong community and everyone is so welcoming and supportive of everyone . . . I thought I'd be really homesick, but I instantly felt warm and comforted and like I'd been here forever. Elon is just such a happy place." So for students who want an education both in and out of the classroom in a welcoming, intimate setting, Elon is the perfect college option.—*Arielle Stambler*

FYI

Three things every student at Elon should do before graduating are: "jump in the fountain (even though you get fined), do the Polar Bear Plunge, and go to a homecoming game."

What surprised me the most about Elon when I arrived was "how friendly Elon's staff was. The woman that checks me out when I get my morning coffee always strikes up a conversation with me and gets me cheerful and excited for my day."

If you come to Elon, you'd better bring "summer dresses, pearls, and gym clothes."

If I could change one thing about Elon, "I'd make it more diverse."

University of North Carolina School of the Arts (formerly known as North Carolina School of the Arts)

Address: 1533 South Main Street, Winston-Salem, NC 27127
Phone: 336-770-3290
E-mail address: admissions@ncarts.edu
Web site URL: www.ncarts.edu
Year Founded: 1963
Private or Public: Public
Religious Affiliation: None
Location: Urban
Number of Applicants: 676
Percent Accepted: 45%
Percent Accepted who enroll: 73%
Number Entering: 224
Number of Transfers Accepted each Year: Unreported
Middle 50% SAT range: M: 480–600, CR: 510–630, Wr: 490–620
Middle 50% ACT range: 19–27

Early admission program EA/ED/None: None
Percentage accepted through EA or ED: NA
EA and ED deadline: NA
Regular Deadline: 1-Mar
Application Fee: $60
Full time Undergraduate enrollment: 722
Total enrollment: 740
Percent Male: 61%
Percent Female: 39%
Total Percent Minority or Unreported: 18%
Percent African-American: 10%
Percent Asian/Pacific Islander: 2%
Percent Hispanic: 5%
Percent Native American: 1%
Percent International: 1%
Percent in-state/out of state: 48%/52%
Percent from Public HS: Unreported

Retention Rate: 77%
Graduation Rate 4-year: 59%
Graduation Rate 6-year: 61%
Percent Undergraduates in On-campus housing: 55%
Number of official organized extracurricular organizations: Unreported
3 Most popular majors: Visual and Performing Arts
Student/Faculty ratio: 8:1
Average Class Size: 7
Percent of students going to grad school: Unreported
Tuition and Fees: $19,857
In-State Tuition and Fees if different: $6,908
Cost for Room and Board: $7,922
Percent receiving financial aid out of those who apply: 77%
Percent receiving financial aid among all students: 49%

Downtown Winston-Salem, North Carolina, is host to over 300 student productions a year in 11 different performance venues on the campus of the University of North Carolina School of the Arts. UNCSA is the public arts conservatory branch of the University of North Carolina System, offering intensive, professional training in visual and performance arts. The undergraduate program is intimate, with an enrollment of 740 students, but the university also encompasses high school and graduate school programs. UNCSA does not provide a liberal arts education. Instead, every aspect of its curriculum is geared toward professional training.

A Professional Conservatory

The university consists of six professional schools dedicated to Dance, Design and Production, Drama, Filmmaking, and Music, each of which offers Bachelor's Degrees in Fine Arts. The general interest of the school's population is in performance and cinematic arts. The largest enrollment is in UNSCA's Filmmaking School followed closely by its school in Music, Design and Production, and Dance. A smaller number of students are enrolled in the School of Drama and in the School of Visual Arts.

Classes at UNCSA often run from 8 a.m. until late at night. General academic courses, such as math, English, and science, are held in the mornings and are followed by art classes. However, "there are very few required classes . . . most of the time only two academics per semester," said one student, adding that "the concentration is not on academics at all, it's one hundred percent on the arts and a lot of students treat it that way." By junior year, many students will have completed their general education requirements and devote their course load entirely to their chosen art.

The curriculum is designed to technically train students, rather than teach only theory, so many classes require hands-on work for a student production. Students assigned to show production will often be in production or rehearsal until 11 p.m. In the School of Film and School of Music, students will often attend film screenings or rehearse outside of their class schedule. "We have very little spare time," said one student. "When we get into show productions, schedule goes out the window."

The intensive workload lasts into the weekend where "during a run of a show . . . you will have tech or rehearsals for 10 out of 12 hours of a workday with 2-hour breaks," said one student. Each student is generally assigned one or two shows per semester although dedicated upperclassmen may be involved with more than 20 shows a year. According to one student, working on show production is "pretty much constant, with a few days to a few weeks off . . . It is what we're here to do." A semester at UNCSA is finished by Intensive Arts, a portion of the semester between Thanksgiving and Winter Break where all academics are dropped and students focus solely on art production.

The school's professional focus means an early edge within the industry. "Very few students don't have jobs when they graduate," said one junior, who cited already receiving industry offers from the professionals that often attend UNCSA productions. "They're coming to these shows and leaving with names," he explained.

Arts (Lover) Magnet

The school concentrates on an intimate academic experience. The student-faculty ratio is 8:1 and 86.4% of UNSCA classes have fewer than 20 students. In art courses, classes sometimes have as few as three students, training under direct supervision from a faculty professional. "This is a specialized place, they treat you like a professional," said one student. All art courses are taught by professionals working in their industry, a faculty requirement. Due to the professionally-geared curriculum, a student in lighting and design spends much more time doing lighting work for shows than in classrooms. Grades often depend on the time committed to a production and on a job well done, said one student.

For film majors, the most popular choice at the university, UNSCA is the only undergraduate program in the country that provides 100% of funding for student films and allows students to begin work on films in the first term. Senior productions are shown at a screening in Los Angeles where students can network with industry professionals. Notable alumni in the entertainment industry include Danny McBride (*Tropic Thunder, Land of the Lost, Up in the Air*) and Paul Schneider (*Lars and the Real Girl, Parks and Recreation*).

Room for Expression

Because of the school's specified concentration, UNSCA is well-equipped with venues and equipment for artists. The school owns 11 performance venues, including three movie theaters and architectural landmarks such as the historic Stevens Center and the modern Watson Chamber Music Hall. For film students, UNSCA also provides a mock studio back-lot, the "Studio Village," which houses production and post-production equipment.

Off-campus, downtown Winston-Salem is a bustling arts community. "It's a dried-up tobacco town," said one student, explaining that, "All of the old warehouses . . . have been turned into lofts and art galleries," said one student. A 'gallery hop' is held on the first Friday of every month where all art galleries are opened and there are performances, food, and other festivities in the streets. Another major aspect is the community theater, which allows students to get work experience off-campus.

The campus itself is located on 74 acres in the downtown Gateway district of Winston-Salem, North Carolina's fourth largest city. Freshmen and sophomores are required to live on campus as long as their residence is more than 25 miles from the college. Students are housed in one of six residence halls which are mostly co-ed and which mix students of various concentrations and class years. "The dorms are pretty nice," said one freshman. "Every dorm has a sink and . . . there are a lot more singles than at other colleges." Every floor of a dorm houses 16 people, 8 of which are assigned to singles.

Underclassmen are also required to participate in a school meal plan. "It's a small selection because we have so few students," said one student, referring to the dining options at UNCSA which consist of a cafeteria and the "Pickle Jar," which provides fast food and snacks. Several retail strips are within walking distance of the campus and many students eat off-campus regularly.

A third of undergraduates move off campus within their last two years. Inexpensive housing geared toward college students is available close to campus and many students rent houses or apartments. Off-campus housing is often within walking distance of academic buildings. Nearby university-owned apartments, which are usually rented by 2-3 students, and houses for rent are popular options as they allow for kitchens and are relatively affordable.

Hipster Haven

During breaks in their schedule, students often gather in Hanes Student Commons, a central building which houses dining, or the "The Hill," a large stretch of grass just outside. Another popular hangout is one of the many sculptures around campus, such as "The Elephant," a collection of abstract rock sculptures set apart from campus buildings. Outside of the school day, university-sponsored social events are rare and students prefer to hang out within dorms or off-campus apartments.

The campus is small and intimate, with an undergraduate population of less than 1,000. One student described the social atmosphere as a "big family" where "by the end your first year, you know pretty much everyone on campus." Half of student enrollment comes from within the state but there are also international students from around the world. Unlike a typical college, there are no sports teams and there is no Greek life although there is a campus mascot, the Fighting Pickle. One student described the campus vibe as "a certain air of creativity and dedication to the work."

Many students own cars which provide easy access to downtown retail districts. The area surrounding UNCSA includes many popular student hangouts, particularly local coffee shops such as Kranky's and Brew Nerds. There are also streets with parks, retail options, and nightclubs as well as a local mall. There are also several local parks and accessible hiking locations which are popular weekend destinations for photographers and other artists. The largest nearby city is Charlotte, North Carolina.

One benefit of attending an arts conservatory is, as one student puts it, "there are a lot of performances all of the time." A popular program is one of UNCSA's major traditions, its annual winter production of *The Nutcracker*. "Every year our ballet students work with the Design and Production and School of Music for downtown and the community," said one student. There are also a few annual school-sponsored social events, most notably a Winter Formal which is held downtown and has a dress-up theme and the end of the year Beaux Arts Ball.

"The school aims to identify potential within students."

Many students often have full schedules from morning until late at night followed by homework. However, more intimate parties can often be found off-campus where students gather in each other's apartments. Students who rent nearby throw house parties which are accessible as long as one has a car. "The party scene is here if you want to partake in it. You don't have to be a part of it and it doesn't get out of hand," said one student. According to school policy, regulations concerning alcohol, tobacco, and drug usage are strictly enforced.

Admissions: Potential is a Must

The university generally receives around 700 applications and has an acceptance rate of 45% (data from 2001–2010). Students can be accepted at UNSCA as early as high school by demonstrating potential for a career in the arts, although acceptance to pre-college programs does not guarantee acceptance to the college. Undergraduate admission emphasizes artistic achievement although transcripts and SAT/ACT scores are also considered. The average SAT of entering freshman was 1113 for Reading and Mathematics and 560 for Writing in 2009. 40% of enrollees ranked in the top 20% of their high school class in 2009 and 70% ranked in the top 40%.

Admission to the schools of Dance, Drama, and Music require a live audition. Auditions are held regionally throughout the winter and spring and at UNSCA. Applicants to the Schools of Design and Production, Filmmaking, and Visual Arts are required to submit a portfolio of work. "The school aims to identify potential within students," said one student. "You don't necessarily need work experience in your major because they teach you everything from the ground up but you do need to show potential."—*Cynthia Hua*

FYI
If you come here, you should bring "a passion for creativity."
If I could change one thing about UNCSA, "I would place the school in a bigger city with more things to do."
How is the social scene? "Students get free tickets into all shows, which run the range from band concerts to theater shows."

North Carolina State University

Address: 203 Peele Hall, Box 7103, Raleigh, NC 27695
Phone: 919-515-2434
E-mail address: undergrad_admissions@ncsu.edu
Web site URL: www.ncsu.edu
Year Founded: 1887
Private or Public: Public
Religious Affiliation: None
Location: Urban
Number of Applicants: 19,503
Percent Accepted: 54%
Percent Accepted who enroll: 43%
Number Entering: 4,547
Number of Transfers Accepted each Year: Unreported
Middle 50% SAT range: M: 560–660, CR: 530–620, Wr: 510–610
Middle 50% ACT range: 23–28
Early admission program EA/ED/None: EA

Percentage accepted through EA or ED: Unreported
EA and ED deadline: 1-Nov
Regular Deadline: 1-Feb
Application Fee: $70
Full time Undergraduate enrollment: 22,133
Total enrollment: 25,246
Percent Male: 56%
Percent Female: 44%
Total Percent Minority or Unreported: 24%
Percent African-American: 8%
Percent Asian/Pacific Islander: 5%
Percent Hispanic: 3%
Percent Native American: 1%
Percent International: 2%
Percent in-state/out of state: 93%/7%
Percent from Public HS: 80%
Retention Rate: 90%

Graduation Rate 4-year: 36%
Graduation Rate 6-year: Unreported
Percent Undergraduates in On-campus housing: 32%
Number of official organized extracurricular organizations: 593
3 Most popular majors: Biology, Management, Mechanical Engineering
Student/Faculty ratio: 18:1
Average Class Size: 25
Percent of students going to grad school: 31%
Tuition and Fees: $17,988
In-State Tuition and Fees if different: $5,153
Cost for Room and Board: $8,536
Percent receiving financial aid out of those who apply: 72%
Percent receiving financial aid among all students: 67%

A land-grant college founded in 1887 primarily as an agricultural school, North Carolina State University is now one of the most important research institutions in the nation. With more than 25,000 undergraduates and nearly 10,000 graduate students, it is the largest school within the University of North Carolina system. With its urban location in the fast-growing city of Raleigh, a strong school spirit in large part due to the Wolfpack, and a strong international reputation as a major research university, North Carolina State is a top destination for those looking for a fulfilling experience—both academic and social—at a large, resourceful university.

Technology and Research

As in all major public institutions of higher learning, North Carolina State is divided into twelve different schools, ten of which are available to undergraduates, including First-Year College, which provides basic educational training to first-year students so that they can be well prepared for more specific programs of study in the future. Another interesting school within North Carolina State is the College of Textiles. It has not only majors in the manufacturing of textiles but also training in related business management topics. Although it does have the traditional liberal arts curriculums, the university is certainly focused on specialized fields in engineering, business, and agriculture. "We are big on technology, so we have a lot of engineers," said one student.

North Carolina Sate offers more than 100 majors, not to mention a number of associate degrees in the School of Agriculture and Life Sciences. These include the traditional fields of Biology and Economics, as well as the highly specialized curriculums of Watershed Hydrology and Biological Oceanography. "Academically, we have everything," said one student. "One of the reasons that I came here is because we have so many different, really specialized majors that are useful for jobs in the future."

The classes at North Carolina State can be very large, especially the introductory classes, which are popular not necessarily because they are particularly good but because everyone has to take them for their major. "The professors can be really impersonal for the big lectures," said one student. "I really recommend small classes if you want to get to know the professors." Of course, it can be relatively difficult for students to enroll in the smaller classes, where students are able to talk more and interact with both their peers and their instructors. This is because there are stricter limits in the number of people per class, thus preventing many interested students, particularly freshmen, from getting into their favorite courses.

> **"One of the reasons that I came here is because we have so many different, really specialized majors that are useful for jobs in the future."**

One important aspect of North Carolina State is that it is a well-known research university. Surely, the large number of students on campus can be intimidating for some people who are more used to small schools, but the benefits of attending a school with research centers and top-notch facilities certainly cannot be ignored. The university is particularly proud of its Centennial Campus, more than 1,000 acres dedicated to house different research facilities, classrooms, and offices. The idea was to build partnerships between North Carolina State and other entities that are interested in education and research, such as government, corporations, and non profit organizations. Students can find many opportunities for work, internship, and academic research on the Centennial Campus, which is still in the process of constructing new buildings and facilities. Of course, the downside of the university's focus on research is that the Centennial Campus, as well as other university facilities, is generally used for engineering and biomedical sciences, which, at the outset, reduces the relative importance of humanities and social sciences departments at North Carolina State.

In *U.S. News & World Report*, North Carolina State is ranked among the top 101 national universities in the United States. The admissions process can be very selective, as nearly half of the applicants are rejected every year. "Just because we are a big state school, it doesn't mean that we are not really selective," said one student. "I feel the people here are very smart and skilled."

Capital of North Carolina

North Carolina State occupies more than 2,100 acres of Raleigh, the state capital and one of the fastest growing cities in the United States. In recent years, the city has become a top destination for businesses, particularly in technology-related industries. It is also considered one of the best places for young professionals. Furthermore, along with Chapel Hill and Durham, home to University of North Carolina and Duke, respectively, Raleigh also forms the famous Research Triangle Park, which is the largest research park in the United States. Therefore, the location of the North Carolina State is already very conducive to students' professional development. "I really like Raleigh," said one student. "It is a lively city."

Given the location, students can find plenty of activities in the city. The array of restaurants, bars, and clubs throughout Raleigh certainly enrich the weekend experiences of students. "I decided to live off campus because the city has so much that I don't have to be limited to the campus," said one student.

Although the majority of upperclassmen live off campus, freshmen generally stay in dorms. After all, living with fellow students in university-provided facilities is often considered one of the most important elements of the college experience. Given the scope of North Carolina State, the dorms vary greatly, ranging from apartment complexes to traditional residential halls. "One of the best things about living in dorms is that you get to meet more people of your year," said one student. "If you are off campus, your neighbor could be anybody, but here in dorms, you have more of a sense of community, which is great." Unlike most colleges that operate a large number of dining facilities, North Carolina State only has three main dining halls. Of course, there are also food courts and a number of stores and eateries easily accessible from the campus. Only freshmen living in dorms are required to have meal plans, and off-campus students generally find meals on their own without going to the university's dining halls.

Wolfpack

For a university that has the size and scope of North Carolina State, sports teams represent an important part of the college experience. The Wolfpack, as the teams are called, play in 24 varsity sports. Since football is played in a stadium of 50,000 spectators, and the basketball games have a capacity of nearly 20,000 fans, these games are quite popular with students, particularly for those with fervent school spirit. As with most teams with long histories, the Wolfpack has a fiery rival in University of North Carolina at Chapel Hill. The basketball teams have played each other more than 200 times and the football teams nearly 100 times, with University of North Carolina having the clear advantage. Fortunately, North Carolina State has found success in the last three football encounters to close the gap.

The party scene is certainly lively at North Carolina State. There are plenty of parties during the weekends, both in students' apartments and in fraternities and sororities. "Weekends are really fun," said one student. "You get to go to the city or just have fun on campus because there are always parties going on."

North Carolina State is certainly one of the top research institutions in the United States. It provides strong technical training to students academically as well as a lively social life during the weekends. For students from North Carolina, the price tag is also relatively low, making the university certainly a good destination for college-bound students.—*Xiaohang Liu*

FYI

If you come to North Carolina State, you'd better bring "a readiness to work."

What is the typical weekend schedule? "Party on Friday and Saturday nights. But make sure you wake up early on Sunday so that you won't be overwhelmed during the week."

Three things every student at North Carolina State should do before graduating are: "take classes outside of your major just for fun, go to a football game, and get to know Raleigh."

University of North Carolina / Chapel Hill

Address: Jackson Hall CB #2200, Chapel Hill, NC 27599-2200

Phone: 919-966-3621

E-mail address: unchelp@admissions.unc.edu

Web site URL: www.unc.edu

Year Founded: 1789

Private or Public: Public

Religious Affiliation: None

Location: Suburban

Number of Applicants: 20,090

Percent Accepted: 32%

Percent Accepted who enroll: 55%

Number Entering: 3,960

Number of Transfers Accepted each Year: 1,286

Middle 50% SAT range: M: 610–710, CR: 590–700, Wr: 590–690

Middle 50% ACT range: 27–31

Early admission program EA/ED/None: EA

Percentage accepted through EA or ED: 42%

EA and ED deadline: 15-Oct

Regular Deadline: 15-Jan

Application Fee: $70

Full time Undergraduate enrollment: 18,579

Total enrollment: 29,390

Percent Male: 40%

Percent Female: 60%

Total Percent Minority or Unreported: 30%

Percent African-American: 9%

Percent Asian/Pacific Islander: 8%

Percent Hispanic: 8%

Percent Native American: 1%

Percent International: 2%

Percent in-state/out of state: 82%/18%

Percent from Public HS: 83%

Retention Rate: Unreported

Graduation Rate 4-year: 86%

Graduation Rate 6-year: Unreported

Percent Undergraduates in On-campus housing: 46%

Number of official organized extracurricular organizations: 557

3 Most popular majors: Social Sciences, Journalism, Biology

Student/Faculty ratio: 14:1

Average Class Size: 15

Percent of students going to grad school: 31%

Tuition and Fees: $26,834

In-State Tuition and Fees if different: $7,008

Cost for Room and Board: $9,470

Percent receiving financial aid out of those who apply: 47%

Percent receiving financial aid among all students: 39%

With strong academics, great athletics, and a pretty campus to boot, the University of North Carolina at Chapel Hill is a great choice for just about any student. This large Southern university does everything big, including its Southern hospitality. So put on your Carolina Blue shirt and come on down!

Is Bigger Better?

Starting with the class of 2010, the university introduced new graduation requirements that are quite extensive. While some students praise the system, saying that it "more fully encapsulates the purpose of a liberal arts education," others point out that changing your major is a difficult feat with all the new requirements and that you might have to stay for an additional semester to complete course work unless you enter with plenty of AP credits. Survey courses are pretty much guaranteed to be 400-person classes. A good way to get a taste of a small class early on is to participate in one of the First Year Seminars. In addition to being small, which is a rare find at UNC, they are generally interesting, tackling subjects such as "U.S.-Cuban Relations." Large sizes of classes aside, students praised the feel of community, as most said they don't view their peers as competition.

The school prides itself on having very strong journalism and business programs, both of which are pretty difficult to get into. With UNC's strong academic reputation also come challenging classes. Grading varies from department to department with some, such as the communications department, being more notorious for grade inflation. Students generally agree that each A requires hard work and is unlikely to be handed out easily. Students warn that the most failed course at UNC is "Calculus 231" (Calculus of One Variable I). In addition, be wary as intro classes such as intro biology, intro statistics, and intro international relations are designed to weed out the people who are not serious about the major. On the other end of the spectrum, for an easy A, students recommend "Race and Ethnic Relations" and most communications classes. As at most schools, it is still the professor that makes the class, and UNC students give high marks to their professors. The professors are generally pretty accessible and open to meeting students. One senior remarked that the professors were always "as helpful as I needed them to be." Professor Ralph Byrns in the economics department is a favorite, drawing crowds even as early as 9:30 in the morning. Additionally UNC is home to several other famous professors, including Professor Christopher Browning, a prominent Holocaust historian, and Professor Andrew Reynolds, who helped write the Afghani and Iraqi constitutions. The academic options are broadened via the very selective Robertson Scholars program, which allows UNC students to take classes not offered at UNC at neighboring Duke University.

Party in the South [Campus]

As a state school, UNC operates under the North Carolina requirement that at least 82 percent of students must be from in-state. For this reason, the rare out-of-state students complain that when they initially arrived on campus, everyone else already knew at least a few people from their high school who also attended. Don't worry about being lonely in this large school, though, as freshman dorms, freshman seminars, and other classes facilitate friendships. And as one student from the Northeast emphasized, the people are very friendly; in fact, he quipped, "It took me a while to get used to."

> "There is crazy school spirit. People here can be a little insane about sports."

The social scene as described by one senior can be split into three categories: the Greek life, the bars and clubs on Franklin Street, and the dorm parties in the suites of South Campus. The underage underclassmen tend to gravitate toward the freshmen-dominated South Campus where the crazy parties are concentrated. Upperclassmen and those with fake IDs can usually be found on Franklin Street, an area that offers a plethora of options. Some of the more popular choices include La Rez, East End, and Top of the Hill. Frats are conspicuous during rush week when a lot of students take advantage of their parties; however, for the remaining part of the year the 16 percent of Greeks on campus are not a very big deal to the rest of the student body. While most people drink, there is no pressure to join in drinking. The practical reality, according to one student, is that the university's priority is to make sure you are safe. For this reason, unless you are being obnoxious or disruptive, the RAs will leave you alone. "RAs are not secret police or anything," one senior explained. For after-party options, students cite the Cosmic Cantina, a Mexican hole in the wall, as a great late-night destination.

See You in the Pit!

The campus is unofficially divided into three areas: North, South, and Middle. Most of the freshmen are housed on South Campus, where suites and large dorms encourage socializing, although there is an integration effort going on that has the administration encouraging first years to move to other parts and mingle with the upperclassmen. While the rest of the campus is characterized by run-of-the-mill dorms, upperclassmen also have the option of living in apartment-style houses in Ram Village. Avery in Middle Campus is cited as the athlete dorm. Students get assigned to dorms via a lottery system based on seniority, although there is always an option of not taking any chances and remaining in the room you currently have. The most popular option of all, however, is living off campus, and 53 percent of students do just that.

The campus draws many compliments from its students, who describe it as "scenic" and full of brick walkways. The only complaint is the never-ending and sometimes disruptive construction due to an ambitious long-term remodeling plan that the university is currently undergoing. The most popular place on campus is the Pit. A central meeting point between the student union, dining hall and a library, the Pit is home to many student organization meetings, people on their way to other destinations and "even occasionally preachers." It is said that all students pass by the Pit at least once a day.

When asked about food, the consensus, as one student summed up, is that the two dining halls on campus are "mediocre at best." However, whenever they become sick of the dining halls, the students can always turn to the endless stream of restaurants on Franklin Street that are bound to satisfy the choosiest of taste buds.

Duke Sucks!

If you are a basketball fan, UNC is the place to be. The Tar Heels bleed Carolina blue and the atmosphere, according to one student, can be described as "mania and fervor" and another added, "There is crazy school spirit. People here can be a little insane about sports." The basketball, baseball, and football teams are successful and draw full crowds to the games. Tickets are in such high demand that the university has a lottery system in place for those who wish to attend. The most anticipated game of the year is, of course, the one against the perennial archrival Duke. A win against Duke is lavishly celebrated by the student body on Franklin Street, where crowds gather to build fires and jump over them in joy. But sports are not confined to only varsity-level talent. The intramural program at the school is also a very popular option. To get the coveted IM champion T-shirt, students compete in a plethora of sports. "There are sports I've never even heard of," claimed one student, perhaps referring to the popular IM underwater hockey. Outside of the sports scene, other extracurriculars also abound, with the Campus Y, a social advocacy umbrella group, and *The Daily Tar Heel* being some of the more popular options. There are also many a cappella groups, and proud students reported that one member participated in the 2009 American Idol competition and advanced to the final 36.

UNC is a great deal on many fronts and a small bill for the North Carolina students. Lucky North Carolina residents take up at least 82 percent of the student population, but the coveted 18 percent left for out-of-state students is well worth the competition. The relaxed Southern atmosphere makes it a pleasant environment even though students warn that it is more conservative and bigger than one might expect. Overall, however, once you get there you are bound to catch at least some of the school spirit. In no time you'll also be chanting: Go, Heels!—*Dorota Poplawska*

FYI

If you come to UNC, you'd better bring "a lot of school spirit."

What is the typical weekend schedule? "Go to the South Point mall on Saturday, at night go to bars and restaurants on Franklin Street, and do homework on Sunday."

If I could change one thing about UNC, I'd "have more small classes."

Three things every student at UNC should do before graduating are: "attend a Carolina-Duke basketball game, rush Franklin Street after beating Duke, and have fro-yo (frozen yogurt) at Yogurt Pump."

Wake Forest University

Address: PO Box 7305,
Reynolda Station,
Winston-Salem, NC 27109
Phone: 336-758-5201
E-mail address:
admissions@wfu.edu
Web site URL: www.wfu.edu
Year Founded: 1834
Private or Public: Private
Religious Affiliation: None
Location: Urban
Number of Applicants: 7,177
Percent Accepted: 40%
**Percent Accepted who
enroll:** 37%
Number Entering: 1,219
**Number of Transfers
Accepted each Year:** 122
Middle 50% SAT range:
M: 620–710, CR: 600–690,
Wr: Unreported
Middle 50% ACT range:
28–31
**Early admission program
EA/ED/None:** EA-ED

**Percentage accepted
through EA or ED:**
Unreported
EA and ED deadline: 15-Nov,
1-Jan
Regular Deadline: 1-Jan
Application Fee: $50
**Full time Undergraduate
enrollment:** 4,657
Total enrollment: 7,162
Percent Male: 48%
Percent Female: 52%
**Total Percent Minority or
Unreported:** 23%
Percent African-American:
7%
**Percent Asian/Pacific
Islander:** 4%
Percent Hispanic: 4%
Percent Native American: 1%
Percent International: 2%
**Percent in-state/out of
state:** 22%/78%
Perocnt from Public HS: 65%
Retention Rate: 94%

Graduation Rate 4-year: 78%
Graduation Rate 6-year: 78%
**Percent Undergraduates in
On-campus housing:** 70%
**Number of official organized
extracurricular
organizations:** 168
3 Most popular majors:
Social Sciences, Marketing,
Biology
Student/Faculty ratio: 11:1
Average Class Size: 14
**Percent of students going to
grad school:** 50%
Tuition and Fees: $41,576
**In-State Tuition and Fees if
different:** No difference
Cost for Room and Board:
$11,410
**Percent receiving financial
aid out of those who apply:**
86%
**Percent receiving financial
ald among all students:**
36%

Just outside of the Raleigh-Durham research triangle, in the green hills of Winston-Salem, North Carolina, lies one of America's premier small colleges, Wake Forest University. The campus is frequently described as "preppy" and has an active Greek life, but the university is extremely committed to both athletics and academics as well, boasting active Division I sports teams and top-notch research facilities. The small class sizes and well-known faculty members—including Maya Angelou—only add to Wake Forest's prestige and Southern charm.

Life at Work Forest

With less than five thousand students, Wake Forest ensures personalized, one-on-one experiences with professors and comfortable class discussions. Students say they "love knowing all of [their] professors on a personal level" and that the faculty members are "so, so helpful" and "always available." One freshman said that her biggest class had sixty students, and juniors and seniors confirmed that large lecture classes were far and few. The university also offers a First-Year Seminar program, which gives freshmen the opportunity to discuss interesting topics with sixteen of their peers and professors who are distinguished in their fields. Applicants interested in research will not be disappointed by Wake's resources, as many current students say the university "has all the resources that are normally found at larger schools."

In addition to the small class sizes, Wake Forest is known for its academic intensity. Students at the school agree that there is truth to the common nickname "Work Forest," and say that while the grading scale can differ from class to class, one does have to put in effort to do well. Attendance and participation factor into one's grade in many classes, and one student noted that "even the less-devoted students have their noses buried in books for at least a couple hours each day." Part of that studying is devoted to fulfilling distribution requirements; before graduation, students are required to take one or two courses in each of five divisions: social sciences, math and natural sciences, fine arts, humanities, and literature. Wake students also have to complete two courses in health and exercise science. Popular majors include Communications and Political Science, and the university's Calloway School of Business and Accountancy has a particularly strong reputation in the field.

WFU also has numerous study-abroad opportunities, with particularly popular programs in England and Venice. Students would say that "about half" of the undergraduate population chooses to study abroad during their four years, and "the administration encourages students to seek out new experiences." Wake Forest also has a prestigious Scholars Program, which awards exceptional students with full-ride scholarships to the university.

Frat Forest?

Although the academics can be challenging, Wake Forest students know the importance of balancing their schedules with fun. "There's a lot of truth to the saying 'work hard, play hard' around here," one student said, explaining that most WFU students go out at least once a weekend and "the campus is lively until four in the morning on Saturdays." Wake Wednesdays are a popular night to go out, followed by "slightly lower-key" Thursdays and "loud and busy" Fridays and Saturdays.

Wake's social scene tends to center on Greek life. Although the more than two dozen fraternities and sororities aren't housed on a traditional Greek Row—instead, they have specific sections of dorms set aside for them, and "lounges" in those areas are designated for parties open to the entire campus. "There's pressure to go Greek," students say, and a typical Saturday night is never complete without a trip to one of the many fraternities for beer and socializing. Although "the lack of diversity of Wake's social scene can get old," one student said, "there's always one thing that redeems it: everyone at Wake seems so spirited and energetic!"

Wake Forest isn't a dry campus, and "most students definitely stick to drinking over heavy drugs." Drinking is common at numerous social events, be it a low-key lounge party or large campus-wide event. The RAs are fairly lenient, and are just there to make sure students are "happy and safe." Although it's much less common, "there are still those who use drugs, with pot being the most common," one student said. There are a few rumors about cocaine use on campus, but drinking clearly remains the most popular social activity.

A Comfortable Community

Wake Forest students take pride in their beautiful North Carolina campus, praising the large magnolia quad in the center of campus and the region's relatively mild weather. Housing options vary and improve as students get older, and are randomly assigned to freshmen or done by lottery for upperclassmen. Upperclassmen housing options include on-campus apartments, many of which feature en suite bathrooms and kitchenettes and are "the high point of on-campus housing." WFU is constantly adding to its housing options, and one of the newer dorms "is almost like a luxury hotel, featuring everything from solar-powered generators to monitors on every floor that keep students informed on daily news."

The small campus fosters "a sense of community that you don't see at bigger schools," and students often praise the university's small size as the source of many campus traditions. During exam week, for example, it's traditional for students and the library staff to "set up pranks and social activities to relieve stress." 2010's festivities included a breakfast buffet and a waterfall of condoms, and "the whole campus spent weeks talking" about the events.

> **"Know professors on a personal level."**

Students agree that to a large extent, the university's close-knit atmosphere stems from its commitment to athletics. One of the first things the freshman class learns during orientation week is the fight song, which can often be heard at the Division I football and basketball games. "It can be competitive to get good seats" at sporting events, and despite the recent disappointing football season, "students still flocked to the games." One of the most well-known Wake Forest traditions arose out of the student body's "tremendous" passion for football; after a big win, students cover the trees on campus in toilet paper in an activity known as "rolling the Quad." It's no surprise that sports are so popular at Wake—the university claims famous athletes like the NBA's Tim Duncan, Chris Paul, and Josh Howard as alums!

One common complaint about the university is that it's not as diverse, ethnically or socio-economically, as the admissions officers would like applicants to believe. "The stereotypes are true," one student said.

"Most Wake students are popped-collar preps" from comfortable backgrounds. However, "cultural groups on campus have become more active recently," and students are open and accepting of all of their peers.

"When you go to a small school, it's all about having a strong sense of community," one student said. From rolling the quad to pulling pranks in the library, it's clear that Wake Forest students are proud to show off that sense of community. Although the university is small in size, its plethora of resources—academic, extracurricular, and social—ensures that any student will be able to find his or her niche in Winston-Salem. Whether it be in the small seminars the school is known for or in the crowd at football and basketball games, Wake's Demon Deacons aren't afraid to show off their school pride.—*Iva Velickovic*

FYI

If I could change one thing about Wake Forest, "I'd mix up the social scene a little bit. If you're into frat parties, Wake is the place for you, but if you're looking for a different way to spend your Saturday nights, you might have to look around a little."

The number one thing that surprised me most when I came to Wake Forest was "how many opportunities it has for the arts, like a student-hosted film festival."

If you come to Wake Forest, you'd better bring "rain boots (the drainage system is awful), but leave your heaviest jacket at home."

North Dakota

Address: 205 Twamley Hall, 264 Centennial Drive Street, Grand Forks, ND 58202-8357

Phone: 800-225-5863

E-mail address: und.enrollmentservices @email.und.edu

Web site URL: www.und.edu

Year Founded: 1883

Private or Public: Public

Religious Affiliation: None

Location: Suburban

Number of Applicants: 4,069

Percent Accepted: 70%

Percent Accepted who enroll: 63%

Number Entering: 2,096

Number of Transfers Accepted each Year: 1,366

Middle 50% SAT range: Unreported

Middle 50% ACT range: 20–25

Early admission program EA/ED/None: None

Percentage accepted through EA or ED: NA

EA and ED deadline: NA

Regular Deadline: Rolling

Application Fee: $35

Full time Undergraduate enrollment: 11,139

Total enrollment: 14,194

Percent Male: 55%

Percent Female: 45%

Total Percent Minority or Unreported: 15%

Percent African-American: 1%

Percent Asian/Pacific Islander: 1%

Percent Hispanic: 1%

Percent Native American: 1%

Percent International: 1%

Percent in-state/out of state: 33%/67%

Percent from Public HS: 92%

Retention Rate: 78%

Graduation Rate 4-year: 54%

Graduation Rate 6-year: Unreported

Percent Undergraduates in On-campus housing: 32%

Number of official organized extracurricular organizations: 230

3 Most popular majors: Business/Marketing, Transportation and Materials Moving, Health Professions

Student/Faculty ratio: 19:1

Average Class Size: 15

Percent of students going to grad school: 18%

Tuition and Fees: $16,767

In-State Tuition and Fees if different: $7,092

Cost for Room and Board: $6,100

Percent receiving financial aid out of those who apply: 66%

Percent receiving financial aid among all students: 53%

Founded in 1883, the University of North Dakota (UND) is the flagship institution of higher learning funded by the state government. Despite being located in a rather unpopulated region of the country, UND is a popular destination for not only students from the state of North Dakota but also students from the rest of the United States, as well as a number of foreign countries. In fact, unlike many other state schools, more than half of the students at UND hail from outside of North Dakota. The second largest employer in the state, UND is also a vital player in the state economy. By providing students with a balanced college experience of exciting social life and good academics, the university is certainly a very good choice for all those who are willing to make the trade-off of staying in a remote part of the country.

Not Just About Flying

More than 10,000 undergraduates are enrolled at UND, along with over 2,500 postgraduates. The university offers a complete set of graduate, professional, and continuing education colleges that cover the educational needs of many types of students. There are ten academic divisions at UND, including the schools of law and medicine. Within these schools, the university offers more than 200 fields of study. The most famous division of UND is the John D. Odegard School of Aerospace Sciences. More than 1,500 students are enrolled in the school, which also has the largest fleet of aircraft dedicated for civilian training. The Grand Forks International Airport serves as the training site for approximately 120 planes. In North Dakota, the United States Air Force has a significant presence. Therefore, it is not surprising the state's main public university is intensely focused on the topic and is one of the premier outer-space research institutions in the country. "The School of Aerospace Sciences is definitely the most prestigious part of UND," said one student. "It is really good for pilot training and space research."

Although the departments in aerospace are considered the most widely recognized divisions of UND, the rest of the academic programs are also very strong. The university has nearly 90 majors. In addition, a large selection of minors is available for entrepreneurial students who would like to enrich their academic experience. The certificate programs can also be useful for students who are looking for pre-professional training in a particular field, and students are generally satisfied with the scope of academia at UND. "I don't feel like the school is missing any important majors," said the student. "Whether you are pre-med or majoring in liberal arts, you will find the programs that suit you."

For a relatively large public school, the degree of interaction between students and professors at UND is strong. Introductory classes can be very large, with more than one hundred people filling lecture halls. However, these courses generally have a number of teaching assistants assigned to help students with their work. These graduate students can be invaluable in helping those who are falling behind as well as teaching more materials to students who would like to study a particular topic in detail. For upper-level classes, the size can be significantly reduced, often with fewer than 20 students per class. In those courses, discussions between students and professors are vital, since much of the teaching is done through conversations and debates rather than lectures.

Prior to graduation, students are required to choose from a list of general education courses. These classes are designed to improve the basic skills of students and offer some background in all major academic fields. The core groups of courses are communication, social sciences, arts and humanities, and mathematics, science, and technology. While some students think the requirements are not very useful, others believe that these courses have introduced them to interesting new topics. "I think the general education requirements are great," said one student. "I never knew I would be so interested in geography after taking a class in it."

> "I never felt overwhelmed here. I think the academics here are pretty relaxed."

Most students are very happy with the workload at UND. The classes tend to be manageable, allowing students to undertake jobs or extracurricular activities during the week, as well as having fun during the weekends. "I never felt overwhelmed here," said one student. "I think the academics here are pretty relaxed."

The Flatland

One of the most important drawbacks for prospective students in choosing UND is the location of the university, particularly for those from outside the state. The winters can be harsh. Those who have little experience with the cold weather may be not too pleasantly surprised during the winter, when the entire campus can be covered with snow. Furthermore, UND is in Grand Forks, more than 70 miles from Fargo, the most important metropolitan area in North Dakota. For those looking to go to major cities several times during the school year, the closest is Winnipeg in Manitoba, Canada, or Minneapolis, both at much more than 150 miles away. "Grand Forks is a small city," said one student. "But that should be what you expect when you come to North Dakota for college."

Despite the issue with the scope of the city, some students do enjoy the remoteness of Grand Forks. "I wanted to go to someplace quiet where you can actually study," said one student. In addition, the small college community creates a sense of safety and closeness, not to mention the fact that there are a number of restaurants and bars around campus where students can socialize outside of the school setting.

The majority of students live off campus, and the freshmen are not required to live in dorms. However, many do choose to live there to get used to the college environment, meet new people, and, of course, have convenient access to the different university facilities. Students are generally satisfied with the school's housing arrangement. There are single-sex residential halls available to students, but most of them are coeducational and arranged in suites. Three main dining centers serve the campus. A number of coffee shops, convenience stores, and food courts are also spread out across the campus to ensure that all students have easy access to dining services.

UND has twelve fraternities and six sororities, and they certainly represent an important part of weekend festivities. For those not interested in the Greek system, students can also find parties around campus in student apartments and houses. However, it must be pointed out that the alcohol policy is relatively strict in on-campus housing.

The National Champions

The university has dedicated significant resources to the men's hockey team, particularly in the construction of the Ralph Engelstad Arena, which seats more than 10,000 spectators. This is in large part due to the popularity of the sport on campus and the immense success of the team over the years, with seven national championships. After a series of reforms in the collegiate sports programs, all teams of UND compete at the NCAA Division I level.

UND students tend to show up in huge numbers to support their hockey team, and it represents an important social venue for students. With a large selection of academic programs and the large number of out-of-state students, UND is certainly a very attractive college choice. Of course, the diversity of the student body and the remoteness of the university are clear disadvantages, but, overall, students are very satisfied with their experience at UND.—*Xiaohang Liu*

FYI
If you come to UND, you'd better bring "many winter coats."
What is the typical weekend schedule? "Go to hockey games. The football games are pretty cool too."
If I could change one thing about UND, I'd "move it south."
Three things every student at UND should do before graduating are: "go to a hockey game against University of Minnesota, have a trip to Canada, and join an extracurricular organization."

Ohio

Antioch College

Address: One Morgan Place, Yellow Springs, OH 45387
Phone: 937-319-6082
E-mail address: admission@antiochcollege.org
Web site URL: antiochcollege.org
Year Founded: 1852
Private or Public: Private
Religious Affiliation: None
Location: Rural
Number of Applicants: 1,204
Percent Accepted: 60%
Percent Accepted who enroll: 15%
Number Entering: 108
Number of Transfers Accepted each Year: Unreported
Middle 50% SAT range: M: 530, CR: 590, Wr: Unreported
Middle 50% ACT range: 22–27
Early admission program EA/ED/None: EA and ED

Percentage accepted through EA or ED: Unreported
EA and ED deadline: 1-Jan, 1-Dec
Regular Deadline: 15-Feb
Application Fee: $40
Full time Undergraduate enrollment: 650
Total enrollment: 650
Percent Male: 40%
Percent Female: 60%
Total Percent Minority or Unreported: 18%
Percent African-American: 16%
Percent Asian/Pacific Islander: Unreported
Percent Hispanic: 1%
Percent Native American: 1%
Percent International: Unreported
Percent in-state/out of state: 34%/66%
Percent from Public HS: Unreported
Retention Rate: 84%

Graduation Rate 4-year: 28%
Graduation Rate 6-year: Unreported
Percent Undergraduates in On-campus housing: Unreported
Number of official organized extracurricular organizations: 16
3 Most popular majors: Business/Marketing, Education, Health Sciences
Student/Faculty ratio: 8:1
Average Class Size: 10
Percent of students going to grad school: Unreported
Tuition and Fees: $27,800
In-State Tuition and Fees if different: No difference
Cost for Room and Board: $7,354
Percent receiving financial aid out of those who apply: 90%
Percent receiving financial aid among all students: 20%

Antioch students are known for their love of a good argument. Their campus, located in Yellow Springs, Ohio, is always politically charged, and its students are always ready to push the envelope, whether they're exploring "radical research on gender" at an annual drag-themed dance party or protesting the new president's curriculum reform. But all Antioch students agree that their school is all the richer for its quirks and its conflicts. One freshman summed up his school like this: "Antioch is a strange, strange place . . . but wonderful nonetheless."

Growing Pains

New academic guidelines have shifted Antioch's focus slightly, with 180 credits needed to graduate and only three required terms in the co-op program. The new academic system consists of "learning communities," in which a chosen set of professors teach a set of classes focused on a certain subject or area. The idea is to unite professors in an interdisciplinary course of study and to promote a core of classes. Yet some students feel that not all professors have responded enthusiastically to the curriculum changes.

"Things are shifting," explained one senior. "A lot of professors aren't entirely pleased with the new academic system. Some of them aren't so keen on participating in it, and we're having a bit of an exodus of professors."

Despite this, many feel that Antioch's changing academic landscape renders it an even more exciting place to spend four years than it was prior to the revamping. "Antioch is changing right now, really quickly," said one senior. "The people who go to this school will have a chance to determine where it goes. If you want to be involved in the rebuilding of a school, the change of an entire academic structure where the community is strong, this is the place to go."

"Co-op"-erating

Antioch students agree that one of their school's unique features is its cooperative education program, designed to give students an opportunity to travel and live independently while still in college. Experiences during co-op term have ranged from helping to run a San Francisco–based theater company to working as a case manager at a mental health residential treatment facility in Pittsburgh to teaching English as a second language at a high school in Chicago. The entire program focuses on the idea of going out into an environment that is utterly unfamiliar.

While the college maintains a list of jobs and opportunities, much of the responsibility for ensuring the program's success lies with the students themselves. The experience was described by one senior as "almost being thrown to the wolves to a certain extent. They don't really help you find housing or adjust to the area at all, although not all of the jobs require you to go out and find your own place." Part of the school's new program, however, has established "co-op communities" in Ohio, New Mexico, and Washington, D.C. These areas enable students to take jobs near groups of other Antioch students and thus act as a sort of support system for each other as they settle in to their temporary homes and communities.

No grades? No problem!

Like everything else about Antioch, academics at the school are unique. In place of letter grades, students receive "narrative evaluations" in their courses. Professors are amenable to providing students with letter grades upon request, but most students say that their peers rarely use this option. This laid-back approach has its benefits and its drawbacks. Some students find that, at times, the pressure-free atmosphere goes hand in hand with a certain laziness for some of their classmates.

"The system really draws people who may not necessarily have done so well in

high school, because they weren't motivated by the way a traditional high school works. But they're very bright people, and Antioch is a place with a lot of bright, critical thinkers," said one senior. "Whether they choose to use that or not . . . that's another matter."

Another student singled out Antioch's size, and in particular the extremely intimate size of the average class, as one of the highlights of attending the school. "Most classes are very small," he said. "If any class is larger than 12 students, I feel like that's too large."

Aside from the environmental studies department and the women's studies department, both popular in a student body known for its liberal, socially, and environmentally conscious students, majors in the excellent communications department are among the most popular. Antiochians are fond of saying that one of their communications professors, Anne Bohlen, "taught Michael Moore how to use a camera."

Costume Parties: What a Drag

Perhaps because few students have cars and because the town of Yellow Springs offers few opportunities for party-seekers, most students said that the social scene on weekends consists entirely of parties on-campus. Antioch students are generally as laid-back about their partying as they are about grades.

Students frequent the costume parties held in the student union each weekend; themes have ranged from "Cowboys and Robots" to "Mystery Prom" to "Jet-Setting Socialites A-Go-Go" to "That's Amazing . . . and Disgusting," for which past revelers have come attired in cellophane or even chocolate pudding. Another perennial favorite is "Gender F**k," an exploration ("it's become more than just a drag ball") of the more radical ideas on gender that "encourages gender-bending to the extreme" and for many students embodies the open, accepting, and ever-inquiring nature of Antioch students regarding their own sexuality. "I think every Antioch student spends some time questioning, 'What gender am I? Am I really male?'" said one student. "This is also a very open community when it comes to transgender students. It's not uncommon to come back to school and see that someone has gotten a sex change."

Aside from these costume parties, however, the social scene on-campus is relatively easygoing and for the most part consists of gathering in friends' rooms or on The Stoop, a popular gathering place near the student union, to drink or smoke. Students described the presence of alcohol and some drugs on-campus, either due to administration policy or due to the makeup of the student body, as a relatively strong force in everyday life. One senior claimed that it was hard to stay away from the drug scene when living on campus, and that at least one student he knew had moved off campus to avoid that aspect of the social scene.

> "It's not uncommon to come back to school and see that someone has gotten a sex change."

Another student, however, said that regardless of the school's lenient alcohol policy, no Antioch student had ever gone to the hospital in her time there and that drugs were easy to avoid. "I do drink, but I don't feel pressured in the slightest," said one freshman.

Passionate About Politics
In general, students feel that the stereotypical Antioch student is not defined by how they party on the weekends—and certainly not by his or her athletic prowess. One student cited school shirts emblazoned with the slogan, "Antioch College: no football since 1929" as an example of the way the school's lack of interest in athletics "is almost a source of pride" on-campus. Rather, Antioch students feel that they are defined by their passions—and usually, by their liberal politics.

One senior described the classic Antioch student as "either the idealistic hippie who spends all their time in the garden talking about auras or the black-clad, angry liberal," while another joked that "if you go to Antioch, you have a few piercings and tattoos and have probably either colored or entirely shaved off your hair at least once in the past year." But all agreed that Antioch students are "ultra, ultra, ultra liberal" and that they love to debate, complain, and protest for the causes about which they feel strongly.

"Any conservative who comes onto campus is pretty quickly driven off," said one student. "People just get so emotional and energetic about their causes and issues, and that's great to see. But sometimes it can end up as these constant clashes between people and personalities, and it can get extremely uncomfortable." Despite students'

concerns with political issues and social injustice, however, one senior girl described the student body as "pretty white."

Perhaps due to the nature of Antioch's community, where "you pretty much know everyone" and everyone's ready to speak their mind and get into a debate with anyone else who does so, few students choose to move off campus at any point in their four years.

From "The Caf" to a Castle
Freshmen and seniors speak of the campus's 140-year-old main building, Antioch Hall, with awe and affection. It was described by one student as "a red brick castle-like building with a copper roof" and praised for "the really amazing view" from its towers by another. The student union, affectionately known as "the Caf," received fewer rave reviews; while one girl maintained that "it's getting a lot better" and another freshman praised "the vegan brownies," students agree that the food (and the hours of operation) are less than ideal.

Aside from the cafeteria, however, the student union is spoken of as a fairly popular gathering place, with one senior singling out the graffiti space in the top floor smoking lounge—one senior estimated that 70 percent of the campus smokes—as a favorite hangout spot.

Despite the amenities on campus, however, one senior recommends bringing a car as a means of occasional escape. "People can go so insane being around the same people on campus all the time," he said. "Bring a car or find a friend who has one pretty soon, so you're not always there in the whirlwind of Antioch drama."

In the end, students concur that "Antioch drama" is part of what makes their school such an unusual and one-of-a-kind place to spend four years. "It can be hard sometimes because of the nomadic nature of Antioch's educational program, but I don't think I could have gone anywhere else," said one senior. And one senior pointed to a common practice among professors as revealing of Antioch's general philosophy. "Professors are fine with you leaving to drive to Washington, D.C., for a protest," he said. "They honestly are more understanding about you going to a protest than about being sick. They want you to get out there and be political, because, after all . . . that's what Antioch's all about."—*Angelica Baker*

FYI

If you come to Antioch, you'd better bring "cigarettes, a strong sense of self, and a backpack. I've basically lived out of a hiking backpack for the past two years."

What is the typical weekend schedule? "Pick up some beer from the local beer shop on Friday, go to the party later on, wake up and go to brunch on Saturday, watch a movie or go into town and thrift shop for your outfit for that night's party . . . then play pool until two or three in the morning and dance your butt off."

If I could change one thing about Antioch, I'd "give us an endowment so we could pay our professors well. So many things that are bad here, are bad because we're such a poor school."

Three things every Antioch student should do before graduating are: "get really angry at a community meeting, go hardcore at Gender F**k, and drink the yellow spring water from the Glen."

Bowling Green State University

Address: 110 McFall Center, Bowling Green, OH 43403
Phone: 419-372-2478
E-mail address: admissions@bgsu.edu
Web site URL: www.bgsu.edu
Year Founded: 1910
Private or Public: Public
Religious Affiliation: None
Location: Rural
Number of Applicants: 11,111
Percent Accepted: 87%
Percent Accepted who enroll: 32%
Number Entering: 3,079
Number of Transfers Accepted each Year: 886
Middle 50% SAT range: M: 450–550, CR: 440–600, Wr: 435–535
Middle 50% ACT range: 19–24
Early admission program EA/ED/None: None

Percentage accepted through EA or ED: NA
EA and ED deadline: NA
Regular Deadline: Rolling
Application Fee: $40
Full time Undergraduate enrollment: 14,862
Total enrollment: 17,874
Percent Male: 47%
Percent Female: 53%
Total Percent Minority or Unreported: 21%
Percent African-American: 10%
Percent Asian/Pacific Islander: 1%
Percent Hispanic: 3%
Percent Native American: <1%
Percent International: 2%
Percent in-state/out of state: 90%/10%
Percent from Public HS: Unreported
Retention Rate: 73%

Graduation Rate 4-year: 33%
Graduation Rate 6-year: 57%
Percent Undergraduates in On-campus housing: 41%
Number of official organized extracurricular organizations: 280
3 Most popular majors: Biology, Psychology, Management
Student/Faculty ratio: 18:1
Average Class Size: 25
Percent of students going to grad school: Unreported
Tuition and Fees: $16,368
In-State Tuition and Fees if different: $9,060
Cost for Room and Board: $7,220
Percent receiving financial aid out of those who apply: 74%
Percent receiving financial aid among all students: 65%

If you're looking for a college town atmosphere, die-hard school spirit, and a relaxed intellectual environment, then Bowling Green State University may be the place for you. With almost 20,000 students, BGSU is filled with tons of different people, opinions, interests, and opportunities. Students are eager to point out that in spite of the relatively small population of the town (around 29,600), Bowling Green doesn't feel that small. Located only 20 miles south of Toledo, the campus is within easy driving distance of larger cities, offering a wide variety of restaurants, events, and clubs, although most students said they usually stay close to campus to participate in the vibrant social scene.

Better than "Normal"

When classes first started in 1914, BGSU was actually called Bowling Green State Normal College, tuition was free, and the only courses offered were education classes for women. The school dropped the "Normal" from its name in 1929, and students today agree that the school is far more interesting than its founding name implies. With over 200 majors and programs offered, a competitive honors curriculum, and a very active study abroad program, BGSU has expanded to offer just about any type of academic environment for its students. And while tuition is no longer free and the campus has long been coed, students say the focus on teacher preparation and the desire to make education affordable are still at the core of BG's academic philosophy. Students agreed that education is still the most popular major, adding that "it seems like everywhere you turn, you meet another future teacher." Indeed, BGSU ranks as a top producer of teachers in the country. With such a high number in one major, it might seem that enrollment in education classes would be competitive. But students said that registering for classes in general is fairly easy. The most frustrating part is getting put on waiting lists, but "with a little determination, it all works out in the end."

No matter what major you decide to pursue, students said BGSU does a good job of offering lots of opportunities to make your education entertaining and affordable with easily accessible resources for fellowships, internships, foreign exchange programs, and scholarships or financial aid. The university can accommodate almost any of your wildest travel plans, with foreign exchange programs in over 30 different countries as well as domestic opportunities for study or work experience. The same generosity with which BG approaches study abroad also translates to their financial aid packages. Nearly 70 percent of students receive financial aid, and the university also offers over $20 million in scholarship money and an extensive work-study program.

Students generally don't talk about their grades or feel a lot of pressure to compete with their classmates. This laid-back atmosphere is to the advantage of self-motivated students, and those in the honors program will find themselves with a demanding schedule no matter what. But others said the relaxed environment makes it almost too easy to forget about classes and only focus on the weekend.

Bleacher Creatures and Dancing Queens

Without a doubt, school pride is an important part of any student's time at BGSU. In the 1970s, a student group of die-hard BGSU Falcons fans dressed up in different Halloween costumes for every hockey game, eventually earning a spot in *Sports Illustrated* as the famous masked "Bleacher Creatures." Today, students channel this school spirit mainly during the annual football game against their archrival, the University of Toledo Rockets, for which fans show up in unusually large numbers. "I never watch football ever, but I've never missed a BG/UT game," one student added. BG has 17 NCAA Division I varsity sports teams to cheer on, and a ton of club sports for anyone to join, including ice hockey, ultimate Frisbee, and lacrosse. At games, students don their school colors, overlooking in the heat of the moment the unsightly combination of murky brown and bright orange.

> "It's nice being able to walk everywhere, and I like that I always run into somebody I know."

In addition to sports events, there are a ton of school-sponsored activities to participate in if athletics doesn't get you going. There are over 300 student-run organizations on campus, and the administration makes it relatively easy to start your own group if your interests aren't already represented. BG students seem more than up for the challenge of spearheading campus events, with student-run social and cultural activities going on "pretty much all the time." Among students' favorites are homecoming, family weekend, sibs-kids weekend, and the dance marathon—student-run events that bring the large campus together and often raise funds for charities and minorities. "I've helped work on the dance marathon for two years now and it's my favorite part of the year," one student said. "It's a really unique experience that the whole student body can come together on." Students can also enjoy theatrical and musical productions at the two large performance halls in the Moore Musical Arts Center, or take a trip to the spacious Fine Arts galleries to see exhibitions from BG student artists.

Another fundamental part of the BGSU lifestyle is the Greek system. Fraternities and sororities abound on campus, with over 43 different houses for students to choose from. About 12% of students opt for the Greek life, while others often attend the parties without choosing to rush.

Each month, BG offers its students close to 300 events and activities, ensuring that there is never a dull moment if you take advantage of the opportunities. Some students said they worried at first about the small-town setting, but the diversity of activities on campus really makes BG come alive so it can feel a lot bigger than the somewhat rural campus seems at first.

Home Sweet Home

BGSU has seven residence halls, some limited to upper- or underclassmen, and all with unique personalities and generally similar accommodations. As a rule, all underclassmen, except those who live at home, must live on campus, but students said they didn't really mind the restriction. Generally, they neither love nor hate the dorms. "The dorms are actually decent," one student said. "They can be pretty small and cramped, though, especially if you're not best buds with your roommate." Generally, the quality and size of the rooms increases as you get older. For example, Founders and Offenhauer (predominately upperclassmen dorms) have air-conditioning, while the all-freshman dorm MacDonald is known for its closet-like bedrooms and sardine lifestyle.

All rooms are equipped with computer connections and cable television access. Each residential hall has its own laundry room, as well as a study area, TV lounge, and computer lab for its students. All the dorms are centrally located on campus, so that you can easily get to all classes by bike or on foot. Shuttle services also are available to take students to main buildings, which they said are especially useful in the winter when it gets "really freakin' cold." Although students are allowed to have cars on campus and many do, the student parking lots are so inconvenient that "you end up walking just about as far as you would have if you hadn't driven in the first place."

Even though Bowling Green is a small town, students said they are never hard-pressed for a place to eat. During the week, students often hang out at the student union, enjoying fast food or the popular Zza's pizza from the food court, a latte from the Starbucks, or a home-cooked meal at the Bowling Greenery. Commons also offers all-you-can-eat-meals, although students warned that the options can often get pretty repetitive, especially at the MacDonald's dining center.

In general, students said living at BG was comfortable and relaxing. "It's safe, friendly, and laid-back," a student said. "It's nice being able to walk everywhere, and I like that I always run into somebody I know."

Close to 18,000 students attend BGSU, making it one of the larger public universities in the country. Only 10 percent of the students are non-residents, with about 500 international undergraduates from 90 countries. At about 21 percent minority, students said diversity is, of course, present on campus but is not a major part of campus life. "I hear a lot of stuff about the preppy frat boys from BG," one student said, "but it's not really like that. That's just the stereotype we get." And with multicultural organizations, hundreds of different student groups, and so many different academic majors, students said diversity of interests is really the main point.

Campus Culture

On the weekends, BGSU's diverse student body really spreads out, with some sticking to the campus events, others partying it up with a few friends, and still others driving out of town, either for a trip home or to livelier club scenes in neighboring cities. Although Bowling Green is a dry campus, with strict enforcement in the residence halls, undergraduate students said underage drinking can thrive at BG as much as at any other college, with the aid of a fake ID, an older friend, or simply a keg at an off-campus party. "If you're underage and you want to drink, it's not hard. You can go to a frat, a bar or club, or just stay in your room and keep it down," one student said. But if drinking's not for you, many students enjoy quieter nights at the movies, the theater, or hanging out in one of the local eateries.

A large number of students do drive out of town on the weekends, either going home if they live close by or visiting friends in Toledo or other nearby towns. Some students said commuting on the weekends can detract from the vibrant social scene BGSU tries hard to create, and that if you stick around, you'll find it can really be an exciting place to be on a Friday night.—*Maggie Reid*

FYI

What is the typical weekend schedule at a place like BGSU? "Friday: pre-game with your friends, go out to a frat or house party, bar hopping, some late night food. Saturday: sleep till noon, do it all again. Sunday: sleep all day and do your homework that's been piling up."

If I could change one thing about BGSU, "it would be the long months of cold, wind, and snow."

Three things every student should do before graduating from BGSU are: "make it to every UT football game, go to at least one frat party, and take advantage of the small, personal environment to really get to know your fellow classmates and your professors." Also, bring "a warm coat for the frigid winters."

Case Western Reserve University

Address: 10900 Euclid Avenue, Cleveland, OH 44106
Phone: 216-368-4450
E-mail address: admission@case.edu
Web site URL: www.case.edu
Year Founded: 1826
Private or Public: Private
Religious Affiliation: None
Location: Urban
Number of Applicants: 7,351
Percent Accepted: 73%
Percent Accepted who enroll: 19%
Number Entering: 1,026
Number of Transfers Accepted each Year: 107
Middle 50% SAT range: M: 620–720, CR: 590–690, Wr: 580–680
Middle 50% ACT range: 26–32
Early admission program EA/ED/None: ED
Percentage accepted through EA or ED: 38%

EA and ED deadline: 1-Nov
Regular Deadline: 15-Jan
Application Fee: $0
Full time Undergraduate enrollment: 4,207
Total enrollment: 8,166
Percent Male: 57%
Percent Female: 43%
Total Percent Minority or Unreported: 25%
Percent African-American: 6%
Percent Asian/Pacific Islander: 17%
Percent Hispanic: 2%
Percent Native American: <1%
Percent International: 4%
Percent in-state/out of state: 54%/46%
Percent from Public HS: Unreported
Retention Rate: 91%
Graduation Rate 4-year: 57%
Graduation Rate 6-year: 78%

Percent Undergraduates in On-campus housing: 78%
Number of official organized extracurricular organizations: 150
3 Most popular majors: Biology, Biomedical Engineering, Business Administration and Management
Student/Faculty ratio: 10:1
Average Class Size: 20
Percent of students going to grad school: Unreported
Tuition and Fees: $35,572
In-State Tuition and Fees if different: No difference
Cost for Room and Board: $10,450
Percent receiving financial aid out of those who apply: 90%
Percent receiving financial aid among all students: 84%

As the product of a merger of two established institutes of science—Case Institute of Technology and Western Reserve University—Case exemplifies the ideal of a technical university where superior academics coupled with a diverse student body provide an enlightening experience.

Academics at Case

Case is famous for its top-ranking science and engineering programs, and ranks perennially in the top 10 undergraduate biomedical engineering programs in the country. Consequently, the majority of students you'll meet at Case will be studying engineering, pre-medicine, and the "hard sciences." However, as one student commented, "Case has been working hard to increase the number of humanities majors."

Case also offers a variety of special programs aimed at students wishing to accelerate through their education, one of the most popular and selective of which is the Pre-Professional Scholars Program. Through PPSP, students are offered conditional placement in Case's graduate schools for law, social work, and dentistry. Competition for a space in the PPSP medicine program is especially intense—only around 20 to 25 students out of an applicant pool of 700 are accepted into the program annually. As a result, a coveted position in the PPSP medicine program becomes one of the most attractive aspects of Case; one pre-med student confessed, "I came to Case because I was accepted into PPSP."

Despite the heavy concentration of students in the sciences and engineering, Case is dedicated to educating their students in all areas, enabling them to become more well-rounded people with diverse interests. Case students are required to explore different areas, such as the arts, the humanities, and the social sciences, as well as courses in "global and cultural diversity."

The number of credits required for majors at Case differ according to department. While the arts and humanities programs require fewer credits and thus allow students more freedom to survey other fields, science and engineering programs require more credits. Though the requirements for science majors seem stringent, students say they leave feeling well prepared. A biomedical engineering major asserted, "The curriculum definitely takes care of every aspect of BME that's necessary, including polymers, imaging and electrics, and biomechanics."

Introductory classes are often lecture-based, with 100 to 300 students in each class. However, Case supplies "Supplemental Instructors" (SIs), who hold review sessions and are known to be "very helpful." As students progress to courses more specific to certain majors, however, typical class size decreases to a cozy 20–30, ensuring more personal attention for each student. Case also requires 16 credits in seminar classes, beginning with the freshman seminar program, SAGES (Seminar Approach to General Education and Scholarship), which is designed to encourage students to "discover . . . the endless opportunities and resources here at Case [as well as] . . . perspectives, passions, and creativity."

Social Scene

There's no question that Case students study hard, but beyond their grueling Sunday through Thursday nights, they also enjoy a vibrant and diverse social scene centered around Case's popular fraternities and sororities. Nearly a quarter of the student body is involved in the Greek scene, and as a result students report that "either you or many of your friends" are fraternity boys or sorority girls. Campus-wide Greek events are commonplace, and one of the most famous is Greek Week, when fraternities and sororities compete in numerous events. Interested students are given the opportunity to get to know their potential brotherhoods or sisterhoods through a series of events, get-togethers, and longer parties before receiving a bid to join.

Although Greek life does compose a large part of Case's social scene, students report that "the Greek community is normally very open." Although some girls complain that it is slightly more difficult to "make a ton of friends as a non-Greek," the majority of students feel that "Greeks are integrated into the campus, and are very inclusive."

While a decent percentage of students at Case come from Ohio, the student body at Case still "embodies diversity in geography, ethnicity, and particularly interests." Consequently, students at Case expect to meet and make friends from varied backgrounds. One student comments, "Sure, we are a nerdy school . . . but most people are socially inclined. I think that [Case] provides opportunities to meet all of the different sorts of people you'd like."

On-campus entertainment consists of performances and events run by a large variety of student groups such as IMPROVment on Friday nights and Spot Night on Wednesday nights, when local bands play. Alcohol is technically banned from campus, but one student reported it is nonetheless "easy to find," though "binge drinking and drugs are not problems on campus."

Case athletics have been increasing in popularity and rank in recent years. The Case football team ended the 2007 season with the school's first University Athletic Association Championship in football. The team was undefeated in 2008 but didn't get far in the NCAA Division III playoffs. Intramural sports, including less traditional events such as dodgeball, are "intense as heck." Three-quarters of the undergraduate body participate in intramurals during their four years at Case.

> "Sure, we are a nerdy school . . . but most people are socially inclined. I think that [Case] provides opportunities to meet all of the different sorts of people you'd like."

Students can also explore the large array of off-campus entertainment. Whether you'd like to go shopping, dining, clubbing, or bowling, there are options accessible on foot or by bus. One of the most popular and unique neighborhoods near Case is Coventry, which can be reached by walking or by "Greenies," the green campus shuttle buses. Coventry is a shopping district with an eclectic mix of stores full of "books, toys, and random cool things" in addition to restaurants offering international cuisine. Sports fans can cheer on the nearby Cleveland Indians and Cavaliers, music aficionados can enjoy their favorite bands at the House of Blues, and window-shoppers can indulge themselves at Beachwood, an upscale mall accessible by bus from campus.

Of course, you can also take advantage of Case's proximity to the University Circle and enjoy masterpieces at the Cleveland Museum of Art, scientific artifacts and displays at Cleveland Museum of Natural History, shows at the Cleveland Play House, and of course the concerts of the world-renowned Cleveland Orchestra at Severance Hall, all within one mile of campus. But when you're traveling to and from locations off-campus at night, be aware that, as with most universities located in urban environments, safety is key. Although Case is currently updating emergency phones and security is "everywhere," "you should [still] definitely be smart about where you go and what you do."

Living at Case

Students are required to live on campus for the first two years of school, unless they live at home and commute. Freshmen dorms are usually doubles located in the "upper three floors of four-storied buildings" and are "fair sized, but without air-conditioning." Students are allowed to choose their own rooms and dorms, pending availability, as well as their own roommates.

Many upperclassmen choose to move off campus, but a significantly larger percentage of them stay on campus due to the recent addition of the "Village at 115." Described as a "swanky hotel" by some, Village at 115 offers the luxury of an apartment with the convenience of living on campus. However, the major complaint about both upperclassmen and underclassmen housing is that "classes are too far away from the dorms."

There are two main dining halls on campus: Fribley (South) and Leutner (North). Students are free to dine at either dining hall, though Fribley is considered better. Flexible meal plans come with "Case cash," which can be used at local restaurants.

The numerous resources and opportunities Case Western Reserve University offers impact its students for a lifetime. Students describe their time at Case as "demanding but rewarding," and with its superior academics and flourishing social scene Case offers its students an ideal environment to enhance their education and social connections.—*Chaoran Chen*

FYI

If you come to Case, you'd better bring "a computer and a warm winter coat."

What is the typical weekend schedule? "Every weekend is different" and "students can generally do whatever they choose," but Friday and Saturday tend to be nights to find a party or enjoy events off campus, whereas Sunday night is reserved exclusively for studying.

If I could change one thing about Case, I'd "make everyone more positive."

Two things every student at Case should do before graduating are: "go to a concert by the Cleveland Orchestra and explore University Circle's museums."

College of Wooster

Address: 847 College Avenue, Wooster, OH 44691
Phone: 800-877-9905
E-mail address: admissions@wooster.edu
Web site URL: www.wooster.edu
Year Founded: 1866
Private or Public: Private
Religious Affiliation: None
Location: Suburban
Number of Applicants: 3,445
Percent Accepted: 81%
Percent Accepted who enroll: 20%
Number Entering: 513
Number of Transfers Accepted each Year: 45
Middle 50% SAT range: M: 540–660, CR: 540–670, Wr: Unreported
Middle 50% ACT range: 23–29
Early admission program EA/ED/None: ED and EA

Percentage accepted through EA or ED: Unreported
EA and ED deadline: 1-Dec, 15-Jan
Regular Deadline: 1-Feb
Application Fee: $40
Full time Undergraduate enrollment: 1,864
Total enrollment: 1,864
Percent Male: 47%
Percent Female: 53%
Total Percent Minority or Unreported: 10%
Percent African-American: 5%
Percent Asian/Pacific Islander: 3%
Percent Hispanic: 2%
Percent Native-American: <1%
Percent International: 5%
Percent in-state/out of state: 39%/ 61%
Percent from Public HS: Unreported
Retention Rate: 88%

Graduation Rate 4-year: 64%
Graduation Rate 6-year: 73%
Percent Undergraduates in On-campus housing: 100%
Number of official organized extracurricular organizations: 130
3 Most popular majors: Psychology, Political Science, English
Student/Faculty ratio: 12:1
Average Class Size: 17
Percent of students going to grad school: 40%
Tuition and Fees: $42,420 comprehensive fee
In-State Tuition and Fees if different: No difference
Cost for Room and Board: Included with tuition
Percent receiving financial aid out of those who apply: 82%
Percent receiving financial aid among all students: 17%

A small liberal arts college with less than 2,000 students, the College of Wooster may not be as well-known as many other similar institutions, but it provides an outstanding education and a supportive intellectual environment to all students. Founded in 1866 and following a mission to educate everyone, Wooster's first PhD was granted to a female student during the 1880s. Today, Wooster focuses only on the undergraduate education of students, and the school is known for its unique Independent Study program, a yearlong senior project that culminates in an oral defense of a thesis in front of a committee. While it seems to be a college with a challenging environment, Wooster also provides an intimate atmosphere that closely supports both the academic and social aspects of student life.

Independence

Being in college means a greater degree of freedom as well as learning about becoming independent. That is exactly what Wooster chooses to foster among its students. The idea is that all students should pursue their own interests at their own initiative. Therefore, one portion of the degree requirement is that everyone must complete three courses of independent study. The first class is generally taken in junior year, during which students learn about research skills and methods. The last two courses are part of the senior thesis where students come up with their own projects. This program traces its beginnings to the 1940s and has since then been both lauded and imitated by many different universities. "I think it can seem really challenging at first," said one student. "But with the support we have here from professors, it becomes a very interesting experience."

Another part of Wooster's goal to foster independence is the availability of student-designed majors. Of course, it has to go through approvals by different levels of the college's bureaucracy to ensure academic vigor and coherence; nevertheless, it is a great way for the more ambitious students to create their personal programs of study instead of following academic plans designed by others. For those not interested in an independent program, there are about 40 majors, not a particularly large number, but that is characteristic of liberal arts schools, where students are expected to achieve a broad range of knowledge. Although the university has pre-professional programs in law, medicine, and engineering, the focus of the college is on liberal arts, which can be somewhat disappointing for all those interested in learning about more practical topics. "I always wanted to take a couple of interesting classes in engineering," said one student. "And I have been very much disappointed, but I guess I should have expected that from a liberal arts school."

> "With the support we have here from professors, [the Independent Study Program] becomes a very interesting experience."

Very interestingly, each major only requires seven to nine courses in the specific department. Therefore, students have greater freedom in choosing their classes. It also means a lengthy list of core requirement classes in which everyone must enroll. Similar to many universities, the required courses include writing, mathematics, foreign languages, and cultural perspectives. In order to graduate, all students must also take a class examining the religious dimension of human interactions. "The required classes are some of the best ones that I have had at Wooster," said one student.

Given the focus on independence, the academic life at Wooster is rather vigorous. Students are expected to work hard in their classes. "There are a lot of smart people here," said one student. "During freshman year, I was really shocked at the amount of work, maybe because my high school was not that demanding." At the same time, professors are very easily accessible. "I think the best thing here is that we are really small, and you can get to know some professors well as long as you try to meet them and talk to them," said one student.

Another advantage of Wooster is the lack of big lectures. For the school, an introductory class of 40 people would be considered very large, compared to large universities that have hundreds of people crammed into a single lecture hall. Therefore, Wooster is able to create an intimate academic atmosphere. Of course, the drawback is that, unlike in large lectures, no one can remain relatively anonymous in a class, and students are expected to participate more in class discussions.

Wooster, the Town

The college is located in Wooster, Ohio, about 50 miles south of Cleveland. It is well known as a college town. Not only is it home to Wooster College, it also includes the Agricultural Technical Institute of the Ohio State University and a major research center on agricultural development. From these institutions, it is clear that the city is highly focused on agriculture, especially in its surrounding areas. Students certainly lament the fact that Wooster lacks the benefits of large cities. "There is not much to do around here, which is exacerbated by the fact that we are in such a small school," said one student. Others, however, believe that Wooster offers a great college town atmosphere that is conducive to learning. "Coming from a big city, I really enjoy the more relaxed life here," said one student.

The great majority of undergraduates live on campus for the entirety of their college education. Only a negligible number of students choose to live elsewhere. The college offers 12 different residential halls. Each floor of the residential hall has a Resident Assistant whose main purpose is to help freshmen settle in and become accustomed to college life. The rooms, like most college dormitories, are very small. "If you have not already, I think you should learn about working outside of your room, because there is not much space," said one student. Most people, however, agree that the residences are adequate, and there is no major complaint about the living arrangement.

The dining services operate two large eateries. In addition, there are two coffee locations and one convenience store. It does not seem to be a large number of options, but considering that the school enrolls fewer than 2,000 students, the dining services certainly provide adequate options for students. "It is not really great food," said one student. "But I have no complaint."

Given the size of the college, students eventually become familiar with a large portion of the undergraduate population. "You get to know not only people of your own year," said one student, "but you are also going to meet plenty of people of other years because we are a very close community." The social life on the weekends, however, can be rather repetitive. Those looking for the nightlife of big cities will be disappointed, especially given the fact that Cleveland is more than an hour away. Surrounding campus, there are a number of bars and clubs, and both the students and the school administration do try to create their own events. However, given the size of the school and the city, it is clear that many students wish they could have access to a greater variety of activities.

An Unknown Gem

The diversity of Wooster is a potential area of improvement for the university. The majority of the student body is white with only a limited number of minorities, though students agree that they have a very tolerant and open-minded campus. In many ways, Wooster is a school that is perhaps not particularly well known, but offers a great intellectual atmosphere that rivals many of the top liberal arts colleges and is certainly a great choice for four years of undergraduate study.—*Xiaohang Liu*

FYI

If you come to Wooster, you'd better bring "a car."
What is the typical weekend schedule? "Doing work during the day, and partying at night."
If I could change one thing about Wooster, I'd "make it a little warmer during winters."
Three things every student at Wooster should do before graduating are: "go to sporting events, hang out at the Underground, and participate in community service."

Denison University

Address: 100 West College, PO Box B, Granville, OH 43023
Phone: 740-587-6276
E-mail address: admissions@denison.edu
Web site URL: www.denison.edu
Year Founded: 1831
Private or Public: Private
Religious Affiliation: None
Location: Suburban
Number of Applicants: 5,181
Percent Accepted: 39%
Percent Accepted who enroll: 29%
Number Entering: 586
Number of Transfers Accepted each Year: 30
Middle 50% SAT range: M: 590–680, Cr: 580–690, Wr: 620–690
Middle 50% ACT range: 26–30

Early admission program EA/ED/None: ED
Percentage accepted through EA or ED: 14%
EA and ED deadline: 1-Nov
Regular Deadline: 15-Jan
Application Fee: $40
Full time Undergraduate enrollment: 2,212
Total enrollment: 2,212
Percent Male: 43%
Percent Female: 57%
Total Percent Minority or Unreported: 18%
Percent African-American: 5%
Percent Asian/Pacific Islander: 3%
Percent Hispanic: 2%
Percent Native American: 1%
Percent International: 5%
Percent in-state/out of state: 43%/57%
Percent from Public HS: 70%
Retention Rate: 93%

Graduation Rate 4-year: 78%
Graduation Rate 6-year: 82%
Percent Undergraduates in On-campus housing: 99%
Number of official organized extracurricular organizations: 156
3 Most popular majors: Communications, Economics, English
Student/Faculty ratio: 11:1
Average Class Size: 19
Percent of students going to grad school: 27%
Tuition and Fees: $32,160
In-State Tuition and Fees if different: No difference
Cost for Room and Board: $8,570
Percent receiving financial aid out of those who apply: 76%
Percent receiving financial aid among all students: 43%

Despite its small size, students at Denison University dream big. With only 2,200 undergraduates, this private liberal arts college has dozens of clubs, offers hundreds of leadership positions, and encourages students to take advantage of these opportunities. And at Denison, they actually do. Indeed, interviewed students said the challenging workload, inclusive party environment and varied extracurricular activities made Denison a place they love.

"Biochemistry and Bluegrass"

"It's just an academically rigorous school," said one sophomore, whose sentiments were repeated by other Denison students. Without a doubt, the academics are demanding, and there does not seem to be an easy class. Students characterized the grading as fair but tough. Even though the school does not have a special honors program, the general academic curriculum provides sufficient difficulty. However, the sophomore added the coursework is "not unbearable or overwhelming. It's definitely manageable."

At Denison, class sizes are extremely small. They range from eight to a maximum of 25 students. One junior said that sometimes "it is hard to get into the classes you want. If you didn't make it, you didn't make it." Yet, most undergraduates agreed the limits on class size foster greater discussion during the class and encourage everyone to participate. Furthermore, Denison requires that professors teach all classes. TAs are only responsible for grading assignments or preparing class demonstrations. According to one senior, the professors "help students feel both challenged and confident." Indeed, many students said that while professors hold them to high standards, they are incredibly approachable and very friendly. The faculty members are there to help the undergraduates, said another senior.

Ever since its inception, Denison offered innovative programs that pushed students to realize their full capacities. According to one senior, Denison offered one of the first women's studies programs in the United States. Currently, the school has a mandatory seminar program that is only open to freshman and offers writing courses in a variety of subjects. The program helps freshmen transition from high school coursework to collegiate level assignments. One student applauded the program as encouraging the pursuit of "self-knowledge."

Certainly, a spirit of independence and student autonomy pervades the student body. Denisonians throw themselves into their coursework, chasing dual degrees in disparate fields. While some students said the academic culture could get overwhelming at times, most undergraduates added that ambition and a genuine interest in learning was universally shared. As one senior said, "At Denison, it's not uncommon to find a Biochemistry and Bluegrass double-major."

City on a Hill

Located in the heart of Licking County, Denison stands alone atop a large hill. If you walk down, at the base you will find Granville, a tiny town with a lot of character. Several students said, "The town is very supportive of Denison. It's a quaint place to be." Wander into Granville, and you can stop for dinner and a pint at Brews or Broadway. Afterwards, walk to Whit's for some delicious frozen custard. For a little variety, try some Mexican food at Taco Dan's. Indeed, many students walk to Granville for a bite to eat or just to relax. While most Denisonians have cars to travel to Columbus, students said it is not a necessity.

After all, the campus itself offers plenty of opportunities for a vibrant social life. Many students hangout and grab food at The Union. Meal plans combine flex dollars—used outside the dining halls—and a swipe system. For your late night cravings, hit up Bandersnatch for milkshakes, coffee or pizza. You surely will be unable to resist a "snagel"—a bagel filled with cream cheese and cinnamon sugar.

Campus Living

As Denison is a 100% residential college, every student lives on campus in one of four quads: North, West, East and South. While dorms do not necessarily improve in seniority, seniors live on North quad in the Sunset apartments. The dormitories have both RAs and HRs (head residents). While Denison is not a dry campus, the RAs and HRs do enforce underage drinking, often resulting in getting "written up." Yet, the policy does not seem too strict. As one freshman said, "[The school] makes sure it's safe rather than restrictive."

This laidback culture results in a fun and lively party atmosphere. The University Programming Council (UPC) hosts an event almost every Friday, according to one senior. During the weekend, "You can almost always find a party to go to." The Sunset apartments are quite popular, as well as the Shaw, Sawyer and Shepardson dorms on East quad. However, students cautioned, "A lot of people can get caught up in [the drinking culture]."

Around 30 percent of students engage in Greek life, even though there are no longer fraternity houses. One freshman noted, "There is a Greek scene on campus, but there's no pressure to be in it. I felt it was something that contributed positively to the atmosphere." However, a junior said she still felt there was a lot of exclusivity surrounding the Greek culture. Regardless, the majority of Denisonians are not directly involved. One student concisely summarized the social life at Denison: "The party scene is not overwhelming. There is something for everyone."

Lead by Example

While Denison certainly emphasizes the importance of academics, students often find as much fulfillment outside of the classroom as inside it. With more than 170 student organizations, ambitious Denisonians can participate in as many facets of extracurricular life as possible. In fact, one senior cautioned that "One of our biggest problems is that everyone is overinvolved. Denison is a campus of over-achievers."

> "Denison is a place with a strong sense of community where I felt I could come and be a leader on campus, make a difference on campus, make a difference in Ohio, and make a difference in the world."

If you can manage to avoid overextending yourself, the vibrant extracurricular life can be enjoyable, students said. Several undergraduates added that because of its small size, Denison offers motivated students the opportunity to become leaders in a multiple areas. Popular groups include the Denison Community Association (DCA)—which is responsible for organizing service opportunities—and the UPC—which brings singers, comedians and lecturers to campus. One student expressed their impact very clearly: "Denison is a place with a strong sense of community where I felt I could come and be a leader on campus, make a difference on campus, make a difference in Ohio, and make a difference in the world." Of course, if these groups, or the other 170 options, are insufficient, students have the independence to create their own group. While Denison is a Division III school, sports pride remains relatively high—especially for men's swimming. While some students said sporting events were "generally well-attended," others said athletics are not emphasized at Denison. One thing undergraduates could agree on was the popularity of the satirical publication *BullSheet* and the student newspaper, *The Denisonian*.

No Shirt? No Shoes? No problem

Naked Week, a tradition started in 2003, "is all about loving the body and being in yourself and being comfortable around others," said one self-confident sophomore. Starting Monday afternoon and lasting the next couple of days, students shed their clothing and run around different parts of campus. The sophomore said last year's Naked Week brought more than 250 runners. Whether you are a willing participant or a curious spectator, the tradition "really builds a sense of community." So, streak on.

If Naked Week is a bit too revolutionary for you, try another famous Denison tradition, Denison Day, known colloquially as D-Day. Sometime in the fall semester, the UPC organizes a daytime carnival and a concert featuring a marquee artist later in the evening. Students say everyone comes out to partake in the festivities and enjoy good music.

On Friday nights, you might find yourself listening to a capella in Swasey Chapel. Perhaps on a sunny spring day, you'll lay outside on A quad relaxing with your friends. Maybe you will even be inside Doane library for a quick study session. The choice is entirely up to you. Indeed, one student captured the ethos of a Denison college experience: "I would characterize it as self-deterministic. It's whatever you can make it." Students have the option to be the architects of their own education. At Denison, they are.—*Adrian Rodrigues*

FYI

What differentiates Denison the most from other colleges is how many different opportunities and experiences you can have. The number of student groups and options is just astounding. There is so much opportunity for students to be involved in as much as they want.

If I could change one thing about Denison, I . . . would make the hill smaller. It takes a long time to walk up and down.

What surprised me the most about Denison when I arrived was everyone's friendliness. Denison is a campus of open and compassionate people. It's a campus where everyone holds doors for others.

Kent State University

Address: 314 University Library, Kent, OH 44242
Phone: 330-672-3000
E-mail address: admissions@kent.edu
Web site URL: www.kent.edu
Year Founded: 1910
Private or Public: Public
Religious Affiliation: None
Location: Suburban
Number of Applicants: 12,325
Percent Accepted: 89%
Percent Accepted who enroll: 35%
Number Entering: 3,831
Number of Transfers Accepted each Year: 920
Middle 50% SAT range: M: 460–590, CR: 460–580, Wr: Unreported
Middle 50% ACT range: 19–24
Early admission program EA/ED/None: None
Percentage accepted through EA or ED: NA

EA and ED deadline: NA
Regular Deadline: 1-Aug
Application Fee: $55
Full time Undergraduate enrollment: 29,227
Total enrollment: 34,056
Percent Male: 39%
Percent Female: 61%
Total Percent Minority or Unreported: 17%
Percent African-American: 9%
Percent Asian/Pacific Islander: 2%
Percent Hispanic: 2%
Percent Native American: <1%
Percent International: Unreported
Percent in-state/out of state: 87%/13%
Percent from Public HS: Unreported
Retention Rate: 71%
Graduation Rate 4-year: 26%

Graduation Rate 6-year: Unreported
Percent Undergraduates in On-campus housing: 35%
Number of official organized extracurricular organizations: 400
3 Most popular majors: Business/Marketing, Education, Health Professions
Student/Faculty ratio: 18:1
Average Class Size: Unreported
Percent of students going to grad school: Unreported
Tuition and Fees: $15,862
In-State Tuition and Fees if different: $8,430
Cost for Room and Board: $7,200
Percent receiving financial aid out of those who apply: 81%
Percent receiving financial aid among all students: 63%

Located in northeastern Ohio, less than a 60-minute drive from Cleveland, Kent State University is one of Ohio's largest with a student population of over 29,000. Nonetheless, Kent State students attest to the availability of resources and closeness within student groups, thereby offsetting many of the traditional drawbacks that students at larger schools tend to deal with. Known, unfortunately, for the tragic shootings of student protestors that happened on campus in 1970, Kent State has since established a reputation as an open university in the midst of a lively college town.

Big School, Small Classes
Considering the number of students on campus, it might be easy to assume that most classes are taught in a large lecture-hall format. Students on campus, however, refuted this notion, saying that while most general elective classes will be "stadium-seated with about 100 to 200 students," many of their other classes, particularly those within their major or freshman writing classes, will likely have less than 40 students.

Regardless of class size, however, most professors make themselves available via office hours, even allowing students to set up individual meetings beyond these times. "They'll work with you to find a time for you to come in to talk to them," a senior said.

Kent State offers over 30 majors, ranging from Integrated Life Sciences to History, and everything in between. "We have a huge nursing program, as well as a huge fashion, merchandising, and design program, and then there's psychology," explained one student when asked to name Kent's three most prominent academic tracks. Kent also allows students to pursue minors in the same disciplines offered as majors, in addition to about 15 minor-only subjects.

Most students take a courseload of 15 credit-hours (equating to 15 hours in class per week), though that can change depending on the difficulty of the student's major. In general, students agree that "for every hour that you're in class, you spend two hours [on work] outside of class." To help ease the pressure of this workload, most Kent students end up working in study groups, which generally consist of friends in similar classes, but occasionally, professors make the effort to actively organize these groups in order to make sure that their students have people to work with. Students interviewed agreed that, at the very least, these groups allow students to meet other people with shared interests.

As for the students looking to push out beyond Kent, Ohio during their college years, Kent State offers many study abroad programs with the most popular ones sending students to Florence, Italy and Geneva, Switzerland every semester.

"Living Learning Communities" and General Housing

Kent State seeks to integrate its student life with its academics by establishing "Living Learning Communities" in which students (beginning with freshmen, up through on-campus upperclassmen) can live in residence halls grouped by major or academic discipline. Through this initiative, Kent State has its sights on "making a large campus feel small," and has even done studies to show that this set-up has actually boosted the GPAs of its students. Though voluntary, many students opt for this arrangement, which divides groups like "A Community of Entrepreneurs" (ACE), "Fine Arts Community" (FAC), and "Public Health Living Learning Community" (PHLLC) into their own distinct buildings and living spaces.

Even so, students still have the option to live in standard on-campus residence halls, which are all staffed with resident advisers and hall councils. Kent State encourages its students to live on campus (arguing that doing so boosts academic performance), but some do make the decision to live off-campus in local apartment complexes.

Kent State's main campus is located in Kent, Ohio, and the majority of the student population attends classes at and lives on this campus; however, satellite campuses are located across Ohio in cities like Ashtabula and Warren for commuter and part-time students.

Clubs for Everyone

Kent State students have several opportunities to join on-campus groups, which include professional, cultural, political, and religious organizations. With so many students, it only makes sense that Kent State boasts hundreds of student organizations. Additionally, several academic majors are affiliated with a related academic group, further encouraging students to explore that which they study in class on a deeper, more profound level.

> **"Barack Obama stopped by Ray's Place when he came—that's where everyone goes."**

Kent, Ohio: College Town.

Right outside Kent State's campus gates lies the city of Kent, which is the quintessential college town. Downtown Kent boasts several popular restaurants, particularly on Main Street. One particular bar, Ray's Place, is a Kent State cultural landmark, and not just for the food and drinks Ray's serves. "Any time a huge band is in town—even Barack Obama stopped by Ray's Place when he came—that's the place where everyone goes," one student said. It doesn't just stop with restaurants though. Kent has everything a college kid could want: shops, theaters, clubs, and bars, all of which are within walking distance from campus and offer student discounts.

The Greek system also plays a feature role in the Kent State social scene. Many of the nation's most prominent fraternities and sororities have chapters and houses at Kent State. Because campus policy regarding parties and alcohol is strictly regulated, the party scene at Kent State largely runs through the Greek system. However, in addition to hosting social functions, the fraternities and sororities at Kent are well-known for their work with various philanthropic projects. "You see the stuff [fraternities and sororities] are doing all over campus; they're always in the *Kent Stater* for the fundraisers they're doing," explained a Kent State senior.

The Golden Flashes

The Kent State Golden Flashes are a major Division I school, and as a result, athletic events are all well-attended (and offer free admission to students). Members of the Mid-American Conference, the Flashes have been particularly successful in football, men's basketball, and baseball in the past few years. Students not on the varsity teams have the traditional opportunities to participate in club or intramural sports, both of which are very popular on campus. The

Student Recreation and Wellness Center is also available for individual athletic activity and exercise.

Big School, Tight Communities
There's no denying that Kent State is significantly larger than most colleges. Though some might be turned off by a student body that tops 20,000, it's important to consider that a college this big affords its students several unique opportunities both inside and outside the classroom. Students have taken it upon themselves to form intimate communities within the school, be it in residential, academic, extracurricular, or general social settings. The academic structure very strongly emphasizes accessibility and support, thereby engaging each student within his or her major on a unique level. Kent State's biggest draw, however, is the city for which it is named. Students rave about the range of activities offered by and proximity of Kent, Ohio. If you're looking for a school with a lot of people and constant activity, give Kent State a look.
—*Marek Ramilo*

FYI
Something that surprised you about Kent State: "I think people are surprised by how big our university is. We're not in a huge city, but we still have a very large campus."
Kent State Bucket List items: "Go to Ray's Place, go sledding behind Taylor Hall, attend all the free concerts that are offered."
Biggest on-campus events: concerts, plays, intramurals, athletic events (particularly against Akron, Kent State's arch-rival).

Kenyon College

Address: Ransom Hall, Gambier, OH 43022 to 9623
Phone: 740-427-5776
E-mail address: admissions@kenyon.edu
Web site URL: www.kenyon.edu
Year Founded: 1824
Private or Public: Private
Religious Affiliation: None
Location: Rural
Number of Applicants: 4,272
Percent Accepted: 34%
Percent Accepted who enroll: 33%
Number Entering: 468
Number of Transfers Accepted each Year: 44
Middle 50% SAT range: M: 610–690, CR: 640–740, Wr: 640–730
Middle 50% ACT range: 28–32
Early admission program EA/ED/None: ED I, ED II

Percentage accepted through EA or ED: 55%
EA and ED deadline: 15-Nov, 15-Jan
Regular Deadline: 15-Jan
Application Fee: $50 (waived for online application)
Full time Undergraduate enrollment: 1,647
Total enrollment: 1,657
Percent Male: 46%
Percent Female: 54%
Total Percent Minority or Unreported: 15%
Percent African-American: 3%
Percent Asian/Pacific Islander: 6%
Percent Hispanic: 5%
Percent Native American: 1%
Percent International: 3%
Percent in-state/out of state: 17%/83%
Percent from Public HS: 54%
Retention Rate: 91%

Graduation Rate 4-year: 85%
Graduation Rate 6-year: 89%
Percent Undergraduates in On-campus housing: 98%
Number of official organized extracurricular organizations: >140
3 Most popular majors: English, Political Science, Economics/International Studies
Student/Faculty ratio: 10:1
Average Class Size: 19
Percent of students going to grad school: 18%
Tuition and Fees: $42,630
In-State Tuition and Fees if different: No difference
Cost for Room and Board: $10,020
Percent receiving financial aid out of those who apply: 88%
Percent receiving financial aid among all students: 35%

I n the picturesque town of Gambier, Ohio, a rural locale with an average 40.3 inches of annual snowfall, sits Kenyon College. A liberal arts Mecca that has drawn progressive-minded students from across the country since 1824, Kenyon's strength is its tight-knit community of around 1,660 students. Kenyon's combined emphasis on academic rigor and out-of-the-box creativity makes it a collegiate paradise for those seeking to explore a variety of interests in a warm and hospitable campus setting—even in winter!

An Intimate Setting

Kenyon couldn't possibly find a more charming setting than Gambier. Every weekend, local Amish families come to sell jam on Middle Path, the gravel trail that runs all the way from the north to south end of the campus. Students bike on the Kokosing Gap Trail, which traverses scenic farm country. Tied to the branches of the Upside Down Tree, so named for its odd appearance in winter, are dozens of pieces of paper on which students write their wishes and dreams. It's common to keep doors unlocked.

Gambier might be idyllic, but there is no short supply of jokes at its expense around campus. One sophomore recommended a trip to the college's observatory in the woods to go stargazing, then added, "There's hardly any light pollution because we're so far from civilization." Students often poke fun at "downtown" Gambier, a block-long string of establishments on Wiggin Street that's hardly a buzzing metropolis—a post office, a bookstore, two restaurants, and a coffee shop students call 'Wiggleground.' Kenyon has just one dining hall, Peirce Hall (though students swear by the aptly named Gambier Grill and NiteBites, a late-night delivery service with legendary Nutella milkshakes). Half of Kenyon students have a car on campus; upperclassmen say occasional drives to Columbus for dinner are a must.

Yet students find that it's the small, intimate nature of Kenyon—and its remoteness—that makes academic and social life so fulfilling. Since the typical class size is 15, students get unique one-on-one attention from professors (there aren't TAs at Kenyon, except in language courses to give students extra help). Many professors live in Gambier, and it's not uncommon for them to invite students over for dinner (or, in the case of one Latin professor, "tea and homemade biscuits"). A freshman interested in East Asian studies said his faculty advisor addresses him as a "friend," and one of his professors even gave out his home phone number so students could ask questions outside office hours. Kenyon's newly elected president, Dr. Sean Decatur, can be found serving waffles at midnight before exam week (an old tradition), and reportedly responds on Twitter to the nickname students gave him—D-Cat.

Though Kenyon students sometimes begrudge their limited dining options, Peirce Hall is the campus' hub, where old and new friends meet. Students say you always see someone you know there, making Kenyon homey (plus, students like that there's no meal plan—it's all-you-can-eat). And though the college's small population can sometimes create problems (a typical complaint: daily post-hookup awkwardness in the dining hall), Kenyon is especially "community-oriented" as a result.

Many students find that they come to love Gambier, which can be a "retreat" from the outside world, allowing students to focus on their studies. And in the words of one senior, "We're all stuck on this hill in the middle of nowhere, so people do become very close."

> "We're all stuck on this hill in the middle of nowhere, so people do become very close."

Traditional School, Progressive People

One sophomore described Kenyon as "a very traditional school for very progressive people." From its neo-gothic architecture to its strict core requirements (requiring students to complete nine two-semester "units" of courses outside their own majors and at least one unit in the natural sciences, social sciences, humanities and fine arts), Kenyon offers the conventional liberal arts approach to higher education. Yet students at Kenyon are uniquely progressive, from their interests to their political views.

Nearly a fifth of Kenyon's 2012 graduating class majored in English, and dorm entryways are covered in posters of award-winning author John Green, a '00 Kenyon grad whose recent book skyrocketed to #1 on the *New York Times* Bestseller List. Students collectively agree that the top floor of Ascension Hall, a study room with comfy couches, looks like a Hogwarts common room. Last year, President Decatur began freshman convocation in the Great Hall by raising a goblet and declaring, "100 points for Gryffindor!" Although students say the math and science departments are strong (Decatur himself was a chemistry professor), the other top majors are psychology, economics and political science.

Because class sizes are so small, Kenyon classes are often hard to get into. "Meanings of Death," a religious studies class taught by iconic professor Royal Rhodes, has a years-long waitlist, with one freshman explaining that freshmen sign up in hopes of getting in junior year. But whether it's by choice, by necessity to fulfill requirements, or by virtue of not getting into top-pick classes, Kenyon students end up taking classes they didn't expect taking. And that's a good thing. According to one senior, students take "a lot of crazy classes," from one devoted entirely to Toni Morrison to one on how animals grow, which often end up defining students' academic lives.

But besides student demand for less traditional classes, there's another reason Kenyon students have gained notoriety as "hipsters": extracurriculars. The largest student group on campus is WKCO, a student-run radio show, which started 67 years ago and now has a hundred—yes, a hundred—DJs. Students can write for an array of literary magazines and online blogs in addition to Kenyon's official newspaper, *The Kenyon Collegian*. The *Kenyon Review*, a nationally acclaimed literary magazine, hosts an annual festival in Gambier. Various a cappella groups perform at "The Horn," a two-story building on campus with an art gallery and a performance space for bands. Kenyon students are also proud of their drama program, with three faculty-directed theater productions and two dance shows on the main stage every year. The program, often listed as one of the best US colleges for aspiring actors, also boasts theater groups from Renegade Theater (for freshman) to Brave Potato (which puts on musicals). And that's not even counting the Improv groups.

Students are also politically progressive. One freshman described Kenyon students as "left-wing and not willing to back down easily from an argument," and estimated there were only a dozen conservative Republicans in his class. The Unity House on campus offers 24-hour support for LGBTQ students, and students praise the college's anti-discrimination policy. Kenyon students also get involved in larger political issues: they recently protested outside Gambier's elementary schools to fight funding cuts to arts programs, and one huge on-campus initiative is to work with local farmers to promote agricultural sustainability. According to a senior leading the initiative, an impressive half of the food served at Peirce is locally grown.

Study Abroad & Cultural Organizations

Though Gambier can be a retreat from the world, Kenyon has a strong international

focus. Over half of students study abroad in their junior year, either through Kenyon programs in England and Rome or through other universities. Many non-international students join cultural organizations focused on Latin America or the Middle East, which organize events promoting a political understanding of those regions.

The International Society, geared at helping international students (four percent of the student body), organizes meetings between incoming freshman and upperclassmen to discuss culture shock. The Center for Global Engagement works with international students to celebrate diversity and helped organize an Eid celebration for Muslim students last year. Still, one international student said he sometimes feels out of place on campus because of his lower-class upbringing in South Africa. "Minority students are very small minorities on campus," he said. "I could probably count on two sets of hands the African American students [in my class]."

But Kenyon's racial and socioeconomic diversity has grown over recent years, with a current 19 percent of students from minority backgrounds and 61 percent receiving financial aid. The recently admitted class is the most diverse in Kenyon's history, showing a change for the better.

The Social Scene

Though a sizeable minority of Kenyon students become members of seven fraternities and four sororities, students maintain that Greek life is "not a huge thing" at Kenyon. Frat and sorority houses are located on the southern edge of campus, almost "buried in the woods," and there isn't any intense hazing, but the Greek houses do throw huge campus-wide parties. Freshmen often attend these "trashier" parties, since counselors monitor freshmen dorms. One popular party is "Shock Your Mom," a spring event where students attend the party in outfits that would shock their mothers, usually resulting in semi-to-total nudity.

Athletes, like members of fraternities and sororities, often end up living in the southern part of campus according to one sophomore. Swimming has a "cult-like" feel around campus—the men's diving and swimming team has won 32 national championships since 1980. So if you're a swimmer dreaming of winning a national championship, look no further. Kenyon's athletic center is also ranked one of the best in the country. Intramural sports are popular, especially Ultimate Frisbee.

Drinking is a major social activity on campus, and Kenyon has a "Good Samaritan" policy, by which students can call Kenyon Safety if a student has alcohol poisoning or needs medical attention without having to worry about getting in legal trouble. Though some students say drugs aren't prominent on campus, others say marijuana use is fairly common. Still, students who don't drink or smoke say they don't feel left out—one freshman who doesn't drink commented, "I feel no pressure to drink, even when I go to parties on Old Campus."

Encore!

Kenyon is full of time-honored traditions. On the last night of freshman orientation, the entire freshman class stands on the steps of the music hall and sings Kenyon's college songs as upperclassmen (and even some professors) look on and jeer. The face-off tests the entering students' school pride and resilience. Four years later, in caps and gowns, the exiting seniors gather to sing again. But this time, only cheers greet them. The emphasis Kenyon College puts on fellowship and continuity binds students together for their college years and long after. As one freshman put it, "Kenyon may not be Hogwarts, but it is a very magical place."—*Abigail Bessler*

FYIs

Three things every student at Kenyon should do before graduating are "go skinny-dipping in the Kokosing River, go to sunset point with a significant other (a bench that overlooks the campus' nature preserve), and take a class that you would never expect yourself to be taking."

If you come to Kenyon, you'd better bring "snow boots. Don't think you can get by with those brown leather fashion boots."

If you come to Kenyon, you'd better leave behind "any prejudices. You're so much more likely to get lectured by a stranger in the dining hall for using an ethnically insensitive term than you are for not knowing which baseball team is winning."

Miami University

Address: 301 South Campus Avenue, Oxford, OH 45056

Phone: 513-529-2531

E-mail address: admission@muohio.edu

Web site URL: www.muohio.edu

Year Founded: 1809

Private or Public: Public

Religious Affiliation: None

Location: Rural

Number of Applicants: 16,772

Percent Accepted: 79%

Percent Accepted who enroll: 24%

Number Entering: 3,236

Number of Transfers Accepted each Year: 522

Middle 50% SAT range: M: 560–660, CR:530–630, Wr: Unreported

Middle 50% ACT range: 24–29

Early admission program EA/ED/None: EA and ED

Percentage accepted through EA or ED: Unreported

EA and ED deadline: 1-Nov (ED), 1-Dec (EA)

Regular Deadline: 1-Feb

Application Fee: $50

Full time Undergraduate enrollment: 14,457

Total enrollment: 16,884

Percent Male: 47%

Percent Female: 53%

Total Percent Minority or Unreported: 10%

Percent African-American: 4%

Percent Asian/Pacific Islander: 3%

Percent Hispanic: 2%

Percent Native-American: 1%

Percent International: 3%

Percent in-state/out of state: 70%/30%

Percent from Public HS: Unreported

Retention Rate: 89%

Graduation Rate 4-year: 70%

Graduation Rate 6-year: 82%

Percent Undergraduates in On-campus housing: 50%

Number of official organized extracurricular organizations: 350

3 Most popular majors: Finance, Marketing, Psychology

Student/Faculty ratio: 15:1

Average Class Size: 31

Percent of students going to grad school: Unreported

Tuition and Fees: $28,385

In-State Tuition and Fees if different: $13,213

Cost for Room and Board: $9,458

Percent receiving financial aid out of those who apply: 68%

Percent receiving financial aid among all students: Unreported

The deceptively named Miami University is not located in Miami, Florida. Rather, it is in Oxford, Ohio. The name came from the Miami Indians who used to live in the area. The tenth public college founded in the United States, Miami University offers "truly the quintessential college experience," said one freshman. Indeed, Miami University offers a combination of solid academics and strong party scene that is "just how I imagined college would be."

Hitting the Books

Miami University has a core curriculum of "Foundation Courses" that are usually taken during the freshman and sophomore years. The requirement is met by taking 36 credit hours in English composition, the fine arts, humanities, and social sciences; cultures; natural sciences; and mathematics, formal reasoning, and technology. While introductory courses are large, the majority of classes are small. "You can really get to know your professors, though maybe less in your freshman year than as an upperclassman," said one junior.

The academic advising system is generally considered "solid." All students have a first-year advisor who lives with them in their dorm. Another advisor replaces the first one when a major is declared during sophomore year. A student's studies in his or her major ends with the Senior Capstone, which is a project designed to combine a liberal arts education with the specialty of a major.

Because preference for class choices is given to athletes, graduate students, and honor students, it can be nearly impossible for freshmen and sophomores to get into certain classes. However, "persistence pays off. If you hang around a class for long enough and talk to the teacher, you can usually find yourself a place," explained one sophomore.

Though "the schoolwork here can basically be as hard as you want to make it," students unanimously agree that the hardest majors are business and pre-med. The Oxford Scholars honors program is also challenging.

Also, Miami University ranks among the top institutions in the nation for the number of students participating in study abroad programs each year (more than 1,500). Many students opt to leave the country for a semester or a year, though the shorter summer programs are another popular option.

A Beautiful Campus

Robert Frost once said that Miami University was "the most beautiful college there ever was," and students take pride in their picturesque campus. "I'm a senior, and I'm still regularly in awe of how beautiful it is here," said one student. The colonial-style brick buildings divide the five sections of campus: the north, south, east, west, and central quads.

Students rave about how well their facilities are maintained. "Everything is kept very clean and pristine—my friends who visit are always surprised at how nicely our buildings are kept," said a sophomore. Dorm quality does vary, though, from mediocre to hotel-like. First-year residence halls are themed and offer theme-related events throughout the year. Types of hall themes include arts, foreign languages, health and wellness, honors and scholars, and leadership. After sophomore year, about 50 percent of students choose to move off campus and into the town of Oxford.

Dining hall food and services are well reviewed by students. Dining halls are located close to residences, and when the cafeterias close, there is a variety of late-night options available from a convenience store in the student center and other locations around campus. Popular off-campus options include the Alexander House, Kona Bistro, and Bagel and Deli.

Greek Life Dominates

Just less than half of the student body is involved with a fraternity or sorority, but students think that it often feels like many more students go Greek. "Being Greek is pretty much the only thing to do here if you want to have a social life," commented one student. "The school is located in a cornfield, and there's pretty much nothing to do but to drink," explained one freshman. "And you're going to drink with your fraternity or sorority." Indeed, the lack of any sort of off-campus scene is what drives so many students into the Greek system. Rushing is an important and stressful time on campus for the prospective Greek community.

Students enjoy the themed parties, semi-formals, and formals thrown by fraternities and sororities, but also insist that the Greek system is useful in other aspects. "Every group does support a cause that benefits the community," said one senior, who then admitted, "It's really all about the parties and socializing." Those few who insist on avoiding Greek life often live on West Campus.

> **"Every fraternity and sorority does support a cause that benefits the community . . . but it's really all about the parties and socializing."**

Aside from fraternities and sororities, there are many extracurricular activities from which to choose, ranging from career-focused groups to volunteer organizations. Intramural sports are also popular, especially broomball, a sport invented at Miami University that is played on ice without skates. Varsity sports are substantially less popular. Attendance at games is sparse, and only hockey games draw crowds.

Welcome to J. Crew U.

Students at Miami University are generally described as thin, blond, and rich. "Everyone drives huge SUVs and is very conservative," said a junior. The student body dresses mostly in clothes from J. Crew and Abercrombie, leading some to nickname Miami University "J. Crew U." The generally white, upper-middle-class student body led one student to complain, "All Miami students are basically the same. It's very overbearing at times." A male student observed that much of the female population is very concerned with health, fitness, and physical appearance. However, one freshman also said that this means "everyone is very good-looking."

Miami's good academic program, beautiful campus, and lively social scene remain attractive despite the homogeneous student body and focus on physical appearance. Students say that in spite of Miami University's shortcomings, they "would definitely come to Miami if they had to do college all over again."—*Erica Rothman*

FYI
If you come to Miami University, you'd better bring "the most recent J. Crew catalog."
What is the typical weekend schedule? "Drink on campus, drink in fraternities and sororities, and drink. Maybe you'll get some work in on Sunday afternoon. . . ."
If I could change one thing about Miami University, I'd "make the school more interested in its athletics."
Three things every student at Miami University should do before graduating are: "play a game of broomball, spend some time abroad, and take pictures of campus to make all your friends at home jealous of how pretty your school is."

Oberlin College

Address: 101 North Professor Street, Oberlin, OH 44074
Phone: 440-775-8411
E-mail address: college.admission@oberlin.edu
Web site URL: www.oberlin.edu
Year Founded: 1833
Private or Public: Private
Religious Affiliation: None
Location: Rural
Number of Applicants: 7,006
Percent Accepted: 33%
Percent Accepted who enroll: 34%
Number Entering: 768
Number of Transfers Accepted each Year: Unreported
Middle 50% SAT range: M: 620–710, CR: 640–740, Wr: 640–730
Middle 50% ACT range: 27–32

Early admission program EA/ED/None: ED
Percentage accepted through EA or ED: 60%
EA and ED deadline: 15-Nov
Regular Deadline: 15-Jan
Application Fee: $35
Full time Undergraduate enrollment: 2,793
Total enrollment: 2,839
Percent Male: 45%
Percent Female: 55%
Total Percent Minority or Unreported: 25%
Percent African-American: 6%
Percent Asian/Pacific Islander: 7%
Percent Hispanic: 5%
Percent Native American: 1%
Percent International: 6%
Percent in-state/out of state: 9%/91%
Percent from Public HS: 60%

Retention Rate: 94%
Graduation Rate 4-year: 65%
Graduation Rate 6-year: Unreported
Percent Undergraduates in On-campus housing: 88%
Number of official organized extracurricular organizations: 125
3 Most popular majors: English, History, Biology
Student/Faculty ratio: 9:1
Average Class Size: 12
Percent of students going to grad school: Unreported
Tuition and Fees: $43,210
In-State Tuition and Fees if different: No difference
Cost for Room and Board: $11,550
Percent receiving financial aid out of those who apply: 61%
Percent receiving financial aid among all students: 60%

Known as a small, freewheeling college with academics among the best and excellent opportunities for music and other arts, Oberlin provides a wealth of academic and extracurricular opportunities. Oberlin is perhaps most distinguished from other schools of its size by its conservatory, which trains musicians and provides students in the college with ample opportunity to play, study, and listen to music, too. Oberlin was founded as a coed school in 1833, and, four years later, it graduated the first women in the country to earn AB degrees. Oberlin was also the first racially integrated college in the nation. Today, Oberlin maintains its welcoming attitude, often drawing students because of its offerings in music and its equal strength in the humanities and sciences.

College and Con

Oberlin students tend to be passionate about academics and care about doing well in classes, but students said the academic atmosphere is mostly relaxed. Students study a lot, but they collaborate rather than compete, except, at times, in the Conservatory, where the nature of performance lends itself to competition. "The Con is pretty damn competitive; the College is really chill," one student said. Students in the Conservatory also take College classes, and College students can study in the Con, though to do so is less common. There are also a fair number of double-degree students who study in both schools.

Students often get to know their professors well. Even in the biggest classes—the most popular introductory science courses can reach up to two hundred students—the professor will always know students' names by the end of the semester. In some smaller classes, individual weekly conferences with the professor are required. Although students often hear stories of others who visit professors' houses or babysit for their kids, one student said relationships with professors "depend on what you make of it."

Oberlin students fulfill distributional requirements known as the 9-9-9 requirement: Nine credits must be completed in each of the social sciences, humanities, and natural sciences. Students complain about the complicated online registration system, which can prevent students from registering in their preferred classes, but getting into classes is easy if students simply go to class on the first day.

Compared to other small liberal arts colleges, Oberlin's science offerings are particularly strong. The school also offers one of the only neuroscience departments among colleges of its size. Biology, politics, neuroscience, and history are among the most popular majors.

Each year, students embark on projects of their choosing during Winter Term. Throughout January, students can work on farms in Costa Rica, tutor students in Oberlin public schools, get an internship, or watch and research movies—pretty much any proposal will be approved, one student said. A small percentage of students stay on campus, while many venture around the world and escape Ohio's cold winter.

Oberlin's Experimental College offers students the opportunity to teach classes. Up to 150 classes, with subjects ranging from steel drums to Korean to the television series *The West Wing*, are offered each term. Each class counts for one credit, and students say ExCo classes are an opportunity not to be missed.

Singing, Soccer, and the 'Sco

Oberlin has varsity athletic teams, but they are far from being a central part of campus life. The teams are rarely successful, and one sophomore counted "booing our sports teams" on a list of ways to be active at Oberlin. While many students love intramurals, varsity athletes "seem like a completely different breed of student," said another sophomore.

Soccer, Frisbee, and Quidditch are among the most popular sports for the casual athlete. According to one Conservatory student, "people like to be active here, surprisingly." To do so, many participate in various kinds of dance; swing dancing and tango are popular activities. Organized dance groups' performances—mostly modern dance—are also very well attended.

Thanks in large part to the Conservatory, music thrives at Oberlin. There are 500 concerts—all free—on campus each year. A capella is very popular and quite competitive. "Everyone plays acoustic guitar and sings and is incredible at those things," one student said. Theatre, too, is very popular, with shows running every weekend.

A majority of students hold jobs on campus, and many work for campus publications or the radio station. The campus newspaper, *The Oberlin Review*, is published weekly. Political activism also draws widespread interest.

> "People here are definitely smart, but I've also noticed a large majority are funny."

Outside of organized extracurricular life, Oberlin students spend a lot of time hanging out with friends in dorm rooms. Oberlin has no fraternities or sororities. Parties are usually held in off-campus houses, but students say they tend to get shut down by campus authorities, sending partygoers back to their rooms later on a Friday or Saturday night. Still, two annual campus-wide parties, the Drag Ball and Safer Sex Night, draw the vast majority of the student population. Safer Sex Night, hosted by the Sexual Information Center, involves scantily clad students and free condoms and works both as an avenue for education about safe sex and an opportunity for a big party. Besides the two big events, it's always easy to find a party because most are publicized on Facebook. The 'Sco, a student-run night club at the Student Union, is another popular weekend destination.

Putting the "Liberal" in Liberal Arts

Oberlin may have a reputation as a hippie school, but students say they were pleasantly surprised to find lots of "normal people." The school has its share of hipsters and vegans, but Obies come in many forms. "It's pretty easy to be yourself here," one student said. "I expected it to be weirder." Oberlin students are not preppy and are generally "artistic, pretty laid back, and intelligent," a student said. "People here are definitely smart, and I've also noticed a large majority are funny," said another student.

The student population is diverse in all respects—except political affiliation. "There are about five people in the Oberlin College Republicans," one student said. Still, students are invested in politics. Students come to Oberlin from around the country and the world. "It's not all white rich kids by any means," one student said, but, according to another, "I wouldn't stress [diversity] as far as Admissions does."

Students say most people on campus drink, though those who don't can still easily find things to do on weekends, especially because of the abundance of performances of every kind. Marijuana smoking, though less dominant, is also a fairly common activity once weekend parties have been busted by authorities. Students say other drugs are rarely encountered on campus.

When the weather is nice, students congregate every Friday afternoon on the grassy Wilder Bowl in a tradition known as TGIF. Most of the campus spends the afternoon hanging out, listening to live music, drinking, and eating. Clubs use the opportunity to advertise, soccer balls and Frisbees abound, musicians pull out the guitars, and gymnasts and jugglers perform. Think stereotypical college catalogue picture on steroids, and in real life.

At Home at Oberlin

Students live in dorms consisting mostly of doubles and closed doubles, which consist of two separated rooms, only one of which connects to the hall. "Freshman dorms are pretty crappy," said one sophomore. But a new freshman dorm is vastly nicer and much coveted. Seniors may enter a lottery to win the chance to live off campus. Students can also opt to live in program houses or village housing, which offers houses on campus, mostly for seniors.

Food at Oberlin received mixed reviews, but it's always possible to find something healthy and good to eat at one of the three dining halls. Oberlin dining halls are also home to one of the greatest things ever to grace a college campus: Fourth Meal. Every night, Sunday through Thursday, from 10:00 to 11:30 pm, dining halls serve a meal. "It's awesome. I wish I had it when I was a kid," one student said.

If one finds the dining halls to be unsatisfactory, one can turn to a co-op. Co-ops often define their members' social lives—one student described them as "self-segregating"—and they provide good food. They're especially popular among vegans, who may find the dining halls' offerings limited.

Oberlin is located in Oberlin, Ohio, which is small but offers good restaurants and coffee shops in close proximity to the College. More adventurous students can drive 40 minutes to Cleveland. About half the students have cars, so one will always have a friend who can drive. Although trips to Cleveland are not frequent—"Cleveland is not exactly a hoppin' hot spot," one student said—the city's museums, including the Rock and Roll Hall of Fame, are well worth the drive.

Students at Oberlin are friendly, especially during the first weeks of the year, when it's common to strike up a conversation with a stranger in the dining hall and—pronto—make a friend. Although school spirit may not be obvious in sports arenas, Obies love their school. As one politics major said, "Students are obsessed with putting the letter O in front of everything."—*Julia Fisher*

FYI

If you come to Oberlin, you'd better bring "a smile, a Frisbee or hackey sack, and an open mind."

What's the typical weekend schedule? "TGIF, dinner, a play or performance, try to go to a party, hang out if that doesn't work. On Saturday, sleep 'til noon, work in Mudd Library, party. On Sunday, homework."

Three things every Oberlin student should do before graduating are: "go to a swing dance, go somewhere cool for Winter Term, go to every concert you can."

Ohio State University, Columbus, Ohio

Address: 190 N. Oval Mall, Columbus, OH 43210

Phone: 614-292-3980

E-mail address: askabuckeye@osu.edu

Web site URL: www.osu.edu

Year Founded: 1870

Private or Public: Public

Religious Affiliation: None

Location: Urban

Number of Applicants: 24,302

Percent Accepted: 68%

Percent Accepted who enroll: 40%

Number Entering: 6,654

Number of Transfers Accepted each Year: 2,198

Middle 50% SAT range: M: 590–700, CR: 540–650, Wr: 540–640

Middle 50% ACT range: 26–30

Early admission program EA/ED/None: None

Percentage accepted through EA or ED: NA

EA and ED deadline: NA

Regular Deadline: 1-Feb

Application Fee: $40

Full time Undergraduate enrollment: 38,521

Total enrollment: 42,082

Percent Male: 53%

Percent Female: 47%

Total Percent Minority or Unreported: 23%

Percent African-American: 6%

Percent Asian/Pacific Islander: 5%

Percent Hispanic: 3%

Percent Native American: <1%

Percent International: 5%

Percent in-state/out of state: 89%/11%

Percent from Public HS: 84%

Retention Rate: 93%

Graduation Rate 4-year: 46%

Graduation Rate 6-year: 71%

Percent Undergraduates in On-campus housing: 25%

Number of official organized extracurricular organizations: 1400

3 Most popular majors: Biology, Finance, Psychology

Student/Faculty ratio: 19:1

Average Class Size: 28

Percent of students going to grad school: Unreported

Tuition and Fees: $24,204

In-State Tuition and Fees if different: $9,309

Cost for Room and Board: $9,180

Percent receiving financial aid out of those who apply: 98%

Percent receiving financial aid among all students: 83%

Forming the crux of the city of Columbus, Ohio, The Ohio State University, or OSU, is an enormous school spilling over with Buckeye spirit. Since its founding in 1873, Ohio State has had ample time to develop a deep-set devotion to its sports teams and a definite (strong) pre-professional feel. It competes in Division I in all sports while also being home to thirteen different programs, ranging from Dental Hygiene and Engineering to Arts and Sciences and Social Work. Despite the size and scope of OSU's campus and student body (1,764 acres and about 42,000 undergrads on its main Columbus campus), the diverse mélange of students all seem to find their own place within the maze, whether through outdoors and sports clubs, academic organizations, or Humans vs. Zombies games. With so many majors, friends, and activities to choose from and so many rowdy Buckeyes games to attend, there's never much time to be bored.

Academics: Structured But With Wiggle Room

With a wagonload of professional schools, over 175 majors, the Personalized Study Program (PSP), and hundreds of specializations and minors to boot, it can be daunting for a freshman to step onto the Oval, the school's main green, without a set path. About 20 percent of frosh come in undecided, but they are immediately helped out by the University Exploration for Individualized Advising and Resources (EXP). The EXP offers orientation, one-on-one appointments, and quarterly outreach to students to help them decide in which direction to proceed. The Senior Bank, a group of former EXP students, is also available for guidance. Once students have become more settled, they have both an advisor and departmental advisor to help them along their way.

OSU boasts over 12,000 courses. Despite its size, almost 75% of first-year courses are fifty students or fewer and only 12% are lectures with enrollment over 100. "In some classes, professors don't teach, and you only get a TA, but once you get over the 400 level and above, you get professors with 30 students in the classes," said a junior. Moreover, outside of the classroom, professors are relatively accessible: "They're really cool, really open, and willing to meet with people for office hours—I've had one or two that make you meet with the TAs, but the TAs are pretty helpful," said a senior.

Students looking for something more can consider joining the Honors or Scholars programs, which involve 14 unique living and learning communities meant to complement students' academic experiences. Though Arts and Sciences is the largest college, "there is absolutely a pre-professional feel—lots of professors go around and do speeches. There are a lot of pre-med, pre-business, pre-law opportunities. There are all kinds of internships with the hospital, business school, and more for each individual major," said one senior.

Popular majors, according to students, include biology, engineering, and nursing. A week of classes involves 15 to 20 credit hours—the amount of time you're in the classroom per week—with two hours of work to be expected, technically, for every hour in class. Though the constant slews of midterms can be drowning, grading is fair; "If you try and put in a solid effort and want an A, then you'll get an A," confirmed a senior in the wildlife division of the School of Environment and Natural Resources.

Several students voiced complaints about the extensive GEC (General Education Curriculum) requirements, which are spread across a variety of disciplines. For example, all students must take four quarters of a language and a certain number of credit hours in areas like quantitative and writing skills. "I had to take an econ class and I'm a wildlife major," said one student, complaining, "You could be a junior until you're in a class for your actual major." A friend of his agreed: "I personally think they're dumb, but you can test out of them." But even if you aren't able to test out, they can be easy enough to fulfill. For example, the History of Rock and Roll counts toward the history GEC, as well as an art history course available online. Other quirky classes students mentioned include: Beer and Wine in Western Culture, Skydiving, Scuba Diving, Yoga, and Boxing, some of these graded on a scale of satisfactory or unsatisfactory rather than counting toward a GPA.

The best thing about the academic system at Ohio State, students widely agreed, is its broad range. "You can pretty much do any major, and there are tons of outside opportunities for all of them," said a sophomore pursuing nursing.

A Place to Get Hands-On and Your Groove On

One of the many benefits of Ohio State is its location just two and half miles from downtown Columbus—a 30-minute stroll or free five-minute bus ride away. Columbus provides extensive work and internship opportunities as well as typical eateries, shopping, and general nightlife, if students are feeling the impetus to wander out of the convenience and comfort of campus.

Ohio State boasts the eighteenth largest research library in North America and is the seventh best public university in research, and many students are applying their knowledge. Through the Field Experience program, students can make use of well-connected faculty and partnerships with organizations in Columbus (and beyond). The opportunities range from work in hospitals and legal offices to local nonprofits and community service groups, and according to students, a good amount of people work or do work-study. In addition, over 1,000 undergraduates receive government or industrial sponsorship for research.

While Columbus certainly has attractive features, students in fact all voiced a preference for keeping their social life closer to campus. "There's a group of people that goes downtown every weekend, but there are enough campus bars that there's no reason to," said one senior. "There are lots of bars on campus, and most are places strict about carding, though a lot of people have fakes," he added. For those uninterested in the bar scene, there's plenty else, including parties in houses, frats, and dorms. The heavy impression of drinking at Ohio State is inaccurate: "If you're not drinking, there's lots of other stuff to do," said a junior. "I know lots of people who don't drink, and you can still go to parties without drinking," he affirmed.

Despite the athletic prowess of the Buckeyes, the athletes are not too dominant on the social scene. "I've seen our president at parties more than I've seen football players," commented one student. The frat scene isn't big either, as most upperclassmen move away from house parties and frat parties, and tend towards smaller bars and off-campus venues.

A Quality and Relaxed Living Atmosphere—Besides the Occasional Zombie

With Ohio State, we're talking about the third largest university in the U.S. It is universes away from the quaint amphitheater of Swarthmore or the cute college towns of Smith and Amherst. With such big numbers, you might expect dorm and dining quality to suffer, but it turns out not to be the case.

Housing is standard, and the school is building several new dorms to get students to stay on campus, since a large number choose to move to apartments off-campus. A senior reported that dorms get nicer as you move up: "If you're a sophomore you can stay in a converted Holiday Inn!" In freshman dorms, there is a male and a female RA on every floor there to support and loosely monitor. "If you're doing something obvious, they have to write you up, but if you are in your room, they aren't going to ask to look in your room, it's not their problem," said a junior. In terms of general campus security, the same general attitude holds. "If you stay out of the street they aren't going to bust you," said a senior. "Not unless it's getting out of control, if you're pouring out on the sidewalk, they'll come. Otherwise they don't care."

As for school dining, you can get food at any time of day, and according to a junior, "the food is great!" At the cafeteria buffets, like Kennedy Commons, the food has apparently just recently improved tenfold, and there are always, of course, plenty of late night nooks around campus.

Major spots on campus include the Shoe,

the nickname for the school stadium, the new Thompson Library, a recently built recreation center, and the student union, which houses a bar, two restaurants, a ballroom, meeting rooms, a theater, fireplaces, study areas, a bank, club offices, student council, and a parking garage. The student union also has a place that provides tickets for events in Columbus, like free music acts and concerts.

At Meer Lake, which one student called "a dirty janky pond with two fountains in the middle of campus," on the Tuesday every year before the Michigan game in November, everybody goes down at night and jumps in. The area is lit up, dorms spray people down and give out hot chocolate, and police stay around to make sure everyone is safe. In the warmer seasons, students gather on "Oval Beach," a popular grassy hang-out in front of the library.

Once in a while a zombie can be spotted roaming the campus, most likely a member of the Humans vs. Zombies club, where zombies and people shooting Nerf guns go about for a whole week across campus. "One of the people on the team even got sponsored by Nerf," informed a student. If that doesn't sound quite like the group for you, there are hundreds of other groups to get involved in, from sports clubs to political associations to publications and whatever else might be imagined. At the Involvement Fair, always on the second day of freshman move-in, crowds of people check out all of the student organizations.

> "It's super diverse—you'll find anybody you can imagine."

Ohio State's miniature city of a student body means that no sweeping generalizations can be made. "It's super diverse—you'll find anybody you can imagine. Groups will hang out in certain areas, but it's not just them or exclusive or anything," said a student. In fact, there are nearly 5,000 international students in the graduate and undergraduate programs, and a quarter of the rest of the student body are from out-of-state. At Ohio State, it's safe to say that there is something available for absolutely everyone, whether that means research opportunities, study-related internships, top-notch varsity and club sports teams, or a group of fellow zombies.—*TaoTao Holmes*

Ohio University

Address: 120 Chubb Hall, Athens, OH 45701-2979
Phone: 740-593-4100
E-mail address: admissions@ohio.edu
Web site URL: www.ohio.edu/admissions
Year Founded: 1804
Private or Public: Public
Religious Affiliation: None
Location: Rural
Number of Applicants: 13,366
Percent Accepted: 85%
Percent Accepted who enroll: 35%
Number Entering: 3,960
Number of Transfers Accepted each Year: 859
Middle 50% SAT range: M: 490–610, CR: 490–610, Wr: 480–590
Middle 50% ACT range: 21–26
Early admission program EA/ED/None: None

Percentage accepted through EA or ED: NA
EA and ED deadline: NA
Regular Deadline: 1-Feb
Application Fee: $45
Full time Undergraduate enrollment: 17,116
Total enrollment: 20,994
Percent Male: 43%
Percent Female: 57%
Total Percent Minority or Unreported: 15%
Percent African-American: 5%
Percent Asian/Pacific Islander: 1%
Percent Hispanic: 2%
Percent Native American: <1%
Percent International: 4%
Percent in-state/out of state: 91%/9%
Percent from Public HS: 85%
Retention Rate: 81%

Graduation Rate 4-year: 48%
Graduation Rate 6-year: 71%
Percent Undergraduates in On-campus housing: 44%
Number of official organized extracurricular organizations: 385
2 Most popular majors: Journalism, Zoology/Animal Biology
Student/Faculty ratio: 19:1
Average Class Size: 15
Percent of students going to grad school: 25%
Tuition and Fees: $18,900
In-State Tuition and Fees if different: $9,936
Cost for Room and Board: $9,753
Percent receiving financial aid out of those who apply: 64%
Percent receiving financial aid among all students: 58%

The oldest institution of higher learning in the state, Ohio University (OU) is located in Athens, a historic city far removed from major metropolitan areas but certainly reminiscent of the quintessential college town. In 1804, the first year of enrollment at OU, only three students entered the university. Today, more than 20,000 undergraduate and postgraduate students are on the campus of OU, which is now more than 1,800 acres. It is a major university with a large number of academic options and an even greater reputation for being one of the top party schools in the nation. The combination of the two certainly makes OU a captivating option for prospective students.

Books Come First?

Given the fact that OU is known for parties and beer, some people may be slightly concerned about the academic quality of the institution. However, according to most students, OU is certainly not a place to slack off for four years. "We have many programs that are highly regarded," said one student. The university is divided into 11 different colleges and schools. Among them, the Scripps College of Communication is considered the strongest institution at OU with top-notch faculty and students in journalism and broadcasting. Furthermore, the engineering school is also known for research in avionics and electronics. Another distinction at OU is that it awards osteopathic medicine degrees, which are very rare in the United States. In addition, thousands of students study in one of the several satellite locations of OU, such as Chillicothe and Lancaster.

OU offers more than 250 programs of study for undergraduates. Therefore, opportunities abound for students. "We might have a reputation of party school," said one student. "But if you look at the academic programs, they are comprehensive and vigorous." Indeed, the university covers everything from early childhood education to industrial engineering.

There is also an Honors Tutorial College at OU. The idea of this program, which is slightly different from that of other universities, is to provide opportunities to teach students through so-called tutorials, or one-on-one sessions, as well as small seminars. Only 220 students in fewer than 30 programs of study are enrolled in this honors program. Students enter through a special application when they apply for freshman admissions to the university. It is a very competitive process and requires on-campus interviews as part of the evaluation for admission into the honors college.

The general education requirements—or, for the lack of simple terms, classes that you must take—are straightforward. Students must complete three tiers. The first tier consists of the most basic skills: mathematics and English composition. Students are placed in mathematics classes based on their standardized test scores or through a placement test at the beginning of the year. The second tier includes different distributional areas, such as science, arts, and humanities. Finally, the third tier is much more flexible—since it depends on the student's discipline—and is mostly designed for upperclassmen.

> "We have many [academic] programs that are highly regarded."

Similar to most universities, the class size diminishes as the course level rises. For most seniors and juniors, classes tend to be fewer than 30 people. Freshmen, on the other hand, are much more likely to experience large lectures of several hundred students. Nevertheless, it is not always a bad thing to be in big lectures, depending on each person's preference. "I enjoy big classes, because I am not really into class discussions," said one student. "Some people like me learn better through listening to what the professors say. Others prefer discussions."

Are the classes difficult? It is certainly dependent on professors and on the students' abilities. For the most part, students believe that their work is manageable. OU has a good academic reputation; therefore, it is not a place to party every hour of the day, but students are generally confident that they can get through most of their schoolwork, while being involved in multiple extracurricular activities or jobs.

OU may not be considered as one of the best colleges in the United States, but it still entered rankings by *U.S. News & World Report* at number 124 for national universities. Therefore, it belongs to the top tier of all colleges in the country and has a competitive admissions process. "I think we have a lot of talented kids at OU," said one student.

Athens

As a small college town, Athens is certainly not as exciting as New York City in terms of the number of activities and social opportunities. On the other hand, Athens is the place to be for one interesting endeavor: ghost hunting.

While it may be hard to believe, different books and television shows have pointed out the small city in southern Ohio as one of the most haunted places on earth. Different folklore stories abound on the witches and spirits that are floating around the city and OU in particular. There is, of course, not much hard evidence to scare anyone away from the city, but it is certainly something worth noting about Athens. To make things even more exciting, OU is home to an asylum known for paranormal activities.

The ghost stories, however, do not seem to faze too many of the 20,000 students at OU, since they choose to attend the school regardless of the unknown spirits. The university requires all freshmen and sophomores to remain in on-campus housing and to use the meal plans. There are more than 40 residential halls at the school, and students are generally satisfied with their living arrangements. Most upperclassmen choose to live off campus in surrounding areas. Those who are not in residences, however, are not concerned with being cut off from friends at the university. After all, most apartments and houses are only a few minutes' walk to the campus, and students mostly crowd into the same neighborhood of Athens.

The dining services operate four main locations as well as a number of smaller cafés. The food is not great, but it's acceptable, just like at most universities. "I hear from people that schools with the best dining halls also become boring to students after a while," said one student. "So I have no complaint. The food gets boring, but that is what I expected when I came here."

What OU does better than dining is partying. Greek life is very important at OU. Fraternities and sororities host large parties. The large number of local bars also represents great places for people to socialize. Alcohol, of course, is an important part of the party scene, but people who do not drink can also feel part of the social life. "I don't think anyone is being forced to drink," said one student. "Whatever your lifestyle is, I think most people are considerate about it."

Bobcats

When people talk about collegiate sports in Ohio, the dominant football team of Ohio State certainly comes to mind. However, OU is also an important force in Division I sports. It features 16 varsity teams in the top division. Women's cross-country and soccer have won more titles than have any other teams of the Mid-Atlantic Conference. Women's field hockey has also been very dominant in recent years, capturing the title in 2009. The biggest rival for OU is Miami University.

As one student pointed out, "We are good at parties and books, so why not come to OU?" That is certainly a question worth asking for any high school seniors, especially those in Ohio who can get a relatively affordable in-state education.—*Xiaohang Liu*

FYI
What is the typical weekend schedule? "There is always a huge party somewhere."
If I could change one thing about OU, I'd "actually try to find some ghosts."
Three things every student at OU should do before graduating are: "enjoy your time here, go to football games, and go see the rest of Ohio if you are not from here."

Ohio Wesleyan University

Address: 61 South Sandusky Street, Delaware, OH 43015
Phone: 740-368-3020
E-mail address: owuadmit@owu.edu
Web site URL: www.owu.edu
Year Founded: 1842
Private or Public: Private
Religious Affiliation: Methodist
Location: Suburban
Number of Applicants: 3,814
Percent Accepted: 66%
Percent Accepted who enroll: 23%
Number Entering: 576
Number of Transfers Accepted each Year: Unreported
Middle 50% SAT range: M: 520–650, CR: 520–640, Wr: Unreported
Middle 50% ACT range: 22–28

Early admission program EA/ED/None: EA and ED
Percentage accepted through EA or ED: Unreported
EA and ED deadline: 15-Dec, 1-Dec
Regular Deadline: 1-Mar
Application Fee: $35
Full time Undergraduate enrollment: 1,948
Total enrollment: 1,967
Percent Male: 48%
Percent Female: 52%
Total Percent Minority or Unreported: 21%
Percent African-American: 5%
Percent Asian/Pacific Islander: 2%
Percent Hispanic: 1%
Percent Native American: 0%
Percent International: 9%
Percent in-state/out of state: 59%/41%
Percent from Public HS: 77%
Retention Rate: 84%

Graduation Rate 4-year: 60%
Graduation Rate 6-year: Unreported
Percent Undergraduates in On-campus housing: 82%
Number of official organized extracurricular organizations: 86
3 Most popular majors: Economics, Pre-med, Psychology
Student/Faculty ratio: 12:1
Average Class Size: 15
Percent of students going to grad school: 32%
Tuition and Fees: $34,570
In-State Tuition and Fees if different: No difference
Cost for Room and Board: $8,030
Percent receiving financial aid out of those who apply: 99%
Percent receiving financial aid among all students: 98%

If you didn't know it was there, you might drive past the tiny town of Delaware, Ohio, population 35,000, without a second glance. But at the core of this small community there is a thriving college with students passionate enough to more than compensate for their low numbers. At Ohio Wesleyan University, you will find a campus that celebrates its Midwestern friendliness, with a close-knit undergraduate community of exceptionally warm and down-to-earth students who make the town worth much more than just a passing glimpse.

A Full Spectrum of Knowledge: OWU and the Liberal Arts Education

When it comes to academics, OWU sends a clear message to its students: education requires knowledge and proficiency in a broad range of areas, which leads to the fairly expansive set of Distributional Requirements. In addition to three classes each in the humanities, social sciences, and natural sciences, students are required to take two semesters of writing-intensive classes, a foreign language, and diversity-geared courses as well as one fine art class and a new one-semester quantitative reasoning requirement. Although this may seem overwhelming, students say that a wide range of interesting classes can fulfill the requirements. One student remarked, "I like to be able to choose classes I like within a department." Others, however, take a different course: "Personally, I don't seek out classes that fill requirements; I just look for classes I find interesting and fulfill requirements along the way."

Nor is it a problem if a student wants a more academically challenging schedule within the OWU environment. The Ohio Wesleyan Honors Program is open to freshmen, based on their high school GPA and standardized test scores, but it is also possible to join later as an upperclassman. One honors student said the program "opens up a lot of interdisciplinary courses" that she would not otherwise have been exposed to, and that while "expectations are higher in terms of quality," the quantity of work does not increase significantly. One student described the program in terms of being "faster and more in-depth," but also noted that "all the majors have difficult courses." Because of this, other students are valuable resources as unofficial advisors when choosing a schedule. Some areas are always difficult, and popular majors including Zoology, Psychology, Education, and Politics

and Government all have their fair share of challenging coursework.

OWU tends to stress sciences over the humanities, although the less scientifically inclined students feel that their smaller programs give them closer relationships with professors who really care about both the material and their students. One English major said that "professors make themselves really available—they take their jobs as teachers very seriously." Professors can focus their full attention on the undergraduates, as one junior remarked: "You get to know the teachers as well as you know the other students." This extends to class work as well, since professors have a strong hand in shaping the curriculum. Because professors teach what they like, students find them engaging, dynamic, and relevant.

Dorm-Dwellers and SLUTs

OWU has all the housing fixtures one might expect in a college setting, but what sets the college apart is its unique cluster of "SLUs," or Small Living Units. The students who decide to take advantage of these themed houses are affectionately referred to as "SLUTs," or Small Living Unit Tenants. Each SLU holds events and lectures that relate to its focus, and they also offer an alternative to the frat party scene. The interests covered by the SLUs are many and varied, some of which are the Women's House, the International House, and the philosophical House of Thought. With so many areas covered, many students find a niche in SLUs. All freshmen live in the dorms along with most sophomores; it is only in the junior year that people begin to move off campus, although even juniors tend to stay. One sophomore noted that OWU is "a very residential campus."

Geography 101

When students live where they eat and study where they sleep, there will understandably be some feeling of claustrophobia. OWU combats these limitations with its unique dumbbell-shaped campus, which has academic buildings on one side with residential housing on the other, connected by a main "highway" called the JAYwalk. The walkway serves as a common meeting-place for students to see and be seen between classes, and it is also flanked by the James A. Young Memorial Library. One sophomore said, "There is a consistent flow of people at certain hours of the day, and most students eat lunch on the JAYwalk." This central hangout is in the middle of an eclectic and architecturally varied campus—students all agree that the mixed architecture lends OWU a distinctly diverse feel.

The Alpha, Beta, Gammas of OWU Social Life

"Wednesday is the new Thursday," remarked one sophomore, when asked about the campus party scene. Other students concur, mentioning Friday and Saturday in addition to Wednesday as the biggest party days at OWU. As for how students get down on those nights, people mentioned a variety of locales: Delaware bars, off-campus apartment parties, SLU parties, and, most frequently, frat parties. One Delta Gamma sister estimated that 30 percent of students are somehow involved in Greek life on campus, and she said that the fraternity and sorority system has a strong presence, especially in the social life of OWU students. Although one senior mentioned that "people party with their own social groups," dance parties tend to bring people together and mix groups.

> "The professors take their jobs as teachers very seriously, and both the students and the faculty are very invested in providing an enriching experience for everyone."

As for the inevitable problems that arise from college partying, students say that the on-campus public safety officers are often willing to let alcohol charges drop if the student is polite. Students applaud the university's decision to charge students for possession rather than consumption, which allows ill students to go to the hospital for help without getting in trouble. While the off-campus police tend to be much stricter, one sophomore says that on university property, "there is an understanding that drinking occurs, and they're more worried about our safety than the fact that we drink."

Crossing the Delaware

If frat parties aren't so appealing, it might be difficult to find something to do on a weekend night. "There's not a lot to do in Delaware," admitted one sophomore, who also noted that "Columbus is a tease because it's not as close as you think it is." Delaware's small size led one senior to remark that "the town exists because the college is here." However, others point to eclectic boutiques and high-quality restaurants as characteristic of their college's hometown. Students generally feel some connection to the town and don't find relations to be particularly hostile, but all mention that there could be quite a bit of improvement. One student noted, "You could go through four years at OWU without meeting people in Delaware, but there are a lot of connections if you look for them."

After the Library Closes

OWU students are dedicated to their academic lives, but they are also committed to many activities outside the classroom. From advocacy groups such as STAND (Students Taking Action Now: Darfur) to warm and fuzzy clubs like Pet Pals, which allows students to work at animal shelters, OWU offers a large variety of extracurriculars, especially given its small size. Highlights include the WCSA, the student government, which is very active and plays a large role in decision-making on campus. Students say that it is easy to get involved with groups as early as freshman year. One sophomore noted, "Attendance can be a problem in terms of turnout, but those who are in the clubs are very dedicated."

Sports also have a large presence in the campus community. Students mention that there is a fair amount of school pride, although potentially somewhat less than at other schools. But people turn out for big games such as Homecoming and rivalry match-ups, and the Division III standing attracts some athletes who want to play in more games. In addition to involvement in a varsity sport, many people decide to play at the intramural or club level. The school has recently worked on the athletic fields and the gym, so there is a clear emphasis on sports as an important part of the school environment and many athletes to reap the benefits.

According to students, the undergrads at OWU are always willing to meet new people and work in different settings. That enthusiasm permeates the entire campus, as one student pointed to the "friendly, open atmosphere" as a major reason she decided to attend OWU. At a place where "the students and the faculty are very invested in providing an enriching experience for everyone," it is important to note that a good quality to bring is the desire to know everyone on campus. One student put it perfectly: "Although there are many different small groups on campus, there is a great sense of a larger community—coming in I had a good feeling about it, and that stuck with me."—*Hannah Jacobson*

FYI

If you come to Ohio Wesleyan, you'd better bring "an umbrella: the weather in Ohio is very unpredictable!"

What is the typical weekend schedule? "Get out of class and take a nap before meeting up with people for dinner and then pre-gaming in a group. Go to at least one party or jump between a few on Friday night. Eat a late lunch on Saturday, go out that night, and worry about homework on Sunday. And sleep a lot: you don't have time to do that during the week!"

If I could change one thing about Ohio Wesleyan, I'd "make it more handicapped accessible."

Three things every student at Ohio Wesleyan should do before graduating are: "go to an SLU party, attend a reception at Professor Olmstead's house, and go to the academic side of campus at night to see the stained-glass windows in Slocum Hall!"

University of Cincinnati

Address: P.O. Box 210091, Cincinnati, OH 45221-0091

Phone: 513-556-1100

E-mail address: admissions@uc.edu

Web site URL: www.uc.edu

Year Founded: 1819

Private or Public: Public

Religious Affiliation: None

Location: Urban

Number of Applicants: 16,972

Percent Accepted: 62%

Percent Accepted who enroll: 37%

Number Entering: 3,875

Number of Transfers Accepted each Year: 1,542

Middle 50% SAT range: M: 510–640, CR: 500–620, Wr: 490 610

Middle 50% ACT range: 22–27

Early admission program EA/ED/None: None

Percentage accepted through EA or ED: NA

EA and ED deadline: NA

Regular Deadline: 1-Jul

Application Fee: $50

Full time Undergraduate enrollment: 18,704

Total enrollment: 22,449

Percent Male: 49%

Percent Female: 51%

Total Percent Minority or Unreported: 22%

Percent African-American: 9%

Percent Asian/Pacific Islander: 3%

Percent Hispanic: 2%

Percent Native American: <1%

Percent International: 2%

Percent in-state/out of state: 90%/10%

Percent from Public HS: Unreported

Retention Rate: 85%

Graduation Rate 4-year: 19%

Graduation Rate 6-year: 54%

Percent Undergraduates in On-campus housing: 20%

Number of official organized extracurricular organizations: 250

3 Most popular majors: Communication Studies/Speech, Communication and Rhetoric, Marketing/ Marketing Management

Student/Faculty ratio: 17:1

Average Class Size: 25

Percent of students going to grad school: Unreported

Tuition and Fees: $23,328

In-State Tuition and Fees if different: $8,805

Cost for Room and Board: $9,780

Percent receiving financial aid out of those who apply: 81%

Percent receiving financial aid among all students: 75%

A prominent public university in Ohio, the University of Cincinnati is home to more than 20,000 undergraduates and 9,000 postgraduates. It also provides important research facilities for the University of Ohio system. Founded in 1819 as an institution focused on medical sciences, the university has now expanded into 14 different schools and is a major player in research, both in technology and in social sciences. With its scope of academic programs and good professional preparation, UC presents an attractive option for students from not only Ohio but also around the world.

A Research Institution

Out of the 20,000 undergraduates, nearly one-third of them are part-time students. This is in part due to the wide range of programs at UC. In fact, the school has a large selection of Associate programs. Furthermore, the university is also home to students in professional schools, doctoral, post-doctoral, and continuing education. "I guess you can say that we meet people of all walks of life at UC," said one student.

The university is divided into 14 different schools, ranging from Applied Health Sciences to Education, Criminal Justice, and Human Services. In addition, there are two regional campuses. The College-Conservatory of Music in particular is known as one of the best in the country. It has a total enrollment of roughly 1,500 and provides a wide range of arts programs, such as music, dance, and electronic media. "[The Conservatory] is definitely the most prestigious school at UC," said one student. Furthermore, some of the university's programs in criminal justice and architecture are also considered among the best in the United States. The College of Nursing is also recognized as the first one to issue baccalaureate degrees in the field. "You will be surprised at how we have quite a few famous departments," said one student.

The university offers more than 300 undergraduate degree programs, a very high number even for a large institution like UC. Students of all tastes can certainly find the appropriate curriculums that satiate their personal interests, as well as preparing them for future endeavors. The different certificate programs also allow students to enrich their academic experiences. "I think we have plenty of majors, too many even, to choose from," said one student.

> "We meet people of all walks of life at UC."

Since many students at UC are using their education directly as a springboard for a specific career path, the university has created the co-op program designed to receive actual professional training and practice as part of their education. In fact, UC has the largest co-op program in the country, and students from many departments, notably engineering, are required to complete different co-op assignments before they can receive their degree. "I really think that it helps you a lot in finding the right career and in actually practicing it," said one student. "The things you learn in classes can be very different from what happens in the real world, so it is nice for you to actually have a hands-on experience."

As in all large universities, the introductory classes can have hundreds of students, and the interactions between students and professors are generally limited in those cases. Nevertheless, particularly for upperclassmen, smaller classes certainly do exist, and the students can have an easier time contacting professors and asking questions. "I found a bunch of accessible professors here," said one student. "I also know that some of my friends really never talk to professors, but I think it is because they never tried." Indeed, building a relationship with one of the many highly knowledgeable professors at UC often depends on initiatives by the students.

Before graduation, students must complete a series of required coursework so that their undergraduate education goes beyond their actual majors. Slightly different from other universities, the requirements at UC are divided into only four categories: critical thinking, effective communications, social responsibility, and knowledge integration. Different courses are classified under those categories. "The requirements are OK," said one student. "I know it is important to learn a little bit of everything."

UC is also one of the most important research institutions in Ohio. Furthermore, unlike many universities that focus research on one specific area, UC has something for everyone. Given its tradition originally as a college of medical education, there is a large array of research centers for cancer, biology, and clinical research. At the same time, it also has the Center for Entrepreneurship Education and Research as well as the Institute for Policy Research, thus providing opportunities for those more interested in business and social sciences.

Cincy

Cincinnati, more fondly known as "Cincy" by some residents, is a major metropolitan area and thus offers the benefits of city living to the students of UC.

Weekend activities are certainly enriched by the location of UC. The city provides its large selection of restaurants, bars, and clubs. Furthermore, for sports enthusiasts, Cincinnati is also home to the National Football League's Bengals and Major League Baseball's Reds. However, it may be difficult sometimes for students to find the time or the energy to go to some of those events in the city. "I am a big Reds fan," said one student. "But when you are in college, you can have so many things to do that you just don't even think of going to a baseball game."

The Greek life is an important part of the party scene at UC. There are over 35 fraternities and sororities, and they contribute a great deal to the parties as well as a number of activities and events on campus. At the same time, those who are not interested in the fraternities and sororities can also find parties in off-campus housing. "It is a big school," said one student. "If you try, you will definitely find a good group of friends."

Since UC is an urban school, the dorms tend to look like big apartment buildings. A significant number of upperclassmen also choose to live off campus, since it is generally easy to find apartments that are not too far from classes, thus allowing students to achieve a great deal of independence without causing much inconvenience. "Based on what I saw from other schools," said one student, "the dorms here are actually pretty good."

The reviews on the dining service, as is the case with most universities, vary greatly. Some people are not impressed at all. Others believe that it is very good. The good news is that UC is in Cincinnati, and plenty of options are available for people who either hate dining hall food or do not participate in the meal plans.

Cheer Cincinnati

The UC Bearcats have a highly successful athletic program. Games by the men's basketball and football teams can often be found on nationally televised broadcasts due to their immense success. The students, of course, are very enthusiastic in their support for the teams, even though the tickets are sometimes hard to find.

UC provides very good programs that combine academic work and practical training. It is also a major research institution, thus giving students the opportunities to make further explorations in their fields. The academics, combined with the urban location, certainly makes UC a college choice worthy of consideration.—*Xiaohang Liu*

FYI
If I could change one thing about UC, I'd "improve the weather somehow."
Three things every student at UC should do before graduating are: "go to sports games, have a trip to Kentucky, and join a club."

Wittenberg University

Address: PO Box 720,
Springfield, OH 45501
Phone: 937-327-6314
E-mail address:
admission@wittenberg.edu
Web site URL:
www.wittenberg.edu
Year Founded: 1845
Private or Public: Private
Religious Affiliation:
Lutheran
Location: Rural
Number of Applicants:
2,887
Percent Accepted: 73%
Percent Accepted who
enroll: 26%
Number Entering: 500
Number of Transfers
Accepted each Year: 69
Middle 50% SAT range:
M: 510–630, CR: 510–610,
Wr: Unreported
Middle 50% ACT range:
22–28
Early admission program
EA/ED/None: EA/ED

Percentage accepted
through EA or ED:
91%/57%
EA and ED deadline:
1-Dec/15-Nov
Regular Deadline: Rolling
Application Fee: $40
Full time Undergraduate
enrollment: 1,894
Total enrollment: 1,909
Percent Male: 51%
Percent Female: 49%
Total Percent Minority or
Unreported: 25%
Percent African-American:
10%
Percent Asian/Pacific
Islander: 2%
Percent Hispanic: 2%
Percent Native American:
<1%
Percent International:
2%
Percent in-state/out of
state: 73%/27%
Percent from Public HS:
Unreported

Retention Rate: 80%
Graduation Rate 4-year: 56%
Graduation Rate 6-year: 57%
Percent Undergraduates in
On-campus housing: 83%
Number of official organized
extracurricular
organizations: 129
3 Most popular majors:
Social Sciences, Biology,
Business/Marketing
Student/Faculty ratio:
Unreported
Average Class Size: 25
Percent of students going to
grad school: Unreported
Tuition and Fees: $36,434
In-State Tuition and Fees if
different: No difference
Cost for Room and Board:
$9,294
Percent receiving financial aid
out of those who apply:
88%
Percent receiving financial
aid among all students:
82%

Nestled within the boundaries of the green Springfield, OH campus, Wittenberg University provides a small, liberal arts college experience unlike many of the larger Universities in the Midwest, while still competing with those powerhouses on the athletic fields. Students enroll into the Witt family, where they are able to bond with their professors and students, which they say leads to a happy, personable campus.

Academics

Witt students describe an intimacy in the classroom that originates in the small class sizes and low teacher-to-student ratio at the University. Every student interviewed mentioned the positives of small, seminar-style classes, making it impossible to get lost in large lecture halls jammed with students. Every class is taught by a member of the faculty, so students learn from professors instead of teaching assistants. One senior pre-law English Literature major said this showed within the department, adding "I get to work closely with professors; the entire English department knows me well, and is always willing to help."

The academic curriculum requires students take classes across a spread of seven academic areas: Integrated Learning; Natural World; Social Institutions; Fine, Performing, and Literary Arts; Religious and Philosophical Inquiry; Western Historical Perspectives; and Non-Western Cultures. Students agree that while they definitely need to plan out their schedules in advance to accommodate these requirements, the necessary range of courses guarantees every student receives the broad liberal arts education that Wittenburg boasts. "It's good that you don't have to pigeonhole yourself within your major," one student said. "They make you branch out and study other parts of the curriculum." He added that, as a humanities major, he had a great time exploring and loved a geology class he checked out in the fall that he would not have taken if not for the requirements. Witt's requirements do more than help students branch out into new subjects—they allow students to learn about themselves as well. One freshman explained how he took an Introductory to American Government course as a way to fill his Social Institutions requirement, and decided to major in Political Science as a result.

> **"It's good that you don't have to pigeonhole yourself within your major."**

In addition to a choosing from one of 35 majors, students can add a minor or take a number of electives. The most popular majors at Witt for the Class of 2011 were Biology/Biological Sciences and Business, with an almost equal number of social science and humanities majors. Witt also offers First-Year Programs (FYP) that cover a range of academic and life skills, catering to individual students' needs so freshmen are on the same page when it comes to things like writing, getting acquainted with Witt, and leadership development skills. Through FYP, students can enroll in a Wittenberg Seminar, or WittSem, which provides a small classroom experience on cool, quirky topics like "Making Coffee."

Over 90 students a year study abroad from Witt, travelling for periods ranging from a few weeks over a break to an entire academic year. While it is not the norm, plenty of students take advantage of the opportunity to travel to places like Italy, China and Spain—over their four years at Witt, almost one in five students will study abroad.

Outside of the Classroom

Any Witt student can tell you the school is proud of its football team. For such a small university, school is a fierce competitor on the football field—Wittenberg has the most wins of any Division III team in the NCAA. "We take it really seriously," one student said, noting that the full stadium often fills up for home games. Football games are a huge social event as well, giving students the chance to create the classic tailgate memories of a large college even though they attend a small one. Over a third of students compete in intercollegiate sports, with 75 percent throwing their hat into the intramural ring. Another student, who plays on the men's lacrosse team, said that he often attends other sports' games because the small student body means everyone has friends to cheer on. The net effect, he concluded, creates a spirited and cohesive group of undergraduates.

Aside from athletics, there are over 120 student organizations at Witt, ranging from the standards like the weekly student newspaper *The Torch* and the Student Senate, to more unique opportunities like the Swing Dance Club and Wittenberg Role-Playing Guild. "Most everyone is involved in at least one thing. It's just so easy because Witt offers something for everyone," one student commented. Another student mentioned that most clubs meet in the evening on weeknights, making it tough for athletes to participate in many organizations, but there are also athletics-centered activities like the Student-Athlete Advisory Committee. There are also a number of multicultural and diversity organizations, including Concerned Black Students, Jewish Culture Club, Hispanic Culture Club, and the Gay-Straight Alliance.

Living On Campus

Wittenberg's campus has the charm of a Northeast, Georgian-style university—the buildings are stately red brick surrounded by plenty of grass and trees. While inside the campus is cozy and comfortable, students rarely venture too far outside into Springfield. Students describe the campus as "extremely beautiful," but one student added that a bubble exists around that beauty, since Springfield itself is "pretty bleak." Students usually live or rent in residences on campus, therefore, and sometimes travel to Columbus, Ohio, which is a forty-minute drive away. Once in Columbus, students will go on dates or check out an Ohio State football game.

> **"Saturday nights are pretty rowdy," he added, "but it's not like people are drinking every day, all the time."**

In addition to the residence halls and houses for rent on campus, many students live in a house for their athletic team or Greek organization. Over 35 percent of students at Witt go Greek, joining one of five sororities or five fraternities that offer quaint living options (from the outside, at least). "There's certain things fraternities and sororities will do that are closed, but they're very open and all about trying to get people to participate," one student said. Another sophomore added that he didn't want to pledge a fraternity as a freshman, but decided to join as a sophomore and found the process both easy and rewarding. Greek organizations make up a significant amount of the partying on campus, but one student called the night scene pretty "chill," adding that many hang out with groups of close friends if they don't feel like going to a rager. "Saturday nights are pretty rowdy," he added, "but it's not like people are drinking every day, all the time."

The school itself does not host many widely-attended organized events, but every spring students flock to WittFest on the Hollow, when the Union Board hires a band to play, though students said they didn't necessarily attend for the music as much as for the chance to hang out with friends and daydrink.

When asked to sum up his experience at Witt, one student said "Great times, small environment, really close, happy people." This seems to be the takeaway for most: students at Witt find their niche in the tight-knit community, where the professors are "always available" and the times are "always good." Witt offers students the resources and attention of a small college, with the football success that lets students experience a sliver of a powerhouse state school. Springfield may seem like an unlikely place to find it, but prospective students looking for a University that becomes a family should tour Wittenberg University and find out it's the right fit.—*Amy Wang*

FYI

What's the typical weekend schedule? "Go to the football game if it's a home game, hang out at the Hollow if it's nice out, catch up on work, and hit a few frat parties."

If I could change one thing about Wittenberg, I'd "make it just a little bit bigger. An extra 500 students would spice up campus life."

Three great themed parties: Hawaiian Night, the Toga Party, and Executive Night

Oklahoma

Address: 219 Student Union, Stillwater, OK 74078
Phone: 405-744-5358
E-mail address: admit@okstate.edu
Web site URL: go.okstate.edu/
Year Founded: 1890
Private or Public: Public
Religious Affiliation: None
Location: Suburban
Number of Applicants: 8,696
Percent Accepted: 81%
Percent Accepted who enroll: 48%
Number Entering: 3,398
Number of Transfers Accepted each Year: Unreported
Middle 50% SAT range: M: 520–630, CR: 490–600, Wr: Unreported
Middle 50% ACT range: 22–28
Early admission program EA/ED/None: None

Percentage accepted through EA or ED: NA
EA and ED deadline: NA
Regular Deadline: Rolling
Application Fee: $40
Full time Undergraduate enrollment: 15,776
Total enrollment: 18,197
Percent Male: 51%
Percent Female: 49%
Total Percent Minority or Unreported: 22%
Percent African-American: 5%
Percent Asian/Pacific Islander: 2%
Percent Hispanic: 3%
Percent Native American: 10%
Percent International: 3%
Percent in-state/out of state: 81%/19%
Percent from Public HS: Unreported
Retention Rate: 78%

Graduation Rate 4-year: 29%
Graduation Rate 6-year: Unreported
Percent Undergraduates in On-campus housing: 44%
Number of official organized extracurricular organizations: 300
3 Most popular majors: Accounting, Aerospace, Agriculture
Student/Faculty ratio: 19:1
Average Class Size: 15
Percent of students going to grad school: Unreported
Tuition and Fees: $15,651
In-State Tuition and Fees if different: $4,305
Cost for Room and Board: $6,680
Percent receiving financial aid out of those who apply: 73%
Percent receiving financial aid among all students: 71%

The most challenging time of the year for most college students is undoubtedly the season when classes have finished, all graded work has been completed, and there is only one hurdle yet to be jumped: finals. And while a typical exam week unfortunately means lots of stress, lots of cramming, and not a lot of sleep, Oklahoma State University has found the perfect cure for the inevitable agony that stands between students and their vacation. Hugs. Lots of unlimited Hugs in the Free Hugs for Finals Week.

And while you might hesitate to judge a school based on hugs, students at OSU believe the hugs during finals week make a broader statement about how the university takes care of its students. Even with a student body exceeding 18,000, all individuals receive the attention and support they need to have a successful college career.

Orange You Going to Study Tonight?

As with any university, Oklahoma State has many different kinds of students. As one junior put it, "There are the thinking people, and the not-quite-as-smart people." Members of both categories spend a fair amount of time studying. A general rule of thumb is to spend two hours studying for every hour of class time. Upperclassmen tend to spend more time studying than freshmen, but "no matter what year you are, or what classes you're taking, you're always going to have time to have fun and chill with your friends, and still make good grades."

So what do OSU students like to study?

Regardless of major, everyone is required to take two courses in each of five general areas—English, math, humanities, social studies, and science. A very popular major is definitely the Business major, while the most difficult ones are Engineering and Pre-Med. OSU's Hotel and Restaurant Administration program is unique and well known across the country.

For applicants who tend to shy away from equations, Oklahoma State is also strong in the humanities. While students who choose one of these majors are definitely in the minority, they often go on to earn graduate degrees in their respective areas of study. One senior said, "You might be a business major because you couldn't really decide on anything else, but if you're a humanities major, you know that's what you want to do."

Regardless of what they choose to study, a great tutoring program is available to all OSU undergrads. For any and every subject, the school provides individual tutoring free of charge. One student who took advantage of this option found it to be rewarding: "The tutors were definitely a big help for a couple of my tougher classes."

It Takes a Village

OSU students are generally pleased with their living situations. The school's arrangements can certainly be characterized as diverse—there are on-campus apartments, lots of quads (four people with singles who share a bathroom and living room), and also more traditional housing. Compared to other large state schools, a surprising number of upperclassmen choose to live on-campus. This is partly because of the recently completed dorm complex called The Village, which consists of six "brand-new, beautiful buildings that pretty much make you love your residential life." Each floor in The Village has a common area furnished with comfy couches and also a community kitchen—perfect for cooking up a late-night snack with some friends.

Integral to residential life at OSU are the Residential Advisors and Community Mentors. While one of their duties is to enforce university rules, these upperclassmen are also there to "make freshmen feel welcome, help them get involved, and generally be a friendly helper." New students will likely form a close relationship with their advisor or mentor, since there is one for every 20 or so students. And as long as you don't get caught in your dorm guzzling a beer, you can expect that relationship to be a rewarding one.

That Rustic Feeling

Anyone who has visited the Oklahoma State campus agrees that it's pleasing to the senses. In terms of architecture, most of the buildings are old and made of bricks, with what one junior called "a little bit of a rustic feel." Another student said she was very fond of her surroundings: "Our campus is really gorgeous, especially in the spring when the flowers are blooming."

While OSU out of necessity has a fairly big campus, students have an easy time of getting from place to place by walking or biking. Conveniently located near the center of campus is Edmon Low Library, a favorite place to study or to wander stacks that contain more than 2.5 million volumes. After hitting the books, students might make a trip to the Colvin Recreation Center, which might best be described as "a glorious piece of workout heaven." The Center is very popular and includes 10 basketball courts, indoor and outdoor swimming pools, an indoor track, and racquetball and volleyball courts.

> "There's not just something for everyone, there are three things for everyone."

Another source of pride for OSU students is the Student Union building. Touted as the largest in the country, it offers a place to relax, hang out with friends, and grab some food. The Union also has the main bookstore and a clothing shop, where you'll find plenty of orange-and-black clothes for your wardrobe.

Fitting In

With about 400 undergraduate organizations, students at OSU find that they have many ways to become active. These include political, cultural, preprofessional, and recreational groups. There are also clubs for each major and many club sports teams. One student said, "There's not just something for everyone, there are three things for everyone."

Oklahoma State also has a vibrant Greek scene. One junior estimated that perhaps one in five students are in fraternities or sororities. He said that going Greek "isn't a necessity, but it is cool if that's what you want to do. And if you don't want to do it, that's fine too." Most students agree that the Greek life is somewhat separated from other social scenes on campus—the frat parties are usually invite-only.

The Oklahoma Two-Step

Oklahoma State undergrads certainly know how to have a good time. When the weekends come around, students like to "hit up the bars on The Strip, maybe go to a party some place off campus, or go out to eat with friends." Popular campus restaurants include the West Side Café and the Service Station, both of which have fast, cheap food. Students craving a more classy setting might dine at the Rancher's Club—an upscale on-campus restaurant that attracts visitors from all over the state.

Much of social life occurs off campus. Stillwater's most well-known dance club is called the Tumbleweed. This unique joint consists of two rooms—one that plays hip/hop and modern tunes, and another that features country music favorites for a line-dancing and two-stepping crowd.

Although Oklahoma State is a dry campus, it's no secret that a majority of students like to relax after a week of classes by downing a few drinks. One popular hangout spot is Eskimo Joe's, a bar and restaurant that is considered the heart of Stillwater. Students often go there on "Thirsty Thursdays," where they can enjoy cheese fries and five-dollar unlimited beer. An OSU senior even joked that "one percent of the beer consumed in the United States is probably consumed in Stillwater."

If students want to get away for the weekend, many choose to visit Tulsa or Oklahoma City, both of which are about an hour away by car. Both cities offer opportunities to go shopping, see a movie, go to a concert, or try out a new restaurant.

It'll Be Bedlam

If there is one thing that all Oklahoma State students can agree on, it's that they love beating OU. The rivalry between these two schools, known as the Bedlam series, is a fierce one with a long history. Students clad in Cowboy orange turn out in huge numbers for the football and basketball games, because "even the people who know nothing about sports love to root against OU."

The chance to see exciting games in packed stadiums against a big rival is only one of many fun opportunities available to students at Oklahoma State. A big school that takes care of the individual, OSU is a comfortable home for its students. And don't forget about the free pancakes.—*Henry Agnew*

FYI
If you come to Oklahoma State, you'd better bring "your party hat."
What is the typical weekend schedule? "Definitely go out on Thursday, hopefully go to class on Friday, then chill with friends, go to the game on Saturday, then hit the books Sunday night."
If I could change one thing about Oklahoma State, I'd "increase student involvement in campus activities."
Three things every student at Oklahoma State should do before graduating are: "eat at Shortcake's diner, play Frisbee on Library Lawn, and go to a Bedlam game and root against the Sooners."

Oral Roberts University

Address: 7777 S. Lewis Avenue, Tulsa, OK 74171
Phone: 918-495-6518
E-mail address: admissions@oru.edu
Web site URL: www.oru.edu
Year Founded: 1963
Private or Public: Private
Religious Affiliation: Christian
Location: Urban
Number of Applicants: 1,127
Percent Accepted: 73%
Percent Accepted who enroll: 58%
Number Entering: 480
Number of Transfers Accepted each Year: Unreported
Middle 50% SAT range: M: 455–570, CR: 465–590, Wr: Unreported
Middle 50% ACT range: 20–26
Early admission program EA/ED/None: None
Percentage accepted through EA or ED: NA

EA and ED deadline: NA
Regular Deadline: Rolling
Application Fee: $35
Full time Undergraduate enrollment: 2,401
Total enrollment: 2,645
Percent Male: 41%
Percent Female: 59%
Total Percent Minority or Unreported: 45%
Percent African-American: 15%
Percent Asian/Pacific Islander: 4%
Percent Hispanic: 6%
Percent Native American: 1%
Percent International: 6%
Percent in-state/out of state: 38%/62%
Percent from Public HS: 75%
Retention Rate: 82%
Graduation Rate 4-year: 54%

Graduation Rate 6-year: Unreported
Percent Undergraduates in On-campus housing: 75%
Number of official organized extracurricular organizations: Unreported
3 Most popular majors: Marketing, Mass Communication, Theology
Student/Faculty ratio: 14:1
Average Class Size: 15
Percent of students going to grad school: 50%
Tuition and Fees: $20,060
In-State Tuition and Fees if different: No difference
Cost for Room and Board: $4,192
Percent receiving financial aid out of those who apply: 87%
Percent receiving financial aid among all students: 85%

Sixty-foot, thirty-ton bronze Praying Hands grace the main entrance to Oral Roberts University, indicating to all visitors that ORU not only offers its students academic guidance from the Ivory Tower, it also directs students to depend on a lifetime of teachings from God. Due to its religious founding, students at the university are encouraged to continually grow academically, physically, *and* spiritually. They are given the unique opportunity to combine a top-notch education with a passionate religious and cultural experience. These aspects of the ORU experience require students to adhere to strict rules such as a dress code as well as to refrain from the partying that is characteristic of your "typical" college experience. Students are also required to participate in mandatory chapel services twice a week so they can continually live out the school founder's vision. Evangelist Oral Roberts claims that God instructed him to found a university based on "God's commission and the holy spirit." Roberts obeyed this mandate and in 1963 opened Oral Roberts University in Tulsa. Few universities can claim that they were built as a result of a message directly from God, but Oral Roberts University is one of the few that can.

Academics

As a Christian school, Oral Roberts University emphasizes students' personal spiritual growth alongside a challenging academic education. Students at Oral Roberts say academics are noticeably "above average" and "top-notch." Students have the option to enroll in one of six undergraduate schools: the College of Arts & Cultural Studies, the College of Science and Engineering, the College of Theology and Ministry, the College of Business, the School of Education, or the Anna Vaughn College of Nursing.

The seven schools vary in difficulty, but all are known to be academically rigorous. According to one student, "The School of Education is very tough. There is a lot required of education majors, but it is a good thing. We have an exceptional program here and it makes the hard work worth it, because

I know I am getting the best, top-of-the-line education." Oral Roberts's Leadership Studies Degree Completion Program (formerly the School of LifeLong Education) provides flexible, quality education programs to adult learners and non-traditional students. The business school is considered "exceptional" and also offers a five-year MBA program. The College of Nursing is also "well-known and hard." Not surprisingly, the theology department is "incredible."

Especially attractive is the Honors Program, which admits 16 to 18 top applicants every year as Fellows. These students enroll in one three-credit hour Fellows Seminar each semester, in addition to one or two other Honors credit courses. Other highly qualified applicants are designated as Honors Program Scholars. Honors students are even invited to live in special dormitory wings with respected quiet hours, and a "quality academic atmosphere."

> The religious atmosphere at Oral Roberts emphasizes a non-competitive academic environment where "everybody would rather help you than compete against you." According to one student, competition is found "only in intramurals," an important part of campus life at ORU.

Faculty and staff at ORU devote themselves to building a university for God by actively participating in the lives of their students. ORU students appreciate this devotion and recognize its contribution to the successful academic environment. According to one undergraduate, "All faculty are extremely willing to go the extra mile for their students." Many students even describe faculty-student relationships as their favorite aspect of ORU academics, specifically noting the "personal help [the students] receive."

In Pursuit of Principled Social Life

ORU has been described as a place where students "get their learning and keep their burning." So life at the university goes well beyond academics. One unique feature of the ORU is an honor code which is taken very seriously and forbids the use of alcohol, tobacco and drugs, as well as lying, cheating, cursing, and premarital sex. The honor code, which is submitted with the application to the university, also requires students to attend all classes and chapel services and to participate in a physical fitness program. Unlike most universities around the country, weekend activities are not centered on drinking. This may be a result of the honor code, or it may just be a result of students' adherence to Christian values. Although drinking is not very common, it does occur, but usually off campus. According to one student, "nobody really drinks in the dorms unless they keep it on the down low." Drugs are even less prevalent than alcohol.

Instead of drinking, students who stay on campus spend their free time playing intramurals and attending dorm and sporting events. Most students do not stay on campus during the weekend. Instead, they tend to visit coffee shops, restaurants, and clubs, as well as commuter students' homes away from campus. Students usually have cars so they can visit these off-campus sites, as "Tulsa does not have a good public transportation system." According to one student, "Tulsa is very boring without a car."

One student said that stereotypical ORU students may be described "as Bible beaters and Jesus freaks but also as hard-working, honest, respected people." While the student population at ORU boasts geographic diversity, in that the school attracts students from 49 states and 70 nations, all students are connected by their faith. "For the most part everybody has a relationship with God, which makes the people pretty much all the same. But as far as culture goes, there is a good mix," said one student.

Living as "Brothers" and "Sisters"

Most students will live in dorms unless they are commuters, married, or over age twenty-five. Students generally do not mind that they are required to live on campus, because it creates a sense of "community spirit." Dorms are divided into wings, and freshmen are randomly assigned to a wing in a single-sex dorm. Each male wing is paired with a specific female wing, and "brother wings" and "sister wings" allow freshmen to meet members of the opposite sex. Brother and sister wings "plan events together, sit together in chapel, and also have designated seats" together in the cafeteria. Freshmen may request a particular dorm if they have had family in that dorm, or they may be recruited by a particular wing. The wings that "recruit, draft on, and initiate people" are similar to fraternities, except the students live in dormitory halls, instead of separate houses elsewhere on campus. One of the oldest and most respected wings on campus is known as YoungBlood. Dorms are also known for their particular personalities. According to one student, "Claudius is the freshman, fun, social dorm. EMR is the fun, manly man's dorm. Michael and Wesley are for more of the pretty boys. Gabby is for the rich girls."

Freshmen generally find it easy to make friends in their own wings, or in their respective brother or sister wing. Additionally, freshmen do not feel excluded from upperclassmen's activities since "everybody is included in whatever is going on." But according to one senior, the upperclassmen have much less free time for socializing. Every floor has an RA and a chaplain. RAs enforce curfews, notify students of events, and maintain general order on the floor. Chaplains provide students with spiritual support.

One thing ORU students all agree on is the strangeness and originality of campus architecture. One student describes it as "space age" and another describes it as "like the Jetsons." Most find it ugly at first, but all agree that it grows on them. Currently, roofs of buildings are being improved and construction for a new student center is underway.

Students generally hang out in and around the cafeteria and at the restaurants on campus, such as the Eagle's Nest or the Internet café. When the weather is nice, they spend time on the quad as well. Favorite places on campus include the Prayer Gardens, surrounding the base of the 200-foot tall Prayer Tower which serves as the visitor's center and the Kenneth H. Cooper Aerobics Center (AC), a two-story building housing athletic facilities and exercise equipment. Located in a very safe neighborhood, ORU offers an extremely safe campus environment. There are no problems between the students and the residents of the surrounding neighborhoods. As one student put it, "They love us."

There is only one cafeteria on campus, but according to a student, it has "good variety. They try hard. You have to be creative sometimes." Another student agrees it is "better than most cafeterias I have eaten in, but it still gets old and is avoided most of the time." Students are required to be on an unlimited, 17-, 14-, or 10-meal per week meal plan and each comes with a certain number of Eagle Bucks that can be used at different restaurants, as well as the coffee shop or bookstore. Even when the students tire of cafeteria food, it is not a problem since Tulsa boasts "a huge restaurant variety—anything and everything you can imagine."

Sports as a Requirement

Oral Roberts University aims to "educate the whole man: spirit, mind, and body. Staying in shape and treating our bodies well is just as important as our mental state." In addition to most students' abstention from alcohol, drugs, and tobacco, students are all required to participate in some sort of physical activity. One way to do this is to participate in a varsity sport. The Oral Roberts Golden Eagles compete in eight Division I sports for both men and women. Though the school is fairly young and school pride and traditions are still developing, sporting events are well-attended. Basketball is especially popular at the 10,000-seat Mabee Center. For students who do not want the time commitment of Division I athletics, intramurals are popular as well. Intramural sports such as basketball, soccer, volleyball, flag football, tennis, badminton, and Ping-Pong are extremely competitive.

> "Staying in shape and treating our bodies well is just as important as our mental state."

Outside of academics and athletics, students have many job opportunities on and off campus. Students are very committed to their extracurricular activities as well. Some students take part in mission trips; others write for the school newspaper, *The Oracle*; and some are involved in community outreach or the Leadership Academy. A unique group called the Student Association allows students to play an active role in the decision-making and programming of the university.

ORU instructs its young people in how to combine morality with worldly endeavors like business and medicine and other professional arenas featured in its academic programs. The university's facilities, high-tech amenities, and space-age architecture contrast greatly with the university's embrace of an old-school mentality concerning academic life. Students all agree that devotion to God comes first; they love being in a strict academic environment where they are given the opportunity to "grow as a Christian." In the words of University Chancellor Roberts (who is son of the university's founder) ORU is a "ministry with a University not a University with a ministry." If you are seeking a spiritual, as well as an academic, collegiate experience, you may be one of the growing number of applicants considering Oral Roberts University.—*Jessica Rubin*

FYI

If you come to Oral Roberts, you'd better bring "flip-flops" and "your Bible . . . I guess."

What's the typical weekend schedule? "Friday: Coffee shops, local concerts at Cain's Ballroom, out to eat and a movie. Saturday: maybe a basketball game or a drive-in movie. Sunday: Church, lunch and a nap. Next, the campus worship service."

If I could change one thing about Oral Roberts, I'd "get rid of the curfew and allow coed dorms" and "get more people to come here!"

Three things every student at Oral Roberts should do before graduating are: "swim in the fountains, run the Howard Run (streaking around Howard Auditorium), and love our President."

University of Oklahoma

Address: 1000 Asp Avenue, Norman, OK 73019-4076

Phone: 405-325-2252

E-mail address: admrec@ou.edu

Web site URL: www.ou.edu

Year Founded: 1890

Private or Public: Public

Religious Affiliation: None

Location: Urban

Number of Applicants: 8,768

Percent Accepted: 85%

Percent Accepted who enroll: 49%

Number Entering: 3,724

Number of Transfers Accepted each Year: 2,514

Middle 50% SAT range: M: 530–670, CR: 510–650, Wr: Unreported

Middle 50% ACT range: 23–29

Early admission program EA/ED/None: None

Percentage accepted through EA or ED: NA

EA and ED deadline: NA

Regular Deadline: 1-Apr

Application Fee: $40

Full time Undergraduate enrollment: 20,892

Total enrollment: 30,303

Percent Male: 47%

Percent Female: 53%

Total Percent Minority or Unreported: 42%

Percent African-American: 5%

Percent Asian/Pacific Islander: 6%

Percent Hispanic: 6%

Percent Native American: 4%

Percent International: 2%

Percent in-state/out of state: 63%/37%

Percent from Public HS: Unreported

Retention Rate: Unreported

Graduation Rate 4-year: 26%

Graduation Rate 6-year: 59%

Percent Undergraduates in On-campus housing: 33%

Number of official organized extracurricular organizations: 338

3 Most popular majors: Health Professions, Business/Marketing, Interdisciplinary Studies

Student/Faculty ratio: 17:1

Average Class Size: 15

Percent of students going to grad school: Unreported

Tuition and Fees: $19,278

In-State Tuition and Fees if different: $8,325

Cost for Room and Board: $8,060

Percent receiving financial aid out of those who apply: 65%

Percent receiving financial aid among all students: 46%

Whether they were fans before college or not, students at the University of Oklahoma, or OU as it is commonly called, love football. The OU campus, located in Norman, Oklahoma, is made up of gorgeous red brick Cherokee-Gothic buildings. As you drive up to the OU campus, the first thing you will see is what one student called the campus "centerpiece": Memorial Stadium. Every year, the Sooners take on archrival University of Texas in the "Red River Rivalry" matchup. While OU sports teams formally call themselves the Sooners, OU actually has two mascots, Boomer and Sooner, whose names ring throughout Memorial Stadium when the sold out stadium performs the

"Boomer, Sooner" chant. The University of Oklahoma was founded in 1890, a full 17 years before Oklahoma became a state. Today, it offers diverse academic options, a vibrant social scene focused on Greek life, and a strong sense of school spirit.

Get to the Greeks

OU students tend to be proud of their extracurricular activities, said one student, especially Greek life. Greek life is an integral part of the OU social scene, as 50 percent of all students belong to one of the 45 Greek organizations scattered around campus. Similar to other large state universities, the rush process for sororities starts a full week before the academic year begins. Freshman women are permitted to move into on-campus housing early so they have some stability during the bustling rush process.

Parties at OU revolve around the Greek organizations and athletics. "Greek life is definitely the number-one social scene on campus and everyone is familiar with each fraternity/sorority even if they are not affiliated with it." Greek organizations will have group parties with other nearby Greeks, date parties, mixers with other Greek organizations, themed parties, and almost always parties following a win from the Sooner football team. While fraternities and sororities allow students to connect with peers early on in the freshman journey and have a dominant presence on campus, there are plenty of other ways to make friends as a freshman. "There are multiple official study rooms in the dorms where people meet and work on homework while connecting with their peers socially," one student said. In fact, students have the opportunity to connect through any of OU's 400 student organizations whether they are interested in sports, chess, politics, or theatre.

Sooner Superfans

Weekends at OU tend to begin on Thursdays with activities peaking on Saturdays and slowing down on Sundays. Off-campus houses and fraternities will start the weekend off with mixers or open parties. "Most people like to go out on Thursday and Friday nights, and the majority go to their respective Greek house if involved," one student said. If there is a football game on Saturday, look out. OU students paint faces, carry flags, and wear as much Crimson and Cream Sooners attire as possible. "The majority of students get season tickets every year," one student said. "Everyone dresses up and looks good for each game."

While the games themselves and long tailgates ahead of time are often weekend highlights, the outcomes of the games are campus mood determinants for the following week. "If the Sooners lose, it's the talk of the campus the whole next week," one student said. "If the Sooners win, it's still the talk of the campus the whole next week." And after a sweet victory, the Sooners throw sweet parties. Many students drink regularly with friends, though the pressure to consume alcohol or drugs depends on what types of people a student surrounds themselves with. "People will completely respect a person's decision to abstain," one student said. OU is a dry campus, so most students go off-campus to take drink. If a student does decide to drink on campus, the punishment from OU is a "strict and harsh" three-strike policy.

Pride in Integrity

OU has a strong academic integrity and ethics policy. "The academic integrity board on campus is extremely strict," one student said. OU is the No. 1 public university in the number of freshman National Merit Scholars enrolled and in the top ten among all public and private universities for the number of freshman National Merit Scholars enrolled with over 700 National Merit Scholars. Honor and distinction also carries weight at OU in signing up for classes. Students who are part of the Honors College, selected based upon high test scores and high school GPA, are able to register for their classes earlier. "As long as you enroll early, you can find a spot in whatever course you want," one student said.

At OU, there is something for everyone to study. Popular majors include pre-med, nursing programs, and psychology; however, business is also a popular major. Some of the more challenging majors include petroleum engineering and aerospace engineering. Sooners' graduation requirements vary based on the major they choose, but generally speaking at least 60 credit hours and a 2.0 GPA are required for graduation. These requirements depend on the major and students may need to take more or less specific courses versus electives depending on what they choose to study. If you are looking to explore something totally new and unusual, you can study Ballet Pedagogy, Costume Technology Emphasis, or Aviation: Air Traffic Management at OU.

Housing Time

All freshman under the age of twenty must live in on-campus housing, but many students choose to move off campus as upperclass-men. "Everyone who's not a freshman lives off campus either in an apartment or a house," one student said. For on-campus housing, there are three main dorms: Adams Center, Walker Center, and Couch Center. Couch has a late night snack food stop called Couch Express that grills popular ham and cheese sandwiches. Walker provides Xcetera, the on-campus convenience store, as well as a large lounge area with pool and ping pong tables on the first floor. Both Walker and Couch have 24-hour computer labs. As for dorm layout, the three towers mentioned each have 12 floors with two wings, one for men and one for women. A keycard is mandatory for entry to each of the two halls per wing and each hall supports roughly 24 rooms, each with two people. A common bathroom area with a toilet, shower and several sinks connects every group of two rooms. Two RAs live per floor of freshman housing, one male and one female. "Some are strict and some are not," one student said. "It's really the luck of the draw." RAs answer questions about life at OU and "inform students of local social events on or off campus."

As with most universities, dining options receive both positive and negative feedback, but Sooners agree there are many options to choose from. Food at Xcetera, the Student Union (or "The Union" as it is commonly called), and the rest of on-campus convenience stores can be purchased with meal points. Crossroads, an all-night restaurant in The Union offers late-night cravings such as Buffalo wings, breakfast food, and a dessert bar with homemade shakes.

For the many that live off campus, a car becomes a necessity. "Almost everyone at OU has a car," one student said. "Some people bike to classes if they're close enough, but most drive their cars the distance every day." The public transportation around Norman is not spectacular, and therefore parking can become a problem with so many student cars.

Bringing a car to campus can also help students travel into Norman for a small college town trip or 15 miles away to Oklahoma City if Sooners want more of a big-city experience.

Looking the Look

While students at OU may like to dress up for Sooners games or for more formal events, most days going to class there's no pressure to dress up. Students are often seen wearing jeans and T-shirts to class, but if you rolled out of bed in your favorite pair of sweat pants, no one would judge you. One thing the Sooners are not is rednecks. When asked about what surprised him most when showing up to OU, one student said "everyone looked normal" and that there were not many "redneck country folks." Many students come to the University of Oklahoma from the Midwest, Oklahoma itself, and rival state Texas, but OU still has international students from over 100 countries as well as representation of all 50 states and 50 unique tribal affiliations.

Regardless of where OU students come from, they bond over school spirit and extracurricular activities more than anything else. Whether it is football, Greek life, the prominent Brothers Under Christ (BUCS) group, or working with your friends at an on-campus restaurant (a fairly popular job), Sooners always find something to bond over while at the University of Oklahoma together.—*Ashton Wackym*

FYI

If you come to the University of Oklahoma, you'd better leave any "clothing bright or burnt orange (which represents Oklahoma State University and the University of Texas respectively)."

One thing you wish you would've known before coming to OU: "Where certain buildings are on campus. It's difficult to find classes sometimes because of how confusing the campus layout can be."

How do you meet people or make friends when first arriving? "Most incoming freshman go to a 3-day retreat on the OU campus during summer called Camp Crimson. It's vital for making friends and getting information on fraternities (which is another big way people make friends on campus). Besides that, it's easy to make friends with people on your floor during your initial days at OU."

University of Tulsa

Address: 800 South Tucker Drive, Tulsa, OK 74104-3189
Phone: 918 631-2307
E-mail address: admission@utulsa.edu
Web site URL: www.utulsa.edu
Year Founded: 1894
Private or Public: Private
Religious Affiliation: Presbyterian
Location: Suburban
Number of Applicants: 4,714
Percent Accepted: 39%
Percent Accepted who enroll: 32%
Number Entering: 671
Number of Transfers Accepted each Year: 282
Middle 50% SAT range: M: 570–700, CR: 560–700, Wr: Unreported
Middle 50% ACT range: 26–32

Early admission program EA/ED/None: None
Percentage accepted through EA or ED: NA
EA and ED deadline: NA
Regular Deadline: Rolling
Application Fee: $35
Full time Undergraduate enrollment: 3,105
Total enrollment: 4,185
Percent Male: 56%
Percent Female: 44%
Total Percent Minority or Unreported: 36%
Percent African-American: 5%
Percent Asian/Pacific Islander: 4%
Percent Hispanic: 4%
Percent Native American: 4%
Percent International: 14%
Percent in-state/out of state: 52%/48%
Percent from Public HS: 78%
Retention Rate: 88%
Graduation Rate 4-year: 48%

Graduation Rate 6-year: 62%
Percent Undergraduates in On-campus housing: 72%
Number of official organized extracurricular organizations: 245
3 Most popular majors: Business/Marketing, Engineering, Visual and Performing Arts
Student/Faculty ratio: 11:1
Average Class Size: 14
Percent of students going to grad school: 23%
Tuition and Fees: $31,126
In-State Tuition and Fees if different: No difference
Cost for Room and Board: $9,464
Percent receiving financial aid out of those who apply: 53%
Percent receiving financial aid among all students: 50%

I n the alphabet of life, the letter "T" stands for many things: tortoise, telepathy, toiletries, tots. But when "t" stands for tenacity, talent, tradition, and togetherness, all in one setting, that is when it also stands for TU, also known as the University of Tulsa. Now, you may be saying to yourself, TU? Did you say TU? Because then should it not be Tulsa University rather than the University of Tulsa? Perhaps yes. Perhaps no. And perhaps this grammatical flip-flop, though perplexing, perfectly demonstrates the small-size/big-time duality which TU actualizes.

Hackedemics

Across the board, TU is habitually known for its challenging academics (especially in the field of engineering). And this can be attractive to strong-minded and/or intelligent young adults (indeed one of every ten students currently enrolled at TU is a National Merit Scholar). But we all know the most attractive attribute about a college to any young adult person is how that education will help him to land an eight-figure salary, become an icon, and/or hack into neighboring governments'

intelligence computers. Yet TU already knows all of that.

The University of Tulsa is "one of six pioneer institutions selected by the National Science Foundation to participate in the Federal Cyber Service Initiative (aka Cyber Corps) to train students for federal careers as computer security experts." This basically translates to "TU receiving $2.7 million to create a band of information security specialists who know how to defend the free world and defend the Internet from hackers." These students come out of the program not only with a degree in computer science and a couple years of their tuition paid for, but also "multiple federal-level computer security certificates as endorsed by the CNSS." They also get a new pick-up line: "Excuse me, I seemed to have dropped my multiple federal-level computer security certificates around here . . ."

However, if computers are not your "bag," TU also receives funding for the "Tulsa Undergraduate Research Challenge," which lets students get involved in advanced research with faculty members as early as their freshman year." It is no wonder that 46 Tulsa students have received Goldwater scholarships since 1995. But the "level of academic strain or prowess is totally dependent on what you want and your major—communication majors have it relatively easy, whereas students with majors like nursing and engineering can easily take up residency in the library."

Classes for Claustrophobics

Come to the University of Tulsa and never feel the restless constriction of cramming into a 500-seat auditorium with a bunch of pungent, pajama-wearing cohorts for the introductory lecture of Rocks for Jocks 101. Why? Because at TU, the average class size is 14 students, 62 percent of classes are under 20 students, and only 1 percent of classes hold 50 or more students. This allows for one-on-one instruction in an environment that "feels like home," an environment where "the teachers become easy friends and mentors, who are so approachable, accommodating, and helpful." Sounds like a little slice of heaven, eh? Except in heaven you do not have to factor in "attendance policies that can lower your grade making it so you can't skip class." In a class of 100, it is possible, but in a class of 12, hiding an absence can prove fruitless. Nonetheless, young adults (local, national, or international) continue to flock to TU in droves, thanks to the attentive faculty, the 10:1 student/teacher ratio, and the fact that "the school is small enough to not feel invisible, but also big enough where you are always meeting new people."

You and Me and Greek Makes Three

This constant confluence of new friendships may in a large part be related to how actively involved the students are within campus organizations. Ninety percent of students participate in some sort of club or organization—the "big ones" being: Young Democrats, FCA, Intramurals, or SA. SA is the Student Association which organizes most of the "big events" on campus, including Homecoming and Springfest—"a week of activities, free stuff, and concerts (Ben Folds, Hanson, 50 Cent, Vertical Horizon, etc.), with amazing tailgating on the 'U' before the football game."

> "The school is small enough to not feel invisible, but also big enough where you are always meeting new people."

Many of the other annual events are held by Greek frats or sororities; most have "philanthropy weeks that are way fun—usually games, competitions, and then parties on the weekends—all to raise money for their chosen organization." A favorite is the Lambda Chi Alpha's LUAU which is a "sand volleyball tourney where they cover a parking lot with sand and anyone can play, it's kinda a big deal." At TU, only about a fifth of the students pledge a fraternity or sorority, making Greek life "an option but not a must." If a frat holds a party or philanthropic event, anyone can attend, "so people do not feel like they have to go Greek in order to have a social life."

In fact, if you want an ample social network, intramurals might be a better bet. Eighty percent of the students partake of the intramural program, and "it is a common dream to win an intramural championship of some sort." The program is run through Collins Fitness Center, a brand-new fitness haven that came about during recent renovations (along with "amazing dorms—LaFortune is the best, the Twin dorms are the worst"). Most students describe the new fitness center as "unreal" though a few add "it is something that some huge rapper would own complete with plasma screens everywhere and every kind of workout machine you can imagine."

Running Backs, Recorders, and Robots

We know TU students love to win academic awards and that they love to play intramurals, but what happens when you combine the two? You get student athletes who love to win and student athletic supporters who love to watch them win! TU basketball games have "long been known as a Tulsa tradition" and "for once, the football team is doing well!" In fact, the Golden Hurricane (or so they are known because of 1. their tendency to "roar through opponents" and 2. Georgia Tech was already known as the tornado) has had recent success not only in football bowl games but also in soccer. But in the words of an insightful fan, "winning is not the best part; the best part is that the school is small enough that you know most of the athletes and this personal connection makes cheering at sporting events or watching them on TV a lot more fun because you are watching your friends."

As touching as that is, what if you do not like watching sports? Not a problem! TU has a large visual and performing arts contingency, and with the city of Tulsa boasting a professional opera company, a national ballet company, and a symphony, the two share an intimate interaction. Often "kids have gotten to fill in with the symphony" and the Tulsa Ballet has adopted a 330-pound "fighting robot" built by TU students for a Battle Bots competition. Fortunately, "the bot had been stripped of its steel spikes and bulletproof panels, allowing it to give a delicate ride to a full-length mirror and interact with the dancers."

Love and Leisure T-Town Style

If you are a TU student your hangout is either the library or the "Ack-Ack." Funnily enough, at TU "the library is almost a social scene; it's fun," and ACAC is similar to a student union and the only place where you can use meal points outside of the cafeteria. Off campus, many students enjoy spending time at Utica Square, a trendy yet quaint outdoor shopping/eating/walking Mecca that is home to Santa's cottage during the winter months and Queenside's bakery year-round ("It has egg salad to die for."). They also enjoy a trip to Philbrook Museum or the Tulsa Rose Garden, "where you can have a picnic at Woodward Park and watch a movie on your laptop."

But what if you are, perhaps, more nocturnal? Where do the creatures of the night hang out? Well, a typical TU Friday night could consist of "going to a bar, then ending back up at a small apartment/house party." Apparently, there used to be more house parties, but because of recent university mandates, "the parties are now being regulated and have significantly decreased in size and quantity; as a result people frequent the bar scene more." The main watering holes are Rehab, Hardwood's, or The Buccaneer (a dive bar affectionately called The Buc). All are located across the street from campus, and "are always offering some kind of beer special or TU student discount." Then there are other, more upscale restaurant/bar districts like Brookside, Cherry Street, or the Riverwalk (also a divine location to go for a jog). If you are not invited to a private apartment party, there are normally language house/frat parties, though those are known to "get kind of old after sophomore or junior year." Dorms also sometimes sponsor functions, and then "there are always City of Tulsa sponsored events like Mayfest or Oktoberfest (one fest has a lot of watercolors and live music and the other fest has a lot of potato pancakes, polka, and beer)." If those combined with Springfest are not enough fests for you, there is even a Harley Motorcycle Festival "where they close down Brookside every year and have a huge party."

But what is a party if one is alone? The dating scene at the University of Tulsa is like a good male/female relationship—discordant. Boys will tell you "it is good, there is a range of different people around and you can find your athletic or partyer or smart person and dates can be as simple as going to a party together." Girls will tell you "it's not bad, there are dating prospects although not too many of quality." But one thing is sure, "it is a small school so there is a clear understanding of who is dating who."

Max Forman once said: "Education seems to be in America the only commodity of which the customer tries to get as little as he can for his money." Apparently, Max Forman has never seen the University of Tulsa, especially during its current booms of a growing international student population, continuing nationally recognized academic award winners, and improving athletic victors. But the special charm of the University of Tulsa is that "as cliché as this sounds, the school feels like one big family," no matter how it orders its name.—*Jocelyn Ranne*

FYI

If you come to TU, you'd better bring "a variety of clothing (for all seasons) because it could be 70 degrees one day and snowing the next, and some cash. Things are expensive on campus, and campus police only know how to do one thing, and that's give out tickets."

What's the typical weekend schedule? "Friday night can start with dinner on Brookside, then parties start around 11 p.m. (most people check out frat row). Saturday you wake up (late) do some homework, check out a sporting event, and then repeat. You do work when you can, but it is mainly partying and catching up on sleep!"

If I could change one thing about TU, "I would get more quick and good food options on campus."

Three things that every TU student should do before graduating are: "camp out on the 'U' (the big U-shaped grassy area in between the dorms, library, and classroom buildings), join an organization, and climb up on the roof of the library to go stargazing."

Oregon

Lewis and Clark College

Address: 10015 SW Terwilliger Boulevard, Portland, OR 97219
Phone: 503-768-6613
E-mail address: admissions@lclark.edu
Web site URL: www.lclark.edu
Year Founded: 1867
Private or Public: Private
Religious Affiliation: None
Location: Urban
Number of Applicants: 5,360
Percent Accepted: 56%
Percent Accepted who enroll: 17%
Number Entering: 507
Number of Transfers Accepted each Year: 68
Middle 50% SAT range: M: 590–680, CR: 610–700, Wr: 590–680
Middle 50% ACT range: 26–31
Early admission program EA/ED/None: EA

Percentage accepted through EA or ED: Unreported
EA and ED deadline: 1-Nov
Regular Deadline: 1-Feb
Application Fee: $50
Full time Undergraduate enrollment: 1,964
Total enrollment: 2,836
Percent Male: 36%
Percent Female: 64%
Total Percent Minority or Unreported: 21%
Percent African-American: 1%
Percent Asian/Pacific Islander: 6%
Percent Hispanic: 5%
Percent Native American: <1%
Percent International: 5%
Percent in-state/out of state: 13%/87%
Percent from Public HS: 76%
Retention Rate: 83%

Graduation Rate 4-year: Unreported
Graduation Rate 6-year: Unreported
Percent Undergraduates in On-campus housing: 67%
Number of official organized extracurricular organizations: 85
3 Most popular majors: Psychology, Visual and Performing Arts, English
Student/Faculty ratio: 13:1
Average Class Size: 20
Percent of students going to grad school: 10%
Tuition and Fees: $33,726
In-State Tuition and Fees if different: No difference
Cost for Room and Board: $8,820
Percent receiving financial aid out of those who apply: 73%
Percent receiving financial aid among all students: 86%

Lewis and Clark students often get to have their cake and eat it too. The beautiful, green campus with astounding views of Mount Hood is only a short bus or bike ride away from the cafes, concerts, food carts, and festivals of Portland. The small size is accompanied by talented and devoted teachers. The students balance passion for their extracurricular activities with dedication to their school work. There is a comfortable "Lewis and Clark bubble," but students are encouraged to develop international perspectives.

Limited Space and Liberal Arts

Large classes are almost unheard of at Lewis and Clark. The average class size is 20, and 85 percent of classes have less than 29 students. These low numbers require many classes to be capped, and this can cause some difficulties. "There are trends in different classes for what's hard to get into and what's not," said one sophomore, but "a lot of the 100 level classes are hard to get into—and art classes, it's really hard to get into art classes." These occasional problems are worth the struggle, however, for small group discussions and personal attention from professors. And they are professors—when college recruitment literature boasts of having "zero graduate assistants," it's not an exaggeration: "even if there are TAs, they just grade papers."

The professors' dedication does not end when class does. Students say that they have never had trouble reaching a professor and that they are very responsive to undergraduate input, and "especially in the higher level classes . . . they don't treat you like just a student. They really care, and really listen." It's hardly surprising then that students are often invited to their teachers' homes for meals or holidays. Academic relationships become "pretty tight-knit."

Students say these relationships can come in handy when tough assignments come along. Not only are professors ready and willing to help solve problems, they will also take students' effort into account when grading. "If you're talking to them and showing them that you're trying really hard, then they see that and grade you according to that," an Environmental Studies major reported. That's not to say that some classes aren't very difficult: "I've gotten A's and I've gotten C's," but for the most part, "it's definitely possible if you put work into it," the student concluded.

One other effect of Lewis and Clark's small size is the somewhat limited number of majors. The college offers 28 majors and nearly as many minors from the arts, humanities, mathematical and natural sciences, and social sciences. Students stress that while it is definitely possible to be a math or science major, the college definitely emphasizes liberal arts, and so choosing Lewis and Clark is "very dependent on what you want to study and what you want to major in." Many students choose to study Economics, possibly because the school offers no business major (although there has been talk of bringing it back). International Affairs is another popular choice, and this can be attributed to a common international focus among the students, faculty, and administration.

International studies of some sort is in fact one of the requirements for graduation. It can be fulfilled through certain classes, but over 60 percent of Lewis and Clark students choose a more adventurous route: study abroad. Students travel to Australia, Japan, Chile, France, Russia, Morocco, Scotland, Kenya, and New Zealand, among others. This puts the student body in a constant state of flux as students leave for and return from trips abroad, but for many that is small price to pay for the once-in-a-lifetime opportunities and experiences.

Aside from the international requirement, the rest of the "core" is fairly predictable and includes languages, creative arts, PE, science, and quantitative reasoning. For diehard liberal arts students living in fear of calculus or physics, there are "Perspectives" classes. In Perspectives on Mathematics or Perspectives on Physics, "you read a lot about math or physics. You don't really study

math and physics," allowing students to branch out and fulfill the requirements without too much grief. The last, or rather first, requirement is the required year-long freshman class, "Exploration and Discovery," which is meant to introduce freshmen to the many areas covered in liberal arts.

Generally Friendly but Self-Aware

Lewis and Clark's small size and relatively large international population facilitate friend groups based on extracurriculars and classes. While small friend groups are common, students emphasize that it isn't cliquey. "It's collections of people who are very, very close friends, but who all hang out with each other anyway," summed up one student. At the beginning of freshman year, people tend to make friends with those living nearest to them, but later, "it depends on what classes you're taking, what activities you're doing." Depending on the range of academic and extracurricular interests, this can lead to a diverse group of friends. "I'm friends with a lot of different people," one sophomore stated. Another student aptly summarized, "It's a weird collection of people all put together in somewhat harmony."

> "It's a weird collection of people all put together in somewhat harmony."

Despite this mixing of social groups, diversity is a big concern. Lewis and Clark's student population is fairly homogeneous when it comes to race, background, and political affiliations. Republican leanings are rare, as are religious conservatives. The school has been attempting to address these issues, but student sentiment indicates that they may be going about it in the wrong way. Never before a sporty school, Lewis and Clark has admitted many more athletes this year. "It's because they want more funding," one student claimed. "It's definitely a different kind of person that's coming in." Other opinions are more blunt: "If we wanted to go to a school for sports, we would go somewhere else."

This is not to imply the Lewis and Clark students don't have school pride—as is appropriate for their liberal reputation, it's just a more self-aware pride than in other places. Attending sporting events might not be as common, especially among the less-athletically-inclined upperclassmen, but "there's school pride but it's like a mocking pride . . . It's mocking but it's also that we own it, we understand it."

What do these self-aware students do if they aren't playing or watching football? As one might expect, activities vary wildly. Many students get involved in the organizing of symposiums, themed events that bring in speakers to give lectures and debates addressing issues like gender or the environment. Others put their creative talents to good use by DJing their own radio shows. Freshmen year is frequently taken up with trying a lot of the various extracurriculars, and people become more committed during sophomore year. It can be harder to stay involved after sophomore year because many upperclassmen move off campus and "getting back for a seven o'clock meeting isn't as worthwhile."

When not participating in clubs and organizations, Lewis and Clark students can often be found in Portland. People go during the week just for the food carts, coffee houses, and festivals. The city is only a short ride away on "the RAZ," a bus that shuttles until 2 am on Fridays and Saturdays. Back on campus, however, "there's always something going on." Students get excited about on-campus dances and theater shows as well as nearby house parties that usually feature student bands. These parties usually have some alcohol or marijuana, but although "it exists at any college," binge drinking isn't a real problem, and neither are hard drugs. Students will also occasionally indulge in alcohol or pot in their dorm rooms with friends, and while the former is technically not allowed unless all present are 21, punishment if caught "depends on the level of what you're doing." Frats are also not a problem—in fact, there aren't any since a wealthy donor stipulated that they be removed, and students don't appear to miss them.

Manor House and Mountain Views

Students are required to live on campus throughout their freshmen and sophomore years, after which most upperclassmen chose to live in nearby houses or in the school's apartment-style living accommodations. Dorms are often themed by floor or by building, so people can live in "language" dorms, "outdoors" dorms, "environmental" dorms, and "substance free" dorms, among others. While each floor does have an RA, their primary function is in providing a sense of community rather than doling out discipline. Rooming is determined by a list of each student's top three choices for freshmen and by a lottery system for all the other years. Unless, that is, students stay in the same room with the same roommate and become "squatters," in which case their rooming is guaranteed. "It's really tough to get a single as a freshman," one student said, and while it's easier for upperclassmen, it's still not by any means ensured.

The buildings on campus are worked on fairly frequently and so all seem new enough, although some are worse than others. For example, "the Forest dorms are the worst in terms of facilities." Apart from dorms, students praise the "really beautiful reflecting pool," "views of downtown and Mount Hood," and the Frank Manor House, the admissions building one student described as "adorable." The library is a popular study spot, and on nice days students can often be found in the campus's designated smoking areas. Another area for meetings is the Student Center, a co-op with food, chairs, and tables, but it has been shut down for a semester with plans to re-open again before the academic year is out.

There is one dining hall, affectionately called "The Bon" after the catering service Bon Appetit. Students report general satisfaction with the food, saying, "people complain about it, but we have good food compared to a lot of other schools." What seems to be more of an issue is the meal plan, which is currently all-you-can-eat but will be shortly changing to a la carte. Students are not allowed to take food out of the dining hall and report that they feel uncomfortable paying ten dollars for what sometimes amounts to "a coffee and a banana." One sophomore concluded, "I wish I could not be on the meal plan, especially because I can't take food out . . . I feel like I'm being watched."

Lewis and Clark students do not claim their school is perfect. They question their administrations' choices about the meal plan, the housing rules, admissions, and class capping. But this refusal to accept the status quo is characteristic of Lewis and Clark's students, who are not happy to let the same mistakes be made again and again. Plus, the administration appears to respond to student opinions and listen to what they have to say. And despite their reservations, Lewis and Clark students claim the beautiful campus, easy access to Portland, small classes, and devoted teachers are things they can't imagine living without: "knowing what I know now, I would *definitely* make the same decision again."—*Erin Maher*

FYI
The typical weekend schedule is "do homework, go into Portland, go to some awesome food cart, go to the coffee shops, sleep in late, have brunch, play board games."
What differentiates Lewis and Clark the most from other colleges is "our cynical self-awareness."
Three things every student should do at Lewis and Clark before graduating are: "win the Bon (the Bon is the cafeteria, and winning it means you're the last person in there), go to the food carts on Hawthorne at 3 a.m. drunk, and fall asleep in front of the library fireplace during a night of intense studying."

Oregon State University

Address: 104 Kerr Administration Building, Corvallis, OR 97331-2106
Phone: 541-737-4411
E-mail address: osuamit@oregonstate.edu
Web site URL: www.oregonstate.edu
Year Founded: 1858
Private or Public: Public
Religious Affiliation: None
Location: Suburban
Number of Applicants: 11,428
Percent Accepted: 81%
Percent Accepted who enroll: 36%
Number Entering: 3,355
Number of Transfers Accepted each Year: Unreported
Middle 50% SAT range: M: 490–610, CR: 460–590, Wr: 450–560
Middle 50% ACT range: 21–26
Early admission program EA/ED/None: EA

Percentage accepted through EA or ED: Unreported
EA and ED deadline: 1-Nov
Regular Deadline: 1-Sep
Application Fee: $50
Full time Undergraduate enrollment: 16,382
Total enrollment: 19,559
Percent Male: 53%
Percent Female: 47%
Total Percent Minority or Unreported: 34%
Percent African-American: 1%
Percent Asian/Pacific Islander: 7%
Percent Hispanic: 5%
Percent Native American: 1%
Percent International: 3%
Percent in-state/out of state: 83%/17%
Percent from Public HS: Unreported
Retention Rate: 83%

Graduation Rate 4-year: Unreported
Graduation Rate 6-year: Unreported
Percent Undergraduates in On-campus housing: 21%
Number of official organized extracurricular organizations: 350
3 Most popular majors: Business, Health, Human Development and Family Studies
Student/Faculty ratio: 25: 1
Average Class Size: 26
Percent of students going to grad school: Unreported
Tuition and Fees: $19,944
In-State Tuition and Fees if different: $6,228
Cost for Room and Board: $9,168
Percent receiving financial aid out of those who apply: 57%
Percent receiving financial aid among all students: 57%

The consensus among students at Oregon State University is that the privilege of being a Beaver is worth the constant rain in Corvallis, Oregon, a quintessential college town settled on the banks of the Willamette River in northwestern Oregon. While many students report much satisfaction with their school choice, many also struggle to define what differentiates OSU from other universities. One student echoed the thoughts of his peers when he called OSU "pretty typical for its size." Still, Oregon State offers top-notch engineering, agriculture and business programs, and those prepared to embrace a small town at the expense of cultural diversity will find a strong sense of community and a spirited atmosphere at Oregon State University.

Freshman Year, Stadium Style
Graduating from Oregon State requires a strong foundation in what the university calls the Baccalaureate Core. While some of these courses focus on basic skills such as mathematics and writing, others are designed to prepare students to participate in

contemporary dialogue on topics such as "Social Processes and Institutions" and "Western Culture." Most students reflect on the "Bacc Core" with positive feelings and enjoy having common ground with all their classmates. In one senior's words, "I found it pretty enjoyable. If the Core weren't in place, most people would never take classes in, for example, 'Difference, Power and Discrimination.'" That said, another consequence of the Core is that the majority of students' classes in the first two years are part of the Core requirements, and therefore tend to be lecture classes. Students complain that these classes often have as many as 400 students and are not as challenging as they would like. Pair these required classes with introductory-level courses for large, popular majors (like those in the College of Business, which also accommodate hundreds of students in large lecture halls) and the early years at OSU can feel very impersonal. Because of a limited number of choices of lower-level Core classes, registration can be a nightmare. Students who fail to plan carefully or register early are sometimes left with no option except to remain at the university a semester or a year longer than planned to get the credits they need. The problem is exacerbated for students in small or new departments. In the words of one sophomore majoring in New Media Communications, "A lot of classes are only offered once a year, so students like me have to plan their schedules very carefully." Four years can also turn into five when students retake classes in which they weren't satisfied with their grade, or change majors multiple times.

Many students choose to attend Oregon State on the strength of its engineering and forestry programs, which are well-respected and have competitive application processes and high standards for accepted students. The university is also home to an Honors College, which offers an Honors degree and smaller classes, lending students a sense of greater intimacy while still providing the broad range of classes available at a large university. OSU's College of Business, already the umbrella for a number of popular majors, recently reorganized itself in a Professional School model and a career-oriented focus, and has become increasingly popular since then. Programs in fashion design and retail management are also favorites and many students consider them to be challenging. A common thread connecting the most popular departments and courses at Oregon State is immediate applicability—students' favorite classes are the ones in which professors impart real-world experience and design a curriculum with potential for direct application to the job market.

Students say they find professors to be accessible and friendly at office hours, and reliable about responding to e-mails. This proves critical for students who take online classes that rely on electronic communication exclusively. Many students use former professors to plug gaps in the academic advising system, which can be hit-or-miss. Advisors are in short supply and "don't like to meet with you very often," one junior said. "We're a large university, so it's easy to fall through the cracks," said another student. Career Services, however, is a bright spot. The office offers a sizable job fair each semester—and occasionally job fairs dedicated exclusively to the very popular engineering programs—and many companies in the Pacific Northwest recruit on campus. Career advisors can also direct students to a one-time class in which students pay eight dollars for training in dining and networking etiquette, as well as to a for-credit class on professional development where students learn the ins and outs of résumé and cover letter writing and practice interviewing.

Geeked Out For Greeks

The Greek system at Oregon State University is flourishing. Greek parties are major social events on weekends, and various Greek houses throw annual themed parties which students, affiliated or not, say they look forward to. OSU's campus is dry only for underage students, and even the Office of Student Conduct and Affairs acknowledges that alcohol is widely used on campus. Students agree that drinking is an ingrained feature of the social experience at the university. In one sophomore's words, "Sure, you can not drink. People will judge you, but you can make that decision." Both the Greek system and house parties are accessible to students of all ages, but the social scene opens up for undergraduates when they turn twenty-one and can access the bars in Corvallis, which are popular hangouts for upperclassmen. One student added that a fun activity for students who don't enjoy structured parties or the bar scene is simply "getting together with friends to have a drink and watch a basketball game."

Students at Oregon State University appreciate the outdoorsy campus atmosphere.

Boating and swimming activities on the Willamette are popular in warm weather, and Corvallis boasts an impressive network of jogging and biking trails. "The ocean's about an hour away, and so are the mountains. You've kind of got it all, and not everyone can say that," one junior said enthusiastically. And of course, with so much rain, the city is perennially green, which makes for "a really pretty campus," another student said. Residents of Corvallis, meanwhile, embrace the university culture and students. "People are friendly when they find out you're a student," one junior noted, and even people not affiliated with the university call themselves Beavers and support the OSU teams.

For all their enjoyment of the area, students make no bones about the size of Corvallis and the attendant dearth of novel things to do. The nearest major retail stores and movie theaters are in Albany, about 15 miles away, which makes a car a necessity. Many students at Oregon State hail from the area and so have an easy time bringing a car to campus, and a less-easy time finding parking. A number of students maintain an even stronger tie to home and choose to live with their parents while attending OSU. These, along with the students who buy houses with friends or lease off-campus apartments, rather than reside in university dorms, make up the majority of the student body. Freshmen are "sort of expected to live in the dorms," one sophomore said; most students plug into social life on campus by way of the friends they make in these early living arrangements. After freshman year, groups of friends move off campus together but stay close to and still spend much time on the campus, which is considered very safe at night. On-campus dining options are more than tolerable, if repetitive, and have flexible hours. Students can use money on their student IDs at a Carl's Jr. on campus, should they really need a culinary escape, and there are numerous fast-food restaurants within walking distance. One senior characterized the Corvallis dining experience as "generally quick, in and out in 10 minutes or less."

Ducks and Beavers, Oh My

As one sophomore put it, "If you're a Duck or a Beaver, you're nothing else." The Ducks, of course, are the OSU rivals at the University of Oregon in Eugene. In preparation for the annual football match between the universities—known fondly as the Civil War game—the state of Oregon divides its allegiances with no looking back. With increasing successes, the Oregon State University football team has the whole of Corvallis behind it, and the baseball team enjoys similar successes and support. The Beaver Dam is a club for student supporters of the OSU Beavers and is one of the most popular clubs on campus, since a one-time $15 fee entitles members to priority seating at games. One student recalled that upon visiting campus, he was struck by "the huge number of people wearing the school colors, more than I'd seen anywhere else."

Student government, in the form of the Associated Students of Oregon State University (ASOSU), is also active and effective, with good access to university administration and much student support. Many students participate in the university's Senate, and students generally appreciate the events the ASOSU brings to campus, including stand-up comedians and a battle of the bands. Recently, a group of professional snowboarders visited the campus and brought their own snow to perform demonstrations. Intramural sports are popular on campus, the most prominent being volleyball and flag football, and many students make frequent use of the athletic facilities in Dixon Recreation Center.

> "The ocean's about an hour away, and so are the mountains. You've kind of got it all, and not everyone can say that."

The OSU administration is proud of the number of cultural houses on its campus, but one member of the Hispanic Cultural Center was quick to point out that having many cultural houses does not necessarily equal diversity. He added, "I guess for someone who's never been in a diverse community before, it could be new and diverse-seeming, but if you come from another culture, it can feel like you've never seen so many white people in one spot." But few students complain of attitudes of intolerance on campus, ostensibly in part because of the explicit inclusion of coursework on diversity in the Bacc Core.

Students at Oregon State University celebrate "a real sense of togetherness," in the words of one student, even if they are unable to identify quite what it is that bonds them or sets them apart. Many students are surprised by "how small the school feels, and how you see people you know everywhere you go," even though the university is home to tens of thousands of students. In short, students who seek what is in many ways the prototypical college experience—a strong football and Greek-oriented culture at a large university—will likely have no regrets about choosing to attend Oregon State University. —*Elizabeth Woods*

FYI

If you come to Oregon State University, you'd better bring "a rain jacket. If you bring an umbrella, the native Oregonians will think you're from California and can't handle the rain."

What's the typical weekend schedule? "Drive to Portland for an afternoon in the city on Saturday, come back for a game Saturday night, stay up late at parties with friends, sleep in and do work on Sunday."

If I could change one thing about Oregon State University, I'd "locate it in a bigger city with more to do."

Three things every student should do at Oregon State University before graduating are: "float the Willamette River, go jogging in the rain, and go to the Civil War football game."

Reed College

Address: 3203 SE Woodstock Boulevard, Portland, OR 97202-8199
Phone: 800-547-4750
E-mail address: admission@reed.edu
Web site URL: www.reed.edu
Year Founded: 1909
Private or Public: Private
Religious Affiliation: None
Location: Urban
Number of Applicants: 3,075
Percent Accepted: 43%
Percent Accepted who enroll: 28%
Number Entering: 373
Number of Transfers Accepted each Year: 82
Middle 50% SAT range: M: 640–710, CR:670–750, Wr: 660–730
Middle 50% ACT range: 30–33
Early admission program EA/ED/None: ED

Percentage accepted through EA or ED: 56%
EA and ED deadline: 15-Nov
Regular Deadline: 15-Jan
Application Fee: $50
Full time Undergraduate enrollment: 1,407
Total enrollment: 1,447
Percent Male: 44%
Percent Female: 56%
Total Percent Minority or Unreported: 44%
Percent African-American: 2%
Percent Asian/Pacific Islander: 6%
Percent Hispanic: 4%
Percent Native American: <1%
Percent International: 5%
Percent in-state/out of state: 13%/87%
Percent from Public HS: 59%
Retention Rate: 90%

Graduation Rate 4-year: 59%
Graduation Rate 6-year: 78%
Percent Undergraduates in On-campus housing: 67%
Number of official organized extracurricular organizations: 130
3 Most popular majors: English, Psychology, Anthropology
Student/Faculty ratio: 10:1
Average Class Size: 15
Percent of students going to grad school: 65%
Tuition and Fees: $42,540
In-State Tuition and Fees if different: No difference
Cost for Room and Board: $11,050
Percent receiving financial aid out of those who apply: 53%
Percent receiving financial aid among all students: 54%

If there's a word to describe Reed College in a nutshell, it would undoubtedly be quirky. A small school in Portland, Oregon, Reed is known for its eclectic student body, intense academic environment, engaged professors, and beautiful campus. Reed is far from a stereotypical college—it has no sororities, fraternities, or football team—and its students like it that way. If you're an open-minded intellectual who doesn't like the prep or jock factor of many other selective schools, you will feel at home at Reed.

An Academic Pressure Cooker

Reed is not a place for the faint of heart: Reedies are quick to admit that their classes are highly demanding. "Just to get by, you need to do a LOT of work," one junior commented. Reed students expect a high workload and are prepared to spend many hours with their noses in their books. "I spend the majority of my time in the library or at a coffee shop, studying," another student remarked. No matter their major, most students said that they tend to stress about their work. "A significant portion of each weekend needs to be devoted to homework if you want to do well," a sophomore lamented.

However, all those hours of work are made more bearable by the college's brilliant and approachable faculty. Thanks to the fact that all classes are taught by professors (there are no TAs at Reed), many students develop close relationships with their teachers. In fact, students tend to call their profs by their first names. "My professors are interested in me both as a person and a student," one junior said. Being invited out for lunch or to a professor's home is not uncommon. "The professors here are unlike those you'll encounter anywhere else," one student said. Reed emphasizes discussion-based classes, so large lectures are uncommon. Students give professors high marks for knowledge of their subjects and the quality of their teaching.

Students say that all majors and classes are considered rigorous, and noted that "easy majors" are virtually nonexistent. That said, science majors are known for being especially challenging, particularly physics. Popular majors include English, Psychology, and Anthropology. The school's specialized International and Comparative Policy Studies major is also highly regarded. Although Reed is better known for its humanities programs, students noted that more and more students are choosing to major in the sciences. The school even has a student-run nuclear reactor on campus, the only one in the country operated primarily by undergraduates.

The required freshman humanities course and the senior thesis are considered two of the school's toughest classes, but students have few complaints about them. Humanities 110, taken by all students during their first year, gives freshman a crash course in the classics, from the *Odyssey* to *Nicomachean Ethics*. "It will kick your butt, but you'll learn how to write a paper," one junior laughed. "Plus, being forced to read all the classics is a good experience, and I don't think I would have done it in my own." Students say the shared pain helps unify the student body and provides a solid academic foundation for their next three years at Reed.

While undoubtedly free-spirited, Reed students are also extremely intellectual and focused students. "Nobody at Reed is here just to get a degree," one junior stated simply. "Everyone is passionate about something, whether it's Russian or biology or linguistics," a sophomore observed. "The one thing we all have in common is that we all love learning and books." Perhaps unsurprisingly, a very high proportion of Reed graduates go on to earn PhDs, particularly in the sciences, history, and political science.

> **"Nobody at Reed is here just to get a degree."**

Students get to show off their non-academic talents during Paideia, an annual event that takes place just before the beginning of spring semester. For about ten days, anyone in the Reed community—including students—can teach a non-credit course in any subject they choose. Although the topics change every year, past offerings have included off-the-wall courses such as "Introduction to Portland Geology" and "Underwater Basket Weaving"—seriously, the class actually exists.

Reed's unusual grading system epitomizes the school's unique approach to education. While students receive written feedback from their professors, students don't learn what their letter grades are unless they request them. Students say this unique approach helps them focus on achieving their personal academic goals rather than earning straight A's—which is unlikely anyway, since the school is famous for not inflating grades. "It's not that Reedies are slackers—just the opposite, actually," one junior said. "It's more that we believe in learning for learning's sake."

Work Hard, Play Hard

It's difficult to describe the stereotypical Reed student. As one junior commented, "We're so different—there just is no average Reed student." While students admit that "there are a lot of hipsters and crunchy-granola types," they are quick to point out "there are still a lot of people who aren't." Students report that there are no traditional social hierarchies or divisions between different types of students. Since Reed has no Greek life or varsity sports program, there are no stereotypical frat guys or jocks, either. Instead, Reed's most popular sports teams are men's Ultimate Frisbee and women's rugby. Students also work up a sweat completing the college's physical education requirement, which they can complete with classes like juggling, sailing, and fencing. The college has a cabin on nearby Mount Hood for students to go skiing during snowy winter weekends.

When they're not at the library, most Reed students spend a lot of time on their extracurricular activities, and the school boasts over eighty student clubs and organizations. Popular groups include the Bike Co-Op and the campus radio station, KRRC. The college is also home to a number of off-beat clubs like Beer Nation, which sets up and runs beer gardens throughout the year, and the Association of Reed Gamers, which hosts biweekly game nights and magic tournaments. Funding for extracurricular organizations is decided by students each semester.

Their heavy workload doesn't stop Reedies from partying, either. The biggest celebration of the year is Renaissance Fayre, or "Renn Fayre," a former Renaissance festival that is now a campus-wide theme party. "Renn Fayre is THE event of the year," one student said. "No one should miss it." "Stop Making Sense," a spring video-dance party, and the Harvest Ball, a Halloween dance, were also cited as favorite annual events.

The school has a reputation for heavy drug and alcohol consumption at parties and other events, so much so that Reed students are sometimes called "Weedies." Students said that while some students do take drugs, most Reedies are not quite so wild. One student described her impression of the campus climate: "It's true that Reedies do like to experiment, and that can include drugs and alcohol. But I've never felt pressured to do anything—people respect your choices." Another shared her belief that "the administration gives us the freedom to make our own choices about our lives, and that extends to drugs and alcohol."

In part because of all the publicity about Reed's permissive drug culture, the administration is now taking measures to discourage substance use. Those who don't want to socialize under the influence can live in Reed's substance-free dorm (nicknamed "Sub-Free") or take part in a range of substance-free activities sponsored by the college. However, the school's liberal Honor Principle, which allows students to behave as they like as long as they don't harm or embarrass another student, means a tough crackdown on alcohol is unlikely. "The idea of the Honor Principle is that it allows us to govern ourselves—we're

given autonomy and want to maintain it," one junior said proudly. Students say the school's policy allows students to discuss drugs and alcohol openly, as well seek help for friends who have had too much, without fear of being punished. The Honor Principle also extends to academics, meaning that students don't need a proctor to take an exam and can take their finals anywhere they please—their rooms, the library, or even the Canyon, a wilderness area in the middle of campus.

Between difficult classes, heavy involvement in extracurricular organizations, and plentiful parties, it's no surprise that Reedies rarely get eight hours of sleep a night. "There's definitely a 'stress culture' at Reed," one student noted. But another said that productive students can have it all: "Just shut up and do your work and you'll be fine."

Eating it Up
Reed's dining hall fare was highly praised. "A lot of Reedies are secret foodies, and the dining hall is pretty good," one student confided. Commons, Reed's cafeteria, won high marks for its variety, especially its meat-free options. "Reed is the friendliest place in the world if you're vegetarian or vegan," a vegetarian student raved. Commons is the only dining hall, but Caffé Paradisio, on the other side of campus, offers sandwiches and other quick bites for those looking for a change of scene.

The one complaint students have about their meal plans is the cost. All students start off the semester with a certain amount of money, known as Commons Cash, that gets used up as they purchase food. Each item costs a certain amount of Commons Cash, meaning students must budget the amount of money they spend at each meal. Many find themselves faced with a dwindling balance before the end of the semester, forcing them to add money to their accounts or seek nourishment in Portland.

However, getting out into the city might not be such a bad thing: despite the Portland's funky, offbeat vibe, students say that they rarely find the time to venture out of the "Reed Bubble." Those that do say it is well worth the short trip off campus. "I don't think most people take advantage of Portland, which is too bad," one junior said. "It's such a young person's city." Those that make it into town often ride a bike, since the city is well-equipped with bike lanes and paths. Students enjoy frequenting the city's many tempting restaurants, including many that are owned or run by Reed alumni. Powell's, the city's largest independent bookstore, is another popular student destination.

Living the Life of the Mind

Reed's buildings are a mix of traditional and modern architecture. The green, wooded campus provides a calm respite from the stress of academic life. Reed students live in a mix of on-campus dorms and off-campus houses. All dorms are co-ed and not separated by grade. Dorms vary in size, age, and desirability, but students say they enjoy the social atmosphere regardless of their location.

After freshman year, students who wish to remain on campus enter a housing lottery or apply to live in a theme dorm or a language house. The Grove, four new houses built in 2008, are known as some of the nicest digs on campus, with Old Dorm Block also earning high praise. "There's not really a bad dorm, and most have really nice amenities. I haven't heard of anyone who hates where they live," one sophomore said. RAs live on each floor and offer advice and study breaks, not supervision. Many upperclassmen move off campus, although most don't stray too far: the majority of off-campus students live within a 10-minute bike ride of the school. The college even offers advice about finding a place to live and navigating the difficulties of off-campus life.

Though they admit that Reed "isn't for everyone" and caution that "Reed favors a kind of maturity that a lot of undergraduates don't have," Reedies couldn't be happier with their college. A visit to campus should help determine if Reed's bohemian, intellectual, silly, and serious atmosphere is a good fit. As one junior said, "Reed will change your life. It's the perfect balance between freedom and structure, independence and rigor. Just be ready to hit the books!"—*Elizabeth Chrystal*

FYI

If you come to Reed, you'd better bring "a solid work ethic and a good pair of rain boots. It rains a lot in the Pacific Northwest!"

The typical weekend schedule is "Friday—unwind, go to at least one on-campus party or dance party at the Student Union (SU); Saturday—go out off-campus; Sunday—spend time doing work you should have been doing Friday and Saturday!"

If I could change one thing about Reed, I would "encourage students to be more involved in the Portland community."

University of Oregon

Address: 1217 University of Oregon, Eugene, OR 97403
Phone: 800-232-3825
E-mail address: uoadmit@uoregon.edu
Web site URL: www.uoregon.edu
Year Founded: 1876
Private or Public: Public
Religious Affiliation: None
Location: Urban
Number of Applicants: 23,012
Percent Accepted: 73%
Percent Accepted who enroll: 11%
Number Entering: 1,812
Number of Transfers Accepted each Year: 2,394
Middle 50% SAT range: M: 500–610, CR: 490–610, Wr: Unreported
Middle 50% ACT range: Unreported
Early admission program EA/ED/None: EA

Percentage accepted through EA or ED: Unreported
EA and ED deadline: 1-Nov
Regular Deadline: 15-Jan
Application Fee: $50
Full time Undergraduate enrollment: 19,528
Total enrollment: 23,342
Percent Male: 47%
Percent Female: 53%
Total Percent Minority or Unreported: 28%
Percent African-American: 2%
Percent Asian/Pacific Islander: 6%
Percent Hispanic: 6%
Percent Native American: 1%
Percent International: 5%
Percent in-state/out of state: 53%/47%
Percent from Public HS: Unreported
Retention Rate: 84%

Graduation Rate 4-year: 65%
Graduation Rate 6-year: Unreported
Percent Undergraduates in On-campus housing: 19%
Number of official organized extracurricular organizations: 250
3 Most popular majors: Social Sciences, Journalism, Business/Marketing
Student/Faculty ratio: 20:1
Average Class Size: 20
Percent of students going to grad school: Unreported
Tuition and Fees: $27,653
In-State Tuition and Fees if different: $8,789
Cost for Room and Board: $9,801
Percent receiving financial aid out of those who apply: 65%
Percent receiving financial aid among all students: 44%

Located in Eugene, the University of Oregon is a big school by numbers and a liberal arts school by heart. Boasting intelligent and approachable professors alongside a powerhouse football program, Oregon is full of school spirit despite the often dismal weather.

Relaxed Academic Environment

Academically, Oregon offers the best of both a large research university and a liberal arts curriculum. With scores of classes to choose from and accessible faculty, students find themselves in a "relaxed academic environment" where they can explore diverse subjects and create close relationships to professors. It is true that for many introduction level classes, students may find themselves surrounded by hundreds of their classmates—one student reported a class of around 500. However, these classes are often tempered with really small discussion sections and a wide range of seminar-style classes.

To encourage students to explore new subjects, Oregon developed a general education curriculum. To earn a typical bachelor's degree, students must take classes in three "areas of human knowledge"—arts and letters, social science, and science. In addition, students interested in a Bachelor of Arts must fulfill a foreign language requirement, and students pursuing a Bachelor of Science must study math. Students find the requirements somewhat irritating, but one student summed them up perfectly. "You end up getting a broader education," she said. "It's annoying, but it's worth it."

With almost 80 majors, finding an interesting subject matter isn't an issue. Students cited the psychology, business, and journalism departments as particularly popular. For ambitious students, there is the opportunity to double major or explore Oregon's scores of minors and several certificates.

In addition, Oregon is home to the Robert D. Clark Honors College, the oldest of its kind. With its separate application and more rigorous admissions process (with an additional essay required), the Clark Honors College is home to 200 or so incoming students each year. They are required to take several different classes and write a thesis to earn a diploma, but they can take advantage of an average class size of 19, student: teacher ratio of 18:1, and a smaller community.

The biggest change from high school academics, students said, was the increased amount of reading and emphasis on tests. However, the professors are there from day one to ease the transition. They encourage students to use them as a resource. One freshman mentioned that "most have quite a few office hours during the week and want to meet with students or help with questions." Some professors offer office hours in cafés. Another offers an even better incentive— students that attend office hours are entered into a drawing whose winners get a dinner with the professor and homemade apple pie. "All the professors I've had are really low-key, laid-back and very approachable," said one student. "Don't get me wrong though; there's always those few who aren't any of these things, but I like to believe and I have experienced that most professors are pretty good," another added.

> **"Within minutes of being on campus, I could just tell that I would be really happy here and I was right."**

All in all, it is not too difficult to do well, if you "do what you're supposed to do, listen in class," and make use of the incredible resources Oregon presents. One student noted that "some classes are pretty difficult and you need to work hard to do well and others are more laid-back. It's really great when you get a schedule with a good mixture."

Outside the Classroom
At the end of the week, Oregon students are pumped to catch up on sleep and have a lot of fun. A typical weekend is very relaxed, with time to hang out with friends and "catch up online with TV shows." Nights often involve partying within the Oregon community. A freshman in a sorority said that sororities and fraternities were "dominant in our life" but didn't have too much of a presence for the rest of campus. That being said, there are many Greek parties over the course of any given weekend.

Oregon is a dry campus, with drinking prohibited within the dorms, fraternities and sororities. With a "Greek police" that goes after those seen holding a beer, students are much more likely to "pre-game" and drink before going to a party. In addition, marijuana is very prevalent on campus, for those who are interested.

Dorms are the center of life for most freshmen, though after a year in the dorms, many upperclassmen move to off-campus apartments. Prior to arriving in Oregon, students fill out surveys indicating their personalities, cleanliness, and music choice, among other things, to help Oregon pair up compatible students. One student said that "dorms are a great way of meeting people . . . during the beginning of the year it's really easy to meet people if you're open to it."

Generally, there are two RAs per hall, whose jobs are to organize activities, keep the peace, and, if you're lucky, make spaghetti dinners. Students described them as "like camp counselors, but less in your face."

Students love the campus, full of "brick buildings, trees, and grass everywhere." One student is particularly a fan of the Frolf (Frisbee golf) course, which "shows the beauty of what is on campus." Oregon is not too big of a school, and while many students have bikes, one student estimated that "at a really slow, leisurely walk" it would take less than 10 minutes to get from her dorm to her farthest class.

Eugene, Oregon, is a small city centered around the university. Students feel very attached to Eugene culture. "The whole town loves the Ducks," one student said. Though homelessness in Eugene is an issue, students describe the campus as pretty safe. "If it's at night, you walk with a friend and make good decisions," said a freshman, who was comforted by the fact that "cops are everywhere, and everything is lit."

There are a couple of dining halls, which have different specialties. Though there is a grocery store nearby, many students see cooking as a "hassle rather than a convenience." Students cited Hamilton's fish tacos, Caron's lamb kabobs, and the New England clam chowder as being particularly good.

Mighty Ducks
Oregon students take pride in the school's stellar athletic program, especially its prowess as a Division I football powerhouse. "Sports are huge here!" one student said, saying that the school is "all about football because we have a good team." Football games

are especially amazing—it is likely that at some point in their Oregon career, many students will boast a Facebook profile picture of them screaming at a football game and wearing a duck mouth.

Besides football, the baseball, volleyball, and lacrosse teams are fan favorites. For those lacking unbelievable athletic skills, many students go running on their own and "everyone does at least one intramural sport."

It's Gray, Not Grey

Located in the Pacific Northwest, Oregon gets plenty of rain. However, don't have too negative an outlook. One student said he was surprised that it hadn't actually rained as much as he expected.

At the end of the day, Oregon is still a big school with over 20,000 students. The concept of a community is still very tricky. "When it comes to sports," one student said, "our community (students and faculty) all comes together and it is quite amazing. When sports are not involved, we could easily just be random strangers to each other."

However, most students don't regret their decision to come to Oregon for a second. One student said that he never expected to go to Oregon. "But within minutes of being on campus, I could just tell that I would be really happy here and I was right."—*Mason Kroll*

FYI

If you come to Oregon, you'd better bring "rain boots and an umbrella."

What surprised me the most about Oregon was "how friendly everyone was."

If I could change one thing about Oregon, I'd "change the rain into sun, because when the sun is out and the weather is somewhat warm, the campus is so beautiful and it is so great being outside."

Willamette University

Address: 900 State Street, Salem, OR 97301

Phone: 503-370-6303

E-mail address: libarts@willamette.edu

Web site URL: www.willamette.edu

Year Founded: 1842

Private or Public: Private

Religious Affiliation: Methodist

Location: Urban

Number of Applicants: 2,983

Percent Accepted: 57%

Percent Accepted who enroll: 19%

Number Entering: 617

Number of Transfers Accepted each Year: 92

Middle 50% SAT range: M: 540–650, CR: 560–670, Wr: 540–650

Middle 50% ACT range: 26–30

Early admission program EA/ED/None: EA

Percentage accepted through EA or ED: 58%

EA and ED deadline: 1-Dec

Regular Deadline: Rolling

Application Fee: $50

Full time Undergraduate enrollment: 2,099

Total enrollment: 2,968

Percent Male: 42%

Percent Female: 58%

Total Percent Minority or Unreported: 38%

Percent African-American: 2%

Percent Asian/Pacific Islander: 6%

Percent Hispanic: 6%

Percent Native American: 1%

Percent International: <1%

Percent in-state/out of state: 27%/73 %

Percent from Public HS: 80%

Retention Rate: 87%

Graduation Rate 4-year: 72%

Graduation Rate 6-year: 73%

Percent Undergraduates in On-campus housing: 71%

Number of official organized extracurricular organizations: 107

3 Most popular majors: Social Sciences, Foreign Lang. & Lit., English

Student/Faculty ratio: 10:1

Average Class Size: 15

Percent of students going to grad school: 27%

Tuition and Fees: $39,012

In-State Tuition and Fees if different: No difference

Cost for Room and Board: $9,350

Percent receiving financial aid out of those who apply: 66%

Percent receiving financial aid among all students: 65%

With majestic brick buildings and a stream running through campus, Willamette University, the first on the West Coast, offers a quintessential liberal arts education in the heart of Salem, Oregon. Willamette students treat college as a time to branch out and discover their passions, from Frisbee to scuba diving. Though the rain-heavy winters can be a bit dreary, close friendships and a glowing community give Willamette students a love of their school and a love of learning.

Emphasis on Inquiry

Students consider the best part of a Willamette education the intimate classroom setting. With an average class size of 15, even popular introductory level classes have no more than 30 students. In such a small class, professors always know their students on a personal basis, encouraging them to ask questions. Professors are "very passionate about what they do," keeping classes interesting and very fluid. "If the conversation takes them elsewhere, they can follow," said one sophomore, who loved the interesting class discussions.

Willamette students also enjoy an extensive class selection, with classes ranging from "Men Looking at Women: a Study of Film" to "Writing Political Humor." Students consider Willamette's music department especially incredible, though they say that music and chemistry majors are notoriously difficult.

Like their counterparts at most liberal arts institutions, Willamette students must complete Gen Ed (general education) requirements, including foreign language, four writing-centered courses, and two Quantitative and Analytical Reasoning courses. In addition, students must take classes in each of six modes of inquiry: Understanding the Natural World; Creating in the Arts; Analyzing Arguments, Reasons, and Values; Thinking Historically; Interpreting Texts; and Understanding Society.

Students are rarely frustrated by these requirements; as many Willamette students initially are undeclared, they use the fulfillment of these requirements as a path to explore their own interests and take classes outside of their comfort zones. In addition, most people go way beyond the requirements, with a large percentage completing either a major and a minor or a double major.

Some students find it difficult for non-majors to get into certain classes, especially arts classes where classes are small and demand is high. However, another student said that with persistence, professors are understanding: "For the most part, if you show up you can get into any class."

> "Everyone kind of knows everyone. Walking to and from class, you'll know every third person."

Workloads can be light or heavy, depending on class selection. "I didn't get into really hard classes, so I have about 2 hours of work a night," one freshman stated. "But I have friends that don't have lives because they have so much homework." Early risers are in for a shock; one student noted, "You don't really go to bed before 10 o'clock." Students who wish to do well must remember to put the proper effort into their classes. "If you study hard and do your homework it will reflect on your grades," one student said. "It's not difficult to get an A, it just means a lot of work."

A Small Pond

"Everyone kind of knows everyone," one student said. "Walking to and from class, you'll know every third person." "People know how you're doing, what you're up to and who you are much more than other, bigger schools," another added. Students find everyone at the school friendly, open-minded and accepting, and feel comfortable to be themselves in every situation. From the beginning, students form close friendships, whether on pre-orientation trips ("Four years later, everyone on those trips are still super bonded," a student said), through classes, or in the dorms.

Dorms are a big part of social life, with weekly activities from midnight munchies every Monday to game nights on Thursdays. Separated mainly into east side and west side, dorms often throw parties and, on Halloween, the Willamette International Studies House even redecorates as a Haunted House. Also, there are some themed ones, such as the outdoor adventure house and a substance-free one. While there are RAs on almost every floor, students agree they are pretty relaxed and chill, not out to get you.

Most people stay on campus over the weekends, but some leave to go home or to concerts in nearby Seattle or Portland (the latter around one hour away). Though there's not much to do in downtown Salem, on- and off-campus parties dominate the weekend social scene. Greek life is very prevalent on campus, but definitely doesn't overtake the rest of the social scene.

While there is a lot of drinking and a good deal of marijuana, a large amount of the student body doesn't drink at all—in fact, two out of the five fraternities are substance-free. School policy on underage drinking is understanding; if students get caught, there is an education system rather than a punishment system. According to a sophomore, students go to a hearing where they think about "how their actions have affected the community, and what they can do to make up for what they've taken from the community."

Sundays are often study days, and students take advantage of the beautiful campus and nearby coffee shops to get their work done. On particularly sunny days, students set up chairs by the Mill Stream (which forms a W in the center of campus) and enjoy the weather. Students especially sing the praises of the Bistro, a student-run coffee shop with a nice vibe that always plays music and sells a bunch of yummy treats. Sunday nights also offer hefty discounts at nearby restaurants, especially at the Ram, an American barbeque "like Outback Steakhouse with less steak and less Australia," said a freshman.

With over 100 clubs and varying levels of commitment, students can find many ways to get involved outside the classroom. Becoming a member of a club is a great way to socialize. One of the biggest on campus is the outdoors club, which offers tons of hiking, camping, and other nature trips. *The Collegian*, Willamette's weekly newspaper, includes staff writers and a slew of contributing writers; anyone can write for it. To get your own show on WU Wire, Willamette's radio station, a sophomore, who hosts shows Wednesday evenings, said that "all you have to do is fill out an application and select your time slot."

If even planning a Hawaiian luau or learning to flame-juggle sounds dull, it is pretty easy to start a club. With a petition signed by at least 10 people, the student body council will fund a new club.

Many students take advantage of Willamette's central location in Salem, across the street from Oregon's capitol building. Internships and community service abound, both in the political arena and in the nearby elementary school and hospital. In fact, students often find local politicians eating in the Willamette dining halls.

Home of the Bearcats

In the early days of the school, Willamette's football coach commented that his team was "as strong as a bear and quick as a cat," thus beginning a long tradition of Bearcat athletics. Though Willamette is no means a sports-dominated school, it boasts 16 Division III teams and lots of school spirit. Especially when playing rival Linfield College, students will show up to the games en masse, often donning red-and-gold shirts given to them in the beginning of the year. One student noted that "your group of friends is from everywhere, and you hang out with pretty much everyone from the school," meaning that it's likely students will be cheering on their friends.

Students not so interested in varsity athletics still have tons of other options, especially in the form of club and intramural sports. Club sports can either be relatively competitive, such as the rugby and ultimate Frisbee teams, or skills building, such as the Juggle/Unicycle club and, for those who wish they were at Hogwarts, the Quidditch club.

Run through an online, Facebook-like system called Athleague, intramurals offer another chance to run around outside. With several traditional leagues and many tournaments (including paper football), students compete for the coveted intramural T-shirt. "If you wear an IM shirt on campus, you're a champion," said one sophomore who already has two under his belt.

Other Cultures Just a Skybridge Away

Nearly 50 years ago, Willamette established a strong connection with a school in Japan, and in 1985, the Tokyo International University in America (TIUA) was created minutes away from campus. Each year, 100–200 foreign exchange students come from Japan to study in America. Though sometimes they may be shy, don't be afraid to branch out; by the end of the year they warm up and some students even request a TIUA roommate. TIUA leads to a huge Japanese presence on campus, whether you're interested in Japanese studies, study abroad in East Asia, or the Japanese cuisine found daily in Kaneko Café (including sushi Tuesdays).

Willamette prides itself on stellar for-credit study abroad opportunities, offering many programs of its own during the school year and breaks and accepting most from other institutions. More than half of the student body engages in some program within their four years at school in countries ranging from Argentina to France to Ghana.

The Willamette Community

Students love living at Willamette. The campus itself is incredibly safe and people often leave their laptops in places for hours at a time and they aren't touched.

Willamette as a community aims to be very socially aware, constantly working hard to be more sustainable and reduce waste, with weekly trayless Tuesdays. In the main cafeteria, students say there is a push for organic and healthy food, and above every entrée lies a list of ingredients. In general, food is surprisingly good, and with a flexible meal plan, students can enjoy the particularly tasty desserts.

The four months of constant rain should not place a deterrent on anyone who wishes to attend Willamette. "As long as you have rain boots and a North Face jacket, you'll be fine," one student advised.

The only time the rain comes into play is on someone's birthday. If you celebrate your birthday at school, make sure to dress appropriately. Your friends will throw you into the nearby stream (the verb that arises is "mill streamed"), which can be fun or very cold, depending on the season. Another campus legend is that if a couple kisses under the star trees (a set of five trees that, when looked at from below, make a star shape), they will get married. "And it's happened a surprising amount of times," one student noted.

Students love the tight-knit and really supportive community that surrounds them every day at Willamette. "Anywhere you go on campus, you'll see a friendly face," one student said. Willamette would be nothing without its collection of interested, aware, and friendly students. "The people are what I like most about it," one student said. "The connections that I've made and the things I've learned from the people I've met at Willamette are definitely what I found to be the most valuable takeaway from college."—*Mason Kroll*

FYI
What surprised me the most about Willamette when I arrived was "the laid-back nature of the professors."
If I could change one thing about Willamette, it would be "its location—Salem's not really an ideal place to have a college."
If you come to Willamette, you'd better bring "rainboots; it rains straight for four months in a row."
Three things every student at Willamette should do before graduating are: "get mill-streamed, try an intramural sport, and appear in the Collegian."

Pennsylvania

Allegheny College

Address: Box 5, 520 North Main Street, Meadville, PA 16335

Phone: 814-332-4351

E-mail address: admissions@allegheny.edu

Web site URL: www.allegheny.edu

Year Founded: 1815

Private or Public: Private

Religious Affiliation: United Methodist

Location: Urban

Number of Applicants: 4,770

Percent Accepted: 58%

Percent Accepted who enroll: 20%

Number Entering: 559

Number of Transfers Accepted each Year: 53

Middle 50% SAT range: M: 540–640, CR: 530–660, Wr: 520–640

Middle 50% ACT range: 23–29

Early admission program EA/ED/None: ED

Percentage accepted through EA or ED: 48%

EA and ED deadline: 15-Nov

Regular Deadline: 15-Feb

Application Fee: $35

Full time Undergraduate enrollment: 2,123

Total enrollment: 2,125

Percent Male: 47%

Percent Female: 53%

Total Percent Minority or Unreported: 14%

Percent African-American: 4%

Percent Asian/Pacific Islander: 3%

Percent Hispanic: 5%

Percent Native American: 0%

Percent International: 3%

Percent In-state/out of state: 55%/45%

Percent from Public HS: 83%

Retention Rate: 87%

Graduation Rate 4-year: 75%

Graduation Rate 6-year: 80%

Percent Undergraduates in On-campus housing: 90%

Number of official organized extracurricular organizations: 95

3 Most popular majors: Biology, Economics, Psychology

Student/Faculty ratio: 12:1

Average Class Size: 17

Percent of students going to grad school: 34%

Tuition and Fees: $36,190

In-State Tuition and Fees if different: No difference

Cost for Room and Board: $11,498

Percent receiving financial aid out of those who apply: 90%

Percent receiving financial aid among all students: 20%

Founded in 1815, Allegheny is one of the oldest colleges in the United States. With a history longer than that of some of the finest and most reputed universities in the country, Allegheny College features a beautiful, pastoral campus with great learning opportunities, for which it earned a place among the top 40 schools in *Colleges that Change Lives*. If you are looking for an excellent liberal arts education and do not mind living in a quiet, small town located hours away from any major cities, consider Allegheny as a potential college choice.

Meadville? Where is That?

Meadville is a small, "post-industrial" town in western Pennsylvania. It is home to a population of only 14,000 people. The closest metropolitan area is Pittsburgh, PA, which is about 90 minutes away. Cleveland, the next nearest city, requires two hours of driving. As a result, although the school offers a quiet learning environment, it certainly has "neither the number nor the quality of activities that can be found in large metropolitan areas." While the Gator Activities Programming invites entertainers to perform on campus, it is obvious that "if you've always wanted to be in a city and have flashing lights and tons of things to do on the weekends, don't bother." Nevertheless, most students agree that "Allegheny has a beautiful campus." The college covers nearly 540 acres, including a natural reserve of 283 acres, as well as 203 acres dedicated to recreation. The campus offers great facilities such as an observatory, an art gallery, and a

TV station, all for a small enrollment of about 2,100 students. With the nearby lakes and state parks, Allegheny is a great place for the enjoyment of nature and tranquility. As one student explained, "If you are looking for a small college in a rural and laid-back community, Allegheny is the place for you."

The college's relationship with Meadville, however, remains rather detached. "There tends to be clash between 'townies' and us Alleghenians," said a student. "But we are truthfully working on the relationship." While most students in the college come from middle-class families, the formerly industrial Meadville has been facing economic difficulties since the 1980s. As a result, Allegheny students are sometimes just seen as "a bunch of rich kids." At the same time, one student remarked, "The campus is rather closed off to the town of Meadville, although there are some students that go to bars and go shopping." There are about 30 restaurants in the area and several small stores. Nevertheless, with the nearest mall about 30 minutes away, "the town doesn't really have anything interesting for us to go there," one senior said.

Despite being in an isolated location, however, the students are very content with the safety of both Allegheny College and Meadville. Few dangerous incidents ever occur in the area, and the students agree that Allegheny is "a peaceful residential campus."

Majorly into Minors

A top-100 liberal arts college according to *U.S. News & World Report*, Allegheny provides its students with a well-rounded academic program. It is a relatively selective school: more than 75 percent of its students were in the top 20 percent of their high schools. The acceptance rate is generally around 60 percent, giving Allegheny a body of capable students. "Academics are the reason that everyone comes here," said a student.

Allegheny is well known for its science departments. "We have one of the best placements into med school in the nation," one Alleghenian said. "Our science departments are very hard. We don't curve grades like other colleges." Despite the belief that humanities and social science classes are less interesting and less difficult than science classes, most students agree that Allegheny "boasts excellent faculty in all fields." The construction of a $23 million state-of-the-art communications and theater

center was completed in the spring of 2009 to help improve the school's reputation in humanities and arts.

The classes are based on hour credits. Most classes are four credits, and the students need 131 credit hours to graduate. People generally take four to five classes per semester. One of the distinctive elements of Allegheny is its requirement of both a major and a minor, or a second major, which helps people to "achieve a more rounded education." The minor cannot be in the same academic division (humanities, natural sciences, and social sciences) as the major, meaning that the students have to take classes in very different fields, thus achieving the goal of a liberal arts education.

The school also has a vigorous set of requirements for its students. In addition to the mandatory classes in humanities, sciences, and social sciences, everyone is required to take three courses on academic planning, starting from second semester of freshman year to the end of sophomore year, to help prepare for the design of their programs of study and their activities. They also need to take three FS seminars during their freshman and sophomore years. These classes focus mostly on improving the students' ability to research and communicate ideas. There are more than 80 different seminars available to the students.

> "I've babysat kids for professors before. We are all equals here and students help professors and professors help students."

By the end of their sophomore year, students choose their majors among the 30 offered by Allegheny. The major requires anywhere from 36 to 48 credit hours and the completion of a junior seminar and a senior project. Students can also make their own major if they can justify the point of having their own course of study. The minor requires 20 credits, 12 of which must be outside the division of the graduation major.

The course load is often agreed to be challenging among Alleghenians. According to one student, "Allegheny College has one of the largest work loads for any class whether it be sciences, social sciences, or humanities. All areas are challenging—and encouraging—which Allegheny College facilitates its students to experience."

2,100 Students, One Tight-Knit Experience

Students at Allegheny maintain close ties with their professors. "Students and professors are all very close," said an Alleghenian. "Professors often invite students to their house for a meal." Indeed, the small classes give plenty of opportunities for the students to interact with the faculty. When asked about the relationship between the students and the faculty, one interviewee said, "I've babysat kids for professors before. We are all equals here and students help professors and professors help students."

The dorms are similar to most colleges. About 86 percent of the students live on campus, with all students except seniors required to do so. According to an Alleghenian, a typical room would be "double 17 by 15, no AC."

"Only the more expensive, new dorms have AC," added another student, who also pointed out that, "Bathroom and shower space is not an issue. There are plenty of those."

Greek life is an important part of Allegheny. Being part of a fraternity or sorority gives sisters and brothers access to a series of activities. Nevertheless, there are plenty of other activities on campus so that the students do not feel left out if they opt out of Greek life. Alcohol is an important part of parties, and it generally can be found by anyone.

Allegheny is trying hard to improve its diversity. Currently, only 14 percent of Alleghenians are ethnic minorities. The administration is making it a priority to recruit more minority applicants.—*Xiaohang Liu*

FYI

If you come to Allegheny, you'd better bring "a Nalgene. We are big on those."
If I could change one thing about Allegheny, I'd "lower the cost of tuition."
Three things every student at Allegheny should do before graduating are "go to Eddie's Footlong for hotdogs, play pool in the Game Room, and take yoga classes."

Bryn Mawr College

Address: 101 North Merion Avenue, Bryn Mawr, PA 19010-2859
Phone: 610-526-5152
E-mail address: admissions@brynmawr.edu
Web site URL: www.brynmawr.edu
Year Founded: 1885
Private or Public: Private
Religious Affiliation: None
Location: Urban
Number of Applicants: 2,150
Percent Accepted: 49%
Percent Accepted who enroll: 35%
Number Entering: 366
Number of Transfers Accepted each Year: 25
Middle 50% SAT range: M: 580–680, CR: 620–730, Wr: 620–720
Middle 50% ACT range: 27–31
Early admission program EA/ED/None: ED

Percentage accepted through EA or ED: 19%
EA and ED deadline: 15-Nov
Regular Deadline: 15-Jan
Application Fee: $50
Full time Undergraduate enrollment: 1,287
Total enrollment: 1,745
Percent Male: 0%
Percent Female: 100%
Total Percent Minority or Unreported: 23%
Percent African-American: 6%
Percent Asian/Pacific Islander: 12%
Percent Hispanic: 4%
Percent Native American: 1%
Percent International: 7%
Percent in-state/out of state: 16%/84%
Percent from Public HS: Unreported
Retention Rate: 90%
Graduation Rate 4-year: 81%

Graduation Rate 6-year: 85%
Percent Undergraduates in On-campus housing: 95%
Number of official organized extracurricular organizations: 94
3 Most popular majors: English, Mathematics, Psychology
Student/Faculty ratio: 8:1
Average Class Size: 16
Percent of students going to grad school: Unreported
Tuition and Fees: $36,540
In-State Tuition and Fees if different: No difference
Cost for Room and Board: $11,520
Percent receiving financial aid out of those who apply: 62%
Percent receiving financial aid among all students: 62%

Located in an ideal location just outside a major metropolis, Bryn Mawr's beautiful campus and motivated student body make it a desirable choice for many young women.

The common trait among all Mawrtyrs, as they're called, is their overwhelming passion for their school.

Smaller Is Better

Academics receive top priority at Bryn Mawr, where they are described as "challenging but so rewarding." Despite the heavy workload, most students could not be happier. The school attempts to prevent a cutthroat environment with a unique honor code forbidding the discussion of grades between students. The honor code is strictly enforced and applies to class rank as well, which is not disclosed until graduation.

The most popular majors are English, Mathematics and Psychology. All students must take a Freshman Liberal Studies Seminar, known as the College Seminar, intended to prepare freshmen for college writing, especially for classes in which papers are required such as English, History, Anthropology and Sociology. In addition to the College Seminar, students must also fulfill core requirements intended to impart a broad liberal arts foundation. These include two labs, two natural sciences, two humanities and two social sciences. One of the best classes is said to be "Identification in Cinema," a film minor/art history major course taught by perennial favorite Homay King. In addition to King, the most popular professors include Mary Louise Cookson, a mathematics professor, and Gary McDonough, director of the Growth and Structure of Cities Program. In addition to Bryn Mawr's extensive course offerings, students have the option of taking classes at nearby Haverford College, Swarthmore College and the University of Pennsylvania.

The school also allows students to design their own Independent major. One student explained, "Any gap you may find in course offerings, you can often work with professors to fill, if you are truly interested and willing to commit to it." Another student knew of friends who had majored in Feminist Studies, Theater Studies, Film, and American Cultural Studies, all as Independent majors.

Unsurprisingly, classes at Bryn Mawr are small. Intimate classes foster intimate student/professor bonds. In addition to office hours, many professors make themselves accessible to students at all hours. Outside of the academic arena, many students babysit for their professors, walk their dogs, or go to their homes for dinner on a regular basis.

Another aspect of classes at Bryn Mawr is their accessibility to all class years. With a few exceptions, classes have a mix of freshmen through seniors. One student praised this feature because it "gave me the opportunity to make friends who were older than me and acted as mentors."

Quiet but Lively

Bryn Mawr's location has a significant impact on its social scene. Students do not bewail its all-female student body because of the coed mingling afforded by the proximity of neighboring colleges Swarthmore and Haverford, with which Bryn Mawr has always enjoyed a close relationship. Haverford tends to have keg parties and dances, and the regular shuttle between the schools makes for easy access to parties.

Students at Bryn Mawr say that underage students looking to drink do not encounter many obstacles. Thursdays and Saturdays are the big party nights on campus, while Fridays are more toned down. "Thursday people party hard, and grin and bear it through their Friday classes," one student explained. When it comes to partying, as with most things at Bryn Mawr, tradition prevails. The biggest party of the year occurs at Halloween. There is usually a themed "East/West party" held in the connected Pembroke East and West dorms. Bryn Mawr and Haverford each host a drag ball, at Haverford in the fall semester and at Bryn Mawr in the spring. Perry House and Radnor, both dorms, are known for throwing good parties. Radnor is sometimes unofficially used as a venue for small bands. According to one student, many of the best parties are after-parties following events like dance performances, culture shows, debate team meets, or a capella concerts.

Beyond the party scene, students hang out in local coffee shops like Cosi or Starbucks or the new coffee shop in town called Milkboy, where local musicians perform and which holds open mike nights. There is a larger Milkboy in an adjacent town two miles away. Both are affiliated with a local record production company of the same name and a current Bryn Mawr student has two albums out on their label. Another option for those interested in the arts is the renovated Bryn Mawr Film Institute, which shows art-house films and has begun cooperating with the Film Studies Department at Bryn Mawr.

For those looking to get away from campus, the local commuter rail system provides easy access to Philadelphia's Art Museum, restaurants and nightlife. The largest mall on the East Coast is 10 minutes from campus.

Most socializing takes place on campus, however, and is associated in some way with academics. One student explains that "while people are definitely social, it's nice to know you won't be the only one in the library on a Friday night." Most students hang out in their halls with friends, or in Canaday Library, which is "open, well-lit, and has sofas everywhere." The café inside, the Lusty Cup, is on the same floor as the 24-hour computing suite, making it a popular study area. A lot of socializing centers around clubs, sports and other extracurriculars because Mawrtyrs tend to be very involved.

Campus Life

At Bryn Mawr "the living is definitely good." Campus architecture is classic Gothic, with beautiful stained-glass windows and imposing stone. The newest dorm, Erdman, was designed by Louis Kahn as a modern Scottish castle. Students live in one of 14 residence halls. The absence of specially designated freshman dorms means that freshman housing can rival senior housing. Every dorm has women from all four years, and there is almost no difference in quality of rooms from freshman to senior year. Many rooms have bay windows, wood paneling and fireplaces; some even have walk-in closets. Campus safety is not a concern. Students feel completely secure, even at night. Bryn Mawr's suburban location means that many students rarely lock their doors or their bikes, and lost wallets have been known to come back to their owners before they were noticed to be missing. Students love the dorms and campus in general, which could explain why 95 percent of the students choose to live on campus.

The food on campus is another reason. The dining halls at Bryn Mawr receive high marks all around. They are "very vegetarian and somewhat vegan friendly." The dining halls are completely student staffed as all freshmen who desire a campus job must start in the dining halls. Outside of the dining halls, there are also many excellent restaurants in the area and in nearby Philadelphia.

Like the classes, dining halls are open to Haverford students as well, but since breakfast ends up being almost only Bryn Mawr women, you get lots of people in pajamas. In many cases, that's how they stay throughout the day. Designer brands can be spotted on campus, but for the most part dress is casual throughout the week. On the weekends students get dressed up and made up, and head out for fun. Though there may not be guys enrolled at Bryn Mawr, there are generally quite a few on campus. The women decide as a floor at the beginning of the year whether their bathroom will be coed. Visiting men are simply expected to act responsibly.

Extracurriculars are another aspect which benefits from the small size of the school. According to one student, "If it isn't here already, you can make it happen." The small size of Bryn Mawr also allows freshmen to play an active role in their extracurricular activities. Student government is one of the largest organizations on campus, along with the Bi-College News, the Haverford-Bryn Mawr newspaper. There is also an active political community, with groups that span the political spectrum. Political groups are extremely active, and there are tons of dance groups (everything from Asian fusion to classical ballet) and a cappella. An active Rainbow Alliance helps to promote an open, accepting atmosphere for LGBT students.

> **"If it isn't here already, you can make it happen."**

The diversity of the student body is universally praised. Students come from all around the country and the world. Campus is described as being virtually "clique-free," and students say that there is no segregation whatsoever. "It's very, very diverse economically, socially, politically and religiously," one student said. Diversity is not only evident in the student body, but openly discussed as well. "We talk about it, a lot," a student explained. This often entails bringing up and discussing problems, as well as acknowledging any failures to address diversity issues within the community.

For all their strengths, Mawrtyrs rarely dominate the athletic field. School spirit is definitely not lacking in the least, but unfortunately that doesn't carry over to achieving many victories. There are exceptions, however. In 2007, Bryn Mawr's coed rugby team won the EPRU Division III championship and competed at nationals. Win or lose, students go out to support their teams (and Haverford's) even at away games. For the nonvarsity athletic types, there are good gym facilities, a pool and plenty of safe places to run around campus. For almost every varsity sport there is a corresponding club team, so anyone can participate.

Tradition Reigns

Bryn Mawr's most distinguishing characteristic may be the Traditions (with a capital T). These are four events held throughout the year, aimed at welcoming the underclassmen into the community. The first Tradition is Parade Night, which welcomes the freshmen to campus with the singing of the school song. Lantern Night follows, each class holding up a lantern of a different color to identify themselves. Third is Hell Week, during which the sophomores get freshmen to do all sorts of crazy things, which the upperclassmen help them evade. Finally, in May the college president rides a horse into campus to begin the May Day celebrations, which focus on the senior class. One unspoken tradition is skinny dipping in the Cloisters, an act inspired by alumna Katharine Hepburn.

There is almost unanimous agreement among Bryn Mawr students that there is no place they would rather be. "So many of my classmates have described their attraction to Bryn Mawr as 'falling in love' or being 'magical,'" one student said. Small classes, a beautiful campus in a great location, and a diverse, passionate student body all make for a nearly ideal college experience. One student described her peers as "amazing." Another remarked that meeting alumnae is like meeting aunts or old family friends because of the shared bond that comes from the Bryn Mawr experience.—*Laura Sullivan*

FYI

If you come to Bryn Mawr, you'd better bring "passion: in studying, partying, rallying and relaxing. We are a pretty devoted-to-our-causes campus."

What's the typical weekend schedule? "Friday: relax if you have no class and go out at night. Saturday: during the day study, play a sport, volunteer, rehearse, work and then party. Sunday: spend far too long at brunch, study for an hour, eat dinner, go to SGA (our student government's open meeting), hang out with friends, stay in the library until midnight."

If I could change one thing about Bryn Mawr, I would "expand the Bryn Mawr bubble to include Philadelphia, get more students involved in off-campus communities."

Three things that every student should do before graduating are: "get sunburned on May Day, join the crowd at 4 a.m. in Guild during finals, and sing good-night to the seniors during Step Sing."

Bucknell University

Address: 701 Moore Avenue, Lewisburg, PA 17837
Phone: 570-577-1101
E-mail address: admissions@bucknell.edu
Web site URL: www.bucknell.edu
Year Founded: 1864
Private or Public: Private
Religious Affiliation: None
Location: Rural
Number of Applicants: 8,024
Percent Accepted: 30%
Percent Accepted who enroll: 40%
Number Entering: 957
Number of Transfers Accepted each Year: 57
Middle 50% SAT range: M: 630–710, CR: 600–680, Wr: 610–700
Middle 50% ACT range: 27–31
Early admission program EA/ED/None: ED

Percentage accepted through EA or ED: 39%
EA and ED deadline: 15-Nov
Regular Deadline: 15-Jan
Application Fee: $60
Full time Undergraduate enrollment: 3,583
Total enrollment: 3,719
Percent Male: 47%
Percent Female: 53%
Total Percent Minority or Unreported: 13%
Percent African-American: 3%
Percent Asian/Pacific Islander: 6%
Percent Hispanic: 4%
Percent Native American: <1%
Percent International: 3%
Percent in-state/out of state: 25%/75%
Percent from Public HS: Unreported
Retention Rate: 95%

Graduation Rate 4-year: 85%
Graduation Rate 6-year: 88%
Percent Undergraduates in On-campus housing: 86%
Number of official organized extracurricular organizations: 150
3 Most popular majors: Biology, Business Administration, Economics
Student/Faculty ratio: 11:1
Average Class Size: 26
Percent of students going to grad school: Unreported
Tuition and Fees: $39,434
In-State Tuition and Fees if different: No difference
Cost for Room and Board: $8,728
Percent receiving financial aid out of those who apply: 62%
Percent receiving financial aid among all students: 58%

With small classes, friendly and accessible professors, and a variety of academic offerings, Bucknell offers students a classic liberal arts experience. Located in central Pennsylvania, its rural setting and small student body foster a close-knit community, while its vibrant Greek scene and wealth of extracurricular activities give students plenty to keep them busy during their time on campus.

Small Classes, Big Opportunities

Bucknell students enjoy a small academic community that allows for close relationships between students and professors. With more than half of the courses containing fewer than twenty students, students are able to interact with their professors and with each other in a more intimate setting. Even the large lecture classes are not overwhelming, with usually about 100 students in the biggest intro-level courses. All freshmen take small "Foundation Seminar Courses" of fifteen students, taught by their academic advisors. "My foundations teacher took ten minutes at the beginning of every class to ask us how we were doing, and he always had great advice," one freshman said. Students describe professors as accessible and always willing to help. "I personally have loved all my professors," one student said. "Though they all have office hours, I mostly just stop by when I'm free and they are always willing to help."

Though a relatively small school, Bucknell has over fifty majors for students to choose from, the most popular of which are management, economics, and psychology. Many students enroll in Bucknell's renowned management and engineering schools, but all undergraduates can take classes in any of the university's schools. In an effort to provide students with a well-rounded liberal arts education, the university requires all students to take a core curriculum, but students said that the requirements are relatively easy to fulfill and still leave plenty of freedom in their schedules.

Most students say that while some classes can be very demanding, the workload is manageable. "I usually have about six hours of work per week, which isn't bad, but I know kids who have up to twenty," said one student, adding that the university recommends three to four hours of work for each hour spent in class, though this is rarely followed. One student noted, "The engineering school is difficult. Those kids are always in their rooms studying." However, like any college, the workload varies depending on the class. Grading at Bucknell is "generally fair," one student said, though some professors are much harder than others. "It's definitely doable to get an A, but it depends on the class. They give teachers a lot of freedom here."

Bison Pride

Even with rigorous academics, students still find time to get involved in a wide range of extracurricular activities. With over 150 clubs and organizations, students can definitely keep busy. "Most people are involved in several organizations, but you can choose the level of involvement you have in each," said one student. Some popular activities include the ACE, which organizes activities and events on campus, and working as a tour guide for the admissions office. Sports are a prominent part of life at Bucknell, with 27 D-1 varsity teams for men and women. "There is a lot of school pride for the sports teams here," one student said. Men's basketball and lacrosse are among the most popular for fans, students said. Despite the intense commitment demanded by D-1 sports, students say that athletes mix well with the rest of the student body.

> " 'Work hard, play hard' seems to be the motto at Bucknell."

Play Hard

"Work hard, play hard" seems to be the motto at Bucknell. Though students have busy schedules balancing academics and extracurricular activities, they still find time to party hard. Students agree that Greek life dominates the social scene, with over 50 percent of sophomores, juniors, and seniors in a fraternity or sorority. Students don't rush until fall of sophomore year, so some of the nightlife for freshmen is restricted to the dorms, but most attend parties hosted by a sorority or fraternity. "That kind of excludes you from a lot of social events," said one freshman, but added that social life gets

much better as you get older. Most students agree that the Greek scene is a mixed bag; while choosing not to pledge a fraternity or sorority can exclude students from certain social events, fraternities and sororities also host parties that non-Greeks can easily attend. "We're kind of out there in the middle of nowhere, so it gives us something to do," said one student.

Even for students not involved in Greek life, there is plenty to do at Bucknell. "I am not in a sorority, and I totally love not being in one," a junior said. "I don't feel like I'm missing out on the party scene at all. Instead of having to go to certain parties and meetings all the time, I can do what I want," she said, adding that with so many friends in sororities, she has a great time attending their parties. Students said the university is trying to change the perception of Greek life on campus, adding a new fraternity in the fall of 2012 and a new sorority in the spring of 2013. "By giving more choices in the number of groups to join, they are hoping to decrease the stereotypes attached to each group," said one upperclassman.

Drinking is a big part of the social scene, most students said. "But if someone chooses not to drink, there's no pressure," one student said. The university has a moderately strict policy regarding alcohol, using a point system to discourage underage and excessive drinking. One to four points are given for a student caught with an open alcoholic beverage, and ten points earns a suspension.

For those who don't want to drink, the school sponsors many activities for the entire student body to enjoy. Concerts, guest speakers, and festivals are among the many university-organized options. "Fall Fest is a really fun event," one student said. "There are country bands playing, a Ferris wheel, free food, it's basically a carnival."

What's a Bucknellian?

"Bucknell is a preppy, white, rich school," said one student of the university's student body. "It is pretty much WASPy East-Coasters." Most students agreed with this characterization. "The perception is that Bucknell is not very diverse. I think this is true to some extent. I would describe the campus as very white and from middle- to upper-class families. But the more you get to know the people here, the more you see that people are more diverse than they appear on the surface," a student said. Students agreed that Bucknellians are generally a friendly breed, and that it is pretty easy to make friends.

Living the Bucknell Life

Nestled in the quaint town of Lewisburg, Pennsylvania, Bucknell boasts a 445-acre campus with redbrick Georgian revival architecture. There are several modern buildings, including the new engineering building, which houses both graduate and undergraduate students. Most students live on campus all four years, though many seniors choose to live in off-campus apartments. The dorms are considered by students to be pretty nice, and they get better as students get older. The freshman dorms, probably the least desirable housing on campus, are "still really nice," said one freshman, adding that though his dorm is old and does not have air conditioning, it is fairly spacious and there is plenty of closet room. Almost all freshmen live in doubles with a roommate assigned to them, with a few living in singles and others in triples or quads. Sophomores generally live in the "mods," which are apartment-style housing, though some live in other dorms around campus. Many juniors live in the "Gateways," which are five buildings containing spacious quads that usually include four bedrooms, a living room, kitchen facilities and their own bathroom. Juniors who are in a fraternity or sorority often live in fraternity houses or Larison Hall, which houses Bucknell's sororities since there are no sorority houses. Though housing is guaranteed for all four years, many seniors choose to live off campus. Bucknellians also have the option of living in small housing communities that include "affinity housing," such as a music house, substance-free living, and a sustainable cooperative. Most dorms do not have any particular personality attached to them, though some are considered "athlete dorms," while others have halls of students from the engineering school. After freshman year, students enter a housing lottery to determine where they will live each year. Bucknell uses a "block-booking" system, which ensures that students can live next to their friends, even if they have different housing lottery numbers.

Bucknellians enjoy a variety of dining options and an assortment of different meal plans to suit their tastes. Students consider the food on campus to be pretty good, ranging from classic cafeteria-style dining to cafes and a "marketplace." Dining plans range from unlimited meals to dining dollar plans, popular for upperclassmen and students living off campus, which allows them to purchase food from on-campus vendors through a debit card system. Bucknell has plenty of options for late-night snackers, with most dining halls remaining open until at least 10pm, and some stay open until after midnight.

Dining halls are only one of the many places on Bucknell's campus where students can gather to hang out. The Lafayette College building, which houses the main cafeteria and a la carte dining options, also includes student space with tables and TVs. "It's the building that you will see everyone you know every time you walk in," one student said. Another student favorite is the library, which has many quiet study spaces as well as its own Starbucks. "You could stay there all day," one student said.

Despite its rural surroundings, Bucknell is a lively community with lots going on. Students juggle rigorous academics, countless extracurriculars, and on top of that, make time to take part in the vibrant social scene Bucknell offers. Above all, students say that what they value most about Bucknell is the tight community it fosters. "It's a small school in a small town," a student said. "But that means we're all having the same experience, and it makes it a much closer community."—*Colleen Flynn*

FYI

If you come to Bucknell you had better bring "good self-esteem; every student on this campus is amazingly talented, and I still hold that Bucknell chooses students at least 50 percent based on looks."

Three things every student at Bucknell should do before graduation are: "go to the Freez and the Campus Theatre, walk around downtown Lewisburg, and go wild at least once!"

My favorite thing about Bucknell is "how easy it is to connect with your professors."

Carnegie Mellon University

Address: 5000 Forbes Avenue, Pittsburgh, PA 15213
Phone: 412-268-2082
E-mail address: undergraduate-admissions@andrew.cmu.edu
Web site URL: www.cmu.edu
Year Founded: 1900
Private or Public: Private
Religious Affiliation: None
Location: Urban
Number of Applicants: 13,527
Percent Accepted: 38%
Percent Accepted who enroll: 29%
Number Entering: 1,465
Number of Transfers Accepted each Year: 59
Middle 50% SAT range: M: 670–780, CR: 620–720, Wr: 620–710
Middle 50% ACT range: Unreported
Early admission program EA/ED/None: ED

Percentage accepted through EA or ED: 17%
EA and ED deadline: 1-Nov
Regular Deadline: 1-Jan
Application Fee: $70
Full time Undergraduate enrollment: 5,998
Total enrollment: 11,064
Percent Male: 59%
Percent Female: 41%
Total Percent Minority or Unreported: 61%
Percent African-American: 5%
Percent Asian/Pacific Islander: 22%
Percent Hispanic: 6%
Percent Native American: 1%
Percent International: 15%
Percent in-state/out of state: 23%/77%
Percent from Public HS: Unreported
Retention Rate: 95%
Graduation Rate 4-year: 70%

Graduation Rate 6-year: 86%
Percent Undergraduates in On-campus housing: 64%
Number of official organized extracurricular organizations: 225
3 Most popular majors: Computer Engineering, Computer Science, Liberal Arts and Sciences
Student/Faculty ratio: Unreported
Average Class Size: 15
Percent of students going to grad school: Unreported
Tuition and Fees: $39,564
In-State Tuition and Fees if different: No difference
Cost for Room and Board: $10,050
Percent receiving financial aid out of those who apply: 75%
Percent receiving financial aid among all students: 64%

S tudents are painting a large fence on the green center of campus. Across from a giant ladder somehow suspended in midair, drama students on break are playing Frisbee. Behind them in the library are engineering students working on problem sets, while others are joking about Monty Python. Carnegie Mellon is a university full of unique traditions with even more interesting people.

Work First

Andrew Carnegie's motto for the campus, "My heart is in the work" certainly describes the student atmosphere. A computer science major said that the engineering department is "notoriously very difficult" and another student commented, "CMU works you hard."

Many students feel that it is "nearly impossible to balance the workload with extracurriculars" and also to have a social life. Several engineering majors commented that, considering the workload and stress, their majors were very "close-knit and helpful,"

and that the departments gave de-stress perks to cope with the workload. Classes are intense and time-consuming, but the skills acquired are invaluable: "We were building things in the first few weeks of college, and it was things that I really wanted to learn" explained an engineering major.

Students at Carnegie Mellon belong to six separate undergraduate colleges: the Mellon College of Science, the Carnegie Institute of Technology, the College of Fine Arts, the College of Humanities and Social Sciences, the Tepper School of Business and the School of Computer Science. Applicants are accepted to one, or sometimes even multiple, specific schools. Some students complained that it is difficult to take courses in other departments because of class size caps. For those students who elect to double major, choosing courses with an interdisciplinary focus is much easier.

Engineering and Computer Science majors consider their requirements to be the most difficult, arguing that the majors in the College of Humanities and Social Sciences are the easiest. The general atmosphere of CMU is that the campus is for engineers and computer scientists, and so other majors are not taken as seriously. To the annoyance of many humanities majors who say that they too have a lot of work, the Humanities department is nicknamed "H and less stress." One Humanities major described a famous course for which students must weight questions by their confidence in their answers, and if having given full weight to an answer that is wrong, they would fail the course. The Music and Drama departments of the College of Fine Arts are well respected. The Music Department hosts faculty from the Pittsburgh Symphony Orchestra and the Drama school was the first drama-degree program of its kind in the US.

CMU highly encourages research regardless of field, and students are not stuck in the vortex of theory. A Business Administration major explained that the business program required students to complete real-life projects involving simulated businesses and in-depth presentations that were very useful for internships. The Career & Professional Development Center is very active for networking and helps students with resumes and interview skills.

What Social Life?

At freshmen orientation, students are instructed to shake hands with people that they don't know. Many students feel that their 'outside of the classroom' education comes from their interesting peers: "CMU students are some of the most genuine people I have ever met," but several students complained of the lackluster social life at CMU.

"I feel that the social life at Carnegie Mellon is what you make of it. I would say at least a quarter of the students hide in their rooms and do nothing but homework and video games. Another quarter of the students do their schoolwork in addition to their clubs and light social activities. The final half attends parties or goes out to bars. The frequency of the latter is totally dependent on the person's ability to handle their schoolwork." The atmosphere can be 'cliquish,' particularly among ethnic groups, and one girl commented: "People find their friend groups and stick with them, which is unfortunate." Students agree that balancing socializing and studying can be difficult, and that while there are many great people at the school, "it is common to only find one or two social events happening on a Friday night." Students must make a marked effort

to socialize. Those who do go out can be found at a fraternity/sorority or house party, drama school production or hang out in their dorms. Students also go out to restaurants and bars close by in Oakland and Squirrel Hill.

Joining a sorority or fraternity "helps many people get through the stress of school and form a sense of community, but this is completely possible to find without Greek life." There are 6 sororities, 11 fraternities and 3 multicultural Greek organizations on campus which together make up about 22% of the university student population. All organizations have a mandated five hours per member service component, but many far surpass this requirement. Though underage drinking is officially not allowed on campus, "as long as you're not stupid you'll be fine" explained one student.

Pittsburgh

The main campus of CMU is separate from downtown Pittsburgh. Students appreciate the privacy of campus and the availability of the city. Pittsburgh is perceived as a relatively safe city with a multitude of cultural options. The closest neighborhoods are Shadyside and Squirrel Hill. The University of Pittsburgh, located in Oakland, is known to have large parties comparable to the lower key events at CMU. While students can show their CMU student ID to use any bus to get around Pittsburgh, a lot of students find themselves staying on-campus a lot—especially during the winter when waiting for buses is nightmarish. Freshman year many RAs plan activities for students to see the numerous museums, concert venues, and parks around Pittsburgh.

The students most involved in the city of Pittsburgh are those involved in service organizations. For example, the EMS organization provides opportunities for students to work alongside Pittsburgh EMS on calls, Strong Women Strong Girls make weekly visits to Pittsburgh Public Schools, and 1000Plus organizes an event every year aiming to get 1000 or more CMU community members to volunteer at an array of sites in the greater Pittsburgh area all on one day.

Square Food and Normal Housing

All freshmen are required to live on campus in dorms with varying levels of space and air conditioning. As students get older, many move off-campus. Almost all CMU sponsored rooms are doubles, and one student said "I don't know anyone who has a single." The converted mansion called "Mudge" is considered the best dorm on campus, which has a courtyard and suites. "Donner" is considered one of the worst dorms because of small, "dingy" rooms and shared bathrooms. The newer dorms have air conditioning.

Much of the upperclassmen housing has a more off-campus feel. These include a series of apartment buildings on 5th Avenue, a small quad of two-story houses, and Greek housing. Those who choose to live off-campus live in either Shady Side or Squirrel Hill, which are within walking distance/a short bus ride from campus. The wireless network on campus is one of the best in the country.

The food "leaves a little to be desired" and is "not great." The meal plan consists of blocks which students must use in the time allotted. Upperclassmen recommend that freshmen buy the most flexible meal plan that allows them to use "DineX," a kind of flex-dollar cash, at Entropy, a campus convenience store. Students complain about both the quality of food and the fact that their money is lost if they do not spend their blocked meals. There are many off-meal plan options nearby and a number of food carts on campus.

Carnival and the Fence

Two of the greatest hallmarks of CMU are "The Fence" and the yearly "Carnival." The painted "Fence" is situated on the middle of the campus green and is a place for organizations to advertise their events. People sleep in tents by the fence and at least two people at a time are required to guard the fence to ward off other students who might paint over their advertisements at night. During warm weather students play music around the Fence and it becomes a kind of gathering place. The Fence is situated in front of the library on the campus green and behind the giant ladder art that is at the front of campus.

Many students are involved in the gubernatory council to plan campus events such as "Carnival." The Spring Carnival is a four-day celebration featuring amusement park rides and concerts. Student organizations build either 1- or 2-story, 18ft by 18ft themed booths, which offer games and prizes. The hallmark event is "buggy," for which students build carbon fiber buggies that people squeeze into and race down the hill behind campus.

Carnival is considered to be the greatest source of school-wide pride for the year.

Andrew Carnegie and his Tartans

The Scottish ancestry of CMU's founder, Andrew Carnegie, has a strong presence on campus. CMU is the only university in the country that offers a major in bagpipes. The Division III football team is named the Tartans and the school mascot is Scotty the Scottish terrier. A Kiltie band and bagpipers play at football games. CMU is not known for its sports teams, and students commented that few attend any sporting events.

Outside of academics, CMU offers "organizations for everyone." With so many interesting people on campus, the environment is described as accepting. One student commented: "Everyone has found at least a few other people who are like them even if they didn't in high school, it's such a diverse group of people."

> "The work is not easy, and the stress culture gets you down, but it definitely pays off. You end up coming out with the tools to do what you want to do."

While there is "a lot of room to gain leadership" through extracurriculars, students find it can be "really difficult to balance schoolwork and staying active in extracurriculars." These activities range from service (1000Plus, Strong Women Strong Girls, Circle K, etc.), to humanitarian aid in terms of constructing safer living environments both domestically and abroad (Habitat for Humanity, Global Brigades, Society of Women Engineers), to social (Fringe, CIA, KGB, Spirit), to musical (Soundbytes, the Originals, Scotch 'n' Soda, etc.). CMU is very supportive of new organizations, and there are clubs for every kind of hobby and/or career interest.

Considering the strains that schoolwork appears to put on social and extracurricular activities, students are positive about their experience, saying, "the work is not easy, and the stress culture gets you down, but it definitely pays off. You end up coming out with the tools to do what you want to do." Students explained that an alumni network of high achieving type-A personalities helped recent graduates line up jobs. — *Dana Schneider*

FYI
If you come to CMU, you'd better bring "an umbrella and a mental state that provides an open mind for the weather changing when you least expect it."
If you come to CMU, you'd better "leave close-mindedness behind. CMU will challenge you, your friends will challenge you, and let's be real here, you are just going to witness a lot of odd things during your time on campus."
What differentiates CMU the most from other colleges is that "technology is really big in all areas of the campus and not just in computer science."

Dickinson College

Address: P.O. Box 1773, Carlisle, PA 17013
Phone: 717-245-1231
E-mail address: admit@dickinson.edu
Web site URL: www.dickinson.edu
Year Founded: 1783
Private or Public: Private
Religious Affiliation: None
Location: Urban
Number of Applicants: 5,349
Percent Accepted: 43%
Percent Accepted who enroll: 27%
Number Entering: 621
Number of Transfers Accepted each Year: 27
Middle 50% SAT range: M: 600–680, CR: 600–690, Wr: 650–720
Middle 50% ACT range: 26–30
Early admission program EA/ED/None: EA and ED

Percentage accepted through EA or ED: 56%
EA and ED deadline: 15-Nov
Regular Deadline: 1-Feb
Application Fee: $60
Full time Undergraduate enrollment: 2,369
Total enrollment: 2,369
Percent Male: 44%
Percent Female: 56%
Total Percent Minority or Unreported: 24%
Percent African-American: 5%
Percent Asian/Pacific Islander: 4%
Percent Hispanic: 4%
Percent Native American: 5%
Percent International: 6%
Percent in-state/out of state: 27%/73%
Percent from Public HS: 61%
Retention Rate: 91%
Graduation Rate 4-year: 78%

Graduation Rate 6-year: 82%
Percent Undergraduates in On-campus housing: 92%
Number of official organized extracurricular organizations: 140
3 Most popular majors: Businss, Political Science, Psychology
Student/Faculty ratio: 12:1
Average Class Size: 13
Percent of students going to grad school: 36%
Tuition and Fees: $35,450
In-State Tuition and Fees if different: No difference
Cost for Room and Board: $8,980
Percent receiving financial aid out of those who apply: 78%
Percent receiving financial aid among all students: 48%

Two blocks from the center square of the historic small town of Carlisle, Pennsylvania, Dickinson College is a similarly historic small school, one with a tight-knit community and an international flair. Here, if students want to study abroad, meet a professor, go to a frat party, and get to know the names of every single one of their classmates, they absolutely can, and will get to do it centered from a preppy campus with historic limestone edifices.

Small Class Sizes and Studies Abroad

At a small school like Dickinson, pride in small class sizes is not uncommon. And at Dickinson, students jump at the opportunity to praise their school for just that reason. Practically no classes have more than a few dozen students, and students say that most classes have even fewer. In part because of this small student body, students find that "professors are easy to talk to and want to know your interests." One student recounted the story of one of his professors: "She knew I was into cellular biology, and she found me a research program to apply to. That's where I spent my summer." Professors are not only friendly, they are invested in the passions of their students at Dickinson.

Dickinson assures that its students respect their school's small class sizes and their professors' involvement with a strict attendance policy in many courses. Completely up to the discretion of the individual courses' professors, students' attendance in class could count for as much as 20 percent of their grade.

As at most colleges, students at Dickinson must complete a range of required courses in different subjects outside of their majors, and this is especially true of studies at a college with such a focus on the liberal arts. Students at Dickinson must participate in a First-Year Seminar, where Dickinsonians beef up their writing skills while exploring topics of their interest, and must take classes in writing, quantitative reasoning, arts and humanities, cross-cultural studies, and physical education activities. Students often find ways to get two requirements over with for the price of one class, but also admit that many do end up waiting until their senior year to rush and complete the distribution requirements. All in all, the courseload at Dickinson seems to be just right for its students. "I'm being challenged, but classes aren't driving me crazy, so it's pretty much right for me," said one sophomore.

Another majorly popular option is Dickinson's study abroad program. Students take the opportunities they have to step away from Carlisle, Pennsylvania, and instead go entirely to a new place and take classes in programs affiliated with Dickinson College in Europe, Asia, Africa, South America, and Australia, for a semester or even for a whole year. Students are often totally immersed in a new culture, as these programs usually house students with host families. The student body is in some way in flux, because after every semester, a large group of students return to campus just as the next group to study abroad leaves to do so, according to one student who is currently abroad.

Limestone Buildings in the Cumberland Valley

While Dickinsonians indeed often leave campus to study overseas, it is not motivated by any dislike of the college's facilities or any lack of visual appeal. From West College, the original building of Dickinson College designed by the architect of the U.S. Capitol building, Benjamin Latrobe, to the Pennsylvania hills and wide open quadrangle, Dickinson students have all they need and manage to feel "right at home in the middle of this beautiful campus," one that is being further beautified by ongoing renovation projects across the College. Students have,

however, a very different opinion about the historic small town that surrounds it. "Carlisle is pretty boring: what you'd expect out of the Cumberland Valley in middle-of-nowhere, Pennsylvania," said one student. Though only 20 minutes from the state's capital in Harrisburg, the town is "really nothing special."

> **"I'm being challenged academically, but classes aren't driving me crazy, so it's pretty much right for me."**

Students have mixed feelings about housing on campus. Though many residence halls were very recently renovated—Adams, Buchanan, Conway, Atwater, Armstrong, and Stuart Halls have been outfitted with new entryways and other modernizations—and upperclassmen residence halls get better, some students wish the halls were bigger, as it seems the residence halls are smaller than the student body actually is.

Situated in small-town Pennsylvania, the demographic makeup of Dickinson College's student body is primarily white, upper-middle-class, and from the Northeast U.S. Many went to private school, and the "preppy" aesthetic is quite popular. Internationalism is not only seen in students' choices of study, however. Much of the diversity seen on Dickinson's campus is not within American students but instead produced by international students.

Greeks in Small-Town PA

Dickinson's party scene is dominated by fraternity parties, which are very popular and open to those who want to attend. It follows that Greek life at Dickinson is hugely popular and that many men choose to pledge fraternities. About 25% of the student body is associated with a Greek organization, which basically translates to slightly less than half of the men being frat brothers. "It's not as important for girls to be in sororities, and they don't get to join until their sophomore year anyway," said one student, who explained that girls are always the first let into frat parties at Dickinson.

And of course, at Dickinson, where Greek life is an all-important social rule and frat parties are the norm, there is a lot of alcohol to be had. The administration at "Drinkinson," as the school is sometimes nicknamed, however, is not pleased by this reality, and has a tough policy against alcohol. Kegs, drinking games, and drinking game–related paraphernalia are prohibited, and some students say that anyone or any frat with a keg will likely be punished, despite some claiming that these strict rules are rarely enforced fully. One junior who had previously worked as a Resident Adviser in the dorms said, "You learn how to hide it and then you just know where and when to drink it," referring to both alcohol during his year as a freshman resident and alcohol during his year as a sophomore RA.

But of course drinking is not the only social scene at Dickinson. Students write *The Dickinsonian*, the campus newspaper, and participate in intramural sports. Other extracurricular groups include foreign language groups (a testament to the multiculturalism of the college) and student government.

Dickinson College gives its students a wide range of experiences in a small package. A close group of friends and classmates getting a liberal arts education, studying in different countries, going to frat parties, challenging themselves academically, and eating delicious food, Dickinsonians have an opportunity unlike many others. And they know that they would do it all over again. —*Connor Moseley*

FYI
If you come to Dickinson, you'd better bring "a Polo shirt."
If I could change one thing about Dickinson, "I'd make it not so preppy and fratty."
What differentiates Dickinson the most from other colleges is "how big the Study Abroad programs are."

Drexel University

Address: 3141 Chestnut Street, Philadelphia, PA 19104
Phone: 215-895-2400
E-mail address: enroll@drexel.edu
Web site URL: www.drexel.edu
Year Founded: 1891
Private or Public: Private
Religious Affiliation: None
Location: Urban
Number of Applicants: 3,823
Percent Accepted: 72%
Percent Accepted who enroll: 45%
Number Entering: 1,238
Number of Transfers Accepted each Year: Unreported
Middle 50% SAT range: M: 560–670, CR: 530–630, Wr: Unreported
Middle 50% ACT range: 20–27
Early admission program EA/ED/None: None

Percentage accepted through EA or ED: NA
EA and ED deadline: NA
Regular Deadline: 1-Mar
Application Fee: $50
Full time Undergraduate enrollment: 10,318
Total enrollment: 17,001
Percent Male: 57%
Percent Female: 43%
Total Percent Minority or Unreported: 27%
Percent African-American: 10%
Percent Asian/Pacific Islander: 13%
Percent Hispanic: 3%
Percent Native American: 1%
Percent International: Unreported
Percent in-state/out of state: 52%/48%
Percent from Public HS: 70%
Retention Rate: 84%
Graduation Rate 4-year: 53%

Graduation Rate 6-year: 60%
Percent Undergraduates in On-campus housing: 35%
Number of official organized extracurricular organizations: 136
3 Most popular majors: Information Science, Mechanical Engineering, Business
Student/Faculty ratio: 15:1
Average Class Size: 14
Percent of students going to grad school: 18%
Tuition and Fees: $27,200
In-State Tuition and Fees if different: No difference
Cost for Room and Board: $11,610
Percent receiving financial aid out of those who apply: Unreported
Percent receiving financial aid among all students: Unreported

Situated in the University City district in the heart of Philadelphia, Drexel University is a private university devoted to intensive education and hands-on training. Although infamous for its not-so-pleasant architecture, Drexel University is more known for its innovative and famous cooperative educational programs across many disciplines in numerous fields. Famous for its engineering, business, and nursing programs, Drexel aims to educate knowledgeable yet practical students who are ready to enter the workforce immediately after graduation.

Co-op and No-op

Academics at Drexel can be overwhelming at times, especially when it comes to deciding what to study. The undergraduate colleges include the College of Information Sciences and Technology, College of Arts and Sciences, College of Engineering, Goodwin College of Professional Studies, LeBow College of Business, Westphal College of Media Arts and Design, and the College of Nursing and Health Professions. All students at Drexel complete the University/College core requirements by taking classes in computing, writing, math, analysis, economics, history, philosophy, political science, humanities, and the fine arts. The core curriculum is rounded off by an early capstone course in The Drexel Experience where students learn about navigating the college experience and transitioning smoothly from high school to college, especially college life in a city like Philadelphia. Classes combine a variety of classroom-based lectures and smaller group sections where students break off into small groups. "The majority of classes can be overwhelmingly large, with a sense of anonymity, but professors are always accessible," says a freshman.

The most popular majors at Drexel include business administration, mechanical engineering, information science, biology, and nursing. The school of engineering is perhaps one of Drexel's most well-known programs with degrees offered in a wide variety of fields and only one of 17 programs nationwide to offer the Bachelor's of Engineering in Architectural Engineering. The engineering curriculum is one of the harder programs on campus, with intensive core studies in engineering sciences and specialization in the many sub-fields of engineering. As one of the country's largest private engineering schools, Drexel students have access to a wide array of resources and help

while still having "accessible professors who all love engineering," as one junior said. What's unique about Drexel's program, however, is the opportunity to work and learn hands-on while still in school. Many Drexel engineering undergraduates chose to co-op, or intern, with an employer while still in school.

Speaking of co-ops, Drexel has one of the largest co-op programs out of all private and public universities in the country that is highly distinguished in education. Students choosing to partake in the co-op spend the year after their sophomore or junior year working full-time, basically interning, for companies, businesses, nonprofits, or other organizations, depending on their intended field of study. While the majority of co-ops take place in the greater Philadelphia region, national and international co-op opportunities are available to "cater to every major, every taste, and every person," noted a sophomore. Prominently featured companies that students work for include but are not limited to: GlaxoSmithKline, Unisys Corporation, Microsoft, Lockheed Martin, Comcast, and QVC. Typical salaries for co-op students can range from $400 per week for those in accounting positions to upwards of $800 dollars per week for chemical engineering positions. Students typically earn anywhere from $11K to $17K during a six-month period during their co-op experience. "It's great to be able to make some money, network, and get real-world work experience while still in school!" a senior reminisced. Perhaps that is the reason why the majority of students opt for the co-op; earning their degree in five years rather than the typical four years at most other institutions. It is also the reason why many employers tend to hire full-time employees from former co-op interns.

In . . . West Philadelphia

Life at Drexel can be as exciting or as tame as one wants it to be. The location in the heart of Philadelphia, with access to major public transportation hubs, allows students to partake in the rich cultural, academic, and entertainment opportunities that The City of Brotherly Love has to offer. Entrenched in University City, Drexel students have the option to, and often do, party at neighboring schools such as the University of Pennsylvania. The party scene often revolves around dorm parties on the weekends with others choosing to hit Center City or surrounding clubs. Of course, as with nearly every college campus, alcohol is a part of the college scene but it's not dominating by any means. In a city rich with arts, entertainment, and restaurants, there are many things to do to suit everyone's tastes.

Philadelphia offers great night life and day life. With its rich history, the city is home to historical landmarks such as the Franklin Court, a Philadelphia tribute to Benjamin Franklin, and the Betsy Ross House. The Liberty Bell is also a popular tourist attraction in addition to Fairmount Park, the largest landscaped urban park in the world with over two hundred statues. Arts and entertainment can be found along the Avenue of the Arts with the Philadelphia Orchestra, Academy of Music, Arden Theater, and the world famous Philadelphia Museum of Art among many others. Shopping ventures at The Gallery at Market East, Chestnut Hill Shops, Liberty Place, Center City, and the Italian Market can be had for a mere subway ride from campus.

> "It's great to be able to make some money, network, and get real-world work experience while still in school!"

Life on campus can feel a little bit claustrophobic. Some students complain of the "institutional" looking buildings that "aren't that great to look at," as a freshman remarked. All freshmen are required to live on campus for their first year. The majority of all students are housed in Calhoun, Caneris, Kelly, Myers, North, Race Street, Towers, and Van Rensselaer Halls. Students in the Pennoni Honors College are singly housed in the brand-new Millennium Hall together as a learning community with their own Honors Lounge. Students may also elect to live with others who have the same academic interests as themselves in learning communities. Each community is housed in a designated area of a residence hall with a common area. Students can choose communities with interests in business, engineering, Honors College, media and design, informational technology, health professions, and a special Sophomore Year Experience community. All residences are in close proximity to the Northside Dining Terrace, Handschumacher Dining Center, and Ross Commons. The two Dining Centers offer typical take-out fare with a variety of choices and Commons offers snacks in addition to full meals. "The food can get a little dull after a while," said a senior. However, most students tend to move off campus and room with their friends in private apartments after freshman year. Still, some stay in university housing.

The Scene

The social scene at Drexel can be a little cliquey, but everyone "seems to be nice," said a junior. Everyone seems to find their group of friends that they stick to for college. The student body can be a little homogenous. "There is a large contingent of international students, but everyone else seems to be white and from the tri-state area," remarked a freshman. However, that's changing as more and more students are attracted to the school, and the recruiting effort to attract these students. Still, if one is looking for a multicultural melting pot on campus, look again. Luckily, Philadelphia offers all of that and more. In spite of the lack of diversity, everyone finds their niche within the larger Drexel community in the numerous clubs, activities, and IM sports. "It is what you make of it," said a senior.

Regardless, one thing is for certain: the Drexel experience is quite a unique one that can be very challenging and rewarding. "You get what you put in," reminisced a senior. The combination of strong business, engineering, and health professions programs coupled with real-world practical experience offered by the co-op program delivers an educational experience that is unlike most.—*Hai Pham*

FYI
If you come to Drexel, you should bring "your party clothes, something homey, and a desire to intern."
If I could change one thing, it would be "adding more diversity."
Three things everyone needs to do before graduating: "Get a cheesesteak from Geno's, frolic in Fairmount Park, and visit the Italian Market."

Franklin and Marshall College

Address: PO Box 3003,
Lancaster, PA 17604-3003
Phone: 877-678-9111
E-mail address:
admission@fandm.edu
Web site URL:
www.fandm.edu
Year Founded: 1787
Private or Public: Private
Religious Affiliation: None
Location: Suburban
Number of Applicants: 5,632
Percent Accepted: 36%
**Percent Accepted who
enroll:** 29%
Number Entering: 589
**Number of Transfers
Accepted each Year:** 42
Middle 50% SAT range:
M: 610–690, CR: 600–690,
Wr: Unreported
Middle 50% ACT range:
Unreported
**Early admission program
EA/ED/None:** ED

**Percentage accepted
through EA or ED:** 57%
EA and ED deadline: 15-Nov
Regular Deadline: 1-Feb
Application Fee: $50
**Full time Undergraduate
enrollment:** 2,164
Total enrollment: 2,164
Percent Male: 48%
Percent Female: 52%
**Total Percent Minority or
Unreported:** 12%
Percent African-American:
4%
**Percent Asian/Pacific
Islander:** 4%
Percent Hispanic: 4%
Percent Native-American:
<1%
Percent International: 9%
**Percent in-state/out of
state:** 34%/66%
Percent from Public HS:
56%
Retention Rate: 94%

Graduation Rate 4-year: 79%
Graduation Rate 6-year: 84%
**Percent Undergraduates in
On-campus housing:** 80%
**Number of official organized
extracurricular
organizations:** 90
3 Most popular majors:
Business, Government,
Biology
Student/Faculty ratio: 10:1
Average Class Size: 19
**Percent of students going to
grad school:** 25%
Tuition and Fees: $38,630
**In-State Tuition and Fees if
different:** No difference
Cost for Room and Board:
$9,870
**Percent receiving financial
aid out of those who apply:**
Unreported
**Percent receiving financial
aid among all students:**
40%

Formed by the 1853 junction between Franklin College, the first bilingual (English and German) and coeducational institution of the country, and Marshall College, founded under the sponsorship of the German Lutheran church, Franklin and Marshall College takes pride in its rich history. Despite the religious affiliations of the past, however, and the inevitable political associations (the students call themselves Diplomats), the Franklin and Marshall College of today is a completely open and secular institution. The varied curriculum, which follows the liberal arts philosophy in nurturing both the arts and the residential college system, fosters a spirit of inclusion and variety.

A Focused Center and a Bounty of Choices

Though F&M specializes in the sciences, students can experience a diverse set of classes and departments before choosing a major. There is a core curriculum, but the university really pushes even first year students to explore every field of study. "I actually enjoy the course requirements because

I am now taking lots of different classes and learning new things I did not know I was interested in," said one student. Students must take classes from each of the three realms of study in the "Foundations" program: Mind, Self, and Spirit; the Natural World; and Community, Culture, and Society. This core provides the base on which upperclassmen build their majors. Most students agree that the focus in the sciences does not hinder the academic curriculum from being characterized as a purely liberal arts curriculum.

Franklin and Marshall is especially notorious for its prestigious pre-med track, although a good portion of students pursue other fields. Because of the exceptionally difficult nature of the pre-med track, many students end up abandoning it. The rate of students committing as pre-meds has indeed decreased exponentially over the years, with a majority of students veering off course to either study other realms of sciences or switching over to the arts and humanities. "If you ask most incoming freshmen they will tell you that they are pre-med but most people end up switching that because the pre-med track is very difficult here," said one freshman.

> "I actually enjoy the course requirements because I am now taking lots of different classes and learning new things I did not know I was interested in."

Furthermore, the solid science courses at Franklin and Marshall do not exclude interesting and unusual classes from a variety of fields. One student said, "I am in a really fun film class right now, and my freshman writing seminar was fun; it was philosophy in film. We also have a foundations course called culture of chocolate where you study chocolate, which is very popular!"

One really exceptional perk of studying at Franklin and Marshall is the low faculty-student ratio of 10:1. Many students said that most of the non-introductory classes they took were generally very small, and that even larger lecture classes do not have more than 50 people. Several also emphasized how accessible and interesting their professors are, and said that research opportunities over the summer, especially in the sciences, are readily available.

Although it is possible to take fun classes and to have casual conversations with the majority of professors, students often complain about their heavy workload. Even those not on the pre-med track admit that the strenuous academic rigor promotes high levels of stress and leaves them with very little free time. "The workload can sometimes be a little overwhelming. Most people will tell you that. In my classes I have a lot of reading every night and pretty lengthy papers," said one student.

A Living Space Between Tradition and Innovation

Students praise F&M for the abundance of open spaces, like Hartman Green, which is often populated with students playing Frisbee, reading, and simply hanging out. As far as campus buildings go, a lot of students mentioned "old main, which is the oldest building and home to the president's office." Freshmen and sophomores are required to live on campus, in accommodations that are generally comfortable, but not exceptionally so. Hallways include both first-year and second-year students, with the latter having

the option of living in doubles or suites. After sophomore year, most students move into the plentiful housing that the school offers across the street. The surrounding area is small and somewhat rural, but provides students with numerous options such as affordable restaurants, interesting shops, and several nighttime bars and clubs. Students tend to eat out a lot even under a budget, because the dining hall food is generally described as not exceptional. At the same time, food is not a major source of complaint, and students say the options are satisfactory. "The dining hall is not my favorite but it is not bad. We have a lot of different options from Kivo, which offers kosher options to a 'make your pizza/pasta' and grill. Dhall is not the only option on campus; we also have Zebis, which is a café, and Pandinis which has many options."

An Intense Social Scene

F&M has an undeniable reputation for the prevalence of cliques and the abundant presence of Greek life. Frats and sororities are not officially recognized, and do not effectively dominate the social scene. There is no expectation to join a frat once you arrive at F&M in order to have a social life, most students agree. The drinking culture is prevalent in a well-defined portion of the student body, and there is a significant division between those who drink and those who don't. Recognizing the ever-increasing trend of heavy drinking on campus, the administration has been particularly strict with alcohol policies over recent years. Police have also reacted strongly—excessively so, many students say—and have been using enforced surveillance methods including the use of undercover agents to break up gatherings. The sports scene is also very popular and almost everyone participates in a sport. The most popular teams are Division III squash, football, and basketball.

Diplomats Different, Diplomats Alike

Most students agree that the population at F&M is not particularly diverse and generally homogeneous, both in terms of background and habits. Most students said that their weekend is composed of "catching up on work and sleep, and going out to parties or frats." All the students are committed to academics, but also fairly involved in extracurricular activities. Socio-economic diversity runs particularly low—almost all the students are wealthy, white, and from the

Northeast. Religious and sexual diversity is also almost nonexistent, although the few representatives of it are particularly outspoken. The gay population, for example, is very visible because it is so unusual. As far as institutions go, there is no substantial representation of these minorities. To that effect, the Hillel center for Jewish life attempts to reach out to students of all faiths. There is diversity in the political scene, students say, but there are no exceptionally vocal factions. With this general dearth in political and social representation, one can imagine that although there is reasonable involvement in extracurricular activities, a lot of people mind their own business and concentrate on their academics. At the same time, the atmosphere on campus is generally friendly and open-minded. "I was just really surprised at how many genuinely nice people there are," said one freshman.

Franklin and Marshall is thus somehow a place of great contradictions, but also of great compromises—it is both a liberal arts college and a science-based institution, it is both an academically focused and a friendly, vibrant hub of activity. Most importantly, Franklin and Marshall is at the same time a school with a history of undeniable weight, which brings with it its own features and traditions, but it also a place with a unique quality of malleability and freedom. Franklin and Marshall is one of those selected few schools that can truly be what you make it—the choice is entirely yours.—*Lavinia Borzi*

FYI

If you come to F&M, you'd better bring: "A good work ethic."

If I could change one thing about F&M, "I'd change the dining hall and more school spirit at sporting events."

One thing you wish you would've known before coming to F&M: "that there would be so much work!"

G e t t y s b u r g   C o l l e g e

Address: 300 North Washington Street, Gettysburg, PA 17325

Phone: 717-337-6100

E-mail address: admiss@gettysburg.edu

Web site URL: www.gettysburg.edu

Year Founded: 1832

Private or Public: Private

Religious Affiliation: Lutheran

Location: Suburban

Number of Applicants: 5,794

Percent Accepted: 37%

Percent Accepted who enroll: 33%

Number Entering: 714

Number of Transfers Accepted each Year: 15

Middle 50% SAT range: M: 610–670, CR: 610–690, Wr: Unreported

Middle 50% ACT range: 27–29

Early admission program EA/ED/None: ED I, ED II

Percentage accepted through EA or ED: 40%

EA and ED deadline: 15-Nov, 15-Jan

Regular Deadline: 1-Feb

Application Fee: $55

Full time Undergraduate enrollment: 2,497

Total enrollment: 2,497

Percent Male: 49%

Percent Female: 51%

Total Percent Minority or Unreported: 10%

Percent African-American: 3%

Percent Asian/Pacific Islander: 1%

Percent Hispanic: 2%

Percent Native American: 1%

Percent International: 4%

Percent in-state/out of state: 22%/78%

Percent from Public HS: 66%

Retention Rate: 92%

Graduation Rate 4-year: 80%

Graduation Rate 6-year: 84%

Percent Undergraduates in On-campus housing: 90%

Number of official organized extracurricular organizations: 140

3 Most popular majors: Management, Political Science, English

Student/Faculty ratio: 11:1

Average Class Size: 18

Percent of students going to grad school: 35%

Tuition and Fees: $37,600

In-State Tuition and Fees if different: No difference

Cost for Room and Board: $9,100

Percent receiving financial aid out of those who apply: 70%

Percent receiving financial aid among all students: 70%

Located in the historic town of Gettysburg, Pennsylvania, Gettysburg College is described by a former student as "one of the most beautiful campuses you will ever see, especially in autumn when the leaves on the trees turn and winter when it's covered with snow." The campus resonates with history. Along with its location near the battlefields, Gettysburg also has an administrative building that was used as a hospital during the Civil War, and is home to the only Civil War Era Studies department.

Though it only has 2,600 students, Gettysburg students make up three quarters of the population of the town of Gettysburg. The downside is that students complain of the city's isolation and lack of diversity, but the small size of this private liberal arts college allows for a close-knit community and ease in meeting people.

Rewarding Rigor

Gettysburg College is a liberal arts college with considerable academic rigor and emphasis on academic honor. Be forewarned that Gettysburg has an extensive General Ed requirement. One senior comments that the requirements "can result in some very annoying experiences, but it can also result in the discovery of a subject that you find fascinating and would never have stumbled upon otherwise." In addition to requiring courses in arts, social and natural sciences, Gettysburg also has an Interdisciplinary Requirement, a First-Year Writing Requirement, and a Language and Cultural Diversity requirement.

Gettysburg has special programs in science, music, and the Civil War, which many Gettysburgians come to the school to study. In fact, students can earn a minor in Civil War Era studies, or just take classes in the department. The Sunderman Music Conservatory offers a degree in music education. Those interested in political science can take classes and hear guest speakers from the Eisenhower Institute. The Garthwait Leadership Center connects students and alumni to leadership opportunities and resources.

At Gettysburg, freshmen can explore various interests and adjust to college academics in the First Year Seminars for incoming freshmen, all capped at 16 students. Ties can easily be formed because classmates from FYS also live near each other in Freshman Dorms.

Faculty members are very well-qualified, most having earned the highest degree in their field. The average class size at Gettysburg is 18. With a student-to-faculty ratio of 11:1, students have opportunities to get to know their professors. Reports one senior, "It is not uncommon to go to a professor's house for a dinner with film majors or to watch the film adaption of a book you read in English." However, because Gettysburg is a small school, the choices of classes are less than at larger ones.

Easy Living

The two primary dining places are Servo and The Bullet Hole. Servo is a dining hall. Describes a student: "It's a fun place to go with a lot of people. My friends from my freshman floor and I would go there all the time." Bullet Hole is smaller, but the food is slightly higher quality, can be selected, and taken to-go. Students can opt for a meal plan or dining dollars. Places to eat off-campus include restaurants like Pizza House or bars.

Students are guaranteed housing all four years at Gettysburg. Generally, housing gets better with seniority. Freshman dorms are evidently not too great: "The freshman dorms are pretty much like prison cells. They are small, have two windows, the walls are just concrete bricks painted white, and you have to share communal bathrooms. It can be rough," says a recent graduate. On the other hand, "Junior and senior year rooms are luxurious. They have their own bathroom, a kitchen, and separate bedrooms," elaborates the graduate. At Gettysburg, there are themes for each house like Theater house and Peace house. Students can also create their own themes, with approval.

Class is Out . . . Greek is In

Greek life is the center of the social scene, and rated very highly by students. Most people on campus go to parties at frats and sororities on Fridays and Saturdays. A building called the Attic is another place people socialize. Open on weeknights, it has "pool tables, a dance floor, and various board games," said a senior.

Gettysburg's range of clubs and activities caters to many interests. Gettysburg has its own student-run TV station, GBURG TV, which "films different events on campus as well as some original programming and broadcasts on its own channel, changing the lineup once a week." Clubs at Gettysburg include anything from "singing and acting, to fencing, political clubs, and reenacting," says a Gettysburgian. Students learn about extracurricular offerings at the activities fair. Newly accepted students can also come to Get Acquainted Day in April to find extracurriculars.

Many at Gettysburg are enthusiastic about club sports and intramurals. A new swimming pool has increased enthusiasm for the swimming team. Football and lacrosse are also widely watched, where students hope for defeat of rival schools Franklin & Marshall and Dickinson. A new gym, open to students from 6 a.m. to 11 p.m., features weight machines, pools, basketball courts, a track, and fitness classes such as zumba and spinning. For students who are not athletes but are interested in playing for a team, there are intramurals. In addition to traditional sports like volleyball, floor hockey, and basketball, Gettysburg Intramurals include less traditional sports like water polo and Quidditch. Different groups can create their own intramural teams. According to a senior, "Often first year halls create a team and different sororities and fraternities as well as groups of friends. There are both coed and single gender varieties."

Historic Paths, Feasts, and More!

Gettysburg first-years take part in the First-Year Walk, which entails walking the same path Abraham Lincoln took to the Gettysburg cemetery where he delivered his famous Gettysburg Address, and listening to a speaker. Another tradition at Gettysburg is OceanFest, where dining halls are closed and students eat varieties of seafood and barbeque outside.

> If you're looking for a small-town vibrant college community with great and caring professors and a plethora of activities and historic traditions, consider Gettysburg College.

Snowball is a dance held every February, and Dog Days are every Monday in the fall, when members of the community bring their dogs for students to play with. On Thanksgiving, dining halls serve Thanksgiving Feast. One student describes: "You get to go to the dining hall with a group of friends and sit at a big table and carve your own turkey and have mashed potatoes, corn, cranberries, and everything else Thanksgiving, including pumpkin pie for dessert. To top it all off staff members, including your professors, serve as the waiters at this event."

The biggest event at Gettysburg is Springfest, where there are activities like "inflatable slides, face paint, balloon animals, boardwalk fries, snowcones, and a live band." If you're looking for a small-town vibrant college community with great and caring professors and a plethora of activities and historic traditions, consider Gettysburg College.—*Catherine Dinh*

FYI
Know that "not all Gettysburgians are obsessed with the Civil War—you don't have to love the Civil War to come here."
What's the typical weekend schedule? "Sleep in, go for a run through the town, go to a movie at the Majestic or a sporting game, attend a party at the Attic or on the lawn, watch a movie with a bunch of friends."
Three things every student at Gettysburg should do before graduating are: "explore the battlefields, eat at the Lincoln Diner & Malt Shop, and sunbathe on Stine Lake."

Haverford College

Address: 370 Lancaster Avenue, Haverford, PA 19041

Phone: 610-896-1350

E-mail address: admissions@haverford.edu

Web site URL: www.haverford.edu

Year Founded: 1833

Private or Public: Private

Religious Affiliation: None

Location: Suburban

Number of Applicants: 3,492

Percent Accepted: 25%

Percent Accepted who enroll: 35%

Number Entering: 315

Number of Transfers Accepted each Year: 89

Middle 50% SAT range: M: 640–740, CR: 650–750, Wr: 650–750

Middle 50% ACT range: Unreported

Early admission program EA/ED/None: ED

Percentage accepted through EA or ED: 35%

EA and ED deadline: 15-Nov

Regular Deadline: 15-Jan

Application Fee: $60

Full time Undergraduate enrollment: 1,169

Total enrollment: 1,169

Percent Male: 46%

Percent Female: 54%

Total Percent Minority or Unreported: 27%

Percent African-American: 8%

Percent Asian/Pacific Islander: 11%

Percent Hispanic: 8%

Percent Native American: <1%

Percent International: 4%

Percent in-state/out of state: 13%/87%

Percent from Public HS: 55%

Retention Rate: 96%

Graduation Rate 4-year: 91%

Graduation Rate 6-year: 93%

Percent Undergraduates in On-campus housing: 99%

Number of official organized extracurricular organizations: 93

3 Most popular majors: Biology/Biological Sciences, General Economics, General English Language and Literature

Student/Faculty ratio: 8:1

Average Class Size: 9

Percent of students going to grad school: 18%

Tuition and Fees: $37,175

In-State Tuition and Fees if different: No difference

Cost for Room and Board: $11,450

Percent receiving financial aid out of those who apply: 41%

Percent receiving financial aid among all students: 42%

Although it was founded by the Religious Society of Friends in 1833, Haverford College does not have a religious affiliation to Quakerism and the roots of the college are not perceived in any way as imposing or hindering to students. Conversely, 'Fordians take pride in the Quaker traditions by embracing their social and academic dimensions and allowing them to inspire a profound sense of mutual care and responsibility in their community.

Uniqueness Through Honor and Customs

Haverford students take great pride in the way the Quaker tradition shapes the college's identity. It is precisely the things about Haverford that may seem most odd to outside observers that 'Fordians praise the most. Students stand firmly by the Honor Code—which is perhaps better described as a philosophy more than as a set of rules—by which they are responsible for their own administration and discipline through mutual understanding. An example of the Honor Code in the academic sphere is the use of self-proctored exams. A freshman said this was the best part of the academic life at Haverford, "I just took a psychology exam in my dorm room while eating a muffin. It makes things so much less stressful." Still, the Honor Code does not transfer solely into a more relaxed academic policy; it creates a sense of trust that underlies the closeness of the community. Although, "as a social code it is kind of a grey area," students agree that it is a big part of what makes Haverford so welcoming and inclusive. As a student stated, "We each hold ourselves responsible and generally don't need to be worried what our peers are doing." Another quirky tradition that students raved about is Customs Week. "Customs Week operates under the guise of giving the freshmen all the information about college they'll need, but its true purpose is to bring them closer together to the people they'll be living with, and make them feel that after a mere few action-packed days, Haverford is home," one student said. A freshman even said that the program makes the transition from high school to the Haverford community seamless. Indeed, the relationships formed during Customs Week remain solid throughout the years and provide the basis for social life at Haverford, adds a senior. And these are not just with other freshmen—the Customs People, defined by the students as upperclassmen, who live in the freshmen dorms but do not have any of the disciplinary roles of RA's, actually form tight friendship bonds with the newcomers. Students say this is why the social life is so inclusive, and there are no great distinctions between upperclassmen and underclassmen—all take pride in their traditions and are deeply committed to upholding the community spirit.

A Wealth of Passion and Academia

Although students say the social scene is very welcoming and "generally everyone is extremely nice here," all agree that academics are definitely a larger part of life at Haverford. Although these do not come in the way of friendships, as there is an unwritten understanding of not sharing grades, they take up a large chunk of people's time and attention. One freshman said that if he could change anything about Haverford, he would make the social life livelier on the weekends. "It gets a little quiet," he said. He would also round up a bit more spirit for Haverford's sports teams, which is notoriously not one of the school's salient features. However, the majority of students interviewed agreed that social life is actually generally satisfying and that it caters to the needs of different people. Given that not every single person at Haverford is a small Jewish kid named Dan, as the famous stereotype dictates, the social scene illustrates the variety of people present on campus. As one student puts it, "We're homogenous enough to forge a strong community, but heterogeneous enough to keep things interesting." There are parties on campus on Saturday nights for those who want to drink, and fun events—organized by the 'Fordians Against Boredom (FAB)—for those who don't. There are plenty of campus-wide dances and the traditional Haverfest, "a festival filled with games, contests, bouncy castles, debauchery, and fuzzy animals." Of this epic event, one student said, "Nobody has an excuse to do work, and it's a great time to just unleash your pent-up energy and anxiety while having a carefree blast with friends." Still, the workload is substantial, and although students say that they generally manage to make time to take part in the plethora of extracurriculars available to

them and to spend time with their friends, it can become very draining. One student admitted that the thing he was most surprised by when he came to Haverford was the amount of work, while another said, "Sometimes the commitments can be overwhelming, and I wish I could just sit around and hang out with friends or dwell on a book more often." At the same time, 'Fordians speak as passionately about their academic life as they do about everything else. One senior said, "My least favorite part of Haverford's academic life is that the work can be so demanding, but I choose my own classes and know what I'm getting myself into." While some think the distributional requirements (3 NA, 3 SO, 3 HU, 1 Quantitative, 1 year of foreign language) can restrain the freedom of "academic experimentation," most are comfortable with them and have had the chance to take fascinating and unusual classes. "Humanimality," "Reading Madness," and "Culture and Crisis in the Golden Age of Athens" are some of the course titles given by the students interviewed. 'Fordians also rave about their professors, both for the quality of their teaching and their accessibility. "One of the reasons people come here is because of the relationships with professors," said a student, explaining that the 8:1 faculty student ratio enables the creation of real interaction both inside and outside of the classroom. As another student gushed, "Haverford manages to hire the nicest professors ever." Likewise, although certain majors, particularly those in math and science, can be dauntingly demanding, there are plenty of resources there to help. "There's the Chem Question Lab, the Math Question Center, and various tutors. Since most professors live on or near campus, they are literally always available if you are struggling as well." The general feeling about academic life, then, seems to be that it is what you make of it. Just as the types of people, which in one student's description are "a little socially awkward," and in another student's description, are "the nicest, quirkiest, least judgmental people you'll ever meet," the academics at Haverford can be heavily daunting or greatly inspiring. No matter their minor criticisms though, all the students interviewed firmly stood by their idea that ultimately the close-knit community and atmosphere of mutual respect and understanding makes it all worth it.

A Bountiful Garden

Although it is their traditions and philosophy that students pride themselves in the most, they did not forget to mention the many attractions of their idyllic campus. The entire campus is an arboretum and boasts massive lawns with an impressive variety of trees, such as the Founder's Green and the Barclay Beach. There is also a duck pond, where it is a tradition to swim in at least once before graduation, even though, as one student said, "the water is kind of disgusting." Another salient feature is the nature trail—in the words of a senior, "I love the nature trail because even though it's on the edges of campus along busy roads, it's wooded and still feels isolated." Despite the enviable woody setting, Haverford is actually not isolated at all. Campus is in a Main Line suburb of Philadelphia and only a 15–20 minute ride from the city. Students hang out regularly at food joints just off campus like Wawa or Chipolte, but most do not venture out into Philadelphia very often. "We're a very active campus," said a senior. Aside from parties and FAB events, there are plenty of extracurriculars to choose from, and Haverford boasts the largest number of a cappella groups per capita in the country. Living spaces are also pretty comfortable. Two new dorms were recently added, Kim Hall and Tritton Hall, and "they didn't expand enrollment, which is nice." While students are generally satisfied with housing, which typically does not substantially improve with seniority, as "freshman dorms are already really nice," most mentioned that the dining hall food is something of a disappointment. However, one student noted, "I like to say that we complain a lot about the food at Haverford because we have nothing else to complain about." 'Fordians have the privilege of a balance between a small, tight community and a spacious, beautiful and livable home. What is most striking about 'Fordians is that ultimately the most glamorous features are not what they rave about—they keep coming back to the simple tenants of their community philosophy and lifestyle.

In the words of one freshman as advice to those wanting to make the most out of the Haverford experience, "Embrace the community, and embrace yourself. You'll be much happier if you pursue what you want to pursue, academically and socially. Haverford has taught me so many things about myself I never would have learned otherwise."

> "Embrace the community, and embrace yourself. You'll be much happier if you pursue what you want to pursue, academically and socially. Haverford has taught me so many things about myself I never would have learned otherwise."

An Experience for All

At first glance, Haverford, with its strongly Quaker roots, is a quieter college experience. But from this quality arises its strengths: a culture of academic trust, easy access to nature, resources to carve one's own desired experience.—*Lavinia Borzi*

FYI
If you come to Haverford, you'd better leave "your 'tude behind. You don't need that. Our honor code applies not just to academics, but to social life as well—our motto is trust, concern, respect."
The biggest college-wide tradition/event at Haverford is Haverfest.
What you need to know to have fun at Haverford: "Take the classes you love, and don't feel intimidated by anyone. Literally everyone is kind and is willing to be your friend."

Lafayette College

Address: 118 Markle Hall, Easton, PA 18042
Phone: 610-330-5355
E-mail address: admissions@lafayette.edu
Web site URL: www.lafayette.edu
Year Founded: 1826
Private or Public: Private
Religious Affiliation: None
Location: Urban
Number of Applicants: 5,716
Percent Accepted: 40%
Percent Accepted who enroll: 28%
Number Entering: 640
Number of Transfers Accepted each Year: 20
Middle 50% SAT range: M: 660, CR: 635, Wr: 630
Middle 50% ACT range: 28.5
Early admission program EA/ED/None: ED
Percentage accepted through EA or ED: 50%

EA and ED deadline: 15-Nov
Regular Deadline: 1-Jan
Application Fee: $65
Full time Undergraduate enrollment: 2,423
Total enrollment: 2,478
Percent Male: 53%
Percent Female: 47%
Total Percent Minority or Unreported: 24%
Percent African-American: 5%
Percent Asian/Pacific Islander: 4%
Percent Hispanic: 6%
Percent Native American: <1%
Percent International: 6%
Percent in-state/out of state: 21%/79%
Percent from Public HS: 70%
Retention Rate: 95%
Graduation Rate 4-year: 85%

Graduation Rate 6-year: 88%
Percent Undergraduates in On-campus housing: 98%
Number of official organized extracurricular organizations: 250
3 Most popular majors: Economics, Government & Law, Psychology
Student/Faculty ratio: 10:1
Average Class Size: 25
Percent of students going to grad school: 26%
Tuition and Fees: $41,358
In-State Tuition and Fees if different: No difference
Cost for Room and Board: $12,362
Percent receiving financial aid out of those who apply: 70%
Percent receiving financial aid among all students: 45%

Lafayette College is a relatively unknown jewel hidden in the woods of Easton, Pennsylvania. A small liberal arts college that emphasizes a focused curriculum of core classes, Lafayette offers 47 different majors across four overarching disciplines: the natural sciences, social sciences, engineering, and humanities, all with a focus on the philosophy of a truly liberal arts education. This unique school with a student body consisting only of undergraduates provides a very focused education with students receiving more individualized attention than those at larger, public universities. Students at Lafayette receive an equitable amount of resources without having to compete with graduate students for attention, money, and advising. The sprawling 110-acre campus provides ample room to live, learn, and grow in a small, yet academically challenging environment.

Academically Speaking

Lafayette College boasts a wide array of classes in 25 fields with hundreds of classes to choose from. Even with these large selections, students are still required to complete 32 credits for a bachelor's degree or 38 credits in engineering in addition to the general "core" requirements. Students must maintain at least a 2.00 GPA in order to graduate. Some courses to expect are the First Year Seminars, English 110, Values and Science/Technology Seminars, and two writing courses in order to fulfill the writing requirement of the bachelor's degree; however, they are left up to the discretion of the faculty depending on students' abilities and entering qualifications. The requirement may seem stiffer than most other schools' but a sophomore noted that "It forces you to really sharpen your ability to communicate an idea intelligently." Indeed, the core curriculum at Lafayette exposes students to many different fields in academia, forcing students out of their comfort zones to explore a truly liberal education. Students may combine two fields in interdisciplinary study, double major, or design their own major in two coordinating departments to fit their educational needs. The new program in policy studies that was created in 2006 allows students to cross traditional majors to combine the fields of management, design, and evaluation of policies and institutions. These and other programs aim to keep Lafayette students "interested and engaged in their education," as one senior remarked.

> **"[The academic requirement] forces you to really sharpen your ability to communicate an idea intelligently."**

Engagement doesn't stop with just interesting classes, but also interesting professors. The relatively small size and low student-to-faculty ratio of the school allows for superb undergraduate focus and attention. Professors take a vested interest in their students' success since they have so few and the student body itself is small. Students generally find professors easy to approach in and out of class for help, guidance, or advice. Although many find this to be a point of comfort, others find it hard to avoid professors or other students on Lafayette's campus. Others complain that the size at times, although homey, feels a little stifling. "You tend to see the same types of people around here," says a freshman.

Leopard Life

In freshman year, all students are required to live on campus. Freshmen are assigned roommates and dorms according to a survey each student fills out before coming to campus. Freshmen are assigned preferences on a first come, first serve basis with South College taking the cake as the most desirable freshman dorm. Rooms are usually adequately spacious with nice amenities owing to recent renovations by the college. Upperclassmen housing is determined by an annual lottery draw where seniors have top pick and the rest picking in subsequent order. Students may choose to live in traditional dorm set-ups or opt to live in special interest housing catering to cultural, language, and academic interests. High honor students, called "McKelvy Scholars," are invited to live in special housing in McKelvy House, and this is a mark of distinction that is bestowed upon only twenty students each year.

Aside from on-campus housing, some upperclassmen choose to live off campus in private apartments or Greek-affiliated fraternity and sorority houses. However, in recent years Lafayette has altered housing policies to lure students back on campus by mandating that students live in college-owned properties. The housing draws for this "off campus" housing are often inundated past capacity with seniors once again getting first pick. These students may be lucky enough to escape the overbearing RAs that some students complain about at Lafayette. "It's like someone is always watching your every move," says a junior. Some feel that the RAs are too strict, too power hungry, or just doing their job. Whichever the case, it seems unanimous that the student body would like to see less overbearing RAs.

Dining at Lafayette complements the housing very well: with variety. There are larger dining halls that accommodate buffet style dining for those on meal plans. Other "student restaurants" like Farinon and Marquis restaurant serve a select variety of retail-style dishes. Food choices range from Italian to Mediterranean, Southern, and many more types of cuisines. Most students seem to be approving of the food quality here due to the many offerings that the college has put together. In freshman year, all students are required to be on the standard full meal plan with twenty-one meals per week. In subsequent years, students may choose from other meal plans according to their choice.

The campus itself is situated on a beautiful suburban landscape in Easton. The actual campus is very well patrolled by campus police and is very safe according to students. However, surrounding neighborhoods are not so friendly so students "have to be smart," says a senior. The Town-Gown relationship between Lafayette and Easton seems to have had some tension in recent years as college parties spill over into adjacent communities, often resulting in unhappy residents. The administration has responded by increasingly cracking down on parties, especially those that serve alcohol.

The Life, the Rivalry

Lafayette and its archrival neighbor, Lehigh University, have a long on-going feud in both academics and sports. Lafayette is not to be taken lightly because despite its small size, all 23 intercollegiate sports are NCAA Division I. Football and basketball seem to dominate the scene here as most other sports' facilities are not on the main grounds of campus. Students gather for the Lafayette-Lehigh game that is played annually in a tradition dating back to almost a century ago. The rivalry between Lehigh and Lafayette is comparable to that between Harvard and Yale, steeped in tradition and time. Students are mostly proud of their school and have some school spirit to show. Aside from athletics, the social scene is split between the frat scene and extracurriculars with the more "jockey" type being drawn to frats. However, with stricter party/alcohol enforcement efforts by the administration, the once thriving Greek scene has dwindled down to about 12 fraternities and sororities. Still, they dominate a sizable chunk of the social scene at Lafayette with 30% of the student population participating. Extracurricular organizations are the other pedestal of Lafayette social life, with many students choosing to do community service with well-known groups such as Engineers Without Borders, pursue academic interests in Academic Club, or explore career-oriented groups such as the Investment Club. Whatever the taste, Lafayette has something for everyone.

Off campus, there aren't too many options open for students. As a result of on-campus party policing, many underclassmen seek out off-campus parties while upperclassmen prefer the town bars. For those seeking big city adventures, Philadelphia is about an hour away by bus or car. Whatever the case, students find ways to keep themselves busy and entertained.—*Hai Pham*

FYI

If you come to Lafayette, you'd better bring "a rug and other home amenities."
What's the typical schedule like? "Classes and homework during the weekdays, party during the weekend (sometimes starting on Wednesday), and relaxing/preparing for class on Sunday."
If you could change one thing what would it be? "The administration here needs to chill out a little more and not take everything so seriously."

Lehigh University

Address: 27 Memorial Drive, West Bethlehem, PA 18015
Phone: 610-758-3100
E-mail address: admissions@lehigh.edu
Web site URL: www.lehigh.edu/admissions
Year Founded: 1865
Private or Public: Private
Religious Affiliation: None
Location: Suburban
Number of Applicants: 11,578
Percent Accepted: 33%
Percent Accepted who enroll: 31%
Number Entering: 1,207
Number of Transfers Accepted each Year: 158
Middle 50% SAT range: M: 640–720, CR: 580–680, Wr: Not Used
Middle 50% ACT range: 28–31
Early admission program EA/ED/None: ED I, ED II

Percentage accepted through EA or ED: 47%
EA and ED deadline: 15-Nov, 15-Jan
Regular Deadline: 1-Jan
Application Fee: $70
Full time Undergraduate enrollment: 4,732
Total enrollment: 7,055
Percent Male: 58%
Percent Female: 42%
Total Percent Minority or Unreported: 22%
Percent African-American: 4%
Percent Asian/Pacific Islander: 6%
Percent Hispanic: 9%
Percent Native American: 0%
Percent International: 5%
Percent in-state/out of state: 25%/75%
Percent from Public HS: Unreported
Retention Rate: 95%

Graduation Rate 4-year: 78%
Graduation Rate 6-year: 87%
Percent Undergraduates in On-campus housing: 69%
Number of official organized extracurricular organizations: 150
3 Most popular majors: Finance, Mechanical Engineering, Psychology
Student/Faculty ratio: 10:1
Average Class Size: 28
Percent of students going to grad school: 34%
Tuition and Fees: $41,060
In-State Tuition and Fees if different: No difference
Cost for Room and Board: $10,840
Percent receiving financial aid out of those who apply: 74%
Percent receiving financial aid among all students: 66%

Bethlehem, Pennsylvania is a pretty unassuming town. It's not known for much, but it's the home of Lehigh University, a middle-sized college known for its engineers, its football team, and its overflowing school spirit. Students at Lehigh know how to excel in the classroom, but they also know when to drop all the textbooks and pick up a bottle. Life at Lehigh is a mix of serious academics and wild parties, of compelling classroom discussions and fun extracurricular activities. As one student put it, "it's the perfect place for someone who wants a well-rounded college experience—nothing too stuffy, not too crazy."

"Work Hard . . ."

While the diversity of student interests and majors at Lehigh has increased over the past few years, one thing has not changed: academics are rigorous and demanding. A psychology major described the student body as "extremely competitive when it comes to academics." Group projects are common, and although they make classes more interesting, they also increase the pressure to outperform your peers. Several students said the level of competition at Lehigh was something high school hadn't quite prepared them for, adding that it took time freshman year to adjust and learn to be more independent when it comes to studying. Despite the somewhat cutthroat tension of Lehigh academics however, students rated their classroom experiences and professors very highly.

One student, a double major in accounting and finance, praised the quality of faculty at Lehigh and said that academics, although challenging, are very fair. "Registration isn't too difficult because if there's ever a class you really want to get in to, you can talk to the professor and your advisor and everyone works hard to accommodate your interests," he said. With a student faculty ration of 10:1, students said it's easy to receive personal attention from professors if you seek it out. The average class size for introsequence classes is 50 to 100 students, while major-specific classes usually have a maximum of 25 to 30 students.

Lehigh has a reputation for being dominated by engineers, and while statistically this is still true, upperclassmen said they've noticed more dynamic interests among incoming classes. Of the five programs that undergraduates can enroll in, the College of Arts & Sciences accounts for 38 percent of the undergraduate population, while the

P.C. Rossin College of Engineering and Applied Science accounts for 35 percent. The engineering school offers eight majors and five integrated programs. The College of Business and Economics is also very popular; 24 percent of undergraduates focus in one of the school's eight majors. Less popular at Lehigh are the Computer Science and Business and Arts and Engineering tracks, which are interdisciplinary programs. The most common majors around campus include accounting, chemical engineering, and mechanical engineering according to one student.

Lehigh's dual degree programs have encouraged students to explore broader interests. A computer science and business (CSB) dual degree student said "the several dual degree programs offered here are very unique to this school." Classes under these programs combine different disciplines, and show students how knowledge from one subject area can be applied to another. The CSB major said economics is his favorite class, because it teaches both macro and micro concepts and relates them back to his computer science lectures. Dual degree programs are perhaps even more competitive than other majors, but students said that once they adjusted to the new academic expectations, they learned to love their classes and professors.

> "We live by the motto 'work hard, party harder.'"

". . . Party Harder!"

Lehigh students might put academics first, but that doesn't mean they don't also prioritize partying. As one student put it, "we live by the motto 'work hard, party harder,' so we get our work done by 9 p.m. every night and then we can go out and have fun." Several students mentioned that Greek life dominates the social scene—over 50 percent of campus population is involved. Fraternity houses are located on top of "the hill," which is a short hike from main campus. Parties also take place in off-campus houses in the city of Bethlehem, and aren't exclusive to weekends. Weekday drinking and drug use are by no means rare.

One freshman also diminished the myth that it's hard for underage students to find alcohol or fun parties at Lehigh. "Although freshmen aren't officially invited anywhere, upperclassmen send out information about parties and then we can pick and choose what we want to do each night," she said. She also added that there are ways to avoid Greek life, as well as drugs and alcohol if you're seeking a different kind of social experience. Most students agreed that although partying is a big part of the Lehigh college experience, they met most of their friends through their residences, classes, or clubs. Even on nights when students aren't at a frat house, social life is typically very active and students will find other "chill" things to do for fun.

Of course while one member of a fraternity confidently said that Lehigh students "choose their own path," a non-partier said there's a lot of pressure to partake and that there have been times when he's felt like an outsider for not wanting to. Social life is oriented around partying, and students typically drink a lot. Partying may be one of the many different lifestyles of Lehigh students, but it's certainly most dominant.

A Beautiful Bubble

Students rave about the architecture and layout of Lehigh's campus. "Campus is literally built into the side of a mountain; the buildings are so pretty and gothic and the forest in the mountain environment just makes this the most beautiful campus on earth," one student said. University Walk and the front lawn are two particularly picturesque spots around campus, and the Linderman Library with its iconic spiral staircase is another favorite building among Lehigh students. Many facilities have been recently renovated, giving campus a good balance of an older, historical feel and a more modern feel, according to a mechanical engineering student.

Lehigh's location in Bethlehem, however, leaves it rather isolated. One student said that unless you have a car, it's hard to go into town to eat or shop, which is one reason that partying is the primary social activity on campus. Still, shuttles to the local mall and plaza run on the weekends, and one student said his goal is to really get to know North and South Bethlehem. "Since we're not in a major city, many people don't think there is much to see and do in town, but actually there's a ton," he said. Of course off-campus areas aren't completely safe, especially after dark, keeping most students on campus.

Luckily, Lehigh dining is rated pretty highly by the student body. Dining halls are equipped with make-your-own sandwich and pasta stations, and serve a good variety of vegetarian and gluten-free options as well. The Upper Court, which accepts dining dollars and serves fast food as well as sushi, salads and Mexican, Chinese and Italian cuisine, is also a popular place to eat according to one student. Nearby pizzerias and the Goose, a famous sandwich shop with a secret menu, are also frequented by Lehigh students, often as a part of campus traditions.

Laugh at Laf

Most students either don't mind or don't notice that Lehigh is isolated, simply because there's so much going on around campus. School spirit is vibrant, especially during Laf week, leading up to the Lehigh-Lafayette football game. The rivalry between these two schools is ranked as one of the top ten college football rivalries by *Sports Illustrated*, so it's no surprise that Lehigh students take their sports and their teams very seriously. One student said his only regret is not living life to the fullest during Laf week, which includes concerts, bed races, and of course, parties. All football games are popular events, with thousands of undergraduates showing up in their Lehigh colors ready to shout their support.

Sports teams and clubs are also one of the more popular extracurricular activities, preceded only by Greek life. Still, undergraduates said that there are opportunities to get involved in different things depending on a student's interests. Volunteering is very common, as is environmental club. In general, students are typically involved in at least one activity outside of their coursework, and many choose to participate in a number of different clubs because it's considered the best way to meet people and make friends. "The great variety of student activities to join helps make a relatively small school feel bigger," one student said.

Students said they chose to come to Lehigh because of its academic reputation, but they fell in love with it because of its campus spirit and traditions, which lends itself to four fulfilling undergraduate years. "Past our hill of frats is this giant star-shaped light called the Bethlehem star, and it's amazing to see it up close in person," one freshman said. "I haven't done it yet because you have to know someone to hop a few fences, but I will get there!"—*Payal Marathe*

FYI

"Three things every student at Lehigh should do before graduating are: get a sandwich from the Goose, see a Lehigh-Lafayette game, and go to the tower at mountaintop in the middle of the night."

"The best college-wide tradition is the Turkey Trot during the week leading up to the Lehigh-Lafayette rivalry football game."

"What surprised me the most about Lehigh when I arrived was how friendly people are here—they'll hold doors for you and smile at you, which I know is a small detail, but I really appreciate that."

Muhlenberg College

Address: 2400 Chew Street, Allentown, PA 18104
Phone: 484-664-3200
E-mail address: admissions@muhlenberg.edu
Web site URL: www.muhlenberg.edu
Year Founded: 1848
Private or Public: Private
Religious Affiliation: Lutheran
Location: Urban
Number of Applicants: 4,876
Percent Accepted: 43%
Percent Accepted who enroll: 28%
Number Entering: 584
Number of Transfers Accepted each Year: 25
Middle 50% SAT range: M: 560–670, CR: 560–670, Wr: 560–670
Middle 50% ACT range: 25–31
Early admission program EA/ED/None: ED

Percentage accepted through EA or ED: Unreported
EA and ED deadline: 1-Feb
Regular Deadline: 15-Feb
Application Fee: $50
Full time Undergraduate enrollment: 2,345
Total enrollment: 2,483
Percent Male: 42%
Percent Female: 58%
Total Percent Minority or Unreported: 27%
Percent African-American: 3%
Percent Asian/Pacific Islander: 2%
Percent Hispanic: 4%
Percent Native American: <1%
Percent International: <1%
Percent in-state/out of state: 22%/78%
Percent from Public HS: 70%
Retention Rate: 90%
Graduation Rate 4-year: 79%

Graduation Rate 6-year: 84%
Percent Undergraduates in On-campus housing: 91%
Number of official organized extracurricular organizations: 100
4 Most popular majors: Business/Commerce, Communication Studies/Speech, Communication and Rhetoric, Psychology
Student/Faculty ratio: 12:1
Average Class Size: 15
Percent of students going to grad school: Unreported
Tuition and Fees: $39,630
In-State Tuition and Fees if different: No difference
Cost for Room and Board: $9,040
Percent receiving financial aid out of those who apply: 80%
Percent receiving financial aid among all students: 46%

A small liberal arts college tucked away in suburban Allentown, Pennsylvania, Muhlenberg College truly offers an intimate college experience. From the quaint 81-acre campus to the modest student population, Muhlenberg is sure to make one feel like part of a small, close-knit community. However, small size doesn't mean small offerings. With over 60 majors and 100 campus organizations to choose from, Muhlenberg offers a sizable array of options for a small school. Students emerge from Muhlenberg with an excellent education, preparation for their career goals, and a stronger sense of self.

Strong Academics, Strong Students

Muhlenberg prides itself on preparing students for whatever challenge they will face, be it graduate school admissions, working towards a career, or simply being better equipped for life. Owing to the College's commitment to a liberal arts education, all students fulfill general education requirements, including two semesters of foreign language study, science, mathematics, physical education, and the fine arts. Fear not, however, as these requirements are aimed at giving a student a well-rounded education. "No one graduates from Muhlenberg with a one-dimensional education," a senior said. "General education requirements are easily fulfilled and allow everyone to actually have a real sense of liberal arts and engage with the liberal arts in their education," a freshman remarked. Students are grounded from the very beginning in the physical sciences, social sciences, and the humanities in order to expose them to academia in both breadth and depth.

The workload at Muhlenberg is also about as diverse as the number of majors the school offers. General introductory classes tend to be fairly easy while more advanced science classes can wrack any genius's brain. "It really depends on the class and the professor. Classes like fitness and wellness are jokes," a freshman said. But do not be misled. Muhlenberg is renowned for its pre-medicine program due to its highly respected science departments. They also have a praised, innovative program in neuroscience that is popular among students and gaining a reputation among academic circles. Pre-med students have a pretty challenging course load that is typical of the pre-med track at any school. Most students can expect to study at least two hours per day for each class; multiplying that by the usual four-class schedule results in about eight hours of study time per day. Some majors allow for less work in the typical homework sense, but more time devoted in the art studio, theater, or dance studio. Even though dance majors are not spending as much time hitting the books as pre-meds, all students at Muhlenberg devote time to their education.

Devoted study doesn't mean there is no room for academic fun. Unusual classes such as "To Hell and Back" and "Bugs and Us" allow students to integrate non-traditional learning into their education with hands-on experiences in interesting subjects of study. Whatever the preference, students are sure to find something that interests them at Muhlenberg. The individualized attention that a small college affords is also an important part of the College experience. Class sizes are usually less than 20, excluding the large introductory science courses, and professors are very accessible. "Most of the professors are really nice and truly want you to succeed," a sophomore said. They can be one of the most valuable resources to students in terms of mastering course material or just building relationships.

What Muhlenberg does lack doesn't come in terms of quality but more so size. Academic departments are generally good, but some departments are undersized due to Muhlenberg's small size as a liberal arts college. Some students complain that although there are many programs offered, there's just not enough of the financial pie to go around for everyone. "Some departments could use expansion," a senior opined. It is apparent that the tradeoff cost for highly individualized attention is a smaller, less extensive program.

Ride the Mule

For a small college, Muhlenberg does have a vibrant social scene on campus. No scene dominates another here; everyone pretty much finds his or her place. Options are plentiful and students usually find what it is they're looking for. Weekends at the 'Berg are filled with variety—there's the frat scene, the usual dorm parties, and many non-partying alternatives. The Muhlenberg Activities Council works hard to put on events during the weekends for those for whom partying isn't their cup of tea. Movies, bowling, concerts, comedians, sports and other events are regularly held for those looking to have good, clean old-fashioned fun.

> "The best part of campus is that it is small, and it is almost impossible to be late getting to classes or appointments."

Of course, alcohol is part of the party scene like at any other school, but at Muhlenberg, it doesn't dominate. Some people drink, and they find it easy to acquire alcohol. Others choose not to drink and find it equally easy to hang out with people who also choose not to drink. Just like alcohol, the Greek life at Muhlenberg is also a selective choice. Only about 20 percent of the student body is involved with Greek life. The school is large enough for people to make many new acquaintances, but small enough so that it doesn't become stifling or overpowering.

A highlight of a small college social scene is the fact that mostly everyone knows each other. People become close with most of their dorm-mates quite quickly due to the sheer amount of time spent interacting with each other. Classmates also quickly become good friends as many within the same major spend much academic time with each other as well. Classes, labs, performances, and more begin to pile up once the semester gets rolling, so it helps to have a core group of study buddies as well as friends. If that's not enough, "everyone on campus seems to be friendly," a freshman observed. There are no social divides between majors, ages, or clubs. The social scene is not cliquey, but at times it can seem very homogenous. "Some people might think that Muhlenberg is a bunch of rich white kids," a senior said, but there are still plenty of opportunities for people to find their place.

Life at the 'Berg

Situated on a hilltop in the West End neighborhood of Allentown, Pennsylvania, Muhlenberg's campus offers old-school, small-town charm alongside the modernity of world-class facilities. Campus grounds are kept pristine throughout the school year. Students praise the gorgeous campus and the relative ease of walking from place to place around campus. "The best part of campus is that it is small, and it is almost impossible to be late getting to classes or appointments," a freshman remarked.

Housing at Muhlenberg can be pretty sweet as well. Even though the college and campus themselves are small, there are still lots of options for housing. Freshmen usually live on campus in one of the three designated freshman dorms with quiet dorms available for those who prefer their dorms to be a quiet study space. Then there are the party dorms for the more socially inclined. Housing is set up in a hall system where students share communal bathrooms in a hall with singles, doubles, and sometimes triples that they share with roommates. Most dorms are equipped with air conditioning while Brown, the all-female dorm, is equipped with 15-foot ceilings and hardwood floors. Others might not get so lucky. But seniors have the additional option to live off campus in suite-style arrangements through the Muhlenberg Independent Living Experience (M.I.L.E.) program. M.I.L.E. houses are owned and operated by the college. They include a kitchen, living room, and multiple bedroom arrangements.

Dining at Muhlenberg is also very diversified. The main dining hall, affectionately known as the Garden Room, serves up traditional cuisine in a buffet-style setting. Choices are usually varied with vegetarian and vegan options consistently available. Aside from the daily hustle and bustle of the dining hall, students may also choose from Sandella's, Cyclone Salads, Freshens Smoothies, Java Joe, and the GQ (General's Quarters), the latter of which serves up late-night munchies. With so much variety, students rarely get bored with the selection at Muhlenberg—but beware, choose wisely as some establishments are better than others depending on taste preferences.

If college food doesn't satiate satisfactorily, there are many restaurants around campus in Allentown. The area around Chew Street is full of businesses catering to the College community. However, town-gown relations aren't the best. Tough neighborhoods located near campus contribute to a divide between "rich" students and their counterparts who actually live in Allentown. Allentown is also just that: a town. Don't expect to find cosmopolitan entertainment options in the immediate area, but Philadelphia is only an hour away while New York City is about two hours away. Students always manage to keep themselves occupied.

Friendly Fro-Yo Fanatics

In all, Muhlenberg students claim they are some of the happiest students to be found in the Tri-State area. From the opening convocation in the chapel to the candlelight ceremony at orientation, students truly feel like an essential part of an academic community. Termed the "caring college" by its denizens, Muhlenberg is home to students known to be diverse in their interests, friends, and goals. Many of them welcome "newbies" with open arms, oftentimes over frozen yogurt, a campus-wide obsession. As much as frozen yogurt is a part of the Muhlenberg culture, so are friendliness and acceptance. If a small, close campus doesn't feel stifling, then Muhlenberg College might be the one for some prospective students. The lack of entertainment options is mostly offset by the proliferation of activities on campus and students are generally happy in spite of the occasional feeling of living in a Muhlenberg bubble.—*Hai Pham*

FYI

Four things everyone should do before graduation are: "eat fro-yo, play in the snow, see a speaker, and go to Hillel's Bagel Brunch."

What's the typical weekend schedule? "People go to parties, hang out in the dorms with their friends, participate in campus events, see a performance, go to the mall, and Sundays are mostly spent studying."

If you come to Muhlenberg you'd better bring "your work ethic, UGGs, and a smile."

If I could change one thing about Muhlenberg, "I would place it somewhere more urban than Allentown."

Penn State University

Address: 201 Shields Building, Box 3000, University Park, PA 16802-1294

Phone: 814-865-5471

E-mail address: admissions@psu.edu

Web site URL: www.psu.edu

Year Founded: 1855

Private or Public: Public

Religious Affiliation: None

Location: Urban

Number of Applicants: 40,714

Percent Accepted: 52%

Percent Accepted who enroll: 31%

Number Entering: 6,540

Number of Transfers Accepted each Year: 108

Middle 50% SAT range: M: 560–670, CR: 530–630, Wr: 540–640

Middle 50% ACT range: Unreported

Early admission program EA/ED/None: None

Percentage accepted through EA or ED: NA

EA and ED deadline: NA

Regular Deadline: 15-Jan

Application Fee: $50

Full time Undergraduate enrollment: 37,486

Total enrollment: 38,630

Percent Male: 55%

Percent Female: 45%

Total Percent Minority or Unreported: 24%

Percent African-American: 4%

Percent Asian/Pacific Islander: 5%

Percent Hispanic: 4%

Percent Native American: 0%

Percent International: Unreported

Percent in-state/out of state: 75%/25%

Percent from Public HS: Unreported

Retention Rate: Unreported

Graduation Rate 4-year: 84%

Graduation Rate 6-year: 88%

Percent Undergraduates in On-campus housing: 37%

Number of official organized extracurricular organizations: 884

3 Most popular majors: Economics, Psychology, Biology

Student/Faculty ratio: 17:1

Average Class Size: 25

Percent of students going to grad school: Unreported

Tuition and Fees: $27,206

In-State Tuition and Fees if different: $15,124

Cost for Room and Board: $9,420

Percent receiving financial aid out of those who apply: 69%

Percent receiving financial aid among all students: 71%

For students looking for a fun and stimulating college experience, this school may be the ticket. With around 40,000 students, Penn State can be the perfect college experience for those seeking a big student body and strong technical programs. Penn State is a land-grant public research university offering undergraduate, graduate, and professional programs. The University features over 160 majors and a wealth of extracurricular activities, which, coupled with a legendary school spirit, can make for a fantastic four years.

University Park, the Place to Be

Penn State actually has 24 campuses spread across the state, with the largest, the University Park campus, located geographically in the middle of Pennsylvania. The University Park campus is the most prestigious and selective of the Penn State locations, having an undergraduate acceptance rate of approximately 52 percent. University Park is comprised of 13 distinct "colleges," including the Colleges of Agricultural Sciences, Arts and Architecture, Business, Communications, and Earth and Mineral Sciences for example.

The University also recently approved a School of International Affairs to be a part of the Dickson School of Law.

Penn State's scientific and research programs are considered the strongest at the university. The meteorology program is particularly well known, as is the College of Agricultural Sciences, having fantastic facilities and a number of livestock. And for the non–technical oriented, the University boasts a breadth of offerings satisfying almost any program you could be looking for. "Pretty much any interest can be pursued given the opportunities here," said one senior. "The wide variety of programs and courses available to students is one of the most appealing aspects of Penn State."

To graduate, students are required to complete Penn State's general education requirements, which consist of 45 credits distributed across disciplines. Undergraduates take classes in the humanities, arts, natural and social sciences, health, communications and quantifications, and physical education. Every year, 1800 students are admitted to the University's Schreyer Honors College, established in 1980. With a mission to "achieve academic excellence with integrity, build a global perspective, and create opportunities for civic engagement and leadership," the Schreyer program offers a curriculum which one student described as "rigorous, and sometimes quite competitive, but manageable." Students in the Schreyer Honors College take classes in both the honors program and the regular college. Key features of the program are generous study-abroad funding and a wealth of internships and co-ops for the ambitious.

Social Scene and Student Life

Asked what some of the most fun activities going on outside of class are, nearly every Penn State student will mention football. The Nittany Lions, as they are called, compete in the NCAA Division I league and are a member of the Big Ten Conference, the United States' oldest Division I college athletic conference. With one of the most tradition-rich football programs in the U.S., PSU games attract huge crowds. "Almost everyone goes to the football games," notes one sophomore. "The tailgates are super popular, especially among underclassman, and are a fantastic way to spend your Saturday."

For students under 21, frat and apartment parties are often the social event of choice in the evenings on the weekends. While local bars aren't known to be strict, they don't have much popularity among underclassmen. "Frats are a big part of the social scene; they're a lot of fun too, for guys that are looking to get involved," said a Penn State freshman. While many students say their weekly workload can be challenging, "people definitely party hard on the weekends." By the numbers, slightly over 20 percent of Penn State students are affiliated with Greek organizations.

Penn State students over 21 can be found enjoying the nightlife on College Avenue, a great college town environment with plenty of restaurants and bars for people to choose from. And for those that aren't heavy partiers, PSU offers plenty of activities and organizations that are known to have fun, substance-free entertainment on weekends. "Movies and concerts are always popular choices," notes one senior.

Beyond football games and nighttime partying, outdoor activities are widespread among University Park students. The beautiful surrounding countryside is ideal for hiking. When cold weather sets in, nearby mountains are prime destinations for PSU skiers and snowboarders. Nearly 250 student clubs and organizations ensure that there are always activities going on and there is always something for everyone. Plenty of community service opportunities exist as well and involve a large portion of the PSU student body.

> "The tailgates are super popular, especially among underclassman, and are a fantastic way to spend your Saturday."

Freshmen are required to live on campus, and students find that the on-campus housing is generally pretty good. "I have no complaints with the Penn dorms, they are more or less what I expected," said one freshman. Nonetheless, a majority of students choose to live off campus in nearby apartments. The meal plan runs on a "pay as you go" point system.

Student Body and Diversity

The vast majority of Penn State students, roughly 75 percent, are residents of Pennsylvania while about 25 percent hail from out of state. While the university's 40,000 strong population certainly has a bit of everything as far as diversity goes, many students note that the student body is relatively more homogenous than other comparable institutions. Asian Americans, Hispanics, and African-Americans combined account for roughly 14 percent of the school.

Nonetheless, Penn State students say that there are niches for everyone, from "jocks to international students, nerds, the frat scene, we represent basically the whole spectrum," said one sophomore.

For a small-town state, Penn State does it big—from a huge student body, to major football games, to a wide range of program offerings encompassing agriculture, law, information science, and everything in between. If you are looking for a strong honors program, fantastic technical majors, a cheaper alternative to private colleges, or just an awesome time, Penn State may be the place for you; there truly is something for everyone.—*Benjamin Prawdzik*

FYI

If you come to Penn State, you'd better bring "a ton of energy and a great attitude."
What's the typical weekend schedule? "Fratting and football!"
What differentiates Penn State most from other colleges is "how many offerings we have here."

Susquehanna University

Address: 514 University Avenue, Selinsgrove, PA 17870
Phone: 570-372-4260
E-mail address: suadmiss@susqu.edu
Web site URL: www.susqu.edu
Year Founded: 1858
Private or Public: Private
Religious Affiliation: Lutheran
Location: Suburban
Number of Applicants: 3,186
Percent Accepted: 70%
Percent Accepted who enroll: 29%
Number Entering: 641
Number of Transfers Accepted each Year: 69
Middle 50% SAT range: M: 520–610, CR: 500–610, Wr: 500–600
Middle 50% ACT range: 22–26
Early admission program EA/ED/None: ED

Percentage accepted through EA or ED: 83%
EA and ED deadline: 15-Nov
Regular Deadline: 1-Mar
Application Fee: $35
Full time Undergraduate enrollment: 2,236
Total enrollment: 2,305
Percent Male: 45%
Percent Female: 55%
Total Percent Minority or Unreported: 13%
Percent African-American: 3%
Percent Asian/Pacific Islander: 1%
Percent Hispanic: 3%
Percent Native American: <1%
Percent International: 1%
Percent in-state/out of state: Unreported
Percent from Public HS: 80%
Retention Rate: Unreported
Graduation Rate 4-year: 79%
Graduation Rate 6-year: 80%

Percent Undergraduates in On-campus housing: Unreported
Number of official organized extracurricular organizations: 128
3 Most popular majors: Business Administration and Management, Communication Studies/Speech Communication and Rhetoric, Creative Writing
Student/Faculty ratio: 13:1
Average Class Size: 16
Percent of students going to grad school: 23%
Tuition and Fees: $35,400
In-State Tuition and Fees if different: No difference
Cost for Room and Board: $9,600
Percent receiving financial aid out of those who apply: 97%
Percent receiving financial aid among all students: 92%

L ocated in the quiet town of Selinsgrove, Pennsylvania, Susquehanna is home to a truly unique student body. Susquehanna boasts all the advantages of a small school; students form tight bonds with each other and cultivate close relationships with their professors. But Susquehanna's breadth of academic options, the faculty's willingness to allow students to create their own major, the new Central Curriculum, and its renowned business and creative writing programs give students at Susquehanna opportunities on par with many larger colleges and universities.

Students at Susquehanna are enthusiastic about everything from their classes to their beautiful surroundings. As one student said, "I love the views. You can see mountains and in the fall everything looks so pretty. It's a beautiful campus." Rumors of haunted buildings and yearly Christmastime readings of "The Night Before Christmas" add to the rich personality of Susquehanna University.

Small and Personalized Classes

When asked about academics at Susquehanna, students praise their small class sizes and friendly professors. At Susquehanna students say that classes have "no more than thirty" students and on average class sizes don't exceed fifteen or twenty. Another student adds that they get even smaller and more personalized "as you get farther into your college education and major."

Although students note that some of the popular classes such as Psych 101, Intro to Film, and certain core science classes, such as geology, fill up very quickly, students do not generally have a problem getting into the classes they want to take. Some "fun classes, like the class about rock music, get filled mostly by seniors, who get first priority in scheduling," but even freshmen and sophomores say that class selection is "not particularly" competitive.

Students note that both the difficulty and quality of a class depends largely on a teacher. One student notes that in some classes, "lack of planning on the professors' part" causes class discussions to go off-topic. But as another student notes, these cases are "exceptions, not the norm." Professors can be tough graders, but one student makes clear that "it isn't all that hard to get an A in most classes if you work hard and put forth the effort."

Susquehanna's nationally ranked Sigmund Weis School of Business is an attractive choice for students aspiring to enter the business world. The program boasts highly qualified faculty and a strong internship program, which gives students real-world experience in their fields.

Students in the Sigmund Weis School have the opportunity to study for a semester in the London Program, where they gain experience in international business environments. One student notes, "Global Business Perspectives is known to be the hardest course. Senior business majors say that if you can make it past that course, you can make it through any business course." Students are teamed up and must complete projects together. At the end of the semester, they make a presentation with analysis and recommendations to real business executives. One student who completed the course said, "It really is a great experience and is a course that is put on your resume after completion."

Not to be outdone is Susquehanna's equally well-regarded creative writing program. One sophomore, a creative writing major, notes that it is "one of the most well-developed and renowned undergraduate programs for creative writing." Students in the writing program enjoy personal attention from a large group of excellent professors, including the campus favorite Tom Bailey, who is "renowned for being likable and very inspiring for freshman writers."

Students in the creative writing program bond and form close friendships over their common interest, and sometimes "make jokes about business majors." However, students from all disciplines tend to get along very well, and as one student enthusiastically said, "I am friends with students in many different majors!" Other strong majors include communications, music, and math. Students regard the science, math, and accounting majors as the most difficult, but it is accepted that "all majors really have their setbacks."

Students in all fields of study regard their professors as "accessible and helpful." Concerning her professors, one student said, "I've felt comfortable and welcome going to office hours or contacting them in emails." Another student said, "I like the fact that my professors are there for me." She added enthusiastically, "They want you to just come in for a quick chat even!"

A recent change in Susquehanna's educational philosophy includes the addition of the Susquehanna Central Curriculum. Intended to provide students with "the skills necessary to succeed in graduate studies and in an increasingly diverse marketplace," the Central Curriculum made its debut in the 2009–2010 academic year. The six main areas of focus in the Central Curriculum are Richness of Thought, Natural World, Human Interaction, Intellectual Skills, Connections, and Capstone. Unique to Susquehanna's Central Curriculum is the requirement that students spend a semester or a shorter amount of time outside of Susquehanna, on a Global Opportunities study abroad program.

In addition, students are required to take

a course following their time abroad, which encourages them to reflect on their experiences studying abroad. South America, Europe, Southeast Asia, and Australia are the most popular destinations, and students receive a lot of funding to either pursue academic goals or volunteer abroad. The Central Curriculum also emphasizes a focus on multiculturalism, ethics, and skill intensives. Unlike the old Core Curriculum, which one student saw as a set of "requirements which could be completed in two years," the Central Curriculum aims to "help you arrange all four of your years" at Susquehanna without limiting academic freedom and flexibility.

Fun but Far

"I sum up our social life like this: We create a lot of fun stuff to do right here on campus because there's not much to do elsewhere besides go to the movies or something."

When asked if Susquehanna students were friendly and outgoing, one student replied "abso-freakin'-lutely." Although a fair number of students, including freshmen, have cars, most students like to stay on campus and go out to restaurants, frat parties, or just chill in their dorms and "make their own fun." The most popular pubs to hit up on weekends are Bots and BJ's, "a local place with great chicken wings."

Restaurants on or near campus include Applebee's, T.G.I. Friday's, Tokyo Diner, and plenty of fast-food places. Many students like to "just go out for a late dinner" and then watch a movie with friends. Trax is an on-campus nightclub that hosts parties and concerts. When asked what he liked most about Trax, one student enthusiastically responded, "Billiards!" and praised the relaxed atmosphere that surrounds the pool tables.

On Saturday nights, students head down to Orange Street, which is "usually where the parties are at," or University Avenue, which is "sort of like frat row." Greek life at Susquehanna is "insignificant" or "huge" depending on who you ask, but according to one student, "about a quarter" of students are involved, and most students go to the frat parties or have friends in the frats.

At Susquehanna, drinking is what you make of it. "Many people do it, but most are fairly safe about it." Students who choose not to drink say that they can have fun with others who are drinking and not feel pressured to partake. One student, discussing the impact of campus drinking on her decision to attend Susquehanna, said "there are PLENTY of people on campus who don't drink. That was important to me when I came here because I didn't drink in high school." However, Susquehanna is, as one student said, a "wet campus," and alcohol can be obtained by students who seek it. Binge drinking only happens on occasion, and "with the exception of pot," drugs are not common at all.

Unique and cherished events on campus are Fall Weekend and Spring Weekend, "with barbecues on the lawn, and games and activities going on." The foam party in the spring is a "fun and anticipated event" in which the on-campus club "gets turned into a foam-filled pit."

Students are described as being "very well off, but a great portion are very down to earth." One sophomore said "I think that overall people have a great, fun, laid-back attitude here; they're rarely competitive." Diversity is generally lacking among the student body, as "most students are white, upper-middle class, and live in the tri-state area." However, Susquehanna has "some interesting nationalities represented by our international students," with lots of exchange students from Asian countries and Russia. Susquehanna's small student body makes it "really easy to meet new people," and students generally say that "everyone is very approachable."

Susquehanna has plenty of variety in housing options. Freshman dorms are generally "pretty small," but they are in "nice buildings and very conveniently located." Freshmen are generally placed in doubles and, on occasion, triples. Freshmen say that they get to know the people in their hall very well, and that "most people leave their doors open and there's always people coming and going."

As a freshman, it is possible to express a preference for housing, but there is no guarantee that students will be placed in the buildings they request. Dorms get better with seniority, as Susquehanna's lottery-based housing system gives priority to seniors. Dorms are known to have different personalities. Smith Hall, the largest freshman dorm, is known for being full of, as one student put it, "rowdy party people." One dorm, Seibert Hall, has a 24-hour courtesy policy, allowing students to concentrate on their work at all hours of the day and live noise-free. Hassinger Hall is full of English and creative writing majors, and Aikens Hall is known for being "in between" in terms of noise level. One junior, recalling the time she spent with friends in the three freshmen dorms her first year, said that "All three are nice!"

> "You can see mountains and in the fall everything looks so pretty. It's a beautiful campus."

Students have the option of pledging and living in frats and sororities, and juniors and seniors sometimes live in suites or townhouses off campus, especially along University Avenue, but most students prefer to remain on campus. There is a house specifically for creative writing majors. Alcohol is allowed in most dorms so long as all members of the dorm are 21 or older.

Susquehanna renovates its buildings often, so "everything looks brand-new." One student described the architecture as "mostly brick-based and very easy on the eyes." Students are excited about the new science building which is, as one student said, "HUGE," and which opened in the Fall of 2010. Seibert Hall is often cited by students as the most aesthetically appealing building on campus, because "it's got these huge white columns out front." Students like to spend their free time on the Degenstein Lawn playing Frisbee, or in one of the many eateries within the Degenstein Campus Center. Charlie's Coffeehouse features movie and bingo nights.

Students are generally very pleased with Susquehanna's cafeteria food. The main dining hall features "more homemade type foods," whereas Benny's Bistro, an alternative to the dining hall at which students can pay with their IDs, offers a tasty, if less healthy, alternative. Students can choose from a variety of different meal plans, ranging from ten to twenty-one meals a week. When asked about the dining hall, one student said, "I think the food is really good there and there is a lot to choose from."

Students are looking forward to the opening of a new Panera in Degenstein Hall as yet another eating alternative. The dining hall has "somewhat flexible" meal hours, but students are generally pleased with the ability to use "flex" points, which allow them to purchase food at Clyde's or Benny's outside of normal meal hours. And of course, T.G.I. Friday's and Tokyo Diner are always popular alternatives.

Students feel "very safe" on campus. As one student said, "it's well lit and I've never felt threatened." Another student added, "I've never heard any horror stories," but just in case, "there are blue light boxes being put up in case there is an emergency." Overall, students at Susquehanna feel not only safe, but very happy. Although the campus can "start to feel a little bit small" by senior year, one student said, "I don't really know why you would live off campus, to be honest. Everything is right here." Another student happily added that "in general, on-campus living is great, and I wouldn't trade it for anything."

Sports and Clubs

At Susquehanna, "there's basically a club for any interest you might have." Students are very active, and are involved in everything from the Belly Dance Circle to the Student Activities Committee (SAC), which organizes weekend events. WQSU, Susquehanna's campus radio station, is the third-largest college radio station in Pennsylvania. It is a very popular organization, and many new student DJ's are trained every year to broadcast their shows across a radius of 90 miles. Students cite publications, SAC, and Greek organizations as some of their most important commitments.

Plenty of students play sports, and although Susquehanna plays in NCAA Division III, "athletics still have a strong presence, with a lot of school spirit."

Among the popular publications on campus are *The Crusader*, Susquehanna's campus newspaper, *Essay*, an on-campus magazine for creative non fiction, and *RiverCraft*, Susquehanna's poetry publication. It is very easy for students at Susquehanna to get involved.

Students easily become a big part of a club or group, and one student enthusiastically discussed his involvement as secretary for the Literature Club and DJ at WQSU. At Susquehanna, there are plenty of opportunities for student employment, and most students hold down at least one job. Students can work on campus, taking shifts in the cafeteria or other dining locations, in the library, at Trax, or as tour guides. Some students work at stores and restaurants off campus.—*Eduardo Andino*

FYI

If you come to SU, you'd better bring "a whiteboard for people to leave you notes on, and a very capable laptop computer with all the most recent updates installed; otherwise, you won't be able to get online in your room with the ethernet cables provided by IT."

What's the typical weekend schedule? "Sleep in late, brunch with friends, maybe get laundry and homework done, then a night out or at an on-campus movie or party."

If I could change one thing about SU, "I'd give the freshmen a lot more say in what classes they take in their first semester, because as it is you just take a small survey and then you're assigned four courses, mostly intended to fulfill curriculum requirements."

Three things every student at SU should do before graduating are: "visit the cemetery at the top of the hill on a clear night and stargaze, go to President Lemon's reading of 'The Night Before Christmas' during finals, and take a class with Dr. Randy Robertson."

S w a r t h m o r e   C o l l e g e

Address: 500 College Avenue, Swarthmore, PA 19081

Phone: 610-328-8300

E-mail address: admissions@swarthmore.edu

Web site URL: www.swarthmore.edu

Year Founded: 1864

Private or Public: Private

Religious Affiliation: None

Location: Suburban

Number of Applicants: 6,041

Percent Accepted: 16%

Percent Accepted who enroll: 40%

Number Entering: 388

Number of Transfers Accepted each Year: 28

Middle 50% SAT range: M: 670–770, CR: 670–760, Wr: 680–770

Middle 50% ACT range: 29–33

Early admission program EA/ED/None: ED

Percentage accepted through EA or ED: 34%

EA and ED deadline: 15-Nov

Regular Deadline: 2-Jan

Application Fee: $60

Full time Undergraduate enrollment: 1,508

Total enrollment: 1,524

Percent Male: 49%

Percent Female: 51%

Total Percent Minority or Unreported: 55%

Percent African-American: 6%

Percent Asian/Pacific Islander: 14%

Percent Hispanic: 11%

Percent Native American: <1%

Percent International: 7%

Percent in-state/out of state: Unreported

Percent from Public HS: 59%

Retention Rate: 96%

Graduation Rate 4-year: 90%

Graduation Rate 6-year: 92%

Percent Undergraduates in On-campus housing: 95%

Number of official organized extracurricular organizations: 138

3 Most popular majors: Biology/Biological Sciences, General Economics, General Political Science and Government

Student/Faculty ratio: 8:1

Average Class Size: 15

Percent of students going to grad school: 21%

Tuition and Fees: $40,816

In-State Tuition and Fees if different: No difference

Cost for Room and Board: $12,100

Percent receiving financial aid out of those who apply: 53%

Percent receiving financial aid among all students: 52%

Tucked away in a quiet Pennsylvania suburb on a campus that is a nationally designated arboretum, Swarthmore boasts a close-knit community of intellectually driven students. With strong Quaker roots and a renowned Honors program, Swarthmore offers top-notch academics in a low-key environment for its student body of 1500. Swatties are passionate about what they do, both inside and outside the classroom. "Everyone has some obscure interest or talent," one freshman said. "People have more than academic interests."

Know Your Teachers

Students praise Swarthmore's small class sizes and the unique level of access they enjoy to professors. Many classes are seminars, capped at a dozen students, and large classes are those that exceed 30. The largest courses are introductory bio and physics, each about 100 students, but a First-Year Seminar program ensures that freshmen get a taste of small class discussions. The college has no teaching assistants, so all classes are led by professors or visiting specialists in a given field.

Professors, many of whom students call by their first names, often invite students to their houses for dinner and make themselves available well beyond office hours to provide assistance. "It's really easy for them to meet you on a night or a weekend, and they're really open to working with you," said one senior.

Swarthmore is best known for its Honors program, which is modeled on Oxford's tutorial system. Students in the program elect an Honors major and minor, enroll in rigorous small seminars, and conclude their studies with an examination by outside experts in their field of study. While about a third of each class pursues Honors, most students opt to double-major or choose a minor regardless. "It's pretty rare that people only have one major," a senior said. "There's almost a sense that people want to combine really different disciplines together for a major/minor combination, like biology and English or computer science and philosophy."

Complementing traditional academic departments, Swarthmore offers interdisciplinary programs such as Interpretation Theory, Cognitive Science, and Peace and Conflict Studies, which can be chosen as minors or developed into a special major. Swarthmore also attracts students with its engineering program, a rarity among liberal arts colleges. Overall, the most popular majors are biology, economics, and political science. The Education Studies department is also very popular, and students cite Introduction to Education as a course not to be missed. "People go into an Intro Ed course and come out wanting to be either an Ed major or a teacher," one freshman said.

While students come to Swat for its academic rigor, the school can seem overwhelming. "There are times when it's very stressful, and I had a friend who said that other schools' final exams periods are like a regular week here," a senior said. Luckily the school provides plenty of resources, from writing associates who look over essays and lab reports to a tutoring program and counseling services. To ease the transition from high school, the first semester of freshman year is pass/fail, a welcome "safety net" for students as they adjust to the quality of work expected of them. Students emphasize that the academic environment is friendly and uncompetitive. "There's not a whole lot of competition amongst students," a junior said. "People are willing to help each other out."

When Classes are Done

After hitting the books during the week, Swatties head out on Thursday and Saturday nights. Though the social scene is varied, ranging from dorm-room parties to a capella performances and comedy shows, there are a few weekly staples. Thursdays are Pub Night at Paces, a student-run café that transforms into a "mini-nightclub" on weekends. Olde Club, an intimate concert venue with "stained glass and a Catholic church kind of feel," hosts student bands or alternative music groups from the local area.

Greek life has a minor presence at Swarthmore, but the campus' two fraternities host popular parties on Saturday nights, including a "graffiti party" where "you go in with a white T-shirt and just draw on each other." The annual Halloween party draws students from nearby Haverford and Bryn Mawr colleges, with which Swat forms a tri-college consortium. There is also an annual winter formal, recently staged as a Harry Potter-esque Yule Ball "decked out with ice sculptures, candles, and a couple of wizard rock groups."

Alcohol is "readily available" on campus, and the school's drinking policy is fairly lenient. As one senior explained, "The administration treats us like adults and isn't trying to bust anybody." Though most students drink, those who do not report no pressure to imbibe. "Social life at Swarthmore is really flexible and accepting," said one senior. "Whatever you want to do, there will be people who want to do it with you, whether it's partying or playing Bananagrams on Friday night."

> "Social life at Swarthmore is really flexible and accepting," said one senior. "Whatever you want to do, there will be people who want to do it with you, whether it's partying or playing Bananagrams on Friday night."

Notable traditions include the Pterodactyl Hunt, a campus-wide role-playing game in which "one team is the Pterodactyls and the other team is the Humans, who try to slay the Pterodactyls," and First and Last Collection, ceremonies held at the beginning and end of a student's college experience in Swat's outdoor amphitheater.

For those who wish to break out of the Swarthmore bubble, Philadelphia is a half-hour ride from the on-campus train station. The school also sponsors free shuttles to the city and to nearby movie theaters and shopping centers. However, student life centers on campus. "Some people go into Philly for a day to explore, but most people stick on campus," a freshman said. "I don't know if we're just lazy or if we love our campus so much, but there's enough going on that we can stay on campus and have a good time."

Life in an Arboretum

Swarthmore's architecture is "eclectic," melding nineteenth-century stonework with modern additions like the LEED-certified Science Center. The campus centerpiece is Parrish Hall, part administrative building and part student residence, which overlooks a grassy lawn and popular hangout known as Parrish Beach. The 399-acre campus also contains the Crum Woods, a forested area with trails and a creek. "People build boats out of various materials and race down the creek" in the annual Crum Regatta.

Ninety-five percent of students live in campus housing, and students forge lasting bonds with their hallmates. Swarthmore has 17 different dorms, which range from a cozy 8-person home to cottage row houses, condo units, and imposing stone edifices. There is no freshmen-only housing; instead, freshmen live on halls alongside sophomores, juniors, and seniors from Day 1. Freshmen all have roommates and typically live in doubles, while juniors and seniors can opt for single rooms.

Students in campus housing are required to be on the meal plan, which provides 14, 17, or 20 meals a week at Sharples, the dining hall. While the food is "pretty solidly mediocre," Sharples serves as an important social area and gathering point. For Screw Your Roommate, in which roommates set each other up on blind dates, couples are told to dress up in matched outfits (Salt and Pepper; Mustard and Ketchup) and meet each other at Sharples. Frat rushing rituals also take place there, such as an applesauce-eating

competition. One junior explains: "Every pledge has to challenge a random person in the cafeteria. They'll put a bowl in their face and say 'go!'" The frats "also make the kids crabwalk around the whole cafeteria and race each other."

Other eating options include a few on-campus coffee shops and restaurants in the Ville, as students call the small town bordering Swarthmore. Student favorites in the Ville include pizza parlor Renato's and Vicky's, a breakfast stop.

Swarthmore has one main athletic facility, which "could stand to be repaired," one varsity athlete said. It includes a fitness center, indoor and outdoor tennis courts, a turf field, a baseball field, a field house, and a pool, all of which are open to varsity and casual athletes alike. Though "academics are emphasized over everything" at Swat, 40 percent of students play varsity, club, or intramural sports. The school fields 22 Division III teams, the most popular of which, Men's Soccer, has had a winning streak in recent years. IM soccer is also popular, as are the Ultimate Frisbee and fencing clubs.

Swatties participate in over 100 clubs and organizations, from the Peaslee Debate Society to dance, music, and theater groups. There are five a capella groups, and dance troupe Rhythm and Motion is quite popular. "Either you sing, dance, or you play something," one junior commented. "Everyone does one of those three things." Many students are members of identity-based groups for various religions, ethnicities, and sexual orientations, which are all under the umbrella Intercultural Center. Swatties also engage in service projects through the Lang Center for Civic and Social Responsibility.

Ultimately, what differentiates Swarthmore from other schools is its tough academics and intimate community. "The fact that we're smaller than most schools means we know a lot more people, and we feel connected to more people at the school," one freshman said. "But at the same time, it's not small because we have so many organizations. If you want to do something, you'll be able to find it, or you can start it. And the smallness keeps the class sizes really small, which is a huge bonus." Students characterize their peers as passionate, friendly, and accepting.—*Antonia Woodford*

FYI

If you come to Swarthmore, you'd better bring "a blanket for lying outside on Parrish Beach and looking at the stars, and a hot water kettle (although they're illegal) for late-night tea parties in your dorm."

If you come to Swarthmore, you'd better not bring "a relationship. Most people break up with people they were dating back home."

The biggest college-wide tradition/event at Swarthmore is "watching *The Graduate* on the very first night before fall classes start. The whole school goes out and sits on the main lawn of the school with a huge projector and watches it."

Temple University

Address: 1801 N. Broad Street, Philadelphia, PA 19122

Phone: 888-340-2222

E-mail address: tudam@temple.edu

Web site URL: www.temple.edu

Year Founded: 1884

Private or Public: Public

Religious Affiliation: None

Location: Urban

Number of Applicants: 17,051

Percent Accepted: 65%

Percent Accepted who enroll: 39%

Number Entering: 4,311

Number of Transfers Accepted each Year: 3,852

Middle 50% SAT range: M: 510–610, CR: 500–600, Wr: 500–600

Middle 50% ACT range: 20–26

Early admission program EA/ED/None: None

Percentage accepted through EA or ED: NA

EA and ED deadline: NA

Regular Deadline: 1-Mar

Application Fee: $50

Full time Undergraduate enrollment: 24,584

Total enrollment: 34,696

Percent Male: 48%

Percent Female: 52%

Total Percent Minority or Unreported: 42%

Percent African-American: 15%

Percent Asian/Pacific Islander: 10%

Percent Hispanic: 4%

Percent Native American: <1%

Percent International: 3%

Percent in-state/out of state: 81%/19%

Percent from Public HS: 73%

Retention Rate: 88%

Graduation Rate 4-year: 36%

Graduation Rate 6-year: 63%

Percent Undergraduates in On-campus housing: 18%

Number of official organized extracurricular organizations: 288

3 Most popular majors: Accounting, Biology/ Biological sciences, Psychology

Student/Faculty ratio: 16:1

Average Class Size: 27

Percent of students going to grad school: Unreported

Tuition and Fees: $21,662

In-State Tuition and Fees if different: $11,834

Cost for Room and Board: $9,550

Percent receiving financial aid out of those who apply: 86%

Percent receiving financial aid among all students: 85%

Temple University resides within Philadelphia, the largest city in Pennsylvania, and the sixth-most populous city in the nation. As a comprehensive public research university that awards degrees up to a doctoral, Temple largely attracts native Pennsylvanians in order to round out its student body of just under 36,000 students. It's the twenty-sixth largest university in America, but students often find that the size does not necessarily become detrimental to their college experience, especially not in historic Philadelphia.

Big Fish in a Bigger Pond

"For the most part I really enjoy my classes. I always feel like I learn at least one new thing in each class," a Temple University freshman informed me. "But they're *so big.*" Like most large public-research universities, Temple's introductory classes range upward of around 100 students at a time. Students say that the class sizes definitely grow smaller as you move further into specialized courses. There are 17 schools within Temple and four professional schools. "I think English, Business, and Communications majors are considered easier and Science and Nursing majors are harder, based on what I've heard," one student noted.

"I might have liked a slightly smaller school because making friends my freshman year was pretty hard. My high school wasn't that small either, but I felt just plain lost most of the time," a student told me, disappointed. There is something for everyone to do here, however. With a student radio that has the second largest audience among Philadelphia's radio stations, an independent weekly newspaper, over 200 student organizations, and a fully-staffed, very popular student government, there is no end in sight when it comes to deciding what to do at Temple.

One complaint that was frequently voiced, however, was the lack of communication that occurred between those attending the institution and those running it. "I really can't stand Temple's poor communication skills between students and administration," a freshman stated. "Granted, the University's huge, but it would still be great to have someone who can answer you when you have problems."

Study abroad options are incredibly organized and therefore extremely popular with the student body. "I went to Temple in Japan," a first-year law student gushed. "It was amazing! I was allowed to take all of the courses Temple offered and wrap up my language study at the same time. Definitely worth it!" It has become increasingly popular to do a summer internship after spending a year at Temple, a semester abroad in the sophomore year, and taking either junior year or post-senior year abroad.

From Brotherly Love to . . . well, Brotherly Love

While often nicknamed the City of Brotherly Love, Philadelphia has lately been getting much more publicity for the violent crime that often occurs off campus. Temple University offers a massive alert system that utilizes text, e-mail, and automatic phone calls, as well as a large and well-organized on-campus police force. There are over 600 security cameras mounted throughout the campus and students as well as faculty and staff are taught early on how to utilize emergency numbers and navigate the Philadelphia area. While students agree that living on campus almost guarantees a safe experience at Temple, one student noted that "Temple is a great school

with a lot of opportunity BUT it's in an awful location and you need to be on top of your game to be able to take advantage of the opportunities." Opportunities include trips into New York City, thanks to Philadelphia's 30th Street Station, which offers access to Amtrak, SEPTA, and New Jersey Transit lines.

That said, most people live off campus despite the danger. "I would rather live on campus because walking alone off campus isn't always safe," said a female student, "but my apartment is pretty nice and cheap, and there's a bunch of students living around me, so I'm not too worried." Those living on campus, numbering around 10,000, tend to gravitate towards Johnson and Hardwick, which are considered to be freshmen-heavy areas to live in and therefore the best dorms to meet new people in. There are often complaints about delinquency of the juvenile kind—frequent pranks, pulled fire alarms, loud and raucous parties going on late into the night on weekdays—but overall, these two buildings are the place to be. White Hall, as the farthest dorm away from campus, is favored by upperclassmen, while the lavish 1300 and Temple Towers buildings are considered to be the best living arrangements if you're willing to spend a little more.

> "Temple is a great school with a lot of opportunity BUT it's in an awful location and you need to be on top of your game to be able to take advantage of the opportunities."

Living in the city of Philadelphia has its perks. Students rave about the shows they get to see, including "arts festivals, plays, movies, and concerts that I never knew existed, and I've lived here for most of my life!" one student exclaimed.

While only 2% of the student body is involved in fraternities or sororities, Greek life at Temple is still large without being in charge. A female junior explained, "I love the frat parties! They're incredibly entertaining and a good way to meet a solid group of guys with pretty much the same values." Most students attend parties thrown at off-campus dormitories or go into clubs around the city. There is definitely something for everyone to do in a city this large.—*Larissa Liburd*

FYI
If you come to Temple University, you'd better leave "your Penn State gear behind."
What's the typical weekend schedule? "Partying. There's always a party."
The biggest college-wide tradition/event at Temple University is "Spring Fling."

University of Pennsylvania

Address: 1 College Hall, Philadelphia, PA 19104

Phone: 215-898-7507

E-mail address: info@admissions.ugao.upenn.edu

Web site URL: www.upenn.edu

Year Founded: 1740

Private or Public: Private

Religious Affiliation: None

Location: Urban

Number of Applicants: 22,645

Percent Accepted: 14%

Percent Accepted who enroll: 66%

Number Entering: 2,370

Number of Transfers Accepted each Year: 328

Middle 50% SAT range: M: 690–780, CR: 660–750, Wr: 680–770

Middle 50% ACT range: 30–34

Early admission program EA/ED/None: ED

Percentage accepted through EA or ED: 31%

EA and ED deadline: 1-Nov

Regular Deadline: 1-Jan

Application Fee: $75

Full time Undergraduate enrollment: 9,865

Total enrollment: 19,842

Percent Male: 49%

Percent Female: 51%

Total Percent Minority or Unreported: 51%

Percent African-American: 6%

Percent Asian/Pacific Islander: 17%

Percent Hispanic: 17%

Percent Native American: <1%

Percent International: 10%

Percent in-state/out of state: 17%/83%

Percent from Public HS: 54%

Retention Rate: 98%

Graduation Rate 4-year: 88%

Graduation Rate 6-year: 94%

Percent Undergraduates in On-campus housing: 62%

Number of official organized extracurricular organizations: 350

3 Most popular majors: Business/Marketing, Social Sciences, Engineering

Student/Faculty ratio: 6:1

Average Class Size: 16

Percent of students going to grad school: 20%

Tuition and Fees: $42,098

In-State Tuition and Fees if different: No difference

Cost for Room and Board: $11,878

Percent receiving financial aid out of those who apply: 82%

Percent receiving financial aid among all students: 46%

Bearing the imprint of Benjamin Franklin, arguably America's most celebrated philosopher, the University of Pennsylvania was imbued with a spirit of liberal thinking and scholarship even before it enrolled its first students. Conceived in 1740 and opened in 1751, Penn has lived up to its goal of providing a practical education devoted to liberal arts, business, and public service. Generally acknowledged as the nation's first true university, it is credited with having developed the first modern liberal arts curriculum. Today, Penn's architecturally varied and attractive 269-acre campus located in West Philadelphia is home to an undergraduate student body that has grown to almost 10,000 students, many of whom are international in origin. Despite its growth, the college has remained true to its original mission since its inception.

Four Schools in One

The academic interests of Penn's undergraduates run the gamut, and despite differences in career plans, all students are completely integrated into the fabric of the college. Nevertheless, successful applicants to Penn enter one of the four schools that together create the undergraduate institution. The largest of the schools is the College of Arts and Sciences, to which over six in 10 students belong, followed by the highly competitive Wharton School of Business, which enrolls about 2,500 Penn students. Wharton is the only undergraduate business school in the Ivy League and has an unparalleled international reputation. The School of Engineering and Applied Science enrolls just slightly fewer students than does the Wharton undergraduate program, and the relatively small but excellent School of Nursing includes approximately 500 undergrads. Thus, Benjamin Franklin's original goal that Penn teach "everything that is practical, and everything that is ornamental" is certainly well-addressed by the broad range of opportunities available to undergraduates here.

The College of Arts and Sciences allows the most freedom of choice of the four schools at Penn. In this undergraduate school at Penn, students are generally required to take between 12 to 14 courses in their major and around 20 outside of their area of concentration. Included in the latter are courses that fulfill distribution requirements. In 2006, the college reduced the number of distributional courses necessary to graduate, with the intention of increasing curricular flexibility. Students must now take one course in each of the following areas: Society, History and Tradition, Arts and Letters, Physical World, Living World, Humanities and Social Sciences, Natural Science, and Math. Within the framework of these disciplines, undergraduates in the College of Arts and Sciences must also fulfill requirements in quantitative reasoning, foreign language, and writing. Noted one sophomore, "Mine was the first class with the new curriculum. My junior and senior friends say that the reduction in distribution requirements makes it much easier to complete your major and still take some great courses that are outside the beaten path." Students preregister for courses, but can change their schedules during a "shopping period." However, noted a junior, "for courses with restricted enrollment, such as seminars, it can be difficult getting in if you have not preregistered, unless someone drops out of the class. Teachers generally try to be accommodating, but they can't always be."

The Wharton School of Business at Penn is world-renowned and the list of its graduates who went on to distinguish themselves in the business world is staggering. It is arguably the best undergraduate business school in the country and, as such, the most competitive of the four schools at Penn in terms of admissions. In contrast to the curriculum of the College of Arts and Sciences, the course of study in this school is much more predetermined. Thirty-seven courses are required to graduate, only two of which

must be taken outside of Wharton. There is theoretically a wide variety of possible "concentrations" available within the context of the Bachelor of Science in Economics degree that is awarded to all students, but the vast majority concentrates in the area of finance.

Penn's School of Engineering and Applied Science, or SEAS, like Wharton, has a fairly fixed curriculum. The course of study is traditional, and most students take classes in math, science, engineering, and little else. "I am very happy with my courses," said one senior. "If I wanted to take Old English poetry, I wouldn't be in SEAS."

The School of Nursing prepares its students for a variety of fields related to nursing and the health sciences. A total of 28 classes in nursing and medicine are required, but there is ample room to take other courses in the College of Arts and Sciences. Students concentrate in one of two programs in the school: Family and Community Health, or Foundational Sciences and Health Systems.

There are many opportunities for interdisciplinary study at Penn, and the school encourages this type of exploration. Students may pursue dual degrees within, for example, the School of Arts and Sciences, or may enroll in one of the joint degree programs at the school. For example, the Huntsman Program in International Studies and Business awards two simultaneous degrees, a Bachelor of Arts in International Studies from the College of Arts and Sciences and a Bachelor of Science in Economics from the Wharton School. The Lauder Institute of Management and International Studies awards an MBA from Wharton and an MA in International Studies from the School of Arts and Sciences.

Academics are rigorous at Penn, and most students put in a good amount of study time. Students are well aware that exams and course grades are curved, especially in the sciences and math, so there is a fair amount of competition among students. In addition, many undergraduates are premed and prelaw. "That alone leads to competition," said a senior, "but I don't think that Penn students are any more cutthroat than preprofessional students at other schools."

Campus in the City
Penn touts the opportunities of its situation in the city of Philadelphia, a bustling metropolis with a long and interesting history. Undergraduates choose to live in a variety

of different types of housing, both on and off campus. Only about 60 percent of undergrads live on campus. Many upperclassmen prefer living off campus in fraternities and sororities or apartments that are generally less expensive than the University housing options.

For those living on campus, there are 11 College Houses, each with its own architectural style, ranging from 24-story high-rise apartment buildings to historic buildings with hardwood floors. Most freshmen live in dorms that surround the Quad. Each facility is home to about 400 students. Dining facilities are in close proximity. Residents of the high-rises have bathrooms and kitchenettes in their suites. In addition to these options are "theme houses" which allow students with similar cultural backgrounds and interests and students with similar academic interests to live together. In addition, fraternities and sororities have been active on campus since the mid-1800s and represent another significant housing option.

Food for Thought

First-year undergraduates are required to enroll in one of four meal plans, all of which include "Dining Dollar$" that can be redeemed at all Penn dining locations, including Starbucks and several on-campus cafés and retail institutions nearby. Upperclassmen who choose to live and eat on campus can choose from among 10 different plans. Dining Dollar$ can be easily added to their accounts. Kosher food is found at Falk Dining Commons and is under Orthodox supervision. In addition, a variety of foods can be purchased at a new "convenience area" in the same facility. The nutritional composition of all meals can be found at kiosks located in each of the dining facilities. Most students do not complain about the food options. "There is always something to fit your dietary needs and preferences," said a sophomore. "And there is an increasing interest in foods that have been grown and prepared with attention to ecological considerations."

An Extracurricular Smorgasbord

Penn boasts a wide array of extracurricular opportunities, including participation on numerous intercollegiate athletic teams. There are 17 men's sports teams and 16 women's teams. In addition, students may participate on intramural teams in 12 sports and on a variety of club sports. Beyond organized sports, huge numbers of students go to the gym on almost a daily basis. The facilities are open

Monday through Thursday from 6 a.m. to 1 a.m., so there is little excuse for being a "couch potato." The gyms are also open on the weekends with less extensive hours.

Many students are involved with the numerous publications on campus as well as student government organizations such as the Undergraduate Assembly, the debate team, and the Model UN. In addition, opportunities to sing, dance, and act abound. There are numerous a cappella groups on campus. "Penn is a real extracurricular smorgasbord," said one senior. "I have done a lot of acting and a lot of writing out of class."

Living in and Giving to West Philadelphia

West Philadelphia provides an active and multiethnic neighborhood for Penn students, as well as tremendous opportunities for community service. But many students voice concerns about their safety on campus, especially its immediate environs. They often point to the great "town-gown" discrepancy between the wealth of the University and the majority of its students and the socioeconomic status of the residents of the surrounding neighborhood. Students call this disparity the "Penn Bubble." "I have been here for three years," stated one student, "and I still feel uncomfortable walking around West Philly at night. I don't like going out alone. But many great universities are located in areas where the underprivileged live. You have to be careful, but there are so many opportunities to get involved. On balance, the neighborhood is really a plus." The University has actively focused on security on campus in recent years.

Penn students actively participate in a wide variety of community service projects. Civic House is the main hub for those interested in such endeavors, providing a liaison between the University and the community. Civic House maintains a community agency database that allows students to locate volunteer organizations that serve the greater West Philadelphia neighborhood.

I'll Drink to That

Like students at the other Ivies, Penn students tend to study hard and play hard. The fraternities and sororities are where a great deal of socializing takes place, especially for the lowerclassmen. Alcohol plays an important role at most weekend parties and it flows more freely in the frats. Most students agree that a significant amount of booze is consumed at Penn. They also note that although there are definite dictates against the availability of alcohol in these venues, the enforcement of such policies is lax. "The RAs and GAs don't allow things to be completely freewheeling," noted one junior, "but they let things go as long as no one gets really out of hand."

> "Many great universities are located in areas where the underprivileged live. You have to be careful, but there are so many opportunities to get involved."

As is the case at many other universities, the social scene generally shifts to private parties in students' apartments during the upperclass years. Many Penn students live off campus as juniors and seniors and are less inclined to spend their weekends at the frat parties.

Beyond the Parties
Philadelphia affords virtually unlimited opportunities for social activities beyond the party scene. Every Thursday, Penn's school newspaper, *The Daily Pennsylvanian*, catalogues the numerous concerts, theatrical performances, and dances that will be taking place that weekend. Most students avail themselves of the city and frequent restaurants, bars, and clubs there. "There are so many things to do in Philly," said a senior. "Sometimes it's nice to get off campus and do some exploring. I am certainly going to miss being in this city after I graduate."

Here's a Toast to Dear Old Penn!
School spirit is alive and well at Penn, and their strong athletic teams reinforce the identification of Penn students with their school. Men's basketball is unquestionably the most popular intercollegiate sport on campus, and Penn's teams have been exceptional in recent years. Games against Princeton, the University's archrival on the court, are packed, and Penn football games have become increasingly popular as well, as a function of the fielding of more competitive teams in recent years.

Penn students traditionally throw toast on the football field after singing a song entitled "Drink a Highball," ever since the drinking age was raised from 18 and most undergraduates could no longer consume the intended cocktail.

. . . As a "Button"
In the center of the Penn campus, there is a huge white button, split asymmetrically, measuring 16 feet in diameter and weighing over 5,000 pounds. Designed by Claes Oldenburg and cast in reinforced aluminum, it faces Benjamin Franklin in front of Penn's Van Pelt Library. According to legend, Benjamin Franklin once popped off a button from his pants after gorging on a huge meal, with the projectile then splitting in two. While the artist himself once remarked that the split in the button divides it into four parts, representing William Penn's original division of Philadelphia into four squares, some argue that it represents the four undergraduate schools at Penn. Others ascribe a variety of other traditions and functions to this sculpture, including as a place to engage in some more risqué public behavior. The Button can, more broadly, be seen as representing a starting point for discussion, inquiry, and debate. Students at Penn have never been accused of not thinking.

When polled, the vast majority of students at this exciting Ivy League university, whose national standing in a variety of published surveys has steadily increased in the last decade, love being students there. The diversity of the student body, the quality of the faculty, the opportunities for extracurricular involvement in a large array of activities, the strong sense of school spirit, and a commitment to the betterment of the surrounding community are but a few of the elements that have made Penn a truly great place to live and study. If you are willing to work hard and find intellectual challenge up your alley, then you may well find that Benjamin Franklin had the right idea when he popped a few buttons while throwing his weight behind the University of Pennsylvania.
—*Jonathan Berken*

FYI
If you come to Penn, you'd better bring "the ability to throw toast like a discus."
What is a typical weekend schedule? "Party like a rock star all weekend long."
If I could change one thing about Penn, I'd "make West Philly safer."
Three things that every student at Penn should do before graduating are: "go see Mask and Wig, read Ben Franklin's autobiography, and have sex under the Button."

University of Pittsburgh

Address: 4227 Fifth Avenue, First Floor Alumni Hall, Pittsburgh, PA 15260
Phone: 412-624-7488
E-mail address: oafa@pitt.edu
Web site URL: www.pitt.edu
Year Founded: 1787
Private or Public: Public
Religious Affiliation: None
Location: Urban
Number of Applicants: 19,056
Percent Accepted: 58%
Percent Accepted who enroll: 32%
Number Entering: 3,710
Number of Transfers Accepted each Year: 1,238
Middle 50% SAT range: M:600–690, CR: 570–680, Wr:560–660
Middle 50% ACT range: 25–30
Early admission program EA/ED/None: None

Percentage accepted through EA or ED: NA
EA and ED deadline: NA
Regular Deadline: Rolling
Application Fee: $45
Full time Undergraduate enrollment: 18,371
Total enrollment: 28,823
Percent Male: 50%
Percent Female: 50%
Total Percent Minority or Unreported: 21%
Percent African-American: 6%
Percent Asian/Pacific Islander: 6%
Percent Hispanic: 6%
Percent Native American: 0%
Percent International: 2%
Percent in-state/out of state: 69%/31%
Percent from Public HS: Unreported
Retention Rate: 90%
Graduation Rate 4-year: 56%

Graduation Rate 6-year: 75%
Percent Undergraduates in On-campus housing: 45%
Number of official organized extracurricular organizations: 450
3 Most popular majors: Marketing, Social Sciences, English
Student/Faculty ratio: 14:1
Average Class Size: 14
Percent of students going to grad school: 39%
Tuition and Fees: $25,540
In-State Tuition and Fees if different: $16,132
Cost for Room and Board: $9,430
Percent receiving financial aid out of those who apply: 68%
Percent receiving financial aid among all students: 55%

Though the University of Pittsburgh is definitely a large research institution, it is anything but impersonal. Pitt's wealth of resources allow students the freedom to pursue very individualized academic and extracurricular interests while supplementing their education with the cultural and professional benefits of living in the energetic city of Pittsburgh.

Academics: Every Man for Himself?

Well-known for its medical and nursing schools, Pitt offers difficult premed and nursing programs that many incoming students take advantage of—at first. "Tons of freshmen come in premed," said one sophomore, "but the science programs are really hard, and not many stick with it." Other popular majors include business, communications, and philosophy, and students say that the creative writing community has a strong support system, as well.

Students praise the University Honors College (UHC) for its flexibility and seemingly limitless opportunities. The UHC has an office in the school's iconic Cathedral of Learning and offers specific classes and a Bachelor of Philosophy degree. However, unlike other universities' honors colleges—which often require membership or enrollment to participate—any student who demonstrates high-caliber work and wants to pursue more rigorous, independent study can reap UHC benefits. In addition to offering small courses like "Ethics and Leadership in Organizations" and a philosophy seminar on the apocalypse, UHC also offers many research and summer opportunities, like the Brackenridge summer fellowships. "Through the Brackenridge fellowship, one of my friends did an analysis of *Leave it to Beaver* as a reflection of social norms," said one senior.

Another special academic option is Pitt's Living Learning Communities. Located on designated floors in Pitt's residence halls, these communities offer students with particular academic or professional interests a way to meet more students like them. In addition, the communities—which range from "Entrepreneurial Experience" to "French Language and Culture"—plan activities to complement each community's focus. Pitt offers learning communities for freshmen without a residential component as well; students in these communities take the same blocks of courses and meet once a week to discuss issues related to their common interest.

Nevertheless, one student said, "The Living Learning Communities are a good idea in theory, but I don't think enough people participate in them for them to be effective." Students agree that most Pitt students are apathetic about the amount of extraordinary opportunities Pitt offers; for example, students say that many people don't take advantage of UHC because they don't seek it out. Students agree that initiative is key to getting what you want from Pitt academics. They praise professors for being very accessible and say that it's fairly easy to take courses outside of one's major. Many students study abroad and emphasize that academic options at Pitt are abundant, though not handed to students on silver platters. "If you initiate independent studies, you can easily work with professors," said one junior politics, philosophy, and economics major. Students say that academics at Pitt tend to be "pretty interdisciplinary" and that professors and departments will work with students' interests, as long as the student takes the initiative. "Not everybody tries to combine departments or propose their own projects, so professors get excited when students do," said one philosophy major.

However, the school's large size means some red tape when it comes to advising and enrolling. While students in the Honors College say they have no problems getting into the courses they want, one junior English major described the online registration process as "very stressful." Another junior complained of the prevalence of night classes, saying, "I've had to take a night class every semester because it's so hard to get into classes." In addition, freshman year courses can be quite large, but by the end of sophomore year, students say that they are happily enrolled in smaller courses.

City Living

Just as Pitt has a wealth of academic opportunities for students to tap into, the University presents students many chances to take advantage of the mid-size city in which it is located. Students rave about PITT ARTS, a program that facilitates on- and off-campus arts experiences, free admission to Pittsburgh's museums, discounted tickets to arts events, and even free Arts Encounters, weekly opportunities for about 30 students to see a show and enjoy a nice dinner for no cost. While getting tickets can sometimes be competitive, one junior said, "If you've never gone, you get first priority, but I don't think very many people know about it."

Students were apathetic about Pitt's dorm life, saying that by junior year, the vast majority move to cheaper off-campus housing in the surrounding neighborhood of Oakland. But that doesn't mean they give up Pitt's great on-campus dining options; the school's meal plan is extremely flexible. For foodies, there is no shortage of popular, inexpensive restaurants in the Oakland area to cater to students' late-night cravings as well. Most local restaurants—including India Garden, an "amazing" student favorite—offer half-priced food after 10 pm. On Thursday, Friday, and Saturday nights before 3:30 A.M., students also recommend heading to T-Rav's BBQ Lab for top-notch homemade barbeque staples.

> **"If you go to Pitt, you're part of Pittsburgh."**

Perhaps because of their shared love of Pittsburgh's successful professional sports teams (the city is home to the Penguins, the Pirates, and the Steelers), Pitt students and Pittsburgh residents get along well. "If you go to Pitt, you're part of Pittsburgh," said one senior. Although residents in Oakland sometimes get a little cranky about students' frequent house parties, many students work in the nearby area and say that Pittsburghers love to chat them up. Moreover, while a lot of students participate in work-study programs on campus, Pitt also allows students to receive academic credit for internships in downtown Pittsburgh, further connecting the University with the community.

Fun and Games

Because of older students' migration to off-campus housing, Pitt's social scene is dominated by house parties. Students say that although there are some good bars in Oakland, most people don't frequent them, and the freshman population dominates attendance at fraternity parties.

But the school's thriving party scene has caused the University some problems. Although students say that the majority drinks, Pitt promotes a zero-tolerance alcohol policy for students under the age of 21, and the policy is strictly enforced (particularly in the dorms near central campus). In fact, some students say that police officers wait at hospitals to cite underage students who show up for alcohol-related medical issues; as a consequence, many students avoid seeking medical attention when they probably should.

Students say that while they value their own extracurricular activities, they often don't interact with students outside of their social groups. In other words, students on the mock trial team hang out with other students on the mock trial team, and students in fraternities and sororities hang out with other students in fraternities and sororities. "I don't think I could tell you who the student body president is," said one sophomore. Students are also not big fans of school-sponsored fun, which might contribute to the University's cliquish tendency. "The school's a huge fan of ice cream socials," said one junior. "No one wants to go to that many ice cream socials."

Despite the variety of social groups on campus, students also say the school doesn't boast significant ethnic diversity. "We like to say that Pitt has the most diverse population of white people that you've ever seen," said one junior communications major. "The city is very diverse, but the school just isn't," she added.

Nevertheless, for students who are willing and excited to explore a variety of academic and social options, the University of Pittsburgh is a great choice. Because the school's opportunities run the gamut from cutting-edge undergraduate scientific research at Pitt's renowned medical school to free tickets to theater performances, all kinds of students can find their niche at Pitt if they know where to look.—*Lauren Oyler*

FYI

If you come to Pitt, you'd better bring "initiative and a love of a Pittsburgh sports team."

What's the typical weekend schedule? "Weekends start on Thursday evenings (unless you're a freshman and someone convinced you to take recitations on Friday). On Fridays, go to a house party and then eat at India Garden or T-Rav's for late-night barbecue. Saturdays, attend a theater performance or visit a museum and then party at night. Sundays, get breakfast at Pamela's Diner and study."

If I could change one thing about Pitt, I'd "make it more diverse and get the cliques to mesh a little bit more."

Ursinus College

Address: PO Box 1000, 601 Main Street, Collegeville, PA 19426-1000

Phone: 610-409-3200

E-mail address: admissions@ursinus.edu

Web site URL: www.ursinus.edu

Year Founded: 1869

Private or Public: Private

Religious Affiliation: None

Location: Suburban

Number of Applicants: 6,192

Percent Accepted: 55%

Percent Accepted who enroll: 16%

Number Entering: 442

Number of Transfers Accepted each Year: 27

Middle 50% SAT range: M: 560–650, CR: 540–650, Wr: 530–650

Middle 50% ACT range: 24–28

Early admission program EA/ED/None: EA and ED

Percentage accepted through EA or ED: Unreported/41%

EA and ED deadline: 1-Dec, 15-Jan

Regular Deadline: 15-Feb

Application Fee: $50/free online

Full time Undergraduate enrollment: 1,802

Total enrollment: unreported

Percent Male: 46%

Percent Female: 54%

Total Percent Minority or Unreported: 25%

Percent African-American: 6%

Percent Asian/Pacific Islander: 7%

Percent Hispanic: 7%

Percent Native-American: 1%

Percent International: <1%

Percent in-state/out of state: 57%/43%

Percent from Public HS: 61%

Retention Rate: 88%

Graduation Rate 4-year: 71%

Graduation Rate 6-year: 74%

Percent Undergraduates in On-campus housing: 95%

Number of official organized extracurricular organizations: 88

3 Most popular majors: Biology, Social Sciences, Psychology

Student/Faculty ratio: Unreported

Average Class Size: 9

Percent of students going to grad school: Unreported

Tuition and Fees: $41,650

In-State Tuition and Fees if different: No difference

Cost for Room and Board: $10,300

Percent receiving financial aid out of those who apply: 84

Percent receiving financial aid among all students: 74%

From day one, students at Ursinus College are placed on an even playing field. All freshmen enter the same rooming lottery, all freshmen are issued Dell laptops, and all freshmen take part in the Common Intellectual Experience (CIE) core curriculum program. But to say that life in Collegeville, Pennsylvania, is ordinary or simple is utterly false. With a lively student body and traditions dating back to the nineteenth century, this small college provides students with the opportunity to work closely with an esteemed faculty and the tools to grow into mature adults who actively explore and question the world around them.

Cooperation and Collaboration

Known for the close relationships between faculty and students, this small college includes a wide range of majors in both the sciences and the humanities. Although Ursinus is known as a popular choice of premed students, the most popular majors for undergraduates are psychology and economics.

But UC has majors for everyone—even dancers—with the addition of dance as a major in recent years.

Part of this collaboration between faculty and students is developed starting from their first days during freshman year, when all Ursinus students participate in the CIE Program—the Common Intellectual Experience. This liberal studies seminar epitomizes the value that the staff at Ursinus puts on the development of conversational skills and well-roundedness of its students. Freshmen are required to take the class for both semesters. Groups of sixteen freshmen address major life questions such as: "What does it mean to be human?"; "How should humans live their lives?"; and "What is the universe and what should our place be within it?" The course was designed so that each freshman student would be reading the same material at the same time, facilitating discussion amongst the entire entering class. By looking at works of art, classical writing, and political theory, professors are leaders but at the same time members of the discussion group. The CIE instructors are from a wide range of disciplines, and this means that there is no expert on the subject; instead, everyone takes part in learning and growth.

Collegeville, PA: Location, Location, Location

Students at Ursinus are not lacking in things to do. With the city of Philadelphia only 30 miles away and free shuttle buses to the city, UC students are not too far away from the Liberty Bell, the Rocky Steps, concerts, and urban life. But even with this at their fingertips, many students say they rarely leave their dorms in the quaint town of Collegeville. With 97% of students living on campus, location of dormitories is a big deal. Students living on campus enter the lottery system to determine their living situation. Older students get preference and the prizes tend to be the restored Victorian-era homes that are located right on campus. But no fear, even for freshmen, the living quarters are definitely not like your stereotypical cinderblock high rise, and most freshmen seem to enjoy the dorm atmosphere.

Thanks to its renowned collection of American arts, the Berman Museum brings a great number of art lovers to Collegeville and Ursinus. Besides the beautiful brick walkways and historic buildings, the campus at UC is enhanced by the famous sculptures from the museum. These statues are all over campus and some of them are extremely realistic. One freshman said that everyone "freaks out" when they see the well-known statue of the old lady who is so lifelike it's "creepy." It is pretty common to see tourists and students taking pictures with the old lady.

Mixin' it Up

According to students, there is hardly any difference socially between upperclassmen and "the new kids." Even juniors and seniors involved in frats do not act superior and this is partially due to all the efforts by the administration at Ursinus to raise school unity and keep all the grades mixed. Therefore, for students of many different ages, a typical night out at Ursinus consists of starting out in the Reimert, which is a residence hall made up of large suites that house some local fraternities and sororities. Although there are only a few nationally recognized Greek organizations on campus, some of the favorite social events of the year for many Ursinus students are joint-hosted by a

fraternity and a sorority, and are always memorable occasions. Students sign up ahead of time, and they are taken on buses off campus where there are big parties at places like firehouses with dancing, music, etc. Students like the Reimert because it is always open and there are always people ready to have a good time. But if you are not at Reimert, then you'll probably start your night off at one of the houses on Main Street, which tend to be known for their great parties as well.

> "The campus and the people at Ursinus are personable and it is almost impossible to get lost in the shuffle."

With all these parties going on, it makes sense to wonder about the drug policy at Ursinus. Students describe the administration as relatively lenient for everyone except those living in freshman dorms, where rules tend to be stricter. As long as you keep the alcohol within the confines of the buildings, trouble tends to stay away—but things become a little trickier when going outside with alcohol. If caught, a common punishment is said to be community service. But even with the party scene at Ursinus, students appreciate the fact that there is not a big drug scene at the school and that students are not typically pressured into doing things which they do not feel comfortable about.

Activities Galore

Some of the most prominent clubs on campus are *The Grizzly* (the student paper), the Campus Activity Board, Student Government, and the Residence Hall Association. According to students, the CAB always has stuff going on in the lounge underneath Wismer Cafeteria such as prerelease movies and casino games. Recently, the Student Council successfully kicked off "Late Night Lower Wismer," where there is popcorn, video games such as Rock Band, a Wii system, a pool table, and karaoke. The Wismer Center is considered a major social center on campus that houses dining facilities, social lounges, a snack bar, and game room. But even with big clubs such as the CAB and *The Grizzly*, it doesn't mean there aren't any obscure or unique organizations in Collegeville. There is a scuba club and a meditation group that meets once a week to "de-stress."

Athletics are also a big part of extracurricular activities at Ursinus, and about 50% of students compete on varsity sports teams. The Bears are part of the Centennial Conference, founded in 1992 for small mid-Atlantic academic institutions, and compete at the NCAA Division III level against schools such as Dickinson, Bryn Mawr, and Johns Hopkins. In fact, in 2006, the Ursinus field hockey team was the Div. III National Champion. Even though the majority of students participate in either varsity or intramural athletics at school, most still say that sports are not the major focus on campus. But even so, UC students are fortunate to have great facilities. With a marvelous fitness center that boasts new machines and an indoor track, students have little reason not to be active.

History and Tradition

According to lore, the tree under which author J. D. Salinger wrote his book *Catcher in the Rye* while he was a student at Ursinus still stands today near the end zone of the football field. A plaque is now placed outside the room where he lived during his time in Collegeville as a student. Ursinus is a place where tradition and history matter. According to campus tour guides, Ursinus was even at one point in the *Guinness Book of World Records* for having the most marriages among students. From the moment undergraduates go through the typical icebreaker games during their first day as freshmen, a sense of unity is apparent, and this lasts through the years. By the time Ursinus students are seniors and ready to graduate, the majority is even comfortable enough with each other to slide down one of the fountains on campus completely naked. Every year there is also an event called Air Band, which is a lip-synch and dance competition for charity. Ursinus's tradition of equality even extends to the technological realm. Since 2000, Ursinus's laptop initiative has provided every student and faculty member with a laptop. Some of the goals of the project are to improve communications between students and faculty, to bolster the sense of community around campus and to provide equal computer access for all students.

It is this sense of togetherness that brings students to Ursinus. Instead of just being a number, students make real connections that last. There is an appreciation for the small, picturesque campus and the welcoming community where everyone is equally appreciated: students, faculty, and staff. According to one sophomore, "The campus and the people at Ursinus are personable and it is almost impossible to get lost in the shuffle."—*Emily St. Jean*

FYI

If you come to Ursinus College, you'd better bring "plenty of snacks because the cafeterias and other eating areas have terrible hours."

What's the typical weekend schedule? "Wake up around 11 or 12, go to brunch until one, study or watch football during the afternoon, dinner, and then out for the rest of the night."

If I could change one thing about Ursinus, I'd change "the school name, because it gets really old hearing people mispronounce the name or make dumb jokes about it."

Three things every student at Ursinus should do before graduating are: "slide down a fountain naked before graduation, take a picture with one of the statues on campus (preferably the old lady), and go to a fraternity-sorority social event."

Villanova University

Address: 800 Lancaster Avenue, Villanova, PA 19085-1672
Phone: 610-519-4000
E-mail address: francesca.reynolds@villanova.edu
Web site URL: www.villanova.edu
Year Founded: 1842
Private or Public: Private
Religious Affiliation: Roman Catholic
Location: Suburban
Number of Applicants: 13,098
Percent Accepted: 45%
Percent Accepted who enroll: 27%
Number Entering: 1,651
Number of Transfers Accepted each Year: 257
Middle 50% SAT range: M: 620–710, CR: 590–680, Wr: Unreported
Middle 50% ACT range: 28–31

Early admission program EA/ED/None: EA
Percentage accepted through EA or ED: 41%
EA and ED deadline: 1-Nov
Regular Deadline: 7-Jan
Application Fee: $75
Full time Undergraduate enrollment: 7,146
Total enrollment: 10,635
Percent Male: 50%
Percent Female: 50%
Total Percent Minority or Unreported: 22%
Percent African-American: 4%
Percent Asian/Pacific Islander: 6%
Percent Hispanic: 6%
Percent Native American: 0%
Percent International: 3%
Percent in-state/out of state: 21%/79%
Percent from Public HS: 55%
Retention Rate: 95%

Graduation Rate 4-year: 82%
Graduation Rate 6-year: 88%
Percent Undergraduates in On-campus housing: 70%
Number of official organized extracurricular organizations: 250
3 Most popular majors: Business/Marketing, Engineering, Social Sciences
Student/Faculty ratio: 11:1
Average Class Size: 22
Percent of students going to grad school: 74%
Tuition and Fees: $41,260
In-State Tuition and Fees if different: No difference
Cost for Room and Board: $10,940
Percent receiving financial aid out of those who apply: 70%
Percent receiving financial aid among all students: 47%

L ocated 12 miles from Philadelphia in suburban Radnor Township, Villanova's lush 254-acre campus is dominated by the spires of St. Thomas of Villanova Chapel. The school was founded by the Order of Saint Augustine in 1842 and is officially Catholic, though students from all denominations now attend. While St. Augustine looms large in Villanova's core curriculum and institutional memory, current students are more preoccupied with something else: the school's stellar basketball team, which has been ranked top-10 in the nation. "If you go to any basketball game or any sporting event, people paint their bodies in blue and wear Villanova shirts; there's a huge amount of school spirit," one freshman said. What distinguishes the school, the student continued, is "school spirit and a commitment to service."

One Campus, Four Schools

Students apply for admission to one of four undergraduate schools: the College of Liberal Arts and Sciences, the School of Business, the College of Engineering, or the College of Nursing. While the College of Liberal Arts and Sciences is the largest, with about half of each incoming class of 1,600, the business and engineering schools are growing more popular, having received competitive national rankings in recent years.

Though each college has its own course requirements, all freshmen take the two-semester core Augustine and Culture Seminar (ACS). "ACS is really just English, but they call it something fancy because we go to a Catholic school," one freshman explained. The course covers literature from Shakespeare to Augustine's "Confessions" and purposely mixes students from different colleges in the same classroom.

Villanova prides itself on its small class sizes, which average about 22 people, students said. While some introductory engineering and nursing lectures can be huge, a first-year business student recalled his surprise at having only 30 students in his largest class, introductory microeconomics. The use of teaching assistants is rare and students find their professors understanding and accessible. "Professors here are very open; they'll invite you to dinner at their house after the last class session," a business student said.

Don't get Caught by VEMS

After a week of classes, students go out on Fridays and Saturdays. Many parties are off campus, leading one freshman to comment that "the party scene doesn't really start until junior year," when students are both allowed to have cars and old enough to frequent bars and clubs in Philadelphia. Other freshmen say that fake IDs are common and that parties closer to campus are not hard to find. Another popular party destination is UPenn, whose alcohol policies are reportedly less stringent than Villanova's.

True to its Catholic roots, Villanova maintains a harsh stance against underage drinking. Resident Assistants (RAs) are required to write up underage students for alcohol possession, and inebriated students who encounter Villanova's Emergency Medical Service team—referred to as "VEMS"—can be put on probation. "They tell you VEMS is student-run and that it won't get you in trouble, but it makes your life shit," one freshman said.

Nightlife aside, students often venture to Philadelphia to shop, eat out, or see a movie. The city is accessible by train (two train lines run through Villanova's campus) or by campus shuttle. The Campus Activities Team organizes everything from trips to Philly for art shows and sports games to on-campus concerts, comedy shows, and karaoke nights. The Connelly Center, a student center and hangout spot, hosts weekly movie screenings and has game tables in its lounges.

Sports, particularly basketball and football games, are a perennial draw for the entire campus community. "Our school has an insane amount of school spirit," one business student said. "People want to go to the basketball game and be surrounded by other Villanova fans. Not just students go; families even bring their small children and come watch the game."

Meet Me at the Oreo

On-campus housing is guaranteed for three years, and students live in one of three locations. All freshmen live on South Campus, in residential halls of doubles and triples, and nursing, engineering, business, and arts and sciences students are all intermingled.

While getting to class from South Campus can be somewhat of a trek, South Campus has its own dining hall, known as the Spit (South Pit), and a supermarket, the Sparket (South Campus Market). Sophomores usually live on Main Campus, home to many academic buildings and another dining hall, and juniors move to apartment houses on West Campus. Most seniors are required to find housing off campus.

The cafeteria fare is "pretty good, for people who aren't too picky," a freshman noted. "It's obviously not as good as home-cooked food, but you can still survive on it." For better food on campus, students can head to the Italian Kitchen, the Corner Grill, or the Belle Air Terrace. The Bartley Exchange, in the business building, has "the best food on campus, but for that one you have to use your wallet, not meal points," another student said. Within walking distance, the surrounding area of Radnor also contains some fast food outlets.

> **"Our school has an insane amount of school spirit. People want to go to the basketball game and be surrounded by other Villanova fans."**

The Connelly Center and the dining halls are popular student hangouts, as is the Pavilion, where the basketball team plays its games. At the center of Main Campus sits the Oreo—"this statue that looks like an oreo"—which serves as both a meeting place and a place for clubs to advertise and recruit new members. Another meeting place is the chapel, whose spires are easily visible from afar. For churchgoing students, Villanova offers frequent masses.

Sports and Service

Among other extracurricular options, many students engage in sports and community service projects. Students who are not varsity athletes often participate in club or intramural sports, depending on their level of commitment. "Any sports club is really popular; any sport that you can think of, there's probably a club for it," a freshman said, whether your passion be Frisbee or Quidditch.

The St. Thomas of Villanova Day of Service is an annual event that sends groups of students, faculty, staff, and alumni into Philadelphia to perform service projects, which range from cleaning and painting old facilities to preparing and serving food in shelters and soup kitchens. Each year Villanova also hosts the largest student-run Special Olympics in the world, which draws over 1,000 athletes for competitions in six Olympic-type sports.

Greek life is a large, though not dominant, part of campus life, with about 40% of students joining a fraternity or sorority. "You see people wearing Greek letters a lot," one student said. "I think people want to join frats even though the school tries to sway kids away from that." However, as there are no Greek houses on campus, they do not overly impact the social scene, students said.

Villanova has been criticized for its lack of diversity; 75% of the student body is white, lending the school the nickname "Vanilla Nova." As one student said, "While there are people of different races and backgrounds, when people think of Villanova they think of a white preppy student, like girls in UGGs and trench coats." The school is no longer monolithically Catholic, however. The school "isn't pressuring kids to conform or change their beliefs at all," one nonreligious student said. "The school is just offering a new way of thinking."—*Antonia Woodford*

FYI

If I could change one thing about Villanova, I would change "the strict policies."

What differentiates Villanova the most from other colleges is "the amount of school spirit that we have."

Three things every student at Villanova should do before graduating are: "go to a basketball game, visit Philadelphia, and do some sort of community service activity, like the Day of Service or the Special Olympics."

Rhode Island

Brown University

Address: 45 Prospect Street, Providence, RI 02912
Phone: 401-863-2378
E-mail address: admission_undergraduate@brown.edu
Web site URL: www.brown.edu
Year Founded: 1764
Private or Public: Private
Religious Affiliation: None
Location: Urban
Number of Applicants: 20,633
Percent Accepted: 14%
Percent Accepted who enroll: 55%
Number Entering: 1,550
Number of Transfers Accepted each Year: 117
Middle 50% SAT range: M: 670–780, CR:650–760, Wr: 660–770
Middle 50% ACT range: 28–33
Early admission program EA/ED/None: ED

Percentage accepted through EA or ED: 36%
EA and ED deadline: 1-Nov
Regular Deadline: 1-Jan
Application Fee: $70
Full time Undergraduate enrollment: 6,095
Total enrollment: 7,909
Percent Male: 48%
Percent Female: 52%
Total Percent Minority or Unreported: 32%
Percent African-American: 7%
Percent Asian/Pacific Islander: 16%
Percent Hispanic: 9%
Percent Native-American: <1%
Percent International: 8%
Percent in-state/out of state: 5%/95%
Percent from Public HS: Unreported
Retention Rate: 97%
Graduation Rate 4-year: 83%

Graduation Rate 6-year: 92%
Percent Undergraduates in On-campus housing: 79%
Number of official organized extracurricular organizations: 400
3 Most popular majors: Biology, Economics, International Relations and Affairs
Student/Faculty ratio: 8:1
Average Class Size: 14
Percent of students going to grad school: Unreported
Tuition and Fees: $37,718
In-State Tuition and Fees if different: No difference
Cost for Room and Board: $10,022
Percent receiving financial aid out of those who apply: 44%
Percent receiving financial aid among all students: 44%

T hese studies fortify one's youth, delight one's old age; amid success they are an ornament, in failure they are a refuge and a comfort." Inscribed in stone upon the Van Wickle Gates, these words reflect an institution steeped in a tradition of individual liberty, tolerance, and freedom. However, don't let Brown's ivy-clad grandeur fool you: this college is also home to a unique freedom of study—no requirements, just the ability to choose exactly where you want to go. Founded in 1764, Brown has fine-tuned this tradition over the last 150 years to establish its place as a sanctuary of intellectual curiosity and freedom of thought.

Still Pretty Laid-Back and Satisfying

Brown affords its students the opportunity to create their own program of study that reflects their own interests, passions, and goals. There are no "majors," in which students only specialize in a particular subject. No one should come to Brown to study unless he or she is willing to combine different experiences and courses, integral to a liberal arts college, to create what they call "concentrations." A concentration is exactly as it sounds—a cohesive focus, more than the sum of its parts. With over 70 concentration programs, students must make a difficult decision by the end of their sophomore year. In many cases, students choose to have two concentrations with many choosing the "11 easy classes" for the economics concentration. One student noted, "We don't think in majors or minors, just concentrations, heavier or lighter ones." Thanks to Brown's flexibility and lack of general requirements, students need only 30 classes to graduate, which is a little under four classes a semester. One junior explained, "This way people can get good at what they do, and I do my own thing." The laid-back requirement or lack thereof exudes an air of freedom and experimentation.

Recently, some departments have required students take specific classes for their concentration, such as an additional math class for the economics concentration. Brown has even implemented an additional WRIT class (writing course) on top of their original one WRIT course requirement. Some students welcome it, explaining, "If people complain, they aren't looking at the real world." Despite these few new requirements, Brown still stays true to its philosophy of giving students the freedom to explore in new fields without the pressure of doing so for the sake of a successful future career. As one student put it, "There's a lot of overlap in concentrations. You run into random people that you would never imagine to be into math or science, and you just remark, 'Wow, these guys are so well-rounded, taking classes having nothing to do with their concentrations.'"

At Brown, students tend to pursue these top three concentrations: International Relations, Biology, or Economics. There are "easy" concentrations like Economics and History—and among the "hard ones" are Engineering and Computer Science. Although Brown has generally been strong in the natural sciences, humanities, and social sciences, the engineering concentration has steadily gained ground and recognition with the advent of its new School of Engineering. For the more ambitious students, Brown offers special programs for students who, in addition to a Brown degree, want to earn a bachelor of fine arts from the equally famed Rhode Island School of Design. Brown even offers early acceptance to Brown's medical school, while completing the regular baccalaureate.

Inside the classrooms, students agree that there are almost too many academic resources to really take advantage of them all, but of course, they are open to whoever is willing to use them. Learning opportunities come from some of the most unexpected places as one sophomore remarked, "Tests are so well written that I learn through tests, realizing how much we learned or haven't learned." These are typical sentiments from Brown students, and this is a result of the efforts of some of the most famous professors. Students should expect to learn from well-known professors, such as Biology professor Ken Miller who recently was a leading witness in the Supreme Court case debating the teaching of evolution in schools. On the other academic spectrum, Professor Deak Nabers's popular class on American literature and film attracts many students. Just as Brown strives to create a sense of freedom in choice among students, Brown also gives free-reign to the types of classes offered, such as a class called "The Simple Art of Murder" or "Belonging and Displacement."

Although most introductory courses can have up to 500 people, most upper classes are seminar-based and capped. Freshmen get the option of applying to highly competitive First Year Seminars, capped at twenty students. One freshman raved about the uniqueness of the seminar courses, such as Rights of Passage—an apt name for any college freshman. Characteristic of many private institutions, the small classroom setting fosters intimate discussions with the professor and other students, and it makes "it easier to really get to know people and to get into the discussion." A junior described the professors at Brown as "very approachable, always offering office hours. Usually, you can email professors and they will respond. Some are up at 3 a.m. in the morning responding to emails."

Because students at Brown tend to "do their own thing," comparing GPAs or staying competitive is not the norm. Although the social sciences and humanities have inflated grades, the sciences like organic chemistry are graded on a curve. Some students opt to take courses Satisfactory/No Credit, which allows students to experiment and "get out of their comfort zone" without worrying too much about number grades. Even though course work can be difficult, "there are students willing to help out, and it's not as competitive as you'd think at an ivy school," said one sophomore.

Being Liberal is the Norm, Being Conservative is a Personal Thing

According to one freshman, "my entire freshman dorm smelled like pot the whole time." Although some caution against giving in to Brown's stereotype of being a "pot-smoking," "hipster-glasses wearing," "tight-jeans flaunting" cohort, students would say there's a ring of truth to that image. With lax policies on alcohol and pot, it is "almost impossible to not know someone who doesn't smoke or drink," as one freshman described. The campus has a very liberal atmosphere, and almost everyone is generally accepted to be a liberal. According to a thick-rimmed glasses-wearing student, "If you deviate from being liberal, you're weird; For example, if a church priest openly protests against gay marriage, students who are a part of the LGBT community will flock out and make out."

In terms of encouraging diversity, students say that the admissions office is doing a good job geographically, but social divisions based on income and ethnicity are sometimes apparent. Some students take note of the large discrepancy between places where people come from, and there is not much anyone can do about that. As one student notes, "I applaud Brown's generous financial aid policy making Brown a dream for low-income students, but some people still don't realize that not everyone starts at the same place."

In terms of the social scene, every club tends to have its own party, while house parties tend to be popular among upperclassmen. Although frat parties do exist, they are limited to attracting eager freshmen or other frat boys. Varsity sports at Brown have their own houses where they can host private parties, which eventually become open parties. With these parties usually the "attractive people dominate the scene" according to one junior. On the other hand, one student quirked, "the Greek scene is relatively small, and frat parties are places you go if you don't have any friends." Moreover, Wednesday is considered college night for a local club named Whisco (formerly known as Fish Co.), and in general, partying begins on Thursday or Friday, while Frats begin on Saturdays. One annual party hosted by the Queer Alliance called "Sex Power God" typifies the free-spirited atmosphere; it's even endorsed by the college. In addition, "Body Chemistry" is another annual tradition, where people wear nothing on weekends. Fortunately for many students, Brown's policies on alcohol and drug use are described as "extremely loose." Lastly, if the local social scene is not satisfying enough, Brown students find it easy to take the bus or train to Boston or New York for the weekend.

What Kind of "Providence?"

Visitors and students who come to Providence notice that Brown is a concentrate of art and thought with colonial-styled architecture and open green space, complete with ivy and impeccable grounds. Brown students these days have adapted their school's "ivy tower" look to their 21st century lifestyles—lounging on the grassy quads, throwing the old pigskin around, crowding around food stands—and it wouldn't be Brown without the occasional hookah.

As with most other private and liberal arts colleges, Brown requires its first-year students to live on-campus. About 600 students live in six connected buildings known as the "freshman zoo." The dorms are arranged in alphabetical order, starting with Archibald house and ending with Poland house that make a "sort of figure eight." The rest of the school lives in dorms that are either a few blocks or a short walk away. Brown assigns almost everyone a roommate, as the rooms are primarily doubles; there are singles scattered throughout, but these are reserved for the RCs or upperclass students. One student said the rooms "are decent, but not as great as I thought." Many freshmen have noted that they made most of their friends in their first-year units, which is made up of forty to sixty students, though one freshman remarked how "there's a lack of community sometimes because there isn't a residential college system." Although making the top 20 happiest colleges in America, one freshman noted that "this year didn't make the happiest campus because people who came in had unrealistic expectations of what happiness is, and anything that makes you unhappy is unnatural." But eventually, after being at Brown for so long, many students say that they become content with their lives and are willing to let things "roll the way things roll." After freshman year, students get a unique housing selection process that allows them to choose the exact room in which they will live in; however, the Housing Lottery determines most on-campus housing assignments.

Brown hosts a long list of campus eateries, but the two main buffet-style dining halls are affectionately coined the "V-Dub" and the "Ratty." Because of the all-you-can-eat dining halls, a lot of doe-eyed freshmen come in exclaiming about the abundance of food, but it goes without saying that the comestibles quickly grow tiring. In order to break the monotony, students head to nearby Thayer Street, which houses a variety of popular food options from famous falafels at East Side Pocket to Antonio's Pizza. And if that doesn't satisfy you, you can easily head downtown for more restaurant options that range from some exotic foods to fine dining choices that "you only eat at when your roommate's parents are in town."

Although the city of Providence has spruced itself up in the last few years, one junior felt that good clubs remain on the run-down side of town. One nice incentive that Brown offers for travel to downtown to its many shops is a free community access trolley that brings students from campus to four main shopping hubs.

New Dart, Get it?

Brown hosts a variety of student-run organizations to balance their academics and free time. One student noted, "Everyone here at Brown seems to be passionate about their extracurricular activities and many times they are completely unrelated." Walking around campus, a freshman recalls how she saw many social activists swinging their signs as if they "seem to be making real reforms, however minor." And of course, Brown's political groups are thriving, especially with the Brown College Democrats widely dominating the scene. One rising junior said, "You know the game Where's Waldo, at Brown we play Where's the Conservative?"

> "At Brown, it is very normal to watch a fashion show with a model dressed as a squat alien who vomited up a plastic envelope-style bag with hands printed on it, a clever play on the 'hand-bag.'"

If you're interested in exploring cultural heritages and learning about race and ethnicity as components of the American Identity, head on over to Brown's Third World Center. A junior heavily involved with the center described it as, "one of the greatest things about Brown, where they run their own program and sponsor lectures" that address all the above issues. The name Third World originates from students who prefer it to the term "minority" because of the negative connotations. One junior explained the name as "originating from the term 'third way' as an alternative to the first and second world, and we use it in the sense of empowerment." The center is "very focused on activism and asks big questions like where we are, where we have been, and where we're all going to have to go," as detailed by an involved sophomore.

Brown students have their share of odd and exciting traditions to complement their free-spirited environment, including the semi-annual "Naked Donut Run" during finals, paying homage to the mythical Josiah S. Carberry, the Professor of Psychoceramics (study of cracked pots), and of course, bringing in performers such as MGMT and Snoop Dogg (Lion) during Spring Weekend. One junior remarked, "If all the nude-themed events weren't enough, a couple of juniors just started a series of workshops and performances called Nudity in Upspace." The nude art performance and the shock value that accompanies it aim to "normalize nudity." Discussions about sexuality and nudity are definitely not hard to come by at Brown. Along the same notion of "liberalness," one senior confided that "At Brown, it is very normal to watch a fashion show with a model dressed as a squat alien who vomited up a plastic envelope-style bag with hands printed on it, a clever play on the 'hand-bag.'"

As a running theme at Brown, students express themselves openly without fear, and many students take pride in this type of atmosphere. As a freshman explained, "Brown is the place to find true freedom of expression." Brown leaves its students with a unique un-structure for their coursework, many esoteric clubs, and a wide-range of activist opportunities to help mold a very Brown college experience.—*Matthew Tran*

FYI

What's the typical weekend schedule? "Weekend starts on Wednesday with Whisco, Thursday night pregame for Friday night, Friday night go out, Saturday frat parties, Sunday sober up."

Three things every student at Brown should do before graduating are: "Ratty challenge, where you swipe in to the Ratty and stay there all day, lunch plus dinner, participate in the naked donut run, sci-li challenge, where you climb a 14-story building/library, and at every floor you take a shot."

What differentiates Brown the most from other colleges is "that it's the chillest Ivy League school."

Rhode Island School of Design

Address: 2 College Street, Providence, RI 02903
Phone: 401-454-6300
E-mail address: admissions@risd.edu
Web site URL: www.risd.edu
Year Founded: 1877
Private or Public: Private
Religious Affiliation: None
Location: Urban
Number of Applicants: 2,511
Percent Accepted: 34%
Percent Accepted who enroll: 47%
Number Entering: 398
Number of Transfers Accepted each Year: 151
Middle 50% SAT range: M:550–670, CR:530–660, Wr: Unreported
Middle 50% ACT range: Unreported
Early admission program EA/ED/None: EA
Percentage accepted through EA or ED: Unreported

EA and ED deadline: 15-Dec
Regular Deadline: 15-Feb
Application Fee: $50
Full time Undergraduate enrollment: 1,882
Total enrollment: 1882
Percent Male: 34%
Percent Female: 66%
Total Percent Minority or Unreported: 49%
Percent African-American: 2%
Percent Asian/Pacific Islander: 14%
Percent Hispanic: 5%
Percent Native-American: <1%
Percent International: 12%
Percent in-state/out of state: Unreported
Percent from Public HS: 60%
Retention Rate: Unreported
Graduation Rate 4-year: Unreported
Graduation Rate 6-year: Unreported

Percent Undergraduates in On-campus housing: 33%
Number of official organized extracurricular organizations: 35
3 Most popular majors: Graphic Design, Illustration, Inustrial Design
Student/Faculty ratio: 11:1
Average Class Size: Unreported
Percent of students going to grad school: Unreported
Tuition and Fees: $27,510
In-State Tuition and Fees if different: No difference
Cost for Room and Board: $7,709
Percent receiving financial aid out of those who apply: Unreported
Percent receiving financial aid among all students: 69%

The Rhode Island School of Design does not offer your "typical" college experience—there are not many sports teams, social life is secondary to schoolwork, and your English teacher might not care if you don't finish your reading assignment because she knows you spent eight hours doing studio work the day before. RISD (pronounced "RIZ-dee") is a serious school for serious art students. Students at RISD, a small campus in Providence, Rhode Island, that is adjacent to Brown University, can major in apparel design, art education, graphic design, industrial design, illustration, textiles, sculpture, glass, or animation, and there are many other options.

The campus is home to approximately 1,900 undergraduates. Students say the relatively low number of students allows for very intimate classes, in which the average size is 13 students.

All RISD freshmen are required to take Foundation Studies, a fundamentals program which consists of three classes: Drawing, Two-Dimensional Design, and Three-Dimensional Design. The program is meant to immerse students in the basics of art and visual design, and to help them explore their options in terms of majors. Freshmen are also given second priority (after seniors) in class selection so that they can experiment with classes before making a final decision on their area of concentration.

RISD is organized on a trimester schedule, which has positives and negatives according to students. Students are only given two weeks off for winter break, but they are also able to take more classes in one year. The second semester, which takes place right after winter break, is also unofficially designated as "relaxation time." According to one RISD junior, no one takes more than two classes during this period in January and February. "Most people only take one class during second semester because the first and third semesters are hardcore," she said.

Liberal arts courses are also required of every student, but they are definitely not the concentration of a RISD education.

According to a RISD sophomore, History of Art and Visual Culture is the most popular liberal arts department and some students even choose to major in this field rather than in a visual art. Students say the most popular visual art department is Illustration because it offers students a great deal of freedom in their studies and concentration. "It's a very open and free department—you can really take it anywhere you want and there aren't a lot of technical restrictions," one RISD junior said. The consensus among RISD students is that the hardest major is architecture, which some students playfully refer to as "archi-torture."

Getting into the class you want can be a nightmare at RISD, mostly because the class sizes are so small. There is also a precise hierarchy of preference in which seniors get first choice during enrollment, freshmen second choice, juniors third, and sophomores are left to fend for themselves at the bottom. As mentioned earlier, freshmen are given second priority so they can explore different classes before they pick their major. "As a sophomore, it was incredibly difficult to get the classes I wanted. I guess it's fair in the long run, but it's still pretty frustrating," a current junior said.

According to interviewed students, the workload at RISD is rigorous to say the least. "There's not a lot of time to sleep because you're spending all night cutting paper, making books, and putting together your portfolio," said one RISD senior. Students also emphasize the necessity of attending class and say you are required to get a note from the nurse if you miss class due to illness, "just like high school." RISD students also have the option of taking classes at Brown, so if a RISD student wants to take a math class, there is nothing stopping her. Beginning in the 2008–2009 academic year, Brown and RISD began to collaborate to offer students a dual degree—the completion of a five-year program will allow students to receive a BA from Brown and BFA from RISD. Participating students must live on both campuses for two years each and must complete both degrees.

> **"There's not a lot of time to sleep because you're spending all night cutting paper, making books, and putting together your portfolio."**

Social life has been a point of contention among RISD students, mostly because the school's social scene is somewhat limited. According to one junior, the amount of work assigned to RISD students makes partying difficult, though some students do go to parties at Brown or to bars. All in all, social life is very much contained within the campus and mostly consists of private parties. "This is not a party school; it's a very serious school. If you're someone who wants to go somewhere with lots of parties and things, RISD probably isn't the school for you," one RISD freshman said. But that is not to say students don't make meaningful relationships or have close friends. A junior said everyone has a very good relationship with almost everyone else simply because the school is so small.

RISD freshmen and sophomores are required to live on campus, and many juniors and seniors choose to do so anyway. Freshmen are housed in the Quad, conveniently located right next to the main dining hall, the Met. Construction was recently completed on 15 Westminster, a new dorm building that also happens to be the location of the main library. Students say the new building is "great," "beautiful," and "centrally located," just a quick walk from the graphic design and illustration building. Housing is done by lottery after freshman year.

Despite the statistic that 66 percent of RISD students are female and 34 percent are male, most students said RISD is very diverse, and that you are able to "meet all sorts of people." There is a large population of international students, especially from Korea.

Student Alliance, the student governing body, is the primary student group on the RISD campus. It meets weekly to discuss student issues, which most recently have included concerns regarding social life at RISD. The Alliance is working to get administrative approval for a student center on campus to increase "hang out" space for students. Other student clubs include a cappella groups and cultural clubs. RISD has two varsity sports, basketball and hockey, both of which compete on the Brown campus. "Sports are not that big of a deal on campus," said one sophomore. "But we still support our teams."

Students describe the food at RISD as "decent" and "pretty good," but they do acknowledge that some dining halls have more options than others. A junior student said the best place to grab a quick bite to eat is the Portfolio Café, located right next to the library in Westminster 15.

The bottom line for students at RISD is their artistic education, and most are more than satisfied with the training they have received at the university. "RISD is the perfect school for me because I'm doing what I love," said one senior. "Make sure you really love this kind of work before you decide to come to RISD."—*Samantha Broussard-Wilson*

FYI
If you come to RISD, you'd better bring "your sketchbook."
What is the typical weekend schedule? "Work, work, and maybe a little extra work before bed."
If I could change one thing about RISD, I'd "give the students more time to sleep."
Three things every student at RISD should do before graduating are "go to a hockey game, explore the coffee shops in Providence, and go on any of the excursions offered, like Newport, New York City, or skiing."

Salve Regina University

Address: 100 Ochre Point Avenue, Newport, RI 02840-4192
Phone: 401-341-2908
E-mail address: sruadmis@salve.edu
Web site URL: www.salve.edu
Year Founded: 1947
Private or Public: Private
Religious Affiliation: Roman Catholic
Location: Suburban
Number of Applicants: 5,256
Percent Accepted: 64%
Percent Accepted who enroll: 15%
Number Entering: 505
Number of Transfers Accepted each Year: 121
Middle 50% SAT range: M: 500–585, CR:500–590, Wr: 500–590
Middle 50% ACT range: 22–26
Early admission program EA/ED/None: EA

Percentage accepted through EA or ED: Unreported
EA and ED deadline: 11-Nov
Regular Deadline: 1-Jan
Application Fee: $50
Full time Undergraduate enrollment: 1,884
Total enrollment: 1,984
Percent Male: 32%
Percent Female: 68%
Total Percent Minority or Unreported: 24%
Percent African-American: 2%
Percent Asian/Pacific Islander: 1%
Percent Hispanic: 3%
Percent Native-American: <1%
Percent International: 1%
Percent in-state/out of state: 16%/84%
Percent from Public HS: Unreported
Retention Rate: Unreported

Graduation Rate 4-year: 63%
Graduation Rate 6-year: 67%
Percent Undergraduates in On-campus housing: 60%
Number of official organized extracurricular organizations: 42
3 Most popular majors: Criminal Justice, Education, Nursing
Student/Faculty ratio: 14:1
Average Class Size: 19
Percent of students going to grad school: Unreported
Tuition and Fees: $32,500
In-State Tuition and Fees if different: No difference
Cost for Room and Board: $11,600
Percent receiving financial aid out of those who apply: 68%
Percent receiving financial aid among all students: 71%

Founded in the mid-twentieth century by the Sisters of Mercy, Salve Regina University is a small Catholic school in Newport, Rhode Island, dedicated to helping people and to the education of students who also strive to achieve this goal. While maintaining one of the best and most competitive nursing programs in the nation, Salve Regina also offers a serious liberal arts education, which ensures its students build a broad academic base—with, of course, a certain Catholic flair—from which to grow.

Nursing and Liberal Arts at a Small Catholic School

When students choose to study at Salve Regina University, they begin by completing a set program of required courses. As the name of the program indicates, Salve Regina's Core Curriculum is at the center of the university's devotion to religious thought and the varied academic pursuits of its students. This curriculum is divided into two major parts: the Common Core Courses, which are a series of five courses that every undergraduate at the university must take (heavily based in writing about literature, philosophy, and religion), and the Core Complement, which requires students to take eleven courses in seven academic fields. Students, on top of this requirement, will complete courses needed to receive a degree in their majors. In part because of the liberal arts nature of the Core Complement, the lower-level and introductory courses in the different departments tend to be some of the most popular courses, and, as one student said, "the general education classes and required classes, along with language classes, are all very competitive to get into." The courses generally are what you expect from a liberal arts school, and many of the more popular courses are in the humanities and social sciences. Unsurprisingly, there are some facets of the university's curriculum that do have "a heavily Catholic" component and this is especially evident in the religion and philosophy courses of the Common Core Curriculum. Almost half of the credits required by the Core Complement must be in the areas of literature, social science, and religious studies.

While there is a well-regarded level of academic diversity on campus, the most popular majors on campus are, "by far, Nursing, Business, and Administration of Justice (ADJ)." Salve's nursing program is one of the top rated in the country, which many attribute to the university's founding principles adopted from the Sisters of Mercy: service to others. It is perhaps because the nursing department has a very low percentage of male students that the university as a whole has a noticeable majority of girls.

At Salve, "faculty members are extremely open and accessible to their students." The average class size is about twenty to thirty students, and the interaction this fosters between students and professors is one of the greatest assets of the university's academic program. "This is the benefit of such a small school." Most classes do not offer curves and the average GPA at Salve is roughly a 3.0.

Living in Mansions

Once freshmen arrive at Salve Regina University, they move into one of three freshman residence halls. The following year, they change scenery and live in one of five sophomore dorms, which are modified Newport mansions. In the underclassmen's dorms, most rooms are large triples and quads with their own bathrooms. Students in the Pell Honors program are given special housing in a Living Learning Community for their first two years. Salve also offers several upperclassman apartment options, and most juniors and seniors live off campus. Resident Assistants in the dorms are on duty fifteen nights each month and act as a connection between the Office of Residential Life and the students. It is a wet campus for age-appropriate dorms and students, according to one RA, "but we do follow strict policies on inappropriate alcohol use in the dorms."

Students at Salve feel safe on campus, which has roaming security patrols 24 hours a day. But they also do not fear stepping off campus and into the city of Newport, Rhode Island. All of downtown Newport is a huge tourist area with "tons of great restaurants and hang-out spots" that students frequent day and night.

A School with a Huge Heart

Most people get involved in multiple clubs and extracurriculars on top of completing Salve's required ten hours before graduation of community service. Newport is "a very popular tourist town with lots of shops and restaurants downtown where most students work." It is also a surf town, and Salve has a surf club where students can learn how to surf while also doing community service such as beach cleanups.

Since there are no fraternities or sororities, athletics and sports teams and members play a huge role in the social aspect of student life at Salve. Soccer and rugby are "the most popular sports, and we have a world champion sailing team," according to one athlete. Every game is packed with eager, supportive fans. "All facilities are top-notch and very well taken care of." The school offers intramural soccer, softball, volleyball, kickball and several others, which are open to all students, and participants say that it does get quite competitive.

Partying, Preppy Style

For some, "athletics completely consume the Salve social life since there are no fraternities." Sports and extracurricular activities in general keep students busy "doing productive activities versus other destructive behaviors," according to one sophomore; this is certainly a goal of the university since it focuses so much on community service and the prevention of destructive behaviors in the social lives of its students.

"As a Catholic school, the administration is very strict on alcohol policies," students say. The first time an underage student is caught with alcohol, the student must pay a $50 fine. Each offense afterwards yields a harsher penalty. This, of course, doesn't stop Salve students from partying the way they want. "I'd say about 80% of students drink," said one student, and drugs are "just about as common as they would be at any other school."

Navigating the social scene might be easier as an upperclassman since they have their group of friends figured out and most have their own houses, and for the same reason, partying (with alcohol) is easier in an upperclassman's off-campus house. On Thursday and Saturday nights, students typically go to dinner downtown or to party at an upperclassman's house. Besides the advantage in social life that older students earn, "it is extremely easy to meet friends as an athlete" but other students do comment on how tough it can be as a non-athlete.

> "It is a small Catholic school with a huge heart. I've never seen such dedicated people and you are engulfed into that culture."

Still, many Salve students seem perfectly content with their school and with their classmates, while being fully aware of their nature. Most students appear to be well-to-do and come from comfortable backgrounds. "Kids dress nicely here," wearing preppy things "such as polos and Sperrys." Salve Regina University's student body is quite noticeably homogeneous. "We are not very diverse at all. Our population is more than predominantly Caucasian," according to one student. And, predictably, the majority of students are in some way members or affiliates of the Catholic Church, although students say "the chapel is small, and only a minority of students do go to Mass."

Beside the New England preppiness and the very-Catholic nature of the school, though, Salve Regina University is home to a different kind of diversity, in the unique lives and studies of its students. Studying in mansions overlooking the Atlantic Ocean, they each get an experience that is quite their own.—*Connor Moseley*

FYI
If you come to Salve Regina, you'd better bring "some polos and some boat shoes."
If I could change one thing about Salve Regina University, "I'd relax the strict dorm policies."
What differentiates Salve Regina University the most from other colleges is "that it is a small Catholic school with a huge heart. I've never seen such dedicated people and you are engulfed into that culture."

University of Rhode Island

Address: 14 Upper College Road, Kingston, RI 02881-1322
Phone: 401-874-7000
E-mail address: admission@uri.edu
Web site URL: www.uri.edu
Year Founded: 1892
Private or Public: Public
Religious Affiliation: None
Location: Rural
Number of Applicants: 14,272
Percent Accepted: 78%
Percent Accepted who enroll: 28%
Number Entering: 2,767
Number of Transfers Accepted each Year: 892
Middle 50% SAT range: M: 470–580, CR: 470–560, Wr: 470–570
Middle 50% ACT range: 21–25
Early admission program EA/ED/None: EA

Percentage accepted through EA or ED: Unreported
EA and ED deadline: 1-Dec
Regular Deadline: 1-Feb
Application Fee: $65
Full time Undergraduate enrollment: 13,093
Total enrollment: 16,294
Percent Male: 47%
Percent Female: 53%
Total Percent Minority or Unreported: 32%
Percent African-American: 6%
Percent Asian/Pacific Islander: 3%
Percent Hispanic: 3%
Percent Native-American: 1%
Percent International: <1%
Percent in-state/out of state: 48%/52%
Percent from Public HS: Unreported
Retention Rate: 81%

Graduation Rate 4-year: 38%
Graduation Rate 6-year: 57%
Percent Undergraduates in On-campus housing: 45%
Number of official organized extracurricular organizations: 100
3 Most popular majors: Business/Marketing, Communications/Journalism, Health Professions
Student/Faculty ratio: 16:1
Average Class Size: 24
Percent of students going to grad school: 50%
Tuition and Fees: $27,454
In-State Tuition and Fees if different: $11,366
Cost for Room and Board: $10,796
Percent receiving financial aid out of those who apply: Unreported
Percent receiving financial aid among all students: Unreported

Because the University of Rhode Island is such a populous institution, students' academic adventures really are as fruitful, difficult, or fun as they make them. There is a lot of freedom, which students can either take advantage of or use to their advantage. Says a senior, "You are allowed to create your own minor as long as you obtain a faculty sponsor and the dean of your respective college's permission."

As for the Classroom . . .

As the larger university is separated into individual subject-specific schools, the most popular of which is the more general College of Arts and Sciences, students are able to dive into whatever it is that they are interested in from the start. Already set on becoming a French restaurateur? Enroll in the College of Business Administration. Whatever your forte may be, there is opportunity after opportunity after opportunities; one can pick and choose between schools, take science classes that draw from real-life trips to magnificent Rhode Island waters, and vary class intensity—from the anonymity of lectures to Honors Program classes. With its broad sampling of students, competition between students varies as well; as with anywhere, some are always going to want to be on top, but the majority work together in a constructive manner. The main academic tension seems to arise between pupils of the hard sciences and those of humanities. There exists an underlying assumption that the former is much more challenging than the latter. If anything, though, comparisons made between the two are done with lightheartedness—not with malice. While there is a selection of smaller discussion-sized classes maxed at 20, they are in high demand; to keep yourself from being one of the many, you should focus on creating some sort of connection with professors, whether during office hours or by talking to Teacher's Assistants. While there definitely is much student support—such as that offered through the Early Alert Program—because the school must cater to the needs of so many students, there is not always a professor on students' backs, making them do their work. How much you prepare for a class really depends on your own self-motivation. Grade-wise, one senior says, "in the physical sciences, it's less about getting an 'A' and more about passing. In the social sciences, it's all about getting an 'A.'"

Social (or Greek) Life?

At the University of Rhode Island, social life flourishes. Students really do come from all different backgrounds; not only racial, but cultural, religious, geographic, and familial. While, as a state school, the majority of students come from around Rhode Island, there is also a good selection from around the country and even the world. Some commute; some dorm. All in all, students' search for others with preferences compatible to theirs tends to be rather straightforward. There is some self-segregation; though people tend to be open with one another, cliques are not obsolete. Sororities and fraternities do take up much of the social life, though one student assures that, "Greek life is more about giving back than drinking."

> "Greek life is more about giving back than drinking."

A Student's Paradise

What isn't there to do in a state with such easy access to all we ever desire: oceans, sun, flora, fauna, rousing cities, beaches, charming towns, and—did I mention water? Because Rhode Island itself is the perfect size for an easy commute, not so long as to require extensive driving, students often go off campus for entertainment—exploring the city, the sand, the wilderness, or just connecting with their peers at parties, club get-togethers, and other organized student gatherings. One of the school's perks is that undergraduates need not live in the dorms to have a lively social life; in fact, because the drug and alcohol policy prohibits the on-campus presence of such substances, many events take place at other locations. In fact, because so many commute, there is just as much of a community off campus as there is on. While some students experiment with dorm life in their initial years, many end up living in their own places; more senior housing, though, is said to be quite the upgrade. Students are not hesitant to give the university's food stellar reviews; one described a typical meal, or shall I say feast, as "omelettes, pancakes, [and] fresh fruit."

Post-Homework

If you're looking for a place to do sports, take a deep breath. Yes, Rhode Island, I will repeat, has pretty much any recreational land formation one could ever want—and students make sure not to miss out on the fun. While many fill their schedules with classic land sports like tennis, hockey, and basketball, there isn't a place more ideal to swim (but where? The choices are many—the pool, the ocean, a pond . . .) or sail. In fact, the University of Rhode Island houses one of the best United States sailing teams. Time commitment varies; if you're really into making sports a huge part of your life, play for a school team; however, don't feel at all pressured—there are a plethora of intramural teams that allow students to de-stress without causing stress. If you're not a sports diehard, there are countless other activities in which you can get involved. Students love their school's theater, close-knit sorority and fraternity groups, fund-raising activities, local community service ventures, and research opportunities.

The University of Rhode Island, as large as it is, has quite the selection of opportunities. There are a lot of students to be met, a lot of clubs to join, a lot of Greek life to become a part of, a lot of activities to pursue, and a lot of things to learn. It is the perfect place for the expansion of one's horizons; make sure you try something new.—*Liliana Cousins*

FYI
If you come to URI, you'd better "leave your parents behind."
Three things every student at URI should do before graduating are "try out the Northwoods Challenge Course [a fun way to exercise alongside friends]; join some of the student organizations; go to Lip Sing ([a] . . . Greek Week event)."
The biggest college-wide tradition/event at URI is "Diversity Week in October."

South Carolina

Clemson University

Address: 105 Sikes Hall, Clemson, SC 29634-5124
Phone: 864-656-2287
E-mail address: cuadmissions@clemson.edu
Web site URL: www.clemson.edu
Year Founded: 1889
Private or Public: Public
Religious Affiliation: None
Location: Rural
Number of Applicants: 16,282
Percent Accepted: 54%
Percent Accepted who enroll: 32%
Number Entering: 2,813
Number of Transfers Accepted each Year: 816
Middle 50% SAT range: M: 587–680, CR: 550–640, Wr: Unreported
Middle 50% ACT range: 25–30
Early admission program EA/ED/None: None

Percentage accepted through EA or ED: NA
EA and ED deadline: NA
Regular Deadline: 1-May
Application Fee: $50
Full time Undergraduate enrollment: 14,713
Total enrollment: 18,317
Percent Male: 54%
Percent Female: 46%
Total Percent Minority or Unreported: 10%
Percent African-American: 7%
Percent Asian/Pacific Islander: 2%
Percent Hispanic: 1%
Percent Native-American: <1%
Percent International: 1%
Percent in-state/out of state: 71%/29%
Percent from Public HS: Unreported
Retention Rate: 92%

Graduation Rate 4-year: 49%
Graduation Rate 6-year: 77%
Percent Undergraduates in On-campus housing: 42%
Number of official organized extracurricular organizations: 292
3 Most popular majors: Biology, Business, Engineering
Student/Faculty ratio: 14:1
Average Class Size: 31
Percent of students going to grad school: Unreported
Tuition and Fees: $24,130
In-State Tuition and Fees if different: $11,108
Cost for Room and Board: $6,556
Percent receiving financial aid out of those who apply: 87%
Percent receiving financial aid among all students: 71%

L ocated on the banks of Lake Hartwell in Clemson, South Carolina, a forty minute drive to the mid-sized city of Greenville and over two hours to Columbia, the capital of South Carolina, Clemson boasts a long history of growth from an agricultural institution to South Carolina's flagship institute of engineering. The Tigers, named for their corresponding mascot, were founded by a relation of John C. Calhoun, and still maintain characteristics of the old South.

The Great Divide: Sciences and the Humanities

Students at Clemson can elect to join one of five colleges at their time of application— Agriculture, Forestry and Life Sciences; Architecture, Arts and Humanities; Business and Behavioral Science; Engineering and Science; and Health, Education and Human Development—though students note that the College of Engineering and Science, in addition to their program in architecture, is the most well known. Combined, the colleges offer a range of majors, from packaging science to food science, yet the majority of the majors are science-centric, with students claiming the most popular majors to be those in biology, business, and engineering. While it may be, according to one student, that "anytime I meet a boy, it's a good guess that he is an engineer," health-centric majors, such as nursing or health science, are also very competitive, particularly concerning getting into classes. Students can also opt to enter the Calhoun Honors College, which requires a separate application process and boasts Freshman Colloquia, small, seminar classes available to freshmen and the option to take "honors" versions of introductory classes. In addition, students within the honors college can enter the "design a course" contest, with recent winners including Graphic Novels.

But, regardless of the college, all students must complete demanding distributional requirements. For example, students in the College of Engineering and Science must complete more than fifteen credits in the humanities and social sciences in order to graduate. Attending a definite "math and science school," students attest that the most difficult majors include engineering and the hard sciences—which make them "work really hard"—in addition to the architecture program. However, students in the parks, recreation and tourism management (PRTM) program have nicknamed it "Party Right Through May," attesting to their relatively light workload. But, when students not in "Party Right Through May" want to opt for an easier workload, they can take "leisure skills" classes, learning about such topics as swing dance, rock climbing, and meditation and relaxation. Other interesting and fun courses include First Aid/CPR. Though class size is dependent on major, students agree that after the large prerequisites and general education requirement classes, the average class size becomes closer to twenty.

Even though Clemson is known for its math and science programs, some students still participate in humanities programs and students assert that a wide gap exists between the science and humanities students. While math and science majors absolutely hate humanities classes, and, said one student, "consider humanities harder," humanities majors regard those in the sciences in an analogous way. As such, students think each other absolutely "crazy" for taking classes on the other side of the gap. However, grading is notably difficult in all departments at Clemson, partly due to the lack of grading curves in many departments, so, as students say, "the amount of work that you put in determines the grades that you get." Fittingly, then, students claim that "it's the student's responsibility to put in the work required to get an A"—the student must show drive and initiative to qualify for help from a professor. A plethora of opportunities abounds for students in need of academic aid, which includes free tutors and the academic success center offering academic coaching and counseling sessions.

Faculty members are lauded by the students as being "extremely accessible" with all having set office hours, but, says one student, "are more than willing to set up appointments outside of those hours." Notable faculty members include David Reinking, a famed researcher analyzing the intersection of technology and literacy.

The Tiger Den

After receiving notifications of their admittance, an incoming freshman can submit a housing application, which has "first-come-first-served" priority rankings. Freshmen, for whom on-campus living is required, as it is for all students under the age of twenty-one, typically live in two-person dorm rooms with communal baths. A few lucky freshmen will have the option to live in apartment-style accommodations owned by the University which are lauded for their spaciousness and private kitchens. Honors students can also choose to reside in Holmes Residential Hall, which offers in-suite bathrooms. Students can also choose to participate in a "living-learning community" to bring together persons who share similar interests, be it community service or behavioral science.

> **"It's the typical Southern university, with dress ranging from the preppy to straight off the farm kind of redneck."**

Though alcohol is strictly prohibited in all of the Freshmen Residence halls, students of age may store alcohol in the University-owned apartments. Smoking, however, is banned in all student housing.

Recent construction at Clemson includes a nearly 100-million-dollar wind turbine testing facility, located in the suburbs of Charleston, South Carolina (a four-hour trip by car from the campus), and a 31-million-dollar renovation to the university's Rudolph E. Lee Hall, which houses the design, architecture, and visual arts program. Emphasizing the university's commitment to the environment, the renovation will include a geothermal heating system and solar panels. Campus largely divides into two sections: central campus and west campus, a gap that can be bridged by a thirty-minute walk. West campus, where most apartment-style residential housing is located, hosts the football stadium, "downtown" Clemson, and most other sports training facilities.

Extracurricular activities are frequently cited by students as a main avenue to making friends at the "very friendly" campus of

Clemson. Whether it's a religious organization such as the Baptist Collegiate Ministry or the primary student publication, *The Tiger*, students use the organizations to build their own niches.

Tigers on the Prowl

Students claim that Greek life is dominant in the social life of the University, but students say that "there are plenty of non-Greek individuals on campus." Nonetheless, few parties take place at Clemson which are not directly related to a fraternity or sorority. However, the majority of the social activity on campus revolves around Thursday to Saturday night, say current students, when students frequent the fraternity houses and bars in the neighboring city of Clemson, in which the university is integrated. And, though, in the past, Clemson was a "suitcase college," most students now stay on campus during the weekends with many students still possessing a car.

Students report that hard drug use on campus is minimal, with only a prevalence of marijuana among some social groups, but that alcohol binge drinking is a problem on campus. And, although alcohol is strictly prohibited on campus—a policy according to students that the administration "does a good job of keeping things under control"—students say that "things can get a little crazy on home games though."

A common complaint of Clemson University centers on the school's relative lack of diversity. Located in the mountains of South Carolina, the University, the students claim, is "predominately white, upper-middle class and 'Protestant.'" Because the University lies along a lake and is only a short thirty-minute drive from the mountains, students say that "the outdoors is a pretty big deal to Clemson." As such, "it's the typical Southern university, with dress ranging from the preppy to straight off the farm kind of redneck," says one current student.

If you are looking for a school with a strong engineering and sciences program in a "small-town" environment with a decidedly southern charm, Clemson is the right school for you. Though the school may suffer from a lack of diversity, it does have a strong sorority and fraternity scene, offering a bevy of social and extracurricular activities.—*John Klement*

FYI
If I could change one thing about Clemson, "I'd change parking . . . They say that no one makes it through four years here without getting a citation."
What differentiates Clemson the most from other colleges "is the excellent location; we're 20 minutes from the lake, 30 minutes from the mountains, 2 hours from Atlanta, 2 hours from Charlotte, . . . 3 hours from the beach. This provides for an unlimited number of fun day trips. Anything you might want to do is totally possible."

F u r m a n　U n i v e r s i t y

Address: 3300 Poinsett Highway, Greenville, SC 29613
Phone: 864-294-2034
E-mail address: admissions@furman.edu
Web site URL: www.furman.edu
Year Founded: 1826
Private or Public: Private
Religious Affiliation: None
Location: Urban
Number of Applicants: 4,414
Percent Accepted: 57%
Percent Accepted who enroll: 30%
Number Entering: 754
Number of Transfers Accepted each Year: 45
Middle 50% SAT range: M: 590–690, CR:590–690, Wr: 580–680
Middle 50% ACT range: 26–30
Early admission program EA/ED/None: ED

Percentage accepted through EA or ED: 56%
EA and ED deadline: 15-Nov
Regular Deadline: 15-Jan
Application Fee: $50
Full time Undergraduate enrollment: 2,801
Total enrollment: 2,970
Percent Male: 43%
Percent Female: 57%
Total Percent Minority or Unreported: 20%
Percent African-American: 7%
Percent Asian/Pacific Islander: 3%
Percent Hispanic: 2%
Percent Native-American: <1%
Percent International: 2%
Percent in-state/out of state: 30%/70%
Percent from Public HS: 63%
Retention Rate: 92%
Graduation Rate 4-year: 80%

Graduation Rate 6-year: 84%
Percent Undergraduates in On-campus housing: 91%
Number of official organized extracurricular organizations: 143
3 Most popular majors: Communications, History, Political Science and Government
Student/Faculty ratio: 11:1
Average Class Size: 18
Percent of students going to grad school: 40%
Tuition and Fees: $34,568
In-State Tuition and Fees if different: No difference
Cost for Room and Board: $8,966
Percent receiving financial aid out of those who apply: 69%
Percent receiving financial aid among all students: 42%

Located on a lush and idyllic 750 acres, visitors and students alike praise Furman University for its friendly community and gorgeous setting. Often compared to a country club, stepping onto the green campus allows views of authentic Virginia-brick buildings centered around a 40-acre lake, which one student called the "literal and also metaphorical, in a sense, soul of campus," in addition to several regularly maintained gardens ready to be explored (at the rose garden, fresh roses are often laid out for students to take home). A tight-knit community, Southern culture, and rigorous academics make for a unique and special college experience.

Hitting the Books

The campus and students who inhabit it may appear idyllically peaceful and beautiful, but the academic schedule is far from relaxed. "It is fair to say that whatever high school you went to did not prepare you for this amount of work," noted one student. "Be prepared to read 30–40 pages for each class every night, and don't be shocked if you receive a C on your first paper." That said, most students called the academic rigor worth the while, and they cited the helpfulness of the faculty. "Most, if not all, of the professors are really genuinely nice people who want you to succeed," reported one sophomore. "That said, they really do expect a lot of you." Furman also offers free tutoring for two hours per week in any subject "and keeps James [the main library on campus] open late, thank God."

Furman also boasts consistently small class sizes, with an 11:1 student:faculty ratio and an average class size of 19. There are no TA's or GA's, meaning that all classes are taught by professors, and the vast majority are small enough to the point where the professors get to know their students personally. "It's not uncommon for a teacher to give you his or her personal phone number," said one senior, "and you'll definitely take at least one class that ventures to the professor's house for a meal or get-together." The small class sizes and involved faculty lead to great opportunities and connections for students, with one Asian Studies and Spanish double major noting the prevalence of study abroad—49% of students study abroad at some point during their experience—and the willingness of many professors to help arrange home stays or internships. Furman also offers the "May experience" each year, a term during which students choose to take a single course. These courses, which range from "Yoga in America" to "Readings in Political Thought" to "Investigative Reporting," are not offered during the normal academic term, and many take place in other parts of the United States or in foreign countries, offering students a totally unique academic opportunity.

> **"Most, if not all, of the professors are really genuinely nice people who want you to succeed. That said, they really do expect a lot of you."**

Another distinct facet of FU academics includes the Cultural Life Programs, or "CLPs." These events occur over 200 times every year, and include academic speakers, artistic performances, or religious services. Some examples include a showing of "Rocky Horror Picture Show," a talk entitled "God and the Big Bang," and a visiting sermon by Reverend Jesse Jackson about "Keeping Hope Alive." Students must attend 32 events in order to graduate.

Classes and academic experiences outside of the classroom permeate so much of campus life that "it's impossible not to care or learn a lot every single day."

After-hours
When they're not studying or attending CLPs, Furman students find other ways to enrich their cultural experiences. Furman remained an officially dry campus for many years, although it has now adjusted to allowing students over 21 to drink "responsibly" in the Vinings and North Village apartments. On-campus parties are relatively sparse, given the strictness of on-campus police officers and the "unduly harsh" consequences for underage students caught drinking; however, many students choose to frequent off-campus fraternity or sorority parties or venture to downtown Greenville, where bars geared towards college-aged students "consistently provide a good time." While some students expressed frustration at the necessity to conceal drinking and to venture off campus to find large parties, others said it created a safer and more positive environment. "There's absolutely no

pressure to drink because so much of it takes place off campus, but at the same time, the parties off campus do involve drinking and are normally really fun," said one non-drinker. "It means that everyone wins."

For those who do choose to partake in the traditional college party scene, the eight fraternities and seven sororities (which host rush at the start of each spring term) provide many events and mixers. 33% of males are in fraternities, and 44% of women are in sororities, so there is no pressure to join, and most of their events are open to non-members as well, though, so rushing is not necessary to ensure attendance. In addition, Greenville has many bars and restaurants geared towards college students. Some frequents include Barley's and The Bait Shack, and many weekend nights begin with students going out to dinner at favorites such as Atlanta Bread Company or Trio A Brick Oven.

Pearls, Bow Ties, and Hospitality
Furman takes pride in its Southern heritage. Most students hail from the Southeast, and "hey, y'all," "yes, ma'am," and "thank you, sir" can be heard throughout campus. Students are proud of their beautiful location and heritage, and laud the general warmth radiating from within their community. "Everyone says hey and smiles all the time, even to people you might not necessarily know very well," said one student. "There's no northern coldness in terms of personality. And everyone watches out for everyone and tries to help out when someone's feeling down." While everyone seems pleased with the gregariousness on campus, many lament the lack of diversity—only 18% of students identify as a racial minority—and the "Republican, conservative Christian mindset seems to be just everywhere." Furman looks like a country club, and many students partake in "country club" lifestyles, with preppy name brands like Lilly Pulitzer and Vineyard Vines promenading through campus, and many spending money on shopping, concerts, or dinners out in Greenville freely. While this is the Furman stereotype and defines a large cross-section of the student body, "it is by no means everyone," and individuals who do not fit the mold are more than capable of finding their own niches and communities.

Joining the Furman Family
The tight-knit community and Southern charm make for a student body brimming with school pride, including a Division 1

athletic program in the Southern Confer-ence. Freshmen, in particular, are introduced to the "Furman Fam" through many social traditions, such as "O Week," or the Orienta-tion at the beginning of their school year, which includes traditional orientation activi-ties intermingled with events like a full-fledged on-campus carnival. During this time, "fur-esh-man" are introduced to the other members of their single-sex hall and the cor-responding brother or sister hall, which often will become their social and familial core for at least the first semester (before rush occurs and other extracurricular activi-ties pick up). Freshmen live in one of six freshmen-only dorms in one of two clusters

(which also includes some upperclassmen dorms): Lakeside and South (or SoHo). Tradi-tionally, SoHo is geared more towards the party crowd and Lakeside more towards "nerds and music majors," but they each have strong communities and each individual dorm has its own distinctive features.

Pala-pride

Furman students are proud both of the physi-cal beauty of their campus and the more inef-fable beauty of academic experiences and positive relationships. Despite the some-times uptight administration and the homo-geneous student body, the Paladins love their lakeside home. —*Caroline Wray*

FYI

If I could change one thing about Furman, I'd "diversify the student body. We need a greater variety of opinions and backgrounds on campus."

Three things every student at Furman should do before graduating are "swim in a fountain, go to My Tie [the annual fall dance], and go to a concert in Greenville."

What surprised me the most about Furman when I arrived was "how tough the academics were, and how happy and fun everyone was in spite of this."

University of South Carolina

Address: Admissions Office, Columbia, SC 29208
Phone: 803-777-7000
E-mail address: admissions-ugrad@sc.edu
Web site URL: www.sc.edu
Year Founded: 1801
Private or Public: Public
Religious Affiliation: None
Location: Urban
Number of Applicants: 18,485
Percent Accepted: 70%
Percent Accepted who enroll: 34%
Number Entering: 4,468
Number of Transfers Accepted each Year: 2,392
Middle 50% SAT range: M: 560–650, CR: 530–630, Wr: Unreported
Middle 50% ACT range: 24–29
Early admission program EA/ED/None: EA

Percentage accepted through EA or ED: 58%
EA and ED deadline: 15-Oct
Regular Deadline: 1-Dec
Application Fee: $50
Full time Undergraduate enrollment: 21,383
Total enrollment: 29,597
Percent Male: 45%
Percent Female: 55%
Total Percent Minority or Unreported: 17%
Percent African-American: 7%
Percent Asian/Pacific Islander: 3%
Percent Hispanic: 3%
Percent Native-American: <1%
Percent International: 1%
Percent in-state/out of state: 64%/36%
Percent from Public HS: Unreported
Retention Rate: 87%
Graduation Rate 4-year: 67%

Graduation Rate 6-year: Unreported
Percent Undergraduates in On-campus housing: 36%
Number of official organized extracurricular organizations: 300
3 Most popular majors: Business/Marketing, Social Sciences, Communications/Journalism
Student/Faculty ratio: 19:1
Average Class Size: Less than 30
Percent of students going to grad school: Unreported
Tuition and Fees: $26,352
In-State Tuition and Fees if different: $10,168
Cost for Room and Board: $8,026
Percent receiving financial aid out of those who apply: 61%
Percent receiving financial aid among all students: 46%

I n spite of initial reservations, "within a week I was obsessed," one senior said of her initial experience at University of South Carolina. This passion seems to extend to most USC students, who sing their school's praises and show their collegiate pride at the drop of a hat or the blow of a whistle. Displays of devotion are especially evident at the popular, and often over the top, football games. But University of South Carolina offers so much more than just grand sporting events. The academic programs, extensive extracurricular choices and an exhausting party scene all contribute to forming a memorable experience that most students, when given the choice, would wish to live all over again.

University 101

Despite USC's large student body, there are few complaints about becoming just a number. The class sizes at the University vary widely from 20 to 300, with intro classes generally on the high end of the spectrum. However, large lectures come equipped with smaller discussion sections to ensure that each student gets personal attention. "I have never taken a class that had more than 50 students," one Honors College student said. Other students praised the numerous options for more intimate academic settings, often citing the professor for "making" the class. One senior raved that "[the professors] have been nothing but awesome," and students have generally described the professorship as being friendly, easily accessible, and diligent to learn the names of all of their students. Among the faculty sit several famous names such as Don Fowler, the former chairman of the Democratic National Committee.

With 14 schools to choose from, the University offers something for everyone. The major unanimously proclaimed as the most sought-after and difficult is the number one, nationally-ranked International Business program. The major accepts only 50 people each year and attracts students from all over the country, as well as many from overseas. South Carolina also offers unique majors such as Sports and Entertainment Management and Hotel and Restaurant Tourism Management. And for the top qualified students of each year, the University features an Honors Program and Capstone Scholars. For freshmen, an atypical class that is offered and sometimes required is University 101, a class that focuses solely on helping students adjust and make the best of university life. Aside from the required English, social science, and history courses (all of which students can place out of), there is a unique assortment of ways students can expand their knowledge, whether by learning how to shag—the dance, that is—or by taking a wine-tasting class or studying Super Bowl commercials (it's actually a class). Overall, the workload itself is deemed manageable. Some students complain about the large amounts of reading they receive, but as one sophomore explained, "People are not missing out on social life."

Where the Beer Is Green and the Beach Is Near

South Carolina offers many great ways to have a good time. Although many students contend that no particular social scene dominates, the Greek parties are the most common ones listed. For the 21-plus crowd (or those with really good IDs), there are the Five Points downtown bars. People usually start going out on Thursday night, especially with Thursday being "college night" in the downtown area.

Even though only about 16 percent of students belong to a sorority or a fraternity, students generally agree that Greek life is "really noticeable." During the first week of school, one of the most prominent things on campus is the excess of flyers inviting people to rush. And students estimate that a majority of the population does rush, especially girls. "During my freshman year, half the kids on my floor rushed," one senior remembered. The Greeks, in addition to hosting regular weekend parties, also organize many exclusive theme parties and are the driving force behind Homecoming week festivities.

Nevertheless, as a senior pointed out, "You can have fun even if you're not Greek." Big annual celebrations include St. Patrick's Day at Five Points, when everything is blocked off from the city and the beer is green. Halloween weekend is "always fun." Many alternative entertainment options are provided by the student-run Carolina Productions. The group organizes main events on campus such as concerts, the Wacky Wednesday Booth that plans something new and fun for each Wednesday at the Student Center, and has even been responsible for bringing Bob Saget to campus. For a more low-key night, there are the dorm parties, which are especially popular for underclassmen. But be forewarned. Despite the abundance of partying on campus, the drinking rules are strict—SLED or undercover officers patrol the area and are quick to enforce the rules. All freshman dorms are labeled dry and all rooms in the upperclassmen dorms in which persons under 21 reside are dry, as well. However, as one freshman observed, "You can drink in the dorm—if you can get away with it." The ability to "get away with it" mainly depends on your RA and on how belligerent you become. One junior pointed out that, although "we are not a dry campus," people are understanding of those who do not drink. As an alternative to partying, many students take weekend trips to the plentiful beaches of Charleston.

Our Stereotypes are Diverse

Many come to South Carolina with the expectation of a crowd of typical Southern girls and frat-guy types. But more often than not, students are pleasantly surprised by the diversity on campus. Although one junior described the day-to-day look as having "a beachy atmosphere—there are shorts and sandals everywhere," there is a greater stylistic range. But it doesn't mean there aren't stereotypes. As one sophomore put it, "You can definitely pick out the Greeks by their clothes, and you can definitely pick out 'emos' by their clothes." Nevertheless, there is a fair amount of geographic and ethnic diversity. Students hail from all 50 states and there is a well-represented international community at South Carolina. Some students acknowledge, however, that the campus often has segregation lines among groups—whites and blacks have their own separate frats and parties. "Walking around campus you [would] think it is segregated," said one student. Students, however, assure that there is no tension on campus, and that the relations among races are by no means "uncivil." Students are making strides to create a more unified collegiate atmosphere, which even in its current state is still generally described as very friendly.

Horseshoes and Pizza Huts

Due to numerous dorm renovation projects, one senior explained that "housing right now is in limbo." Still, all freshmen are required to live on campus, spread out between the freshman-only dorms, many of which are single-sex with strict visitation rules for prospective guests of the opposite sex. All freshman dorms feature suite-style rooms (two double bedrooms, a common room and a bathroom). Due to dorm renovations, the upperclassmen are not guaranteed housing. However, this lack of guarantee is not a major problem; many, if not most, upperclassmen

prefer off-campus housing—especially at the nearby university-exclusive apartment complexes. For those who choose to stay on campus, there are several coed options, including Roost, which mainly houses athletes, and the "Green Dorm," a completely environmentally friendly habitat. The University also offers several themed communities such as the French community, the Spanish community (where they speak only the language of affiliation), the International community, and the Music community. Currently, the University is building a multimillion-dollar Research community. The Greeks, especially in their sophomore year, often opt to reside in the multimillion-dollar houses that populate the Greek Village. All students are able to bring cars, and it seems like all do. Parking, or lack thereof, is the most common complaint heard from the students. "To get to class on time, you have to get there 30 minutes before to find a spot to park," one student warned.

> "Everyone here is obsessed with football, even those who are not athletic."

USC students vote the campus food as "most likely to make you gain the Freshman 15." There are five dining halls, including the Russell House, which serves both as the student union and the grand marketplace or main dining hall. Dining options include everything from a salad bar to an overabundance of fast food chains like Burger King, Chick-fil-A, Taco Bell, and Pizza Hut, where students can use their meal plans. Luckily, Columbia houses many privately owned restaurants that, all in all, "give the city more character."

The campus itself is pretty, with a smattering of modern industrial buildings, many newly renovated buildings, and—of course—the Horseshoe with "an old, traditional, Southern feel to it." The Horseshoe—you guessed it—is shaped like a horseshoe and serves as the main, grassy hangout area for students looking to picnic or play Frisbee. Most importantly, the campus is regarded as safe. "Considering the size of this university, they have done a good job of protecting us," one student praised. Call boxes which are located throughout campus (you can't turn around without seeing at least one) serve as emergency call services. A shuttle service also operates on campus.

The Loyal Gamecocks

Many students at South Carolina "rely on organizations to find [their] niche," a senior observed. Some of the more prominent groups include Student Government, the Triple A's (Association of African-Americans), and Carolina Productions. For the politically aspirant, there are the College Republicans and Young Dems; for the journalistically inclined, there is *The Daily Gamecock;* and for the socially focused, there are 15 sororities and 22 frats from which to choose.

If all else fails, the uniting theme of the University seems to be sports. Club and intramural sports serve as competitive, but very fun, alternatives to varsity. But perhaps the most popular way to be involved in the athletic life is actually just attending the varsity games. South Carolina's talented teams are fun to watch and support. The baseball and basketball games are both very well attended, but football remains king. People fight for tickets, which sell out almost immediately. "Everyone here is obsessed with football, even those who are not athletic," one sophomore declared. The annual game against archrival Clemson is among the most exciting and is preceded by the Tiger Burn—a pep rally and ceremonial burning of a papier-mâché Clemson Tiger. The proud Gamecocks attend the games dressed in their best—pearls, cocktail dresses, blazers, and bow ties. The tailgates begin at noon and last for about five or more hours until the game begins. The Gamecocks are known for their loyalty; they cheer loudly until the last minute, win or lose.

It is easy to get swept up in the enthusiasm of the football crowd of the always-filled-to-the-brim Williams-Brice Stadium. Such an exhilarating feeling is a good reflection of the mentality of South Carolina University's students. Any initial reservations incoming students might have are quickly replaced by feelings of school pride and affection. Because whether it be the campus, the vast array of extracurriculars or the friendly people, it is good to be a Gamecock.—*Dorota Poplawska*

FYI

If you come to South Carolina, you'd better bring "Rainbows (sandals that everyone wears) and dressy clothes for those football games."

What is the typical weekend schedule? "Thursday attend college night at Five Points and party on Friday. Saturdays are dominated by tailgates and football games that take up all day. Catch up on work Sunday after sleeping in or going to church."

If I could change one thing about South Carolina, I'd "add more parking spaces."

Three things every student at South Carolina should do before graduating are "go to Five Points, stay till the end of a football game, and get to know a professor on a more personal basis."

Wofford College

Address: 429 North Church Street, Spartanburg, SC 29303-3663
Phone: 864-597-4130
E-mail address: admission@wofford.edu
Web site URL: www.wofford.edu
Year Founded: 1854
Private or Public: Private
Religious Affiliation: United Methodist
Location: Urban
Number of Applicants: 2,442
Percent Accepted: 62%
Percent Accepted who enroll: 28%
Number Entering: 431
Number of Transfers Accepted each Year: 34
Middle 50% SAT range: M: 590–680, CR: 560–680, Wr: 550–650
Middle 50% ACT range: 22–28
Early admission program EA/ED/None: ED

Percentage accepted through EA or ED: 70%
EA and ED deadline: 15-Nov
Regular Deadline: 1-Feb
Application Fee: $35
Full time Undergraduate enrollment: 1,506
Total enrollment: unreported
Percent Male: 53%
Percent Female: 47%
Total Percent Minority or Unreported: 17%
Percent African-American: 6%
Percent Asian/Pacific Islander: 3%
Percent Hispanic: 3%
Percent Native-American: 0%
Percent International: 1%
Percent in-state/out of state: 59 %/41%
Percent from Public HS: 65%
Retention Rate: 87%
Graduation Rate 4-year: 77%

Graduation Rate 6-year: 82%
Percent Undergraduates in On-campus housing: 94%
Number of official organized extracurricular organizations: 111
3 Most popular majors: Biology, Business/Marketing, Foreign Languages
Student/Faculty ratio: 11:1
Average Class Size: 18
Percent of students going to grad school: 39%
Tuition and Fees: $34,270
In-State Tuition and Fees if different: No difference
Cost for Room and Board: $9,375
Percent receiving financial aid out of those who apply: 79%
Percent receiving financial aid among all students: 63%

Wofford College offers a tight-knit community and strong teacher-student relationships for a student body that is smaller than that of many high schools. With approximately 1,600 students, Wofford reserves its solid liberal arts education for a select group of students. Its location in the traditional South impacts student culture; students say that Greek life "dominates" on campus, with over half of students taking part. Wofford also stands out for its Division I Athletics. With such a small student body, "one in six guys plays football." Yet pearls, sports, and prep don't diminish the fact that Wofford is widely respected for its premedicine program and "many students go into politics" after graduation. The college boasts state-of-the-art, apartment-style housing for upperclassmen, complete with private bedrooms, full-size kitchens, and large balconies. Students also praise the school's unique January interim, a one-month period in which students bond over esoteric classes, creative projects, and travel abroad.

Is There a Doctor in the Classroom?

Opened in 1854 and still affiliated with the Methodist Church, Wofford has remained small by choice. The administration reportedly has no plans to expand enrollment, but instead plans to concentrate on providing a select group of students with a strong education in the humanities, arts, and sciences. Students said that "the small class sizes are really nice." One student warned, however, that due to Wofford's size, "there is not a wide variety of classes." Professors are especially accessible and maintain an "open door policy," according to students. "I didn't expect the professors to be so understanding, but they are like high school teachers in that sense. They want to help you out." Students said that teachers learn every student's name almost immediately, are very approachable through emails and office hours, and generally take attendance before each class. Wofford remains committed to providing students with a true "liberal arts" education, requiring undergrads to take courses in humanities, science, fine arts, foreign language, philosophy, culture, math, religion, and physical education. These requirements ensure that, by the end of their first two years, students acquire a breadth of knowledge and take some classes they normally would not have considered. Students are also required to complete four interim projects. The month of January is designated as Interim, a time between the two regular semesters when students can research, travel, take an internship, or work on an independent project. Because many students study abroad during one or more interim, Wofford has received national recognition for the percentage of students who spend term time in other countries. Students can travel with professors to retrace World War II battles through Budapest and Normandy beach, study ecotourism in Belize, and much more. Interim projects on campus can include courses such as "Class, Gender, and Race in Disney's Magic Kingdom" or "Golf for Beginners and in American Culture." Internship projects and service learning can even take you to Capitol Hill for a month. The Interim permits and encourages teachers and students to explore the new and untried. "Everyone gets really excited," a student said. "It's much more relaxed than school, and you get time to hang out with your friends more." An added boon, most interim projects are graded Pass/Fail.

Among the popular majors at Wofford are biology, business economics, foreign languages, political science, history, and English. "Business Economics is seen as a fairly easy program," one student said, "and sociology is picked on for having the easiest major." But "in general everyone respects each other because every major requires a lot of time and effort." The science department is reported to be particularly strong. One student said that, as a physics major, "people tend to hold me in somewhat (unwarranted) high regard because there are so few of us. I have a class this semester where I am the only student in the class." But there is no doubt that the sciences and particularly the biology major are "top-notch" at Wofford and many students go on to medical school.

A Smart Investment
Successful alumnae and high post-graduation satisfaction rates secured Wofford a spot within Forbes' 2013 top 50 "Return on Investment List" (www.forbes.com). Some students attribute these high levels of approval to College efforts to provide students with high-quality facilities and services. Wofford's program called FYI (First Year Interface) allows freshmen to meet and greet via social media. After sharing profiles, photos, bedtimes, and partying habits on the site, Wofford lets students who hit it off become roommates. Students may also contact members of the Student Life staff with questions about what to expect when preparing to come to Wofford. But the College does not only use technology to help its students acclimate to campus: in 2002, Wofford began the Novel Experience—a program that asks incoming students to read an assigned novel over the summer and to write essays prior to arrival in Spartanburg. In early September, a town-gown exercise takes place when student groups and professors are assigned to eat at local restaurants through a lottery, discussing the novel over dinner. About a week later, the author comes to campus for a special address. "It was nice to get dressed up and go out to dinner with your class," one student said. "I think it enhances your intellectual conversations outside of the classroom." Rising freshmen also have the option to attend a program called the Summit. This program takes place before the start of school, and new students spend one day at a summer camp and go whitewater rafting. "It's where you first meet most of the people you come to hang out with."

Dorm Life: A Necessary Experience
An online lottery system sorts all dorm assignments and seniority is recognized. The two freshman dorms each accommodate both men and women, although on separate halls or even floors. Marsh Hall—one freshman dorm—is known as "particularly miserable, crazy, and disgusting all at the same time. But all in all, a necessary experience." A student who lives in Greene Hall, the other freshman dorm, said that "It's not the best but it's not terrible. I'm perfectly happy." All students living in dorms have the convenient advantage of a five- or 10-minute walk to classroom buildings. "If I wake up late at 9:20 I can still get to a 9:30 class." On the way, students enjoy the shade of many oak trees or stop to lounge on the benches near the central campus field. Students "literally cannot wait" to receive coveted spots in College-owned apartments called "The

Village" as upperclassmen. Freshly renovated houses purchased by the College, these dwellings feature cable television, high speed Internet, and spacious living/dining/kitchen areas. They are also the site of late-night partying after fraternity parties come to a close. Campus is "much safer" than the surrounding areas in Spartanburg. According to students, "it's kind of a rough town in places" and "people tend to stay within the 'Wofford bubble.'"

Frat Row, Football, and More

"Greek life at Wofford is huge" and more than 50 percent of the student body is Greek. The fraternity row (location on campus for fraternity houses and called "the row" by students) is the dominant social scene on campus. It's a popular site for a shaving cream fight and "you can't miss out on slip-and-slide at the row." "Greek life defines your social life on the weekends, although it isn't too demanding otherwise, and all of the parties are open to everyone." One of the most talked-about days of the year is Fountain Fest when freshman boys find out which fraternity they're pledging. A popular celebration follows: students spray each other with paint on the lawn and then jump into a giant fountain afterwards. "Greek life is not hard to get involved in," one student said, "just about anyone who wants to get involved can." Many students attend home football games on Saturdays during the fall and tailgates before the games. "The games aren't huge," a student said. "They're very relaxed but fun, especially when we win." The College-sponsored Spring Weekend offers festivities for the entire campus, and is a time when "you should party extremely hard." In addition to the popular varsity athletic teams, like men's and women's basketball, "we have an ultimate Frisbee team and a fly fishing organization—which is funded by the school for their equipment and trips." One student called it "a sweet gig."

> "There's always a comfortable setting. You just raise your hand if you have a question and the teacher will answer you."

"Spartanburg is a quality college town," and students do often take advantage of its restaurants, movie theater, numerous shops, and bars "We'll go into Spartanburg to eat

sometimes, but we're on campus the majority of the time," one student said. Students readily participate in community service at Wofford through a variety of outlets. Greek organizations sponsor philanthropy projects throughout the year, and several classes require students to engage with Spartanburg through service learning. Wofford is located in "an underprivileged area, so we interact with the community in a variety of ways," a student said. Wofford reportedly hosts two events during the school year for children in the area to attend. "There is a definite emphasis on helping out Spartanburg," one student said. Prominent student groups on campus include Campus Ambassadors, students who volunteer their time to give tours to prospective students, the Fellowship of Christian Athletes (FCA), the Campus Union (student council), and Reformed University Fellowship (a Christian ministry group). The Outdoors Club is another option for bikers, hikers, and climbers. "Most students are passionate about the clubs they are involved in" and "each group has their fanatics."

Southern Culture with a "Place for Everyone"

Although "Wofford is typically viewed as a white, conservative school," students say all types of students can find a place on campus. Although students are often characterized as "particularly preppy and from 'old money' families or parents with white-collar careers," a growing percent of the population does not fit this mold. "In terms of dress, there's really everything," one student said. "It's preppy when people actually get dressed up, but it's not overwhelming." Only about 10 percent of the school is made up of minority students. Despite a lack of ethnic diversity, students said that there is definitely geographic diversity. "There seems like there are as many out-of-state students as there are in-state." In addition, religious diversity is becoming more prevalent at Wofford. "Most students are Christian but not in an overbearing way, and there are definitely other religions." Students also said that the political climate on campus is definitely conservative, but students are not extremely outspoken about it. Most students praise the effects of the school's southern culture. "Part of being in the south is that everyone is so nice," one student said. "Everyone is looking out for their reputation as well, especially because it's a small school, and word gets around fast. No one is really sleeping around or doing the stuff you hear about at other colleges." The "frat look" is very popular with "Sperrys, khakis, and sunglasses with Croakies making a dominant appearance all over campus" and "pastel colors are worn by both guys and girls." Students said that you can always expect a smile and a "hello" when passing others on campus. "It's a really tight-knit community," a student said. "I haven't met a single person that I don't like. It's extreme to say, but it's true." The same mentality translates to the classroom where "there's always a comfortable setting. You just raise your hand if you have a question and the teacher will answer you."

"Student are Proud to Be at Wofford"

Any school that takes as much pride in its history as Wofford does is bound to have unique traditions. Old Main was the foundational building of the University and features a misspelled plaque that reads "benificent" rather than "beneficent." For Wofford students, rubbing the mislaid "i" brings them luck on exams. If you're a student who desires personal attention at a small liberal arts college and hopes for the benefits of an incredible network of alumni—"who are always there to offer jobs to the next graduates"—Wofford's luck is just waiting to rub off on you.—*Hailey Winston*

FYI

If you come to Wofford, you'd better bring "sunglasses with Croakies, polo shirts, pearls, and a flask."

What's the typical weekend schedule? "A sports game or workout during the day. Next, dinner or a movie with friends and then to fraternity row all night."

Three things every student at Wofford should do before graduating are "swim in the fountain after jumping in the mud on Guys' Bid Day, ring the bell in the Old Main building, and date someone."

South Dakota

University of South Dakota

Address: 414 East Clark Street, Vermillion, SD 57069
Phone: 605-677-5434
E-mail address: admissions@usd.edu
Web site URL: www.usd.edu
Year Founded: 1862
Private or Public: Public
Religious Affiliation: None
Location: Rural
Number of Applicants: 3,499
Percent Accepted: 89%
Percent Accepted who enroll: 37%
Number Entering: 1,248
Number of Transfers Accepted each Year: 1,427
Middle 50% SAT range: M: 460–580, CR: 460–550, Wr: Unreported
Middle 50% ACT range: 20–26
Early admission program EA/ED/None: None

Percentage accepted through EA or ED: NA
EA and ED deadline: NA
Regular Deadline: Rolling
Application Fee: $20
Full time Undergraduate enrollment: 7,473
Total enrollment: 9,970
Percent Male: 39%
Percent Female: 61%
Total Percent Minority or Unreported: 14%
Percent African-American: 2%
Percent Asian/Pacific Islander: 1%
Percent Hispanic: 1%
Percent Native-American: 3%
Percent International: 1%
Percent in-state/out of state: 64%/36%
Percent from Public HS: 94%
Retention Rate: 72%
Graduation Rate 4-year: 20%

Graduation Rate 6-year: 44%
Percent Undergraduates in On-campus housing: 32%
Number of official organized extracurricular organizations: 130
3 Most popular majors: Business/Marketing, Psychology, Health Professions
Student/Faculty ratio: 18:1
Average Class Size: 24
Percent of students going to grad school: Unreported
Tuition and Fees: $8,924
In-State Tuition and Fees if different: $7,209
Cost for Room and Board: $6,543
Percent receiving financial aid out of those who apply: 65%
Percent receiving financial aid among all students: 58%

The University of South Dakota (USD) is the only comprehensive institution of higher learning that offers law, medical, business, and fine arts schools in the state of South Dakota. The state's oldest university, USD is home to over 6,000 undergraduates and 1,800 graduate and professional students. The school offers everything from associate degrees to doctorates. The location of the university in Vermillion, South Dakota, may leave something to be desired, but it remains a very attractive college choice given the number of academic options, especially for in-state students looking for a good education at a relatively affordable price.

College Standardized Tests

USD is divided into seven different schools: the College of Arts and Sciences, Beacom School of Business, School of Education, College of Fine Arts, School of Health Sciences, School of Law, and Sanford School of Medicine. Most undergraduates are in the College of Arts and Sciences, where the majority of majors are found. However, for those who are looking for more specialized programs of study, the other schools certainly offer plenty of options. Moreover, the presence of graduate programs allows the more ambitious undergraduates to take a number of graduate classes, which can be highly rewarding for in-depth study of different topics. "We have a lot of options," said one student. "That is a plus in coming to USD."

The university offers 132 majors and minors, ranging from the traditional tracks in Finance, Business, and Biology to the more specialized ones, such as Alcohol and Drug

Studies. The most popular majors are those in business, education, and health care, and many students partake in the preprofessional preparations. After all, a large percentage of students at USD are looking to follow particular professional tracks and make use of their college education for preparing for graduate studies. The preprofessional programs include not only the traditional pre-medicine and prelaw curricula, but also less frequently seen programs, such as pre-occupational therapy and pre-chiropractic. "A lot of people are pre-something," said one student. "And we have a lot of really good programs specifically for those students."

> **"Most of the professors that I met have been really nice and actually happy to talk to students."**

Although USD is the flagship state university, it is rather small in scale with fewer than 10,000 students. As a result, it creates an intimate academic atmosphere. For the most part, the faculty welcomes interactions with students. The introductory classes are often conducted in large lecture halls, but students have access to a number of small classes where professors and students debate, discuss, and come to conclusions together on a variety of topics. "I have no problem talking to professors," said one student. "Most of the professors that I met have been really nice and actually happy to talk to students." As freshmen tend to have difficulties finding small classes, a program called First Year Experience provides a select number of students with small seminars as well as preferential treatment in enrolling in a number of popular courses. At the same time, the Honors Program is another way to receive more personalized attention in smaller classes and more in-depth investigation of topics.

One feature of USD is the requirement that students take standardized tests during their college years. All undergraduates must take the Collegiate Assessment of Academic Proficiency and achieve a satisfactory grade on the exam. From the outset, it may seem like a nerve-racking experience, especially since the test is divided into writing, reading, mathematics, and sciences and must be completed for a student to graduate. However, it is certainly nothing too worrisome for students. It makes sure that students have a minimal grasp of basic skills needed in a college graduate, and most people have

no difficulty passing the exam. Even for those who fail the standardized test, they can retake it within a year in order to remain at the university. "It is not a big deal," said one student. "I don't even know why they have it." In addition, prior to the exams, the students would already have completed a number of required courses in mathematics, sciences, composition, and humanities. Therefore, most people are well prepared to be successful at these tests.

Students generally have favorable opinions of the coursework at USD. Students are not overworked. People have time to enjoy a good social life, even during some weekdays. "I think if you manage your courses right, you will definitely have time to do a lot of other things than schoolwork," said one student.

College Town

Vermillion, where USD is located, is a rural, corn-growing city of approximately 10,000 residents. Given the university population of around 10,000 students, it is easy to imagine the importance of the university and the lack of anything particularly exciting within the city limits. Furthermore, Vermillion is also removed from any other metropolitan areas. "It's pretty boring here," said one student. "You can't find anything to do here. We do have a few restaurants and bars around campus, but that's it." The only well-known feature of the city to outsiders is the National Music Museum, which contains some world renowned collections of musical instruments. "The good part of Vermillion is that it is quiet," said one student.

Students in the first two years must live on campus in one of the residential halls. The rooms are small and not particularly attractive to students, and most of them move off campus after their first two years to the surrounding areas. "The off-campus housing is bigger and easy to find," said one student. Nevertheless, some students think that living in dorms helps them greatly in acclimating to the social and academic environment. "I got to meet a lot of people," said one student. "And when you live in dorms, you don't have to worry about taking care of your housing and food." The dining services offer meal plans for those who eat almost every meal on campus and those who simply eat lunches during weekdays at one of the campus dining locations, and the facilities are located conveniently for students.

The university has a very strict alcohol policy, which is another reason students forgo on-campus living. Most of the weekend festivities occur in off-campus apartments and houses, as well as fraternities and sororities. Finding a hangout or party place during the weekends is certainly difficult, but students should expect to find it within the USD community. "There is not much beside USD at Vermillion," said one student. 'The whole place is pretty boring. Some people go to Sioux Falls for the weekends to find more things to do."

The National Champions

USD's varsity teams have recently been reclassified into NCAA Division I, thus offering top-level athletics for students. A unique aspect of the football team is that the games are played in a dome instead of an open-air stadium, a testament to the cold weather of South Dakota. For football games, the dorms can be very loud and intimidating for opposing teams. More than 120 extracurricular organizations are also available, thus offering even more socializing opportunities.

USD certainly has its drawbacks: small town, cold weather, and strict alcohol policies. The diversity of the student body is certainly another area for potential improvement for the school, as the number of minority students remains small, despite the university's efforts to increase diversity. However, USD also offers a great variety of academic programs and presents students with a balanced social and academic life.—*Xiaohang Liu*

FYI
If you come to USD, you'd better bring "a car."
What is the typical weekend schedule? "Parties start on Thursday and end on Saturday. Sometimes you can even get by not doing too much study on Sunday."
If I could change one thing about USD, I'd "let people hold parties in dorms."
Three things every student at USD should do before graduating are "join a frat, go to the dome for a game, and visit Sioux Falls."

Tennessee

Rhodes College

Address: 2000 North Parkway, Memphis, TN 38112
Phone: 901-843-3700
E-mail address: adminfo@rhodes.edu
Web site URL: www.rhodes.edu
Year Founded: 1848
Private or Public: Private
Religious Affiliation: Presbyterian
Location: Urban
Number of Applicants: 5,598
Percent Accepted: 45%
Percent Accepted who enroll: 20%
Number Entering: 502
Number of Transfers Accepted each Year: 20
Middle 50% SAT range: M: 590–690, CR:590–700, Wr: 580–680
Middle 50% ACT range: 26–30
Early admission program EA/ED/None: ED and EA

Percentage accepted through EA or ED: Unreported
EA and ED deadline: 1-Nov (ED), 15-Nov (EA)
Regular Deadline: 15-Jan
Application Fee: $45 (waived for online application)
Full time Undergraduate enrollment: 1,695
Total enrollment: 1,712
Percent Male: 42%
Percent Female: 58%
Total Percent Minority or Unreported: 26%
Percent African-American: 7%
Percent Asian/Pacific Islander: 5%
Percent Hispanic: 3%
Percent Native-American: 1%
Percent International: 4%
Percent in-state/out of state: 27%/73%
Percent from Public HS: 50%

Retention Rate: 88%
Graduation Rate 4-year: 75%
Graduation Rate 6-year: 82%
Percent Undergraduates in On-campus housing: 73%
Number of official organized extracurricular organizations: 82
3 Most popular majors: Biology, Business, English
Student/Faculty ratio: 10:1
Average Class Size: 15
Percent of students going to grad school: 33%
Tuition and Fees: $36,154
In-State Tuition and Fees if different: No difference
Cost for Room and Board: $8,976
Percent receiving financial aid out of those who apply: 96%
Percent receiving financial aid among all students: 92%

Nestled in the heart of Memphis, Rhodes College mixes the calm of a small liberal arts college with the hustle of an urban center, enclosed in an oasis of Gothic architecture. For students at Rhodes, having fun is just as important as working hard. Students gain intense academic experiences in a close-knit community, while also enjoying a vibrant social scene.

Professor by Day, Drinking Buddy by Night

Rhodes holds firmly to the values of a liberal arts school, emphasizing the study of diverse disciplines through a set of core requirements, and is centered around small, discussion-based classes. Students at Rhodes begin their education by fulfilling "foundation requirements," which, as one student described, "represent what the administration deems to be the pillars of the liberal arts ideal." These include the expected writing and history classes as well as a more unique program that divides students into one of two tracks, both of which comprise three classes. "Search" surveys Western thought and philosophy, guiding students through a rigorous examination of the Great Books curriculum, while "Life" focuses on a literary study of religious scripture such as the Torah and the Bible. While devoting so many classes to requirements may seem limiting, the majority of students interviewed felt like the program was a good use of time. One sophomore who had completed the Search track said, "I really enjoyed the comprehensive nature of the foundation requirements. They helped integrate my classes, and it was interesting when something I had learned in history came up the next week in my English class."

The low student-faculty ratio at Rhodes has an immense impact on campus culture. Nearly all classes have fewer than 20 students, and faculty members are known for being readily accessible and willing to help students. One student even claimed that she had the cell phone number of each of her teachers in the event of a last-minute question. Not only had every student interviewed met with professors and attended office hours, but many had even interacted with their teachers outside of the academic setting. A senior described his personal experiences with Rhodes faculty. "I've been to professors' homes for dinner, I've played trivia games with professors, and I've even gone to bars with them." This unusually close relationship between students and faculty reinforces the liberal arts mind-set shaping the Rhodes experience.

The Soup Kitchen May Be More Crowded than the Stadium

Rhodes, although a small college with a narrower range of activities than some schools, encourages passion for the extracurricular activities it does sponsor. The school is well known for its mock trial team, frequently appearing in the national tournament and holding the second most national titles.

> "I've been to professors' homes for dinner, I've played trivia games with professors, and I've even gone to bars with them."

Also prominent are the school's abundant service organizations. Students at Rhodes respond enthusiastically to service challenges. One freshman said, "I've made a lot of my closest friends through working at a soup kitchen once a week. It's really the only time I ever go into Memphis, so it can be an exciting escape from the hustle of campus." The emphasis on service complements the campus' intense Greek life, with fraternities and sororities organizing many service projects.

While "Rhodents" tend to be very committed to their extracurricular activities, Rhodes culture does not embrace the tradition of spectator sports. A senior said, "I've never been to a football game here. Even if I go to tailgate, no one ever seems to go to the actual game." The small student body makes it extremely easy to play a sport at Rhodes,

leading to an unusually large number of student athletes, according to one student, which may contribute to the lack of a football culture. "So many people are involved that it's hard to find time to watch other sports." Students don't seem to regret the lack of enthusiasm for football, though, and are content with the highly successful intramural program.

Go Greek or Go Home

Greek life is a major part of the social scene at Rhodes. About 50 percent of the students on campus are part of a sorority or a fraternity, and many of the major parties have some affiliation with a house. According to one senior, the rush process for girls is much more intimidating and organized than for boys. However, "a huge number of girls rush every year," she said. For those students not wishing to pursue Greek life, or who wish to be involved socially outside of their fraternities or sororities, there are other options for social interaction. One junior said, "My friends consist of people that I am in similar organizations with, people that share my major, and close friends from freshman year." Because of the small size of the college, however, several students noted that Rhodents tend to form cliques with their close groups of friends.

Even if you don't choose to go Greek, many social activities do involve alcohol. One senior categorized Rhodes' social scene as "get drunk, go crazy." While students said that alcohol use is prevalent on Rhodes' campus, another senior noted that "it's not a big deal if you don't drink at all; people respect that." While a wide range of opinions of alcohol use on campus exists within the student body, the College states that it supports and expects behavior of its students that is "legal, responsible, healthy, and reflective of our community values." An important part of Rhodes' Social and Alcohol Policy is its Good Samaritan Statement, which precludes a student from getting penalized for calling help for an intoxicated person.

Because of Rhodes' location in midtown Memphis, however, students have plenty of off-campus options for entertainment. Many choose to go downtown to Beale Street where they can enjoy live jazz in clubs and bars such as B.B. King's or Silky O'Sullivan's. Most students have cars, as public transportation is not easily available or easy to use.

The Land of the Lynx

When students arrive at Rhodes for their freshman year, they are randomly sorted into a dorm, and unless they specifically request someone, randomly assigned a roommate. For freshman and sophomore years, students are required to live on campus, but can choose to move off campus for junior and senior years. Some of the dorms are themed—there is a biological sciences dorm, as well as a British Studies dorm—but the quality of the Gothic-style dorms is relatively uniform. According to several upperclassmen, housing gets markedly better with seniority. According to one student, "Our dorm life in general is pretty nice . . . juniors and seniors have the option of living in on-campus apartments that are quite coveted." While some students choose to move off campus, about three-fourths of Rhodents remain on campus all four years.

The food at Rhodes is not, according to many students, one of the highlights of the Rhodes experience. One student complained that "there aren't very many options and what's available often isn't very healthy."

When on-campus options are not appealing, students often go into the city of Memphis to find good food options. "Memphis as a city has so much to offer, that it seems odd to eat on campus much," said one student. However, a meal plan is required for all students living on campus.

Between meals and living spaces, there are plenty of places around campus for students to hang out. The Lynx Lair, a student-center type location, has not only food options but also air hockey and Ping-Pong tables. Another busy student hub is the Middle Ground, a coffee shop by the library. The bustling activity in these social hubs reflects on Rhodes' atmosphere as an excellent choice for those who want an active social life. A balanced combination of academic rigor through intense discussion classes and social vitality through Greek organizations, Rhodes is a "work hard, play hard" school that fulfills any prospective student's liberal arts dream.—*Natasha Thondavadi and Anjali Balakrishna*

FYI

If you come to Rhodes College, you'd better bring "your tie and blazer. Be ready to dress up."
What's the typical weekend schedule at Rhodes? "Party Friday. Party Saturday. Work all Sunday."
Three things every student at Rhodes College should do before graduating are "ride the lynx statue, go to Beale Street, and take a picture in the fountain."

University of Tennessee / Knoxville

Address: 320 Student Service Building, Circle Park Drive, Knoxville, TN 37996-0230
Phone: 865-974-1000
E-mail address: admissions@utk.edu
Web site URL: www.tennessee.edu
Year Founded: 1794
Private or Public: Public
Religious Affiliation: None
Location: Urban
Number of Applicants: 12,824
Percent Accepted: 74%
Percent Accepted who enroll: 47%
Number Entering: 4,214
Number of Transfers Accepted each Year: 1,954
Middle 50% SAT range: M: 530–640, CR: 530–640, Wr: Unreported
Middle 50% ACT range: 24–29
Early admission program EA/ED/None: None

Percentage accepted through EA or ED: NA
EA and ED deadline: NA
Regular Deadline: 1-Dec
Application Fee: $30
Full time Undergraduate enrollment: 21,393
Total enrollment: 30,312
Percent Male: 51%
Percent Female: 49%
Total Percent Minority or Unreported: 19%
Percent African-American: 8%
Percent Asian/Pacific Islander: 3%
Percent Hispanic: 3%
Percent Native-American: <1%
Percent International: 1%
Percent in-state/out of state: 88%/12%
Percent from Public HS: Unreported
Retention Rate: 84%
Graduation Rate 4-year: 29%

Graduation Rate 6-year: Unreported
Percent Undergraduates in On-campus housing: 35%
Number of official organized extracurricular organizations: 450
3 Most popular majors: Business/Marketing, Journalism, Psychology
Student/Faculty ratio: 15:1
Average Class Size: 25
Percent of students going to grad school: Unreported
Tuition and Fees: $25,298
In-State Tuition and Fees if different: $8,456
Cost for Room and Board: $8,480
Percent receiving financial aid out of those who apply: 60%
Percent receiving financial aid among all students: 58%

Knoxville, a small city in the heart of mountainous East Tennessee, is home to the state's major University, the University of Tennessee at Knoxville. At UTK, the scenic surroundings and the urban feel blend for a collegiate environment where students bleed Volunteer orange, party hard, and get their work done.

A Wide Range of Workloads and Habits

At UTK, academic rigor spans a wide range. Depending on which major you choose, the class difficulty and time commitment to class increases. One freshman said he spends about 5 hours a week on homework, while upperclassmen said it is often the high reading workload that takes up their time. Certain majors, such as nursing, engineering, architecture, and accounting, are considered to be more work-intensive majors, while English, psychology, and geography seem to have lighter workloads. "If I didn't study at least a couple hours every

day, I would get behind very quickly," said one junior accounting major.

Large lecture classes are often curved, "especially freshman level courses to help newer students transition to college," said one sophomore. It is possible to get straight As in every course, said one junior, but such a feat is not the average goal of UTK students.

Big School, Big Choices

As to be expected at a large university, students say it is difficult to make connections with professors, especially as underclassmen. One freshman cited the lack of intimacy with professors as one of his least favorite aspects of UT academics. Some classes, especially general freshmen lectures like History or Natural Sciences, can have over 200 students in them. But as students begin to take specialized classes in their majors, class size decreases and professor involvement increases. Even as an underclassman, though, it's possible to be enrolled in classes of around 20 students, said one freshman.

Despite the lack of personal attention, students tend to appreciate the opportunities that do come out of being at a large state school. "I really enjoy the wide variety of majors and programs that you can choose at UT," said one senior. Students have the option to take interesting elective classes in areas ranging from Japanese horror films to the history of rock 'n' roll.

Because of its location near the Oak Ridge National Laboratories, science research plays a substantial role in campus life. UT's campus is also home to the "Body Farm," a collection of corpses arranged in various positions used by medical and anthropology students to study forensics.

Good Ole Rocky Top

Greek life plays a major role on UT's campus, with frat parties being one of the main weekend activities for students. The fraternities have a row of houses on campus, while sororities do not. The most popular fraternities, Pike, Sigma Chi, Kappa Sigma, and SAE often throw big theme parties like Casino Date party or "Lifestyles of the Rich and Famous," amongst others. The rush process, which occurs during the first few weeks of the fall semester, is notoriously more stressful and structured for sororities than fraternities, said one junior girl. However, some students noted that Greek life is not as big a deal at UT's campus as it is at other SEC schools. Greeks on UT's campus do express pride in their fraternities and sororities, often sporting clothing with their letters on it. In addition to hosting parties, Greek organizations are involved with a lot of philanthropic work on campus.

For most students social life happens off campus—a short walk from school in downtown Knoxville is "The Strip," a row of bars and clubs that are the center of UTK weekend activity. UT's campus itself is supposed to be dry—but as one freshman said, "that's the biggest joke I've ever heard." Campus police are strict when it comes to alcohol and are fairly prominent around the school. The school's zero-tolerance drug policy is very strictly enforced, said one sophomore. Drugs are present on campus, but students said they don't feel pressured to participate.

For students who don't wish to participate in typical "party" activities, UT hosts a number of weekend events to keep students occupied. One freshman noted, "UT always has a lot to do for the weekends." The Campus Entertainment Board brings in performers, from magicians to speakers, and the University Center often screens movies for free for students. Market Square, another social center in downtown Knoxville, has a number of delicious restaurants which students frequent. Additionally, because the majority of students at UT are Tennessee natives, many choose to go home for the weekends. At UT, people are easy to meet, and friendly, said one junior. "Always! It's a Southern thing." While Greek life is a major way to meet people on campus, students find that the majority of their friends come from classes and freshman dorm life. However, some students do notice the lack of diversity on campus, both racially and politically. And often, this lack of diversity results in discomfort with the unfamiliar. "Our university has had and still has a lot of problems with diversity, whether they admit it or not. People are really hesitant about ANYTHING they're not familiar with," one senior said. But for students who do represent minority populations on campus, this lack of diversity often leads to interesting conversations and friendships. "I'm biracial and Muslim, which at times gets very interesting, in a good way, because we are in the Bible Belt, and a large majority of campus is involved in some form of religious ministry or organization," said one junior boy. Most students seem to be able to find their niche in UT's social scene, and as one sophomore described it, UT is a "great place to live and learn."

Dorm Decisions

All freshmen who live less than 50 miles away from UT are required to live on campus for their first year. Before arriving on campus, students enter their dorm preferences online through UT's housing website and are assigned to a dorm. One freshman described the housing for first years as "tight but comfortable." The dorms come in a variety of styles—there are double rooms with a floor bathroom shared with around 20 other students as well as suite-style arrangements with a bathroom for a group of four students. If students have friends that are also going to UT, they can make arrangements to live with them throughout their time at school. The best freshmen dorms, South Carrick, Humes, North Carrick, and Reese, surround the "Presidential," a large quad central to campus. Students in the Honors program live in a separate dorm.

Many upperclassmen, though, choose to live off campus, where apartments can be found for around $400 to $450 per month. One of the major neighborhoods that UT students live in is called "Fort Sanders"—this residential area is also one of the main social hubs on campus. Because housing here is so popular, though, there is often a waiting list.

The Campus Bubble
As one junior said, "UT's campus is not pretty." The buildings, often a mixture of architectural designs, do not seem to have any sort of consistency—but while students sometimes pine for a more aesthetically pleasing campus, the collegiate atmosphere at UT is definitely palpable. "The Hill," the oldest part of campus that houses the school's math and science facilities, is noted for looking the most consistent. There are several central locations around campus where students congregate. Freshmen tend to hang out around the Presidential Courtyard, near their housing and cafeteria, while students in all years frequent the amphitheater, where student groups often organize events. Probably the most popular spot on campus, though, is the University Center, where students can get food, play games, and attend special events. One junior noted a particular bizarre hangout spot—an outdoor vent that emits heat. "People stand over it, even when it's sub-freezing outside, and talk, smoke, and laugh," he said.

Because of UT's heavy emphasis on sports, the exercise facilities are especially popular. "T-Rec," the University's big student gym, has state-of-the-art workout machinery as well as an indoor track, four basketball courts, three racquetball courts, intramural fields, and an indoor and outdoor pool.

Students generally feel safe on UT's campus—however the area around campus is often the target of crime. The Fort is notorious for being the most dangerous spot that students frequent.

Good Eats On and Off Campus
With five cafeterias and numerous restaurants on campus, students have a wide range of culinary options. Two of the dining halls have recently been renovated, and at the University Center, students can eat at popular chains such as Chik-fil-A and Subway. Students have a choice of five different meal plans, which incorporate "bonus bucks" to be used in the restaurants on campus. But it is the off-campus options that really make the UT culinary experience. One sophomore said "The hardest part isn't finding somewhere good to eat in Knoxville; it's deciding between all the great restaurants!"

> "People are always friendly and easy to meet at UT. It's a Southern thing!"

The restaurants in Knoxville range from "BBQ joints featured on Food Network to modern fusion restaurants and cafes." The Strip—the weekend social hub—is also lined with food options representing many types of cuisine and price ranges. Often, local restaurants like to show their UT pride, giving dishes University-based names.

Bleeding Volunteer Orange
At UT, students have no shortage of extracurricular options—"there are literally hundreds of clubs and organizations to get involved with at UT, all ranging from academic, to student government, to religious and ethnic groups." Because of the school's size, students are able to find organizations that appeal to them. According to one sophomore, "just about everything you want to join or be a part of is available." Apart from student groups, about one half of the student body has a job.

But it is UT Volunteer Athletics that unifies the student body throughout the year. Football and basketball are the most popular sports on campus—a sea of orange packs the 100,000 seat Neyland Stadium on the weekends during football season. "Game days in Knoxville in football season make UT the place to be," said one junior. The athletes are considered "minor celebrities" on campus, and tend to hang out with each other, but athletics are nonetheless a pride of the whole student body. Students belt "Rocky Top" during events, take part in the Vol Walk to the games, and tailgate enthusiastically.

Ultimately, UT is a school with an "emphasis on tradition and school spirit." Students are motivated by a number of elements on campus—whether it's sports, Greek life, or academics—and this blend creates a diverse community that allows each Volunteer to find his or her place and college life.—*Anjali Balakrishna*

FYI

If you come to UT, you'd better bring something orange.

What differentiates UTK the most from other colleges is that game day is a holiday and an all-day event.

Three things every student at UTK should do before graduating are 1. Paint the Rock. 2. Go to the Vol Walk before a Home Football game. 3. Memorize "Rocky Top" and the "Alma Mater."

University of the South (Sewanee)

Address: 735 University Avenue, Sewanee, TN 37383-1000

Phone: 931-598-1000

E-mail address: admiss@sewanee.edu

Web site URL: www.sewanee.edu

Year Founded: 1857

Private or Public: Private

Religious Affiliation: Episcopal

Location: Rural

Number of Applicants: 2,481

Percent Accepted: 62%

Percent Accepted who enroll: 25%

Number Entering: 401

Number of Transfers Accepted each Year: 39

Middle 50% SAT range: M: 580–670, CR: 580–690, Wr:570–680

Middle 50% ACT range: 26–30

Early admission program EA/ED/None: ED

Percentage accepted through EA or ED: 66%

EA and ED deadline: 15-Nov

Regular Deadline: 1-Feb

Application Fee: $45

Full time Undergraduate enrollment: 1,455

Total enrollment: 1,536

Percent Male: 46%

Percent Female: 54%

Total Percent Minority or Unreported: 16%

Percent African-American: 4%

Percent Asian/Pacific Islander: 2%

Percent Hispanic: 2%

Percent Native-American: 0%

Percent International: 1%

Percent in-state/out of state: 24%/76%

Percent from Public HS: Unreported

Retention Rate: 88%

Graduation Rate 4-year: 77%

Graduation Rate 6-year: Unreported

Percent Undergraduates in On-campus housing: 93%

Number of official organized extracurricular organizations: Unreported

3 Most popular majors: Social Sciences, English, History

Student/Faculty ratio: 11:1

Average Class Size: Unreported

Percent of students going to grad school: Unreported

Tuition and Fees: $32,292

In-State Tuition and Fees if different: No difference

Cost for Room and Board: $9,226

Percent receiving financial aid out of those who apply: 69%

Percent receiving financial aid among all students: 33%

Amid castles and gardens in a small town in sunny East Tennessee, the students of the University of the South at Sewanee forge close academic and social bonds that will last them a lifetime. Sewanee offers a distinctive liberal arts education focused on encouraging students to explore the wide intellectual world before them, as well as a lively social environment on and off campus that is a product of Sewanee students' love for their school, their peers and their traditions.

A liberal arts education

Sewanee's academic culture is focused on arts and humanities for the most part, and is reading- and writing-intensive, students said. However, the liberal arts college requires students to complete a fairly extensive set of core requirements across several subjects like language, sciences, English, and math. But rather than being restrictive, students agree, the requirements encourage them to try out new things and explore learning for the sake of learning, in the spirit of a true liberal arts education. One freshman still working out his academic path says that "the system is good for me because I don't really know what I want to do yet . . . I'm taking diverse classes and finding subjects I really do like." To encourage students to experiment academically, Sewanee does not require its students to declare a major until the end of their sophomore year. According to one senior, one thing that made the requirements a bit "frustrating" at times is that they, as well as certain other classes, "offer a broad base along the [academic] canon," rather than preparing students for the specialization to come in graduate school. The emphasis on a broader, liberal arts–based education at Sewanee, for all its merits, tends to make seniors "nervous on the job front."

As far as rigor at Sewanee, one senior warns, "you have to be ready to work hard"— especially if you want to join the ranks of the Order of the Gownsmen, a society of students who have achieved a certain GPA average, and are entitled to participate in some of the oldest of the university's traditions, such as the huge gowning ceremony, encouraging university-wide changes through OG committees and even wearing their gowns to class. Some students added that while the rigor level is "just above average," "you get out what you put into it; there's personal responsibility on each student" to get the education he or she wants.

Faculty Relationships

Inexperienced teaching assistants and bored professors, say students, are completely nonexistent at Sewanee. Students interviewed were in agreement that their professors are always engaged with their students and classes, regardless of the level of the class. The university has a distinctive academic policy that all sections of every class are taught by an actual member of faculty, reflecting the close direct bond between faculty and students. One senior says, "the students and professors get very close here. I like it that they treat students as equals when working with them."

The classes themselves also take on the intimate and close-knit feel of the college. Most classes are discussion-based, and one senior said in his four years at Sewanee, he hasn't had a single class larger than 30 students. This is not an unusual experience at Sewanee, with almost 70% of classes under 20 students; professors thus have the opportunity to engage personally with all of their students. One freshman said he was surprised but grateful that his English professor went out of her way several times to get him to participate in class discussion at the beginning of the year when he felt too shy to get his word in. It's a mixed blessing though, says a senior. "They can definitely tell when you're not prepared— and they will make you participate."

Because everyone at the university— students, administration, staff, and faculty— lives in the proximity of the small, remote town, academic relationships blend well into personal ones, said a junior. For example, in many of her classes, professors have given out their addresses and personal cell phone numbers on the first day of class. Almost all students interviewed said they have met professors outside of class at casual places like the dining hall or the popular coffee house Stirling's. "They not only act as academic mentors, but also mentors at life," the junior said.

Student to Student

It's the little things that make Sewanee the nurturing, close community that it is, says one freshman, when asked about his impression of the people at Sewanee. For one, everyone greets each other when passing on campus. "Even something as simple as a 'hello' on the sidewalk makes you feel welcomed. It encourages a living sense of community," he says. One policy on campus, which is respected though not strictly enforced, is that students should not talk or text on their phones, or have earbuds in when walking from class to class. It's a little "Southern hospitality" strengthened by the intellectual bonds they share.

> "Everyone greets each other when passing on campus."

Despite the friendly character of the campus, broader inclusion has historically been more of a challenge for Sewanee. The student body is "majority white, Southern, upper middle-class American," notes a senior, who happens to be one of only three male Latino students at the college. Recently, however, "several student organizations have been working to raise awareness of cultural groups on campus." The admissions office has also been pursuing outreach and recruitment programs locally to draw in more minority students. Although students acknowledge that from the outside, Sewanee seems preppy, white, and conservative, the community is actually "accepting," "open," and "fun."

Small Town, Big Campus

But Sewanee is more than the institution itself. Because Sewanee is so remote, students feel the town and the college are "totally integrated." One student explains the strong legacies at Sewanee: "The professors all live here, their kids go to school in town, and many complete the legacy and go to Sewanee eventually." Also, says one student, "some professors work on projects with students and even are in student-led organizations."

The isolated nature of Sewanee "makes everyone focus on their academic and campus life," says one student. But when drawn more to "civilization," students have to make the hour-long drive to get to the mall or closest city, Chattanooga. 75% of students on campus own cars, so "it's not hard to get a ride anywhere," says a carless freshman. Even on the relatively large campus, though, it can be hard to get from point A to point B on time. "For some classes, I've needed to go by bike to be on time," says one junior. "I really wish there were a public transportation system." Another drawback of living in a rural area, adds a senior, is that "if we were in a larger city, we could intern during the year, but that's not an option that's open to us."

The various dorms and houses at Sewanee are structured by interest, rather than arranged arbitrarily. Students can live in the larger dormitories for more general interests, like science or foreign language, or can live in smaller house communities, like the Bairnwick Women's Center. One senior who lives there says it's "old, charming, and I live with only eight other people, so there's a lot of freedom and responsibility. It feels like a home as opposed to the typical dorm." Though segregated in relation to academic or extracurricular interest, students of all class years live together, with a system that groups underclassmen with upperclassman mentors in lieu of RAs. As one senior says, "you get to make a bunch of friends in different classes and we're there to give you advice." On the other hand, it sometimes gets "annoying when freshman act, you know, 'freshman-y'."

Get it to the Greek

"There isn't much to do out here so . . ." is how most students begin their description of the party scene at Sewanee. Without popular clubs, theaters, and bars associated with urban college towns, "Greek life is the main social outlet here," says one student; he, like 70% of Sewanee students, is in a Greek organization on campus. However, students are quick to add that the fraternity and sorority scene at Sewanee is distinctive from that of other colleges. For one, "every student is welcome in any fraternity or sorority party—we have an open-door policy here," says a fraternity member. Another sorority member adds that there is a heavy emphasis on community service in these organizations, and they are major contributors to Sewanee's reputation for civic involvement. But there's no denying that "a lot of drinking goes on at Sewanee," and it is in some sense associated with Greek life. While policies about alcohol in public and not causing major disturbances on campus are "enforced to a reasonable extent" by the administration, students say that drinking is a part of the university culture. "We balance working hard with playing hard here," says a junior. One freshman, who is a non-drinker, says that he attends the frats "sometimes, to see people," but has also found other things to do on weekends that don't involve alcohol, like hanging out in the game room or catching a movie in a dorm.

Outside of frat houses, there are many other social gathering places on and off campus. There are various centers for different activities and organizations where people meet, and the library courtyard and dining hall are always packed with socializing students. Students describe Sewanee's "downtown" with a chuckle. More of a modest commercial strip just off campus, it does offer students a place to go grocery shopping and have a coffee without making the considerable haul to the next town's mall.

Southern Comforts

One of the major social centers on campus throughout the day, students agree, is McClurg, the sole dining hall. This year, the college has committed to improving the quality of the food for students on the meal plan, turning one of the major drawbacks to living at Sewanee into one of the major benefits. Upperclassmen say that "you can taste the difference." Another notes that "they try to stick to locally produced ingredients (some of which are actually grown on the campus farm), and it's better and healthier." Another of Sewanee's draws is its beautiful and historic campus buildings and gardens. The Princeton Review ranked Sewanee the #1 most beautiful campus in the country in 2010, one senior cites proudly, and in the fall and spring, students say the greenery on campus is "truly gorgeous." The Gothic-style buildings, surprisingly enough, are at the cutting edge of ecological sustainability. One senior describes the All Saints' Church, a campus landmark, as "the most beautiful place on Earth." Students also take advantage of the sprawling 13,000-acre "Domain" surrounding the campus, which the college owns to preserve the rich forests, mountains, and waters for recreational and educational use. Students say hiking, mountain biking, and canoeing on Lake Cheston are just part of their weekend routines. "Sewanee is huge on outdoor activity," one student says.

After Class

Extracurricular activities are a critical part of life at Sewanee, just as much as studying and socializing. "Most students are involved with at least one or two extracurriculars, some many more," attests a junior. Greek organizations "really feel different here than they do in other places," says a senior. The culture of service at the college, possibly stemming from its Christian roots, runs strong through the frats and sororities. "We take advantage of the community we have here to organize all the volunteer work that we do," says a senior. Also padding Sewanee students' résumés are the many other student- and university-run organizations like publications, cultural groups, and theater performances. Though one freshman was crestfallen upon learning that there was no musical theater at Sewanee, he was hopeful that he could "maybe try to start it up next year, since you can do that at Sewanee if you want to." The Sewanee Outing Program, run by the administration, is a hugely popular opportunity for students to take full advantage of the Domain, says one senior.

Sports are an important, though not central, part of the Sewanee identity and pride. Students admit that while football (Division III) is the most popular sport and "getting a lot better," it hasn't historically been the best team. Student-athletes can participate in various club and intramural sports, including crew, cycling, fencing, and the extremely successful rugby team.

Campus Customs

It's the series of traditions, routines, and formalities Sewanee students have that make the school unique. Tradition runs strong at the historic university, and contributes to a sense of belonging, says a freshman adjusting to the community. For example, it's not uncommon to see students dressed up when they go to class; even during finals season or on rough mornings, it's rare to see sweatpants or slippers in classrooms, say students. "It shows a level of respect for the professors," say students. Semi-formal attire is also common at sports games. But the tradition goes deeper than formalities. Legend has it that "guardian angels live at the gates" of Sewanee, and follow students to protect them as they leave campus if they summon them by tapping the top of the car. On returning, students tap it again to "release the angel."—*Christopher Taylor*

FYI
If you come to Sewanee, you'd better bring "bug spray and a raincoat—the weather here's crazy." Also a "bowtie and a blazer, at least."
The biggest college-wide tradition/event at Sewanee is "the passing 'Hello'" and "the Order of the Gownsmen ceremony."
What's the typical weekend schedule? "Friday nights to the frats, Saturdays there are outing trips, sports games, and after parties, and on Sundays we wind down and sometimes go to church."

Vanderbilt University

Address: 2305 West End Avenue, Nashville, TN 37203
Phone: 615-322-7311
E-mail address: admissions@vanderbilt.edu
Web site URL: www.vanderbilt.edu
Year Founded: 1873
Private or Public: Private
Religious Affiliation: None
Location: Urban
Number of Applicants: 21,811
Percent Accepted: 18%
Percent Accepted who enroll: 41%
Number Entering: 1,600
Number of Transfers Accepted each Year: 376
Middle 50% SAT range: M: 690–770, CR: 670–760, Wr: 660–750
Middle 50% ACT range: 30–34
Early admission program EA/ED/None: ED

Percentage accepted through EA or ED: 32%
EA and ED deadline: 1-Nov
Regular Deadline: 3-Jan
Application Fee: $50
Full time Undergraduate enrollment: 6,879
Total enrollment: 12,714
Percent Male: 51%
Percent Female: 49%
Total Percent Minority or Unreported: 37%
Percent African-American: 9%
Percent Asian/Pacific Islander: 6%
Percent Hispanic: 6%
Percent Native-American: 1%
Percent International: 6%
Percent in-state/out of state: 14%/86%
Percent from Public HS: Unreported
Retention Rate: 96%
Graduation Rate 4-year: 89%

Graduation Rate 6-year: Unreported
Percent Undergraduates in On-campus housing: 85%
Number of official organized extracurricular organizations: 329
3 Most popular majors: Social Sciences, Engineering, Foreign Languages and Literature
Student/Faculty ratio: 8:1
Average Class Size: 16
Percent of students going to grad school: 36%
Tuition and Fees: $41,996
In-State Tuition and Fees if different: No difference
Cost for Room and Board: $13,560
Percent receiving financial aid out of those who apply: 86%
Percent receiving financial aid among all students: 50%

Vanderbilt University, located in Nashville, Tennessee, blends strong academics with a vibrant social scene and a touch of "Southern hospitality." Whether they're studying or partying, students at this medium-size, private co-educational university are enthusiastic about their school, the quality of the education, and the wide range of opportunities available to them at "Vandy," both inside and outside the classroom. With six graduate and professional schools, Vanderbilt University is a true research institution that attracts motivated students from all over the world. Students in the four undergraduate schools have many resources at their disposal, including a renowned faculty. Vanderbilt was ranked 17th in *U.S. News and World Report*'s list of National Universities in 2011.

No 'Easy A's'

The five most popular majors at Vanderbilt are Economics, Political Science, English, Psychology, and Spanish, though many students double major. One student said it feels like "everybody and their mom" majors or double-majors in Economics. Undergraduates can choose between 70 majors in the College of Arts & Science, the School of Engineering, the Peabody College of Education and Human Development, and the Blair School of Music. Students apply to a specific school, but once you are at Vanderbilt you can change your school, or "flip" as the students say. Vanderbilt's requirements are flexible enough to allow students to explore a wide range of interests. "I've gotten to try almost every discipline that interests me," said a junior. Undergraduate students, other than freshmen, also have the option of studying abroad, and around 40 percent of the junior class studies abroad each year. Class size at Vanderbilt is small—78 percent of undergraduate classes have fewer than 30 students and 91 percent have fewer than 50—encouraging an engaged student population. The student-to-faculty ratio is eight to one, so students have easy access to accomplished faculty members, 97 percent of whom have terminal degrees.

The undergraduate curriculum in the College of Arts & Sciences, Achieving Excellence in Liberal Education (AXLE), provides students with a well-rounded liberal arts education. Students must fulfill a series of distribution requirements in a wide range of disciplines, including three courses in Mathematics and Natural Science, one of which must be a laboratory science course. General chemistry and calculus are common freshmen courses, but they are known for being very difficult. "Calculus is one of the most failed classes here," said one freshman. "There are people who take it three times."

One unique freshman requirement at Vanderbilt is Vanderbilt Visions. "We meet once a week for a semester with a randomly assigned group of students, a faculty member and student mentor," said one freshman. Visions groups discuss the issues and challenges related to college life and foster a sense of community among freshmen. "I met one of my really good friends through Visions," said one student.

Grading at Vanderbilt can be hard, particularly in larger lecture classes where the grade is dependent upon the curve. "You can get an A if you work your butt off," said a sophomore. But professors are "incredibly accessible." Through Vanderbilt's "Online Access to Knowledge intranet system," more commonly referred to as OAK, students can make appointments with professors. Expect to spend your Sunday hitting the books if you want to do well, as "pretty much everyone will be seen in the library" for the day.

Work Hard, Play Harder
While academic expectations are high at Vanderbilt, students do not let their studies get in the way of having some fun. "You study, study, study until you get burnt out and then you drink, drink, drink, drink, drink," said one student. From parties on Greek Row to the bars on the two-block 'Nashvegas Strip' downtown, students at Vanderbilt are never without a place to have a good time.

Downtown Nashville is only a mile and a half away from the Vanderbilt campus. "It's a five-minute car ride and there is tons of stuff to do in the city," said one student. Vanderbilt's proximity to downtown enables students to take advantage of all the "Music City" has to offer. Each April, Vanderbilt hosts Rites of Spring, a two-day concert that has recently featured artists such as Kid Cudi, Ben Harper, The Flaming Lips, and K'NAAN. "It's the best day of the year," said a junior.

With 40 percent of students involved in Greek life, frat parties dominate the social scene. "You got your top 40 music and people dancing on top of each other," said a junior. Fraternity parties are technically open to the entire campus, but while a "girl can show up anywhere, it's not as easy for boys. As a boy you either better be Greek or you better have friends who are Greek." For "Formal Weekend," fraternities take trips to Panama City, Pensacola, Myrtle, and other towns for a weekend of beach parties.

But there is plenty to do closer to campus too. West End Avenue and Hillsborough Village boast a wide array of dining options, including "quaint little ice cream and coffee shops." A number of restaurants and bars are also close to campus.

> **"It's a very smart school but not a nerdy school."**

Students are very involved in extracurricular activities outside of Greek life, from the student newspaper, *The Vanderbilt Hustler*, to intramural sports and various performance groups. Religious organizations are particularly active on campus. While one junior commented that "the majority of Vanderbilt students overcommit and under-deliver" he also added that he met some of his closest friends through joining clubs.

With such a strong basketball team, it's no surprise that sports are popular on campus. "The gym is always full," said one sophomore. Tailgating football games is also a favorite weekend activity. "It's a blast and a half," said a student. "I rarely watch the football game, but I hate it when football season ends."

Students said there is truth in some of the school's social stereotypes. For example, Southern hospitality is alive and well at Vanderbilt. "The atmosphere is really friendly. Everyone holds the door, says hi and makes an effort to be very polite," said one student. Additionally, the female population is known for being attractive and fashionable, and many girls join sororities their second semester. "People just sort of assume you're in [a sorority]," said one student. "Being in one is the norm." However, Vanderbilt is by no means a homogenous environment. "I remember thinking when I first visited, 'it's not as white as I thought it would be,'" said one freshman. "There's more diversity than people think." Indeed, only 30 percent of

Vanderbilt students come from the South. Thirty-seven percent of the 2011–2012 student body were minority students. Admissions is need-blind, 50 and 61 percent of students receive some amount of financial aid.

Living in the Vanderbubble

The original Vanderbilt campus was constructed in the late 19th century. Known for its beautiful trees, it was designated a national arboretum in the 1980s. Vanderbilt's architecture is "bricks on bricks," with grassy lawns that are strewn with tanning students every spring.

Vanderbilt freshmen all live together on the Peabody Campus, or "the Commons." This site, a National Historic Landmark with six LEED-certified green dorms, was renovated in 2006. "All the dorms are either brand-new or newly renovated," said a freshman student. "The brand-new ones are actually like hotels." Roommates either find each other through Facebook, or take a simple survey to get paired up according to sleep schedule and cleanliness.

Friendships are primarily formed in the dormitories. "Just having all the freshman together made it really easy to get to know people," said a freshman student. No alcohol is permitted on the freshman campus, but students said this policy is not well enforced. The level of supervision varies greatly depending on the RA. The RAs at Vanderbilt are very involved in student life, sometimes organizing "salsa lessons, Glee marathons and waffle nights," said a student. Many upperclassmen dorms have clear stereotypes. "McGill is the hipster dorm, the antithesis of frats and sororities. Cole is full of sorority girls," one junior said.

Vanderbilt is in the process of moving towards a residential college system. In the meantime, while the Kissam Quadrangle, one of the six residential areas, is being renovated, the school is looking to purchase additional housing space and also "encouraging students to move off campus," said a sophomore.

Vanderbilt University is a prestigious option for students seeking an academically and socially enriching college experience on a beautiful campus. Vanderbilt's graduate schools provide excellent research opportunities for undergraduate students, and the school's proximity to Nashville and over 300 student organizations mean that there is something for everyone to do on weekends, even if the frat scene is not for you. Vanderbilt students stay busy, balancing challenging but rewarding academics with an active social life. If you want to get a good education *and* have a good time, Vanderbilt is a great college to consider.—*Sophie Gould*

FYI

If you come to Vanderbilt, you'd better bring "12 sundresses, cowboy boots, pastels, and Sperry topsiders."

Three things every student at Vanderbilt should do before graduating: "go to a Fraternity Formal, tailgate, and go line dancing in Nashville."

What differentiates Vanderbilt the most from other colleges is "the incredibly smart but incredibly social people. It's a very smart school but not a nerdy school."

Texas

The history of Baylor University began before Texas even entered the Union as a state. In fact, its official establishment in 1845 was chartered by the then-Republic of Texas. Over one and a half centuries later, Baylor has become not only a well-respected academic institution, but also the largest Baptist-affiliated university in the world, with a total of over 14,000 students. Furthermore, due to its dedication to research activities across all disciplines, Baylor has also emerged as a highly regarded global university, attracting students and faculty from around the world.

No-nonsense Academics

The quality of education offered by Baylor is widely recognized as one of the best in the country. *U.S. News & World Report* recently ranked Baylor as the 75th best national university. In 2007, *Relevant* magazine listed the university as the best Christian college in the country. This means competitive students and challenging academics. "Surely, finding easy classes is not that hard, and sometimes it depends on what you want to achieve in college," said one senior. "But overall, the classes are hard and make you work quite a bit."

Baylor students are also keen on boasting about the range and number of academic opportunities. After all, the University provides 151 different areas of study, not to mention the fact that it also offers 50 study-abroad programs, a rarity even among the largest academic institutions in the United States. Given Baylor's status as a leading research university, undergraduate students who seek to enrich themselves even further can easily gain exposure to the numerous in-depth research projects on campus.

In addition, the undergraduate education at Baylor goes far beyond the traditional liberal arts subjects. The University is divided into 11 different schools, and eight of them—ranging from the customary Arts and Sciences to the Hankamer School of Business to the School of Social Work—have degree-granting programs for undergraduates. Several certification programs are also available for those who seek to link their education directly to future employment, like students who are planning for a career in teaching. "The School of Education is great here at Baylor," affirmed one student. "It gives a lot of opportunities to students to have field experiences and do some actual teaching in classrooms. It prepares us well for our careers."

As its Baptist affiliation would suggest, Baylor maintains considerable emphasis on Christianity in the education of students. The core curriculum that everyone must fulfill before graduation reflects this religious commitment by requiring students to attend Chapel regularly during at least two semesters. Furthermore, everyone must take two specific religion classes: Introduction to Christian Scripture and Introduction to Christian Heritage. "I particularly enjoyed my religion classes. I now know so much more about what it means to be a Christian," one student explained.

The rest of the curriculum varies significantly, given the large differences between majors. However, as in most universities of similar academic vigor, students are required to take classes in a variety of fields, such as English, foreign language, and mathematics. These skills are deemed highly valuable regardless of major. "The required classes can be a pain, but I feel I learned a lot of new things from them," said one student.

Life in Waco

Located on the south side of Waco, Texas, Baylor is generally considered an urban school, but its surroundings are certainly more reminiscent of the suburbs, with low-rise apartments and small houses. Although Waco does employ a large number of commuters, it is certainly not a major metropolitan area and has been suffering from urban decay for several decades. Nevertheless, efforts are now underway, with the help of Baylor, to revive the city. On the other hand, students do not necessarily feel it is

necessary to be part of Waco, and prefer staying on campus. "We have a very big university," one student said. "So I don't feel the need to go to the city, which doesn't have much anyway."

Life on Campus

Freshmen are required to live on campus, unless they live with their parents in McLennan County or have extenuating circumstances such as being married or having dependents. In applying for housing, students can ask for a specific roommate and indicate residential hall preferences. Although there is no guarantee that these requests will be honored, students certainly have a degree of control over their living arrangements. "The rooms are reasonable," one student said. "I have been to dorms of my friends at other colleges, and, compared to them, I think Baylor's housing is not bad." Nevertheless, upperclassmen tend to move off campus to the many surrounding apartments. This means that only about 40 percent of the students are currently living in university facilities; however, Baylor has recently indicated that it recognizes the importance of campus living to education and aims to improve the number of students living on campus.

> **"You will learn a lot about Texas during your time at Baylor."**

As a Baptist university, the way students behave certainly reflects Christian values. Alcohol, for example, is strictly monitored on campus. Therefore, many parties happen off of University property. Baylor has more than 40 fraternities and sororities, making them an important part of the social scene. For those uninterested in Greek life or alcohol, many other options are also available, especially the different artistic and sporting performances where many people gather and socialize. Furthermore, unlike at most universities in the country, another major and well-attended weekend activity is church. "Of course people go to church on Sundays," one student said. "At the end of the day, this is a Christian university, and going to church is essential for many people here."

Baylor Bears

Baylor, like many other large Texan universities, is a major force in collegiate athletics. The Bears, named after the school mascot, participate in the Big 12 Conference, a highly competitive and prestigious conference of NCAA Division I. Although the football team has not been very successful due to the quality of its adversaries, the games still attract large crowds and are famous for the Baylor Line, made entirely of a large number of freshmen wearing yellow football jerseys cheering for the team and intimidating the opponents.

The more successful programs include the baseball team, which regularly provides quality players to Major League Baseball; the women's basketball team; and the track and field team, which is known to have produced one of the most celebrated sprinters in recent memory, world-record holder Michael Johnson. The most outstanding team award, however, probably goes to the tennis team, which has been winning consecutive titles since 2005. "Our teams are very good, so it is only natural that sports are big at Baylor," one student concluded. "The teams and the crowd help us to have a strong school spirit," added another.

Diversity in a Baptist Institution

One of the major factors that may turn away many prospective applicants is the image of a heavily religious university that focuses on proclaiming Christian values. Undoubtedly, Baylor does have a strong emphasis on religion. In fact, its mission statement unambiguously affirms that the goal of the institution is to combine Christianity with academic excellence. "My religion is important to me," one student explained. "That is why I chose to come here." The requirement of Chapel attendance clearly shows that the school is deeply committed to teaching students about not only religion, but also faith.

On the other hand, Baylor's student body does have substantial diversity, at least for a school of such strong religious affiliation. Minority students account for roughly 35 percent of the total enrollment, a considerable number for most universities. At the same time, more than 80 countries are represented on campus, and the school enrolls about 200 international students. Furthermore, despite the preaching of Christian values, there are a small number of non-Christians. "I know people who are atheists here," said one student. "As long as you can stand having plenty of pious people around you, I don't think you will find it really hard to get by." One drawback, however, is that the University is predominantly Texan in nature. In fact, four out of five students come from the Lone Star State. "You will learn a lot about Texas during your time at Baylor," affirmed one student.

Baylor is unique. With its combination of qualities and weaknesses, students choose to attend this school for a particularly large variety of reasons. Sometimes it is because Baylor is academically industrious. Sometimes it is because of Baylor's religious traditions. Sometimes it is the school spirit. Regardless of their reasons, most students are happy about their choice. Surely the strong emphasis on Christian values and the location in Waco may turn away some potential suitors. At the end of the day, however, Baylor remains a top destination for students from around the world.—*Xiaohang Liu*

FYI
If you come to Baylor, you'd better bring a "work ethic."
What is the typical weekend schedule? "Parties, but you have to make sure that you will get up in the morning on Sunday for church."
If I could change one thing about Baylor, I'd "make more upperclassmen live on campus."
Three things every student at Baylor should do before graduating are "visit Dallas, study abroad, and go to as many sports games as you can."

Rice University

Address: MS 17 PO Box 1892, Houston, TX 77251-1892
Phone: 713-348-7423
E-mail address: admission@rice.edu
Web site URL: www.rice.edu
Year Founded: 1912
Private or Public: Private
Religious Affiliation: None
Location: Urban
Number of Applicants: 12,393
Percent Accepted: 21%
Percent Accepted who enroll: 36%
Number Entering: 949
Number of Transfers Accepted each Year: 106
Middle 50% SAT range: M: 690–790, CR: 650–750, Wr: 660–760
Middle 50% ACT range: 30–34
Early admission program EA/ED/None: ED

Percentage accepted through EA or ED: 32%
EA and ED deadline: 1-Nov
Regular Deadline: 1-Jan
Application Fee: $70
Full time Undergraduate enrollment: 3,475
Total enrollment: 3,529
Percent Male: 52%
Percent Female: 48%
Total Percent Minority or Unreported: 57%
Percent African-American: 7%
Percent Asian/Pacific Islander: 21%
Percent Hispanic: 11%
Percent Native-American: <1%
Percent International: 10%
Percent in-state/out of state: 53%/47%
Percent from Public HS: Unreported
Retention Rate: Unreported
Graduation Rate 4-year: 79%

Graduation Rate 6-year: 92%
Percent Undergraduates in On-campus housing: 77%
Number of official organized extracurricular organizations: 215
3 Most popular majors: Biology, Economics, Psychology
Student/Faculty ratio: 6:1
Average Class Size: 6
Percent of students going to grad school: 41%
Tuition and Fees: $34,900
In-State Tuition and Fees if different: No difference
Cost for Room and Board: $12,270
Percent receiving financial aid out of those who apply: 53%
Percent receiving financial aid among all students: 62%

W ith its cleanly manicured lawns, lush green vegetation, and park-like atmosphere, one would hardly guess that Rice University is located just a few miles from downtown Houston, Texas. As one of the nation's top universities, it offers students an unmatched education in addition to a beautiful learning environment.

"We Study a Lot"

In describing Rice, one student said, "You will work so hard here. The students I know could not work more if they wanted to." Even those who choose to take the easier route must fulfill Rice's academic requirements, which can vary in intensity depending on the major and the number of AP credits an individual has coming in. There are three areas of distributional requirements—the humanities, the social sciences, and the natural sciences. Students point out that the requirements have their "ups and downs," but one student said it is beneficial, since "taking classes outside of your major really helps to open your mind." Many students take a lot

of science courses regardless, but there are complaints about the "perfectionist pre-meds." It is common for students to continue their research at Rice over the summer. One of Rice's most well-known programs is the Rice-Baylor program, which guarantees acceptance to Baylor College of Medicine, the largest medical center in the country, located "right across the street." However, the program only accepts approximately 14 undergrads per year. Unfortunately, many pre-med students do not have the luxury of going abroad—a hefty sacrifice, considering that about half the University's students do so for at least a semester.

In terms of getting into classes, freshmen often have the most difficulty procuring a spot for the more coveted lectures. The upside for freshmen is that general education classes such as introductory humanities tend to be capped, so they range from 20 to 30 people. Other introductory courses, including biology, chemistry, physics, and constitutionalism, are generally quite large, "which for Rice isn't that big—maybe 100 students." One Rice freshman bragged that "my smallest class is an amazing Introduction to Theater class, which only has about 10 students." Upper-level courses are extremely small at Rice; typically less than 20 to 30 people. One upperclassman said, "I had four classes with fewer than 10 students last year."

While most Rice students are committed to their studies, few deny that some majors are harder than others. Mathematics, physics, and computer science top the list of most demanding majors. However, "every discipline at Rice has very serious students, and those are the ones that study the most—it doesn't depend on the major." "You will spend your four years at this school either working or feeling like you should be working." This deep commitment to academics and intensive studying does have its payoff, however. "There's a deeper level of satisfaction here than at most other schools because we know that 'excellence' should be hard to achieve (and that things can only get easier)."

The workload is more bearable when students have the opportunity to take classes from famous professors like Dennis Huston, a humanities teacher famous for lectures in which "he spits out obscenities left and right." People actually camp out in front of the registrar's office to ensure a spot in Huston's public speaking class. Bombs and Rockets, a class about the "Politics of American National Security," is another hot ticket. And these classes don't disappoint, with enjoyable assignments to hold students' interest. One premed student was assigned the task of creating artificial blood for one of his science courses.

Grade inflation doesn't seem to be a prominent concern at Rice, where students joke about its prevalence at Ivy League schools. Some classes, such as chemistry, do have what are called "redemption points." In this system, if a student's score on a portion of the final exam is better than that on a test from the beginning of the year, the earlier test score replaces final questions pertaining to the earlier test, resulting in the higher grade.

For all their positive attributes, academics at Rice do have some drawbacks. One student noted that some "professors and classes are not as liberal-artsy or teaching-focused as advertised. You get a lot of indifferent professors and big lecture classes, especially in the math and science departments." For more difficult classes, recitation sessions taught by the TAs are offered. Students seem to have mixed feelings about TAs, some complaining that they only muddle the information and that it can be "really hard to understand" those with foreign accents. This is not always the case, however, and one student praised the grad students at Rice, calling one of her TAs "better than the professor." Whatever the case may be, "between the office hours of the TAs and professors, you can always get help if you need it."

Studying Aside

Rice isn't all brains and no beer (despite its Greek-free status). "Even though Rice students are hardworking, you can find a lot of students that like to party a lot." Although most parties serve up alcohol, there are "always other things to do," one student emphatically pointed out, and nondrinkers are not at all ostracized. "I can't imagine a more accepting social scene." The residential colleges throw a lot of the parties. Well-known bashes include the Annual Night of Decadence, "which is basically a nude party"; Disorientation (at the end of orientation week); and the Tower Party. Late-night games of powderpuff football or just "chilling" with card games or a movie are options for those students who just want to veg out. The dating scene (or lack thereof) at Rice is often blamed on the common stereotype that "most of us guys tend to be shy," one male Rice student explained. And the males' shyness only works to their disadvantage, since "there's a good amount of cute girls on campus." The verdict is still out, however, because other Rice students feel that "you're either in a very serious relationship or you're not dating anyone at all."

Instant Family

The social life at Rice is supplemented by the University's "amazing" residential college system. About 400 people (100 from each grade) live in each of nine colleges, providing an instant family atmosphere ingrained in freshmen from the start of "a great orientation week." Freshmen from each college are divided into groups of eight to 10 students during "O-Week." "You're really tight with them from the start and you do all your activities with your group," a student explained. The colleges "make a very concerted effort to put people from very different backgrounds and with very different interests in each group," one student said. And yes, the residential colleges definitely do have different personalities, students said, which "are all brainwashed into us during our orientation week." Most students are positive about the system and their experience. One student noted that the system is like "the best parts of a fraternity and a dorm all put together." And don't worry about meeting people outside of your residential college. Classes, parties, or common friends are all ways to extend your social circle, although it does "take a little bit more effort."

Each college has its own master and staff of associates. The master is a tenured professor at the University and handles academic and personal matters, in addition to organizing social events. He or she lives and eats with the students in the residential college. The associates are faculty members, most of whom live outside of Rice, except for the two associates who reside in each college. They provide academic advice and help direct students' career choices.

Dorms vary from college to college, but most students would agree that none are terrible. Rooms range from singles to quads, most of which are located on coed floors and share single-sex bathrooms. There are more singles in the newer colleges, but there's no reason to fear being lonely—usually four singles comprise a suite, with its own common room and bathroom. And don't worry about playing your music too loudly: the RA system is fairly lenient and the RAs "tend to be really cool here and enjoy hanging out with us."

> **"The education you receive outside the classroom at Rice is what makes me feel like I could have never been happy anywhere else."**

Each college has its own dining hall, and though the quality varies, overall the food at Rice is "good by college standards." Even seniors opt to eat in the dining halls because "one of the great things about the college system is that students from all classes interact on a daily basis (primarily at lunch)." On Saturday nights, the cafeterias are closed for all students—a mixed blessing because "it forces one to go off campus." And there are more than enough places to choose from, with a great range in price and quality. When the clock strikes two in the morning, Taco Cabana, "a better, cheaper version of Taco Bell," is the place to be for post-party munchies. House of Pies is another Rice novelty.

A World Away

What's green, flat, and pretty all around? Why, the campus of Rice University, of course. It features beautiful landscaping and sprawling quads that students said "people are actually encouraged to walk on," although some prefer to utilize the plush grass for napping. The main local attraction is Rice Village, an outdoor mall with a mix of franchises and independent retailers that is "packed with restaurants." But who wants to walk when you can hitch a ride with any of the estimated 40 percent of Rice students who have cars on campus? Beyond campus, Houston has so much to offer, including the Theater District, Chinatown, and the Galleria, a "really famous, really large mall," but one student did lament the insular nature of the school. The hedges that surround the "spacious campus sometimes make Rice students forget that there's the city of Houston and even an entire world outside Rice." When they do get outside, favorite Rice bar hangouts in Houston include Bar Houston, Brian O'Neil's, Brock's Bar, and Two Rows. Little Woodrow's is another popular bar in the Village (along with Brian O'Neil's). Luckily for students not blessed with the luxury of wheels, a rail system makes getting places a bit easier. Last year, Rice's president implemented "Passport to Houston," so now all undergraduates can ride the light rail for free, "which makes going to bars, baseball games, and restaurants downtown, as well as the museum district and apartment complexes, very easy."

Outside the Classroom

"The education you receive outside the classroom at Rice is what makes me feel like I could have never been happy anywhere else," one student said. "People game, take salsa lessons, play ultimate Frisbee," and do anything to "enrich themselves," another said of the extracurricular scene at Rice. Although some organizations are more "official" than others, "as long as you have a group of people with a common shared idea, it can be made into an official club." The Cabinet, Parliament, and Diet among others are the names of residential college student governments, and these are a popular activity, even more than their counterpart, the official University student government. Future journalists can take a stab at writing for Rice's widely read newspaper, *The Thresher*.

High participation rates show more than just an interest to beef up résumés. "Everybody does their own thing," and they are appreciated for it. One student went so far as to say that "Rice people will change your life."

Although Rice's athletics are not the pinnacle of the University, the school's baseball team won the College World Series in 2003, made the NCAA tournament in 2006, and advanced to the NCAA Super Regionals. Rice students don't just cheer for the champs, though. A surprising number of people attend the football games "even though we're quite pathetic," one student said. College sports are another popular option—teams from various residential colleges compete against one another for the President's Cup. Although there are separate workout facilities for varsity athletes, the general public facility "pales in comparison to Duke's," as one student put it. "You're probably going to have to wait for cardio equipment anytime in the afternoon or evening, and most mornings as well. But the Board of Trustees has stated that a new Rec Center is a priority."
—*Laura Sullivan*

FYI

If you come to Rice you'd better bring "water balloons for O-Week, Beer Bike, and general mayhem."

What is the typical weekend schedule? "A lot of studying and a lot of procrastinating with your friends either partying, going out in Houston, or hanging out at your college."

If I could change one thing about Rice, I'd "help the premeds relax."

Three things every student at Rice should do before graduating are "support their powderpuff team, explore Houston without a car, and advise during O-Week (it's more fun for the advisers than for the freshmen, shhh!)."

Southern Methodist University

Address: PO Box 750181, Dallas, TX 75275-0181
Phone: 214-768-3417
E-mail address: enrol_serv@smu.edu
Web site URL: www.smu.edu
Year Founded: 1911
Private or Public: Private
Religious Affiliation: Methodist
Location: Urban
Number of Applicants: 8,239
Percent Accepted: 59%
Percent Accepted who enroll: 30%
Number Entering: 1,476
Number of Transfers Accepted each Year: 558
Middle 50% SAT range: M: 580–680, CR:560–670, Wr: 560–660
Middle 50% ACT range: 25–30
Early admission program EA/ED/None: EA

Percentage accepted through EA or ED: Unreported
EA and ED deadline: 1-Nov
Regular Deadline: 15-Mar
Application Fee: $60
Full time Undergraduate enrollment: 5,944
Total enrollment: 6,192
Percent Male: 47%
Percent Female: 53%
Total Percent Minority or Unreported: 30%
Percent African-American: 5%
Percent Asian/Pacific Islander: 6%
Percent Hispanic: 10%
Percent Native-American: <1%
Percent International: 6%
Percent in-state/out of state: 51%/49%
Percent from Public HS: 61%
Retention Rate: 89%

Graduation Rate 4-year: 58%
Graduation Rate 6-year: 73%
Percent Undergraduates in On-campus housing: 33%
Number of official organized extracurricular organizations: 180
3 Most popular majors: Economics, Finance, Psychology
Student/Faculty ratio: 12:1
Average Class Size: 16
Percent of students going to grad school: Unreported
Tuition and Fees: $34,990
In-State Tuition and Fees if different: No difference
Cost for Room and Board: $13,215
Percent receiving financial aid out of those who apply: 75%
Percent receiving financial aid among all students: 71%

Many Southern Methodist University students are frustrated with the stereotypes associated with common perceptions of their beloved school, complaining that "everyone assumes because we go to SMU we must be rich and Southern." But never fear. "SMU is really working to change its image from 'Southern Millionaires' University' to an academically charged, more demanding and well-respected and recognized university," asserted one proud Mustang. And while there are elements of that academic millionaires' club that still linger on campus (one sophomore insisted that every girl should know to bring "a Lilly Pulitzer dress and pearls" to school), this is not by any means all that SMU has to offer. "SMU has top-notch academics, opportunities, professors, location, and students," one senior explained.

Life on a Movie Set

SMU offers nationally recognized programs in fields ranging from business to dance. Although the offerings are rigorous, requirements are flexible enough to allow students to double major, to pick up minors, or to participate in one of the many study-abroad programs that SMU offers. But between the wide variety of academic programs and extensive extracurricular involvements, students must quickly learn to balance their time. One Mustang observed, "There is always something to do, but the library is also always packed!"

> "It's 'SMU tailgating.' People have big-screen TVs, satellite dishes, leather couches, and other ridiculous tailgating items."

"First-years" (never call them "freshmen"!) are required to live on campus. There are a number of different housing options, including an Honors dorm. "I enjoy on-campus living because I don't have to drive much unless I'm going out to eat or shopping," a sophomore RA said. "It's nice being close to all of my classes." Another Mustang chimed in that he "loved living in the dorms! It can get a little loud in the freshman dorms at times, but it is essential to the freshman experience." After first year, the housing choices expand immensely. Sophomore males may decide to move into their fraternity houses (girls have to wait until their junior year to live in the sorority houses), but there are also on-campus

as well as off-campus apartments ("It's not cheap, but it's very doable"), and of course, various on-campus residence halls and houses.

The on-campus eating options, centered around the offerings of Umphrey Lee Center, are enough to keep most Mustangs happy. Its pasta bar has a loyal following amongst students, as do the omelets at Mac's Place. In general, on-campus dining offers enough variety that at least one item will please every student's palate. And, for at least one first-year, there's more than enough to keep her happy. "It's all pretty delicious," she said.

But even if the beauty of SMU is not in its dining halls, then the breathtaking campus landscape more than makes up for it. "The whole thing is amazing!" one senior raved. Another added, "It's like a movie campus!" Indeed, the school takes full advantage of the sunny Dallas weather. "The groundskeepers change all the flowers in the flower beds once a month so they're always in season and beautiful." All of this is encased in what one Mustang described as the "Highland Park Bubble." Highland Park, one of the wealthiest neighborhoods in Dallas, surrounds the campus. And while this may make things expensive for students, it also provides them with "small-town shops and little diners." Furthermore, it provides an outstanding level of safety on campus. "I literally walked from one end of the campus to the other at midnight and felt extremely safe," one sophomore said. Indeed, thanks to the fact that the campus lies within the jurisdiction of four different police forces (Highland Park, neighboring University Park, SMU Campus Police, and the Dallas Police), students are well protected at all times.

TVs and Tailgating

On the surface, there is a large element of homogeneity within the student body. "SMU is really conservative. It's kind of like a scaled-down version of UGA or Ole Miss," one sophomore noted. However, there is a subtle streak of diversity that quickly becomes apparent upon closer investigation. For example, the campus boasts far more religious diversity than a school with the word "Methodist" in its name would be expected to have, with 28 religious groups, including Hillel, the Hindu Club, the Baha'i Club, and the Muslim Student Association, operating under the office of the campus chaplain. As one junior explained, "I would say the majority of campus often feels predominantly Christian. However, when you really start to meet people and talk to them, you will find out just how diverse we all really are."

There are a number of ways to get involved in athletics on campus, from intramural sports to the varsity level. And although the school is successful in a number of different sports, football is an undeniable favorite at SMU. Some students complained that this favoritism can be to the detriment of other sports. "Our men's soccer team is ranked number one in our conference, and many people do not have any interest."

Still, there's something to be said for the enthusiasm amongst students when it comes to supporting their football team. Aside from the requisite body-painting and jersey-wearing, Mustangs list tailgating amongst their favorite SMU traditions. Sure, this may sound like a relatively common pastime for a college campus, but don't be fooled. As one first-year explained, "It's 'SMU tailgating.' People have big-screen TVs, satellite dishes, leather couches, and other ridiculous tailgating items." Indeed, tailgating draws crowds of Mustangs, alumni, and other fans to the "Boulevard," the road that runs north to south through the center of campus. Groups such as fraternities, sororities, and even different colleges rent out the red and blue tents that line the Boulevard to wait for the game to begin, aided by the large, digital countdown clocks that are scattered throughout the crowd. "Seeing friends, the free food, and the whole aspect of body-painting with fraternity brothers right before the game makes the whole experience a great one."

Going Greek

Despite the fact that only about one third of Mustangs are members of a fraternity or sorority, it is also true that Greek life has a disproportionately strong presence on campus. "At SMU Greek life is huge," one sorority sister asserted. "The school, particularly the admissions office, tries to play it down. But in reality, as proven by statistics, it is the students that are in sororities and fraternities that have the highest average GPA and are the most involved in other programs on campus."

But the Greek system's visibility does not end there. The rush process virtually takes over the entire campus during the week before the start of spring semester in January. Rushees return early to SMU in order to participate in a full week of rush activities, described across the board as "intense." Sorority rushees, for example, have to dress for a different theme each day, whether it be business casual or formal. At the end of the rush process, all accepted sorority rushees participate in a "Pig Run," which requires the girls, dressed identically in white tops and jeans, to run from the center of campus to Sorority Row, all the while cheered on by the new fraternity pledges. And the enthusiasm extends well past rush. "In the spring everything kind of revolves around Greek life because everyone is so excited about it," a sophomore said.

The process is taken extremely seriously, to the point that potential pledges are not even allowed to interact with Greek members in the fall semester, for fear that groups will attempt to unfairly lure hapless first-years into their sororities or fraternities. A small percentage of students, however, may take the process a little too seriously. "There's people who talk about girls transferring because they didn't get the house they wanted," one Mustang remarked, but later admitted to not knowing "how true that is."

The prominence of fraternities and sororities on campus often calls into question the issue of drinking on campus. In fact, aside from tailgates (at which those 21 and older wear bands indicating that they can drink), SMU is a dry campus. Campus police are strict in enforcing the rules. Students do have the option of going both to fraternity parties and to the bars surrounding campus, and many actively take advantage of these opportunities. But at the same time, there are more than enough opportunities for those who choose to stay on campus and not to drink. "SMU does a great job of providing many things to do, such as sneak peek previews for upcoming movies." At times, Southern Methodist University may live up to its reputation as "where rich white kids go to become Greek, party, and find their spouses." But that is far from all the school has to offer. From academics to tradition, SMU provides its students with the opportunity to have a world-class education within the "movie campus" that SMU calls home.—*Stephanie Brockman*

FYI

If you come to SMU, you'd better bring "a sundress for tailgating if you're a girl, and a polo shirt if you're a boy."

What is the typical weekend schedule? "Sleep almost all day on Saturday, wake up in time to tailgate, go pregame and then tailgate, and then go to sleep. Sundays, sleep in, shop, and do some studying."

If I could change one thing about SMU, I'd "dispel the negative stereotypes and rumors about SMU. I think many strong and focused students buy into the rumors and therefore believe SMU would not be a good fit for them."

Three things every student at SMU should do before graduating are "go to Plucker's (a local restaurant with GREAT wings) late night, take 'Crime and Delinquency' with Richard Hawkins, and explore, and probably get lost in, downtown Dallas."

Texas A&M University

Address: P.O. Box 30014, College Station, TX 77843-3014

Phone: 979-845-3741

E-mail address: admissions@tamu.edu

Web site URL: www.tamu.edu

Year Founded: 1876

Private or Public: Public

Religious Affiliation: None

Location: Rural

Number of Applicants: 23,407

Percent Accepted: 69%

Percent Accepted who enroll: 46%

Number Entering: 7,447

Number of Transfers Accepted each Year: 2,295

Middle 50% SAT range: M: 570–680, CR: 530–650, Wr: 510–620

Middle 50% ACT range: 24–30

Early admission program EA/ED/None: None

Percentage accepted through EA or ED: NA

EA and ED deadline: NA

Regular Deadline: 15-Jan

Application Fee: $60

Full time Undergraduate enrollment: 36,016

Total enrollment: 39,148

Percent Male: 52%

Percent Female: 48%

Total Percent Minority or Unreported: 28%

Percent African-American: 3%

Percent Asian/Pacific Islander: 5%

Percent Hispanic: 16%

Percent Native-American: <1%

Percent International: 2%

Percent in-state/out of state: 97%/3%

Percent from Public HS: 87%

Retention Rate: 91%

Graduation Rate 4-year: 41%

Graduation Rate 6-year: 77%

Percent Undergraduates in On-campus housing: 24%

Number of official organized extracurricular organizations: 725

3 Most popular majors: Biological and Physical Sciences, Multi-Interdisciplinary Studies, Operations Management and Supervision

Student/Faculty ratio: 19:1

Average Class Size: 26

Percent of students going to grad school: Unreported

Tuition and Fees: $19,726

In-State Tuition and Fees if different: $5,296

Cost for Room and Board: $8,200

Percent receiving financial aid out of those who apply: 76%

Percent receiving financial aid among all students: 64%

"From the outside looking in, you can't understand it. And from the inside looking out, you can't explain it." This expression is often used to describe life at Texas A&M University, located in College Station, Texas. Aggies, as the students are called, bleed maroon and white, and school spirit is contagious. Texas A&M is "the perfect school for anyone who loves sports, especially loud, rowdy ones." Students become part of the Aggie family the minute they start Fish Camp, an orientation program for freshmen, and their ties to the school and to their classmates last a lifetime.

Aggie Academics

Texas A&M, the oldest public university in Texas, is comprised of approximately 39,000 undergraduate students enrolled in one of ten colleges. Given the number of students, "freshman core classes, which are about 200–250 students, are always hard to get into." However, as Aggies progress further and further into their academic careers, they are allowed to register early, before classes fill up with students. When students begin narrowing their field of interest, it becomes easier to enroll in classes because "there are less people vying for space." According to one freshman, "I've never really heard of anyone not getting the classes they wanted, other than people wanting to get the small, easy 'core requirement classes.' Eventually everyone gets the classes they want."

Students typically find classes engaging, and it is easy to find courses tailored towards special interests. According to one senior, "The most interesting class I've taken is a seminar called the Academy for Future International Leaders. It focuses on international leadership, the challenges that our world is facing, and some of the skills our generation will need to solve these tough problems." Texas A&M has many highly regarded professors, like Dr. Ben Welsh, who teaches "Management 105, one of the most popular courses in the state of Texas." Professor Amy Austen is internationally famous, and the "College Station, Galveston, and Qatar Texas A&M campuses all have very large fan clubs in her honor."

Texas A&M is known for its Business and Engineering Schools, and admission to these programs is very competitive. A large number of students pursue coursework in health-related majors as well as sports management. Other popular majors include petroleum engineering, business, biomedical sciences, architecture, and kinesiology. Additionally, Aggies are given the opportunity to receive a military-based education during their college years as members of the Corps of Cadets. This student organization has endured ever since the university's founding, a time when all enrolled students were required to partake in military training.

Other programs that have withstood the test of time are those in the school's College of Agriculture and Life Sciences. According to one Aggie, "Our agricultural studies are great here since we started out as a farming school." In fact, the A&M of Texas A&M used to stand for "agricultural and mechanical." Majors in this department range from agribusiness to dairy science to recreation, park, and tourism science. The term "Aggie" is a direct reference to the school's history as an agricultural school.

Aggies who are unsure of what they want to major in can apply for admission to the General Studies program. General Studies students take classes that fulfill their core curriculum requirements while exploring potential degree plans. Students select a major upon the completion of sixty hours (equivalent to about four to five semesters of coursework).

Campus Life in College Station

Texas A&M's campus sprawls over 500 acres. There are numerous points of interest on campus, including the George (H.W.) Bush Presidential Library and Museum, and the Cushing Memorial Library. The Memorial Student Center, the student union, has been dubbed the campus "living room," and many concerts, lectures, and cultural programs are put on in conjunction with the MSC Student Programs Office. The Memorial Student Center has undergone a $100 million renovation project, and reopened during the summer of 2012. According to one student, "The campus itself is fairly pretty, but most of the buildings here are big concrete boxes. They all look the same."

The majority of housing on campus is divided into two communities, the Northside or the Southside. The Southside is comprised of newer dorms and is home to Commons, a popular complex made up of four connected dorms. There are configurations available for all personal preferences and budgets. Aggies can also choose to live in on-campus university apartments, while students in the Corps of Cadets are required to live in corps housing. However, according to one student, "There is only room for 8,000 students on campus or about one-fourth of the student body. Basically you live on campus as a freshman and move off your sophomore year." Most students do opt to move off-campus after freshman year but "as long as you get your papers in on time, you should be able to secure housing."

> "For us here at A&M, it's not just a spirit, it's how you live; it becomes part of your life."

Student meal plans are available for both students living on and off campus. The Sbisa Dining Center is a popular place for students to dine. Aggies can also get food from commercial chains like Chick-fil-A on their meal plans. Off campus, students flock to the Dixie Chicken, a restaurant/bar on Northgate. According to one freshman, "It's known as 'the Chicken,' and it's pretty much an institution in Aggieland. People carve their names in the wooden wall and tables everywhere; it's got a great atmosphere and feel to it."

Gig 'em Ags!

Texas A&M University is a sports lover's paradise. Aggies love football, and the games in the fall are great socializing and unifying events on campus. At Texas A&M, Yell leaders lead the students instead of cheerleaders at the football games. Students participate in Midnight Yell, "a yell practice held (at midnight) the night before a home football game," explains one Aggie. "Students gather at Kyle Field to practice yells, bring a date, and 'mug down' or get a kiss when the lights go off for a few seconds."

Students love camping out to pull tickets for the games. Aggies pitch tents outside the football stadium and play football or board games all night long. It's a great way "to meet so many fun people, and it's a miracle if you see the inside of your tent before 4 a.m. since you have to wake up at 6:15 a.m. at the latest to start standing in line to get your tickets." As one student exclaimed, "One time my tentmates and I were woken up at 5:30 in the morning by hurricane force winds and about thirty-five-degree weather, but it is something I would do again."

Aggies agree that all students should attend at least one "t.u." game. As one Aggie explains it, "The t.u. game is the game against the University of Texas, known as t.u. to Aggies because there are technically many universities of Texas." Students rave about the "amazing energy" and love with which the "third deck of the stadium (which is solid concrete and steel) noticeably vibrates under the Aggies' feet from the volume of the students' voices." The cheers of the fans can be heard at Northgate, which is about a mile away from Kyle Field. Students used to light a Bonfire before the big game until 1999 when 12 students were tragically killed during construction. Currently, students organize the Bonfire and hold it off-campus each year.

When Aggies are not cheering on their teams, they can probably be found at one of the many dance halls in College Station. A large number of students go to three main dance halls: Daisy Dukes ("Dukes"), Hurricane Harry's ("Harry's"), or the Hall of Fame ("the Hall"). Aggies also enjoy going out to Northgate at night to hit the TAMU bars.

According to students, "The Greek scene is not really that big here." As one Aggie explains, "'Fraternity Row' is fairly far from campus, and their parties are never really broadcasted." At Texas A&M, "everyone is so active that the Greeks are just another thing that some people are involved in." Girls in sororities "love it but it does not consume their lives."

Students at Texas A&M have a love/hate relationship with a school of TAMU's size. As one Aggie puts it, "You meet so many kinds of people. Truly. Yes, more than 90 percent of the student body is from Texas, but there are so many types of 'Texans' that I never knew." Students enjoy getting to know people they would have never met otherwise. However, some students lament "it's hard to meet and keep a good group of people." Oftentimes, Aggies find they're good friends with people in their major because they take all the same classes. As one freshman explains, "My incoming freshman class numbers 8,200. That means with approximately 200 school days a year, I can meet ten new people in my class every day of the school year and not meet all of them in four years." Most students appreciate that TAMU is so big that there is a niche for everyone. As one Aggie explains, "You meet plenty of people, but you just have to go the extra mile to actually be close with them because there are just so many people here."

Twelfth Man Traditions

Students at Texas A&M are active in over 700 different student organizations. Freshmen enjoy getting to know one another in Freshman Leadership Organizations or FLOs. Each FLO has a different focus, and they offer students the opportunity to assume leadership positions and to organize and execute projects. Students agree that it is easy to start a new club. *The Battalion*, the daily newspaper at TAMU, keeps students in the know with what is happening on campus. According to one Aggie, "The Corps of Cadets is perhaps the most prominent organization on campus. It's essentially the heart of the school."

Texas A&M is famous for its traditions that bond students, both past and present alike. "For us here at A&M," elaborates one Aggie, "it's not just a spirit, it's how you live; it becomes part of your life." The Aggie Ring is possibly one of the most famous traditions. "It's arguably the most well-recognized collegiate ring and has started conversations between strangers all over the world," according to an Aggie senior. Students participate in the activity known as ring dunking. As one student explains, "It's a celebration the day one receives his/her ring. He/she drops it in a pitcher (usually of beer, but most other drinks can be substituted), and the recipient drinks the pitcher as fast as possible to get to the bottom."

Tradition is something Aggies are introduced to when they first decide to enroll at Texas A&M. Incoming freshmen go through an orientation program called Fish Camp. At Fish Camp, freshmen bond with other freshmen and learn about where they will call home for the next four years. As one freshman put it, "After I went through Fish Camp (known to outsiders as brainwashing) being an Aggie was just as much a part of me as being Asian or American. I've talked for hours trying to explain, but I know it's something that someone just has to experience."

Students at Texas A&M are proud of the history of their school. Aggies acknowledge, "We obviously cannot all know each other, but just being Aggies usually creates a mutual understanding or bond, what we call the Aggie Family." When it comes to traditions, Aggies agree, "Honestly, there are too many to count or explain. TAMU is a school built on tradition. So many things here have been in effect for 100 years, and if someone tries to change them, it could cause an uproar." From their beloved mascot, Reveille, also known as the First Lady of Aggieland, to Aggie Muster, a service put on every year in April to honor the Aggies that have fallen that year, students at Texas A&M love and respect their institution. One Aggie explains, "It is a place unlike any other in my opinion. I know some people call it a cult, and honestly, I thought the same thing. What I, and others, didn't realize is that it is just Texas A&M."—*Alexa Sassin*

FYI

If you come to TAMU, you'd better bring: "Your cowboy boots, your Southern hospitality, lots of maroon, a love of A&M football, and nothing that's remotely close to burnt orange."

What's the typical weekend schedule? "In the fall, Friday nights involve going over to a friend's house for a while and then heading to Midnight Yell Practice. On Saturday, students get ready for the game, go to tailgates, stand and yell throughout the football game, and then disperse all over College Station afterward. Sundays are the day of rest."

If I could change one thing about TAMU: "I'd create a better music scene, outside of country-western music, which is plentiful."

Three things every student should do before graduation are: "Have a burger at the Dixie Chicken, put a penny on the statue of Lawrence Sullivan Ross before an exam for good luck, and 'mug down' at Midnight Yell Practice."

Texas Christian University

Address: 2800 S. University Drive, Fort Worth, TX 76129
Phone: 817-257-7490
E-mail address: admissions@tcu.edu
Web site URL: www.tcu.edu
Year Founded: 1873
Private or Public: Private
Religious Affiliation: Christian Church, Disciples of Christ
Location: Urban
Number of Applicants: 14,085
Percent Accepted: 53%
Percent Accepted who enroll: 25%
Number Entering: 1,826
Number of Transfers Accepted each Year: 826
Middle 50% SAT range: M: 530–650, CR: 520–630, Wr: 520–630
Middle 50% ACT range: 23–29
Early admission program EA/ED/None: EA

Percentage accepted through EA or ED: Unreported
EA and ED deadline: 1-Nov
Regular Deadline: 15-Feb
Application Fee: $40
Full time Undergraduate enrollment: 7,539
Total enrollment: 7,853
Percent Male: 41%
Percent Female: 59%
Total Percent Minority or Unreported: 26%
Percent African-American: 5%
Percent Asian/Pacific Islander: 2%
Percent Hispanic: 10%
Percent Native-American: 1%
Percent International: 5%
Percent in-state/out of state: 75%/25%
Percent from Public HS: 65%
Retention Rate: 88%
Graduation Rate 4-year: 54%

Graduation Rate 6-year: 69%
Percent Undergraduates in On-campus housing: 50%
Number of official organized extracurricular organizations: 200
3 Most popular majors: Business Administration and Management, Public Relations, Advertising, and Applied Communication
Student/Faculty ratio: 13:1
Average Class Size: 27
Percent of students going to grad school: 22%
Tuition and Fees: $32,400
In-State Tuition and Fees if different: No difference
Cost for Room and Board: $10,410
Percent receiving financial aid out of those who apply: 79%
Percent receiving financial aid among all students: 78%

Buried in the heart of the Lone Star State, Texas Christian University embodies much of the Deep South. Proud of their football, their Greek life, and their school, students at TCU would not choose to attend any other college.

The Perfect Fit

Texas Christian University offers its students a well-rounded liberal arts education that allows students to experiment with classes outside of their major in the first couple years. The core curriculum, which consists of credits in the humanities, social sciences, natural sciences, fine arts, mathematics, writing, and oral communication as well as a Heritage, Mission, Vision, and Values requirement with emphases on religion, culture, and history, forces students to step outside of their comfort zone. There is also a religious requirement at TCU that requires students to take one religious class during their four years, although they may choose to take more than one. Students, however, are complimentary of the chance to expand their horizons. "They try to create really well-rounded students," said one student. "It has me taking some really weird classes, but it's really cool." This student, who is a mechanical engineer, said he is also taking classes in cultural language, study of the Bible and world regional geography.

In addition, students at TCU must complete their majors' requirements. One sophomore explained that "people in 'technical' majors like nursing or engineering have it much tougher than the liberal arts majors." Students name biology, physics, mathematics, chemistry, accounting/finance, engineering, and nursing as the difficult majors, and advertising/public relations, communications, interior design, and nutrition as the less demanding ones.

The Neeley School of Business houses the most competitive majors, while hardcore studiers are found racing along the premed track. One student interviewed who is a business major said that so far, classes are living up to expectations. He characterized them as "challenging but also reasonable." TCU also offers a highly praised Honors Program, which awards early class registration to students invited to the program upon acceptance to TCU, as well as those who prove themselves capable by first semester grades. In order to stay in the Honors Program, students must fulfill additional class requirements. Many pursue the Chancellor's Leadership Program and specialized programs in the business school in place of the generalized honors curriculum. Texas Christian University strives to maintain small classes of 30 to 40 students. "It's the feel of having a big university with plenty of majors, and at the same time small classes," one student said. One freshman said that none of his classes have had more than 40 students, but that some of the bigger lectures can have many students.

Professors at Texas Christian University are acclaimed by their students. One student interviewed said that he has liked all of his professors so far and praised them for having a sense of humor. Even in a subject that is traditionally viewed as dry and boring, like calculus, this student said his professor was "hilarious."

Living It Up

TCU party life is divided in two ways: underclassmen and upperclassmen, and Greeks and non-Greeks. Underclassmen go to frat parties, house parties, and mixers on the weekends, while upperclassmen prefer bars. However, obtaining alcohol is not much of a problem for anyone at TCU, even for those who are underage.

Since the University is a Christian school, there are many non-drinkers and more alternative social venues for them to enjoy. "I would say that everyone has some sort of religious background," one student said. Another student interviewed said that there are as many fraternity options as there are Christian organizations. A number of concert venues are near campus, and the TCU theater has scheduled performances on most weekends. Further, the Bass Performing Arts Hall provides musical performances, and the Programming Council, part of the student government, plans movies and concerts for students. There is a student center on campus with a ballroom.

Most campus-wide events at TCU are hosted by independent or Greek organizations. One student said that the campus is over 50% Greek and contributes a good deal

to the social life on campus. "I would say Greek life is a pretty big presence, the southern background has a lot to do with it," said one student. The rush process consumes a large amount of student energy. However, another added that which fraternity or sorority you decide to join is strictly a matter of preference. "You find what you want with the Greek thing," said one freshman who is a member of the Beta Theta Pi fraternity. The parties are usually fun and girls are rarely charged for admission or drinks. Most often, it's the fraternity members who fund alcohol purchases and theme parties, the best of which come at Halloween, Christmas, and the end of the year—barring any police presence. Students said that a fraternity or a sorority usually has a mixer on party nights and if you know someone in the Greek organization, parties are easy to attend. Fraternities and sororities also have their annual events which can be a lot of fun, one student added. In addition, big campus concerts are a crowd pleaser. One student said that Blake Shelton came to campus this year for a concert.

The dating life at TCU is mixed. One student said that while he has a girlfriend, he found that most people who enter college do so single. He said that it is perfectly normal to be in a relationship and for those who are single, there is plenty of nightlife where students can meet other people.

Although diversity may be slightly stunted since the school is right in the middle of Texas, students did not seem to feel like the school was significantly hindered in this respect. There are a lot of Texas-born students at TCU, said one student who was from Massachusetts, but there are also students from across the country he continued. He did add however that, "It's not as diverse as other schools I've visited or Ivy League schools."

Living Conditions

Students were complimentary of the living conditions at TCU. "The dorms here are amazing," one student interviewed said. "Of all the schools I've visited, these are the nicest dorms and just about every dorm on campus is that way." TCU has a separate endowment dedicated to landscaping, so you can be sure that the physical campus is beautiful—and safe. The police are easily accessible, and TCU has an all-male organization called "Froggie-Five-O" that gives rides to girls when they have to walk at night. According to one student, mainly upperclassman men can sign up for a job with

"Froggie-Five-O" and drive golf carts around campus to pick up female students after 9 P.M.

Despite the friendly security services, most upperclassmen move off campus to enjoy apartment or house set-ups and lower prices. One student said, "All freshmen have to live on campus, they request sophomores live on campus, and most juniors and seniors live off campus."

Most students, even residents, eat a fair number of meals off campus, because there are a number of off-campus dining options within walking distance of campus and there are few options for dining on campus. The main dining hall on campus is "Good for college cafeteria food," according to one student. He also mentioned a number of other on-campus dining options. There is a sports café near the main cafeteria that serves burgers to students from 9–12 on school nights. Student can use their meal swipes at the sports café. There is also a coffee shop with sandwiches on campus.

As for off-campus eateries there is Joe T. Garcia's and Italian Inn, where the waiters serve and entertain.

Texas Is for Football

"In the fall, it's all about football," one student said.

Football is the most popular spectator sport at Texas Christian University. The Horned Frogs won the Poinsettia Bowl in 2008, but lost in the Fiesta Bowl in 2010. In 2011 they redeemed themselves with a win in the Poinsettia Bowl, but most recently, in 2012, they lost in the Buffalo Wild Wings Bowl. TCU has recently transitioned into the Big 12, a change that students are excited about. The football team draws much school spirit from students and alumni alike. In fact, TCU's traditional spectator chant, "Riff Ram Bah Zoo," is one of the oldest cheers in college history. "It's a really big football school especially in the last 10 years, just about every student goes to the football games," a student said. Another student who is on the football team, said that players glean a lot of media attention, which is exciting.

Unique to TCU are the Purple Hearts, a student organization that helps lure high school football players to the University. For more recreational athletes, IM sports are prevalent at TCU, and the Campus Recreation Center offers state-of-the-art athletic equipment.

TCU students are very involved in numerous extracurricular activities. Many in the student body work part-time jobs, and most are identified by their extracurricular activities. Social organizations, performance groups, intramurals, academic organizations, and service organizations are the most popular. The most heralded organization is Frog Camp, an orientation trip for freshmen for which upperclassmen are leaders. Also highly touted are the Student Government Association, Order of Omega Greek honors society, sports appreciation organizations, and the "eleven40seven" journal of written and visual arts.

Texas Tradition

One thing is clear: TCU is a university bathed in tradition. Along with legendary cheers, students are indoctrinated by a wealth of myth when they accept admission to the school. For example, if you kiss the nose of the iron Horned Frog statue, you will have good luck. The bodies of Addison and Randolph Clark (TCU's founders) are actually cremated inside their bronze statues. It is tradition to raise your right hand and make the horned frog sign with your fingers when the chapel bell rings the alma mater. Another noted that President Lyndon B. Johnson himself broke the ground for the Sid Richardson Science Building when it was built in the seventies.

TCU is a place that people fall in love with, from its glorious oaks to its cheesy mascot: "People take a lot of pride from being Frogs—we're the only Horned Frogs in the nation!"

At the end of the day, students at TCU bleed purple. Full of traditions and football, major requirements and experimental courses, off-campus eating and on-campus eating, when students graduate from TCU they stay forever frogs—*Monica Disare*.

FYI
Biggest college tradition: Football in the fall!
Things I learned my first year: "It is nice to take classes outside of your major and comfort zone. Even a world history class may help a mechanical engineer."
Important notes: Although Greek life is big on campus, since TCU is a Christian school, there are just as many Christian activities on any given night.

Texas Tech University

Address: P.O. Box 45005,
  Lubbock, TX 79409-5005
Phone: 806-742-1480
E-mail address:
  admissions@ttu.edu
Web site URL: www.ttu.edu
Year Founded: 1923
Private or Public: Public
Religious Affiliation: None
Location: Urban
Number of Applicants:
  16,143
Percent Accepted: 72%
**Percent Accepted who
  enroll:** 37%
Number Entering: 4,338
**Number of Transfers
  Accepted each Year:**
  2,818
Middle 50% SAT range:
  M: 520–620, CR: 490–590,
  Wr: 460–570
Middle 50% ACT range:
  22–26
**Early admission program
  EA/ED/None:** None

**Percentage accepted
  through EA or ED:** NA
EA and ED deadline: NA
Regular Deadline: 1-May
Application Fee: $50
**Full time Undergraduate
  enrollment:** 21,258
Total enrollment: 33,000
Percent Male: 56%
Percent Female: 44%
**Total Percent Minority or
  Unreported:** 23%
Percent African-American:
  4%
**Percent Asian/Pacific
  Islander:** 3%
Percent Hispanic: 14%
Percent Native-American:
  1%
Percent International: 1%
**Percent in-state/out of
  state:** 96%/4%
Percent from Public HS:
  84%
Retention Rate: 80%
Graduation Rate 4-year: 27%

Graduation Rate 6-year:
  54%
**Percent Undergraduates in
  On-campus housing:** 26%
**Number of official organized
  extracurricular
  organizations:** 399
3 Most popular majors:
  Health and Physical
  Education, Mechanical
  Engineering, Psychology
Student/Faculty ratio: 18:1
Average Class Size: 15
**Percent of students going to
  grad school:** Unreported
Tuition and Fees: $13,185
**In-State Tuition and Fees if
  different:** $4,875
Cost for Room and Board:
  $7,527
**Percent receiving financial
  aid out of those who apply:**
  46%
**Percent receiving financial
  aid among all students:**
  44%

Red Raiders, austere landscape of the South Plains, and an unrivaled school spirit: They only paint a small yet iconic portion of the picture in Texas Tech University. Enrolling over 31,000 students, with over 17 varsity teams in 11 sports—one of the founders of the Big 12 Conference—offering over 150 degree programs, Texas Tech has continued to place its mark as one of the top public schools in the great state of Texas. The Spanish Renaissance–style buildings—sitting on a 1,839-acre campus—have been described "as one of the most beautiful campuses in the nation." Despite being a large public University, students at Texas Tech agree that their university can still retain the feel of a small liberal arts institution. Not only is Texas Tech vast in size, but also in variety. Students have the chance to leverage Texas Tech's emerging research facilities, explore diverse student groups, and of course, attend the much anticipated football games.

Academics on the Upswing

Students say they are generally happy with the courses offered at Tech, but deciding which classes to take can be a bit of a headache. Students criticized the advising program, claiming that the academic advisors "don't always help them make the right decisions when choosing classes or professors." While one student remarked that his interactions with advisors "left something to be desired," others reported that advisors can actually be helpful. Since the beginning of the spring 2013 semester, Texas Tech students can now leverage a new technology, Visual Skill Builder—when advisors are less than helpful—to plan their schedules for the semester.

Small classes tend to give students the most positive academic experiences at Texas Tech. Introductory classes, particularly in popular departments like business, engineering, family consumer sciences, and English, may have 400 or more students. One student called his experiences in these classes "disappointing, because faculty members are only sometimes accessible and not as often as I'd like." Upper-level classes, however, which contain between 35 and 50 students, are "more satisfying."

Regardless of class size, professors can be available, offering regular, frequent office hours. Students also praised Tech's academic atmosphere. "Even though getting into classes is very competitive, after that process things become more chill," said one student. "The professors and students are, surprisingly, friendly and helpful."

One student highlighted Tech's recent academic improvement and potential for future growth. He said that while "he wants the university to improve its image to improve student marketability," the school has made a lot of progress, as a greater number of small classes are offered and the quality of professors improves. In fact, the University has just completed a new business building and is currently working on a new petroleum engineering building. One Texas Tech organization, Upward Bound, which aids low-income first-generation students, received a federal grant of $2.5 million to be used over the next five years. One student remarked, "We're excited about the changes coming."

At Large in Lubbock

Most students at Texas Tech, especially non-freshmen, live off campus. With over fourteen residence halls, three-suite-style halls, and one apartment complex, university housing has become increasingly convenient, simple, and "sometimes worry free." Students said high-quality off-campus housing is relatively easy to find, even though there are new dorms. In addition to the three apartment complexes across the street from campus, students also live in a residential neighborhood south of campus known as "Tech Terrace." Other popular apartment complexes may be found farther away from campus, but travel to and from these locations usually requires a bus trip.

The University requires that freshmen live on campus, and most students claimed that the experience of living in a dorm was valuable. One student noted that even though she moved off campus by sophomore year, she was "grateful" for her on-campus experience because it was "a good way to interact with people you normally might not interact with." Students also have the option of living on specially assigned Intensive Study or Substance-Free floors (although technically, alcohol and other drugs are prohibited in all dorms).

Student attitudes are generally positive, but not extremely enthusiastic, about the town of Lubbock. One student said that she wished she were "in a bigger city, although I love Lubbock because of the small, tight-knit community." Students say that the town is safe, and there is a separate university police force that "wanders around campus often." One student explained, "You either love Lubbock or you hate it, because there's not a whole lot to do except get involved with things on campus and in the town."

Gregarious Greeks

Getting involved is what Tech students do best. Whether it's involvement in a community outreach program, writing for Tech's newspaper, *The Daily Toreador*, or membership in a service sorority or fraternity, there is no shortage of extracurricular pursuits at Texas Tech.

While Tech's over 400 student organizations cater to a variety of interests, Greek organizations are especially popular. "Greek life is really big, whether you're in it or not," said one student. Fraternities and sororities throw most of the parties at Tech, although because so many students live off campus, non-Greek house parties are common as well. Greek students pointed out that by joining a fraternity or sorority, you are not only part of the single organization, but also a member of the greater Greek community at Tech. One fraternity member noted that "Because Lubbock is so small, you could go to any bar and see many of your friends." Students at Tech are also attracted to Greek life for its service component, and some choose to join service sororities, which place an even greater emphasis on philanthropy. A student who joined both a Greek sorority and a non-Greek service sorority pointed out that while she enjoys Greek life, she has made closer friends through the service sorority because of its smaller size and more personal atmosphere.

The Center for Campus Life, which is the central office for all registered organizations on campus, is located in the Student Union Building. The Student Union, which houses a bookstore, places to eat, a theatre, study rooms, meeting rooms, TVs, and a computing assistance center, has been especially popular among students. One enthusiastic senior remarked, "there are so many great fast food joints in the Student Union!"

The Center for Campus Life also provides a host of entertainment programs and events that range from concerts, interactive games, and movies to more academic-oriented programs like workshops and lecturers. TAB, the Tech Activities Board, also organizes events such as open mike nights, bowling, and foreign film screenings for those looking for an alternative to the Greek life. When football season is in play, countless students participate in RaiderGate, co-hosted by the student government, which is Texas Tech's version of tailgating, complete with live music and barbecue.

A "Dry" Town

Though Lubbock is a "dry" town and liquor stores are prohibited, bars are exempted from this law. In fact, Lubbock has a colorful bar scene—Bleacher's Sports Café, The Library, Rocky's, and Timmy's are student favorites. Because there is "absolutely no alcohol on campus," students drive to an area called the Strip (apparently modeled after Las Vegas) outside of town in order to purchase liquor. One student complained how, "It would be much more convenient to buy alcohol at a local liquor store." While a lot of "house parties go on Friday and Saturday nights," in any case, students agreed that nondrinkers do not feel uncomfortable at Tech.

Red Raiders in a Red State

Students agree that the political climate at Tech and in Lubbock is "very conservative." One student put it this way: "If Obama is not your arch-nemesis, then you're part of the minority." However, an officer of the University Democrats pointed out that liberal students are more common than you might expect, adding that liberalism is "an underground thing." One outspoken female noted how, "feminism is still unaccepted in a place such as Texas Tech."

The student body at Tech is not very diverse, although students claim that the school is taking steps to increase racial diversity. While there is a Gay Straight Alliance at Tech, students agree that the gay community is not very visible. Of the 37 religiously affiliated student organizations at Tech, 30 are Christian groups. One student pointed out that Bible studies are common and well-attended at Tech. Another student agreed that Christian groups are plentiful on campus but added that non-Christians "can still hang out and have fun with Christians." One senior

remarked, "it's more diverse now, compared to 2009" when he first entered as a freshman.

> "Just wait for your first football game, and you'll love it here, seriously."

Tech Takes the Field

Texas Tech is known for its high-caliber sports teams and enthusiastic fans. Cheering on the Red Raiders at football and basketball games is a central part of the Tech experience. Texas Tech recently introduced their new Raiders head coach Kliff Kingsbury, second youngest in college football history. "With Coach Kingsbury, there's no doubt what kind of offense the Red Raiders will run now; he'll be the one to turn our record around." The pregame festivities alone are impressive, with fraternities, sororities, alumni groups, and even local rodeos sponsoring tailgates. "Just wait for your first football game, and you'll love it here, seriously," exclaimed one senior. On the Thursday before a game day, students decorate a statue of Will Rogers and his horse, Soapsuds, with red crepe paper. Even without the streamers, this Tech landmark is full of Tech pride. The horse's behind points straight in the direction of Tech's biggest rival, Texas A&M.

Non-varsity athletes at Tech are not just devoted fans; they are devoted players. Tech students are passionate about intramural sports, and since the expansion of the Student Recreation Center, IMs are more popular than ever. Student organizations, Greek organizations, and dorms field IM teams, and, as one student explained, "Everybody plays; everybody wants to be the best." The Rec Center offers classes, workshops, and even massage therapy.

In the classroom, on the football field, or in the community, Red Raiders are proud to be part of the growth and improvement that characterizes Texas Tech. With a wide array of academic offerings, facilities that are constantly improving, and a rich extracurricular scene, Texas Tech is gaining popularity with Texans and non-Texans alike.—*Kathleen Reeves and Matthew Tran*

FYI

What surprised me the most about Texas Tech when I arrived was "that I did not expect that people here to be this nice, since it's the west, you know."

The biggest college-wide tradition/event at Texas Tech is "Football, Rock The Plaza, and Intramural Sports."

What's the typical weekend schedule? "Wednesday: Hit up a bar called South Beach; Thursday: Go to the Depot District of town; Friday: Hear a country band play at Wild West; Saturday: Football game day! Afterwards, head to a house party or the bars. Sunday: Wake up, spend all day at the library."

Trinity University

Address: One Trinity Place, San Antonio, TX 78212-7200
Phone: 210-999-7207
E-mail address: admissions@trinity.edu
Web site URL: www.trinity.edu
Year Founded: 1869
Private or Public: Private
Religious Affiliation: None
Location: Urban
Number of Applicants: 4,507
Percent Accepted: 61%
Percent Accepted who enroll: 23%
Number Entering: 636
Number of Transfers Accepted each Year: 37
Middle 50% SAT range: M: 590–680, CR: 570–680, Wr: Unreported
Middle 50% ACT range: 26–31
Early admission program EA/ED/None: EA and ED
Percentage accepted through EA or ED: Unreported

EA and ED deadline: EA: 1-Dec, ED: 1-Nov
Regular Deadline: 1-Feb
Application Fee: $50
Full time Undergraduate enrollment: 2,388
Total enrollment: 2,431
Percent Male: 46%
Percent Female: 54%
Total Percent Minority or Unreported: 38%
Percent African-American: 3%
Percent Asian/Pacific Islander: 7%
Percent Hispanic: 13%
Percent Native-American: <1%
Percent International: 7%
Percent in-state/out of state: 71%/29%
Percent from Public HS: 64%
Retention Rate: 89%
Graduation Rate 4-year: 69%

Graduation Rate 6-year: 79%
Percent Undergraduates in On-campus housing: 74%
Number of official organized extracurricular organizations: 130
3 Most popular majors: Business Administration/Management, English, Foreign Languages and Literature
Student/Faculty ratio: 9:1
Average Class Size: 16
Percent of students going to grad school: 34%
Tuition and Fees: $31,176
In-State Tuition and Fees if different: No difference
Cost for Room and Board: $10,966
Percent receiving financial aid out of those who apply: 94%
Percent receiving financial aid among all students: 87%

Trinity University in San Antonio, Texas, has more than just a stunning hilltop campus that offers students a view of the whole of San Antonio, including the downtown area and the hill country. The university offers all the perks of a large, bustling city while still fostering the growth of a tight-knit undergraduate community. With only 2,600 students and a serious undergraduate focus, Trinity is ideal for students looking for a relatively small private university with a strong liberal arts curriculum. The facilities at Trinity cater to every interest from humanities to sciences and everything in between. Trinity has a rich history of community traditions, which are certain to make every student feel like a part of the close community in the heart of Texas.

Hard Work Pays Off

When students graduate from Trinity, they have "had a taste of pretty much everything that is offered." The broad knowledge base possessed by Trinity graduates is due to the Common Curriculum that the university places great emphasis on. According to one student, Trinity just wants "to make sure you're really well-rounded." There are a wide variety of credits that students must get in areas such as Cultural Heritage, Arts and Literature, Human Social Interaction, Natural Science and Technology, Basic Computer Skills, Foreign Language, Lifetime Fitness, Mathematics and Quantitative Reasoning. In addition, freshmen are required to take a First Year Seminar and a Writing Workshop, one each semester, to make sure they have a solid English foundation to carry them through the duration of their college education. Even though some students might consider the task of completing so many general requirements daunting, one freshman said that the Trinity curriculum is nice because "you can get your core classes done whenever."

With 39 majors and 52 minors, Trinity has plenty of options for every student to explore beyond the Common Curriculum. The only problem, as one senior put it, is that the general requirements plus the requirements for individual majors "can add up to be a lot." Of all the majors offered at Trinity, Business and Communications are the two most popular ones. In addition, many students choose to major in one of the modern languages, including Spanish, French, German, Chinese, and Russian. Even though the Common Curriculum combined with a major is a substantial amount of work, one student noted, "[Trinity is] regarded very highly . . . because it's so much work."

Students believe that overall Trinity provides quite a solid liberal arts education with a significant amount of work to boot, but some students say that there are definitely certain departments that give out more work than others. One upperclassman said, "It depends a lot on your major how the workload is." Most students say that science majors tend to be the ones that have heavier workloads, especially the Biochemistry major. Similarly, students add that the individual science classes at Trinity also tend to be the most difficult. A freshman said that Integrative Bio I was her most difficult class and was "impossible to do well in."

Of course, for every "impossible" class to avoid at Trinity, there are plenty of classes that students love to take, including Asian Religions and Classical Rhetorical Theory, which students say are two of the most interesting classes on campus. For freshmen who love the humanities, the HUMA 1600 Readings from Western Culture course presents students with the opportunity to immerse themselves in a comprehensive overview of Western literature while simultaneously knocking out both the First Year Seminar and Writing Workshop in the same semester. Students looking for an easy class will want to head straight to Russian Studies and Cultures, which is considered "a blow-off course for seniors." Regardless of what level of class a student is looking for, from "impossible" to "blow-off" courses, Trinity has something to suit every interest.

Students Who Live Together, Stay Together

Trinity is, at its heart, a strong community dedicated to forging relationships between students where 79 percent of undergraduates live on campus. In order to reinforce the community feel, all freshmen, sophomores, and juniors are required to live in Trinity's residence halls, and 30 percent of seniors choose to live on campus as well. The freshman housing is assigned randomly "with the exception of people who request to be on certain 'themed' halls." An upperclassman said that these "themed" residences are not very big but allow students to live with others who share similar interests, such as language immersion and substance-free living. Freshmen who take the HUMA course at Trinity are offered housing with their classmates so that they can have peer study sessions and share ideas with one another more easily. At the end of freshman year, the rising sophomores are randomly assigned numbers that allow them to choose housing, with the lowest numbers going first when choosing their rooms. Once students are juniors, the housing system changes, and they are allowed to choose housing based on the number of hours they have, which helps to reinforce the strong academic nature of Trinity.

Right from the outset, Trinity aims to make its freshmen feel as welcome as possible, beginning with a New Student Orientation program that lasts for one week before classes start. The period of orientation allows students to meet their fellow classmates and bond with them before their lives are overcome with the rigorous academic culture of the university. During the rest of the year, the university sponsors other events, such as Hallympics, in which the residence halls go head-to-head to compete in athletic competitions. Events like Hallympics help to cultivate the feelings of friendship and closeness that many Trinity students say is a very important part of their college experience.

Hitching a Ride

The larger city of San Antonio is highly accessible to members of the Trinity community because the majority of students on campus have cars. It is difficult to get around the surrounding area without a car because the public transportation in San Antonio is fairly scant. With all the highways and the long distances between local attractions, students need some method of transportation to allow them to explore the local bars, clubs, restaurants, and other venues in the city. If students don't happen to have a car, it's not a huge problem, students say. As one senior put it, "If you don't have [a car], then you'll definitely know someone who does and can give you a ride."

Work Hard, Play Hard

While students at Trinity love their traditions, they have mixed feelings about the Greek scene. One student added that Greek life is not as big of a part of the Trinity social scene because many students would rather participate in groups such as academic frats, Trinity University Volunteer Action Community, a community service group, and Alpha Phi Omega, a community service fraternity, than spend all their time absorbed in the Greek system. One senior noted that interest in Greek life "seems to be more dominant with the girls." So fraternities and sororities are available at Trinity, but they do not dominate the campus completely. One student said that one good aspect of Trinity's Greek scene is that there is plenty of time to "get accustomed to the school before pledging to a group . . . for the rest of your Trinity years." She said that rush happens during the first semester, and pledging does not occur until the spring, leaving a lot of time in between to make sure the Greek system is a good fit for the students who are thinking of entering into it.

"Work hard, play hard (but smart)."

Of course, the fraternities and sororities that are on campus throw lots of parties. One student noted, "Anyone can find a party whenever they want, but they're pretty boring." Another student said that at parties "you'll find first years through seniors from all over campus." She also noted that after students turn 21, they start to frequent local bars instead of frat parties, visiting bars such as Bombay Bicycle Club and Broadway 5050. With parties and bars comes the drinking culture on campus, which students call "very healthy." One student said that Trinity students "work hard, play hard (but smart)." She added that one of the great things about Trinity is that the administration knows the students are going to drink and makes sure

they are safe about it. "Trinity teaches us to be smart, but if something goes wrong, to always call for help," she said. Trinity is not a "dry" campus, and students over 21 are allowed to keep beer and wine in their dorm rooms.

Tradition Keeps a Campus Lively

When students need a break from all of their intense studying, they can turn to the traditions that make Trinity so unique and fun. When a student has a birthday at Trinity, there is often the usual birthday fare—parties, friends, and presents—but what makes birthdays at Trinity extra special is Miller Fountain. Students' friends will kidnap them on their birthday and throw them into the fountain, an experience that is rarely forgotten, especially when a student has a winter birthday.

Another Trinity tradition is known as Calvert Ghosts and happens on Halloween. According to one student, the "freshmen who live in Calvert Hall run around naked on campus," creating an unforgettable Halloween memory for everyone who witnesses the streak. Students also identified the annual library rave as an important tradition and a great way to release pent-up stress. During finals week, hundreds of students take a study break and spontaneously break out dancing in the middle of the library. For a more tame tradition, students can attend Vespers, which is the most widely attended event at Trinity. Vespers is a hallmark event on Trinity campus when the President of the university and the Vice Presidents allow students to come to their homes and "enjoy food, drink, and each other." One senior said that Vespers is "the best way to de-stress a little before finals and a wonderful way to get into the Christmas spirit."—*Christina Hull*

FYI
If I could change one thing about Trinity, I'd "make sure there were campus dogs in addition to our campus cats."
Three things that every student should do before graduating are "go to the library rave, go to Vespers, and get thrown in the fountain."
What differentiates Trinity the most from other colleges is "our close relationships with our professors."

University of Dallas

Address: 1845 East Northgate Drive, Irving, TX 75062
Phone: 972-721-5266
E-mail address: ugadmis@udallas.edu
Web site URL: www.udallas.edu
Year Founded: 1956
Private or Public: Private
Religious Affiliation: Roman Catholic
Location: Urban
Number of Applicants: 1,041
Percent Accepted: 91%
Percent Accepted who enroll: 40%
Number Entering: 376
Number of Transfers Accepted each Year: 81
Middle 50% SAT range: M: 530–650, CR: 550–700, Wr: 540–680
Middle 50% ACT range: 24–30
Early admission program EA/ED/None: EA

Percentage accepted through EA or ED: 35%
EA and ED deadline: 1-Dec
Regular Deadline: 1-Mar
Application Fee: $40
Full time Undergraduate enrollment: 1,322
Total enrollment: 2,843
Percent Male: 49%
Percent Female: 51%
Total Percent Minority or Unreported: 31%
Percent African-American: 1%
Percent Asian/Pacific Islander: 4%
Percent Hispanic: 16%
Percent Native-American: <1%
Percent International: 2%
Percent in-state/out of state: 45%/55%
Percent from Public HS: 43%
Retention Rate: 82%
Graduation Rate 4-year: 46%

Graduation Rate 6-year: 56%
Percent Undergraduates in On-campus housing: 55%
Number of official organized extracurricular organizations: 35
3 Most popular majors: Biology, Business, English
Student/Faculty ratio: 10:1
Average Class Size: 25
Percent of students going to grad school: 25%
Tuition and Fees: $27,500
In-State Tuition and Fees if different: No difference
Cost for Room and Board: $9,326
Percent receiving financial aid out of those who apply: 96%
Percent receiving financial aid among all students: 93%

Amidst the wide variety of colleges and universities in the greater Dallas area, the University of Dallas stands out for its combination of academic rigor and traditional Catholic sensibilities. With a strong emphasis on the Western canon, a comprehensive core curriculum, and a wildly popular study-abroad program in Rome, UD offers its students a structured, traditional education that will serve them well both in and out of the classroom.

Nerdy to the Core

UD has a reputation for being, as one student puts it, a "nerdy" school because of its comprehensive set of requirements known as the core curriculum. The UD core is mostly made up of twenty courses (over two years) that allow students to engage directly with the texts that shape the foundations of Western thought. This curriculum covers philosophy, theology, history, literature, politics, economics, mathematics, science, art, and foreign language. Classes in the Core typically average a class size of 17. In addition, undergraduate students are either enrolled in the Constantin College of Liberal Arts, the College of Business, or the School of Ministry. Graduate students in the Braniff Graduate School of Liberal Arts also follow a similar Core Curriculum.

English is one of the most popular majors at UD, despite the large amounts of reading, writing, and memorization it requires. Psychology is also a favorite, even though majors have to complete a thesis over 100 pages long to graduate. Language and math majors are universally less popular.

No matter what you're majoring in, classes at UD seem to be challenging all around. As one student explains, "UD is hard, a lot harder than the other schools my friends go to . . . you can't find an easy class to shrug off." Though the University is generous with academic and athletic scholarships, they are difficult to maintain: "The academic demands for retaining any scholarships . . . are rigorous, so many students aren't able to slack off even if they don't care." Adding to the academic intensity, there is a very strict attendance policy at UD—missing four classes automatically means that you are dropped from the course. Luckily, students have the support of the faculty to guide them through the rough waters of UD academics; most students are happy with their professors, saying that they are "very accessible— they want you to contact them when you need them." Some popular ones include English professor Father Robert Maguire and economics teacher William Doyle, who help UD kids achieve their "number one goal" of truly learning and internalizing the material that they grapple with.

TGIT: Thank God It's Thursday

Of course, there is much more to life at UD besides its standout academic program. While sports admittedly "aren't the focus of UD," students enjoy participating in and cheering on the teams that they have, including the men's rugby and basketball teams, whose games draw a huge following. Support for women's teams is a little "less vigorous," but both genders play baseball, soccer, and lacrosse. The newly renovated athletic center also provides lots of resources for students to stay in shape, including trainers and state-of-the-art equipment. Overall, as one student puts it, sports are "compatible" with the typical UD student way of life, even if they don't dominate it.

While there are approximately 35 extracurricular activities and clubs in which UD kids can participate, the consensus is that "club life isn't too popular in general, [since] a lot of students are busy studying." However, the student government and activities committee is large and attracts more and more people to its ranks in hopes of increasing the popularity of its events. Since there are no sororities or fraternities, on-campus social life at UD seems to revolve around parties in upperclassmen apartments either on campus or across the street in a group known as "Old Mill." Though some students say that "Student Apartment kids tend to stick to themselves," the parties they throw attract partygoers from all over the UD community. As one girl explains, "Younger and older students intermingle, making it easy for there to always be a party to go to if you have the right connections."

> "Students are true to what they believe, kind and caring, and the farthest from a fake crowd you will ever find."

UD is a wet school, meaning that drinking is tolerated and prevalent throughout campus. While the drinking scene "never really gets out of control," one student admits that "technically, drinking policy is according to the law of the state of Texas, and if you get caught underage, you do get in trouble." Drinkers "tend to stick together" and congregate either at various parties or at a campus bar and grill called the Rathskeller that is actually on the student meal plan. For those who prefer their weekends dry, the student government sponsors a weekly event known as TGIT ("Thank God It's Thursday"), during which students party and dance to live music without the addition of alcohol.

Living in "the Convent"

Socially, UD provides a safe, friendly environment in which students can get to know each other. Despite the small size of the school (nearly 1,300 students), most students claim that its nurturing environment is a help rather than a hindrance. "It's super easy to meet people your first semester, mostly because the school is so small . . . you immediately find your group of friends and settle in for the haul," said one junior. Diversity is a bit lacking at UD, since "most kids are white, hail from a Catholic (or at least Christian) household, and hold the same basic beliefs in common." However, some students claim that "there is a fair amount of diversity in religions and races," emphasizing that the University recognizes the importance of diversifying the student body and is making a conscious effort to do so. Either way, there is no lack of community at UD. As one junior raves, "That's one thing I love about this school . . . absolutely one hundred percent of [students] are genuine. Students are true to what they believe, kind and caring, and the farthest from a fake crowd you will ever find."

All full-time undergraduates at UD fall under a mandatory residence requirement. The UD residential community is made up of seven halls, each of which has its own unique character. Freshmen and sophomores must live on campus in specific dorms, only one of which is coed. The prevalence of same-sex living "though it may seem like a bother, is actually pretty fun . . . dorm spirit is [awesome]." Of the eight dorms, the all-male Gregory and all-girl Jerome are known as the "party dorms," and Catherine, by contrast, is sometimes called "the Convent." All of them, however, have at least two RAs who are "strict" and "are pretty serious about their roles." While some upperclassmen continue to live on campus after sophomore year, most move to the Old Mill apartments across the street or into those in the Student Apartment complex, which are "a lot nicer . . . there's usually a waitlist to get in." The architecture on campus is "not very pretty to look at, but it serves its purpose"—some of UD's architectural standouts include the Braniff Memorial Tower, which is a "landmark for the University" and the newer Art Village, in which a whole group of buildings is "put on stilts, so . . . they pretty much [look like] they're in the trees."

All UD students who live on campus must be on a meal plan, and freshmen can choose between 14- or 19-meal-per-week plans. After freshman year, you can choose between plans of 19, 14, or 10 meals, and the declining balance can be used at the Rathskeller, which is located below the campus's only dining hall in the Haggar University Center. Most upperclassmen tend to get either the lowest amount of meals or no plan at all, since food-wise, "some days are better than others." Others are less diplomatic, saying, "Let's just put it this way—one of the most popular groups on Facebook is 'I starve myself to go to UD.' No one goes here for the dining services." Despite the lack of gourmet options, the dining hall and student center remains one of the central hangout locations on campus.

Dallas to Rome

Since there's "not much to do on campus," many UD students spend their weekends enjoying the restaurants and club scene in the surrounding Texas area. The town of Irving itself is "a little scruffy" and not quite as nice as the school itself, yet town-gown relations are so calm as to be almost nonexistent, as one student describes: "Some people that live 15 minutes from the University have never even heard of it." To really get a taste of college town life, students recommend heading into the bigger city of Dallas itself for the best bar, shopping, and restaurant scenes. They agree, however, that "[since] most places are a few miles away . . . if you want to hang out outside of campus, you need a car." Whether you want to party in downtown clubs, shop in the popular West End or Las Colinas districts, or just grab dinner and a movie with friends, Dallas offers a plethora of opportunities for fun and relaxation off campus.

Perhaps the most well-known component of life at UD and the one that draws in the most students is its Rome program. Most sophomores spend at least one semester studying at UD's campus at Due Santi, just 20 minutes away from Rome itself. For many UD students, Rome is the highlight of their college career, as they take classes in subjects like ancient architecture and travel throughout Italy and Greece on weekends to see the very monuments they study. The Rome program, with its synthesis of Western tradition and Catholic values, and its application of the concepts learned in the classroom to real life, is the epitome of what makes the University of Dallas "a real, true, Catholic, strenuous liberal arts education that will influence all aspects of students' lives."—*Alexandra Bicks*

FYI
If you come to Dallas, you'd better bring: "a formal gown, cowboy hat, and boots."
If I could change one thing about Dallas, I'd: "Make it a little bigger, and pretty up some of that architecture."
Three things everyone should do before graduating are: "[Participate in] all the activities you can, go to Rome, and attend mass at the Cistercian Abbey of Our Lady of Dallas."

University of Houston

Address: 4400 University Drive, Houston, TX 77204-2023
Phone: 713-743-1010
E-mail address: admissions@uh.edu
Web site URL: www.uh.edu
Year Founded: 1927
Private or Public: Public
Religious Affiliation: None
Location: Urban
Number of Applicants: 13,322
Percent Accepted: 70%
Percent Accepted who enroll: 39%
Number Entering: 3,637
Number of Transfers Accepted each Year: 5,687
Middle 50% SAT range: M: 510–620, CR:470–580, Wr: Unreported
Middle 50% ACT range: 20–25
Early admission program EA/ED/None: None

Percentage accepted through EA or ED: NA
EA and ED deadline: NA
Regular Deadline: 1-Apr
Application Fee: $50
Full time Undergraduate enrollment: 22,624
Total enrollment: 30,688
Percent Male: 52%
Percent Female: 48%
Total Percent Minority or Unreported: 76%
Percent African-American: 17%
Percent Asian/Pacific Islander: 25%
Percent Hispanic: 25%
Percent Native-American: <1%
Percent International: 3%
Percent in-state/out of state: 97%/3%
Percent from Public HS: 92%
Retention Rate: 82%
Graduation Rate 4-year: 15%

Graduation Rate 6-year: 46%
Percent Undergraduates in On-campus housing: 15%
Number of official organized extracurricular organizations: 415
3 Most popular majors: Business Administration and Management, Psychology, Social Sciences
Student/Faculty ratio: 23:1
Average Class Size: 25
Percent of students going to grad school: Unreported
Tuition and Fees: $18,601
In-State Tuition and Fees if different: $9,211
Cost for Room and Board: $8,318
Percent receiving financial aid out of those who apply: 79%
Percent receiving financial aid among all students: 61%

Located in the Deep South, the University of Houston Cougars spend their four years living in nice warm weather in the comfort of southern hospitality. Centered in downtown Houston, Texas, students enjoy the temperate climate that rarely drops below freezing temperatures, along with the many quality opportunities that prepare them for the professional world. Because Houston is one of the largest cities in the country, students are in an ideal position to find research opportunities and land internships. With their unique number of academic colleges, drawing a large number of commuters, University of Houston remains unmatched among state universities in terms of student background diversity against the backdrop of the very diverse city of Houston. Quality academics, such as opportunities from the Honors College, and a large diverse student body provide for nearly every degree and extracurricular interest.

An Academic College Just For You

With over 120 majors and minors, more than 40 cutting-edge research centers, a well-known honors college along with many other specialized colleges, a student at the University of Houston would be hard-pressed to find something he or she couldn't do or didn't love. Students at the University embrace the opportunity to explore and apply to the University's 12 academic colleges including Honors College. Colleges like College of Liberal Arts and Social Sciences and College of Natural Sciences and Mathematics provide a mere glimpse at the incredible variety of academic offerings available to the Cougars.

One famous and interesting college that students can claw their way into is the Conrad N. Hilton College of Hotel and Restaurant Management. As one of their more "weird" colleges, students have agreed that the rigor is much the same as the University's other colleges. Underscoring its reputation as a world leader in "hospitality education" is Hilton College's "experiential-learning opportunities." In addition to the traditional courses in accounting and economics, students in this college must complete a minimum of 600 hours of total industry work experience. These practicum hours provide a great opportunity to explore "different facets of the industry, expand your knowledge, and discover your ideal career path," as one junior explained. The Gerald D. Hines College of Architecture is known for offering its students a platform of integrated disciplines, where students and faculty work together in a studio-centric curriculum, supported by a premier digital fabrication facility. The C. T. Bauer College of Business ranks as one of the leading business schools in Texas, attracting students "from over 70 countries." The Colleges of Optometry and Pharmacy have also gained renown across the states. Their graduate program for doctoral studies in literature has made the top lists, even "drawing James Franco to apply."

The Honors College is a "point of pride" at University of Houston, recently raised to tier one research institution status, making it one of three public in Texas and only one in Houston. In line with its reputation, the Honors College has been pioneering a model of excellence in undergraduate education. The Honors College, as a highly selective program, enrolls approximately 500 students each year to study "great books and have great conversations," as one freshman noted. Students in Honors College are required to take a two-semester course titled "The Human Situation," which draws upon and examines texts from the Greek, Roman, Hebrew, Christian, and Islamic cultures of antiquity. Although the course load and rigor tend to be more than the average, students enrolled in this college gain access to many benefits. One sophomore remarked how, compared to non-Honors College classes, "Honors classes are smaller with more face time with the professors, and my classmates are much more motivated than the average UofH student." The Honors College offers students many specialized classes for all majors, priority registration, accessible faculty, a special student community, personal advisors, and distinction among other perks.

At the University of Houston, all bachelor degrees are required to take a 42-hour core curriculum. The core curriculum includes ten categories: communications, mathematics, reasoning, American history, government, humanities, visual and performing arts, natural sciences, social sciences, and writing. But even with these requirement categories, students don't feel "limited in what they can or cannot explore at UofH." One senior looking back noted that she "was very grateful for the core requirements, because it made me take really fascinating classes I would have never thought of taking."

Approachable Professors and Accessible Courses

Although many students choose to major in business, management, marketing, and related support services, they can specialize in more unusual majors as well. The University of Houston has recently introduced a major in biomathematics, a rapidly growing field. There is a consensus around campus that many of the science and engineering courses are rather difficult, while many of the humanities courses, "such as philosophy or sociology are easy and very basic." In the chemistry department, Professor Simon Bott, a well-known and beloved professor, teaches the introductory courses in chemistry, which attracts many students. According to one freshman, "In addition to having a British accent, Professor Bott teaches you to really think. He seriously cares about his students." It also isn't surprising that many professors are very helpful and approachable. "It's not uncommon to see professors rent out rooms under their name to student groups, even when it's not their responsibility" said a club president. Students agree that while many introductory courses can have up to a few hundred people in them, most professors are willing to stay later after class for more than 30 minutes for questions. In one important observation, students frequently spot their president, Renu Khator, walking about campus and occasionally entering classrooms. As one junior explained, "She chats with us about what we're learning, and she really gets into student life." And if that wasn't remarkable, students have also noted how their president will respond to all emails within two days. In other words, students agree that faculty and professors are always willing to listen.

Reputation of Diversity and Commuters

The University of Houston has been at the forefront of encouraging diverse applicants to apply. With students coming from across

Texas, all over the nation, and 137 different countries, University of Houston ranks as the second most ethnically diverse research institution in the nation. As one student put it, "there's no *majority* here. It's really diverse." Many students agree that the combination of Houston being the most diverse city and the University's generous financial aid has contributed to the overall college diversity.

Many Houstonians consider the University of Houston a "commuting university unlike other colleges." Students choose to commute for a variety of reasons—most due to the financial incentive of living at home and its proximity to the University. At the same time, many students who do commute may face up to a "one-hour commute," but as one junior put it, "the University of Houston is worth the long commute." The fact that University of Houston caters to commuters also has other benefits and affords its students greater freedom of mobility. Students cite how this kind of University lends itself to "generating more opportunities and internships because of commuting." According to one senior, "Probably about 60–75% of the student body has cars, and every morning, we literally fight for parking spots." The situation is, nonetheless, improving with the current construction of a new parking garage in addition to their existing three. Despite the large commuting population, the University, student groups, and social scene is "very accommodating, hosting many events on Thursdays."

Housing for Non-Commuters
For students who cannot stand the commute, the University of Houston offers a wide-array of on-campus housing options with varying quality. One of the older and less desirable dorms is Moody Towers. Generally, dorm assignments are "first-come first-serve," and as one student explained, "When there are no other dorms options left, you choose Moody Towers. You can literally see pipes on the ceilings coming out." Fortunately, there are better options. Last year "Cougar Village" opened up its doors to mainly freshmen and is known to "not only be very nice, but also very affordable." Sophomores, juniors, and seniors have a tendency to choose the "Quads," which are also nice and include the preferred Honors dorms. Students who opt for a more apartment- or condominium-style dorm can choose to stay in the Calhoun Lofts. If the housing options don't suit you, one senior reported,

"Ordinarily, juniors and seniors would move off campus and find apartments anyways." Although the campus is located nearby "the third ward, which is definitely not safe," the campus itself is safe and full of friendly Cougars, but of course, administrators warn students to retain some common sense when traveling.

On campus, the University offers its students two meal plans from two cafeterias in addition to many other commercial fast food outlets that are located underground, "which is a must-go place," remarked one student. Many students prefer to dine in "Moody Towers, because of the delicious buffet, from chicken subs to Italian noodles." On the other hand, the "Cougar Place" received very poor reviews from students.

If You Want, We Got
At the University of Houston, students head clubs that cater to an assortment of interests, and even one student commended how, "If UofH doesn't have the group, it's very easy to start one." Depending on the type of club, the students can be "very committed or very relaxed." Martial arts clubs have found a certain niche at the University that attracts students from all sorts of disciplines, including Kendo and Kung Fu. Nerf war clubs and foam sword clubs have also gained an interesting following. Pre-professional clubs have also managed to attract a constant stream of students from each individual academic college. In terms of recreation, the University's Rec Center features seven basketball courts, an entire room devoted to indoor soccer, second floor for machines and cycling, a big swimming pool, and a rock-climbing wall. Students are rarely ever short of activities to do at the university.

In recent years, University of Houston athletics have made great strides, drawing large crowds of students to Cougar home games. Explained one junior, "You go to a home game and you see a sea of red with people yelling Go Coogs with a personal hand sign!" Baseball, basketball, and football play in tier-one collegiate leagues. One student reported, "If you're not quick it's easy to find out that those tickets to these sports games are sold out." But all those denied game tickets still have numerous intramurals to attend.

Live it up, H-Town Style
Outside of the classroom, most Cougars spend time at nearby off-campus houses

for parties or in downtown for the food, dancing, and comedy scene. Many students take advantage of a convenient light rail nearby called the METRORail, which connects students to different parts of downtown.

Many students find the light rail handy as the go-to choice to reach the many clubs, entertainment venues, and fine dining experiences in Houston. The city's dining scene has been heating up lately with the opening of three marvelous restaurants—Oxheart, Underbelly, and Uchi—placing on national best-restaurant lists. Because many students own cars and because of the University's location, students are afforded easy access to many of Houston's hot spots, including "Chinatown for karaoke and tapioca; fashionable Montrose, catering to a lot of yuppies; and the ever-popular shopping center near Rice University." And for students who crave culture, the Houston Museum District contains a renowned coterie of institutions that include the Menil Collection, Rothko Chapel, Museum of African American Culture, Houston Museum of Natural Science, and the Asia Society Texas Center—among many other offerings of the Museum District. To round out the options in downtown, the Theater District also offers discounts for students. As one junior put it, "Houston is a big place to explore, and there's a surprising number of things to do!"

> "You will have the time of your life, meet new people, experience new things, and also have those lifelong friendships that you will hold dearly for life."

When it comes to drinking, University of Houston administrators can be tough, however, on those planning to hold parties, as one student revealed. "Because there is a strict rule on drinking, you must register parties with the reservation office or the University's police station when you serve alcohol. They sometimes even send out agents to check and see if safety procedures are being followed." It is also well known that the University has a no-tolerance policy for those caught drinking underage or those serving underage drinkers. But even with these tight policies on the social scene, one junior noted that at the University of Houston, "You will have the time of your life, meet new people, experience new things, and also have those lifelong friendships that you will hold dearly for life."—*Matthew Tran*

FYI
If you come to the University of Houston, you'd better bring a parking permit.
"What surprised me the most about the University of Houston when I arrived was the diversity."
If you come to the University of Houston, "you'd better leave all your other college gear behind or you'll get *massacred* by Dr. Bott."

University of Texas / Austin

Address: 2400 Inner Campus Drive, Austin, TX 78713-8058
Phone: 512-471-3434
E-mail address: NA
Web site URL: www.utexas.edu
Year Founded: 1883
Private or Public: Public
Religious Affiliation: None
Location: Suburban
Number of Applicants: 27,237
Percent Accepted: 47%
Percent Accepted who enroll: 54%
Number Entering: 7,275
Number of Transfers Accepted each Year: 3,134
Middle 50% SAT range: M: 580–700, CR: 530–670, Wr: 530–670
Middle 50% ACT range: 25–31
Early admission program EA/ED/None: None

Percentage accepted through EA or ED: NA
EA and ED deadline: NA
Regular Deadline: 1-Dec
Application Fee: $60
Full time Undergraduate enrollment: 38,420
Total enrollment: 51,195
Percent Male: 47%
Percent Female: 53%
Total Percent Minority or Unreported: 52%
Percent African-American: 5%
Percent Asian/Pacific Islander: 17%
Percent Hispanic: 17%
Percent Native-American: <1%
Percent International: 4%
Percent in-state/out of state: 92%/8%
Percent from Public HS: Unreported
Retention Rate: 92%
Graduation Rate 4-year: 48%

Graduation Rate 6-year: 76%
Percent Undergraduates in On-campus housing: 20%
Number of official organized extracurricular organizations: 900
3 Most popular majors: Social Sciences, Communication/Journalism, Business/Marketing
Student/Faculty ratio: 18:1
Average Class Size: 14
Percent of students going to grad school: Unreported
Tuition and Fees: $32,506
In-State Tuition and Fees if different: $9,794
Cost for Room and Board: $10,422
Percent receiving financial aid out of those who apply: 64%
Percent receiving financial aid among all students: 49%

When you step onto the sunny campus of the University of Texas, you will immediately know that you are "deep in the heart of Texas." It has been said that everything is bigger in Texas, and this assessment certainly applies to UT. With a campus sprawling over 400 acres, 16 different colleges and schools, 90 research units, and 2,500 dedicated full-time faculty members, UT has the resources to provide for the 50,000 people that comprise its student body. UT students can pursue 100 majors in more than 170 fields of study, take part in the tradition of Longhorn football, and enjoy the vast array of political opportunities and musical performances that can only be found in Austin. The university's ability to combine tradition, excellence, and exploration make it the perfect choice for someone who is looking for a big school that provides learning experiences both inside and outside the classroom.

Learning Longhorn Style

Academics at UT have something for everyone. Many freshmen are admitted directly to a major in one of the university's 11 undergraduate colleges or schools and begin taking classes in that school when they arrive in the fall. Additionally, students who are undecided on their major can enter UT through the School of Undergraduate Studies so that they may have more time to pick a major. Freshmen who began UT during the fall 2010 semester and beyond are required to enroll in a signature course and earn a certain number of "flags" in different academic areas. Signature Courses are first-year-only classes like "Spies, Espionage, and Treason" and "Offensive Art" that help freshmen with college-level writing, research, speaking, and discussion skills. Flags are distributional requirements that ensure students are exposed to courses in a variety of areas such as leadership and ethics, quantitative reasoning, and ethnic diversity.

Even though hundreds of people often attend Intro level courses, UT students agree that faculty members are very accessible. One freshman's professor "met with students one-on-one after the first test to help the students prepare better on the next test." With office hours multiple times a week, professors are more than willing to talk to students in their "cozy offices." All freshmen have the opportunity to carve out a smaller community at UT, whether it is through the multiple honors programs or through the First Year Interest Groups. Freshman honors programs range from business to engineering to Plan II. Plan II is one of the most respected and selective honors programs in the country that "gives students the opportunity to take a broad range of classes within the Liberal Arts school such as Philosophy, Tutorial Courses, Plan II Physics, and World Literature." Admission to this program requires a separate application. While explaining Plan II as a degree is "difficult and confusing to others," students rave that Plan II students have "a great group of people overlooking the program that are very involved in students' lives." The First Year Interest Groups or FIGS are ways for "students who are not in an honors program to form tight-knit groups with other students," a freshman explained.

UT has nine Nobel Prize winners and two Pulitzer Prize winners on its faculty. Students unanimously consider School of Communication's Professor John Daly's Interpersonal Communications course to be one of the best the university has to offer. Other classes that draw crowds are courses for business and premed students, two of UT's most popular majors. While the campus itself has plenty to offer academically, many Longhorns take advantage of one of UT's 650 study abroad programs. One UT student advised, "If you want to study abroad, think about where you want to go early on and plan accordingly." UT's top study abroad destinations include the United Kingdom, Spain, and Italy.

Life Around the Forty Acres

With a school of UT's size, there is not enough room for everyone to live on campus. However, there are housing options to suit everyone's needs, with 14 dorms on campus and multiple off-campus private dorms. The most famous dorm on campus is Jester, which houses 3,200 students alone. It is so big that it even has its own zip code! Students are encouraged to fill out housing applications along with their applications to the university, and many send in deposits before they are accepted to the school. For those who live off-campus, there is a UT-operated shuttle that helps students get around UT's sprawling campus. The shuttle gets high marks, as one freshman explains, because "you rarely have to wait longer than 10 minutes for the bus to arrive."

UT has an extensive array of dining halls and places to eat on campus. Students praise the variety of foods to eat, with vegan and vegetarian options at every meal. For breakfast, students enjoy making waffles with the waffle machine. As one Longhorn summed it up, "I wouldn't say the food is so delicious that I would never get sick of it, but the food tastes much better than I had expected!"

Longhorns–Keeping Austin Weird

UT students rave about all there is to see and do, both on campus and in and around the city of Austin. UT is home to the world's first photograph, some of the artwork of Frieda Kahlo, and the Blanton Museum, the largest college art museum in the country. History-loving students and visitors alike enjoy the Lyndon Baines Johnson Presidential Library, the most visited presidential library in the United States. The university has welcomed speakers like the Dalai Lama, Barack Obama, Bill Gates, and Al Gore, as well as performers like Jerry Seinfeld and Kanye West in recent years. Students agree that a visit to the Harry Ransome Center is a "must before graduation." Some of the items this cultural archives center contains include a Gutenberg Bible, manuscripts of Ernest Hemingway, and the collections of Woody Allen. Longhorns also enjoy the Texas Revue, the university-wide talent show.

As one senior put it, "The best thing about UT is the variety. There is truly something for everyone." There are over 900 student organizations on campus. Students agree that the best way to make the most of your time at UT is to get involved on campus. Warned one junior, "If you don't get involved, you might run the risk of getting lost in the crowd."

The city of Austin is consistently ranked as one of the most livable cities in America. According to one UT junior, "The city is so driven and energized by our university." Students with interests in politics love that they can intern at the Capitol of Texas. Additionally, Longhorns are committed to the environment, and they have made great strides to make their campus more sustainable and eco-friendly. "I have not met anyone, including my conservative mother, who doesn't love Austin," explained one UT senior. With all of its resources, Austin acts as UT's biggest classroom.

Every year, thousands of music lovers descend upon the "Live Music Capital of the World" for the annual Austin City Limits Music Festival. The South by Southwest Conference exposes students to original music, independent films, and emerging technologies every year. The legendary Cactus Café in the Texas Union is one of the most intimate live music venues in the country.

Students do find the lack of green space on campus frustrating. However, "surrounding Austin helps make up for it with venues like Lady Bird Lake and Zilker Metropolitan Park." Longhorns enjoy taking a break from classes and spending time on the lake. Weekend trips often involve visits to the deep Texas Hill Country. Austin boasts an average daily temperature of about 70 degrees and more than 300 days of sunshine each year, so Longhorns take advantage of the more than 50 miles of hike and bike trails just minutes from campus. Students also enjoy visiting the "famous yet infamous 6th street downtown."

Hook 'em, Horns

At UT, football isn't just a game, it's a way of life. Students spend Saturdays in the fall packing into the 90,000-seat Darrell K. Royal-Texas Memorial Stadium to cheer their beloved Longhorns to victory. Students unanimously agree that the Red River Rivalry game against OU in Dallas's Cotton Bowl is an event not to be missed. UT fans have a lot to cheer for, as the Longhorns have claimed 47 total national championships.

Students are united by their love of singing "The Eyes of Texas" at athletic events and seeing the Tower lit burnt orange.

Another important aspect of UT life is the Greek system. While a large number of students "go Greek," those who decide not to are still invited to attend the parties. Students enjoy going to fraternity parties on Friday and Saturday nights. Much of UT's social life is centered around Greek-hosted social events, but in a community of 50,000 people, there is always something to do that is not Greek-related.

> **"I have not met anyone, including my conservative mother, who doesn't love Austin."**

Students at UT are passionate about all aspects of their collegiate life. UT "definitely combines academics, athletics, and a social scene." Despite all the different activities, interests, and goals of the gigantic student body, all Longhorns are united by the fact that they truly bleed burnt orange. Students initially have to work to carve out a community for themselves by taking the initiative to meet their professors and get involved on campus. According to one Longhorn junior, "Things won't just come to you unless you work for them. I've found, though, that there is a great payoff to this initial investment."
—*Alexa Sassin*

FYI

If you come to UT, you'd better bring some "burnt orange clothes, cowboy boots, and a pair of walking shoes because the campus is big."

What's the typical weekend schedule? "Thursday night: go downtown to Sixth Street. Friday: Go to class and get a little homework done. Head to West Campus to partake in whatever is going on that night. Grab some late night Kerby Lane queso or a Big Bite 'phat sandwich.' Saturday: Tailgate with friends before the football game and then cheer on the Longhorns to victory. Later that evening, attend parties hosted by the Greek community. Sunday: Grab breakfast at Juan in a Million. Attend extracurricular meetings. Hit the books and get ready for the school week ahead."

If I could change one thing about UT, I'd: "make more parking available to students."

Three things every student at UT should do before graduation are: "1. Attend the OU/Texas football game. 2. Take a tour of the Tower. 3. Go downtown and explore all Austin has to offer, like the Austin City Limits Music Festival, Sixth Street, and Lady Bird Lake."

Utah

Brigham Young University

Address: A-153 ASB, Provo, UT 84602
Phone: 801-422-2507
E-mail address: admissions@byu.edu
Web site URL: www.byu.edu
Year Founded: 1875
Private or Public: Private
Religious Affiliation: Church of Jesus Christ of Latter-Day Saints
Location: Urban
Number of Applicants: 10,182
Percent Accepted: 68%
Percent Accepted who enroll: 77%
Number Entering: 6,500
Number of Transfers Accepted each Year: 1,500
Middle 50% SAT range: M: 570–680, CR: 550–670, Wr: Unreported
Middle 50% ACT range: 25–30
Early admission program EA/ED/None: None

Percentage accepted through EA or ED: NA
EA and ED deadline: NA
Regular Deadline: 1-Feb
Application Fee: $30
Full time Undergraduate enrollment: 30,000
Total enrollment: 32,992
Percent Male: 51%
Percent Female: 49%
Total Percent Minority or Unreported: 11%
Percent African-American: <1%
Percent Asian/Pacific Islander: 3%
Percent Hispanic: 3%
Percent Native-American: <1%
Percent International: 3%
Percent in-state/out of state: 33%/67%
Percent from Public HS: Unreported
Retention Rate: Unreported
Graduation Rate 4-year: 21%
Graduation Rate 6-year: 54%

Percent Undergraduates in On-campus housing: 11%
Number of official organized extracurricular organizations: 390
3 Most popular majors: Business, Education, Social Sciences
Student/Faculty ratio: 23:1
Average Class Size: 25
Percent of students going to grad school: Unreported
Tuition and Fees: Member of The Church of Jesus Christ of Latter-day Saints: $4,080, Non-member of The Church of Jesus Christ of Latter-day Saints: $9,160
In-State Tuition and Fees if different: No difference
Cost for Room and Board: $6,460
Percent receiving financial aid out of those who apply: 54%
Percent receiving financial aid among all students: 20%

Set on 560 pristine acres in Provo, Utah, Brigham Young University offers a strong academic education in a beautiful environment. With its religious affiliation with the Church of Jesus Christ of Latter-Day Saints, BYU is certainly not your typical college. One of the most significant differences that you might notice is the policy against drinking—and the students' willing adherence to it.

Integrated Secular and Spiritual Education

BYU is known for strong academics, and the reputation is well-deserved. Students say there is a pretty heavy workload, but that they always find time to have fun. A student, reflecting on his and his friends' academic schedules, said, "it's not extreme unless you make it that way." Students are also very satisfied with the range of classes offered for every interest at every level. They say that some of the strongest and most popular majors are in business and marketing, education, and social sciences.

The most distinctive aspect of BYU lies in the university's religious affiliation with the Church of Jesus Christ of Latter-Day Saints. Academically, the philosophy of BYU is that truth comes from God, so secular learning and spiritual learning are parts of a whole. Often, students defer enrollment, taking a gap year to do missionary work in a foreign country. Other students attend BYU for their freshman year, and then take a year or two off to complete a mission. The missions also act as immersion programs, allowing students to experience a new and foreign culture. Forty-five percent of students go on mission trips, adding to the international cultural awareness of the campus.

As part of its undergraduate degree requirements, BYU has a University Core consisting of 18 requirements that are divided into five categories: Doctrinal Foundations; The Individual and Society; Skills; Arts, Letters, and Sciences; and Electives. The Doctrinal Foundations requirements include studying the Book of Mormon, the New Testament, and Doctrine and Covenants. These contribute to the 14 credit hours of required religion coursework throughout a student's time at BYU. Every Tuesday, BYU holds Devotionals and forums where students can go to listen to and meet prominent figures in the Church, world leaders, and scholars. Professors in other subjects at the University are encouraged to make connections between their material and religion as well.

Housing and Food
Also, because the Church owns the university, operating costs, tuition, and fees are greatly subsidized, and many students receive full merit-based scholarships. As a result, students laugh about how "food is more expensive than tuition." Meal options for BYU students vary greatly. There are a large variety of places on campus where meal cards can be used, from Cannon Commons, the cafeteria, to the fancy Skyroom Restaurant on the top floor of the student center or the Jamba Juice on campus. Students can also use points from their meal plans to buy groceries from the Creamery.

Students have the options of apartment-style living with in-suite kitchens as well as a foreign language residence where students commit to only speak a selected foreign language while in their apartments. The housing policies at BYU reflect the University's emphasis on chastity. The dorms at BYU are separated by gender with restrictions on people of the opposite sex being in housing buildings after 1:30 a.m. on Fridays and after midnight on all other days. These policies are actually a part of the Honor Code, which dictates specific visiting hours for each individual dorm and even off-campus housing for single students.

Fun without Alcohol
One significant characteristic that distinguishes BYU from other universities is the spirit and atmosphere of the students' social life. BYU has an honor code that students and faculty alike take very seriously. Among the provisions of the Honor Code are the typical "be honest" and "respect others," but there is also a rule that men must be clean-shaven at all times. The one policy that is most prominently evident—and often shocking to students at other universities—is abstinence from alcohol and caffeine, as dictated by Mormon beliefs.

For many schools, students' social activities will often involve drinking, and it can even be hard to imagine a university where alcohol is not present. But at BYU, students embrace the policy, arguing instead that "it's great for social life." One student said, "People are more creative about things to do because there needs to be more to a party than just an open cooler."

> "People are more creative about things to do because there needs to be more to a party than just an open cooler."

Instead, students have fun at events like dances run by the student government, often multiple times a week, that have themes like swing, '80s, and country. Students say there are always people hanging out in the dorms and around campus. At later hours at night, though, students migrate to outside the dorms because of the gender restrictions on housing buildings. In terms of interaction between the sexes, students say that one of the biggest myths about BYU—namely that students go to BYU to get married—is not that far off the mark. One student noted that students do marry earlier than at other colleges.

Sports and Leisure
BYU's symbol is a giant white "Y" on the mountain above the school. Yes, the mountain is above the school. Students are extremely active in sports, especially skiing and snowboarding. BYU's intramural sports program is very popular, and creative adjustments are made to promote participation. One student remarked, "My favorite weird one is inner-tube water polo. The idea is to make the game more accessible to people who aren't amazing swimmers."

Apart from intramural sports, BYU competes in the NCAA's Division I Mountain West Conference. The university's varsity sports are competitive, with its football and men's basketball teams ranked fairly high. Other sports in which BYU's Cougars are a major force are volleyball, rugby, and soccer.

People of Provo

Perhaps it is the beauty and peacefulness of Provo that causes it, but the people at BYU are very friendly. One freshman explained, "When you walk past someone here that you don't know, they always say hi instead of awkwardly looking away like anywhere else. It's weird for a few days, but after that, it's wonderful." Additionally, BYU's huge expanse of a campus creates a very serene and isolated environment for students. Many students said that BYU is such a safe place and the students are so respectful toward one another that they don't worry about nodding off to sleep on the grass with their laptops next to them: "The crime report section of the paper is a big joke."

As might be expected by the school's religious affiliation, the vast majority of students are Mormon. At the same time, the Mormon population is largely distributed throughout the world, with the majority living outside of the United States. As a result, even though BYU's student body is religiously homogenous, cultural diversity is not completely lacking. BYU also has a focus in international studies, offering courses in over sixty languages. About one third of the student body is enrolled in foreign language courses during any given semester, a proportion that is four times the national average, and BYU's Russian program is one of the largest in the nation.

BYU provides its students with an academic and social environment that is really unlike that of any other university. While restrictions abound, from the dress code to an emphasis on chastity, students love their beautiful school and the unique experience it gives them.—*Michelle Yu*

FYI

If you come to BYU, you'd better bring "a snowboard or skis, and a razor if you're a guy."

What is the typical weekend schedule? "At least one dance and a well-organized group date, normally something silly and free/cheap."

If I could change one thing about BYU, I'd "loosen the dress code and un-restrict dorm visiting hours."

Three things every student at BYU should do before graduating are "hike the Y, take a dance class, and attend all of the devotionals and forums."

University of Utah

Address: 201 South 1460 East, Salt Lake City, UT 84112
Phone: 801-581-7281
E-mail address: admissions@sa.utah.edu
Web site URL: www.utah.edu
Year Founded: 1850
Private or Public: Public
Religious Affiliation: None
Location: Urban
Number of Applicants: 8,364
Percent Accepted: 83%
Percent Accepted who enroll: 40%
Number Entering: 3,110
Number of Transfers Accepted each Year: 2,753
Middle 50% SAT range: M: 510–630, CR: 490–630, WR: 490–610
Middle 50% ACT range: 21–27
Early admission program EA/ED/None: None

Percentage accepted through EA or ED: NA
EA and ED deadline: NA
Regular Deadline: 1-Apr
Application Fee: $45
Full time Undergraduate enrollment: 23,371
Total enrollment: 30,819
Percent Male: 53%
Percent Female: 47%
Total Percent Minority or Unreported: 28%
Percent African-American: 1%
Percent Asian/Pacific Islander: 5%
Percent Hispanic: 5%
Percent Native-American: 1%
Percent International: 6%
Percent in-state/out of state: 80%/20%
Percent from Public HS: Unreported
Retention Rate: 83%
Graduation Rate 4-year: 20%

Graduation Rate 6-year: 51%
Percent Undergraduates in On-campus housing: 13%
Number of official organized extracurricular organizations: 154
3 Most popular majors: Social Sciences, Business/Marketing, Journalism
Student/Faculty ratio: 15:1
Average Class Size: 30
Percent of students going to grad school: Unreported
Tuition and Fees: $21,389
In-State Tuition and Fees if different: $6,763
Cost for Room and Board: $6,699
Percent receiving financial aid out of those who apply: Unreported
Percent receiving financial aid among all students: Unreported

At the feet of the Wasatch Mountains and in the heart of Salt Lake City, the University of Utah, in many ways, offers the best of the West. Motivated students will find it offers all the intellectual challenge they are looking for, and it is an unusual example of a large university where student input matters a great deal. Those seeking a friendly, small-town feel in the setting of a large university and who are willing to forego cultural diversity will find a happy home at the University of Utah.

Hidden Opportunities for Challenge

Students of all levels of seniority agree that it can be easy to coast at the University of Utah ("the U," to those in the know), since there is a strong flow of student-to-student information about which are the easiest classes and most lenient professors. Several of the largest majors also require many large lecture classes—which tend to be the easiest—and relatively few small seminar-style classes. Those same large lecture classes are the paths to general education credits for many students, few of whom struggle to fulfill the

distributional requirements. Many students take advantage of this opportunity to get outside their discipline for a painless foray into Survey of Jazz or Introduction to Music, for example.

At the same time, students hoping to be challenged will not be disappointed if they are willing to do their own legwork. The University divides its academic disciplines into colleges, including an Honors College, which offers Honors Degree and Honors Certificate options to accepted applicants. The University has expanded the honors program in the last several years, and students who take part sing praises of more engaged professors, more classroom discussion, and assignments that are, in one student's words, "more open-ended, rather than 'Answer 10 questions from the book.'" The U is also very willing to accept credit for advanced high school classes and even "life experience." One senior remarked with candor, "I knew it was going to be an okay education that would qualify me for graduate school, but the opportunities available surprised me, and I've been very impressed."

There can be no doubt that the University

of Utah is a research institution where science is king. The University's engineering and premedical programs are regarded as the most challenging, and the students in them as the "smartest" at the University. Many students at the U come expressly to take advantage of the science faculty and facilities, and Engineering, Biology, and Chemistry are popular majors. Changing majors and double majoring are very common at the U, so many students have experience in both the sciences and the humanities—departments that are located on opposite sides of the very large campus—and have an easy time finding common academic ground. But students do feel a stark disparity in department funding, with the sciences garnering the majority of state grants to the school. The Utah Science Technology and Research (USTAR) program is a special initiative that directs state funding to scientific research initiatives that program directors hope will result in company and job creation in the state of Utah. The University also continues to draw national attention for its cardiology division and such faculty as geneticist Mario Capecchi, who won the 2007 Nobel Prize in Physiology or Medicine and is a source of pride for students in all disciplines.

> "I knew it was going to be an okay education that would qualify me for graduate school, but the opportunities available surprised me, and I've been very impressed."

The U is well connected to Salt Lake City, where the majority of University of Utah alumni remain after graduation. Many students benefit from the Career Services office, which has access to a strong network of internship and job opportunities in the city. Academic advising is markedly less popular. Students complain of advisors recommending classes that are too easy or unnecessary for their major. Some intrepid students supplement their advising needs: "When the advisors aren't helpful, I turn to former professors. Every time I've wanted to meet with a professor, they've made time for me," explained one student. Faculty at the U is broadly regarded as friendly, accessible, and generally interested in the success and satisfaction of their students. Bad professors are weeded out of the undergraduate teaching body through

student advisory committees' input or through dwindling class sizes that speak for themselves.

Alternatives to Mom and Dad's House

The phrase "commuter campus" is deeply entrenched in University of Utah students' vocabulary. An overwhelming majority of students live off campus, and because much of the student body is from the Salt Lake City area, many live with their parents. Similarly, many students come into the U with the same group of friends they had in high school, and socialize primarily with that group. Those who choose not to live with their parents often find off-campus housing—which is generally cheap in the area around campus—with their network of high school friends. Meanwhile, on-campus housing presents opportunities for students who want to look outside their high school crowd. The University, the International Olympic Committee, and Salt Lake City joined to rebuild University housing when the city hosted the 2002 Winter Olympics and used residence halls for athletes' housing. Dorms are now spacious, and located in one of the prettiest parts of campus. "The residence buildings are red brick, and it's really nice when you can be in your dorm room, and then walk 5 or 10 minutes and be on the trails where you can walk or hike," said one junior.

Freshmen living on campus are required to buy a meal plan, but upperclassmen housing often includes kitchens. Few students at the U have complaints about the quality of the food, but many find its repetition disappointing. As the U undertakes extensive property development—including renovations of many class buildings and the Marriott Library and construction of a new Student Life Building to replace the Field House as the home of student recreation—the administration is increasingly focusing on taking the University in a greener, more renewable direction. On-campus and off-campus students alike enjoy the social benefits of two fraternity and sorority systems at the University of Utah. The first is the traditional Greek system common to many large universities. "Greek row" is as close to the University proper as it could be while remaining nominally off campus, and therefore exempt from the University's well-enforced dry campus policy. Parties on Greek row are a weekend activity that draws even off-campus students. The other system of fraternities and sororities is an outgrowth of the large number of practicing members of the Church of Jesus Christ of Latter-Day Saints at the U, who make up about half the student body. "The LDS Institute, across the street from campus, is a big hangout," said one student. "They have their own activities and their own version of the Greek system."

Students often occupy themselves outside class at the Gateway, an open-air promenade in downtown Salt Lake City with restaurants and a movie theater, and on nearby ski slopes such as Alta, Snowbird, and Park City, the last of which hosted numerous Winter Olympics events and boasts, in one student's opinion, "the best snow in the world." The OneLove Ski and Snowboard Club and the Utah Freeskier Society are two of the largest student groups on campus. While students do need transportation to the slopes, a car is not a real necessity for taking part in most activities around Salt Lake City. The city is home to a well-developed bus system and light rail, both of which run in and around the campus and are free to University of Utah students. But because so many students come from the area and live off campus, many have cars, so parking near the U is competitive.

Social goings-on at the U are accessible to students of all years and ages. Because the University is home to a large "non-traditional" student population, including older-than-average and married students, many undergraduates find that, in the words of one senior, "They have no idea what year people are," so all comers are welcome at social events.

"I Am a Utah Man, Sir, and Will Be Till I Die; Ki! Yi!"

Recent sports seasons have been good to the University of Utah Utes, which is good news for students at the U, and for residents of much of the Salt Lake City valley, which divides its fervent allegiance between the University of Utah and nearby rival Brigham Young University (BYU). Utah fans sign up in droves to be part of the Mighty Utah Student Section (the MUSS, taken from a line in the school song), which has a waiting list. Membership entitles students to prime seating at Utah games, and one member describes it as "the best rush you could ever

have. Since we are a dry campus, where else are you going to get 5,000 students together at a game to cheer and have a good time?"

The MUSS has done much to address worries about lackluster student involvement at the U. Club officers can be hindered, when organizing events, by the volume of students who live off campus, many of whom also work 20–40 hours per week, and so do not endeavor to participate in the hundreds of student groups on campus. Those students who are involved on campus have undertaken efforts to raise student awareness of the extracurricular opportunities at the U. One such effort is the U Book, a brainchild of the Student Alumni Board. The U Book contains information about various student groups, 50 University of Utah traditions, including athletic events like Homecoming and the Utah-BYU football game, places to visit on campus and around Salt Lake City, and annual student events like the Hunger Banquet.

Still, the size and influence of the Associated Students at the University of Utah (ASUU)—the school's student government—are especially noteworthy given the challenges of engaging a geographically spread out student body with diverse interests. A relatively large number of students take part and most of the remaining student body is well informed about current issues up for debate. ASUU efforts also produce results. A recent example is the Graduation Guarantee, under which the University guarantees that by fulfilling a series of advising requirements, all incoming freshmen and transfer students will graduate in four years, or the University will pay for or waive the remaining requirements for graduation. The University approved and began implementing the Guarantee shortly after the ASUU passed the student initiative.

The University of Utah adheres to and helps define the libertarian spirit that prevails in much of Utah. Students define the course and rigor of their own education, and many find that what they learn is immediately applicable in the work force; they work together to govern themselves as much as possible, and many remain in the Salt Lake City area and continue to engage with the U as donors, board members, and die-hard Ute fans. In the words of a nostalgic second-semester senior, "I didn't expect to feel this way, but I want to come back, and I want to support my school."—*Elizabeth Woods*

FYI

If you come to the University of Utah, you'd better bring "your skis and good walking shoes to get around campus."

What is the typical weekend schedule? "Go to a concert or other student performance Friday night, sleep in Saturday and have a leisurely brunch with friends, head to the MUSS tailgate and then the football game, and spend the rest of the night at after parties."

If I could change one thing about the University of Utah, I'd "have more people live on campus, to create more of a community."

Three things every student should do before graduating are "join the MUSS, spend time in the Wasatch Mountains, and finish the U Book."

Vermont

Bennington College

Address: One College Drive, Bennington, VT 05201
Phone: 800-833-6845
E-mail address: admissions@bennington.edu
Web site URL: www.bennington.edu
Year Founded: 1932
Private or Public: Private
Religious Affiliation: None
Location: Rural
Number of Applicants: 1,057
Percent Accepted: 62%
Percent Accepted who enroll: 29%
Number Entering: 190
Number of Transfers Accepted each Year: 56
Middle 50% SAT range: M: 560–660, CR: 620–720, Wr: 646–768
Middle 50% ACT range: 24–28
Early admission program EA/ED/None: ED

Percentage accepted through EA or ED: 60%
EA and ED deadline: 15-Nov
Regular Deadline: 3-Jan
Application Fee: $60
Full time Undergraduate enrollment: 618
Total enrollment: 618
Percent Male: 34%
Percent Female: 66%
Total Percent Minority or Unreported: 17%
Percent African-American: 2%
Percent Asian/Pacific Islander: 2%
Percent Hispanic: 3%
Percent Native-American: <1%
Percent International: 4%
Percent in-state/out of state: 4%/96%
Percent from Public HS: 59%
Retention Rate: 89%
Graduation Rate 4-year: 45%

Graduation Rate 6-year: 59%
Percent Undergraduates in On-campus housing: 98%
Number of official organized extracurricular organizations: 21
3 Most popular majors: Drama, English, Visual and Performing Arts
Student/Faculty ratio: 9:1
Average Class Size: 15
Percent of students going to grad school: Unreported
Tuition and Fees: $38,270
In-State Tuition and Fees if different: No difference
Cost for Room and Board: $10,680
Percent receiving financial aid out of those who apply: 87%
Percent receiving financial aid among all students: 77%

Located in the Green Mountains of southwestern Vermont, Bennington College boasts 300 wooded acres, five acres of tilled farmland, 15 acres of wetland, 80 species of trees and 121 species of birds. How's that for diversity?

Small and remote, Bennington attracts an equally intellectually diverse range of students, who come for the individualized academics and the intimate campus—not to mention the theme parties.

Flex Your Academic Muscle

Bennington's academic system is unique. There are no majors at Bennington; instead, students develop a "focus" or a "concentration" themselves with large input from a faculty adviser. Focuses can range from the more traditional, such as mathematics, to the absolutely untraditional, such as storytelling. With the help of a faculty adviser, students plan their course load to best suit their focus, a method called the Plan Process.

Some students relish this academic freedom, saying that it forces you to really "think about your education" and engage in your academic career. For example, one student, who is focusing on "painting and education," said he planned his course load to involve a lot of sciences so he could learn things like the chemistry used to make paint pigment. A junior with a focus in literature said, "The best students are the ones who do take advantage of the flexibility." Indeed, students agreed that the best academic careers are the ones that are cross-disciplinary, to use all of Bennington's resources.

But while many students laud this different

take on academics, others say it encourages floundering, and in fact sometimes attracts "terrifically unmotivated" students. "No one is forced to get specific, so everyone is doing everything," one junior said. "Freedom is good for some people, but for most it is just too much." Along with no majors, grades are also optional at Bennington, with narrative evaluations available as an alternative option. Those with grad school plans typically opt for grades, but many other students opt out, helping to contribute to the somewhat misguided perception of Bennington as a "slacker school."

The most popular concentrations at Bennington are the visual arts, dance, writing, and language programs. In fact, much of modern dance was developed at Bennington, whose program was founded by pioneer Martha Graham. The current faculty boasts many literature standouts, and a recent project brought a group of South African leaders to campus to lead classes in the social sciences.

> **"I feel like the main thing you learn at Bennington is how to educate yourself."**

Because of the "planning" system's built-in one-on-one time with faculty members, and because of the small size of the school, students are very close to professors. "I call most professors by their first name," said the student concentrating in painting and education. Other students say they frequently have lunch with their professors, and know their families. But again, this closeness seems to be a double-edged sword; some students complained that professors are almost "too nice," and as a result there is a kind of pressure to befriend all your professors to get ahead. "Something that goes hand in hand with extremely personal relationships is that there is favoritism."

One of the biggest draws to Bennington is the Field Work Term (FWT), a seven-week winter term during which students take internships at various institutions across the country and the world. An annual requirement for graduation, the FWT provides the opportunity to work at places such as the San Francisco Museum of Modern Art, the Pittsburgh Zoo, and Houghton Mifflin Publishing Company. Many students enjoy the FWT as an opportunity not only to apply what they've learned to the real world, but also to take a break from life at Bennington's small and remote campus.

Do-It-Yourself Extracurriculars

Although it is a small campus, Bennington offers any extracurricular group you might want—if you're willing to create it. Because it is such a small school, most clubs come and go, with students forming new ones every year. Long-term groups include the school newspaper; the literary magazine *Silo*; the campus radio station, WHIP; and the perennially popular Outing Club, which sponsors skiing, horseback riding, rock climbing, and hiking trips in the neighboring Green Mountains. There are also community service groups, including the Student Action Network (SAN) and the Community Outreach Leadership Team (COLT). One current club, sure to be a keeper, is Sugar Bush, in which students make maple syrup from nearby trees.

If you're looking for sports at Bennington, though, you're out of luck. As one junior bluntly puts it, "Why would anyone interested in sports come to Bennington?" There are no varsity sports teams, and the only club team is coed soccer, which has been known to play nearby high schools. And forget about intramurals. (Students have recently started a dodgeball team, though.) Instead, Bennington students focus their energy on the great outdoors, the free fitness classes, and the "great" rec center—complete with climbing wall and sauna.

The Birthplace of the Theme Party

What Bennington may lack in athletics, it surely makes up for in theme parties. "Bennington is pretty much the birthplace of the theme party," one arts concentrator said. Another seconded, "You'll pretty much never go to a party at Bennington that isn't a theme party." Popular parties in the past have included pirates versus ninjas, Pigstock (a pig roast with live music), the "office party," and the huge roller-disco party, Rollerama. Every year, the college puts on SunFest, a music festival on the central lawn featuring 10 to 15 bands during the day. The recent addition of MoonFest the night before is also popular.

Although theme parties are truly the dominant social scene, there are a few other outlets for those not wanting to get dressed up. The campus brings in two to three live bands each week, most of which are small, indie-rock groups, most famously the White Stripes. There is also the occasional unthemed house party, though those are few and far between.

Drinking and drugs are both prevalent at Bennington, though not out of control. "Drugs are in your face if you look for them, they are not in your face if you do not," one male junior said. "They don't dominate the social scene. Parties are still fun if you aren't into that stuff—no one is going to force them on you, or think you're not cool if you're not into them."

From Colonial to Co-op
Bennington's version of student housing is as unique as its take on academics. Bennington offers five types of housing: a drug-free house on campus, an organic co-op off campus, colonial houses, 1970s modern houses, and 2001 contemporary houses. Each house accommodates 25 to 30 students and is managed by two students selected by their peers. These students run Sunday evening "coffee houses" to discuss community issues or just to chat. Students across the board describe Bennington housing as "amazing." Not only are the houses beautiful, but the system guarantees that you'll end up living with your friends—and guarantees a single for junior and senior years.

Students are less unequivocally enthusiastic about the meal plan. Though the food is good by college standards, with plenty of vegetarian and meat options, all students must be on the same three-meal-a-day meal plan for all four years. So even though most houses come equipped with a kitchen, students rarely eat anywhere but the dining hall.

In fact, for the most part, students rarely venture far off the Bennington campus.

Many students have cars, and thanks to a "ride board," rides are easy to find, but most choose to stay on what they consider a "really self-sufficient campus." That campus, while intellectually and increasingly socioeconomically diverse, is noticeably lacking in ethnic or cultural diversity. "It is sad," one student said. "This is one thing Bennington is—and needs to be—working on." The campus also has an overwhelming majority of women, running to around 66 percent of the undergraduate population. Female students say that this ratio is not as much of a problem as you might think, however, especially since they can meet people much more easily during the Field Work Term. "Ultimately people still have boyfriends, people still meet people."

If students are really itching to meet more people, they can go to nearby Hampshire or Williams Colleges. Most, however, stay in the area of North Bennington—the "ridiculously New England" town where Bennington College is actually located—or Bennington, a larger city. One especially nice aspect of such a remote lifestyle is that students never have to worry about their safety: "Vermont feels like the safest place in the world. I never worry."

Overall, a Bennington education is what you choose to make of it. It is unique, to be sure, but it is that unusual character that allows many students to flourish. For those expecting an easy ride, however, Bennington is not the place, nor is it the place for those who need much hand-holding: "I feel like the main thing you learn at Bennington is how to educate yourself."

And how to throw a damn good theme party.—*Claire Stanford*

FYI
If you come to Bennington, you'd better bring "roller skates, costumes, and false eyelashes."
What's the typical weekend schedule? "Some sort of 'thirsty Thursday' celebration, class Friday, Friday night find out who is having a party in their room. Galavant around after, maybe see what band is playing. Saturday night, dress up in whatever you can find that remotely fits the theme of whatever party is going on, and get drunk. Sunday, recover."
If you could change one thing about Bennington I'd "only admit students who would be terribly excited."
Three things every student should do before graduating are "go in the catacombs, take a private tutorial, and run naked across the Commons lawn."

M a r l b o r o　C o l l e g e

Address: P.O. Box A, 2582 South Road, Marlboro, VT 05344-0300
Phone: 802-258-9236
E-mail address: admissions@marlboro.edu
Web site URL: www.marlboro.edu
Year Founded: 1946
Private or Public: Private
Religious Affiliation: None
Location: Rural
Number of Applicants: 459
Percent Accepted: 68%
Percent Accepted who enroll: 30%
Number Entering: 93
Number of Transfers Accepted each Year: 55
Middle 50% SAT range: M: 510–650, CR: 590–690, Wr: 640–720
Middle 50% ACT range: 24–32
Early admission program EA/ED/None: EA and ED

Percentage accepted through EA or ED: Unreported
EA and ED deadline: ED: Dec. 1; EA: Feb. 1
Regular Deadline: 15-Feb
Application Fee: $50
Full time Undergraduate enrollment: 330
Total enrollment: 330
Percent Male: 43%
Percent Female: 57%
Total Percent Minority or Unreported: 13%
Percent African-American: <1%
Percent Asian/Pacific Islander: 6%
Percent Hispanic: 4%
Percent Native-American: 1%
Percent International: 1%
Percent in-state/out of state: 10%/90%
Percent from Public HS: 70%
Retention Rate: 73%

Graduation Rate 4-year: Unreported
Graduation Rate 6-year: Unreported
Percent Undergraduates in On-campus housing: 80%
Number of official organized extracurricular organizations: 22
3 Most popular majors: English, Social Sciences, Visual & Performing Arts
Student/Faculty ratio: 8:1
Average Class Size: 8
Percent of students going to grad school: Unreported
Tuition and Fees: $32,180
In-State Tuition and Fees if different: No difference
Cost for Room and Board: $9,040
Percent receiving financial aid out of those who apply: Unreported
Percent receiving financial aid among all students: Unreported

Located in rustic Vermont, a 20-minute drive from the nearest town, Marlboro College offers its students an academic sanctuary in the midst of the New England mountains and greenery. With a small student body and a focus on the outdoors and schoolwork, Marlboro provides an intimate environment perfect for those looking for a unique and self-driven collegiate experience.

An Intense Learning Environment

Marlboro, with its lack of athletics and scarcity of extracurricular activities, is primarily a learning-driven college. Students unanimously concur that most non-class time is spent on schoolwork. "It's a really rigorous setting," one junior said. "People just do work all the time. It really affects the social scene." Another junior agreed, "Work *is* our extracurricular activity."

The academic program is lauded as extremely strong all around. Classes are small, with most classes consisting of about 10

students: "Eighteen students in a class is huge." If students are interested in a topic not offered, one-on-one tutorials can be arranged with professors in fields such as Arabic or fiction writing. There are no required classes except for a writing seminar that must be completed during freshman year.

Because of the small classes and intellectual environment, it is easy for students to form strong bonds with the faculty members leading their classes. "It's up to the students to enhance the faculty-student bond," one junior explained. Another student said professors often eat in the dining hall and are for the most part extremely "affable and approachable." But another student pointed out the one downfall of small classes: students who don't do the reading generally stand out. "You can't hide," said one senior. "Professors will call you if you don't show up for class."

Classes are divided into five basic categories: humanities, social sciences, natural sciences, world studies, and arts. In general, the humanities and literature departments are seen as the strongest, though there is also a notable "film culture," and political science is a very popular concentration. The math and science departments are "growing," though most students concede that those programs are slightly weaker. Recent additions to campus include the Serkin Arts Center and a new World Studies building.

Students choose a self-designed Plan of Concentration (known as "the Plan") to complete their studies at Marlboro. The plan can take many different forms: anything from a 120-page paper to an architectural model to writing a musical. Junior year is spent designing the Plan, and the project is executed during senior year. "Everything culminates in the Plan," one junior said.

> **"Work *is* our extracurricular activity."**

Though most find the academic experience "intense" and "wonderful," for others it can be a little overbearing. "It can definitely be too much for some people," a junior said. In general, though, students say they appreciate the unique structure because it creates a noncompetitive atmosphere, with the focus more on the "academic process." Some people transfer out, one sophomore said, because of the heavy workload, as they look for a college experience where the learning is "less individually driven."

An Intimate Community

The extremely small student body—there are only slightly over 300 students enrolled—makes for a unique collegiate social life. There are rarely huge on-campus parties, and there are no frats or sororities to host gatherings. "Most of our parties are pretty mellow," one junior said. "People will dance; there will be a band playing; people will drink and smoke."

For some students, though, living in such isolation can be restricting. "It kind of feels like we're living in a bubble," a senior said. Brattleboro, the nearest town, does offer "cool coffeehouses and a co-op, which everyone loves because we're all hippies." Students also get off campus to participate in numerous outdoor activities in the surrounding Vermont mountains and lakes.

Despite the lack of prominent social activities, one junior said it was easy to find ways to have fun. "You just have to make things happen," she said. "There's not the consistent night life that you might find at a large university, but there's usually a few big parties every year and things to do."

Students at Marlboro tend to be of a certain mold. Most students hail from the mid-Atlantic states and New England. A senior summed up the typical Marlboro student: "We tend to be white, of a similar socioeconomic category, and—in general—people who didn't fit in during high school." The small community also means that everyone knows everyone's business. "You can't really avoid the gossip," one freshman said.

Dorms, "Cottages," and a Barn-Turned-Building

The dorms that house Marlboro students reflect the intimate feel of the campus. The dorms are "really small," one senior said—each of the nine on-campus residence halls houses roughly 12 to 30 students, with roughly 80 percent of students living on campus. In general, the rooms are large, though some of the rooms are arranged in an unusual fashion—some freshmen complained about having to live in triples.

While housing is guaranteed for freshmen, it is not guaranteed for the next three years. Typically, 50 or so students (usually sophomores) are forced to live off campus each year. The off-campus dormitories—only a quarter-mile away from central campus—offer an appealing option due to their intimate feel (students described them as "little cottages"). Other students choose to live in Brattleboro in an apartment. One senior who lives in Brattleboro said she enjoys the change of pace after living on the close-knit Marlboro campus for three years: "There's a huge art and music scene."

There are residential advisers in every dorm, though they do not often take on the disciplinarian role. "No one is policing you," a sophomore said. Instead, RAs serve as resources for students and are able to offer advice and answers.

In general, the campus itself is "pretty rustic." A junior said, "The landscape is definitely really nice with all the white buildings, though the architecture could use some work." The on-campus dorms—each built in a slightly different era—are marked by a variety of architecture styles. The main classroom building is a converted barn, and the campus center—marked by its huge wooden rafters—was designed by a student for his Plan.

Food Complaints, Pride, and Broomball

One thing that all Marlboro students seem to agree on is the unappealing food on campus. There is one dining hall on campus and one basic meal plan for all students. A "big issue on campus" according to one junior, the food is a constant source of consternation for students. "There is just no selection whatsoever," one junior said. Though some students said the food was passable and not as bad as it was made out to be, many students have taken to creating their own food options. Many students said the lack of vegetarian and vegan options forced even the most devout vegetarians to start eating meat again; vegetarians currently have the option of filling out forms to request chicken or fish.

In general, as one junior put it, "extracurriculars don't really exist" at Marlboro. Unlike at other schools, where there are certain clubs that exist from year to year, students at Marlboro start up new clubs each year based on interests, which may fizzle and change at any given point in the year. "You can make happen pretty much whatever you want here," one senior said.

"Pride"—the campus shorthand for the Gay-Straight Alliance—is considered the most prominent on-campus organization.

Music ensembles tend to attract a fair number of students as well. Many students also join committees to help plan events and deal with other Marlboro-related issues.

While there are no official sports teams, the club soccer team is a source of school pride, as the student body often comes out to support the soccer squad. Frisbee and fencing are other popular sports. The Outdoor Program also plans many trips and excursions every year. Every winter, the whole school participates in a "broomball" tournament—a kind of makeshift hockey game—on the frozen pond on campus, at which school spirit and enthusiasm is often at its highest.

Marlboro College certainly stands out from the endless list of colleges because of its small size and intense academic atmosphere. Though some students said it becomes suffocating and small at times, most students appreciate the closeness of the campus and the bonds they are able to form with faculty. As one student put it, "A typical Marlboro student is one who is interested in his or her education and wants to play a role in it."—*Josh Duboff*

FYI

If you come to Marlboro, you'd better bring "a winter coat, motivation, and a stick of deodorant."
What is the typical weekend schedule? "Eat brunch, read a few books, go to the pond/sledding, eat dinner, read more, party, dance, listen to music, have some good conversations, go to bed."
If I could change one thing about Marlboro, I'd "give the school a lot more money."
The three things every student should do before graduating from Marlboro are "play broomball, skinny-dip in South Pond, and get to know each other well."

Middlebury College

Address: The Emma Willard House, Middlebury, VA 05753-6002

Phone: 802-443-3000

E-mail address: admissions@middlebury.edu

Web site URL: www.middlebury.edu

Year Founded: 1800

Private or Public: Private

Religious Affiliation: None

Location: Suburban

Number of Applicants: 7,823

Percent Accepted: 17%

Percent Accepted who enroll: 44%

Number Entering: 576

Number of Transfers Accepted each Year: Unreported

Middle 50% SAT range: M: 640–740, CR: 630–740, Wr: 640–740

Middle 50% ACT range: 29–33

Early admission program EA/ED/None: ED

Percentage accepted through EA or ED: 27%

EA and ED deadline: 1-Nov

Regular Deadline: 1-Jan

Application Fee: $65

Full time Undergraduate enrollment: 2,422

Total enrollment: 2,422

Percent Male: 50%

Percent Female: 50%

Total Percent Minority or Unreported: 41%

Percent African-American: 5%

Percent Asian/Pacific Islander: 10%

Percent Hispanic: 7%

Percent Native-American: 1%

Percent International: 12%

Percent in-state/out of state: 5%/95%

Percent from Public HS: 52%

Retention Rate: 95%

Graduation Rate 4-year: 88%

Graduation Rate 6-year: 92%

Percent Undergraduates in On-campus housing: 97%

Number of official organized extracurricular organizations: 100

3 Most popular majors: Economics, English, Psychology

Student/Faculty ratio: 9:1

Average Class Size: 16

Percent of students going to grad school: Unreported

Tuition and Fees: $49,210

In-State Tuition and Fees if different: No difference

Cost for Room and Board: Included with tuition

Percent receiving financial aid out of those who apply: 48%

Percent receiving financial aid among all students: 79%

I ndoors and outdoors, in and out of class, Middlebury College offers quirky, fun, and meaningful programs for students willing to take advantage of all that is available on this cozy yet exuberant campus. While the natural beauty of the surrounding Green Mountains and the frigid and pretty Vermont environment humbles the self-proclaimed "outdoorsy-type" of student, the focus and rigor of the academic curriculum similarly humbles students who find themselves at home in the classroom—and the zany thing about Middlebury is that these two categories of students are not mutually exclusive.

Parlez-vous Français?

Breadth and depth are the cornerstones of academics at Middlebury. While Middlebury does not stipulate a core curriculum, it nevertheless ensures its students obtain wide academic exposure through its distributional requirements. Students must take courses in seven out of eight academic categories: literature, the arts, philosophical and religious studies, historical studies, physical and life sciences, deductive reasoning and analytical processes, social analysis, and foreign language. Middlebury also emphasizes an international perspective; to that end, it requires students to take courses in four categories as part of a cultures and civilizations requirement: one in Africa, Asian, or Latin American culture, one comparing cultures and civilizations, one in European culture, and one in North American culture. A freshman seminar and a writing course are also required to graduate. "All the requirements seem daunting at first, but by the time you're finishing up you wish you could take more," a senior admitted. Another senior added, however, that she wished at times she hadn't needed to take so many distributional courses, because it prevented her from taking more interesting courses.

As far as majors go, economics, political science and English are very popular on campus, with psychology and environmental studies not far behind. "It's a fairly typical spread of majors," one student reported, "but everyone takes at least a couple of cool courses completely unrelated to their major." And around 15 percent of students are double majors; "a lot of people come to Middlebury wanting to do everything; some keep it up all four years, but others decide a double major is not for them," one recent double majoring graduate said.

> **"All the requirements seem daunting at first, but by the time you're finishing up you wish you could take more."**

Middlebury's course offerings are as strong and wide as you would expect, with two particular strengths that students point to. The first are their language classes; the college boasts a world-renowned language program that encourages study abroad and intensive immersion programs. The other are courses available during "J-term," a one-month interim period between the fall and spring semesters during which students take one course, which may range from "Chinese Painting" to "Combinatorial Games and Puzzles."

Students enjoy a "love-hate relationship" with their courses; "most are fairly demanding, but nearly all are interesting in one way or another," according to one student. Class sizes vary depending on subject, with large introductory lectures filled with 70 or more students; over 40 percent of courses, however, have between 6 and 15 students. These small class sizes are ideal for interacting with professors, who, "for the most part, are sage and know how to convey their material in unique ways." Professors understand the demands placed on students, and most set a "reasonable" amount of work. But this does not preclude some students from feeling overwhelmed, particularly in courses where reading can "seriously accumulate, to the point that you can't keep up with it all," reported a junior pursuing an English major. Still, students agreed that "the vast majority of students love their academic experience at Middlebury, despite the rough moments that occasionally pop up."

Something in Common[s]

The core of residential life at Middlebury lies in its "commons" system, which creates communities in and out of the classroom by assigning students enrolled in a particular freshman seminar to live in the same commons, or dorm building. The five commons compete against each other in intramural sports, and many students identify strongly with their smaller community. Others point to the disparity between colleges; "there's a marked difference between the quality of housing in some of the commons," one student reported. All commons have residential buildings, a dining hall, and host various speakers and events throughout the year. Students can, for the most part, readily change commons and their corresponding housing, though many students find their closest friends in their assigned commons and hence have no desire to change. One student said, "I think of my commons as my family unit—it's my home, I wouldn't think of leaving it." Unsurprisingly, the majority of students live on-campus all four years.

While some students characterize Middlebury as a "resort—Club Midd" for its excellent overall accommodations, housing does tend to vary around campus. And the quality of housing increases with seniority, by most reports; freshmen tend to get basic singles and suites while seniors live in spacious apartment-like suites, complete with common rooms and kitchens. "If I were to choose between my suite and those of all my friends at other colleges around the country, I'd pick my suite any day of the week, and I'm sure my friends would too," one junior said.

It is not only housing that is described in superlative terms by Middlebury students; the food, often locally produced, is too. Students praise the basic meal plan, which allows them unlimited access to dining halls. Two freshmen credited the plan for the "freshman 15" they have both put on. Another student said the staff was particularly attentive to students' cravings; she cited an example of her best friend pointing out the lack of a certain food in the dining hall to the chef, who cooked it the very next day. Of course, the nature of dining halls situated within commons means that dinner-table conversations can be just as interesting as the food that is actually on the dinner table itself.

Beyond campus, good food is in abundance. Students particularly appreciate the freshness and taste of produce available in rural Vermont. Not so appreciated, however, is the dearth of options to satisfy late night pangs of hunger, with staples like pizza and Chinese not readily available.

If none of the other food options takes

your fancy, you can always turn to Vermont's beloved Ben and Jerry's ice cream!

At the Extremes
If Middlebury students are studying hard during the day, you can expect many will be hard at work in the myriad extracurricular organizations in the evenings, and drinking hard on the weekends. "Students take things to the extreme, whatever it is they happen to be doing," said one student. And they do things in characteristically quirky style.

Take social life, for instance. Rather than the frats that dominate many other college campuses, Middlebury has social houses, coed groups of students who throw parties, and a number of local bars frequented by upperclassmen. More zany, however, are the themed dance parties that routinely take place; themes range from contra dance parties, in which couples folk dance in two facing lines of indefinite length, to neon dance parties. More routine is the prevalence of alcohol, which students say is big on campus, whether at small dorm parties or larger parties.

Because of the small campus, there are invariably familiar faces that pop up at every party. Students consider this a mixed blessing. "It's awesome that no matter where you go on the weekend, you'll know someone, but on the other hand, it can get a bit awkward depending on the person and situation," one student said.

Of course, there are alcohol-free alternatives aplenty to fill up your free time, with concerts, movies, and other activities organized throughout the term. According to one student, "there's never a free moment; even when you don't have class and aren't doing some extracurricular, there's always stuff going on around campus."

Extracurricular activities are likewise extremely varied. The proactive student can participate in a comprehensive array of organizations, ranging from the Big Sky Society, celebrating the state of Montana, to Bobolinks, a coed a cappella group. One student who has founded his own club said, "If there is no club wacky or adventurous enough to satisfy your tastes, you can simply start one up!" Like at any other college, there are varying levels of commitment; some people choose to prioritize studies over other activities, while others spend the majority of their time with extracurricular clubs.

As for the people that make up these organizations, the self-proclaimed "Midd Kids," they are a motley bunch, as would be expected of an unconventional college like Middlebury. "There is no typical student here," one student offered, but went on to describe a good number of students as extroverted and very much suited to the outdoors. Another student added that there was definitely a "hippie streak" among students at Middlebury, with the rural setting and mix of interesting people augmenting the already open-minded class.

Though Middlebury prides itself on its international student body—students can name friends from all over the world—some are less satisfied by the diversity on campus. "It seems outwardly that we're very diverse, but when you get here, you realize students largely conform to several, predominantly middle-to-upper class stereotypes," one junior commented.

A Community Too Cozy?
At the heart of the Middlebury experience is the intimate community, both of scholars and of friends. This is largely due to the rural setting of the college, with little reason to go off campus save skiing or grocery shopping, and a secure, cozy environment almost free from criminal danger and theft. The same sense of security translates into the Honor Code that students hold dear, which manifests itself in professor-free exams. According to one student, "everybody is bound to each other, so we respect each other and keep each other in check." Even in terms of social life, there is a "symbiotic" relationship between people, with everyone invariably going to each other's events.

Shared values permeate other areas of student life too, with most students holding liberal views and caring for the natural environment that surrounds them. "It can seem quite homogenous, but I guess that's what happens when people are so close and converse together all the time," one student said. Still, that sense of community is what so many Middlebury students first call to mind when they think of their college, and will hold dear long after they leave. "It really is an amazing place—I think every time I see the sun rise over the mountains of all those before me and with me who see the same sight, who are lucky to be part of that same beautiful beginning."—*James Lu*

FYI

If you come to Middlebury, you'd better bring "heaps of flannel."

If you come to Middlebury, you'd better leave "your sun-tan lotion" behind.

If I could change one thing about Middlebury, I'd "get kids to go to Burlington or Boston more often, to get a better view of the world."

Three things every student at Middlebury should do before graduating are "streak, experiment with veganism, and cross-country ski."

University of Vermont

Address: South Prospect Street, Burlington, VT 05405-0160

Phone: 802-656-3131

E-mail address: admissions@uvm.edu

Web site URL: www.uvm.edu

Year Founded: 1791

Private or Public: Public

Religious Affiliation: None

Location: Suburban

Number of Applicants: 22,365

Percent Accepted: 71%

Percent Accepted who enroll: 15%

Number Entering: 2,472

Number of Transfers Accepted each Year: 873

Middle 50% SAT range: M: 550–640, CR: 540–640, Wr: 540–640

Middle 50% ACT range: 24–29

Early admission program EA/ED/None: EA

Percentage accepted through EA or ED: 75%

EA and ED deadline: 1-Nov

Regular Deadline: 15-Jan

Application Fee: $55

Full time Undergraduate enrollment: 11,593

Total enrollment: 13,554

Percent Male: 42%

Percent Female: 58%

Total Percent Minority or Unreported: 12%

Percent African-American: 1%

Percent Asian/Pacific Islander: 2%

Percent Hispanic: 2%

Percent Native-American: <1%

Percent International: 1%

Percent in-state/out of state: 25%/75%

Percent from Public HS: Unreported

Retention Rate: 86%

Graduation Rate 4-year: 54%

Graduation Rate 6-year: 69%

Percent Undergraduates in On-campus housing: 51%

Number of official organized extracurricular organizations: 200

3 Most popular majors: Social Sciences, Business/Marketing, Environmental Science

Student/Faculty ratio: 17:1

Average Class Size: 19

Percent of students going to grad school: 23%

Tuition and Fees: $34,424

In-State Tuition and Fees if different: $14,784

Cost for Room and Board: $9,708

Percent receiving financial aid out of those who apply: 80%

Percent receiving financial aid among all students: 63%

University of Vermont, known commonly as UVM (an abbreviation of its Latin name, Universitas Viridis Montis), is one of the oldest universities around—the 23rd to be founded in the U.S. and one of the original eight Public Ivies. While it has its roots deep in the college tradition, UVM is one of the most forward-looking schools in terms of environmentalism and clean energy. Its student center, the Dudley H. Davis Center, was the first in the U.S. to receive U.S. Green Building Council LEED (Leadership in Energy and Environmental Design) Gold certification. The lights in all of the newest dorms are constantly turning themselves off, and just down the road in the bustling metropolis of Burlington, there are plenty of natural foods at the local co-ops for students to cook up in their apartments, which are often strung with colorful lines of prayer flags. While the Greek scene barely makes it onto the radar, the Outing Club is easily the most active group on campus. According to students, almost everyone hikes, and people are always trying to get outside, whether to bike, ski, or play broomball. After all, Burlington, a thriving college town, has been named the healthiest city in the U.S. for two years running. Between rigorous academics, constant outdoor athletics, and quirky annual traditions, UVM students are consumed with a robust enthusiasm for life that is sure to infect any newcomer on campus.

Lots of Schools, Lots of Learning

UVM is home to a number of undergraduate colleges, including the College of Nursing and Health Sciences, the College of Agriculture and Life Sciences, The School of Business Administration, the College of Engineering and Mathematics, and of course, the College of Arts and Sciences. While the College of Arts and Sciences is the largest, there is a significant number of students spread across the others as well, especially in engineering. Within the College of Arts and Sciences, majors in the social sciences draw the biggest numbers. The quality and rigor of academics are difficult to generalize, and according to students, they are dependent on the particular school. A sophomore said that his engineering program was challenging, but good, and all of the future health care programs are popular, especially given the opportunity to work right alongside the on-campus hospital, Fletcher Allen Health Care.

Some students complain about boring prerequisites during the first two years, though they agree that after those are over classes greatly improve. "But that's stereotypical of a bigger school," commented a junior. A political science major reiterated that his first classes were huge lectures without a lot of individual instruction but that the classes shrunk as he continued. The average class size, said a student, seems to be around 30 or so students. "I have one class with 150, and one with 10," she pointed out. There are also two elective-like requirements called "diversity classes" that are "kind of a bummer" but fairly easy to fulfill.

With nearly 10,000 undergraduates scampering about a whole slew of various schools, students are still able to get individual attention. Each student receives an academic advisor, generally one of his or her professors, as part of the teacher advisory program. "I think the advising system is great—[advisors are] like parents if you need help with things," said a junior. Advisors can help students choose their classes and can point out the right professors to talk to and students generally take advantage of professors' office hours to seek extra help or advice. "All the faculty that I've had have been really approachable and easy to ask questions," shared a current freshman. A

senior reflected, "A lot of the teachers I've had really like teaching. Only one seemed totally there obviously to do research."

For students looking to mix it up a little bit, UVM offers a bunch of less mainstream subjects. There are classes on figure skating, ballroom and African dance, hip hop, and scuba certification. "There are also a ton of cool, weird-ish outdoors classes, like classes structured around our area with field trips that take advantage of things like geological sites," said a senior.

Students hit the books hard for most of the week, working Monday through Thursday, often taking a break on Friday and Saturday, and then occupying the library from wall to wall on Sunday to prepare for the new week ahead. The academic community embodies diligence, but also a healthy, balanced lifestyle, because, come Saturday, the books are on the shelves and it's time to get outside!

Hiking and Skiing and Broomball, Oh my!

UVM has a huge population of environmentally friendly, conscious people. As a sophomore clarified, "It's not like a bunch of hippies, but clean-cut environmental people, and easily the most visible group on campus." A love for the environment seems to go hand in hand with a love for the outdoors, because come weekend, a lot of students choose to spend their time with the Outing Club. Tucked up in Vermont, groups have the chance go hike Mount Mansfield or climb in the White Mountains. In the winter, practically the entire school relocates to the mountains to strap on their skis and snowboards. "In the cold, miserable dark winter months, [non-UVM students] are usually depressed, but we have skiing—so everyone's usually pretty happy," said a junior.

"There are a lot of communities people are wicked passionate about," said a junior. Intramurals, unsurprisingly, draw a large crowd, as well as club sports. The Frisbee team and Kayaking Club are particularly popular. "If you want to do something," commented a student, "there's probably someone who will do it with you." And while everyone hikes and skis and plays sports, UVM's real pastime is broomball. It's essentially like hockey, but minus the skates, and it's played year-round in the rink. In addition to all the physical action, students participate in a lot of activist and community service organizations, as well as political and literary groups and UVM's two competing weekly newspapers. Many students also take on-campus jobs (of which there are "tons") or find part-time employment off-campus, such as at a Burlington clothing store or local farm.

In terms of UVM's varsity sports culture, students, on the whole, only care about three teams: skiing, basketball, and hockey. "Hockey is huge, so our hockey team—they're gods, they're awesome," said a freshman. The rest of the sports are "just kind of pushed to the side."

Each year, there are also a few highly anticipated events that almost everyone takes part in. On the last day of classes at the end of each semester there is a massive naked run. In celebration of Halloween, there is also a pumpkin festival and pumpkin race—which involves students climbing into 600 pound pumpkins and kayaking them across the lake.

Especially for the outdoors type, there are ample activities for entertainment and excitement when it's time to take a break from the books. "If you're an outgoing person you'll jump in and get a lot of friends," said a senior. However, while extracurriculars can often keep people busy, and students are usually highly dedicated to what they do outside of the classroom, they still, for the most part, put academics first.

Party, Ski, Study

The UVM campus is proof that healthy and happy go hand in hand. "Everyone here is really nice—it's hard to meet a jerk. Maybe it's the Vermont attitude," said a sophomore. That said, the majority of students at UVM are from out of state. "That's cool, and you meet a lot of people, but it's definitely predominantly white. It attracts a similar type of person, so there's not a lot of diversity," said a student. Most everyone in the community tends to get along, and on evenings on the weekend there's always something to do and someone with whom to do it. "You can go out and drink if you want, go watch a show or movie or music downtown, or see a presentation by a faculty member," said a senior. "It's the most eclectic type of community I've ever been a part of. There's a spot for everyone."

The college is always organizing dances and there are lots of house parties. The fraternity scene is rather mellow, with fewer than ten frats that all have a very low-key reputation. "UVM is really strict about hazing and that stuff. It's the total opposite of bigger schools," said a junior. "You might be part of Greek life, but that doesn't define you at all." The frats also only throw big parties on certain occasions, like Halloween, and for these, attendance requires tickets that need to be purchased from a member of the fraternity. "The only thing I've heard frats being active in is with community service in Burlington," said another student. "It's pretty hard to make it into a frat party—quite selective. Most people party elsewhere." Bars in town are really hard to get into unless students are 21. As a result, most students turn to off-campus gatherings, which for underclassmen is often dependent on knowing juniors and seniors who live in houses and apartments. "The first month or two of school, it was hard to find parties, because I didn't know that many upperclassmen. But that didn't last long," said a freshman. According to her, there's not a big difference in social life between upper- and lowerclassmen.

UVM has a dry campus, so freshman dorms rarely get rowdy. Most people drink, but dorms aren't conducive to all-out parties. That said, drinking on campus is not too strict. "If you're smart you can drink in your dorms. You have to be caught three times before you get in real trouble. It's pretty low-key," said a freshman. It also often depends on the RA. According to one freshman, his RA is very professional in the dorm, but they've partied together off campus. Smoking is also relatively prominent, but in terms of treatment toward students, the administration focuses on students' safety more than it does on cracking down. There are blue lights with emergency buttons spread all over campus, and students feel absolutely secure both on campus and in Burlington. "UVM preaches being safe—it's a really great, supporting community," said one student.

Earthy Crunchy Vermont Livin'

There seems to be a common misconception that, hidden away in Vermont, the campus is surrounded by a bunch of cows and trees. However, a trip up to Burlington quickly debunks such myths. "I had this friend visit. He thought my dorm would be at the end of a dirt road—[non-UVM students] forget there's a town, and awesome musicians and performers that come," said a junior. With the lively small city of Burlington just a 15-minute walk from campus, students are not short of art, music, and culture. Burlington has "a pretty prevalent downtown . . . a really progressive city, but pretty small," according to a sophomore. Another student described it as "super artsy, and straight-up awesome." The city is studded with charismatic coffee shops, independent boutiques, places to eat, and a huge farmer's market. "The town is mostly students; it definitely has that college town vibe," said a junior. Nearby Champlain College students also frequent Burlington.

UVM students seem pretty satisfied with their housing. Freshmen and sophomores generally live on campus, but after that, almost everyone moves into apartments. The regular freshman dorms on central campus were described by one newbie as "shoe-box dorms that are pretty old-school." However, he and other freshmen who opted to reside in applied housing (such as living with other members of a specific college, like Engineering, or interest groups, such as environmental or community service) ended up in really nice dorms with suite-style living. Program housing is far better than regular assigned housing—the dorms are larger, nicer, in a better location, and better equipped than the generic dorm setup.

> "We have everything you could probably need. When I talk to my friends who go to more traditional state schools, I feel like you're getting a more unique experience in total education here that you just don't get elsewhere."

As for food, students provide mixed reviews. There are two dining options: unlimited and points. With unlimited, you can get as much as you want from the campus dining halls; with points, you can use meal points to eat at other places, like a marketplace, pub, burrito joint, and even a Ben and Jerry's. "The points plan is *definitely* the way to go, you just have to make sure you don't run out," said a sophomore. There are three places to use the unlimited meal swipe, and they all provide various vegetarian and vegan options. "I think dining hall food is delicious," said a senior. "A lot of the dining halls get produce from the local businesses, and there are themed nights once in a while." He does, however, cook a fair amount in his apartment. Many off-campus students get a CSA farm share (a community-supported agriculture arrangement), which provides fresh veggies and fruit from local farms. In addition to a handful of regular supermarkets, there's also a co-op supermarket downtown that specializes in local produce. "It's like Whole Foods on crazy steroids," a student described.

The campus, with all of its separate schools, has a lot going on. There are a lot of cool places to hang out outside, like the outdoor amphitheaters, and the Davis Center is the social crux. Everyone is constantly passing through; there are plenty of places to snack, play pool or ping pong, and check out frequent programmed events. There are also two libraries—a larger, older one, and a smaller, brand-new one. A notable section of campus is a beautiful street lined with old, antique buildings that is part of the English department. But while campus is nice, students are more preoccupied with either studying, poking around Burlington, or hitting the mountains for a good hike or ski. There's a poster that shows a picture of Burlington with the line, "Have it all, every day." According to a student, this poster makes him think of UVM itself. "It totally applies. We have everything you could probably need. When I talk to my friends who go to more traditional state schools, I feel like you're getting a more unique experience in total education here that you just don't get elsewhere." From broomball and mountain vistas to environmentalism and political activism, all in a community of diverse academic interests and pursuits, UVM sure does seem to have it all.
—*Tao Tao Holmes*

FYI

If you come to UVM, you'd better bring "Your skis or snowboard, a bicycle, and flannel, and you'd better leave your Hummer behind."

Three things every student at UVM should do before graduating are "1) do the Naked Bike Ride (though normally everyone runs) 2) go on an Outing Club trip and see some part of beautiful Vermont, and 3) eat a Ben & Jerry's Vermonster all by yourself."

Virginia

College of William and Mary

Address: PO Box 8795, Williamsburg, VA 23187-8795
Phone: 757-221-4223
E-mail address: admission@wm.edu
Web site URL: www.wm.edu
Year Founded: 1693
Private or Public: Public
Religious Affiliation: None
Location: Suburban
Number of Applicants: 11,636
Percent Accepted: 34%
Percent Accepted who enroll: 35%
Number Entering: 1,386
Number of Transfers Accepted each Year: 356
Middle 50% SAT range: M: 620–710, CR: 630–730, Wr: 610–720
Middle 50% ACT range: 27–32
Early admission program EA/ED/None: ED

Percentage accepted through EA or ED: 50%
EA and ED deadline: 1-Nov
Regular Deadline: 1-Jan
Application Fee: $60
Full time Undergraduate enrollment: 5,850
Total enrollment: 7,300
Percent Male: 45%
Percent Female: 55%
Total Percent Minority or Unreported: 23%
Percent African-American: 7%
Percent Asian/Pacific Islander: 8%
Percent Hispanic: 8%
Percent Native-American: 1%
Percent International: 2%
Percent in-state/out of state: 59%/41%
Percent from Public HS: Unreported
Retention Rate: 94%

Graduation Rate 4-year: 90%
Graduation Rate 6-year: Unreported
Percent Undergraduates in On-campus housing: 67%
Number of official organized extracurricular organizations: 378
3 Most popular majors: Business Administration, Psychology, Government
Student/Faculty ratio: 11:1
Average Class Size: 22
Percent of students going to grad school: Unreported
Tuition and Fees: $29,116
In-State Tuition and Fees if different: $10,246
Cost for Room and Board: $8,030
Percent receiving financial aid out of those who apply: 82%
Percent receiving financial aid among all students: 58%

The College of William and Mary, founded in 1693, is the second-oldest university in the United States. As its tour guides are quick to tell you, it was the college that Thomas Jefferson attended, the college where George Washington was chancellor, and the college that gave birth to the Phi Beta Kappa society in 1776. Yet William and Mary isn't all about tri-corner hats and resting on past laurels, despite its location in touristy Colonial Williamsburg. What distinguishes William and Mary nowadays, aside from having Sandra Day O'Connor as its chancellor, is its reputation for academic excellence. *U.S. News & World Report* ranked it first among public universities for undergraduate teaching. Results like that have many students here proudly embracing their label of being a "public Ivy." But William and Mary isn't just about staying locked in the library. The school has a beautiful campus, a successful football team, and serious cash flow from recent donations, donations that are funding a number of renovations and new buildings all around campus.

A Public Ivy

Most students agree that academics take precedence. According to one student, "At William and Mary, it's cool to be smart. People here are a different kind of intelligent." Students must complete 120 credits to graduate, and the average course counts for three or four credits. In addition, students must also fulfill the GERs, or General Education Requirements, which include one course in mathematics and quantitative reasoning; two courses in the natural sciences;

two courses in the social sciences; three courses in world cultures and history; one course in literature or art history; two credits in creative or performing arts; and one course in philosophical, religious, or social thought. Classes at W&M vary in size but all generally fall into one of three categories. The largest are introductory lectures with 100 to 250 people, and the smallest are seminars capped at 15, with classes of 25 to 35 people in between. All freshmen are required to take a freshman seminar; these are generally praised. Students register by class year in a relatively painless process.

William and Mary also rewards its incoming overachievers (generally the top 7 percent of each class) with its James Monroe Scholar Program. In addition to having one of the best dorms on campus (Monroe Hall) reserved exclusively for freshman Monroe Scholars, they get first pick in freshman seminars, have a chance to apply for a $1,000 grant for the summer after freshman year, and are guaranteed $3,000 for an independent project the summer after their sophomore or junior years. Of him to whom much is given, however, much is expected. In an already intense academic environment, the Monroes feel the pressure even more than most.

Among the 50 or so concentrations offered at William and Mary, there is the usual mix of easy and difficult majors. Some of the usual suspects like geology, psychology, and anthropology are popular with the less academically motivated crowd, while biology, chemistry, physics, and computer science are some of the hardest, and most well taught, majors. For those interested in economics, W&M offers a business major affiliated with its business school. For all their stellar reputation, one student believes W&M's academics are actually underrated. "I don't think people are quite aware of how good they are," he explained. Perhaps part of what makes the academics so good is that, for the most part, classes are taught by full professors. In four years, one senior could recall having been taught by a TA only once. Students also give the professors rave reviews, calling them approachable, interested, and "brilliant."

Partying at a Deli?

Students bring the same passion to social activities as they do to their classes. "The same people who hide out in Swem all week and study, party on the weekends (and during the week)." So what do William and Mary students do when they're not in the newly renovated library? Options abound. Student organizations, which number over 400, are popular, and most people belong to at least one or two clubs: "In all honesty I can say that W&M is where the kids who were involved in high school come to be even more involved in college." There are numerous performing arts and a cappella groups; several publications like the *DoG Street Journal* (referencing Duke of Gloucester Street, the main drag for students and locals) and the *Flat Hat*, W&M's weekly student newspaper; a number of Christian groups; and a whole host of others, from the chess club to the Russian club. Many students' social lives revolve around their organizations, as many clubs sponsor a number of parties and formals. Athletics, of course, play a big part in school life, as was especially the case a few years ago, when the Tribe football team made it all the way to the NCAA I-AA semifinals. Stands were more crowded than they had been in years, and Tribe Pride promises to stay inflated for years to come.

Greek organizations play a large role in the campus social scene as well. According to the W&M administration, 25 percent of undergrads are involved in Greek life, but according to one frat brother, the majority of those students belong to exclusive social service frats, evidence of W&M's passion for volunteerism. "Students praise volunteerism and community service as cool things to do." The school boasts the largest chapter in the country of Alpha Phi Omega and the largest collegiate service fraternity, and the governor recently visited campus to commend W&M for its commitment to service.

The percentage of people who live in traditional party-oriented frat houses is much smaller, and continues to shrink as frats lose their charters or housing by violating alcohol or other policies. The school has attempted to crack down on underage drinking in recent years, but students still manage to circumvent the system. Although the school requires that fraternity parties serving alcohol receive advance approval from the administration, "people can and do drink at the frats." Pregaming in dorm rooms is also popular among underclassmen.

For upperclassmen, off-campus parties, held by clubs, sports teams, or even Greek members living off campus, are popular. Because of regulations, there are no bars near W&M, but several so-called "delis" in the area reportedly serve the same purpose. In recent years, the delis have started to card more strictly, but for the persistent, alcohol is still available. Since "the most popular of the delis tends to rotate throughout the year," the reputations tend to depend on who and when you ask. The "nicest" of these delis is the Green Leafe, which has Mug Night every Sunday, when you can bring in a mug and they'll fill it with beer for a small price. College Delly, now under new ownership, is also popular and, last spring, Paul's was "the place to go." Aside from the delis, however, students report that there really isn't much off-campus nightlife, though there's always plenty to do on campus. In addition to the party scene, more toned-down events include forums with a host of visiting speakers: "In my years at the College I've seen Ralph Nader and Jon Stewart (he's an alum of ours), and even Kofi Annan and Supreme Court Justice Antonin Scalia."

Multinational Neighbors

In terms of housing, many students stay on campus all four years; as one student said, "I think people stay living on campus because it's very convenient and we have a really tight community." The dorms, which, with a few exceptions, are all coed, are generally pretty nice. Yates, Monroe, and Barret may be a little better than average, and Jamestown North and South are so far away that people dread getting placed there, but the halls are actually in decent shape. The housing system revolves around a lottery that most agree "ends up being pretty fair." Freshman housing is generally pretty good, and friends made in freshman halls often end up being friends for all four years. For those into foreign languages, W&M offers the opportunity to live in houses geared toward a specific language, whether it be Russian, Spanish, or French. Each house has a tutor from one of the countries where the language is spoken and hosts various cultural events. The language houses provide a warm, tight-knit community.

Dining services at William and Mary were significantly better before a budget crisis a few years ago led to cutbacks in quality. The university is, however, trying to remedy this: the main dining hall, "the Caf," recently received a facelift, with improvements including "amazing" food and an Internet café. Students can still find other good-quality offerings around, such as the daily-made sushi, which one student describes as "not sketchy. It's really good." When the options feel limited, though, students can take a walk around town and find plenty of ways to spice up their dining. Local restaurants like the Fat Canary, Aromas, Trellis, and the Cheese Shop receive good ratings, though the ones in the tourist part of colonial Williamsburg are pretty pricey. There are also two convenience stores open 24-7 in Williamsburg, including the Wawa, without which "students would go crazy."

What really sets William and Mary apart from most colleges, in the opinion of several students, is the sheer beauty of its campus. When these students talk about how spectacular their campus looks, they don't just mean the sites that every William and Mary tour guide points out: the colonial architecture of Old Campus, the famous Sunken Gardens, or even the Crim Dell pond with its storied bridge. (Supposedly, any couple who kisses on the bridge has to get married unless one of them throws the other one off.) These students mean places that are far less touristy, like the amphitheater at Lake Matoaka, which a couple of students said was the most beautiful place they had ever been in their lives.

> "At William and Mary, it's cool to be smart. People here are a different kind of intelligent."

The students at William and Mary are aware of its history and traditions. As one student said, "We all know that the Wren Building is the oldest academic building in the country still in use, almost all of us can recite the great history of our college, and almost all of us know the chorus to the alma mater. Our big tradition events such as the Yule Log and Convocation Ceremonies are incredibly crowded and bring us together."

One of the most interesting traditions at W&M is the Triathlon: swimming the Crim Dell pond, streaking the length of the Sunken Gardens, and jumping the Governor's Mansion wall to complete the garden maze inside, all in the same night. True triathletes complete the entire thing nude. It is not uncommon to see people streaking the Sunken Gardens on a typical weekend in the wee hours of the morning. "Some students are so gung-ho as to complete the triathlon not once but many times!"

So in the end, what does William and Mary have to offer? It has a beautiful campus, and thanks to a number of donations it is also poised to complete a number of major renovations. People here are generally pretty studious folks, with a grasp on tradition. If you're looking for a gorgeous place to live and an Ivy League–level education for a public school price, the College of William and Mary is the place for you.—*Laura Sullivan*

FYI

If you come to William and Mary, you'd better bring "a camera."

What's the typical weekend schedule? "Friday: UCAB event/party at a frat; Sat.: sleep in, study some, football game, or other athletic event, dance party; Sun.: study day/stay in."

If I could change one thing about William and Mary, it would be "the food; on-campus food leaves much to be desired, but that's why God created Wawa."

Three things that every student at William and Mary should do before graduation are "camp out and sleep under the stars in the Sunken Gardens (beware of streakers, Matoaka Ampitheater may be a safer bet), take a class in the Wren Building, and complete the triathlon."

George Mason University

Address: 4400 University Drive, Fairfax, VA 22030
Phone: 703-993-2400
E-mail address: admissions@gmu.edu
Web site URL: www.gmu.edu
Year Founded: 1972
Private or Public: Public
Religious Affiliation: None
Location: Urban
Number of Applicants: 12,943
Percent Accepted: 63%
Percent Accepted who enroll: 31%
Number Entering: 2,497
Number of Transfers Accepted each Year: 4,068
Middle 50% SAT range: M: 520–610, CR: 500–600, Wr: Unreported
Middle 50% ACT range: 22–26
Early admission program EA/ED/None: EA

Percentage accepted through EA or ED: 18%
EA and ED deadline: 1-Nov
Regular Deadline: 15-Jan
Application Fee: $70
Full time Undergraduate enrollment: 18,589
Total enrollment: 29,803
Percent Male: 47%
Percent Female: 53%
Total Percent Minority or Unreported: 37%
Percent African-American: 16%
Percent Asian/Pacific Islander: 16%
Percent Hispanic: 6%
Percent Native-American: <1%
Percent International: 4%
Percent in-state/out of state: 90%/10%
Percent from Public HS: 85%
Retention Rate: 84%
Graduation Rate 4-year: 41%

Graduation Rate 6-year: 59%
Percent Undergraduates in On-campus housing: 25%
Number of official organized extracurricular organizations: 250
3 Most popular majors: Accounting, Political Science, Speech and Rhetorical Studies
Student/Faculty ratio: 15:1
Average Class Size: 23
Percent of students going to grad school: Unreported
Tuition and Fees: $22,476
In-State Tuition and Fees if different: $7,512
Cost for Room and Board: $7,360
Percent receiving financial aid out of those who apply: 59%
Percent receiving financial aid among all students: 34%

Although George Mason University was established less than forty years ago, it offers something for everyone. Not only does GMU offer unique classes such as African Dance, the educational experience is also distinguished by its easily accessible world class professors. Overall, George Mason features a diverse student population, which is reflected in the myriad extracurricular clubs on campus. Last but not least, having the nation's capital less than an hour away opens the door to wide assortments of internship opportunities for students looking to further pursue their interests.

Location, Location, Location

George Mason has always prided itself in its proximity to Washington, D.C. Its convenient location attracts local students as well as students from all over the nation and the world.

Having D.C. just a metro ride away means not only an abundance of internship opportunities unavailable anywhere else but also exciting off-campus excursions. If students are interested in politics, criminal justice, or working at government agencies, Capitol Hill and FBI Headquarters etc. are all nearby, making internships a lot easier. On weekends, many students from neighboring cities commute home to spend time with friends or family. Unfortunately, since a large portion of students stream into surrounding cities, the campus is not as lively as others where all the students stay on campus. Nevertheless, "If you get the chance to stay on the weekend, there is always something to do whether it's on or off campus," said one freshman.

While D.C. offers city excitement, the campus has its own social scene as well. Greek life is the more dominant social scene on campus with its constant stream of frat parties and sorority events. However, because George Mason is such a diverse campus, there are other prominent student organizations as well. Religious groups such as Catholic Campus Ministry or Campus Crusade for Christ are well known. The anime club is also popular and famous for its Halloween Party. While the variety in social scenes mirrors the diversity of campus, one thing that unites the diverse campus is Mason Madness, George Mason's version of March Madness. The Patriot Center, George Mason's stadium, offers students free tickets and consequently brings everyone together for home basketball games. They even have "fight cheers." According to one alum, when Mason was in the final 4 in 2006, "it was like the entire campus was one big family coming out to support each other."

Campus Life

Although many students choose to live in off-campus apartments and even freshmen are not required to live on campus, many students enjoy dorm life. Freshman dorms are divided into three separate locations though the main one is "President's Park." First year students are usually assigned to singles, doubles, triples or quadruples. These dorm rooms are maintained by a janitorial staff who regularly cleans the shared bathrooms. Moreover, there are Residential Advisers (RAs) on every floor. Before rooming assignments are made, students take a quiz in order to be paired with an RA, who serves as a counselor and advisor. They are there not only to answer questions but also to plan bonding activities such as floor dinners. While they are not super strict

with regards to rules, according to one student, they do take students' problems and concerns very seriously. After freshman year, students have the option of keeping their room, in which case they would not have to go through the housing lottery. Otherwise, students who decide to live on campus receive a lottery number according to the amount of academic credits they have accumulated to determine the order of choosing. When the student's turn comes, he/she has a slotted time to go online to select his/her room. On campus, sophomores, juniors and seniors usually live in apartment-style dorms that are complete with a kitchen.

But students who do not live in dorms with kitchens need not worry. At George Mason there is plenty of good food, from dining halls to chain restaurants. The newly opened Southside is a popular buffet-styled dining hall where students pay a fee to eat all they want. The George W. Johnson Center is a campus hotspot because it has a plethora of food options from Chick-fil-A to a Chinese restaurant. On its other floors, there is also a computer lab, mail service, and a library, fulfilling all of a student's needs. According to one junior, "when I sit in the food court I feel like I'm at the center of college life." George Mason offers three different types of meal plans to cater to different eating habits. Block and Traditional allow for a fixed amount of meals per semester and per week respectively. There is also the Ultimate, which is unlimited. Besides meal swipes, students can also have Mason Money, which is money that is put on the student's Mason ID and can be used in most restaurants and cafés around campus.

Adventure Classes and Dance Time

Students are very satisfied with the selection of classes offered. If you're looking for more fun and adventurous classes like as Rock Climbing, Trap and Skeet Shooting, Snowboarding, Scuba Diving, and Coastal Kayaking, George Mason is the place for you. "Students rarely sign up for these classes because they require lab and equipment fees and don't meet any specific degree requirements," a senior reported. On the upside, he said they are fairly easy to get into, though he hasn't taken any of these classes himself.

Students seem to enjoy the dance classes offered at GMU. "The most fun class I've taken was Intro to Modern Dance," a senior said. She plans to take African Dance next semester. "Dance classes are fun and a way to get in a good workout," a recent grad who took tap dance recounted.

There are also interesting classes like Criminology or Semester at the Smithsonian where students meet at the National Zoo and work behind the scenes with scientists and zookeepers in the labs and exhibits.

Furthermore, Mason also offers classes like University 100, which helps students adjust from high school to university life and is mandatory for students living in the Living Learning Community (LLC).

> "Everyone at Mason was always very friendly and helpful. Whenever I had a problem or a question there was always someone willing to help or who knew someone who could."

A senior mentioned that she particularly enjoyed the creative writing courses at Mason. "Most classes aren't hard to get into, as long as you sign up on time," another senior recounted.

Personal Attention

The advisors and professors are great resources for GMU students. Overall, students say that most of the faculty members are accessible through phone or e-mail and respond relatively quickly. "Everyone at Mason was always very friendly and helpful," said a recent grad. "Whenever I had a problem or a question there was always someone willing to help or who knew someone who could." Sometimes teachers even allow one-on-one time with each student, for extra and more personal meetings with the teacher. "It really helps, especially if you really need extra time outside of class," a junior said. Since classes are usually fairly small, students are able to get some one-on-one time with the professors in class as well.

Some students interviewed praised the teachers as very easy to talk with, saying, "They know the struggles students go through and will work with you through your assignments." However, there were some mixed reviews. "A few professors will ignore student e-mails and avoid office hours," a freshman said. "Some are friendly, some are not, but you can find out before signing up for a class by checking ratemyprofessors.com or the teaching evaluations posted on the GMU Web site."

Students say they find there are many resources available for their academic needs. "At any time I could go into the math tutoring center or the writing center to get help with homework," a senior said. Students who need more help in other subjects can go to that department, which sends an e-mail to all departmental majors who are interested in private tutoring.

Mason students have no complaints about early classes. They find that the classes are scheduled at nice times. "I've always had the opportunity to have great schedules," a senior said. A freshman reported, "The academics here are challenging, but easy to get through because of the professors always presenting help."

Out of the Classroom

There are also many clubs and organizations on campus. From the Hockey team to the Drama club to rowing there is something for everyone. There is even an underwater polo team! Yet the men's basketball team remains the most famous team on campus.

Mason's proximity to the nation's capital also draws in students who hope to work for the government as its location lends itself to federal internships. One freshman said, "I want to eventually join the FBI and Mason is close to FBI HQ, CIA HQ, NCIS HQ, and many other government agencies."

GMU would be a great choice for all students looking for a school that is at once academically and socially enriching. More than that, the location of the university guarantees adventures on campus and a whole new world of opportunities just a train ride away in Washington, D.C.—*Sharon Yin and Jenny Dai*

FYI

If you come to George Mason, you'd better bring an open mind. "This school is so diverse that it is difficult to get by if you aren't tolerant of different types of people of different races, ethnicities, cultures, and sexual orientations."

What's the typical weekend schedule? "Weekends could be just as active as the weekdays. I'd either hang out with friends on campus or we could head into D.C. for a hockey game or to visit the monuments. There was always something to do."

If I could change one thing about GMU: "I would say the biggest drawback to Mason is that a lot of people leave campus on the weekend. Usually they go home, or to visit friends at nearby schools."

Hampden-Sydney College

Address: P.O. Box 667, Hampden-Sydney, VA 23943
Phone: 800-755-0733
E-mail address: admissions@hsc.edu
Web site URL: www.hsc.edu
Year Founded: 1775
Private or Public: Private
Religious Affiliation: Presbyterian
Location: Rural
Number of Applicants: 1,553
Percent Accepted: 64%
Percent Accepted who enroll: 32%
Number Entering: 333
Number of Transfers Accepted each Year: 18
Middle 50% SAT range: M: 515–610, CR: 500–610, Wr: 480–590
Middle 50% ACT range: 20–26
Early admission program EA/ED/None: EA and ED

Percentage accepted through EA or ED: Unreported
EA and ED deadline: 15-Nov
Regular Deadline: 1-Mar
Application Fee: $30
Full time Undergraduate enrollment: 1,120
Total enrollment: 1,120
Percent Male: 100%
Percent Female: 0%
Total Percent Minority or Unreported: 13%
Percent African-American: 4%
Percent Asian/Pacific Islander: 1%
Percent Hispanic: 1%
Percent Native-American: <1%
Percent International: 2%
Percent in-state/out of state: 68%/32%
Percent from Public HS: 58%
Retention Rate: 79%

Graduation Rate 4-year: 61%
Graduation Rate 6-year: 66%
Percent Undergraduates in On-campus housing: 94%
Number of official organized extracurricular organizations: 50
3 Most popular majors: Economics, History, Government and Foreign Affairs
Student/Faculty ratio: 10:1
Average Class Size: 15
Percent of students going to grad school: 20%
Tuition and Fees: $28,250
In-State Tuition and Fees if different: No difference
Cost for Room and Board: $9,228
Percent receiving financial aid out of those who apply: 98%
Percent receiving financial aid among all students: 54%

Nestled into the heart of Virginia, Hampden-Sydney College is a neat collection of Federal-style brick buildings where, as its motto states, "good men and good citizens are formed." This all-male institution has stood outside of Farmville since its founding in 1775 as a place where young men come together both to work and to party.

Core Curriculum

When freshmen arrive on campus, they must begin taking classes to fulfill requirements in a foreign language, Western studies, the arts, science, and rhetoric. Students are also required to pass a rhetoric proficiency exam by the end of their junior year. Once students get out of these core requirements, grades tend to be lower as the school is adamantly against grade inflation, a student said. "Teachers say if you earn an A at Hampden Sydney you have truly earned that grade compared to bigger universities that heavily curve their students' grades." True to its Liberal Arts core curriculum, the most popular majors on campus are Economics, History, and Government and Foreign Affairs.

"People who come to Hampden-Sydney enjoy a small, close-knit community that makes you feel like you have a place in your school's culture. Hampden-Sydney allows you to find out a lot about yourself and is very helpful with fulfilling your dreams and aspirations because the whole community invests something into each and every student, which can't be found at larger universities."

Frat Circle

When asked about the social life at Hampden-Sydney, every student named Greek life as the center. A typical night will take most students to "Frat Circle," where most of the eleven fraternities have their houses on campus. "Most parties take place from Thursday night to Saturday night," a student said. "They usually consist of a live band of some sort and free house beer." The bands are generally influenced by Motown or classic rock, students said, but the one constant is beer. Most parties are open to all students, though one student cautioned that "house beer on the other hand gets to be stingy when big crowds arrive."

Sports teams are the other major social component on campus, although Greek life and athletics often go hand-in-hand. "[A] typical weekend schedule involves either a baseball game or football game on Saturday, followed by a celebration down on 'frat circle'," one student said. Greek Week in the spring is one of the most-anticipated weeks of the year.

Girls?

With a total enrollment of 1,120 and not a single girl in the lot, one could reason that the fairer sex is a rarity at Hampden-Sydney. According to students, however, that could not be further from the truth. A forty-five-minute drive away sits Sweet Briar College, Hampden-Sydney's all-girl sister school. The ladies of Sweet Briar are also often able to come to parties even on Thursday nights, as they do not have classes on Friday. Most of the girls who frequent Hampden-Sydney come from closer to home, according to one student. Longwood University is just 10 miles away in Farmville, and the 40–60 male-to-female ratio helps to pull Longwood women to Hampden-Sydney. Police activity is also more relaxed in relation to parties at Hampden-Sydney, as one student said that "Hampden-Sydney is in a little bubble that allows us to get away with a lot of parties that wouldn't be able to happen at Longwood."

Preppy Fashion

A student said that, "a lot of people do dress in a preppy fashion; most of the backgrounds of the students are from small private high schools and families that make a decent living considering the tuition for the school." He added that the college has made an effort to promote diversity in the last ten years, but 83 percent of the student body still self-identifies as Caucasian. Students are said to be laid-back and approachable on campus, which one student said is due to the "tight community that allows you to know most of the people." Another student said that the lack of stratification between the different grades makes the environment more welcoming. He added that "freshmen hang out and study with seniors just as often as they do with other freshmen. In the eyes of a Hampden-Sydney student, all students are equal."

A Question of Honor

Steeped in the Southern tradition of honor, the honor code is taken very seriously by much of the student body. "The honor code is taken very seriously on campus," one student said. "It's a one and done kind of deal and people won't hesitate to bring you in front of the honor code." He added that cooperation on assignments happens often to "lower the difficulty of the classes," but that students take care to avoid cheating. Another student disagreed, arguing that the honor code is often over-hyped. "The honor code is spoken by some as a sacred and unbreakable law; however, many of the students take advantage of the 'honor code' and act as if no such thing ever existed." Crime on campus, on the other hand, is almost nonexistent and most theft comes from outside of the Hampden-Sydney community. One student felt so secure that he stated, "I personally haven't locked my door while I'm on campus for theft reasons."

A Whole New Level

Those who went to an all-boy's high school can relate to H-SC, but the college expects its students to perform at a college level. Hampden-Sydney also takes brotherhood to the next level. Both the camaraderie and the academic expectations fulfill the school motto that the boys who enter the college leave as men.

At a 1,100 person school, the all-male student body creates an atmosphere where, "everyone pretty much knows everyone for the most part." That closeness creates a bond that lasts well beyond graduation.
—*Charles Condro*

FYI

The biggest college-wide tradition/event at Hampden-Sydney College is "The Game," or the annual football showdown between the Tigers and rival Randolph-Macon College.

The best place to go for late-night food? "Cookout (new in town)," is a fast-food chain from North Carolina known for its cheap prices, hush puppies, and a wide variety of thick milkshakes.

How do you meet people or make friends when first arriving? "You meet people through Freshman Orientation, Sports teams, Fraternities, individual class (because they are so small)."

Hollins University

Address: PO Box 9707,
Roanoke, VA 24020-1707
Phone: 540-362-6401
E-mail address:
huadm@hollins.edu
Web site URL:
www.hollins.edu
Year Founded: 1842
Private or Public: Private
Religious Affiliation: None
Location: Urban
Number of Applicants:
651
Percent Accepted: 84%
**Percent Accepted who
enroll:** 35%
Number Entering: 193
**Number of Transfers
Accepted each Year:** 50
Middle 50% SAT range:
M: 490–620, CR: 500–670,
Wr: 490–620
Middle 50% ACT range:
21–28
**Early admission program
EA/ED/None:** ED

**Percentage accepted
through EA or ED:**
Unreported
EA and ED deadline: 1-Dec
Regular Deadline: 1-Feb
Application Fee: $35
**Full time Undergraduate
enrollment:** 799
Total enrollment: 1,049
Percent Male: 1%
Percent Female: 100%
**Total Percent Minority or
Unreported:** 9%
Percent African-American:
8%
**Percent Asian/Pacific
Islander:** 2%
Percent Hispanic: 3%
Percent Native-American:
<1%
Percent International: 2%
**Percent in-state/out of
state:** 52%/48%
Percent from Public HS: 77%
Retention Rate: 73%
Graduation Rate 4-year: 57%

Graduation Rate 6-year: 59%
**Percent Undergraduates in
On-campus housing:** 80%
**Number of official organized
extracurricular
organizations:** 46
3 Most popular majors:
Communication and Media
Studies, English Language
and Literature, General
Psychology
Student/Faculty ratio: 10:1
Average Class Size: 13
**Percent of students going to
grad school:** 22%
Tuition and Fees: $25,110
**In-State Tuition and Fees if
different:** No difference
Cost for Room and Board:
$9,140
**Percent receiving financial
aid out of those who apply:**
97%
**Percent receiving financial
aid among all students:**
93%

Among the few things you can expect from Hollins University is the absence of male students. This small all-women's school prides itself on its unconventional classes and quirky traditions, in addition to its diverse and accepting student body. If you come to Hollins, prepare to "leave behind your conceptions of what a college education should be."

Ladies and the Liberal Arts

As a liberal arts university, Hollins places a strong focus on the humanities. Freshmen take mandatory freshman seminars, and prior to graduation students must satisfy the distributional requirements that comprise "Education Through Skills and Perspectives" (ESP), a general education program which includes disciplines like modern language and scientific inquiry. The school is known for its creative writing program, which hosts a number of conferences and literary festivals throughout the year. Classes are small, with twelve or fewer students in each and a student-faculty ratio of approximately 9:1. Because of their small size, lectures "turn into seminars," and rarely exceed thirty students. Students say the workload is manageable, but math, science, and pre-med classes have a reputation for being particularly difficult.

The Hollins academic calendar runs on a "4-1-4" schedule: two four-month semesters, with a four-week January term, called "J-term." During J-term, students can pursue internships offering free room and stipends in Roanoke, Washington D.C., and New York, or study abroad. Students say that Hollins makes studying abroad a "no-brainer," offering classes in Greece, Spain, France and numerous other countries, and offers substantial scholarships and financial aid. Another option for J-term is taking a quirky, unconventional class on campus. Topics have spanned the gamut from "Julie and Julia and Me: French Cooking and Food Culture for Everyone" to "The Road Trip in Photography," in which students embark on a month-long road trip, taking pictures.

Hollins faculty hold required office hours, and are eager to meet with students outside of class, whether for dinner or advice. Many professors have houses on campus in "Faculty Row," and it is not uncommon to see them walking their dogs or with their children in the cafeteria. Faculty members also participate in Tinker Day, in addition to other student-organized events on campus.

Each student at Hollins must commit to an honor code, which permits student-monitored exams. Professors will occasionally assign take-home tests or papers that count for test grades, and trust that their students will work on them independently. Hollins also makes use of an independent final exam schedule. Students are given liberty to select, within a five-day period with three slots per day, the dates on which they would prefer to take their exams.

One Big Sorority

Freshman dorms have air-conditioning, unlike the other, more historic dorms on campus. Rooms are fairly large, and there is one communal bathroom on each hall. Three halls and two communal spaces comprise each floor, in addition to two laundry rooms and a kitchen. After their first semester, students may apply to live in one of Hollins' specialty houses, each with its own theme. In the Spanish house, for example, students may only speak Spanish in the common room, and there is the Otaku house for students interested in anime. Students may switch houses, depending on their interests. Each house has "family time," but none are known for being "cliquey."

The Moody Dining Hall has a vegan station, in addition to a salad and hummus bar. Food is locally grown, and students "always have options." Students seeking a quick bite can head to the Rat café, which serves sandwiches and fries between meals, or the bookstore cafeteria. Both are popular meeting places, as is the Wyndham-Robertson library.

Hollins holds two formal dances: the Fall Formal (Winter Ball), and Spring Cotillion, both open to all students. Students also host class events for their "big sisters" in other years, closed to members of their two graduating classes. The Near East Fine Arts (NEFA) group hosts themed parties—to celebrate the Hollins production of "The Vagina Monologues," the theme was "What would your vagina wear?" Other campus-wide activities include Zumba and yoga, local band performances, and movie nights. There are no sororities or fraternities on campus, but "the entire campus ... is like one big sorority," said one student.

An Active Life After Class

On the weekends, students can take the shuttle to downtown Roanoke to visit art spaces, attend concerts, and take advantage of student discounts while shopping, although one admits it "isn't really much of a college town." Students also attend parties on campus and at nearby colleges Virginia Tech and Hampden-Sydney. Other popular activities include volunteering and attending student productions.

Hollins students are particularly committed to working and playing in the great outdoors. Popular organizations include the Hollins Outdoor Program (HOP), which sponsors backpacking trips up the Appalachian Trail, fishing, canoeing, horseback riding, and rock climbing in the Hollins gymnasium. Incoming freshman can participate in the five-day Wilderness Orientation Program, led by the HOP director and Hollins students, which provides opportunities for recreation at nearby Camp Roanoke. At this Division III school, many girls are involved with sports, particularly tennis and riding. There are no club sports, but students participate in intramurals, and two terms of physical education are mandatory.

> "The beauty of Hollins . . . [is how] everyone respects that people have different interests and different ways of looking at the same thing . . . Hollins is the place you can most be yourself."

Students are heavily involved in their extracurricular pursuits. Political and community activism is characteristic of the majority of Hollins students. Popular clubs include the College Democrats and College Republicans, OUTloud, the gay-straight alliance, and the Feminist Majority Leadership Alliance (FMLA), which promotes women's equality. SHARE, the community service organization, hosts a service trip to Jamaica each spring. Freya, another such organization, is a selective society that performs anonymous service. Publications at Hollins include *Hollis Columns*, the campus newspaper, *Cargoes* and *The Album*, both literary magazines, and *Cyborg Griffin*, another literary magazine with a focus on fantasy and science fiction. A radio channel, Hollins Entertainment Radio (HER), was launched in 2012.

Students at Hollins take pride in their "different" traditions. On the annual Tinker Day, Hollins' largest college-wide tradition, classes are canceled. Seniors bang pots and pans in dorm hallways to wake up the underclassmen, and all students congregate in Moody for Krispy Kreme donuts. Dressed in silly costumes, they spend the day hiking up Tinker Mountain, and eat fried chicken and chocolate cake at the top.

Although Hollins has a reputation for being a "pearl girl" school with primarily conservative, white students, the school has made strides toward celebrating student diversity. Students come to Hollins from around the country, and the school hosts study-abroad students from locales like Nepal and Gaza. There are global interest and international clubs for students interested in exploring other cultures, and the Cultural and Community Engagement Department hosts a large number of cultural events throughout the year. Additionally, the "Global Village" specialty house sponsors events typical to the various cultures to which its students belong. Students also say that the school is proud of its particularly large and open LGBTQ community, with "every day a gay pride day."

Not every student chooses Hollins with the intention of attending a women's college, but students say they grow to love Hollins' welcoming sisterhood and campus. As one student put it, "the beauty of Hollins . . . [is how] everyone respects that people have different interests and different ways of looking at the same thing . . . Hollins is the place you can most be yourself."—*Jennifer Gersten*

FYI
If you come to Hollins, you'd better bring "confidence and an open mind."
If I could change one thing about Hollins, "I would change the way the school markets itself. It seems like a school full of conventional, preppy girls, but Hollins is full of different kinds of girls. It's hard to say that there's a Hollins type."
Three things every student at Hollins should do before leaving are "climb Tinker Mountain, live in specialty housing, and study abroad."

James Madison University

Address: Sonner Hall, MSC 0101, Harrisonburg, VA 22807
Phone: 540-568-5681
E-mail address: admission@jmu.edu
Web site URL: www.jmu.edu
Year Founded: 1908
Private or Public: Public
Religious Affiliation: None
Location: Suburban
Number of Applicants: 19,245
Percent Accepted: 65%
Percent Accepted who enroll: 32%
Number Entering: 3,956
Number of Transfers Accepted each Year: 659
Middle 50% SAT range: M: 540 630, CR: 520–620, Wr: 520–620,
Middle 50% ACT range: 22–26
Early admission program EA/ED/None: EA

Percentage accepted through EA or ED: 46%
EA and ED deadline: 1-Nov
Regular Deadline: 15-Jan
Application Fee: $40
Full time Undergraduate enrollment: 16,916
Total enrollment: 18,454
Percent Male: 40%
Percent Female: 60%
Total Percent Minority or Unreported: 14%
Percent African-American: 4%
Percent Asian/Pacific Islander: 5%
Percent Hispanic: 2%
Percent Native-American: <1%
Percent International: 1%
Percent In-state/out of state: 71%/29%
Percent from Public HS: Unreported
Retention Rate: 91%
Graduation Rate 4-year: 66%

Graduation Rate 6-year: 81%
Percent Undergraduates in On-campus housing: 36%
Number of official organized extracurricular organizations: 328
3 Most popular majors: Finance, Health and Physical Education, Psychology
Student/Faculty ratio: 16:1
Average Class Size: 26
Percent of students going to grad school: 35%
Tuition and Fees: $9,229
In-State Tuition and Fees if different: $3,482
Cost for Room and Board: $7,690
Percent receiving financial aid out of those who apply: 54%
Percent receiving financial aid among all students: 52%

Located in the town of Harrisonburg, Virginia, James Madison University offers a variety of educational opportunities and extracurricular activities to cater to a diverse student body. With a friendly social vibe, an engaged student body and excellent dining food, JMU also provides students with a comfortable experience at a reasonable tuition.

The Human Community

JMU has a diverse range of academic offerings under eight academic colleges and across 69 majors. Many students choose to take courses at the School of Media Arts and Design, the Department of Nursing, and the College of Business. The latter is ranked third in the country in the ratio of graduate starting salaries to tuition. All students are also required to fulfill general education requirements under the core academic program, called "The Human Community." The requirements are organized into different areas, including "Human Questions and Contexts" and "Wellness Domain."

A junior said one of JMU's key strengths is its array of unique classes, recalling a theater class she took in which the students staged a production of *Twelfth Night*. The University also offers classes that examine esoteric topics such as Appalachian Literature.

Grading policy varies from department to department, and a junior said the workload is manageable, though she added that "in order to get an A in a class, you've definitely got to be willing to do some work." Professors can grade strictly, and will sometimes curve grades to reach a bell curve in every class. Still, students agree professors are generally very accessible at JMU. "I frequent the bioscience building and can meet professors as long as they're not busy and are in their office," a biology major said.

Beyond the Classroom

JMU has an especially open and sociable student body of 17,000 undergraduates. "The campus at JMU is amazingly friendly and diverse to the sense that you can find a group of people that are also interested in the obscure hobby you have," a student said. "You will often see people hold doors open for each other in any part of campus, in any building." Upperclassmen are more than willing to give freshmen advice when they seem lost or confused. Though the student body itself is not very diverse, with an 81 percent Caucasian population, students said the campus is "accepting and very open-minded."

> "The campus at JMU is amazingly friendly and diverse in the sense that you can find a group of people that are also interested in the obscure hobby you have."

JMU also has a vibrant and diverse extracurricular scene, including over 350 student organizations and around 20 fraternities and sororities, as well as many school-sponsored events. "Everyone I know is involved in at least one club, team, or extracurricular," a junior said. Student groups range from an opera guild to the Society of Automotive Engineers, providing students with the opportunity to pursue any interest they might have. Extracurricular activities also allow students to build more friendships, and a student who joined the university's pre-med organization and a Jewish group said she met many of her friends through those groups. In addition to joining student groups, many students also hold part-time jobs, usually working in labs, libraries, or with dining services.

Football and basketball are the most popular sporting events at JMU. Recently, Bridgeforth Stadium was renovated to raise its capacity to 25,000 fans. "Every game day, rain or shine, all of JMU's parking lots are full with tailgaters," a student said. The biggest football rivals are the University of Richmond and the College of William and Mary. The Harrisonburg community as a whole generally supports the sports scene. As one student described, "on game days, businesses all over Harrisonburg are decked out in purple and gold."

Sushi and other benefits

Most underclassmen live on-campus and then move off-campus in their junior or senior years. Students are generally enthusiastic about the diversity and quality of the food options at JMU's all-you-can-eat dining hall, which include sushi, crepes and Mexican cuisine. The dining facilities operate many retail facilities and eateries outside of the dining halls. One frequently mentioned locale is the Dog Pound, a popular late-night eatery that satisfies cravings for foods such as pizza, hot dogs, and nachos.

There are several meal plans offered, including "commuter plans" for students living off campus. Many of them stay on one of these smaller meal plans because it is easier for them to grab lunch while on campus during the day. One student noted that there are also many popular outside eateries within walking distance of campus, such as the chain Jimmy John's Gourmet Sandwiches, and Cookout, which serves fresh hamburgers and shakes.

JMU offers numerous academic and extracurricular opportunities while supporting a vibrant social scene. Though some students say the experience may seem overwhelming at times with students scrambling to find spots in popular classes, choosing between hundreds of extracurricular activities, or making time on the weekend to attend sporting tailgates and hang out with friends, in the end students can always rely on their peers for a helping hand.—*Molly Ma*

FYI
Three things every student at JMU should do before graduating are climb the rock wall, attend a home football game, and yell "JMU" at a tour group just to hear them yell "duuuuukes" back.
What is an example of the biggest campus-wide traditions each year? Throwing streamers at football games after touchdowns.
"My favorite part of the experience was being able to meet my now best friends that have been through many things with me."

Randolph College

Address: 2500 Rivermont Avenue, Lynchburg, VA 24503
Phone: 434-947-8100
E-mail address: admissions@randolphcollege.edu
Web site URL: www.randolphcollege.edu
Year Founded: 1891
Private or Public: Private
Religious Affiliation: Methodist
Location: Urban
Number of Applicants: 734
Percent Accepted: 90%
Percent Accepted who enroll: 25%
Number Entering: 163
Number of Transfers Accepted each Year: 53
Middle 50% SAT range: M: 500–600, CR: 500–610, Wr: Unreported
Middle 50% ACT range: 23–27

Early admission program EA/ED/None: EA
Percentage accepted through EA or ED: 73%
EA and ED deadline: 1-Dec
Regular Deadline: 1- March
Application Fee: $35; online application is free
Full time Undergraduate enrollment: 499
Total enrollment: 517
Percent Male: 34%
Percent Female: 66%
Total Percent Minority or Unreported: 36%
Percent African-American: 9%
Percent Asian/Pacific Islander: 2%
Percent Hispanic: 5%
Percent Native-American: 1%
Percent International: 13%
Percent in-state/out of state: 58%/42%
Percent from Public HS: 75%

Retention Rate: 79%
Graduation Rate 4-year: 66%
Graduation Rate 6-year: 66%
Percent Undergraduates in On-campus housing: 91%
Number of official organized extracurricular organizations: 40
3 Most popular majors: Biology, Political Science, Psychology
Student/Faculty ratio: 7:1
Average Class Size: 6
Percent of students going to grad school: 31%
Tuition and Fees: $29,866
In-State Tuition and Fees if different: No difference
Cost for Room and Board: $10,386
Percent receiving financial aid out of those who apply: 99%
Percent receiving financial aid among all students: 96%

Randolph College, formerly Randolph-Macon Women's College, began a new chapter of its 120-year history. In fall of 2007, this small liberal arts college admitted its first coeducational class. The school also has fulfilled its plans to release a new, enhanced curriculum. Yet with all these dramatic changes, the school insists that "the essential elements of the Randolph-Macon experience will remain constant."

A Close-Knit Community

Randolph College is described as a "gorgeous" college, set against the backdrop of the Virginia hills, and it is distinctive for its classic redbrick buildings and a matching redbrick wall that surrounds the entire campus. Students are required to live on campus for their full four years. "I like that everyone lives here," said one student. "We have such a wonderful sense of community, and it only takes five minutes to get from one part of campus to another." Most people have "no real complaints" about the living situation, as the rooms are larger than those at many other

colleges and each of the dorm buildings has a unique attribute such as air-conditioning, elevators, larger rooms, a better location, or extended quiet hours. Freshman dorms are assigned based on student preference forms, and upperclassmen draw for rooms in spring. Most of the dormitories are divided proportionally among the classes (except for the senior dorm and the mostly freshmen dorm) in order to facilitate and encourage interaction among upperclassmen and underclassmen. One senior commented, "My first year, I had so many upperclassmen coming into my room, welcoming me, letting me borrow books, telling me about professors, giving me tips, asking me about my clubs . . . people just take you under their wing!"

Another student commented, "It's really easy to meet people here because it's such a small school. There is only one dining hall and everyone has the same set meal plan, so sometimes people will stay at dinner for hours, just talking. Of course there are a couple of cliques, but there will be groups in any community and no one is exclusive."

Students say they met their friends through athletics, clubs, classes, or freshman orientation groups. "There are a ton of mixers," said one student. "You'd have to live in a hole not to have any friends at [Randolph]. And that's not possible to do here, either!" The college is very geographically diverse and boasts a large international student population, but ethnic diversity could use some improvement. "We could use more diversity, but I'm glad that we're at least as diverse as we are now," said one student. "It brings a lot to the classroom to have so many different vantage points."

From Homework to Happy Hour

The academics at Randolph are rigorous, to say the least. Students have a variety of requirements to fulfill, spanning such subjects as religion, philosophy, English, physical education, and a lab science. "Because of the liberal arts requirements, I get exposed to a lot of classes that may not be my strengths," commented one student. "But if you come in with an open mind and you push yourself to do well, they're really great." The most popular majors are psychology, politics, biology, and English, and if students can't find a major that suits them among the list of more than 25 possibilities, they always have the opportunity to design their own major. Most students agree, "All the majors are difficult—[Randolph] definitely doesn't give anything out for free." Registration is based on seniority and usually people are satisfied with the system, but the popularity of certain majors (particularly biology), the limited selection of classes, and the small class size can sometimes make it difficult to get into certain courses. Class size varies from 4 or 6 students to 30, although the average is 12. Workload, too, varies and depends on the class, the professor, and the preparation of the students. While one described it as "pretty heavy compared to other colleges," another observed, "It's not too different from high school AP classes. It can be overwhelming at first, but it's definitely manageable." Said one student, "Standards are fairly high, but there's no animosity within the classroom. People just want to do their own personal best."

According to many students, grading can be stringent. "We have a saying here: 'Anywhere else it would have been an A,'" said one. "I don't know if that's true, or if that's just us complaining about it." Still, student-faculty relations are "amazing. There's a lot of interaction with professors, especially on independent research projects." Another said, "A lot of professors have students babysitting,

house-sitting, pet-sitting, whatever!" Most professors have an open-door policy, where students can come by and talk or ask questions even if it's not during office hours. "Professors want students to do well," noted one junior. The faculty is also highly involved in student extracurricular life, participating in award shows or other activities and often attending a Macon Community Happy Hour. Overall, students appreciate their professors and their academic opportunities, believing that the rigor of the curriculum is "worth it, because we're working hard for our education and becoming stronger in the process."

We Like to Party?

The extracurricular activity at Randolph is centered around a wide variety of student clubs and organizations. "We're very involved in our clubs," said one student. "We're always out to save the world in one form or another." Several of the larger groups include Amnesty International, the Environmental Club, the Black Students Alliance, various religious organizations, language clubs, and the Macon Activities Council, which brings in speakers and musicians and organizes events such as horseback riding or whitewater rafting. There are also multiple drama productions, musical ensembles, and a whole host of other clubs. "We have upwards of 100 clubs for a student body of only 1,150 people, if that gives you any idea of how important clubs are to us," one student said.

> "You'd have to live in a hole not to have any friends at [Randolph]. And that's not possible to do here, either!"

Varsity athletics, however, has a slowly growing following, thanks to the college's recent infusion of males. In fact, nearly half of the male students are varsity athletes. "The people involved are really dedicated and the faculty is supportive, but I don't know how much attention the student body pays to the WildCats," said one student athlete. Intramural sports are not big; most students get their exercise by working out on their own, lifting weights or going running. A large majority of students have jobs on campus, especially since many of them participate in the work-study program.

As far as the weekend social scene is concerned, Randolph is not a party school. "We go off campus to party," one student said. "I'd say that on the weekends, almost half the campus goes home or goes to another college to party, while the other half stays behind to do work or club stuff." Another student said that weekend socializing can consist of a variety of activities such as drinking in people's rooms, going to a movie or out to dinner, going to see guest speakers or musicians, or going out to a club. "One club across the street has Wednesday college night, but generally, there's not a whole lot to do in Lynchburg," commented one sophomore. "Occasionally an organization on campus will host a bigger party, but for the most part people stick to smaller groups in rooms." One famous annual celebration is the "Never-Ending Weekend," with Friday night being the Tacky Party (the name is self-explanatory) and Saturday night being Fall Formal. Weekend activities in the surrounding town are limited, since Lynchburg "is not really a college town, so you have to drive to get to a movie theatre and most good restaurants." When asked to comment on the town's relationship with the college, one student responded, "We're definitely a separate community, but the town respects Randolph students and they have no real reason to complain about us because we're not a party school."

Daisy Chains and Pumpkin Parades

One particularly distinctive tradition at Randolph is the inter-class rivalry. Students identify themselves as "evens" or "odds," depending on the year of their graduation, and they enthusiastically participate in a vast collection of activities—such as water balloon fights and painting each other's banners—associated with the even-odd rivalry. "Sister classes" (freshmen/juniors and sophomores/seniors) have a strong connection, and they show their support for one another during Ring Week, when freshmen give small gifts to the juniors and create a scavenger hunt for them to find their class rings, and the Pumpkin Parade, where each senior receives a pumpkin carved by a sophomore. Right before graduation, sophomores make a huge daisy chain and pass it to the seniors. The class rivalry is even physically built into the school: a special staircase in the main lobby has one side for evens and one side for odds, and if a student goes up or down the wrong side, rumor has it that she won't graduate on time.

Randolph is certainly not for everyone. But for those who are willing to brave the tough academics and enjoy a somewhat quieter social scene, the college offers a vibrant community of dedicated, intelligent students who are working to better themselves and their society. One senior's final comment was, "It's a wonderful place. I've been exceedingly happy with what I've experienced there in the past four years."—*Lindsay Starck*

FYI
If you come to RC, you'd better bring "a whole lot of class spirit for the even-odd rivalry!"
What's the typical weekend schedule? "Relax, maybe party a bit or take a trip off-campus, then hit the books on Sunday."
If I could change one thing about RC, I'd "have more faculty available so that it's easier to get into popular or required classes."
Three things every student at RC should do before graduation are "join a club or several of them, ring the bell in Main Hall, and participate in the traditional Dell Run (running naked across the Greek-style ampitheater)."

Sweet Briar College

Address: P.O. Box 1052, Sweet Briar, VA 24595
Phone: 800-381-6142
E-mail address: admissions@sbc.edu
Web site URL: www.sbc .edu
Year Founded: 1901
Private or Public: Private
Religious Affiliation: None
Location: Rural
Number of Applicants: 606
Percent Accepted: 0.84
Percent Accepted who enroll: 36%
Number Entering: 180
Number of Transfers Accepted each Year: Unreported
Middle 50% SAT range: M:468–580, CR:500–620, Wr: 490–592
Middle 50% ACT range: 21–26
Early admission program EA/ED/None: None

Percentage accepted through EA or ED: NA
EA and ED deadline: NA
Regular Deadline: 1-Feb (rolling)
Application Fee: $40
Full time Undergraduate enrollment: 723
Total enrollment: 747
Percent Male: 3%
Percent Female: 97%
Total Percent Minority or Unreported: 17%
Percent African-American: 5%
Percent Asian/Pacific Islander: 2%
Percent Hispanic: 5%
Percent Native-American: <1%
Percent International: 2%
Percent in-state/out of state: 51%/49%
Percent from Public HS: 72%
Retention Rate: 76%

Graduation Rate 4-year: 70%
Graduation Rate 6-year: 72%
Percent Undergraduates in On-campus housing: 90%
Number of official organized extracurricular organizations: 61
3 Most popular majors: Biology, Business Management, Psychology
Student/Faculty ratio: 7:1
Average Class Size: 13
Percent of students going to grad school: 24%
Tuition and Fees: $30,620
In-State Tuition and Fees if different: No difference
Cost for Room and Board: $11,100
Percent receiving financial aid out of those who apply: 91%
Percent receiving financial aid among all students: 93%

Nestled in rural Virginia, approximately 11 miles away from Lynchburg, is Sweet Briar College, one of the nation's premier liberal arts and sciences colleges for women. With 3,250 acres, two lakes, and a 130-acre riding center, Sweet Briar's campus serves as a historical environment for its students to grow and learn. With small classes, interesting courses, and helpful professors, Sweet Briar girls rave about the academics and relationships they establish with professors and fellow students.

Professors as Friends

Students interviewed cited the school's small class sizes as a draw to Sweet Briar. The average class size is around 13 students with about 25 students filling the largest class rosters, which are primarily for introductory courses. The small classes "facilitate great class discussion; everyone gets a chance to contribute, and your professors really get the chance to know you as a person and a friend," a sophomore said.

Students interviewed all agreed that Sweet Briar professors are very accessible and helpful. They cited professors Gmail chatting at 3 a.m. to help students with Latin and instructors encouraging students to send drafts of papers. "Our professors work with us to not only study the material, but also put it into real-world context," a junior said, adding that the hands-on and experience driven academics help Sweet Briar thrive as a school. In addition, it is not uncommon for professors to invite students to their homes for dinner. "I have made some connections of a lifetime with many of my professors during my time as a Sweet Briar student," a sophomore said.

Due to Sweet Briar's small enrollment, the number of courses offered is less than the number offered by larger universities, a freshman said, but some of Sweet Briar's majors are "designable" for students to pursue specific aspects and concentrations. Yet, Sweet Briar offers fascinating classes like "Myth, Legends, and Their Retelling English,"

"Historic Preservation in Virginia," and "Sacraments and Civil Unions." Some classes, such as one seminar offered recently, reflecting on where America stands 10 years after 9/11, are a mixture of two course subjects like international affairs and English, while others include field trips. One sophomore recounted how in the "Intro to Archaeology" course she took freshman year the class went to an 18th or 19th century house site on campus to participate in the ongoing archeological dig for credit. "On Families Weekend, I even took my parents with me; they're still talking about it," she said. The professors and small student body create a pleasant community feel at Sweet Briar. One student commented, "The most surprising thing to me about Sweet Briar was the community. I was shocked at how tightly knit and helpful everyone was."

Tap Clubs and Dances

Listed as one of the top ten most preppy colleges by *The Official Preppy Handbook*, Sweet Briar's official colors are pink and green. Sweet Briar's brother school, Hampden-Sydney College, placed third on the Handbook's list. Yet, Sweet Briar does not host sororities or the Greek system. Instead, the 11 tap clubs are the dominant social setting, said one freshman, who added that they are Sweet Briar's version of sororities. Tap clubs, which are invitation-only clubs, each admit new members differently. New members are often associated with a mentor called a "Mom," and tap clubs often have lineages just like the family system in Greek sororities. "It is a huge deal to be tapped into a Club and the fact that you've been chosen becomes part of your SBC identity," a freshman said.

Each tap club's membership is based on various aspects from focusing on theatre and comedy to emphasizing service and areas of academic study. But if you are not part of a tap club, Sweet Briar's open community allows many groups to join together for activities and social gatherings, one junior said. StARs (Student Activities Representatives) and the student-run Campus Events Organization work with Residence Life to plan awesome campus-wide events every week, a sophomore said. Whether it is "drive-in style" movie nights out on the lawn, "Girls' Night Out" at a fun restaurant in Lynchburg, rock climbing and hiking opportunities, or shuttles to Ballroom Dancing Classes at VMI, there are always plenty of ways to stay busy, she added.

Each year, Sweet Briar hosts a Founder's Day dance. Open to alumni and their guests, the dance gives attendees the chance to come back and reminisce at their picturesque alma mater. Sweet Briar often also holds a Winter Mixer with a neighboring school, like Hampton-Sydney College or Virginia Military Institute (VMI), a junior said.

Sweet Briar also has more frequent parties, commonly referred to as "Boathouse parties" almost every Thursday night. Different clubs and organizations hold these events, which usually have a fun theme like "Last Friday Night" or "Barbie," a freshman said, adding that boys from other schools are sometimes invited to attend. "They can get crazy, but we're not a party campus . . . when your big party is on a *Thursday*, you know that's not what we're about," a sophomore said.

Off Campus Weekends

On weekends, many students leave campus said four students interviewed. One sophomore estimated about half the campus departs for other locations. "Because we're an all-women's college, if you want to meet guys, you need to go out and find them," a sophomore said, adding that "Sweet Briar is not a party school; but if you want to party, there are plenty of larger, co-ed schools in the area."

> "The most surprising thing to me about Sweet Briar was the community. I was shocked at how tightly knit and helpful everyone was."

A popular destination for the weekend is Sweet Briar's brother school, Hampden-Sydney College in Farmville, Va., about 60 miles away. Other popular collegiate choices include neighboring schools like VMI and UVA, a sophomore said. Others venture into the city of Lynchburg, which is approximately 20 miles away from campus, to go to interesting shops, restaurants, galleries, and other attractions. Those who remain on campus study, participate in events on campus, and have their own fun.

Steeped in Tradition

According to students, Sweet Briar is a school heavily defined by history and immersed in history, legends and other stories. The college was named after the former Sweet Briar plantation, and the school's founding in honor of the plantation owner's daughter who died of illness at 16 years of age leads to ghost stories that float around campus, and annual Halloween ghost tours are fun, a sophomore said.

Sweet Briar girls also come together in support of their sport teams. Though the season dictates which sport students follow the most, students find a lot of pride in Sweet Briar's varsity sports. "They all have a big following, and campus pride is definitely prominent during sport seasons," a junior said. In particular, Sweet Briar's equestrian team is nationally ranked and the school's most well known team, a sophomore said.

Another tradition is the Big Sister-Little Sister program where each freshman is assigned a junior "Big Sister" to help her acclimate to her new home-away-from-home. Students say this tradition of having a mentor, advisor, and friend helped them transition into college.

And the campus itself is steeped in tradition and history. The National Register of Historic Places designated 21 buildings on Sweet Briar's campus as a National Historical District. One sophomore said she finds the library her favorite place on campus— "it's definitely one of the most beautiful places on campus." Still, many students find the outdoors, which is filled with rolling hills, trails, lakes and more breathtaking spots, as stunning as the historical buildings. Sweet Briar's girls can see these views from their dorms, as almost every dorm room has a view of the Blue Ridge mountain area. "I feel so blessed to be so close to nature; a lot of people don't get that chance, especially at college," another sophomore added.
—*Sharon Yin*

FYI

If you come to Sweet Briar, "you'd better bring a positive attitude, pearls, puffy paint, and anything pink or green!"

If you come to Sweet Briar, "you'd better leave negative attitudes and laziness behind."

Three things every student at Sweet Briar should do before graduating are "spend some time down at the Boathouse (on one of Sweet Briar's lakes), ride the horses, go to dinner at a professor's house."

University of Richmond

Address: 28 Westhampton Way, University of Richmond, VA 23173

Phone: 804-289-8640

E-mail address: admissions@richmond.edu

Web site URL: www.richmond.edu

Year Founded: 1830

Private or Public: Private

Religious Affiliation: None

Location: Suburban

Number of Applicants: 7,970

Percent Accepted: 33%

Percent Accepted who enroll: 29%

Number Entering: 781

Number of Transfers Accepted each Year: 138

Middle 50% SAT range: M: 610–700, CR: 580–690, Wr: 580–690

Middle 50% ACT range: 28–31

Early admission program EA/ED/None: ED

Percentage accepted through EA or ED: 39%

EA and ED deadline: 15-Nov

Regular Deadline: 15-Jan

Application Fee: $50

Full time Undergraduate enrollment: 3,000

Total enrollment: 3,555

Percent Male: 47%

Percent Female: 53%

Total Percent Minority or Unreported: 40%

Percent African-American: 7%

Percent Asian/Pacific Islander: 5%

Percent Hispanic: 5%

Percent Native-American: 0%

Percent International: 9%

Percent in-state/out of state: 18%/82%

Percent from Public HS: 61%

Retention Rate: 91%

Graduation Rate 4-year: 82%

Graduation Rate 6-year: 87%

Percent Undergraduates in On-campus housing: 90%

Number of official organized extracurricular organizations: 275

3 Most popular majors: Business/Marketing, Social Sciences, English

Student/Faculty ratio: 8:1

Average Class Size: 16

Percent of students going to grad school: 25%

Tuition and Fees: $43,170

In-State Tuition and Fees if different: No difference

Cost for Room and Board: $9,250

Percent receiving financial aid out of those who apply: Unreported

Percent receiving financial aid among all students: Unreported

Located in a lush landscape near the James River, the University of Richmond offers arguably one of the most beautiful campuses in the country. But don't let the seemingly serene environment of UR fool you. Throughout their four years at UR, Richmond students are kept busy by a multitude of academic, social, and extracurricular activities. When the freshmen arrive on campus, they will be pleasantly surprised by the welcoming and friendly atmosphere and quickly delve into the unique opportunities offered by UR.

Only at Richmond

Bloomberg Businessweek recently ranked the Robins School of Business as the 15th best undergraduate business program in the country. Thus it's no surprise that business is one of the most popular majors and students can choose to focus on accounting, business administration, or economics. UR also offers a unique interdisciplinary major: leadership studies. Students apply in their second year for admission into the Jepson School of Leadership Studies, where they will study a variety of subjects including economics, history, literature, philosophy, and psychology. While all the majors are challenging in their own right, they are not overwhelming. "I haven't heard of any major being especially hard, but many of them are quite competitive," said a sophomore. "Premedicine biology, for example, has a laid-out plan for all four years so it's hard if you do not start early." Sophomores can also design unique fields of study by creating their own interdisciplinary studies major.

Richmond students must complete the General Education curriculum, which covers art, history, language, natural sciences, social analysis, symbolic reasoning, and First Year Seminar courses. In addition, everyone at UR has to take The Core Course, which examines common human problems through a combination of philosophy and literature. Prior to graduation, students must also complete three-part Wellness classes that aim to promote academic success and a healthy lifestyle. Another unique academic program UR offers is the Bonner Scholars Program, which pairs up students with local non-profit organizations and lets them engage in social issues that interest them. About 25 students in each class are selected as Bonner Scholars and they commit ten hours each week toward community service. In return, the students receive a renewable $2,500 scholarship.

Most Richmond students agree that classes are not easy. "There are no really easy classes in general, as you progress anywhere the classes get harder and more challenging," one junior said. Many students complain about the calculus courses, which are required for getting into the business school, as well as the lab sciences. One student describes the typical workload as "150 to 450 pages of reading a week and then a paper every other week with a couple of smaller assignments in between." With a student-faculty ratio of 8:1, most students find it very easy to engage with the professors and receive help. "The teachers will help with papers or tell you where to go to get help," one freshman noted. The average class size is around 15 people and most classes are less than 20 people, which helps to foster discussions in an intimate environment. Getting into certain classes is competitive especially as a first year student. The basic classes always fill up quickly and you should always have alternates. Sometimes, the professors are willing to help out and accept students into closed classes.

Outside the Classrooms

Richmond students balance out their busy academic life by actively pursuing a myriad of student groups. The most popular groups are the 15 active fraternity and sorority chapters, with 37 percent of the undergraduates affiliated with a Greek group. "The dominant social scene is probably the frat parties, whether in a lodge (fraternity house) or at an apartment," one freshman explained. "However, you don't need to join the frat to go." People usually go out Thursday, Friday, and Saturday nights. The upperclassmen live in on-campus apartments, which also host a lot of parties on those nights. Students agree that while the majority of people drink, there are large numbers of people who do not and students are capable of finding other events to attend on the weekend.

But Greek life isn't the only activity that Richmond students are heavily involved with. UR boasts over 250 student-run clubs and organizations, covering a wide range of subjects from academics to sports to visual and performing arts. Time commitments toward these groups are entirely up to the students. "Extracurricular involvement depends on what groups you join and the time you have," one student said. "If you can't attend the meetings but still want to be part of the group, that works, too."

Like many other liberal arts colleges,

sports do not play a very important role at UR and student enthusiasm is not very high. Football and basketball are probably the most popular ones. Tailgating, which is a social event by itself, during football season tends to bring out a lot of students, many of who never actually make it into the stadium or simply leave at half time. "There is pride amongst the people who attend the games, but outside the sports arenas, there is not an outstanding amount of pride for the sports teams," a freshman said.

> "The school surprised me in how welcoming it was to incoming freshmen and how well it helped people transition from high school to college."

Even though UR is located within the suburbs, it is close enough to Richmond that students can get off campus and explore the surroundings. The James River is a great spot for swimming and sunbathing in the afternoon as well as for the running and biking trails. However, many students choose to stay on campus and do not venture into the city too often despite free transportation services offered by the University. Many students have cars to escape the confines of the campus. "There is plenty to do without leaving the campus," one junior explained. "But if you do want to leave campus for a while, there are plenty of rides available."

On Campus Perks
In recent years, UR renovated several existing buildings and added a new residence hall as well as a planned business school building set to open this spring. The University expanded the Robins Stadium from a soccer and track complex to a multi-purpose stadium that will now serve the football, lacrosse, soccer and track and field teams. In 2006, the Gottwald Center for the Sciences, which hosts the biology, chemistry and physics departments, underwent a $37 million expansion that provided brand-new equipment and facilities for students and faculties. As part of UR's effort to expand the internationalization of the school, the Carole Weinstein International Center was constructed and helps to match students with nearly 80 study abroad programs. "The International Center is very open and has many places to sit and relax," one freshman said.

The dining hall, affectionately known as "D-Hall," provides another place for friends to hang out. Though students are generally satisfied with the quality of food served at the Heilman Dining Center, many complain about the lack of variety. "The main dining hall has everything and nothing," one junior said. "There are many choices, but the choices do not change ever and get boring after a while." In addition to D-Hall, there are many other dining options on campus available to students. Tyler's Grill is great for a quick sandwich or breakfast snack, and it has a weekly special to change things up. One student compared the Grill to a "healthy McDonalds: very quick and tastes good." The Celllar offers great dinner choices with take-out options and also doubles as a bar, letting students grab drinks without leaving the campus. There is a large selection of restaurants on Broad Street in downtown Richmond, about a 20-minute drive from campus.

The Weinstein Center for Recreation and Wellness is also a popular destination for students. It has a three-court gymnasium, an indoor track, six-lane swimming as well as racquet and squash courts. "The gym is clean, well-kept and extensive," one freshman said. Other student favorites include the Whitehurst building and the centrally located Commons, which spans across Westhampton Lake and provides a restaurant, a smoothie bar, TVs and game systems and plays movies on the weekend.

A View to the Lake
While students have the option to move off campus, most choose to stay in one of the 14 residence halls or the on-campus apartments. Freshmen are housed in single-sex dorms: Dennis, Marsh or Wood Halls for men and Lora Robins Court or Moore Hall for women. "The freshman dorms are really nice," one freshman said. "They get cleaned almost every day and are bigger than the dorms at many colleges I have seen." Several coed residence halls are also available to upperclassmen and learning communities, where people live together because they are all interested in one topic. Freshmen are assigned dorms by the housing department while upperclassmen can either participate in a lottery for dorms or request a town house-styled apartment. There are also RAs assigned to each freshmen residence and students said that they try to help out whenever they can and keep the hall running smoothly without becoming overly involved in people's lives. The Westhampton Lake divides the residence

halls and legend has it that whoever kisses on the gazebo that connects the two sides of the lake are bound to marry each other.

There are also many traditions that students eagerly observe and participate in. At the beginning of the year, the freshmen class collectively participates in the honor code signing ceremonies—Proclamation for women and Investiture for men—that officially recognize them as members of the University. Held at a hotel in downtown Richmond, the annual Ring Dance is a formal event celebrating the junior women, who can bring family and friends as well as

a date with them to the dance. During graduation weekend, the entire graduating class circles around the Westhampton Lake as part of a candlelight ceremony.

Richmond students are excited to be where they are and ready to take advantage of the plethora of opportunities available to them. Their enthusiasm for academics and extracurricular activities can be matched at very few places. As one freshman said, "The school surprised me in how welcoming it was to incoming freshmen and how well it helped people transition from high school to college."—*Jimin He*

FYI

If you come to UR, you'd better bring "comfortable shoes for walking around and knowledge of calculus."

What's the typical weekend schedule? "Generally people eat brunch between 12 and 1 pm. On Saturdays the football games are in the afternoon with tailgates before them. Then you go out Saturday night and wake up late on Sunday and do homework the rest of Sunday."

If I could change one thing about UR, it would be "making scheduling easier, especially for first-year students."

University of Virginia

Address: PO Box 400160, Charlottesville, VA 22904-4160
Phone: 434-924-0311
E-mail address: undergradadmission@virginia.edu
Web site URL: www.virginia.edu
Year Founded: 1819
Private or Public: Public
Religious Affiliation: None
Location: Urban
Number of Applicants: 17,798
Percent Accepted: 33%
Percent Accepted who enroll: 52%
Number Entering: 3,434
Number of Transfers Accepted each Year: 858
Middle 50% SAT range: M: 630–740, CR: 610–720, Wr: 610–720
Middle 50% ACT range: 28–32
Early admission program EA/ED/None: EA

Percentage accepted through EA or ED: Unreported
EA and ED deadline: 1-Nov
Regular Deadline: 1-Jan
Application Fee: $60
Full time Undergraduate enrollment: 15,762
Total enrollment: 24,297
Percent Male: 46%
Percent Female: 54%
Total Percent Minority or Unreported: 31%
Percent African-American: 6%
Percent Asian/Pacific Islander: 13%
Percent Hispanic: 13%
Percent Native-American: <1%
Percent International: 6%
Percent in-state/out of state: 71%/29%
Percent from Public HS: 75%
Retention Rate: 97%

Graduation Rate 4-year: 84%
Graduation Rate 6-year: 91%
Percent Undergraduates in On-campus housing: 41%
Number of official organized extracurricular organizations: 604
3 Most popular majors: Social Sciences, Engineering, Business/Marketing
Student/Faculty ratio: 16:1
Average Class Size: 16
Percent of students going to grad school: 80%
Tuition and Fees: $35,898
In-State Tuition and Fees if different: $11,576
Cost for Room and Board: $9,240
Percent receiving financial aid out of those who apply: 47%
Percent receiving financial aid among all students: 34%

Founded in 1819 by Thomas Jefferson, the University of Virginia is rich with tradition and history dating back to its creation by the man who would become the third President of the United States. Since its founding, UVa has revolutionized the American university, as it was the first to offer courses of study in subjects such as philosophy, architecture, and political science. UVa's tradition of breaking tradition dictates that no student is a "freshman" or a "senior," but simply a first-year, second-year, third-year, or fourth-year. Students call their campus "the Grounds," and often refer to UVa as very simply "the University."

The University

The undergraduate program of the University of Virginia is divided into seven schools, including the Engineering School, the Architecture School, the Nursing School, the McIntire School of Commerce, the Curry School of Education, the Batten School of Leadership and Public Policy, and the College of Arts and Sciences. Each of the University's schools has different requirements for graduation, and they are often specific to a student's major. The College of Arts and Sciences requires that students complete 120 credits to graduate, including 12 credits in sciences and mathematics, six in humanities, six in social sciences, three in history, and three in non-Western perspectives. Students as well must complete a foreign language requirement and a writing requirement. Upon entry to UVa, a small number of students, selected by the University from a pool of those specifically nominated by their high schools, are named Jefferson Scholars, and receive a full scholarship for four years of tuition, room, board, books, and other expenses. Echols Scholars, who get priority over the rest of the undergraduate body when scheduling courses, are also automatically selected during the admissions process. These students have the chance to create their own Interdisciplinary Major program, and are housed in the same first-year dormitories.

By far, the most popular major in the College is Economics, "mostly populated by those who were denied entry into the McIntire School of Commerce," as reported by one fourth-year. Some of the most difficult majors traditionally include Mechanical Engineering, Commerce, and Biochemistry. Another student illustrated this difficulty: "For example, to receive a C in Dr. Grisham's Biochemistry lecture class, he states

that for every hour that students spend in class per week, they must work for a total of three hours outside of class. This totals to 9 hours outside of class for a C—you do the math." However, there are always "gut" classes, like every other university, as well as very popular classes "because the professor is just great." One more recent addition to the list of popular classes is "Gaga for Gaga," which one student described as "a legitimate class, despite accusations otherwise, where the students and professor use Lady Gaga as a launching point for discussing issues of gender and sexuality in modern society."

Students say that the workload for these classes is considerable but always manageable. "Just as any other large university, it takes a fair amount of self-discipline and initiative to stand out and do well at UVa. A student's workload is strictly dependent on his future aspirations and competitive drive," one student commented. One fourth-year student who transferred to UVa noted, "I had to get used to writing 20- to 45-page papers instead of five pages . . . but the workload obviously depends on the class and it's not very hard to adapt."

Students often find adapting to a high-work environment is easy because the professors are very helpful and readily accessible. One student said "professors are keen to the needs of their students and are very supportive." Faculty members are described as "friendly, available, and helpful." Professors are "very responsive to email" and provide very valuable help during office hours. The University strives to make the interaction between students and faculty closer and more active, and has implemented a program in which a student can "take any professor out to lunch and UVa funds will pick up your tab."

Amidst the tradition embedded in UVa culture, the University also promotes honor in all aspects of social and academic life through the Honor System. Student-governed, the Honor System places a lot of trust in the students, but treats all academic and behavioral infractions as equal under the infamous "single sanction": dismissal from the University. Some students find the code to be "frightening and fair." One student said, "Though cheating still exists at the University, the threat of expulsion and the effectiveness of honor trials in expelling students at UVa make doing so unattractive enough where it is kept to a minimum."

Wahoo!

Of course, UVa students must work hard to stand out in class, but all the hard work done during the week gives way to parties and release in this university that is more than 30 percent Greek.

> **"People here just seem to have an air of integrity, and the Honor System is merely a reflection of the collective atmosphere."**

While the mascot of UVa is officially the Cavalier, the "Wahoo" has long been a popular name for those attending the University, and Charlottesville has earned the nickname "Hooville" from the presence of UVa's Wahoos. This moniker comes from the name of the wahoo fish, which can supposedly drink its weight in water. "There is alcohol everywhere, and it's surprising how many UVa students actually do drink like a fish." However, one student said, "there are those who do not drink (including me) and they can still have fun, especially if they avoid the crazy-partier types."

With the prevalence of Greek life at the University, there is a party to be found every night of the weekend, but still most students restrict themselves to partying from Thursday through Saturday nights, spending the weeknights on coursework. For Wahoos, including one fourth-year athlete, who are not fans of fraternity parties, "there are over 10 bars open 7 days a week on the Corner (the popular name for a row of shops, bars, and eateries on the corner of a nearby block) in walking distance from any area on campus."

Grounds

On the Grounds, old, renovated, and new buildings retain "Thomas Jefferson's unique flair for architecture. UVa is a World Heritage Site for a reason. It's stunning and one of a kind," according to one first-year housed on UVa's campus.

First-years live on Grounds and are randomly assigned to the Old Dorms or the New Dorms. Old Dorms—"small," non-air-conditioned two-person doubles—are "often highly sought after for their proximity to central Grounds, even though students no longer have a choice." New Dorms, which "despite renovations are not as new as the common name implies," are larger and suite-styled. One drawback of the New Dorms is their distance from the center of campus. However, they are rather close to the largest dining hall and "some lucky suites are air-conditioned." Each floor on Old Dorms and each pair of ten-person suites in New Dorms has an RA. Students say that their RAs are often rather relaxed, "but some are very strict about enforcing school policies."

After their first year, many students move off of Grounds, with 50 percent of second-years living off-campus. Many move to fraternity or sorority houses, and others move to one of the residential colleges. The residential colleges, including Hereford, Brown, and the International Residential College (IRC), "are social communities and tend to each have a basic principle, like 'odd' or 'artsy' or 'diverse,' that describes them very well." One resident of Brown described the college as "eccentric, quirky, fun, and friendly"— qualities of a community that are ensured by a long application requiring essays responding to such ridiculous topics as "Backpacking across Europe, you manage to irrevocably offend an entire village. In retaliation, an old gypsy woman puts a curse on you, making you fall in love with a refrigerator. Explain your newfound love to your parents with utmost sincerity." Hereford, while much farther from campus, is usually a very culturally and socially diverse community. Its residents request Hereford for the chance to live in a diverse community of their choosing, in lieu of the regular first-year housing which offers no choice between Old Dorms and New Dorms. In addition, "about half of the International Residential College's residents are international students and the other half American." IRC partners with local community service organizations so that its students can get more involved in local and global service.

Students who live on campus say that the dining hall food is "less than perfect, but still rather good: B-plus." The few complaints about dining facilities are centered on the sometimes long lines. There are three main dining halls, spaced roughly evenly on the Grounds. The newest, Observatory Hill Dining Hall, is right next to New Dorms, and is a "very social experience," according to one first-year. Runk Dining Hall, which is rather far from much of Grounds "serves arguably the best food on Grounds." Students with meal plans can use "Plus Dollars" to shop at restaurants near campus, like Domino's and Starbucks, and can eat at on-Grounds food courts like Pavilion and Crossroads, which have restaurants like Chik-fil-A and Sbarro.

"After first year, some students do not opt in for a meal plan and either prepare or purchase their own meals in restaurants along the Corner or on campus," according to one student who described the life of students who live off-campus.

While the University's bus system "does a really great job of getting you around Grounds to wherever you need to be," many second-, third-, and fourth-years who live off-Grounds have cars. The few who do drive away from UVa on the weekends "go back home to visit their family in Virginia (since most are in-state)."

The "Conservative Stronghold"

Since UVa is a public university, it accepts primarily in-state students, and the "wealth in Northern Virginia in the suburbs of D.C. in counties such as Fairfax and Prince William" has led to a stereotype of the UVa student as white, "preppy, conservative, upper-middle class, wearing polo shirts and khaki pants." While some students see this as reality and are upset that "some people seem close-minded," others are refreshed to see Charlottesville as "one of the most open-minded places in all of Virginia," and find that in the University, there is "significant ethnic and cultural diversity despite the relative lack of geographic diversity." The latter students often find that the UVa community is "open and embracing" to those of different socioeconomic backgrounds, as well as those of different sexual orientations and gender identities.

Wah-Hoo-Wah, Hoo-Rah-Ray, U-V-A!

The University of Virginia is rife with history and tradition, and this translates into intense devotion to and pride in the University's extracurricular activities, sports, and overall community. People are "very dedicated" to their extracurricular activities, which include debate in the Jefferson Society, volunteerism with the Madison House, writing for such publications as *The Cavalier Daily*, or university-wide organizations of students and clubs with the University Judiciary Committee, the Honor Committee, and Student Council: "the Big Three."

Besides some work-study jobs and "working in some capacity at a bar," most Wahoos are too busy with their academic life and their extracurricular life to have jobs.

Attending sports games and other athletic events is a huge way that students at UVa show school spirit. While "just about every sports team besides the football team does extremely well," especially men's and women's soccer, lacrosse, swimming, and tennis, one Cavaliers football fan said, "We dress up for no apparent reason but tradition, pre-game, and scream our hearts out even though we know we'll probably lose, and I think that says a lot about our school spirit." Besides the football games, "huge crowds show up for the champion soccer team's games and basketball games and get to see some great athletic success there as well."

Imbued in the tradition of the University are a great many secret societies. Most of these societies' operations are philanthropic in nature, but, according to one student, the different organizations of community-minded students "have different styles of secrecy." The IMPs are very public with their identities, but keep their generally altruistic actions well hidden from view. The Zs are very public about their community service, but choose to keep their identities secret until graduation. Members of the 7 Society, however, are secret until death. The philanthropy of these groups is carried out in very secretive and exciting ways, as one first year recounted that "at Convocation, the President of the University's address to all the first-years on the Lawn, the 7 Society planted letters in one speaker's hand and under the seventh seat in the seventh row, revealing that the society had donated several thousand dollars to the first-years' graduating class."

As a listen to UVa's de facto alma mater, "The Good Ole Song," will make clear, the sense of community and school pride that saturates the University is unquestionable. One Wahoo said that he would make the decision to choose UVa over other universities "every time, without question. The University is my home."—*Connor Moseley*

FYI

If you come to UVa, you'd better leave behind "the words 'freshman,' 'sophomore,' 'junior,' and 'senior.'"

If I could change one thing about UVa, "I'd change the time when first-years have to submit applications for their second-year housing—way too early in October or November, before people get to know each other and make good decisions."

Three things every student at UVa should do before graduating are "streak the lawn, make out in the tunnels below the Rotunda while it's raining, and give Dean Groves a high-five."

Virginia Polytechnic Institute & State University

Address: 201 Burruss Hall, Blacksburg, VA 24061
Phone: 540-231-6267
E-mail address: vtadmiss@vt.edu
Web site URL: www.vt.edu
Year Founded: 1872
Private or Public: Public
Religious Affiliation: None
Location: Rural
Number of Applicants: 21,201
Percent Accepted: 67%
Percent Accepted who enroll: 40%
Number Entering: 5,205
Number of Transfers Accepted each Year: 1,536
Middle 50% SAT range: M: 580–680, CR: 540–640, Wr: 540–630
Middle 50% ACT range: Unreported
Early admission program EA/ED/None: ED

Percentage accepted through EA or ED: 55%
EA and ED deadline: 1-Nov
Regular Deadline: 15-Jan
Application Fee: $60
Full time Undergraduate enrollment: 23,690
Total enrollment: 31,006
Percent Male: 58%
Percent Female: 42%
Total Percent Minority or Unreported: 23%
Percent African-American: 3%
Percent Asian/Pacific Islander: 7%
Percent Hispanic: 7%
Percent Native-American: <1%
Percent International: 2%
Percent in-state/out of state: 69%/31%
Percent from Public HS: Unreported
Retention Rate: 91%

Graduation Rate 4-year: 52%
Graduation Rate 6-year: 53%
Percent Undergraduates in On-campus housing: 37%
Number of official organized extracurricular organizations: 600
3 Most popular majors: Engineering, Biology, Business
Student/Faculty ratio: 17:1
Average Class Size: 30
Percent of students going to grad school: 49%
Tuition and Fees: $24,480
In-State Tuition and Fees if different: $10,509
Cost for Room and Board: $6,856
Percent receiving financial aid out of those who apply: 55%
Percent receiving financial aid among all students: 42%

Virginia Polytechnic Institute and State University, often referred to as VT or Virginia Tech, is home to more than 23,000 undergraduates. Located in Blacksburg, Virginia, the university draws much of its student body from Virginia. Here students not only get a great education, but they also are immersed with school spirit and surrounded by amazing food options.

Hokies Seek Academic Success

"The biggest thing for me that differentiates VT from other schools is our engineering fair." Every semester, VT gathers about 50 companies that are there to hire engineers for internships and co-ops. This allows students to bypass online searching for jobs; rather they just go and hand out résumés and schedule interviews on campus. Many have found paid summer internships through this event.

Students are excited by the span of classes to take. With nearly 3,000 students, World Regions is often regarded as one of the largest classes at VTech. Many students enjoyed this class and noted it as one of their favorite courses taken. The class is popular with good reason—it's once a week, a core curriculum class, and is taught by an interesting professor.

Other classes students interviewed highlighted include Intro to Acting, Human Sexuality, and Cryptography. Classes vary in how difficult they are to get into at VT. Some of the large classes have over 2,700 students and are easy to get into, while others like Intro to Acting, which is significantly smaller, is much more difficult.

Students are happy to be learning at VT. "I love going to class and learning new ways to think and considering new perspectives on things," a junior said. A sophomore noted that she felt she was getting a great education. While students pointed out they don't like the stress of exams, they feel prepared for the real world when they graduate. Hokies point out that the staff is very well qualified.

One of the downsides of a large school is that not all classes are taught by professors—some are taught by graduate students. "At first I didn't like that graduate students teach some of my classes, but I haven't found it to be a problem." Most students find faculty accessible. All teachers have "set office hours and are more than willing to make separate appointments if their office hours conflict with your schedule," a sophomore said.

Hokie Pride

Despite a large student body, they're all connected by school spirit. "We take our Hokie pride seriously," a junior said. Hokies have an immense amount of school pride. "I think by far Virginia Tech has the best school spirit out there," a sophomore said.

VT pride is also obvious in the surrounding Blacksburg area and alumni who continue to be Tech fans for life. "Once a Hokie, always a Hokie. I can say with full confidence that there is no other school like us and there is really nothing like being a Hokie," a junior said.

Everything relates back to the school's motto "Ut Prosim" which means "That I may serve." A current junior described a visit to Virginia Tech her senior year of high school: "I was amazed at how many people were wearing Virginia Tech gear. It was literally a sea of maroon and orange." She said she felt an instant connection with other students. "Every time I step foot outside I realize how lucky I am to be here."

One of the dominant social scenes is at Hokie athletics when the whole community is involved and school spirit comes out in number and intensity. "The football games in Lane Stadium and the basketball games in Cassel Colosseum are intense with pride and everyone goes all out to support our Hokies," a sophomore said.

Greek life is also a major part of the social scene. Around 20 percent of Hokies participate in Greek life. Some students look to Greek organizations to provide parties. "Frats can host crazy parties," a sophomore said. There are also coed fraternities and the sororities that organize activities ranging from volunteering at animal shelters to going on cruises together.

Pomp and Circumstance

Virginia Tech abounds with traditions. One famous annual event is a huge snowball fight for the first snowfall. Corps play against Civilians. VTech is one of the few public universities that maintain a corps of cadets. "Despite the larger number of civilians, the Corps uses strategy and usually wins. It's really fun to have everyone out on the drill field in the snow!" a junior said.

Another tradition is jumping up and down to Enter Sandman when the football team comes out. "Everyone is jumping and if you're not, you're forced to anyway because the entire stadium is shaking," a sophomore said. "I heard at the ACC Championship we shook the press box."

The big tradition at Virginia Tech for the juniors is the annual Ring Dance. Established by the Class of 1935, the dance has been held in subsequent years in the spring. There is a catered dinner banquet on the Friday before the dance, and then on Saturday the dance is held. The Corps of Cadets march in to form the Class' roman numerals, and dates exchange rings and see their rings for the first time. There is also a Military Ball and the Navy Ball for the Corps of Cadets every year.

There are annual parties for everybody, from the ballroom dancers to the salsa dancers to the grinders, a sophomore stated. "With such a large school if you have a five percent interest in a group, that's more than enough to host large events."

> **"We are especially spirited. It's one of the reasons that I chose to come."**

One Large Campus

Most Hokies enjoy the size of the campus and the students. "My favorite part of campus is the Drill Field," a junior said. "I think it is what makes our campus stand out. I love walking across it going to and from class, watching the Corps of Cadets marching and students wearing Maroon and Orange with pride."

Others enjoy Lane Stadium because football games are the highlight of the year, while others revel in the size of the student population. "There's so many people that you just meet everyone and know there's still so many different people to meet."

Another benefit of a large campus is that there are clubs for everything—"Skydiving, skiing, snowboarding, surfing, chess, math, obscure Indian culture, renaissance, etc." There are also clubs for most majors.

There are also various singing groups: Juxtaposition (all male a cappella), Solstice (all female a cappella). "The VTU (Virginia Tech Union) arranges for the awesome concerts and entertainment we have at Tech," a junior said. Virginia Tech's clubs host many large events such as Relay For Life.

Though many VTech students come from

Virginia, not many go home on weekends, as there is so much fun and events to go to at VTech. According to a sophomore, "No one goes home, unless sick or visiting others." Many students stay on campus because their friends are on campus and since sporting events are often on weekends.

Housing Options and Yummy Food

Freshmen are required to live on campus. Housing is selected in a lottery system based on seniority. There are special housing requests that you can opt into (i.e. the Galileo dorm is half full of engineers). After freshman year, most live off campus. There are around 5,000 freshmen and approximately 9,000 slots for on campus housing.

Dorms typically have one RA for each floor or hallway who serves as a mentor. "They basically make sure you have a pleasant living experience on campus and that you stay out of trouble," a sophomore stated. The RAs are there for students to talk to, get advice from, and to enforce housing rules when needed.

The strictness of the RA is dependent on the RA. "I've heard stories of RAs who enforced curfew and made random checks, and I've heard of RAs who regularly took the kids out to parties," a sophomore said. "Personally, I still party with my RA."

Those in sororities and fraternities can live in the Oak Lane community, which is considered on campus housing but is more of a home with brothers or sisters. Food gets top marks at VT—it's rated #1 for campus food in the country. "Virginia Tech has the best dining service in the country, our food is unbelievable," a junior said. They have steak, lobster, and salmon options at the five main dining halls. There is also an additional express dining hall, kiosks, and a few small places here and there where students can get food.

"I can pretty much think of anything I want and I'll be able to get it at least one place on campus," a sophomore said.

Hokies report there is a new dining hall being built on the academic side of campus for those who live off-campus and don't want to hike across the drill field to get food between classes.

To pay for the food, students sign up for a certain amount of money and it's put on a Hokie Passport. The food is priced and when students swipe their Hokie Passport, they get 50 percent off the price and the money is taken off their card.

With all Virginia Tech has to offer, it's no surprise students from all over the nation flock there to get an undergraduate education. The students are full of spirit and the school is so full of traditions, making VT a destination to learn and create friendships for life.—*Sharon Yin & Jenny Dai*

FYI
If you come to VT, you'd better leave behind "anything UVa related, or there will be serious consequences!"
What is the typical weekend schedule? "Parties are usually on Friday and Saturday nights, studying and sleep in the time between."
Three things every student at VT should do before graduating: "go to a football game, Ring Dance, and live off-campus."

Washington & Lee University

Address: 204 West
Washington Avenue,
Lexington, VA 24450-2116
Phone: 540-458-8710
E-mail address:
admissions@wlu.edu
Web site URL: www.wlu.edu
Year Founded: 1749
Private or Public: Private
Religious Affiliation: None
Location: Rural
Number of Applicants: 6,487
Percent Accepted: 18%
**Percent Accepted who
enroll:** 42%
Number Entering: 494
**Number of Transfers
Accepted each Year:** 13
Middle 50% SAT range:
M: 660–740, CR 650–740,
Wr: 650–730
Middle 50% ACT range:
29–32
**Early admission program
EA/ED/None:** ED
**Percentage accepted
through EA or ED:** 44%

EA and ED deadline: 15-Nov
Regular Deadline: 2-Jan
Application Fee: $50
**Full time Undergraduate
enrollment:** 1,793
Total enrollment: 2,196
Percent Male: 52%
Percent Female: 48%
**Total Percent Minority or
Unreported:** 17%
Percent African-American:
3%
**Percent Asian/Pacific
Islander:** 3%
Percent Hispanic: 3%
Percent Native-American:
0%
Percent International: 3%
**Percent in-state/out of
state:** 12%/88%
Percent from Public HS:
94%
Retention Rate: 94%
Graduation Rate 4-year:
Unreported
Graduation Rate 6-year:
Unreported

**Percent Undergraduates
in On-campus housing:**
60%
**Number of official organized
extracurricular
organizations:** Unreported
3 Most popular majors:
Social Science,
Business/Marketing, Foreign
Lang. & Lit.
Student/Faculty ratio:
Unreported
Average Class Size:
23
**Percent of students going to
grad school:** 27%
Tuition and Fees: $41,927
**In-State Tuition and Fees if
different:** No difference
Cost for Room and Board:
$10,687
**Percent receiving financial
aid out of those who apply:**
81%
**Percent receiving financial
aid among all students:**
47%

As its name suggests, Washington and Lee University is steeped in history and shaped by two of America's greatest leaders, George Washington and Robert E. Lee.

Since it was founded in 1749, the board of trustees has renamed the institution three times before settling on its current name in 1870 after Lee's death. Though it is a traditional Southern institution with a dominating Greek life, Washington and Lee's student body has a lot of geographical diversity, which, as one sophomore from Texas put it, "is not as Southern as I thought it would be." Located in a small town in Lexington, Virginia (about 3 ½ hours southwest of Washington, D.C.), Washington and Lee is the central focus of the town, making Lexington a "quaint and safe" college town for all students. What distinguishes Washington and Lee over other small liberal arts schools are its traditions, most notably the "speaking tradition" and the Honor Code. Moreover, the size fosters a really strong sense of community. As one sophomore put it, "I feel like I know the names of almost everyone here."

Work Hard

Washington and Lee has a rigorous academic program which often requires students to spend quite a bit of time in the library. One student said that she has never been in a class with more than 30 people. She couldn't even imagine a class having more than 40 people. But because of these small classes, one sophomore noted that it puts pressure on kids to step up to the plate and participate. Instead of having a midterm and a final that makes up your grade for the term, students at Washington and Lee also have frequent homework and papers. Teachers have time to grade students' work because they don't have that many students in their classes. Additionally, one student said, "most classes aren't curved because they don't want students to compete. That mentality discourages cut-throat competitiveness."

There are three terms at Washington and Lee (fall, winter and spring). During fall and winter terms, students usually take four classes. But during spring term, students immerse themselves into one class. According to one student, "everyone loves spring term." Students can also join the Journalism or Business school if they want to concentrate on one of those subjects. You don't need to apply for these schools, so anyone can do it. Students at Washington and Lee really value the constant communication with their professors. One sophomore said, "It's really easy to stay over the summer and do research with professors. You can make your own experience here because there are so many options." Though most students at Washington and Lee rave about the classroom life, one student did say that she was disappointed with all of the requirements for majors (the business major in particular).

Play Hard

After long days and nights in the library during the week, Washington and Lee students definitely know how to have fun. Like most Southern schools, the social life at Washington and Lee is centered around fraternities and sororities. "Almost everyone is in a frat or a sorority," one sophomore said. But another student added that "Greek life is very welcoming here. There are no closed parties. Anyone can walk into Frats." One freshman also said that upperclassmen are very welcoming to freshman at parties. While freshmen live in freshman dorms and eat in the dining hall, sophomores live in their fraternity's or sorority's houses and eat in their fraternity's or sorority's dining hall. But one student said "you can eat in whatever house you want. It's not exclusive."

Be a Gentleman

When Robert E. Lee became president of Washington and Lee in 1865, he established what is now known as the Honor Code in order to encourage men to "behave like gentlemen." Though the institution began admitting women in 1985, the Honor Code still has a huge presence at the school, dictating almost everything students do. While there are no written rules, no "dos" or "don'ts," an executive committee comprised entirely of students determines whether or not a student has violated the Honor Code. Violations can be anything from speeding to more serious offenses such as plagiarism and cheating, which lead directly to expulsion if the student is found guilty. While one student noted that the honor code "makes people cautious of working together on assignments," she added that this doesn't mean that Washington and Lee is a "cut-throat" environment. Because of the Honor Code's strong presence on campus, teachers often give students closed-book take-home tests and even allow students to pick up their final exams to complete at their own convenience. Once students turn in their assignments, they have to sign their name to ensure that they have upheld the Honor Code. Additionally, one freshman said, "There's a huge sense of trust on campus. You can leave anything anywhere without worrying that someone would take it." When asked how many people actually follow the Honor Code, a sophomore said, "definitely 99 percent." She added, "it works because you pick the school knowing about the Honor Code and you take pride in it."

> "There's a huge sense of trust on campus. You can leave anything anywhere without worrying that someone would take it."

Washington and Lee students also take pride in another aspect of chivalry known as the "speaking tradition." The small undergraduate population (around 1,800 students) fosters a real sense of community that is strengthened by this tradition which encourages everyone to say hi to each other whenever you pass someone on a path or in the hallway. "Everyone is really friendly," one freshman said. "With this tradition, it's not weird to say hi to someone you don't know. It just works really well with our small school."

"Lex Vegas"

Well, Lexington, Virginia isn't exactly Las Vegas, but it definitely has its perks. One student described Lexington as a "historic town with plenty of good restaurants and shops." Another added that it's great for college kids because it has the basic necessities and it's really safe. A lot of juniors and seniors move off campus and live in apartments in Lexington. One sophomore also insisted that all students must explore Lexington and the surrounding area during their four years at Washington and Lee. "There are the Blue Ridge mountains and hiking and camping and tubing all really close to campus. It's one of the prettiest parts of the country." The Honor System also extends into the town. A sophomore said, "If you're ever short of money when you're buying something, stores and restaurants in the town trust that kids from Washington and Lee will always pay them back."—*Charlotte Dillon and Madeline McMahon*

FYI
If you come to Washington and Lee, you'd better leave "liberal points of view" behind.
What's the typical weekend schedule? "Pregame, party until 2, brunch on Sunday, work in the library."
Three things every student at Washington and Lee should do before graduating are "go to a sporting event; streak the Collonade; visit the Robert E. Lee chapel; go to homecoming."

Washington

Evergreen State College

Address: 2700 Evergreen Parkway NW, Olympia, WA 98505

Phone: 360-867-6170

E-mail address: admissions@evergreen.edu

Web site URL: www.evergreen.edu

Year Founded: 1971

Private or Public: Public

Religious Affiliation: None

Location: Urban

Number of Applicants: 1,725

Percent Accepted: 96%

Percent Accepted who enroll: 33%

Number Entering: 537

Number of Transfers Accepted each Year: 1,281

Middle 50% SAT range: M: 460–580, CR: 510–640, Wr: 470–610

Middle 50% ACT range: Unreported

Early admission program EA/ED/None: None

Percentage accepted through EA or ED: NA

EA and ED deadline: NA

Regular Deadline: 1-Mar

Application Fee: $50

Full time Undergraduate enrollment: 4,090

Total enrollment: 4,467

Percent Male: 46%

Percent Female: 54%

Total Percent Minority or Unreported: 31%

Percent African-American: 5%

Percent Asian/Pacific Islander: 3%

Percent Hispanic: 6%

Percent Native-American: 2%

Percent International: 1%

Percent in-state/out of state: 74%/26%

Percent from Public HS: 65%

Retention Rate: 71%

Graduation Rate 4-year: 51%

Graduation Rate 6-year: 57%

Percent Undergraduates in On-campus housing: 20%

Number of official organized extracurricular organizations: 62

3 Most popular majors: Social Sciences, Humanities, Multi/Interdisciplinary Studies

Student/Faculty ratio: 23:1

Average Class Size: 25

Percent of students going to grad school: 21%

Tuition and Fees: $18,090

In-State Tuition and Fees if different: $6,909

Cost for Room and Board: $9,000

Percent receiving financial aid out of those who apply: 0.5

Percent receiving financial aid among all students: 57%

Founded in 1971 to balance the geographical distribution of public universities in the State of Washington, Evergreen State College is a liberal arts institution that caters mostly to undergraduates, though there are also a small number of postgraduates in the masters programs. It has a reputation of being politically liberal, which is certainly the case as most students are left leaning. However, a large part of its liberal reputation is also because Evergreen State was founded as an alternative institution, much different from other schools. The best-known feature of Evergreen State is that it does not give out grades. Instead, students receive narrative-style evaluations by professors. Therefore, all students only get comments on their performances, not an actual letter or number. However, far beyond the grading system, Evergreen State is every bit different from most other colleges in the country.

Hard Working Yet No Grade

As an experimental college, Evergreen State already has a long history of doing things differently from others. The most intriguing part of the college, however, is still the unique grading system. After all, following years of laboring for a high GPA in high school, it may seem inconceivable for many college freshmen to find themselves without having to worry about scoring a certain number of points on a test. That is the beauty of Evergreen State. It allows students to focus on learning something from their classes instead of trying to get through tests and papers to obtain a reasonable score. Therefore, at Evergreen State, learning comes before grading. Although the lack of grading may seem simply strange, people at Evergreen State believe that it actually approaches what happens in the real world. Most employers do not give a single number to people to determine whether they should be retained, promoted, or fired. They take a broader view of what the employee has achieved. The same works at Evergreen. At the end of each course, professors meet with the student about his or her performance. They provide a detailed narrative of the student's work. In addition, the student also has the opportunity to provide self-evaluation of performance, not to mention offering critiques of the professors. "I think the evaluation process at Evergreen State is the best part of my experience," said one student. "There is less stress and more learning."

One of the reasons for the narrative evaluation is that courses are taken differently at Evergreen State. At the majority of universities, students major in a field by taking individual classes in a single department. Although there may be a few required courses, most students end up with a collection of individual classes without being able to make the linkage between them. Therefore, students enroll in programs, which are a series of classes on a theme, not a single topic. Professors from different disciplines teach the programs. Students therefore have a better appreciation of how academic fields are actually interrelated.

Students can also create their own area of study called Learning Contracts, in which students, after completing a few prerequisites, can simply decide to study on their own. Of course, a faculty member follows the student closely to provide advice and to ensure that the person is actually doing the work.

Given the necessity for professors to provide individual comments and the type of close interaction needed during classes, academic programs at Evergreen State have fewer than 25 people per session. "I love being able to study in smaller groups," said one student. "Large lectures at other schools make you go to sleep, but here, everything is so interactive."

From the outset, there would seem to be little incentive for students to work hard. After all, there is no grading. However, it is important to point out that there is still a transcript, which will have commentaries by the professors. That is the way employers or graduate schools will evaluate the students. Therefore, it is still important for students to do their work and try to do the best they can in classes. "We actually work a lot," said one student. "When I first came here, I thought that we could all slack off. But then I realized that we have a demanding curriculum, and there is a lot of pressure from your peers to professors to do well and participate in class."

> **"Most people are liberal here, but it does not mean that we are completely intolerant of conservative ideas."**

Even though Evergreen State is a small college, there are also plenty of research opportunities, especially in environment-related fields. In addition, the school encourages students to undertake internships and acquire work experiences, some of which can be converted into academic credits.

The Capital of Washington

Olympia is a small city of about 42,000 people. Nevertheless, it is one of Washington's cultural centers and the state's capital. As is expected of state capitals, the city provides a large number of cultural activities, such as fine art and theater, and parks. "Olympia is a very nice city," said one student. "We are definitely not a big place like Seattle, but we have our own identities." The city also has a collection of restaurants and bars around campus, which are certainly valuable for students in search of something to do during weekends. Furthermore, as one student pointed out, as the state capital, Olympia "feels like a highly intellectual city."

Most students live off campus while attending Evergreen State. Many people choose to do so because they come from nearby areas and live at home—since it is a public university, the majority of students are from the state. At the same time, many people choose to live in the blocks surrounding the college to have a more independent experience. A considerable number of freshmen, however, choose to spend their first year on campus. The school designates specific buildings for freshmen so that they can meet each other and create a sense of first-year community. Students are placed into either singles or doubles.

The dining services operate five locations, including two convenience stores. Most students agree that the food is satisfactory. "We don't have that many choices, but the food is good," said one student. "If you don't like it, you can always find other places around campus." The college has four dining plans for freshmen and five voluntary plans for other students, as well as faculty and staff.

The social activities often happen on campus. Since many off-campus students can be spread out, dorms are excellent places to host parties. The school is not extremely severe in monitoring the students' party scene, as long as no one does anything outrageous within the dorms.

Outside of Classrooms

Evergreen State is certainly not known for its sports teams. It has nine varsity intercollegiate teams. "Sports teams are definitely not big here," said one student. "Some people go to the games once in a while, but not often." Student clubs, on the other hand, abound and provide excellent opportunities to acquire a new interest or simply meet new people. As to the belief that Evergreen State is extremely liberal, one student remarked, "Most people are liberal here, but it does not mean that we are completely intolerant of conservative ideas."

Evergreen State is very different from other colleges, and so are the student experiences. In many ways, attending Evergreen State is a slightly risky move. Some people may truly enjoy a school without grades and big lectures. Others may prefer a more traditional college experience. Nevertheless, for all those willing to try something novel, something different, Evergreen State may be the answer for you.—*Xiaohang Liu, Paul Treadgold*

FYI

If you come to Evergreen State, you'd better bring "an umbrella."
What is the typical weekend schedule? "Party in dorms, concerts in Olympia, and homework."
If I could change one thing about Evergreen State, I'd "make it rain less."

University of Puget Sound

Address: 1500 North Warner Street, Tacoma, WA 98416-1062
Phone: 800-396-7191
E-mail address: admission@ups.edu
Web site URL: www.ups.edu
Year Founded: 1888
Private or Public: Private
Religious Affiliation: None
Location: Suburban
Number of Applicants: 5,580
Percent Accepted: 52%
Percent Accepted who enroll: 19%
Number Entering: 625
Number of Transfers Accepted each Year: 154
Middle 50% SAT range: M: 560–660, CR: 570–680, Wr: 560–670
Middle 50% ACT range: 26–30
Early admission program EA/ED/None: ED
Percentage accepted through EA or ED: 82%

EA and ED deadline: 15-Jan
Regular Deadline: 15-Jan
Application Fee: $50
Full time Undergraduate enrollment: 2,582
Total enrollment: 2,867
Percent Male: 43%
Percent Female: 57%
Total Percent Minority or Unreported: 21%
Percent African-American: 1%
Percent Asian/Pacific Islander: 6%
Percent Hispanic: 6%
Percent Native-American: 1%
Percent International: 1%
Percent in-state/out of state: 18%/82%
Percent from Public HS: 75%
Retention Rate: 85%
Graduation Rate 4-year: 70%

Graduation Rate 6-year: 76%
Percent Undergraduates in On-campus housing: 58%
Number of official organized extracurricular organizations: Unreported
3 Most popular majors: Social Sciences, Business/Marketing, Foreign Language and Literature
Student/Faculty ratio: 12:1
Average Class Size: 18
Percent of students going to grad school: Unreported
Tuition and Fees: $38,720
In-State Tuition and Fees if different: No difference
Cost for Room and Board: $10,020
Percent receiving financial aid out of those who apply: 87%
Percent receiving financial aid among all students: 66%

Located near the cities of Tacoma and Seattle and the natural landmarks of Mount Rainier and Puget Sound, University of Puget Sound gives its students a unique experience that is both urban and rural. With a variety of social and academic areas to explore, Puget Sound offers all the opportunities of a larger university while structuring its academics and extracurriculars around what is most important: a personal experience for each and every student.

A Unique Introduction

Students' holistic experiences at University of Puget Sound begin as soon as they step foot on campus. Puget Sound's unique three-part orientation is called Prelude, Passages and Perspectives. It introduces students to the environmental, academic, and community-oriented aspects of the university. Students are first given a taste, or "Prelude," of Puget Sound academics with a sample of a typical day of classes. Then, during "Passages," students are sent on a camping trip in Hood Canal, three hours away from campus. Through three days of hiking through the wilderness, watching the sunrise from the top of a mountain, and gathering around huge bonfires, students learn to appreciate the natural beauty surrounding Puget Sound and develop bonds with their fellow students. One student recounted, "There is a special kind of bonding that takes place when you spend three days backpacking in the wilderness without a shower." The third segment, "Perspectives: Urban Plunge," demonstrates Puget Sound's involvement with the Tacoma community. In "Perspectives," students engage in service projects ranging from cleaning the Puget Sound to working with mentally disabled people. These three components let students experience three important parts of a Puget Sound education: environment, academics and community.

Small College Treatment, Large College Selection

As a liberal arts college, University of Puget Sound encourages its students to explore numerous academic fields outside of their own majors. In order to fulfill the core requirements, which consist of eight different courses in different academic areas, students must take at least one core course every semester over their four years at Puget Sound. However, the university's unique core class system makes it simple to find classes that fulfill the core requirements and that interest students from every major by offering these classes in almost every department. For instance, one potential English major claimed, "I can fulfill my math core requirement with a class in the philosophy department."

Although the ways through which students can fulfill their core requirements are numerous, some students may find it difficult to get the exact classes that they want. Course scheduling for freshmen is a laborious process because some popular classes fill up quickly or are offered in only a couple of time slots. As a result, some students may find it difficult to "take the classes [they] need to take while fitting them into a feasible schedule."

Once students get into their desired classes, however, they are likely to find a unique and personal experience. The majority of courses at Puget Sound consist of classes with fewer than 25 students, and each student should expect to pay attention in every class. Because of the small class sizes, one student noted, "people attend class and pay attention to the discussion because, when there is no back row, sleeping is not an option." Similarly, students expect to receive personal attention from their professors. As one student reported, when she began to pay less attention in class, her professor e-mailed her, writing, "I noticed that your in-class participation has dropped off a little, and I wanted to say that I value your opinion very much and encourage you to talk." Eager to ensure that each of their students performs well, professors are available for assistance outside of class, by office hours, or by e-mail appointments. In addition, professors encourage students to meet with them on other subjects. For example, one student said, "I spent one afternoon going over a German test and the meeting ended with us talking about places in Washington to go spelunking."

Although teachers want their students to do well, good grades are by no means easily achieved at Puget Sound. One student says, "In one of my classes the professor told us that A's were reserved for perfect work only." However, getting good grades is not impossible. Students agree that professors grade fairly. One student said, "I have never felt cheated out of the grade I deserved, nor have I felt I've gotten good grades when I least deserved them."

Daring You to Try Something New

Extracurriculars at Puget Sound are numerous and diverse, from political clubs such as

Young Democrats and Young Republicans to entertainment groups such as the Circus Club. Puget Sound is not a sports school—in the words of one student, "You won't find 10,000 students at the football games"—but on the whole its athletic teams are competitive. Among the most competitive of the Division III teams are the swim team—the women's team is ranked number one in the region—the women's soccer team, and the crew team. For those who would rather participate than observe, Puget Sound intramurals are extensive and popular as well.

The variety in Puget Sound's extracurriculars dares the University's students to try something new. One of the most popular extracurricular groups at Puget Sound is the Repertory Dance Group (RDG). A no-cut campus dance troupe that performs one show every semester, RDG is composed of expert and novice dancers and choreographers of every style. The most unique extracurricular activities at Puget Sound, however, take advantage of its proximity to natural reserves. One of the most popular activities is Puget Sound Outdoors, which organizes "reasonably priced outdoors trips like weekend backpacking trips, ski trips, rock climbing trips, etc." Puget Sound even has its own student-run equipment rental shop, the Expeditionary (affectionately called the Expy), which equips students for outdoor excursions from camping to cross-country skiing.

At Puget Sound, not only are students encouraged to try a variety of extracurriculars, they are also given motivation to pursue them. The unique system of credits at Puget Sound awards 0.25 credits for certain co-curricular activities. For instance, students majoring in Communication Studies may earn activity credits for participating in competitive forensic programs like the National Parliamentary Debate Association (NPDA) debate.

Of Castles and Cafés

University of Puget Sound is located in a suburban neighborhood. Puget Sound has taken advantage of the area near the University and purchased houses surrounding the campus for student living. Consequently, many juniors and seniors live in these on-campus houses instead of dorms. However, off-campus housing in the neighborhood is also abundant.

On-campus housing is available in the form of themed houses and residence dorms, many of which have distinct personalities. For instance, Todd/Phibs is the unofficial "party dorm." Puget Sound's official themed dorms are not, as one student described it, the "look, all the potheads live together" unofficial kind. For example, Harrington features the official Healthy Options floor, and Schiff Hall houses the Outdoors dorm. Themed on-campus houses like the Comic House and House of Ramen line the famous "Theme Row."

Campus food at Puget Sound, like typical cafeteria food, can get tiring. However, students consistently boast of its variety. With sandwich lines and theme nights, there is usually something worth trying. Other on-campus restaurants, such as the Oppenheimer Café ("the OC"), Diversions Café, and the Cellar, which serves late-night pizza and ice cream, give students several dining and snacking options no matter what time of day or night they want to eat. Puget Sound is also very vegetarian-friendly and has been rated by PETA as one of the top 10 universities for most vegetarian options. For those who still want to dine off campus, there are numerous choices. Silk Thai offers delicious Thai cuisine. Farrelli's and Garlic Jim's pizza are popular, and cafés like the Mandolin and Rosewood Cafés serve delicious sandwiches and other simple fare. Puget Sound's proximity to Tacoma gives students ample opportunity to explore the city's best restaurants.

> "I spent one afternoon going over a German test and the meeting ended with us talking about places in Washington to go spelunking."

Student opinion on campus security varies depending on who is asked. While some contend that they have "never felt unsafe on campus" and emphasize that there have been "no crimes and no thefts," others say that they feel uncomfortable walking alone at night. However, students know that security is always available to escort students both on and off campus.

Puget Sound 101: How to Change the World

Appropriate to its proximity to nature and its devotion to the outdoors, Puget Sound is a university that makes sustainability one of its priorities. For example, the university participates in numerous sustainable programs around campus, such as the vermicomposting program, which is run by Students for a

Sustainable Campus in conjunction with Dining Services and turns the University's food waste into fertile soil by using red worms. Puget Sound's eco-friendly beliefs also manifest in its mascot. While the Puget Sound athletic teams are called the "Loggers," the university's official mascot has changed from a logger to a grizzly bear, "Grizz." As one student reports, "Grizz is our mascot, because at such an eco-friendly school, we felt a logger was too unsustainable . . . we take our sustainability very seriously." In addition to sustainability, Puget Sound students have been passionate about many other domestic and international issues, such as the 2012 presidential election and the genocide in Darfur. As part of the "number one liberal college feeder into the Peace Corps," Puget Sound students are, as one student describes, "the ones who will change the world."

For the student who is passionate about resolving current issues, University of Puget Sound offers a personalized education and numerous opportunities to explore in academics, extracurriculars and life experience. As one student put it, Puget Sound is "for dedicated, intelligent, outdoorsy, active, passionate, open-minded people. [It] will give you a unique education [and] teach you to think in a forward, global way."—*Chaoran Chen*

FYI

If you come to UPS, you'd better bring "your hiking boots and rain slicker."

What's the typical weekend schedule? "Friday night, prepare for a hiking trip or find a party; Saturday night, watch a movie or hang out with friends; Sunday, wake up late and do homework."

If I could change one thing about UPS, I'd "find a way to encourage ethnic diversity on campus."

Three things every student at UPS should do before graduating are "spend a weekend in the mountains, devise a plan to steal the Hatchet, and participate in the Repertory Dance Group."

University of Washington

Address: 1410 Northeast Campus Parkway, Box 355852, Seattle, WA 98195

Phone: 206-543-2100

E-mail address: Visit website to submit questions

Web site URL: www.washington.edu

Year Founded: 1861

Private or Public: Public

Religious Affiliation: None

Location: Suburban

Number of Applicants: 17,777

Percent Accepted: 57%

Percent Accepted who enroll: 46%

Number Entering: 5,497

Number of Transfers Accepted each Year: 2,173

Middle 50% SAT range: M: 570–690, CR: 520–650, Wr: 520–640

Middle 50% ACT range: 24–30

Early admission program EA/ED/None: None

Percentage accepted through EA or ED: NA

EA and ED deadline: NA

Regular Deadline: 1-Dec

Application Fee: $60

Full time Undergraduate enrollment: 29,302

Total enrollment: 56,949

Percent Male: 47%

Percent Female: 53%

Total Percent Minority or Unreported: 54%

Percent African-American: 3%

Percent Asian/Pacific Islander: 29%

Percent Hispanic: 29%

Percent Native-American: 2%

Percent International: 10%

Percent in-state/out of state: 84%/16%

Percent from Public HS: Unreported

Retention Rate: 92%

Graduation Rate 4-year: 48%

Graduation Rate 6-year: 74%

Percent Undergraduates in On-campus housing: 25%

Number of official organized extracurricular organizations: 550

3 Most popular majors: Social Sciences, Biology, Business/Marketing

Student/Faculty ratio: Unreported

Average Class Size: 24

Percent of students going to grad school: 44%

Tuition and Fees: $28,310

In-State Tuition and Fees if different: $10,826

Cost for Room and Board: $9,000

Percent receiving financial aid out of those who apply: Unreported

Percent receiving financial aid among all students: Unreported

Nestled between the Cascade and Olympic Mountain ranges, the University of Washington embraces its Seattle location by combining its background as a prominent research institution with a "relaxed, West Coast atmosphere." With three campuses, two seasons, tons of people, and an array of food, the University of Washington is characterized by numbers. But Huskies who don't let the numbers overwhelm them are guaranteed a fulfilling college experience.

Living in Husky Territory

UW is a large university, with nearly 57,000 undergraduate and graduate students on three campuses. The main location is in Seattle, with smaller satellite campuses in Bothell and Tacoma. Despite rumors to the contrary, Seattle is far from being the rain capital of the nation: its annual precipitation is actually less than that of Houston, New York and Philadelphia! The city's rainy reputation derives from the region's overcast skies and constant light drizzle during the winter months. One current student said Seattle experiences two seasons, not four—rainy and beautiful.

All three campuses serve an incredibly diverse student body, offering both day and evening classes for either full-time or part-time students. With a combination of gorgeous architecture and natural beauty—looking at Mt. Rainier over a clear day from Drumheller Fountain or enjoying the annual blooming of cherry blossoms in The Quad are among students' favorite part of the Seattle campus—there's more than enough space to go around on this 700-acre school.

In the Lecture Hall

With over 1,800 undergraduate courses offered every quarter, incoming freshmen could feel slightly overwhelmed. Freshmen may choose to join the FIG (Freshman Interest Group) program, where small groups of freshmen with similar academic interests share the same courses during their first quarter. One student involved in a FIG said they made the transition "a little bit easier" both socially and academically. The UW Honors Program is also highly regarded, though a junior stressed that the program's diverse and interesting classes can be hard to get into.

Don't be surprised if many classes during your freshman year are on the higher end of the student-to-faculty ratio: first quarter lectures can often have over 500 students.

Introductory courses also tend to have stricter grading than higher-level courses. "The main purpose of many of the intro classes is to 'weed out' those students who cannot handle the workload," a sophomore said. This is even more apparent in competitive programs like engineering, computer science and the biological sciences. However, once a student becomes more involved in a department, the focus is more on the material and the learning process. "I didn't expect the professors to be as open to students as they were," one student explained. "They really made an effort to get to know us, so it wasn't at all impersonal." For certain majors, students must apply to their program after a year or two of study—for some majors, a high GPA is often necessary—which one student said meant "a stressful first few years."

The academics at the UW are extremely varied, as the requirements for graduation differ from college to college. The most competitive programs include the business school, the architecture school, and the college of engineering. The science majors are also widely cited as being difficult, due to the UW's top-tier medical school and the large number of students who enroll for its stellar scientific research facilities. Many other majors do not have any prerequisites for admission or a competitive admissions process. Several students testified to the discrepancy between the science and the humanities programs: "I have friends who take communications and history classes and they can easily get [a GPA of] 3.6 or 3.7," said a sophomore, "while science majors often have GPAs an entire point lower." Students recommended Comparative History of Ideas, International Studies and Near Eastern Languages and Civilization as being unique and intriguing majors, although they said the UW is largely perceived as a science and engineering-based school.

Among UW's 3,600-plus faculty are six Nobel Laureates, a National Book Award Winner, and 43 members of the National Academy of Sciences, not to mention many other widely renowned scholars and scientists. Freshman seminars offer incoming students the opportunity to establish a relationship with these faculty members while exploring their fields of study. But don't get too excited, a sophomore warns, as "in all honesty, the school is so big it is really hard to identify famous professors. There are celebrity profs, you just have to be part of the department to realize it." The competition for popular classes varies depending on the department, but as one student noted, "if you're a good enough student and stubborn enough, you can get into anything." Registration, though, was often cited as a "massive headache" for most students, with a randomized computer system and limited spots in high-demand classes often resulting in a rough or incorrect schedule that can be hard to change.

Dorm Life and Coffee Breaks

Most UW students live on campus for their freshman year, and switch to off-campus housing as an upperclassman. Although the dorms are always full, many students said on-campus housing is expensive, and a majority of students end up either commuting to campus or renting a house or apartment nearby. The Greek system occupies the neighborhood immediately to the north of campus, with 27 frats and 16 sororities owning off-campus houses. The area north of Greek Row, Ravenna, is a popular spot for students to live, as well as Wallingford, the neighborhood immediately across the freeway from the U-District. Despite the slightly higher rent, the U-District is a vibrant, diverse neighborhood, filled with cheap eateries, popular hangouts, and cool stores.

When it comes to dining, Huskies claim that UW has "the best campus food service in the country." The meal plan is fairly simple, as students place a certain amount of money in their dining accounts to spend like cash. Dining services are available in most dorms, with one dorm even featuring a Papa John's on the ground floor. But even though there are dining halls all over campus, most UW students also choose to take advantage of the ubiquitous coffee shops and cheap ethnic restaurants in the nearby U-District, which range from Vietnamese to Mexican.

With so much of the undergraduate student body hailing from Washington State, the campus can feel empty on Saturdays when students go home for the weekends. While the bus system may be difficult to navigate, it is free for students because part of their tuition goes toward a bus pass that allows for free rides on all Seattle public transportation. With the Sea-Tac airport, the ferry docks, and the Amtrak train station only a bus ride away, most UW students find they can travel fairly conveniently without needing a car. Light rail now connects Sea-Tac to downtown Seattle, transit that will be expanded to young and hip Capitol Hill and then the U-District in coming years.

Size Matters

"UW is a very self-directed university," one student noted. "You need to know what you want in order to get it. Because it's so big, no one does it for you." With over 25,000 undergraduates on the Seattle campus alone, many incoming freshmen worry that they will become a nameless face in the crowd, and several students said the first few months on campus can feel overwhelming. But current students repeatedly declared that friends are easy to find, and with "over 500 student groups, there's always something going on!"

Most students begin to associate with a certain social circle early in their college experience, often drawn from where they live in their first quarter at the UW. Social life at the UW is fairly segregated between the Greeks, the dorm kids and students who live off campus. Greek life is largely insular, and the Greeks are sometimes described as preppier than the rest of campus, wearing "the type of clothes you'd expect to find at an East Coast boarding school." One student cited the social groups as the main difference between underclassmen and upperclassmen; the older students tend to already have their social circles established and are less receptive to forming new friendships than the incoming freshmen.

There are over 550 student clubs on campus, ranging from living groups to multicultural societies to political associations to groups that some see as "just plain weird." Students listed a medley of different organizations, ranging from the Filipino American Student Association and Habitat for Humanity to the Amateur Porn Club and the Peanut Butter and Jelly Club. Many students dedicate a lot of time to their organizations, and define their social groups within those groups. But other students aren't involved in extracurricular activities at all, instead devoting most of their time to schoolwork, jobs or their social life. As one student put it, "you can only have two of the four: grades, parties, extracurriculars or a job." Most jobs tend to be located in the U-District as waiters or clerks, or on campus as an RA or tutor. Many Huskies also have internships in Seattle during the year, particularly upperclassmen.

There are also many options for nighttime activities. The residence halls throw a weeklong extravaganza called "Winterfest," complete with casino nights, dances and bonfires. The annual "Powwow" and "Spring Cruise," in addition to the Greeks' annual Homecoming and "Anchor Splash" parties,

Washington 893

are also highly anticipated school events. On the weekend, upperclassmen party more at bars or houses, while freshmen tend to flock to the larger frat parties.

Sleepless in Seattle

Given the UW's proximity to downtown Seattle, there's always something for students to do farther from campus, as well. As the music capital of the Pacific Northwest, Seattle hosts a large number of concerts throughout the year. The city is also home to an endless array of bars and clubs—many students end up commuting to nearby Capitol Hill, known for its young, gay crowd—giving students plenty of opportunities to explore the city beyond the campus. The school's proximity to both the Cascade Mountains and Puget Sound leads to many fun weekend trips—one student said she often took the local ferry to the San Juan islands, a common destination for outdoor-oriented students, while another said he went snowboarding at nearby Steven's Pass nearly every weekend between December and April. Seattle itself is a fascinating city, home to Starbucks, Microsoft, Amazon, REI, and Nintendo, among other major companies, and is consistently rated one of America's highest cities on a quality of living scale.

UW's student body represents the complete spectrum of attitudes toward drinking: some students go out every night of the week to drink, while other students never touch alcohol. Students claim that, depending on one's social circle, there is usually not a lot of pressure to drink. Because the residence halls enforce a strict alcohol and drug policy, which includes probation and mandatory alcohol counseling following minor violations, most drinking takes place off campus.

Husky Fitness and Pride

Since Seattle is associated with an image of fitness, it comes as no surprise that the University of Washington is also recognized as one of the top athletic programs in the country. It is not unusual for the 10 men's and 11 women's varsity teams to earn national honors. If you are more inclined to cheer from the stands, Huskies hold the gold standard for the student cheering sections: "I've never screamed so hard in my life," one student said about attending UW football games. All sports events except basketball and football are free for students, and the university usually provides free transportation to venues as well. During the fall, volleyball and football dominate the athletic scene, and the "campus literally shuts down on football Saturday." During the annual Apple Cup, thousands of current and former UW Huskies flock to the football stadium to cheer their school to victory over archrival Washington State. During the winter, die-hard basketball fans camp outside the gym for days before games even if they already have tickets—just to show their support! This student section is one of the best in the country; affectionately called the "Dawg Pack," this group of devoted fans even has its own locker in the men's locker room.

For the non-varsity athletes, there is a state-of-the-art gym called the "IMA." It has an elevated running track, a 5,000-square-foot weight room, over 300 machines, four basketball courts, racquetball, squash and tennis courts, a pool, saunas, and an indoor climbing wall. Free for all students, the gym also offers a diverse array of fitness classes, over 30 club sports, and the Dawg Bites Sports Café. Intramural sports are also a popular activity, ranging from very competitive to purely recreational. Examples include innertube basketball, ultimate Frisbee, rowing, and bowling. Meeting up with friends to go to the IMA, one student said, is pretty common across campus.

The University of Washington and the surrounding area can cater to the interests of all 43,000 undergraduate and graduate students, whether athletes, baristas, scholars, or ski bums. One student's comment in particular emphasized the enthusiasm characteristic of all Huskies: "I love the UW. It's a fantastic education, I get exposed to a huge amount of cutting-edge research, and there are so many opportunities I don't know where to start!"—*Nick Defiesta*

FYI
If you come to UW, you have to bring "an umbrella."
If I could change one thing about UW, I'd "change food prices on campus. The meal plan is a horrible deal."
What's the typical weekend schedule? "Friday: head to a party on Greek Row or at a friend's house. Saturday: pregame with friends and head to the football game then go out again after you recover. Sunday: get up and do all the work you put off during the rest of the weekend!"

Washington State University

Address: 370 Lighty Student Services Building, Pullman, WA 99164-1067

Phone: 888-468-6978

E-mail address: admissions@wsu.edu

Web site URL: www.wsu.edu

Year Founded: 1890

Private or Public: Public

Religious Affiliation: None

Location: Rural

Number of Applicants: 12,478

Percent Accepted: 69%

Percent Accepted who enroll: 39%

Number Entering: 3,288

Number of Transfers Accepted each Year: 3,907

Middle 50% SAT range: M: 500–610, CR:480–580, Wr: 470–570

Middle 50% ACT range: 21–26

Early admission program EA/ED/None: None

Percentage accepted through EA or ED: NA

EA and ED deadline: NA

Regular Deadline: Rolling

Application Fee: $50

Full time Undergraduate enrollment: 21,816

Total enrollment: 26,308

Percent Male: 50%

Percent Female: 50%

Total Percent Minority or Unreported: 30%

Percent African-American: 2%

Percent Asian/Pacific Islander: 6%

Percent Hispanic: 6%

Percent Native-American: 1%

Percent International: 3%

Percent in-state/out of state: 90%/10%

Percent from Public HS: 99%

Retention Rate: 84%

Graduation Rate 4-year: 40%

Graduation Rate 6-year: 69%

Percent Undergraduates in On-campus housing: 33%

Number of official organized extracurricular organizations: 200

3 Most popular majors: Business, Social Sciences, Communication

Student/Faculty ratio: 15:1

Average Class Size: 16

Percent of students going to grad school: 38%

Tuition and Fees: $22,077

In-State Tuition and Fees if different: $10,799

Cost for Room and Board: $9,662

Percent receiving financial aid out of those who apply: 68%

Percent receiving financial aid among all students: 52%

Going to Washington State University might only last a few years of your life, but being a Cougar is a lifetime commitment. It involves a ferocious pride for your school and a willingness to don crimson whenever physically possible.

"WSU has a ridiculous amount of school pride, to the point of violence," explained a freshman. She added, "I wouldn't be walking the streets wearing anything purple or gold during Apple Cup week," referring to the historic rivalry with the University of Washington.

Although the school's atmosphere of school pride and spirit may permeate the air as you walk around campus, there are other reasons why the overall experience is intoxicating, to say the least.

Academics? Oh yeah. . .

Although simply being a Cougar is an experience in itself, WSU academics are rigorous, high caliber, and stimulating. *U.S. News and World Report* has consistently ranked WSU among the nation's top public research universities, and more than 200 fields of study are offered. Perhaps most impressive is WSU's communications program, which is ranked by Radio and Television News Directors survey in the top four in the nation. The Communications major is one of the most popular majors on campus, and Agricultural Science, Sports Management, and Education are also popular.

Science classes are no joke—most students say pre-med classes are the toughest, while general education requirements can be the easiest "as long as you stay caught up on the reading," says one freshman.

Students say their least favorite part about Coug academics is the giant classes. "You're just a number at WSU," lamented one freshman. Still, professors are more than willing to help and provide resources outside of class. The New Student Programs helps orient students to their new environment and make a smooth transition into college. Freshmen say these programs have helped them adjust to WSU's rigorous academic demands.

Although the academic workload may be challenging and time consuming, going to WSU involves much more than just going to class.

Greeks and Athletes

It's the social life that distinguishes WSU from most other universities. One freshman, who said she was anxious about getting lost in such a big school, says she is surprised how she is "meeting so many people who are nice and welcoming." Another student said she is continually surprised with the school's welcoming environment and the constant stream of activities throughout the day.

> **"WSU has a ridiculous amount of school pride, to the point of violence."**

The Greek scene is very involved, though students stress it is not necessarily the dominant social activity on campus. There are ways for anybody to be involved as long as they are friendly. "It's very easy to meet people, join a club, and be social in classes," says one freshman.

"Thirsty Thursday"

Like most schools, Friday and Saturday nights are a popular time for people to go to fraternities, house parties, or watch movies in the dorms. However, a particularly interesting day is "thirsty" Thursday, when people usually party and walk up Greek Row. So is there much drinking on campus? Oh yeah. But the only people who get blackout drunk are those guys whose only goal *is* to intoxicate themselves as quickly as possible. Some, but not all, students describe binge drinking as a serious problem. Although drinking is present at most parties, students say there is not necessarily negative pressure to drink. However, since students describe drinking as a social event, most people choose to participate.

Careful though, because alcohol is only allowed in the dorms if you're over 21, and there are Residential Advisors (RAs) to make sure everything runs smoothly in the dorm. Students say that generally, RAs are very understanding.

Pullman: Middle of Nowhere

Fret not that eastern Washington is not very populated; amenities on campus are very accommodating. The newly renovated CUB (Compton Union Building) is one of the main places to meet people on campus, and the distinct clock tower glows crimson at night. There are advantages to a small town. "Everyone in town is a Coug, and [towns-people] love the college," said one freshman. And since Pullman is so small, students describe it as a very safe campus. WSU basically *is* Pullman. But don't expect you'll be living in a palace.

"The food is extremely mediocre," explained one freshman.

Pay attention to dorm policies: the earlier freshmen send in their confirmation to attend WSU, the higher they are ranked on the dorm choice priority list. There are older "hill halls" that are mostly either girl or boy dorms built in the 1900s, and newer dorms built around the 1960s that are co-ed. The dorms near Bohler Gym (the gym for athletes only) are usually full of athletes so they can get to their gym quickly.

All dorms are age diverse, so freshmen could be living close to seniors.

ExtraCoug activities

"Extracurricular activities are open to anyone willing to try out," said one freshman. Intramural sports, especially soccer and ultimate Frisbee, are both popular and competitive.

Many people have jobs on campus, especially in the dining halls.

Look to *The Daily Evergreen*, the campus newspaper, for daily news and sports updates. Because there are so many ways to be involved, most people are involved in some sort of club activity. The football team is always supported by the student body, regardless of their record.

Coming to WSU is more than an investment in your education—it's an investment in your life. Every day is an adventure, with new people and exciting activities. Perhaps most important, the people you meet at WSU will be your lifelong friends. Being a Coug is for life.—*Mitchell Murdock*

FYI
"If I could change one thing about WSU, I'd open up the Greek system to be more inviting to the rest of the school."
The typical weekend schedule: "You wake up Saturday morning around 1:00 p.m. (don't worry, they serve breakfast until 2:00 on the weekends). Then, you talk to your friends about what the hell happened last night and then lay in bed all day in order to recover in time for Saturday night's activities. Eventually, get on your party clothes and walk up to Greek Row with your group of friends and get ready for a long night."
The biggest college-wide tradition is "the Apple Cup! Go Cougs!"

Whitman College

Address: 345 Boyer Avenue, Walla Walla, WA 99362
Phone: 509-527-5176
E-mail address: admission@whitman.edu
Web site URL: www.whitman.edu
Year Founded: 1883
Private or Public: Private
Religious Affiliation: None
Location: Rural
Number of Applicants: 3,096
Percent Accepted: 47%
Percent Accepted who enroll: 28%
Number Entering: 415
Number of Transfers Accepted each Year: 60
Middle 50% SAT range: M: 610–720, CR: 610–720, Wr: 610–710
Middle 50% ACT range: 27–31
Early admission program EA/ED/None: ED
Percentage accepted through EA or ED: 80%

EA and ED deadline: 15-Nov
Regular Deadline: 15-Jan
Application Fee: $50
Full time Undergraduate enrollment: 1,555
Total enrollment: Unreported
Percent Male: 43%
Percent Female: 57%
Total Percent Minority or Unreported: 32%
Percent African-American: 2%
Percent Asian/Pacific Islander: 9%
Percent Hispanic: 9%
Percent Native-American: 1%
Percent International: 4%
Percent in-state/out of state: 62%/38%
Percent from Public HS: 75%
Retention Rate: 93%
Graduation Rate 4-year: 84%
Graduation Rate 6-year: 85%

Percent Undergraduates in On-campus housing: 67%
Number of official organized extracurricular organizations: 60
3 Most popular majors: Social Sciences, Biology, Visual and Performing Arts
Student/Faculty ratio: 10:01
Average Class Size: 16
Percent of students going to grad school: Unreported
Tuition and Fees: $40,496
In State Tuition and Fees if different: No difference
Cost for Room and Board: $10,160
Percent receiving financial aid out of those who apply: 74%
Percent receiving financial aid among all students: 54%

Whitman College, located in the small town of Walla Walla, Washington, is defined by its small size, abundance of extracurricular activities and friendliness of its students. "Whitties," as Whitman students call themselves, are typically laid-back and politically liberal, with equal passion for outdoor activities and educational experiences.

The First Few Weeks
Orientation events and pre-orientation outdoor trips make it easy for students to break the ice and get to know each other. On top of that, Whitman College is known for the general friendliness of its students. One freshman remarked: "The thing that was easiest was making new friends . . . I feel like I know a ton of people already."

The Student Body
Whitman students define themselves as "very accepting." One freshman noted that students who are not accepting of other types of people find themselves on the outside of social circles. However, the Whitman

student body is not racially diverse. Furthermore, although there is a significant presence of international students, internationals all live in a dorm together. One student said: "[International kids] all make friends with each other but don't really integrate a bunch into the rest of the school." "The majority of Whitman students are middle- or upper-class white kids," said one student. Whitman is also not politically diverse, leaning far to the left. Despite the racial and political homogeneity, Whitman's students vary widely in terms of religion, prompting spirited in-class discussions of religion.

The Passion for Learning

Whitman students balance their naturally social demeanors with hard work and academic discipline. Whitties' passion for learning is demonstrated in a variety of majors, most students choose majors in the college of arts and sciences, with a conspicuously high number opting for studies in biology or performing arts. Whitties are also given the option to create their own majors; one current senior has created his own major in global health. Students at Whitman are given all the academic attention they crave, with the biggest classes capping at 40 students. The professors are "unbelievable" and "very knowledgeable" even in freshman year, said one student, "and will just get better as [my field of study] becomes more specialized." Professors are "engaging in the classroom . . . they do a really good job keeping the classes interactive." Regular classes such as environmental science and geology are supplemented in some cases by field trips in which students and professors go off-campus to study their topics in the real world.

One of Whitman's many academic requirements is a freshman seminar called "Encounters." The class is seen as both a strength and weakness of Whitman; since the teachers are selected from a variety of departments, including chemistry and Spanish, knowledge of and enthusiasm for the curriculum varies widely. One student said that the success of the program depends on which teacher one gets for his section.

Although professors are available when they are sought out, "they don't go out of their way to find out who their students are in big classes," said one Whittie. Reviews of professors at Whitman are somewhat mixed: Some seem enthusiastic and engaged, while others lack knowledge of their subject. Still, Whitman students view their professors positively, for the most part.

One of Whitman's academic weaknesses, according to its students, is the language department. Across the board, foreign languages are seen to be lacking in both the professors and the curricula.

The Typical "Whittie"

"There is an expectation of open-mindedness at Whitman," remarked one student. Another Whittie said: "Everyone there has to be weird to a certain extent. If you aren't comfortable being weird, you probably shouldn't go [to Whitman]." Whitties do warn that students who would describe themselves as materialistic, high-maintenance or unfriendly might find Whitman to be a difficult place. One student also noted: "If you're not comfortable being weird to a certain extent, you probably shouldn't go to Whitman." Another remarked, "99 percent of the people at Whitman are happy, bubbly, and want to have a conversation at all times."

The Social Scene

Sororities and fraternities account for a large part of Whitman's social scene, with almost forty percent of girls and more than fifty percent of boys involved in Greek life. "Sororities at Whitman are unlike any other sororities I've heard about," said one freshman girl. "There are no high expectations . . . you make it what you want it to be." Greek life becomes "a network of support" for its members.

Many students say they have made their best friends through IM sports, club teams, and extracurricular activities such as improv. For example, rock-climbing is "huge" at Whitman, and one student said that she fell in love with the community that it provided. Whitman students take their intramurals more seriously than students at other schools. One student remarked that her Whitman experience has been defined by her participation on the Ultimate Frisbee team.

The Grub

Whitman's two dining halls are "very accommodating" for vegetarians, and the dining staff makes an effort to spice up the cuisine. One dining hall is set up with tables for four or five people each; the other has long tables designed for communal eating, which makes it easy to see lots of friends during mealtimes. However, the meal plan is not flexible. According to one freshman boy, the meal plan is too strict, allotting only one hour each for lunch and dinner.

> **"Other people say they're having a good time at college. We're having an *ecstatic* time at Whitman."**

Meeting at meals, competing in intramurals, and learning together in their small courses, Whitties are excited to get to know their classmates. The happiness and friendliness of Whitman students are unmistakable: "Other people say they're having a good time at college. We're having an *ecstatic* time at Whitman."

I chose Whitman because: "It meant I didn't have to choose between awesome outdoor experiences and great academics. I could have both at the same time."

FYI
If you come to Whitman, you'd better bring: "A climbing harness, a plant, and slippers."
If I could change anything at Whitman, I'd: "create more quiet study spaces in which to work. The library is so loud that I often get distracted!"
The typical Whitman student looks like: "A nerdy hippie, wearing a Patagonia puffy jacket, a flannel, Carhartt pants, and Birkenstock with socks, and carrying a mason jar of tea."
Whitman is different from high school because: "No one cares about drama. We aren't competing with each other, and no one wants to spread rumors or talk about gossip."

West Virginia

Marshall University

Address: One John Marshall Drive, Huntington, WV 25655
Phone: 304-696-3160
E-mail address: admissions@marshall.edu
Web site URL: www.marshall.edu
Year Founded: 1837
Private or Public: Public
Religious Affiliation: None
Location: Suburban
Number of Applicants: 2,409
Percent Accepted: 83%
Percent Accepted who enroll: 83%
Number Entering: 1,661
Number of Transfers Accepted each Year: 762
Middle 50% SAT range: M: 440–560, CR: 450–560, Wr: 440–550
Middle 50% ACT range: 19–25
Early admission program EA/ED/None: None

Percentage accepted through EA or ED: NA
EA and ED deadline: NA
Regular Deadline: Rolling
Application Fee: $30
Full time Undergraduate enrollment: 8,904
Total enrollment: 13,562
Percent Male: 45%
Percent Female: 55%
Total Percent Minority or Unreported: 11%
Percent African-American: 6%
Percent Asian/Pacific Islander: 1%
Percent Hispanic: 2%
Percent Native-American: 1%
Percent International: 1%
Percent in-state/out of state: 74% / 26%
Percent from Public HS: Unreported
Retention Rate: 71%
Graduation Rate 4-year: 44%

Graduation Rate 6-year: Unreported
Percent Undergraduates in On-campus housing: Unreported
Number of official organized extracurricular organizations: 100
3 Most popular majors: Business, Education, Liberal Arts
Student/Faculty ratio: 19:1
Average Class Size: 25
Percent of students going to grad school: 27%
Tuition and Fees: $11,702
In-State Tuition and Fees if different: $4,598
Cost for Room and Board: $7,210
Percent receiving financial aid out of those who apply: 68%
Percent receiving financial aid among all students: 44%

For the many West Virginia residents on campus, Marshall University can seem like a larger version of high school: a familiar environment surrounded by classmates they have known since kindergarten. While this can contribute to a lack of diversity on campus, Marshall is able to boast accessible professors, brand-new facilities, and a tight-knit community available to students who live both on and off campus.

One Class at a Time

All students must satisfy the requirements of the Marshall Plan, which is composed of a course or two in mathematics, science, computer literacy, writing, multicultural studies, international studies, and a senior capstone experience involving both oral and written presentations. Although the Plan is considered more annoying than demanding, many students would like to see changes to these general education requirements or at least a decrease in the time they must devote to them. Furthermore, several students, particularly those who commute, complained of not having enough time for electives. And at the same time, many of the "coolest" electives are only offered through the Marshall Community and Technical College. "I don't want to sacrifice the authenticity of regular Marshall courses for the coolness of the technical school ones," said one senior.

Although the Marshall Plan consumes large portions of students' academic hours, one psychology major said that he loves the freedom within his major. "You don't really have to take a lot of hours in your major," he said. Many students concentrate in business or nursing, but other departments also receive praise from students. "Take as many history classes as you can. Those have the best professors," one student said, while another described his first-year experience in the music department as "amazing." Science majors are generally regarded as more difficult, and those students not in the science departments bemoan a lack of opportunities in humanities and social sciences. The University seems to propel this perspective, having unveiled the Robert C. Byrd Biotechnology Science Center in 2006.

Nevertheless, students agree that the workload at Marshall is not strenuous. "I would definitely apply myself more if I were in a more intense academic environment," one senior said. Students said that many professors implement curves, and one freshman laughed when she was asked about the difficulty of the course load. "My favorite thing about Marshall is how easy my classes are," she said. "But Drinko Library is always packed."

However easy the classes are, Marshall University does attract talented students with not only the promise of intimate student-teacher interaction but also financial incentives. The University offers myriad scholarships, particularly for in-state students, based on ACT scores and a cumulative GPA. There is also the prestigious Yeager Scholarship, which provides tuition, room and board, a semester abroad for foreign language study, a summer program at Oxford University in the United Kingdom, and convenient benefits like early registration for classes.

Living the Dream
Many West Virginia residents view Marshall and its rival, West Virginia University, as the only college options. The West Virginia state government encourages this idea with a scholarship called the PROMISE. The result is a student population that is overwhelmingly homogenous and can often make out-of-state students feel like outsiders. Most in-state students continue associating with their friends from high school, so it can be difficult for out-of-state students to acclimate. However, students say that the social scene at Marshall depends greatly on the living situations.

Marshall requires students to live in dorms for the first two years on campus. However, the two-year rule only applies to those living

outside of a 50-mile radius, so commuters have very different opinions of Marshall and its social scene. Students who live in the dorms rate Marshall as much more diverse, and they praise the quality of freshman dorms. When asked if rooms get better with seniority, one freshman said, "No, not at all." This is because Marshall recently constructed new buildings designed just for freshmen, and the additions are expected to attract more students to on-campus living.

> **"The most political that the campus gets is during elections for Mr. and Miss Marshall."**

There exists a thriving off-campus life as well. Many students live in designated off-campus apartments and enjoy more freedom than those who opt for dormitory living, probably because of the strict dry policy enforced by on-campus housing authorities.

Eat, Drink, and Be Merry
One student who had lived in the small city her entire life commented that "Huntington is the place to be if you want to go to church, go out to eat, or get totally drunk." Being located in what the Centers for Disease Control and Prevention recently named the unhealthiest city in America does have advantages. The city of Huntington recently constructed a complex called Pullman Square that caters to college students looking for both daytime and nighttime fun. Pullman Square offers restaurants, a movie theater, an independent bookstore, a comedy club, shops, and plenty of parking for all the commuters.

Students also frequent Huntington's numerous bars and nightclubs. One student spoke passionately about "quarter-pitcher night" at the Eager Beaver, while others never miss an opportunity to go "club-hopping" on Friday and Saturday nights. In addition, Marshall has a large Greek scene that provides weekend parties for the entire community.

Students praise the number of extracurricular options available to Marshall students. One freshman noticed that students are "very committed" to their extracurricular activities, particularly those that are entirely student-run. There are plenty of activities and resources available for religious students in particular, but those looking for political activism should search elsewhere. "The most political that the campus gets is during elections for Mr. and Miss Marshall," said one senior. The student newspaper, *The Parthenon*, is extremely popular on campus, and most students are kept up-to-date by reading it.

"We Are Marshall."

Sports also have a dominant presence on campus. Excitement abounds during football season, and students are dedicated to their football team, the "Thundering Herd," known to provide quality players to the NFL. The Marshall basketball program also gets significant attention, particularly during the Marshall-WVU game, which brings a large audience of both current students and alumni. "There is a ton of school pride," said one sophomore. "Go Herd!" he added.

Nothing better illustrates the closeness of the Marshall campus than the sentimentality associated with the plane crash that killed almost the entire football team, coaching staff, and some fans in November of 1970. Often called the "worst sports-related disaster in United States history," the tragedy continues to affect students, staff, and area residents. The Memorial Fountain that commemorates the catastrophe is not only considered one of the "prettiest" parts of campus, but also the most meaningful.

The overall atmosphere at Marshall University can be summed up by the school's motto, "We Are Marshall." This sentiment is a testimony to the enormous pride that students, faculty and alumni feel about their school. The recent renovations and additions demonstrate that Marshall is expanding, and many students see their school changing from being known as a commuter school to becoming a leading university in the near future.—*Lauren Oyler*

FYI

If you come to Marshall, you'd better bring "a ton of green clothes."

What is the typical weekend schedule? "On Wednesdays, it's quarter-pitcher night at Eager Beaver. Thursdays and Fridays are frat parties or clubbing. Saturday is football or basketball games. Then on Sunday, go to church and start studying."

If I could change one thing about Marshall, I'd "decrease the number of requirements of the Marshall Plan."

Three things every student at Marshall should do before graduating are "eat the peach pie at Harless, take advantage of the Marshall Artist Series, and see *We Are Marshall* to understand the school's history."

West Virginia University

Address: PO Box 6009, Morgantown, WV 26506-6009
Phone: 304-293-2121
E-mail address: go2wvu@mail.wvu.edu
Web site URL: www.wvu.edu
Year Founded: 1867
Private or Public: Public
Religious Affiliation: None
Location: Rural
Number of Applicants: 15,094
Percent Accepted: 86%
Percent Accepted who enroll: 39%
Number Entering: 5,034
Number of Transfers Accepted each Year: 1,765
Middle 50% SAT range: M: 480–580, CR: 460–560, Wr: Unreported
Middle 50% ACT range: 21–26
Early admission program EA/ED/None: None

Percentage accepted through EA or ED: NA
EA and ED deadline: NA
Regular Deadline: 1-Aug
Application Fee: $25
Full time Undergraduate enrollment: 22,303
Total enrollment: 29,306
Percent Male: 54%
Percent Female: 46%
Total Percent Minority or Unreported: 14%
Percent African-American: 4%
Percent Asian/Pacific Islander: 2%
Percent Hispanic: 2%
Percent Native-American: <1%
Percent International: 1%
Percent in-state/out of state: 46%/54%
Percent from Public HS: Unreported
Retention Rate: 84%
Graduation Rate 4-year: 56%

Graduation Rate 6-year: Unreported
Percent Undergraduates in On-campus housing: 23%
Number of official organized extracurricular organizations: 300
3 Most popular majors: Business, Interdisciplinary Studies, Journalism
Student/Faculty ratio: 23:1
Average Class Size: 25
Percent of students going to grad school: Unreported
Tuition and Fees: $17,844
In-State Tuition and Fees if different: $5,674
Cost for Room and Board: $8,404
Percent receiving financial aid out of those who apply: 59%
Percent receiving financial aid among all students: 49%

W est Virginia University is better known for its football and basketball teams than academics, but this nationally ranked party school certainly offers much more than just a good time outside of classes.

All Play and No Work?

Despite its reputation as a party school, students at WVU actually do study. Popular majors include business, communications and journalism, and engineering, but many students take advantage of WVU's more esoteric programs, such as Exercise Physiology or Textiles, Apparel and Merchandising. By the time students are juniors, they apply to a specific college within the University, such as the Perley Isaac Reed School of Journalism, the College of Human Resources and Education, or the Eberly College of Arts and Sciences. WVU also offers over 60 minors, including a great variety of disciplines such as Native American Studies, Conservation Ecology, and Pest Management.

In addition to the broad range of majors and minors offered, WVU students love the large number of class choices. The only drawback is the size of classes. "All of my classes this semester are too big," said one sophomore majoring in chemistry. "I'm talking 250 or so students." Although the classes do become progressively smaller with seniority, many students feel that they have trouble choosing a major because "lecture hall classes are impossible to pay attention in."

Because the school is so large, many students receive relatively little advising. All students must complete the requirements of the General Education Curriculum (GEC), which ultimately takes up about one third of each student's course schedule. Although students are assigned an academic advisor, one freshman said she didn't even know she had to complete the GEC and "expected much more help with scheduling" from the advisors.

The Honors College at WVU provides a more intimate learning environment for students who have demonstrated academic prowess throughout high school. The Honors Program allows students to graduate with honors as well as take small classes that are unheard of for students not in the program. These courses, which are capped at 20 students, are offered in departments ranging from microbiology to theater. They make it possible for honors students to engage in discussions and debate with their professors and peers. Students in the Honors Program say that they don't know what they would do without the additional benefits of the program, which include better housing, priority course registration, and more easily available study abroad opportunities. In return, students must complete at least 24 credit hours of Honors courses and maintain a high GPA.

> **"WVU is like being a kid trying to do a jigsaw puzzle at a carnival."**

On the other hand, the Honors program at WVU reportedly lacks academic diversity. Students claim that the number of science majors in the Honors College is significantly disproportional to the number of science majors in the overall undergraduate population. "The only time I hear anyone talking about humanities is when they are trying to fill GECs," said one sophomore in the Honors College. This disparity contributes to the overarching belief around campus that social sciences and humanities are easy. "Whenever I'm at a party and tell people that I'm a biology major, people cringe," said one junior. "They usually follow up with something like 'Oh, that's so hard. I could never do that.'"

Country Roads
Located in the Mountain State, WVU's campus boasts great opportunities for hiking, which may be required to get to classes. West Virginia has two campuses, the Evansdale campus and the Downtown campus. To connect them, the University constructed a monorail system, called the Personal Rapid Transit (PRT). While riding the PRT remains a uniquely Mountaineer experience, students' overall impressions of the PRT are negative. "The PRT is like a roller coaster for little children," one WVU junior said.

Running from 6:30 a.m. to 10:15 p.m. on weekdays, 9:30 a.m. to 5:00 p.m. on Saturdays, and closed on Sundays, the PRT schedule is not designed for convenience. It is also known to break down frequently, leaving students without cars stuck on their respective campuses. Even students who do

have cars have trouble getting around because parking is "severely limited."

Instead of solving the parking or the PRT problem, many students would prefer that the University somehow unify the two campuses, which are separated by about one and a half miles. While the Downtown campus is known as the heart and soul of WVU, the Evansdale campus has many necessary resources as well, including many athletic facilities, making transportation between the two campuses unavoidable. One freshman complained that the dual campus structure of WVU makes it "impossible to see anyone."

The West Virginia hills are also considered inconvenient by some students. There is even a Facebook group called "I Got 99 Problems and 82 of them are the Steps by the Life Science Building," dedicated to commiserating about the hilly terrain at WVU. However, the hills are also beloved by students. Active students utilize the area's natural landscape by hiking, walking, or jogging on trails located next to the Monongahela River. They can also make frequent visits to Coopers Rock State Forest, make use of the nearby ski resorts, and enjoy whitewater rafting.

Take Me Home
Ironically, the dorms at WVU are unwaveringly dry, even for students over the age of 21. The school's policy on alcohol in the dorms is strict: All students found drinking in the dorms will be written up and fined. Students looking to drink need not search far, however, for an off-campus house party or a bar. Because Greek life is not particularly important on campus, students say that the social scene at WVU truly revolves around Morgantown's bounty of bars and clubs, frequented by students every night of the week. On the other hand, the easy access can be problematic when finals approach. The dilemma of juggling the bustling social scene and academics contributes to WVU's relatively low freshman to sophomore retention rate, and one sophomore estimated that "probably 95 percent" of the student body drinks.

For those not looking to imbibe, WVU has Up All Night, a weekly event that takes place in the Mountainlair, the student union on the Downtown campus. Each Thursday, Friday, and Saturday night beginning at 7 p.m., the Mountainlair is transformed into Up All Night, where students can get free food, watch movies, go bowling, and enjoy myriad other activities. Although many students view Up All Night as a way to sober up after a long night of drinking, it is still lauded as one of the country's best weekend alternatives to the "college party scene."

The school also sponsors another entertainment event called FallFest. Every year the University welcomes students back to campus with a huge outdoor concert featuring several headlining bands. This event is so impressive that it even attracts students from rival Marshall University, whose students are often willing to make the two-and-a-half-hour drive from southern West Virginia to enjoy big-name acts at WVU.

Sports are also an essential part of student life at WVU. With sports teams that consistently rank among the top 25 in the nation, loyal Mountaineer fans look forward to game days with passion. On Saturday mornings in the fall, fans in gold and blue shirts flock to the Pit for unforgettable tailgates before moving on to Milan Puskar Stadium, where they cheer on the Mountaineers in what is usually a spectacular football game. School spirit is also palpable during the basketball season, when Mountaineer fans religiously follow NCAA Division I rankings to see if their team prevails.

Students are envious of the "sweet" athletic facilities reserved for varsity athletes, but the Student Rec Center is more than adequate for non-athletes. Boasting everything from standard exercise equipment to a 50-foot climbing wall, badminton courts, and an elevated track, the Student Rec Center is home to WVU's intramurals, which are fairly popular among students.

To the Place I Belong

"My economics professor really said it best," commented one junior majoring in accounting. "He said 'WVU is like being a kid trying to do a jigsaw puzzle at a carnival.' You can get the education at WVU that you could get anywhere, but there is so much going on around you that it's really a test to see if you can concentrate, which is something I think is unique. It probably prepares you for the real world better than a lot of places in that sense." The majority of students are proud of their school and their Mountaineers. Students are known to sing along to John Denver's "Country Roads," which is usually done at sporting events. This is because, to them, WVU really is "home."—*Lauren Oyler*

FYI

If you come to West Virginia, you'd better bring "an appreciation for beer."

What is the typical weekend schedule? "Go out to bars or an off-campus party on Thursday and Friday, wake up early for a tailgate on Saturday, cheer on the Mountaineers, and have a victory celebration on Saturday night."

If I could change one thing about West Virginia, I'd "bring the two campuses together."

Three things every student at West Virginia should do before graduating are "walk down High Street to see all the crazy parties, go to a football game at Milan Puskar Stadium, and see Coopers Rock."

Wisconsin

Beloit College

Address: 700 College Street, Beloit, WI 53511
Phone: 608-363-2500
E-mail address: admiss@beloit.edu
Web site URL: www.beloit.edu
Year Founded: 1846
Private or Public: Private
Religious Affiliation: None
Location: Urban
Number of Applicants: 2,248
Percent Accepted: 63%
Percent Accepted who enroll: 24%
Number Entering: 362
Number of Transfers Accepted each Year: 25
Middle 50% SAT range: M: 560–690, CR: 570 700, Wr: Unreported
Middle 50% ACT range: 25–30
Early admission program EA/ED/None: EA
Percentage accepted through EA or ED: Unreported

EA and ED deadline: 1-Dec
Regular Deadline: 15-Jan
Application Fee: $35
Full time Undergraduate enrollment: 1,388
Total enrollment: 1,388
Percent Male: 44%
Percent Female: 56%
Total Percent Minority or Unreported: 13%
Percent African-American: 4%
Percent Asian/Pacific Islander: 3%
Percent Hispanic: 4%
Percent Native-American: <1%
Percent International: Unreported
Percent in-state/out of state: 22%/78%
Percent from Public HS: 78%
Retention Rate: 89%
Graduation Rate 4-year: 72%

Graduation Rate 6-year: 78%
Percent Undergraduates in On-campus housing: 95%
Number of official organized extracurricular organizations: 95
3 Most popular majors: Creative Writing, Sociology, Anthropology/Political Science
Student/Faculty ratio: 11:1
Average Class Size: 15
Percent of students going to grad school: 40%
Tuition and Fees: $31,540
In-State Tuition and Fees if different: No difference
Cost for Room and Board: $6,696
Percent receiving financial aid out of those who apply: 80%
Percent receiving financial aid among all students: 62%

O n a beautiful autumn day in the small rural town of Beloit, Wisconsin, just fifty miles due south of Madison, you can find Beloit College students taking part in a host of activities ranging from playing ukuleles on the steps outside their dorm room entryways, to throwing Frisbees throughout their wooded forty-acre campus, or even "LARPing," also known as Live Action Role Playing, on the green.

With a unique campus atmosphere in which students categorize their classmates as "really weird and not at all afraid to be," "really opinionated," and "quirky," most Beloitians tend to agree that their school draws students who are looking for opportunities to follow their own path.

Curriculum with an Arts Emphasis

Limited to a maximum of 4.75 credits each semester (considered a heavy course load), students at Beloit College typically take four classes worth one credit each and supplement these with .5 credit classes and .25 credit classes. These classes are more geared toward encouraging students to pursue interests that aren't necessarily strictly academic. Beloitians often take performance-based classes, such as music or theater, in these 0.25 and .5 credit spots. "I'm taking a .25 credit this semester called Jazz Improv Group, and there's a group practice when we meet for an hour once a week and then we also have a half-hour mini-lesson," one freshman said.

"It's been a great experience for me to improve my saxophone skills."

Although students are required to take three courses designated "writing courses," one quantitative reasoning course, and a social science course to foster "intercultural literacy" over the course of their four years, some students say they have found it easy to pursue their own academic interests and are even provided the opportunity to design their own major. One senior said he enjoyed all of the core classes he took except for calculus. "A lot of students' experiences with the core courses depend on who teaches it," he added. "I have had both phenomenal teachers and not-so-great ones."

In addition to required courses in the aforementioned three areas, students are encouraged to explore other disciplines as part of Beloit's liberal arts philosophy by taking at least one course in each of the following five domains during their first four semesters: conceptual and foundational systems, artistic and creative practices, social analysis of human behavior, science inquiry into the physical and biological universe, and textual cultures and analysis. While some students appreciate the wide range of classes they take through these requirements, some express frustration. "I think there are a lot of holes you have to jump through to graduate," one sophomore said. Another freshman added: "It has seemed overly complicated and, with five domains of classes to take, there are a lot of things that seem to be unnecessary."

Outside of the typical class requirements, Beloitians must complete a "Liberal Arts in Practice" experience after their fourth semester. "This experience goes along with the learning-by-doing model that I think is really embraced here," one junior said. "Having the ability to explore is key here at Beloit. I've had friends who have done off-campus studies for their 'Liberal Arts in Practice,' and others who have done research and others who have done community service. What makes this place unique is that you can just be you." All seniors also complete some type of capstone experience during their final year at Beloit.

An Expansive Learning Experience

On the whole, students at Beloit say they like that most classes feature interactive components and a little less than three-fourths of all classes have fewer than twenty students. Several students highly recommended one course titled "U.S. Elections, Special Interest Groups, and Campaigns," taught by Georgia Duerst-Lahti. Professor Duerst-Lahti teaches the course every midterm and presidential election cycle, and students in the class gave very positive reviews. In fact, two chose to become Fall Fellows for President Obama's presidential campaign because of their class experience. "It was a total blast, and has opened up opportunities for me that I've never dreamed of," one senior in the class said. Another class that three students all praised was "Whiteness," a course in the anthropology department taught by Lisa Anderson, who is known throughout campus as an expert in analyzing how interracial relations play out on Beloit's campus and in society as a whole. "So many from so many years have told me to take this class, and I'm so happy that I did," one sophomore said.

Another professor who has become highly regarded among students is Biology Professor Marion Fass, who students say has had an enormous influence on youth movements in health awareness. Although there are high SGI's in Beloit, most schools are against having sex education, and Fass, who also created the Health and Society major at Beloit, has taken huge steps to improve birth control methods in these schools. "She has made a significant impact on so many student lives, and she's really all about networking," one senior who took Fass's class "Emerging Diseases" said. Fass also teaches Health, Medical Care, and Soceity.

Extending the learning-by-experience mantra embraced at Beloit, students in a class called "Chicago Public Schools in Context" said it was one that all Beloitians should consider taking. Two professors worked in collaboration with each other to teach the system of education, the history of education, and how urban education has developed. "I don't know how to explain it, but I just learned so much so quickly," said one junior majoring in the sciences who took the class as an elective. "We went to Chicago during the week of October break and went into Chicago Pubic Schools, did research, and saw things outside of the classroom. All twelve of us in the class were so interested in public schooling and you could see that. It's been my favorite class."

In addition to extending classroom experiences, Beloitians also praise the school because of its strong support to students looking to go abroad for a summer or a full semester of even a full year. "I know at least four students who have actually spent an entire year away from campus. It's totally possible to do that here," said one junior. In addition to study-abroad programs, students believe Beloit embraces the idea of putting liberal arts into practice through summer experiences. Another junior spent this past summer in a program called Adventure Grants, which provides money to support educationally constructive programs for students.

> "Getting into the community and doing something—I think that's something that Beloit stands for and practices."

Given the diverse range of interests, most say there isn't a typical Beloit student or characteristics that you could assign to most students. While many students major in some type of science class, most are not strictly involved in science. One junior majoring in Health and Society, a major unique to Beloit, said that most of her friends who are science majors are also heavily interested in the social sciences or foreign languages. And, with the ability to create one's own major at Beloit, the student added that a lot of people mix foreign languages with biology especially, and doing something like "International Engineering" would not be uncommon. "A lot of people find themselves in a science major and then for some reason or another also move to a different major. That's not difficult here. I feel like I've touched so many different academic majors—political science, Spanish, anthropology, sociology, and psychology," said the same junior, who assumed she wanted to be a doctor when she first started at Beloit. After working at Camp Heartland with individuals affected by AIDS the summer after her sophomore year, decided she liked the philosophical aspects of disease more and switched to her current major, Health and Society.

A "Local" Feel to Campus
Outside of the classroom, with over 60 clubs on campus, most students agree that, by halfway through their first semester, they feel welcome. Freshmen said that they have found the overall atmosphere to be inviting and friendly during their first three months. "It's a tiny campus so you will see new people everyday, but you still have a tight-knit group of friends also," one freshman said. "I actually lost my phone this past week, and I didn't even need it."

Split into two distinct sections, the Beloit college campus features a strictly residential side and another half referred to as the "educational side," where most academic buildings are located. When they're not engaging in extracurriculars or working for classes, Beloitians frequent the Coffee House, more affectionately referred to as the "C-House," located on the residential side of campus. Another coffee house on the opposite side of campus, Java Joint, is more oriented toward providing a place for students to study, with coffee and lunch food served.

The C-House offers students food and games like pool and fooseball on the first floor, and then live music performances on the basement level. "It gives a sort of barryfeel," said one freshman, who has been to two concerts at the C-House in his first semester. "We've had people come in from all over to play at C-House," one senior noted. "There's been a mix of student bands and prominent artists, probably 90% outside artists and 10% people from campus." In addition to performances at the C-House, many students said one of the highlights of the fall semester is the Folk and Blues Festival, where professional bands come in to play for two nights in October.

Freedom to Let Loose
Most Beloit students also say they find the drinking philosophy at Beloit to be pretty unique compared to what they have heard at other colleges. "The administration's motto is that, at Beloit, we're going to treat you, students, like adults and, if you do drink, then drink responsibly, like adults." one freshman said. Residential Advisors and security personnel do not actively check students and no retributions are handed out, and several students said that drinking thus becomes the most prominent part of social life on campus. "The culture here is kind of geared toward getting drunk and having a good time on the weekends," one freshman noted. "Normally, some frats throw a party and everybody goes to that on Saturday. Friday nights are a little more chill, and oftentimes people just go from dorm party to dorm party throughout an evening." Students said that the approach to drinking is part of the liberal approach that the administration takes with regards to the residential aspect of being at colleges. "For the most part, they leave us alone on the residential side of campus," one senior said when he reflected on his past four years. "It's up to you to figure out what you want to do with your

social life. If you act like an adult, they'll treat you like one." Another junior added that the drinking culture isn't much different than at any other college. "It's nothing out of the ordinary in terms of what people do at college to have fun. They leave us alone to do what we want within reason. As long as people aren't being irresponsible, it's fine."

When asked what they would like to see changed about their college, many students expressed disappointment over the fact that many people don't take much interest in supporting Beloit sports teams. "The athletic side of the community is very serious but there's a surprisingly little amount of school pride, and that's something us athletes have tried to stir up to revitalize the program," one senior who runs cross country and track said. "We just brought in a men and women's lacrosse team this past year, and in the spring they'll make their debut, so I think we're trying to improve the sports culture here. It goes hand in hand with a renovation of the track stadium, which was at least 3.7 million dollars." Thirty percent of students participate in varsity athletics àt Beloit, which competes in Division III.

Competitive but Satisfactory Housing

Students are typically matched with a roommate their freshman year, and most freshmen are usually situated in a particular area close to the main dining hall and one specific freshman dorm building called 840. After their freshmen year, Belotians typically branch out without any restrictions on places to live. "A lot of seniors tend to live in townhouses or haven/wood rooms, which are harder to get into than regular dorms. They are usually highly coveted on campus. There are usually four students per town house—four singles with one common kitchen, bathroom, and living area," one

senior living in a fraternity said. Two sets of townhouses are located on campus, totaling approximately 100 for the college's nearly 1,400 undergraduates.

However, not only seniors live in these townhouses. "If you have buddies that aren't in the same year but want to live together, then the lottery system could give it to one guy, who then chooses who he wants to live with," the senior added. "What a lot of people like to do is have one senior get the house, because they are often given priority in the lottery, and then have junior friends live in it and pass it down to people that way from year to year."

Students looking to live outside of the dorms or these townhouses also have the option of choosing special-interest housing, with houses ranging from academic-focused houses like the Anthropology House and Geology House to club houses like the LGBT House. Beloitians are required to live on campus for six semesters, and nearly all students live on campus using one of these options during their entire college career.

On the whole, most Beloitians say they're happy with the housing situation. "I think that Beloit does a really good job at putting people on the same floor that have similar interests with each other," one freshman said. "They do a really good job of creating tight-knit communities, which they emphasize by keeping us on campus for six semesters." Students also say they feel pretty safe on campus in the residential area, but the surrounding area can be "a little rough." "As long as you're not being careless, you should be fine," one senior said. "The worst thing that has happened to a student here was being robbed."

Beloit, in short, is a college its students do not regret choosing. Beloit truly tries to satisfy its undergraduates, treating them as adults, broadening academic horizons, and fostering community.—*Jonathan Reed*

FYI
What surprised me most about Beloit when I arrived was "how unafraid people are to talk about their own lives."
Three things you have to do before you graduate are: "take a class with Lisa Anderson, attend Spring Day (where Beloit gives students the day off and a carnival comes to campus), and take in a concert at C-House."

Lawrence University

Address: P.O. Box 599, Appleton, WI 54912-0599
Phone: 800-227-0982
E-mail address: excel@lawrence.edu
Web site URL: www.lawrence.edu
Year Founded: 1847
Private or Public: Private
Religious Affiliation: None
Location: Suburban
Number of Applicants: 2,618
Percent Accepted: 59%
Percent Accepted who enroll: 25%
Number Entering: 414
Number of Transfers Accepted each Year: 68
Middle 50% SAT range: M: 610–720, CR: 590–720, Wr: 610–690
Middle 50% ACT range: 27–31
Early admission program EA/ED/None: EA and ED
Percentage accepted through EA or ED: 39%

EA and ED deadline: 15-Nov for EA, 1-Dec for ED
Regular Deadline: 15-Jan
Application Fee: $40
Full time Undergraduate enrollment: 1,503
Total enrollment: 1,503
Percent Male: 46%
Percent Female: 54%
Total Percent Minority or Unreported: Unreported
Percent African-American: 4%
Percent Asian/Pacific Islander: 2%
Percent Hispanic: 1%
Percent Native-American: <1%
Percent International: Unreported
Percent in-state/out of state: 27%/73%
Percent from Public HS: Unreported
Retention Rate: 90%

Graduation Rate 4-year: 63%
Graduation Rate 6-year: 79%
Percent Undergraduates in On-campus housing: 97%
Number of official organized extracurricular organizations: 130
3 Most popular majors: Biology, History, English
Student/Faculty ratio: 9:1
Average Class Size: 15
Percent of students going to grad school: 22%
Tuition and Fees: $33,264
In-State Tuition and Fees if different: No difference
Cost for Room and Board: $6,957
Percent receiving financial aid out of those who apply: 66%
Percent receiving financial aid among all students: Unreported

Lawrence University's 84 acres in Wisconsin barely contain the vibrancy and excitement of the 1,500 students that bring the school to life. Lawrence is renowned for its music conservatory, and a sizeable percentage of students choose to follow its five-year double-degree program for a Bachelor of Music and Bachelor of Arts. At the same time, the close, intimate atmosphere of its liberal arts curriculum provides the opportunity for budding English and Biology majors alike to shine. And as if that wasn't enough, Lawrence students regularly go on retreats to Björklunden (pronounced "Bee-york-lun-den"), an estate on the shore of Lake Michigan, for seminars and weekend trips and to enjoy nature at its most beautiful. "I had my choice of so many schools," one sophomore said, "and I picked Lawrence because it had everything I could ask for."

So a Connie and a Bio major are in a Frosh Studies class . . .

The hallmark of any Lawrentian's education is the Freshman Studies program, which every professor teaches and all students take in their first year at school: "It's unique to Lawrence, because all the freshmen read the same works, which cross different disciplines . . . so the curriculum covers works mostly from literature but also from science and math, history, and of course, music." One student mentioned looking at Martin Luther King Jr.'s "I Have a Dream" speech alongside John Coltrane's song "Alabama" and realizing with her classmates that the two texts shared the same rhythms and cadences: "It was just fascinating to uncover things like that, that you would never notice outside of the classroom!"

The distributional requirements are a writing-intensive and speaking-intensive class, a quantitative class, classes with elements of diversity, a lab science class, a humanities class, a social science class, a fine arts class, a semester of a foreign language (or its equivalent), and a year of Freshman Studies. An English major noticed that "especially with the 'diversity' classes, the distributional requirements encourage people to have a broad view of the foundations of our world. Dead white males have been powerful forces, yes, but there's so much more than that." Classes are on the small side, and one student said she was surprised when her roommate was in a chemistry lecture class with 60 students, "and I had just never heard of anything that big at Lawrence. Classes are usually closer to 15 or 20, but they get smaller as you take more advanced courses."

Lawrence's music conservatory adds a unique twist to the school, and a significant number of students take classes at the Con, as it is called. One student considering a degree in music spent her free hours in a new way: "My workload is a different kind because I'll practice for several hours every day rather than reading books and writing papers or working in a lab." Still, she added, the amount of work is not unreasonable: "I've heard about people pulling all-nighters, but usually it's their fault because they've been putting off something too long."

With such small classes, professors focus on students and strive to make the work interesting. "In Music Theory we each wrote our own four-part chorales and then had people in that class perform them on their respective instruments . . . Viola was a really popular instrument," said a viola player from that class. Geology classes have also gone out into Wisconsin's geologic deposits, and students have dug up rather sizeable artifacts.

Life in between Brewed Awakenings and Björklunden!

When Lawrentians are not hard at work (and most of them do have some time to relax on weeknights), they take the time to enjoy themselves. On weekend afternoons, people usually go to a coffee shop in Appleton "and pretend to work while socializing and enjoying the day." Most students are split between the smaller, cozier Brewed Awakenings and the slightly more posh Copper Rock with its high ceilings, exposed brick walls, and cool art. "On weekend nights, there's usually one or two main parties that have been advertised, usually at the theme house or frat house," so the campus tends to split into the "party" groups and the "relaxed" groups. When asked about parties, one underclassman said, "The Coop's Nearly Naked parties are really neat—the point is to be creative and dress in anything other than clothing. We've even had dresses made out of juice boxes."

True to Lawrence's focus on music, the all-around coolest frat on campus is Sinfonia, a music fraternity that is almost all brass and percussion, with a lot of jazz musicians. "They provide the music for all their parties, and I just think that's really cool," said a staff writer for the school paper.

"If I had to nail down a stereotypical Lawrence student," said the writer, "it would be a music nerd. Nice, yes, but nerdy. There are definitely jocks on campus, though, and both groups have their female counterparts." On a 1-to-10 scale, Lawrence students rate an eight for all-around attractiveness. Downer Commons, where most students tend to eat, has three rooms that segment the student body in an interesting way: "A lot of the huge jocks sit in the A room, probably because it's closer to the food. The 'cool and alternative' people, including the outdoorsy people, sit in B, because it gets the best sunlight. And people who want peace and quiet sit upstairs in C, but everybody talks to them because the soft-serve ice cream machine is upstairs!" Lucinda's Dining Hall, the smaller dining facility, is a dining hall with an amazing view of the Wisconsin landscape that Lawrence borders. A vending machine is being added to the Con, and "now Connies won't ever go outside the Con again," joked a musician.

> "I had my choice of so many schools and I picked Lawrence because it had everything I could ask for."

Almost all students live on campus, with a very small handful of super seniors, or fifth-year students in the double-degree program, living in apartments. A major part of dorm life is theme housing, "a hot-button issue every spring. The validity of the Swing (Dancing) House and SoundBoard House are the topics of much debate, in comparison to the Comp-Sci House, the GLOW (Gay, Lesbian, or Whatever) House and the oft-discussed but never realized French House." While most floors are single-sex, "coed floors are creeping slowly onto campus." The Lawrence campus is small enough that news often spreads over Saturday and Sunday brunch at Downer.

On some weekends, for a change of pace, students can go to Björklunden to explore the beautiful 425-acre estate that the University owns along Lake Michigan on the Door County peninsula. There is a lodge, and often student concerts are performed there. Different student groups go each weekend, and some students manage to go two or three times per term. Many students would tell you that a memorable part of a weekend at Björklunden is the food. It's a weekend of nonstop eating, and the food is a nice break from cafeteria food. A notable treat is Chef Steve's famous bread pudding.

One Lawrence student said that, even in the cold of winter, "Lawrence is a bit like Lake Wobegon (which makes sense since we're pretty close to Minnesota), because all the women are strong, all the men are good looking, so all us students are above average." With such a tight-knit community, an intimate liberal arts curriculum, nightlife as cozy as the town of Appleton, and the wild beauty of Wisconsin all around, how could any student *not* pick Lawrence?—*Jeffrey Zuckerman*

FYI

If you come to Lawrence University, you'd better bring "an active love of music."

What is a typical weekend schedule? "Friday: dinner at the Coop, concert, dance party. Saturday: yoga, Farmer's Market, study until your friend's recital, dance party. Sunday: brunch, studying, and maybe another recital, SoundBoard at the coffeehouse in the evening."

If I could change one thing about Lawrence University, "I'd spend more time at Björklunden."

Three things every student at Lawrence University should do before graduating are "visit the cupola on top of Main Hall, answer phones all night during the Great Midwest Trivia Contest, and spend all Saturday attending student recitals."

Marquette University

Address: P.O. Box 1881, Milwaukee, WI 53201-1881	**Percentage accepted through EA or ED:** NA	**Graduation Rate 6-year:** 77%
Phone: 414-288-7302	**EA and ED deadline:** NA	**Percent Undergraduates in On-campus housing:** 51%
E-mail address: admissions@marquette.edu	**Regular Deadline:** 1-Dec	**Number of official organized extracurricular organizations:** 250
Web site URL: www.marquette.edu	**Application Fee:** $0	
Year Founded: 1881	**Full time Undergraduate enrollment:** 8,142	**3 Most popular majors:** Communication, Business,
Private or Public: Private	**Total enrollment:** 11,062	Biomedical Sciences/
Religious Affiliation: Roman Catholic Jesuit	**Percent Male:** 48%	Journalism
Location: Suburban	**Percent Female:** 52%	**Student/Faculty ratio:** 15:1
Number of Applicants: 19,500	**Total Percent Minority or Unreported:** 17%	**Average Class Size:** 16
Percent Accepted: 34%	**Percent African-American:** 5%	**Percent of students going to grad school:** 41%
Percent Accepted who enroll: 29%	**Percent Asian/Pacific Islander:** 4%	**Tuition and Fees:** $28,680
Number Entering: 1,950	**Percent Hispanic:** 5%	**In-State Tuition and Fees if different:** No difference
Number of Transfers Accepted each Year: 350	**Percent Native-American:** 1%	**Cost for Room and Board:** $9,680
Middle 50% SAT range: M: 550–660, CR:540–630, Wr: 530–640	**Percent International:** 2%	**Percent receiving financial aid out of those who apply:** 92%
	Percent in-state/out of state: 43% / 57%	
Middle 50% ACT range: 24–29	**Percent from Public HS:** 54%	**Percent receiving financial aid among all students:** 74%
Early admission program EA/ED/None: None	**Retention Rate:** 93%	
	Graduation Rate 4-year: 58%	

The largest private university in the state of Wisconsin, Marquette University is also one of the most important Jesuit universities in the country. Marquette certainly has a strong Catholic character and incorporates theological classes into the university's curriculum. Of course, this does not mean that Marquette focuses on religious training. It is in fact a well-respected institution of higher learning in a large number of fields, ranking among the top 100 national universities by the *U.S. News & World*

Report. Most students tend to have a very good academic and social experience, making it a great college choice.

A Different Approach to Learning

At the outset, Marquette is very typical of universities of similar scope. It is divided into 12 different colleges and schools. Of course, a number of them, such as the Schools of Law and Management, are only available to graduate students. However, the university certainly has a large selection of programs to satisfy almost any academic pursuit. Indeed, for undergraduates, the university offers a long list of programs in engineering, business, communications, health sciences, nursing, and liberal arts, not to mention a number of preprofessional curricula to help those planning for graduate school. "I think we do have a lot of choices at Marquette," said one student. "The College of Business Administration, especially, has a lot of options." The university has more than 100 majors offered, as well as a good selection of minors. The majors in communications and business are highly popular. For those who are not sure about majors, they are not alone. In fact, about 20 percent of students are unsure about the precise direction of their studies and need to take a number of classes at Marquette before deciding on a major.

What is different about Marquette is its Core of Common Studies, which is similar to most universities' general education requirements. In order to provide a well-rounded education, students must all complete courses in certain topics. Marquette, given its Catholic traditions, has a very extensive list of required fields, ranging from the usual mathematics and social sciences to areas such as rhetoric and theology. The idea of taking classes in theology may not be very amenable to a number of less than religious students, but these theology courses are in fact basic introductions to the Bible and the Christian faith. "The requirements in theology are not there to make you become a priest," said one student. "They can actually be really interesting in teaching you about the history of Catholicism." Furthermore, the university also requires classes about other cultures to establish better global understanding.

Students are generally satisfied with the class sizes at Marquette, which offers a combination of hundred-people lectures and small discussion-based seminars. According to students, both types of classes are important in a college education. "Going to a bigger lecture is totally different from sitting in a small class with twelve people," said one student. "I don't know which one is better, but you will definitely get a chance to do both at Marquette." Of course, freshmen tend to be stuck with larger classes, if only due to the large number of people enrolling in introductory courses.

> "I think Milwaukee is great. It is not really stressful like New York, but it has all the attractions of a big city, and Marquette is right in the center of it."

The workload is also manageable, but students should remember not to overload their schedule. "You should try to find a balance between easy and difficult classes," said one student. "If you are already taking two hard courses, you should choose a couple of easy ones to balance them out." Another issue is to find the equilibrium between extracurricular activities and academics. "Because we have so many organizations, you can be involved in too many of them and forget about your classes," said one student.

Students are also happy with their access to professors. They can go to office hours, and course instructors are happy to have informal chats with students on topics beyond academics. "Most professors are really helpful, and they can give you all kinds of advice on classes, careers, everything," said one student.

At the Center of Brew City

Marquette's location is one of the best assets of the university. Milwaukee is one of the 30 largest cities in the United States in terms of population. In addition, it is also a city of college students, serving as the location of more than a dozen colleges and universities. Marquette is very close to downtown Milwaukee, thus offering students the chance of having access to the numerous cultural activities of the city. In addition, given the high level of economic activities in Milwaukee, students have an easier time finding jobs and internships in the area that can accompany their studies. "I think Milwaukee is great," said one student. "It is not really stressful like New York, but it has all the attractions of a big city, and Marquette is right in the center of it."

Marquette offers nine different residential

halls, most of which are modern high- to midrises, in accordance with an urban setting. The freshmen rooms tend to be small and cramped, but the quality of accommodations improve as students rise in seniority. "You have to be patient and wait until the last couple of years to have nicer housing," said one student. "But then again, you might no longer be living on campus after sophomore year." In fact, a large number of upperclassmen leave dorms to enjoy greater freedom in nearby off-campus housing. There is more space and certainly fewer restrictions on student activities. "You can definitely find pretty good off-campus housing nearby at a reasonable price," said one student. "So there is less incentive to stay in dorms after freshman year."

Marquette operates five dining halls from early morning into late night. In addition, each residential hall has a store mostly used for snacks and drinks. "There is nothing great about the food," said one student. "But it is definitely good enough for you to get by on during the school year." For those who have difficulties with the dining services, it is important to remember that Marquette is in a city, and there are restaurants of all types around the university.

Weekend activities vary for students. Some people prefer fraternities and sororities, which hold big, theme parties. Others go to local bars and clubs. For those uninterested in drinking, there are plenty of shows and events to attend around Milwaukee, not to mention the proximity to Chicago. "There are so many things to do here," said one student. "I just wish I had more time during the weekends."

Like Pros

Marquette is known for one of the most successful men's basketball programs in the country. The Golden Eagles have produced a large number of players in the National Basketball Association and qualify for the NCAA Division I Tournament almost every year. The games are some of the best-attended college basketball events in the country. "Basketball is huge here," said one student. "When March comes around, everyone is infected with a basketball craze." In fact, the Golden Eagles play at Bradley Center, which is the home to none other than Milwaukee's professional team, the Bucks.

With the Golden Eagles, Marquette certainly has a great deal of school spirit. Of course, the university also derives pride from its Catholic tradition. Some students do complain that the university is not sufficiently diverse. Most students come from Wisconsin and the surrounding Midwestern states and are predominantly white. However, the university is certainly working toward making Marquette better known and more attractive to those outside of the region. Ultimately, the university has strong academics, good location, and fun social life, three great selling points to prospective students.—*Xiaohang Liu*

FYI
If you come to Marquette, you'd better bring "some winter clothing."
What is the typical weekend schedule? "Basketball games and frat parties."
Three things every student at Marquette should do before graduating are "go to mass, go to
   Chicago, and make sure that you show up to as many basketball games as possible. Some people
   would pay a fortune to see some of the games."

University of Wisconsin / Madison

Address: 716 Langdon Street, Madison, WI 53706-1481
Phone: 608-262-3961
E-mail address: onwisconsin@admissions.wisc.edu
Web site URL: www.admissions.wisc.edu
Year Founded: 1848
Private or Public: Public
Religious Affiliation: None
Location: Urban
Number of Applicants: 25,522
Percent Accepted: 57%
Percent Accepted who enroll: 41%
Number Entering: 5,927
Number of Transfers Accepted each Year: 2,119
Middle 50% SAT range: M: 620–750, CR: 530–670, Wr: 580–680
Middle 50% ACT range: 26–30
Early admission program EA/ED/None: None

Percentage accepted through EA or ED: NA
EA and ED deadline: NA
Regular Deadline: 1-Feb
Application Fee: $44
Full time Undergraduate enrollment: 30,555
Total enrollment: 42,595
Percent Male: 47%
Percent Female: 53%
Total Percent Minority or Unreported: 21%
Percent African-American: 2%
Percent Asian/Pacific Islander: 6%
Percent Hispanic: 6%
Percent Native-American: 1%
Percent International: 6%
Percent in-state/out of state: 63%/37%
Percent from Public HS: Unreported
Retention Rate: 93%
Graduation Rate 4-year: 49%

Graduation Rate 6-year: 80%
Percent Undergraduates in On-campus housing: 25%
Number of official organized extracurricular organizations: 700
3 Most popular majors: Social Sciences, Biology, Business/Marketing
Student/Faculty ratio: 17:1
Average Class Size: 29
Percent of students going to grad school: 48%
Tuition and Fees: $25,415
In-State Tuition and Fees if different: $9,665
Cost for Room and Board: $7,780
Percent receiving financial aid out of those who apply: 55%
Percent receiving financial aid among all students: 35%

The University of Wisconsin-Madison, a school of 30,000 undergraduates, is one of the top public universities in the nation, known for stellar academics, a powerhouse football team, and a lively party environment. Students find Madison to be a perfect college town, despite the cold winter weather. Wisconsin challenges students to grow independent, taking the big school and breaking it down into small, Badger communities.

Work Hard

Wisconsin is divided up into nine schools and colleges, including the very strong School of Business and the liberal arts-style College of Letters and Science. With over 100 majors, it is not too difficult for students to find something they are interested in, whether it is the popular science, psychology, and business majors or the more wacky ones, like Dairy Science. Within the colleges there are various general education requirements, including two quantitative reasoning and communication classes for the College of Letters and Science, but students don't find them too frustrating. "Most people do it anyway," one student noted.

Students with the most credits are given priority when choosing classes, meaning that it is sometimes difficult for underclassmen to get into the classes they want to take. However, with so many options to choose from, students don't think it's hard to find an interesting class.

Especially for freshmen, a majority of classes may be lectures, which can include more than 400 people. Often, the professors put the notes online, which students find enormously helpful. In one student's sociology class, there are 420 students, but the class is coupled with a 10-person discussion section to ensure maximum understanding. However, the same student shared her public speaking seminar with just 12 other students.

Professors, like any school, are largely good, but vary on the class. For some classes, they are very interesting, though on the other hand, some find it difficult to keep the lecture hall engaged. One student said her professor was "really into the class, always joking and having fun with everyone." However, students say the TAs are really good, which, according to one student, "is almost more important than the professor."

Wisconsin has a somewhat strange grading system. Students can obtain the following grades in their courses: A, A/B, B, B/C, C, D or F. This can be a detriment or a benefit depending on the person. For an A- student it is particularly frustrating, when a 91 on a test is counted the same as a 87.

Those seeking more of a challenge can apply for the College of Letters and Science honor program, which can involve honors in the liberal arts, honors in a specific major, or both. As a member of the honors program, students can test themselves academically and grow closer to professors. One freshman said she took a class with 17 other people from a professor who usually lectures to hundreds of students.

For freshmen, it is a big transition from high school. Yes there is more reading and the workload increases, but freshmen receive an "overwhelming amount of independence," one student said. Because of big lectures and less one-on-one time with professors, students have to be more proactive with their college experience. "There's so much I don't know about still," said a freshman. "I have to figure things out on my own."

Play Hard

"Students study so much during the week," one student said. "We work really hard, and we earn it for the weekends." While for some, the weekend starts on Tuesdays, for many students Thursday night is the beginning of the fun. The bar scene is huge, even for minors: "Fake IDs are pretty crucial," one student said. "Don't expect to get away with any old one—it has to be good." Students also go to house parties, fraternities and sororities.

According to one student, Greek life is no longer dominating on campus since they got in trouble a few years ago. Many students join fraternities or sororities to "make a school of 40,000 a little smaller," said one sorority member.

There are a few famous parties that take place throughout the year, but the two biggest are the Mifflin Street Block Party and the State Street Halloween Party. Mifflin occurs the week before finals and involves the complete takeover of the street. Halloween lasts at least three nights, meaning three nights of costumed brouhaha, with music, concerts, and tons of fun. The party takes place on State Street, which leads from Bascom Hill, a hub of Wisconsin academics, to the state capitol.

Life in Madison

Students consider Madison, the capital of Wisconsin, the perfect college town. "It's not a huge city, but it's a lot bigger than what I'm used to," said one Wisconsin native. "There's always so many different things going on." Another student added: "With Madison you get a small-town college feel while still having that big-time college experience." Madison is home to lots of concerts, many of which take place at the Majestic Theater, and scores of restaurants serving all types of cuisine. For parents' weekend, Tornado is a great place to go, where you can find the "best steak of your life," one student said. After a night of late partying—or studying—students often head over to Ian's Pizza, which has lines out the door at two in the morning. "It's really nice that everything is close," one student said. "The capitol is right here. The lake is right here. We have natural trails and a downtown with interesting food."

> **"With Madison you get a small-town college feel while still having that big-time college experience."**

With the state capitol right next to campus, Madison offers countless opportunities to get involved in local politics. Many student organizations are involved with lobbying (and following around) local politicians. One student said, "We're so close, so we have a big influence on the government." Many students, especially political science majors, take on an internship through the year to get a taste of civil service. Other internship opportunities arise from the sciences. As Wisconsin is a research-based college, lots of students are involved in medical internships, sometimes paid, which they keep throughout their college career. According to one student, about half of the students have jobs—including those paid internships—which can range from the ordinary (dining hall worker) to the more fun (scoring intramural sports).

Your own Wisconsin Community

Wisconsin has over 500 student organizations on campus, so there is always something to get involved in. Many students view clubs and extracurriculars as not only a way to pursue passions outside the classroom, but also to make Wisconsin feel smaller. "There are lots of options," one student said. "If you want it, it's here." One example of this is intramurals. There are dozens of IM sports to participate in, from volleyball to broomball to Ultimate Frisbee, and they are very low stress. One student noted: "They're as competitive as you want them to be. I have some friends who just have fun with them."

Most freshmen live in dorms, though upperclassmen generally move off campus. Students consider the dorms a smaller community and quickly bond with others on their floor. There are two areas of dorms: Lakeshore ("secluded, quiet, and nature-y") and Southeast (closer to downtown with more of a party reputation). Every year, there is a huge snowball fight between the two. "It's pretty intense," one freshman said.

Bucky Badger
In the early days of Wisconsin, the mascot at football games was a live badger. When it proved too dangerous and uncontrollable, an art student had an idea—she crafted a papier-mâché head for the original Bucky the Badger student costume. As a mascot for a Big Ten powerhouse football school, Bucky makes it to every game, but he is definitely not alone.

On Game Days, Wisconsin students wake up early, dress in red, and walk together to the huge Camp Randall Stadium. They are soon surrounded by "the entire town" of Madison natives; one student noted that "everyone comes to football games. They take a lot of pride in the school." The student section, a sea of red, stands up for the entire game. At the end of the third quarter, House of Pain's song, "Jump Around" begins to play. According to one freshman, "the entire student section goes up and down and goes absolutely nuts." The so-called fifth quarter is a continuation of the rumpus, which is an entire quarter of more jumping and singing about Wisconsin. "You finally feel like this huge school is coming together as one, with everyone in one location," one student said.

Sconnies and Coasties
When first arriving at Wisconsin, there is some tension between the Wisconsin natives ("Sconnies") and those from out-of-state ("Coasties"). One Coastie from Los Angeles mentioned an incident when she was trying out for the club water polo team, saying that "they look down on you when they see where you're from and what you're wearing." A Sconnie said that Coasties "bring more of a city atmosphere, party habits, and different clothes. They're a little more wild than Wisconsin people." Though there is some self-segregation, the two groups generally "mix pretty well." "I have lots of Coastie friends," one Wisconsin-native said.

"People are extremely friendly," said one student. "Every single flight home I've been on, I've met someone who went to Wisconsin. Everyone who goes there loves it and wants to talk about it." It is easy to make new friends, whether through dorms, classes, or extracurriculars.

The Polar Plunge
Standard dress, at least during winter, is a staple Wisconsin sweatshirt, UGGs, and a North Face jacket. According to some, it is not that big of a deal. "I expected this freezing terrain. When I came, it was absolutely beautiful," one student said. However, some brave students undertake the polar plunge, jumping into the freezing cold water of Lake Mendota. Somewhere, apparently, there is a list of all students that ever accepted the challenge. "I hope I have it in me," one student said.

But despite the frigid winter months, students are generally happy they chose to be Badgers. "Madison has always been a dream school for me," one student said. Another noted, "I wanted to be in a school that had a big-spirited athletic environment while still excelling academically."

Students say that almost everyone at Wisconsin loves it, and it's easy to see why. Wisconsin is a perfect school for students looking to obtain a great education in a place where school pride, especially in athletics, is a dominant force. Though students have to be more independent academically and socially, they learn to break Wisconsin up into smaller communities, making great friends in the process. Spending four years at Wisconsin, students can get the parties, college town and fun of a traditional college experience.—*Mason Kroll*

FYI
Three things every student at Wisconsin should do before graduating are: "complete the polar plunge, storm the field, and go to a hockey game."

If you come to Wisconsin, you'd better bring "snowboots. Don't think your UGGs can last in the snow—you have to do a penguin waddle to keep dry."

If I could change one thing about Wisconsin, I'd "make there be less students per professor—you really have to go out and make an effort to talk to a professor."

Wyoming

Not many universities can claim a location at 7,200 feet. Amidst mountain ranges and grassy plains, the height only adds to the remote, yet urban setting of the University of Wyoming, one that most students come to love. With the University of Wyoming being the only big college in the state, the University continually draws fans to cheer for the brown and gold.

The State University

With just over 10,000 undergraduates claiming their loyalty to UW, many students feel that the size is perfect. One sophomore commented that the student body population is "the perfect size, enabling individual attention and creating an atmosphere for better learning, but also big enough to see unfamiliar faces." Like any university, the class sizes vary with specialization. While introductory courses can range anywhere from 200 to 500 students, the higher-level courses cater to crowds of 30 students or less.

At U of Wyoming, one will find most students looking to major in Business Administration or Education, but don't be fooled: Wyoming offers a variety of fun areas of study. "In order to fulfill the physical education requirement, I've known people who have taken Ballroom Dancing, Ballet, and even Tai Chi," one senior said. The University of Wyoming offers strong honors programs and boasts fantastic engineering and research science departments. In order to qualify for the honors program at Wyoming, high school students must have a minimum 3.7 GPA, at least a 1,240 total score on the

SAT, or composite ACT scores of at least 28. Honor students are required to take five honors courses throughout their time at UW, two freshman year and one each of the three remaining years. One student at UW commented that the course load is "pretty manageable, but continues to get more difficult as you go. The honors classes and the science courses are amongst the most challenging."

A Little Too Small

Similar to many campuses, most students at Wyoming usually move off campus after freshman year. For those students still on campus, their housing options include Wyoming's six dorm buildings located at the center of campus, "Prexy's Pasture." With the ability to move off campus, approximately 50 percent of sophomores do so along with almost all the juniors and seniors. "It's sort of a rite of passage to be able to live off campus. Although it's nice to live close to classes, living off campus is really liberating: no restrictions and no RAs," commented one Wyoming senior. As far as the architectural style of the University is concerned, students find it somewhat uninviting. The cement façades seem to emphasize the barren winter months. However, the University is undergoing "a lot of renovation and is committed to modernizing all of campus."

For those students still living on campus, the dining halls are one of Wyoming's best features: "The dining halls are all renovated and the food offered by UW is actually really good. There's a lot of variety and the food is pretty fresh," one freshman noted. Open until 10:30 p.m., the dining halls resemble more of a food court than a dining hall. Off-campus students don't have to miss out. Local businesses are able to serve Wyoming students through the use of their WyoOne ID cards. Thus, all students can take advantage of a late-night slice of pizza or cup of coffee with the swipe of a card.

A Separate Place

Students can feel a true sense of community in Laramie. With only 25,000 people occupying the small town, more than half are students. As great as a small-town community may feel, it can be a bit restricting. "Laramie is about a two-hour drive from anywhere. Most students will usually stay on campus," one sophomore said. But most students do have cars, so the possibility for escape is always there. When on campus,

upperclassmen mostly hit the bar scene, with Lovejoy's Bar and Grill and Altitude Chophouse & Brewery being two favorites. Underclassmen usually either attend the usual frat parties or make their way to the athletes' houses. Because many upperclassmen live off campus, the underclassmen "don't really intermingle regularly with juniors and seniors unless they are a part of the same team or organization," one junior said. The University of Wyoming has a strict policy against alcohol in the dorms and really tries to curb underage drinking, but "alcohol is very accessible" nonetheless. The big event all students can look forward to is the annual Beach Party that one on-campus frat puts on. "The frat actually drags sand in and transforms the entire house into a beach. It's pretty fun; everyone goes," one sophomore said.

> "I think the fact that the entire state of Wyoming is behind the university and all of its programs means a lot to the students here."

Although it is hard for some students to feel so isolated, Laramie has many other kinds of attractions, including its breathtaking scenery. The surrounding areas include everything from grassy plains to rocky climbing areas. With a mountainous landscape in the background, many students rock climb, hike, or even ski at Snowy Range or Happy Jack. On weekends, many students set aside a day to head up to the mountains and get some fresh air.

Saddle Up for the Gold and Brown

With an overall student body of over 12,000, many students find their niches in diverse activities. Varsity athletics are valued highly. With football and basketball bringing in the biggest crowds, other sports draw supportive crowds as well. "As a swimmer at Wyoming, I am proud to say that we bring in more spectators at home meets than any other school in our conference," remarked one junior. Wyoming also emphasizes an active lifestyle by providing 18 different club sports, involving nearly 6,000 students, faculty, and staff. UW's Half Acre Gym is a "hot spot to hang out and one of the most noteworthy buildings on campus." Life at UW is one of comfort. Many students will show up to class in sweats and sometimes pajamas.

The general feel is that the atmosphere is easygoing and laid-back, but where school spirit is concerned, the Cowboys and Cowgirls find themselves very well supported.

Nowhere Else

Students across the nation have school pride; that's a given. But for students at the University of Wyoming, it's deeper than that. The community involvement is really treasured, and the people are friendly. "First and foremost, I go to the University of Wyoming. I think the fact that the entire state of Wyoming is behind the university and all of its programs means a lot to the students here. Also, I think that the small community brings the students here closer together."
—*Taylor Ritzel*

FYI

If you come to the University of Wyoming, you'd better bring a "big winter coat and anything that protects you from the wind."

What is the typical weekend schedule? "Party Fridays, sleep and climb Saturdays, party Saturday nights, and study on Sundays."

If I could change one thing about the University of Wyoming, I'd "get rid of the wind. The weather can be really nice on any given day, but the wind ruins the day."

Three things every student at the University of Wyoming should do before graduating are "ski at Snowy Range, attend a home UW football game, and hike Vedauwoo."

Canada

Despite Canada's image as a country of winter storms and glaciers, thousands of American students cross the border every year to seek an education from their country's northern neighbor. The reasons for this northbound move range from low tuition to beautiful landscape to high educational standards. Given the numerous advantages of attending Canadian universities, it is certainly worthwhile for American students to take a close look.

Money Matters

One important factor in choosing which college to attend is money. In that respect, Canadian universities, which are all public, have significant advantages over their American counterparts. The tuition rates at the most expensive schools are generally below $8,000 for Canadians. Even for American citizens, the average rate hovers below $20,000, much cheaper than the price tags of many universities in the United States, which are rapidly approaching $40,000.

Another major expense that students will face, the cost of living, depends greatly on location—living in Toronto is certainly more expensive than, say, Wolfville, Nova Scotia, but it is still cheaper than a number of cities in the United States. American students in need of financial aid can apply for Stafford loans from the federal government, even if they study in Canada. Both merit- and need-based scholarships are also available.

The low fees, however, come with a disadvantage. Funding for universities in Canada depends on the government. This means that they tend to have fewer resources than many private institutions in the United States. In general, however, the overall impact of tight government funding on the quality of education is minimal, especially for undergraduates.

A Whole Different Country

Each Canadian province maintains its own system of higher education. For example, in Quebec, most students attend a post-secondary program called a College of General and Vocational Education (CEGEP) prior to enrollment in universities, making the academic programs more specialized. In fact, unlike many American universities, which encourage students to study in a wide range of subjects, Canadian schools tend to place greater emphasis on career preparation.

Most American students studying in Canada choose to attend one of the major research universities, creating the perception that undergraduate education in Canada is always within large, impersonal institutions located in urban centers. While it is true that the better-known universities, such as McGill University and the University of Toronto, enroll tens of thousands of undergraduate and graduate students, there are plenty of smaller, predominantly undergraduate schools housing only a few thousand students, very similar to liberal arts colleges in the United States. Choices abound for those who would like to escape the noise of bustling cities and settle in the countryside.

One aspect of college life that Canada fails to offer is school spirit. Although students wear their college gear and cheer for their sports teams, their attachment to their schools is not as strong as in the United States, many students say. This is in part because intercollegiate sports are not as important in Canada. Youngsters who aspire to become professional athletes mostly rise through junior leagues instead of collegiate competitions. Furthermore, the large number of students in off-campus housing diminishes the sense of community in many universities.

Getting in

The admissions process in Canada places greater emphasis on grades and standardized test scores than do American universities. Although extracurricular activities and achievements outside of school are also considered, academic performance significantly outweighs everything else. Many schools even set cutoff limits for SAT scores and high school GPAs. Of course, this is not universal, and different schools have different policies regarding admissions.

Studying in Canada for non–Canadian citizens requires a student visa, which is easy to obtain once the student is admitted.

Just like those in the United States, Canadian universities attract thousands of students from around the world every year. The cold weather and the differences in college life may turn away many American students, but given its quality of education and affordability, Canada is certainly a great destination for college students and deserves strong consideration.—*Xiaohang Liu*

Carleton University

Address: 1125 Colonel By Drive, 315 Robertson Hall, Ottawa, ON K1S 5B6 Canada
Phone: 613-520-3663
E-mail address: liaison@admissions.carleton.ca
Web site URL: www.carleton.ca
Year Founded: 1942
Private or Public: Private
Religious Affiliation: None
Location: Urban
Number of Applicants: 15,934
Percent Accepted: 73%
Percent Accepted who enroll: 43%
Number Entering: 5,000
Number of Transfers Accepted each Year: 830
Middle 50% SAT range: Unreported
Middle 50% ACT range: Unreported
Early admission program EA/ED/None: None

Percentage accepted through EA or ED: NA
EA and ED deadline: NA
Regular Deadline: Rolling
Application Fee: $85 (Canadian dollars)
Full time Undergraduate enrollment: 20,746
Total enrollment: 23,161
Percent Male: 50%
Percent Female: 50%
Total Percent Minority or Unreported: Unreported
Percent African-American: Unreported
Percent Asian/Pacific Islander: Unreported
Percent Hispanic: Unreported
Percent Native-American: Unreported
Percent International: 8%
Percent in-state/out of state: 1% from U.S.
Percent from Public HS: Unreported
Retention Rate: Unreported

Graduation Rate 4-year: Unreported
Graduation Rate 6-year: Unreported
Percent Undergraduates in On-campus housing: 15%
Number of official organized extracurricular organizations: 78
3 Most popular majors: Unreported
Student/Faculty ratio: 2:1
Average Class Size: 9
Percent of students going to grad school: Unreported
Tuition and Fees: $14,936 Canadian
In-State Tuition and Fees if different: $4,794 Canadian
Cost for Room and Board: $7,247 Canadian
Percent receiving financial aid out of those who apply: Unreported
Percent receiving financial aid among all students: Unreported

Located in the heart of Canada's national capital, Carleton University offers both a taste of French-Canadian culture and a thriving political environment for aspiring public servants. The city is rich with eclectic offerings—national museums, memorials, heritage sites and scene walkways. In the long winters, students find refuge from the cold through a variety of activities, from skating in the Rideau Canal, the world's largest skating rink, to shopping at the historic Byward Market. Known for its professional programs in journalism, architecture, engineering, and public affairs, Carleton has overcome its past reputation as "Last Chance U."

Work Ready

Founded in 1942, Carleton was Ontario's first private, non-denominational college. It is a public university offering more than 65 programs, among which the most reputed are its engineering, humanities, and public affairs departments. The Faculty of Public Affairs and Policy Management encompasses some of the university's most prestigious majors, from its selective journalism program to its popular political science curriculum, which serves as a training ground for many of the country's budding politicians. The university prides itself in co-operative education and internship programs that prepare students for the workforce following graduation. Students in engineering, public affairs and policy management, architecture and select science and humanities programs are eligible to apply for the co-operative education program alongside their initial application to the school. If they are successful, they have the opportunity to obtain up to 20 months of work experience prior to graduation. Many students take advantage of the school's proximity to Parliament and other governmental headquarters by seeking internship placements at federal institutions. Carleton's criminology and criminal justice track, for instance, is quite popular and gives its students the opportunity to intern with attorneys, policy analysts, police officers, victim counselors, and so on.

For those who are inclined toward more traditional forms of education, Carleton also offers a four-year, interdisciplinary Bachelor of Humanities degree centered on the Western canon. Students undertake a thorough study of the likes of Plato, Homer, Virgil, Shakespeare, Moliere, and Kant. Despite its breadth, the program is often dismissed by its pre-professional counterparts as "easy" and "basically for people who have less of a clue about what they want to do with themselves than people studying the arts." The latter refers to the ArtsOne track for first-years who have yet to choose a major when they arrive on campus. The program is separated into different "clusters" containing four courses each of a central theme. Each cluster contains one hundred students with identical course schedules, allowing them to establish a distinct peer group within the larger scale of the university. Meanwhile, Carleton's journalism program is lauded as one of the best in Canada, with opportunities for students to complete apprenticeships in print or broadcast media.

Snowed In

During the long Canadian winter, Ottawa's cold weather keeps many students indoors, where they find refuge in their tight-knit dorm communities. All the on-campus residences are situated in a "residence village," where students live in buildings based on their year. At the center of all the dorms is the Residence Commons, where students convene to dine at the cafeteria or simply hang out. While most students opt to live off campus after first year, those who remain attested to the convenience of staying in residence: "Once you get to your second or third year, you get an apartment style dorm with a kitchen, so you don't have to stay on the meal plan," said a second-year student. "Plus all your classes are within walking distance." These facilities are not available to everyone, however: Residential spaces are limited after first year and are given to students based on their grades and the availability of the rooms they seek.

> "Once you get to your second or third year, you get an apartment style dorm with a kitchen, so you don't have to stay on the meal plan."

The resources provided in the dorms make the transition into university easy. Even though most freshmen adapt quickly to "a different city with a different lifestyle," the residence fellows in each building ensure that no one is falling behind and serve as point-people for struggling underclassmen. "It's like having a big sister or big brother on your floor"—except when it comes to late-night partying or drinking, the fellows do not make any compromises. They exercise a large amount of authority over the inhabitants of the building, and work to maintain silence when it is needed.

When the students do go outside, the neighboring downtown area provides an array of options. In the summer, there is a beach a mere bus ride away, and an assortment of outdoor restaurants overlooking the canal and the river on the other side. Popular nighttime haunts include Union Station club and the center of the residence village, where there is often dancing and games.

A Capital Rivalry

Carleton maintains a fierce but friendly rivalry with its fellow capital higher education institution, the University of Ottawa. The neighboring schools' basketball teams face off on the courts every year, although

Carleton's Ravens have generally triumphed with five consecutive national titles at the Canadian Interuniversity Sport (CIS) tournament from 2002 and 2007, and again in 2009. The city's cold climate makes it an ideal destination for winter sports, so it is not a surprise that the CU Ski and Snowboard Club is one of the most popular sports organizations on campus. The school's "hip-hop community, ski and snowboard community and drinking community (party people)" come together every fall, when the organization hosts a large hip-hop show complete with ski and snowboard move screenings.

Sporting events aside, Carleton and U Ottawa also have an intellectual rivalry. During frosh week, when newly-minted freshmen descend on the city, frosh groups from both universities compete against each other in a large fundraising activity held downtown. When it comes to club activities, there is the same mindset of competition. While Carleton's Model United Nations team is ranked first in Canada, they derive as much joy from beating U Ottawa as they do from winning the top spot. As one student said, "Our goal is always to get more awards than [U Ottawa]."

Like the flame that burns in front of the Parliament Building, Carleton University students' abiding pride for their school stays alive long after graduation. Those who are passionate about Canadian politics and ready to tackle the work world will find a home in Carleton.—*Yanan Wang*

FYI
If you come to Carleton, you'd better bring . . . a Canada goose jacket and some skates.
If I could change one thing about Carleton, "I'd . . . make the allotment of funds more even—engineering students receive a lot more funding than those in other programs, which is frustrating."
Three things every student at Carleton should do before graduating are . . . have a beaver tail (Canadian-based pastry chain), go skating on the Canal, and attend a Carleton vs. U Ottawa basketball game.

McGill University

Address: 845 Sherbrooke Street West, Montreal, QC H3A 2T5 Canada
Phone: 514-398-3910
E-mail address: admissions@mcgill.ca
Web site URL: www.mcgill.ca
Year Founded: 1821
Private or Public: Public
Religious Affiliation: None
Location: Urban
Number of Applicants: 20,391
Percent Accepted: 54%
Percent Accepted who enroll: 43%
Number Entering: 4,781
Number of Transfers Accepted each Year: 933
Middle 50% SAT range: M: 640–720, CR: 640–740, Wr: 650–720
Middle 50% ACT range: 29–31
Early admission program EA/ED/None: None
Percentage accepted through EA or ED: NA

EA and ED deadline: NA
Regular Deadline: 15-Jan
Application Fee: $80 Canadian
Full time Undergraduate enrollment: 20,459
Total enrollment: 29,585
Percent Male: 40%
Percent Female: 60%
Total Percent Minority or Unreported: Unreported
Percent African-American: Unreported
Percent Asian/Pacific Islander: Unreported
Percent Hispanic: Unreported
Percent Native-American: Unreported
Percent International: 19%
Percent in-state/out of state: 9% from the U.S.
Percent from Public HS: Unreported
Retention Rate: 92%
Graduation Rate 4-year: 68%
Graduation Rate 6-year: 83%

Percent Undergraduates in On-campus housing: 11%
Number of official organized extracurricular organizations: 150
3 Most popular majors: Business/Commerce, Political Science, Psychology
Student/Faculty ratio: 16:1
Average Class Size: 15
Percent of students going to grad school: Unreported
Tuition and Fees: $15,420 Canadian
In-State Tuition and Fees if different: $1,868 Canadian within Quebec; $5,378 within Canada
Cost for Room and Board: $12,948 Canadian
Percent receiving financial aid out of those who apply: Unreported
Percent receiving financial aid among all students: Unreported

I f you're looking for a truly international college experience, look no further than McGill University in Montreal, Quebec. While the Canadian university system is not well known in the United States, the caliber of students that McGill attracts from all over the world and its emphasis on undergraduate studies make it a top-tier international institution. Founded in 1821 by James McGill, a prominent Montreal merchant, this publicly funded university boasts a diverse student body, a cosmopolitan setting, and, as a result of recent efforts, top research facilities.

Parlez-vous français?

Located in Montreal, the second-largest French speaking city in the world, McGill is one of only three English-language universities in the province of Quebec. Most students do not consider McGill to be a "bilingual school." "If you want to immerse yourself in French, Montreal is a great place to start, but if you don't want to learn a word, it's not a problem," said a junior political science major. With the exception of the Faculty of Law, students are not required to speak or learn French. However, the influence and presence of French and francophone culture is integral to the McGill experience. As one senior said, "It's wonderful to hear a mix of French and English being spoken on campus since it truly gives the cultural experience I was looking for." Since 1964, students in all faculties have had the option to write exams and papers in either English or French. While less-than-perfect *français* is not a problem in the classroom, don't attempt to use developing language skills in the streets of Montreal: "If you try to speak French the Montrealers will respond in English—they know a fakie when they hear one."

Eleven Faculties

Given McGill's international campus culture, it is only fitting that McGill has a very diverse student body where international students are a significant presence. Close to 20 percent of McGill's student body is comprised of international students, a third of which are American. These students are attracted to McGill for its European feel, diverse culture, and the relatively reasonable tuition. Since 1996, McGill has been following the Ministry of Education, Leisure and Sports guidelines by exempting qualified international students from paying certain tuition fees. Due to this financial policy, more and more American students are expressing an interest in McGill and other Canadian schools close to the border.

In order to meet the interests of this diverse, multilingual student body, McGill has 11 different departments called faculties. Unlike most American universities, prospective students apply to each faculty, rather than applying to the university as a whole. Some of these faculties include the Schulich School of Music, the Faculty of Dentistry, and the Desautels Faculty of Management. A third of all students are enrolled in the Faculty of Arts, while the Centre for Continuing Education, the Faculty of Science, and the Faculty of Engineering all enroll around 10 percent each. Some students complain that the mandatory introductory classes in each of these faculties can result in 500 person lectures that are "impersonal" and "intimidating." However, one upperclassman claimed that "it gets better after those entry-level courses." Once students are done with the requirements, there are many thought-provoking and unique electives to choose from.

The "Rez"

McGill's main campus is situated in downtown Montreal by Mount Royal, a beautiful park enjoyed by students and denizens of Montreal for its walking trails. It is close to the metro stations of McGill and Peel, often filled with off-campus students. Once you enter through the Roddick Gates, you are surrounded by a refreshing mix of gray limestone architecture and trees, where it is easy to forget that you are in the bustling business district of Montreal.

The second campus, the Macdonald Campus, is home to the natural sciences such as the Faculty of Agricultural and Environmental Science and the School of Dietetics and Human Nutrition. The Macdonald Campus has a hands-on approach to learning and focuses on preparing

students for careers in science and technology.

> **"If you want to immerse yourself in French, Montreal is a great place to start, but if you don't want to learn a word, it's not a problem."**

Unlike those at many American colleges, after their first year, McGill students do not stay in residence halls, colloquially known as "rez." Although accepted first-year students are guaranteed on-campus housing, due to the limited space, upperclassmen are expected to find housing off campus. A freshman at McGill reports that living in residence "is definitely a great way to meet people, but it can get pretty loud in the hallways sometimes." There are four main rezes you can live in. Most freshmen live in Upper Rez (officially Bishop Mountain Residences). Royal Victoria College is a women's university turned women's-only residence hall. Solin Hall is an apartment-style residence four metro stops away from central campus. The most coveted residence is New Residence Hall. New Rez was originally a four-star hotel, and students describe it as being superior in décor, space, and food. "They have sushi, steak, whatever you want, basically," says one former inhabitant of New Rez.

Beware of the McGill Bubble

Finding off-campus housing can be a bit of a hassle for McGill students. Although there are many university-owned apartments, some students have trouble finding off-campus housing due to strict housing markets and rising rents in the areas near campus. The section of Montreal dubbed McGill Ghetto, an area east of the campus, seems to be growing in popularity among McGill students. Despite the complications of living off campus, most upperclassmen like living on their own: "Unlike a lot of U.S. schools, McGill really lets you be an adult. I am 21; I can make my own food."

Another reason why students love living off campus is because they can explore the city of Montreal. "There is really no shortage of things to do in Montreal!" gushed one literature major. The city provides something different for every taste. For those who enjoy bar- and club-hopping, the streets of St. Laurent, St. Denis, and Ste. Catherine are lively with students on the weekends.

For those who prefer a more relaxing scene, there are many jazz venues and lounges to be discovered. Students describe the people of Montreal and McGill as very accepting and tolerant, and the city as very gay-friendly. Because the city and the university are so integrated, many students warn of getting caught in the "McGill Bubble." One senior said, "Since I am always surrounded by students, I don't have a sense of living in a 'real-world' community."

Because so many students live off campus, most of the weekend activities take place off campus as well. The drinking age in Quebec is 18, so throughout their McGill career, students have easy access to bars, pubs, and alcohol. There are also several on-campus events that are not to be missed. In the warmer month of September, students flock to the lower field to partake in the outdoor open-air pub commonly known as OAP. Another event fondly looked back on is Frosh, the first week of freshman year. "Basically a week of non-stop drinking and debauchery," reminisced one sophomore.

A Society of Students

If McGill students mostly reside off campus, what do they do on campus? In a school with more than 20,000 undergraduates, one of the ways in which McGill students form communities amongst themselves is through clubs. There are over 150 student clubs and organizations to choose from. Students can be involved in everything from performance art to political action. Through some of these clubs, McGill students contribute to the community as well. Healthy Minds is an organization devoted to visiting children in hospitals, and Santropol Roulant is a student-run organization that delivers over 100 hot meals a day to housebound senior citizens.

The core of all of these student activities is the University Centre on the main campus. The William Shatner University Centre is a place for students to hang out with their friends, watch TV, play foosball, and hold club meetings. Named after William Shatner, alumnus and actor of *Star Trek* fame, the facility includes a food court, a legal clinic, a pub, and a lounge, all run by the Students' Society of McGill University. The SSMU is a student union that not only serves as an umbrella organization for many student activities but also serves as the voice of the student body. "I appreciate the efforts that SSMU goes through to makes sure our needs and voices are heard by the administration," said one senior. "It definitely brings the McGill student body together."—*Lee Komeda*

FYI
If you come to McGill, "you'd better bring a Canadian phone, a strong liver, and a good work ethic."
What's the typical weekend schedule? "A lot of reading and essay writing but also a lot of fun! On Saturdays you can head down to St. Laurent, St. Denis, or Ste. Catherine streets to have dinner with friends, then go to a bar, a club, or a relaxing lounge. On Sundays you can take in a gallery show, go to a concert, or stroll down to the Old Port for a glass of wine."
If I could change one thing about McGill, I'd "make the final examination dates part of the syllabus (we wait until November, which makes booking a ticket home for Christmas costly)."
Three things every student at McGill should do before graduating are "get trashed during Frosh Week, go to Winter Carnival, enjoy OAP in September."

McMaster University

Address: Gilmour Hall Room 108, 1280 Main Street W. Hamilton, Ontario, L8S4L8 Canada

Phone Number(s): 905-525-9140

E-mail address: macadmit@mcmaster.ca

Web site URL: www.mcmaster.ca

Year Founded: 1887

Private or Public: Public

Religious affiliation: None

Location: Suburban

Number of Applicants: Unreported

Percent Accepted: Varies by Program

Percent Accepted who enroll: Varies by Program

Number Entering: Unreported

Number of Transfers Accepted each Year: Unreported

Middle 50% SAT range: Minimum score of 580 for Critical Reading and 520 for Math

Middle 50% ACT range: Minimum score of 27

Early admission program (EA/ED/None): None

Percentage accepted through EA or ED: NA

EA/ED deadline: NA

Regular Deadline: 9-Feb

Application Fee: Varies by Program

Full time Undergraduate enrollment: 20,600

Total enrollment: 27,337

Percent Male: Unreported

Percent Female: Unreported

Total Percent Minority or Unreported: Unreported

Percent African-American: Unreported

Percent Asian/Pacific Islander: Unreported

Percent Hispanic: Unreported

Percent Native-American: Unreported

Percent International: Unreported

Percent in-Country/out of Country: Unreported

Percent from Public HS: Unreported

Retention Rate: Varies by program

Graduation Rate (4-year): Unreported

Graduation Rate (6-year): Unreported

Percent in On-campus housing: Unreported

Number of official organized extracurricular organizations: Unreported

3 Most popular majors: Varies by program

Student/Faculty ratio: Varies by program

Average Class Size: Varies by program

Percent of students going to grad school: Unreported

Tuition and Fees: CA$13,693–$20,611 for visa students

In Province Tuition and Fees (if different): Unreported

Cost for Room and Board: Dependent on residence and meal plan

Percent receiving Financial aid, first-year (out of those who apply): Unreported

Percent of Undergraduates Receiving Financial Aid: Unreported

McMaster University lies in Hamilton, Ontario, and is one of the most prestigious Canadian universities, ranking fifth in Canada. The university boasts outstanding science programs and excellent research opportunities, particularly in medicine.

A happy student body

According to the *Globe and Mail*'s Canadian University Report of 2013, McMaster has among the most satisfied student populations, only lagging behind University of Western Ontario among large universities. McMaster has a rapidly growing student body of over 20,000 undergraduate students.

Students said the university has an academically-focused student body, with an average entering grade of 84.3 percent and a 75 percent cutoff for admissions. Employment opportunities are relatively easy to come by after graduation—96 percent of undergraduates are employed within two years of graduating.

McMaster students also often participate in various extracurricular activities to relax from their studies. Although McMaster's sports scene is not very prominent, the football team placed the best in the nation in 2012. Students also describe a lively social scene

A scientific approach

McMaster has a strong teaching faculty of 900 professors, and is ranked as one of the best universities in quality of teaching and learning among large Canadian universities. It also has excellent research opportunities for students, with the highest research income-to-faculty ratio in the country. McMaster attempts to promote a "problem-based" approach to teaching by offering small "Inquiry" courses to students starting in first year. In these classes, students are work in groups of 20 with the guidance of a professor as they try to solve problems on their own, rather than watch traditional lectures.

Like other Canadian universities, McMaster does not carry a liberal arts emphasis, so students enter specific programs in their field of interest and tend to specialize rapidly.

Students agree that the university is much more oriented toward the sciences at the expense of its humanities and social sciences, with a strong and highly competitive health sciences program.

An insular campus

Many students are satisfied with life on McMaster's campus. A large pedestrian campus with 56 buildings, McMaster is surrounded by a quiet, residential neighborhood.

McMaster offers its students pre-paid meals, and students are generally pleased with the quality of the food. "If you are on campus, you are never more than five minutes away from a meal," a student added.

In Ontario, one can enjoy the province's drinking age of 19, and students can easily find parties on or off campus. Although McMaster's party scene is less prominent than its peers', students say they still easily find opportunities to relax and socialize.

The university has excellent research opportunities for students, with the highest research income-to-faculty ratio in the country.

However, a recent campus-capacity study found that the university is severely overcrowded, and received criticism in particular for neglecting its social sciences and humanities facilities, which are currently in the aging arts quad. A new liberal arts building is slated to open in 2015.

Although the University is minutes from downtown Hamilton, most students choose to stay on campus, as downtown Hamilton has little to offer relative to more major cities like Toronto. For those who do wish to explore beyond campus, there are plenty of hiking and mountain biking trails nearby, including at the Bruce Trail, the Niagara Escarpment and the Waterfront Trail.

With academic rigor and a high quality of student life, McMaster is a great choice for students looking to pursue a science degree in Canada.—*Clinton Wang*

FYI
What is an example of the biggest campus-wide traditions each year? "Going to the Marauders football game at Homecoming."
If I could change one thing about McMaster, "I'd change the student registration system. It doesn't work at all, and it causes a lot of headaches for students."
"My favorite part of the experience was the camaraderie amongst students. Even though the academics can be intense, especially in health sciences, there's not too much competition, and many students are willing to help each other and collaborate."

Queen's University

Address: Gordon Hall, 74 Union Street, Kingston, ON K7L 3N6 Canada
Phone: 613-533-2218
E-mail address: admission@queensu.ca
Web site URL: www.queensu.ca
Year Founded: 1841
Private or Public: Public
Religious Affiliation: None
Location: Urban
Number of Applicants: 25,403
Percent Accepted: 42%
Percent Accepted who enroll: 31%
Number Entering: 3,246
Number of Transfers Accepted each Year: Unreported
Middle 50% SAT range: Unreported
Middle 50% ACT range: Unreported
Early admission program EA/ED/None: None

Percentage accepted through EA or ED: NA
EA and ED deadline: NA
Regular Deadline: 16-Feb
Application Fee: $135 Canadian
Full time Undergraduate enrollment: 16,038
Total enrollment: Unreported
Percent Male: 40%
Percent Female: 60%
Total Percent Minority or Unreported: Unreported
Percent African-American: Unreported
Percent Asian/Pacific Islander: Unreported
Percent Hispanic: Unreported
Percent Native-American: Unreported
Percent International: 9%
Percent in-state/out of state: 18%/72%
Percent from Public HS: Unreported
Retention Rate: Unreported
Graduation Rate 4-year: Unreported

Graduation Rate 6-year: Unreported
Percent Undergraduates in On-campus housing: Unreported
Number of official organized extracurricular organizations: 200
3 Most popular majors: Business/Commerce, General Sport and Fitness Administration/Management
Student/Faculty ratio: 16:1
Average Class Size: 26
Percent of students going to grad school: Unreported
Tuition and Fees: $15,980 Canadian
In-State Tuition and Fees if different: unreported
Cost for Room and Board: $10,110 Canadian
Percent receiving financial aid out of those who apply: Unreported
Percent receiving financial aid among all students: Unreported

O ne of the earliest institutions of higher learning in Canada, Queen's University is also one of the most prestigious schools in the country. It is a research university of more than 20,000 undergraduates and postgraduates—a rather small number by Canadian standards—and provides top-notch education to all of its students. For American students, Queen's may not be as readily recognized as schools such as the University of Toronto or McGill University, but the quality of education and the number of research opportunities certainly rival many of its better known counterparts. Queen's is not situated in the great metropolises of Toronto or Montreal, but its location in Kingston, Ontario, offers students both the sense of a college town and the conveniences of a decent-size city.

The Faculty

The terms used in Canada to describe different divisions of a university can sometimes baffle American students. Whereas universities in the United States are often divided into separate schools and colleges, in Canada, this type of division is often known as faculty. For example, Queen's is divided into five separate faculties, the Faculty of Arts and Sciences, the Faculty of Applied Science, the Faculty of Law, the Faculty of Education, and the Faculty of Health Sciences. In addition, the university also has its School of Business, School of Graduate Studies and Research, and Theology College. As a result, students have easy access to a large number of courses in different fields. "I think Queen's does a really good job of making sure that there are classes for people of any interest," said one student.

Another difference between Canadian and American universities is the specificity of majors in Canada. While many colleges in the United States also have unique and specialized majors, Canadian undergraduate programs can be in a very specific field, such as Commerce or Geographic Information

Science. For American students who are mostly familiar with the limited number of majors available at liberal arts colleges, the undergraduate programs in Canada can surprise quite a few people at the beginning. However, this also means that the education often provides better professional training and more in-depth teaching of different topics, which can be highly valuable for students.

The number of students in a class varies greatly. In the introductory classes, hundreds of freshmen can be crammed into a single lecture hall. However, that is normal for both Canadian and American universities, especially those with relatively large student populations. The drawback is that it can be difficult to maintain concentration in those classes. "Paying attention in those classes or even showing up to some of them is a big challenge for me," said one student. Of course, students in higher level courses eventually find themselves in much smaller classes. Some of the classes for seniors can have fewer than a dozen students.

The grading system for Canadian schools is also different from the United States. Instead of the letter grading system of A, B, C, D, and F, Canadians use numbers from zero to 100. The good part is that it differentiates those within grades. For example, someone with an A in a class could be scoring 90 on tests, while another with the same letter grade can have 100 on everything. This way, the numerical system helps to better differentiate students. On the other hand, some students may become too concerned with a few points in their grade. "I don't really care about the difference between 80 and 82, but some people do, and I think they spend too much time trying just to raise one or two points," said one student.

The admissions process in Canada can also be unfamiliar to American students. Luckily, given the large number of Americans going north to seek a good education at a relatively affordable price, Queen's has its own special admissions process for American high school students, which is mostly similar to college applications in the United States. Unlike American schools that typically do not have minimum requirements, Queen's admissions office does provide numbers for the minimal GPA and standardized test scores. The combined critical reading and math scores on the SAT should be above 1,200, and students must maintain a high school grade of B-. If the student decides to use ACT, the score must

be at least 26. In addition, the requirements are also different depending on the specific programs to which the student is applying. Just to offer an idea on the admissions standards, the average grade of first-year students from Canada is 87 percent, equivalent of an A to A- in the letter grade system.

> "Queen's does a really good job of making sure that there are classes for people of any interest."

Limestone City

Kingston is known as the Limestone City for the simple fact that it has a large number of limestone buildings. The campus is therefore very beautiful with many historic, neo-gothic structures, not unlike many of the Ivy League institutions on the East Coast of the United States. The city approximates a suburban environment with mostly low rises and large open spaces. Kingston does have a college town atmosphere, however, given that most of the economic activities are linked to universities, government, or hospitals.

One issue for many students in choosing Canadian schools is the weather. For the majority of students, however, the weather is actually not bad at all, but that is mostly because they are Canadians who come from areas north of Kingston. According to an American student, "It is what I expected: cold and long winters, but then again it is not that different from places like Minnesota or the Midwest."

The university offers 16 different residence buildings spread around campus, though the majority of them are located in the southwest corner of the university. The rooms are generally very small, but they do have the basic furniture needed by students. After freshman year, many students choose to live off campus. Most of the time, a group of friends get together and rent a small house in the area, generally at a reasonable price that is competitive with the price of rooms at the university. Queen's has three main dining halls as well as seven retail food outlets. The quality of food is not great, but that is expected of college dining. "I had siblings who went to different universities," said one student. "So I sort of knew that food in dining halls gets repetitive very quickly."

Perhaps one thing for American students to look forward to in Canada is the legal drinking age of 19 instead of 21 in the United

States. Alcohol is certainly part of college life in Canada, and most people have easy access to it given the low age limit. However, the school does have strict policies limiting alcohol on campus. Of course, a number of bars surround the university, so finding places to drink and socialize is certainly not difficult during weekends. As a result, parties typically occur outside of university residences and in off-campus housing.

A Canadian Ivy

Although hockey is certainly the most important sport in Canada, to the delight of American students, the Queen's football team does draw big and fervent crowds. In many ways, Queen's is quite similar to an Ivy League university. It has a great reputation both domestically and internationally. It provides top-notch academic opportunities to students, and it provides a historic college town atmosphere. While the tuition is much lower for Canadians than for Americans, Queen's still provides an excellent education at an affordable price. Therefore, it is certainly a school to consider for all those willing to brave the cold of Canadian winters.—*Xiaohang Liu*

FYI

If you come to Queen's, you'd better bring "a big coat."

What is the typical weekend schedule? "Relax after a long week."

If I could change one thing about Queen's, I'd "make it easier to get to Toronto."

Three things every student at Queen's should do before graduating are "Go to football games, join a club, and go to the music festival here."

University of British Columbia

Address: Room 2016, 1874 East Mall, Vancouver, BC V6T 1Z1, Canada

Phone: 604-822-3014

E-mail address: www .publicaffairs.ubc.ca/about

Web site URL: www.welcome .ubc.ca

Year Founded: 1908

Private or Public: Public

Religious Affiliation: None

Location: Urban

Number of Applicants: 18,773

Percent Accepted: 49%

Percent Accepted who enroll: 49%

Number Entering: 5,017

Number of Transfers Accepted each Year: Unreported

Middle 50% SAT range: Unreported

Middle 50% ACT range: Unreported

Early admission program EA/ED/None: None

Percentage accepted through EA or ED: NA

EA and ED deadline: NA

Regular Deadline: 28-Feb

Application Fee: $60 Canadian

Full time Undergraduate enrollment: 30,170

Total enrollment: 38,811

Percent Male: 47%

Percent Female: 53%

Total Percent Minority or Unreported: Unreported

Percent African-American: Unreported

Percent Asian/Pacific Islander: Unreported

Percent Hispanic: Unreported

Percent Native-American: Unreported

Percent International: 7%

Percent in-state/out of state: 2% from U.S.

Percent from Public HS: Unreported

Retention Rate: 92%

Graduation Rate 4-year: Unreported

Graduation Rate 6-year: Unreported

Percent Undergraduates in On-campus housing: 20%

Number of official organized extracurricular organizations: 250

3 Most popular majors: Biological and Physical Sciences, Computer and Information Sciences, Psychology

Student/Faculty ratio: 15:1

Average Class Size: 9

Percent of students going to grad school: 50%

Tuition and Fees: $5,168 Canadian

In-State Tuition and Fees if different: $23,690 Canadian

Cost for Room and Board: $6,650 Canadian

Percent receiving financial aid out of those who apply: Unreported

Percent receiving financial aid among all students: Unreported

Students at the University of British Columbia are happy to talk about the benefits of a global education at UBC, and they don't just mean those that come from crossing the Canadian border. From a wealth of international students to the resources of one of the top 20 public schools in the world to the close proximity of Vancouver and Whistler, UBC has a lot of reasons to make even its very large student population proud.

Different Faculties and a Diverse Faculty

When applying to UBC, students must choose which of the schools, or faculties, they are interested in. For applicants looking for a liberal arts style education, this would be the popular Faculty of Arts, but others may be more interested in the Faculty of Sciences (or the Saunder School of Business, or the Faculty of Education, or the Faculty of Forestry, and so on). Unlike in most American universities, switching between faculties is not easy: "You apply to a faculty and you stay in it."

Requirements and difficulty vary between faculties. The Faculty of Arts requires its students to take classes in arts and sciences, but it is still considered to have a workload that is "not as heavy, mainly because there are way fewer labs." Conversely, "[Saunder School of] Business has a heavy workload, [the Faculty of] Science is really heavy," one student in the Faculty of Arts noted.

Regardless of area of interest, prospective students should know that "Canada does grades differently than the States." New freshmen might be thrilled to learn that 90 to 100 percent is an A+ and B's don't even start until under 80 percent, but they soon learn that while "everything is on an easier scale . . . it's a lot more difficult to attain than in high school." At UBC, even high-achieving students can feel proud of a B.

UBC is an undeniably very large school, and this does lead to some very large classes, especially at the introductory level. Students say that class sizes in the first year are "between 100 and 200, probably about 150," but "as you take more specialized classes it gets smaller." This doesn't mean that individual attention is impossible to come by. While professors are "primarily there for their research purposes and teaching courses is not their concern," UBC students are not too worried by their professors' lack of availability. Students find the large number of TAs to be "really, really good," and "very knowledgeable."

Social Lives: Legal, and Less-than-Legal

First years soon recognize that their huge classes are not the best way to make friends, so many of those who live on campus turn to their residences. Residence halls have not just a concentration of people, but also sponsored activities and parties to help residents meet and bond. Totem Park Residence in particular is known as a hot-spot of on-campus culture on the weekends.

Another common stop for nightlife is the "on-campus pub, called the Pit Pub, that's really popular on Wednesdays." Frats do exist at UBC, and while they are "the same in terms of trashy environments," they are not as popular as their American counterparts. Perhaps this is because so many students live outside the residence halls and "a lot of people just don't even come to campus on weekends." For these students, and for those looking for something outside of UBC, Vancouver has big draw. While not all activities in the city are alcohol-related, "it's pretty popular to go out since the drinking age here is 19."

Possibly to combat the increased availability of alcohol, the university has prohibited drinking games on campus, but students say that "people still do them, but the administration doesn't like the promotion of binge drinking." In the dorms, RAs aren't known to be particularly tough on alcohol usage, and both in residences and outside of them, much of students' socializing involves drinking.

If not drinking, then what? Well, casual marijuana use is another common social activity, and one student reported that "pretty much . . . everyone smokes weed." Harder drugs are far less ubiquitous.

Substances need not be the only outlets for student life, however. Intramural sports are popular, although varsity sports are not "particularly followed." Clubs and organizations also work to provide other outlets for interaction, such as the popular Ski and Board Club that subsidizes ski passes and provides weekly transportation to Whistler or the Film Society that offers cheaper movie tickets. Go Global, a group that assists students in studying abroad, is another popular option, and for many international students or recent Canadian immigrants, ethnic and cultural groups provide a home away from home. These groups also throw events, some for members only and some for the general population.

The social scene and student population is filled with individuals who are, overall, friendly, politically very liberal, and mainly upper-middle class in spite of the quite affordable price tag, which students have attributed to the increased tuition costs for international students (who number at over 5,000 and come from more than 140 countries due to the school's active recruiting abroad). Despite this increased diversity, UBC is perceived by students as "about 40 percent Asian," a fact which gives it the nickname, "University of a Billion Chinese," and causes some less-than-politically-correct individuals to even refer to Vancouver, Canada as "Hongcouver, Japanada."

> **"Canada does grades differently than the States."**

In-Demand Dorms and Beyond

Unlike at many other schools, UBC's freshmen are not required to live on campus. In fact, the university doesn't have room to house all of their first years. Incoming freshmen fill out an online application for one of the two freshmen residence complexes, but "only a fraction of people get into residences," and this creates "a wait-list of, like, 3,000 people." Those who do get in find Totem Park or Place Vanier to be convenient and comfortable residences. Dorms can be singles, doubles, triples, or quads, and feature a nearby lounge, study area, and gym. These complexes also have one RA on each floor.

Totem Park and Place Vanier also contain the only two "specific cafeteria dining areas." Food reviews were mixed, with students describe the dining halls as having "a good variety," but also complaining that "the food kind of gets old," and "it's pretty expensive." Overall, as one student put it, "if you

are conscious and willing to put a little more effort into it you can get a good meal. However, outside of these dining halls there are "a lot of places to eat on campus . . . and a lot of places you can use your meal card." Many students eschew all of those options in favor of cooking for themselves.

There are more living options for upperclassmen, including dorms that feature suite-style living with shared kitchen and common areas. In spite of this, most students choose (or are forced, because of lack of space) to leave campus after their first year. Only about one-fifth of the undergraduate student population lives on campus. The other four-fifths tend to find that commuting isn't difficult, especially with Vancouver's extensive bus service.

Students living or hanging out in Vancouver might need to exercise a little more caution when walking around at night, but students on campus feel safe. There are occasional problems along the outside of campus and "there's been the occasional poster put up saying to be careful," but most students are happy with programs like Safewalk that will dispatch two people to accompany anyone on a late-night trip to the library or back to their residence.

Campus buildings are varied, but not always in a good way. Study areas tend to be well-liked, possibly because they're well-lit, "really nice modern study areas [with] lots of glass." Thankfully for fans of these spots, the libraries are open for long periods, and "quite often during exams they're open 24 hours." UBC's main physical draw is not its architecture but the natural surroundings, which are "incredibly picturesque."

Some students make the trip across the border for the mountains, forests, and natural beauty, while others might be drawn by UBC's international outlook or stellar academic programs. No matter what brings students to UBC, they will find a large community ready to learn, play, and enjoy their undergraduate years at the University of British Columbia.—*Erin Maher*

FYI

Three things every student at UBC should do before graduating are: "Storm the Wall, vandalize the engineering "E" sign, watch the sunset at Wreck Beach (it's a nude beach on the edge of campus but students rarely strip)."

If I could change one thing about UBC, I'd: "add more study space, since during exams, study space is super hard to find because everyone is on campus studying (even though the majority of students commute)."

If you come to UBC, you'd better bring: "rainboots, an umbrella, and a bike (to get around because campus is so big)."

University of Toronto

Address: 25 King's College Circle, Toronto, ON M5S 1A1 Canada
Phone: 416 978-2190
E-mail address: admissions.help@utoronto.ca
Web site URL: www.utoronto.ca
Year Founded: 1827
Private or Public: Public
Religious Affiliation: None
Location: Suburban
Number of Applicants: 60,776
Percent Accepted: 67%
Percent Accepted who enroll: Unreported
Number Entering: Unreported
Number of Transfers Accepted each Year: Unreported
Middle 50% SAT range: Unreported
Middle 50% ACT range: Unreported
Early admission program EA/ED/None: None

Percentage accepted through EA or ED: NA
EA and ED deadline: NA
Regular Deadline: 1-Mar
Application Fee: $80 Canadian
Full time Undergraduate enrollment: 58,182
Total enrollment: Unreported
Percent Male: 45%
Percent Female: 55%
Total Percent Minority or Unreported: Unreported
Percent African-American: Unreported
Percent Asian/Pacific Islander: Unreported
Percent Hispanic: Unreported
Percent Native-American: Unreported
Percent International: 10%
Percent in-state/out of state: 3% from U.S.
Percent from Public HS: Unreported
Retention Rate: Unreported
Graduation Rate 4-year: Unreported

Graduation Rate 6-year: Unreported
Percent Undergraduates in On-campus housing: 30%
Number of official organized extracurricular organizations: 250
3 Most popular majors: Unreported
Student/Faculty ratio: Unreported
Average Class Size: Unreported
Percent of students going to grad school: 34%
Tuition and Fees: Dependent on major
In-State Tuition and Fees if different: NA
Cost for Room and Board: $7,000
Percent receiving financial aid out of those who apply: Unreported
Percent receiving financial aid among all students: Unreported

Lying in the heart of Canada's economic and cultural capital, the University of Toronto is widely considered the best and most prestigious university in the country. U of T's location and reputation make it appealing to students from around the world, and the admissions standards are more relaxed than those of some of the most prestigious universities in the United States. But don't be fooled by the high acceptance rate—despite the lively social scene, the academics can be intense. U of T offers students of all calibers opportunities to challenge themselves and engage in their interests on both academic and extracurricular levels, though a student needs to take initiative to excel.

An Intense Academic Experience

The University offers several hundred undergraduate programs and has limited distributional requirements, providing first year students with the flexibility to immediately pursue a narrow academic focus. By spring semester of their first year, U of T students must select a major, minor or specialist program. The specialist track is offered for a range of fields and has double the requirements of the equivalent major for that field. Incoming students who know exactly what they want to do often opt for a specialist program, where they can actively pursue their interests in great depth, while others have a chance to explore, potentially choosing a double major or major-minor combination. More ambitious students can combine a specialist program with a second major or minor by increasing their course load during the school year and taking summer courses.

U of T has high standards in many subject areas across the sciences, arts and humanities, perhaps driven in part by its infamously low curves in many large classes, which have drawn complaints of grade deflation.

"Most profs at U of T design their evaluations to be really hard to make sure they can challenge and distinguish between the students on the higher end of the mark distributions," a fourth-year student said. "As long as they've got a nice bell curve they can then adjust everyone's mark until the average is around 67 percent." With the curve set this low for many popular courses, there may be large gaps in grades among even the best students, while the worst students may fail their courses and even enter academic probation. Science and engineering programs are also notorious for their hefty coursework, and students said the difficulty of the course material isn't as problematic as the sheer amount of readings and preparatory work. "It can be pretty easy to fall behind," a second-year student said. "The profs expect you to do a lot of things on your own without reminders, so although they give you a lot of resources and extra help to work with, [many] people don't really feel motivated to stay on top of things."

> **"The opportunities are definitely there, but you'll have to go after them yourself."**

Class sizes are generally quite large, though they range from fewer than 30 for music seminars to well over 1,000 in some introductory courses. As a result, some students complain about being treated like numbers, particularly given the competition for high grades. Students described the professors as very passionate about their subjects, and many have impressive credentials, including a large number of science professors from the Royal Society of London. Many students also find that professors are willing to help students who have the initiative to seek them out for office hours and extra tutorials, though they will not pamper struggling students who do not actively pursue these opportunities. "The opportunities are definitely there, but you'll have to go after them yourself," one student said. "Nobody will babysit you." Though U of T gives students exposure to what is at times a cutthroat and unsupportive environment, other students view their college careers as good practice "so we get to know what the real world is like."

Scattered Social Interactions

The 58,000 undergraduates that comprise U of T's student body vary widely in terms of their personalities, attitudes and interests, allowing most students to easily find their own niche, though students looking to interact with a variety of well-rounded peers may be disappointed. Students can explore a large number of extracurricular activities and social events both on campus and in the city. From cultural associations to music groups to sports teams and clubs, student groups for all different interests abound on campus. Research opportunities in state-of-the-art facilities are also quite readily available to undergraduate students who have the initiative to approach professors.

Unfortunately, some students say that U of T doesn't provide the best environment for making friends. "You really do have to make an effort to find friends in extracurricular activities since most of the people you sit with in lecture halls will be complete strangers, and the diversity can sometimes make it hard to find common ground," a first-year student said. "Even if you get a person's name you generally won't be seeing them for many hours a week, and most people have very busy schedules." Colleges assign students in the same academic department to a First Year Learning Community (FLC), which helps students form study groups that often also become social groups—but outside FLCs and student organizations, he said social interactions are often scattered. "There are a lot of commuters, people who are always busy or have their faces buried in a textbook."

A Metropolitan Campus

With a large immigrant population, Toronto offers a large variety of authentic cuisines from around the world, and U of T's main campus is located right next to Chinatown. 50 percent of Toronto's population is foreign-born, and U of T reflects this diversity in its student body, attracting a large number of international students, particularly from Asia and the United States. Toronto has a vibrant nightlife, and while a great deal of parties and social events happen on campus, students often go to local restaurants and pubs and make use of the frequent cultural events in the city. "You can always find something exciting to do on any night, and living in the middle of downtown is a big part of that," a fourth-year student said, "though you'll definitely have to sacrifice either sleep or grades in the process."

The main St. George campus is highly accessible via subway and streetcar systems, and many students opt to live off campus to save money, whether commuting from home or renting apartments or rooms in the city. Residential college life and dorm style varies from college to college, and most students find the accommodations satisfactory. Each residence has its own characteristics, as students are sorted partly by program and partly by their responses to a housing survey. A clear divide emerges between those residences that are hubs for social activity and those that are tranquil and more conducive to study. There are also two satellite campuses, in Scarborough and Mississauga, which provide a suburban environment and feature smaller class sizes, but have a more limited range of courses.

Besides its top-notch academics and facilities, U of T provides students with the rare opportunity to appreciate the diversity of a student body drawn from all different countries, backgrounds and personalities, and experience a truly international, dynamic city. For students who enjoy city life, want to challenge themselves and have initiative, U of T would be a great destination.
—*Clinton Wang*

FYIs

What surprised me the most about UT when I arrived was "the sheer diversity of students, many of whom come from countries you'd otherwise only hear about on the Internet."

One thing you wish you would've known before coming: "Admission standards can be deceiving, since academic standards are incredibly tough."

The biggest college-wide tradition/event at UT is the "campus-wide all-nighter series before finals!"

Three things every student at UT should do before graduating are "get involved in research, experience Toronto's nightlife, and eat at every food truck parked along St. George Street."

University of Waterloo

Address: 200 University Avenue, West Waterloo, ON N2L 3G1 Canada
Phone: 519-888-4567
E-mail address: admissions@uwaterloo.ca
Web site URL: www.uwaterloo.ca
Year Founded: 1957
Private or Public: Public
Religious Affiliation: None
Location: Urban
Number of Applicants: 37,113
Percent Accepted: 50%
Percent Accepted who enroll: 31%
Number Entering: 5,762
Number of Transfers Accepted each Year: 3,165
Middle 50% SAT range: Unreported
Middle 50% ACT range: Unreported
Early admission program EA/ED/None: None
Percentage accepted through EA or ED: NA

EA and ED deadline: NA
Regular Deadline: 12-Jan
Application Fee: $110 Canadian
Full time Undergraduate enrollment: 24,599
Total enrollment: unreported
Percent Male: 56%
Percent Female: 44%
Total Percent Minority or Unreported: Unreported
Percent African-American: Unreported
Percent Asian/Pacific Islander: Unreported
Percent Hispanic: Unreported
Percent Native-American: Unreported
Percent International: 8%
Percent in-state/out of state: 3% from U.S.
Percent from Public HS: Unreported
Retention Rate: Unreported
Graduation Rate 4-year: 79%

Graduation Rate 6-year: Unreported
Percent Undergraduates in On-campus housing: Unreported
Number of official organized extracurricular organizations: 150
3 Most popular majors: Unreported
Student/Faculty ratio: 3:1
Average Class Size: Unreported
Percent of students going to grad school: 70%
Tuition and Fees: Dependent on major
In-State Tuition and Fees if different: NA
Cost for Room and Board: Dependent on residence plan
Percent receiving financial aid out of those who apply: Unreported
Percent receiving financial aid among all students: Unreported

Nestled in the quiet college town of Waterloo, Canada, the University of Waterloo has made great strides as an undergraduate institution since its founding a mere 57 years ago. The school, which has been named Canada's "most innovative university" by Maclean's magazine for 19 years in a row, keeps its students busy with a combination of rigorous academics and a renowned co-op program. Opportunities at the University of Waterloo, and students who seek them, are never in short supply.

Rigorous Academics with Real-World Applications

Those interested in attending the University of Waterloo must be prepared to work—both inside and outside of the classroom. With most students competing for top jobs through the university's prestigious cooperative education program, grades are taken very seriously, and many studious Waterloo Warriors are known to forgo extracurricular activities to achieve that all-important 4.0. These particularly serious students are known as "keeners"—an oft-repeated refrain on campus that describes those whose scholarly doggedness keeps them at the top of the curve at all times. "I don't really like the competitive vibe," said one first-year student. "You often hear people saying things like 'Oh my gosh, you're so keen!' or 'You're keening!,' but sometimes being keen isn't such a good thing." Although she admits that she finds her peers' ambition daunting at times, she also expressed gratitude for supportive upper-years, many of whom are happy to help freshmen in need.

In terms of workload, Waterloo endorses the two-for-one model: two hours of studying for each hour of class. For the average student with four to five classes each term, this totals to about 30 hours of studying a week. "The work is challenging enough that it motivates you to work hard and accomplish it," said a third-year accounting student who expressed satisfaction over the school's academic rigour. "It's definitely manageable. It makes you think outside the box and keeps you humble."

Famed for its School of Accounting, Computer Science and Math departments, the University of Waterloo aims to integrate academics with vocational and professional training. The Co-operative Education & Career Services (CECS) at the university connects students to employers and alumni. Student enrolled in co-op alternate between terms of school and terms of work in fields relevant to their studies. Work terms generally last for four months, and co-op students will graduate with the same amount of academic terms as a non-co-op student, in addition to two years of work experience. Although it means that they will take five years to complete their bachelor's degree instead of the traditional four, 56 percent of the undergraduate population choose to enroll in co-op because of the practical, hands-on experiences it provides. One student said that co-op gave Waterloo graduates a large advantage over their competitors from other colleges because "we already have 16 months of work experience [by graduation]," she said. "No other school can compete with us in terms of preparation for the work world." Indeed, with degrees such as Math and Chartered Accounting and Financial Analysis and Risk Management, Waterloo has a reputation for being a vocational school for the academically inclined. This is perhaps to the detriment of their social sciences and humanities programs, as one student noted, "Waterloo is an engineering, math, and computer science school."

Thus, for the technically and mathematically minded, a University of Waterloo education and degree can reap large rewards. Because Waterloo is the only school in Canada that is recognized by the Institute of Chartered Accountancy, aspiring chartered accountants can work toward the hours necessary for a CA designation while they are still in school. As for jobs that are found through the co-op program, many students land starting positions with prestigious corporate firms. One upper-year, who worked for Ernst & Young during his first work term, said that the experience not only gave him insight into the world of public accounting, but also that he learned how to collaborate with his colleagues, who treated him "like an actual member of the team as opposed to just doing miscellaneous office tasks." The student also noted that while the work terms only last for four months at a time, co-op students are treated like and given the benefits of full-time employees, giving them the chance and incentive to deeply immerse themselves in the working environment.

Living and Learning Communities

When choosing which residential buildings to live in first year, students have the choice to opt for Living-Learning Communities, in which they are matched up with students in the same departments as them. The school's housing Web site states, "Many of your neighbours are also your classmates." One first-year student, who lives in a Living-Learning Community in a small residence called Village One, said that she also has a peer leader, an upper-year student in the same program as the freshmen she mentors.

As for social space, many students hold parties in their residential buildings, but drinking is kept to a minimum because alcohol consumption by minors (the legal drinking is age in Ontario is 19) is strictly prohibited. This rule is enforced by the residence dons, who give out warnings and fines to students who "come stumbling in drunk or are caught with alcohol in their rooms." Nevertheless, Waterloo is a "live" place, as one upper-year said. The residence dons, senior students in charge with building a strong residence community, plan casual social gatherings such as Tostito Tuesdays and games of Assassin, a foam dart-gun game. Each year, the Waterloo Student Council also hosts a range of larger events, including a concert at the beginning of the term that has featured the likes of Marianas Trench, Lights, and Down with Webster. For business students, the School of Accounting and Financing organizes banquets and conferences to give students a chance to network and learn about new opportunities in the industry, and in early November, the Math department holds a Math-Hatter's Ball.

> **"Most years, we hire more students out of Waterloo than any other university in the world."—Bill Gates**

For the most part, extracurricular life is dominated by large organizations such as the School of Accounting and Finance and the DECA Business Club. Accordingly, some students have expressed discontent over their social interactions being limited to people within their area of study. One first-year Computer Science major commented that his friends were almost all in the Computer Science department as well, because they take the same classes and live in the same residence building. An Accounting student described the Accounting and Financial Management and Math/CA departments as very small communities: "It's like a high school where everyone knows

everyone." The tight-knit atmosphere can make students feel more comfortable within such a large school, but it also has its downsides. "People tend to gossip a lot, so you really have to watch what you do," said the same student.

Current students praise Waterloo for its open environment, which allows students to make connections with ease. "Random people I sit next to somehow become very, very good friends three years later," one student remarked. "You meet one person, and through six degrees of separation, you end up meeting someone else." Because they are so academically focused, however, Waterloo students add a quirky twist to their social interactions. "There are a lot of smart people at Waterloo," one student said. "I look around, and there are all these Sheldons [from *The Big Bang Theory*]! They're really smart, but socially awkward as well."

Waterloo being the acclaimed computer science school that it is, students attest that for those who prefer to stay in, there is no shortage of "geekier" activities to partake in. "There are some hardcore gamers at Waterloo," said one student. One popular activity is partaking in LAN parties: gatherings of students who bring their computers into one room and play multiplayer video games. The school's Starcraft team is ranked second in the world, and a League of Legends tournament is held on campus every year. The university's reputation as a training ground for future computer programmers and software developers is nothing to scoff at; during a campus visit in 2005, Bill Gates said, "Most years, we hire more students out of Waterloo than any other university in the world."

Out and About Town

Waterloo is the quintessential college town (except for the goose poop pervasively found on the ground!): Home to both the University of Waterloo and Wilfred Laurier University, the town features many services aimed at students, who make up the majority of its population. Around the school, there are several local bars and restaurants that cater to students at night and on the weekends. A popular hangout is Morty's, which is famous for its wing's nights on Mondays and Thursdays. Moreover, cultural delicacies abound, with a nearby plaza of Chinese, Korean, Japanese, and Indian restaurants just a few blocks away. For those who prefer a more casual atmosphere, there is McGinnis Frontrow: a restaurant and sports bar that students say is great for a post-game drink (it doesn't hurt that the legal drinking age in Ontario is 19). If these eclectic options don't satisfy, there is plenty of variety in the cafeteria, where frozen rice lunches, aloe drinks and even sushi can be found.

For students looking to gain valuable work experience prior to graduation and entering the job market, the University of Waterloo provides some of the best career-matching services in Canada. Among public universities, it is among the most rigorous academically and has been widely recognized for its cutting-edge innovation. Those who have no qualms with sacrificing a bit of their social life in favor of academic and professional pursuits will find a home at Waterloo.—*Yanan Wang*

FYI

If you come to Waterloo, you'd better bring "an umbrella, goose poop-proof shoes and a month's supply of McDonald's (they're far from campus!)."

What is the typical weekend schedule? "A little bit of studying, a lot of time with friends and catching up on sleep."

If I could change one thing about Waterloo, I'd "add more classical gothic buildings and some decent Internet in our math and computers building."

University of Western Ontario

Address: 1151 Richmond Street, London, ON N6A 3K7 Canada
Phone: 519-661-2111
E-mail address: publications@uwo.ca
Web site URL: www.uwo.ca
Year Founded: 1878
Private or Public: Public
Religious Affiliation: None
Location: Suburban
Number of Applicants: 27,652
Percent Accepted: 59%
Percent Accepted who enroll: 36%
Number Entering: 5,871
Number of Transfers Accepted each Year: Unreported
Middle 50% SAT range: Unreported
Middle 50% ACT range: Unreported
Early admission program EA/ED/None: None
Percentage accepted through EA or ED: NA

EA and ED deadline: NA
Regular Deadline: 1-Jun
Application Fee: $105 Canadian
Full time Undergraduate enrollment: 20,524
Total enrollment: 24,943
Percent Male: 41%
Percent Female: 59%
Total Percent Minority or Unreported: Unreported
Percent African-American: Unreported
Percent Asian/Pacific Islander: Unreported
Percent Hispanic: Unreported
Percent Native-American: Unreported
Percent International: 4%
Percent in-state/out of state: 1% from U.S.
Percent from Public HS: Unreported
Retention Rate: Unreported
Graduation Rate 4-year: Unreported
Graduation Rate 6-year: Unreported

Percent Undergraduates in On-campus housing: Unreported
Number of official organized extracurricular organizations: 100
3 Most popular majors: Unreported
Student/Faculty ratio: Unreported
Average Class Size: Unreported
Percent of students going to grad school: Unreported
Tuition and Fees: $13,050 Canadian
In-State Tuition and Fees if different: No difference
Cost for Room and Board: $6,941 Canadian
Percent receiving financial aid out of those who apply: Unreported
Percent receiving financial aid among all students: Unreported

Western University is one of Canada's most famous universities, as well as among the happiest. Though Western isn't at the top of most Canadian university rankings, what it lacks in its graduate programs and certain departments is more than made up for in the overall quality of the undergraduate education and experience. Indeed, a 2012 *Globe and Mail* student survey ranked Western as the best Canadian university in terms of recreation and athletics, and the best large one in terms of student satisfaction and work-play balance—a fitting outcome given its reputation as a laid-back party school. For students looking for a fun and dynamic undergraduate experience in Canada, Western may be the perfect destination.

A big campus in a small city

Western is located in London, a city halfway between Toronto and Detroit. Students are only somewhat satisfied with the city, and acknowledge the "Western bubble" that limits students' experiences in the city beyond campus. Even though most upperclassmen live off-campus or commute from home, many students still don't feel particularly attached to their city. "It doesn't help that Western's campus is so massive," quipped one student. 86 percent of graduates leave London after graduation, many choosing to work in Toronto.

Western boasts great residential facilities, and first-year students can enjoy spacious suites with a kitchen and multiple bathrooms. Residential life is also highly social and students looking for a party never need look far. The campus also features bustling bars and clubs, and Greek organizations can offer an important socializing venue off-campus for first-year students looking for alcohol—an aspect that has generated hostility from the administration.

Still, a student warned against making too much of the "party school" reputation—most parties are held on weekends and resident assistants do enforce quiet hours in the dorms. Students can always find places in residence to study in peace (except during exam week), and there are a few who do seem to study or work all the time.

The extracurricular scene is as vibrant and diverse as any other, though two niches that are especially prominent are fashion shows and athletics. Western's varsity sports teams, the Mustangs, perform particularly well in football and hockey. Intramurals are also popular and range from futsal to inner tube water polo.

Campus food is expensive but diverse and mostly healthy—indeed, a student said more first-years seem to lose weight rather than gain weight, let alone the freshman 15. Students often choose to pack a lunch or cook instead, and those living off campus often take advantage of London's numerous restaurants.

> A *Globe and Mail* student survey ranked Western as the best Canadian university in terms of recreation and athletics, and the best large one in terms of student satisfaction and work-play balance.

Superior teaching and stress-free learning

Western's academic experience may be determined in large part by one's major. Its elite, challenging business program and academically rigorous engineering program contrast with more laid-back programs in the arts and humanities. Western's engineering department has grown rapidly in recent years, rising to 5th in Canada ahead of the more famous programs at the University of Waterloo and University of Toronto, and engineering students may have over five hours of class each day lasting as late as 10 p.m. to show for the program's intensity. HBA students at the prestigious Richard Ivey School of Business are also expected to maintain both strong academics and intense extracurricular involvement. But most students, including those in Ivey or engineering, said they felt the academic demands of their program were manageable and relatively stress-free.

As at other large Canadian universities, most introductory classes are lectures of hundreds of students, and underclassmen find that they have little opportunity to interact with professors and find individual academic guidance, though *Globe and Mail* surveys find that Western still outperforms other universities in quality of instruction, class size and student-faculty interaction. A fourth-year student said that in order to find any help you need, you only need the initiative to approach professors and TAs during office hours, or find support at the tutoring center—both resources that only few students take advantage of. He added that higher-level classes are much smaller and allow students to easily find a professor to interact and work with.

As well, underclassmen get to engage in classes and research opportunities that may be rare for undergraduates at other universities. "Every week, I get to dissect human cadavers in anatomy lab," one student said. "It's the coolest thing I've ever done." Most undergraduates also have the flexibility to pursue their passions through electives— one interviewee is taking judo classes for credit—and many find the time to engage in extracurricular activities outside of class.

For those looking for a rewarding undergraduate life in Canada, Western is certainly a strong choice. The university combines a satisfying academic experience with abundant opportunities for leisure, socialization or pursuit of extra-curricular activities and passions.—*Clinton Wang*

FYI
What differentiates UWO the most from other colleges is "the quality of our non-academic student life. The sports scene in particular is fantastic, and school spirit is always high."
If I could change one thing about UWO, "I'd increase the study spaces. It's impossible to find a study spot during exam period, and none of the libraries are open 24 hours."
What you should know to have fun at UWO: "Work hard, play hard!"

Index